The Booth Catalogue

Collect GB First Day Covers

30th Edition

A reference catalogue of all
Great Britain First Day Issues

Compiled and Edited by
Jeffrey H. Booth
Garth Denman

Published by:
First Day Publishing Company
P.O. Box 11, Arundel
West Sussex BN18 9SS. England

Rare KEVII First Day Post Card

Royalty Post Cards are the subject of the Special Feature in this 30th Edition of the catalogue. The presentation starts on page 160.

King Edward VII did not come to the throne until he was 60 years old! This fine first day Post Card has the new 1902 halfpenny Stamp nicely tied on the reverse side.

Index to the 30th Edition
Collect GB First Day Covers
The Booth Catalogue

Selected Philatelic Gems throughout the catalogue

Introduction to the 30th Edition

Welcome to the 30th edition of The Booth Catalogue

In the new catalogue we have continued the tradition of presenting a sixteen page full colour Feature. This time it is on Royalty Post Cards and we hope that the great selection of first day Cards will prove to be of interest to all. The Colour Feature starts on page 160.

In recent years there has been a marked increase in the number of sponsored handstamps and in the use of cds postmarks. Since the early 90's many new issues have taken a full page to present them. We have always listed all handstamps individually in the past, but if we want to continue to see the catalogue as an easy to carry reference guide, the time has come to catalogue these in a different way - at least for the Commemorative Issues.

From 1990 onwards we have started to list all Commemorative Issues sponsored handstamps by total number rather than by describing them individually. With very few exceptions, all of these handstamps now have the same catalogue price, which makes it easier to adopt this solution going forward. We are still able to identify all new issue handstamps in detail and invite readers to write to us with any questions they might have on a particular Stamp Issue or handstamp.

The popular GB Overprints Section has been updated and the checklist of Pre-release and Missing Colours covers has been kept for the 30th Edition. Also, make sure you don't miss the many 'Gems' pages featured at random throughout the catalogue.

The 30th edition runs to 464 pages and includes thousands of postmark listings and illustrations, along with many pages of GB first day cover illustrations. Prices have been updated and all new Issues added to the catalogue. The listings start with the Uniform 4d Post Issue of December 5th, 1839 and from then on we have tried to list every known new Issue and to catalogue all postmarks up to 2010. There are still a few gaps in the Queen Victoria and Edward VII sections, where the problem is one of establishing the 'real' first day of issue. We are adding to these sections all the time, but collectors are invited, as always, to write with any comments or additional information on these early Issues.

We hope that you will enjoy reading and referring to the new edition of our catalogue, which we and many of our readers, believe to be the leading published authority on GB First Day Covers today. Our publication is distributed throughout the UK through retailers and the Stamp Trade. Enquiries and comments are always welcome, please write to the address given at the front of the catalogue in the first instance, or email us at jhbfdc@gmail.com.

All prices in the catalogue are for
clean covers, with undamaged stamps
and clear postmarks.

Anything less is worth less!

Introduction to the 30th Edition

Postmarks, Illustrated Covers and 'Official' Covers

We still say the proper place for a Stamp is on an envelope! But it needs to be cancelled with a clear and clean (tidy) first day postmark to qualify as a First Day Cover. Prices given are for such cancellations, on neat undamaged envelopes, or post cards as the case may be. Given the demands of most Collectors today, covers dating from 1901 onwards, which do not conform to these requirements, are worth considerably less than the value shown in this catalogue.

Neat hand addressed covers are acceptable alternatives to printed, rubber stamped, or typed ones, up until the end of 1963 for Commemoratives and up to the time of the Machin Head Issue, which started in 1967, for Definitives; from 1958 for Regionals and from 1957 for Booklets, etc. Beyond these dates most hand addressed covers are worth only some 20% of the catalogue price. Exceptions are made in the case of the rare cancellations, with a catalogue value of £85 or more. For all such cancellations a neat hand addressed cover is an acceptable alternative, with only minor loss of catalogue value.

On the question of plain or illustrated covers, prices are given for both where applicable, but from 1937 onwards all Commemoratives are priced as illustrated (picture plus text) or display (printed text only) covers. The same applies for Definitives, starting with the May 1951 KGVI issues and for Regionals from their beginning in 1958. As far as Booklet Panes, etc, are concerned cachet covers (usually text only, applied by rubber stamp) are acceptable for the earlier issues of the mid 1950's and early 1960's, as indicated in the catalogue.

We have tried to limit handstamp and cds listings, particularly for the issues of the last twenty years, to those which are relevant to the actual Stamp Issue concerned. In recent years there have been – and still are – a number of first day postmarks which really have nothing at all to do with the Stamp Issue itself. We see little reason to list any of these totally unrelated postmarks.

Our View on 'Official' Covers

Some years ago the term 'official covers' started to appear and was used to describe any fdc where the cover designer and postmark sponsor were the same. It has always seemed inappropriate to us to catalogue these at a higher price than covers where the cover designer and the postmark sponsor are not the same person.

Every first day postmark after all is sponsored and made available, via Royal Mail, for everyone to use without further charge. So why pay a premium for one cover design over another? It should be remembered that we catalogue Stamps and postmarks, not cover designs.

The discussion continues and currently these modern 'official 'covers – now starting to be called 'sponsored' – are being sold at a premium. Maybe this is as it should be, but we remain unconvinced and prefer to make no variation in pricing between the different types of cover design. If the postmark was only available to the sponsor – which is not the case – then things would be different!

We'll keep you 'posted' on this tricky question...

Introduction to the 30th Edition

Advance Information on New Stamp Issues and First Day Postmarks

The British Philatelic Bulletin, published monthly by Royal Mail, gives much complete advance information on all new GB Stamp Issues - Commemoratives, Definitives, Regionals, Booklets, etc. The British Postmark Bulletin, published by Royal Mail every two weeks, illustrates in advance all special postmarks that have been designed and sponsored for each and every forthcoming GB Stamp Issue.

Covers with special sponsored first day postmarks can usually be ordered through a local Stamp Dealer, or from most postmark sponsors themselves. The Post Office Philatelic Bureau in Edinburgh also offers first day postmarks for each new Stamp Issue. For those who like to prepare their own covers and then have them stamped with a special postmark, Royal Mail offers such a service, known as the re-posting facility, to Collectors and Dealers alike through five Special Handstamp Centres. These are located in London, South Shields, Birmingham, Cardiff, and Glasgow as follows:

Special Handstamp Centres:

London Special Handstamp Centre
Royal Mail, Mount Pleasant, Farringdon Road, LONDON, EC1A 1BB.

Northern England Special Handstamp Centre
South Shields D.O., Keppell Street, SOUTH SHIELDS, NE33 1AA.

Midland Special Handstamp Centre
Birmingham Mail Centre, St. Stephens Street, BIRMINGHAM, B6 4AA.

Wales & The West Special Handstamp Centre
Royal Mail, 220-228 Penarth Road, CARDIFF, CF11 8TA.

Scotland & Northern Ireland Special Handstamp Centre
Rutherglen D.O., Duchess Place, Rutherglen, GLASGOW, G73 1BT.

Forces Post Office
Philatelic Bureau, BFPO, West End Road, Ruislip, Middlesex HA4 6DQ.

For general information on all Handstamp Centres there is a central phone number 08457 740 740.

For information on sponsoring a special handstamp contact Royal Mail Handstamp Liaison, 21 South Gyle Crescent, Edinburgh EH12 9PB. Telephone 0845 071 2000.

Collecting Different Postmarks on Modern Covers

There are four main types of postmark listed in the catalogue for most issues. These are priced, as appropriate, for each new series of Stamps. The four postmark types are:

- Special (sponsored) Handstamps
- 'First Day of Issue' Handstamps (all issued by Royal Mail)
- Circular Date Stamps (known as cds)
- Slogan cancellations (up to 1996)

Special Handstamps – These can be in any shape and can be designed and sponsored by any individual or organisation. Such postmarks are made available at a designated Special Handstamp Centre, once approved. Details are published in the British Postmark Bulletin. Covers can be sent to the Handstamp Centre to receive the special postmark as part of the Post Office re-posting facility. Special sponsored handstamps are very popular with Collectors today.

First Day of Issue Handstamps (FDI) – These are circular postmarks incorporating the words 'First Day of Issue', the date and a town. They are done by Royal Mail and used across the country in main Post Offices on the day of issue of new Stamps. FDI's are only catalogued where the town is relevant to the Issue.

Circular Date Stamps (cds) – Also known as Counter Date Stamps. These are postmarks available through Post Offices, but only applied on the day of issue on new stamps if one of the priority services is used, i.e. Special Delivery. There is no re-posting service offered for these postmarks and items have to be handed in (not sent) at the Post Office in question. This is one of the reasons why cds are usually catalogued higher than special handstamps or FDI postmarks.

Slogan Postmarks – These were available up to 1996, when Royal Mail stopped offering a reposting service for these.

There is also a fifth group known as Royal Mail permanent handstamps. These were redesigned and first put into use in March 1997. There are currently between 40-50 of these handstamps, each one with the words Royal Mail and the name of a major city and local landmark illustration. They are available for all new Stamp Issues from the relevant Special Handstamp Centre.

Photocopy Cover Service of Postmarks in the new Catalogue

Photocopies of actual covers with most postmarks listed in this catalogue are available from the Publishers. There is a 50p charge per b&w photocopy, plus postage, towards the research and administrative costs involved in offering this service to Collectors.

It is important to always try to collect first day covers with relevant postmarks!

Introduction to the 30th Edition

Pricing Additions and General Comments on New Royal Mail Products

First Day Covers Signed by the Stamp Designer

Covers with one or more Stamps signed by the Stamp designer are worth a 20% premium over catalogue prices.

Control Numbers and/or Cylinder Numbers

Covers showing these are worth a 20 – 25% premium over catalogue prices.

Personality signed First Day Covers

Modern covers signed by a well known personality, with relevance to the Stamp Issue, are worth a premium over catalogue prices.

Postal Stationery Update 1972 – 1982

A new Section has been added at the end of the catalogue. This covers the period 1972 to 1982. Postal Stationery covers, prior to 1972, continue to be listed in the Definitives Section of the catalogue.

Generic Sheets / Commemorative Sheets

These new products from Royal Mail, usually 10 or 20 copies of a single stamp + a series of Labels, have proved difficult to track and to catalogue. Often the subject and/or date of release does not do tie in with any particular Stamp Issue. We have tried to track and catalogue these Sheets, but inevitably a few have been missed. In the next catalogue we will list all of them, probably together in a subsection of the QEII Commemoratives.

Modern Smilers Sheets

These are sheets of usually 20 copies of a single Stamp, plus blank Labels, which anyone can order personalised. Basically we have not found a way to properly catalogue these.

A Comment on cds postmarks

With all the Post Office closures of recent years, we have lost many of the classic/traditional cds postmarks. As a result it has become more and more difficult to find appropriate cds, for each new Stamp Issue.

Until such time as better information on what cds are left and who is servicing them becomes available, we have decided to stop trying to list individual cds. From mid 2008 onwards for this edition of the catalogue we, in most cases, have priced cds under the general heading of 'any relevant cds'. We hope that the situation will become clearer in due course, allowing us to go back to doing an individual listing of cds for each new Issue.

Introduction to the 30th Edition

Short Glossary of Terms

cds - Everyday circular or counter date stamp

fdi - First day of issue

fdc - First day cover

h/s - Handstamp

m/c - Machine cancel

Perfs - Perforations

Phos - Phosphor

pmk - Postmark

wmk - Watermark

BPO - British Post Office

BFPS - British Forces Postal Service

cachet cover - Text applied to envelope by rubber stamp

commemorative cover - Envelope designed to commemorate something, but not necessarily a first day issue of stamps

display cover - Text only printed on envelope

illustrated cover - Printed illustration on envelope, with text usually

handstamp - Cancellation usually of specially designed postmark.

Closing Comments

We are always looking for ways to further improve the catalogue and we hope you like the additions that we have made this time. In this edition, among other things, we have increased the QV Section and also added a new Section on updating Postal Stationery 1972/82. In terms of special Colour Features we have so far covered: Overprints, Hand Painted Covers, Blocks on fdc, Royal Anniversaries, the 1929 PUC Issue, 1924/25 Wembleys, KEVIII, The 1951 Festival of Britain and in this edition Royalty Post Cards.

The catalogue continues to progress and we are encouraged by readers comments on the usefulness and authority of the catalogue as a work of reference. We hope you will enjoy reading the 30th edition and that it will prove to be both helpful and informative throughout your stamp collecting year.

Finally, readers comments on any aspect of the catalogue are always welcome. So why not send us an email with your thoughts at some point during the coming year!

Give a friend a copy of our catalogue and get them started on collecting Stamps - *this year!*

QV Issues - Selected Covers

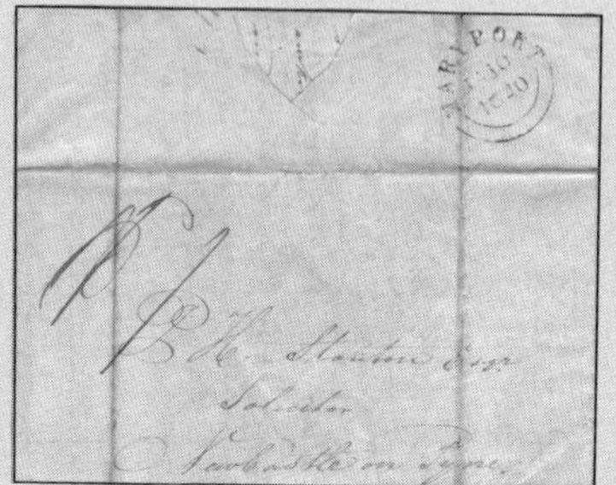

Uniform Penny Post. January 10, 1840

Stampless Envelope. May 6 1840

Penny Black. May 6, 1840

Mulready Envelope. May 6, 1840

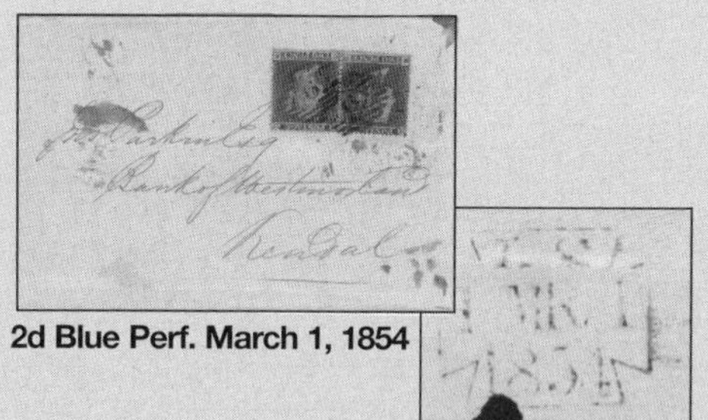

2d Blue Perf. March 1, 1854

1d Brown & 2d Blue. Feb 22, 1855

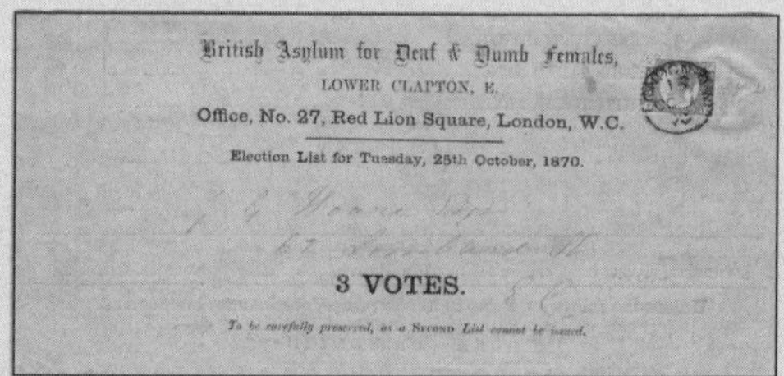

Halfpenny Stamp. October 1, 1870

QUEEN VICTORIA

Queen Victoria came to the throne on June 20th, 1837. The 1d Black, the first postage stamp in the world was issued May 6, 1840. QV reigned for 63 years! She died on January 22nd, 1901. All QV first day covers are scarce and dates for some issues difficult to confirm.

1. 1839, 5th December

Uniform 4d Post

1a Entire with date stamp, or manuscript '4' in red or black on letter dated 5th December 1839 .... **£750.00** ☐

The first serious attempt to introduce a uniform postal rate and the prelude to Rowland Hill's introduction of the penny post the following year.

1b Last day of previous rate, December 4, 1839.. **£600.00** ☐

1c Last day of Uniform 4d Post. January 9, 1840 .... **£550.00** ☐

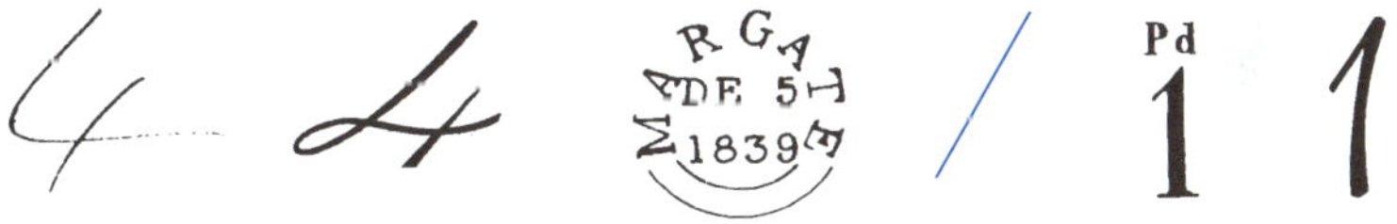

2. 1840, 10th January

Uniform 1d Post

Entire with date stamp and 1d (paid) mark .... **£750.00** ☐

First day of universal penny postage rate.

3. 1840, 6th May

The Penny Black

1d Black Imperf. with Maltese Cross cancel and date stamp .... **£35,000.00** ☐

First ever postage stamp.

4. 1840, 6th May

Stampless Envelope

Stampless envelope, postmarked Paid May 6, 1840 .... **£750.00** ☐

5. 1840, 6th May

The Mulready Envelope or Wrapper

5a 1d Mulready with Maltese Cross cancel and date stamp (usually on reverse) ..... **£4,000.00** ☐

5b Examples are known used between 1-5 May .... **from £15,000.00** ☐

5c 2d Mulready with Maltese Cross cancel and date stamp .... **£50,000.00** ☐

(5b and 5c seen in Auction 1998.)

6. 1840, 8th May

The 2d Blue Imperf.

2d Blue Imperf with Maltese Cross cancel and date stamp .... **£75,000.00** ☐

2d Blue Imperf with Maltese Cross, May 9 date stamp .... **£40,000.00** ☐

QV Issues • 1854-1880

7. 1854 – 1855

The 2d Blue Perf.

7a	2d Blue Perf 16, Plate 4, watermark small crown	Issue Date	1.3.1854	**£4,500.00**	☐
7b	2d Blue Perf 14, Plate 4, watermark small crown	Issue Date	22.2.1855	**£4,500.00**	☐
7c	2d Blue Perf 14, Plate 5, watermark small crown	Issue Date	5.7.1855	**£4,500.00**	☐
7d	2d Blue Perf 14 or Perf 16, Plate 5, wmk large crown	Issue Date	20.7.1855	**£4,500.00**	☐
7e	2d Blue Perf 16, Plate 6, watermark large crown	Issue Date	1.2.1858	**£4,500.00**	☐

8. 1855-1883

Surface Printed Issues. 2½d – 2/- Values

Stamps were (pre)released during this period, without proper regard for the official planned dates.

8a	2½d Rosy Mauve, Plate 1, Wmk Anchor	Issue Date	1.7.1875	**£3,500.00**	☐
8b	2½d Rosy Mauve, Plate 3, Wmk Orb	Issue Date	4.5.1876	**£3,000.00**	☐
8c	2½d Blue, Plate 17, Wmk Orb	Issue Date	5.2.1880	**£3,000.00**	☐
8d	3d Rose, Plate 2, Wmk Emblems	Issue Date	1.5.1862	**£3,000.00**	☐
8e	4d Carmine, Plate 1, Wmk Small Garter**	Issue Date	31.7.1855	**£5,000.00**	☐
8f	4d Carmine, Plate 1, Wmk Medium Garter	Issue Date	25.2.1856	**£4,000.00**	☐
8g	4d Vermillion, Plate 15, Wmk Large Garter	Issue Date	1.3.1876	**£4,000.00**	☐
8h	6d Lilac, Plate 1, Wmk Emblems	Issue Date	21.10.1856	**£3,500.00**	☐
8i	6d Lilac, Plate 4, Wmk Emblems	Issue Date	20.4.1864	**£3,500.00**	☐
8j	6d Lilac, Plate 5, Wmk Emblems	Issue Date	7.3.1865	**£3,500.00**	☐
8k	6d Lilac, Plate 6, Wmk Spray	Issue Date	26.6.1867	**£3,500.00**	☐
8l	6d Lilac, Plate 8, Wmk Emblems	Issue Date	8.3.1869	**£3,500.00**	☐
8m	6d Chestnut, Plate 11, Wmk Spray	Issue Date	12.4.1872	**£3,500.00**	☐
8n	6d Pale Buff, Plate 11, Wmk Spray	Issue Date	19.10.1872	**£3,500.00**	☐
8o	6d Grey, Plate 13, Wmk Spray	Issue Date	31.3.1874	**£3,500.00**	☐
8p	8d Orange, Plate 1, Wmk Large Garter	Issue Date	11.9.1876	**£3,500.00**	☐
8q	9d Straw, Plate 4, Wmk Emblems	Issue Date	1.12.1865	**£5,000.00**	☐
8r	10d Red-Brown, Plate 1, Wmk Spray	Issue Date	1.7.1867	**£5,000.00**	☐
8s	1/-Green, Plate 1, Wmk Emblems	Issue Date	1.11.1856	**£5,000.00**	☐
8t	1/-Green, Plate 8, Wmk Spray	Issue Date	1.9.1873	**£5,000.00**	☐
8u	2/-Brown, Plate 1, Wmk Spray	Issue Date	27.2.1880	**£6,000.00**	☐

8n Seen off cover (with certificate) in 2009. Value £2,750

** First ever Surface Printed Stamp!

I D
LONDON
12 AP
72

m L
LONDON
JY 1
75

m A
LONDON
MY 4
76

LONDON.W.C.
7
OC 1
70

If you have any QV first day cover not listed here, preferably with an issue date confirmed in Gibbons, please write and let us know, together with a scan of the cover, of course. Then, subject to careful study, we will list it in the next catalogue.

QV Issues • 1870-1890

9. 1870, 1st October

Halfpenny Postage

The first day of the Halfpenny printed paper rate and Halfpenny printed post card.

9a ½d Rose Red (small format) with tied cds or other postmark **£1,250.00**

The small format ½d (the "Bantam") usually occurs on an official printed voting form for the British Asylum for Deaf & Dumb Females. It is rarely seen on any other cover.

9b ½d Printed Post Card (small format) with cds or other postmark **£750.00**

9c ½d Printed Post Card (larger format) with cds or other postmark **£850.00**

10. 1880, 1st January

Penny Venetian Red

1d Venetian Red, with tied cds or other postmark **£5,500.00**

11. 1881.

New Issues

1d Lilac, Die 1, Watermark Crown, with tied postmark, ... 12.7.1881 ...... **£10,000.00**

This was the first stamp to carry the words Postage & Revenue

1/- Orange-Brown, with tied postmark, ... 24.5.1881 ...... **£3,750.00**

12. 1887-1900

Q.V. Jubilee Issue

12a 4½d Carmine, with tied cds .... 15.9.1892 ...... **£3,750.00**

12b 5d Purple and Blue, with tied cds .... 1.1.1887 ...... **£3,000.00**

12c ½d Blue-Green, with tied cds .... 17.4.1900 ...... **£1,750.00**

13. 1888, 1st February

£1 Brown-Lilac

£1 Brown-Lilac, watermark three orbs, tied cds **£7,000.00**

This stamp was sold off cover with clear postmark in 1992 (cat. £4,500).

14. 1890, 16th May and 2nd July

Uniform Penny Postage Jubilee

The Post Office produced an illustrated envelope and insert card for this occasion, possibly the first souvenir first day cover ever produced in Great Britain! A special handstamp (No.2) was used to cancel mail on July 2nd. Four souvenir handstamps (nos. 3-6) were also designed for the Jubilee, but less use was made of these on the first day in addition to the postally valid No.2 handstamp.

14a Jubilee Envelope, South Kensington special h/s No.2 (small size £70) **£50.00**

14b Jubilee Card, South Kensington special h/s No.2, large size (small size £80) **£60.00**

14c Jubilee Envelope with July 2 cds postmark **£150.00**

14d Envelope or card bearing all five special handstamps Nos. 2 - 6 .... **£180.00**

Covers/cards bearing one or more of handstamps Nos. 3-6 are valued at £75

14e Envelope or card bearing all six special handstamps. Nos. 2 (both sizes) - 6 .... **£225.00**

14f Guildhall 1d Red printed Post Card, with 16 May '90 special Guildhall h/s No.1 .... **£70.00**

2 sizes

QV Issues - Selected Covers

Last Day of use Maltese Cross.
April 30, 1844

First Halfpenny Post Card.
October 1, 1870

Signed Black Harry Furniss Card & Envelope. 1890

Penny Post Jubilee Envelope.
cds July 2, 1890

One Penny Carmine Letter Card.
February 11, 1892

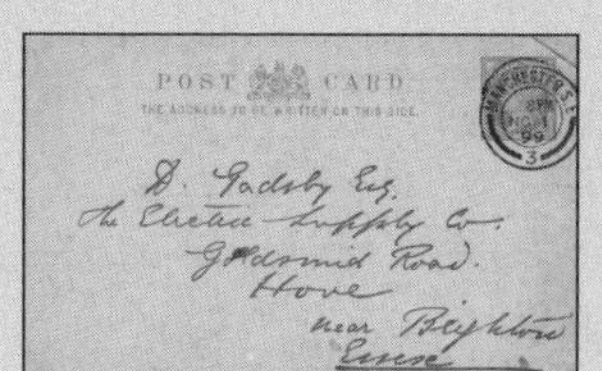

Halfpenny Red-Brown Post Card.
November 1, 1899

Halfpenny Blue-Green Stamp (2).
April 17, 1900

Queen Victoria Issues are now very difficult - and expensive - to find on first day of issue. As such they are very collectable and their value continues to increase year after year. Definitely a sound investment!

QV Issues • 1892-1901

15. 1892, 11th February
Penny Letter Card
1d Pale Carmine printed on pastel blue card, Huggins LCP1, any tied postmark ...**£1,750.00** ☐

16. 1892, 1st April
Postal Union Post Card
1d Red printed on thin buff card, Huggins CP27, any tied postmark ....**£1,750.00** ☐

16A. 1895, 21st January
Halfpenny Inland Court Size Post Card
½d Brown on buff card, Huggins CP29a, any postmark ....**£1,750.00** ☐

17. 1899 - 1901
Halfpenny Post Cards
17a ½d Red-Brown on thin buff card 1.11.99, Huggins CP31a, any postmark............**£1,650.00** ☐
17b ½d Green on thick white card 1.1.01, Huggins CP38a, any postmark..................**£1,450.00** ☐

More Memorable QV dates...

1840, 16th January
Parliamentary Privilege Envelope
First Day of Issue

1841, January
1d Mulready Envelope
Withdrawn from sale

1841, 10th February
1d red-Brown. Imperf.
Printed from 'black' plate on blued paper
First Day of Issue. Confirmed in Gibbons.
Not seen on cover.

1841, 10th February
1d Pink Embossed Envelope
First Day of Issue
Seen in Grosvenor Auction 2009

1844
Mulready 1d and 2d Letter Sheets
Withdrawn from use

1855, 31st July
Surface Printed Stamps
First Day of Issue

1841, 6th January
Registered Letter
First recorded Day of Use

1841, April
2d Mulready Envelope
Withdrawn from sale

1841, 10th February
Maltese Cross in Black
First Day of Use

1844, 30th April
Maltese Cross Cancellation
Last Day of Use - in red or black
See cover on opposite page

1854, 28th January
Henry Archer Trial Perforation
First Day of Use

1855
Stamped to Order Stationery
First Introduced

18h

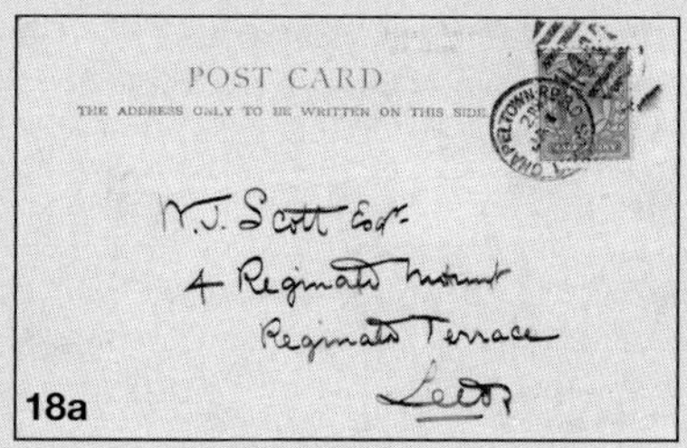
18a

18c

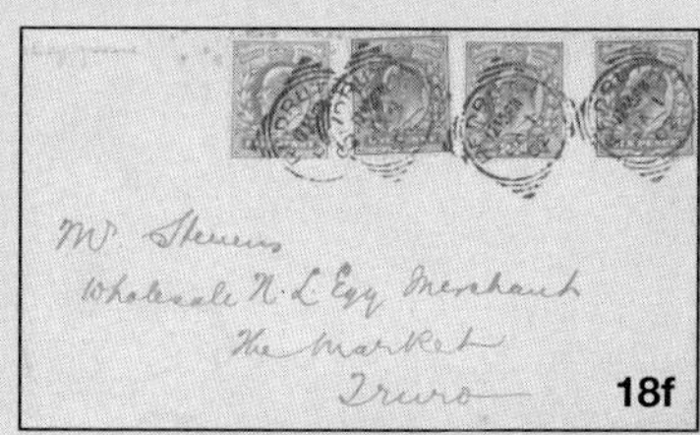
18f

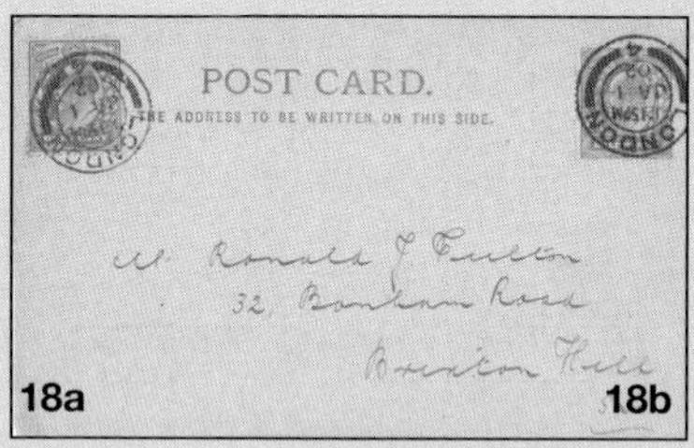
18a 18b

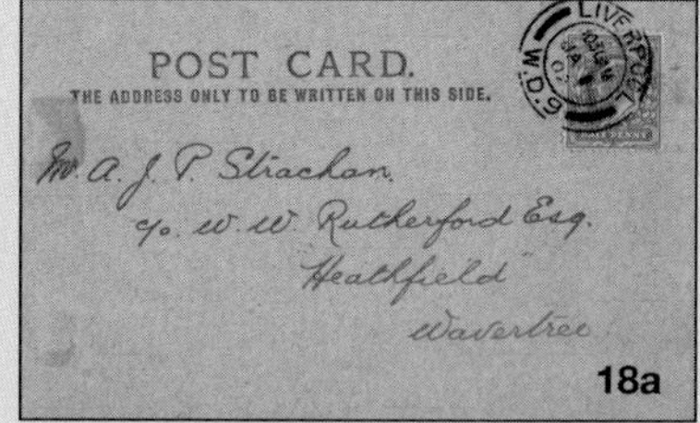
18a

19

KING EDWARD VII

Edward VII, born in 1841, came to the throne at the age of 60 and reigned for nine years, Jan 1901 - May 1910. He was a much travelled man and was often referred to as Edward the Peacemaker. Relatively few stamps were issued during his short reign.

18. 1902, 1st January
First Definitive Issue

18a ½d Green on plain envelope or post card, cds postmark .... **£150.00** ☐
18b 1d Red on plain envelope or post card, cds postmark .... **£150.00** ☐
18c 1d Red on Sandringham, Norfolk printed card with Sandringham cds .... **£515.00** ☐
18d 2½d Blue on plain envelope, cds postmark .... **£375.00** ☐
18e 6d Purple on plain envelope, cds postmark .... **£600.00** ☐
18f All four stamps on one cover, cds postmark .... **£1,400.00** ☐
18g Set on plain cover, with Parliament St. cds .... **£1,800.00** ☐
18h Royalty Picture postcard, with ½d Green, any postmark .... **£465.00** ☐
7d seen off cover in 1996, dated Aug 1, 1912 - first day Somerset printing

SANDRINGHAM JA 1 02 — PARLIAMENT ST C JA 1 02 S.W. — LONDON 12.30 PM OC 1 08 FS8 — WOODFORD GREEN NO 1 09

19. 1908, 1st October
First Penny Postage to the USA
Special commemorative envelope published by the Junior Philatelic Society.
Printed in black, with 1902 1d Red stamp cancelled OC.1.08 .... **£250.00** ☐

20. 1909, November - December
4d De La Rue Printing

20a 4d Orange, Perf. 14, De La Rue printing ....Issue Date 1.11.09 .... **£2,500.00** ☐
20b 4d Orange-Red, Perf. 14, De La Rue printing ....Issue Date 1.12.09 .... **£2,500.00** ☐
Both stamps seen off cover in 1999 and valued at £1,650.00 each.

21. 1911, July
Harrison & Sons Printing*. Perf 14. Imperial Crown wmk

21a 2½d Bright Blue ....Issue Date 10.7.11 .... **£2,250.00** ☐
21b 4d Bright Orange ....Issue Date 12.7.11 .... **£2,500.00** ☐

22. 1911, September - October
Harrison & Sons Printing*. Perf 15x14. Imperial Crown wmk

22a Halfpenny Dull Green, ...Issue Date 30.10.11 .... **£2,500.00** ☐
Seen on cover in 2005
22b 1d Rose-Red, ...Issue Date 4.10.11 .... **£2,500.00** ☐
Seen on cover in 2005
22c 3d Purple-Lemon, ...Issue Date 18.9.11 .... **£2,500.00** ☐
Seen off cover in 1992 and valued at £1,750

*When Harrison & Sons took over the Inland Revenue stamp printing contract from De La Rue on January 1st, 1911, it was apparent that insufficient stocks of stamps were available. So despite the King's death the previous year, further printings were made by Harrison & Sons, using the original KEVII plates!

23. Not assigned.

The Definitive Issue of King Edward VII is well documented by Stanley Gibbons and others. Dates are given by them for all values, colours and printings (De La Rue and Harrison). However, few values have been seen on first day cover.

KGV Issues - Selected Covers

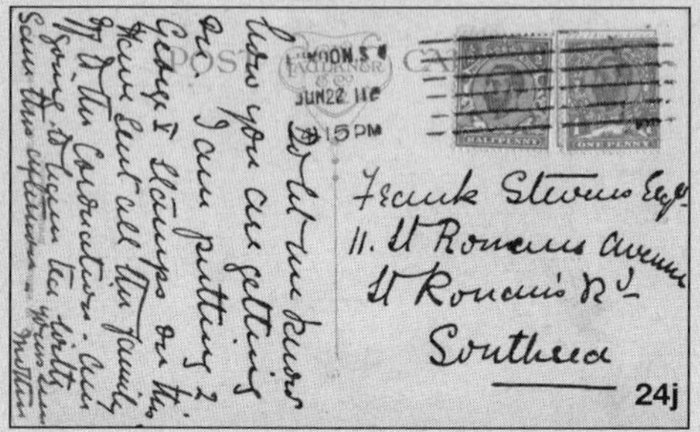

24j

24b

24c 24i

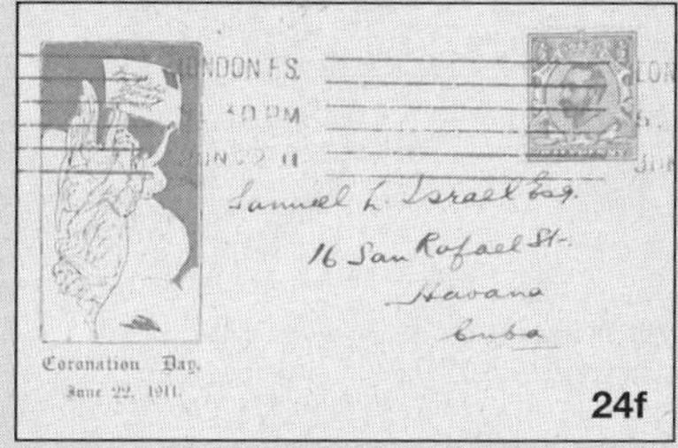

24f

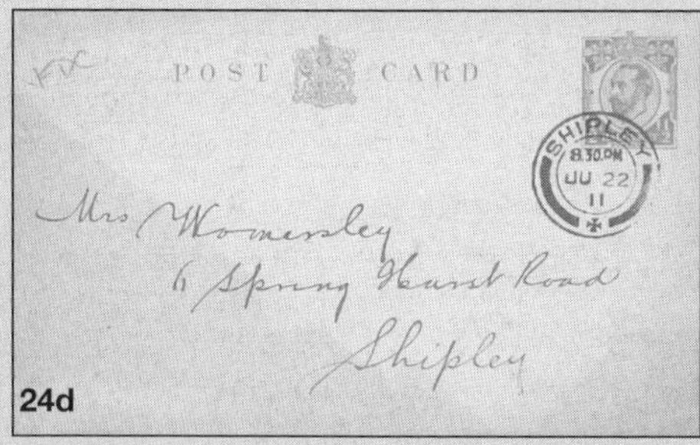

24d

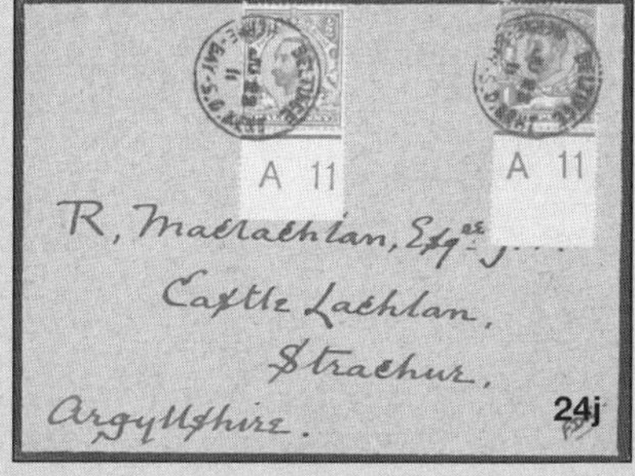

24j

24a

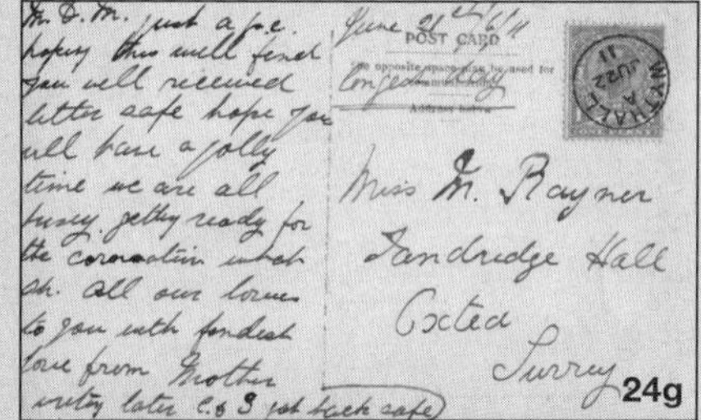

24g

KING GEORGE V

George V was born in June 1865. He came to the throne on May 6th, 1910 and was crowned on June 22nd, 1911. KGV reigned for 26 years. His Silver Jubilee was held on May 6th, 1935. He died on January 20th, 1936. King George V was a keen philatelist.

24. 1911, 22nd June

Coronation Day (Downey Head) Definitives

24a	½d Green, plain envelope or post card, any postmark	£75.00 ☐
24b	½d Green, plain envelope, Westminster Abbey cds	£3,000.00 ☐
24c	½d Green on illustrated Coronation post card, machine cancel	£350.00 ☐
24d	½d Printed post card, any postmark	£150.00 ☐
24e	½d Printed post card with ½d and 1d Stamps added, any pmk	£250.00 ☐
24f	½d Junior Philatelic Society envelope, machine cancel	£300.00 ☐
24g	1d Red, plain envelope or post card, any postmark	£60.00 ☐
24h	1d Red, plain envelope, Westminster Abbey cds	£3,500.00 ☐
24i	1d Red on illustrated Coronation post card, machine cancel	£400.00 ☐
24j	½d and 1d both on one envelope, any postmark	£160.00 ☐

24b and 24g together on one cover £6,000.

WESTMINSTER ABBEY B JU 22 11

MANCHESTER 8. 30 PM JUN 22 11A

The September 1911 Coronation Aerial Post

The first official mail carrying flight by an aeroplane was made at Allahabad in India in February 1911. It was organised by Captain Walter S. Windham RN. On his return to the UK soon afterwards, it was he who organised the first UK Aerial Post between Hendon and Windsor in September of the same year.

A specially designed post card and envelope was prepared and pre-stamped with the new KGV ½d and 1d postage stamps. These were the rates in force at the time. Only the special souvenir card and envelope (in various colours) was authorized to be carried on the First UK Aerial Post flights. A special handstamp was designed for the event.

The cost of the pre-stamped post card was set at 6½d and the commemorative envelope at 1/1d. Special mail boxes were set up in London (postmark Dies 1-4) and at Hendon (postmark Dies 5-6) for posting the pre-stamped post cards and letters.

Special 'privilege' commemorative post cards and envelopes with the design in violet were also prepared. These were not available to the general public and are thus both scarce and valuable.

The first London to Windsor flight took place on September 9, 1911. The first Windsor to London flight is postmarked September 16, 1911, it actually took place on Sunday, September 17.

See page 20 for selected covers and page 22 for pricing.

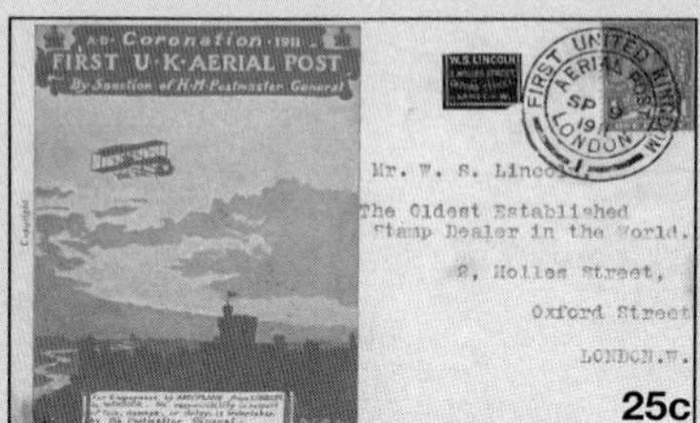

25c

25c

25a

25e

25g

25g

violet 25d

violet 25h

violet 25f

violet 25b

KGV Issues - Selected Covers 1912/14

30a

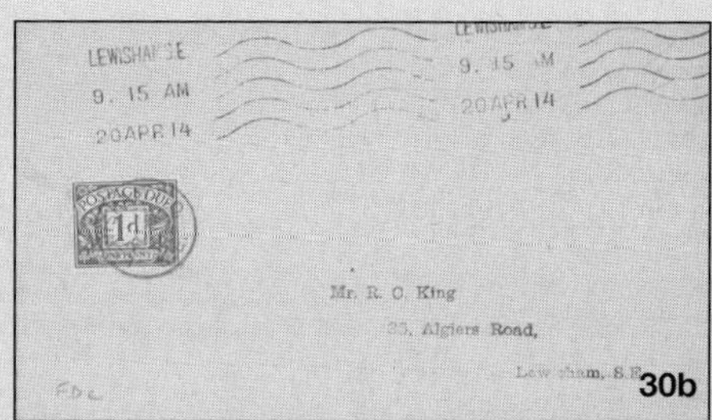

30b

30c

27

28a

28c

28c 28e

28h

KGV Issues • 1911 - 1912

25. 1911, 9th September

First UK Aerial Post. London-Windsor

25a ½d Green Coronation stamp, commemorative post card, (red-brown/dark brown/olive) with special First United Kingdom Aerial Post, London handstamp .... **£85.00** ☐

25b ½d on 'privileged' violet post card, with special handstamp .... **£700.00** ☐

25c 1d Red Coronation stamp on commemorative envelope (scarlet/purple-brown/deep green/ deep brown/red-brown) special First United Kingdom Aerial Post, London h/s .... **£100.00** ☐

25d 1d on 'privileged' violet envelope, with special handstamp .... **£675.00** ☐

1911, 16th September

First UK Aerial Post. Windsor-London

25e ½d Green Coronation stamp, commemorative post card, (olive-green) with special First United Kingdom Aerial Post, Windsor handstamp .... **£90.00** ☐

25f ½d on 'privileged' violet post card, with special handstamp .... **£625.00** ☐

25g 1d Red Coronation stamp on commemorative envelope (olive-green) with special First United Kingdom Aerial Post, Windsor handstamp .... **£115.00** ☐

25h 1d on 'privileged' violet envelope, with special handstamp .... **£650.00** ☐

These are important commemorative covers (not first day covers), marking the beginning of Air Mail service in the UK. See page 19 for more details.

---

26. 1912, 1st January

Redrawn Downey Head Definitives

½d and 1d values with crown watermark .... **£1,500.00** ☐

Single value on cover with cds postmark .... **£850.00** ☐

1912, 2nd October

The Last Downey Head Issue

½d or 1d value, with multiple cypher watermark, cds postmark .... **£850.00** ☐

27. 1912, 25th January

Wilkinson Experimental Meter Mail

Envelope with Meter Mark and London E.C. cds (last day £250) .... **£300.00** ☐

The original Wilkinson machine, modified by the Post Office, was used experimentally from January 25th to August 31st, 1912. It is considered to be the forerunner of meter mail, which was finally introduced in 1922.

See Special Feature on Royalty Post Cards on pages 160 – 176

KGV Issues • 1912 - 1924

28. 1912-1913

The Profile Head Definitives, Watermark Royal Cypher

28a	½d Green, plain envelope, any postmark	Issue Date	17.1.13	**£1,250.00**	☐
28b	1d Red, plain envelope, any postmark	Issue Date	8.10.12	**£1,000.00**	☐
28c	1½d Brown, plain envelope, any postmark	Issue Date	15.10.12	**£850.00**	☐
28d	2d Orange, plain envelope, any postmark	Issue Date	20.8.12	**£2,000.00**	☐
28e	2½d Blue, plain envelope, any postmark	Issue Date	18.10.12	**£850.00**	☐
28f	3d Violet, plain envelope, any postmark	Issue Date	9.10.12	**£2,000.00**	☐
28g	4d Grey, plain envelope, any postmark	Issue Date	15.1.13	**£2,000.00**	☐
28h	5d Brown, plain envelope, any postmark	Issue Date	30.6.13	**£3,500.00**	☐
28i	6d Purple, plain envelope, any postmark	Issue Date	1.8.13	**£3,000.00**	☐
28j	7d Olive, plain envelope, any postmark	Issue Date	1.8.13	**£3,000.00**	☐
28k	8d Black on Yellow, plain envelope, any postmark	Issue Date	1.8.13	**£3,000.00**	☐
28l	9d Grey-Black, plain envelope, any postmark	Issue Date	30.6.13	**£3,500.00**	☐
28m	10d Turquoise, plain envelope, any postmark	Issue Date	1.8.13	**£3,000.00**	☐
28n	1/- Bistre-Brown, plain envelope, any postmark	Issue Date	1.8.13	**£3,000.00**	☐

These are very rare covers. The 1½d and 2½d were issued during the International Stamp Exhibition in London and usually have a special Exhibition handstamp cancel. The 5d and 9d are known on one cover and are valued at £4,000. The 1½d and 2½d also exist on one double dated cover, value £2,750.

At least one set of this Issue is known on piece.
These are valued at 70% of the above catalogue prices.

---

29. 1913, 30th June

Waterlow 'Sea-Horses' High Values

2/6d Brown, plain cover, any tied postmark .... **£3,500.00** ☐

Seen off cover in 1993 and 1995, valued at £2,350.

No first day dates have been confirmed for the other three high values, all issued in 1913.

30. 1914, 20th April

The First Ever Postage Dues

30a	½d Green, plain envelope or post card, tied cds	**£750.00**	☐
30b	1d Red, plain envelope or post card, tied cds	**£500.00**	☐
30c	2d Black, plain envelope, tied cds	**£700.00**	☐
30d	5d Brown, plain envelope, tied cds	**£2,500.00**	☐
30e	4d Blue, plain envelope with tied cds, 23rd December 1920	**£3,500.00**	☐

31. 1924, 23rd April

British Empire Exhibition, Wembley

1d Red and 1½d Brown, set on one or two plain covers

31a	Set with Empire Exhibition, Wembley Park 1924 handstamp	**£265.00**	☐
31b	Set with Empire Exhibition, Wembley Park 1924 slogan, machine cancel	**£250.00**	☐
31c	Set with Palace of Industry special Exhibition handstamp (single value £350)	**£750.00**	☐
31d	Set with Palace of Engineering Special Exhibition h/s (single value £375)	**£850.00**	☐
31e	Set on Harmers display cover, Exhibition machine cancel	**£325.00**	☐
31f	1d Red on Exhibition Picture Post Card, slogan or handstamp cancel	**£300.00**	☐

KGV Issues - Selected Covers 1924/25

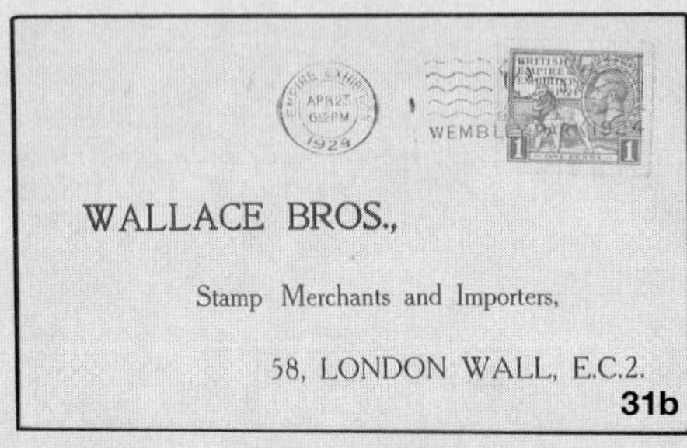

31b

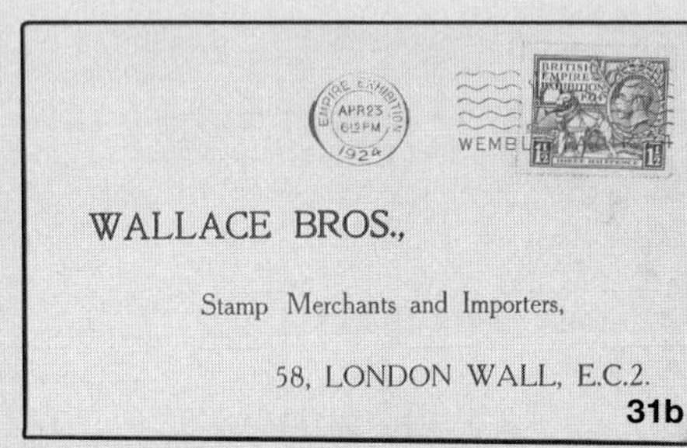

31b

31e

31c

31b

33c

33b

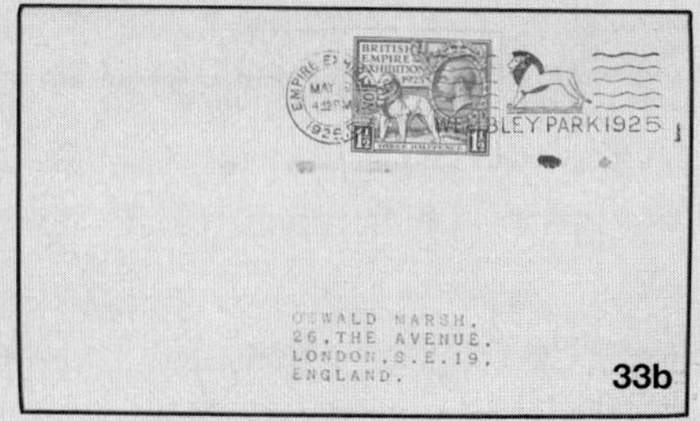

33b

KGV Issues - Selected Covers 1924/29

32a

32f

32d

32c

35f

35g

35a

35a

32. 1924, 23rd April

Postal Stationery of the 1924 Exhibition

32a 1d Printed post card, Exhibition machine cancel (handstamp **£160**) **£145.00** ☐
32b 1d Printed post card, Palace of Industry handstamp **£250.00** ☐
32c 1½d Printed UPU post card, Exhibition machine cancel (handstamp **£150**) **£200.00** ☐
32d 1½d Printed letter card, Exhibition machine cancel (handstamp **£160**) **£180.00** ☐
32e 1½d Printed letter card, Palace of Industry Exhibition handstamp **£275.00** ☐
32f 1½d Printed envelope, Exhibition machine cancel (handstamp **£160**) **£145.00** ☐

33. 1925, 9th May

British Empire Exhibition, Wembley

1d Red and 1½d Brown, set on one or two plain covers

33a With Empire Exhibition, Wembley Park 1925 handstamp **£1,350.00** ☐
33b With Empire Exhibition, Wembley Park 1925 slogan cancel **£1,250.00** ☐
33c With Palace of Industry special Exhibition handstamp (single value £900) **£1,900.00** ☐
33d Exhibition picture post card, with 1d value, machine cancel **£700.00** ☐
33e 1d Red on Souvenir Telegram with Govt. Pavilion handstamp **£2,850.00** ☐

34. 1925, 9th May

Postal Stationery of the 1925 Exhibition

34a 1d Printed post card, Exhibition machine cancel **£350.00** ☐
34b 1½d Printed UPU post card, Exhibition machine cancel **£425.00** ☐
34c 1½d Printed letter card, Exhibition machine cancel **£350.00** ☐
34d 1½d Printed envelope, Exhibition machine cancel **£325.00** ☐

35. 1929, 10th May

Universal Postal Union Congress, London

35a ½d Green, 1d Red, 1½d Brown, 2½d Blue, plain cover, any postmark **£350.00** ☐
35b With London Chief Office, registered handstamp **£550.00** ☐
35c With PUC Congress special handstamp **£1,000.00** ☐
35d With PUC Congress special handstamp on Congress envelope* **£1,500.00** ☐
35e With PUC Congress registered oval cancel **£2,000.00** ☐
35f PUC Congress Card, low values set, PUC handstamp **£2,000.00** ☐
35g PUC Congress Card + ½d + 1d PUC h/s first day, 1½d + 2½d PUC h/s last day **£3,500.00** ☐
35h £1 on plain cover, any postmark **£5,750.00** ☐
35i £1 on plain cover with PUC Congress special handstamp **£8,250.00** ☐
35j £1 on PUC envelope, with PUC postmark **£8,500.00** ☐
35k Full set of five values on plain cover, or matching covers, any postmark **£6,750.00** ☐
35l Large size printed PUC writing paper, all five values, PUC handstamp **£7,500.00** ☐
35m Small size printed PUC note paper, all five values, PUC handstamp **£8,600.00** ☐
35n Small size printed PUC note paper, four low values, PUC handstamp **£1,400.00** ☐

*There were two types of Congress envelope, one was plain white with embossed flap, the other was brown with printed text on front and on flap. The Congress closed on June 28, 1929.

KGV Issues • 1934 - 1936

36. 1934-1936

The Photogravure Definitives

36a ½d Green, plain cover, any postmark ....Issue Date 19.11.34..........**£12.50** ☐
36b ½d Green, plain cover, London F.S. Air Mail cds ....Issue Date 19.11.34 ....**£85.00** ☐
This was the first day of 3d overseas air mail. Covers had 2½d postage added.
36c 1d Scarlet, plain cover, any postmark ....Issue Date 24.9.34..........**£12.50** ☐
36d 1½d Brown, plain cover, any postmark ....Issue Date 20.8.34..........**£12.50** ☐
36e 1½d Brown on illustrated Railway Air Services cover................Issue Date 20.8.34..........**£40.00** ☐
36f 1½d Brown small format thinner paper, plain cover.............Issue Date 31.7.35........**£200.00** ☐
36g 2d Orange, plain cover, any postmark ....Issue Date 21.1.35..........**£25.00** ☐
36h 2d Orange on printed cachet cover, any postmark ....Issue Date 21.1.35..........**£40.00** ☐
36i 2½d Blue, plain cover, any postmark ....Issue Date 18.3.35..........**£30.00** ☐
36j 3d Violet, plain cover, any postmark ....Issue Date 18.3.35..........**£40.00** ☐
36k 2½d and 3d on one plain cover, any postmark ....Issue Date 18.3.35..........**£85.00** ☐
36l 4d Grey-Green, plain cover, any postmark ....Issue Date 2.12.35..........**£95.00** ☐
36m 5d Brown, plain cover, any postmark ....Issue Date 17.2.36 **£1,350.00** ☐
36n 9d Olive-Green, plain cover, any postmark ....Issue Date 2.12.35........**£185.00** ☐
36o 4d and 9d on one plain cover, any postmark ....Issue Date 2.12.35........**£275.00** ☐
36p 4d and 9d on one plain cover, George St. cds ....Issue Date 2.12.35........**£800.00** ☐
36q 10d Blue, plain cover, any postmark ....Issue Date 24.2.36 ....**£1,000.00** ☐
36r 1/- Brown, plain cover, any postmark ....Issue Date 24.2.36 ....**£1,000.00** ☐
36s Complete set on one cover (with all dates). Posted nine times!...............................**£3,500.00** ☐
The ½d, 1d, 1½d, and 2d values exist on Alcock Philatelic Advisor illustrated covers. These are scarce and add 300% to above catalogue values. Any value with Kingston postmark add 50%.

36A. 1934, 16th October

2/6d Brown Sea-Horse, Re-engraved

36Aa 2/6d Brown Sea-Horse, Swansea cds or Huddersfield cds ....**£3,500** ☐

---

37. 1935, 7th May

Silver Jubilee Issue

37a ½d Green, 1d Red, 1½d Brown, 2½d Blue, one or more plain covers, any pmk.............**£80.00** ☐
37b With Windsor, cds or machine cancel (single value £50) ....**£200.00** ☐
37c With London SW1, cds or machine cancel ....**£150.00** ☐
37d With Royal Parade, Yorks cds ....**£200.00** ☐
37e Set on one or more commemorative covers, any postmark..**£450.00** ☐
37f Same with Windsor, cds or machine cancel (single value **£135**) ....**£750.00** ☐
37g With London SW1, cds or machine cancel ....**£600.00** ☐
37h Any value on KGV Royalty post card, any postmark...**£185.00** ☐
37i 1½d value on Lusitania commemorative cover, any postmark ....**£195.00** ☐
37j Booklet stamps ½d, 1d, 1½d, plain cover, any postmark...**£225.00** ☐
Forgeries exist on Westminster Stamp Co (nonembossed) cover. Value £55.

37f

37e

37e

37e

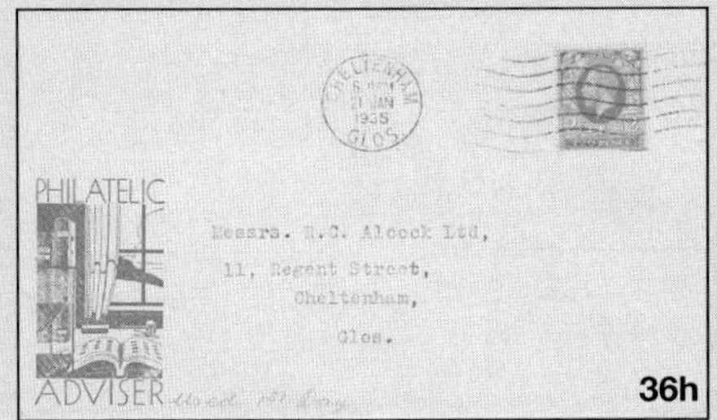

36h

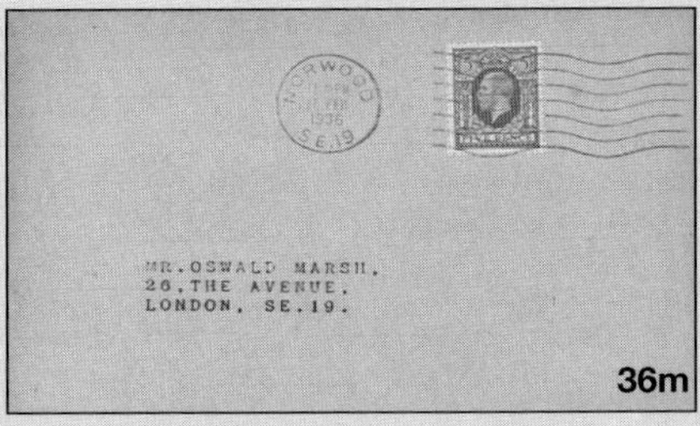

36m

36q

36r

KEVIII Issues - Selected Covers 1936

38f

38j

38f

38j

38f

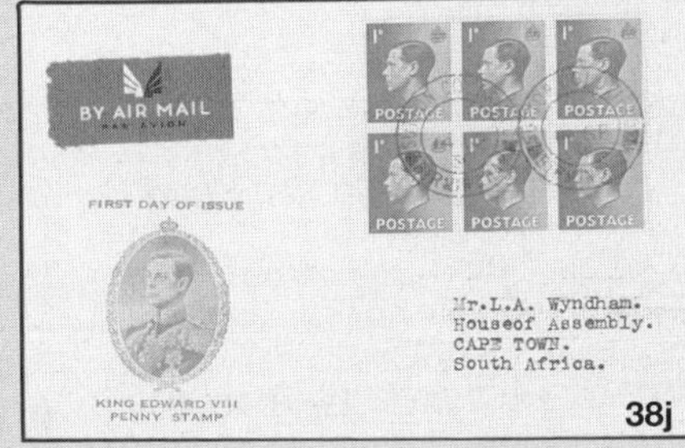

38j

38b

38i

KING EDWARD VIII

Edward VIII came to the throne on January 20th, 1936. He abdicated just over 10 months later in favour of his brother Albert (King George VI) on December 10th, 1936. As Duke of Windsor he married Mrs. Simpson on June 3rd, 1937 in France.

38. 1936, 1st and 14th September

New Definitives

38a ½d Green, 1½d Brown, 2½d Blue on plain cover, any pmk......Issue Date 1.9.36 ....**£8.00** ☐
38b On plain cover, King Edward Banff cds ....Issue Date 1.9.36 ......**£110.00** ☐
38c On plain or display cover, Windsor cds ....Issue Date 1.9.36 ......**£165.00** ☐
38d On plain cover, Queen Street, or King Street cds ....Issue Date 1.9.36 ......**£150.00** ☐
38e On plain cover, Kingston, or Charlton Kings cds.....................Issue Date 1.9.36 ......**£145.00** ☐
38f On commemorative cover, any postmark ....Issue Date 1.9.36 ......**£125.00** ☐
38g With Kingstanding cds ....Issue Date 1.9.36 ......**£210.00** ☐
38h 1d Red on plain cover or post card, any postmark ....Issue Date 14.9.36 ....**£12.00** ☐
38i On plain cover, King Edward Banff cds, or Windsor cds ....Issue Date 14.9.36 ......**£125.00** ☐
38j On commemorative cover, any postmark ....Issue Date 14.9.36 ......**£145.00** ☐
38k ½d Green or 1d Red on KEVIII illustrated (portrait) post card, any pmk ....**£175.00** ☐

---

39. 1936, 26th October

New Definitives Overprint Issue

Morocco Agencies British - 1d, 2½d values: Morocco Agencies French - 1d, 1½d values
Morocco Agencies Spanish - ½d, 1d, 1½d, 2½d: Tangier (British currency) - ½d, 1d, 1½d

39a Complete set as above, eleven values, on one plain cover, with British Foreign Post Office cancel ....**£60.00** ☐
39b Complete set on four separate plain covers, with British Foreign P.O. cancel..............**£65.00** ☐
39c Set of eleven values on four Selfridges printed philatelic post cards ....**£70.00** ☐

40. 1936, 10th December

Announcement of Abdication

40a Set of 4 stamps on plain cover, any postmark...**£35.00** ☐
40b Set on plain cover, King Edward Banff cds ....**£90.00** ☐
40c Set on plain cover, House of Commons, or Windsor cds..**£185.00** ☐
40d Set on illustrated cover, any postmark (Windsor cds **£215**) ....**£110.00** ☐

All of these are abdication covers and not first day covers of the four definitive stamps. Plain covers dated 11th December, the first day of abdication, also exist and are catalogued with the full set of stamps at £20.00

1937, 3rd June

Wedding Day. Monts, France

Any Illustrated cover, with French stamp and Monts cds ....**£35.00** ☐
Any Illustrated cover, with any GB stamp and Windsor cds ....**£50.00** ☐

Photocopies of actual covers with most postmarks listed in this catalogue, are available from the Publishers! See Introduction for details and cost.

KGVI Issues - Selected Covers 1937/51

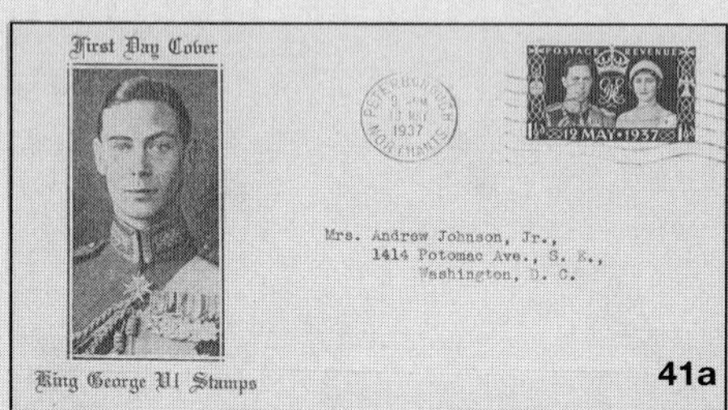

41a

42g

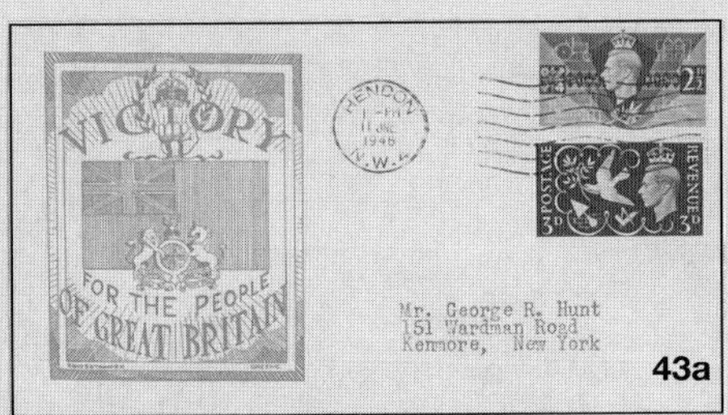

43a

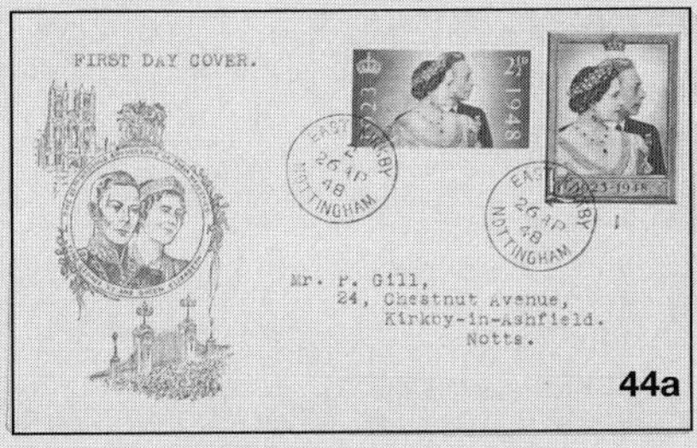

44a

46d

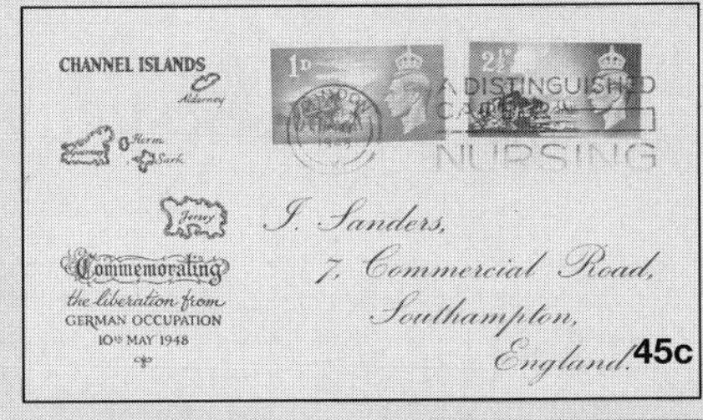

45c

47a

48d

KING GEORGE VI

Commemoratives

From the very beginning of King George VI reign, many different illustrated covers were produced for all new commemorative stamp issues. These were done privately, primarily by dealers, and were widely available to collectors at the time - and still today. As a result plain covers of KGVI commemorative issues have little value, and therefore are not catalogued, with a few exceptions and special postmarks.

41. 1937, 13th May

Coronation Issue 1½d Brown

41a	Commemorative (illustrated) cover, any postmark	**£25.00** ☐
41b	Commemorative (display text) cover, any postmark	**£168.00** ☐
41c	Coronation Goodwill Flight cover, flown by Dick Merrill from USA and back	**£36.00** ☐
41d	Commemorative cover, Windsor cds or machine cancel	**£168.00** ☐
41e	Any commemorative cover, London SW1 machine cancel	**£35.00** ☐
41f	Any commemorative cover, Kingston, Kingsley or Kingston Vale cds	**£55.00** ☐
41g	Souvenir Coronation post card, any postmark	**£60.00** ☐
41h	Commemorative cover, St. George (Exeter) cds, or George Town cds	**£78.00** ☐
41i	Commemorative cover, King Street, or George St. (Aberdeen) cds	**£78.00** ☐
41j	Commemorative cover, Ville au Roi, Guernsey cds	**£85.00** ☐
41k	Hampton Court Camp, Kensington Gardens Camp, any cover	**£195.00** ☐
41l	Pirbright Camp cds, any cover (Regents Park Camp cds **£60**)	**£190.00** ☐
41m	Windsor Castle cds, any cover	**£230.00** ☐
41n	King Edward Hospital Fund Coronation cover, in full colour, South Kensington cds	**£260.00** ☐

There were over 200 different display/commemorative covers produced for this issue!

42. 1940, 6th May

Centenary of First Adhesive Postage Stamp

½d Green, 1d Red, 1½d Brown, 2d Orange, 2½d Blue, 3d Violet

42a	Set on commemorative cover, Stamp Centenary Bournemouth handstamp	**£47.50** ☐
42b	With 27th Philatelic Congress, Bournemouth handstamp	**£100.00** ☐
42c	With Stamp Centenary (Red Cross), London handstamp in red	**£55.00** ☐
42d	Set with any other postmark on commemorative cover	**£35.00** ☐
42e	Set on 2 Mulready copy envelopes, 27th Philatelic Congress handstamp	**£160.00** ☐
42f	Set on Perkins Bacon cover (black or blue), Stamp Centenary London h/s	**£87.50** ☐
42g	Set on Chalmers illustrated cover, with Arbroath, or Dundee Angus cds	**£185.00** ☐
42h	Set on plain cover, printed address (British Pavilion NY Worlds Fair). London cds	**£40.00** ☐
42i	Set with Bournemouth (Pavilion) cds, any cover (single stamp **£75**)	**£275.00** ☐

Full set with Pavilion pmk seen in 2003

KGVI • Commemoratives 1946-48

43. 1946, 11th June
Victory Issue 2½d Blue, 3d Violet

43a Set on commemorative cover, any postmark .... **£45.00** ☐
43b With "Don't Waste Bread ..." slogan cancel .... **£75.00** ☐
43c With London Chief Office ECI postmark .... **£60.00** ☐
43d With any Jersey or Guernsey postmark .... **£80.00** ☐
43e With House of Commons cds .... **£135.00** ☐
43f Set on cachet cover or covers, with "Canadian Overseas P.D." special UK cds .... **£150.00** ☐

44. 1948, 26th April
Royal Silver Wedding 2½d Ultramarine, £1 Blue

44a Set on commemorative cover, any postmark .... **£325.00** ☐
44b Set on two matching commemorative covers .... **£285.00** ☐
44c Set on one or two government envelopes, with House of Commons cds .... **£425.00** ☐
44d Set on plain cover, George Town, Jersey cds .... **£285.00** ☐
44e 2½d only on commemorative cover, any postmark .... **£20.00** ☐
44f £1 only on commemorative cover, any postmark (on plain cover £65) .... **£200.00** ☐
44g Set on plain cover, any postmark (Duke of York's School cds £150) .... **£80.00** ☐
44h 2½d on plain cover, Buckingham Palace cds .... **£225.00** ☐

45. 1948, 10th May
Channel Isles Liberation, 3rd Anniversary 1d Scarlet, 2½d Blue

45a Set on commemorative cover, any British postmark .... **£30.00** ☐
45b With "British Industries Fair ..." machine cancel .... **£110.00** ☐
45c With "A Distinguished Career - Nursing" machine cancel .... **£75.00** ☐

Any of the above postmarks on plain covers would be valued at 50% of catalogue price.
Please refer to Early Channel Isles section for Guernsey and Jersey cancellations

46. 1948, 29th July
Olympic Games, Wembley
2½d Blue, 3d Violet, 6d Purple, 1/- Brown

46a Set on commemorative cover, any postmark .... **£30.00** ☐
46b With Olympic Games slogan cancel .... **£45.00** ☐
46c With Wembley, Middlesex handstamp .... **£55.00** ☐
46d With both slogan cancel and Wembley handstamp .... **£75.00** ☐
46e With Wembley registered cds (see below). Nos 11-16 used at Games .... **£110.00** ☐
46f With Wembley, Middx machine cancel .... **£60.00** ☐
46g 6d Air letter, with Olympic Games slogan cancel .... **£35.00** ☐
46h Set plus the five Monaco Olympic Games stamps, on one illustrated cover .... **£165.00** ☐

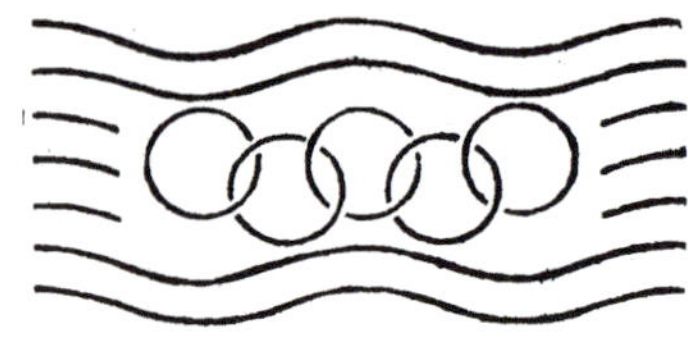

KGVI • Commemoratives 1949-51

47. 1949, 10th October
Universal Postal Union, 75th Anniversary
2½d Blue, 3d Violet, 6d Purple, 1/- Brown

47a Set on commemorative cover, any postmark .... **£55.00** ☐
47b With London Chief Office EC1 cds .... **£95.00** ☐
47c With Balmoral Castle registered handstamp .... **£110.00** ☐
47d Post card of UPU Statue, Bern. Any value, any postmark .... **£80.00** ☐

48. 1951, 3rd May
Festival of Britain, London 2½d Scarlet, 4d Ultramarine

48a Set on commemorative cover, any postmark .... **£30.00** ☐
48b With London S.E.1 postmark .... **£45.00** ☐
48c With Glasgow or Belfast cds .... **£60.00** ☐
48d With Battersea machine cancel, or Battersea cds .... **£65.00** ☐
48e With Festival of Britain slogan, cancelled in Cardiff .... **£400.00** ☐
48f With Field Post Office cds, usually on British Forces Iraq cover .... **£65.00** ☐
48g Set on souvenir card, any postmark .... **£80.00** ☐

The Festival Engineering Exhibition was held in Glasgow and the Festival Industry /Agriculture Exhibition was held in Belfast.

48h Set with May 4th special Festival handstamp .... **£12.50** ☐
48i Set with May 4th special Festival machine cancel .... **£18.50** ☐

These special Festival cancels were not available for use on the issue day of the Stamps. The Exhibition itself opened on May 4th, 1951.

Valuation Guide for GB Blocks of 4 on fdc

1840 to 1900 - three times the single fdc value
1902 to 1936 - two and a half times the single fdc value
1936 KEVIII - twice the single fdc value
1937 to 1951 - twice the single fdc value
1952 to date - one and a half times the single fdc value

KGVI • Definitives 1937-48

Few illustrated covers were available for the early KGVI Definitives. Most prices are therefore for plain covers, as indicated in the text, for issues prior to 1950.

49. 1937 - 1939, 1947

First Low Value Definitives

49a	½d Green, 1d Red, 2½d Blue on commemorative cover	10.5.37	**£20.00**	☐
49b	With Windsor machine cancel (Parliament St **£75**)	10.5.37	**£125.00**	☐
49c	With Kingstanding Road cds, Kingston Vale cds, or King St cds	10.5.37	**£60.00**	☐
49d	With Hampton Court Camp special registered h/s	10.5.37	**£75.00**	☐
49e	With Kensington Gardens Camp special registered cds	10.5.37	**£85.00**	☐
49f	1½d Brown on commemorative cover, any postmark	30.7.37	**£35.00**	☐
49g	1½d Brown on plain cover, any postmark	30.7.37	**£5.00**	☐
49h	1½d Brown with Sandringham, Norfolk (registered) cds	30.7.37	**£65.00**	☐
49i	2d Orange and 3d Violet on commemorative cover, any pmk	31.1.38	**£85.00**	☐
49j	Same on one or two plain covers, any postmark	31.1.38	**£18.00**	☐
49k	4d Grey-Green and 5d Light Brown, on one or two plain covers	21.11.38	**£25.00**	☐
49l	4d and 5d on plain cover, Windsor, Berks cds	21.11.38	**£150.00**	☐
49m	6d Light Purple on plain cover, any postmark	30.1.39	**£30.00**	☐
49n	7d Green and 8d Carmine, on one or two plain covers	27.2.39	**£35.00**	☐
49o	9d Olive-Green, on plain cover, any postmark	1.5.39	**£75.00**	☐
49p	10d Turquoise, on plain cover, any postmark	1.5.39	**£80.00**	☐
49q	11d Plum, on plain cover, any postmark	29.12.47	**£35.00**	☐
49r	11d on illustrated cover, any postmark	29.12.47	**£90.00**	☐
49s	1/- Brown, on plain cover, any postmark	1.5.39	**£80.00**	☐
49t	9d, 10d, 1/- all on one plain cover, any postmark	1.5.39	**£250.00**	☐
49u	Set of 14 values on one cover, plus Coronation stamp. Posted eight times!		**£1,800.00**	☐
49v	½d, 1d, 1½d from 2/- Booklet, plain cover	21.8.37	**£450.00**	☐

York Town and two Kingston postmarks exist for most values and are worth 50% over above prices.

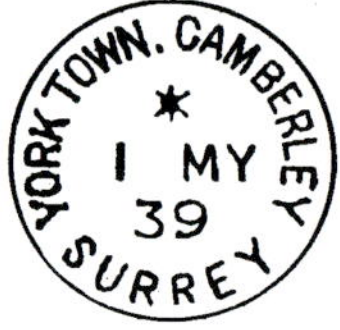

50. 1939-1941

Postal Stationery

50a	1½d Brown printed envelope (small size)	Issue Date	2.3.39	**£35.00**	☐
50b	1½d Brown letter card	Issue Date	26.1.40	**£27.50**	☐
50c	1½d Brown printed envelope (standard size)	Issue Date	29.4.40	**£32.00**	☐
50d	2½d Blue letter card	Issue Date	24.7.40	**£35.00**	☐
50e	2½d Blue printed envelope (standard size)	Issue Date	15.10.40	**£35.00**	☐
50f	2½d Blue prisoner of war air mail letter	Issue Date	21.7.41	**£47.50**	☐
50g	4½d Burgundy printed registered envelope	Issue Date	30.4.40	**£40.00**	☐

51. 1939-1942, 1948

The Arms High Values

51a	2/6d Brown, plain cover, any postmark	Issue Date	4.9.39	**£950.00**	☐
51b	2/6d Yellow-Green, plain cover, any postmark	Issue Date	9.3.42	**£750.00**	☐
51c	5/- Red, plain cover, any postmark	Issue Date	21.8.39	**£400.00**	☐
51d	10/- Dark Blue, plain cover, Northern Ireland cds	Issue Date	3.10.39	**£2,250.00**	☐
51e	10/- Dark Blue, any England/Scotland/Wales pmk	Issue Date	30.10.39	**£1,750.00**	☐
51f	10/- Ultramarine, plain cover, any postmark	Issue Date	30.11.42	**£2,000.00**	☐
51g	£1 Brown, plain cover, any postmark	Issue Date	1.10.48	**£140.00**	☐

The 10/- Dark Blue seems to have been released in Northern Ireland ahead of the rest of the U.K.

KGVI • Definitives 1941-51

52. 1941-1942

Low Value Definitives - Pale Colours

52a ½d Pale Green, plain cover, any postmark ....Issue Date 1.9.41............**£15.00** ☐
52b On display cover, any postmark ....Issue Date 1.9.41............**£50.00** ☐
52c 1d Pale Scarlet, plain cover, any postmark ....Issue Date 11.8.41............**£15.00** ☐
52d On display cover, any postmark ....Issue Date 11.8.41............**£50.00** ☐
52e 1½d Pale Brown, plain cover, any postmark ....Issue Date 28.9.42............**£40.00** ☐
52f On display cover, any postmark ....Issue Date 28.9.42............**£65.00** ☐
52g 2d Pale Orange, plain cover, any postmark ....Issue Date 6.10.41............**£25.00** ☐
52h On display cover, any postmark ....Issue Date 6.10.41............**£55.00** ☐
52i 2½d Pale Ultramarine, plain cover, any postmark ....Issue Date 21.7.41............**£25.00** ☐
52j On display cover, any postmark ....Issue Date 21.7.41............**£60.00** ☐
52k 3d Pale Violet, plain cover, any postmark ....Issue Date 3.11.41............**£80.00** ☐
52l On display cover, any postmark ....Issue Date 3.11.41 ....**£115.00** ☐

Kingston postmarks exist for all of the above values and are worth £20 over prices above.

53. 1950, 2nd October

4d Definitive Colour Change

53a 4d Light Ultramarine, plain cover, any postmark..**£18.00** ☐
53b With Kingston cds cancel ....**£50.00** ☐
53c On illustrated cover, any postmark..**£85.00** ☐

54. 1951, 3rd May

Festival Low Value Definitives - Colour Change

½d Orange, 1d Blue, 1½d Green, 2d Brown, 2½d Red

54a Set on plain cover, any pmk (**£5**), on illustrated cover, any pmk ....**£40.00** ☐
54b Set on plain cover with Kingston cds cancel ....**£45.00** ☐
54c Set on plain cover with House of Commons SWI cds, or Parliament St cds ....**£80.00** ☐
54d Set on illustrated cover(s), Festival of Britain, Cardiff slogan ....**£425.00** ☐
54e Set on illustrated cover, Battersea cds ....**£100.00** ☐
54f Set on illustrated cover, Windsor cds or machine cancel ....**£160.00** ☐
54g 1/- Booklet stamps on illustrated cover, any postmark ....**£350.00** ☐

55. 1951, 3rd May

Festival High Value Definitives

2/6d Green, 5/- Red, 10/- Blue, £1 Brown

55a Set on one or more plain covers, any postmark ....**£85.00** ☐
55b Set on one or more illustrated covers, any postmark ....**£650.00** ☐
55c Set on illustrated cover, Battersea cds or machine cancel ....**£950.00** ☐
55d Set on plain cover(s), Windsor cds/reg. cds, or machine cancel ....**£1,250.00** ☐
55e Set plus the five Festival low values, all on one plain cover ....**£100.00** ☐
55f Same all on one illustrated cover, any postmark ....**£750.00** ☐

Items 55e or 55f with the two Festival commemoratives added, are worth 15% over catalogue price.

WINDSOR * 3 MY 51 BERKS

REGISTERED 3 MY 51 1 WINDSOR BERKS.

WINDSOR 10-AM 3 MAY 1951 BERKS.

---

56. 1951, 3rd May

New (Festival) Postal Stationery

56a 2d Brown printed post card, any postmark..**£35.00** ☐
56b 2½d Red printed envelope, any postmark ....**£32.00** ☐
56c 2½d Red printed letter card, any postmark..**£38.00** ☐

KGVI Issues - Selected Covers 1937/42

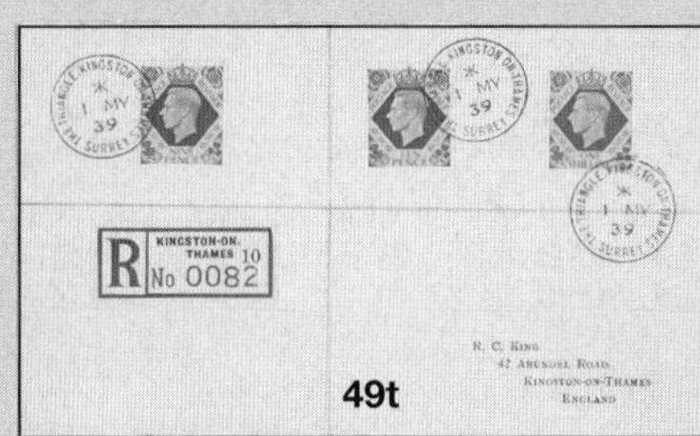

KGVI Issues - Selected Covers 1939/51

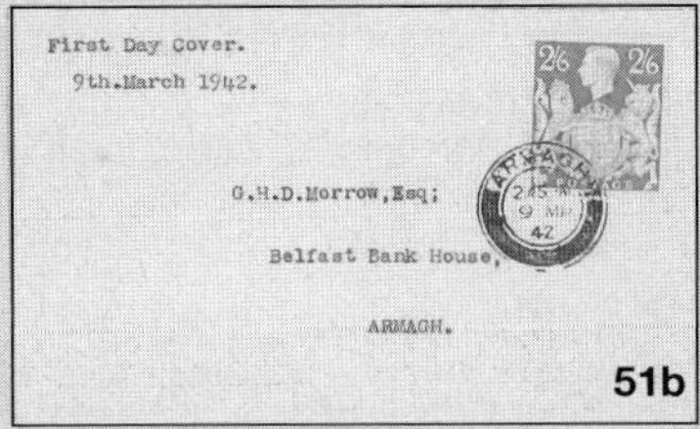

51b

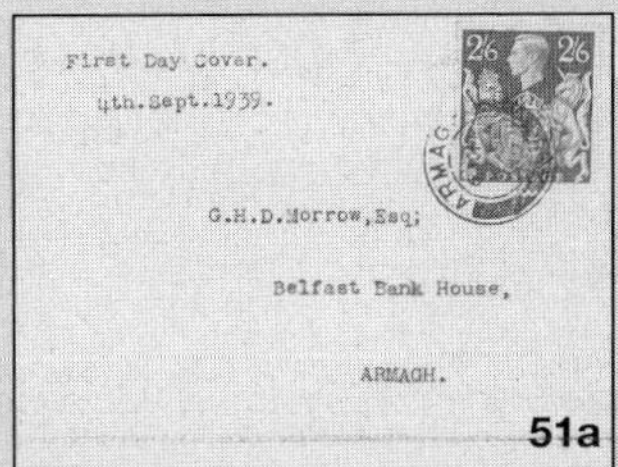

51a

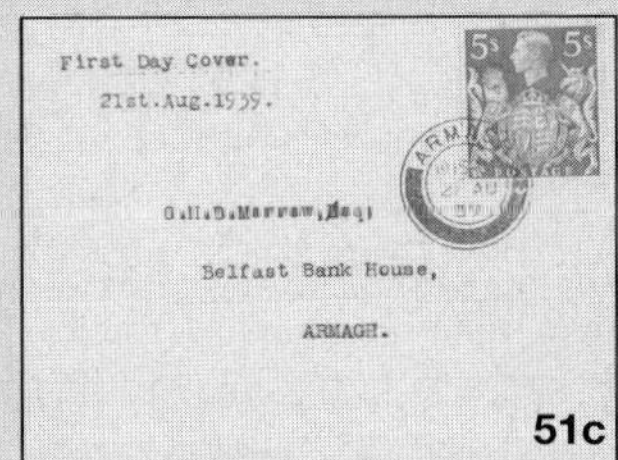

51c

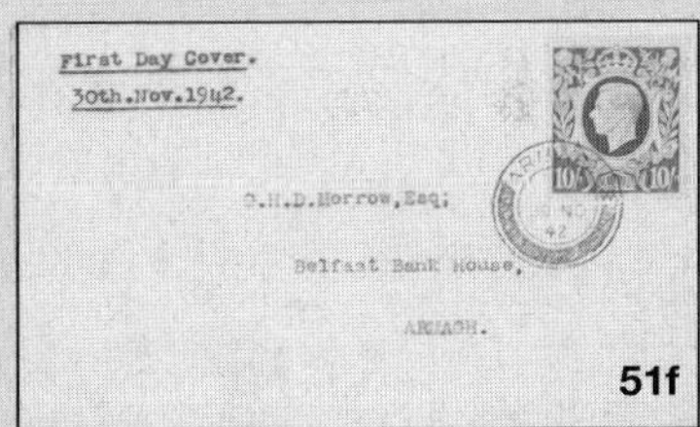

51f

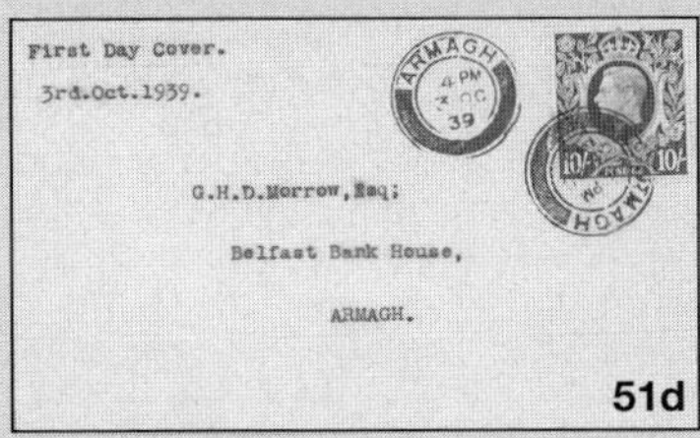

51d

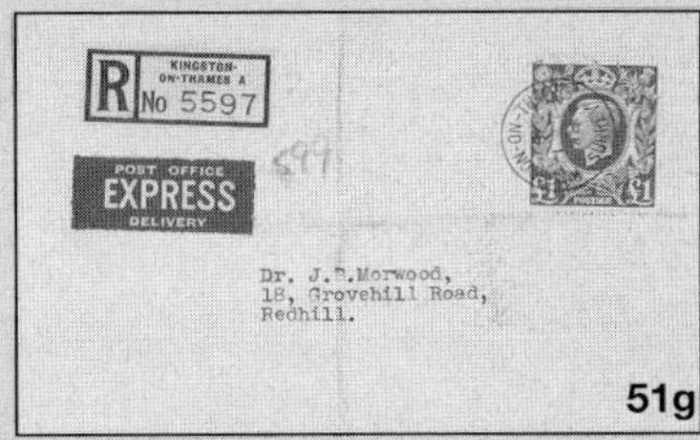

51g

54a

55b

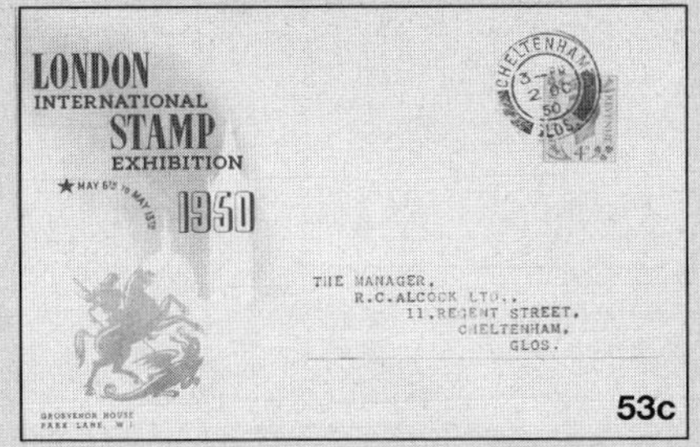

53c

Gems • 1948 BMA Overprint Set

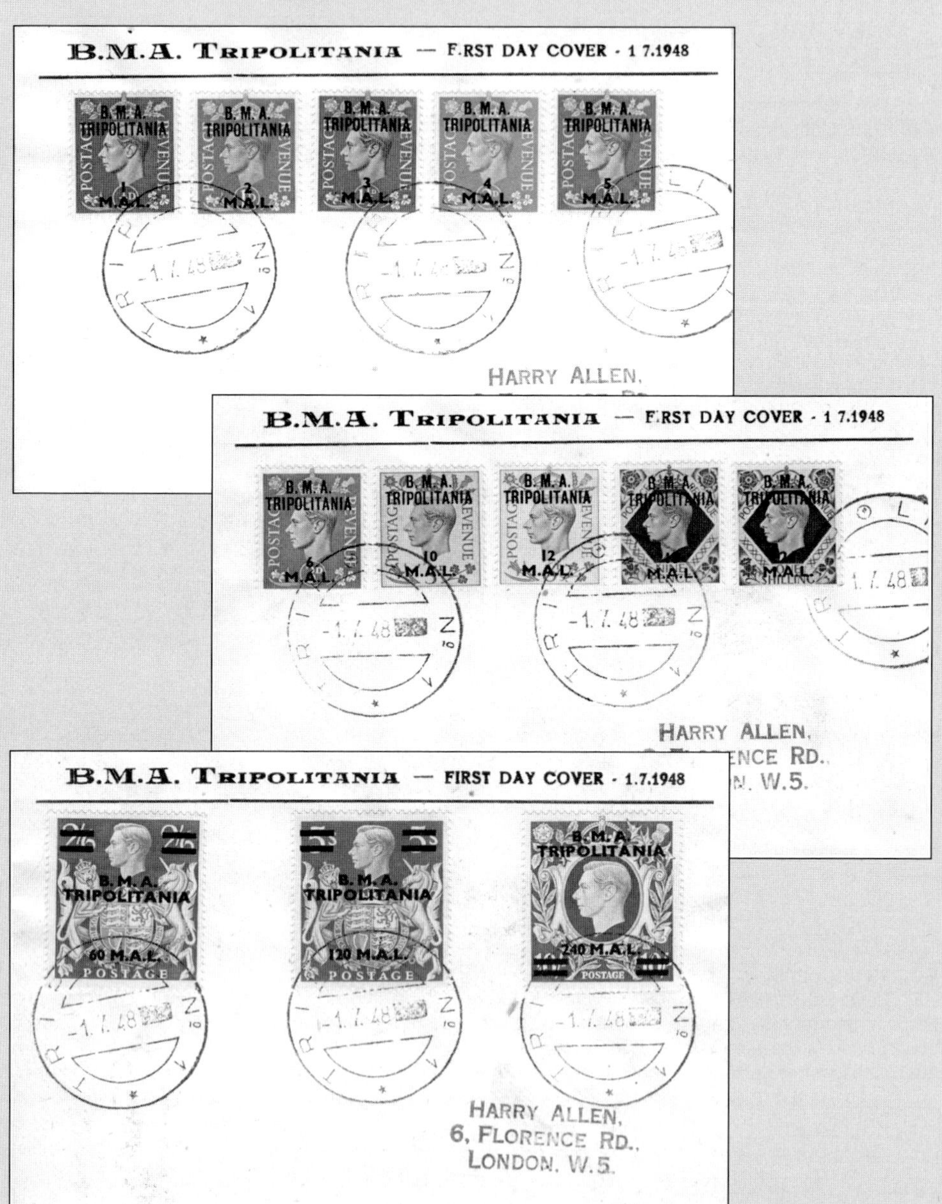

Scarce British Military Administration Set for Tripolitania, First Day Cover July 1st, 1948.

KGVI • Channel Isles

GUERNSEY 1940-48

57. 1940, 27th December

The 2d Orange Bisects, Provisional Issue

57a KGVI Definitive 2d Orange, plain cover or post card, any local postmark .... **£40.00** ☐
57b KGVI Centenary 2d Orange, plain cover or post card, any local postmark .... **£30.00** ☐
57c KGV Gravure 2d Orange, plain cover or post card, any local postmark .... **£90.00** ☐
57d KGV Royal Cypher 2d Orange, plain cover or post card, any local postmark .... **£125.00** ☐

Covers were also done with the KGVI 1d definitive or 1d Centenary stamp added and as such are worth an extra 40% over the above catalogue values. The bisecting of 2d stamps was authorised because of the shortage of 1d stamps on the Island.

58. 1941 -1944

Guernsey Arms Definitives

58a ½d Green, plain cover or post card ....Issue Date 7.4.41 .... **£5.00** ☐
58b ½d Green, display cover or post card ....Issue Date 7.4.41 .... **£40.00** ☐
58c 1d Scarlet, plain cover or post card ....Issue Date 18.2.41 .... **£5.00** ☐
58d 1d Scarlet, display cover or post card ....Issue Date 18.2.41 .... **£40.00** ☐
58e 2½d Ultramarine, plain cover or post card ....Issue Date 12.4.44 .... **£17.50** ☐
58f 2½d Ultramarine, display cover ....Issue Date 12.4.44 .... **£65.00** ☐
58g All three stamps on one plain cover, posted three times .... **£90.00** ☐

The above set, plus the Centenary bisect on one plain cover, each stamp with first day cds, £160.00. The same four stamps plus the 1948 Liberation pair on the reverse, all stamps on one cover, each with first day cancel £185.00.

Bank Note Paper

58h ½d Green, plain cover or post card ....Issue Date 11.3.42 .... **£275.00** ☐
58i 1d Scarlet, plain cover or post card ....Issue Date 9.4.42 .... **£85.00** ☐

59. 1946, 11th June

Victory Issue (GB Stamps) on Channel Isles Commemorative Cover

59a 2½d Blue and 3d Violet with Alderney cds .... **£95.00** ☐
59b With Sark cds .... **£110.00** ☐
59c With any Guernsey postmark .... **£65.00** ☐

60. 1948, 10th May

Liberation, 3rd Anniversary

60a 1d Scarlet and 2½d Ultramarine, plain cover, Guernsey postmark .... **£5.00** ☐
60b Set on commemorative cover, Guernsey postmark .... **£30.00** ☐
60c On commemorative cover, Sark cds .... **£65.00** ☐
60d On commemorative cover, Alderney cds .... **£60.00** ☐
60e Set with Sark or Alderney cds on plain cover .... **£20.00** ☐

All prices in this catalogue are for clean covers, with undamaged stamps and clear postmarks.

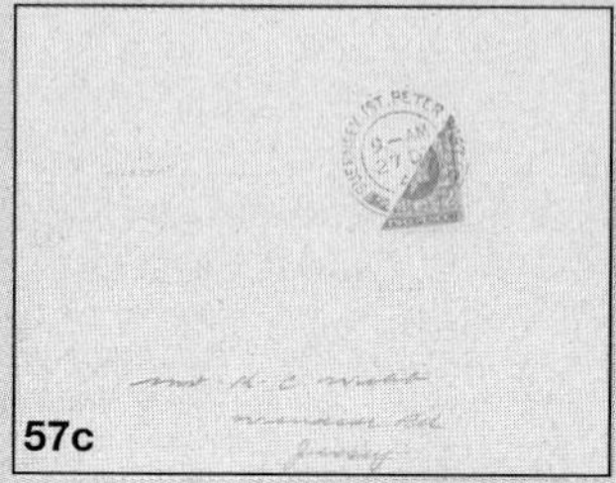
57c

57d

58b

58d

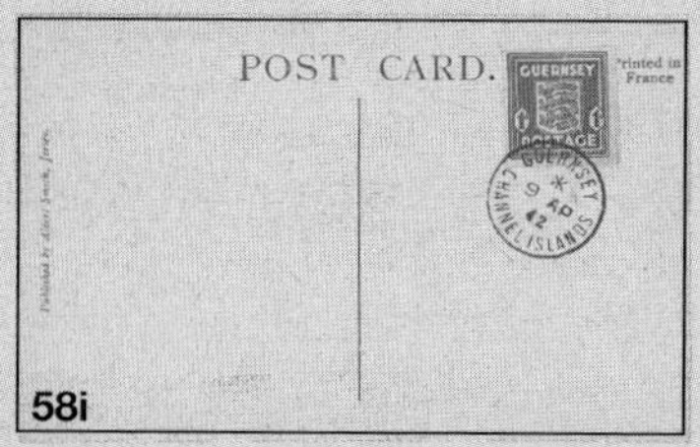

58i

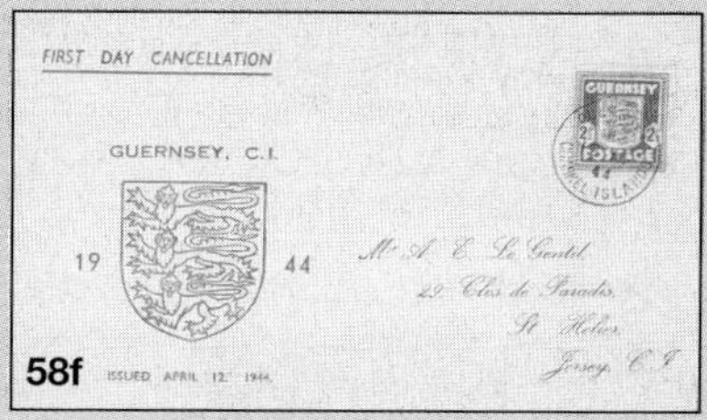

58f

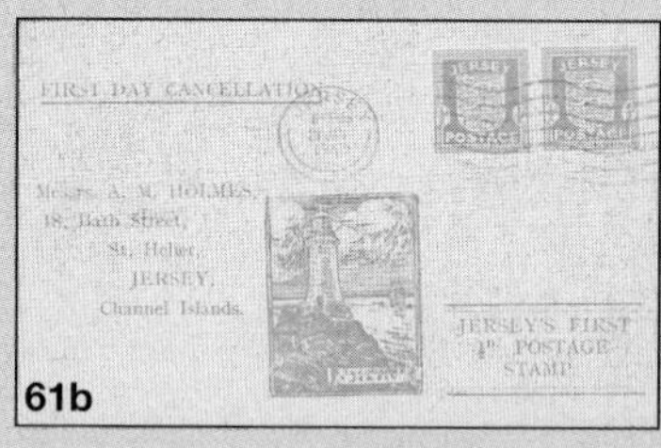

61b

61d

62k

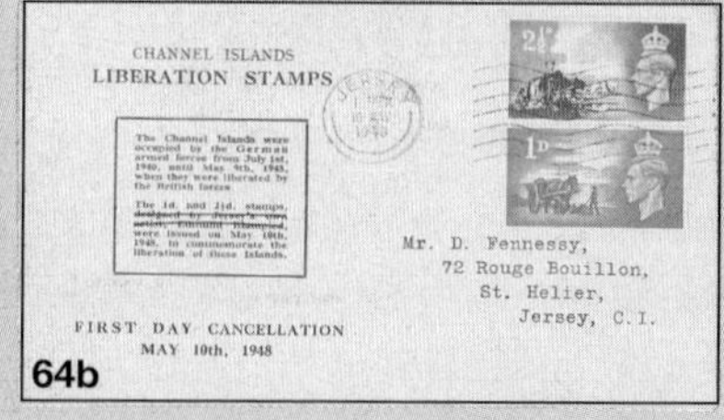

64b

KGVI • Channel Isles

JERSEY 1941-48

61. 1941-1942
Jersey Arms Definitives

61a	½d Green, plain cover or post card	Issue Date 29.1.42	£5.00 ☐
61b	½d Green, display cover or post card	Issue Date 29.1.42	£40.00 ☐
61c	1d Scarlet, plain cover or post card	Issue Date 1.4.41	£5.00 ☐
61d	1d Scarlet, display cover or post card	Issue Date 1.4.41	£40.00 ☐
61e	Both stamps on plain cover, posted twice		£60.00 ☐
61f	Complete sheet ½d Green, each stamp cancelled	Issue Date 29.1.42	£285.00 ☐
61g	Complete sheet 1d Scarlet, each stamp cancelled	Issue Date 1.4.41	£285.00 ☐

62. 1943, June
Jersey Views Set

62a	½d Green and 1d Scarlet on 1 or 2 plain covers/ post cards	Issue Date 1.6.43	£15.00 ☐
62b	Same on display cover(s) or display post card(s)	Issue Date 1.6.43	£30.00 ☐
62c	½d, 1d gutter pairs on two covers	Issue Date 1.6.43	£55.00 ☐
62d	1½d Brown and 2d Orange on 1 or 2 plain covers/post cards	Issue Date 8.6.43	£25.00 ☐
62e	Same on display cover(s) or display post card(s)	Issue Date 8.6.43	£40.00 ☐
62f	1½d, 2d gutter pairs on two covers	Issue Date 8.6.43	£65.00 ☐
62g	2½d Blue and 3d Violet on 1 or 2 plain cover(s) post cards	Issue Date 29.6.43	£30.00 ☐
62h	Same on display cover(s) or display post card(s)	Issue Date 29.6.43	£50.00 ☐
62i	2½d, 3d gutter pairs on two covers	Issue Date 29.6.43	£75.00 ☐
62j	Set on three covers with German Eagle and Swastika handstamp, any cds		£150.00 ☐
62k	Set on one cover, each stamp with first day cds		£85.00 ☐
62l	Full sheets, any value, with one or more first day cancels		£225.00 ☐
62m	Last Day Cover. Jersey Views, plus Guernsey Arms and Banknote pair, plus Jersey Arms, all on one display cover dated 13 April 1946. Any Guernsey or Jersey cds		£60.00 ☐

63. 1946, 11th June
Victory Issue (GB Stamps) on Channel Isles Commemorative Cover

63a	2½d Blue and 3d Violet, Jersey "Don't Waste Bread ..." slogan cancel	£125.00 ☐
63b	Set with any Jersey postmark	£65.00 ☐

64. 1948, 10th May
Liberation, 3rd Anniversary

64a	1d Scarlet and 2½d Ultramarine, plain cover, Jersey postmark	£5.00 ☐
64b	Set on commemorative cover, Jersey postmark	£30.00 ☐
64c	Complete sheet of each value, cancelled with Gorey, Jersey cds, or other	£600.00 ☐
64d	Complete sheet of each value, cancelled with George Town, Jersey cds	£950.00 ☐

Gems • 1953 Coronation Day Pre-Release

Unique QEII Pre-release cover, June 2nd

Buckingham Palace cds on a Palace embossed envelope. Whilst this postmark is known on fdc, this is believed to be the only Buckingham Palace Pre-release cds – and it is on a Palace envelope!

QUEEN ELIZABETH II

Commemoratives

Queen Elizabeth II succeeded to the throne in February 1952. She was crowned on June 2nd 1953. As the current monarch she has been on the throne for over 53 years. During this time Royal Mail (the Post Office) has made much progress in terms of GB stamp design and the marketing of philatelic products.

Pre-Decimal Issues

Illustrated covers were widely available for all commemorative issues, starting with the Coronation in 1953. Catalogue prices from here on are for clean illustrated covers with the full set of stamps as issued, unless otherwise stated. Hand addressed illustrated covers are acceptable up to 1965, but from 1966 onwards prices are for covers with typed or printed addresses or neat printed labels. An exception is made to this rule in the case of a rare postmark with a value of over £75.

65. 1953, 3rd June
Coronation Issue 2½d Red, 4d Ultramarine, 1/3d Green, 1/6d Grey-Blue

65a Full set on commemorative cover, any postmark (pre-release June 2nd **£200**) ....**£30.00** □
65b With London postmark ....**£45.00** □
65c With 'Long Live the Queen' slogan cancel, any office ....**£60.00** □
65d With 'Long Live the Queen' slogan, London F.S or London SW1 ....**£85.00** □
65e With Buckingham Gate, Queen Street, Queen's Head, or Queensferry cds ....**£125.00** □
65f On one or more covers with 'Long Live the Queen' slogan, Windsor ....**£300.00** □
65g Set on commemorative cover with Henlow Camp cds ....**£330.00** □
65h Set on commemorative cover with Windsor cds or reg. oval handstamp ....**£250.00** □
65i Set on commemorative cover with Arundel cds ....**£190.00** □
65j With Buckingham Palace cds (pre-release June 2nd Coronation Day **£2,750**) .....**£1,500.00** □
65k Set on commemorative cover with Windsor Castle cds ....**£1,250.00** □
65l Set on commemorative cover with Sandringham cds ....**£1,200.00** □
65m Set on Qantas Coronation cover, London F.S. slogan ....**£185.00** □
65n 2½d, 4d on Qantas air letter, London F.S. postmark ....**£55.00** □
65o Coronation air letter, with printed 6d red, London slogan (Windsor slogan **£50**) ....**£20.00** □
65p Set on Coronation Souvenir letter card, London cds ....**£85.00** □
65q 2½d only on set of ten regional Coronation envelopes ....**£125.00** □
65r Coronation post cards – scene or portrait, single stamp (2½d cat. **£20**) ....**£35.00** □

Qantas covers are usually franked with only one of the 2½d, 1/3d or 1/6d values, these are catalogued at £25 each. Qantas covers are very rare with the 4d value or with the full set.

Please refer to notes at the beginning of this catalogue for additional information

QEII • Commemoratives 1957-60

66. 1957, 1st August

World Scout Jubilee Jamboree 2½d Red, 4d Ultramarine, 1/3d Green

66a Set on Illustrated cover, any postmark .... **£17.50** ☐
66b With Sutton Coldfield slogan cancel (slogan with town name **£38**) .... **£25.00** ☐
66c With Sutton Coldfield cds .... **£150.00** ☐
66d Cover overprinted 'Royal Visit August 3rd', full set , Sutton Coldfield slogan 3.8.57. .**£45.00** ☐
66e 2½d on cover for First British Megaton Trial 1957, BFPO Christmas Island cds .... **£65.00** ☐
66f Set on plain cover with BFPO Christmas Island cds .... **£80.00** ☐

67. 1957, 12th September

46th Inter-Parliamentary Conference 4d Ultramarine

67a 4d stamp on illustrated cover, any postmark.......... **£65.00** ☐
67b With 46th Parliamentary Conference, London SWI special handstamp .... **£95.00** ☐
67c With Northern Parliament, Belfast cds .... **£265.00** ☐
67d With House of Commons or House of Lords cds.......... **£285.00** ☐
67e Air letter with 6d red overprinted, special conference handstamp .... **£45.00** ☐

68. 1958, 18th July

Sixth British Empire and Commonwealth Games

3d Lilac, 6d Purple-Red, 1/3d Green

68a Set on illustrated cover, any postmark .... **£35.00** ☐
68b With Games slogan cancel, Cardiff.......... **£80.00** ☐
68c With Games slogan cancel, Llanberis.......... **£90.00** ☐
68d With Games slogan cancel, Barry. .... **£85.00** ☐
68e Set on illustrated cover, Empire Games Village, Barry registered postmark .... **£385.00** ☐
68f Same with Empire Games Village, Barry cds, or Mobile P.O. cds.......... **£280.00** ☐

---

69. 1960, 7th July

Tercentenary of Establishment of the General Letter Office

3d Lilac, 1/3d Green

69a Set on illustrated cover, any postmark .... **£37.50** ☐
69b With Lombard Street, or London Chief Office cds .... **£80.00** ☐
69c With International Postal Conference, Eastbourne 1960 slogan cancel .... **£150.00** ☐
69d The Postal History Society cover showing Henry Bishop, the first PMG in 1660, Lincoln machine cancel. .... **£200.00** ☐

QEII • Commemoratives 1960-61

70. 1960, 19th September

1st Anniv. European Postal & Telecommunications Conference (Europa)

6d Green and Purple, 1/6d Brown and Blue

70a	Set on illustrated cover, any postmark	**£35.00** ☐
70b	With Lombard Street, or London Chief Office cds	**£80.00** ☐
70c	With Norwich, Norfolk cds	**£85.00** ☐
70d	With House of Commons SW1 cds	**£85.00** ☐

71. 1961, 28th August

Centenary of Post Office Savings Bank

2½d Black and Red, 3d Brown and Violet, 1/6d Red and Blue

71a	Set on illustrated cover, any postmark	**£40.00** ☐
71b	With Blythe Rd. B.O., West Kensington W.14, cds	**£275.00** ☐
71c	With Lombard St. B.O. (London Chief Office EC cds **£150**)	**£87.50** ☐
71d	With any London postmark	**£60.00** ☐
71e	With West Kensington W.14/machine cancel	**£265.00** ☐

72. 1961, 18th September

European Postal & Telecommunications Conference (CEPT)

2d Orange and Brown, 4d Mauve and Blue, 10d Green and Blue

72a	Set on illustrated cover, any postmark	**£5.00** ☐
72b	With European Conference, Torquay slogan cancel	**£10.00** ☐
72c	With London Chief Office EC cds	**£35.00** ☐
72d	With Torquay cds	**£42.00** ☐
72e	With Post Office Savings Bank 1861-1961 slogan cancel	**£190.00** ☐

73. 1961, 25th September

Seventh Commonwealth Parliamentary Conference

6d Purple and Gold, 1/3d Green and Light Blue

73a	Set on illustrated cover, any postmark	**£20.00** ☐
73b	With any London postmark	**£35.00** ☐
73c	With Parliamentary Conference, London SW, slogan cancel	**£65.00** ☐
73d	With Gresham House EC2 cds	**£75.00** ☐
73e	Set with House of Commons cds	**£275.00** ☐
73f	Set with House of Lords cds	**£260.00** ☐

Please refer to the Index on page 3 for a complete listing of all Reigns covered in the Catalogue.

QEII • Commemoratives 1962-63

Starting with the National Productivity Issue of November 14th, 1962 all new stamp issues were produced both with and without phosphor bands. Relatively small quantities of stamps were printed with phosphor bands, and their distribution limited to places such as Southampton, where special sorting machinery was installed. The phosphor coating of all stamps finally came in to being with the British Paintings Issue of July 10th, 1967. For the period November 1962 - April 1967 both Phosphor and Non-Phosphor (ordinary) first day illustrated covers are listed.

74.	1962, 14th November **National Productivity Year** 2½d Green and Carmine, 3d Light Blue and Violet, 1/3d Multi-Colour	**Non-Phos**	**Phos**
74a	Set on illustrated cover, any postmark	**£45.00** ☐	**£75.00** ☐
74b	With National Productivity Year, London slogan	**£65.00** ☐	**£137.50** ☐
74c	With Southampton 'T' machine cancel		**£120.00** ☐
74d	With Export and Prosper, London NWI slogan	**£335.00** ☐	
74e	Both Non-Phos and Phos sets on one illustrated cover, any pmk		**£180.00** ☐

LONDON E.C. 7 15PM 14 NOV 1962 D

NATIONAL PRODUCTIVITY YEAR NOVEMBER 1962-63

75.	1963, 21st March **Freedom From Hunger** 2½d Pink, 1/3d Yellow		
75a	Set on illustrated cover, any postmark	**£30.00** ☐	**£35.00** ☐
75b	With Freedom From Hunger Week, London slogan	**£45.00** ☐	**£50.00** ☐
75c	With Stampex Tenth Anniversary special handstamp	**£85.00** ☐	**£80.00** ☐
75d	With Christchurch, Hants cds	**£50.00** ☐	
75e	With Southampton 'T' machine cancel		**£47.50** ☐
75f	Both Non-Phos and Phos sets on one illustrated cover, any pmk		**£80.00** ☐
75g	Set on special Stampex cover, Stampex or FFH postmarks	**£75.00** ☐	**£85.00** ☐

FREEDOM FROM HUNGER WEEK 17-24 MARCH 1963

QEII • Commemoratives 1963

		Non-Phos	Phos
76.	1963, 7th May **Paris Postal Conference Centenary** 6d Green and Mauve		
76a	6d on illustrated cover, any postmark	**£12.00** ☐	**£20.00** ☐
76b	With Dover Packet Service, Dover special h/s	**£30.00** ☐	**£450.00** ☐
76c	With 'First Day of Issue' envelope cancellation	**£20.00** ☐	**£25.00** ☐
76d	On Dover Philatelic Society cover, Dover Packet Service h/s There are four different versions of this cover.	**£35.00** ☐	**£475.00** ☐
76e	With "Norwich Addresses Need Postal Codes", Norwich slogan	**£150.00** ☐	
76f	With Southampton 'T' machine cancel		**£35.00** ☐
76g	6d Non-Phos and Phos on one illustrated cover, any postmark		**£45.00** ☐

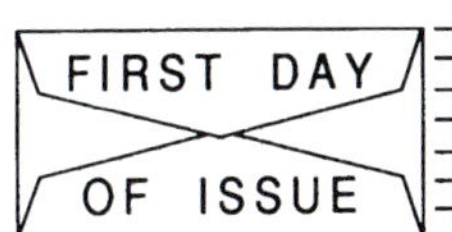

		Non-Phos	Phos
77.	1963, 16th May **National Nature Week** 3d Light Brown, 4½d Brown		
77a	Set on illustrated cover, any postmark	**£20.00** ☐	**£25.00** ☐
77b	Same with envelope design, 'First Day of Issue' cancel	**£25.00** ☐	**£35.00** ☐
77c	With Brownsea Island, Poole special handstamp	**£95.00** ☐	**£115.00** ☐
77d	With Selborne cds	**£100.00** ☐	**£115.00** ☐
77e	With Forest Row, or Colliers Wood cds	**£120.00** ☐	**£150.00** ☐
77f	With Southampton 'T' cancel		**£30.00** ☐
77g	Both Non-Phos and Phos on one illustrated cover, any pmk		**£65.00** ☐

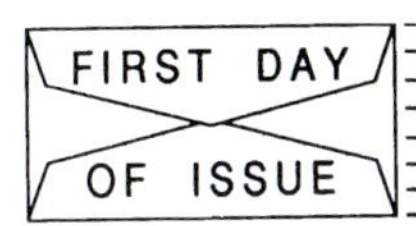

		Non-Phos	Phos
78.	1963, 31st May **9th International Lifeboat Conference** 2½d Blue and Red, 4d Blue and Brown, 1/6d Blue and Yellow		
78a	Set on illustrated cover, any postmark	**£25.00** ☐	**£30.00** ☐
78b	With Lifeboat Conference, Edinburgh slogan cancel	**£75.00** ☐	**£85.00** ☐
78c	With Lifeboat Conference slogan, London cancel	**£50.00** ☐	**£65.00** ☐
78d	With envelope design, 'First Day of Issue' cancel	**£40.00** ☐	**£45.00** ☐
78e	With Battersea or Edinburgh cds	**£90.00** ☐	**£100.00** ☐
78f	With Walmer, Cromer, Stonehaven cds, or any Lifeboat station	**£100.00** ☐	**£115.00** ☐
78g	With Culdrose cds (air sea rescue base)	**£100.00** ☐	**£120.00** ☐
78h	With Southampton 'T' cancel		**£45.00** ☐
78i	Both Non-Phos and Phos on one illustrated cover, any pmk		**£80.00** ☐

QEII • Commemoratives 1963-64

		Non-Phos	Phos
79.	1963, 15th August **Red Cross Centenary Congress** 3d Red and Lilac, 1/3d Red and Grey, 1/6d Red and Blue		
79a	Set on illustrated cover, any postmark	£30.00 ☐	£45.00 ☐
79b	With Red Cross Centenary slogan, London or other cancel	£75.00 ☐	£100.00 ☐
79c	With West Wellow cds	£110.00 ☐	£125.00 ☐
79d	With envelope design, 'First Day of Issue' cancel	£45.00 ☐	£60.00 ☐
79e	With Southampton 'T' cancel		£70.00 ☐
79f	Both Non-Phos and Phos on one illustrated cover, any pmk		£125.00 ☐

		Non-Phos	Phos
80.	1963, 3rd December **Commonwealth Pacific Cable (Compac)** 1/6d Blue		
80a	1/6d on illustrated cover, any postmark	£25.00 ☐	£30.00 ☐
80b	With envelope fdi cancel, London	£30.00 ☐	£35.00 ☐
80c	With envelope fdi cancel and Philatelic Bureau h/s*	£45.00 ☐	£50.00 ☐
80d	With Southampton cds	£50.00 ☐	£55.00 ☐
80e	With Southampton 'T' cancel		£50.00 ☐
80f	Both Non-Phos and Phos on one illustrated cover, any pmk		£65.00 ☐
80g	1/6d on (Philart) illustrated card, London cds		£50.00 ☐

*The Philatelic Bureau in London designed its own circular postmark for the first time with this issue.

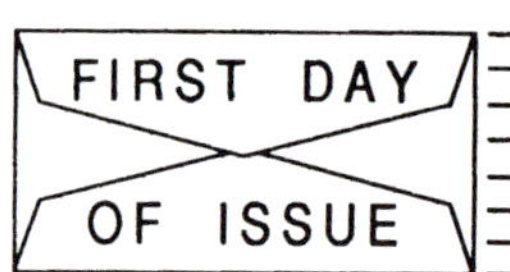

In 1964 the Post Office introduced the first circular 'First Day of Issue' handstamp – and have used it in one form or another on nearly all issues since. The same year the Post Office started to produce its own first day envelopes, beginning with the 1964 Shakespeare issue, and with five exceptions in 1965 and only one in 1966, they have done so for every new stamp issue since.

		Non-Phos	Phos
81.	1964, 23rd April **Shakespeare Festival** 3d Violet, 6d Olive, 1/3d Dark Brown, 1/6d Dark Blue, 2/6d Blackish Brown The 2/6d was only issued in a Non-Phos variety		
81a	Set on illustrated cover, any postmark	£10.00 ☐	£12.00 ☐
81b	With Stratford-upon-Avon FDI handstamp	£16.00 ☐	£18.50 ☐
81c	With Shakespeare 400th Anniversary special handstamp	£40.00 ☐	£45.00 ☐
81d	With Shakespeare Anniversary Year slogan cancel	£800.00 ☐	£900.00 ☐
81e	With Reading FDI large circular handstamp	£75.00 ☐	
81f	With Field Post Office 1050 cds		£65.00 ☐

QEII • Commemoratives 1964

81g	On Shakespeare Show Centre cover, 400th Anniversary h/s	**£60.00** ☐	**£75.00** ☐
81h	Both Non-Phos and Phos on one illustrated cover, FDI or special handstamp		**£75.00** ☐
81i	Non-Phos set with 2/6d Black variety, Stratford FDI, GPO cover	**£100.00** ☐	
81j	Single value with 'envelope' FDI, plus Stratford machine cancel	**£20.00** ☐	**£20.00** ☐
81k	Set on one or more covers, Stratford-upon-Avon cds	**£140.00** ☐	**£175.00** ☐

---

82. 1964, 1st July

20th International Geographical Congress, London

2½d Green and Grey, 4d Rose and Black, 8d Black and Green, 1/6d Black and Brown

82a	Set on illustrated cover, any postmark	**£15.00** ☐	**£20.00** ☐
82b	With Philatelic Bureau, London handstamp	**£25.00** ☐	**£35.00** ☐
82c	With London FDI handstamp	**£25.00** ☐	**£35.00** ☐
82d	With envelope design FDI, Greenwich postmark	**£300.00** ☐	**£325.00** ☐
82e	With South Kensington SW7 cds	**£145.00** ☐	**£160.00** ☐
82f	Both Non-Phos and Phos on one illustrated cover, any postmark		**£80.00** ☐

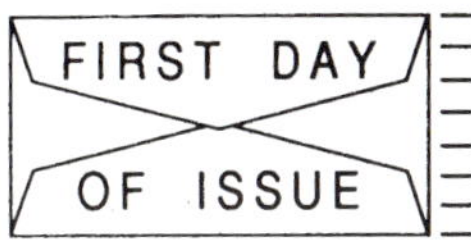

---

83. 1964, 5th August

10th International Botanical Congress, Edinburgh

3d Violet and Blue, 6d Green and Pink, 9d Orange and Yellow, 1/3d Olive and Yellow

83a	Set on illustrated cover, any postmark	**£25.00** ☐	**£30.00** ☐
83b	With Botanical Congress, Edinburgh, Thistle special h/s	**£225.00** ☐	**£260.00** ☐
83c	With Philatelic Bureau handstamp	**£30.00** ☐	**£45.00** ☐
83d	With Edinburgh FDI	**£20.00** ☐	**£30.00** ☐
83e	With Edinburgh cds	**£30.00** ☐	**£45.00** ☐
83f	With Kew Gardens cds	**£210.00** ☐	**£225.00** ☐
83g	With Richmond and Twickenham cds	**£100.00** ☐	**£120.00** ☐
83h	With Primrose Valley, or Spalding cds	**£185.00** ☐	**£225.00** ☐
83i	With Forest Row cds, or Wood Green cds	**£160.00** ☐	**£175.00** ☐
83j	With Richmond and Twickenham envelope FDI slogan	**£185.00** ☐	**£215.00** ☐
83k	Both Non-Phos and Phos on one illustrated cover, any pmk		**£85.00** ☐

All prices in this catalogue are for clean covers, with undamaged stamps and clear postmarks.

QEII • Commemoratives 1964-65

84. 1964, 4th September

Opening of Forth Road Bridge 3d Blue and Violet, 6d Blue and Red-Brown

		Non-Phos	Phos
84a	Set on illustrated cover, any postmark	£10.00 □	£15.00 □
84b	With North Queensferry special handstamp	£45.00 □	£125.00 □
84c	With South Queensferry special handstamp	£30.00 □	£80.00 □
84d	With Philatelic Bureau handstamp	£20.00 □	£25.00 □
84e	With Edinburgh FDI handstamp	£17.50 □	£25.00 □
84f	With Balmoral Castle cds	£215.00 □	£225.00 □
84g	With South Queensferry, West Lothian cds	£100.00 □	£125.00 □
84h	With North Queensferry, Fife cds	£120.00 □	£130.00 □
84i	Both Non-Phos and Phos on one illustrated cover, any pmk		£55.00 □

---

85. 1965, 8th July

Sir Winston Churchill Commemoration

4d Black and Brown, 1/3d Black and Grey

		Non-Phos	Phos
85a	Set on illustrated cover, any postmark	£5.00 □	£8.00 □
85b	With London FDI handstamp	£10.00 □	£12.50 □
85c	With Philatelic Bureau handstamp	£10.00 □	£12.50 □
85d	With Bladon, Oxford FDI	£20.00 □	£25.00 □
85e	With First Day of Issue - Westminster, London slogan	£110.00 □	£130.00 □
85f	With Churchill, Oxford or Bristol cds	£90.00 □	£100.00 □
85g	With South Woodford E.18 cds	£135.00 □	
85h	With Marlborough cds (Bladon cds **£145**)	£240.00 □	
85i	With any British Forces or Field P.O. cds, or Dover cds	£60.00 □	£65.00 □
85j	With House of Commons cds	£80.00 □	£85.00 □
85k	With House of Lords cds	£140.00 □	£160.00 □
85l	Both Non-Phos and Phos on one illustrated cover, any postmark		£60.00 □

FIRST DAY
OF ISSUE
WESTMINSTER

Don't miss the

Royalty Post Cards Special Feature!

See pages 160 - 176

New Listing for

Pre-Release and Missing Colours

See pages 458 - 461

QEII • Commemoratives 1965

		Non-Phos	Phos
86.	1965, 19th July **700th Anniversary of Simon de Montfort's Parliament** 6d Olive-Green, 2/6d Black and Grey The 2/6d stamp was only issued in a Non-Phos variety.		
86a	Set on illustrated cover, any postmark	**£10.00** ☐	**£10.00** ☐
86b	With London FDI handstamp	**£20.00** ☐	**£20.00** ☐
86c	With Leicester or Oxford FDI cancel	**£35.00** ☐	**£40.00** ☐
86d	With Philatelic Bureau FDI cancel	**£15.00** ☐	**£17.50** ☐
86e	With Evesham FDI cancel	**£35.00** ☐	**£35.00** ☐
86f	With Evesham cds (Lincoln cds, Dover cds **£75**)	**£125.00** ☐	**£125.00** ☐
86g	With House of Commons cds, or machine cancel	**£110.00** ☐	**£110.00** ☐
86h	With House of Lords cds	**£130.00** ☐	**£130.00** ☐
86i	With Parliament St. cds, or Lewes cds	**£90.00** ☐	**£85.00** ☐
86j	Both Non-Phos and Phos on one illustrated cover, any postmark		**£60.00** ☐

		Non-Phos	Phos
87.	1965, 9th August **Salvation Army Centenary** 3d Grey-Blue, 1/6d Red and Orange		
87a	Set on illustrated cover, any postmark	**£20.00** ☐	**£25.00** ☐
87b	With Nottingham FDI cancel	**£70.00** ☐	**£75.00** ☐
87c	With London EC FDI cancel (London ECI cds **£100**)	**£40.00** ☐	**£45.00** ☐
87d	With Portsmouth Philatelic Society cancel	**£100.00** ☐	**£110.00** ☐
87e	Both Non-Phos and Phos on one illustrated cover, any postmark		**£75.00** ☐

		Non-Phos	Phos
88.	1965, 1st September **Centenary of Lister's Discovery of Antiseptic Surgery** 4d Grey and Black, 1/- Blue and Black		
88a	Set on illustrated cover, any postmark	**£8.00** ☐	**£10.00** ☐
88b	With Glasgow or Edinburgh FDI cancel	**£50.00** ☐	**£55.00** ☐
88c	With 'First Day of Issue' Paddington, envelope design cancel	**£140.00** ☐	
88d	With 'First Day of Issue' Edinburgh, envelope design cancel	**£130.00** ☐	**£150.00** ☐
88e	With Paddington or Glasgow cds	**£130.00** ☐	**£165.00** ☐
88f	With Royal Infirmary, Edinburgh cds	**£200.00** ☐	**£225.00** ☐
88g	With 4th Bach Festival, Bath slogan	**£235.00** ☐	**£265.00** ☐
88h	With Commonwealth Arts Festival slogan, any office	**£220.00** ☐	**£250.00** ☐
88i	Set on Royal Infirmary of Edinburgh cover, Edinburgh FDI pmk	**£70.00** ☐	**£75.00** ☐
88j	Set on Warner-Lambert (makers of Listerine) cover, Kingston FDI	**£45.00** ☐	
88k	With Eyam, Sheffield special handstamp	**£250.00** ☐	
88l	Both Non-Phos and Phos on one illustrated cover, any postmark		**£55.00** ☐

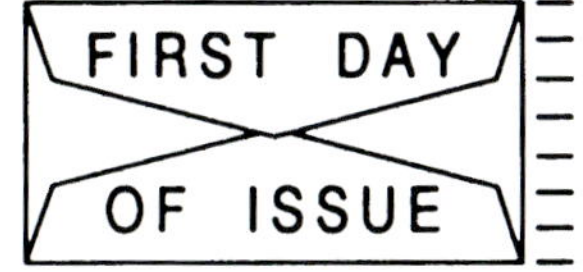

65e

66b

67b

68d

69c

70a

71b

72b

73c

74b

75b

76b

77d

78b

79b

80b

81b

82d

83b

84g

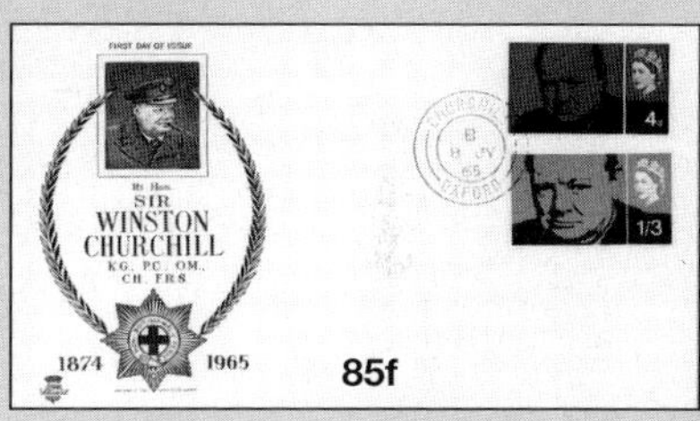

85f

86g

87a

JOSEPH LISTER
OF ISSUE
Alan G. Nicholls Esq.,
136 Park Road,
Chiswick,
LONDON, W.4.
FIRST DAY COVER-COMMEMORATIVE ISSUE
88c

BACH
BATH
Mr. F.B. Leadbetter,
112, Packard Avenue
MEDFORD,
Massachusetts, 02155,
U.S.A.
1/6
89d

13 SEP 65
4d
9d
Battle of Britain 1940
GPO FIRST DAY COVER
90c

Post Office
Communications
Tower
LONDON
1965
LONDON, W.
8 OCT 1965
FIRST DAY OF ISSUE
W.R. Fry, M.D.,
426, William St.,
London,
Ontario,
Canada.
91b

LEICESTER PHILATELIC SOCIETY
1906-65
SEMPER
EADEM
1/6
D WEBSTER ESQ
26 ALBERT RD
ASHFORD
MIDDX
92d

INTERNATIONAL
TELECOMMUNICATIONS
UNION
1865 CENTENARY 1965
LONDON W.C.
15 NOV 1965
FIRST DAY OF ISSUE
JOHN LISTER LTD.
186, SHAFTESBURY AVE
LONDON W.C.2.
93b

FIRST DAY COVER
DUMFRIES
THE FRIEND OF MAN-TO VICE ALONE A FOE
ROBERT BURNS
1759-1796
COMMEMORATIVE ISSUE
Robert Burns House in Dumfries
1/3
94b

WESTMINSTER
2/6
900th ANNIVERSARY
OF THE FOUNDATION OF
WESTMINSTER ABBEY
1066–1966
FIRST DAY COVER
Alan G. Nicholls Esq.,
The Medical Mailing Company Ltd.,
The Mailing House,
Leeland Road,
LONDON, W.13.
95d

Pictorial
Issue
2 MAY 1966
FIRST DAY COVER
96c

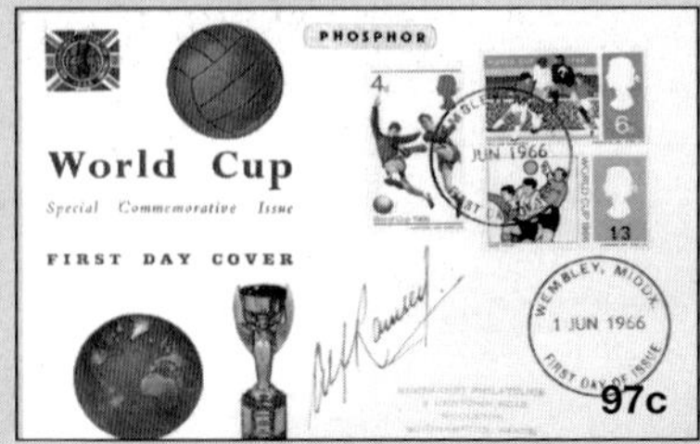
PHOSPHOR
World Cup
Special Commemorative Issue
FIRST DAY COVER
1 JUN 1966
WEMBLEY, MIDDX
FIRST DAY OF ISSUE
97c

98b

99b

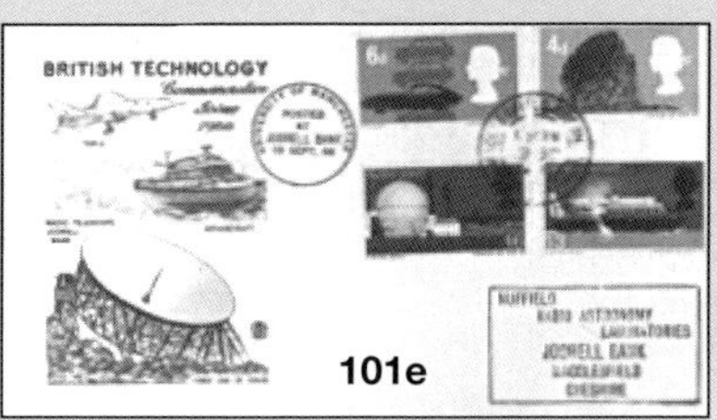

101e

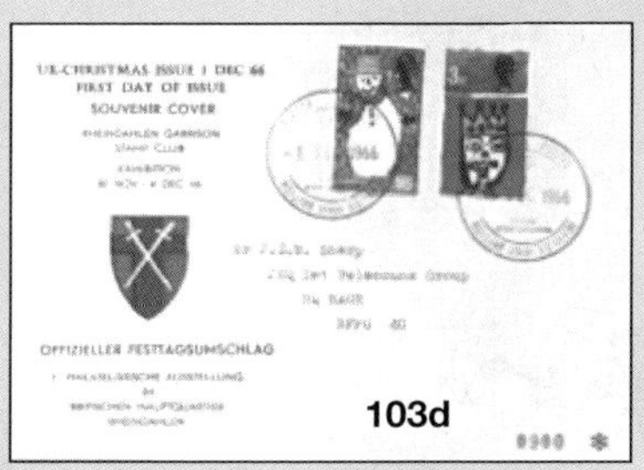

103d

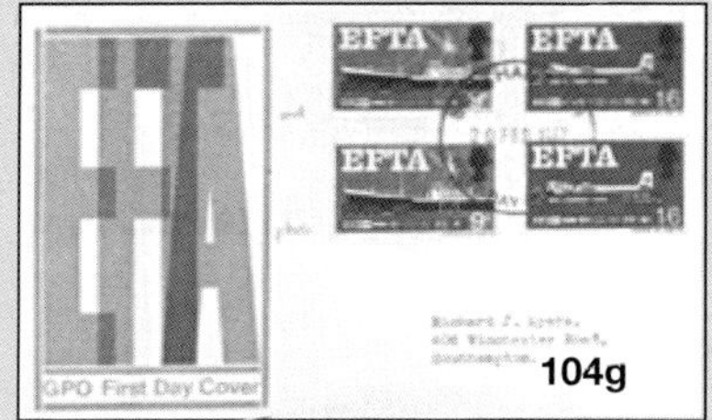

104g

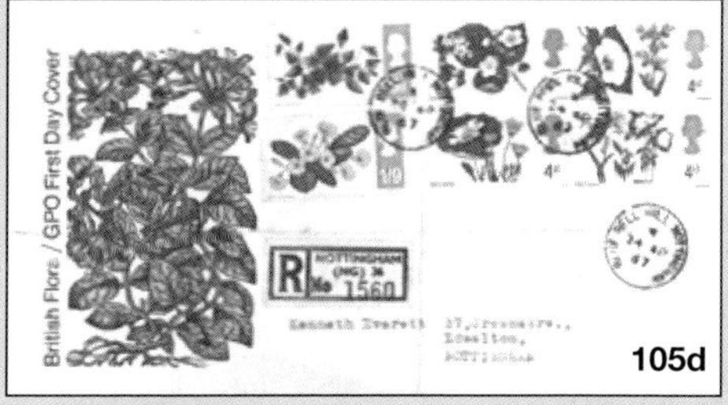

105d

106e

107d

102b

QEII • Commemoratives 1965

89. 1965, 1st September

Commonwealth Arts Festival 6d Black and Orange, 1/6d Black and Violet

		Non-Phos	Phos
89a	Set on illustrated cover, any postmark	£16.00 ☐	£20.00 ☐
89b	With London, Glasgow, Liverpool or Cardiff FDI cancel	£35.00 ☐	£40.00 ☐
89c	With Stratford-on-Avon cds, on Arts Centre cover	£125.00 ☐	
89d	With 4th Bach Festival slogan, Bath	£525.00 ☐	
89e	With Commonwealth Arts Festival slogan, any Office	£525.00 ☐	£585.00 ☐
89f	Both Non-Phos and Phos on one illustrated cover, any postmark		£60.00 ☐
89g	Arts Festival and Lister Sets on same cover, any pmk	£60.00 ☐	£65.00 ☐

90. 1965, 13th September

25th Anniversary of Battle of Britain

4d Se-tenant Block of Six, 9d Violet, 1/3d Blue and Grey

		Non-Phos	Phos
90a	Complete set on illustrated cover, any postmark	£15.00 ☐	£17.50 ☐
90b	With London FDI cancel	£20.00 ☐	£25.00 ☐
90c	With Biggin Hill, Westerham Kent large cds (small cds **£140**)	£90.00 ☐	£100.00 ☐
90d	With Philatelic Bureau handstamp	£20.00 ☐	£25.00 ☐
90e	With Dover cds, or Churchill cds	£70.00 ☐	£76.00 ☐
90f	With RAF Waddington, or any other RAF cds	£130.00 ☐	£145.00 ☐
90g	With Halifax or Lancaster cds	£130.00 ☐	£140.00 ☐
90h	Both Non-Phos and Phos on one illustrated cover, any postmark		£60.00 ☐

91. 1965, 8th October

Opening of the Post Office Tower

3d Blue and Bronze, 1/3d Green and Blue

		Non-Phos	Phos
91a	Set on illustrated cover, any postmark	£6.00 ☐	£7.50 ☐
91b	With London W, FDI handstamp	£18.00 ☐	£20.00 ☐
91c	With Philatelic Bureau handstamp	£12.50 ☐	£15.00 ☐
91d	With Gt. Portland St. cds		£120.00 ☐
91e	On Leicester Philatelic Society cover, with special h/s	£70.00 ☐	£75.00 ☐
91f	Both Non-Phos and Phos on one illustrated cover, any postmark		£45.00 ☐

92. 1965, 25th October

20th Anniversary United Nations/International Co-Operation Year

3d Orange and Blue, 1/6d Blue and Purple

		Non-Phos	Phos
92a	Set on illustrated cover, any postmark	£10.00 ☐	£12.00 ☐
92b	With London SW FDI handstamp	£20.00 ☐	£25.00 ☐
92c	With Int. Co-Operation Year, Reading special slogan	£500.00 ☐	£525.00 ☐
92d	Set on Leicester Philatelic Society cover, with special cancel	£75.00 ☐	£85.00 ☐
92e	Set with House of Commons SWI cds	£50.00 ☐	£60.00 ☐
92f	Both Non-Phos and Phos on one illustrated cover, any postmark		£50.00 ☐

QEII • Commemoratives 1965-66

		Non-Phos	Phos
93.	1965, 15th November **International Telecommunications Union Centenary** 9d Violet and Pink, 1/6d Blue and Pink		
93a	Set on illustrated cover, any postmark	£15.00 ☐	£18.00 ☐
93b	With London FDI handstamp	£20.00 ☐	£25.00 ☐
93c	With Helston, Cornwall cds (Goonhilly Downs)	£290.00 ☐	£320.00 ☐
93d	Both Non-Phos and Phos on one illustrated cover, any postmark		£50.00 ☐

		Non-Phos	Phos
94.	1966, 25th January **Robert Burns Commemoration** 4d Burns Portrait, 1/3d Burns Portrait		
94a	Set on illustrated cover, any postmark	£5.00 ☐	£8.00 ☐
	With one of eight special Post Office sponsored handstamps:		
94b	Alloway, Ayr, Dumfries, Edinburgh, Glasgow or Kilmarnock	£15.00 ☐	£18.50 ☐
94c	Greenock or Mauchline h/s	£35.00 ☐	£40.00 ☐
94d	Set on Burns Memorial Fund cover, any postmark	£25.00 ☐	£30.00 ☐
94e	Set on the Greenock Philatelic Society cover, Greenock h/s	£40.00 ☐	£47.50 ☐
94f	Set on the Kilmarnock Burns Club cover, Kilmarnock h/s	£20.00 ☐	£25.00 ☐
94g	Set on the Burns Federation cover, Kilmarnock handstamp	£20.00 ☐	£25.00 ☐
94h	Set with Burns Statue, Ayr 3 cds	£260.00 ☐	£280.00 ☐
94i	With St. Andrews, Fife cds	£35.00 ☐	
94j	Both Non-Phos and Phos on one illustrated cover, any postmark		£38.00 ☐

The eight special GPO handstamps were available in two sizes, except for Greenock and Mauchline which came in the larger size only. Both sizes are very collectable and are priced equally.

		Non-Phos	Phos
95.	1966, 28th February **900th Anniversary of Westminster Abbey** 3d Westminster Abbey, 2/6d Henry VII Chapel The 2/6d stamp was only issued in a Non-Phos variety		
95a	Set on illustrated cover, any postmark	£5.00 ☐	£7.50 ☐
95b	With London SW FDI handstamp	£20.00 ☐	£20.00 ☐
95c	With Philatelic Bureau handstamp	£12.50 ☐	£15.00 ☐
95d	With First Day of Issue Westminster, London SWI cancel	£135.00 ☐	£115.00 ☐
95e	With Westminster Abbey 900th Anniversary slogan	£150.00 ☐	£130.00 ☐
95f	With House of Commons cds	£120.00 ☐	£110.00 ☐
95g	With House of Lords cds	£135.00 ☐	£120.00 ☐
95h	With Buckingham Palace cds	£150.00 ☐	£150.00 ☐
95i	Set on souvenir Westminster Abbey post card, any FDI postmark	£100.00 ☐	
95j	Both Non-Phos and Phos on one illustrated cover, any postmark		£45.00 ☐

FIRST DAY OF ISSUE WESTMINSTER

WESTMINSTER ABBEY 900 th ANNIVERSARY YEAR

QEII • Commemoratives 1966

		Non-Phos	Phos
96.	1966, 2nd May **British Landscapes** 4d Sussex Scene, 6d Antrim Scene, 1/3d Harlech Scene, 1/6d Cairngorms Scene		
96a	Set on illustrated cover, any postmark	£8.00	£10.00
96b	With Philatelic Bureau handstamp	£10.00	£12.00
96c	With Lewes, Sussex FDI handstamp	£60.00	£70.00
96d	With Harlech, Merioneth FDI handstamp	£80.00	£90.00
96e	With Coleraine, Co. Londonderry FDI handstamp	£80.00	£90.00
96f	With Grantown-on-Spey, Morayshire FDI handstamp	£95.00	£110.00
96g	With Forest Row, Sussex cds	£90.00	£115.00
96h	With Antrim, Coleraine, Harlech or Grantown cds	£130.00	£140.00
96i	Set of 4 covers each with single stamp and appropriate FDI h/s	£40.00	£50.00
96j	Both Non-Phos and Phos on one illustrated cover, any postmark		£50.00

		Non-Phos	Phos
97.	1966, 1st June **World Cup Football Competition** 4d, 6d, 1/3d, Football Players		
97a	Set on illustrated cover, any FDI postmark	£10.00	£12.00
97b	With Philatelic Bureau handstamp	£18.50	£22.00
97c	With Wembley, Middx FDI handstamp	£30.00	£40.00
97d	With First Day of Issue, Harrow & Wembley 'envelope' cancel	£70.00	£75.00
97e	Set with Birmingham, Liverpool, Manchester, Middlesborough, Sheffield or Sunderland FDI cancel - cup matches played here (cds + 20%)	£30.00	£30.00
97f	Set with World Cup City Sheffield ... slogan cancel	£550.00	
97g	Set with World Cup Sunderland slogan (4d only **£150**)	£275.00	
97h	Both Non-Phos and Phos on one illustrated cover, any postmark		£50.00

		Non-Phos	Phos
98.	1966, 8th August **British Birds** 4d Se-tenant Block of Four Birds		
98a	Set in block of four on illustrated cover, any FDI postmark	£12.50	£15.00
98b	With Philatelic Bureau handstamp	£25.00	£30.00
98c	Both Non-Phos and Phos on one illustrated cover, any postmark		£50.00

		Price
99.	1966, 18th August **World Cup Football – England Winners, Wembley** 4d England Winners. Issued in Non-Phos variety only	
99a	4d on illustrated cover, any FDI postmark	£5.00
99b	With Harrow & Wembley FDI handstamp	£17.50
99c	With Harrow & Wembley black cds (purple cds **£35**)	£32.00
99e	With Birmingham, Liverpool, Manchester, Middlesborough, Sheffield or Sunderland FDI cancel (cup matches played here)	£22.50
99f	With any Field Post Office cds	£12.50
99g	World Cup Willie post card, any fdi postmark	£25.00

		Price
100.	1966, 1st June and 18th August **World Cup Football Competition Issue + England Winners** Combined cover with all stamps and both dates (Non-Phos or mixed)	
100a	Harrow & Wembley FDI handstamps	£250.00
100b	Any other FDI handstamps	£70.00

QEII • Commemoratives 1966

101. 1966 19th September

British Technology

4d Jodrell Bank, 6d British Cars, 1/3d Hovercraft, 1/6d Windscale Reactor

		Non-Phos	Phos
101a	Set on illustrated cover, any postmark	£5.00 ☐	£6.50 ☐
101b	With Philatelic Bureau handstamp	£12.00 ☐	£15.00 ☐
101c	With Birmingham, Coventry, Manchester or Oxford FDI cancel	£22.50 ☐	£27.50 ☐
101d	With Carlisle, Luton, Newport or Portsmouth FDI cancel	£22.50 ☐	£30.00 ☐
101e	With Macclesfield, Cheshire cds, plus Jodrell Bank cachet	£160.00 ☐	£200.00 ☐
101f	With 1945-1966 Remploy 21st Anniv, London slogan	£65.00 ☐	£80.00 ☐
101g	Hovercraft SRN 6 post card with 1/3d stamp, any FDI cancel	£20.00 ☐	
101h	Set of 4 covers each with single stamp and appropriate FDI pmk	£30.00 ☐	£40.00 ☐
101i	Both Non-Phos and Phos on one illustrated cover, any pmk		£50.00 ☐

102. 1966, 14th October

900th Anniversary of the Battle of Hastings

6 x 4d Se-tenant, 6d, 1/3d, Bayeux Tapestry Scenes

		Non-Phos	Phos
102a	Full set on illustrated cover, any postmark	£5.00 ☐	£6.00 ☐
102b	With Posted from the Battlefield, Battle, Sussex handstamp	£12.00 ☐	£15.00 ☐
102c	With Battle or Hastings FDI handstamp	£10.00 ☐	£12.50 ☐
102d	With Philatelic Bureau handstamp	£10.00 ☐	£12.00 ☐
102e	With Guernsey or Jersey FDI handstamp	£27.50 ☐	
102f	With Battle, Sussex cds (Normandy cds, or Harold Hill cds **£200**)	£65.00 ☐	
102g	Les Isles Normandes 1066-1966, Guernsey or Jersey slogan	£385.00 ☐	£400.00 ☐
102h	4d Stamp only, Hastings Popular with Visitors since1066, slogan	£40.00 ☐	£45.00 ☐
102i	Same with Hastings... slogan on plain cover, 4d only	£30.00 ☐	£35.00 ☐
102j	Both Non-Phos and Phos on one illustrated cover, any postmark		£60.00 ☐

103. 1966, 1st December

First Ever GB Christmas Issue 3d King, 1/6d Snowman

		Non-Phos	Phos
103a	Set on illustrated cover, any postmark	£2.00 ☐	£2.50 ☐
103b	With Philatelic Bureau handstamp	£7.50 ☐	£10.00 ☐
103c	With Bethlehem small FDI handstamp	£9.00 ☐	£10.50 ☐
103d	With BFPS 1000 h/s, Rheindahlen Stamp Exhibition, Germany	£35.00 ☐	£40.00 ☐
103e	With Nasareth or Bethlehem cds (St Nicholas cds **£100**)	£275.00 ☐	£285.00 ☐
103f	Both Non-Phos and Phos on one illustrated cover, any postmark		£40.00 ☐

Don't miss the Special Feature on Royalty Post Cards.
Pages 160 - 176

104. 1967, 20th February

European Free Trade Association (EFTA)

9d Sea Freight, 1/6d Air Freight

No.	Description	Non-Phos	Phos
104a	Set on illustrated cover, any postmark	£2.00 ☐	£3.00 ☐
104b	With Philatelic Bureau handstamp	£7.00 ☐	£8.50 ☐
104c	With House of Commons cds, House of Lords cds	£50.00 ☐	£60.00 ☐
104d	With Hull, Grimsby, or Newcastle cds	£20.00 ☐	£25.00 ☐
104e	With NATO, Portmeirion, special handstamp	£45.00 ☐	£50.00 ☐
104f	With Ship Early Through the Port of London Slogan	£190.00 ☐	£200.00 ☐
104g	Both Non-Phos and Phos on one illustrated cover, any postmark		£35.00 ☐

105. 1967, 24th April

British Wild Flowers

4 x 4d Se-tenant of Wild Flowers, 9d Dog Violets, 1/9d Primroses

No.	Description	Non-Phos	Phos
105a	Set on illustrated cover, any postmark	£4.00 ☐	£6.00 ☐
105b	With Philatelic Bureau handstamp	£8.50 ☐	£10.00 ☐
105c	With Kew Gardens, Richmond, or Kew, Richmond cds	£145.00 ☐	£155.00 ☐
105d	With Blue Bell Hill, Nottingham cds	£175.00 ☐	£185.00 ☐
105e	With Primrose St., Alloa cds	£175.00 ☐	£185.00 ☐
105f	With Flore Northants cds, or Hawthorn Wilts cds	£175.00 ☐	£185.00 ☐
105g	With Forest Row cds, Hedgend cds, or Flowery Field cds	£42.00 ☐	£47.50 ☐
105h	Both Non-Phos and Phos on one illustrated cover, any postmark		£55.00 ☐

Starting with the 1967 Paintings issue the Non-Phos stamp variety was dropped, and all commemorative stamps from then on were Phosphor coated.

106. 1967, 10th July

British Paintings

4d Thomas Lawrence, 9d George Stubbs, 1/6d L.S. Lowry

106a	Set on illustrated cover, any postmark	£5.00 ☐
106b	With Philatelic Bureau handstamp	£10.00 ☐
106c	With London WC FDI handstamp	£10.00 ☐
106d	With Bishop Auckland FDI handstamp (Manchester FDI h/s **£15**)	£45.00 ☐
106e	Art on Stamps Exhibition, London special handstamp	£35.00 ☐

107. 1967, 24th July

Sir Francis Chichester's World Voyage 1/9d Gipsy Moth IV

107a	1/9d on illustrated cover, any postmark	£2.50 ☐
107b	With Philatelic Bureau special handstamp	£9.00 ☐
107c	With Greenwich or Plymouth special handstamp	£12.00 ☐
107d	With Barnstaple FDI handstamp (Barnstaple cds **£30**)	£16.00 ☐
107e	With Chichester FDI handstamp (Chichester Rd cds **£225**)	£14.50 ☐
107f	On Outward Bound Trust large cover, House of Commons cds	£25.00 ☐
107g	With Hull – Gateway to Europe, slogan cancel	£85.00 ☐
107h	With Ship through the Port of London slogan	£115.00 ☐

QEII • Commemoratives 1967

108. 1967, 19th September

British Discovery and Invention

4d Radar, 1/- Penicillin, 1/6d Jet Engine, 1/9d Television.

108a	Set on on illustrated cover, any postmark	**£5.00**	☐
108b	With Philatelic Bureau handstamp	**£6.50**	☐
108c	With HMS Discovery Exhibition special handstamp, London	**£18.50**	☐
108d	With Penicillin Discovered 1928, Paddington special handstamp	**£25.00**	☐
108e	With Coventry, Hounslow, Paddington or Plymouth FDI	**£25.00**	☐
108f	With Helensburgh, Brechin, Darvel or Coventry cds	**£150.00**	☐
108g	With Benenden Chest Hospital, Cranbrook cds	**£350.00**	☐
108h	With First Day of Issue, Paddington, 'envelope' design postmark	**£115.00**	☐

This was the last GB commemorative issue to bear a watermark.

---

109. 1967, 18th October and 27th November

Christmas Issue

4d Madonna and Child, 3d and 1/6d Adoration of the Shepherds

109a	4d on illustrated cover, any postmarkIssue Date	18.10.67	**£1.00**	☐
109b	4d with Philatelic Bureau handstamp	Issue Date 18.10.67	**£3.00**	☐
109c	4d with Bethlehem, Llandeilo FDI handstamp	Issue Date 18.10.67	**£5.00**	☐
109d	4d with First Day of Issue, Bethlehem, 'envelope' pmk	Issue Date 18.10.67	**£12.00**	☐
109e	4d with St. Nicholas, Guildford cds	Issue Date 18.10.67	**£75.00**	☐
109f	4d with Jericho, Lancs cds, or Bethlehem cds	Issue Date 18.10.67	**£165.00**	☐
109g	3d and 1/6d on illustrated cover, any postmark	Issue Date 27.11.67	**£2.00**	☐
109h	3d and 1/6d with Philatelic Bureau handstamp	Issue Date 27.11.67	**£4.00**	☐
109i	3d and 1/6d with Bethlehem, Llandeilo FDI handstamp	Issue Date 27.11.67	**£5.50**	☐
109j	3d and 1/6d with First Day of Issue, Bethlehem 'envelope' pmk	27.11.67	**£75.00**	☐
109k	3d and 1/6d with 'First Ever Christmas present...', Coleraine slogan	27.11.67	**£335.00**	☐
109l	3d only on New Life souvenir post card, First Ever Christmas slogan	27.11.67	**£90.00**	☐
109m	3d and 1/6d with Bethlehem, Llandeilo cds	27.11.67	**£230.00**	☐
109n	3d and 1/6d with See Christmas Illuminations, Cheltenham slogan	27.11.67	**£345.00**	☐

Double Dated Covers:

109o	Set with two Bethlehem, Llandeilo FDI handstamps, on one cover	**£32.00**	☐
109p	Set with two Philatelic Bureau handstamps, on one cover	**£27.50**	☐
109q	Set with two matching postmarks, any office, on one cover	**£18.50**	☐

All prices in this catalogue are for clean covers, with undamaged stamps and clear postmarks.

110. 1968, 29th April

British Bridges

4d Tarr Steps, 9d Aberfeldy Bridge, 1/6d Menai Bridge, 1/9d M4 Viaduct

110a	Set on illustrated cover, any postmark	£3.00 ☐
110b	With Philatelic Bureau Special handstamp	£8.50 ☐
110c	With Bridge, Kent special handstamp (Bridge cds **£225**)	£9.50 ☐
110d	With First Day of Issue, Bridge, Canterbury ‘envelope’ cancel	£85.00 ☐
110e	With First Day of Issue, Menai Bridge, ‘envelope’ cancel	£80.00 ☐
110f	With First Day of Issue, Aberfeldy, Perth ‘envelope’ cancel	£85.00 ☐
110g	With Chiswick W.4. plus wavy line, machine cancel	£165.00 ☐
110h	With Perth or Exeter FDI handstamp	£20.00 ☐
110i	With Aberfeldy or Menai cds (single stamp **£35**)	£145.00 ☐
110j	With Chiswick or Dulverton cds (single stamp **£40**)	£190.00 ☐
110k	Set of four covers, each with single stamp and appropriate postmark	£42.50 ☐

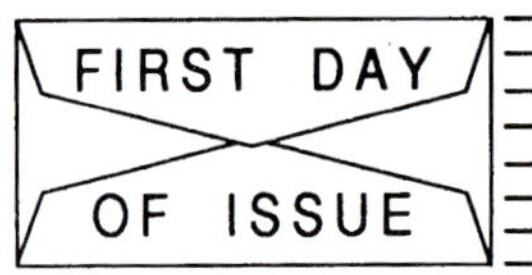

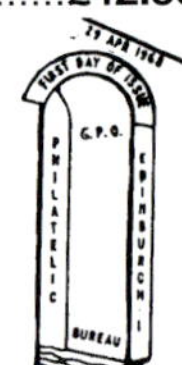

111. 1968, 29th May

British Anniversaries

4d TUC, 9d Mrs. Pankhurst, 1/- RAF, 1/9d Captain Cook

		Single Stamp	**Full Set**
111a	4d with TUC 100, Manchester special handstamp	£3.00 ☐	£75.00 ☐
111b	4d with P.O. Engineering Union, Ealing handstamp	£20.00 ☐	£250.00 ☐
111c	4d with Manchester FDI handstamp	£3.00 ☐	£17.50 ☐
111d	9d with Aldeburgh, Suffolk, special handstamp	£5.00 ☐	£75.00 ☐
111e	9d with London FDI handstamp	£3.00 ☐	£15.00 ☐
111f	9d with House of Commons cds	£12.00 ☐	£65.00 ☐
111g	1/- with Hendon FDI, London NW4 special handstamp	£4.00 ☐	£75.00 ☐
111h	1/- with Digby Aerodrome, Lincoln cds	£17.50 ☐	
111i	1/- with Field Post Office 1027 cds	£15.00 ☐	
111j	1/- with RAF Escaping Society, BFPO 1067 handstamp	£12.50 ☐	£190.00 ☐
111k	1/- with 50th Anniversary, RAF Leuchars handstamp	£12.50 ☐	£190.00 ☐
111l	1/- with RAF 50th Anniversary, Fylingdales RAF PO cancel	£12.50 ☐	£200.00 ☐
111m	1/- with RAF College Cranwell, Sleaford handstamp	£15.00 ☐	£235.00 ☐
111n	1/- with 50th Anniversary RAF Medmenham, RAF PO cancel	£12.00 ☐	£190.00 ☐
111o	1/- with any other RAF Station, RAF Post Office cancel	£10.00 ☐	£135.00 ☐
111p	1/9d with Whitby FDI, Yorkshire special handstamp	£4.00 ☐	£80.00 ☐
111q	1/9d with Bi-Centenary Captain Cook, Whitby slogan pmk	£30.00 ☐	£180.00 ☐
111r	Full set with Philatelic Bureau handstamp		£10.00 ☐
111s	Full set with House of Commons, or House of Lords cds		£65.00 ☐

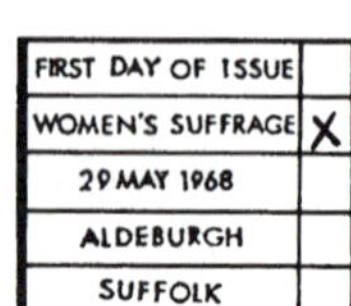

POST OFFICE ENGINEERING UNION
29 · MAY · 68
Ealing W.5.

QEII • Commemoratives 1968-69

112. 1968, 12th August

British Paintings

4d Portrait of QEI, 1/- Portrait of Pinkie, 1/6d St. Mary LePort, 1/9d The Hay Wain

112a	Set on illustrated cover, any postmark	**£2.00**
112b	With Philatelic Bureau handstamp	**£8.00**
112c	With Philatex 68 Woburn, Bletchley special handstamp	**£26.50**
112d	With Portsmouth & District Philatelic Society handstamp	**£42.00**
112e	With First Day of Issue slogan - London WI, London SE or Hatfield	**£42.00**
112f	With Parish Church Restoration, Kettering special handstamp	**£42.00**
112g	With Ipswich, Bristol, Bath or Salisbury FDI handstamp	**£12.00**
112h	With Greenwich, Blackheath or Richmond (Yorks) cds	**£225.00**
112i	With rare East Bergholt, Essex cds (1/9d stamp only **£65**)	**£435.00**
112j	With Windsor Castle, Windsor cds	**£175.00**
112k	Set of four covers, each with appropriate stamp and postmark	**£20.00**

FIRST DAY OF ISSUE 1 2 AUG 1968 BRISTOL

WINDSOR CASTLE WINDSOR 12 AU 68 BERKS.

EAST BERGHOLT B 12 AU 68 COLCHESTER. ESSEX

PORTSMOUTH & DISTRICT 12 AUG 1968 PHILATELIC SOCIETY

---

113. 1968, 25th November

Christmas Issue 4d Rocking Horse, 9d Doll's House, 1/6d Train Set

113a	Set on illustrated cover, any postmark	**£1.00**
113b	With Philatelic Bureau handstamp	**£4.50**
113c	With Bethlehem, Llandeilo FDI handstamp	**£8.00**
113d	With Selfridges Christmas Toy Fair handstamp	**£18.50**
113e	With Bethlehem 'envelope' FDI cancel (4d only **£20**)	**£60.00**
113f	HMS Hermes, BF 1074 PS handstamp	**£110.00**

FIRST DAY OF ISSUE 25 NOV 1968 BETHLEHEM LLANDEILO, CARMS.

SELFRIDGES Christmas toy fair 25 NOV 1968 LONDON W.1.

LLOYD'S OF LONDON NEW COFFEE HOUSE OPENED 1769 15 JAN 1969 LONDON EC3

CUTTY SARK STAMP DAY 15 JAN 1969 GREENWICH S.E.10

114. 1969, 15th January

British Ships 5d QEII, 3 x 9d Se-tenant, 2 x 1/- Se-tenant, Ships of the Past

114a	Set on illustrated cover, any postmark	**£4.00**
114b	With Philatelic Bureau handstamp	**£12.50**
114c	With Cutty Sark Stamp Day, Greenwich handstamp	**£32.00**
114d	With Lloyd's of London, New Coffee House handstamp	**£90.00**
114e	With Bristol, Liverpool, Portsmouth or Plymouth FDI handstamp	**£25.00**
114f	With Belfast, Glasgow, Newcastle or Hull FDI handstamp	**£22.50**
114g	With London SE, London EC or Southampton FDI handstamp	**£18.50**
114h	With Bristol, Plymouth, Southampton or Hull cds	**£80.00**
114i	With Clydebank or Nelson Place, Broadstairs cds	**£250.00**
114j	With Greenwich S.E.10. 'envelope' FDI cancel	**£95.00**
114k	With First Day of Issue, Great Britain W2, 'envelope' cancel	**£62.00**
114l	With Maritime Mail, London cds	**£245.00**
114m	Set of 6 covers, each with single stamp and appropriate postmark	**£24.50**

115. 1969, 3rd March

First Flight of the Concorde

4d, 9d, 1/6d, Different Views of the Concorde

115a	Set on illustrated cover, any postmark	£5.00 ☐
115b	With Philatelic Bureau handstamp	£15.00 ☐
115c	With Filton, Bristol FDI handstamp	£25.00 ☐
115d	With Filton FDI, plus French Concorde stamp with fdi 2.3.69 h/s	£190.00 ☐
115e	With Filton FDI and Conseil de l'Europe 10.3.69 h/s	£40.00 ☐
115f	With Hounslow, Middx FDI handstamp (Heathrow Airport)	£35.00 ☐
115g	With Filton FDI, plus French 20th Anniversary Concorde h/s 2.3.89	£40.00 ☐
115h	With Field Post Office 975 cds, (Signals Regiment postal service)	£30.00 ☐
115i	With Bristol cds	£45.00 ☐
115j	With Farnborough cds	£85.00 ☐
115k	With House of Commons cds	£60.00 ☐

116. 1969, 2nd April

Notable Anniversaries

5d Alcock and Brown, 9d Europa/Cept Emblems, 1/- ILO Emblem, 1/6d NATO Flags, 1/9d First UK/Australia Flight.

		Single Stamp	Full Set
116a	5d with 50th Anniv. Non-Stop Trans-Atlantic Flight, Manchester h/s	£3.50 ☐	£35.00 ☐
116b	5d with Manchester FDI handstamp	£2.50 ☐	£25.00 ☐
116c	5d with Hoverlloyd Inaugural Flight, Ramsgate handstamp	£10.00 ☐	
116d	5d with Doncaster Grammar School Centenary handstamp	£5.00 ☐	£165.00 ☐
116e	5d with Manchester Airport Salutes Alcock and Brown slogan	£50.00 ☐	
116f	9d with London or Torquay FDI handstamp	£2.50 ☐	£14.00 ☐
116g	9d with London FDI, plus Conseil de l'Europe handstamp	£10.00 ☐	
116h	1/- with London FDI handstamp	£2.00 ☐	£14.00 ☐
116i	1/6d with NATO HQ, NATO SHAPE, or any other BFPS cancel	£12.00 ☐	£250.00 ☐
116j	1/9d with Hounslow FDI handstamp (there are two types)	£4.00 ☐	£25.00 ☐
116k	1/9d with Hounslow FDI, plus 1919-69 h/s and label	£25.00 ☐	
116l	Full set on one cover, any postmark		£4.00 ☐
116m	Full set on one cover with Philatelic Bureau handstamp		£8.50 ☐
116n	Set of five covers, each with appropriate stamp and postmark		£16.50 ☐

Remember, from 1966 onwards, most hand addressed Commemorative covers are worth only 20% of catalogue prices.

QEII • Commemoratives 1969

117. 1969, 28th May

British Cathedrals

4 x 5d Se-tenant, Durham, York, Canterbury, Edinburgh Cathedrals
9d St. Paul's Cathedral, 1/6d Liverpool Metropolitan Cathedral.

117a	Set on illustrated cover, any postmark	**£3.00** ☐
117b	With Philatelic Bureau handstamp	**£7.00** ☐
117c	With Philatex St. Paul's, London EC handstamp	**£22.50** ☐
117d	With York Minster handstamp	**£30.00** ☐
117e	With Metropolitan Cathedral, Liverpool handstamp	**£27.50** ☐
117f	With German British Culture Week, BFPS 1078 handstamp	**£45.00** ☐
117g	With Croeso 69, Towyn handstamp	**£37.50** ☐
117h	With Ulster Recruiting, BFPS 1085 handstamp	**£42.00** ☐
117i	With London EC FDI handstamp	**£15.00** ☐
117j	With Canterbury, Durham, Edinburgh, Liverpool or York FDI h/s	**£15.00** ☐
117k	With Durham or Alcester cds (Winchester cds **£50**)	**£67.50** ☐
117l	Set of 6 covers, each with appropriate stamp and postmark	**£15.00** ☐

---

118. 1969, 1st July

Investiture of the Prince of Wales

3 x 5d Caernarvon Castle Views, 9d Celtic Cross, 1/- Prince Charles

118a	Set on illustrated cover, any postmark	**£2.00** ☐
118b	Same with Day of Investiture, Caernarvon, (Philatelic Bureau) h/s	**£6.50** ☐
118c	With Margam Abbey, Port Talbot handstamp	**£120.00** ☐
118d	With Talyllyn Railway, Towyn Station handstamp	**£47.50** ☐
118e	With Greetings ... Reilfford Talyllyn, Tywyn h/s – all in Welsh	**£42.00** ☐
118f	With Nettleham, Lincoln handstamp	**£110.00** ☐
118g	With BFPS 1000 handstamp (Caernarvon Field P.O.)	**£125.00** ☐
118h	With Croeso 69 Investiture Day, Cardiff handstamp	**£120.00** ☐
118i	With Investiture Day, Caernarvon, 'envelope' cancel	**£265.00** ☐
118j	With Windsor FDI or London SW FDI handstamp, or any Forces P.O. cds	**£15.00** ☐
118k	With Buckingham Palace or Windsor Castle cds	**£285.00** ☐
118l	With House of Commons or House of Lords cds	**£65.00** ☐
118m	With Wales Tomorrow Exhibition, Cardiff slogan	**£160.00** ☐

Single stamp with any one of 118g/118h/118i/118m postmark above is worth £30.00.

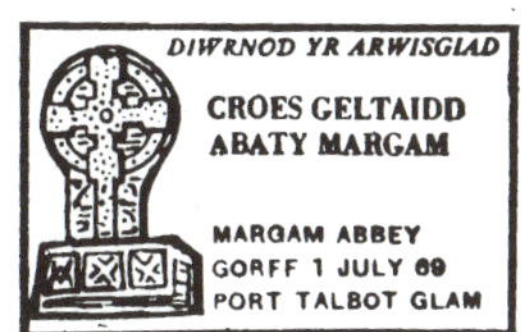

QEII • Commemoratives 1969

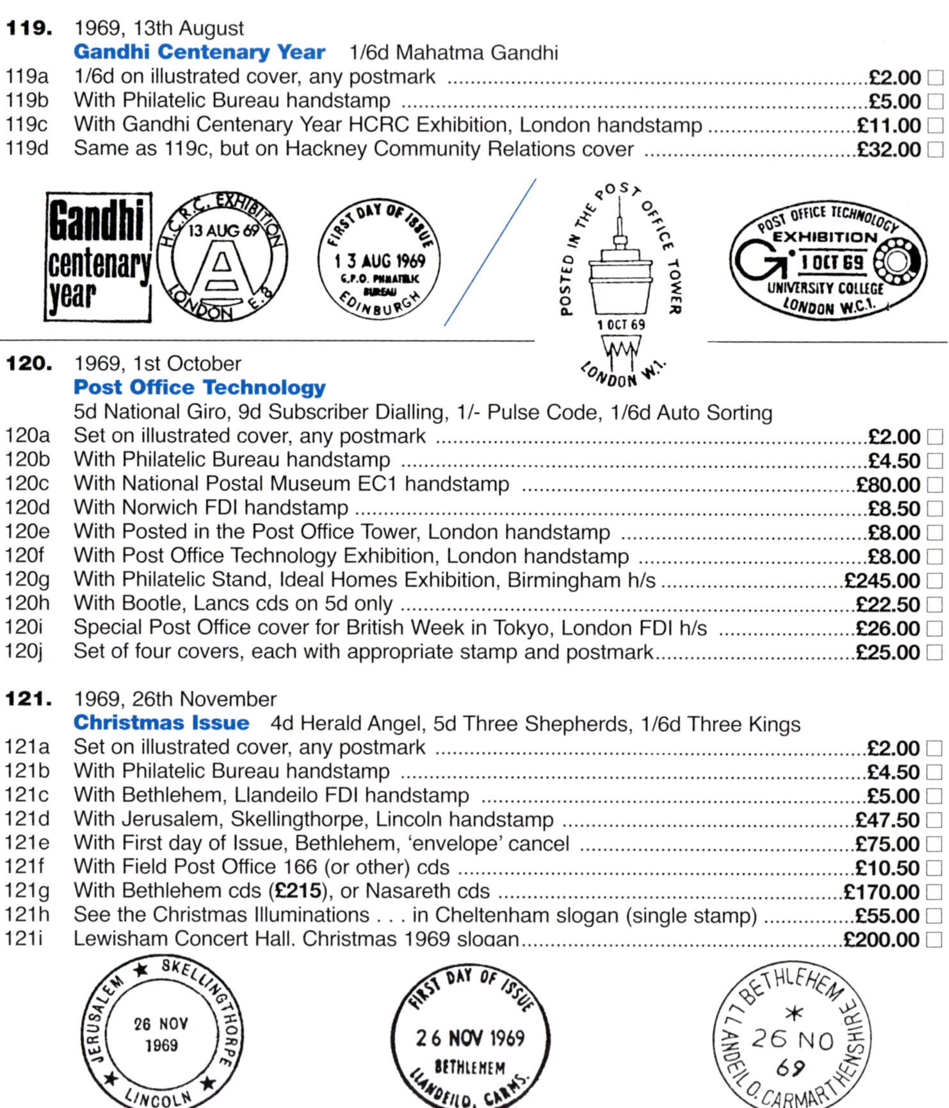

119. 1969, 13th August
Gandhi Centenary Year 1/6d Mahatma Gandhi

119a	1/6d on illustrated cover, any postmark	**£2.00** ☐
119b	With Philatelic Bureau handstamp	**£5.00** ☐
119c	With Gandhi Centenary Year HCRC Exhibition, London handstamp	**£11.00** ☐
119d	Same as 119c, but on Hackney Community Relations cover	**£32.00** ☐

120. 1969, 1st October
Post Office Technology
5d National Giro, 9d Subscriber Dialling, 1/- Pulse Code, 1/6d Auto Sorting

120a	Set on illustrated cover, any postmark	**£2.00** ☐
120b	With Philatelic Bureau handstamp	**£4.50** ☐
120c	With National Postal Museum EC1 handstamp	**£80.00** ☐
120d	With Norwich FDI handstamp	**£8.50** ☐
120e	With Posted in the Post Office Tower, London handstamp	**£8.00** ☐
120f	With Post Office Technology Exhibition, London handstamp	**£8.00** ☐
120g	With Philatelic Stand, Ideal Homes Exhibition, Birmingham h/s	**£245.00** ☐
120h	With Bootle, Lancs cds on 5d only	**£22.50** ☐
120i	Special Post Office cover for British Week in Tokyo, London FDI h/s	**£26.00** ☐
120j	Set of four covers, each with appropriate stamp and postmark	**£25.00** ☐

121. 1969, 26th November
Christmas Issue 4d Herald Angel, 5d Three Shepherds, 1/6d Three Kings

121a	Set on illustrated cover, any postmark	**£2.00** ☐
121b	With Philatelic Bureau handstamp	**£4.50** ☐
121c	With Bethlehem, Llandeilo FDI handstamp	**£5.00** ☐
121d	With Jerusalem, Skellingthorpe, Lincoln handstamp	**£47.50** ☐
121e	With First day of Issue, Bethlehem, 'envelope' cancel	**£75.00** ☐
121f	With Field Post Office 166 (or other) cds	**£10.50** ☐
121g	With Bethlehem cds (**£215**), or Nasareth cds	**£170.00** ☐
121h	See the Christmas Illuminations . . . in Cheltenham slogan (single stamp)	**£55.00** ☐
121i	Lewisham Concert Hall, Christmas 1969 slogan	**£200.00** ☐

Pre-Release Covers have again been included in the catalogue and are priced in a separate section beginning on page 458. We clearly cannot present a complete list since only covers we have actually seen are included. With Pre-Release covers there is often more than one date and readers are invited to submit copies of covers missing from our List.

122. 1970, 11th February

British Rural Architecture

5d Fife Harling, 9d Cotswold Stone, 1/- Welsh Stucco, 1/6 Ulster Thatch

122a	Set on illustrated cover, any postmark	£2.00 ☐
122b	With Philatelic Bureau handstamp	£4.00 ☐
122c	With Aberaeron, Cardiganshire FDI handstamp	£10.00 ☐
122d	With Belfast, Dunfermline, Edinburgh or Gloucester FDI h/s	£10.00 ☐
122e	With Cirencester, Glos cds	£78.00 ☐
122f	With Bibury, Culross, or Chipping Camden cds	£98.00 ☐
122g	With Auchtermuchty, Fife cds (5d value only)	£25.00 ☐
122h	With Holywood, Co. Down cds (1/6d value only)	£25.00 ☐
122i	With Keep Britain Green, 1970 . . .Conservation Year	£180.00 ☐
122j	Set of 4 covers with appropriate stamp and postmark	£12.00 ☐

123. 1970, 1st April

General Anniversaries

5d Declaration of Arbroath, 9d Florence Nightingale,
1/- Co-Op Alliance, 1/6d Mayflower, 1/9d Herschel Telescope.

No.	Description	Single Stamp	Full Set
123a	5d with Arbroath, Angus FDI handstamp	£5.00 ☐	£50.00 ☐
123b	5d with British Anniversary Stamps, Canterbury h/s	£3.50 ☐	£22.00 ☐
123c	9d with Crimean War BFPS 1206 handstamp	£20.00 ☐	£330.00 ☐
123d	9d with Florence Nightingale Hospital, London h/s	£5.00 ☐	£65.00 ☐
123e	9d with Florence Nightingale 150th Birthday Exhibition h/s	£5.00 ☐	£45.00 ☐
123f	9d with 150th Anniversary Florence Nightingale BFPS 1121	£20.00 ☐	£185.00 ☐
123g	9d with 150th Anniversary Florence Nightingale BFPS 1205	£25.00 ☐	£240.00 ☐
123h	1/- with London Co-Op Golden Year, London handstamp	£7.50 ☐	£275.00 ☐
123i	1/- with World HQ International Co-Op Alliance, London h/s	£6.00 ☐	£230.00 ☐
123j	1/- with London WI FDI handstamp	£4.00 ☐	£12.50 ☐
123k	1/- with Rochdale, Lancs FDI handstamp	£4.00 ☐	£20.00 ☐
123l	1/6d with Southampton or Plymouth FDI or cds handstamp	£3.00 ☐	£12.50 ☐
123m	1/6d with Mayflower '70, Scrooby, Yorks handstamp	£25.00 ☐	£230.00 ☐
123n	1/6d with Boston, Lincs FDI handstamp	£12.00 ☐	£20.00 ☐
123o	1/9d with Sir William Herschel, First President RAS, Slough h/s	£5.00 ☐	£75.00 ☐
123p	1/9d with London WI FDI handstamp, or Slough FDI handstamp	£5.00 ☐	£15.00 ☐
123q	1/9d with Immingham, Grimsby cds	£20.00 ☐	£78.00 ☐
123r	1/9d with Plymouth or Boston Mayflower 70 slogan	£32.50 ☐	
123s	Full set on one cover with Philatelic Bureau handstamp		£7.00 ☐

QEII • Commemoratives 1970

124. 1970, 3rd June

Literary Anniversaries

4 x 5d Block of Dickens Characters, 1/6d Grasmere/Wordsworth

124a	Set on illustrated cover, any postmark	£3.00 ☐
124b	With Philatelic Bureau handstamp	£5.50 ☐
124c	With Broadstairs FDI handstamp	£16.00 ☐
124d	With Portsmouth or Rochester FDI handstamp	£16.00 ☐
124e	With Cockermouth FDI handstamp	£32.00 ☐
124f	With Chigwell, Essex E78 handstamp	£60.00 ☐
124g	With Dickens Centenary, Old Curiosity Shop handstamp	£22.00 ☐
124h	With Charles Dickens Winterbourne handstamp	£60.00 ☐
124i	With Dickens Fellowship, Broadstairs Branch, handstamp	£56.00 ☐
124j	With Dickens Centenary, Pickwick, Corsham handstamp	£80.00 ☐
124k	With First Day of Issue, Broadstairs, 'envelope' cancel	£95.00 ☐
124l	With Ambleside or Grasmere cds	£180.00 ☐
124m	With Portsmouth cds	£82.50 ☐
124n	Set on 2 covers, each with appropriate stamp(s) and postmark	£8.50 ☐

---

125. 1970, 15th July

9th British Commonwealth Games, Edinburgh

5d Running, 1/6d Swimming, 1/9d Cycling

125a	Set on illustrated cover, any postmark	£2.00 ☐
125b	With Philatelic Bureau handstamp	£4.00 ☐
125c	With Edinburgh FDI handstamp	£11.00 ☐
125d	With Edinburgh, Gt. Britain, 'envelope' FDI cancel (single stamp **£20**)	£67.50 ☐
125e	With Edinburgh machine cancel	£28.50 ☐
125f	With National Postal Museum slogan	£80.00 ☐
125g	With Edinburgh Mobile Post Office cds	£135.00 ☐

There were several non-related and Army cancellations used on July 15th, 1970.

Please read the notes at the beginning of this catalogue by way of general information.

QEII • Commemoratives 1970

126. 1970, 18th September

Philympia International Stamp Exhibition

5d – 1840 1d Black, 9d – 1847 1/- Green, 1/6d – 1855 4d Carmine

126a	Set on illustrated cover, any postmark	£2.00 ☐
126b	With Philatelic Bureau handstamp	£4.00 ☐
126c	With London WI FDI handstamp	£8.00 ☐
126d	With National Postal Museum, London handstamp	£65.00 ☐
126e	With Philympia Day, London, multi color cancel	£6.00 ☐
126f	With First Flight Philympia Day, Calne, Wilts h/s (5d stamp only £35)	£125.00 ☐
126g	With First Flight Philympia Day, Bembridge IOW h/s (5d stamp only £35)	£125.00 ☐
126h	With House of Commons SW1, or House of Lords cds	£50.00 ☐
126i	With Buckingham Palace SW1 cds	£85.00 ☐
126j	With International Stamp Exhibition, Philympia 70 slogan	£545.00 ☐
126k	With British Forces Postal Service 1136 h/s, on REME cover	£75.00 ☐
126l	With Field Post Office 552 (or other) cds, on BFPS cover	£20.00 ☐
126m	With Olympia W.14 cds	£275.00 ☐

PHILYMPIA DAY

LONDON 18 SEPT 70

127. 1970, 25th November

Christmas Issue 4d, 5d, 1/6d, Religious Christmas Scenes

127a	Set on illustrated cover, any postmark	£2.00 ☐
127b	With Philatelic Bureau handstamp	£4.00 ☐
127c	With First Day of Issue, Bethlehem, Llandeilo handstamp	£7.50 ☐
127d	With Lilleshall Parish Church, Lilleshall, handstamp	£185.00 ☐
127e	With Forces/Field Post Office handstamp (85, 142, etc.), on BFPS cover	£22.50 ☐
127f	With Bethlehem, Llandeilo cds	£275.00 ☐
127g	With First Day of Issue, Bethlehem, Llandeilo 'envelope' cancel	£135.00 ☐

Milestones in Early Post Office History

See page 180 for some fascinating facts covering the period 1482-1898!

BRITISH DISCOVERY
SIR ALEXANDER FLEMING
PENICILLIN
penicillium notatum
1928
108d
DISTA

CHRISTMAS ISSUE
FIRST DAY COVER
109p
Stanley A. Garnett., F.R.P.S.L.
5, Fairview Road.
Timperley, Altrincham.
CHESHIRE.

BRITISH BRIDGES
FIRST DAY COVER
110e

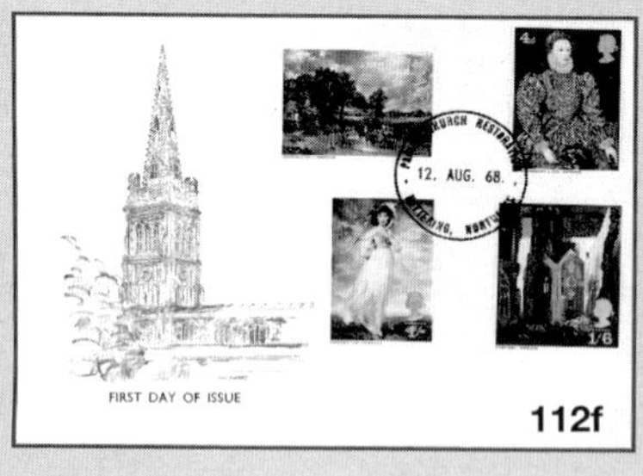
12. AUG. 68.
FIRST DAY OF ISSUE
112f

Christmas 1968
FIRST DAY OF ISSUE
25 NOV 1968
BETHLEHEM
Jeffrey H. Booth Esq.,
23, Hamilton Avenue,
PYRFORD. WOKING.
Surrey.
113c

FIRST DAY OF ISSUE
BRITISH SHIPS
1969
First Day
LLOYD'S OF LONDON
NEW COFFEE HOUSE OPENED 1769
15 JAN 1969
LONDON EC3
114d

LIAISON EUROPÉENNE
FILTON - CONSEIL DE L'EUROPE
CONCORDE FIRST FLIGHT
1969
FIRST DAY COVER
EUROPA FDC SERVICE
115e

- 2 APR 1969
HOUNSLOW, MIDDLESEX
IMPORTANT ANNIVERSARIES
First Day Cover
116j

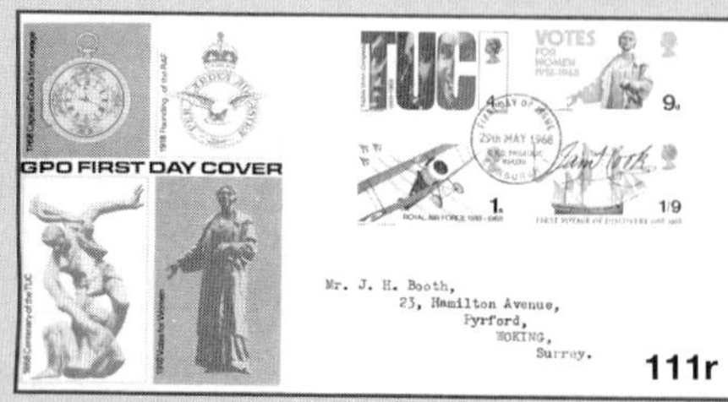
GPO FIRST DAY COVER
TUC
VOTES FOR WOMEN
29th MAY 1968
Mr. J. H. Booth,
23, Hamilton Avenue,
Pyrford,
WOKING,
Surrey.
111r

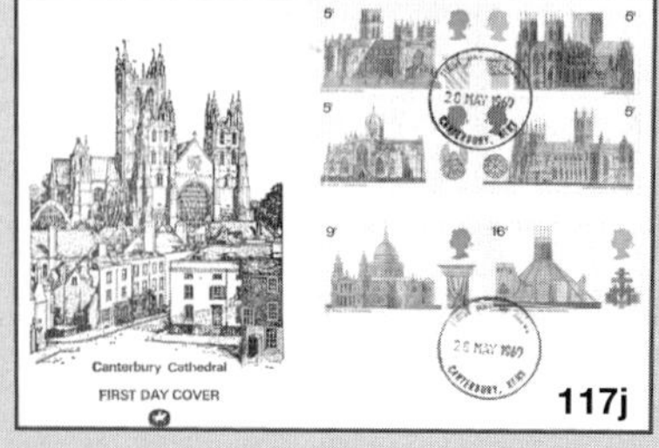
Canterbury Cathedral
FIRST DAY COVER
29 MAY 1969
117j

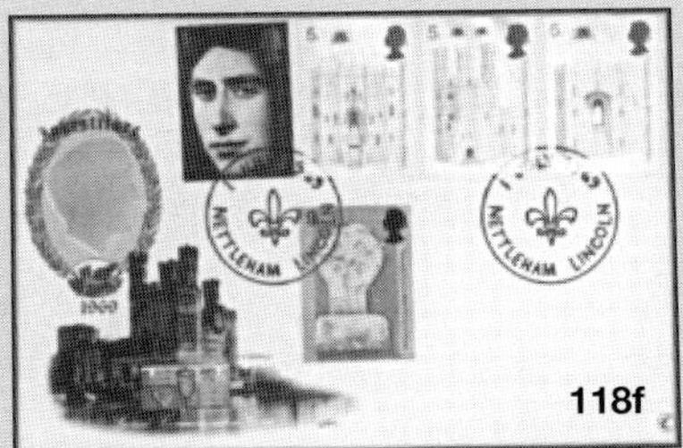

118f

119d

120e

121d

123e

125c

128i

129e

138d

136e

First Day Cover Albums

Albums tailor-made for cover collectors

Stanley Gibbons cover albums are designed to meet the needs of today's first day cover collectors and postal historians alike. All feature high-capacity padded PVC binders, each gold blocked on the spine and contain polypropylene leaves, which do not crease, degrade or tear easily, protect against UV light and contain black insert cards.

New Pioneer

A great value single cover album available in red, green or black with 20 leaves to hold 40 covers up to 9.25 x 5.125 inches (234.95x130.175mm).
Capacity 30 leaves.

R3510	New Pioneer Album (20 leaves)	£14.95
R3511	Extra leaves (per 10)	£4.95

New Classic

A compact deluxe single cover album available in deep blue or maroon with 20 reinforced, easy-access leaves to hold 40 covers up to 5 x 9 inches plus two matching index leaves and a leaf compression clip.

R3525	New Classic Album (20 leaves)	£16.75
R3526	Extra leaves (per 10)	£5.85
R3519	Slipcase	£6.85
R3525-SC		Album & Slipcase £20.75

Malvern

An excellent fully-padded 4-ring double cover album in blue, green, red or black. Contains 19 double leaves to hold 8.75 x 5 inch (222.25x127mm) covers and one single pocket leaf measuring 8.75 x 10.25 inches (222.25x260.35mm).

R3588	Malvern Album (20 leaves)	£14.95
R3593	Extra double leaves (per 10)	£6.85
R3594	Extra single leaves (per 10)	£6.85
R3590	Malvern Slipcase	£8.85
R3588-SC		Malvern Album with Slipcase
£23.50		

SG Major

The top-of-the-range album for that really special collection. Features a luxury padded maroon or deep blue peg-fitting binder, 15 reinforced double pocket and 5 single pocket leaves to hold 70 covers and two matching index leaves measuring 253 x 275mm.

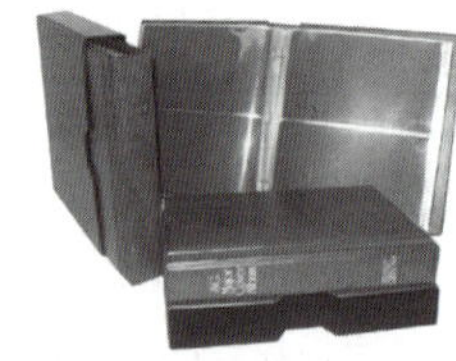

R3550	SG Major Album (20 leaves)	£24.50
R3551	Extra double leaves (per 10)	£8.85
R3552	Extra single leaves (per 10)	£8.85
R3554	SG Major Slipcase	£9.85
R3550-SC	SG Major Album and Slipcase £31.50	

Prices subject to change. Correct as of September 2009.

Order on FREEPHONE 0800 611 622 (UK only)
Stanley Gibbons Publications, 7 Parkside, Christchurch Road, Ringwood, Hampshire BH24 3SH
www.stanleygibbons.com **+44 (0)1425 472 363**

Catalogue prices are for clean illustrated covers, unless otherwise stated, with the full set of stamps as issued. All covers should have typed or printed addresses, or neat labels (not hand addressed). All prices reflect this requirement. Most hand addressed covers are valued at only 20% of catalogue prices.

Decimal Issues

128. 1971, 16th June
Ulster Paintings 3p T.P. Flanagan, 7½p Tom Carr, 9p C. Middleton

128a	Set on illustrated cover, any postmark	**£2.00**
128b	Same with Philatelic Bureau handstamp	**£4.00**
128c	With First Day of Issue slogan, cancelled at Armagh, Ballymena, Cookstown, Coleraine, Enniskillen, Newry, Omagh, or Portadown	**£155.00**
128d	With First Day of Issue slogan, cancelled at Londonderry.	**£45.00**
128e	With First Day of Issue slogan, cancelled at Belfast.	**£8.50**
128f	With 53rd Philatelic Congress ... Ulster Paintings Day, Norwich slogan	**£67.50**
128g	With Ulster 71 Botanic Gardens, Belfast handstamp	**£80.00**
128h	With Dungiven, Hilltown, or Newcastle cds (set of 3 covers **£110**)	**£35.00**
128i	With Northern Parliament, Belfast cds	**£90.00**
128j	With Field Post Office 1029 cds. Recruiting in Ulster illustrated card	**£55.00**
128k	Set of 3 covers, each with one stamp only and appropriate cds postmark (Dungiven, Hilltown, Newcastle)	**£70.00**
128l	Same, each with one stamp and any other appropriate postmark	**£37.50**

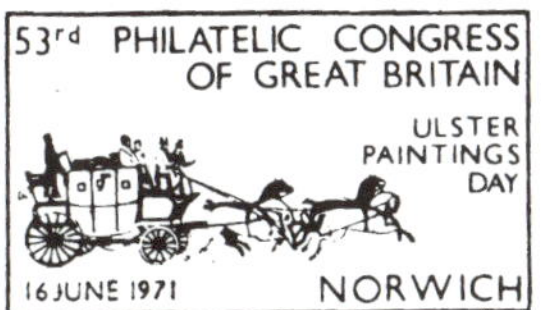

129. 1971, 28th July
Literary Anniversaries 3p John Keats, 5p Thomas Gray, 7½p Sir Walter Scott

129a	Set on illustrated cover, any postmark	**£4.00**
129b	With Philatelic Bureau handstamp	**£6.00**
129c	With First Day of Issue, London EC handstamp	**£9.00**
129d	With Thomas Gray Bi-Centenary, Stoke Poges handstamp.	**£42.50**
129e	With John Keats, Shanklin 1819 handstamp	**£128.00**
129f	With Edinburgh FDI handstamp	**£16.00**
129g	With Melrose cds (single 7½p stamp **£12**)	**£165.00**
129h	With Field Post Office 949 cds or other, on BFPS cover	**£15.00**
129i	Set on 3 covers, each with appropriate stamp and postmark	**£12.50**

The Thomas Gray, Stoke Poges cancellation is sometimes accompanied by a 'Carried by mail coach' red handstamp. This adds £15.00 to the value of the cover with full set.

QEII • Commemoratives 1971

130. 1971, 25th August

General Anniversaries 3p British Legion, 7½p City of York, 9p Rugby Football

130a Set on illustrated cover, any postmark .... **£3.00** ☐
130b With Philatelic Bureau handstamp .... **£6.00** ☐
130c With First Day of Issue, Maidstone handstamp (3p only **£4**) .... **£16.00** ☐
130d With First Day of Issue, York handstamp (7½p only **£3**) .... **£18.50** ☐
130e With First Day of Issue, Twickenham handstamp (9p only **£5**) .... **£18.50** ☐
130f With British Legion 50th Anniversary BFPS 1182 handstamp .... **£230.00** ☐
130g With any Field Post Office (949, 1029 or other) cds, on BFPS cover .... **£22.50** ☐
130h With Rugby Football Union Centenary Year, Rugby, rectangular h/s .... **£190.00** ☐
130i With Rugby Football Union Centenary, Twickenham, oval handstamp .... **£190.00** ☐
130j With Rugby FDI handstamp .... **£34.00** ☐
130k With Richmond & Twickenham cds .... **£62.00** ☐
130l Set of 3 covers, each with appropriate stamp and postmark .... **£12.50** ☐

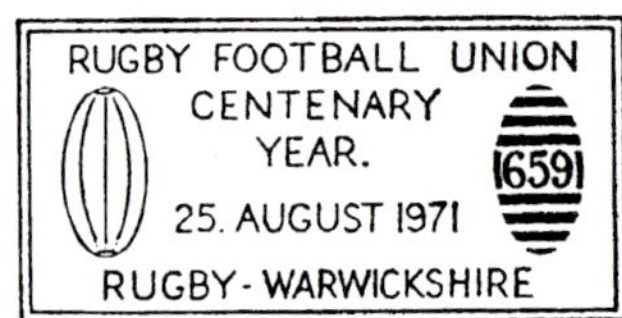

131. 1971, 22nd September

British Architecture – Modern Universities

3p Aberystwyth, 5p Southampton, 7½p Leicester, 9p Essex

131a Set on illustrated cover, any postmark .... **£4.00** ☐
131b With Philatelic Bureau handstamp .... **£6.00** ☐
131c With Aberystwyth special First Day of Issue handstamp .... **£17.50** ☐
131d With Southampton special First Day of Issue handstamp .... **£17.50** ☐
131e With Leicester special First Day of Issue handstamp .... **£17.50** ☐
131f With Colchester special First Day of Issue handstamp .... **£17.50** ☐
131g With Welsh/ English double circle FDI handstamp (various Welsh towns) .... **£14.00** ☐
131h With Field Post Office 949 cds, or other, on BFPS cover .... **£15.00** ☐
131i With Opening Postal Management College, Rugby, double ring handstamp .... **£200.00** ☐
131j Set on 4 covers each with appropriate stamp and postmark .... **£11.50** ☐

SOUTHAMPTON
FIRST DAY OF ISSUE
22 SEP 1971

132. 1971, 13th October

Christmas Issue 2½p, 3p, 7½p, Stained Glass Images, Canterbury Cathedral

132a Set on illustrated cover, any postmark .... **£4.00** ☐
132b With Philatelic Bureau handstamp .... **£6.00** ☐
132c With Bethlehem, Llandeilo special handstamp .... **£12.00** ☐
132d With First Day of Issue, Canterbury special handstamp .... **£12.00** ☐
132e With Field Post Office 949 cds or other, on BFPS cover .... **£9.00** ☐

All QEII Definitives are listed in date order from page 350

QEII • Commemoratives 1972

133. 1972, 16th February

British Polar Explorers

3p Ross, 5p Frobisher, 7½p Hudson, 9p Scott

133a	Set on illustrated cover, any postmark	£6.50 ☐
133b	With Philatelic Bureau handstamp	£10.00 ☐
133c	With First Day of Issue, London WC special handstamp	£11.00 ☐
133d	With Plymouth, Devon FDI handstamp	£17.50 ☐
133e	With Greenwich B.O., SE.10 cds	£130.00 ☐
133f	With Gravesend, Kent cds (7½p stamp only £15)	£120.00 ☐
133g	With Reykjavik, Iceland BFPS cds FPD 376	£560.00 ☐
133h	Set on 4 covers each with appropriate stamp and postmark	£25.00 ☐

---

134. 1972, 26th April

General Anniversaries

3p Tutankhamun, 7½p Coastguard, 9p Vaughan Williams

134a	Set on illustrated cover, any postmark	£3.00 ☐
134b	With Philatelic Bureau handstamp	£5.00 ☐
134c	With Treasures of Tutankhamun Exhibition, London handstamp	£38.00 ☐
134d	With First Day of Issue, London EC circular handstamp	£7.50 ☐
134e	With Vaughan Williams Centenary, Down Ampney handstamp	£38.00 ☐
134f	With HM Coastguard 1822-1972, Bideford, Devon handstamp	£38.00 ☐
134g	3p value with Treasures of Tutankhamun British Museum, London WC cancel	£42.00 ☐
134h	Set on 3 covers, each with appropriate stamp and postmark	£12.00 ☐

GB Overprints on fdc – see pages 454-457

Photographs of most GB Overprints listed can be seen in the 1998/99 edition of the Collect GB First Day Covers catalogue.

All prices in this catalogue are for clean covers with undamaged stamps and clear postmarks.

Gems • 1971 Ulster Paintings

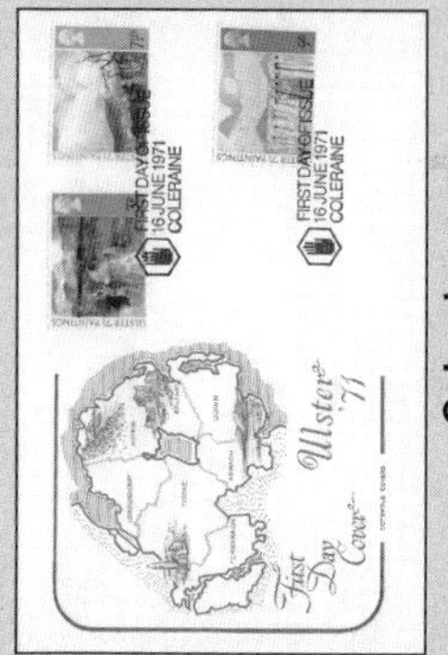

Coleraine

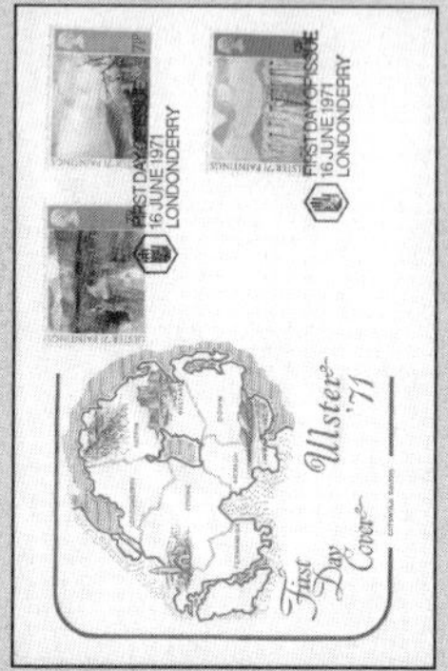

Londonderry

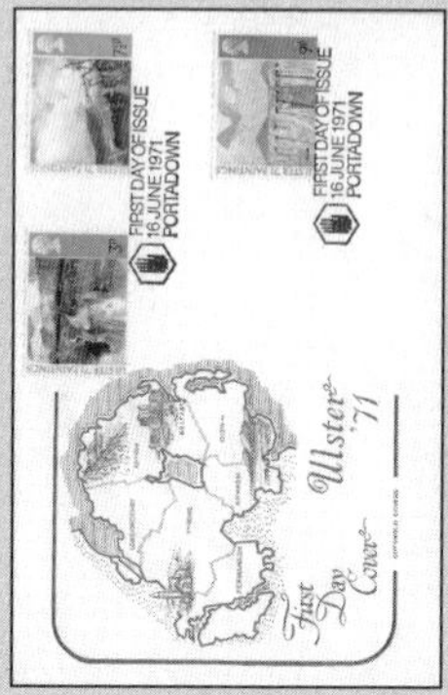

Portadown

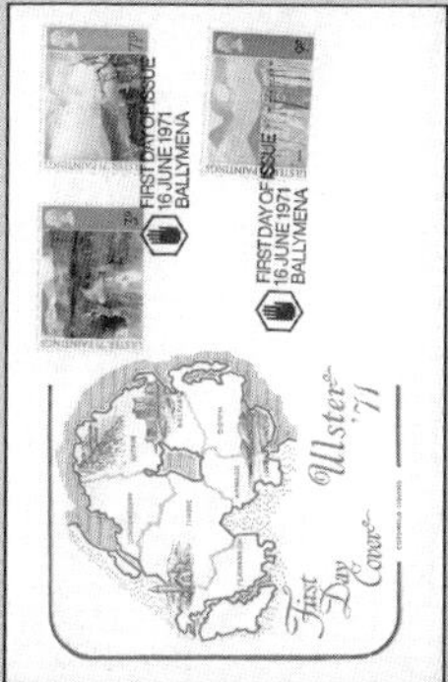

Ballymena

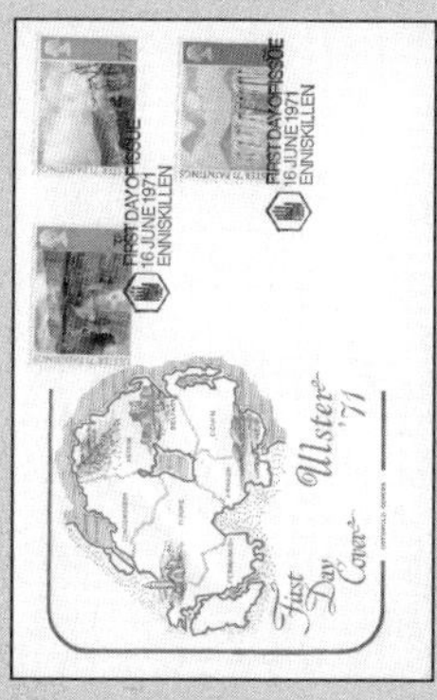

Enniskillen

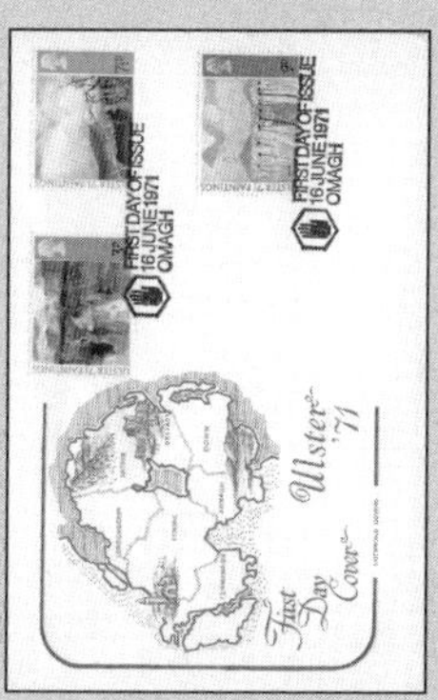

Omagh

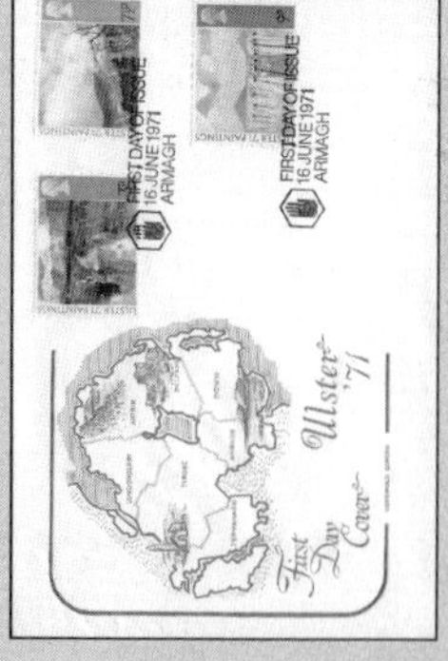

Armagh

Cookstown

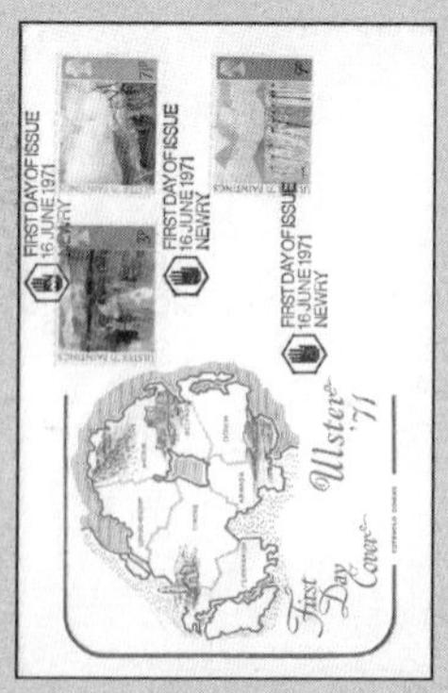

Newry

Set of 9 Key fdi Postmarks

QEII • Commemoratives 1972

135. 1972, 21st June

British Architecture - Village Churches

3p Greensted, 4p Earls Barton, 5p Letheringsett, 7½p Helpringham, 9p Huish Episcopi

135a Set on illustrated cover, any postmark .... **£5.00** ☐
135b With Philatelic Bureau handstamp .... **£7.00** ☐
135c With First Day of Issue, Canterbury circular handstamp .... **£8.50** ☐
135d With World's Oldest Wooden Church, Greensted, Essex handstamp .... **£37.50** ☐
135e With Village Churches Earls Barton, Northampton handstamp .... **£30.00** ☐
135f With Village Churches, Letheringsett, Holt, Norfolk handstamp .... **£35.00** ☐
135g With Village Churches, Helpringham, Sleaford, Lincs handstamp .... **£35.00** ☐
135h With First Day of Issue Exhibition, Huish Episcopi, Langport h/s .... **£35.00** ☐
135i With Parish Church of St. Mary, Langley, Slough, Bucks handstamp .... **£165.00** ☐
135j With St. Augustine's Church, Kilburn, London NW6 handstamp .... **£165.00** ☐
135k With Festival of Berkswell, Coventry handstamp .... **£170.00** ☐
135l With Earls Barton cds (Church Street cds **£200)** .... **£130.00** ☐
135m Set on 5 covers, each with appropriate stamp and postmark .... **£20.00** ☐

---

136. 1972, 13th September

BBC and Marconi Broadcasting Anniversaries

3p BBC Microphones, 5p BBC Loudspeaker, 7½p BBC TV Camera, 9p Marconi Transmitter

136a Set on illustrated cover, any postmark .... **£4.00** ☐
136b With Philatelic Bureau handstamp .... **£6.00** ☐
136c With First Day of Issue, London WI special handstamp .... **£10.50** ☐
136d With Chelmsford, Essex, or Brighton FDI cancel .... **£26.00** ☐
136e With Marconi-Kemp Wireless Experiments, Chelmsford handstamp .... **£37.50** ☐
136f With 75th Anniversary Marconi's First Wireless, Flatholm handstamp .... **£35.00** ☐
136g With Humberside Home Service Philatelic Display, Hull handstamp .... **£75.00** ☐
136h With 21st Anniv. World/British Relay TV Network, Gloucester handstamp .... **£75.00** ☐
136i With 75th Anniv. Adoption of Wireless in British Army, BFPS 1326 .... **£75.00** ☐
136j With BBC 50th Anniversary, Pebble Mill, Birmingham handstamp .... **£415.00** ☐
136k With BBC Radio Leicester, First Local Radio Station, 5th Anniversary Year, Leicester handstamp on 3 BBC stamps only .... **£65.00** ☐
136l With any Field Post Office cancel on BFPS cover .... **£16.50** ☐
136m With BBC Radio Brighton 202 metres, Brighton slogan .... **£455.00** ☐
136n Set on 2 or more covers, each with appropriate stamp and postmark .... **£12.50** ☐

BBC Pebble Mill covers come in two versions, one with full illustration and the other with BBC logo only (catalogue £160.00).

21st Anniversary 1951-1972
First World And
British Relay TV
Network Opened-Gloucester
13 Sept 1972
Gloucester

QEII • Commemoratives 1972-73

137. 1972, 18th October

Christmas Issue

2½p, 3p, 7½p, Angels – Based on early Italian Paintings

137a	Set on illustrated cover, any postmark	£3.00 ☐
137b	With Philatelic Bureau handstamp	£6.50 ☐
137c	With First Day of Issue, Bethlehem slogan cancel	£10.00 ☐

138. 1972, 20th November

Silver Wedding Anniversary

3p, 20p, Queen Elizabeth and Duke of Edinburgh

138a	Set on illustrated cover, any postmark	£2.00 ☐
138b	With Philatelic Bureau handstamp	£5.00 ☐
138c	With First Day of Issue, Windsor, Berks, special handstamp	£8.50 ☐
138d	With Royal Silver Wedding, Westminster Abbey special handstamp	£16.50 ☐
138e	With Commemorating the Royal Silver Wedding, BF 1307 PS h/s	£47.50 ☐
138f	With National Postal Museum handstamp in brown	£16.50 ☐
138g	With any Field Post Office cds on BFPS cover (1340 or other)	£45.00 ☐
138h	With 16th/5th Queen's Royal Lancers, BF 1922 PS handstamp	£52.00 ☐
138i	With Buckingham Palace cds	£165.00 ☐
138j	With House of Commons, or House of Lords cds	£47.50 ☐
138k	With Windsor Castle, Windsor Berks cds	£195.00 ☐

139. 1973, 3rd January

European Communities

3p, 2 x 5p Se-tenant, Map Made from Nine Jigsaw Puzzle Pieces

139a	Set on illustrated cover, any postmark	£4.00 ☐
139b	With Philatelic Bureau handstamp	£6.00 ☐
139c	With Dover or Folkstone FDI handstamp	£12.00 ☐
139d	With Southampton FDI handstamp	£10.00 ☐
139e	With New Parcel Office, Southampton handstamp	£57.50 ☐
139f	With Pas-de-Calais cds and Paquebot marking	£45.00 ☐
139g	With Dover or Folkstone FDI, but with Paquebot marking added	£42.00 ☐
139h	With Brennan Torpedo, BF 1343 PS handstamp	£42.00 ☐
139i	With Conseil de l'Europe, Strasbourg cds	£18.50 ☐
139j	With House of Commons cds	£57.50 ☐
139k	With House of Lords cds	£62.50 ☐
139l	With Harwich cds	£62.50 ☐

Commissioning
of new
Parcel Office
3 Jan 73
SOUTHAMPTON

PAQUEBOT

QEII • Commemoratives 1973

140. 1973, 28th February
Tree Planting Year 9p Oak Tree

140a Set on illustrated cover, any postmark .... **£3.00** ☐
140b With Philatelic Bureau handstamp .... **£6.00** ☐
140c With Royal Horticultural Hall, London, Stampex 73 handstamp .... **£12.50** ☐
140d With Hatfield Broad Oak Exhibition, Herts handstamp .... **£22.50** ☐
140e With Tree Planting Year, Westonbirt Arboretum handstamp .... **£22.50** ☐
140f With Three Oaks cds (Oakham cds **£85**) .... **£130.00** ☐
140g With Stampex h/s or Sevenoaks cds .... **£25.00** ☐

141. 1973, 18th April
British Explorers
2 x 3p Se-tenant Livingstone/Stanley, 5p Drake, 7½p Raleigh, 9p Sturt

141a Set on illustrated cover, any postmark .... **£5.00** ☐
141b With Philatelic Bureau handstamp .... **£10.00** ☐
141c With Drakes Island Adventure Centre, Devon handstamp .... **£35.00** ☐
141d With Sir Walter Raleigh Exhibition, Budleigh Salterton handstamp .... **£35.00** ☐
141e With Welsh/English Denbigh FDI (Stanley born here) handstamp .... **£38.50** ☐
141f With Forces Post Office 79, or other cds .... **£8.50** ☐
141g With Gloucester FDI (Sturt buried here) handstamp .... **£48.50** ☐
141h With Plymouth, Devon FDI handstamp .... **£25.00** ☐
141i With Blantyre, Glasgow FDI (Livingstone born here), handstamp .... **£42.00** ☐
141j With Livingstone, West Lothian cds (3p pair **£60**) .... **£110.00** ☐
141k Set on 2 or more covers, each with appropriate stamp and postmark .... **£12.00** ☐
141l 3p Se-tenant with Livingstone-Stanley Philatelic Exhibition, 19 April, Denbigh h/s ..... **£10.00** ☐

142. 1973, 16th May
Centenary of County Cricket 3p, 7½p, 9p, Furness Sketches of W.G. Grace

142a Set on illustrated cover, any postmark .... **£4.00** ☐
142b With Philatelic Bureau handstamp .... **£6.00** ☐
142c With Lords, London NW FDI handstamp .... **£8.00** ☐
142d With 100 Years English County Cricket Exhibition, Lords, London h/s .... **£16.50** ☐
142e With Birthplace of W.G. Grace, Downend, Bristol handstamp .... **£27.50** ☐
142f With County Cricket Centenary, Chelmsford, Essex handstamp .... **£32.50** ☐
142g With Yorkshire v Hampshire, Headingley, Leeds handstamp .... **£32.50** ☐
142h With HQ Sussex County Cricket Club, Hove, Sussex handstamp .... **£32.50** ☐
142i With HQ Surrey County Cricket Club, Kennington handstamp .... **£32.50** ☐

142j With The Birthplace of English Cricket, Hambledon, Hants handstamp .... £60.00 ☐
142k With Munich BFPS 1400 IBRA Exhibition handstamp .... £67.50 ☐
142l With Hambledon cds .... £110.00 ☐
142m With any of the following FDI handstamps: Bristol, Cardiff, Derby, Canterbury, Birmingham, Leicester, Manchester, Northampton, Southampton, Taunton, Worcester, Nottingham. Each .... £12.50 ☐
142n Complete set of 18 TCCB Cricket Club covers, produced by Stamp Publicity of Worthing, each with full set of stamps and relevant postmark (12 FDI and 6 special handstamps). The set .... £200.00 ☐

143. 1973, 4th July

British Paintings 3p, 7½p Sir Joshua Reynolds; 5p, 9p Sir Henry Raeburn

143a Set on illustrated cover, any postmark .... £3.00 ☐
143b With Philatelic Bureau handstamp .... £6.00 ☐
143c With 250th Birthday Sir Joshua Reynolds, London W.I. handstamp .... £15.00 ☐
143d With Plymouth or London FDI handstamp .... £14.00 ☐
143e With Edinburgh FDI handstamp .... £16.50 ☐
143f With any Forces Post Office cds on BFPS cover .... £8.50 ☐
143g With Raeburn Place, Edinburgh cds .... £65.00 ☐
143h With Douglas, Isle of Man or Whitehaven, Cumberland FDI handstamp .... £46.00 ☐

July 4th 1973 was the last day of British Postal Administration in the Isle of Man.

144. 1973, 15th August

400th Anniversary Inigo Jones

2 x 3p Se-tenant, 2 x 5p Se-tenant; Works by Inigo Jones

144a Set on illustrated cover, any postmark .... £3.00 ☐
144b With Philatelic Bureau handstamp .... £6.00 ☐
144c With London WC FDI handstamp .... £7.50 ☐
144d With 400th Anniversary Inigo Jones, Newmarket handstamp .... £17.50 ☐
144e With Inigo Jones Exhibition, Wilton, Salisbury handstamp .... £17.50 ☐
144f With any Forces Post Office cds, on BFPS cover .... £8.50 ☐
144g With Inigo Jones Banqueting House, Whitehall slogan cancel .... £460.00 ☐

QEII • Commemoratives 1973

145. 1973, 12th September
19th Commonwealth Parliamentary Conference
8p, 10p, Palace of Westminster

145a Set on illustrated cover, any postmark .... **£3.00** ☐
145b With Philatelic Bureau handstamp .... **£5.00** ☐
145c With Parl. Conference, Houses of Parliament, London SW1 handstamp .... **£8.50** ☐
145d With London FDI handstamp .... **£7.50** ☐
145e With House of Commons, or House of Lords SWI cds .... **£85.00** ☐
145f With Buckingham Palace SWI cds .... **£125.00** ☐

146. 1973, 14th November
Royal Wedding 3½p, 20p, Princess Anne and Mark Phillips

146a Set on illustrated cover, any postmark .... **£3.00** ☐
146b With Philatelic Bureau handstamp .... **£5.00** ☐
146c With Westminster Abbey, London SW1 handstamp .... **£6.50** ☐
146d With First Day of Issue, Windsor, Berks handstamp .... **£7.50** ☐
146e With Royal Wedding Celebrations, Great Somerford, handstamp .... **£16.00** ☐
146f With Queens Dragoon Guards, Royal Wedding BF 1434 PS h/s .... **£26.00** ☐
146g With any Field Post Office cds (309 or other), on BFPS cover .... **£17.50** ☐
146h With The Chinese Exhibition, London W1 h/s, with Wedding cachet .... **£40.00** ☐
146i With Sandhurst, Camberley cds .... **£32.50** ☐
146j With Great Somerford, Chippenham, Wilts cds .... **£32.50** ☐
146k With Buckingham Palace, SW1 cds .... **£170.00** ☐
146l With Windsor Castle, Windsor, Berks cds .... **£185.00** ☐
146m With House of Commons, or House of Lords SW1 cds .... **£40.00** ☐

147. 1973, 28th November
Christmas Issue 5 x 3p Se-tenant, 3½p, Good King Wenceslas Carol

147a Set on illustrated cover, any postmark .... **£2.00** ☐
147b With Philatelic Bureau handstamp .... **£5.00** ☐
147c With Welsh/English FDI, Bethlehem, Llandeilo handstamp .... **£9.50** ☐
147d With 141st Anniv. Birth of Lewis Carroll, Daresbury handstamp .... **£185.00** ☐
147e Set of 6 covers, each with one stamp and the Lewis Carroll, Daresbury h/s .... **£145.00** ☐

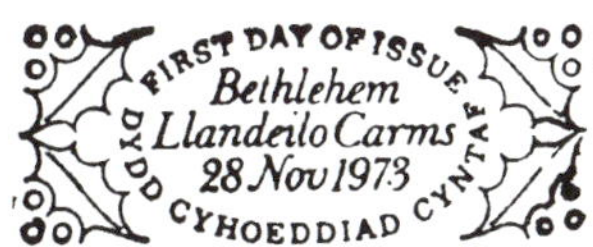

Gems • Two Rare QEII Covers

Buckingham Palace cds.
The best by far of all postmarks for the 1953 Coronation Issue.

1966 - the very first GB Christmas Stamps.
Bethlehem – the best by far of all postmarks for this Issue.

QEII • An Editorial Comment

All About Postmarks.

Royal Mail continue to publish their excellent booklet entitled All About Postmarks. This is an informative guide on the subject of postmarks and postmarking. As such it is a recommended read for all first day cover Collectors.

The booklet summarises the key elements of postmarking and answers many frequently asked questions on the subject. The main chapters are:

- What is a Postmark?
- Postmarks in general postal use
- Special handstamps
- How to obtain different postmarks
- Postmark rules
- Sponsoring a special handstamp

All About Postmarks is published by Royal Mail and is available from the Philatelic Bureau in Edinburgh at the time of writing.

Investing in GB First Day Covers.

Stocks and Shares don't do so well these days but Stamp values continue to climb. Stamps do not seem to be affected by all the usual market forces and it's fair to say that rare and expensive first day covers make an excellent investment.

If one is considering investing in GB first day covers, then go for the older Issues – QV, KEVII, KGV. Ideally hold them for a few years for the best return – and the good news is that they rarely go down in value!

With over 40 years experience we are always happy to advise on GB first day cover investing.

148. 1974, 27th February
British Trees 10p Horse Chestnut

148a 10p stamp on illustrated cover, any postmark .... **£3.00** ☐
148b With Philatelic Bureau handstamp .... **£6.50** ☐
148c With Stampex, London Royal Horticultural Hall SW1 handstamp .... **£12.00** ☐
148d **Double Dated Cover:** 1974 10p Tree stamp with FDI postmark on 1973 cover with 9p Tree stamp and FDI postmark .... **£85.00** ☐

FIRST DAY OF ISSUE · PHILATELIC BUREAU EDINBURGH · 27 FEB 74 ·

STAMPEX 27 FEB 1974 LONDON 1974 ROYAL HORTICULTURAL HALL SW1

---

149. 1974, 24th April
200th Anniversary First Fire Service Legislation
3½p, 5½p, 8p, 10p, Early Fire Engines

149a Set on illustrated cover, any postmark .... **£3.50** ☐
149b With Philatelic Bureau handstamp (Winsor fdi **£25**) .... **£6.50** ☐
149c With First Open Day Avon County Fire Brigade, Bristol handstamp .... **£30.00** ☐
149d With Binns Philatelic and Fire Services Exhibition, Sunderland h/s .... **£44.00** ☐
149e With Inaugural Ceremony Cambridgeshire Fire Rescue Service h/s .... **£40.00** ☐
149f With Lansing Bagnall 25 years at Basingstoke handstamp .... **£215.00** ☐
149g With any Forces Post Office cds (79 and others), on BFPS cover .... **£10.00** ☐
149h With London SE1, Cambridge, Bristol or Sunderland FDI handstamp .... **£17.50** ☐
149i With 'The Fire Brigade Needs Men of Courage', Northern Ireland slogan .... **£575.00** ☐
149j Set of 4 covers, each with single stamp and different relevant postmark .... **£8.00** ☐
149k Set with Burnt House Lane, Exeter cds .... **£530.00** ☐
149l With Hose, Melton Mowbray cds .... **£275.00** ☐
149m With Tooley Street, SE1 cds, or Windsor Castle cds! .... **£285.00** ☐
149n With House of Commons, or House of Lords SWI cds .... **£47.50** ☐

The Post Office cover exists with 'Merryweather' overprint at the top left and Bureau cancellation of the stamps. Catalogue value **£15.00**.

INAUGURAL CEREMONY CAMBRIDGESHIRE FIRE AND RESCUE SERVICE 24 APRIL 1974 CAMBRIDGE

Lansing Bagnall 25 YEARS AT BASINGSTOKE HAMPSHIRE 1949-1974 APRIL 24th 1974

first day of issue UPU centenary 12 JUNE 74 PHILATELIC BUREAU EDINBURGH

150. 1974, 12th June
Centenary Universal Postal Union
3½p P & O Packet, 5½p Farman Biplane, 8p Mail Van, 10p Flying Boat

150a Set on illustrated cover, any postmark .... **£3.00** ☐
150b With Philatelic Bureau special handstamp .... **£6.50** ☐
150c With Internaba cachet on P.O. cover, Bureau handstamp .... **£10.50** ☐
150d With Universal Postal Union 100th Anniversary, Southampton h/s .... **£16.50** ☐
150e With National Postal Museum, London EC1 handstamp in brown .... **£65.00** ☐
150f With Windsor or Southampton FDI handstamp .... **£18.00** ☐
150g With Chief Office, London EC1 handstamp .... **£18.00** ☐
150h With Field Post Office FPO 955 cds, or other, on BFPS cover .... **£12.50** ☐
150i With London F.S. cds .... **£32.50** ☐
150j With Windsor Castle cds .... **£185.00** ☐
150k Set on 4 covers, each with appropriate stamp and postmark .... **£8.00** ☐

QEII • Commemoratives 1974

151. 1974, 10th July

Great Britons - Medieval Knights

4½p Robert the Bruce, 5½p Owain Glyndwr, 8p Henry V, 10p The Black Prince

151a	Set on illustrated cover, any postmark	£3.50 ☐
151b	With Philatelic Bureau handstamp	£7.00 ☐
151c	With Robert the Bruce, Dunfermline Abbey, Fife handstamp	£38.50 ☐
151d	With 700th Anniv. Birth of Robert the Bruce, Bannockburn, Stirling h/s	£38.50 ☐
151e	With Welsh/English Owain Glyndwr's Parliament House handstamp	£38.50 ☐
151f	With Royal Tournament BF 1974 PS handstamp on tournament cover	£78.00 ☐
151g	With Canterbury, Dunfermline, Gwent or Windsor FDI handstamp	£16.50 ☐
151h	With Normandy, Guildford, Surrey cds	£87.50 ☐
151i	With Calais Maritime cds and Paquebot cachet (8p stamp only **£20**)	£165.00 ☐
151j	With Cardross Dumbarton cds, 4½p stamp only, or Woodstock cds, 10p stamp	£28.00 ☐
151k	With Glyndyfrdwy, Merioneth cds, 5½p stamp only	£28.00 ☐
151l	With House of Commons or House of Lords SWI cds	£36.00 ☐
151m	With Buckingham Palace SW1 cds	£87.50 ☐
151n	Set on 4 covers, each with one stamp and appropriate (different) postmark	£12.50 ☐

152. 1974, 9th October

Centenary of the Birth of Sir Winston Churchill

4½p, 5½p, 8p, 10p, Photographs of Sir Winston

152a	Set on illustrated cover, any postmark	£3.50 ☐
152b	With Philatelic Bureau handstamp	£7.00 ☐
152c	With First Day of Issue, Blenheim, Woodstock handstamp	£10.50 ☐
152d	With First Day of Issue, House of Commons, London handstamp	£10.50 ☐
152e	With Centenary Exhibition, Somerset House, London handstamp	£52.00 ☐
152f	With Oldham, Churchill's First Constituency handstamp	£28.00 ☐
152g	With Churchill Centenary, Woodford Green, Essex handstamp	£26.50 ☐
152h	With Sir Winston Churchill, RAF Honnington BF1874 PS handstamp	£32.00 ☐
152i	With Tunbridge Wells, Kent FDI and 'Posted at Chartwell' cachet	£32.00 ☐
152j	With Dover, or other Cinque Ports FDI handstamp	£18.00 ☐
152k	With Churchill, (Oxford or Bristol) cds	£150.00 ☐
152l	With House of Commons cds	£110.00 ☐
152m	With House of Lords cds	£125.00 ☐
152n	With Bladon, Oxford cds or Woodstock, Oxford cds	£147.50 ☐
152o	With Sandhurst, Camberley cds (Rye cds **£60**)	£85.00 ☐
152p	With Marlborough or Winston cds	£225.00 ☐
152q	With Normandy, Guildford, Surrey cds	£97.50 ☐
152r	With Windsor Castle or Buckingham Palace cds	£100.00 ☐
152s	Set on 4 covers, each with different stamp and relevant postmark	£20.00 ☐

Two Winston Churchill Centenary souvenir sheets, with postal validity, were prepared for the November 9th, 1974 Southampton stamp fair. One sheet has a printed 3p blue and the other a printed 4½p light blue stamp. With Southampton cds these are catalogued at **£22** each.

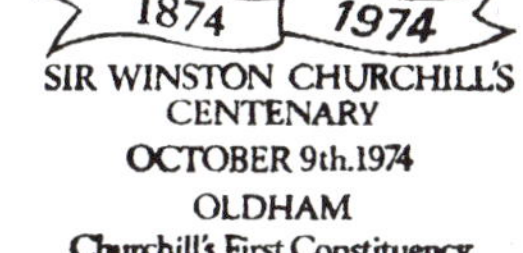

QEII • Commemoratives 1974-75

153. 1974, 27th November
Christmas Issue 3½p, 4½p, 8p, 10p, Church Roof Bosses

153a Set on illustrated cover, any postmark **£3.00**
153b With Philatelic Bureau handstamp **£5.50**
153c With Welsh/English Bethlehem, Llandeilo handstamp **£8.00**
153d With The Collegiate Church Exhibition, Ottery St. Mary handstamp **£27.50**
153e With St. Helen's Church Centenary, Great Hospital, Norwich h/s **£27.50**
153f With The Salvation Army Christmas Supermarket, Tunbridge Wells handstamp **£87.50**
153g With Norwich, Worcester or York FDI handstamp (cds **£40**) **£26.50**
153h With any British Forces P.O. cds, on BFPS cover **£10.50**

154. 1975, 22nd January
Charity Stamp 4½p +1½p Invalid in Wheelchair

154a 4½p +1½p stamp on illustrated cover, any postmark **£2.00**
154b With Philatelic Bureau handstamp **£4.00**
154c With Kettering, Northants FDI plus Winged Fellowship Trust cachet **£14.00**
154d With Aylesbury, Bucks, FDI (Stoke Mandeville hospital) **£18.00**
154e With Oxford FDI (Oxfam HQ) **£16.50**
154f With 'Tenovus Cares' Cardiff special cancel **£295.00**
154g With Menphys Love the Handicapped, Leicester or Wigston slogan **£97.50**
154h With 'Barnardo's Cares', Hounslow slogan cancel **£295.00**
154i With Stoke Charity, Winchester, Hants cds **£295.00**

155. 1975, 19th February
British Painters - J.M.W. Turner 4½p, 5½p, 8p, 10p, Turner Paintings

155a Set on illustrated cover, any postmark **£3.50**
155b With Philatelic Bureau handstamp **£6.50**
155c With First Day of Issue - London WC special h/s (two sizes) **£7.50**
155d With Petworth or Turners Hill cds **£187.50**
155e With Harwich cds on 5½p stamp **£28.00**
155f With Turner, Royal Academy slogan **£35.00**

QEII • Commemoratives 1975

156. 1975, 23rd April

European Architectural Heritage Year

2 x 7p Se-tenant Edinburgh, 8p Greenwich, 10p Windsor, 12p London

156a Set on illustrated cover, any postmark **£3.50** ☐
156b With Philatelic Bureau handstamp **£8.00** ☐
156c With Chester Heritage City handstamp **£26.50** ☐
156d With Corinium 1900 Heritage, Cirencester handstamp **£37.50** ☐
156e With 500 years St. Georges Chapel, Windsor handstamp **£22.00** ☐
156f With National Trust for Scotland, Edinburgh handstamp **£36.00** ☐
156g With Wilton House Open Day, Wilton Salisbury handstamp **£37.50** ☐
156h With Edinburgh, Windsor, Chester or London SE FDI handstamp **£16.00** ☐
156i With European Architectural Heritage Year, Leicester, slogan cancel **£380.00** ☐
156j With Chester Heritage City, Chester, slogan cancel **£340.00** ☐
156k With Windsor Castle cds **£147.50** ☐
156l With Greenwich B.O. S.E.10 cds (Dartmouth Row cds **£280**) **£225.00** ☐
156m Set on 5 covers, each with appropriate stamp and postmark **£16.00** ☐

157. 1975, 11th June

Sailing Centenaries 7p Dinghies, 8p Keel Boats, 10p Yachts, 12p Multihulls

157a Set on illustrated cover, any postmark **£3.00** ☐
157b With Philatelic Bureau handstamp **£6.00** ☐
157c With 'Arphila 75 Paris' cachet and Bureau handstamp **£10.50** ☐
157d With Royal Thames Yacht Club Bi-Centenary, London handstamp **£16.00** ☐
157e With Royal Dorset Yacht Club Centenary, Weymouth handstamp **£16.00** ☐
157f With any Field Post Office (51 or other) cds, on BFPS cover **£8.50** ☐
157g With Hastings, East Sussex FDI **£22.00** ☐
157h With Newport, Woking, Plymouth, Southampton or Weymouth FDI **£22.00** ☐
157i With Cowes I.O.W. cds **£110.00** ☐
157j With Rye, West Wittering, or Burnham-on-Crouch cds **£84.00** ☐
157k With House of Commons cds (they have a Yacht Club!) **£50.00** ☐
157l Set on 4 covers, each with single stamp and different relevant postmark **£10.50** ☐

158. 1975, 13th August

150th Anniversary First Public Steam Railway

7p, 8p 10p, 12p, Famous Engines

158a Set on illustrated cover, any postmark **£3.50** ☐
158b With Philatelic Bureau handstamp **£7.00** ☐
158c With Darlington - First Day of Issue 'ticket' handstamp **£12.50** ☐
158d With Stockton - First Day of Issue 'ticket' handstamp **£12.50** ☐
158e With Shildon - First Day of Issue 'ticket' handstamp **£14.50** ☐
158f With Return of Steam, 10th Anniv, Buckfastleigh handstamp **£24.00** ☐
158g With Royal Engineers 70th Anniv. Longmoor Military Railway BF1396 PS h/s **£24.00** ☐
158h With Railway Festival, Wylam, Northumberland, birthplace of G. Stephenson **£36.00** ☐
158i With Torbay Steam Railway, 25th Anniv., Paignton, Devon h/s **£24.00** ☐
158j With Stockton and Darlington Railway Jubilee, Shildon slogan **£415.00** ☐
158k With Stockton and Darlington Railway Anniversary, Darlington slogan **£415.00** ☐
158l With Ravenglass and Eskdale Railway Centenary slogan* **£260.00** ☐

QEII • Commemoratives 1975

158m With Brighton, East Sussex FDI, Bluebell Railway cover and cachet .... **£30.00** ☐
158n With Bournemouth or Swindon FDI cancel .... **£30.00** ☐
158o With Crewe, York, or Paddington FDI cancel .... **£22.00** ☐
158p With North East T.P.O. (Travelling Post Office), or any other TPO cds .... **£42.50** ☐
158q With Wylam cds (birthplace of George Stephenson) .... **£95.00** ☐
158r With Caerphilly cds (10p stamp **£25**) .... **£75.00** ☐
158s With Welshpool cds .... **£46.00** ☐
158t With any Forces Post Office cds, on BFPS cover .... **£16.00** ☐

*The Ravenglass and Eskdale railway slogan cover usually has only one stamp and is catalogued as such at **£35**

13 AUG. STOCKTON ON-TEES CLEVELAND 1975 FIRST DAY OF ISSUE

RETURN OF STEAM 10th ANNIVERSARY YEAR 13 AUG 75 13 AUG 75 BUCKFASTLEIGH ○ DEVON

13 AUG. DARLINGTON CO DURHAM 1975 FIRST DAY OF ISSUE

62nd Inter-Parliamentary Conference 3 SEP 1975 Royal Festival Hall LONDON SE1

159. 1975, 3rd September

Inter-Parliamentary Union Conference 12p Palace of Westminster

159a 12p stamp on illustrated cover, any postmark .... **£2.00** ☐
159b With Philatelic Bureau handstamp .... **£4.00** ☐
159c With 62nd Inter-Parliamentary Conference, Royal Festival Hall h/s .... **£8.00** ☐
159d With House of Commons SW1 cds .... **£57.50** ☐
159e With House of Lords SW1 cds .... **£65.00** ☐
159f With Parliament St. B.O. cds .... **£60.00** ☐
159g With Evesham cds .... **£80.00** ☐
159h **Double dated cover**, with both 1975 and 1973 Parl. Conference stamps, FDI pmks .... **£78.00** ☐

160. 1975, 22nd October

Bicentenary of Jane Austen

8½p, 10p, 11p, 13p, Characters from Jane Austen Novels

160a Set on illustrated cover, any postmark .... **£3.00** ☐
160b With Philatelic Bureau handstamp .... **£5.50** ☐
160c With First Day of Issue, Steventon, Hants handstamp .... **£7.50** ☐
160d With Steventon, Hants handstamp plus mail coach cachet on official cover .... **£12.00** ☐
160e With Jane Austen Bicentenary Exhibition, Bath handstamp .... **£16.00** ☐
160f With Jane Austen Bi-Centenary 1775-1975, Hampshire. This slogan was used together with a cds at Alton, Basingstoke, Southampton and Winchester. Each .... **£350.00** ☐
160g With Alton, Hants cds (Steventon, Hants cds **£150**) .... **£127.50** ☐
160h With Winchester or Chawton cds .... **£137.50** ☐

Jane Austen 1775-1975 Bicentenary Exhibition 22nd Oct 1975 Bath

FIRST DAY OF ISSUE STEVENTON BASINGSTOKE HANTS 22 OCT 1975

FIRST DAY OF ISSUE · DYDD CYHOEDDIAD CYNTAF BETHLEHEM LLANDEILO DYFED · 26 NOV 1975

ANGEL HILL, SUTTON * 26 NO 75 SURREY

161. 1975, 26th November

Christmas Issue 6½p, 8½p, 11p, 13p, Angels with Musical Instruments

161a Set on illustrated cover, any postmark .... **£3.00** ☐
161b With Philatelic Bureau handstamp .... **£5.00** ☐
161c With Welsh/English FDI Bethlehem, Llandeilo handstamp .... **£6.50** ☐
161d With Angel Hill, Surrey cds .... **£218.00** ☐

QEII • Commemoratives 1976

162. 1976, 10th March

Centenary of First Telephone Communication

8½p, 10p, 11p, 13p, People using the Telephone

162a Set on illustrated cover, any postmark .... **£3.00** ☐
162b With Philatelic Bureau handstamp .... **£4.50** ☐
162c With Post Office Museum, Taunton, Somerset handstamp .... **£8.00** ☐
162d With Boston, Edinburgh, or Hull FDI handstamp .... **£17.50** ☐
162e With Samaritans Distress Despair, Bognor slogan cancel .... **£360.00** ☐
162f With Hope Street, Edinburgh cds .... **£165.00** ☐

163. 1976, 28th April

British Social Reformers 8½p Mining - Hepburn, 10p Work Conditions - Owen, 11p Child Labour - Shaftesbury, 13p Prison Reform - Fry

163a Set on illustrated cover, any postmark .... **£3.00** ☐
163b With Philatelic Bureau handstamp .... **£5.00** ☐
163c With Durham, Folkstone, Norwich or Rochdale FDI handstamp .... **£20.00** ☐
163d With Lanark, New Lanark, or Wimborne cds .... **£112.00** ☐
163e With Brixton or Parkhurst cds .... **£87.50** ☐
163f With Pelton or Shaftesbury cds .... **£154.00** ☐
163g With Newton or Norwich cds .... **£60.00** ☐
163h With House of Commons or House of Lords cds .... **£38.00** ☐
163i Set of 4 covers, each with appropriate stamp and postmark .... **£16.00** ☐

164. 1976, 2nd June

Bicentennial of American Independence 11p Benjamin Franklin

164a 11p on illustrated cover, any postmark .... **£2.00** ☐
164b With Philatelic Bureau handstamp .... **£4.00** ☐
164c With Interphil cachet and Bureau handstamp .... **£14.00** ☐
164d With American Bicentennial, American Museum, Bath handstamp .... **£14.00** ☐
164e With The 1776 Exhibition, Greenwich, London handstamp .... **£14.00** ☐
164f With USA Independence Bicentenary, Washington oval handstamp .... **£14.00** ☐
164g With 58th Philatelic Congress of GB, Plymouth, Devon handstamp .... **£22.50** ☐
164h With Bicentennial of American Independence, BF 1776 PS handstamp .... **£14.00** ☐
164i With Plymouth, Boston or Cambridge FDI handstamp .... **£16.00** ☐
164j With Buckingham Palace cds, or Bunker's Hill cds .... **£148.00** ☐
164k With Sulgrave, Banbury cds .... **£68.00** ☐
164l With House of Commons or House of Lords cds .... **£40.00** ☐
164m With Dallas, Denver, New York, or Washington cds* .... **£130.00** ☐

*These are all places in England, but far better known in America!

QEII • Commemoratives 1976

165. 1976, 30th June

Centenary of Royal National Rose Society

8½p, 10p, 11p, 13p, Different Varieties of Roses

165a	Set on illustrated cover, any postmark	£3.00 ☐
165b	With Philatelic Bureau handstamp	£6.00 ☐
165c	With Royal National Rose Society, Oxford handstamp	£14.00 ☐
165d	With Royal National Rose Society, St. Albans handstamp	£14.00 ☐
165e	With Year of the Rose, Bath handstamp	£15.00 ☐
165f	With Year of the Rose, Northampton handstamp	£15.00 ☐
165g	With Royal Norfolk Show, Norwich handstamp	£32.00 ☐
165h	With Tunbridge Wells FDI, plus Sissinghurst Castle cachet	£22.50 ☐
165i	With The Mothers' Union Centenary, London SWI handstamp	£68.00 ☐
165j	With Kew Gardens cds	£175.00 ☐
165k	With Glamis, Forfar cds	£112.00 ☐
165l	With Buckingham Palace cds	£90.00 ☐
165m	With Rose, Truro cds or Rose Cottage, Hull cds	£165.00 ☐
165n	With Rosebush, Rose Lane, Rosebranch, or Rosebank cds	£90.00 ☐

166. 1976, 4th August

British Cultural Traditions

8½p Archdruid, 10p Morris Dancer, 11p Scots Piper, 13p Welsh Harpist

166a	Set on illustrated cover, any postmark	£3.00 ☐
166b	With Philatelic Bureau handstamp	£5.00 ☐
166c	With Welsh-English FDI, Cardigan handstamp	£6.00 ☐
166d	With Bristol Morris Men 25th Anniv. Bristol handstamp	£10.00 ☐
166e	With Eisteddfod 1176-1976 Cardigan, Dyfed oval handstamp	£10.00 ☐
166f	With Thaxted, Braemar or Llangollen cds	£60.00 ☐
166g	With Bristol or Padstow cds, or Exeter FDI handstamp	£40.00 ☐
166h	With Abingdon, Bampton, Abbots Bromley or Britannia cds	£45.00 ☐

There are many other places that can be related to this issue - Corwen, Carmarthen, Headington Quarry, Chipping Campden, and possibly more. All of these are catalogued at £35.00 on illustrated covers.

BRISTOL MORRIS MEN
25TH ANNIVERSARY
4TH AUGUST 1976 · BRISTOL

Remember, from 1966 onwards, most hand addressed Commemorative covers are worth only 20% of catalogue prices.

Gems • Two Fine QEII Covers

1961 Post Office Savings Bank
Blythe Rd. West Kensington. The best postmark!

1964 International Botanical Congress
Rare Kew Gardens cds

QEII • Commemoratives 1976-77

167. 1976, 29th September
William Caxton - 500th Anniv. Printing in England
8½p Woodcut, 10p Typestyles, 11p Chess Board, 13p Printing Press

167a Set on illustrated cover, any postmark .... **£3.00** ☐
167b With Philatelic Bureau handstamp .... **£6.00** ☐
167c With First Day of Issue, London SW1 special handstamp .... **£7.50** ☐
167d With William Caxton Exhibition, British Library, London handstamp .... **£17.50** ☐
167e With Centenary De Montfort Press, Leicester handstamp .... **£17.50** ☐
167f With 500 Years British Printing, Westminster SW1 handstamp .... **£17.50** ☐
167g With NATSOPA Celebrates ... London SEI handstamp .... **£17.50** ☐
167h With British Philatelic Exhibition, London W1 handstamp .... **£17.50** ☐
167i With 500 Anniversary of Printing, Plymouth, Devon handstamp .... **£17.50** ☐
167j With Paper & Printing Study Group Celebrates ..., London SE1 handstamp .... **£17.50** ☐
167k With Royal Charter Quincentenary, Cheltenham handstamp .... **£37.50** ☐
167l With Canterbury, Cambridge, Plymouth, Manchester, Sunderland FDI h/s .... **£14.00** ☐
167m With Caxton, Fleet Street, or Abingdon cds .... **£115.00** ☐
167n With House of Commons SW1 cds (Tenterden cds **£85**) .... **£65.00** ☐

---

168. 1976, 24th November
Christmas Issue
6½p, 8½p, 11p, 13p Embroideries from Victoria and Albert Museum

168a Set on illustrated cover, any postmark .... **£3.00** ☐
168b With Philatelic Bureau handstamp .... **£6.00** ☐
168c With Bethlehem, Llandeilo handstamp .... **£7.50** ☐
168d With A Tonic to the Nation, V&A Museum, London handstamp .... **£25.00** ☐
168e With Pompeii Exhibition, Royal Academy, London handstamp .... **£25.00** ☐
168f With 75 Anniv. 1st British Corps, Aldershot BF 1901 PS handstamp .... **£30.00** ☐
168g With Angel Hill, Sutton cds .... **£55.00** ☐
168h With Pincushion, Boston, Lincs cds .... **£60.00** ☐

169. 1977, 12th January
Racquet Sports 8½p Tennis, 10p Table Tennis, 11p Squash, 13p Badminton

169a Set on illustrated cover, any postmark .... **£3.00** ☐
169b With Philatelic Bureau handstamp .... **£6.00** ☐
169c With Squash Rackets Association, Founded in 1928, Harrow handstamp .... **£12.00** ☐
169d With Badminton Association, Badminton, Avon handstamp .... **£12.00** ☐
169e With Birmingham, Hastings or Warwick & Leamington FDI handstamp .... **£17.50** ☐
169f With Woodside Parade, Wimbledon, or Wimbledon SDO cds .... **£195.00** ☐
169g With Wimbledon Park, Wimbledon SW19 cds .... **£225.00** ☐

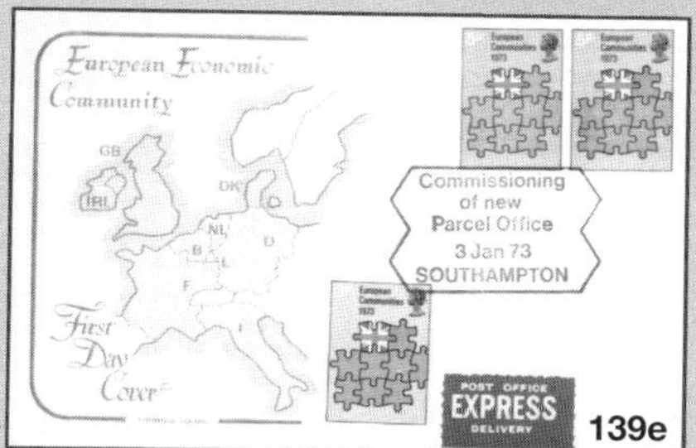

139e

159e

142j

167e

152h

164b

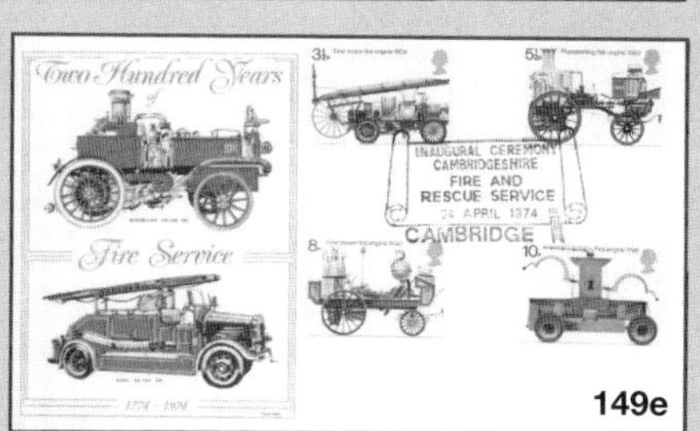

149e

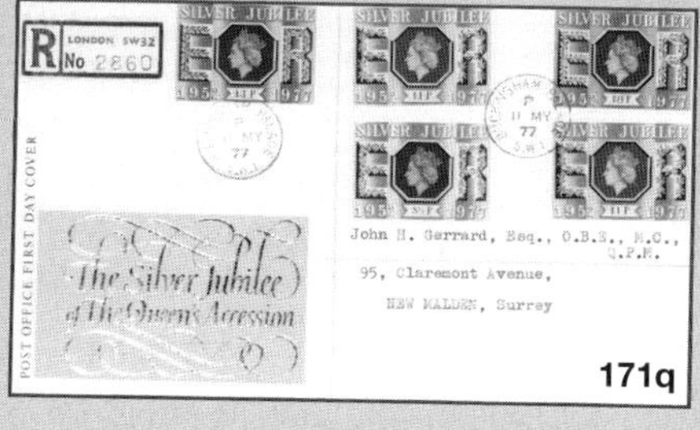

171q

157d

169d

170. 1977, 2nd March
Centenary Royal Institute of Chemistry
8½p Steroids, 10p Vitamin C, 11p Starch, 13p Salt

170a	Set on illustrated cover, any postmark	£2.50 ☐
170b	With Philatelic Bureau handstamp	£4.50 ☐
170c	With Royal Institute of Chemistry, London WC handstamp	£8.50 ☐
170d	With Stampex, London SW1 handstamp	£10.50 ☐
170e	With Starch Derivatives for Industry, Battersea SW11 handstamp	£9.00 ☐
170f	With any Field Post Office (659 or other), on BFPS cover	£6.50 ☐
170g	With Birmingham or Liverpool FDI handstamp	£12.50 ☐
170h	With Wigton, Cumbria, or Gravesend, Kent cds	£60.00 ☐
170i	With Barton, Richmond N. Yorks cds	£65.00 ☐
170j	With Haworth, Keighley W. Yorks cds	£67.50 ☐
170k	With Martin, Lincoln, or Martin, Hants cds	£67.50 ☐

171. 1977, 11th May
Silver Jubilee of the Queen's Accession 8½p, 10p, 11p, 13p, Queens Head Profile

171a	Set on illustrated cover, any postmark	£2.50 ☐
171b	With Philatelic Bureau handstamp	£4.50 ☐
171c	With First Day of Issue, Windsor, Berks special handstamp	£5.00 ☐
171d	With Hayling Island P.S. Silver Jubilee, Havant handstamp	£27.50 ☐
171e	With Jubilee Exhibition, Bath England handstamp	£16.00 ☐
171f	With Croydon Celebrates Queen's Silver Jubilee, Croydon handstamp	£16.00 ☐
171g	With Royal Jubilee Exhibition, British Library handstamp	£16.00 ☐
171h	With St. Martin-in-the-Fields, Silver Jubilee, London handstamp	£16.00 ☐
171i	With Duke of Edinburgh's Award, London handstamp	£12.50 ☐
171j	With Stamp of Royalty Exhibition, Glasgow handstamp	£15.50 ☐
171k	With Exercise Makefast XXV, Chatham, BF1952PS handstamp	£15.50 ☐
171l	With Stamp Collecting Promotion Council, Festival Hall handstamp	£15.50 ☐
171m	With Philatelic Exhibition, Weymouth & Portland handstamp	£17.50 ☐
171n	With Kings Lynn Norfolk FDI, plus Sandringham cachet	£32.50 ☐
171o	With Belfast or Aberdeen FDI handstamp	£18.00 ☐
171p	With Silver Jubilee slogan London, Edinburgh, Belfast or Cardiff	£125.00 ☐
171q	With Buckingham Palace cds	£180.00 ☐
171r	With Windsor Castle, Windsor Berks cds	£190.00 ☐
171s	With House of Commons or House of Lords cds	£35.00 ☐
171t	With Queen's Parade or Queen's Head cds	£40.00 ☐
171u	With Jubilee Fields or Jubilee Oak cds	£32.50 ☐
171v	With Silver Link or Jubilee Crescent cds	£32.50 ☐
171w	With Queen Elizabeth Ave, Walsall W. Mids cds	£55.00 ☐
171x	Souvenir Letter Card, issued by Stamp Collecting Promotion Council 8½p stamp with SCPC overprinted in dots, plus SCPC handstamp	£32.00 ☐

172. 1977, 8th June

Commonwealth Heads of Government Meeting

13p Gathering of Nation

172a Set on illustrated cover, any postmark **£2.00**
172b With Philatelic Bureau handstamp **£4.00**
172c With First Day of Issue, London SW special handstamp **£4.50**
172d With Beating Retreat, BF 8677 PS handstamp **£25.00**
172e With House of Commons cds (Queen Elizabeth Ave cds **£25**) **£55.00**
172f With House of Commons machine cancel **£25.00**
172g With House of Lords cds **£65.00**
172h With Buckingham Palace or Windsor Castle cds **£85.00**

There were many other postmarks used on the date of this issue, but they are not considered strictly relevant and have therefore not been listed.

---

173. 1977, 15th June

Queens Silver Jubilee, Additional Value - New Postage Rate

9p Queens Head Profile

173a 9p Stamp on illustrated cover, any postmark **£2.00**
173b With Philatelic Bureau handstamp **£3.50**
173c With First Day of Issue, Windsor Berks special handstamp **£4.00**
173d With Jubilee Exhibition, North Devon handstamp **£11.00**
173e With City of Leicester, Silver Jubilee, EIIR Leicester handstamp **£11.00**
173f With Borough of Blackburn, Silver Jubilee, Lancashire handstamp **£11.00**
173g With The Royal Image, City of Bristol Museum handstamp **£25.00**
173h With Croydon Celebrates the Queen's Silver Jubilee, Croydon handstamp **£11.00**
173i With Nuneaton Borough Council Silver Jubilee, Nuneaton handstamp **£11.00**
173j With A Royal Jubilee Exhibition, British Library handstamp **£11.00**
173k With Silver Jubilee Exhibition, Trafalgar Square, London handstamp **£11.00**
173l With Buckingham Palace SW1 cds **£80.00**
173m With Windsor Castle, Windsor, Berks cds **£85.00**
173n With Jubilee Fields or Jubilee Oak cds **£22.50**
173o With Queen's Parade or Queen's Head cds **£20.00**
173p With Queen Elizabeth Ave, Walsall W. Mids cds **£17.50**
173q With Silver Link or Jubilee Crescent cds **£20.00**
173r With House of Commons or House of Lords cds **£16.00**
173s With The Queen's Silver Jubilee Appeal, London (and other P.O.s) **£22.50**
173t With Queen's Silver Jubilee Philatelic Exhibition Cardiff **£25.00**
173u With Queen's Silver Jubilee Philatelic Exhibition Edinburgh **£25.00**
173v With Portsmouth and Southsea slogan cancel, Portsmouth **£32.00**
173w With Silver Jubilee International Air Tattoo slogan (various P.O.s) **£52.50**
173x With Review of the Fleet, Portsmouth & Southsea slogan **£28.50**

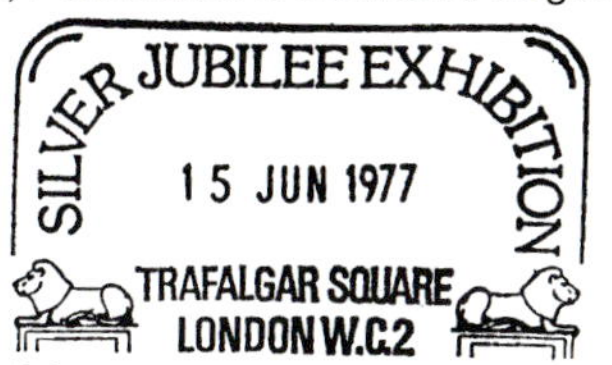

NUNEATON BOROUGH COUNCIL
SILVER JUBILEE
1952 EIIR 1977
15th JUNE 1977
NUNEATON · WARWICKSHIRE

QEII • Commemoratives 1977

174. 1977, 11th May/15th June
Queens Silver Jubilee - Double Dated Covers

174a	Philatelic Bureau 11th May and 15th June	£34.00 ☐
174b	With special handstamp 11th May and 15th June	£42.00 ☐
174c	With cds 11th May and 15th June	£55.00 ☐
174d	Any mix of handstamp and slogan/cds	£37.50 ☐

175. 1977, 5th October
British Wildlife 5 x 9p Se-tenant. Hedge Hog, Hare, Red Squirrel, Otter, Badger

175a	Set on illlustrated cover, any postmark	£3.00 ☐
175b	With Philatelic Bureau postmark	£6.00 ☐
175c	With Badger Beer, Blandford, 200 Anniv. handstamp	£12.50 ☐
175d	With Bear Steps, Shrewsbury handstamp	£12.50 ☐
175e	With Norfolk Wildlife in Trust, Norwich handstamp	£12.50 ☐
175f	With Educational Open Day,Port Lympne Wildlife, Hythe handstamp	£10.50 ☐
175g	With 11-13 Broadcourt, Covent Garden handstamp	£10.50 ☐
175h	With Otterferry or Haresfield cds	£45.00 ☐
175i	With Forest Row or Hedge End cds, or Ottery St. Mary cds	£30.00 ☐
175j	With Badgers Mount or Squirrels Heath cds	£65.00 ☐
175k	With Harewood, Foxton or Otterbourne cds	£45.00 ☐
175l	With Nettleham cds (Nature Conservation Society)	£37.50 ☐

176. 1977, 23rd November
Christmas Issue 5 x 7p Se-tenant, 9p, Twelve Days of Christmas

176a	Set on illlustrated cover, any postmark	£2.50 ☐
176b	With Philatelic Bureau special handstamp	£5.00 ☐
176c	With Silver Jubilee Christmas Greetings, from Blackpool h/s	£25.00 ☐
176d	With Welsh/English Bethlehem, Llandeilo handstamp	£6.00 ☐
176e	With Cambridge FDI	£18.00 ☐
176f	With Partridge Green, Horsham, or House of Lords SWI cds	£46.00 ☐
176g	With Pear Tree cds (three different offices)	£55.00 ☐
176h	Set of 12 Fleetwood covers (12 Days of Christmas) each with different FDI h/s	£48.00 ☐
176i	Collect through the British Philatelic Bureau slogan	£65.00 ☐

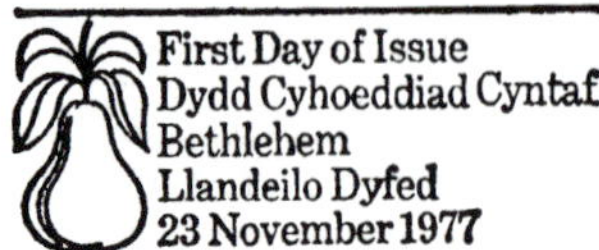

177. 1978, 25th January
Energy Resources 9p Oil, 10½p Coal, 11p Natural Gas, 13p Electricity

177a	Set on illustrated cover, any postmark	£3.00 ☐
177b	With Philatelic Bureau handstamp	£5.50 ☐
177c	With Institute of Fuel, Golden Jubilee Year, London W1 handstamp	£11.00 ☐
177d	With Forties Field, BP Contribution to Energy, Aberdeen handstamp	£11.00 ☐
177e	With Oil is Precious, Save it, Melton Mowbray, Leicester handstamp	£16.50 ☐
177f	With Coal is Precious, Save it, Ellistown, Leicester handstamp	£16.50 ☐
177g	With West Sole Field, BP Contribution to Energy, Hull handstamp	£14.00 ☐
177h	With SEGAS, a part of British Gas, Croydon Surrey handstamp	£16.50 ☐
177i	With KW Claymore 'A', Project Management Team, Peterhead h/s	£48.00 ☐
177j	With 21 Years British Nuclear Electricity, Dungeness handstamp	£12.50 ☐
177k	With Gulf Oil League, Speedway 50th Anniv., London handstamp	£16.00 ☐
177l	With Coalville, Selby, Grangemouth, Cruden Bay, or Bacton cds	£67.50 ☐
177m	With Seascale cds	£100.00 ☐

178. 1978, 1st March
British Architecture - Historic Buildings
9p Tower of London, 10p Holyroodhouse, 11p Caernarvon Castle, 13p Hampton Court

178a	Set on illustrated cover, any postmark	£2.00 ☐
178b	With Philatelic Bureau handstamp	£5.00 ☐
178c	With First Day of Issue, London EC special handstamp	£5.50 ☐
178d	With Britain's Royal Heritage, Hampton Court Palace, Kingston h/s	£10.50 ☐
178e	With Her Majesty's Tower of London, BF 900 PS handstamp	£10.50 ☐
178f	With British Architecture, British Library, London WC handstamp	£10.50 ☐
178g	With Stampex Silver Jubilee, London SW1 handstamp	£12.50 ☐
178h	With Portland 900th, Dorset, England handstamp	£22.00 ☐
178i	With Wells Cathedral 800th Anniv. Wells, Somerset handstamp	£12.50 ☐
178j	With Welsh/English First Day of Issue, Caernarfon Gwynedd h/s	£10.00 ☐
178k	With Hampton Court, England's Oldest Tennis Court, Kingston h/s	£11.00 ☐
178l	With Kings Lynn, Norfolk FDI, plus Sandringham cachet	£28.50 ☐
178m	With Holyrood, Edinburgh cds	£62.00 ☐
178n	With House of Commons or House of Lords cds	£36.00 ☐

179. 1978, 1st March
British Architecture - Miniature Sheet, London 1980, First Min. Sheet

179a	Miniature Sheet on illustrated cover, any postmark	£3.00 ☐
179b	With Philatelic Bureau handstamp	£6.00 ☐
179c	With First Day of Issue, London EC special handstamp	£6.50 ☐
179d	With Britain's Royal Heritage, Hampton Court Palace, Kingston h/s	£16.50 ☐
179e	With Her Majesty's Tower of London, BF 900 PS handstamp	£16.50 ☐
179f	With British Architecture, British Library, London WC handstamp	£16.50 ☐
179g	With Stampex Silver Jubilee, London SW1 handstamp	£16.50 ☐
179h	With Portland 900th, Dorset, England handstamp	£25.00 ☐
179i	With Wells Cathedral 800th Anniv. Wells, Somerset handstamp	£20.00 ☐
179j	With Welsh/English First Day of Issue, Caernarfon Gwynedd h/s	£12.00 ☐
179k	With Hampton Court, England's Oldest Tennis Court, Kingston h/s	£16.00 ☐
179l	With Kings Lynn, Norfolk FDI, plus Sandringham cachet	£32.50 ☐
179m	With Holyrood, Edinburgh cds	£60.00 ☐
179n	With House of Commons or House of Lords cds	£32.50 ☐

Covers with the set of stamps and the miniature sheet add 20% to combined value.

QEII • Commemoratives 1978

180. 1978, 31st May
25th Anniversary of the Queen's Coronation
9p State Coach, 10½p St. Edward's Crown, 11p The Orb, 13p Imperial Crown

180a Set on illustrated cover, any postmark .... **£3.00** ☐
180b With Philatelic Bureau handstamp .... **£5.00** ☐
180c With First Day of Issue, London SW1 special handstamp .... **£5.50** ☐
180d With 1953 Coronation 1978, The British Library, London handstamp .... **£8.00** ☐
180e With 25 Anniv. RAF Hospital Wegberg, BF 1612 PS handstamp .... **£27.50** ☐
180f With 25th Anniv. Coronation Queen Elizabeth II, RAF Wattisham BF 1953 PS h/s .... **£9.00** ☐
180g With Lewis's Celebrate 21 Years in Bristol handstamp .... **£26.00** ☐
180h With 31 May 1978 Mint, Sutton, Surrey handstamp .... **£26.00** ☐
180i With Visit of HRH Prince of Wales, Newton Aycliffe handstamp .... **£26.00** ☐
180j With Official Opening HRH Prince of Wales, Newcastle handstamp .... **£26.00** ☐
180k With 60th British Philatelic Federation Congress, Worthing handstam .... **£26.00** ☐
180l With Caernarfon Gwynedd, pictorial castle handstamp .... **£26.00** ☐
180m With Coronation Anniversary Exhibition, Cameo Stamp Centre, London .... **£9.00** ☐
180n With Union of Post Office Workers Conference, Blackpool handstamp .... **£28.50** ☐
180o With QEII 25 Anniv. Coronation RHDR railway cover and handstamp .... **£9.00** ☐
180p With Windsor, Berks FDI handstamp .... **£12.50** ☐
180q With Kings Lynn, Norfolk FDI, plus Sandringham cachet .... **£28.00** ☐
180r With Kings Lynn, Norfolk FDI, plus Kings Lynn cachet .... **£28.00** ☐
180s With Buckingham Palace SW1, cds .... **£160.00** ☐
180t With Windsor Castle, Windsor Berks cds .... **£170.00** ☐
180u With Coronation Road or Coronation Square cds .... **£26.50** ☐
180v With Queen Elizabeth Ave, Walsall cds .... **£25.00** ☐
180w With Scone, Perth cds .... **£170.00** ☐
180x With House of Commons or House of Lords cds .... **£35.00** ☐
180y **Double dated covers.** 1953 Coronation set on illustrated cover, any pmk, with 1978 Coronation Anniversary set on reverse, Windsor or other FDI .... **£92.00** ☐

---

181. 1978, 5th July
Centenary of the Shire Horse Society
9p Shire Horse, 10½p Shetland Pony, 11p Welsh Pony, 13p Thoroughbred

181a Set on illustrated cover, any postmark .... **£3.00** ☐
181b With Philatelic Bureau handstamp .... **£5.50** ☐
181c With First Day of Issue, Peterborough handstamp .... **£6.00** ☐
181d With World Dressage Championships, Goodwood handstamp .... **£22.00** ☐
181e With Courage Shire Horse Centre, Maidenhead, Berks handstamp .... **£12.00** ☐
181f With The Royal Show, Kenilworth, Warwickshire handstamp .... **£17.50** ☐
181g With Tribute to the Horse, Shire Horse Drive, York handstamp .... **£14.00** ☐
181h With The Sport of Kings, Brighton handstamp .... **£16.00** ☐
181i With Home of the Derby, Epsom, Surrey handstamp .... **£14.00** ☐
181j With RNLI Clacton, Clacton-on-Sea, Essex handstamp .... **£26.00** ☐
181k With Horses of Britain, The British Library, London handstamp .... **£12.00** ☐
181l With Shetland Pony Stud Book Society, Shetland handstamp .... **£17.50** ☐

181m With Horses on Stamps Exhibition, Havering Park Riding School .... £16.00 ☐
181n With MGM logo and Ars Gratia Artis, London W1 handstamp .... £22.50 ☐
181o With Bournemouth FDI (Horse Brasses Museum) .... £26.00 ☐
181p With Welsh/English FDI, Aberystwyth, plus Pony Express cachet .... £34.00 ☐
181q With Kings Lynn, Norfolk FDI, plus Royal Studs cachet .... £27.50 ☐
181r With Ascot, Berks cds .... £95.00 ☐
181s With Aintree or Epsom Downs cds .... £95.00 ☐
181t With Horse Fair, Shireoaks or Riding Mill cds .... £32.00 ☐
181u With Studlands, Newmarket, Suffolk cds .... £45.00 ☐
181v With Blackhorse, Horsebridge or Horsington cds .... £25.00 ☐
181w With Lerwick cds, (Great Yarmouth cds **£52**) .... £82.50 ☐
181x With Darley cds .... £62.50 ☐

182. 1978, 2nd August

Cycling Centenaries 9p, 10½p, 11p, 13p, Various Types of Bicycle

182a Set on illustrated cover, any postmark .... £2.50 ☐
182b With Philatelic Bureau handstamp .... £4.50 ☐
182c With First Day of Issue, Harrogate handstamp .... £5.00 ☐
182d With TI Raleigh World's Largest Bicycle Manufacturer, Nottingham h/s .... £8.50 ☐
182e With BCF Centenary International Meeting, Leicester handstamp .... £8.50 ☐
182f With TI Raleigh Tour de France Winners, Nottingham handstamp .... £8.50 ☐
182g With Guildford FDI, (plus Posted at Mount Browne cachet **£28**) .... £26.00 ☐
182h With Coventry FDI (first British bicycle production in 1870) .... £36.00 ☐
182i With Dumfries FDI (first UK production) .... £46.50 ☐
182j With Charlbury, Godalming or Meriden Coventry cds .... £92.00 ☐
182k With Raleigh, Cornwall cds .... £230.00 ☐
182l With Driver, Mind that Bike, Reading, Berks slogan cancel .... £115.00 ☐
182m With Driver, Mind that Bike, Brighton, Sussex Coast slogan cancel .... £115.00 ☐

Improved Postal Stationery Coverage from 1972

Postal Stationery is covered in the body of the catalogue up to 1971. From 1972 onwards we have added a detailed listing in a separate section at the end of the catalogue.

QEII • Commemoratives 1978-79

183. 1978, 22nd November

Christmas Issue 7p, 9p, 11p, 13p, Carol Singers of the Past

183a Set on illustrated cover, any postmark **£2.00**
183b With Philatelic Bureau handstamp **£4.50**
183c With Welsh/English FDI Bethlehem, Llandeilo handstamp **£5.00**
183d With London Borough of Havering, Music for All handstamp **£9.00**
183e With History of Philately Exhibition, Warwick handstamp **£9.00**
183f With 50 Years of Broadcasting Carols, Kings College, Cambridge **£9.00**
183g With Carols for Christmas, British Library, London WC handstamp **£9.00**
183h With 50 years of Rotary in Clacton, Essex handstamp **£20.00**
183i With Parish of Dalgety, Dalgety Bay, Dunfermline, Fife handstamp **£8.00**
183j With Meet Your Post Office, Dunfermline, Fife handstamp **£25.00**
183k With Oxford or Dover FDI handstamp **£12.50**
183l With Windsor FDI (First English Christmas Tree in 1848) **£37.50**
183m With Nasareth, Caernarfon, Gwynedd cds **£72.00**
183n With Hollybush, Fir Tree or Fairy Cross cds **£36.50**
183o With Boars Head, Wigan cds **£87.50**

184. 1979, 7th February

British Dogs

9p English Sheepdog, 10½p Springer Spaniel, 11p Highland Terrier, 13p Irish Setter

184a Set on illustrated cover, any postmark **£2.00**
184b With Philatelic Bureau handstamp **£4.50**
184c With First Day of Issue, London SW special handstamp **£5.00**
184d With Spillers Congratulate the Kennel Club, Crufts Exhibition, London **£8.00**
184e With Exeter District FDI, plus Guide Dogs for the Blind Association cachet **£26.00**
184f With Windsor, Berks FDI handstamp **£25.00**
184g With London W1 FDI (Canine Defence League HQ) **£28.00**
184h With MLO Redhill FDI on PDSA special series cover **£32.00**
184i With Battersea FDI handstamp **£18.50**
184j With Barking, Essex cds **£28.00**
184k With Battersea Park Road cds **£78.00**
184l With Black Dog, or Hounds Hill cds, (Dogsthorpe cds **£36**) **£80.00**
184m With Dog Kennel Lane or Isle of Dogs cds **£125.00**
184n With Dog & Gun, Liverpool cds **£130.00**

185. 1979, 21st March

British Spring Flowers 9p Primrose, 10½p Daffodil, 11p Bluebell, 13p Snowdrop

185a Set on illustrated cover, any postmark **£2.00**
185b With Philatelic Bureau handstamp **£4.50**
185c With Royal Botanic Gardens Kew, Richmond Surrey handstamp **£9.00**
185d With Floral City Exhibition, Bath handstamp **£9.00**
185e With Nat. Assoc. Flower Arrangement Socs., Penzance handstamp **£7.50**
185f With Nat. Assoc. Flower Arrangement Socs., Isles of Scilly handstamp **£7.50**
185g With 20th Anniversary Founders Day, Bluebell Railway, Uckfield h/s **£10.00**
185h With Rural Blisworth Exhibition, Northampton handstamp **£12.00**

185i	With WI (Women's Institute) Canterbury, Kent handstamp	£17.00 ☐
185j	With Bath Europe's Floral City, Bath Avon slogan cancel	£98.00 ☐
185k	With Spalding 21st Flower Parade, Spalding Lincs slogan cancel	£98.00 ☐
185l	With Kew Gardens, Richmond Surrey cds	£115.00 ☐
185m	With Blue Bell Hill, Huddersfield cds	£60.00 ☐
185n	With Flowery Field, Hyde Cheshire cds	£52.50 ☐
185o	With Primrose, Jarrow cds	£62.50 ☐
185p	With Spring Gardens, Lancs cds, (Isles of Scilly cds £27.50)	£45.00 ☐
185q	With Botanic Gardens, Belfast cds	£55.00 ☐
185r	With Field Post Office handstamp, on BFPS cover	£10.00 ☐

---

186. 1979, 9th May

Direct Elections to the European Assembly

9p, 10½p, 11p, 13p, Hands Placing Flags into Ballot Boxes

186a	Set on illustrated cover, any postmark	£3.00 ☐
186b	With Philatelic Bureau handstamp	£5.50 ☐
186c	With London SW First Day of Issue handstamp	£6.50 ☐
186d	With First British European Parliamentary Elections, London h/s	£7.50 ☐
186e	With Strasbourg, Leicester's Twin City, Leicester handstamp	£7.50 ☐
186f	With National Stamp Week, Europa Day, Cameo London h/s	£7.50 ☐
186g	With Entente Cordiale, Stowmarket handstamp	£230.00 ☐
186h	With Folkestone, Kent FDI handstamp	£8.00 ☐
186i	With First Day Worth Valley Railway Letter Service, Keighley	£12.00 ☐
186j	With House of Commons cds	£27.50 ☐
186k	With House of Lords cds	£35.00 ☐
186l	With Newhaven, Harwich, or Dover cds	£17.50 ☐
186m	With Newhaven, Paquebot cds	£17.50 ☐
186n	With Dieppe, Seine-Maritime cds (French!)	£18.50 ☐
186o	With Northern Parliament, Belfast cds	£35.00 ☐
186p	With Parliament St. BO SW1 cds	£22.50 ☐
186q	With any Field Post Office cds, on BFPS cover	£6.50 ☐
186r	With Are You on the Voters List - Check Now, Lincoln slogan	£565.00 ☐
186s	**Double dated covers.** 1973 European Communities + Direct Elections, any pmks	£60.00 ☐

Please read the notes at the beginning of this catalogue for general information.

Gems • 1966 Birds. Missing Legs!

Legless Birds! Missing Brown.

Two Dramatic Missing Colour fdc's
Catalogued at £600 each - phos or plain.

See Missing Colours new listing on pages 460 - 461

187. 1979, 6th June
Horse Racing - Derby Bicentenary
9p Epsom 1936, 10½p Aintree 1839, 11p Newmarket 1793, 13p Windsor 1684

187a	Set on illustrated cover, any postmark	**£2.50** ☐
187b	With Philatelic Bureau handstamp	**£5.00** ☐
187c	With First Day of Issue, Epsom Surrey, special handstamp	**£5.50** ☐
187d	With Newberry Show, Newberry Berks handstamp	**£8.00** ☐
187e	With Kiplingcotes, England's Oldest Horse Race, York handstamp	**£8.00** ☐
187f	With Derby 200, Epsom Surry handstamp	**£6.50** ☐
187g	With Headquarters Jockey Club, Newmarket handstamp	**£6.50** ☐
187h	With Derby 200 Exhibition, Royal Academy, London handstamp	**£6.50** ☐
187i	With any Forces Post Office handstamp, on BFPS cover	**£6.50** ☐
187j	With Chigwell School 1629-1979, Chigwell, Essex handstamp	**£11.00** ☐
187k	With Derbyshire Festival, Matlock handstamp	**£11.00** ☐
187l	With Codesort comes to Liverpool, or Manchester cancellation	**£8.50** ☐
187m	With Kings Lynn, Norfolk FDI, plus The Royal Studs cachet	**£26.50** ☐
187n	With Liverpool, Derby or Doncaster FDI handstamp (Windsor FDI **£17**)	**£12.50** ☐
187o	With Come Racing at Great Yarmouth slogan cancel	**£85.00** ☐
187p	With Aintree, or Epsom Downs cds (Tattenham Corner cds **£130**)	**£87.50** ☐
187q	With Ascot, Newmarket, or Windsor cds	**£78.00** ☐
187r	With Derby, Studlands, Stud Farm or Horse Fair cds	**£36.50** ☐
187s	With Buckingham Palace, or Windsor Castle cds	**£87.50** ☐

188. 1979, 11th July
International Year of the Child
9p, 10½p, 11p, 13p, Designs based on Drawings from Children's Books

188a	Set on illustrated cover, any postmark	**£2.50** ☐
188b	With Philatelic Bureau handstamp	**£5.00** ☐
188c	With Beatrix Potter Lived in Near Sawrey, Ambleside handstamp	**£9.00** ☐
188d	With Alice in Wonderland, Inspired by our Town, Llandudno handstamp	**£12.00** ☐
188e	With Methuen Commemorate Centenary of E.H. Shepard, Hartfield handstamp	**£8.00** ☐
188f	With Year of the Child, Wokingham, Berks handstamp	**£11.00** ☐
188g	With International Year of the Child, Westminster Cathedral handstamp	**£11.00** ☐
188h	With 1979 The Year of the Child and Cub Country Year, Birkenhead	**£11.00** ☐
188i	With Yardley Primary School, Chingford, London handstamp	**£11.00** ☐
188j	With The Hospital for Sick Children, Great Ormond Street, London WCI h/s	**£16.50** ☐
188k	With Care for Mother & Baby, Life Care and Housing Trust, Leamington h/s	**£36.50** ☐
188l	With New Parks Boys School, Leicester handstamp	**£11.00** ☐
188m	With Lewis Carroll Society, Daresbury, Warrington handstamp	**£11.00** ☐
188n	With 1979 Anniversaries, British Library, London handstamp	**£11.00** ☐
188o	With Any Forces Post Office handstamp (42 or other), on BFPS cover	**£6.50** ☐
188p	With NSPCC, Bethlehem, Llandeilo handstamp	**£9.50** ☐
188q	With The Kent & East Sussex Railway Children's Day, Tenterden	**£9.50** ☐
188r	With Palitoy Diamond Jubilee, Leicester handstamp	**£25.00** ☐
188s	With Royal Tournament 1979, BF 1979 PS handstamp	**£12.50** ☐

QEII • Commemoratives 1979

188t With Edinburgh, Hartfield, Ilford, or Oxford FDI handstamp .... £15.00 □
188u With Childs Hill or Child Okeford cds .... £55.00 □
188v With Playing Place, Truro, Cornwall cds .... £70.00 □
188w With Hartfield, East Sussex, or Ilford, Essex cds .... £35.00 □
188x With Far Sawrey, Ambleside, Cumbria cds .... £78.00 □
188y With Barnardo's Cares About Children, Ilford Essex slogan .... £68.00 □
188z With Give a Child a Home 448624 Leeds Social Services slogan .... £115.00 □

189. 1979, 22nd August
Centenary Death of Sir Rowland Hill 10p Sir Rowland Hill, 11½p Postman 1839, 13p London Postman 1839, 15p Uniform Postage 1840

189a Set on illustrated cover, any postmark .... £2.50 □
189b With Philatelic Bureau handstamp .... £4.50 □
189c With First Day of Issue, London EC special handstamp .... £5.00 □
189d With Rowland Hill, Kidderminster, Worcestershire handstamp .... £7.50 □
189e With Rowland Hill Centenary Commemorative Mail Coach Run, Kidderminster .... £7.50 □
189f With Rowland Hill Centenary Commemorative Mail Coach Run, Birmingham .... £7.50 □
189g With Bath Postal Museum, Rowland Hill Centenary Exhibition, Bath h/s .... £7.50 □
189h With Sir Rowland Hill Centenary Exhibition, Kidderminster Art Gallery, WFDC h/s .... £7.50 □
189i With 1979 Anniversaries, British Library London WC handstamp .... £10.00 □
189j With Bruce Castle Museum, Tottenham N17 handstamp .... £11.00 □
189k With Rowland Hill Centenary, Commemorative Delivery, Rayleigh h/s .... £11.00 □
189l With Sir Rowland Hill 1795-1879, Warwick handstamp .... £7.50 □
189m With Sir Rowland Hill 1795-1879 Coventry handstamp .... £7.50 □
189n With Sir Rowland Hill 1795-1879 Stratford-upon-Avon handstamp .... £7.50 □
189o With any Field Post Office cds (994 or other), on BFPS cover .... £4.50 □
189p With Haddo House & Country Park Now Open, Aberdeen handstamp .... £10.00 □
189q With Pier Centenary, Bournemouth handstamp (on Philatex cover) .... £62.00 □
189r With National Postal Museum, London EC1 handstamp .... £7.00 □
189s With Chief Office London EC, handstamp .... £8.00 □
189t With Brighton, East Sussex or Sanquhar, Dumfriesshire FDI handstamp .... £8.00 □
189u With Kidderminster FDI handstamp, or cds postmark .... £10.00 □
189v With Int. Stamp Exhibition Earls Court, London 1980, 6-14 May slogan .... £82.00 □
189w With Hampstead, Hampstead Heath, or Belsize Park NW3 cds .... £35.00 □
189x With Rowland's Castle cds or Bruce Grove cds .... £26.50 □
189y With House of Commons cds or House of Lords cds .... £27.50 □
189z With Buckingham Palace SW1 cds .... £82.00 □

190. 1979, 26th September
150th Anniversary Metropolitan Police
10p, 11½p, 13p, 15p, Day-to-Day Duties of the Police

190a Set on illustrated cover, any postmark .... **£2.50** ☐
190b With Philatelic Bureau handstamp .... **£4.50** ☐
190c With First Day of Issue, London SW special handstamp .... **£5.00** ☐
190d With Port of London Police, London E16 handstamp .... **£11.50** ☐
190e With Royal Air Force Police, Bruggen BF 1665 PS handstamp .... **£11.50** ☐
190f With HQ West Yorkshire Metropolitan Police, 150 Years, Wakefield h/s .... **£8.00** ☐
190g With Metropolitan Police, New Scotland Yard, London SW1 handstamp .... **£6.00** ☐
190h With Devon & Cornwall Constabulary Exhibition, Exter handstamp .... **£9.00** ☐
190i With 1979 Anniversaries, The British Library, London handstamp .... **£9.00** ☐
190j With Sir Robert Peel, Tamworth Commemoration handstamp .... **£9.00** ☐
190k With Crook, Co. Durham, or Constable Burton, N.Yorks cds .... **£45.00** ☐
190l With Field Post Office 999, on Yorks Police or BFPS cover .... **£50.00** ☐
190m With Bow Street cds .... **£87.50** ☐
190n With Hendon cds, Tamworth cds (Wapping E1 cds, or Bury cds **£50**) .... **£32.50** ☐
190o With Law, Lanarkshire cds, or Constable Road cds .... **£55.00** ☐
190p With House of Commons, or House of Lords cds .... **£37.50** ☐

191. 1979, 24th October
Sir Rowland Hill – Miniature Sheet
10p +11½p +13p +15p, Block of 4 in Miniature Sheet Presentation

191a Set on illustrated cover, any postmark .... **£2.50** ☐
191b With Philatelic Bureau handstamp .... **£4.50** ☐
191c With First Day of Issue, London EC special handstamp .... **£5.00** ☐
191d With Sir Rowland Hill Director/Chairman London Brighton Railway h/s .... **£8.00** ☐
191e With Cartoonists Club Honour the Post Office, Horley Surrey handstamp .... **£8.00** ☐
191f With National Postal Museum, London EC1 handstamp .... **£8.50** ☐
191g With Chief Office, London EC1 handstamp .... **£8.50** ☐
191h With Bruce Castle Museum, Tottenham N17 handstamp .... **£24.50** ☐
191i With 1979 Anniversaries, The British Library, London handstamp .... **£8.50** ☐
191j With Kidderminster cds, or FDI handstamp .... **£11.00** ☐
191k With Sanquhar, Dumfriesshire FDI handstamp .... **£8.50** ☐
191l With Hampstead NW3 cds (Rowland's Castle cds **£28**) .... **£18.50** ☐
191m With House of Commons, or House of Lords cds .... **£18.50** ☐
191n With International Stamp Exhibition Earls Court, London 1980, 6-14 May h/s .... **£75.00** ☐
191o **Double Dated Covers:** Rowland Hill stamps plus miniature sheet, both dates .... **£60.00** ☐

192. 1979, 21st November
Christmas Issue 8p, 10p, 11½p, 13p, 15p, Traditional Scenes from the Nativity

192a	Set on illustrated cover, any postmark	£2.00 ☐
192b	With Philatelic Bureau handstamp	£4.50 ☐
192c	With First Day of Issue, Bethlehem, Llandeilo handstamp	£5.00 ☐
192d	With Int. Year of the Child, Stamp and Coin Christmas Exhibition, Coventry	£7.50 ☐
192e	With 1954-1979 Christmas, 25th Anniv. After the Ball, Blackpool	£7.50 ☐
192f	With Christmas, The British Library, London WC handstamp	£7.50 ☐
192g	With Father Christmas Special, Kent & East Sussex Railway handstamp	£7.50 ☐
192h	With BIPEX 79, November 21 London SW handstamp	£8.00 ☐
192i	With Romney Hythe and Dymchurch Railway Salutes ... Christmas Lights	£8.00 ☐
192j	With Centenary of The War Cry 1879-1979, London EC4 handstamp	£8.00 ☐
192k	With any Field Post Office cds (716 or other), on BFPS cover	£6.00 ☐
192l	With Windsor, Berks FDI handstamp	£18.50 ☐
192m	With Windsor Castle, Windsor Berks cds	£57.50 ☐
192n	With Nasareth, Caernarfon cds	£48.00 ☐
192o	With Shepherds Bush, Holy Island, or Angel Hill cds	£17.50 ☐
192p	With Central Milton Keynes, Xmas Shopping as it should be slogan	£115.00 ☐

Listing of Pre-release Covers

See pages 458 - 459

Listing of Missing Colours on fdc

See pages 460 - 461

QEII • Commemoratives 1980

193. 1980, 16th January

British Birds 10p Kingfisher, 11½p Dipper, 13p Moorhen, 15p Yellow Wagtails

193a	Set on illustrated cover, any postmark	£2.00
193b	With Philatelic Bureau handstamp	£4.50
193c	With First Day of Issue, Sandy, Beds handstamp	£5.00
193d	With Leicester & Rutland Ornithologist Society, Leicester handstamp	£6.50
193e	With The West Midland Bird Club 51st Anniv. Birmingham handstamp	£6.50
193f	With Cotswold Wildlife Park 10th Anniv. Burford, Oxford handstamp	£6.50
193g	With Wildfowl Trust Martin Mere, Liverpool handstamp	£6.50
193h	With Wildfowl Trust Washington, Tyne & Wear handstamp	£6.50
193i	With Wildfowl Trust Peakirk, Peterborough handstamp	£6.50
193j	With Wildfowl Trust Arundel, West Sussex handstamp	£6.50
193k	With Wildfowl Trust Slimbridge, Gloucester handstamp	£6.50
193l	With RSPB Pioneers in Bird Protection, Sandy, Beds h/s (large pink)	£6.50
193m	With RSPB Pioneers in Bird Protection, Sandy, Beds h/s (smaller pmk)	£22.00
193n	With Hull Natural History Society Centennial Year, Hull handstamp	£7.50
193o	With 1880-1980 Essex Field Club Centenary, Chelmsford, Essex handstamp	£7.50
193p	With NNT Celebrates 1880 Wild Birds Protection Act, Norwich, Norfolk h/s	£7.50
193q	With Wintertime, The British Library, London WC handstamp	£12.50
193r	With any Forces Post Office cds (1677 or other), on BFPS cover	£8.00
193s	With Sandy, Beds cds	£48.00
193t	With House of Commons or House of Lords cds	£32.00
193u	With Fair Isle, Shetland cds	£47.50
193v	With Partridge Green, Birds Edge, Heron Cross, Swallownest cds	£27.50
193w	Wren's Nest, Wing or Eagle cds	£27.50

194. 1980, 12th March

150th Anniversary Liverpool and Manchester Railway

5 x 12p Se-tenant, Complete Train of 1830 Era

194a	Set on illustrated cover, any postmark	£2.00
194b	With Philatelic Bureau handstamp	£4.50
194c	With First Day of Issue, Manchester or Liverpool handstamp	£5.00
194d	With TPO Exhibition, Crewe handstamp	£8.00
194e	With Codesort Comes to Liverpool, or Manchester handstamp	£15.00
194f	With The Great Railway Exposition, Liverpool Rd. Station, Manchester h/s	£8.50
194g	With Newton-Le-Willows, Earlstown, Merseyside handstamp	£8.50
194h	With Main Line Steam Trust Celebrates 150 Years Mail by Rail, Leics h/s	£8.50
194i	With Haverings Own Railway Celebrates 150 Years Mail by Rail handstamp	£8.50
194j	With Bressingham Steam Museum, Diss, Norfolk handstamp	£8.50
194k	With The Railway Age 150th Anniversary, Coventry handstamp	£8.50
194l	With 80th Anniversary Rother Railway, Tenterden, Kent handstamp	£8.50
194m	With Wintertime, The British Library, London WC handstamp	£15.00
194n	With Bournemouth & Poole FDI handstamp (railway museum)	£26.00
194o	With Bradford W. Yks. FDI handstamp (Worth Valley Railway)	£26.00
194p	With Colchester FDI (Stour Valley Railway Preservation Society)	£26.00
194q	With Great Western T.P.O. UP cds	£27.50

194r With Northwestern T.P.O. NT Down cds .... **£27.50** ☐
194s With East Anglian T.P.O. DN-PE SECT., or UP-PE SECT cds .... **£27.50** ☐
194t With East Anglian T.P.O. Down cds .... **£27.50** ☐
194u With Down Special T.P.O. cds or Up Special T.P.O. cds .... **£27.50** ☐
194v With Norwich-London T.P.O. cds .... **£27.50** ☐
194w With Rainhill, Prescot cds .... **£38.00** ☐
194x With Crowthorne Station cds .... **£27.50** ☐
194y With The Rocket, Liverpool cds .... **£62.00** ☐
194z With To London 1980 by Rail, BF 1682 PS cancellation .... **£8.50** ☐
194aa With Liverpool to Manchester 150 Years of Mail by Rail, Liverpool slogan .... **£55.00** ☐
194bb With Liverpool to Manchester 150 Years of Mail by Rail, Manchester slogan .... **£55.00** ☐

Other T.P.O. cancellations are known in addition to those above. Catalogue value from **£20** up.

195. 1980, 9th April
London 1980 International Stamp Exhibition
50p Montage of Famous London Buildings

195a 50p stamp on illustrated cover, any postmark .... **£2.00** ☐
195b With Philatelic Bureau handstamp .... **£4.50** ☐
195c With First Day of Issue, London SW special handstamp .... **£5.00** ☐
195d With London Tourist Board, Visit London 1980, Victoria, London SW1 h/s .... **£7.50** ☐
195e With Stampway to London Exhibition, Cameo Stamp Centre handstamp .... **£7.50** ☐
195f With National Postal Museum, London EC1 brown handstamp .... **£9.50** ☐
195g With Springtime, British Library, London WC handstamp .... **£8.00** ☐
195h With any Forces Post Office cds, on BFPS cover .... **£5.50** ☐
195i With G.B. Major Errors Exhibition, Warwick handstamp .... **£8.00** ☐
195j With West Country-Liverpool Royal Mail by Air, Exeter handstamp .... **£8.00** ☐
195k With House of Commons or House of Lords cds .... **£17.50** ☐
195l With Earls Court BO, London SW5 cds .... **£62.00** ☐
195m With Collect British Stamps, World's Greatest Hobby, Leicester slogan .... **£45.00** ☐
195n With International Stamp Exhibition, Earls Court London 1980, Leeds slogan .... **£62.00** ☐
195o With Trafalgar Square Branch Office handstamp .... **£10.00** ☐

Remember, most modern hand addressed covers
are worth only 20% of catalogue prices.

QEII • Commemoratives 1980

196. 1980, 7th May
London 1980 – Miniature Sheet 75p Miniature Sheet

196a Miniature sheet on illustrated cover, any postmark .... **£2.00** ☐
196b With Philatelic Bureau handstamp .... **£4.00** ☐
196c With First Day of Issue, London 1980, London SW handstamp .... **£4.50** ☐
196d With First Day of Issue, Kingston-upon-Thames handstamp .... **£4.50** ☐
196e With Post Office Day London 1980, Int. Stamp Exhibition, London .... **£6.50** ☐
196f With Royal Opera House, Covent Garden, London WC handstamp .... **£7.50** ☐
196g With 1880 Centenary Appeal 1980, Youth Clubs, London SE5 handstamp .... **£7.50** ☐
196h With any Forces Post Office cds (961 or other) .... **£7.50** ☐
196i With Leicester Philatelic Society 75 Anniversary, Leicester handstamp .... **£7.50** ☐
196j With Supersonically to London 1980, British 7580 PS handstamp .... **£7.50** ☐
196k With Springtime, British Library, London WC handstamp .... **£11.00** ☐
196l With London Stamp Fair, London SW1 handstamp .... **£7.50** ☐
196m With Stamps Magazine Pays Tribute to London 1980, Brentwood h/s .... **£7.50** ☐
196n With House of Commons or House of Lords cds .... **£26.00** ☐
196o With Earls Court Exhibition B.O. SW5 cds .... **£65.00** ☐
196p With Earls Court B.O. London SW5 cds .... **£60.00** ☐
196q With Collect British Stamps, Worlds Greatest Hobby slogan .... **£36.00** ☐
196r **Double Dated Covers:** The April 9th 50p Stamp and the May 7th. 75p Miniature Sheet on one cover, both with relevant postmarks, from .... **£42.50** ☐
196s With Imperforate Pane, any postmark .... **£3,250.00** ☐

---

197. 1980, 7th May
London Landmarks 10½p Buckingham Palace, 12p Albert Memorial, 13½p Opera House, 15p Hampton Court, 17½p Kensington Palace

197a Set on illustrated cover, any postmark .... **£2.00** ☐
197b With Philatelic Bureau handstamp .... **£4.00** ☐
197c With First Day of Issue, London 1980, London SW handstamp .... **£4.50** ☐
197d With First Day of Issue, Kingston-upon-Thames handstamp .... **£4.50** ☐
197e With Post Office Day London 1980, Int. Stamp Exhibition handstamp .... **£8.00** ☐
197f With London Stamp Fair, London SW1 handstamp .... **£8.00** ☐
197g With Supersonically to London 1980, British Forces 7580 PS handstamp .... **£8.00** ☐
197h With Royal Opera House, Covent Garden, London WC handstamp .... **£8.00** ☐
197i With 1880 Centenary Appeal 1980, Youth Clubs, London SE5 handstamp .... **£8.00** ☐
197j With any British Forces Post Office cds (Berlin or other) .... **£8.00** ☐
197k With Leicester Philatelic Society 75 Anniversary, Leicester handstamp .... **£8.00** ☐
197l With Stamps Magazine Pays tribute to London 1980, Brentwood h/s .... **£8.00** ☐
197m With Springtime, British Library, London WC handstamp .... **£10.00** ☐
197n With London SW FDI or Kingston-upon-Thames FDI handstamp .... **£6.50** ☐
197o With Buckingham Palace SW1 cds (Buckingham Gate **£48**) .... **£115.00** ☐
197p With Earls Court BO cds .... **£50.00** ☐
197q With House of Commons or House of Lords cds .... **£34.00** ☐
197r **Double Dated Covers:** April 9th 50p Stamp plus May 7th Miniature Sheet **and** May 7th London Landmarks set. All three issues on one cover (any 2 issues **£46**) ... **£80.00** ☐

QEII • Commemoratives 1980

198. 1980, 9th July

Famous Women Novelists (Europa)

12p Charlotte Bronte, 13½p George Eliot, 15p Emily Bronte, 17½p Mrs. Gaskell

198a	Set on illustrated cover, any postmark	**£2.00** ☐
198b	With Philatelic Bureau handstamp	**£4.00** ☐
198c	With First Day of Issue, Haworth, Keighley, W. Yorks handstamp	**£4.50** ☐
198d	With Leicester Writer's Club Celebrates its 27th Year, Leicester handstamp	**£7.00** ☐
198e	With Elizabeth Gaskell, Chelsea, London SW3 handstamp	**£7.00** ☐
198f	With Dent Commemorate the Achievement of Charlotte and Emily h/s	**£7.00** ☐
198g	With George Eliot Centenary, Nuneaton, Warwickshire handstamp	**£7.00** ☐
198h	With The Elms, Country Home of George Eliot, Rickmansworth	**£7.00** ☐
198i	With International Society Commemorates Mrs. Gaskell, Manchester h/s	**£6.50** ☐
198j	With Summertime, British Library, London WC handstamp	**£8.50** ☐
198k	With any Field Post office h/s (1980 or other) on BFPS cover	**£7.50** ☐
198l	With William Shakespeare, Stratford-upon-Avon, Warwickshire h/s	**£15.50** ☐
198m	With Altrincham, Cheshire FDI, or Manchester FDI handstamp	**£14.00** ☐
198n	With Inkpen, Newbury, Berks cds, or Knutsford, Cheshire cds	**£25.00** ☐
198o	With Haworth, Keighley cds or Cranford, Kettering cds	**£27.50** ☐
198p	With Thornton, Bradford cds or Chilvers Coton cds	**£27.00** ☐
198q	With Knutsford, Mrs. Gaskell's Cranford-Historic Town, Great Future slogan	**£52.00** ☐
198r	With missing 'p' on 12p, any postmark	**£25.00** ☐

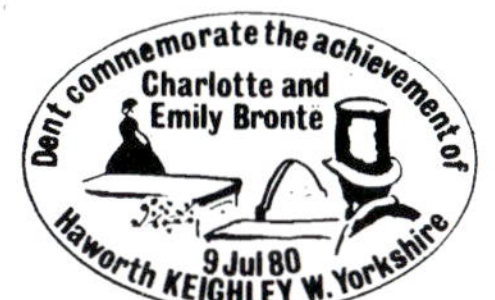

---

199. 1980, 4th August
80th Birthday HM Queen Elizabeth The Queen Mother
12p Portrait Photograph by Norman Parkinson

199a 12p Stamp on illustrated cover, any postmark .... **£1.50** ☐
199b With Philatelic Bureau handstamp .... **£2.50** ☐
199c With First Day of Issue, Glamis Castle, Forfar handstamp .... **£3.00** ☐
199d With HM Queen Elizabeth the Queen Mother 80th, York handstamp .... **£7.50** ☐
199e With HM Queen Elizabeth The Queen Mother 80th, Windsor handstamp .... **£7.50** ☐
199f With First Day Covers of Royalty Exhibition, Leicester handstamp .... **£7.50** ☐
199g With HM Queen Elizabeth The Queen Mother 80th, Hitchin, Herts h/s .... **£7.50** ☐
199h With In Honour 80th Birthday HM Queen Mother, Walmer Castle h/s .... **£7.50** ☐
199i With HM Queen Elizabeth The Queen Mother 80th, London SW1 h/s .... **£7.50** ☐
199j With St. Paul's Walden Flower Festival, Hitchin, Herts handstamp .... **£7.50** ☐
199k With St. Mary's Church, Birthday Greetings from Ware, Herts handstamp .... **£7.50** ☐
199l With HM Queen Mother, Happy Birthday, British Library, London WC h/s .... **£7.50** ☐
199m With Her Majesty Queen Elizabeth, The Queen Mother, BF 8080 PS h/s .... **£7.50** ☐
199n With A Royal Birthday, Grand Theatre Blackpool handstamp .... **£7.50** ☐
199o With Hitchin Salutes The Queen Mother, Hitchin, Herts handstamp .... **£7.50** ☐
199p With Poppy Appeal Cares All Year Round, Richmond handstamp .... **£7.50** ☐
199q With London SW FDI or Windsor FDI handstamp .... **£12.00** ☐
199r With Forces Help Society 80th Anniversary, London SW3 .... **£5.00** ☐
199s With Kings Lynn FDI plus Sandringham cachet .... **£16.00** ☐
199t With Isle of Man Queen Mother Crown Minted in Sutton slogan, various pmks .... **£22.50** ☐
199u With Buckingham Palace SW1 cds .... **£140.00** ☐
199v With Windsor Castle, Windsor Berks cds .... **£155.00** ☐
199w With House of Commons SW1 cds .... **£30.00** ☐
199x With House of Lords SW1 cds .... **£30.00** ☐
199y With Mey, Thurso Caithness cds .... **£37.50** ☐
199z With Glamis, Forfar Angus cds .... **£37.50** ☐
199aa With Queen Elizabeth Ave cds .... **£22.50** ☐
199bb With First Day of Issue, Bournemouth-Poole slogan .... **£22.00** ☐

200. 1980, 10th September
British Conductors
12p Henry Wood, 13½p Thomas Beecham, 15 Malcolm Sargent, 17½p John Barbirolli

200a Set on illustrated cover, any postmark .... **£2.00** ☐
200b With Philatelic Bureau handstamp .... **£4.00** ☐
200c With First Day of Issue, London SW special handstamp .... **£4.50** ☐
200d With Royal Opera House, British Conductors, London WC2 handstamp .... **£7.50** ☐
200e With The Malcolm Sargent Cancer Fund for Children, London SW3 h/s .... **£7.50** ☐
200f With Famous British Conductors, Bedford handstamp .... **£7.50** ☐
200g With Birmingham CBSO Diamond Jubilee handstamp .... **£7.50** ☐
200h With TI Commemorates the CBSO Diamond Jubilee, Birmingham h/s .... **£7.50** ☐
200i With Anaesthesia Royal Festival Hall, London SE1 handstamp .... **£7.50** ☐
200j With 50th Anniv. BBC Symphony Orchestra, Royal Albert Hall handstamp .... **£7.50** ☐
200k With Sponne School 550th Anniversary, Towcester handstamp .... **£8.50** ☐

200l	With Guildhall School of Music Centenary, London EC2 handstamp	£7.50 ☐
200m	With Fairfield Croydon Wednesday 10 September 1980 handstamp	£7.50 ☐
200n	With Conductors of the Hallé, Manchester handstamp	£7.50 ☐
200o	With Sir Thomas Beecham Birthplace, St. Helens handstamp	£7.50 ☐
200p	With 1980 Promenade Concerts, Royal Albert Hall London	£7.50 ☐
200q	With The Royal Philharmonic Orchestra, Royal Festival Hall handstamp	£7.50 ☐
200r	With Leicester Symphony Orchestra, Sir Malcolm Sargent, Leicester h/s	£7.50 ☐
200s	With Sir Thomas Beecham, Rossall School, Fleetwood Lancs handstamp	£7.50 ☐
200t	With Any Field Post Office cds (318 or other) on BFPS cover	£7.50 ☐
200u	With Summertime, British Library, London WC handstamp	£8.50 ☐
200v	With Ashford Kent FDI or London SW7 FDI handstamp	£12.50 ☐
200w	With Hitchin Herts, Stamford Lincs, or Ashford Kent cds	£18.00 ☐
200x	With St. Helens or Southampton Row cds	£18.00 ☐
200y	With Marylebone W1 or New York, Lincoln cds	£18.00 ☐

The Malcolm Sargent
Cancer Fund
for Children
10th September 1980
LONDON S.W.3.

---

201. 1980, 10th October

British Sports Centenaries

12p Athletics, 13½p Rugby, 15p Boxing, 17½p Cricket

201a	Set on illustrated cover, any postmark	£2.00 ☐
201b	With Philatelic Bureau handstamp	£4.00 ☐
201c	With First Day of Issue, Cardiff special handstamp	£4.50 ☐
201d	With 100th Anniversary Amateur Athletic Assn, Crystal Palace handstamp	£7.50 ☐
201e	With 100th Anniversary Amateur Boxing Assn, Wembley handstamp	£7.50 ☐
201f	With London Union of Youth Clubs Salutes London Sportsmen handstamp	£7.50 ☐
201g	With Middlesex CCC 1980 County Champions, Gillette Cup handstamp	£7.50 ☐
201h	With WRU Centenary, Cardiff Arms Park oval handstamp	£7.50 ☐
201i	With The Saints, Northampton oval handstamp	£7.50 ☐
201j	With St. John Ambulance, Manchester Centre handstamp	£7.50 ☐
201k	With A Century of Tests 1880-1980, Kennington Oval handstamp	£7.50 ☐
201l	With King Henry VIII Rugby Centenary, Coventry handstamp	£7.50 ☐
201m	With Centenary 1880-1980 Tour, Centenary Test, Lord's handstamp	£7.50 ☐
201n	With Leicester Football Club Centenary 1880-1980, Leicester h/s	£7.50 ☐
201o	With any Forces Post Office handstamp (42 or other), on BFPS cover	£7.50 ☐
201p	With Autumntime, British Library, London WC handstamp	£7.50 ☐
201q	With Post Office XI v Cricket Writers/Vic Lewis XI, Lord's handstamp	£9.00 ☐
201r	With Oxford, Rugby or Twickenham FDI handstamp	£11.00 ☐
201s	With Marylebone BO, Murrayfield, Neath or Hambledon cds	£36.00 ☐
201t	With Kennington, The Oval, Box, or Jump cds	£37.50 ☐

202. 1980, 19th November
Christmas Issue 10p, 12p, 13½p, 15p, 17½p, Traditional Christmas Decorations

202a	Set on illustrated cover, any postmark	£2.50 ☐
202b	With Philatelic Bureau handstamp	£4.00 ☐
202c	With First Day of Issue, Bethlehem, Landeilo handstamp	£4.50 ☐
202d	With Norway's Christmas Gift, Trafalgar Sq. Christmas Tree handstamp	£7.50 ☐
202e	With Merry Christmas, Hollybush, Ledbury handstamp	£7.50 ☐
202f	With Christmas Carols, Ivybridge, Devon handstamp	£7.50 ☐
202g	With The Regent Street Association Wish You a Very Happy Christmas h/s	£7.50 ☐
202h	With 1980 Christmas, British Library, London WC handstamp	£7.50 ☐
202i	With Leicester Fire Service, Annual Charity Appeal, Leicester handstamp	£7.50 ☐
202j	With any Forces Post Office handstamp, on BFPS cover	£7.50 ☐
202k	With 950 Years of Worship, Waltham Abbey handstamp	£7.50 ☐
202l	With Commonwealth Christmas Stamps Exhibition handstamp	£7.50 ☐
202m	With Glastonbury, or Holy Island cds	£28.00 ☐
202n	With Fairy Cross, Holly Bush, or Star cds	£18.00 ☐
202o	With Magdalen, Ivychurch, or Ivybridge cds	£15.00 ☐
202p	With Bethlehem, Llandeilo, or Nasareth cds	£35.00 ☐
202q	With Everyone's Shopping by Post...London slogan	£40.00 ☐

203. 1981, 6th February
Folklore (Europa) 14p, 18p, 22p, 25p, Traditional Folklore Scenes

203a	Set on illustrated cover, any postmark	£2.00 ☐
203b	With Philatelic Bureau handstamp	£4.00 ☐
203c	With First Day of Issue, London WC special handstamp	£4.50 ☐
203d	With Valentines at the British Library, London WC handstamp	£7.50 ☐
203e	With My Valentine, Lover Salisbury, Wilts handstamp	£7.50 ☐
203f	With Headington Quarry Morris Dancers, Centuries of Tradition handstamp	£7.50 ☐
203g	With The Dunmow Flitch, Little Dunmow, Essex handstamp	£7.50 ☐
203h	With Valentine's Day Cards Exhibition, Leicester handstamp	£7.50 ☐
203i	With Folklore Robin Hood Society Exhibition, Nottingham handstamp	£7.50 ☐
203j	With English Folk Song & Dance Soc. Folk Festival, London handstamp	£7.50 ☐
203k	With 70th Anniversary Thaxted Morris Men, Thaxted, Essex handstamp	£7.50 ☐
203l	With Padstow cds	£16.00 ☐
203m	With Headington Quarry or Thaxted Dunmow cds	£27.50 ☐
203n	With Gretna Green, Carlisle cds, or Lover cds	£45.00 ☐
203o	With Robin Hood or Tintagel cds	£28.00 ☐

QEII • Commemoratives 1981

204. 1981, 25th March
International Year of Disabled People
14p Guide Dog, 18p Sign Language, 22p Wheelchair, 25p Foot Painting

204a	Set on illustrated cover, any postmark	£2.00 ☐
204b	With Philatelic Bureau handstamp	£4.50 ☐
204c	With First Day of Issue, Windsor special handstamp	£5.00 ☐
204d	With Arthritis Care, International Year of Disabled People, London SW1 h/s	£7.50 ☐
204e	With MS Exeter and District Branch, Exeter handstamp	£7.50 ☐
204f	With Stoke Mandeville Hospital National Special Unit, Aylesbury h/s	£7.50 ☐
204g	With Daily Mail 1981 Ideal Home Exhibition, Earls Court handstamp	£7.50 ☐
204h	With Coventry Sports Association - Charity Walk for the Disabled h/s	£7.50 ☐
204i	With Leicestershire Committee Commemorates Int. Year of Disabled h/s	£7.50 ☐
204j	With Guide Dogs Golden Jubilee, Wallasey handstamp	£7.50 ☐
204k	With Cambridge & District Hard of Hearing Assn., Cambridge handstamp	£7.50 ☐
204l	With Le Court, First Cheshire Home, Petersfield Hants handstamp	£7.50 ☐
204m	With Stars for the Disabled, Activities of Daily Living, Peterborough h/s	£7.50 ☐
204n	With Disabled Drivers Motor Club, London W3 handstamp	£7.50 ☐
204o	With Year of Disabled People, Oaklands PH School, Salford handstamp	£7.50 ☐
204p	With Menphys Celebrate International Year for Disabled Persons, Leicester	£7.50 ☐
204q	With any Forces Post Office handstamp, on BFPS cover	£7.50 ☐
204r	With March Philatelic Displays, British Library, London WC h/s	£7.50 ☐
204s	With RAF Headley Court Medical Rehabilitation Unit, BF 1726 PS	£7.50 ☐
204t	With Carters Commemorates International Year of Disabled People, Westbury	£7.50 ☐
204u	With Diamond Jubilee, London SW1, The Royal British Legion h/s	£7.50 ☐
204v	With International Year of Disabled People, Toynbee Hall, London E1 h/s	£7.50 ☐
204w	With Stoke Mandeville, Leeds or St. Dunstans cds	£30.00 ☐
204x	With Midhurst W. Sussex or Oswestry Salop cds	£32.00 ☐
204y	With 1981 IYDP 'Can Disabled People Go Where You Go?' Dumfries slogan	£45.00 ☐
204z	With The British Deaf Association Cares, Carlisle slogan	£45.00 ☐
204aa	With 1981 IYDP St. Loyes College, Exeter machine cancel	£60.00 ☐

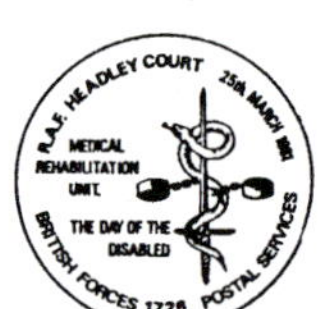

205. 1981, 13th May
British Butterflies
14p Tortoiseshell, 18p Large Blue, 22p Peacock, 25p Chequered Skipper

205a	Set on illustrated cover, any postmark	£2.00
205b	With Philatelic Bureau handstamp	£4.50
205c	With First Day of Issue, London SW special handstamp	£5.00
205d	With British Butterfly Conservation Soc. Sherbourne, Dorset handstamp	£7.50
205e	With British Butterfly Conservation Soc. Quorn, Loughborough handstamp	£7.50
205f	With British Butterfly Conservation Soc. Burton, Cheltenham handstamp	£7.50
205g	With British Naturalist Assoc. Woodwalton, Huntingdon handstamp	£7.50
205h	With Leicestershire Museums, British Butterflies Exhibition, Leics h/s	£7.50
205i	With Nottinghamshire Trust Nature Conservation, Purchase of Eakring h/s	£7.50
205j	With Worldwide Butterflies 21st Anniversary, Compton House, Sherborne	£7.50
205k	With Margaret Fountaine Exhibition, Castle Museum, Norwich handstamp	£7.50
205l	With National Butterfly Museum, Bramber Steyning, W. Sussex h/s	£7.50
205m	With Wildfowl Trust, Slimbridge Gloucester handstamp	£7.50
205n	With May Philatelic Displays, British Library, London WC handstamp	£10.00
205o	With Peacock Cross cds or Quorn Leics cds	£32.00
205p	With Nettlebed, Henley-on-Thames, or Nettleham, Lincoln cds	£18.50
205q	With National Butterfly Museum, First Year at Bramber slogan	£52.00
205r	With any Forces Post Office handstamp (98 or other) on BFPS cover	£6.50

GB Overprints on fdc .... pages 454 - 457
Pre-Release Covers .... pages 458 - 459
Missing Colours on fdc .... pages 460 - 461
Postal Stationery Supplement .... pages 462 - 463

Improved Postal Stationery Coverage from 1972

Postal Stationery is covered in the body of the catalogue up to 1971.
From 1972 onwards we have added a detailed listing
in a separate section at the end of the catalogue.

QEII • Commemoratives 1981

206. 1981, 24th June
The National Trusts 14p Scotland, 18p England, 20p Wales, 22p N. Ireland, 25p Scotland

206a Set on illustrated cover, any postmark .... **£2.00** ☐
206b With Philatelic Bureau handstamp .... **£4.50** ☐
206c With First Day of Issue, Glenfinnan handstamp .... **£5.00** ☐
206d With First Day of Issue, Keswick special handstamp .... **£5.00** ☐
206e With The National Trust for Scotland, Glenfinnan handstamp .... **£7.50** ☐
206f With Giant's Causeway, Bushmills Co. Antrim handstamp .... **£7.50** ☐
206g With Stackpole Head, Pembroke Dyfed handstamp .... **£7.50** ☐
206h With Lyke Wake Walk, RAF Fylingdales BF 1739 PS handstamp .... **£7.50** ☐
206i With St. Kilda 25 Years, British Forces 1750 Postal Service handstamp .... **£7.50** ☐
206j With National Trust for Scotland, St. Kilda, Western Isles handstamp .... **£7.50** ☐
206k With National Trust, Derwentwater, Keswick handstamp .... **£7.50** ☐
206l With Friends of the Earth 10th Anniversary, Olympia, London handstamp .... **£7.50** ☐
206m With June Philatelic Displays, British Library, London WC handstamp .... **£7.50** ☐
206n With Institute of Geological Sciences, Causeway Coast Exhibition handstamp .... **£7.50** ☐
206o With Lingholm Gardens Open Day, Keswick, Cumbria handstamp .... **£7.50** ☐
206p With National Trust Leicester Centre, Staunton Harold, Leicester .... **£7.50** ☐
206q With The National Trust, Scotland 50th Anniversary, Charlecote handstamp .... **£8.50** ☐
206r With Tintagel Cornwall cds, or Alfriston cds .... **£26.00** ☐
206s With Haslemere, Wisbech or Lower Shiplake cds .... **£30.00** ☐
206t With Glenfinnan, Stackpole or Causeway Head cds .... **£27.50** ☐
206u With Culross or Barmouth cds .... **£20.00** ☐
206v With any Forces Post Office handstamp (1724 or other), on BFPS cover .... **£10.50** ☐

207. 1981, 22nd July
The Royal Wedding 14p, 25p, Prince Charles and Lady Diana Spencer

207a The pair on illustrated cover, any postmark .... **£1.50** ☐
207b With Philatelic Bureau handstamp .... **£3.50** ☐
207c With First Day of Issue, London EC special handstamp .... **£4.00** ☐
207d With English/Welsh FDI, Caernarfon Gwynedd handstamp .... **£4.00** ☐
207e With Commemorating the Royal Wedding, Althorp, Northampton handstamp .... **£11.00** ☐
207f With Congratulations from the East of England Show, Peterborough handstamp .... **£8.00** ☐
207g With Royal Wedding Celebrations, Leicester handstamp .... **£8.00** ☐
207h With Windsor, Berks 22 JUL 1981 large pictorial handstamp .... **£14.00** ☐
207i With Royal Wedding Greetings, Canterbury handstamp .... **£12.00** ☐
207j With Royal Wedding Celebration, Cameo Stamp Centre London handstamp .... **£8.00** ☐
207k With Commemorating Royal Wedding, RAF Clement Danes, BF 1932 PS h/s .... **£12.00** ☐
207l With Royal Wedding, St. Paul's Cathedral, London EC4 handstamp .... **£8.00** ☐
207m With The Bride and Groom! Royal Wedding Day Toast, St. Paul's handstamp .... **£8.00** ☐
207n With Loyal Greetings from Watton-at-Stone, Hereford handstamp .... **£8.00** ☐
207o With Royal Wedding Stamp Exhibition, Exeter handstamp .... **£8.00** ☐
207p With Royal Wedding Year, 800th Anniv. of Chingford Old Church handstamp .... **£8.00** ☐
207q With July Philatelic Displays, British Library, London WC handstamp .... **£10.00** ☐
207r With First Prince of Wales Proclaimed at Lincoln Cathedral 1301, Lincoln handstamp .... **£9.00** ☐
207s With 1981-82 Mayor's Charity, City of Exeter handstamp .... **£9.00** ☐
207t With Marriage Prince of Wales and Lady Diana Spencer, Caernarfon Castle h/s .... **£8.00** ☐
207u With The Royal Tournament, BF 1805 PS handstamp .... **£10.50** ☐

207v With Royal Wedding, St. Paul's London EC4, large handstamp .... **£8.00** ☐
207w With Loyal Greetings from Lullingstone Silk Farm, Sherborne handstamp .... **£8.00** ☐
207x With Canoe '81 ... Celebrates the Royal Wedding, Nottingham handstamp .... **£10.00** ☐
207y With Windsor FDI, or Kings Lynn Norfolk plus Sandringham cachet .... **£20.00** ☐
207z With Sanquhar, Dumfriesshire cds on special Wedding cover .... **£12.50** ☐
207aa With Buckingham Palace SW1 cds (Windsor Castle cds **£190**) .... **£180.00** ☐
207bb With Tetbury, Glos cds .... **£34.00** ☐
207cc With House of Commons or House of Lords cds .... **£32.50** ☐
207dd With Princetown, Prince Charles Ave, or Prince of Wales Ave cds .... **£28.00** ☐
207ee With Caernarfon, Charlestown, or St. Pauls cds .... **£26.50** ☐
207ff With Prince Charles Lady Diana Isle of Man Crowns, Sutton Surrey slogan .... **£36.00** ☐
207gg With Royal Westminster Exhibition, Parliament Sq. London slogan .... **£100.00** ☐
207hh With TSB Exhibition of Royal Pageantry, Hagley Hall slogan .... **£85.00** ☐
207ii With London EC FDI plus specially minted Crown Coin .... **£22.00** ☐
207jj **Double Dated Covers** with July 22nd plus July 29th (Wedding Day) cancellations .... **£27.50** ☐

208. 1981, 12th August
Duke of Edinburgh's Award Scheme 14p Expeditions, 18p Skills, 22p Service, 25p Recreation

208a The set on illustrated cover, any postmark .... **£2.00** ☐
208b With Philatelic Bureau handstamp .... **£4.50** ☐
208c With First Day of Issue, London W2 special handstamp .... **£5.00** ☐
208d With Duke of Edinburgh's Award 1956-1981, Edinburgh handstamp .... **£7.00** ☐
208e With Duke of Edinburgh's Award 1956-1981, London EC4 handstamp .... **£7.00** ☐
208f With Duke of Edinburgh's Award 1956-1981, Cardiff handstamp .... **£7.00** ☐
208g With Duke of Edinburgh's Award 1956-1981, London SW1 handstamp .... **£7.00** ☐
208h With Duke of Edinburgh's Award 1956-1981, Belfast handstamp .... **£7.00** ☐
208i With Duke of Edinburgh's Award, 85th Squadron, Winchmore Hill handstamp .... **£7.00** ☐
208j With Duke of Edinburgh's Award, County of Devon, South Devon handstamp .... **£7.00** ☐
208k With Duke of Edinburgh's Award, RAF Halton CR Expedition, BF 1740 PS h/s .... **£7.00** ☐
208l With Leicestershire Girl Guides Association ... Duke of Edinburgh's Award h/s .... **£7.00** ☐
208m With August Philatelic Displays, British Library, London WC handstamp .... **£8.00** ☐
208n With Cardiff Searchlight Tattoo handstamp BF 1747 PS handstamp .... **£8.00** ☐
208o With 25th Anniversary Duke of Edinburgh's Award, Hull handstamp .... **£8.00** ☐
208p With Royal Mail House, Wakefield Official Opening, W. Yorks handstamp .... **£8.00** ☐
208q With Military Tattoo, Edinburgh handstamp .... **£12.00** ☐
208r With Windsor, Berks FDI handstamp .... **£15.00** ☐
208s With Edinburgh or Phillipstown cds .... **£27.50** ☐
208t With Buckingham Palace cds (Windsor Castle cds £125) .... **£115.00** ☐
208u With Pathfinder Village, Exeter, Devon cds .... **£26.00** ☐
208v With Okehampton or Duffus Elgin cds .... **£18.00** ☐
208w With Duke of Edinburgh's Award Crowns, Minted in Sutton, slogan .... **£35.00** ☐
208x With any Field Post Office handstamp (980 or other), on BFPS cover .... **£6.50** ☐

QEII • Commemoratives 1981

209. 1981, 23rd September
Fishing Industry 14p, 18p, 22p, 25p, Four Different Fishing Methods

209a	Set on illustrated cover, any postmark	£2.00 ☐
209b	With Philatelic Bureau handstamp	£4.50 ☐
209c	With First Day of Issue, Hull special handstamp	£5.00 ☐
209d	With Fishing Fleets of Brixham, South Devon handstamp	£7.00 ☐
209e	With Centenary Celebration, Deep Sea Fishermen Mission, Aberdeen h/s	£7.00 ☐
209f	With International Fisheries Exhibition, Catch 81, Falmouth handstamp	£7.00 ☐
209g	With In the Heart of Scotland's Fishing Industry, Buckie, Banff handstamp	£7.00 ☐
209h	With Fishermans Year, Fishmongers Company, London EC4 handstamp	£7.00 ☐
209i	With Ocean Tapestry, RAF St. Mawgan, BF 1741 PS handstamp	£7.00 ☐
209j	With Leicester and District Amalgamated Society of Anglers Anniv. h/s	£7.00 ☐
209k	With Centuries of Trading, Billingsgate London EC3 handstamp	£7.00 ☐
209l	With Manchester Weather Centre Commem 21 Years Service to Fishing	£7.00 ☐
209m	With September Philatelic Displays, British Library, London WC h/s	£7.00 ☐
209n	With any Field Post Office handstamp (980 or other) on BFPS cover	£6.00 ☐
209o	With The Harbour, Paignton, or Hull, or Fishguard cds	£16.00 ☐
209p	With Grimsby, Lowestoft or Great Yarmouth FDI handstamp	£15.00 ☐
209q	With Stafford cds, Six Bells cds, or The Wharf cds	£35.00 ☐
209r	With Lighthouse cds, or Hastings ... for all Seasons slogan cancel	£60.00 ☐

210. 1981, 18th November
Christmas Issue 11½p, 14p, 18p, 22p, 25p, Designs from Childrens Paintings

210a	Set on illustrated cover, any postmark	£2.00 ☐
210b	With Philatelic Bureau handstamp	£4.50 ☐
210c	With First Day of Issue, Bethlehem, Llandeilo handstamp	£5.00 ☐
210d	With A Very Happy Xmas From the Big 'C' Appeal, Norwich handstamp	£7.00 ☐
210e	With Seasons Greetings to HRH Princess of Wales, Regent St. h/s	£7.00 ☐
210f	With Association of Friends of Leicester Cathedral ... Merry Christmas h/s	£7.00 ☐
210g	With Greetings from Stamp Magazine, Croydon Surrey handstamp	£7.00 ☐
210h	With Christmas 1981, Church of St. Mary-at-Hill, London EC3 handstamp	£7.00 ☐
210i	With Children's Christmas Book Show, Blackwells, Oxford handstamp	£7.00 ☐
210j	With Children First, Canterbury Kent handstamp	£7.00 ☐
210k	With England v Hungary, World Cup Xmas 1981, Wembley handstamp	£10.00 ☐
210l	With November Philatelic Displays, British Library, London WC handstamp	£10.00 ☐
210m	With Angel Hill, Holy Island, or St. Nicholas cds	£17.50 ☐
210n	With Bethlehem, Llandeilo cds	£27.50 ☐
210o	With Nasareth, Gwynedd cds	£27.50 ☐
210p	With Kings Road, Star, or Trinity House cds	£14.00 ☐
210q	With any Forces Post Office handstamp on BFPS cover	£6.00 ☐

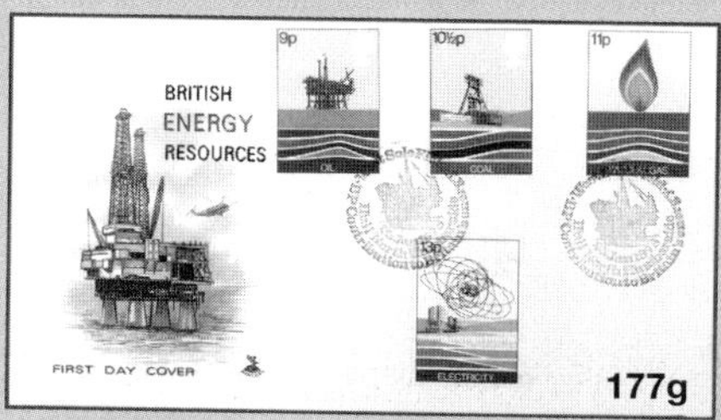

177g

178e

189g

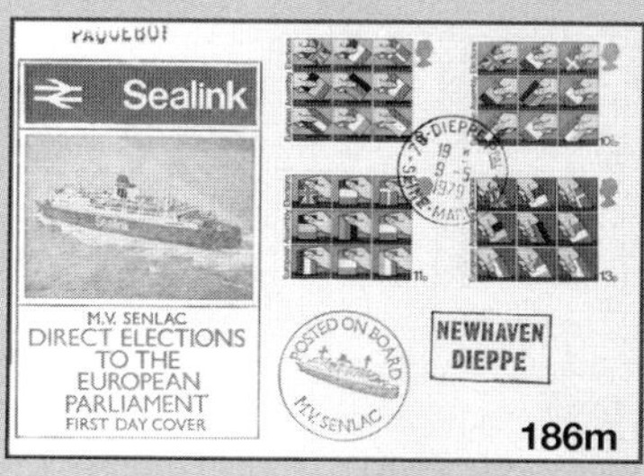

186m

200p

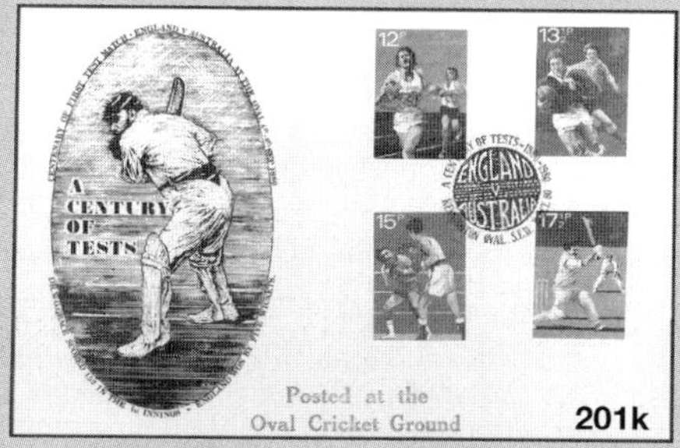

201k

205b

207u

212b

217b

QEII • Commemoratives 1982

211. 1982, 10th February

Charles Darwin Centenary

15½p, 19½p, 26p, 29p, Darwin with Galapagos Animals and Skulls

211a	Set on illustrated cover, any postmark	**£2.00**
211b	With Philatelic Bureau handstamp	**£4.50**
211c	With First Day of Issue, Shrewsbury special handstamp	**£5.00**
211d	With Charles Darwin Centenary, Man of Vision, London SW7 handstamp	**£7.00**
211e	With Voyage of HMS Beagle 150th Anniversary, Plymouth Devon handstamp	**£7.00**
211f	With Charles Darwin Westminster Abbey, London SW1 handstamp	**£7.00**
211g	With Darwin Centenary, RSPB Protects Wild Birds, Sandy, Beds handstamp	**£7.00**
211h	With Charles Darwin, 1809-1882, Cambridge handstamp	**£7.00**
211i	With Charles Darwin Centenary 1809-82, London NW1 handstamp	**£7.00**
211j	With Down House, The Charles Darwin Memorial, Downe, Kent handstamp	**£7.00**
211k	With Charles Darwin 1809-1882, Shrewsbury handstamp	**£7.00**
211l	With HMS Beagle, 150th Anniversary of the Great Voyage, BF 1762 PS h/s	**£7.00**
211m	With Charles Darwin 1809-1882, Slimbridge Gloucester handstamp	**£7.00**
211n	With Maer Hall Tribute to Charles Darwin, Newcastle, Staffs handstamp	**£8.00**
211o	With February Philatelic Displays, British Library, London WC handstamp	**£10.00**
211p	With Darwen Lancs, or Downe Kent cds	**£20.00**
211q	With Shrewsbury, Shropshire cds	**£20.00**
211r	With Plymouth or Falmouth cds	**£24.00**
211s	With Lizard or Piltdown cds	**£30.00**

212. 1982, 24th March

Youth Organisations

15½p Boys Brigade, 19½p Girls Brigade, 26p Boy Scout, 29p Girl Guide

212a	Set on illustrated cover, any postmark	**£2.00**
212b	With Philatelic Bureau handstamp	**£4.50**
212c	With First Day of Issue, London SW handstamp	**£5.00**
212d	With First Day of Issue, Glasgow handstamp	**£5.00**
212e	With Girl Guides Assoc. London SW1 handstamp	**£7.00**
212f	With Youth Activities, St. Donats Castle, Llantwit, Major, S. Glamorgan h/s	**£11.00**
212g	With 75th Anniversary of Scouting, Caterham Surrey handstamp	**£7.00**
212h	With Lord Baden Powell Memorial, Westminster Abbey, London SW1 h/s	**£7.00**
212i	With Eighteen in 82, National Youth Bureau, Leicester handstamp	**£7.00**
212j	With The Girls Brigade, London SW6 handstamp	**£7.00**
212k	With Youth Organisations Young Enterprise, Folkstone, Kent handstamp	**£7.00**
212l	With 75th Anniversary of Scouting, Glasgow handstamp	**£7.00**
212m	With First For Boys, London SW6 handstamp	**£7.00**
212n	With Year of the Scout Celebrations, Peterborough handstamp	**£7.00**
212o	With Scouts Anniversary St. Marys 8th Hendon, London NW4 handstamp	**£7.00**
212p	With 1982 Year of the Scout, British Scout Movement W. Europe, BF 1742 PS h/s	**£8.00**
212q	With Loughborough District Scouts Celebrate Year of the Scout, Leics handstamp	**£7.00**
212r	With Nat. Association of Youth Clubs 70th Anniversary, Leicester handstamp	**£7.00**
212s	With Scouting for Boys by BP, Baden-Powell House, London SW7 h/s	**£7.00**
212t	With March Philatelic Displays, British Library, London WC handstamp	**£12.00**
212u	With Darlington, Co Durham FDI h/s, on Railway Year of Scout cover	**£12.50**

212v With Fleur-de-lis, Gwent cds .... **£100.00** ☐
212w With Pathfinder Village, Exeter, Devon cds .... **£32.00** ☐
212x With West Hampstead, London NW cds .... **£26.00** ☐
212y With Chingford E.4. or The Camp, or Guide cds .... **£26.00** ☐
212z With House of Lords SW1 cds .... **£25.00** ☐
212aa With 'Scouts Help Others' slogan - London SWI or Chingford (or other **£18**) .... **£27.50** ☐

213. 1982, 28th April
British Theatre (Europa)
15½p Ballet, 19½p Pantomime, 26p Theatre, 29p Opera

213a Set on illustrated cover, any postmark .... **£2.00** ☐
213b With Philatelic Bureau handstamp .... **£4.50** ☐
213c With First Day of Issue, Stratford-upon-Avon handstamp .... **£5.00** ☐
213d With Theatre Royal Bath, Restoration Project, Bath handstamp .... **£6.50** ☐
213e With Arts Theatre 1936-82, Cambridge handstamp .... **£6.50** ☐
213f With Shakespeare Memorial at Southwark Cathedral, London SE1 handstamp .... **£6.50** ☐
213g With 250th Anniversary, Royal Opera House, Covent Garden, London WC h/s .... **£6.50** ☐
213h With Barbican Centre, Where the Arts come to life, London EC2 handstamp .... **£6.50** ☐
213i With Worthing Operatic Society Founded 1902, Worthing, West Sussex h/s .... **£6.50** ☐
213j With Mercury Theatre Tenth Anniversary, Colchester, Essex handstamp .... **£6.50** ☐
213k With Theatre Royal 225 Years, Norwich, Norfolk handstamp .... **£6.50** ☐
213l With New Theatre Hull, 150th Anniversary of Historic Building, Hull h/s .... **£6.50** ☐
213m With John Gay 250th Death Anniversary, Westminster Abbey, London SW1 h/s .... **£6.50** ☐
213n With Royal Shakespeare Theatre, 50th Anniversary, Stratford-upon-Avon h/s .... **£6.50** ☐
213o With 50 Golden Jubilee Festival Final, Pitlochry, Perthshire handstamp .... **£6.50** ☐
213p With William Shakespeare, Stratford-upon-Avon, Warwickshire handstamp .... **£15.00** ☐
213q With The Queens Theatre Stamp Exhibition, Hornchurch, Essex handstamp .... **£7.50** ☐
213r With Leicester Drama Society Celebrate their Diamond Jubilee, Leicester h/s .... **£7.50** ☐
213s With Royal Air Force Central Band, 62nd Anniv. BF 1773 PS handstamp .... **£10.00** ☐
213t With any Forces Post Office h/s (8282 or other), on BFPS cover .... **£7.50** ☐
213u With Tavistock Repertory Company, Golden Jubilee 1932-1982, London NI h/s .... **£7.50** ☐
213v With Stratford-upon-Avon, Barnstaple, or Great Yarmouth cds .... **£16.00** ☐
213w With Ben Johnson Road, or Macduff cds .... **£26.00** ☐
213x With The Harlequin, or Clowne cds .... **£26.00** ☐
213y With Broadway or Hollywood cds .... **£22.50** ☐
213z With Shakespeare St. Padham, or Globe Rd E1 cds .... **£27.50** ☐
213aa With Eden Court, Inverness, Theatre of the Highlands slogan .... **£36.00** ☐
213bb With Theatr Clwyd, Mold, Clwyd handstamp .... **£26.00** ☐
213cc With Dickens Festival, Rochester 3-6 June slogan .... **£98.00** ☐

QEII • Commemoratives 1982

214. 1982, 16th June
Maritime Heritage 15½p Henry VIII, 19½p Blake, 24p Nelson, 26p Fisher, 29p Cunningham

214a	Set on illustrated cover, any postmark	£2.50 ☐
214b	With Philatelic Bureau handstamp	£4.50 ☐
214c	With First Day of Issue, Portsmouth special handstamp	£5.00 ☐
214d	With Royal Mail Maritime Heritage Cruise, Penarth S. Glamorgan h/s	£8.00 ☐
214e	With National Maritime Heritage Year, Stamp Exhibition, Exeter handstamp	£8.00 ☐
214f	With The Mountbatten Memorial Trust, Broadlands, Romsey handstamp	£8.00 ☐
214g	With Britannia's Maritime Heritage, Dartmouth, South Devon handstamp	£8.00 ☐
214h	With Maritime England Year, Poole, Dorset handstamp	£8.00 ☐
214i	With Axe Valley Maritime '82, Seaton, Devon handstamp	£8.00 ☐
214j	With Lloyd's Register of Shipping, London EC3 handstamp	£8.00 ☐
214k	With Cinque Ports Exhibition, Dover, Kent handstamp	£8.00 ☐
214l	With Leicester Sea Cadet Corps Celebrates Maritime Heritage Year, Leics	£8.00 ☐
214m	With Captain Cooks Endeavour Salutes Admiral Nelson's Victory, Whitby h/s	£8.00 ☐
214n	With 180th Anniversary, Captain Flinders RN Discovery of Port Lincoln h/s	£8.50 ☐
214o	With Peru Joint Services Hovercraft Expedition, BF 1956 PS h/s	£14.00 ☐
214p	With National Maritime Museum, Greenwich SE10 handstamp	£8.00 ☐
214q	With Worshipful Company of Shipwrights, City of London EC2 h/s	£12.00 ☐
214r	With National Postal Museum, Army Bag handstamp in red	£12.00 ☐
214s	With Centenary 1882-1982, British Forces 8282 Postal Service h/s	£12.00 ☐
214t	With Birthplace Horatio Nelson, Burnham Thorpe, Norfolk handstamp	£8.00 ☐
214u	With Weymouth & Portland Chamber of Commerce, Dorset handstamp	£8.00 ☐
214v	With any Field Post Office handstamp (911 or other), on BFPS cover	£8.00 ☐
214w	With The Historic Ship Collection, St. Katharine's Dock, London E1 h/s	£8.00 ☐
214x	With Over 250 Years of Maritime Heritage, Lloyds of London handstamp	£8.00 ☐
214y	With The Missions to Seamen, Serving Seafarers since 1856, Hants h/s	£8.00 ☐
214z	With 35th Anniversary Formation RAF Maritime Branch BF 1779 PS	£14.00 ☐
214aa	With Maritime England Year, The Missions to Seamen, Stratford h/s	£8.00 ☐
214bb	With Nottinghamshire Lifeboat Appeal, Nottingham handstamp	£8.00 ☐
214cc	With Trafalgar Square Philatelic Counter, (Nelson) handstamp	£16.00 ☐
214dd	With Norwich Philatelic Counter handstamp, plus Castle Museum cachet	£8.50 ☐
214ee	With Portsmouth FDI handstamp or cds, plus HMS Victory cachet	£16.50 ☐
214ff	With Nelson, Lancs, or Burnham Thorpe, Norfolk cds	£24.00 ☐
214gg	With Bridgewater, Somerset cds or FDI handstamp	£11.00 ☐
214hh	With Blake's Corner, Blake Street, or Nelson Portsmouth cds	£17.50 ☐
214ii	With Cunningham Cres. Bournemouth, or Fishers Pond, Eastleigh cds	£14.00 ☐
214jj	With Trafalgar, Victory Street, or Naval Barracks Chatham cds	£24.00 ☐
214kk	With Clyde Submarine Base, Hellensburg cds	£16.00 ☐
214ll	With The Docks, The Quarterdeck, or Flotta Orkney cds	£20.00 ☐
214mm	With Falkland, Greenwich, or Westward Ho, Devon cds	£17.50 ☐
214nn	With House of Commons or House of Lords cds	£25.00 ☐
214oo	With Buckingham Palace SW1 cds	£85.00 ☐
214pp	With Fleet Mail Office FPO cds, Portsmouth or Devonport	£52.00 ☐
214qq	With Maritime Bristol, The start of many an adventure, Bristol slogan	£75.00 ☐
214rr	With See the Spectacular Tall Ships in Southampton slogan	£55.00 ☐

A complete catalogue Index appears on page 3

QEII • Commemoratives 1982

215. 1982, 23rd July

British Textiles 15½p 1883 Fabric Design, 19½p 1906 Design, 26p 1929 Design, 29p 1949 Design

215a	Set on illustrated cover, any postmark	£2.00 ☐
215b	With Philatelic Bureau handstamp	£4.50 ☐
215c	With First Day of Issue, Rochdale special handstamp	£5.00 ☐
215d	With Arkwright Anniversary, Cromford Mills, Matlock, Derbyshire h/s	£8.00 ☐
215e	With William Morris Exhibition, Water House Lloyd Park, London E17 h/s	£8.00 ☐
215f	With Textiles On Stamps Exhibition, Liberty Regent Street, London W1 h/s	£8.00 ☐
215g	With Leek-Centre of the Textile Industry, Leek, Staffs handstamp	£8.00 ☐
215h	With Sir Richard Arkwright 250th Anniv. Arkwright House, Preston h/s	£8.00 ☐
215i	With The Textile Institute 1910-1982, Manchester handstamp	£8.00 ☐
215j	With Coldharbour Mill, Uffculme, Cullompton, Devon handstamp	£8.00 ☐
215k	With Royal School of Needlework RSN, Princes Gate, London SW7 h/s	£8.00 ☐
215l	With School of Textiles, 99 Years in Leicester, Leicestershire handstamp	£8.00 ☐
215m	With Leicester & District Knitting Industry Association, Leicester h/s	£8.00 ☐
215n	With Centenary British Forces Postal Service, BF 8282 PS handstamp	£8.00 ☐
215o	With British Philatelic Federation 64th Congress, Southampton handstamp	£8.00 ☐
215p	With Royal Tournament, BF 1840 PS handstamp	£8.00 ☐
215q	With Textile Exhibition, Bradford Industrial Museum, Bradford handstamp	£8.00 ☐
215r	With Polytechnic Huddersfield, Textile Design Education, Huddersfield h/s	£8.00 ☐
215s	With Hockley Mill, World's First Mechanised Cotton Mill, Nottingham	£8.00 ☐
215t	With Harris, Worstead, Cotton Tree, or Weaver Lodge cds	£15.00 ☐
215u	With Cherry Orchard, Silk St., Wool or Tweed Road cds	£16.00 ☐
215v	With Forest Road, Hammersmith, Preston, or Walthamstow cds	£14.00 ☐
215w	With Hall-Ith-Wood, Bolton, Lancs cds (Spinning Mule invention)	£26.00 ☐
215x	With Coggeshall, Draperstown, or Bobbers Mill cds	£15.00 ☐

There are several other postmarks that can be associated with this issue. Pricing from **£10**.

This is the 30th Edition of the Collect GB First Day Covers catalogue

We hope that you are enjoying it and find it useful in developing your own collection. Don't forget that we now include sections on Overprints, Pre-release covers and Missing Colours. These can all be found in the last part of the catalogue.

216. 1982, 8th September
Information Technology
15½p Communications Development, 26p Modern Technology

216a	Set on illustrated cover, any postmark	**£2.00** ☐
216b	With Philatelic Bureau handstamp	**£3.50** ☐
216c	With First Day of Issue, London WC special handstamp	**£4.00** ☐
216d	With Information Technology Year, Bedford handstamp	**£7.00** ☐
216e	With Information Technology Year, UMIST Manchester handstamp	**£7.00** ☐
216f	With Best of Prestel, The First Year, Martlesham Heath handstamp	**£7.00** ☐
216g	With University of Leicester Celebrates Information Technology 82 h/s	**£7.00** ☐
216h	With Information Technology Year, The National Electronics Centre, London	**£7.00** ☐
216i	With Open Days, Broadlands, Romsey, Hants handstamp	**£7.00** ☐
216j	With Computertown, Croydon, Surrey handstamp	**£7.00** ☐
216k	With 10th Anniversary Royal Air Force Control Centre BF 1787 PS	**£7.00** ☐
216l	With 2nd Anniversary Intelpost, Head Post Office, London E1 handstamp	**£7.00** ☐
216m	With 25 Years Artificial Earth Satelites, Jodrell Bank, Cheshire handstamp	**£7.00** ☐
216n	With Ashville College Joins the Computer Age Exhibition, Harrogate h/s	**£8.00** ☐
216o	With any BFPO postmark, 1788, 8282, 1882 and others	**£8.50** ☐
216p	With New Invention, Willenhall cds	**£15.00** ☐
216q	With Taunton, Somerset cds (British Telecom Museum)	**£15.00** ☐
216r	With Mawgan, Mullion, or Helston cds (Goonhilly Downs)	**£15.00** ☐
216s	With Totnes cds or Norwich FDI handstamp	**£13.50** ☐
216t	With Martlesham, Woodbridge cds (BT research centre)	**£28.50** ☐

A few other cds postmarks can be associated with this issue. Prices from **£10**.

217. 1982, 13th October
British Motor Industry
15½p Austin, 19½p Ford, 26p Jaguar, 29p Rolls-Royce

217a	Set on illustrated cover, any postmark	**£2.50** ☐
217b	With Philatelic Bureau handstamp	**£4.50** ☐
217c	With First Day of Issue, Birmingham special handstamp	**£5.00** ☐
217d	With First Day of Issue, Crewe special handstamp	**£5.00** ☐
217e	With 2nd Anniversary Metro, World Trade Center, London E1	**£9.50** ☐
217f	With National Motor Museum, Beaulieu, Hampshire handstamp	**£9.50** ☐
217g	With Sixty Years of Jaguar Cars, Coventry handstamp	**£9.50** ☐
217h	With 60th Anniversary Austin 7, Brooklands, Weybridge handstamp	**£9.50** ☐
217i	With Heritage Collection Car Design Exhibition, Brentford, Middx h/s	**£9.50** ☐
217j	With Motor Cycle & Car Museum, Stanford Hall, Leicester handstamp	**£9.50** ☐
217k	With Year of the Car 1982, Motoring Anniversaries, Woodford h/s	**£9.50** ☐
217l	With Worshipful Company of Coachmakers and Coach Harness, London	**£9.50** ☐
217m	With Rolls-Royce Enthusiasts Club 1957-1982 Towcester, Northants h/s	**£9.50** ☐
217n	With 35 Years of Silverstone Circuit, Silverstone, Towcester handstamp	**£9.50** ☐
217o	With Dagenham Home of Ford & Dagenham Motors, From Model T to Sierra	**£9.50** ☐
217p	With Commemorating the Millionth New Ford Escort, Halewood, Liverpool	**£9.50** ☐
217q	With Ford Sierra Launch Day, Ford Chippenham, Wilts handstamp	**£9.50** ☐
217r	With 70th Anniversary of Motor Transport, Royal Flying Corps BF1789 PS	**£9.50** ☐

217s With any Forces Post Office handstamp (98, 8282 or other), on BFPS cover **£9.50** ☐
217t With 45 Anniversary Nuffield College, Oxford handstamp **£9.50** ☐
217u With Transport Centenary 1882-1982, Chesterfield, Derby handstamp **£9.50** ☐
217v With Crewe or Manchester FDI handstamp **£12.50** ☐
217w With Ford, Liverpool or Shrewsbury cds, or Austin Plymouth cds **£22.50** ☐
217x With Dagenham, Halewood, Longbridge (Leyland cds £26) **£22.50** ☐
217y With Saltley, Foleshill, Crewe, Brighton or Knightsbridge cds **£20.00** ☐
217z With Birmingham N.E.C. cds and Motor Show cachet **£80.00** ☐
217aa With Alwalton, Amersham, Beaulieu, or Bentley (Surrey or Yorks) cds **£20.00** ☐
217bb With Trafford Park, Manchester cds and Model T cachet **£47.50** ☐
217cc With R.A.C. London cds **£460.00** ☐
217dd With Lanchester, Vauxhall, Silverstone, or Dunlop cds **£25.00** ☐
217ee With Hella of Banbury Motor Show Exhibition, Banbury or Oxford slogan **£65.00** ☐

FORD MOTOR COMPANY LIMITED.
HALEWOOD, LIVERPOOL
COMMEMORATING
THE MILLIONTH
NEW FORD ESCORT
13 OCTOBER 1982

---

218. 1982, 17th November

Christmas Issue

12½p, 15½p, 19½p, 26p, 29p, Scenes from Traditional Carols

218a Set on illustrated cover, any postmark **£3.00** ☐
218b With Philatelic Bureau handstamp **£4.50** ☐
218c With First Day of Issue, Bethlehem, Llandeilo handstamp **£5.00** ☐
218d With I Saw Three Ships Exhibition, Hythe, Kent handstamp **£7.50** ☐
218e With A Christmas Carol Exhibition, Dickens House, London WC1 h/s **£7.50** ☐
218f With Seasons Greetings, Cutty Sark Christmas 1982, London SE10 h/s **£7.50** ☐
218g With The Salvation Army, Wish You a Happy Christmas, Leicester h/s **£7.50** ☐
218h With Good King Wenceslas Christmas 82, Salisbury, Wilts handstamp **£7.50** ☐
218i With Seasons Greetings, Norwich Cathedral, Norwich, Norfolk handstamp **£7.50** ☐
218j With We Three Kings, Christmas 1982, Star Glenrothes, Fife h/s **£7.50** ☐
218k With Sir Christopher Wren, East Knowle, Salisbury handstamp **£14.00** ☐
218l With any Forces Post Office handstamp (8282 or other), on BFPS cover **£8.50** ☐
218m With Bethlehem, Llandeilo, or Nasareth, Caernarfon cds **£26.00** ☐
218n With Star, Starcross, Ivychurch, Shepherd's Hill, or Shepherdswell cds **£18.00** ☐
218o With Kingsworthy, St. Nicholas, Holy Island, Noel Rd, or Hollybush cds **£18.00** ☐

There are a few other cds pmks which relate to the Christmas theme. Prices from **£10**.

Readers comments are always welcome.

QEII • Commemoratives 1983

219. 1983, 26th January
British River Fish
15½p Salmon, 19½p Pike, 26p Trout, 29p Perch

219a Set on illustrated cover, any postmark .... **£2.00** ☐
219b With Philatelic Bureau handstamp .... **£4.00** ☐
219c With First Day of Issue, Peterborough special handstamp .... **£4.50** ☐
219d With Izaac Walton Tercentenary, River Itchen, Winchester handstamp .... **£8.50** ☐
219e With Izaac Walton Tercentenary, Stafford handstamp .... **£8.50** ☐
219f With Redditch, 400 Years of Fishing Tackle handstamp .... **£10.50** ☐
219g With Fishing the Teign, Newton Abbot, Devon handstamp .... **£10.50** ☐
219h With National Anglers Council, Izaac Walton Tercentenary, London h/s .... **£9.00** ☐
219i With Over 100 Years of Salmon Fishing, Salmon Leap, Coleraine h/s .... **£9.00** ☐
219j With London Anglers' Association, Walthamstow, London E17 handstamp .... **£9.00** ☐
219k With The Pike Anglers Club of Great Britain, Norwich, Norfolk handstamp .... **£9.00** ☐
219l With Izaac Walton 1593 - 1683, Stafford handstamp .... **£9.00** ☐
219m With Celebrating the Return of the Salmon, Thames Water, London h/s .... **£9.00** ☐
219n With Make the Most of Your Waterways, British Waterways Board, London .... **£9.00** ☐
219o With The Birmingham Anglers Association Ltd, Birmingham handstamp .... **£10.50** ☐
219p With Douglas Bader Angling Club 1970 - 1983, Leicester handstamp .... **£10.50** ☐
219q With Cinq Ports Angling Society, 60th Anniversary, Hythe, Kent h/s .... **£9.00** ☐
219r With History of the House of Hardy Exhibition, Pall Mall London h/s .... **£9.00** ☐
219s With Display of River Fish, Salisbury, Wilts handstamp .... **£10.50** ☐
219t With 40th Anniversary RAF Stafford Angling Club, BF 1798 PS h/s .... **£8.50** ☐
219u With 14th Anniversary Tisbury Fish Farm, Romford, Essex handstamp .... **£9.50** ☐
219v With The Salmon Leap,Troutbeck, Pyke Hill or Pyke Road cds .... **£20.00** ☐
219w With Fleet Street, Winchester, or Itchen cds .... **£24.00** ☐
219x With Walton-on-Thames, Walton, or Stafford cds .... **£24.00** ☐
219y With Coldstream, Fishlake, Freshwater, or River cds .... **£18.00** ☐

A few other cds postmarks can be related to this issue. Prices from **£10**.

Valuation Guide for GB Blocks of 4 on fdc

1840 to 1900 - three times the single fdc value
1902 to 1936 - two and a half times the single fdc value
1936 KEVIII - twice the single fdc value
1937 to 1951 - twice the single fdc value
1952 to date - one and a half times the single fdc value

220. 1983, 9th March

Commonwealth Day

15½p Tropical Island, 19½p Desert, 26p Farmland, 29p Mountain Range

220a Set on illustrated cover, any postmark **£2.00**
220b With Philatelic Bureau handstamp **£4.00**
220c With First Day of Issue, London SW special handstamp **£4.50**
220d With Royal Commonwealth Society Founded 1868, London WC2 h/s.... **£7.50**
220e With Mahatma Gandhi, Romsey, Hants handstamp.... **£7.50**
220f With 35th Commonwealth Anniv., World Trade Centre, London E1 h/s.... **£7.50**
220g With Commonwealth Institute, The First Twenty One Years, London W8 .... **£7.50**
220h With Association of Cricket Umpires, 30 Years, Leicester handstamp.... **£7.50**
220i With Geographical Magazine, A Window on the World, London SW7 h/s.... **£7.50**
220j With The Wilberforce Council, William Wilberforce 150th Anniv. Hull h/s **£7.50**
220k With 68th Anniv. Formation No. 24 Commonwealth Squadron BF1799 PS **£7.50**
220l With any Forces Post Office handstamp, on BFPS cover.... **£7.50**
220m With 215th Anniversary Capt. Cook's Voyages of Discovery, Whitby h/s **£7.50**
220n With Buckingham Palace SW1 cds (Gleneagles, Perth cds **£65**).... **£90.00**
220o With House of Commons or House of Lords cds **£40.00**
220p With Parliament St, or Kensington High St B.O. W8 cds **£22.00**
220q With Windsor FDI handstamp, or Queen Elizabeth Ave cds.... **£16.50**
220r With Blantyre, Melbourne Road, Falkland, or Toronto cds **£16.50**
220s With Imperial Ave, Leicester, or Union Road, Exeter cds.... **£14.00**

A few other cds postmarks can be related to this issue. Prices from **£10**.

221. 1983, 25th May

Engineering Achievements (Europa)

16p Humber Bridge, 20½p Thames Flood Barrier, 28p Iolair-Emergency Support Vessel

221a Set on illustrated cover, any postmark **£2.00**
221b With Philatelic Bureau handstamp **£4.00**
221c With First Day of Issue, Hull special handstamp **£4.50**
221d With Celebrating Engineering Achievements, AUEW London SE15 h/s.... **£7.00**
221e With Humber Bridge - Opened 17 July 1981, Barton on Humber h/s.... **£7.00**
221f With Ten Years of Engineering Achievement, Thames Flood Barrier London **£7.00**
221g With 2 Years A Tribute to British Engineering, Humber Bridge, Hull h/s **£7.00**
221h With UDI. Taking technology to greater depths, Aberdeen handstamp **£7.00**
221i With British Shipbuilders, Iolair, London SW7 handstamp **£7.00**
221j With The GLC Thames Barrier, Protecting London, Woolwich SE7 h/s **£7.00**
221k With Institute of Mechanical Engineers, London SW1 handstamp **£7.00**
221l With Telecom Technology Showcase, London EC4 handstamp **£7.00**
221m With Bristol Philatelic Counter (bridge design) handstamp **£7.00**
221n With Commemorating the CTH Joint Venture, Thames Flood Barrier h/s **£7.00**
221o With Institution of Civil Engineers, London SW1 handstamp **£7.00**
221p With Dan Air 30 Years Experience, London Gatwick, West Sussex h/s **£7.00**
221q With Printing - shares the fruits of Human Genius, Slough, Berks h/s **£7.00**
221r With The Harrier Birthplace, Kingston upon Thames, Surrey handstamp **£7.00**
221s With No. 2 School of Technical Training, RAF Cosford BF 1806 PS **£7.00**
221t With BP Contribution. Iolair A British Engineering Achievement, Aberdeen h/s.... **£7.00**
221u With Silvertown cds and Charlton cds (2 covers). The pair.... **£26.00**

221v	With Hessle cds and Barton-on-Humber cds (2 covers). The pair	£32.00 ☐
221w	With Ironbridge, Telford cds, or New Bridge, Dover cds	£24.00 ☐
221x	With Woolwich B.O. cds (Southside of Thames Barrier)	£14.00 ☐
221y	With Cleveland, Dundee, Clydebank, Cruden Bay, or Telford cds	£14.00 ☐
221z	With New Invention, or Eagle cds	£14.00 ☐
221aa	With Port Glasgow cds (where Iolair was built)	£45.00 ☐
221bb	With GLC Thames Barrier Protecting London, Charlton/Woolwich slogan	£32.00 ☐
221cc	With Collect British Stamps, Your Humberside Philatelic Link, Hull slogan	£52.00 ☐

A few other cds postmarks can be related to this issue. Prices from **£10**.

222. 1983, 6th July

The British Army 16p, 20½p, 26p, 28p, 31p, Five Different Army Regiments

222a	Set on illustrated cover, any postmark	£2.00 ☐
222b	With Philatelic Bureau handstamp	£5.00 ☐
222c	With First Day of Issue, Aldershot special handstamp	£5.50 ☐
222d	With The British Army Series, BF 1983 PS handstamp	£10.00 ☐
222e	With Soldier Print Society Exhibition, Military Uniforms, Worthing h/s	£10.00 ☐
222f	With Ensign Miniatures Model Soldier Exhibition, Lincs handstamp	£10.00 ☐
222g	With Regimental Stamp Display, Philatelic Counter, Glasgow handstamp	£10.00 ☐
222h	With Blenheim Palace, Woodstock, Oxford handstamp	£10.00 ☐
222i	With Duke of Edinburgh's Royal Regimental Museum, Wilts handstamp	£10.00 ☐
222j	With The Royal Military Academy, Serving to Lead...Sandhurst handstamp	£10.00 ☐
222k	With 12th Anniversary National Army Museum, London SW3 handstamp	£10.00 ☐
222l	With Duke of Yorks Royal Military School, 180th Anniv., Dover handstamp	£10.00 ☐
222m	With Rheindalen Allied Marches, BF 1810PS handstamp	£10.00 ☐
222n	With The Parachute Regiment 1942-1983, BF 2000 PS handstamp	£10.00 ☐
222o	With 75th Anniversary of the TA in Wales, BF 1908 PS handstamp	£10.00 ☐
222p	With Richard III 500th Anniversary Celebrations, Middleham handstamp	£14.00 ☐
222q	With Irish Guards 1900-1983, BF 1900 PS handstamp	£10.00 ☐
222r	With The Royal Green Jackets 1966-1983, BF 1800 PS handstamp	£10.00 ☐
222s	With The Royal Scots (The Royal Regt.), BF 0350 PS handstamp	£10.00 ☐
222t	With The Royal Welch Fusiliers, BF 0294 PS handstamp	£10.00 ☐
222u	With Any Forces/Field Post Office handstamp, on BFPS cover	£20.00 ☐
222v	With The Queen's Own Hussars, Silver Jubilee, Warwick handstamp	£10.00 ☐
222w	With Aldershot, Catterick, Sandhurst, or Salisbury cds	£20.00 ☐
222x	With Waterloo, Wellington, or Marlborough cds	£20.00 ☐
222y	With Yorktown, Battlefield, Gun Hill, Battle or Bunkers Hill cds	£20.00 ☐
222z	With Edinburgh, Winchester, Hightown, or Broadway cds	£20.00 ☐
222aa	With Buckingham Palace SW1 cds (Windsor Castle **£90**)	£80.00 ☐
222bb	With The Army 1914-82 National Army Museum, London slogan	£35.00 ☐
222cc	With Join the Territorial Army, 75th Anniversary, Northampton slogan	£510.00 ☐

A few other cds postmarks can be related to this issue. Prices from **£10**.

QEII • Commemoratives 1983

223. 1983, 24th August

British Gardens

16p 20th Century, 20½p 19th Century, 28p 18th Century, 31p 17th Century

223a Set on illustrated cover, any postmark .... **£2.00** ☐
223b With Philatelic Bureau handstamp .... **£4.50** ☐
223c With First Day of Issue, Oxford special handstamp .... **£5.00** ☐
223d With The Queen's Gardens, Croydon, Surrey handstamp .... **£9.00** ☐
223e With Capability Brown 1716-1783, Kirkharle, Newcastle Upon Tyne h/s .... **£9.00** ☐
223f With League of Friends, The Grange Biddulph, Stoke-on-Trent handstamp .... **£9.00** ☐
223g With The National Trust Sissinghurst Castle, Sissinghurst Kent h/s .... **£9.00** ☐
223h With The National Trust for Scotland, Pitmedden Ellon, handstamp .... **£9.00** ☐
223i With Blenheim Palace, Woodstock, Oxford handstamp .... **£9.00** ☐
223j With Capability Brown 1715-1783, Kew Gardens, Richmond handstamp .... **£9.00** ☐
223k With Capability Brown 200th Anniversary, Claremont Surrey handstamp .... **£9.00** ☐
223l With Roses in August, Syon Park, Brentford Middx handstamp .... **£9.00** ☐
223m With A Celebration of English Gardens, London SW1 handstamp .... **£9.00** ☐
223n With Capability Brown - Bicentenary Hampton Court, Surrey handstamp .... **£9.00** ☐
223o With Capability Brown at Bowood, 220th Anniv., Bowood, Calne h/s .... **£9.00** ☐
223p With National Trust for Scotland, Crathes Castle, Banchory handstamp .... **£9.00** ☐
223q With 30th Anniversary RAF Memorial Gardens, Runnymede, BF1814 PS .... **£12.50** ☐
223r With The National Trust, Lyme Park, Disley, Cheshire handstamp .... **£9.00** ☐
223s With Lancelot Capability Brown 1716-1783, Fenstanton handstamp .... **£9.00** ☐
223t With Kew Gardens, Richmond cds .... **£40.00** ☐
223u With Botanic Gardens, Belfast cds .... **£35.00** ☐
223v With Biddulph, Woodstock, Udny Ellon, or Sissinghurst cds .... **£22.00** ☐
223w With Glamis, Petworth, or Harewood cds .... **£16.50** ☐
223x With Mayfair W1, Fenstanton, or Newcastle cds .... **£16.50** ☐
223y With Rose Cottage, Shrublands, or The Allotments cds .... **£16.50** ☐
223z With Back Beautiful Britain, London SW1 (slogan used at various P.O.'s) .... **£42.50** ☐
223aa With Your Garden Isle is Beautiful, Keep it Tidy, Isle of Wight slogan .... **£48.00** ☐
223bb With Chamber of Commerce, See Devizes in Bloom slogan .... **£45.00** ☐

A few other cds postmarks relate to this issue. Prices from **£12**.

224. 1983, 5th October

British Fairs

16p, 20½p, 28p, Fairground Scenes. 31p Early Produce Fair

224a Set on illustrated cover, any postmark .... **£2.00** ☐
224b With Philatelic Bureau handstamp .... **£4.00** ☐
224c With First Day of Issue, Nottingham special handstamp .... **£4.50** ☐
224d With Turner's Musical Merry-Go-Round, Still Going Strong, Northants h/s .... **£9.00** ☐
224e With Showmen's Guild of G.B. Honouring British Fairs, Middx handstamp .... **£9.00** ☐
224f With Rowell Lions, First Year, Rothwell, Kettering Northants handstamp .... **£9.00** ☐
224g With Butchers Charitable Institution, Bartholomew Fair, London h/s .... **£9.00** ☐
224h With Goose Fair, Tavistock, Devon handstamp .... **£9.00** ☐
224i With Chipperfields Circus 300 Years, London EC handstamp .... **£9.00** ☐
224j With Priory Church of St Bartholomew the Great, London EC handstamp .... **£9.00** ☐

224k	With Goose Fair 1983, Nottingham handstamp	**£9.00** ☐
224l	With 80th Anniversary World's First Air Fair, BF 1815 PS handstamp	**£12.50** ☐
224m	With any Field Post Office handstamp, on BFPS cover	**£8.50** ☐
224n	With Fairfield Croydon 21st Birthday, Croydon Surrey handstamp	**£9.50** ☐
224o	With British Philatelic Federation 65th Congress, Bath handstamp	**£14.00** ☐
224p	With Widecombe-in-the-Moor cds, (Scarborough cds **£16**)	**£27.50** ☐
224q	With Appleby-in-Westmorland, Tavistock, or Cambridge cds	**£15.00** ☐
224r	With St. Giles Oxford, Borough High St SE1, or London Chief Office cds	**£20.00** ☐
224s	With Winchester, Horse Fair Rugeley, or Fair Isle cds	**£17.50** ☐
224t	With Big Top cds, on Big Top Circus cover	**£17.50** ☐

There are several more cds postmarks which relate to this issue, especially those of towns with traditional involvement in fairs or the circus. Prices range from **£10**.

225. 1983, 16th November

Christmas Issue

12½p, 16p, 20½p, 28p, 31p, Peace on Earth Designs

225a	Set on illustrated cover, any postmark	**£2.00** ☐
225b	With Philatelic Bureau handstamp	**£4.00** ☐
225c	With First Day of Issue, Bethlehem, Llandeilo handstamp	**£4.50** ☐
225d	With Winchester Cathedral, Christmas 1983, Winchester handstamp	**£8.00** ☐
225e	With Peace and Goodwill, Nasareth, Caernarfon Gwynedd	**£8.00** ☐
225f	With Peace on Earth, Goodwill Toward Men, Peacehaven handstamp	**£8.00** ☐
225g	With 1350th Anniversary Lyminge Parish Church, Lyminge Kent h/s	**£8.00** ☐
225h	With 50th Anniversary Rededication Minster Gatehouse, Sheppey h/s	**£8.00** ☐
225i	With Leicestershire Society for the Blind 1858-1983, Leicester handstamp	**£8.00** ☐
225j	With Christmas Greetings, St. Mary-le-Strand, London WC2 handstamp	**£8.00** ☐
225k	With Seasons Greetings, Telecom Technology Showcase, London EC4	**£8.00** ☐
225l	With Nasareth or Bethlehem cds	**£32.00** ☐
225m	With St. Nicholas, Holy Island, Star, or Peacehaven cds	**£17.50** ☐
225n	With Hastings - A Resort for All Seasons, slogan cancel	**£98.00** ☐

A few other cds postmarks can be related to this issue. Prices from **£12**.

Improved Postal Stationery Coverage from 1972

Postal Stationery is covered in the body of the catalogue up to 1971. From 1972 onwards we have added a detailed listing in a separate section at the end of the catalogue.

226. 1984, 17th January
Heraldry - College of Arms Quincentenary
16p College of Arms, 20½p Richard III, 28p Earl Marshall, 31p City of London

226a Set on illustrated cover, any postmark .... **£2.00** ☐
226b With Philatelic Bureau handstamp .... **£4.00** ☐
226c With First Day of Issue, London EC special handstamp .... **£4.50** ☐
226d With Heraldry Society Celebrates the College of Arms 1484-1984 h/s .... **£8.50** ☐
226e With College of Arms Quincentenary, London EC4 handstamp .... **£8.50** ☐
226f With The Arthurian Legend, Camelot Tintagel, Cornwall handstamp .... **£8.50** ☐
226g With 400th Anniv. Deputy Norroy, King of Arms, Visit to York handstamp .... **£8.50** ☐
226h With Richard III born 1452, Fotheringhay Castle, Peterborough .... **£8.50** ☐
226i With 50 Years Post Office Stamp Printing, High Wycombe handstamp .... **£11.00** ☐
226j With Heraldry, Guildhall, City of London handstamp .... **£8.50** ☐
226k With London, Financial Capital of the World, London EC handstamp .... **£8.50** ☐
226l With Richard III Society, Quincentenary Celebrations, Leicester h/s .... **£8.50** ☐
226m With Marks & Spencer Centenary Year handstamp .... **£8.50** ☐
226n With Spencer of Althorp Commemorating 475 Years, Northants h/s .... **£8.50** ☐
226o With Richard III Celebration, Scarborough N. Yks handstamp .... **£8.50** ☐
226p With Coat of Arms Granted in 1890, Belfast handstamp .... **£8.50** ☐
226q With Coat of Arms Granted in 1906, Cardiff handstamp .... **£8.50** ☐
226r With Coat of Arms Granted in 1975, Edinburgh handstamp .... **£8.50** ☐
226s With Friary Meux, Kings Arms & Royal Godalming Exhibition handstamp .... **£8.50** ☐
226t With 65th Anniversary of Award of 1st RAF Badge, BF 1826 PS h/s .... **£12.00** ☐
226u With Post Office Philatelic Counter Opened 17 Jan 1984, Lincoln .... **£20.00** ☐
226v With National Postal Museum London EC1, plus London FS Air Mail cds .... **£15.00** ☐
226w With Berkswell Parish Church Restoration, Coventry handstamp .... **£15.00** ☐
226x With any Field Post Office handstamp, on BFPS cover .... **£10.00** ☐
226y With Arundel, York, Chester, or Canon St. London cds .... **£22.50** ☐
226z With The Barony, St. George's Cross, or Fleur-de-Lis cds .... **£22.50** ☐
226aa With Stratford-upon-Avon FDI on Arms of Shakespeare cover .... **£22.50** ☐
226bb With Middleham or Bosworth cds .... **£28.00** ☐

A few other cds postmarks can be related to this issue. Prices from **£12**.

227. 1984, 6th March
British Cattle 16p Highland Cow, 20½p Chillingham Bull, 26p Hereford Bull, 28p Welsh Bull, 31p Irish Moiled Cow

227a Set on illustrated cover, any postmark .... **£2.00** ☐
227b With Philatelic Bureau handstamp .... **£5.00** ☐
227c With First Day of Issue, Oban Argyll handstamp .... **£5.50** ☐
227d With The Last Stronghold of the Chillingham Bull, Alnwick handstamp .... **£9.50** ☐
227e With The Royal Veterinary College, London NW1 handstamp .... **£9.50** ☐
227f With Farming, The Backbone of Britain, London SW1 handstamp .... **£9.50** ☐
227g With Earls Court, Home of Royal Smithfield Show, London SW5 h/s .... **£9.50** ☐
227h With Welsh Black Cattle Society, Caernarfon Gwynedd handstamp .... **£9.50** ☐
227i With The Irish Moiled Cattle Society, Founded 1926, Co. Down handstamp .... **£9.50** ☐
227j With Hereford Herd Book Society, Hereford handstamp .... **£9.50** ☐
227k With Dairy Crest Honours British Cattle, Crewe handstamp .... **£12.00** ☐
227l With Home of Chillingham Wild Cattle, Chillingham, Alnwick handstamp .... **£9.50** ☐

227m With Farmers Weekly Golden Jubilee, Sutton, Surrey handstamp .... **£9.50** □
227n With Centenary of the Highland Cattle Society, Edinburgh handstamp .... **£9.50** □
227o With any Field Post Office handstamp, on BFPS cover .... **£9.50** □
227p With 25th Anniversary Granting Freedom of Entry, RAF Hereford, BF1828 .... **£11.00** □
227q With The Martyrs Tolpuddle, Dorset handstamp (TUC Congress 1984) .... **£14.00** □
227r With Rare Breeds Survival Trust, Stoneleigh, Kenilworth handstamp .... **£9.50** □
227s With Butchers Charitable Institution, Salute 30th Anniv. London h/s .... **£9.50** □
227t With British Friesan Cattle Society, Rickmansworth, Herts handstamp .... **£9.50** □
227u With Chateau Impney Highland Cattle Herd, Droitwich handstamp .... **£17.50** □
227v With Stampex, London SW1 handstamp .... **£15.00** □
227w With Livestock Show, Tring, Herts handstamp .... **£17.50** □
227x With Oban, Argyll cds, or Kyle cds (Red Cow cds **£28**) .... **£25.00** □
227y With Hereford, Lincoln, Chillingham, or Caernarfon cds .... **£20.00** □
227z With Cowes, Black Bull, or Horn St cds (Cattle Market cds **£28**) .... **£25.00** □
227aa With Bull Bay, Bull Farm, Cowplain, or Oxen Park cds .... **£25.00** □

A few other cds postmarks can be related to this issue. Prices range from **£10**.

228. 1984, 10th April

Urban Renewal 16p Liverpool, 20½p Durham, 28p Bristol, 31p Perth

228a Set on illustrated cover, any postmark .... **£2.00** □
228b With Philatelic Bureau handstamp .... **£4.00** □
228c With First Day of Issue, Liverpool special handstamp .... **£4.50** □
228d With Commercial Street Redevelopment, Perth handstamp .... **£8.00** □
228e With Urban Renewal, City of Durham handstamp .... **£8.00** □
228f With Urban Renewal BDP, London W1 handstamp .... **£8.00** □
228g With The Year of Building CIOB, Ascot, Berks handstamp .... **£8.00** □
228h With Abbey National Building Society, Garden Festival, Liverpool h/s .... **£8.00** □
228i With International Garden Festival, Liverpool handstamp .... **£8.00** □
228j With Bush House, Arnolfini Gallery, Bristol handstamp .... **£8.00** □
228k With RIBA 150th Anniversary, Yorkshire Region handstamp .... **£8.00** □
228l With International Garden Festival, Landscape Institute, Liverpool h/s .... **£8.00** □
228m With Covent Garden Market 1634-1984, London WC handstamp .... **£8.00** □
228n With RIBA 150 Years, Festival of Architecture,London W1 handstamp .... **£8.00** □
228o With LAING Development & Construction Celebrates, Durham h/s .... **£8.00** □
228p With St. John the Evangelist 1834-1984, Stratford EI5 handstamp .... **£8.00** □
228q With The Wigan Pier Project, Wigan, CG & Co Birmingham handstamp .... **£16.50** □
228r With Festival of Architecture, Urban Renewal in City of London, Guildhall h/s .... **£12.00** □
228s With Dundee Institute of Architects Centenary 1984, Dundee handstamp .... **£12.00** □
228t With London Docklands Enterprise Zone, Isle of Dogs handstamp .... **£8.00** □
228u With Letchworth the First Garden City, Letchworth, Herts handstamp .... **£8.00** □
228v With Colchester Castle Restoration, Colchester handstamp .... **£27.50** □
228w With any Field Post Office handstamp (1835 or other), on BFPS cover .... **£9.00** □
228x With Durham, Liverpool, Ascot, Letchworth, or Isle of Dogs cds .... **£15.00** □
228y With International Garden Festival, Liverpool '84 slogan .... **£25.00** □

QEII • Commemoratives 1984

229. 1984, 15th May

Europa Issue 16p, 20½p, Se-tenant pairs. Anniversary Logo and Abduction of Europa

229a Set on illustrated cover, any postmark .... **£2.00** ☐
229b With Philatelic Bureau handstamp .... **£4.00** ☐
229c With First Day of Issue, London SW special handstamp .... **£4.50** ☐
229d With Sealink, Britain's Bridge with Europe, Folkestone handstamp .... **£8.00** ☐
229e With 1606-1984 Dover Harbour Board, Dover, Kent handstamp .... **£8.00** ☐
229f With Europa Stamp Exhibition, Europe House, London E1 handstamp .... **£8.00** ☐
229g With 35th Anniversary Formation of NATO, BF 1949 PS handstamp .... **£15.00** ☐
229h With any Forces Post Office handstamp, on BFPS cover .... **£8.00** ☐
229i With European Election 84, London SW1 handstamp .... **£8.00** ☐
229j With Second British European Parliamentary Elections, London h/s .... **£8.00** ☐
229k With Parliament St. BO SW1 cds .... **£17.50** ☐
229l With Harwich, Dover, Folkestone, Newhaven, or Weymouth cds .... **£15.00** ☐
229m With House of Commons or House of Lords cds .... **£32.00** ☐
229n With Folkestone/Newhaven/Boulogne/Dieppe/Calais cds, with Paquebot .... **£20.00** ☐

---

230. 1984, 5th June

Economic Summit, London

31p Lancaster House, London SW1

230a 31p stamp on illustrated cover, any postmark .... **£2.00** ☐
230b With Philatelic Bureau handstamp .... **£3.00** ☐
230c With First Day of Issue, London SW special handstamp .... **£3.50** ☐
230d With London Welcomes the Economic Summit, London EC1 h/s .... **£6.50** ☐
230e With Economic Summit, London SW1 handstamp .... **£6.50** ☐
230f With British Philatelic Cover Producers Association, London SW1 h/s .... **£6.50** ☐
230g With London Economic Summit, London SW1 handstamp .... **£6.50** ☐
230h With National Postal Museum, UPU Exhibition handstamp .... **£12.00** ☐
230i With Institute of London Underwriters Centenary, London EC3 h/s .... **£6.50** ☐
230j With Any Forces Post Office handstamp (551, 1016 or other), BFPS cover .... **£6.50** ☐
230k With Summit (Littleborough or Heywood), Lancs cds .... **£22.50** ☐
230l With Stock Exchange BO, London EC2 cds .... **£27.50** ☐
230m With Parliament St. B0, SW1 cds .... **£25.00** ☐
230n With House of Commons SW1 cds or machine cancel .... **£30.00** ☐
230o With Lombard St. BO, London EC3 cds .... **£32.00** ☐
230p With Lancaster, or Pound cds .... **£20.00** ☐
230q With Dollar cds .... **£50.00** ☐

231. 1984, 26th June
Greenwich Meridian Centenary
16p Earth, 20½p English Channel, 28p Greenwich, 31p Airy's Telescope

231a	Set on illustrated cover, any postmark	**£2.00** ☐
231b	With Philatelic Bureau handstamp	**£4.00** ☐
231c	With First Day of Issue, London SE10 special handstamp	**£4.50** ☐
231d	With British Horological Institute, Newark, Notts handstamp	**£8.00** ☐
231e	With British Astronomical Association, London W1 handstamp	**£8.00** ☐
231f	With Meridian Day Celebration, Swavesy, Cambridge handstamp	**£10.50** ☐
231g	With Captain Cook...Round the World use of Marine Chronometer, Whitby h/s	**£10.00** ☐
231h	With Geographical Magazine Salutes Greenwich Meridian Centenary h/s	**£8.00** ☐
231i	With Centenary of the Greenwich Meridian, East Lindsey, Lincolnshire h/s	**£10.50** ☐
231j	With Meridian Centenary Peacehaven, Newhaven Sussex handstamp	**£12.50** ☐
231k	With 0°00'00" Meridian Road, Boston Lincolnshire handstamp	**£12.50** ☐
231l	With John 'Longitude' Harrison, Copley Gold Medallist 1749 handstamp	**£12.50** ☐
231m	With Centenary of the World's Prime Meridian, Greenwich SE10 h/s	**£8.00** ☐
231n	With Royal Naval College Greenwich, Meridian Centenary, London SE h/s	**£10.50** ☐
231o	With Greenwich Mean Time, London EC4 handstamp	**£18.00** ☐
231p	With Meridian Day, Meridian County Primary School, Cambridge h/s	**£12.50** ☐
231q	With The UK Time Standard, National Physical Laboratory, Middlesex h/s	**£10.00** ☐
231r	With 1884 Longitude Zero 1984, Somersham, Huntingdon, Cambs h/s	**£12.50** ☐
231s	With Lloyds List 1734-1984 Greenwich, London SE10 handstamp	**£10.50** ☐
231t	With Royal Naval Staff College, 65th Anniversary, BF 1838PS handstamp	**£12.50** ☐
231u	With any Forces Post Office handstamp (1016 or other), on BFPS cover	**£8.00** ☐
231v	With Greenwich, or Herstmonceux cds	**£22.00** ☐
231w	With Alnwick, or Chingford cds	**£17.50** ☐
231x	With Globe Road, or The Chart, Oxted cds	**£17.50** ☐
231y	With Playford, or Hartland (Clock Face cds **£40**)	**£25.00** ☐
231z	With House of Commons SW1 cds	**£25.00** ☐
231aa	With Meridian Centre, Peacehaven cds	**£145.00** ☐

232. 1984, 31st July

The Royal Mail

16p Se-tenant strip of 5. Bath, Exeter, Norwich, Liverpool, Edinburgh - Mail Coaches

232a Strip of five on illustrated cover, any postmark .... **£2.00** ☐
232b With Philatelic Bureau handstamp .... **£4.00** ☐
232c With First Day of Issue, Bristol special handstamp .... **£4.50** ☐
232d With Bath Mail Coach Commemorative Run, Bath, Avon handstamp .... **£7.50** ☐
232e With Worshipful Company of Coachmakers, London WC2 handstamp .... **£7.50** ☐
232f With Royal Mail Commemoration, The Holyhead Mail, Holyhead handstamp .... **£7.50** ☐
232g With Golden Age of Coaching, Bath handstamp .... **£7.50** ☐
232h With Liverpool Mail Coach, Liverpool h/s, or the Islington Society, London N1 h/s .... **£7.50** ☐
232i With The Interlink Express Parcels Co. Commemorative Run, Bristol h/s .... **£7.50** ☐
232j With North Eastern Parcel Centre, Washington, or UPU Exhibition, NPM London h/s .. **£17.50** ☐
232k With Manchester-Altrincham Mail Coach Run, Manchester handstamp .... **£7.50** ☐
232l With Royal Mail Transport 1784-1984, Leicester handstamp .... **£7.50** ☐
232m With 65th Anniversary British Airways Mail Service, BF 1845 PS handstamp .... **£7.50** ☐
232n With any Forces Post Office handstamp (980 or other), BFPS cover .... **£7.50** ☐
232o With London Chief Office EC1, or P.O. Tram, Blackpool handstamp .... **£12.00** ☐
232p With Islington, Newmarket, Thatcham, Winterslow, or Moffat cds .... **£15.00** ☐
232q With Bath, Exeter, Norwich, Edinburgh, or Liverpool cds .... **£15.00** ☐
232r With Fleet Street, Bristol, Marlborough, or Salisbury cds .... **£15.00** ☐
232s With Collect British Stamps, slogan cancel. Lincoln or Cleveland .... **£35.00** ☐
232t With Be Properly Addressed, Post Code it! Hull slogan cancel .... **£48.00** ☐

233. 1984, 25th September

50th Anniversary of the British Council

17p Medical Education, 22p The Arts, 31p Technical Training, 34p Reading

233a Set on illustrated cover, any postmark .... **£2.00** ☐
233b With Philatelic Bureau handstamp .... **£4.00** ☐
233c With First Day of Issue, London SW handstamp .... **£4.50** ☐
233d With Centenary of the Oxford English Dictionary, Oxford handstamp .... **£7.50** ☐
233e With The British Council 50th Anniversary, London SW handstamp .... **£7.50** ☐
233f With RBPD Serving Asia, Africa & Middle East, Sutton, Surrey handstamp .... **£7.50** ☐
233g With William Shakespeare, Stratford-upon-Avon, Warwicks handstamp .... **£7.50** ☐
233h With Ausipex 84, 1st Australian Stamp Exhibition, Melbourne, Derby h/s .... **£7.50** ☐
233i With any Forces Post Office handstamp (1850 or other), on BFPS cover .... **£7.50** ☐
233j With Walton St, Southampton St., or St. James's cds .... **£16.50** ☐
233k With Melbourne, Oxford, or Burgh Norwich cds .... **£14.00** ☐

234. 1984, 20th November

Christmas Issue

13p, 17p, 22p, 31p, 34p, Scenes from the Nativity

234a Set on illustrated cover, any postmark .... **£2.00** ☐
234b With Philatelic Bureau handstamp .... **£4.50** ☐
234c With First Day of Issue, Bethlehem, Llandeilo handstamp .... **£5.00** ☐
234d With Glastonbury Abbey, Glastonbury, Somerset handstamp .... **£8.50** ☐
234e With Christmas, Isle of Iona handstamp .... **£8.50** ☐
234f With Christmas Greetings Theatre Royal, Stratford E15 handstamp .... **£8.50** ☐
234g With Christmas Greetings 1984, World Trade Center, London E1 h/s .... **£8.50** ☐
234h With Christmas 1984, Weybridge, Surrey handstamp .... **£8.50** ☐
234i With Seasons Greetings, Telecom Technology Showcase, London EC4 .... **£12.50** ☐
234j With The Lindisfarne Gospels, Holy Island, Berwick-upon-Tweed h/s .... **£8.50** ☐
234k With Christian Heritage Year, Ely, Cambs. handstamp .... **£8.50** ☐
234l With Christian Heritage Year, Durham handstamp .... **£8.50** ☐
234m With Christian Heritage Year, Norwich handstamp .... **£8.50** ☐
234n With Christian Heritage Year, Liverpool handstamp .... **£8.50** ☐
234o With Bethlehem, or Nasareth cds .... **£22.00** ☐
234p With Holy Island, Glastonbury, or St. Nicholas cds .... **£16.00** ☐
234q With Star, Shepherd's Bush, or Shepherd's Hill cds .... **£14.00** ☐
234r With Hastings - a resort for all seasons slogan cancel .... **£45.00** ☐
234s With Halfpenny Green, Christmas 1984, Dudley slogan cancel .... **£58.00** ☐
234t **Christmas Discount Booklet.** 13p x 2 with Star underprint, any postmark .... **£8.50** ☐

Collecting First Day Covers

increases one's knowledge of both history and geography on the way. Better GB Covers are a good investment too. Remember, no hand addressed, relevant postmarks and clean/ tidy covers whenever possible.

QEII • Commemoratives 1985

235. 1985, 22nd January
Famous Trains 17p, 22p, 29p, 31p, 34p, Legendary Steam Locomotives

235a Set on illustrated cover, any postmark .... **£2.50** ☐
235b With Philatelic Bureau handstamp .... **£5.00** ☐
235c With Philatelic Bureau handstamp, plus Orient Express cachet .... **£8.00** ☐
235d With First Day of Issue, Bristol handstamp .... **£6.00** ☐
235e With The Firefly Project, Swindon handstamp .... **£15.00** ☐
235f With Swindon, The Great Western Town, 150th Anniversary of GWR h/s .... **£15.00** ☐
235g With York Station, Rail Riders World, York handstamp .... **£15.00** ☐
235h With Famous Trains, Golden Arrow, Victoria Station, London h/s .... **£15.00** ☐
235i With 150th Anniversary of GWR, The Flying Scotsman, London h/s .... **£15.00** ☐
235j With 150th Anniversary of GWR, The Cheltenham Flyer, Glos h/s .... **£15.00** ☐
235k With 150th Anniversary of GWR, The Golden Arrow, Dover handstamp .... **£15.00** ☐
235l With 150th Anniversary of GWR, The Cornish Riviera, Paddington h/s .... **£15.00** ☐
235m With 150th Anniversary of GWR, The Royal Scot, Euston Station h/s .... **£15.00** ☐
235n With 150th Anniversary of GWR, The Cornish Riviera, Penzance h/s .... **£15.00** ☐
235o With Congratulations from the Great Western Royal Hotel, Paddington h/s .... **£15.00** ☐
235p With GWR 150, Paddington Stn., London W2 handstamp .... **£15.00** ☐
235q With 150th Anniversary of GWR, King George V, Hereford handstamp .... **£22.00** ☐
235r With 150th Anniversary, GWR, Didcot, Oxon handstamp .... **£15.00** ☐
235s With GWR Preservation Group, Southall Railway Centre handstamp .... **£15.00** ☐
235t With National Railway Museum, Famous Trains, York handstamp .... **£20.00** ☐
235u With Scotrail, Edinburgh Welcomes Flying Scotsman, Edinburgh h/s .... **£20.00** ☐
235v With Scotrail, Glasgow Welcomes The Royal Scot, Glasgow handstamp .... **£20.00** ☐
235w With The Flying Scotsman, Pride of Doncaster handstamp .... **£15.00** ☐
235x With Steamtown Railway Museum, Famous Trains, Carnforth handstamp .... **£15.00** ☐
235y With Railway Loco's, Royal British Legion, Maidstone handstamp .... **£15.00** ☐
235z With North Staffordshire Rly. Co., Tribute to Famous Trains, Leek h/s .... **£15.00** ☐
235aa With VS Orient Express stops at Denham Station, Uxbridge handstamp .... **£24.00** ☐
235bb With any Forces Post Office handstamp (1857 or other), BFPS cover .... **£14.50** ☐
235cc With any T.P.O. cancellation (Up, Down, Night, Special) .... **£27.00** ☐
235dd With Euston, Paddington, or Kings Cross B.O. cds .... **£28.50** ☐
235ee With Didcot, Saltash, Doncaster, or Carnforth cds .... **£27.50** ☐
235ff With Penzance, Edinburgh, Glasgow, Dover, or Cheltenham cds .... **£24.00** ☐

A few other cds postmarks can be related to this issue. Prices from **£12**.

---

236. 1985, 12th March
Insects - Centenary Royal Entomological Society Charter
17p Bumble Bee, 22p Ladybird, 29p Cricket, 31p Stag Beetle, 34p Dragonfly

236a Set on illustrated cover, any postmark .... **£2.50** ☐
236b With Philatelic Bureau handstamp .... **£5.00** ☐
236c With First Day of Issue, London SW handstamp .... **£5.50** ☐
236d With Nature Conservation, Hummer, Sherborne, Dorset handstamp .... **£15.00** ☐
236e With Stamp Bug Club, 5th Anniversary, High Wycombe handstamp .... **£14.00** ☐
236f With British Insects, Natural History Museum, London SW7 handstamp .... **£9.00** ☐
236g With A.E.S. Golden Jubilee, Feltham, Middlesex handstamp .... **£9.00** ☐
236h With Writhlington School, Radstock, Avon handstamp .... **£14.00** ☐
236i With Robert Hooke, The Minute Anatomist, Freshwater I.O.W h/s. .... **£12.50** ☐

236j	With Selborne Society Centenary 1885-1985, Alton, Hants handstamp	**£12.50** ☐
236k	With Centenary of Charter of Royal Entomological Society, London h/s	**£9.00** ☐
236l	With Centenary of Charter of Royal Entomological Society, Meadow Bank h/s	**£9.00** ☐
236m	With Enfield Butterfly Centre, British Insects Exhibition, Enfield h/s	**£12.50** ☐
236n	With Pestalozzi Children's Village Trust, Hastings E. Sussex handstamp	**£35.00** ☐
236o	With 21st Anniversary Scottish Wildlife Trust, Edinburgh handstamp	**£12.50** ☐
236p	With 1980-1985 I am Five, Bugford, Dartmouth, Devon handstamp	**£20.00** ☐
236q	With any Field Post Office handstamp (1862 or other) on BFPS cover	**£10.50** ☐
236r	With Selborne, Alton, Hants cds	**£20.00** ☐
236s	With South Kensington SW7 cds, or Buckfastleigh cds	**£20.00** ☐
236t	With Bugbrooke, St. Bees, or Nettleham cds	**£20.00** ☐

A few other cds postmarks can be related to this issue. Prices from **£10**.

237. 1985, 14th May

British Composers (Europa) 17p Handel, 22p Holst, 31p Delius, 34p Elgar

237a	Set on illustrated cover, any postmark	**£2.50** ☐
237b	With Philatelic Bureau handstamp	**£4.00** ☐
237c	With First Day of Issue, Worcester special handstamp	**£4.50** ☐
237d	With British Composers, GLC Royal Festival Hall, London SE1 handstamp	**£10.00** ☐
237e	With St. Pauls Cathedral, 850 Years of Music, City of London handstamp	**£10.00** ☐
237f	With European Music Year, Gustav Holst, Cheltenham, Glos handstamp	**£10.00** ☐
237g	With Delius Festival, St. George's Hall, Bradford W. Yorkshire handstamp	**£10.00** ☐
237h	With George Frederic Handel 1685-1759, Westminster Abbey, London h/s	**£10.00** ☐
237i	With 1975-1985 Holst Birthplace Museum, Cheltenham handstamp	**£10.00** ☐
237j	With 300th Anniversary Handel's Birthday, Covent Garden, London WC h/s	**£10.00** ☐
237k	With Sir Edward Elgar, First Professor of Music, University of Birmingham	**£12.00** ☐
237l	With Stagenhoe Park, Home of Sullivan, Centenary of Mikado, Hitchin h/s	**£10.00** ☐
237m	With European Music Year, National Postal Museum EC1 handstamp	**£12.00** ☐
237n	With European Music Year, High Wycombe, Bucks handstamp	**£12.00** ☐
237o	With European Music Year, Sir Michael Tippett 80th Birthday handstamp	**£10.00** ☐
237p	With Lennon & McCartney, Classic Composers of Today, Liverpool h/s	**£12.00** ☐
237q	With Scottish National Orchestra, SNO Music Week 85, Aberdeen h/s	**£10.00** ☐
237r	With Scottish National Orchestra, SNO Proms 85, Dundee handstamp	**£10.00** ☐
237s	With Leicester Philharmonic Society Centenary Season, Leicester	**£10.00** ☐
237t	With St. David's Hall, National Concert Hall of Wales, Cardiff handstamp	**£10.00** ☐
237u	With 128th Anniversary, Royal Military School of Music, BF 2128PS h/s	**£10.00** ☐
237v	With any Forces/Field Post office handstamp on BFPS cover	**£10.00** ☐
237w	With Lower Broadheath, or Pittville cds	**£17.50** ☐
237x	With Limpsfield, Chichester, Malvern or Lowesmoor cds	**£17.50** ☐
237y	With Whitwell, or University Bradford, West Yorks cds	**£17.50** ☐
237z	With CBSO Proms 1945-1985, Town Hall, Birmingham slogan cancel	**£52.50** ☐
237aa	With The Bradford Delius Festival, May 20-26, Bradford slogan cancel	**£52.50** ☐

238

QEII • Commemoratives 1985

238. 1985, 18th June
Safety at Sea
17p Lifeboat, 22p Lighthouse, 31p Satellite, 34p Buoys

238a	Set on illustrated cover, any postmark	**£2.50** ☐
238b	With Philatelic Bureau handstamp	**£4.00** ☐
238c	With First Day of Issue, Eastbourne, E. Sussex handstamp	**£4.50** ☐
238d	With Sealion Shipping, Tenth Anniversary, City of London handstamp	**£10.00** ☐
238e	With Lifeboat Dedication, Cromer, Norfolk handstamp	**£10.00** ☐
238f	With 200 Years Safety at Sea, Maritime Museum, Greenwich handstamp	**£10.00** ☐
238g	With 200th Anniversary Earliest Lifeboat Design, Lowestoft, Suffolk h/s	**£10.00** ☐
238h	With Grace Darling Museum, Bamburgh, Northumberland handstamp	**£10.00** ☐
238i	With Lifeboat Display, Poole, Dorset handstamp	**£10.00** ☐
238j	With The Plimsoll Line, Bristol handstamp	**£10.00** ☐
238k	With 50th Anniversary The Geographical Magazine, London SW7 h/s	**£10.00** ☐
238l	With Spurn Head Lifeboat, 175th Year 1810-1985, Hull handstamp	**£10.00** ☐
238m	With Global Maritime, Safety at Sea, London WC2 handstamp	**£10.00** ☐
238n	With Schermuly celebrates Safety at Sea, Greenwich SE10 h/s	**£10.00** ☐
238o	With Lukins Patent Lifeboat Design, 200th Anniversary, Hythe h/s	**£10.00** ☐
238p	With The Lighthouse Club, Whitley Bay, Tyne & Wear handstamp	**£10.00** ☐
238q	With Appledore RNLI Lifeboat Station, Brideford, Devon handstamp	**£10.00** ☐
238r	With Nore Lightship, Historic Ship Collection, London E1 handstamp	**£10.00** ☐
238s	With Berwick-upon-Tweed Lifeboat Service 1835-1985 handstamp	**£12.00** ☐
238t	With Bamburgh, Hythe, or Little Dunmow cds	**£17.50** ☐
238u	With Poole, or Redcar cds	**£17.50** ☐
238v	With Cromer, Dover, or Whitley Bay cds	**£17.50** ☐
238w	With R.N. Air Stn. Culdrose or Yeovilton cds, any other Air-Sea Rescue Station	**£27.50** ☐
238x	With Beacon, or Six Bells cds	**£17.50** ☐
238y	With Lighthouse cds, Hawes cds	**£28.00** ☐

R.N. AIR STN. CULDROSE – JU 18 85 – HELSTON. CWLL.

BAMBURGH 18 JU 85 NORTHUMBERLAND

LIFE-BOAT DISPLAY · 18 JUN 85 · POOLE · DORSET

THE PLIMSOLL LINE
TF F T S W WNA L R
18 JUNE 1985, BRISTOL

---

239. 1985, 30th July
Royal Mail, 350 Years of Service
17p Datapost, 22p Rural Postbus, 31p Parcel Post, 34p Letter Post

239a	Set on illustrated cover, any postmark	**£2.50** ☐
239b	With Philatelic Bureau handstamp	**£4.00** ☐
239c	With First Day of Issue, Bagshot, Surrey handstamp	**£4.50** ☐
239d	With Royal Mail 350 Exhibition, Bristol handstamp	**£10.00** ☐
239e	With 350th Anniversary of the Post Office, Bath Postal Museum h/s	**£10.00** ☐
239f	With 350th Anniv. Thomas Witherings, Chief Postmaster 1635 handstamp	**£10.00** ☐
239g	With Records of 350 Years, Post Office Archives, London SE1 h/s	**£10.00** ☐
239h	With Royal Mail 350 Years, London Post, London EC1 handstamp	**£10.00** ☐
239i	With Royal Mail 350 Years of Service to the Public, London EC h/s	**£10.00** ☐
239j	With Royal Mail SEPR Postcards, First Day of Sale, Bagshot handstamp	**£10.00** ☐
239k	With Royal Mail SEPR Postcards, First Day of Sale, Windsor handstamp	**£10.00** ☐
239l	With North Eastern Parcel Centre, Royal Mail Parcels, Washington h/s	**£17.50** ☐
239m	With National Postal Museum, London EC1 handstamp	**£17.50** ☐
239n	With National Postal Museum, 350 Years of Service to the Public, London h/s	**£10.00** ☐

QEII • Commemoratives 1985

239o	With Post Paid, 100 Years in the City of London, Healey and Wise h/s	**£10.00** ☐
239p	With 5th Anniversary Intelpost, Head Post Office, London E1 handstamp	**£10.00** ☐
239q	With UCW - A Public Service Union, Clapham, London SW4 handstamp	**£10.00** ☐
239r	With any Forces/Field Post Office (382 or other) on Postal & Courier cover	**£12.50** ☐
239s	With Bagshot, Lombard Street, or Mount Pleasant cds	**£22.50** ☐
239t	With House of Commons or House of Lords SW1 cds	**£26.00** ☐
239u	With Buckingham Palace SW1 cds	**£55.00** ☐
239v	With Stock Exchange, or Cannon Street cds	**£22.50** ☐
239w	With Sanquhar, or Hornchurch cds (Letter, Enniskillen cds **£36**)	**£22.50** ☐
239x	With Royal Mail 350 Years Service... In Business to Serve You, slogan	**£25.00** ☐
239y	**Discount Booklet** 17p x 2 with 'D' underprint, any postmark	**£8.00** ☐

240. 1985, 3rd September

The Arthurian Legend 17p, 22p, 31p, 34p, Scenes Based on Le Morte D'Arthur

240a	Set on illustrated cover, any postmark	**£2.50** ☐
240b	With Philatelic Bureau handstamp	**£4.00** ☐
240c	With First Day of Issue, Tintagel, Cornwall handstamp	**£4.50** ☐
240d	With King Arthurs Avalon, Glastonbury, Somerset handstamp	**£9.50** ☐
240e	With Land of Arthur Exhibition of Celtic Legend, Glastonbury handstamp	**£9.50** ☐
240f	With Morte D'Arthur, Mere, Warminster, Wilts handstamp	**£9.50** ☐
240g	With The Great Hall, Winchester, Hants handstamp	**£9.50** ☐
240h	With Legendary Camelot, Old Post Office, Tintagel, Cornwall handstamp	**£9.50** ☐
240i	With The Legendary Camelot, Winchester, Hants handstamp	**£9.50** ☐
240j	With Arthurian Legend, The Sword & The Stone, St. Paul's London h/s	**£9.50** ☐
240k	With St. Margaret's Church, Caxton's Morte D'Arthur, London h/s	**£9.50** ☐
240l	With any Field/Forces Post Office handstamp (2340 or other), BFPS cover	**£9.50** ☐
240m	With Tintagel, Silchester, or Camelford cds	**£17.50** ☐
240n	With Glastonbury, Bamburgh, Bodmin, or Winchester cds	**£17.50** ☐
240o	With Merlin's Bridge, Lancelot Place, or King Arthurs Way cds	**£25.00** ☐
240p	With Caxton, Knights Road, or South Cadbury cds	**£17.50** ☐

All prices in this catalogue are for clean covers, with undamaged stamps and clear postmarks.

QEII • Commemoratives 1985

241. 1985, 8th October

British Film Year

17p Sellers, 22p Niven, 29p Chaplin, 31p Leigh, 34p Hitchcock

241a Set on illustrated cover, any postmark .... **£2.50** ☐

241b With Philatelic Bureau handstamp .... **£4.00** ☐

241c With First Day of Issue, London WC special handstamp .... **£4.50** ☐

241d With British Film Year, David Niven Campaign MNDA, Northampton h/s .... **£12.00** ☐

241e With Goldcrest British Film Year, London W1 handstamp .... **£12.00** ☐

241f With Fifty Years 1935-1985, National Film Archive, London W1 handstamp .... **£12.50** ☐

241g With British Film Year, Leicester Sq., London WC2 round handstamp .... **£12.00** ☐

241h With British Film Year, Leicester Square, London W.C.2 oblong h/s .... **£12.00** ☐

241i With Alfred Hitchcock Exhibition, Alfred Hitchcock Hotel, Leytonstone h/s .... **£12.00** ☐

241j With British Film Year, Richmond, Surrey handstamp .... **£12.00** ☐

241k With Equity Celebrates British Film Year, Harley Street, London handstamp .... **£12.00** ☐

241l With British Film Year, Bradford, W. Yorshire handstamp .... **£12.00** ☐

241m With National Postal Museum Film Festival, London EC1 handstamp .... **£12.50** ☐

241n With British Film Year MCMLXXXV, London W1 handstamp .... **£12.00** ☐

241o With Leytonstone, Walworth, Southsea, or London SW1 cds .... **£15.00** ☐

241p With any Film Studio cds, such as Elstree, Ealing, Denham, Bray. .... **£20.00** ☐

241q With Hollywood, Shepperton or Star cds .... **£20.00** ☐

---

242. 1985, 19th November

Christmas Issue 12p, 17p, 22p, 31p, 34p, Five Pantomime Characters

242a Set on illustrated cover, any postmark .... **£2.50** ☐

242b With Philatelic Bureau handstamp .... **£4.50** ☐

242c With First Day of Issue, Bethlehem, Llandeilo handstamp .... **£5.00** ☐

242d With The Traditional Home of English Pantomime, Drury Lane handstamp .... **£10.00** ☐

242e With Christmas Greetings, Telecom Technology Showcase, London h/s .... **£10.00** ☐

242f With Cinderella at the Palladium, London W.I. handstamp .... **£10.00** ☐

242g With London S.W.I., 19 Nov '85, pictorial (Palace Guards) handstamp .... **£10.00** ☐

242h With Mother Goose Pantomime, Famous Over 250 Years, Ashford, Kent h/s .... **£10.00** ☐

242i With Nottingham Theatre Royal Presents Aladdin, Nottingham h/s .... **£10.00** ☐

242j With Peace on Earth, Sewardstone Evangelist Church, Christmas '85 h/s .... **£10.00** ☐

242k With any Forces Post Office handstamp, on BFPS cover .... **£10.00** ☐

242l With Bethlehem cds (Nasareth cds **£24**) .... **£27.50** ☐

242m With Clowne, or The Harlequin, or Whittington cds .... **£16.50** ☐

242n With Holy Island, Star, or St. Nicholas cds .... **£18.00** ☐

242o **Christmas Booklet** 12p x 2 with Star underprint, any postmark .... **£8.50** ☐

A few other cds postmarks can be related to this issue. Prices from **£10**.

QEII • Commemoratives 1986

243. 1986, 14th January
Industry Year 17p Energy, 22p Health, 31p Steel, 34p Agriculture

243a	Set on illustrated cover, any postmark	**£2.50** ☐
243b	With Philatelic Bureau handstamp	**£4.00** ☐
243c	With First Day of Issue, Birmingham special handstamp	**£4.50** ☐
243d	With Industry Year BP London EC2 handstamp	**£10.50** ☐
243e	With Farming, The Industry that Feeds the Nation, Wheatacre handstamp	**£8.00** ☐
243f	With Ironbridge, Birthplace of Industry, Telford handstamp	**£8.00** ☐
243g	With Industry Year 1986, British Steel, London SEI handstamp	**£12.50** ☐
243h	With Purveyor of Flour, Hovis Centenary 1886-1986, Windsor handstamp	**£15.50** ☐
243i	With Osram a Leading Light in Industry Year '86, Wembley handstamp	**£15.50** ☐
243j	With All Industrious People Are Happy, Lewis Carroll, Oxford handstamp	**£8.00** ☐
243k	With RTH Rank Taylor Hobson, Centenary - Industry Year, Leicester h/s	**£8.00** ☐
243l	With The Workers Playground Since 1840, Blackpool, Lancs handstamp	**£8.00** ☐
243m	With 1976: A breakthrough in ulcer therapy, Welwyn Garden City h/s	**£15.00** ☐
243n	With Steel Smelters' Assoc. I.S.T., 1886-1986, Confederation, London WC1 h/s	**£12.50** ☐
243o	With World Leading Energy Technology, Aberdeen handstamp	**£12.50** ☐
243p	With 70th Anniversary British Aerospace Companies, BF 2105PS h/s	**£11.00** ☐
243q	With any Forces/Field Post Office handstamp, on BFPS cover	**£7.50** ☐
243r	With NEC Birmingham, Ironbridge, Clydebank, or Cruden Bay cds	**£12.50** ☐
243s	With Greenock, Sunderland, or Sheffield cds	**£16.00** ☐
243t	With Pill, Bakewell, or Furnace cds (Steel City, or Steel cds **£22**)	**£16.00** ☐

STEEL CITY HOUSE H 14 JA 86 SHEFFIELD

FIRST DAY OF ISSUE BIRMINGHAM INDUSTRY Matters 14 JANUARY 1986

BRITISH PHILATELIC BUREAU EDINBURGH FIRST DAY OF ISSUE Thanks to INDUSTRY 14 JANUARY 1986

IRONBRIDGE BIRTHPLACE OF INDUSTRY 14 JAN 1986 TELFORD·TF8 7JS

244. 1986, 18th February
Halley's Comet 17p Halley as a Comet, 22p Giotto, 31p Text, 34p Comet Orbit

244a	Set on illustrated cover, any postmark	**£2.50** ☐
244b	With Philatelic Bureau handstamp	**£4.00** ☐
244c	With First Day of Issue, London SE10 special handstamp	**£4.50** ☐
244d	With Halley's Comet Society 1986, London SE10 handstamp	**£8.50** ☐
244e	With Islington, Home of Halley, Salutes his Comet, London handstamp	**£8.50** ☐
244f	With Edmond Halley Born 1656 at Haggerston, London E2 handstamp	**£8.50** ☐
244g	With London Planetarium Celebrates Return of Halley's Comet h/s	**£8.50** ☐
244h	With Old Royal Observatory, Happy Returns to Halley, Greenwich h/s	**£8.50** ☐
244i	With Giotto, Halley's Comet Interceptor, Bristol handstamp	**£8.50** ☐
244j	With Halley's Comet Interceptor, Giotto Encounter Day, Filton handstamp	**£8.50** ☐
244k	With The Return of Halley's Comet, British Interplanetary Society h/s	**£8.50** ☐
244l	With A Return of Halley's Comet, Star Winscombe, Avon handstamp	**£8.50** ☐
244m	With Return of Halley's Comet, Royal Greenwich Observatory, Hailsham	**£8.50** ☐
244n	With Commemorating Skynet AA Satellite, BF 2109PS handstamp	**£8.50** ☐
244o	With any Forces/Field Post Office handstamp on BFPS cover	**£8.50** ☐
244p	With Filton, Shoreditch, or Islington cds	**£20.00** ☐
244q	With Helston, Macclesfield, or Hartland cds	**£20.00** ☐
244r	With Greenwich, Herstmonceux, or Battle cds	**£20.00** ☐
244s	With Star Glenrothes, or Seven Sisters Rd cds	**£15.00** ☐

QEII • Commemoratives 1986

245. 1986, 21st April

60th Birthday of Queen Elizabeth II

17p Se-tenant Pair, 34p Se-tenant Pair. Portraits of the Queen

245a	Set on illustrated cover, any postmark	**£2.50** ☐
245b	With Philatelic Bureau handstamp	**£4.00** ☐
245c	With First Day of Issue, Windsor special handstamp	**£4.50** ☐
245d	With Commemorating HM The Queen's 60th birthday, London SW1 h/s	**£8.50** ☐
245e	With Loyal Greetings, The City of London, London EC handstamp	**£8.50** ☐
245f	With Radio Times Congratulates HM The Queen, 60th Birthday h/s	**£8.50** ☐
245g	With Lombard North Central PLC, 17 Bruton St., Birthplace of The Queen	**£8.50** ☐
245h	With Her Majesty The Queen's Birthday, London SW1 handstamp	**£8.50** ☐
245i	With Her Majesty The Queen's Birthday, Balmoral, Crathie, Aberdeenshire	**£8.50** ☐
245j	With Her Majesty The Queen's Birthday, Sandringham, Norfolk handstamp	**£8.50** ☐
245k	With Her Majesty The Queens Birthday, Windsor, Berks handstamp	**£8.50** ☐
245l	With Happy Birthday to our Patron EIIR, London SW1 handstamp	**£8.50** ☐
245m	With HM Queen Elizabeth II - 60th Birthday, Bruton St. London W1	**£8.50** ☐
245n	With Southend Salutes Queen's 60th Birthday, Southend-on-Sea h/s	**£8.50** ☐
245o	With Birthday Greetings, London SW1 handstamp	**£8.50** ☐
245p	With Royal British Legion, Happy Birthday to our Patron, London h/s	**£8.50** ☐
245q	With Many Happy Returns, National Postal Museum, London EC1 h/s	**£9.00** ☐
245r	With 60th Birthday HM The Queen, Lord High Admiral BF 2113 PS h/s	**£8.50** ☐
245s	With 50th Anniversary of the Queen's Flight BF 2106 PS handstamp	**£8.50** ☐
245t	With any Forces/Field Post office handstamp, on BFPS cover	**£8.50** ☐
245u	With Windsor Philatelic Counter or FDI handstamp	**£15.00** ☐
245v	With Federation of Women's Institutes Denman College W.I., Chichester h/s	**£12.50** ☐
245w	With Buckingham Palace SW1 cds (SW1 Perm h/s-Palace design **£18**)	**£130.00** ☐
245x	With Windsor Castle, Berks cds	**£150.00** ☐
245y	With House of Commons, or House of Lords cds	**£30.00** ☐
245z	With Windsor, Berks cds, or Windsor Park cds	**£25.00** ☐
245aa	With Mount Street B.O., or Badminton cds (Crathie cds **£24**)	**£15.00** ☐
245bb	With Queen Elizabeth Ave, Queensway, or Queens Parade cds	**£20.00** ☐

A few other cds postmarks, such as Queens Rd, can be related to this issue. Prices from **£10**.

246. 1986, 20th May

Nature Conservation (Europa) 17p, 22p, 31p, 34p, Four Species at Risk

246a	Set on illustrated cover, any postmark	**£2.50** ☐
246b	With Philatelic Bureau handstamp	**£4.00** ☐
246c	With First Day of Issue, Lincoln special handstamp	**£4.50** ☐
246d	With Royal Society for Nature Conservation, London EC4 handstamp	**£9.50** ☐
246e	With Royal Society for Nature Conservation, London W1 handstamp	**£9.50** ☐
246f	With RSPB 'Endangered Species', Sandy, Beds handstamp	**£9.50** ☐
246g	With Cornish Wildlife CTNC, Truro handstamp	**£9.50** ☐
246h	With Barn Owl Endangered Species, Owlsmoor, Camberley h/s	**£9.50** ☐
246i	With Hampshire and I.O.W. Naturalists Trust, Romsey, Hants handstamp	**£9.50** ☐
246j	With Friends of the Earth, London EC1 (Hawk 200 Godalming **£10**) h/s	**£9.50** ☐
246k	With The Wildfowl Trust 1946-1986, Slimbridge, Gloucester handstamp	**£9.50** ☐

246l	With British Herpetological Soc. Conservation Exhibition, Studland h/s	**£9.50** ☐
246m	With Caring for the Countryside Ramblers Association, London h/s	**£9.50** ☐
246n	With Species at Risk, The Lady's Slipper Orchid, Grassington h/s	**£10.50** ☐
246o	With Life & Landscape on the Norfolk Broads, 1886-1986 Norfolk h/s	**£9.50** ☐
246p	With Striving to Protect Species at Risk, Romsey, Hants handstamp	**£10.50** ☐
246q	With any Field/Forces Post Office handstamp (2116 or other), BFPS cover	**£9.00** ☐
246r	With Nettleham Lincs, or Selborne Hants cds	**£16.50** ☐
246s	With Aviemore, Beddgelert, or Regents Park cds	**£16.50** ☐
246t	With Owlsmoor, Eagle, Otterburn, or Frog Island cds	**£16.50** ☐
246u	With Lincs & S. Humberside Trust, Nature Conservation – Lincoln slogan	**£80.00** ☐
246v	With Lincs & S. Humberside Trust, Nature Conservation – Doncaster slogan	**£80.00** ☐
246w	With Natureland Marine Zoo, Skegness, 21st Anniversary slogan	**£80.00** ☐

A few other cds postmarks can be related to this issue. Prices from **£9**.

---

247. 1986, 17th June

900th Anniversary of the Domesday Book

17p Peasants, 22p Freeman, 31p Knight, 34p Feudal Lord

247a	Set on illustrated cover, any postmark	**£2.50** ☐
247b	With Philatelic Bureau handstamp	**£4.00** ☐
247c	With First Day of Issue, Gloucester special handstamp	**£4.50** ☐
247d	With Domesday Survey 900 Years, Battle, E. Sussex handstamp	**£9.50** ☐
247e	With Blackwells Children's Bookshop, Domesday Exhibition, Oxford h/s	**£9.50** ☐
247f	With The Great Hall, Winchester, Hants. Domesday 900 handstamp	**£9.50** ☐
247g	With Domesday 900th Anniversary, Domesday 1086-1986, London h/s	**£9.50** ☐
247h	With 70th Anniversary - Cub Scouts, Medieval Pageant, Worthing h/s	**£9.50** ☐
247i	With Hereward Country, Isle of Ely, Cambridge handstamp	**£9.50** ☐
247j	With Freemen of England, Oswestry, Shropshire handstamp	**£9.50** ☐
247k	With Medieval Life Stamps Designed by Tayburn, Edinburgh or London h/s	**£12.50** ☐
247l	With Stamplink 86, Portsmouth handstamp, plus Paquebot cachet	**£12.50** ☐
247m	With Domesday Book MLXXXVI, Winchester, Hants handstamp	**£9.50** ☐
247n	With Domesday, Chapter House, Abbey of St. Peter, Gloucester h/s	**£9.50** ☐
247o	With 900th Anniversary of Domesday Survey, Exeter, Devon handstamp	**£9.50** ☐
247p	With Hereward Country, Peterborough handstamp	**£9.50** ☐
247q	With any Field/Forces Post Office handstamp (2116 or other) on BFPS cover	**£8.50** ☐
247r	With Crofters Act 1886-1986, Edinburgh or Inverness handstamp	**£11.00** ☐
247s	With Kingsholm cds (Winchester, or Battle cds **£18)**	**£55.00** ☐
247t	With Chancery Lane, London WC2 cds	**£24.00** ☐
247u	With Cherbourg Normandy Paquebot, or Jersey Paquebot cds	**£26.00** ☐
247v	With Hereward Country, Fen Heritage & Legend, Peterborough/Cambridge	**£80.00** ☐

A few other cds postmarks can be related to this issue. Prices from £10 - £18.

248. 1986, 15th July

13th Commonwealth Games

17p Athletics, 22p Rowing, 29p Weightlifting, 31p Shooting, 34p Hockey

248a	Set on illustrated cover, any postmark	£2.50 ☐
248b	With Philatelic Bureau handstamp	£4.00 ☐
248c	With First Day of Issue, Edinburgh special handstamp	£4.50 ☐
248d	With Commonwealth Games, Mac, Edinburgh handstamp	£9.00 ☐
248e	With Scottish Brewers Welcome XIII Commonwealth Games, Edinburgh h/s	£9.00 ☐
248f	With Amateur Rowing Association, ARA, London, W6 handstamp	£9.00 ☐
248g	With Amateur Athletic Association, London SW1 handstamp	£9.00 ☐
248h	With Legion Youth & Sports, Royal British Legion, London SW1 h/s	£9.00 ☐
248i	With 6th World Hockey Cup for Men, National Hockey Centre, London h/s	£9.00 ☐
248j	With Waltham Forest Salutes London Youth Games, London E17 h/s	£9.00 ☐
248k	With Home of British Rowing, Henley-on-Thames, Oxfordshire handstamp	£9.00 ☐
248l	With The Royal Tournament, British Forces 2118 Postal Service h/s	£14.50 ☐
248m	With Commemorating 21st Anniversary, Cosford Arena BF2119 PS h/s	£18.00 ☐
248n	With any Field Post Office cds on BFPS cover	£8.50 ☐
248o	With Henley-on-Thames, or Bisley cds (Willesden cds **£16**)	£16.50 ☐
248p	With Edinburgh cds, or any of the other seven Games venues	£16.50 ☐
248q	With Mobile Post Office 2, Edinburgh (Games Village)	£135.00 ☐

A few other cds postmarks can be related to this issue. Prices from **£10**.

FIRST DAY OF ISSUE EDINBURGH 15 JULY 1986

COMMONWEALTH GAMES 1986 Mac © EDINBURGH

AMATEUR ROWING ASSOCIATION ARA 15 JULY 1986 LONDON W6

HOME OF BRITISH ROWING 15 JULY '86 HENLEY-ON-THAMES OXFORDSHIRE

---

249. 1986, 22nd July

Royal Wedding 12p, 17p, Prince Andrew and Sarah Ferguson

249a	Set on illustrated cover, any postmark	£2.00 ☐
249b	With Philatelic Bureau handstamp	£3.50 ☐
249c	With First Day of Issue, London SW1 handstamp	£4.00 ☐
249d	With Congratulations HRH Prince Andrew, Sarah Ferguson, Dummer h/s	£7.00 ☐
249e	With The Royal Wedding, Westminster Abbey, London S.W.I. h/s	£7.00 ☐
249f	With The Royal Wedding, Congratulations XIII Commonwealth Games h/s	£7.00 ☐
249g	With The Lewis Carroll Society Salutes The Royal Wedding, Oxford h/s	£7.00 ☐
249h	With Loyal Greetings from York, York handstamp	£7.00 ☐
249i	With Royal Wedding, Westminster Abbey, London SW1 handstamp	£7.00 ☐
249j	With Royal Wedding Greetings, Windsor, Berks handstamp	£7.00 ☐
249k	With Debretts, Recording Royal History across the centuries, London h/s	£26.50 ☐
249l	With The Royal Wedding, London EC4 handstamp	£7.00 ☐
249m	With The Royal Wedding ... Congratulations, Westminster Abbey, London	£7.00 ☐
249n	With Congratulations from The Village of Dummer, The Royal Wedding h/s	£7.00 ☐
249o	With Loyal Greetings From Lullingstone Silk Farm, Sherborne, Dorset h/s	£7.00 ☐
249p	With Woman's Weekly, 75th Anniv. Year, London SE1 handstamp	£7.00 ☐
249q	With The Royal Tournament, BF 2118 PS handstamp	£7.00 ☐
249r	With any Forces/Field Post Office handstamp (2120 or other)	£7.50 ☐
249s	With Buckingham Palace SW1 cds	£135.00 ☐
249t	With Windsor Castle, Berks cds (Windsor, Windsor Park cds **£16**)	£150.00 ☐
249u	With House of Commons or House of Lords cds	£22.50 ☐

249u With London SWI Permanent handstamp (Palace) .... **£9.00** ☐
249v With Windsor Philatelic Counter handstamp .... **£9.00** ☐
249w With Ascot, Dummer, or Kelso cds .... **£16.50** ☐
249x With RN Air Stn. Culdrose, Helston cds .... **£12.50** ☐

A few other cds postmarks can be related to this issue. Prices from **£10**.

250. 1986, 19th August

Commonwealth Parliamentary Conference

34p Stylised Cross on Ballot Paper

250a 34p Stamp on illustrated cover, any postmark .... **£1.50** ☐
250b With Philatelic Bureau handstamp .... **£3.50** ☐
250c With First Day of Issue, London SW1 special handstamp .... **£4.00** ☐
250d With St. Margaret's Parish Church of House of Commons, London SW1 h/s .... **£7.00** ☐
250e With Commonwealth Parliamentary Assoc. 32nd Conference, London h/s. .... **£7.00** ☐
250f With Commonwealth Parliamentary Conference, Houses of Parliament, London .... **£7.00** ☐
250g With House of Commons SW1 cds (Gleneagles Hotel **£16**) .... **£45.00** ☐
250h With House of Lords SW1 cds (Kensington High St. **£10**) .... **£48.00** ☐
250i With Buckingham Palace SW1 cds .... **£78.00** ☐

A few other cds postmarks can be related to this issue. Prices from **£10**.

Special Feature!

Royalty fdc Post Cards

A total of 134 Post Cards are illustrated, running from KEVII to KGV, KEVIII, KGVI and finally QEII.

In this edition of the Catalogue we have prepared a special 16 page full colour presentation on these fdc Post Cards.

All is revealed on pages 160-176.

QEII • Commemoratives 1986

251. 1986, 16th September

The Royal Air Force 17p, 22p, 29p, 31p, 34p, Famous Commanders and Aircraft

251a	Set on illustrated cover, any postmark	£3.00 ☐
251b	With Philatelic Bureau handstamp	£5.00 ☐
251c	With First Day of Issue, Farnborough handstamp	£5.50 ☐
251d	With 50th Anniversary The RAF, Scampton, Lincoln handstamp	£12.50 ☐
251e	With 46th Anniversary Battle of Britain, BF 2123 PS handstamp	£12.50 ☐
251f	With 50th Anniversary Reorganisation Royal Air Force, BF 2114 PS h/s	£12.50 ☐
251g	With RAFA Andover, Hants handstamp	£12.50 ☐
251h	With 46th Anniversary of the Battle of Britain, Uxbridge handstamp	£10.50 ☐
251i	With Hawkinge Aerodrome ... Fifty Years of the Spitfire handstamp	£12.50 ☐
251j	With 50th Anniversary of the Spitfire 1936-1986, Eastleigh, Hants h/s	£12.50 ☐
251k	With Kenley Aerodrome Salutes The RAF, Kenley, Surrey handstamp	£12.50 ☐
251l	With Marx Memorial Library, Spain 1936-39 Exhibition, London h/s	£12.50 ☐
251m	With Newark-on-Trent Salutes The RAF, Newark, Notts handstamp	£12.50 ☐
251n	With British Philatelic Federation, 68th Congress, Norwich handstamp	£12.50 ☐
251o	With Duxford Aviation Society, Duxford Airfield, Duxfield, Cambs h/s	£12.50 ☐
251p	With Cranwell, Sleaford Lincs, or Biggin Hill cds	£26.00 ☐
251q	With Digby, Manston, Hawkinge, or Oakington cds	£26.00 ☐
251r	With any RAF Station P.O. cds (Cosford, Duxford, etc)	£22.50 ☐
251s	With House of Commons or House of Lords cds	£25.00 ☐
251t	With Pathfinder Village, or Lancaster cds	£22.50 ☐
251u	With any Forces/Field Post Office cds	£24.00 ☐

A few other cds postmarks can be related to this issue. Prices from **£18**.

---

252. 1986, 18th November

Christmas Issue 13p, 18p, 22p, 31p, 34p, Customs and Legends of Christmas

252a	Set on illustrated cover, any postmark	£2.50 ☐
252b	With Philatelic Bureau handstamp	£4.50 ☐
252c	With First Day of Issue, Bethlehem, Llandeilo handstamp	£5.00 ☐
252d	With Christmas Greetings, St. Margaret's Westminster, London SW1 h/s	£8.50 ☐
252e	With The Glastonbury Thorn, Christmas 1986, Glastonbury, Somerset h/s	£8.50 ☐
252f	With The Hebrides Tribute, Christmas, Stornoway, Isle of Lewis	£8.50 ☐
252g	With The Devil's Knell, All Saint's Church, Dewsbury handstam	£8.50 ☐
252h	With Christmas Greetings, Folkestone, Kent handstamp	£8.50 ☐
252i	With English Folk Dance & Song Society Celebrate Christmas handstamp	£8.50 ☐
252j	With Christmas Hereford 18 November '86 handstamp	£8.50 ☐
252k	With Happy Christmas, Telecom Technology Showcase, London h/s	£12.00 ☐
252l	With Seasons Greetings to all Railway Societies, London handstamp	£15.00 ☐
252m	With Bethlehem or Nasareth cds	£16.00 ☐
252n	With Glastonbury, Hereford, or Dewsbury cds	£15.00 ☐
252o	With Star, Holy Island, or St. Nicholas cds	£15.00 ☐

STORNOWAY
ISLE OF LEWIS
OUTER HEBRIDES
18 NOVEMBER
1986

253. 1986, 2nd December
Christmas Issue 12p The Glastonbury Thorn, 13p 'Discount' Stamp

253a 12p Stamp on illustrated cover, any postmark .... **£1.00** ☐
253b With Philatelic Bureau handstamp .... **£3.00** ☐
253c With The Glastonbury Thorn, Glastonbury SC, Somerset handstamp .... **£5.50** ☐
253d With Happy Christmas, Telecom Technology Showcase, London h/s .... **£8.50** ☐
253e With Christmas, Glastonbury, Somerset handstamp .... **£6.50** ☐
253f With The Glastonbury Thorn, Christmas 1986, Glastonbury handstamp .... **£6.50** ☐
253g With Christmas Greetings from Biggin Hill, BF 2130 PS handstamp .... **£7.50** ☐
253h With Bethlehem or Nasareth cds .... **£20.00** ☐
253i With Star, Holy Island, St. Nicholas, or Glastonbury cds .... **£15.00** ☐
253j With Happy Christmas, The Post Office slogan cancel (any office) .... **£15.00** ☐
253k **13p Discount Sheet** The 13p discount stamp was issued in a sheet of 36 stamps (two half sheets of 18 stamps, with a perforated double gutter in the middle). The full sheet was sold with a 36p discount. The 13p in half sheet form on FDC (18 x 13p) is catalogued at .... **£24.00** ☐
253l **Double Dated Covers** With Nov. 18th set, plus Dec. 2nd 12p, any postmark .... **£36.00** ☐

Covers with postmarks a-j above often have the 13p discount stamp (single or pairs) added, since it was released on the same day. The 13p discount stamp is exactly the same as the one released on November 18th, except that it has a five pointed star printed on the gum side. Covers with the discount 'star' 13p stamp added are worth an additional £2.50.

---

254. 1987, 20th January
Flowers 18p Blanket Flower, 22p Thistle, 31p Echeveria, 34p Crocus

254a Set on illustrated cover, any postmark .... **£2.00** ☐
254b With Philatelic Bureau handstamp .... **£4.00** ☐
254c With First Day of Issue, Richmond, Surrey handstamp .... **£4.50** ☐
254d With 1987 Opening the New Conservatory, Royal Botanic Gdns, Kew h/s .... **£8.00** ☐
254e With Stephen Thomas - Flora & Fauna Exhibition, Ovingdean h/s .... **£8.00** ☐
254f With National Assocn. of Flower Arrangement Societies, London h/s .... **£8.00** ☐
254g With Lindley Library, Royal Horticultural Society, Westminster, London h/s .... **£8.00** ☐
254h With Chelsea Flower Shows, Royal Horticultural Society, Chelsea, London SW3 .... **£8.00** ☐
254i With Wisley Gardens, Royal Horticultural Society, Wisley, Woking h/s .... **£8.00** ☐
254j With Westminster Shows, Royal Horticultural Society, London SW1 h/s .... **£8.00** ☐
254k With GQT 1947-1987 BBC Manchester handstamp .... **£9.00** ☐
254l With KEB Horticultural Society, London ECIA IAA handstamp .... **£9.50** ☐
254m With Flowers, Flore, Northampton handstamp .... **£9.50** ☐
254n With Royal College of Art 1837-1987, London SW7 handstamp .... **£10.50** ☐
254o With any Field/Forces Post Office (2150 or other) handstamp .... **£8.50** ☐
254p With Kew Gardens, Richmond cds .... **£30.00** ☐
254q With Botanic Gardens, Belfast cds .... **£30.00** ☐
254r With Ripley, Sissinghurst, or Royal Hospital Chelsea cds .... **£17.50** ☐
254s With St. Bees, Flowery Field, Thistle Hill, or Spring Gardens cds .... **£16.00** ☐

QEII • Commemoratives 1987

255. 1987, 24th March
Sir Isaac Newton
18p, 22p, 31p, 34p, Treatise from Newton's "Mathematical Principles of...Philosophy"

255a	Set on illustrated cover, any postmark	£2.00 ☐
255b	With Philatelic Bureau handstamp	£4.00 ☐
255c	With First Day of Issue, Woolsthorpe, Lincs handstamp	£4.50 ☐
255d	With Isaac Newton, Grantham handstamp	£8.00 ☐
255e	With Old Royal Observatory, Sir Isaac Newton 1642-1727, Greenwich h/s	£8.00 ☐
255f	With Apple's Tenth Anniversary, Hemel Hempstead, Herts handstamp	£12.00 ☐
255g	With Sir Isaac Newton 1642-1727, Trinity College, Cambridge h/s	£8.00 ☐
255h	With Sir Isaac Newton, President of the Royal Society, London h/s	£8.00 ☐
255i	With The George Celebrates Newton's Tercentenary, Grantham h/s	£8.00 ☐
255j	With Sir Isaac Newton, Science Museum - London S.W.7 handstamp	£8.00 ☐
255k	With Sir Isaac Newton 1642-1727, Woolsthorpe, Grantham handstamp	£8.00 ☐
255l	With Newton (Cambridge, Swansea, or Wisbech) cds	£15.00 ☐
255m	With Trinity St, Cambridge cds, or Colsterworth, Grantham cds,	£15.00 ☐
255n	With House of Commons SW1 cds (Newton was Cambridge MP)	£16.00 ☐
255o	With Regent St, London cds or Kensington, London cds	£12.50 ☐
255p	With Greenwich, London cds	£15.00 ☐
255q	With any Forces/Field Post Office cancellation (2151 or other)	£7.00 ☐

256. 1987, 12th May
British Architects in Europe (Europa)
18p Ipswich, 22p Paris, 31p Stuttgart, 34p Luxembourg

256a	Set on illustrated cover, any postmark	£2.00 ☐
256b	With Philatelic Bureau handstamp	£4.00 ☐
256c	With First Day of Issue, Ipswich special handstamp	£4.50 ☐
256d	With The Clore Gallery, British Architects in Europe, London SW1 h/s	£8.00 ☐
256e	With RIBA Royal Charter 1837-1987, London W1 handstamp	£8.00 ☐
256f	With British Architects in Europe, London W1 handstamp	£8.00 ☐
256g	With British Architects in Europe, RIBA Community Architecture h/s	£8.00 ☐
256h	With Heritage & Progress, Willis Faber, Ipswich handstamp	£8.00 ☐
256i	With Ipswich, or Ascot cds (New Buildings cds **£32**)	£12.50 ☐
256j	With Town Centre, or Gt. Portland St. cds	£12.50 ☐
256k	With 200th Anniv. granting Royal Warrant to Royal Engineers, BF 1987 PS h/s	£15.00 ☐

QEII • Commemoratives 1987

257. 1987, 16th June

Centenary St. John Ambulance 18p - 1887, 22p - 1940, 31p - 1965, 34p - 1987

257a	Set on illustrated cover, any postmark	**£2.50** ☐
257b	With Philatelic Bureau handstamp	**£4.00** ☐
257c	With First Day of Issue, London EC1 handstamp	**£4.50** ☐
257d	With St. John Ambulance Brigade Centenary, Hyde Park, London SW1 h/s	**£8.50** ☐
257e	With World's 2nd Oldest Division, St. John Ambulance, Heywood, Lancs h/s	**£8.50** ☐
257f	With St. John Ambulance Brigade, London SW1 handstamp	**£8.50** ☐
257g	With St. John's Gate, SJA Centenary Exhibition, London EC1	**£8.50** ☐
257h	With St. John Ambulance, St. Margaret's Hospital, Epping, Essex h/s	**£8.50** ☐
257i	With 100th Anniversary St. John Ambulance, Stansted, Essex handstamp	**£8.50** ☐
257j	With Ashford, Woolwich, Stansted, or Margate cds	**£15.00** ☐
257k	With St. John's. (Ipswich, Bradford or Worcester) cds, or St. John's Chapel cds	**£18.00** ☐
257l	With Harrow, London EC, or Coventry cds	**£15.00** ☐

A few other cds postmarks can be associated with this issue. Prices from **£10**.

258. 1987, 21st July

Scottish Heraldry 18p, 22p, 31p, 34p, Heraldry Ancient and Modern

258a	Set on illustrated cover, any postmark	**£2.00** ☐
258b	With Philatelic Bureau handstamp	**£4.00** ☐
258c	With First Day of Issue, Rothesay, Isle of Bute handstamp	**£4.50** ☐
258d	With Tercentenary Revival of Order of the Thistle, Edinburgh handstamp	**£8.50** ☐
258e	With Mary Queen of Scots, Fotheringhay, Peterborough handstamp	**£8.50** ☐
258f	With Visit of Duke & Duchess of York, York handstamp	**£8.50** ☐
258g	With Scottish Heraldry, Bannockburn, Stirling handstamp	**£8.50** ☐
258h	With Royal Scottish Academy, Edinburgh handstamp	**£8.50** ☐
258i	With Scottish Heraldry, Dunkeld, Perthshire handstamp	**£8.50** ☐
258j	With Lord Cameron of Balhousie, Knight of the Thistle handstamp	**£8.50** ☐
258k	With any Forces/Field Post Office handstamp (2142 or other)	**£10.00** ☐
258l	With Glasgow Herald, Scotland's Newspaper, Scottish Heraldry handstamp	**£14.00** ☐
258m	With Scottish Heraldry, Drum Castle, Banchory, Kincardineshire	**£8.50** ☐
258n	With Scottish Heraldry, Crathes Castle, Banchory, Kincardineshire	**£8.50** ☐
258o	With Rothesay, or Banff, or Edinburgh cds	**£16.50** ☐
258p	With Scone, Perthshire cds (Holyrood, Edinburgh cds **£22**)	**£45.00** ☐
258q	With House of Lords or House of Commons cds	**£20.00** ☐
258r	With Thistle Hill, or St. Andrews, or Bannockburn cds	**£20.00** ☐

A few other cds postmarks can be related to this issue. Prices from **£10**. The Philatelic Bureau handstamp was used in two sizes, the standard 30mm and a smaller 28mm size (cat. **£14**).

QEII • Commemoratives 1987

259. 1987, 8th September

150th Anniversary Accession of Queen Victoria

18p, 22p, 31p, 34p, Portraits of QV and 19th Century Achievements

259a	Set on illustrated cover, any postmark	**£2.50** ☐
259b	With Philatelic Bureau handstamp	**£4.00** ☐
259c	With First Day of Issue, Newport, Isle of Wight handstamp	**£4.50** ☐
259d	With CPF Victorian Britain, Edensor Bakewell, Derbyshire handstamp	**£8.50** ☐
259e	With Marconi's first wireless transmission to France, Chelmsford h/s	**£8.50** ☐
259f	With Victorian Britain VA, London SW7 handstamp	**£8.50** ☐
259g	With Queen Victoria 1837-1901, London SW1 handstamp	**£8.50** ☐
259h	With Victorian Britain, Windsor, Berks handstamp	**£8.50** ☐
259i	With Mrs. Beeton's A Great Tradition Since 1858, London W1 handstamp	**£22.00** ☐
259j	With Victorian Britain, Balmoral, Ballater, Aberdeenshire handstamp	**£8.50** ☐
259k	With Calderdales Victorian Inheritance, Halifax, W. Yorkshire handstamp	**£20.00** ☐
259l	With National Postal Museum, London EC1 handstamp	**£12.00** ☐
259m	With Southampton Victorian Post Office handstamp	**£16.00** ☐
259n	With National Trust for Scotland, Places of Historic Interest handstamp	**£8.50** ☐
259o	With Henry Archer, Victorian Stamps & Railway Pioneer handstamp	**£17.50** ☐
259p	With any British Forces Postal Service handstamp (2156 or other)	**£10.00** ☐
259q	With Queen Victoria Road, Prince Consort Rd, or Victoria Road cds	**£18.00** ☐
259r	With South Kensington B.O. SW7 cds (QV Birthplace)	**£15.00** ☐
259s	With Balmoral Castle cds (Windsor Castle cds **£165**)	**£325.00** ☐
259t	With Buckingham Palace SW1 cds	**£154.00** ☐
259u	With House of Commons or House of Lords cds	**£20.00** ☐
259v	With S. Kensington, Beaconsfield, or Bamburgh cds	**£16.00** ☐
259w	With St. Margaret's Bay, Dover, Kent cds	**£35.00** ☐
259x	With Millwall, Maida Vale London, or Cowes cds	**£16.00** ☐

260. 1987, 13th October

British Studio Pottery 18p Leach, 26p Fritsch, 31p Rie, 34p Coper

260a	Set on illustrated cover, any postmark	**£2.00** ☐
260b	With Philatelic Bulletin handstamp	**£4.00** ☐
260c	With First Day of Issue, St. Ives, Cornwall handstamp	**£4.50** ☐
260d	With Studio Pottery, Potters Corner, Ashford, Kent handstamp	**£8.50** ☐
260e	With Designed and Photographed by Tony Evans, Shrewsbury	**£8.50** ☐
260f	With Craftsmen Potters Assocn., London W1 handstamp	**£8.50** ☐
260g	With Studio Pottery VA, London SW7 handstamp	**£8.50** ☐
260h	With any British Forces Postal Service (2154 or other) handstamp	**£8.50** ☐
260i	With Chelsea SW3, or Bathwick Street, Bath cds	**£14.00** ☐
260j	With St. Ives, Barlaston, or South Kensington cds	**£14.00** ☐
260k	With Marble Arch, Frome, or Poplar London cds	**£14.00** ☐
260l	With Potters Bar, Potters Road, or Pottery Road cds	**£15.00** ☐
260m	With Stennack, St. Ives cds	**£32.00** ☐

QEII • Commemoratives 1987-88

261. 1987, 17th November
Christmas Issue 13p, 18p, 26p, 31p, 34p, Christmas as Seen by a Child

261a	Set on illustrated cover, any postmark	£2.50
261b	With Philatelic Bureau handstamp	£4.50
261c	With First Day of Issue, Bethlehem, Llandeilo handstamp	£5.00
261d	With Christmas, Toys Hill, Westham, Kent handstamp	£9.50
261e	With Happy Christmas from Hamleys, The Finest Toyshop, London h/s	£9.50
261f	With Merry Christmas, Telecom Technology Showcase, London h/s	£12.50
261g	With Christmas, Christleton, Chester handstamp	£9.50
261h	With Christmas, Christmas Common, Oxford handstamp	£9.50
261i	With 175th Anniversary Year, Birth of Charles Dickens, Portsmouth h/s	£9.50
261j	With Holy Cross Church, Pattishall, Towcester handstamp	£9.50
261k	With any Forces Post Office BFPS cancel (2157 or other)	£10.00
261l	With Bethlehem, Llandeilo, Dyfed, or Nasareth cds	£27.50
261m	With St. Nicholas, or Star cds	£14.00
261n	With Playing Place, Noel Road, or Snows Hill cds	£14.00
261o	With Holy Island, Berwick on Tweed cds	£14.00
261p	With Christmas Shopping is Fun! Nottingham slogan	£140.00
261q	**Discount Miniature Sheet** 13p, with Star printed over gum, any postmark	£6.00
261r	Half-Sheet of 18 x 13p with Star Underprint, Star Gwynedd handstamp	£25.00
261s	With Holy Island cds	£27.50

262. 1988, 19th January
Bicentenary of Linnean Society
18p Bull-rout Fish, 26p Waterlily, 31p Berwick's Swan, 34p Morels

262a	Set on illustrated cover, any postmark	£2.00
262b	With Philatelic Bureau handstamp	£4.00
262c	With First Day of Issue, Burlington House of London W1 handstamp	£4.50
262d	With Linnean Society 1788-1988, London W1 handstamp	£8.50
262e	With Wildfowl Trust, Swan Lake, Arundel, Sussex	£8.50
262f	With Wildfowl Trust, Welney, Wisbech, Cambs handstamp	£8.50
262g	With British Natural History, Waterside, Darwen, Lancs	£8.50
262h	With any BFPS handstamp (2157 or other)	£8.50
262i	With Kew Gardens, or Slimbridge cds	£25.00
262j	With Fleur-de-Lis, Blackwood, Gwent cds	£22.00
262k	With Swanpool, Hanley Swan, or Abbotsbury cds	£15.00
262l	With Norwich cds, Broadwick St. London cds, or Holloway cds	£12.50
262m	With Gotenburg, Sweden cds and paquebot marking	£60.00

A few other cds postmarks could be related to this issue, prices from **£10**.

QEII • Commemoratives 1988

263. 1988, 1st March

400th Anniversary of The Welsh Bible

18p Rev. Morgan, 26p William Salesbury, 31p Bishop Davies, 34p Bishop Parry

263a	Set on illustrated cover, any postmark	**£2.50**
263b	With Philatelic Bureau handstamp	**£4.00**
263c	With First Day of Issue, Ty Mawr, Wybrnant, Gwynedd handstamp	**£4.50**
263d	With Bible Society St. David's Day, Welsh Bible, St. Asaph, Clwyd h/s	**£8.50**
263e	With Welsh Bible 1588-1988, Ty Mawr Wybrnant, Gwynedd handstamp	**£8.50**
263f	With The Welsh Bible, Caernarfon Castle, Caernarfon, Gwynedd h/s	**£8.50**
263g	With Translators of Welsh Bible, St. Asaph, Clwyd handstamp	**£8.50**
263h	With Y Beibl Yn Gymraeg 1588-1988, Llanhaeadr-Yn-Mochnant h/s	**£8.50**
263i	With Spring Stampex, London SW1 handstamp	**£12.00**
263j	With St. David's, Haverfordwest, Dyfed cds, or Bethlehem cds	**£20.00**
263k	With Llanrhaeadr Ym, Oswestry, Salop cds	**£14.00**
263l	With St. Asaph, Clwyd cds, or Llandaff, Cardiff cds	**£14.00**
263m	With House of Commons or House of Lords SW1 cds	**£25.00**
263n	With Penmachno, Betws-Y-Coed, Gwynedd cds	**£14.00**
263o	With 150th Anniv. Sasra, Scripture Readers Association, BF 2159 PS h/s	**£8.50**
263p	With Llansannan Denbigh, Conway, or Cwm cds	**£14.00**
263q	With Jesus is Alive! slogan, used at various offices	**£65.00**

A few other cds postmarks can be associated with this issue. Prices from **£10**.

264. 1988, 22nd March

Sporting Activities 18p Gymnastics, 26p Skiing, 31p Tennis, 34p Football

264a	Set on illustrated cover, any postmark	**£3.00**
264b	With Philatelic Bureau handstamp	**£4.00**
264c	With First Day of Issue, Wembley special handstamp	**£4.50**
264d	With The Lawn Tennis Association, 100th Anniversary, London W14	**£8.50**
264e	With Record Holders Liverpool FC, 16 Championship Wins, Liverpool h/s	**£8.50**
264f	With Record Holders Arsenal FC, Division One 1919-1988, London h/s	**£8.50**
264g	With Record Holders Tottenham Hotspur, European Trophy, Tottenham h/s	**£8.50**
264h	With "A Question of Sport" Celebrates Sport on Stamps, Manchester h/s	**£8.50**
264i	With Manchester United, The Club With It's Own Museum, Manchester h/s	**£8.50**
264j	With Preston North End Football Club, Preston, Lancs handstamp	**£8.50**
264k	With 130th Anniversary of Lawn Tennis at Edgbaston, Edgbaston h/sp	**£8.50**
264l	With 100, 1888-1988 British Gymnastics, Slough handstamp	**£10.50**
264m	With 100 Years League Football, Wolves, Wolverhampton handstamp	**£8.50**
264n	With 100 Years League Football, Aston Villa, Birmingham handstamp	**£8.50**
264o	With 100 Years League Football, Everton Current Champions h/s	**£8.50**
264p	With 100 Year Ago Accrington FC, Founder Members of the League h/s	**£8.50**
264q	With any BFPS handstamp (2161 or other)	**£8.50**
264r	With Leamington Spa, Edgebaston, or Wimbledon cds	**£16.50**
264s	With Slough Bucks, Lytham St. Annes, Lancs, or Eccleston St. SW1 cds	**£15.00**
264t	With Wembley Park cds (Wembley B.O. cds **£12**)	**£26.00**

A few other cds postmarks can be related to this issue. Prices from **£10**.

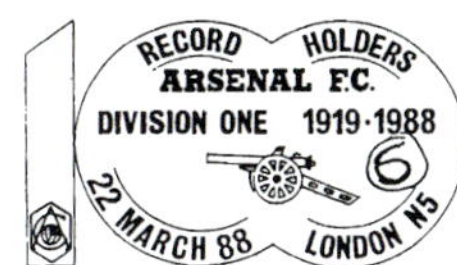

QEII • Commemoratives 1988

265. 1988, 10th May

Transport and Communications (Europa)

18p Mallard Train, 26p Liner 'Queen Elizabeth', 31p Glasgow Tram, 34p HP42 Plane

265a Set on illustrated cover, any postmark .... **£2.50** ☐
265b With Philatelic Bureau handstamp .... **£4.00** ☐
265c With First Day of Issue, Glasgow special handstamp .... **£4.50** ☐
265d With 50th Anniversary Launch of RMS Queen Elizabeth, London h/s .... **£8.50** ☐
265e With Designed by Carroll Dempsey & Thirkell, London WC1 handstamp .... **£10.00** ☐
265f With National Postal Museum, London EC1 handstamp .... **£8.50** ☐
265g With The Jessop Collection, Diss, Norfolk handstamp .... **£8.50** ☐
265h With Mallard 50th Anniversary, Rail Riders, York handstamp .... **£8.50** ☐
265i With Lloyd's of London 1688-1988, Tercentenary London EC3 h/s .... **£10.00** ☐
265j With The New Museum of Transport, Glasgow handstamp .... **£8.50** ☐
265k With 50th Anniversary Imperial Airways, Rochester, Kent handstamp .... **£8.50** ☐
265l With 50th Anniversary Year, RMS Queen Elizabeth, Southampton h/s .... **£8.50** ☐
265m With Railways and the Post Exhibition. National Postal Museum h/s .... **£8.50** ☐
265n With TGWU Celebrates Historic Transport Stamps, London SW1 h/s .... **£8.50** ☐
265o With TPO 150 Anniversary 1838-1988, Peterborough handstamp .... **£8.50** ☐
265p With Sheffield & Rotherham Railway 1838-1988, Sheffield handstamp .... **£10.00** ☐
265q With 50th Anniversary World Record Mallard 88, NRM, York h/s .... **£8.50** ☐
265r With 60th Anniversary Opening of Croydon Airport Terminal, BF2162 PS h/s .... **£8.50** ☐
265s With any BFPS handstamp (2165 or other) .... **£8.50** ☐
265t With Illustrated (the stamps) by Andrew Davidson, Bromley, Kent h/s .... **£11.00** ☐
265u With Glasgow, Southampton, or York cds .... **£15.00** ☐
265v With Cricklewood, or Doncaster cds .... **£15.00** ☐
265w With Berkhamstead cds (Croydon cds £25) .... **£15.00** ☐
265x With Mosspark, Glasgow cds, or Essendine cds .... **£15.00** ☐
265y With Clydebank, Dumbartonshire, or any TPO cds. .... **£15.50** ☐
265z With Crewe-Peterborough T.P.O., or any Up/Down T.P.O. .... **£17.50** ☐
265aa With Only Fools Play on Railway Lines slogan (various towns) .... **£32.00** ☐

A few other cds postmarks can be related to this issue. Prices from **£10**

Remember, most hand addressed covers are worth only 20% of catalogue prices.

QEII • Commemoratives 1988

266. 1988, 21st June

Australian Bicentenary 18p Se-tenant Pair, 34p Se-tenant pair

266a	Set of both Se-tenant pairs on illustrated cover, any postmark	£2.50	☐
266b	With Philatelic Bureau handstamp	£4.00	☐
266c	With First Day of Issue, Portsmouth special handstamp	£4.50	☐
266d	With The Bicentenary of Australia, 1788-1988, London SW1 handstamp	£8.50	☐
266e	With Australian Bicentenary, 1788-1988, Wedgwood, Barlaston handstamp	£8.50	☐
266f	With Capt. Cook Museum Commemorates Australian Bicentenial h/s	£8.50	☐
266g	With Australian Bicentenary 1788, Portsmouth, Hants handstamp	£8.50	☐
266h	With Links with Australia, Amy Johnson, Queen of the Air, Hull handstamp	£8.50	☐
266i	With Australian Bicentenial, London EC handstamp	£10.00	☐
266j	With Australian Bicentenary, 'Botany Bay', Enfield, Middx	£8.50	☐
266k	With any BFPS postmark (2177, 2178 or other)	£9.00	☐
266l	With Great Britain Cricketing Links, 200th Anniversary, Australia 1788-1988, Lords, London NW8, or any one of the following: Headingley, The Oval, Old Trafford, Edgbaston, or Trent Bridge handstamp	£12.50	☐
266m	With House of Commons SW1 cds	£32.00	☐
266n	With House of Lords SW1 cds	£35.00	☐
266o	With Hambledon, Downend, Wimbledon, or Liverpool cds	£15.00	☐
266p	With Stratford-upon-Avon, Portsmouth, or Whitby cds	£15.00	☐
266q	With Botany Bay, Melbourne, or Sidney Rd. Exeter cds	£17.50	☐
266r	**Double Dated Covers** Both sets of stamps (English and Australian) on one cover, or on matching covers. Two different Country postmarks	£36.00	☐
266s	Same with matching postmarks (i.e. Brighton Sussex/Brighton Victoria)	£46.00	☐

There are several other postmarks which can be related to this issue. Prices are from **£10**.
This issue was released jointly by the British Post Office and Australia Post. The Queens head was not used on the Australian stamps and the currency was changed also. Double dated covers were done by several dealers as were pairs of matching covers. This was the first ever joint issue by the British Post Office.

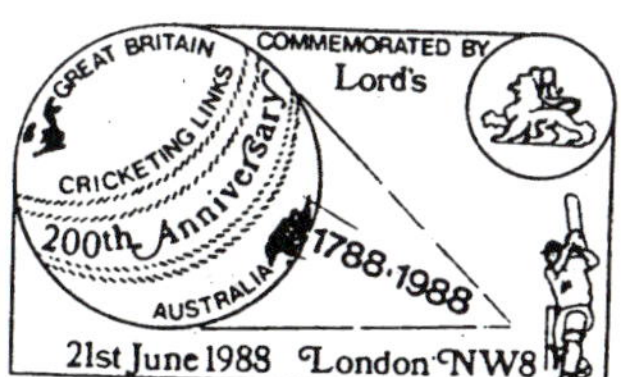

All prices in this catalogue are for clean covers, with undamaged Stamps and clear postmarks.

Royalty Post Cards - Special fdc Colour Feature

Introduction

Our fdc colour feature in the new catalogue presents Royalty Post Cards, starting on the first three pages with King George V and his Coronation back in 1911. Many different fine Post Cards were produced at the time by the Tuck company and others. Then comes the Silver Jubilee of 1935, on two pages, with some great portrait shots of the King.

King Edward VIII is next, again with some fine portrait shots, but alas too few. This is followed by a good selection for King George VI, starting with the first definitives, then the Coronation, one stamp from the 1946 Victory Issue and finally the Silver Wedding Issue of 1948.

For Queen Elizabeth II many wonderful photographs were done, by Dorothy Wilding in particular, and these were reproduced for both the Coronation in 1953 and for the first definitive Stamp Issue started in December 1952. Here we present a broad selection of great Royalty Post Cards over six pages, covering both Stamp Issues.

It has taken quite a few years to put this collection of Royalty fdc Post Cards together, but it has proved well worth while and we hope you will enjoy looking through the wide selection presented here.

We recognize that it is difficult to read the postmarks on many of the Post Cards shown here. However, if you would like to receive a full size photocopy of the reverse of any fdc Card in this Feature, please let us know.

> This is our ninth Special Feature! We started back in 1994 with Selected Overprints, then came Hand Painted Covers. This was followed by Blocks of Four and in 1997, for our 25th Edition of the catalogue, we made a complex presentation of 25th Anniversaries from different years. Next came the 1929 PUC Issue plus a more detailed look at GB Overprints. In the 27th Edition we featured the 1924/25 Wembley Issues and in the following Edition we did sixteen pages on Edward VIII. Finally in the 29th Edition we presented the 1951 Festival of Britain. So here we are at the ninth Special Feature with a very colourful presentation of Royalty fdc Post Cards.

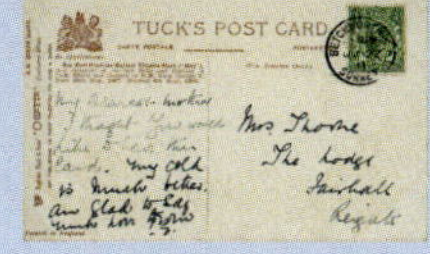

King George V Coronation 1911. First Definitives

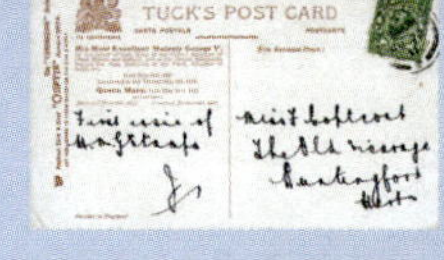

King George V Coronation 1911. First Definitives

King George V Coronation 1911. First Definitives

Royalty Post Cards - Special fdc Colour Feature

King George V Silver Jubilee 1935

King George V Silver Jubilee 1935

May 6, 1935 was the 25th anniversary of King George V accession to the throne. A special set of four Silver Jubilee Stamps was issued by the Post Office the following day. The Stamps were designed by Barnett Freedman, a pre-eminent artist of the day, who beat out Harold Nelson and Edmund Dulac among others, in the design competition. The Stamps were printed in photogravure by Harrison & Sons Ltd.

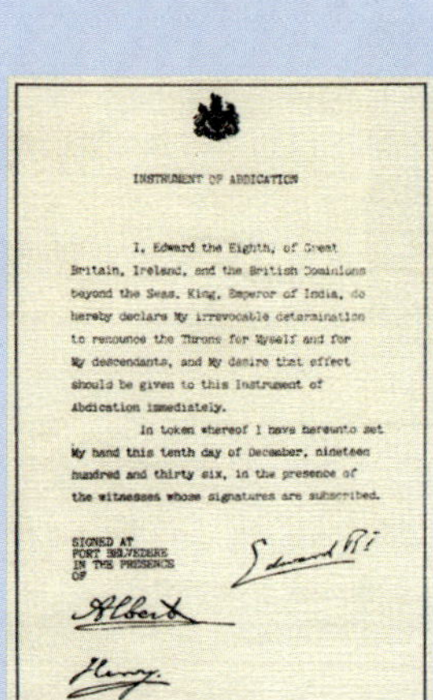

INSTRUMENT OF ABDICATION

I, Edward the Eighth, of Great Britain, Ireland, and the British Dominions beyond the Seas, King, Emperor of India, do hereby declare My irrevocable determination to renounce the Throne for Myself and for My descendants, and My desire that effect should be given to this Instrument of Abdication immediately.

In token whereof I have hereunto set My hand this tenth day of December, nineteen hundred and thirty six, in the presence of the witnesses whose signatures are subscribed.

SIGNED AT FORT BELVEDERE IN THE PRESENCE OF

Edward RI

Albert

Henry

George.

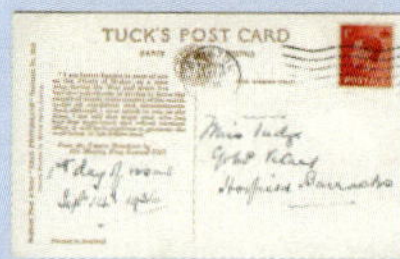

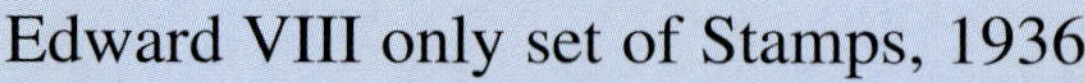

Edward VIII only set of Stamps, 1936

Shown above is a copy of The Instrument of Abdication by which Edward VIII renounced the throne of England. He signed the Document as Edward RI (Rex Imperator) and it was witnessed by his brothers, Albert(who became KGVI), Henry (Duke of Gloucester) and George (Duke of Kent). A moment in history.

King George VI First Definitives and Coronation Issue, 1937

Royalty Post Cards - Special fdc Colour Feature

King George VI Coronation 1937

Royalty Post Cards - Special fdc Colour Feature

Royalty Post Cards - Special fdc Colour Feature

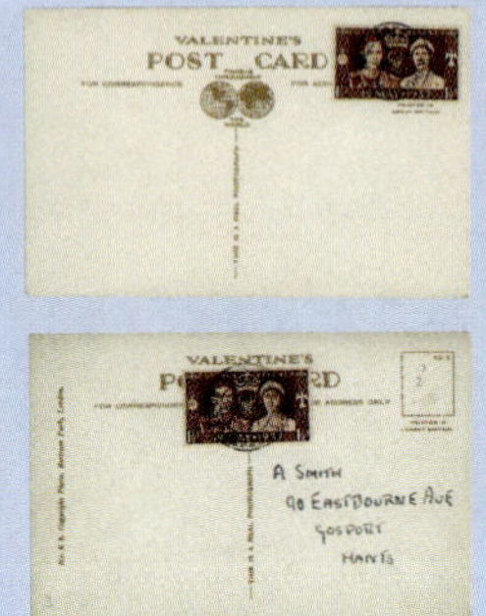

King George VI Coronation/Victory/Silver Wedding Issues
1937/1946/1948

Royalty Post Cards - Special fdc Colour Feature

Queen Elizabeth II Coronation Issue. June 3, 1953
Followed by the First Definitive Issue, 1952/54

Royalty Post Cards - Special fdc Colour Feature

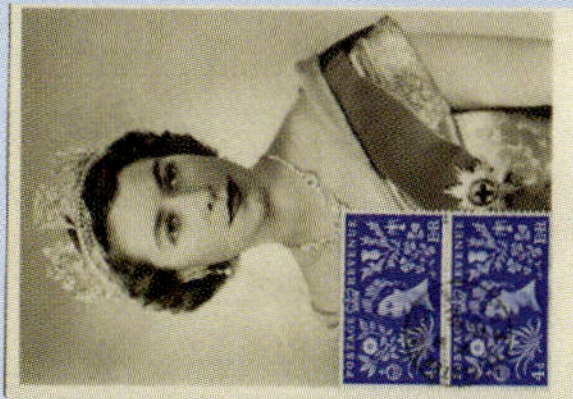

Royalty Post Cards - Special fdc Colour Feature

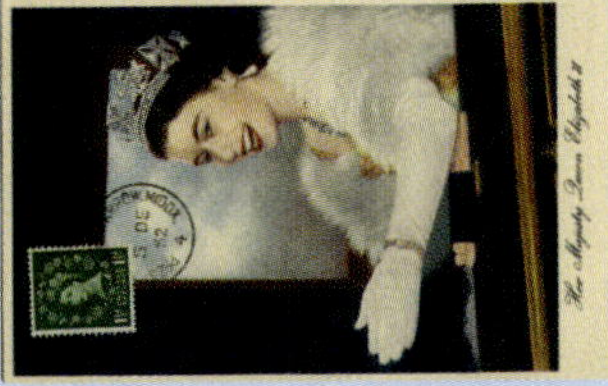

Royalty Post Cards - Special fdc Colour Feature

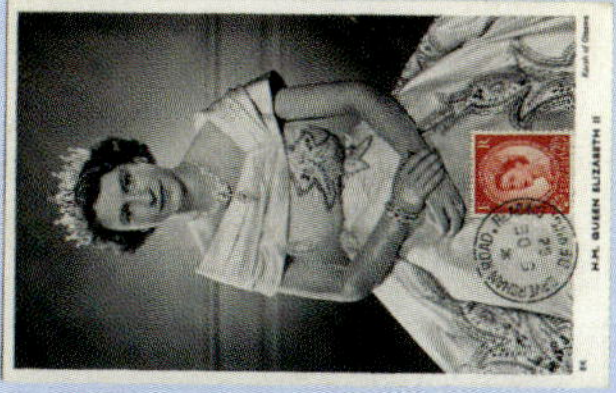

Royalty Post Cards - Special fdc Colour Feature

End of Special fdc Colour Feature

QEII • Commemoratives 1988

267. 1988, 19th July
400th Anniversary Spanish Armada
18p Se-tenant strip of 5. Different Locations of the Armada off the British Isles

267a Se-tenant strip of 5 x 18p stamps on illustrated cover, any postmark .... **£2.50** ☐
267b With Philatelic Bureau handstamp .... **£4.00** ☐
267c With First Day of Issue, Plymouth special handstamp .... **£4.50** ☐
267d With The Spanish Armada 1588, Tilbury, Essex handstamp .... **£9.50** ☐
267e With The Spanish Armada, Tilbury, Essex handstamp .... **£9.50** ☐
267f With Armada 400 Yrs 1588-1988, Plymouth handstamp .... **£11.00** ☐
267g With Armada 400, Plymouth, Devon handstamp .... **£9.50** ☐
267h With Armada 400, The Battle of Gravelines, Dover, Kent handstamp .... **£9.50** ☐
267i With 400th Anniv. Sighting of Armada by 'HM Navy Royal', BF2179 PS h/s .... **£9.50** ☐
267j With Armada Anniversary, Tavistock, Devon handstamp .... **£9.50** ☐
267k With First Armada 400 Beacon, The Lizard, Cornwall handstamp .... **£11.00** ☐
267l With Royal Naval College, Armada Anniversary, Greenwich handstamp .... **£9.50** ☐
267m With Spanish Armada, Effingham, Leatherhead, Surrey handstamp .... **£9.50** ☐
267n With John Hurleston, Mariner, Chester handstamp .... **£9.50** ☐
267o With The Royal Tournament, Earls Court 1988, BF 2181 PS handstamp .... **£10.00** ☐
267p With Portsmouth or Plymouth Philatelic Counter handstamp .... **£25.00** ☐
267q With Calais cds, or Dover cds, plus paquebot markings .... **£30.00** ☐
267r With Sandwich cds, or London S.E.I. FDI (maritime museum) .... **£17.50** ☐
267s With House of Commons, or House of Lords cds .... **£25.00** ☐
267t With Tilbury, Portland, or Drakes Broughton cds .... **£17.50** ☐
267u With Tavistock, Greenwich, The Lizard, or Effingham cds .... **£20.00** ☐
267v With 400th Anniv. of Spanish Armada, Plymouth/Truro/Penzance slogan .... **£65.00** ☐
267w With Drake, Plymouth cds (Plymouth cds **£20**) .... **£240.00** ☐
267x With Maritime Mail, London cds (Tobomory or Fair Isle cds **£26**) .... **£110.00** ☐

A few other cds postmarks can be related to this issue. Prices from **£15**.

268. 1988, 6th September
Centenary of Edward Lear 19p, 27p, 32p, 35p, Verses by Lear and Lear Signature

268a Set on illustrated cover, any postmark .... **£2.50** ☐
268b With Philatelic Bureau handstamp .... **£4.00** ☐
268c With First Day of Issue, London N7 special handstamp .... **£4.50** ☐
268d With Edward Lear Centenary, Knowsley, Liverpool handstamp .... **£8.50** ☐
268e With Birthplace of Edward Lear 1812-1888, Holloway, London N7 h/s .... **£8.50** ☐
268f With Centenary of Edward Lear, Learmouth, Northumberland handstamp .... **£8.50** ☐
268g With Designed by The Partners, Edward Lear 1812-1888, London ECI h/s .... **£8.50** ☐
268h With Knowsley from Menagerie to Safari Park, Prescot, Merseyside h/s .... **£8.50** ☐
268i With any BFPS postmark (2173 or other) .... **£10.00** ☐
268j With Holloway N7, Knowlsey, Camden Town, or Theobalds Road cds .... **£15.00** ☐
268k With Regents Park, or Regents Park Rd. cds .... **£16.00** ☐

A few other cds postmarks can be related to this issue. Prices from **£12**.

QEII • Commemoratives 1988

269. 1988, 27th September

Edward Lear Centenary Miniature Sheet of all Four September 6th Stamps

269a Miniature Sheet on illustrated cover, any postmark .... £3.00 ☐
269b With Philatelic Bureau handstamp .... £4.50 ☐
269c With First Day of Issue, London N22 handstamp .... £5.00 ☐
269d With Edward Lear Centenary, Stampex, London SW handstamp .... £10.00 ☐
269e With Centenary of Edward Lear, Learmouth, Northumberland handstamp .... £10.00 ☐
269f With Edward Lear Centenary, Knowsley, Liverpool handstamp .... £10.00 ☐
269g With Autumn Stampex/BPE, London SW1 handstamp .... £12.00 ☐
269h With Birthplace of Edward Lear 1812-1888, Holloway, London h/s .... £10.00 ☐
269i With Stampway to the World, Liverpool Museum handstamp .... £15.00 ☐
269j With any BFPS postmark (2182 or other) .... £10.00 ☐
269k With Alexandra Park Rd. N.10, Muswell Hill cds .... £20.00 ☐
269l With Holloway B.O. N7 cds .... £20.00 ☐
269m With Knowsley, Prescot, or Derry Hill cds .... £20.00 ☐
269n With Regents Park Rd., or Regents Park cds .... £20.00 ☐
269o With Autumn Stampex/BPE, Royal Horticultural Hall, London slogan .... £25.00 ☐
269p With British Philatelic Bulletin, 25th Anniversary, London EC slogan .... £28.00 ☐
269q **Double Dated Covers** with both Sept 6th and 27th issues, any pmk .... £42.00 ☐

270. 1988, 15th November

Christmas Issue 14p, 19p, 27p, 32p, 35p, Christmas Card Scenes from The Nativity

270a Set on illustrated cover, any postmark .... £2.50 ☐
270b With Philatelic Bureau handstamp .... £5.00 ☐
270c With First Day of Issue, Bethlehem, Llandeilo handstamp .... £5.50 ☐
270d With Victorian Christmas Cards, Postling, Hythe, Kent handstamp .... £9.00 ☐
270e With Happy Christmas, Telecom Technology Showcase, London EC4 h/s .... £12.50 ☐
270f With The Christmas Card Mailcoach Run, Bath, or Luton handstamp .... £9.00 ☐
270g With The Christmas Card Mailcoach Run, Box, Corsham, Wilts h/s .... £9.00 ☐
270h With St. Alban the Martyr, Northampton handstamp .... £9.00 ☐
270i With Saint Dunstan Millennium Year 988-1988, Canterbury handstamp .... £10.00 ☐
270j With Royle Royle Royle, London N.I. handstamp .... £12.50 ☐
270k With York Minster Commemoration handstamp .... £9.00 ☐
270l With Cartmel Priory 1188-1988, 800 Years of Worship, Cumbria h/s .... £12.00 ☐
270m With Stampway to the World, Liverpool Museum handstamp .... £12.50 ☐
270n With Christmas Greetings, Guinea Pig Club, BF 2184 PS handstamp .... £9.00 ☐
270o With Lancelot Place SW7, or Bath, Avon cds .... £12.00 ☐
270p With Holy Island, Star, Noel Rd, or Shepherds Bush cds .... £15.00 ☐
270q With Angel Hill, St. Nicholas, or Nasareth, Gwynedd cds .... £20.00 ☐
270r With Washington Red Apples, The Bigger Christmas Crunch! slogan .... £26.00 ☐
270s With 13p instead of 14p error, any postmark .... £5,750.00 ☐

QEII • Commemoratives 1989

271. 1989, 17th January

Sea Birds - Centenary of the RSPB

19p Puffin, 27p Avocet, 32p Oystercatcher, 35p Gannet

271a	Set on illustrated cover, any postmark	**£2.50** ☐
271b	With Philatelic Bureau handstamp	**£4.00** ☐
271c	With First Day of Issue, Sandy, Bedfordshire handstamp	**£4.50** ☐
271d	With Leics & Rutland Ornithological Society handstamp	**£9.00** ☐
271e	With First Day of Issue, City of London EC handstamp	**£9.00** ☐
271f	With Bass Rock, Britain's most famous Gannet Colony handstamp	**£9.00** ☐
271g	With British Sea Birds, Dungeness, Romney Marsh, Kent handstamp	**£9.00** ☐
271h	With Lundy Island, Bristol Channel, Bideford, Devon handstamp	**£9.00** ☐
271i	With St. Kilda, Britain's Largest Puffin Colony, Benbecula handstamp	**£9.00** ☐
271j	With Action for Birds, 100 Years Sandy Beds, The RSPB handstamp	**£9.00** ☐
271k	With any Forces/Field Post Office BFPS handstamp (2194 or other)	**£9.00** ☐
271l	With Sandy, Beds cds, or Fair Isle, Shetland cds	**£18.00** ☐
271m	With Didsbury Village cds, or Snettisham cds	**£18.00** ☐
271n	With House of Commons cds (Wild Bird Protection Act)	**£20.00** ☐
271o	With Slimbridge, Gloucester cds (Tring cds **£36**)	**£18.00** ☐

A few other cds postmarks can be related to this issue. Prices vary from **£10**.

---

272. 1989, 31st January

Greetings Stamps (Booklet)

19p x 5 Se-tenant strip, Rose/Cupid/Boat/Fruit/Teddy Bear

272a	19p Se-tenant strip on illustrated cover, any postmark	**£3.50** ☐
272b	With Philatelic Bureau handstamp	**£6.50** ☐
272c	With First Day of Issue, Lover, Salisbury handstamp	**£7.50** ☐
272d	With Greetings from Flowery Fields, Hyde, Cheshire handstamp	**£14.00** ☐
272e	With Greetings from The Teddy Bear Museum, Ironbridge handstamp	**£14.00** ☐
272f	With St. Valentine Patron Saint of Lovers, Lover, Salisbury handstamp	**£14.00** ☐
272g	With Portsmouth Philatelic Counter handstamp (ship design)	**£15.00** ☐
272h	With Commission 'Postes', CEPT, Edinburgh handstamp	**£18.50** ☐
272i	With Lover, Salisbury Wilts, or Gretna Green, Carlisle cds	**£25.00** ☐
272j	With Greet, or Greetland cds	**£25.00** ☐
272k	With Bearpark, Rose, Cowes, Seaside, Flowery Field, or Orchard cds	**£25.00** ☐
272l	With any Field/Forces Post Office BFPS handstamp (2192 or other)	**£15.00** ☐

Complete Booklet Pane of 10 stamps (19px5x2) adds £6.00 to above prices.

273. 1989, 7th March

Food & Farming Year

19p Vegetables & Fruit, 27p Meat & Fish, 32p Dairy, 35p Cereals

273a	Set on illustrated cover, any postmark	£2.50 ☐
273b	With Philatelic Bureau handstamp	£4.00 ☐
273c	With First Day of Issue, Stoneleigh, Kenilworth handstamp	£4.50 ☐
273d	With Ministry of Agriculture, Fisheries and Food, 100 Years 1889-1989, London	£8.50 ☐
273e	With BVA Animal Welfare Foundation, London W1 handstamp	£8.50 ☐
273f	With British Food & Farming, Isle of Grain, Rochester, Kent handstamp	£8.50 ☐
273g	With Purveyors of Flour Since 1886, Hovis, Windsor, Berks handstamp	£8.50 ☐
273h	With 150th Anniversary RASE, Stoneleigh, Warks handstamp	£8.50 ☐
273i	With 50th Anniversary, Women's Land Army, BF2195 PS handstamp	£8.50 ☐
273j	With Isle of Grain, Rochester, or Wheatley, Oxford or Farmers, Dyfed cds	£16.50 ☐
273k	With Cheddar, Somerset, or Ham, Richmond cds, or Stilton cds	£16.50 ☐
273l	With Stoneleigh, Cirencester, or The Orchards, Wigston cds	£16.50 ☐
273m	With Sheepscombe, Stroud, or Bewcastle cds	£18.50 ☐
273n	With Corn Exchange cds, Leek cds, or Bramley cds	£16.50 ☐

A few other cds postmarks can be related to this issue. Prices from **£10**.

Early Post Office History

1482 Messenger Relays set up to carry Royal Despatches

1516 Sir Brian Tuke appointed Master of the King's Post

1635 First Postal Act establishing rates and confirming state monopoly

1635 Postal service made available to the public

1653 John Manley appointed Postmaster General - he paid £10,000 in auction for the position!

1660 Henry Bishop takes over as Postmaster General (he paid £21,500 to get the job!)

1661 The 'Bishop Mark' is introduced (the first UK postmark)

1680 William Dockwra Penny Post started in London

1711 Act to unify postal operations throughout the U.K.

1784 First Mail Coach run - Bristol to London

1830 First mail by rail - Liverpool to Manchester

1837 Rowland Hill Postal Reform pamphlet published

1838 First Travelling Post Office introduced

1840 Uniform Penny Postage

1840 First Postage Stamp - The Penny Black - issued

1840 Mulready pre-paid envelopes introduced

1841 Embossed envelopes issued

1861 Post Office Savings Bank Act Passed

1870 Post Cards introduced (Austria was first in 1869)

1874 Universal Postal Union Act signed in Switzerland

1876 Telephone introduced in UK

1881 Postal orders introduced

1882 Reply Post Card introduced

1883 First parcel post

1890 Penny Post Jubilee

1892 Letter Cards introduced

1894 First picture post cards created

1897 Jubilee celebrations. Postage rates reduced!

1897 Delivery to every home in the country!

1898 First time Post Office motor vans used

QEII • Commemoratives 1989

274. 1989, 11th April

Anniversaries 19p x 2 Se-tenant; Education and European Parliament, 35p x 2 Se-tenant; PTT Congress and IPU Conference

274a Set of Both Se-tenant Pairs, illustrated cover, any postmark **£2.50**
274b With Philatelic Bureau handstamp **£4.00**
274c With First Day of Issue, SW London Letter District handstamp **£4.50**
274d With Strasbourg-Leicester Twin City, Leicester handstamp **£9.00**
274e With 26th World Congress P.T.T.I., London W1 handstamp **£9.00**
274f With Third Direct Elections, European Parliament, Downing St. handstamp **£9.00**
274g With Inter Parliamentary Union, Centenary Conference, London SW1 h/s **£9.00**
274h With Weston Favell Upper School, Northampton handstamp **£9.00**
274i With Centenary Derbyshire County Council 1889-1989, Matlock h/s **£9.00**
274j With any Forces/Field Post Office BFPS handstamp (2179 or other) **£9.00**
274k With House of Commons or House of Lords cds **£30.00**
274l With Pas de Calais cds plus Paquebot handstamp, or Dover plus Paquebot **£18.00**
274m With any famous School or University pmk (Eton, Oxford, etc.) **£15.00**
274n With College Road cds, or London SW1 cds **£12.50**
274o With Brighton cds, or Telephone House cds (NATO 40th Anniv slogan **£95**) **£18.00**

There are several other postmarks that can be related to this issue, as well as some non specific slogan cancellations. These range widely in price from **£10-£20**.

275. 1989, 16th May

Games & Toys (Europa)

19p Plane & Train, 27p Building Blocks, 32p Board Games, 35p Robot, Boat, etc.

275a Set on illustrated cover, any postmark **£2.50**
275b With Philatelic Bureau handstamp **£4.00**
275c With First Day of Issue, Leeds special handstamp **£4.50**
275d With Childrens Toys & Games, Toys Hill, Westerham handstamp **£8.50**
275e With The Teddybears Picnic, Ironbridge, Telford Salop handstamp **£8.50**
275f With Pollock's Toy Museum, London W1 handstamp **£8.50**
275g With Putting Children First, NSPCC London EC1 handstamp **£8.50**
275h With Lewis Carrol 1832-1898, Oxford handstamp **£8.50**
275i With National Postal Museum Uniform Exhibition, London EC h/s **£8.50**
275j With any Forces/Field Post Office BFPS handstamp (2200 or other) **£8.50**
275k With Playing Place, Truro, or Regent St. London W1 cds **£16.50**
275l With Swansea, Waddington, or Hornby cds **£16.50**
275m With Winsor Castle cds (Queen's Dolls House kept here) **£70.00**
275n With Medway & Swale, Child Safety, Medway slogan **£32.00**
275o With Save the Children Week, 70 Years of Saving Children slogan **£45.00**

276. 1989, 4th July
Industrial Archaeology
19p Ironbridge, 27p Tin Mine, 32p Cotton Mill, 35p 1,000ft. long Aqueduct

276a	Set on illustrated cover, any postmark	**£2.50** ☐
276b	With Philatelic Bureau handstamp	**£4.00** ☐
276c	With First Day of Issue, Telford special handstamp	**£4.50** ☐
276d	With Pontcysyllte Aqueduct, Llangollen, Clwyd handstamp	**£8.50** ☐
276e	With New Lanark Conservation, Lanark handstamp	**£8.50** ☐
276f	With Our Industrial Heritage, Preserved by the National Trust, St. Agnes h/s	**£8.50** ☐
276g	With Birthplace of British Industry, The Ironbridge Gorge Museum h/s	**£8.50** ☐
276h	With Isambard Kingdom Brunel, Industrial Pioneer, Bristol handstamp	**£8.50** ☐
276i	With Water Powered Mills at New Lanark, Lanark handstamp	**£8.50** ☐
276j	With Over 300 Years of Water Power, Aberdulais Falls, Neath h/s	**£8.50** ☐
276k	With Killiecrankie 1689-1989, Tercentenary, National Trust Scotland h/s	**£10.00** ☐
276l	With Bradford, or Bolton Philatelic Counter handstamp	**£18.50** ☐
276m	With any Forces/Field Post Office BFPS handstamp (2201 or other)	**£8.50** ☐
276n	With New Lanark cds, St. Agnes cds, or Ironbridge cds	**£16.00** ☐
276o	With Langholm, Dumfries or Froncysyllte cds	**£16.00** ☐
276p	With Arkwright, Newtown, or Liverton Mines cds	**£12.50** ☐
276q	With Collect British Stamps, Bradford Postshop, Bradford slogan	**£30.00** ☐
276r	With Aveling Barford (Machines) Ltd. The Earthmovers, Leicester slogan	**£26.50** ☐

A few other cds postmarks can be related to this issue. Prices from **£10**.

QEII • Commemoratives 1989

277. 1989, 25th July
Industrial Archaeology - £1.40 Miniature Sheet

277a	Miniature Sheet on illustrated cover, any postmark	**£3.00** ☐
277b	With Philatelic Bureau handstamp	**£4.00** ☐
277c	With First Day of Issue, New Lanark handstamp	**£4.50** ☐
277d	With Ironbridge, Birthplace of British Industry, Telford handstamp	**£8.50** ☐
277e	With Association for Industrial Archaeology, AIA, Ironbridge handstamp	**£8.50** ☐
277f	With Water Powered Mills at New Lanark, Lanark handstamp	**£8.50** ☐
277g	With The Pontcysyllte Aqueduct, Llangollen, Clwyd handstamp	**£8.50** ☐
277h	With Killiecrankie 1689-1989 Tercentenary, National Trust Scotland h/s	**£8.50** ☐
277i	With Our Industrial Heritage, Preserved by the National Trust, Pool h/s	**£8.50** ☐
277j	With Bradford, Bolton or Bristol Philatelic Counter handstamp	**£16.50** ☐
277k	With any Forces/Field Post Office BFPS handstamp (1968 or other)	**£10.00** ☐
277l	With New Lanark cds, St. Agnes cds, or Ironbridge cds	**£16.50** ☐
277m	With Langholm, Dumfries, or Froncysyllte cds	**£15.00** ☐
277n	With Arkwright, Newtown, or Liverton Mines cds	**£15.00** ☐
277o	With Collect British Stamps, Bradford Postshop, Bradford slogan	**£26.00** ☐
277p	With Aveling Barford (Machines) Ltd. The Earthmovers, Leicester slogan	**£30.00** ☐
	A few other cds postmarks can be related to this issue. Prices from **£10**.	
277q	**Double Dated Covers** July 4th Set and July 25th Min. Sheet, one cover, any pmk.	**£36.00** ☐

Gems • A Wonderful Unique QEII fdc Cover

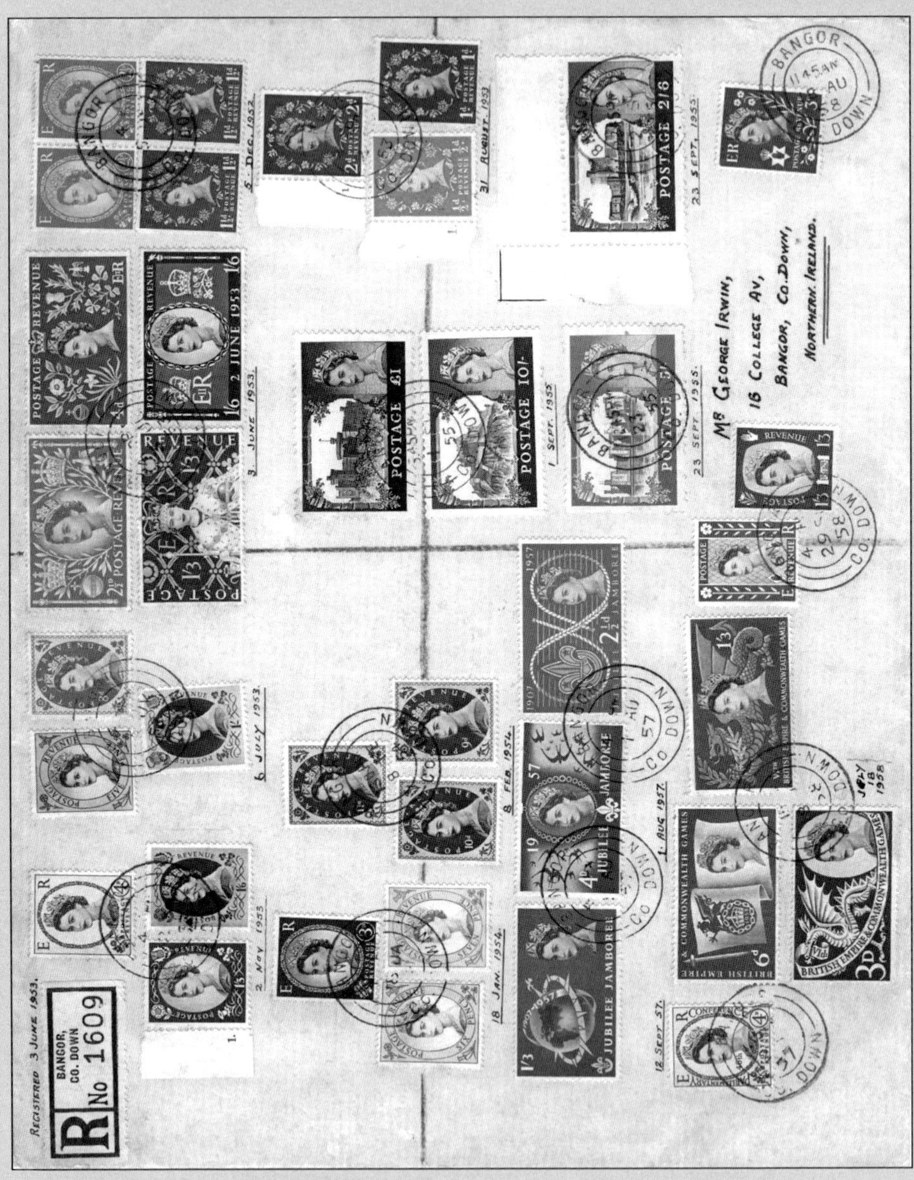

Fourteen different fdc postmarks!
Not possible to do this today...

QEII • Commemoratives 1989

278. 1989, 5th September
150th Anniversary Royal Microscopical Society
19p Snowflake, 27p Fly, 32p Blood Cells, 35p Microchip

278a	Set on illustrated cover, any postmark	**£2.50** ☐
278b	With Philatelic Bureau handstamp	**£4.00** ☐
278c	With First Day of Issue, Oxford special handstamp	**£4.50** ☐
278d	With Year of the Microscope, RMS 1839-1989, Oxford handstamp	**£8.50** ☐
278e	With Year of the Microscope Exhibition at Science Museum, London h/s	**£8.50** ☐
278f	With Cambridge Instruments, 25 Years in Scanning ... Cambridge h/s	**£9.00** ☐
278g	With Dr. Robert Hooke 1635-1703, Author Micrographia, I.O.W h/s	**£8.50** ☐
278h	With The Year of the Microscope 1989, London SW7 handstamp	**£8.50** ☐
278i	With Royal Microscopical Society, Oxford handstamp	**£8.50** ☐
278j	With IMLS 19th Triennial Conference, Warwick University handstamp	**£9.50** ☐
278k	With The Year of the Microscope, Cambridge handstamp	**£8.50** ☐
278l	With Marconi Electronic Devices, Microtechnology in Space, Lincoln h/s	**£8.50** ☐
278m	With any Forces/Field Post Office BFPS handstamp (2209 or other)	**£10.00** ☐
278n	With Oxford, Regent St. WI, or Whitechapel cds	**£12.50** ☐
278o	With South Kensington SW7, or Freshwater cds	**£12.50** ☐
278p	With Army Blood Supply Depot, 50 Years of Blood Transfusion slogan	**£25.00** ☐
278q	With Europe Against Cancer Year 1989 slogan	**£26.50** ☐

A few other cds postmarks can be related to this issue. Prices from **£10**.

ARMY BLOOD SUPPLY DEPOT
50 YEARS OF BLOOD TRANSFUSION
1939 1989

---

279. 1989, 17th October
The Lord Mayor's Show 20p Se-tenant strip of 5, Lord Mayor's Procession

279a	20p Strip on illustrated cover, any postmark	**£2.50** ☐
279b	With Philatelic Bureau handstamp (carried in Parade **£8**)	**£4.00** ☐
279c	With First Day of Issue, London EC4 handstamp	**£4.50** ☐
279d	With The Lord Mayor 800th Anniversary, City of London, London EC h/s	**£8.50** ☐
279e	With 800th Anniv. City of London Lord Mayor 1189-1989, London EC h/s	**£8.50** ☐
279f	With Dick Whittington Thrice Lord Mayor of London, London EC h/s	**£8.50** ☐
279g	With Richard Whittington's Birthplace, Pauntley, Glos handstamp	**£10.00** ☐
279h	With 800th Anniversary Lord Mayor's Show 1989, London EC handstamp	**£8.50** ☐
279i	With Autumn Stampex/BPE 1989, London SW1 handstamp	**£8.50** ☐
279j	With National Postal Museum - SWL 90, City of London EC handstamp	**£8.50** ☐
279k	With any London EC cds (EC1 - EC4)	**£12.00** ☐
279l	With Whittington, Lichfield cds	**£22.00** ☐

A few other cds postmarks can be related to this issue. Prices from **£10**.

QEII • Commemoratives 1989

280. 1989, 14th November
Christmas Issue
15p, 15+1p, 20p+1p, 34p+1p, 37p+1p, Architecture of Ely Cathedral

280a	Set on illustrated cover, any postmark	**£2.50** ☐
280b	With Philatelic Bureau handstamp	**£4.00** ☐
280c	With First Day of Issue, Bethlehem, Llandeilo handstamp	**£4.50** ☐
280d	With First Day of Issue, Ely handstamp	**£4.50** ☐
280e	With The Christmas Mailcoach Run, Cambridge - Ely Cathedral handstamp	**£8.50** ☐
280f	With Christmas 1989, Ely, Cambs handstamp	**£8.50** ☐
280g	With 800th Anniversary The Norman Nave, Ely Cambs emblem h/s	**£8.50** ☐
280h	With 800th Anniv. The Norman Nave, Ely Cambs circular handstamp	**£8.50** ☐
280i	With Christmas Greetings, HM Ships Abroad, BF2214PS handstamp	**£10.00** ☐
280j	With Christmas 1989 Gloucester handstamp	**£8.50** ☐
280k	With Thomas Invites You, Nene Valley Railway Santa Specials handstamp	**£11.00** ☐
280l	With Merry Christmas Telecom Technology Showcase, London handstamp	**£10.00** ☐
280m	With 450th Anniv. of Dissolution of Whitby Abbey, Whitby Yorks handstamp	**£11.00** ☐
280n	With Nasareth, Angel Hill, or Holy Island cds	**£15.00** ☐
280o	With Ely, Cambs cds, or Tonbridge, Kent cds	**£15.00** ☐
280p	With Walsingham, Norfolk cds or Stoke Charity, Hants cds	**£15.00** ☐
280q	With any Forces/Field Post Office BFPS handstamp (2212 or other)	**£10.00** ☐
280r	With Forty Years of Unicef cards, Belfast slogan	**£22.50** ☐
280s	With BBC Children in Need Appeal, Hull M10 slogan	**£25.00** ☐
280t	With Choose Charity Stamps, Show You Care slogan	**£26.00** ☐
280u	With Luton Carol Aid '89, Luton slogan	**£45.00** ☐

A few other cds postmarks can be related to this issue. Prices from **£15**.

For a complete listing of all sections in this catalogue, please refer to the Index on page 3.

QEII • Commemoratives 1990

Royal Mail is producing more new Stamp Issues and variations than ever before. As we see it there are several important implications in this policy for the first day cover Collector:

- Stretching the Collector's pocket financially and maybe to breaking point.
- Making it difficult for young new would-be Collectors to keep up financially
- Not helping to improve the future value of such new Issues

Short term it must be helping Royal Mail total sales value, otherwise they surely would not do it! But there is no doubt that fewer Issues would create better long term value, which is what the fdc Collector wants.

As we see it all of these frequent Stamp Issues on first day cover, with any one of the many commemorative handstamps available (all through Royal Mail), have about the same catalogue value. We have therefore decided that from 1990 onwards we will stop trying to list/describe every relevant commemorative handstamp per Issue and just indicate the number done per Issue instead - all with the same value! Royal Mail handstamps will continue to be priced separately. We will also continue to list cds, since price differences do occur for these.

This decision will contribute importantly to keeping the catalogue to a manageable size going forward. Collectors clearly need to be able to carry it comfortably and easily when going to Stamp Shows, Club Meetings, etc.

QEII • Commemoratives 1990

281. 1990, 10th January

150th Anniversary Uniform Penny Post

15p, 20p, 29p, 34p, 37p Queen Elizabeth/Queen Victoria Profile Heads

281a Set on illustrated cover, any postmark .... **£2.50** ☐
281b With First Day of Issue, Philatelic Bureau handstamp .... **£5.00** ☐
281c With First Day of Issue, Windsor handstamp .... **£5.50** ☐
281d With any one of some 12 additional relevant commemorative handstamps .... **£12.00** ☐
281e With Fleet Street or Sanquhar cds, or Windsor, Berks cds .... **£25.00** ☐
281f With Arbroath, Angus cds, or Bath, Avon cds .... **£16.50** ☐
281g With Queen Elizabeth Ave, or Queen Victoria Road cds or Kidderminster cds .... **£16.00** ☐
281h With House of Commons or House of Lords cds .... **£35.00** ☐
281i With Buckingham Palace SWI cds (Windsor Castle cds **£85**) .... **£75.00** ☐
281j On 1890 Jubilee envelope or insert card, any postmark .... **£64.00** ☐
281k With Collect British Stamps - World's Greatest Hobby slogan .... **£27.50** ☐
281l With Collect British Stamps, York, Lincoln, Bradford Philatelic Counter slogan .... **£27.50** ☐
281m With Stampway to the World slogan (various offices) .... **£85.00** ☐

A few other cds postmarks (and slogans) can be related to this issue. Prices from **£15**.

282. 1990, 23rd January

150th Anniversary RSPCA

20p Kitten, 29p Rabbit, 34p Duck, 37p Puppy

282a Set on illustrated cover, any postmark .... **£2.50** ☐
282b With First Day of Issue, Philatelic Bureau handstamp .... **£4.50** ☐
282c With First Day of Issue, Horsham handstamp .... **£5.00** ☐
282d With any one of some 6 additonal relevant commemorative handstamps .... **£11.50** ☐
282e With Battersea or Battersea Park Rd SW11 cds .... **£22.00** ☐
282f With Horsham, West Sussex cds (RSPCA HQ) .... **£16.00** ☐
282g With Bunny, Isle of Dogs, Ducklington, Catfield, or Dog Kennel Lane cds .... **£22.00** ☐

Several other pmks (mainly Dog and Cat related) are relevant to this issue. Prices from **£14**.

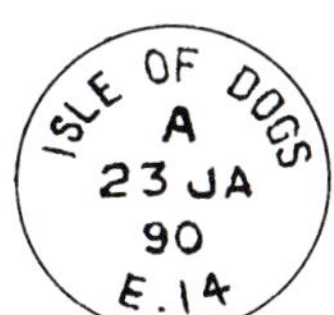

All prices in this catalogue are for clean covers, with undamaged stamps and clear postmarks.

QEII • Commemoratives 1990

283. 1990, 6th February

Greetings Stamps - Second Issue

20p x 10 Se-tenant, Featuring Famous Smiles

283a Set on illustrated cover, any postmark .... **£3.00** ☐
283b With First Day of Issue, Philatelic Bureau handstamp .... **£5.00** ☐
283c With First Day of Issue, Giggleswick, North Yorkshire handstamp .... **£5.50** ☐
283d With any one of some 4 additional relevant commemorative handstamps .... **£15.00** ☐
283e With Oxford, Ulverston, or Laughterton cds .... **£22.50** ☐
283f With Constable Road, Constable Burton, or Law cds .... **£22.50** ☐
283g With Giggleswick, Greet, or Bow St. cds .... **£22.50** ☐
283h With Catfield, Pudsey, Laurel Lane, Bearpark, or Big Top cds .... **£22.50** ☐
283i With Collect British Stamps, Lincoln slogan .... **£36.00** ☐
283j With Take A Bite Out Of Crime, Newcastle slogan .... **£36.00** ☐

A few other cds postmarks can be related to this issue. Prices from **£15**.

---

284. 1990, 6th March

Europa 1990 - Historic Buildings

20p x 2 Buildings in London and Glasgow, 29p Edinburgh, 37p Glasgow

284a Set on illustrated cover, any postmark .... **£2.50** ☐
284b With First Day of Issue, Philatelic Bureau handstamp .... **£4.00** ☐
284c With First Day of Issue, Glasgow handstamp .... **£4.50** ☐
284d With any one of some 9 additional relevant commemorative handstamps .... **£9.50** ☐
284e With Glasgow, Edinburgh, or Alexandra Park Rd cds .... **£12.50** ☐
284f With 'There's A Lot Glasgowing On In 1990', Cultural Capital of Europe .... **£25.00** ☐
284g With Collect British Stamps - World's Greatest Hobby slogan .... **£25.00** ☐
284h With Collect British Stamps, Bradford or Lincoln slogan .... **£25.00** ☐

Write to us if you have questions on Commemorative handstamps for any QEII Stamp Issue.

285. 1990, 10th April

The Queen's Awards to Industry

20p x 2 Se-tenant and 37p x 2 Se-tenant, Export and Technology Award Emblems

285a Set on illustrated cover, any postmark .... **£2.50** ☐
285b With First Day of Issue, Philatelic Bureau handstamp .... **£4.00** ☐
285c With First Day of Issue, SW London Letters District handstamp .... **£4.50** ☐
285d With any one of some 6 additional relevant commemorative handstamps .... **£10.50** ☐
285e With Tufton Street SW1 cds (Awards Office) .... **£16.00** ☐
285f With Buckingham Palace cds, or Windsor Castle cds .... **£75.00** ☐
285g With Queen Elizabeth Ave, Walsall, or New Invention cds .... **£16.00** ☐
285h With Stamp World London 90, Alexandra Palace, Bristol slogan .... **£25.00** ☐
285i With Invest in Sunderland . . . Enterprise Zone slogan .... **£25.00** ☐

A few other cds postmarks can be related to this issue. Prices from **£12**.

286. 1990, 3rd May

Penny Black Anniversary

£1 Miniature Sheet - Britannia Design, with 1990 20p + 1d Black Replica

286a	Miniature Sheet on illustrated cover, any postmark	**£2.50**	☐
286b	With First Day of Issue, Philatelic Bureau handstamp	**£4.00**	☐
286c	With First Day of Issue, City of London handstamp	**£4.50**	☐
286d	With First Day of Issue, Alexandra Palace, London N22 handstamp	**£10.00**	☐
286e	With any one of some 19 additional relevant commemorative handstamps	**£10.00**	☐
286f	With Britannia, or Kidderminster cds	**£12.50**	☐
286g	With Queen Elizabeth Ave, or Victoria Road cds	**£12.00**	☐
286h	With Alexandra Park Rd. N.10, or Wood Green N.22 cds	**£12.50**	☐
286i	With Buckingham Palace SW1 cds	**£50.00**	☐
286j	With Windsor Castle cds (Windsor cds **£55**)	**£120.00**	☐
286k	With House of Commons or House of Lords cds	**£37.50**	☐
286l	With Sanquhar, or Fleet Street EC4 cds	**£12.50**	☐
286m	With Stamp World London 90, Visit Alexandra Palace slogan	**£20.00**	☐
286n	With complete Imperforate Pane, any postmark	**£7,000.00**	☐

There are a number of other postmarks and slogan cancellations that were in use on May 3rd 1990. Many of these can be related generally to this issue. Prices vary from **£10**.
The International Stamp Exhibition London N22 cancellation at Stamp World on Opening Day was used in two different sizes - 29mm and 33mm in diameter.

287. 1990, 5th June

150th Anniversary Kew Gardens

20p, 29p, 34p, 37p, Trees and Buildings at Kew

287a	Set on illustrated cover, any postmark	**£2.50**	☐
287b	With First Day of Issue, Philatelic Bureau handstamp	**£4.00**	☐
287c	With First Day of Issue, Kew, Richmond handstamp	**£4.50**	☐
287d	With any one of some 8 additonal relevant commemorative handstamps	**£8.50**	☐
287e	With Kew Gardens MSPO cds	**£27.50**	☐
287f	With Royal Botanic Gardens Kew, Open 150 Years, Royal Mail slogan	**£46.00**	☐
287g	With Richmond, Twin Towns Celebrations 1990, Twickenham slogan	**£25.00**	☐

A number of tree type cds postmarks can be related to this issue. Prices from **£20**.

See the Introduction for a comment on Signed Covers

288. 1990, 10th July
150th Anniversary Thomas Hardy
20p Thomas Hardy Portrait

288a	20p Stamp on illustrated cover, any postmark	**£1.00**	☐
288b	With First Day of Issue, Philatelic Bureau handstamp	**£2.50**	☐
288c	With First Day of Issue, Dorchester handstamp	**£3.00**	☐
288d	With any one of some 9 additonal relevant commemorative handstamps	**£7.50**	☐
288e	With Dorchester cds	**£14.00**	☐
288f	With Puddletown cds	**£14.00**	☐
288g	With Fordington cds	**£14.00**	☐

There are other West Country postmarks that relate to Hardy's many novels. These are worth **£10** each.

289. 1990, 2nd August
90th Birthday HM The Queen Mother
20p, 29p, 34p, 37p, Portraits of The Queen Mother

289a	Set on illustrated cover, any postmark	**£2.50**	☐
289b	With First Day of Issue, Philatelic Bureau handstamp	**£4.00**	☐
289c	With First Day of Issue, City of Westminster SW1 handstamp	**£4.50**	☐
289d	With any one of some 20 additional relevant commemorative handstamps	**£10.00**	☐
289e	With Glamis, or Forfar or Mey cds,	**£20.00**	☐
289f	With Bowes, Whitwell cds	**£12.50**	☐
289g	With Windsor or Barnard Castle cds	**£12.50**	☐
289h	With Windsor Castle cds	**£125.00**	☐
289i	With Buckingham Palace SW1 cds	**£120.00**	☐
289j	With House of Commons or House of Lords cds	**£30.00**	☐
289k	With York cds, Queen Elizabeth Ave. cds, or Queens Rd cds	**£17.50**	☐

A few other cds postmarks can be related to this issue. Prices from **£12**.

Photocopies of actual covers with most postmarks listed in this catalogue, are available from the Publishers.

290. 1990, 11th September

Gallantry - 50th Anniversary of the George Cross

20p x 5, British Gallantry Medals and Crosses

290a	Set on illustrated cover, any postmark	**£2.50**
290b	With First Day of Issue, Philatelic Bureau handstamp	**£4.00**
290c	With First Day of Issue, City of Westminster SW1 handstamp	**£4.50**
290d	With any one of some 16 additional relevant commemorative handstamps	**£11.50**
290e	With St. George's Cross, Glasgow cds	**£22.00**
290f	With St. George, Bristol, or Victoria Road SW1 cds	**£20.00**
290g	With Sandhurst, Portsmouth, or any RAF station cds	**£20.00**
290h	With House of Commons or House of Lords cds	**£20.00**
290i	With Buckingham Palace SWI cds (Windsor Castle cds **£65**)	**£55.00**
290j	With Waterloo, Normandy, Battle, Biggin Hill, or Battlefield cds	**£30.00**
290k	With Churchill, Oxford/Bristol, or Dunkirk, Notts cds	**£20.00**

A few other cds postmarks can be related to this issue. Prices from **£11**.

---

291. 1990, 16th October

Centenary British Astronomical Association

22p, 26p, 31p, 37p, Man's Exploration and Understanding of Space

291a	Set on illustrated cover, any postmark	**£2.50**
291b	With First Day of Issue, Philatelic Bureau handstamp	**£4.00**
291c	With First Day of Issue, Armagh handstamp	**£4.50**
291d	With any one of some 11 additional relevant commemorative handstamps	**£10.00**
291e	With Greenwich, Cambridge, Armagh, or Macclesfield cds	**£18.00**
291f	With Albermarle St. WI, Southern Cross, or Helston cds	**£16.00**
291g	With Amesbury, Starcross, Herstmonceau, or Newton cds (Meridian cds **£18**)	**£16.00**

A few other cds postmarks can be related to this issue. Prices from **£10**.

---

292. 1990, 13th November

Christmas Issue

17p Snowman, 22p The Christmas Tree, 26p Carols, 31p Tobogganing, 37p Skating

292a	Set on illustrated cover, any postmark	**£2.50**
292b	With First Day of Issue, Philatelic Bureau handstamp	**£4.50**
292c	With First Day of Issue, Bethlehem, Llandeilo handstamp	**£5.00**
292d	With any one of some 10 additional relevant commemorative handstamps	**£10.00**
292e	With St. Nicholas, Jerusalem St. or Holy Island cds	**£17.50**

292f With Playing Place, Hollybush, Jericho, or Noel Road cds .... **£17.50** ☐
292g With Nasareth cds .... **£22.50** ☐
292h **Christmas Booklet.** 2 x 17p (Stamps with straight edge top & bottom), any postmark..**£8.00** ☐

---

293. 1991, 8th January

Dogs - Centenary Cruft's Dog Show

22p, 26p, 31p, 33p, 37p, Paintings of Dogs by George Stubbs

293a Set on illustrated cover, any postmark .... **£2.50** ☐
293b With First Day of Issue, Philatelic Bureau handstamp.. **£4.50** ☐
293c With First Day of Issue, Birmingham handstamp.. **£5.00** ☐
293d With any one of some 12 relevant commemorative handstamps .... **£10.50** ☐
293e With NEC Birmingham cds (Cruft's Dog Show).. **£20.00** ☐
293f With Isle of Dogs, Dog Kennel Lane, or Black Dog cds .... **£22.50** ☐
293g With Battersea, Battersea Park Rd, or Barking cds.. **£20.00** ☐
293h With Portman Square, Stubbs Cross, or Royal College St. cds .... **£15.00** ☐
293i With Pawprints Appeal, Tel 0782 577282, Stoke-on-Trent slogan .... **£22.50** ☐
293j With Take a Bite Out of Crime, Newcastle slogan .... **£22.50** ☐

A few other cds postmarks can be related to this issue. Prices from **£12**.

---

294. 1991, 5th February

Greetings Stamps - Third Issue

10 First Class NVI Stamps, each Featuring a Good Luck Symbol

294a Set of 10 Stamps on illustrated cover, any postmark .... **£3.00** ☐
294b With First Day of Issue, Philatelic Bureau handstamp.. **£5.00** ☐
294c With First Day of Issue, Greetwell, Lincs handstamp .... **£5.50** ☐
294d With any one of some 6 relevant commemorative handstamps .... **£12.00** ☐
294e With Luckington, Ducklington, or Swallow Nest cds .... **£18.50** ☐
294f With Greet, Star, Starcross, Bridge, or Wing cds.. **£18.50** ☐

There are a few other cds postmarks that can be related to the Good Luck Symbols in the stamps. These are worth from **£15.**

QEII • Commemoratives 1991

295. 1991, 5th March
British Scientific Achievements
22p Electricity, 22p Computer, 31p Radar, 37p Jet Engine

295a	Set on illustrated cover, any postmark	**£2.50** ☐
295b	With First Day of Issue, Philatelic Bureau handstamp	**£4.00** ☐
295c	With First Day of Issue, South Kensington, London SW1 handstamp	**£4.50** ☐
295d	With any one of some 17 relevant commemorative handstamps	**£10.50** ☐
295e	With Daventry, Cranwell, or New Invention cds	**£17.50** ☐
295f	With Albermarle Street, or Exhibition Road cds	**£17.50** ☐
295g	With Totnes, or Brechin cds (Lutterworth or Weedon cds **£22**)	**£17.50** ☐
295h	With Loughborough Univ. of Technology, 25 Anniv, Loughborough slogan	**£18.50** ☐
295i	With Philips - A Hundred Years Ahead (Various Offices) slogan	**£18.50** ☐

There are a few other cds postmarks that can be related to this issue. Prices from **£15**.

296. 1991, 26th March
Greetings Stamps - Fourth Issue
10 First Class NVI Stamps, each Featuring a Famous Smile

296a	Pane of 10 stamps on illustrated cover, any postmark	**£3.00** ☐
296b	With First Day of Issue, Philatelic Bureau handstamp	**£5.00** ☐
296c	With First Day of Issue, Laughterton, Lincs handstamp	**£5.50** ☐
296d	With any one of some 7 relevant commemorative handstamps	**£12.00** ☐
296e	With Greet, Laughterton, or Giggleswick cds	**£15.00** ☐
296f	With Clowne, Puncheston, or Ulverston cds	**£15.00** ☐
296g	With Constable Road, or Queens Head cds	**£15.00** ☐
296h	With Catsfield, Catford, or Bearpark cds	**£15.00** ☐

26 MAR 1991

Wish you were here!

Post Office History – More Early Dates

See also page 180

1902	First GPO Telephone Exchange opened
1905	Official parcel post to USA
1908	First Penny Postage to USA
1911	First official air mail (Hendon-Windsor)
1918	Penny Post letter rate abandoned!
1920	Union of Post Office Workers formed
1927	Post Office London Underground Railway Opened

QEII • Commemoratives 1991

297. 1991, 23rd April

Europe in Space (Europa)

22p and 37p each in Se-tenant Pairs. Illustrations by Folon

297a	Set on illustrated cover, any postmark	£2.50 ☐
297b	With First Day of Issue, Philatelic Bureau handstamp	£4.00 ☐
297c	With First Day of Issue, Cambridge handstamp	£4.50 ☐
297d	With any one of some 11 relevant commemorative handstamps	£10.00 ☐
297e	With Cambridge, Comberton, S. Lamberth Rd., or Greenwich cds	£12.50 ☐
297f	With Macclesfield, or Helston cds	£15.00 ☐
297g	With Star, Eye, or The Rocket cds	£17.50 ☐

298. 1991, 11th June

Sport - World Student Games, Rugby World Cup

22p Fencing, 26p Hurdling, 31p Diving, 37p Rugby

298a	Set on illustrated cover, any postmark	£2.50 ☐
298b	With First Day of Issue, Philatelic Bureau handstamp	£4.00 ☐
298c	With First Day of Issue, Rugby handstamp	£4.50 ☐
298d	With First Day of Issue, Sheffield handstamp	£4.50 ☐
298e	With any one of some 12 additional relevant commemoraative handstamps	£10.00 ☐
298f	With Twickenham, Cardiff, Murrayfield, or Rugby cds (Rugby FDI **£12**)	£18.00 ☐
298g	With Sheffield, or Birmingham cds	£18.00 ☐
298h	With Cardiff, Just Capital, Cardiff slogan	£22.50 ☐
298i	With Visit The RFU Shop at Twickenham, Twickenham slogan	£22.50 ☐
298j	With Birmingham Welcomes 97th Session of I.O.C. slogan	£20.00 ☐
298k	With Loughborough, University of Technology, 25th Anniv. slogan	£16.50 ☐

Other relevant pmks include towns where the different Events took place... **£18** each.

299. 1991, 16th July

9th World Rose Congress, Belfast

22p Hybrid Tea, 26p Climbing Rose, 31p Mountain Rose, 33p Floribunda Rose, 37p China Rose

299a	Set on illustrated cover, any postmark	**£2.50** ☐
299b	With First Day of Issue, Philatelic Bureau handstamp	**£4.00** ☐
299c	With First Day of Issue, Belfast handstamp	**£4.50** ☐
299d	With any one of some 13 relevant commemorative handstamps	**£10.00** ☐
299e	With Kew Gardens, or Glamis Forfar cds	**£25.00** ☐
299f	With Botanic Gardens, Belfast, or Rose, Truro cds	**£25.00** ☐
299g	With Rosemarket, Rosebush, or Roseland cds (Royal Hospital **£18**)	**£18.50** ☐
299h	With Chipping Campden, Rosehill or Newtonards cds	**£16.00** ☐
299i	With Beechwood Place. Shopping in Full Bloom, High St. Cheltenham slogan	**£20.00** ☐
299j	With Belfast 1991. A year and place to be proud of, Belfast slogan	**£18.50** ☐

There are several other 'Rose' postmarks that can be related to this issue. Prices from **£12**.

300. 1991, 20th August

150th Anniversary Use of the Word Dinosaur

22p Iguanodon, 26p Stegosauros, 31p Tyrannosauros, 33p Protoceratops

300a	Set on illustrated cover, any postmark	**£2.50** ☐
300b	With First Day of Issue, Philatelic Bureau handstamp	**£4.00** ☐
300c	With First Day of Issue, 150 Years ... Plymouth circular handstamp	**£4.50** ☐
300d	With any one of some 9 relevant commemorative handstamps	**£10.00** ☐
300e	With Dorchester, Cuckfield, or Maidstone cds	**£20.00** ☐
300f	With Plymouth, Owen Rd, or Exhibition Road SW7 cds	**£20.00** ☐
300g	With Ness, or The Lizard cds	**£20.00** ☐

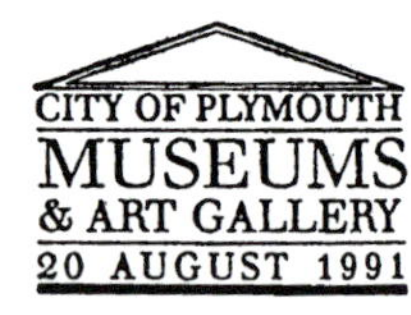

All QEII Definitives, Dues, Regionals, Booklets, Coils, Graphites and variations in Phosphors, Watermarks, Perfs, Gum Types, Papers, etc. are in one comprehensive section, in chronological order, starting on page 350.

QEII • Commemoratives 1991

301. 1991, 17th September

Maps - Bicentenary of the Ordnance Survey

24p, 28p, 33p, 39p, Hamstreet in 1816, 1906, 1959, 1991 respectively

301a	Set on illustrated cover, any postmark	£2.50 ☐
301b	With First Day of Issue, Philatelic Bureau handstamp	£4.00 ☐
301c	With First Day of Issue, SU 14 38, Southampton handstamp	£4.50 ☐
301d	With amy one of some 13 relevant commemorative handstamps	£10.00 ☐
301e	With Maybush, Southampton, or Seething Lane, London cds	£15.00 ☐
301f	With Hamstreet, Kent or Pathfinder Village cds	£20.00 ☐
301g	With House of Commons or House of Lords SW1 cds	£25.00 ☐
301h	With John O'Groats, Land's End, or Ordnance Rd cds	£25.00 ☐

A few other cds postmarks can be related to this issue. Prices from **£14**.

---

302. 1991, 12th November

Christmas Issue

18p, 24p, 28p, 33p, 39p, From Manuscript in Bodleian Library, Oxford

302a	Set on illustrated cover, any postmark	£2.50 ☐
302b	With First Day of Issue, Philatelic Bureau handstamp	£4.00 ☐
302c	With First Day of Issue, Bethlehem, Llandeilo handstamp	£4.50 ☐
302d	With any one of some 13 relevant commemorative handstamps	£10.00 ☐
302e	With Jerusalem Street, Rhymney cds	£14.00 ☐
302f	With Nasareth or St. Nicholas cds	£17.50 ☐
302g	With Angel Hill, or Holy Island cds	£17.50 ☐
302h	With Exeter or Oxford cds	£16.00 ☐
302i	**Christmas Booklet:** 18p vertical pair with margin top and bottom, any pmk	£8.00 ☐

A few other cds postmarks can be related to this issue. Prices from **£14**.

Please read the notes
at the beginning of this catalogue
for general background information.

303. 1992, 14th January

Wintertime

18p Deer, 24p Hare, 28p Fox, 33p Redwing Thrush, 39p Welsh Sheep

303a Set on illustrated cover, any postmark .... £3.00 ☐
303b With First Day Issue, Philatelic Bureau handstamp .... **£4.50** ☐
303c With First Day of Issue, Brecon handstamp .... **£5.00** ☐
303d With First Day of Issue, Europe '92, City of London handstamp .... **£5.00** ☐
303e With any one of some 11 additional relevant commemorative handstamps .... **£12.00** ☐
303f With Birds Edge or Wing cds .... **£18.00** ☐
303g With Foxhole, or Fox Lane, or Foxton cds .... **£18.00** ☐
303h With Sheepridge or Brecon cds .... **£18.00** ☐
303i With Haresfield or Harewood cds .... **£18.00** ☐
303j With Deerpark, or Old Deer cds .... **£18.00** ☐
303k With Forest Row, East Sussex, or Winter Road cds .... **£18.00** ☐
303l With Sheepscombe cds .... **£28.00** ☐

There are a few other cds postmarks that can be related to this issue. Prices from **£14**.

---

304. 1992, 28th January

Greetings Stamps - Fifth Issue

10 x 1st Class NVI Stamps on the theme of Memories

304a Pane of 10 Stamps on illustrated cover, any postmark .... **£3.00** ☐
304b With First Day of Issue, Philatelic Bureau handstamp .... **£5.00** ☐
304c With First Day of Issue, Whimsey, Gloucestershire handstamp .... **£5.50** ☐
304d With any one of some 7 additional relevant commemorative handstamps .... **£10.00** ☐
304e With Kings Road, or Portobello Road cds .... **£15.00** ☐
304f With Greet, Birmingham, or Lover, Salisbury cds .... **£15.00** ☐
304g With Keyworth, Rose, Letter, Bala, or Seaside cds .... **£15.00** ☐

There are a few other cds postmarks that can be related to this issue and these are worth **£12**.

---

305. 1992, 6th February

40th Anniversary of the Queen's Accession

24p x 5 Se-tenant, Different Portraits of the Queen

305a Se-tenant Strip on illustrated cover, any postmark .... **£2.50** ☐
305b With First Day of Issue, Philatelic Bureau handstamp .... **£4.00** ☐
305c With First Day of Issue, Buckingham Palace, 40th, London SW1 h/s .... **£4.50** ☐
305d With First Day of Issue, City of London EC handstamp .... **£4.50** ☐
305e With any one of some 18 additional relevant commemorative handstamps .... **£10.00** ☐

305f With Buckingham Palace SW cds .... **£125.00** ☐
305g With Windsor Castle cds (Sandringham cds **£140**) .... **£130.00** ☐
305h With Windsor, Windsor Great Park cds (Scone cds **£15**) .... **£17.50** ☐
305i With Heathrow, Canterbury, Catterick, or Aldershot cds .... **£17.50** ☐
305j With House of Commons or House of Lords SW1 cds .... **£25.00** ☐
305k With Queen Elizabeth Ave, Walsall cds .... **£17.50** ☐

A few other cds postmarks relate to this important stamp issue. Prices from **£15**.

---

306. 1992, 10th March

Centenary of Alfred, Lord Tennyson

24p, 28p, 33p, 39p Tennyson and Characters from his Poems

306a Set on illustrated cover, any postmark .... **£2.50** ☐
306b With First Day of Issue, Philatelic Bureau handstamp .... **£4.00** ☐
306c With First Day of Issue, Isle of Wight handstamp .... **£4.50** ☐
306d With any one of some 11 relevant commemorative handstamps .... **£10.00** ☐
306e With Tintagel, Tetford, or Winchester cds .... **£15.00** ☐
306f With Haslemere, or Freshwater cds .... **£15.00** ☐
306g With House of Lords SW1 cds .... **£38.00** ☐
306h With Tennyson Road, or Tennyson Ave cds .... **£18.00** ☐

307. 1992, 7th April

Europa Issue

24p Columbus, 24p Olympics, 24p Para Olympics, 39p Operation Raleigh, 39p Expo '92

307a Set on illustrated cover, any postmark .... **£2.50** ☐
307b With First Day of Issue, Philatelic Bureau handstamp (CEPT logo) .... **£4.00** ☐
307c With First Day of Issue, Liverpool handstamp .... **£4.50** ☐
307d With any one of some 12 additional relevant commemorative handstamps .... **£10.00** ☐
307e With Maritime Mail, London I.S., large cds .... **£18.50** ☐
307f With Croydon, or Wandsworth cds .... **£15.00** ☐
307g With Chelsea, Stoke Mandeville, or Liverpool cds .... **£15.00** ☐
307h With New York, Boston, Raleigh, or Westward Ho! cds .... **£15.00** ☐

A few other cds postmarks can be related to this issue. Prices from **£12.**

308. 1992, 16th June

350th Anniversary Battle of Edgehill

24p Civil War Pikeman, 28p Drummer, 33p Musketeer, 39p Standard Bearer

308a Set on illustrated cover, any postmark .... **£2.50** ☐
308b With First Day of Issue, Philatelic Bureau handstamp .... **£4.00** ☐
308c With First Day of Issue, Banbury, Oxfordshire handstamp .... **£4.50** ☐
308d With any one of some 16 additional relevant commemorative handstamps .... **£10.00** ☐
308e With Hull, Huntingdon, Castle Blvd, Battle, or Southwell cds .... **£20.00** ☐
308f With House of Commons or House of Lords SW1 cds .... **£30.00** ☐
308g With Buckingham Palace SW1 cds .... **£35.00** ☐
308h With Naseby, Marston, Worcester, Edgehill, or Battlehill Portadown cds .... **£20.00** ☐
308i With Hull Festival 1992, Hull MLO slogan cancel .... **£22.50** ☐
308j With The Storming of Preston, Battle and Pageant, Preston slogan .... **£28.00** ☐

Philatelic Gems!

A number of first day cover Philatelic Gems are illustrated throughout the catalogue, starting with:

Inside covers, pages 40, 44, 78, 84, 93, 104, 184, 223, 231 and 363.

QEII • Commemoratives 1992

309. 1992, 21st July

150th Anniversary Sir Arthur Sullivan

18p, 24p, 33p, 39p, Scenes from Gilbert & Sullivan Comic Operettas

309a	Set on illustrated cover, any postmark	**£2.50** ☐
309b	With First Day of Issue, Philatelic Bureau handstamp	**£4.00** ☐
309c	With First Day of Issue, D'Oyly Carte, Birmingham handstamp	**£4.50** ☐
309d	With any one of some 19 additional relevant commemorative handstamps	**£11.00** ☐
309e	With Penzance, Paignton, or Birmingham cds	**£18.00** ☐
309f	With London I.S. Maritime Mail, large cds, or machine cancel	**£18.00** ☐
309g	With West End, Co. Antrim cds, or Tempo, Co Fermanagh cds	**£18.00** ☐
309h	With House of Commons or House of Lords cds	**£26.00** ☐

There are a few other cds postmarks that relate to this issue. Prices from **£12**.

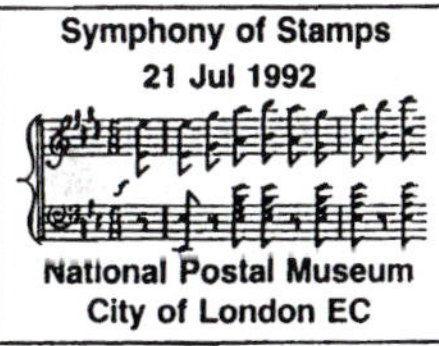

310. 1992, 15th September

The Green Issue

24p Acid Rain, 28p Ozone Layer, 33p Greenhouse Effect, 39p Bird of Hope

310a	Set on illustrated cover, any postmark	**£2.50** ☐
310b	With First Day of Issue, Philatelic Bureau handstamp	**£4.00** ☐
310c	With First Day of Issue, Torridon handstamp	**£4.50** ☐
310d	With any one of some 22 additional relevant commemorative handstamps	**£10.00** ☐
310e	With Balham, Islington or Glasshouses York cds	**£16.50** ☐
310f	With Forest Green, The Green, Hopes Green, or Greenside cds	**£16.50** ☐
310g	With Kew Gardens cds, or Green Island, Co. Antrim cds	**£20.00** ☐
310h	With House of Commons or House of Lords cds	**£20.00** ☐
310i	With Rainhill, Sunnyside, Globe Road, or World's End cds	**£15.00** ☐
310j	With Leicester, Britain's First Environment City, Leicester slogan	**£20.00** ☐
310k	With Skegness is So Bracing, Skegness slogan cancel	**£20.00** ☐

There are a few more cds postmarks that relate to this issue. Prices form **£15**.

Remember, most modern *hand addressed* covers are worth no more than 20% of catalogue prices.

220c

239b

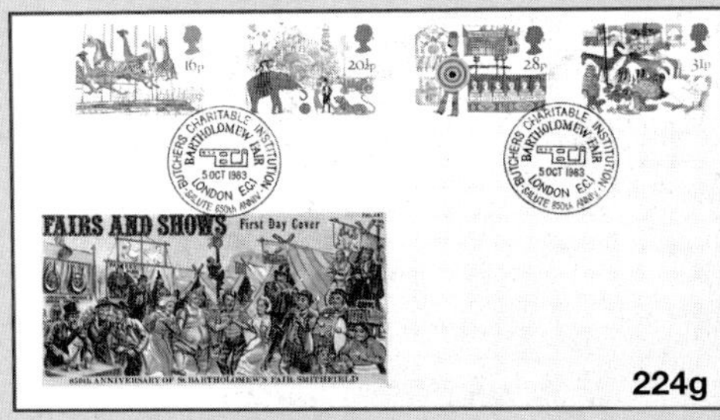

224g

245k

226c

251e

231c

257b

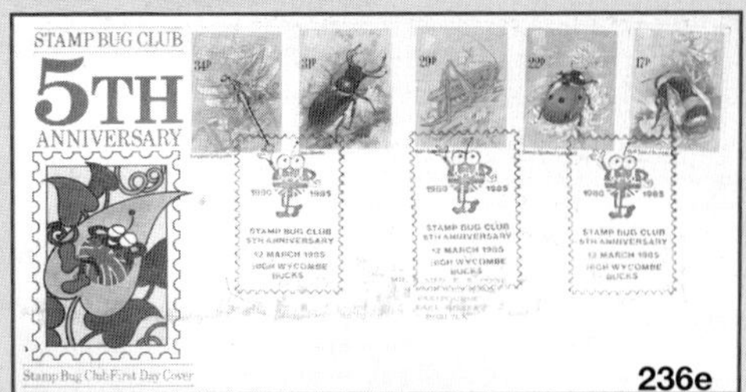

236e

259b

266

286

267

300

277

298

271

308

287

309

QEII • Commemoratives 1992

311. 1992, 13th October
Single European Market
24p Artist's Interpretation of a Star

311a 24p Stamp on illustrated cover, any postmark .... **£1.00** ☐
311b With First Day of Issue, Philatelic Bureau handstamp .... **£3.00** ☐
311c With First Day of Issue, Westminster handstamp .... **£4.00** ☐
311d With First Day of Issue, Europe '92, City of London handstamp .... **£4.00** ☐
311e With any one of some 8 additonal relevant commemorative handstamps .... **£8.00** ☐
311f With House of Commons, or House of Lords cds .... **£20.00** ☐
311g With Parliament St., London SW1, or Birmingham cds .... **£15.00** ☐
311h With Dover, Folkestone, Newmarket, or Calais cds .... **£15.00** ☐

There are a few more cds postmarks that relate to this issue. Prices from **£15**.

312. 1992, 10th November
Christmas Issue
18p, 24p, 28p, 33p, 39p, Stained Glass Scenes of The Nativity

312a Set on illustrated cover, any postmark .... **£2.50** ☐
312b With First Day of Issue, Philatelic Bureau handstamp .... **£4.00** ☐
312c With First Day of Issue, Pangbourne handstamp .... **£4.50** ☐
312d With any one of some 23 additional relevant commemorative handstamps .... **£11.00** ☐
312e With Holy Island, Nasareth, or St. Nicholas cds .... **£15.00** ☐
312f With Star, Starcross, Hollybush, or Noel Road cds .... **£15.00** ☐
312g With Pangbourne, Bibury, Porthcawl or Leatherhead cds .... **£15.00** ☐
312h With Church, St. Mary's, Ely, or Canterbury cds .... **£15.00** ☐
312i With Happy Christmas ... Inverness, or Wick slogan cancel .... **£30.00** ☐
312j With Leeds Lights Up, 9 Miles of Illuminations slogan .... **£25.00** ☐
312k With "Jesus is Alive" Manchester slogan .... **£180.00** ☐
312l **Christmas Booklet** 18p x 2 on display cover, any of above handstamps .... **£6.00** ☐

Write to us if you have questions on Commemorative handstamps for any QEII Stamp Issue.

QEII • Commemoratives 1993

313. 1993, 19th January

600th Anniversary of Abbotsbury Swannery

18p Mute Swan, 24p Cygnet, 28p Pair of Swans, 33p Swan's Nest, 39p Mute Swan

313a Set on illustrated cover, any postmark .... **£2.50** ☐
313b With First Day of Issue, Philatelic Bureau handstamp .... **£4.00** ☐
313c With First Day of Issue, Abbotsbury, Dorset handstamp .... **£4.50** ☐
313d With First Day of Issue, London handstamp (swan design) .... **£4.50** ☐
313e With any one of some 16 additional relevant commemorative handstamps .... **£11.00** ☐
313f With Action for Birds, Bedford slogan .... **£25.00** ☐
313g With Abbotsbury, Egham, Sandy, Slimbridge, or Comber cds .... **£25.00** ☐
313h With Swanpool, Swanland, Old Swan, Thetford, or Waterside cds .... **£25.00** ☐

There are a few other cds postmarks that can be related to this issue. Prices from **£15**.

314. 1993, 2nd February

Greetings Stamps - Sixth Issue

10 x 1st Class NVI Stamps, Characters from Children's Books

314a Pane of 10 Stamps on illustrated cover, any postmark .... **£3.00** ☐
314b With First Day of Issue, Philatelic Bureau handstamp .... **£5.00** ☐
314c With First Day of Issue, Greetland handstamp .... **£5.50** ☐
314d With First Day of Issue, London handstamp (hooter/horn) .... **£5.50** ☐
314e With any one of some 10 additional relevant commemorative handstamps .... **£11.00** ☐
314f With Greet, Oxford, Far Sawrey, or Rupert St. cds .... **£16.50** ☐
314g With Brighten Your Mail, Use Colourful Greetings Stamps slogan .... **£25.00** ☐
314h With Cumbria Will Work For You, Carlisle slogan .... **£18.00** ☐

A few other cds postmarks can be related to this issue. Prices from **£12**.

This is the 30th Edition of the Collect GB First Day Covers catalogue

We hope that you are enjoying it and find it useful in developing your own collection. Don't forget that we now include sections on Overprints, Pre-release covers and Missing Colours. These can all be found in the last part of the catalogue.

QEII • Commemoratives 1993

315. 1993, 16th February

Marine Timekeepers

24p, 28p, 33p, 39p, John Harrison's No.4 Chronometer

315a Set on illustrated cover, any postmark .... **£2.50** ☐
315b With First Day of Issue, Philatelic Bureau handstamp .... **£4.00** ☐
315c With First Day of Issue, Greenwich handstamp .... **£4.50** ☐
315d With First Day of Issue, John Harrison 1693-1776, London handstamp .... **£4.50** ☐
315e With any one of some 14 additional relevant commemorative handstamps .... **£10.00** ☐
315f With New Crofton, New Invention, or Hampstead cds .... **£12.00** ☐
315g With Quarterdeck, Chart, or Clock House cds .... **£15.00** ☐
315h With Greenwich, Marine Parade, or Clock Face cds .... **£17.50** ☐
315i With Maritime Mail, London machine cancel, plus handstamp .... **£25.00** ☐
315j With Meridian Centre, Newhaven Sussex cds .... **£42.00** ☐
315k With Swatch, Swatch the World slogan .... **£240.00** ☐

A few other cds postmarks can be related to this issue. Prices from **£12**.

---

316. 1993, 16th March

14th World Orchid Conference

18p, 24p, 28p, 33p, 39p. Illustrations of Five Different Orchids

316a Set on illustrated cover, any postmark .... **£2.50** ☐
316b With First Day of Issue, Philatelic Bureau handstamp .... **£4.00** ☐
316c With First Day of Issue, Glasgow handstamp .... **£4.50** ☐
316d With First Day of Issue, London handstamp (Orchids) .... **£4.50** ☐
316e With any one of some 12 additional relevant commemorative handstamps .... **£12.00** ☐
316f With Kew Gardens, Botanic Gardens (Belfast or Ripley) cds .... **£25.00** ☐
316g With Royal Hospital, Chelsea cds, or Flore, Northants cds .... **£20.00** ☐
316h With Sandyford or Glasgow, Glasshouses or Bloomfield cds .... **£20.00** ☐
316i With Marie Curie Daffodil Day ... slogan (various offices) .... **£16.00** ☐
316j 33p stamp with the year 1993 omitted, any postmark .... **£40.00** ☐

All prices in this catalogue are for clean covers, with undamaged stamps and clear postmarks.

QEII • Commemoratives 1993

317. 1993, 11th May

Art in the 20th Century (Europa)

24p Moore, 28p Bawden, 33p Spencer, 39p Nicholson

317a	Set on illustrated cover, any postmark	£2.00 ☐
317b	With First Day of Issue, Philatelic Bureau handstamp	£3.50 ☐
317c	With First Day of Issue, London SW handstamp	£4.00 ☐
317d	With First Day of Issue, London handstamp (sculpture)	£4.00 ☐
317e	With any one of some 11 additional relevant commemorative handstamps	£9.00 ☐
317f	With Castleford, Cookham, Braintree, or Denham Green cds	£12.00 ☐
317g	With Much Hadham, Trafalgar Sq., Tufton St., or Pembroke St. cds	£12.00 ☐
317h	With Albermarle St, or Moore cds	£15.00 ☐
317i	With Kew Gardens cds	£20.00 ☐
317j	With Royal Mail Supports The Arts is Magic Festival, Glasgow slogan	£25.00 ☐
317k	With Barnes Cray School Arts Week, May 17-21, Dartford slogan	£25.00 ☐

There are a few other cds postmarks that can be related to this issue. Prices from **£9**.

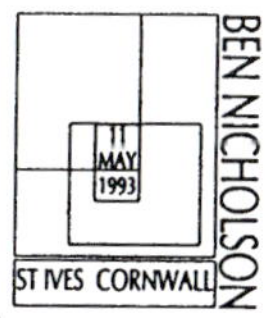

318. 1993, 15th June

Roman Britain - 1950th Anniversary

24p Claudius, 28p Hadrian, 33p Roma, 39p Christ

318a	Set on illustrated cover, any postmark	£2.00 ☐
318b	With First Day of Issue, Philatelic Bureau handstamp	£3.50 ☐
318c	With First Day of Issue, Dydd Cyhoeddi Cyntaf, Caerllion handstamp	£4.00 ☐
318d	With First Day of Issue, London handstamp (columns)	£4.00 ☐
318e	With any one of some 17 additional relevant commemorative handstamps	£10.00 ☐
318f	With Roman Road, or Occupation Rd cds (Roman Way cds **£25**)	£14.00 ☐
318g	With Camp, Villa Rd, Wallsend, Garrison, or The Forum cds	£14.00 ☐
318h	With North/East/South/West Gate cds	£14.00 ☐
318i	With Fort Augustus, Watling St, or Wall Hexham cds	£14.00 ☐
318j	With Colchester, Sandwich, or Heddon-on-the-Wall cds	£15.00 ☐
318k	With Bredgar, Caerleon, or Southampton Row cds	£15.00 ☐
318l	With Britannia, Ermine, Fishbourne, or York cds	£15.00 ☐
318m	With Christian Aid Week, May 17-22 slogan	£36.00 ☐

All QEII Definitives are listed in chronological order from page 350.

319. 1993, 20th July

Inland Waterways Bicentenary

24p Narrow Boats, 28p Humber Keels, 33p Horse-Drawn Boats, 39p Fishing & Puffer Boats

319a Set on illustrated cover, any postmark .... **£2.00** ☐

319b With First Day of Issue, Philatelic Bureau handstamp .... **£3.50** ☐

319c With First Day of Issue, Gloucester handstamp .... **£4.00** ☐

319d With First Day of Issue, London handstamp (barge) .... **£4.00** ☐

319e With any one of some 15 additional relevant commemorative handstamps .... **£10.00** ☐

319f With Locks Bottom, or Locks Lane cds .... **£17.50** ☐

319g With Keadby, Brecon, Ardrishaig, Braunston, or Brentford cds .... **£17.50** ☐

319h With Stainforth, Abergavenny, or Bellanoch cds .... **£17.50** ☐

319i With Ellesmere Port cds (Inland Waterways Museum) .... **£17.50** ☐

319j With House of Commons or House of Lords cds .... **£32.00** ☐

320. 1993, 14th September

Autumn Season 18p, 24p, 28p, 33p, 39p. Seasonal Fruits.

320a Set on illustrated cover, any postmark .... **£2.50** ☐

320b With First Day of Issue, Philatelic Bureau handstamp .... **£4.00** ☐

320c With First Day of Issue, Taunton handstamp .... **£4.50** ☐

320d With First Day of Issue, London handstamp (acorns) .... **£4.50** ☐

320e With any one of some 8 additional relevant commemorative handstamps .... **£10.00** ☐

320f With Kew Gardens cds .... **£25.00** ☐

320g With The Orchards, Pear Tree, or Mountain Ash cds .... **£20.00** ☐

320h With Chestnut Grove, Chestnut Terrace, or Berry Hill cds .... **£20.00** ☐

320i With Hazel Grove, Rowanburn, or Woodlands cds .... **£20.00** ☐

A few other cds postmarks can be related to this issue. Prices from **£15**.

321. 1993, 12th October

Sherlock Holmes Centenary

24p x 5 Se-tenant. Scenes from Five Sherlock Holmes Stories.

321a Se-tenant strip on illustrated cover, any postmark .... **£2.50** ☐

321b With First Day of Issue, Philatelic Bureau handstamp .... **£4.00** ☐

321c With First Day of Issue, 221B Baker St, London NW1 handstamp .... **£4.50** ☐

321d With First Day of Issue, Autumn Stampex, London SW1 handstamp .... **£4.50** ☐

321e With any one of some 19 additional relevant commemorative handstamps .... **£12.50** ☐

321f With Crowborough, South Norwood, or Baker Street cds .... **£30.00** ☐

321g With Holmes Chapel, Crook, Minstead and Beckenham cds .... **£30.00** ☐

QEII • Commemoratives 1993

321h With Post Office Investigation Dept, 200 Years of Service slogan .... £30.00 ☐
321i With Autumn Stampex, RH Halls, London SW1 slogan .... £27.50 ☐
321j With Please control your dog slogan .... £45.00 ☐
There are a few other cds postmarks that can be related to this issue. Prices from **£20**.

---

322. 1993, 9th November

Christmas Issue - 150th Anniversary Dickens Christmas Carol

19p, 25p, 30p, 35p, 41p. Characters from A Christmas Carol

322a Set on illustrated cover, any postmark .... £2.50 ☐
322b With First Day of Issue, Philatelic Bureau handstamp .... £4.00 ☐
322c With First Day of Issue, Bethlehem, Llandeilo handstamp .... £4.50 ☐
322d With First Day of Issue, City of London handstamp (hat) .... £4.50 ☐
322e With First Day of Issue, London handstamp (cracker) .... £4.50 ☐
322f With any one of some 20 additional relevant commemorative handstamps .... £10.00 ☐
322g With Broadstairs, Gads Hill, Rochester, or Portsmouth cds .... £16.50 ☐
322h With St.Nicholas, Nasareth or Holy Island cds .... £16.50 ☐
322i With Do your Christmas Shopping at Rainbow Stores slogan cancel .... £22.00 ☐
322j **Christmas Booklets** 19p or 25p x 2 on display cover, any postmark .... £6.00 ☐

For a complete listing of all sections in this catalogue, please refer to the Index on page 3.

323. 1994, 18th January

The Age of Steam –1825 to 1968

19p, 25p, 30p, 35p, 41p, Steam Engines of the 1960's

323a	Set on illustrated cover, any postmark	£2.50 ☐
323b	With First Day of Issue, Philatelic Bureau handstamp	£4.00 ☐
323c	With First Day of Issue, York handstamp	£4.50 ☐
323d	With First Day of Issue, Bridge of Orchy, Dalmally handstamp	£4.50 ☐
323e	With First Day of Issue, London handstamp (railway signal)	£4.50 ☐
323f	With any one of some 22 additional relevant commemorative handstamps	£12.00 ☐
323g	With The Rocket, Stephenson Sq, or Rainhill cds.	£18.50 ☐
323h	With Kings Cross, Euston Centre, or Paddington cds	£18.50 ☐
323i	With Carnforth, Didcot, Saltash, or Mallaig cds.	£18.50 ☐
323j	With any Railway Station postmark or T.P.O. cds	£20.00 ☐
323k	With Derby, Swindon, Quainton, or Bright St. cds	£15.00 ☐
323l	With British Philatelic Bulletin...slogan cancel	£15.00 ☐

324. 1994, 1st February

Greetings Stamps - Seventh Issue

10 x 1st Class NVI Stamps on the theme of Messages

324a	Pane of 10 Stamps on illustrated cover, any postmark	£3.00 ☐
324b	With First Day of Issue, Philatelic Bureau handstamp	£4.50 ☐
324c	With First Day of Issue, Penn, Wolverhampton handstamp	£5.00 ☐
324d	With First Day of Issue, London (pigeon) handstamp	£5.00 ☐
324e	With amy one of some 10 additional relevant commemorative handstamps	£12.00 ☐
324f	With Rupert Street, Bearsden, Paddington, or Biggleswade cds	£18.00 ☐
324g	With Catshill, Bunny, Eagle or Bearpark cds	£18.00 ☐
324h	With Letter, Penn, Oxford, or Greet cds	£18.00 ☐
324i	With Write Now, Say it Better in a Letter slogan cancel	£25.00 ☐

325. 1994, 1st March

25th Anniversary Investiture of the Prince of Wales

19p, 25p, 30p, 35p, 41p, Paintings by Prince Charles

325a	Set on illustrated cover, any postmark	£2.50 ☐
325b	With First Day of Issue, Philatelic Bureau handstamp	£4.00 ☐
325c	With First Day of Issue, Caernarfon bi-lingual handstamp	£4.50 ☐
325d	With First Day of Issue, London handstamp (ensign)	£4.50 ☐
325e	With any one of some 18 additional relevant commemorative handstamps	£10.50 ☐
325f	With Buckingham Palace SWI cds	£75.00 ☐
325g	With Windsor Castle cds	£80.00 ☐
325h	With House of Commons or House of Lords SWI cds	£25.00 ☐
325i	With Windsor, Caernarfon, or Nettleham cds	£16.00 ☐
325j	With Tetbury, Wales, St. David's Road, or St David's cds	£16.00 ☐

325k With Prince Charles Avenue, Mount Charles, or Princeville cds .... **£16.00** ☐
325l With Le Shuttle, 35 mins Folkestone to Calais slogan .... **£20.00** ☐

A few other cds postmarks can be related to this issue. Prices from **£12**.

326. 1994, 12th April

Centenary of the Pictorial Postcard

19p, 25p, 30p, 35p, 41p, Comic Seaside Postcard Designs

326a Set on illustrated cover, any postmark .... **£2.50** ☐
326b With First Day of Issue, Philatelic Bureau handstamp .... **£4.00** ☐
326c With First Day of Issue, Blackpool handstamp .... **£4.50** ☐
326d With First Day of Issue, London handstamp (Tower Bridge) .... **£4.50** ☐
326e With any one of some 8 additional relevant commemorative handstamps .... **£11.00** ☐
326f With Sands, Sandy, The Pier, or Beach cds .... **£17.50** ☐
326g With Broadbottom, Holmfirth, or North or South Shore Blackpool cds .... **£17.50** ☐
326h With Giggleswick, Crab Lane, Greet, or Puncheston cds .... **£14.00** ☐
326p With Seaside, Seaview, Pratts Bottom, or Tower Hill cds .... **£20.00** ☐
326j With Broadstairs, Scarborough, Brighton, or Southend cds .... **£17.50** ☐

A few other cds postmarks can be related to this issue. Prices from **£12**.

327. 1994, 3rd May

Official Opening of the Channel Tunnel

25p and 41p pairs, Lion and Cockrel Extending Hands

327a Set on illustrated cover, any postmark .... **£2.50** ☐
327b With First Day of Issue, Philatelic Bureau handstamp .... **£4.00** ☐
327c With First Day of Issue, Folkestone handstamp (coastline/tunnel) .... **£4.50** ☐
327d With First Day of Issue, Folkestone handstamp (Big Ben/Eiffel Tower) .... **£4.50** ☐
327e With First Day of Issue, London handstamp (tunnel) .... **£4.50** ☐
327f With any one of some 17 additional relevant commemorative handstamps .... **£11.00** ☐
327g With The Link, Terminus Rd, Cheriton, or Folkestone cds .... **£16.50** ☐
327h With Kings Cross, Waterloo, or Ashford cds .... **£16.50** ☐
327i With Calais Rd, French St, or Undercliff cds .... **£16.50** ☐
327j With le Shuttle, 35 Minutes Folkestone to Calais slogan .... **£18.00** ☐

A few other cds postmarks can be related to this issue. Prices from **£12**.

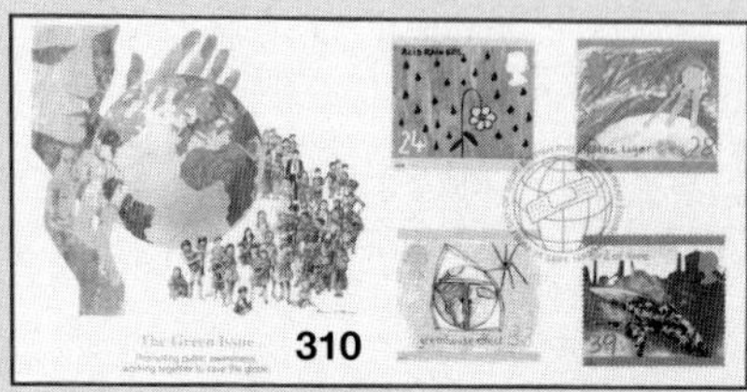
The Green Issue
310

13th October 1992
THE SINGLE MARKET
WESTMINSTER LONDON SW1
311

BETHLEHEM
DYFED
312

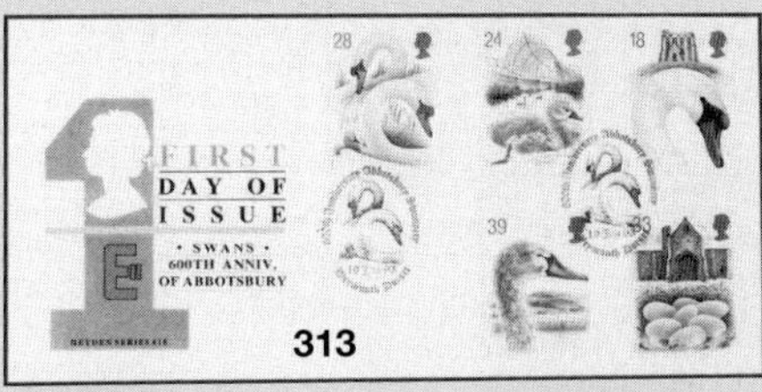
FIRST
DAY OF
ISSUE
• SWANS •
600TH ANNIV.
OF ABBOTSBURY
313

First Day Cover
314

John Harrison
PLYMOUTH DEVON
MARINE TIMEKEEPERS
315

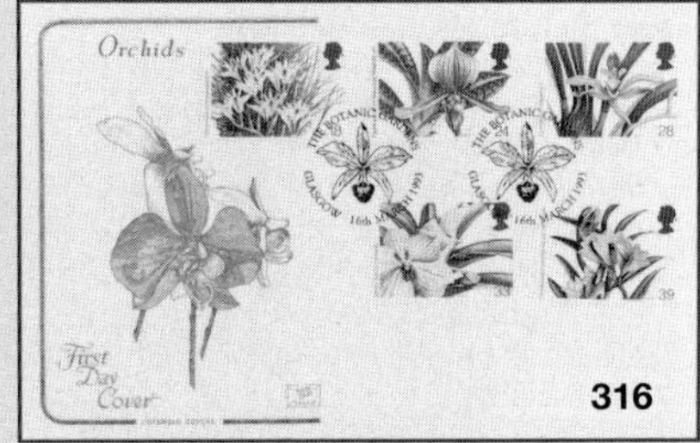
Orchids
First Day Cover
316

Art in the 20th Century
317

318

The Grand Union Canal
319

The Age of Steam
The Northumbrian engine 1830
323

Summer Green Turning Brown
Autumn Leaves Falling Down
320

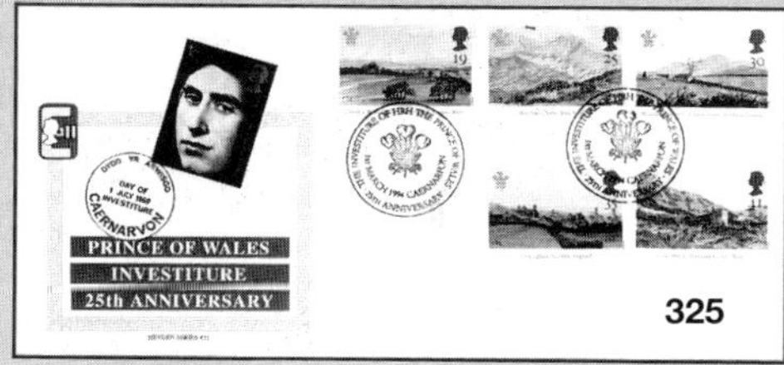

325

Sherlock Holmes Anniversary
321

Blackpool Tower Centenary
326

A Christmas Carol
Bob Cratchit and Tiny Tim
322

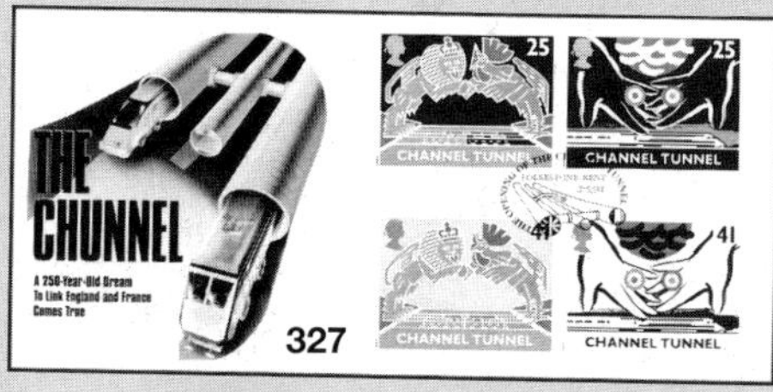

327

GREETINGS from RUPERT
324

328

328. 1994, 6th June
50th Anniversary of D-Day
25p x 5 Se-tenant, Scenes from D-Day Landings

328a	Se-tenant strip on illustrated cover, any postmark	**£2.50** ☐
328b	With First Day of Issue, Philatelic Bureau handstamp	**£4.00** ☐
328c	With First Day of Issue, Portsmouth handstamp	**£4.50** ☐
328d	With First Day of Issue, London handstamp (Spitfire)	**£4.50** ☐
328e	With any one of some 32 additional relevant commemorative handstamps	**£11.00** ☐
328f	With Bulford Barracks, Salisbury cds	**£17.50** ☐
328g	With Normandy, Battle, or Victory Street cds	**£20.00** ☐
328h	With Churchill, Montgomery, or Trenchard Lines cds	**£20.00** ☐
328i	With any RAF Station postmark	**£17.50** ☐
328j	With Battlefield, Portsmouth, Southampton, or Boston cds	**£15.00** ☐
328k	With House of Commons or House of Lords SW1 cds	**£35.00** ☐
328l	With European Parliament Elections... London SW1 slogan	**£18.00** ☐

A few other cds postmarks can be related to this issue. Prices from **£15**.

329. 1994, 5th July
250th Anniversary of the First Golf Tournament
19p, 25p, 30p, 35p, 41p, Famous Scottish Golf Courses

329a	Set on illustrated cover, any postmark	**£2.50** ☐
329b	With First Day of Issue, Philatelic Bureau handstamp	**£4.50** ☐
329c	With First Day of Issue, Turnberry handstamp	**£5.00** ☐
329d	With First Day of Issue, London handstamp (Golfers)	**£5.00** ☐
329e	With any one of some 15 additional relevant commerative handstamps	**£12.50** ☐
329f	With St. Andrews, Turnberry, Gullane, or Troon, Carnoustie cds	**£35.00** ☐
329g	With Leith, Ballybogy, or any Club cds	**£32.00** ☐
329h	With The Green, The Links, Fairway, or Golf Road cds	**£32.00** ☐
329i	With Par, Gleneagle Hotel, Eagle cds (Caddy cds **£150**)	**£38.00** ☐
329j	With Edinburgh or Glasgow cds	**£15.00** ☐

A few other cds postmarks can be related to this issue. Prices from **£15.**

This is the 30th Edition of the

330. 1994, 2nd August
Summertime
19p Welsh Show, 25p Wimbledon, 30p Cowes, 35p Lord's, 41p Braemar

330a	Set on illustrated cover, any postmark	**£2.50**
330b	With First Day of Issue, Philatelic Bureau handstamp	**£4.00**
330c	With First Day of Issue, Wimbledon handstamp	**£4.50**
330d	With First Day of Issue, London handstamp (Tennis)	**£4.50**
330e	With any one of some 34 additional relevant commemorative handstamps	**£10.00**
330f	With Wimbledon Woodside, Wimbledon SDO, or Wimbledon Park cds	**£12.00**
330g	With Hambledon, Marylebone, Cowes, or Braemar cds	**£15.00**
330h	With Summerhouse, Summertown, or Summerseat cds	**£15.00**
330i	With Pavilion, Bowling, or Over cds	**£15.00**
330j	With Builth Wells or St. Johns Wood cds	**£15.00**
330k	With Birthplace George Williams, Founder YMCA ... Dulverton slogan	**£18.00**

There are a few other cds postmarks that can be related to this issue. Prices from **£12**.

331. 1994, 27th September
Medical Discoveries (Europa) 25p, 30p, 35p, 41p, Medical Diagnostic Techniques

331a	Set on Illustrated cover, any postmark	**£2.50**
331b	With First Day of Issue, Philatelic Bureau handstamp	**£4.00**
331c	With First Day of Issue, Cambridge handstamp	**£4.50**
331d	With First Day of Issue, London handstamp (microscope)	**£4.50**
331e	With any one of some 15 additional relevant commemorative handstamps	**£9.00**
331f	With Royal Infirmary Glasgow cds	**£30.00**
331g	With Benenden Chest Hospital, or Orthopaedic Hospital Oswestry cds	**£20.00**
331h	With Pill, Glasgow cds, Cambridge cds, Healing, Grimsby cds	**£17.50**

A few other cds postmarks can be related to this issue. Prices from **£14**.

Modern first day covers signed by a well known personality, with relevance to the Stamp Issue, are worth a premium over catalogue prices.

QEII • Commemoratives 1994-95

332. 1994, 1st November
Christmas Issue 19p, 25p, 30p, 35p, 41p, Children's Nativity Plays

332a	Set on Illustrated cover, any postmark	£2.50 ☐
332b	With First Day of Issue, Philatelic Bureau handstamp	£4.00 ☐
332c	With First Day of Issue, Bethleham, Llandeilo handstamp	£4.50 ☐
332d	With First Day of Issue, London handstamp (star)	£4.50 ☐
332e	With any one of some 15 additional relevant commemorative handstamps	£10.00 ☐
332f	With St Nicholas, Nasareth, Holy Island, Jerusalem St, or Noel Road cds	£20.00 ☐
332g	With Star, Starcross, Hollybush, or Angel Hill cds	£20.00 ☐
332h	With Walt Disney's Snow White slogan cancel	£30.00 ☐
332i	**Christmas Booklets** 19p or 25p on display cover, any postmark	£7.00 ☐

---

333. 1995, 17th January
Cats Issue 19p, 25p, 30p, 35p, 41p, Neighbourhood Cats

333a	Set on illustrated cover, any postmark	£2.50 ☐
333b	With First Day of Issue, Philatelic Bureau handstamp	£4.00 ☐
333c	With First Day of Issue, Kitts Green handstamp	£4.50 ☐
333d	With First Day of Issue, London handstamp (cat)	£4.50 ☐
333e	With any one of some 20 additional relevant commemorative handstamps	£12.50 ☐
333f	With Catsfield, Catfield, Catshill, Catbrook, Catworth, or Catforth cds	£16.50 ☐
333g	With Mousehole, Penzance cds or Earls Court, London cds	£16.50 ☐
333h	With Horsham,West Sussex cds (RSPCA HQ)	£18.50 ☐

Other Cat related cds pmks can be associated with this issue. Prices from **£12**.

Don't forget that we now include sections on Overprints, Pre-release covers and Missing Colours on fdc. These can all be found in the last part of the catalogue.

QEII • Commemoratives 1995

334. 1995, 14th March

Springtime 19p, 25p, 30p, 35p, 41p, 3-D Sculptures of Plants and Leaves

334a	Set on illustrated cover, any postmark	**£2.50** ☐
334b	With First Day of Issue, Philatelic Bureau handstamp	**£4.00** ☐
334c	With First Day of Issue, Springfield handstamp	**£4.50** ☐
334d	With First Day of Issue, London handstamp (leaf)	**£4.50** ☐
334e	With First Day of Issue, St. Albans, Herts handstamp	**£4.50** ☐
334f	With any one of some 10 additional relevant commemorative handstamps	**£10.00** ☐
334g	With Springhill, Spring Corner, Leaves Green, or Kew Gardens cds	**£16.50** ☐
334h	With Swallownest, Wrens Nest, or Birdbrook cds	**£16.50** ☐

A few other cds postmarks can be related to this issue. Prices from **£12**.

335. 1995, 21st March

Greetings Stamps - Eighth Issue

10 x 1st Class NVI Stamps on the theme of Works of Art

335a	Pane of 10 Stamps on illustrated cover, any postmark	**£2.50** ☐
335b	With First Day of Issue, Philatelic Bureau handstamp	**£5.00** ☐
335c	With First Day of Issue, Lover handstamp	**£5.50** ☐
335d	With First Day of Issue, London handstamp (clown)	**£5.50** ☐
335e	With any one of some 13 additional relevant commemorative handstamps	**£12.50** ☐
335f	With Letter, Penn, Greet, Lover, or Clowne cds	**£14.50** ☐
335g	With Gretna Green, Greetland, or Playing Place cds	**£14.50** ☐
335h	With Please control your dog when Mail is delivered, Gloucester slogan	**£22.00** ☐

A few other cds postmarks can be related to this issue. Prices from **£12**.

336. 1995, 11th April

Centenary of the National Trust

19p, 25p, 30p, 35p, 41p, Various Aspects of the National Trust

336a Set on illustrated cover, any postmark .... **£2.50** ☐
336b With First Day of Issue, Philatelic Bureau handstamp .... **£4.00** ☐
336c With First Day of Issue, Alfriston handstamp .... **£4.50** ☐
336d With First Day of Issue, London handstamp (oakleaves) .... **£4.50** ☐
336e With any one of some 22 additional relevant commemorative handstamps .... **£10.00** ☐
336f With Alfriston, Tintagel, Bushmills, London SW1 cds .... **£17.50** ☐
336g With Send a little happiness, Post A Card This Easter slogan cancel .... **£20.00** ☐

Several other cds postmarks can be related to this issue. Prices from **£12**.

337. 1995, 2nd May

Peace and Freedom Anniversaries (Europa)

19p British Red Cross, 25p, 30p United Nations, 19p, 25p Victory Celebrations

337a Set on illustrated cover, any postmark .... **£2.50** ☐
337b With First Day of Issue, Philatelic Bureau handstamp .... **£4.00** ☐
337c With First Day of Issue, London SW handstamp .... **£4.50** ☐
337d With First Day of Issue, London handstamp (V50 design) .... **£4.50** ☐
337e With First Day of Issue, VE Day, London EC4 handstamp .... **£4.50** ☐
337f With any one of some 23 additional relevant commemorative handstamps .... **£10.00** ☐
337g With House of Commons or House of Lords SW1 cds .... **£45.00** ☐
337h With Buckingham Palace SW1 cds .... **£45.00** ☐
337i With Windsor Castle cds .... **£48.00** ☐
337j With Peacehaven, Churchill, Battle, or Victory St. cds .... **£18.50** ☐
337k With Any RAF Station, Battlefield, Normandy, or Portsmouth cds .... **£18.50** ☐

A few other cds postmarks can be related to this issue. Prices from **£12**.

338. 1995, 6th June

Science Fiction 25p, 30p, 35p, 41p, Illustrations of H.G. Wells Novels

338a Set on illustrated cover, any postmark .... **£2.50** ☐
338b With First Day of Issue, Philatelic Bureau handstamp .... **£4.00** ☐
338c With First Day of Issue, Wells handstamp .... **£4.50** ☐
338d With First Day of Issue, London (HG Wells) handstamp .... **£4.50** ☐
338e With First Day of Issue, Bonnybridge, Scotland handstamp .... **£4.50** ☐
338f With any one of some 13 additional relevant commemorative handstamps .... **£10.00** ☐
338g With Bromley, Wells, Worlds End, or Globe Road cds .... **£17.50** ☐

338h With The Rocket, New Invention, Clockface, or Nomansland cds .... **£17.50** ☐
338i With Woking, Star, Star Road, or Exhibition Road SW7 cds .... **£17.50** ☐
A few other cds postmarks can be related to this issue. Prices from **£12**.

339. 1995, 8th August

Opening of The Replica Globe Theatre, London

25p x 5 Se-tenant strip, South Bank Theatres between 1592 and 1614

339a Set on illustrated cover, any postmark .... **£2.50** ☐
339b With First Day of Issue, Philatelic Bureau handstamp .... **£4.00** ☐
339c With First Day of Issue, Stratford-on-Avon handstamp .... **£4.50** ☐
339d With First Day of Issue, London handstamp (masks) .... **£4.50** ☐
339e With First Day of Issue, Glamis, Forfar, Scotland handstamp .... **£4.50** ☐
339f With any one of some 14 additional relevant commemorative handstamps .... **£11.00** ☐
339g With Reading, Stratford-upon-Avon, or London SE1 cds .... **£15.00** ☐
339h With Globe Road, Playford, Playing Place, or Shakespeare St cds .... **£15.00** ☐
A few other cds postmarks can be related to this issue. Prices from **£12**.

QEII • Commemoratives 1995

340. 1995, 5th September

Communications History

19p, 25p Rowland Hill, 41p, 60p Marconi

340a	Set on illustrated cover, any postmark	**£2.50** ☐
340b	With First Day of Issue, Philatelic Bureau handstamp	**£4.00** ☐
340c	With First Day of Issue, London EC handstamp	**£4.50** ☐
340d	With First Day of Issue, Rowland Hill, Father of the Postage Stamp, London h/s	**£4.50** ☐
340e	With British Philatelic Bureau, Rowland Hill Fund, Edinburgh handstamp	**£10.00** ☐
340f	With any one of some 17 additional relevant commemorative handstamps	**£10.00** ☐
340g	With Rowland, Rowland's Castle, or Rowland's Gill cds	**£15.00** ☐
340h	With Kidderminster, Chelmsford, or Bath cds	**£15.00** ☐
340i	With Sandbanks, The Lizard, or Mullion cds	**£16.50** ☐

341. 1995, 3rd October

Rugby League Centenary

19p H. Wagstaff, 25p G. Risman, 30p J. Sullivan, 35p B. Batten, 41p B. Bevan

341a	Set on illustrated cover, any postmark	**£2.50** ☐
341b	With First Day of Issue, Philatelic Bureau handstamp	**£4.00** ☐
341c	With First Day of Issue, Headingley, Leeds handstamp	**£4.50** ☐
341d	With First Day of Issue, Rugby League Centenary, London handstamp	**£4.50** ☐
341e	With First Day of Issue, Huddersfield handstamp	**£4.50** ☐
341f	With any one of some 18 additional relevant commemorative handstamps	**£11.00** ☐
341g	With any major Rugby League town cds.	**£15.00** ☐
341h	With Rugby, Playing Place, Wembley Park, or Wembley cds	**£16.00** ☐
341i	With Halifax Rugby League Centenary slogan	**£45.00** ☐

All prices in this catalogue are for clean covers, with undamaged stamps and clear postmarks.

Anything less is worth less!

Gems • 1929 Set on PUC Postal Stationery

Full Set on ***Small Size*** PUC Postal Stationery.
We believe only two copies exist!

QEII • Commemoratives 1995-96

342. 1995, 30th October

Christmas Issue

19p, 25p, 30p, 41p, 60p, European Red Robin Scenes

342a Set on illustrated cover, any postmark .... **£2.50** ☐
342b With First Day of Issue, Philatelic Bureau handstamp .... **£4.00** ☐
342c With First Day of Issue, Bethlehem Llandeilo handstamp .... **£4.50** ☐
342d With First Day of Issue London handstamp (Robin) .... **£4.50** ☐
342e With any one of some 19 additional relevant commemorative handstamps .... **£10.00** ☐
342f With St. Nicholas, Nasareth, Jerusalem St., Noel Road, Angel Hill cds .... **£16.50** ☐
342g With Holy Island, Star, Starcross or Hollybush cds (Robin's Lane cds **£24**) .... **£16.50** ☐
342h **Christmas Booklets** 19p, 25p or 60p x 2 on display cover, any postmark .... **£7.00** ☐

343. 1996, 25th January

Robert Burns Bicentenary

19p Burns Poem, 25p, 41p, 60p Burns Songs

343a Set on illustrated cover,any postmark .... **£2.00** ☐
343b With First Day of Issue, Philatelic Bureau handstamp .... **£4.00** ☐
343c With First Day of Issue, Dumfries handstamp .... **£4.50** ☐
343d With First Day of Issue, Dunfermline, Scotland handstamp .... **£4.50** ☐
343e With First Day of Issue, London handstamp (plume/scroll) .... **£4.50** ☐
343f With any one of some 20 additional relevant commemorative handstamps .... **£10.00** ☐
343g With Burns Statue, Ayr 3 cds .... **£20.00** ☐
343h With Mauchline, Alloway, Dumfries, Kilmarnook cds .... **£12.00** ☐
343i With any other Scottish town cds .... **£10.00** ☐
343j With Robert Burns, Celebrate the Legend slogan .... **£38.00** ☐

344. 1996, 26th February

Greetings Stamps - Ninth Issue

10 x 1st Class NVI Stamps on Cartoon Themes

344a Pane of 10 Stamps on illustrated cover, any postmark .... **£3.00** ☐
344b With First Day of Issue, Philatelic Bureau handstamp .... **£4.50** ☐
344c With First Day of Issue, Titterhill . . . Ludlow handstamp .... **£5.00** ☐
344d With First Day of Issue, London handstamp (face/text) .... **£5.00** ☐
344e With any one of some 16 additional relevant commemorative handstamps .... **£12.00** ☐
344f With Greet, Greetwell, Greetland, or Greete cds .... **£15.00** ☐
344g With Penn, Wrightington, Inkpen, Laughterton, or Laughton cds .... **£15.00** ☐
344h With Walt Disney World slogan .... **£17.50** ☐

345. 1996, 12th March

50th Anniversary Wildfowl & Wetlands Trust

19p Muscovy Duck, 25p Lapwing, 30p Goose, 35p Bittern, 41p Whooper Swan

345a	Set on illustrated cover, any postmark	**£2.50** ☐
345b	With First Day of Issue, British Philatelic Bureau handstamp	**£4.00** ☐
345c	With First Day of Issue, Slimbridge, Gloucester handstamp	**£4.50** ☐
345d	With First Day of Issue, London handstamp (bird)	**£4.50** ☐
345e	With any one of some 15 additional relevant commemorative handstamps	**£10.00** ☐
345f	With any Trust related cds postmark, such as Arundel, Slimbridge, etc.	**£18.00** ☐
345g	With Goose Green, Ducklington, Swanpool or Swanland cds	**£15.00** ☐

---

346. 1996, 16th April

Centenary First British Public Cinema Show

19p Odeon Harrogate, 25p Olivier/Leigh, 30p Ticket, 35p Pathé, 41p Odeon Manchester

346a	Set on illustrated cover, any postmark	**£2.50** ☐
346b	With First Day of Issue, Philatelic Bureau handstamp	**£4.00** ☐
346c	With First Day of Issue, London WC2 handstamp	**£4.50** ☐
346d	With First Day of Issue, Cinema 100 Premiere, London handstamp	**£4.50** ☐
346e	With First Day of Issue, Aberfeldy Perthshire, Scotland handstamp	**£4.50** ☐
346f	With any one of some 24 additional relevant commemorative handstamps	**£10.00** ☐
346g	With Shepperton, Elstree, Bray, Denham Green, Ivor Heath, or Ealing cds	**£15.00** ☐
346h	With Harrogate, Hollywood, Manchester, or London WC2 cds	**£15.00** ☐

First Day Publishing Company, c/o Star, Glenrothes

347. 1996, 14th May

British Football Legends

19p Dixie Dean, 25p Bobby Moore, 35p Duncan Edwards,
41p Billy Wright, 60p Danny Blanchflower

347a	Set on illustrated cover, any postmark	**£2.50** ☐
347b	With First Day of Issue, Philatelic Bureau handstamp	**£4.00** ☐
347c	With First Day of Issue, Wembley or Manchester handstamp	**£4.50** ☐
347d	With First Day of Issue, London handstamp (Footballer)	**£4.50** ☐
346e	With any one of some 31 additional relevant commemorative handstamps	**£12.00** ☐
347f	With Wembley or Wembley Park cds	**£17.50** ☐
347g	With any of the above Football towns cds	**£15.00** ☐
347h	With Snickers, Proud to Support Euro '96 slogan	**£17.00** ☐

---

348. 1996, 9th July

Centenary Modern Olympic Games

26p x 5 Se-tenant. Five Olympic Athletes

348a	Set on illustrated cover, any postmark	**£2.50** ☐
348b	With First Day of Issue, Philatelic Bureau handstamp	**£4.00** ☐
348c	With First Day of Issue, Much Wenlock handstamp	**£4.50** ☐
348d	With First Day of Issue, London handstamp (Olympic Torch)	**£4.50** ☐
348e	With any one of some 27 additional relevant commemorative handstamps	**£10.00** ☐
348f	With Wembley or Wembley Park cds, Wandsworth, Runwell or Speedwell cds	**£18.50** ☐
348g	With Croydon or Stoke Mandeville cds	**£18.50** ☐

> **The successful campaign to revive the Olympic Games was started in France by Baron Pierre de Coubertin late in the 19th century. The first of the modern Olympic Games opened on March 24th, 1896 in Athens.**

QEII • Commemoratives 1996

349. 1996, 6th August

20th Century Women of Achievement (Europa)

20p D. Hodgkin, 26p Margot Fonteyn, 31p E. Frink, 37p D. du Maurier, 43p M. Hartman

349a	Set on illustrated cover, any postmark	**£2.50** ☐
349b	With First Day of Issue, Philatelic Bureau handstamp	**£4.00** ☐
349c	With First Day of Issue, Fowey handstamp	**£4.50** ☐
349d	With First Day of Issue, London handstamp (Symbol)	**£4.50** ☐
349e	With any one of some 21 additional relevant commemorative handstamps	**£10.00** ☐
349f	With Reigate, Thurlow, or Birmingham cds	**£12.50** ☐
349g	With Egypt (Cornwall), Lady, or Shipston on Stour cds	**£12.50** ☐
349h	With Par, or Fowey cds	**£12.50** ☐

350. 1996, 3rd September

50 Years of Children's Television

20p Muffin The Mule, 26p Sooty, 31p Stingray, 37p The Clangers, 41p Dangermouse

350a	Set on illustrated cover, any postmark	**£2.50** ☐
350b	With First Day of Issue, British Philatelic Bureau handstamp	**£4.00** ☐
350c	With First Day of Issue, Alexandra Palace, London handstamp	**£4.50** ☐
350d	With First Day of Issue, London handstamp (Children/TV)	**£4.50** ☐
350e	With any one of some 18 additional relevant commemorative handstamps	**£10.00** ☐
350f	With Playing Place, Jubilee, Box, Teddington, or Alexandra Park Road cds	**£15.00** ☐
350g	With Grange Hill, or Blackpool cds	**£15.00** ☐
350h	With Your Friends in the North, BBC Look North slogan cancel	**£17.00** ☐

GB Overprints on fdc

We have again priced these important issues on pages 454 - 457. They make a great addition to any GB first day cover collection.

Photographs of most GB Overprints listed can be seen in the 1998/99 edition of the Collect GB First Day Covers catalogue.

329

334

330

335

331

336

332

337

333

338

The Globe Theatre around 1615
339

COMMUNICATIONS
GUGLIELMO MARCONI
SIR ROWLAND HILL
340

Get a kick out of collecting
Rugby League Football
The Heyden fdc Series
CENTENARY
RUGBY LEAGUE
FOOTBALL
341

Merry Christmas
342

Wee, fleeket, cowran, tim'rous beastie,
SCOTS, WHA HAE WI WALLACE BLED
THE BURNS FEDERATION
343

1996
GREETINGS
STAMPS
with love * happy birthday * miss you * please write back
344

The Wildfowl & Wetlands Trust
RNLI OFFICIAL FIRST DAY COVER No147
345

LEIGH
OLIVIER
THAT
HAMILTON WOMAN!
MUSEUM
346
Celebrating British Cinema Centenary

Collect GB First Day Covers 1996
Winning new Readers. That's our goal!
347
First Day Publishing Company c/o Wembley, Middx.

Kodak
Atlanta 1996
Olympic Games Centenary
348

QEII • Commemoratives 1996

351. 1996, 1st October

Classic Sports Cars. Centenary First British Built Car

20p Triumph TR3, 26p MG TD, 37p Austin-Healey, 43p Jaguar XK120, 63p Morgan

351a	Set on illustrated cover, any postmark	**£2.50** ☐
351b	With First Day of Issue, British Philatelic Bureau handstamp	**£4.00** ☐
351c	With First Day of Issue, Beaulieu, Brockenhurst handstamp	**£4.50** ☐
351d	With First Day of Issue, London E1 handstamp (steering wheel)	**£4.50** ☐
351e	With First Day of Issue, London handstamp (car)	**£4.50** ☐
351f	With any one of some 40 additional relevant commemorative handstamps	**£10.00** ☐
351g	With any car manufacturing town cds (Longbridge, etc.)	**£15.00** ☐
351h	With Redcar, Cargo, Carr (N. Ireland), Carr Bank, or Carr Hill cds	**£22.00** ☐
351i	With Beaulieu, Birmingham NEC, or Silverstone cds	**£22.00** ☐
351j	With Austin, Bentley, Ford, Healey, Leyland, or Dunlop cds	**£20.00** ☐
351k	With Morris Green, Humber Road, Morganstown, or Fender cds	**£20.00** ☐
351l	With Royal Automobile Club, London SW1 handstamp	**£45.00** ☐

This issue also celebrated the Centenary of the London to Brighton car rally

---

352. 1996, 28th October

Christmas Issue

2nd Class NVI, 1st Class NVI, 31p, 43p, 63p, Biblical Nativity Scenes

352a	Set on illustrated cover, any postmark	**£2.50** ☐
352b	With First Day of Issue, British Philatelic Bureau handstamp	**£4.00** ☐
352c	With First Day of Issue, Bethlehem, Llandeilo handstamp	**£4.50** ☐
352d	With First Day of Issue, London handstamp (star)	**£4.50** ☐
352e	With any one of some 18 additional relevant commemorative handstamps	**£9.50** ☐
352f	With Jerusalem, Nasareth, Bethlehem, or St. Nicholas cds	**£16.00** ☐
352g	With Mary Park, Noel Road, Angel Hill, Star, or Holy Island cds	**£15.00** ☐
352h	With Shepherd's Bush, Shepherdswell, Holytown, or Threekingham cds	**£15.00** ☐
352i	**Christmas Booklets** 1st or 2nd x 2 on display cover, any postmark	**£8.00** ☐

Please read the notes at the beginning of this catalogue by way of general information

1. The Umm Said Post Office opened February 1st, 1956.

353. 1997, 6th January
Greetings Stamps -Tenth Issue. Featuring Flower Drawings
10 x 1st Class NVI Stamps

353a	Pane of 10 Stamps on illustrated cover, any postmark	**£3.00** ☐
353b	With First Day of Issue, British Philatelic Bureau handstamp	**£4.50** ☐
353c	With First Day of Issue, Kew, Richmond Surrey handstamp	**£5.00** ☐
353d	With First Day of Issue, London handstamp (flower)	**£5.00** ☐
353e	With any one of some 15 additional relevant commemorative handstamps	**£11.00** ☐
353f	With Kew Gardens cds, or Botanic Gardens Belfast cds	**£22.00** ☐
353g	With Bloomfield cds, Chelsea cds, Belfast cds, Rose cds, or Flowery Field cds	**£17.50** ☐
353h	With Penn cds, Greet cds, or Letters cds	**£17.50** ☐

354. 1997, 21st January
The Great Tudor. 450th Anniversary of Henry VIII
Se-Tenant Strip of Six 26p Stamps (Wives), 26p (Henry VIII)

354a	Set of 7 Stamps on illustrated cover, any postmark	**£2.50** ☐
354b	With First Day of Issue, British Philatelic Bureau handstamp	**£4.50** ☐
354c	With First Day of Issue, Hampton Court, East Molesey handstamp	**£5.00** ☐
354d	With First Day of Issue, London handstamp (shield)	**£5.00** ☐
354e	With any one of some 29 additional relevant commemorative handstamps	**£10.00** ☐
354f	With Greenwich cds, Windsor cds, Hampton cds, or Hampton Wick cds	**£16.00** ☐
354g	With Henry Street cds, Tudor Drive cds, Tower Hill cds, or E. Molesey cds	**£16.00** ☐
354h	With Windsor Castle cds	**£125.00** ☐

There are a few other cds postmarks that can be related to this issue, from **£14**.

Valuation Guide for GB Blocks of 4 on fdc

1840 to 1900 - three times the single fdc value
1902 to 1936 - two and a half times the single fdc value
1936 KEVIII - twice the single fdc value
1937 to 1951 - twice the single fdc value
1952 to date - one and a half times the single fdc value

355. 1997, 11th March
Missions of Faith
26p and 37p St. Columba, 43p and 63p St. Augustine

355a	Set on illustrated cover, any postmark	**£2.50** ☐
355b	With First Day of Issue, Philatelic Bureau handstamp	**£4.00** ☐
355c	With First Day of Issue, Isle of Iona handstamp	**£4.50** ☐
355d	With First Day of Issue, London handstamp (fish)	**£4.50** ☐
355e	With First Day of Issue, Durham handstamp	**£4.50** ☐
355f	With First Day of Issue, St. Albans handstamp	**£4.50** ☐
355g	With any one of some 17 additional relevant commemorative handstamps	**£9.50** ☐
355h	With Canterbury cds, Isle of Iona cds, or Holy Island cds	**£14.50** ☐
355i	With St. Columb cds, St. Columb Rd cds, All Saints cds, or St. Cross cds	**£14.50** ☐

Postal Rate Changes since the Introduction of the Two Tier Postal System in 1968

Date	1st class	2nd class	Date	1st class	2nd class
Sept. 16, 1968	*5d*	*4d*	Sept. 5, 1988	*19p*	*14p*
Feb. 15, 1971	*3p*	*2½p*	Oct. 2, 1989	*20p*	*15p*
Sept. 10, 1973	*3½p*	*3p*	Sept. 17, 1990	*22p*	*17p*
June 24, 1974	*4½p*	*3½p*	Sept. 16, 1991	*24p*	*18p*
Mar. 17, 1975	*7p*	*5p*	Nov. 1, 1993	*25p*	*19p*
Sept. 29, 1975	*8½p*	*6½p*	July 8, 1996	*26p*	*20p*
June 13, 1977	*9p*	*7p*	April 26, 1999	*26p*	*19p*
Aug. 20, 1979	*10p*	*8p*	April 27, 2000	*27p*	*19p*
Feb. 4, 1980	*12p*	*10p*	May 8, 2003	*28p*	*20p*
Jan. 26, 1981	*14p*	*11½p*	April 1, 2004	*28p*	*21p*
Feb. 1, 1982	*15½p*	*12½p*	April 7, 2005	*30p*	*21p*
April 5, 1983	*16p*	*12½p*	April 3, 2006	*32p*	*23p*
Sept. 3, 1984	*17p*	*13p*	April 2, 2007	*34p*	*24p*
Nov. 4, 1985	*17p*	*12p*	April 7, 2008	*36p*	*27p*
Oct. 20, 1986	*18p*	*13p*	April 6, 2009	*39p*	*30p*

Reposting facility for Slogan Postmarks withdrawn

Royal Mail stopped offering this service at the end of October 1996. Thus making it nearly impossible to get fdc's with a slogan machine cancellation anymore.

356. 1997, 21st April
QEII Golden Wedding Anniversary
26p and 1st Class NVI Definitive Format Stamps. Printed in Gold.

356a	Set on illustrated cover, any postmark	**£2.00** ☐
356b	With First Day of Issue, Philatelic Bureau handstamp	**£3.50** ☐
356c	With First Day of Issue, Windsor handstamp	**£4.00** ☐
356d	With First Day of Issue, London handstamp (Lions)	**£4.00** ☐
356e	With any one of some 15 additional relevant commemorative handstamps	**£8.50** ☐
356f	With Queen Elizabeth Ave. cds, Queens Parade cds, or Queens Road cds	**£17.50** ☐
356g	With House of Commons or House of Lords, London SW1 cds	**£17.50** ☐
356h	With Buckingham Palace, London SWI cds	**£145.00** ☐
356i	With Windsor Castle, Windsor Berks cds (Windsor cds **£16**)	**£120.00** ☐
356j	With Edinburgh cds, Queensway cds, Queens Head cds	**£17.50** ☐

---

357. 1997, 13th May
Tales of Terror (Europa)
26p Dracula, 31p Frankenstein, 37p Jekyll & Hyde, 43p Hound of the Baskervilles

357a	Set on illustrated cover, any postmark	**£2.50** ☐
357b	With First Day of Issue, Philatelic Bureau handstamp	**£4.00** ☐
357c	With First Day of Issue, Whitby handstamp	**£4.50** ☐
357d	With First Day of Issue, London handstamp (Frankenstein)	**£4.50** ☐
357e	With any one of some 19 additional relevant commemorative handstamps	**£9.50** ☐
357f	With Horrabridge cds, Princetown cds, Whitby cds or Purfleet cds	**£12.50** ☐
357g	With Marlow cds, Hindehead cds, or Westbourne cds	**£12.00** ☐
357h	With Hyde cds, Houndsditch cds, Elstree cds, or Edinburgh cds	**£12.50** ☐

All QEII Definitives, Dues, Regionals, Booklets, Coils, Graphites and variations in Phosphors, Watermarks, Perfs, Gum Types, Papers, etc. are in one comprehensive section, in chronological order, starting on page 350.

QEII • Commemoratives 1997

358. 1997, 10th June

Architects of the Air. British Aircraft Designers.

20p Mitchell – Spitfire, 26p Chadwick – Lancaster, 37p Bishop – Mosquito
43p Carter – Meteor, 63p Camm – Hawker Hunter

358a	Set on illustrated cover, any postmark	**£2.50** ☐
358b	With First Day of Issue, Philatelic Bureau handstamp	**£4.00** ☐
358c	With First Day of Issue, Duxford, Cambridge handstamp	**£4.50** ☐
358d	With First Day of Issue, London handstamp (airplane)	**£4.50** ☐
358e	With any one of some 34 additional relevant commemorative handstamps	**£12.00** ☐
358f	With Cranwell cds, Duxford cds, Farnborough cds, or Lancaster cds	**£15.00** ☐
358g	With Leuchars cds, Scampton cds, Marham cds, or Marston cds	**£14.00** ☐
358h	With Lossiemouth cds, Biggin Hill cds, Southampton cds, or Coningsby cds	**£15.00** ☐

Several other cds postmarks can be related to this issue. Prices from **£12**

---

359. 1997, 8th July

All the Queen's Horses

20p St. Patrick, 26p Thompson, 43p James, 63p River Star. Horses Names

359a	Set on illustrated cover, any postmark	**£2.50** ☐
359b	With First Day of Issue, Philatelic Bureau handstamp	**£4.00** ☐
359c	With First Day of Issue, Windsor, Berks handstamp	**£4.50** ☐
359d	With First Day of Issue, London handstamp (drum)	**£4.50** ☐
359e	With any one of some 16 additional relevant commemorative handstamps	**£10.00** ☐
359f	With Victoria St. cds, Windsor cds, or Lancelot Place cds	**£14.50** ☐
359g	With Blackhorse cds, Queen's Drive cds, or Guardhouse cds	**£14.50** ☐
359h	With Buckingham Palace cds	**£60.00** ☐

A few other cds postmarks can be related to this issue. Prices from **£12**

First Day Covers signed by the Stamp Designer

Covers, with one or more Stamps, signed by the designer are worth a 20% premium over catalogue prices.

360. 1997, 12th August

Centenary National Federation of Sub-Postmasters

20p Haroldswick, 26p Painswick, 43p Beddgelert, 63p Ballyroney. Post Offices

360a	Set on illustrated cover, any postmark	£2.50 ☐
360b	With First Day of Issue, Philatelic Bureau handstamp	£4.00 ☐
360c	With First Day of Issue, Wakefield handstamp	£4.50 ☐
360d	With First Day of Issue, London handstamp (envelope)	£4.50 ☐
360e	With any one of some 19 additional relevant commemorative handstamps	£9.50 ☐
360f	With Shoreham-by-sea cds, Wakefield cds, or Kirkgate cds	£16.00 ☐
360g	With Beddgelert cds, Ballyroney cds, Haroldswick cds, or Painswick cds	£14.50 ☐
360h	With Tintagel cds, Sanquhar cds, Letters cds, or any TPO cds	£14.50 ☐

---

361. 1997, 9th September

Enid Blyton Centenary

20p Noddy & Big Ears, 26p Famous Five, 37p Secret Seven
43p Faraway Tree, 63p Malory Towers

361a	Set on illustrated cover, any postmark	£2.50 ☐
361b	With First Day of Issue, Philatelic Bureau handstamp	£4.00 ☐
361c	With First Day of Issue, Beaconsfield handstamp	£4.50 ☐
361d	With First Day of Issue, London handstamp (children)	£4.50 ☐
361e	With any one of some 18 additional relevant commemorative handstamps	£11.00 ☐
361f	With Beaconsfield cds, Blyton cds, East Dulwich cds, or Beckenham cds	£16.50 ☐
361g	With Child's Hill cds, Playing Place cds, Fiveways cds, or Fivehead cds	£16.50 ☐
361h	With Corfe Castle cds, Cove Bay cds, Cherry Tree cds, or St. Clare cds	£15.00 ☐
361i	With Mount Nod, Bickley cds, or Pollok cds	£15.00 ☐

Philatelic fdc Gems!

A number of rare first day cover Philatelic Gems are illustrated throughout the catalogue. These can be seen on pages: inside covers, 40, 44, 78, 84, 93, 104, 184, 223, 231 and 363.

362. 1997, 27th October

Christmas Issue. 150th Anniv. of the Christmas Cracker

2nd NV1, 1st NV1, 31p, 43p, 63p, Santa and Crackers

362a	Set on illustrated cover, any postmark	£2.50 ☐
362b	With First Day of Issue, Philatelic Bureau handstamp	£4.00 ☐
362c	With First Day of Issue, Diwrnod Cyhoeddi Cyntaf, Bethlehem handstamp	£4.50 ☐
362d	With First Day of Issue, London handstamp (Santa)	£4.50 ☐
362e	First Day of Issue, Birmingham handstamp (Santa)	£4.50 ☐
362f	With any one of some 19 additional relevant commemorative handstamps	£10.00 ☐
362g	With St. Nicholas cds, Nasareth cds, Jerico cds, or Holy Island cds	£14.50 ☐
362h	With Angel Hill cds, Noel Road cds, Jerusalem St cds, or Hollybush cds	£14.50 ☐
362i	With Smith House cds, Norwich cds, Starcross cds	£12.50 ☐

363. 1997, 13th November

The Queen's Golden Wedding

20p & 43p Wedding Portrait 1947, 26p & 63p Snowdon Portrait 1996

363a	Set on illustrated cover, any postmark	£2.50 ☐
363b	With First Day of Issue, Philatelic Bureau handstamp	£4.00 ☐
363c	With First Day of Issue, Fifty Years, Golden Wedding, London SW1 handstamp	£4.50 ☐
363d	With First Day of Issue, London handstamp (doves)	£4.50 ☐
363e	With First Day of Issue, Golden Wedding 1947–1997, Birmingham handstamp	£4.50 ☐
363f	With any one of some 31 additional relevant commemorative handstamps	£10.00 ☐
363g	With Windsor, Berks cds, or Windsor Great Park cds	£12.50 ☐
363h	With Edinburgh cds, Duke St cds, Queen's Road cds	£16.00 ☐
363i	With Queen Elizabeth Ave cds, Royal Parade cds	£16.00 ☐
363j	With Balmoral cds, Wedmore cds, Brittania cds	£16.00 ☐
363k	With Buckingham Palace cds (Windsor Castle cds **£185**)	£150.00 ☐
363l	With House of Commons or House of Lords cds	£35.00 ☐
363m	**Christmas Booklets** 1st or 2nd x 2 on display cover, any postmark	£8.00 ☐

Remember, from 1966 onwards, most hand addressed Commemorative covers are worth no more than 20% of catalogue prices.

WOMEN OF ACHIEVEMENT
Lifeboats
Royal National Lifeboat Institution
349

354
450th Anniversary Henry VIII

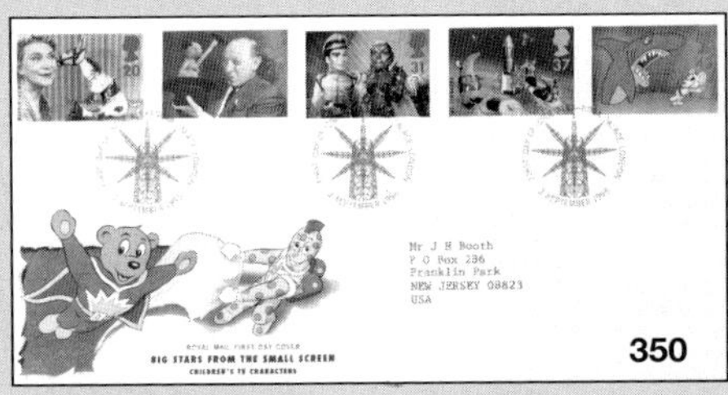
Mr J H Booth
P O Box 236
Franklin Park
NEW JERSEY 08823
USA
BIG STARS FROM THE SMALL SCREEN
350

St. Columba in Stained Glass. Iona Abbey.
355

The Daily Telegraph
Motor Show
351

CLASSIC
TALES OF
HORROR
TALES OF TERROR · WHITBY
13 MAY 1997
357

1996
CHRISTMAS
ISSUE
352

Supermarine Spitfire
358

353
with love * happy birthday * miss you * please write back

50th ANNIV.
BRITISH
HORSE SOCIETY
The Queen's Horses
359

361
Enid Blyton 100th Anniversary Born August 11, 1897
Noddy
Famous Five
Secret Seven
Faraway Tree
Malory Towers
Enid Blyton Children's Books
360
Centenary National Federation Sub Postmasters
CHRISTMAS GREETINGS
RNLI OFFICIAL FIRST DAY COVER No.166
Lifeboats
Royal National Lifeboat Institution
362
MERRY CHRISTMAS
363
SILVER WEDDING
Royal Golden Wedding Anniversary
The Queen's Golden Wedding
1961-1997
365

365
DIANA PRINCESS OF WALES
Collect GB First Day Covers 1997
First Day Publishing Company, c/o Kensington

364
Endangered Species - The Song Thrush

366

367
LIGHTHOUSES EDDYSTONE ANNIV
300TH ANNIVERSARY
EDDYSTONE
LIGHTHOUSE

364. 1998, 20th January

Endangered Species

20p Dormouse, 26p Lady's Slipper Orchid, 31p Song Thrush, 37p Ram's Horn Snail, 43p Mole Cricket, 63p Devil's Bolete

364a	Set on illustrated cover, any postmark	£3.00 ☐
364b	With First Day of Issue, British Philatelic Bureau handstamp	£4.50 ☐
364c	With First Day of Issue, Selbourne, Alton handstamp	£5.00 ☐
364d	With First Day of Issue, London handstamp (Butterfly)	£5.00 ☐
364e	With First Day of Issue, Birmingham handstamp (Panda)	£5.00 ☐
364f	With any one of some 23 additional relevant commemorative handstamps	£12.00 ☐
364g	With Selbourne cds, Kew Gardens cds, Regents Park Rd cds	£16.00 ☐
364h	With Mousehole cds, Snailbeach cds, Otterburn cds, Molehill Green cds	£15.00 ☐
364i	With Whale Hilll cds, Dolphin Holme cds, Eagle cds, Devils Bridge handstamp	£15.00 ☐
364j	With Godalming cds, South Kensington cds, Grassington cds, Lincoln cds	£15.00 ☐
364k	With The Science Museum cds, Attenborough cds, Botanic Gardens cds	£16.00 ☐

365. 1998, 3rd February

Diana, Princess of Wales

5 x 26p Se-tenant. Portraits of Diana

365a	26p Se-tenant strip on illustrated cover, any postmark	£2.50 ☐
365b	With Diana Princess of Wales, Philatelic Bureau handstamp	£4.00 ☐
365c	With First Day of Issue, Kensington handstamp	£4.50 ☐
365d	With any one of some 41 additional relevant commemorative handstamps	£10.00 ☐
365e	With Kensington High St. cds, Great Brington cds	£50.00 ☐
365f	With Rose cds, Spencer Road cds, Spencers Wood cds, Princess Street cds	£22.00 ☐
365g	With Wales cds, Paris Avenue cds, Memorial Road cds	£22.00 ☐
365h	With House of Commons, or House of Lords SW1 cds	£30.00 ☐
365i	With Buckingham Palace cds, Windsor Castle cds (£90)	£65.00 ☐
365j	With Sandringham cds	£85.00 ☐

All prices in this catalogue are for clean covers, with undamaged stamps and clear postmarks.

366. 1998, 24th February

The Queen's Beasts. 650th Anniversary Order of the Garter

5 x 26p Se-tenant. Featuring Heraldic Beasts

366a	26p Se-tenant strip on illustrated cover, any postmark	**£2.50** ☐
366b	With First Day of Issue, Philatelic Bureau handstamp	**£4.00** ☐
366c	With First Day of Issue, London SW1 handstamp (3 lions)	**£4.50** ☐
366d	With First Day of Issue, London handstamp (lion)	**£4.50** ☐
366e	With First Day of Issue, Birmingham handstamp (horseman)	**£4.50** ☐
366f	With any one of some 29 additional relevant commemorative handstamps	**£10.00** ☐
366g	With Kew Gardens cds, Reigate cds, York cds, or Richmond cds	**£12.50** ☐
366h	With Beaufort cds, Greyhound cds, Falcon Lodge cds, Falconwood cds	**£12.50** ☐
366i	With Eagle cds, Lion Green cds, Black Bull cds, Blackhorse cds	**£12.50** ☐
366j	With Boars Head cds, King's Stag cds, Talbot Road cds, Beast Bank cds	**£12.50** ☐
366k	With Broadway cds, Royal Parade cds, King Edward's Drive cds	**£12.50** ☐
366l	With Windsor cds, or Windsor Great Park cds, or Oxford cds	**£15.00** ☐
366m	With Queens Road cds, Clarence Rd cds, or St. Georges cds	**£12.50** ☐
366n	With House of Commons, or House of Lords SW1 cds	**£27.50** ☐
366o	With Buckingham Palace SW1 cds (Windsor Castle **£100**)	**£90.00** ☐

There are a few other cds postmarks that can be related to this issue. From **£10**.

Readers comments are always welcome.

Write to us if you have questions on Commemorative handstamps for any QEII Stamp Issue.

QEII • Commemoratives 1998

367. 1998, 24th March

300th Anniversary Eddystone Lighthouse

20p St. John's Point, 26p Smalls, 37p Needles, 43p Bell Rock, 63p Eddystone

367a	Set on illustrated cover, any postmark	**£2.50**
367b	With First Day of Issue, Philatelic Bureau handstamp	**£4.00**
367c	With First Day of Issue, Plymouth handstamp	**£4.50**
367d	With First Day of Issue, London handstamp (lighthouse)	**£4.50**
367e	With First Day of Issue, Birmingham handstamp (lighthouse)	**£4.50**
367f	With any one of some 28 additional relevant commemorative handstamps	**£11.00**
367g	With Lighthouse cds, Winstanley cds, Six Bells cds, Beacon Hill cds	**£15.00**
367h	With Totland Bay cds, Plymouth cds, Killough cds, or Dale cds	**£12.50**
367i	With Arbroath cds, Fair Isles cds, St. Mary's cds, Downpatrick cds	**£12.50**
367j	With Lightwater cds, Seething Lane cds, Beacon cds, Sandbanks cds	**£12.50**
367k	With Penzance cds, or any Lifeboat Station in the UK	**£15.00**

368. 1998, 23rd April

British Comedians

20p T. Cooper, 26p E. Morecambe, 37p J. Grenfell, 43p L. Dawson, 63p P. Cook

368a	Set on illustrated cover, any postmark	**£2.50**
368b	With First Day of Issue, Philatelic Bureau handstamp	**£4.00**
368c	With First Day of Issue, Morecambe handstamp	**£4.50**
368d	With First Day of issue, Ho Ho Ha Ha Ha Hee Hee, London handstamp	**£4.50**
368e	With First Day of Issue, Birmingham handstamp (glasses/stars)	**£4.50**
368f	With any one of some 32 additional relevant commemorative handstamps	**£11.00**
368g	With Morecambe cds, Torquay cds, Caerphilly cds, Collyhurst cds	**£16.00**
368h	With Clowne cds, Laughterton cds, Giggleswick cds, Goonhaven cds	**£16.00**
368i	With Cookston cds, Coopers Rd cds, Grenfell Rd cds	**£16.00**

30p stamp instead of 37p, any postmark **£1,500**

The complete catalogue Index appears on page three.
All reigns listed from Queen Victoria to date.

QEII • Commemoratives 1998

369. 1998, 23rd June

Celebrating 50 Years of the National Health Service

20p Blood Donors, 26p Prescriptions, 43p New Babies, 63p Outpatients

369a	Set on illustrated cover, any postmark	**£2.00** □
369b	With First Day of Issue, Philatelic Bureau handstamp	**£3.50** □
369c	With First Day of Issue, Tredegar handstamp	**£4.00** □
369d	With First Day of Issue, London handstamp (NHS 50)	**£4.00** □
369e	With First Day of Issue, Birmingham handstamp (surgeons)	**£4.00** □
369f	With any one of some 25 additional relevant commemorative handstamps	**£10.00** □
369g	With Pill cds, any hospital P.O.– Benenden, Oswestry, Edward VII, etc cds.	**£12.50** □
369h	With Healing cds, Glasgow Royal Infirmary cds	**£14.00** □

There are a few other cds postmarks that can be associated with this issue. From **£10**

WILLIAM BEVERIDGE
1879 - 1963
Father of the National Health Service
23 June 1998
WESTMINSTER SW1

---

370. 1998, 21st July

Magical Worlds! Children's Fantasy Books

20p JR Tolkien, 26p CS Lewis, 37p E. Nesbit, 43p M. Norton, 63p Lewis Carroll

370a	Set on illustrated cover, any postmark	**£2.50** □
370b	With First Day of Issue, Philatelic Bureau handstamp	**£4.00** □
370c	With First Day of Issue, Oxford handstamp	**£4.50** □
370d	With First Day of Issue, London handstamp (dragon)	**£4.50** □
370e	With First Day of Issue, Birmingham handstamp	**£4.50** □
370f	With any one of some 28 additional relevant commemorative handstamps	**£11.00** □
370g	With Daresbury cds, Oxford cds, Birmingham cds, Belfast cds	**£14.50** □
370h	With Headington, Guildford, or Leighton Buzzard cds	**£14.50** □
370i	With Lewis Road, Lewisham, or Llandudno cds	**£14.50** □
370j	With Childs Hill, Lilliput, Paradise cds	**£14.50** □

This issue also celebrated the centenaries of CS Lewis and Lewis Carroll.

Modern QEII First Day Covers need to have a *relevant* commemorative or cds postmark. Without this they are of little value in today's market place.

QEII • Commemoratives 1998

371. 1998, 25th August
Celebrating The Notting Hill Carnival (Europa)
20p, 26p, 43p, 63p. Photos from the Masquerade Parade

371a	Set on illustrated cover, any postmark	£2.50 ☐
371b	With First Day of Issue, British Philatelic Bureau handstamp	£4.00 ☐
371c	With First Day of Issue, London W11 handstamp	£4.50 ☐
371d	With First Day of Issue, London handstamp (sax/drums)	£4.50 ☐
371e	With First Day of Issue, Birmingham handstamp	£4.50 ☐
371f	With any one of some 21 additional relevant commemorative handstamps	£10.00 ☐
371g	With Kingston, Lewes, Lerwick, or Durham cds	£12.50 ☐
371h	With Jamacia St. Road, The Parade, or W. India Dock cds	£12.50 ☐
371i	With Notting Hill, Leicester, or Portobello Road cds	£12.50 ☐

The Notting Hill Carnival is the largest street carnival in Europe. Started in 1964, it takes place every August Bank Holiday weekend and is an impressive display of artistic expression and dazzling costumes.

---

372. 1998, 29th September
Speed Records. Anniversary Malcolm Campbell
20p Bluebird, 26p Sunbeam, 30p Babs, 43p Railton, 63p New Bluebird

372a	Set on illustrated cover, any postmark	£2.50 ☐
372b	With First Day of Issue, Philatelic Bureau handstamp	£4.00 ☐
372c	With First Day of Issue, London handstamp (steering wheel)	£4.50 ☐
372d	With First Day of Issue, Pendine handstamp	£4.50 ☐
372e	With First Day of Issue, Birmingham handstamp	£4.50 ☐
372f	With any one of some 31 additional relevant commemorative handstamps	£11.00 ☐
372g	With The Drive, RAC, Heath Road cds	£15.00 ☐
372h	With Mansell Road, Seagrave, Campbelltown cds	£15.00 ☐
372i	With Beaulieu, Chislehurst, Weybridge cds	£16.00 ☐
372j	With Silverstone, Brooklands, Thruxton cds	£16.00 ☐
372k	With Pendine, Coniston, Windermere cds	£16.00 ☐

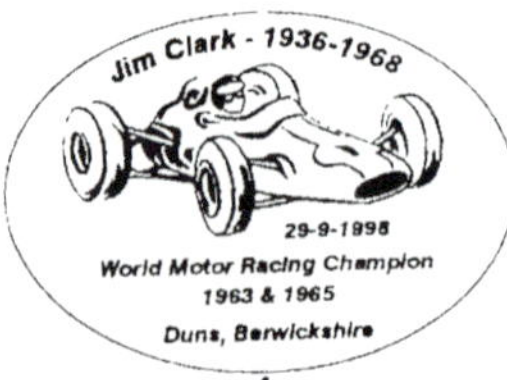

QEII • Commemoratives 1998-99

373. 1998, 2nd November

Christmas Issue - Angels

20p, 26p, 30p, 43p, 63p.Christmas Angels

373a	Set on illustrated cover, any postmark	**£2.50** ☐
373b	With First Day of Issue, Philatelic Bureau handstamp	**£4.00** ☐
373c	With First Day of Issue, …Bethlehem, Llandeilo handstamp	**£4.50** ☐
373d	With First Day of Issue, London handstamp (angel)	**£4.50** ☐
373e	With First Day of Issue, Birmingham handstamp	**£4.50** ☐
373f	With First Day of Issue, non pictorial version	**£4.50** ☐
373g	With any one of some 22 additional relevant commemorative handstamps	**£11.00** ☐
373h	With Angel Hill, Nasareth, Holy Island cds	**£13.50** ☐
373i	With Noel Road, Godshill, Jerusalem St cds	**£13.50** ☐
373j	With St. Nicholas, Jerico, Starcross cds	**£13.50** ☐
373k	**Christmas Booklets** 20p or 26p x 2 on display cover, any postmark	**£9.00** ☐

374. 1999, 12th January

Millennium Stamps - The Inventors' Tale

20p Timekeeping, 26p Steam Power, 43p Photography, 63p Computers

374a	Set on illustrated cover, any postmark	**£2.00** ☐
374b	With First day of Issue, Philatelic Bureau handstamp	**£4.00** ☐
374c	With First Day of Issue, Greenwich, London SE handstamp (0 degrees)	**£4.50** ☐
374d	With First Day of Issue, Greenwich, London SE handstamp	**£4.50** ☐
374e	With any one of some 39 additional relevant commemorative handstamps	**£10.00** ☐
374f	With Meridian Centre cds, Greenwich cds, Salisbury cds	**£12.50** ☐
374g	With New Crafton cds, The Science Museum cds, Bressingham cds	**£12.50** ☐
374h	With Lacock cds, James Watt Dock cds, Talbot Rd cds	**£12.50** ☐
374i	With New Invention cds, Clockface cds, or The Rocket cds	**£15.00** ☐

QEII • Commemoratives 1999

375. 1999, 2nd February

Millennium Stamps - The Travellers' Tale

20p Jet travel, 26p Liberation by Bike, 43p Linking the Nation, 63p Cook's Endeavour

375a	Set on illustrated cover, any postmark	**£2.00** ☐
375b	With First day of Issue, Philatelic Bureau handstamp	**£4.00** ☐
375c	With First Day of Issue, Coventry (A to B) handstamp	**£4.50** ☐
375d	With First Day of Issue, Coventry handstamp	**£4.50** ☐
375e	With First Day of Issue in English/Welsh text (A to B), Coventry handstamp	**£4.50** ☐
375f	With First Day of Issue in English/Welsh text, Coventry handstamp	**£4.50** ☐
375g	With any one of some 44 additional relevant commemorative handstamps	**£10.00** ☐
375h	With Marton-in-Cleveland cds, Lutterworth cds, Portsmouth cds	**£12.50** ☐
375i	With Heathrow Terminal 4 cds, Heathrow Airport cds, Filton cds, any TPO cds	**£12.50** ☐
375j	With Whitby cds, Raleigh cds, The Rocket cds, or Byker cds	**£15.00** ☐

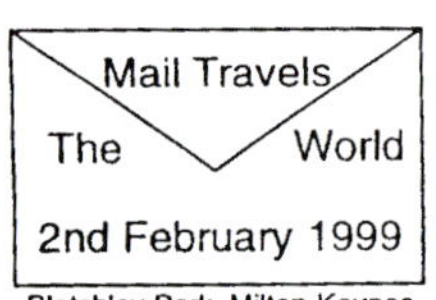

376. 1999, 2nd March

Millennium Stamps - The Patients' Tale

20p Vaccination, 26p Nursing, 43p Penicillin, 63p Test-tube Baby

376a	Set on illustrated cover, any postmark	**£2.00** ☐
376b	With First day of Issue, Philatelic Bureau handstamp	**£4.00** ☐
376c	With First Day of Issue, Oldham handstamp (grapes)	**£4.50** ☐
376d	With First Day of Issue, Oldham handstamp	**£4.50** ☐
376e	With First Day of Issue in English/Welsh text, Oldham handstamp (grapes)	**£4.50** ☐
376f	With First Day of Issue in English/Welsh text, Oldham handstamp	**£4.50** ☐
376g	With any one of some 37 additional relevant commemorative handstamps	**£10.00** ☐
376h	With Fleming Way cds, Cow Hill cds, Eye cds	**£12.50** ☐
376i	With Berkeley cds, West Wellow cds, Benenden cds	**£12.50** ☐
376j	With Oldham cds, Darvel cds, Paddington cds, or Harrow cds	**£12.50** ☐
376k	With Pill cds, Healing cds, Well cds, or Ward End cds	**£15.00** ☐

Write to us if you have questions on Commemorative handstamps for any QEII Stamp Issue.

QEII • Commemoratives 1999

377. 1999, 6th April

Millennium Stamps - The Settlers' Tale

20p Migration to Scotland, 26p Pilgrim Fathers, 43p Destination Australia, 63p Migration to UK

377a	Set on illustrated cover, any postmark	**£2.00** ☐
377b	With First day of Issue, Philatelic Bureau handstamp	**£4.00** ☐
377c	With First Day of Issue, Plymouth handstamp (UK map)	**£4.50** ☐
377d	With First Day of Issue, Plymouth handstamp	**£4.50** ☐
377e	With First Day of Issue in English/Welsh text, Plymouth handstamp (UK map)	**£4.50** ☐
377f	With First Day of Issue in English/Welsh text, Plymouth handstamp	**£4.50** ☐
377g	With any one of some 29 additional relevant commemorative handstamps	**£10.00** ☐
377h	With Melbourne cds, St. Andrews Cross cds, West India Dock cds	**£12.50** ☐
377i	With The Barbican Plymouth cds, Jamaica Road cds, Sydney Road cds	**£12.50** ☐
377j	With Settle cds, Seaforth cds, Pilgrims Hatch cds, Paradise cds	**£12.50** ☐
377k	With Boston cds, Plymouth cds, Portsmouth cds, or New England cds	**£15.00** ☐

An attractive Stamp Searchers cover for the Millennium Settlers' Tale Issue

Countdown to the New Millennium!

QEII • Commemoratives 1999

378. 1999, 4th May

Millennium Stamps - The Workers' Tale

19p Weaver's Craft, 26p Mill Towns, 44p Shipbuilding, 64p City Finance

378a Set on illustrated cover, any postmark.......... **£2.00** □
378b With First day of Issue, Philatelic Bureau handstamp.......... **£4.00** □
378c With First Day of Issue, Belfast handstamp (clock hand).......... **£4.50** □
378d With First Day of Issue, Belfast handstamp.......... **£4.50** □
378e With First Day of Issue in English/Welsh text, Belfast handstamp (clock hand).......... **£4.50** □
378f With First Day of Issue in English/Welsh text, Belfast handstamp.......... **£4.50** □
378g With any one of some 30 additional relevant commemorative handstamps.......... **£10.00** □
378h With Lombard Street cds, Oldham cds, Worsted cds, Shotton cds.......... **£12.50** □
378i With Belfast cds, Arkwright Town cds, Clyde Bank cds.......... **£12.50** □
378j With Pounds cds, Wool cds, Cotton Tree cds, Woolpit cds.......... **£15.00** □

---

379. 1999, 1st June

Millennium Stamps - The Entertainers' Tale

19p Freddie Mercury, 26p Bobby Moore, 44p Dr. Who, 64p Charlie Chaplin

379a Set on illustrated cover, any postmark.......... **£2.00** □
379b With First day of Issue, Philatelic Bureau handstamp.......... **£4.00** □
379c With First Day of Issue, Wembley handstamp (star).......... **£4.50** □
379d With First Day of Issue, Wembley handstamp.......... **£4.50** □
379e With First Day of Issue in English/Welsh text,Wembley handstamp (star).......... **£4.50** □
379f With First Day of Issue in English/Welsh text, Wembley handstamp.......... **£4.50** □
379g With any one of some 38 additional relevant commemorative handstamps.......... **£10.00** □
379h With Aldeburgh cds, West End cds, Hollywood cds, or Rock cds.......... **£12.50** □
379i With Shepherds Bush cds, Wembley cds, Moore cds or Cult cds.......... **£12.50** □
379j With Walworth cds, or Walworth Road cds.......... **£12.50** □

Don't forget that we now include sections on Overprints, Pre-release covers and Missing Colours on fdc. These can all be found in the last part of the catalogue.

QEII • Commemoratives 1999

380. 1999, 15th June

Royal Wedding

26p, 64p Prince Edward and Miss Sophie Rhys-Jones

380a Set on illustrated cover, any postmark .... **£1.50** ☐
380b With First day of Issue, Philatelic Bureau handstamp .... **£4.00** ☐
380c With First Day of Issue, Windsor handstamp (E&S) .... **£4.50** ☐
380d With First Day of Issue, Windsor handstamp .... **£4.50** ☐
380e With First Day of Issue in English/Welsh text, Windsor handstamp (E&S) .... **£4.50** ☐
380f With First Day of Issue in English/Welsh text, Windsor handstamp .... **£4.50** ☐
380g With any one of some 20 additional relevant commemorative handstamps .... **£10.00** ☐
380h With Windsor cds, Bagshot cds, Brenchley cds, or Edward St. cds .... **£12.50** ☐
380i With Windsor Castle cds **(£75)**, or Buckingham Palace cds .... **£65.00** ☐

Double dated covers June 15 and 19 (Wedding Day) are worth £12

381. 1999, 6th July

Millennium Stamps - The Citizens' Tale

19p Equal Rights, 26p Right to Health, 44p Right to Learn, 64p First Rights

381a Set on illustrated cover, any postmark .... **£2.00** ☐
381b With First day of Issue, Philatelic Bureau handstamp .... **£4.00** ☐
381c With First Day of Issue in English/Welsh text, Newtown Powys h/s (stick man) .... **£4.50** ☐
381d With First Day of Issue in English/Welsh text, Newtown Powys handstamp .... **£4.50** ☐
381e With any one of some 28 additional relevant commemorative handstamps .... **£10.00** ☐
381f With Egham cds, Manchester cds, New Lanark cds .... **£12.50** ☐
381g With Newtown cds, Salisbury cds, Parliament St cds .... **£12.50** ☐
381h With House of Commons cds .... **£16.50** ☐

382. 1999, 3rd August

Millennium Stamps - The Scientists' Tale

19p Decoding DNA, 26p Darwin's Evolution, 44p Faraday's Electricity, 64p Newton Telescope

382a	Set on illustrated cover, any postmark	**£2.00** ☐
382b	With First day of Issue, Philatelic Bureau handstamp	**£4.00** ☐
382c	With First Day of Issue, Cambridge handstamp (rings)	**£4.50** ☐
382d	With First Day of Issue, Cambridge handstamp	**£4.50** ☐
382e	With First Day of Issue in English/Welsh text, Cambridge handstamp (rings)	**£4.50** ☐
382f	With First Day of Issue in English/Welsh text, Cambridge handstamp	**£4.50** ☐
382g	With any one of some 29 additional relevant commemorative handstamps	**£10.00** ☐
382h	With Downe cds, Albermarle St cds, Cambridge cds, Colsterworth cds	**£12.50** ☐
382i	With Faraday Ave cds, Newton cds, New Invention cds, Science Museum cds	**£15.00** ☐

383. 1999, 11th August

Solar Eclipse - £2.56 Miniature Sheet

4 x 64p Scientists' Tale Stamp

383a	Set on illustrated cover, any postmark	**£2.00** ☐
383b	With First day of Issue, Philatelic Bureau handstamp	**£4.50** ☐
383c	With First Day of Issue, Falmouth handstamp (eclipse)	**£5.00** ☐
383d	With First Day of Issue, Falmouth handstamp	**£5.00** ☐
383e	With First Day of Issue in English/Welsh text, Falmouth handstamp (eclipse)	**£5.00** ☐
383f	With First Day of Issue in English/Welsh text, Falmouth handstamp	**£5.00** ☐
383g	With any one of some 14 additional relevant commemorative handstamps	**£12.00** ☐
383h	With Falmouth cds, Greenwich cds, Newton cds, Science Museum cds	**£15.00** ☐
383i	With St. Ives cds, Ringland cds, Shade or Blackshade cds	**£15.00** ☐
383j	With complete Imperforate Pane, any postmark	**£5,000.00** ☐

384. 1999, 7th September

Millennium Stamps - The Farmers' Tale

19p Strip Farming, 26p Mechanical Farming, 44p The Potato, 64p Satellite Agriculture

384a	Set on illustrated cover, any postmark	£2.00 ☐
384b	With First day of Issue, Philatelic Bureau handstamp	£4.00 ☐
384c	With First Day of Issue, Laxton, Newark handstamp (tractor)	£4.50 ☐
384d	With First Day of Issue, Laxton, Newark handstamp	£4.50 ☐
384e	With First Day of Issue in English/Welsh text, Laxton, Newark h/s (tractor)	£4.50 ☐
384f	With First Day of Issue in English/Welsh text, Laxton, Newark handstamp	£4.50 ☐
384g	With any one of some 29 additional relevant commemorative handstamps	£10.00 ☐
384h	With Farmers cds, Laxton cds, Bull Farm cds	£12.50 ☐
384i	With Kenilworth cds, Cattle Market cds, Isle of Grain cds	£12.50 ☐

385. 1999, 5th October

Millennium Stamps - The Soldiers' Tale

19p Robert the Bruce, 26p The Civil War, 44p World Wars, 64p Peace-keeping

385a	Set on illustrated cover, any postmark	£2.00 ☐
385b	With First day of Issue, Philatelic Bureau handstamp	£4.00 ☐
385c	With First Day of Issue, London SW handstamp (dove)	£4.50 ☐
385d	With First Day of Issue, London SW1 handstamp	£4.50 ☐
385e	With First Day of Issue in English/Welsh text, London SW handstamp (dove)	£4.50 ☐
385f	With First Day of Issue in English/Welsh text, London SW1 handstamp	£4.50 ☐
385g	With any one of some 40 additional relevant commemorative handstamps	£10.00 ☐
385h	With Bannockburn cds, Wargrave cds, Battle cds, or Naseby cds	£12.50 ☐
385i	With Peacehaven cds, The Barracks cds, Guardhouse cds, or Sandhurst cds	£12.50 ☐
385j	With Churchill cds, Dunkirk cds, Battlefield Road cds, or Aldershot cds	£12.50 ☐

386. 1999, 2nd November
Millennium Stamps - The Christians' Tale
19p Wesley's Hymn, 26p King James' Bible, 44p St Andrews Cathedral, 64p First Christmas

386a	Set on illustrated cover, any postmark	**£2.00** ☐
386b	With First day of Issue, Philatelic Bureau handstamp	**£4.00** ☐
386c	With First Day of Issue, St Andrews, Fife handstamp (star)	**£4.50** ☐
386d	With First Day of Issue, St Andrews, Fife handstamp	**£4.50** ☐
386e	With First Day of Issue in English/Welsh text, St Andrews, Fife h/s (star)	**£4.50** ☐
386f	With First Day of Issue in English/Welsh text, St Andrews, Fife handstamp	**£4.50** ☐
386g	With any one of some 32 additional relevant commemorative handstamps	**£10.00** ☐
386h	With Nasareth cds, Holy Island cds, St. Andrews cds, or James Street cds	**£12.50** ☐
386i	With Jerusalem St. cds, Christchurch cds, Angel Hill cds, or Epworth cds	**£12.50** ☐
386j	**Christmas Booklets** – 19p or 26p x 2 on display cover, any pmk	**£9.00** ☐

387. 1999, 7th December
Millennium Stamps - The Artists' Tale
19p World of the Stage, 26p World of Music, 44p World of Literature, 64p New Worlds

387a	Set on illustrated cover, any postmark	**£2.00** ☐
387b	With First day of Issue, Philatelic Bureau handstamp	**£4.00** ☐
387c	With First Day of Issue, Stratford-upon-Avon handstamp (figure)	**£4.50** ☐
387d	With First Day of Issue, Stratford-upon-Avon handstamp	**£4.50** ☐
387e	With First Day of Issue in English/Welsh text, Stratford-upon-Avon h/s (figure)	**£4.50** ☐
387f	With First Day of Issue in English/Welsh text, Stratford-upon-Avon handstamp	**£4.50** ☐
387g	With any one of some 35 additional relevant commemorative handstamps	**£10.00** ☐
387h	With Stratford upon Avon cds, Theatre Square cds, Theatre cds, or Glynde cds	**£12.50** ☐
387i	With Rochester cds, Globe Road cds, Poets Field cds, or The Galleries cds	**£12.50** ☐
387j	With Ben Johnson Road cds, Broadstairs cds, Gainsborough cds, or Mcduff cds.	**£12.50** ☐

388. 1999, 14th December

Millennium Timekeeper - £2.56 Miniature Sheet

4 x 64p Stamps in block - Stamps Show Midnight GMT Getting Closer and Closer

388a	On illustrated cover, any postmark	£2.00 ☐
388b	With First day of Issue, Philatelic Bureau handstamp	£4.50 ☐
388c	With First Day of Issue, Greenwich, London SE h/s (Millennium Timekeeper)	£5.00 ☐
388d	With First Day of Issue, Greenwich, London SE handstamp	£5.00 ☐
388e	With First Day of Issue in English/Welsh text, Millennium Timekeeper, Greenwich h/s	£5.00 ☐
388f	With First Day of Issue in English/Welsh text, Greenwich, London SE h/s	£5.00 ☐
388g	With any one of some 22 additional relevant commemorative handstamps	£12.00 ☐
388h	With Clockface cds, Clockhouse Parade cds, Greenwich cds, or Meridian Centre cds	£15.00 ☐

389. 2000, 18th January

Millennium Issue - Above and Beyond

19p Owl Trust, 26p Space Science Centre, 44p Torrs Walkway, 64p Seabird Centre

389a	Set on illustrated cover, any postmark	£2.00 ☐
389b	With First Day of Issue, Philatelic Bureau handstamp	£4.00 ☐
389c	With First Day of Issue, Muncaster, Ravenglass handstamp (paper plane)	£4.50 ☐
389d	With First Day of Issue, Muncaster, Ravenglass handstamp	£4.50 ☐
389e	With any one of some 26 additional relevant commemorative handstamps	£10.00 ☐
389f	With Owlsmoor cds, North Berwick cds, Ravenglass cds, or New Mills cds	£12.50 ☐
389g	With Greenwich cds, Leicester cds, Macclesfield cds, or Starcross cds	£12.50 ☐

In to the New Millennium!

QEII • Commemoratives 2000

390. 2000, 1st February

Millennium Issue - Fire and Light

19p Beacon, 26p Welsh Railway, 44p Dynamic Earth Project, 64p Croydon's Skyline

390a Set on illustrated cover, any postmark .... **£2.00** ☐
390b With First Day of Issue, Philatelic Bureau handstamp .... **£4.00** ☐
390c With First Day of Issue, Edinburgh (3' 10' W) handstamp .... **£4.50** ☐
390d With First Day of Issue, Edinburgh handstamp .... **£4.50** ☐
390e With any one of some 24 additional relevant commemorative handstamps .... **£10.00** ☐
390f With Croydon cds, Edinburgh cds, Kings Cross cds, or Caernarfon cds .... **£12.50** ☐
390g With Beacon Hill cds, Beacon Lough cds, Beacon cds, or Burnt House Lane cds **£12.50** ☐
390h With Ffestiniog cds, Porthmadog cds, Millennium Dome cds .... **£12.50** ☐

391. 2000, 7th March

Millennium Issue - Water and Coast

19p Turning the Tide, 26p Pondlife Centre, 44p Parc Arfordirol, 64p Portsmouth Harbour

391a Set on illustrated cover, any postmark .... **£2.00** ☐
391b With First Day of Issue, Philatelic Bureau handstamp .... **£4.00** ☐
391c With First Day of Issue in English/Welsh text, Llanelli handstamp (seaside) .... **£4.50** ☐
391d With First Day of Issue in English/Welsh text, Llanelli handstamp .... **£4.50** ☐
391e With any one of some 27 additional relevant commemorative handstamps .... **£10.00** ☐
391f With Portsmouth cds, Prescott cds, Durham cds, or Llanelli cds .... **£12.50** ☐
391g With Seaside cds, Seaside Lane cds, Waterside cds, or Waterbeach cds .... **£12.50** ☐
391h With Frogpool cds, Frogmore cds, The pond cds, or Freshwater cds .... **£12.50** ☐

371

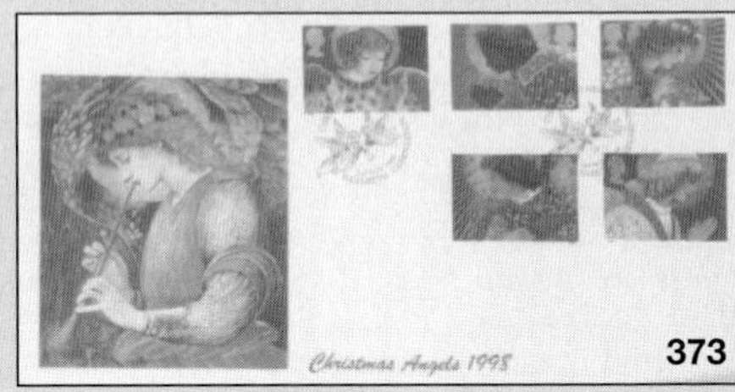

373

377

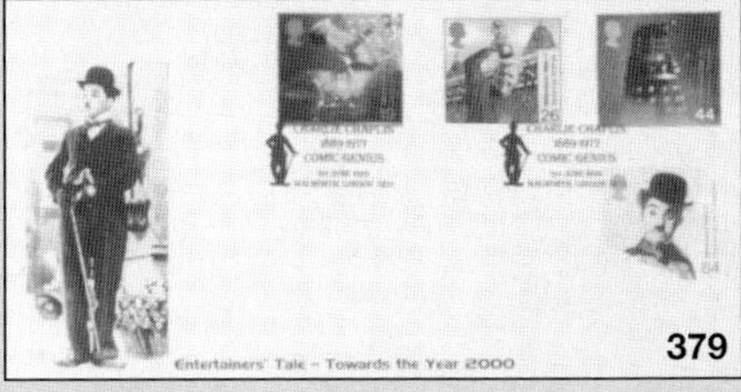

379

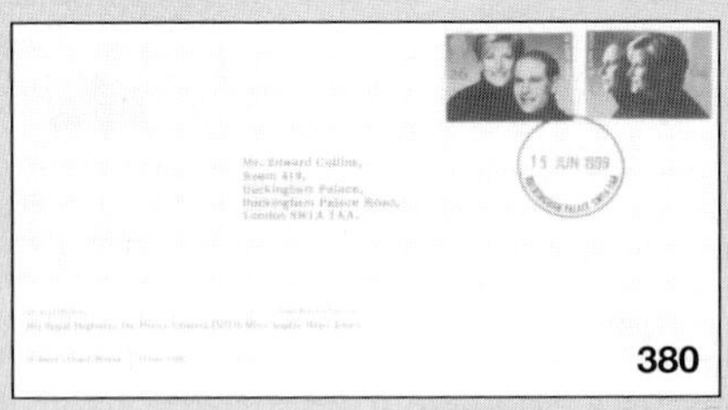

380

381

384

385

387

386

390

393

397

399

400

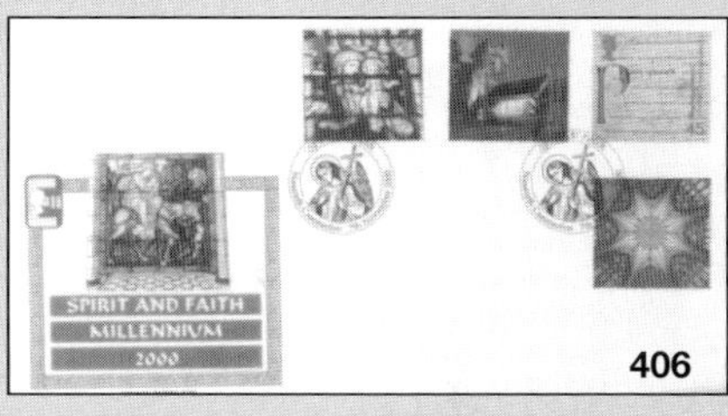

406

408

411

418

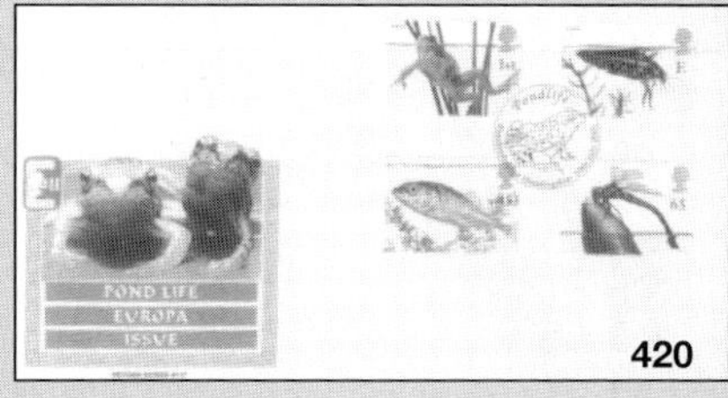

420

392. 2000, 4th April
Millennium Issue - Life and Earth
2nd ECOS Ballymena, 1st Web of Life, 45p Earth Center, 65p Project SUZY

392a	Set on illustrated cover, any postmark	£2.00 ☐
392b	With First Day of Issue, Philatelic Bureau handstamp	£4.00 ☐
392c	With First Day of Issue, Doncaster handstamp (dandelion)	£4.50 ☐
392d	With First Day of Issue, Doncaster handstamp	£4.50 ☐
392e	With any one of some 29 additional relevant commemorative handstamps	£10.00 ☐
392f	With Regents Park Rd cds, Ballymena cds, Doncaster cds, or Middlesbrough cds	£12.50 ☐
392g	With Kew Gardens cds, Botanic Gardens Belfast cds, Denaby Main or Freshwater cds	£12.50 ☐

393. 2000, 2nd May
Millennium Issue - Art and Craft
2nd Ceramica Museum, 1st Tate Modern, 45p Cycle Network, 65p The Lowry Complex

393a	Set on illustrated cover, any postmark	£2.00 ☐
393b	With First Day of Issue, Philatelic Bureau handstamp	£4.00 ☐
393c	With First Day of Issue, Salford (2' 18' W) handstamp	£4.50 ☐
393d	With First Day of Issue, Salford handstamp	£4.50 ☐
393e	With any one of some 27 additional relevant commemorative handstamps	£10.00 ☐
393f	With Salford cds, The Galleries cds, Seaburn cds	£12.50 ☐
393g	With Raleigh cds, Byker cds, Manchester cds, or Dumfries cds	£12.50 ☐
393h	With Stoke on Trent cds, Pottery Road cds, Hanley cds, Barlestone cds, Dresden cds	£12.50 ☐

All QEII *Definitives* are listed in order from page 350

394. 2000, 22nd May

Stamp Show 2000. Smilers £2.95 Sheetlet.

Ten 1st Stamps + Labels. Stamps first issued in 1991 as Greetings Stamps

394a Sheetlet on illustrated cover, any postmark .... **£2.00** ☐
394b With First Day of Issue, Earls Court, London SW5 handstamp .... **£4.50** ☐
394c With The Stamp Show 2000, Earls Court, London SW5 handstamp .... **£5.00** ☐
394d With The Stamp Show 2000, Art & Entertainment, Earls Court, London h/s .... **£5.00** ☐
394e With any one of some 14 additional relevant commemorative handstamps .... **£10.00** ☐

395. 2000, 23rd May

Stamp Show 2000. £2.08 Her Majesty's Stamps Miniature Sheet

(New £1 adapted from 1953 Coronation Stamp + 4 x 1st Millennium Definitive)

395a Miniature Sheet on illustrated cover, any postmark .... **£2.00** ☐
395b With First Day of Issue, Philatelic Bureau handstamp .... **£4.00** ☐
395c With First Day of Issue, City of Westminster, London SW1 handstamp .... **£4.50** ☐
395d With First Day of Issue, London SW1 handstamp .... **£4.50** ☐
395e With any one of some 12 additional relevant commemorative handstamps .... **£10.00** ☐
395f With Earls Court cds, Windsor cds, Queen Elizabeth Ave cds, or Queen St cds... **£15.00** ☐
395g With Buckingham Palace cds (**£120**), or Windsor Castle cds .... **£140.00** ☐

All prices in this catalogue are for clean covers, with undamaged stamps and clear postmarks.

396. 2000, 26th May

Stamp Show 2000. Millennium £2.70 Retail Booklet

(2 x Millennium 1st Commems - Space Centre, Web of Life + 8 x Millennium 1st Defs)

396a	Retail Booklet on illustrated cover, any postmark	**£2.00** ☐
396b	With First Day of Issue, Philatelic Bureau handstamp	**£3.00** ☐
396c	With First Day of Issue, Leicester handstamp (arms)	**£4.00** ☐
396d	With First Day of Issue, Leicester handstamp	**£4.00** ☐
396e	With any one of some 9 additional relevant commemorative handstamps	**£10.00** ☐
396f	With Stamp Show 2000 cds	**£12.50** ☐

397. 2000, 6th June

Millennium Issue - People and Place

2nd Millennium Greens, 1st Gateshead Bridge, 45p Mile End Park, 65p On The Line

397a	Set on illustrated cover, any postmark	**£2.00** ☐
397b	With First Day of Issue, Philatelic Bureau handstamp	**£4.00** ☐
397c	With First Day of Issue, Gateshead (1' 37' W) handstamp	**£4.50** ☐
397d	With First Day of Issue, Gateshead handstamp	**£4.50** ☐
397e	With any one of some 31 additional relevant commemorative handstamps	**£10.00** ☐
397f	With Gateshead cds, Greenwich cds, Mile End cds, or Meridian Centre cds	**£12.50** ☐
397g	With Bridge cds, The Green cds, Playing Place cds	**£12.50** ☐

Control Numbers and/or Cylinder Numbers

Covers showing these are worth a premium of 20% - 25%

QEII • Commemoratives 2000

398. 2000, 4th July

Millennium Issue - Stone and Soil

2nd Strangford Stone, 1st Pennine Trail, 45p Fife Cycle Ways, 65p Changing Places

398a Set on illustrated cover, any postmark .... **£2.00** ☐
398b With First Day of Issue, Philatelic Bureau handstamp .... **£4.00** ☐
398c With First Day of Issue, Killyleagh (5' 41' W) handstamp .... **£4.50** ☐
398d With First Day of Issue, Killyleagh handstamp .... **£4.50** ☐
398e With any one of some 23 additional relevant commemorative handstamps .... **£10.00** ☐
398f With Glenrothes cds, Killyleagh cds, Strangford cds, or Bluebell Hill cds .... **£12.50** ☐
398g With Stone cds, Stonesfield cds, Southport cds, or Kingdom Centre Glenrothes cds ... **£12.50** ☐
398h With Hadfield cds, Digswell cds .... **£12.50** ☐

399. 2000, 1st August

Millennium Issue - Tree and Leaf

2nd Millennium Yews, 1st Eden Project, 45p Ardingly Seed Bank, 65p Scotland Forest

399a Set on illustrated cover, any postmark .... **£2.00** ☐
399b With First Day of Issue, Philatelic Bureau handstamp .... **£4.00** ☐
399c With First Day of Issue, St. Austell (44' 7' W) handstamp .... **£4.50** ☐
399d With First Day of Issue, St.Austell handstamp .... **£4.50** ☐
399e With any one of some 28 additional relevant commemorative handstamps .... **£10.00** ☐
399f With Ardingly cds, St. Austell cds, Kew Gardens cds, or Woodlands Park cds...... **£12.50** ☐
399g With Eden cds, Yew Tree cds, Oaktree Rd cds, or Four oaks cds .... **£12.50** ☐
399h With Ash cds, Firtree cds, Pinewoods cds .... **£12.50** ☐

QEII • Commemoratives 2000

400. 2000, 4th August
100th Birthday HM The Queen Mother
$1.08 Miniature Sheet (4 x 27p Royal Family Portraits)

400a	Miniature Sheet on illustrated cover, any postmark	**£1.50**	☐
400b	With First Day of Issue, Philatelic Bureau handstamp	**£4.00**	☐
400c	With First Day of Issue (Clarence House...), London SW1 handstamp	**£4.50**	☐
400d	With First Day of Issue, London SW1 handstamp	**£4.50**	☐
400e	With any one of some 47 additional relevant commemorative handstamps	**£10.00**	☐
400f	With Windsor cds, Windsor Great Park cds, Clarence Road Windsor cds	**£12.50**	☐
400g	With Royal Parade cds, Queen Elizabeth Ave cds, Prince Charles Ave, or Whitwell cds	**£12.50**	☐
400h	Bowes cds, Glamis cds, Mey cds, Rye cds, Hastings cds, or Hundred House cds	**£12.50**	☐
400i	With Buckingham Palace cds (**£200**), or Windsor Castle cds	**£220.00**	☐

401. 2000, 4th August
100th Birthday HM The Queen Mother. £7.03 Prestige Stamp Book. 4 Panes
(6 x Scottish 2nd Defs + 2 x Scottish 65p Defs), (9 x 1st Millennium Definitive)
(Miniature Sheet 4 x 27p Royal Portraits), (4 x 27p Queen Mother, from Miniature Sheet)

401a	All 4 entire Panes with any of the previous h/s, or combinations thereof	**£24.00**	☐
401b	With any of the previous cds postmarks, or combinations thereof	**£34.00**	☐
401c	With Buckingham Palace cds (Windsor Castle **£265**)	**£250.00**	☐

402. 2000, 5th September
Millennium Issue - Mind and Matter
2nd Wildscreen Bristol, 1st Norfolk/Norwich Project, 45p Millennium Point, 65p SCRAN

402a	Set on illustrated cover, any postmark	**£2.00**	☐
402b	With First Day of Issue, Philatelic Bureau handstamp	**£4.00**	☐
402c	With First Day of Issue, Norwich (1' 18' E) handstamp	**£4.50**	☐
402d	With First Day of Issue, Norwich handstamp	**£4.50**	☐
402e	With any one of some 24 additional relevant commemorative handstamps	**£10.00**	☐
402f	With Birmingham cds, Bristol cds, Norwich cds, or Edinburgh cds	**£12.50**	☐

Readers comments are always welcome.

403. 2000, 5th September

Millennium 54p Retail Booklet

(2 x 1st Se-tenant Stamps - Pennine Trail, Eden Project)

403a	With Millennium Booklet, St Austell, Cornwall handstamp (pattern)	£6.00	☐
403b	With Millennium Booklet, St Austell, Cornwall handstamp (crest)	£6.00	☐
403c	With Millennium Booklet, St Austell, Cornwall handstamp	£6.00	☐
403d	With Millennium Booklet, Trans Pennine Trail, Liverpool handstamp	£6.00	☐
403e	With Pennine Trail - from coast to coast, Barnsley handstamp	£6.00	☐
403f	With Garden of Eden, St. Austell, Cornwall handstamp	£6.00	☐
403g	With Eden Project, St. Austell, Cornwall handstamp	£6.00	☐

404. 2000, 3rd October

Millennium Issue - Body and Bone

2nd Dome Body Zone, 1st Hampden Park, 45p Bath Spa Complex, 65p Newcastle Centre

404a	Set on illustrated cover, any postmark	£2.00	☐
404b	With First Day of Issue, Philatelic Bureau handstamp	£4.00	☐
404c	With First Day of Issue, Glasgow (4 15'W) handstamp (skeleton hand)	£4.50	☐
404d	With First Day of Issue, Glasgow handstamp	£4.50	☐
404e	With any one of some 26 additional relevant commemorative handstamps	£10.00	☐
404f	With Millennium Dome cds, Newcastle cds, Bath cds, or Greenwich cds	£12.50	☐
404g	With Hampden Park cds, Glasgow cds, The Ball cds,	£12.50	☐
404h	With Spa View cds, Bathpool cds, Bathwick cds, or Coldbath cds	£12.50	☐

405. 2000, 3rd October

'Customised' Christmas Stamps. 2 Sheets

(20 x 19p Robin (1995) + 20 labels), (10 x 1st Father Christmas (1997) + 10 labels)

405a One of each Stamp with label attached, any postmark .... **£2.00** ☐
405b With Happy Christmas, Hollybush, Ayr handstamp.......... **£7.00** ☐
405c With Happy Christmas, Christmas Common, Oxford handstamp.......... **£7.00** ☐
405d With 1st Customised Christmas Stamps, Bethlehem, Llandeilo handstamp .... **£7.00** ☐
405e With Full Sheet - 20 x 19p any handstamp.......... **£10.50** ☐
405f With Full Sheet - 10 x 1st any handstamp.......... **£9.00** ☐
405g With Robbins Lane cds (both stamps **£9**), either Sheet .... **£18.00** ☐

All Body and Bone October 3rd handstamps, except the 3 Royal Mail pmks, were also available for this Issue, price **£6** each.

406. 2000, 7th November

Millennium Issue - Spirit and Faith

2nd Suffolk Cathedral, 1st Church Floodlighting, 45p St Patrick Centre, 65p York Plays.

406a Set on illustrated cover, any postmark .... **£2.00** ☐
406b With First Day of Issue, British Philatelic Bureau handstamp.......... **£4.00** ☐
406c With First Day of Issue, Downpatrick (5' 43' W) handstamp (wreath on door) .... **£4.50** ☐
406d With First Day of Issue, Downpatrick handstamp .... **£4.50** ☐
406e With any one of some 28 additional relevant commemorative handstamps.......... **£10.00** ☐
406f With York cds, Downpatrick cds, Bury St. Edmunds cds, or Nether Stowey cds ... **£12.50** ☐
406g With Holy Island cds, Nasareth cds, Angel Hill cds, Christchurch or Norwich cds. **£12.50** ☐
406h **Christmas Booklets** – 1st or 2nd x 2 on display cover, any postmark .... **£10.00** ☐

See the Introduction for details of Handstamp Centres

QEII • Commemoratives 2000

407. 2000, 5th December

Millennium Issue - Sound and Vision

2nd Ringing in Millennium, 1st Year of the Artist, 45p Canolfan Cardiff, 65p Talent & Skills

407a Set on illustrated cover, any postmark .... **£2.00** ☐
407b With First Day of Issue, British Philatelic Bureau handstamp .... **£4.00** ☐
407c With First Day of Issue in bilingual (welsh) text, Caerdydd Cardiff (3' 11' W) h/s..... **£4.50** ☐
407d With First Day of Issue, Cardiff Caerdydd handstamp .... **£4.50** ☐
407e With any one of some 30 additional relevant commemorative handstamps .... **£10.00** ☐
407f With Sheffield cds, Cardiff cds, Loughborough cds, or The Galleries cds .... **£12.50** ☐
407g With Foundry Lane cds, Bell Lane cds, Six Bells cds, or Eye cds .... **£12.50** ☐

408. 2001, 16th January

Hopes for the Future. Last of the 25 Millennium Commemorative Issues

2nd Nature Children, 1st Listen to children, 45p Teach Children, 65p Children's Freedom

408a Set on illustrated cover, any postmark .... **£2.00** ☐
408b With First Day of Issue, Philatelic Bureau handstamp .... **£4.00** ☐
408c With First Day of Issue (cut out figures), Hope, Hope Valley handstamp....... .... **£4.50** ☐
408d With First Day of Issue, Hope, Hope Valley handstamp .... **£4.50** ☐
408e With any one of some 24 additional relevant commemorative handstamps .... **£10.00** ☐
408f With Hope cds, High Holborn cds, The Harlequin cds, ... **£12.50** ☐
408g With Playing Place cds, Child's Hill cds, Kidsgrove cds .... **£12.50** ☐

Write to us if you have questions on Commemorative handstamps for any QEII Stamp Issue.

409. 2001, 6th February

Occasions Stamps

1st Love, 1st Thanks, 1st ABC(Baby), 1st Welcome, 1st Cheers

409a Set on illustrated cover, any postmark .... £2.00 ☐
409b With First Day of Issue, Philatelic Bureau handstamp .... £4.00 ☐
409c With First Day of Issue (pigeon), Merry Hill, Wolverhampton handstamp .... £4.50 ☐
409d With First Day of Issue, Merry Hill, Wolverhampton handstamp .... £4.50 ☐
409e With any one of some 16 additional relevant commemorative handstamps .... £10.00 ☐
409f With Lover cds, Greet cds, Silver Link cds, or Silverstone cds .... £12.50 ☐
409g With Silvertown, Silverdale cds, Silver End cds .... £12.50 ☐

410. 2001, 13th February

Cats and Dogs. Self-adhesive

10 x 1st Class Stamps. Photographs of Five Cats and Five Dogs

410a Set on illustrated cover, any postmark .... £2.00 ☐
410b With First Day of Issue, Philatelic Bureau handstamp .... £4.50 ☐
410c With First Day of Issue (paw print), Petts Wood, Orpington handstamp .... £5.00 ☐
410d With First Day of Issue, Petts Wood, Orpington handstamp .... £5.00 ☐
410e With any one of some 28 additional relevant commemorative handstamps .... £11.00 ☐
410f With Isle of Dogs cds,Horsham cds, Barking cds, or Battersea cds .... £14.00 ☐
410g With Dog Kennel Lane cds, Catsfield cds, Catshill cds, or Catford cds .... £14.00 ☐
410h With Dog and Gun cds, Pant cds, Pett cds, Yapton cds, or Terriers cds .... £14.00 ☐

Modern first day covers signed by a well known personality,
with relevance to the Stamp Issue,
are worth a premium over catalogue prices.

QEII • Commemoratives 2001

411. 2001, 13th March

The Weather

19p Rain, 27p Sunshine, 45p Storms, 65p Very Dry

411a Set on illustrated cover, any postmark .... **£2.00** ☐
411b With First Day of Issue, Philatelic Bureau handstamp .... **£4.00** ☐
411c With First Day of Issue, Fraserburgh handstamp (umbrella) .... **£4.50** ☐
411d With First Day of Issue, Fraserburgh handstamp .... **£4.50** ☐
411e With any one of some 29 additional relevant commemorative handstamps .... **£10.00** ☐
411f With Fair Isle, Bracknell, Reading, Rainham, Rainhill, or Fog Lane cds .... **£12.50** ☐
411g With Fraserburgh, Sunnyhill, Sunnyfields, Sunniside, or Sunnybrow cds .... **£12.50** ☐
411h With Gale Street, Thunder Lane, Freezywater, Frosterley, or Puddletown cds .... **£12.50** ☐

412. 2001, 13th March

The Weather. £1.56 Miniature Sheet

Same Weather Stamps - 19p, 27p, 45p, 65p - in block of 4
All Weather Stamps handstamps and cds were available for use with the Miniature Sheet.
Catalogue values are the same as for the Weather Stamps, issued on the same day.

---

413. 2001, 10th April

Submarines. Centenary Royal Navy Submarine Service

2nd Vanguard, 1st Swiftsure, 45p Unity, 65p Holland Class

413a Set on illustrated cover, any postmark .... **£2.00** ☐
413b With First Day of Issue, Philatelic Bureau handstamp .... **£4.00** ☐
413c With First Day of Issue, Portsmouth handstamp (insignia) .... **£4.50** ☐
413d With First Day of Issue, Portsmouth handstamp .... **£4.50** ☐
413e With any one of some 29 additional relevant commemorative handstamps .... **£10.00** ☐
413f With Barrow-in-Furness, Clyde Submarine Base, Gosport, or Devonport cds .... **£12.50** ☐
413g With Clydebank, Chatham, Holland On Sea, Drake, or Six Mile Bottom cds .... **£12.50** ☐

QEII • Commemoratives 2001

414. 2001, 17th April

Submarines. £1.62 NVI Booklet. Self-adhesive

(2 x 1st Submarine Stamp + 4 x 1st Definitive)

414a	With Self Adhesive Stamps, Barrow in Furness handstamp	£7.00 ☐
414b	With Submarines, NVI Booklet, Barrow-in-Furness handstamp	£7.00 ☐
414c	With Submarines, NVI Booklet, Chatham, Kent handstamp	£7.00 ☐
414d	With Submarine, NVI Booklet, Gosport handstamp	£7.00 ☐
414e	With R.N.Submarine Service Centenary, Faslane, Helensburgh handstamp	£7.00 ☐
414f	With R.N.Submarine Service Centenary, Gosport, Hampshire handstamp	£7.00 ☐
414g	With 100th Anniversary Year, Royal Navy Submarine Service, Vickerstown, Barrow-in-Furness	£7.00 ☐
414h	With 50th Anniversary of the Loss of HM Submarine Affray...Gosport, Hampshire h/s	£7.00 ☐
414i	With Barrow-in-Furness cds, Clyde Submarine Base cds, Gosport cds	£12.50 ☐
414j	With Drake cds, Holland On Sea cds, Applecross cds	£12.50 ☐

415. 2001, 15th May

Buses. Classic British Double-Deckers

Five 1st Class Stamps Featuring 16 Buses - in Se-tenant Strip

415a	Set on illustrated cover, any postmark	£2.00 ☐
415b	With First Day of Issue, Philatelic Bureau handstamp	£4.00 ☐
415c	With First Day of Issue, Push Once, Covent Garden, London WC2 handstamp	£4.50 ☐
415d	With First day of Issue, London WC2 handstamp	£4.50 ☐
415e	With any one of some 31 additional relevant commemorative handstamps	£10.00 ☐
415f	With Leyland cds, Paddington cds, Victoria Street cds, London cds, or Tuckingmill cds	£12.50 ☐
415g	With Terminus Road cds, Coach Road cds, Trafford Park cds, Busby or Park Royal cds	£12.50 ☐

416. 2001, 15th May

Buses. £1.35 Miniature Sheet Five 1st Class Buses Stamps

All Buses Stamps handstamps and cds were available for use with the Miniature Sheet Catalogue values are the same as for the Buses Stamps, issued on the same day.

Write to us if you have questions on Commemorative handstamps for any QEII Stamp Issue.

417. 2001, 5th June

Occasions Stamps. Sheet of 20 Stamps

Re-issue of February 2001 Stamps, each with Label. 5 x 1st Class NVI Stamps in 4 Rows

417a Set of 5 1st Class NVI Stamps with labels, any postmark .... **£2.00** ☐
417b With Lover, Salisbury handstamp .... **£7.50** ☐
417c With Letters, Lochbroom, Garve handstamp .... **£7.50** ☐
417d With Lover cds, Greet cds, Silverstone cds .... **£12.00** ☐
417e With Silver Link cds, Silver Street cds, Silverdale cds .... **£12.00** ☐
417f Complete Sheet of 20 Stamps, with either handstamp .... **£20.00** ☐
417g Complete Sheet of 20 Stamps, with any cds .... **£28.00** ☐

---

418. 2001, 19th June

Fabulous Hats

1st Toque Hat, E Butterfly Hat, 45pTop Hat, 65p Spiral Hat

418a Set on illustrated cover, any postmark .... **£2.00** ☐
418b With First Day of Issue, Royal Mail, Tallents House, Edinburgh handstamp .... **£4.00** ☐
418c With First Day of Issue,Thoroughly Modern Millinery, Ascot handstamp .... **£4.50** ☐
418d With First Day of Issue, Ascot handstamp .... **£4.50** ☐
418e With any one of some 21 additional relevant commemorative handstamps .... **£9.00** ☐
418f With Ascot cds, Derby cds, Hatfield cds, Hatt cds, or Hatton cds .... **£12.00** ☐
418g With Carnaby Street cds, Luton cds, Busby cds, or Silk Street cds .... **£12.00** ☐

---

419. 2001, 3rd July

Smilers. £1.35 Generic Sheet

Reprint of five 1st Class NVI Smiles Stamps with New Labels

1st Teddy Bear, 1st Laughing Policeman, 1st Dennis The Menace, 1st Mona Lisa, 1st Clown

Stamps with different labels previously issued May 2000, March 1991, February 1990

419a Set of 5 Stamps plus labels, with Smilers, Greetwell, Lincoln handstamp .... **£8.50** ☐
419b With Smile with Mr. Punch, Covent Garden, London handstamp .... **£8.50** ☐

Remember, from 1966 onwards,

most hand addressed Commemorative covers

420. 2001, 10th July
Pond Life (Europa Issue)
1st Common Frog, E Gt. Diving Beetle, 45p Three-spined Stickleback, 65p Hawker Dragonfly

420a	Set on illustrated cover, any postmark	**£2.00** ☐
420b	With First Day of Issue, Royal Mail, Tallents House, Edinburgh handstamp	**£4.00** ☐
420c	With First Day of Issue, Oundle, Peterborough handstamp (beetle)	**£4.50** ☐
420d	With First Day of Issue, Oundle, Peterborough handstamp	**£4.50** ☐
420e	With any one of some 21 additional relevant commemorative handstamps	**£9.00** ☐
420f	With The Pond cds, Pond Park cds, Watermeadow cds, Waterside cds, or Frogmore cds	**£12.00** ☐
420g	With Fishlake cds, Fishpool cds, Riverbank cds, Lake cds, or Oundle cds	**£12.00** ☐

421. 2001, 4th September
Punch & Judy. Se-tenant
1st Policeman, 1st Clown, 1st Mr. Punch, 1st Judy, 1st Beadle, 1st Crocodile

421a	Set on illustrated cover, any postmark	**£2.00** ☐
421b	With First Day of Issue, Royal Mail, Tallents House, Edinburgh handstamp	**£4.00** ☐
421c	With First Day of Issue, Blackpool handstamp (bucket & spade)	**£4.50** ☐
421d	With First Day of Issue, Blackpool handstamp	**£4.50** ☐
421e	With any one of some 22 additional relevant commemorative handstamps	**£10.00** ☐
421f	With The Beach cds, The Pier cds, Seaside cds, or South Shore Blackpool cds	**£12.50** ☐
421g	With Constable Road cds, Clowne cds, Norwich cds, or Blackpool cds	**£12.50** ☐

All QEII Definitives are listed in chronological order from page 350

422. 2001, 4th September
Punch & Judy. £1.62 Booklet. Self-adhesive
(1st Mr. Punch, 1st Judy + 4 x 1st Class Definitives)

422a With Self Adhesives, Covent Garden, London handstamp .... **£7.50** ☐

In addition, all Punch & Judy handstamps and cds were available for use with this Booklet. Catalogue values are the same as for the Punch & Judy Stamps, issued same day.

---

423. 2001, 2nd October
The Nobel Prize. Nobel Institute Centenary
2nd Chemistry, 1st Economic Sciences, E Peace, 40p Physiology or Medicine, 45p Literature, 65p Physics

423a Set on illustrated cover, any postmark .... **£2.50** ☐
423b With First Day of Issue, Royal Mail, Tallents House, Edinburgh handstamp .... **£4.00** ☐
423c With First Day of Issue, Cambridge handstamp (prize categories) .... **£4.50** ☐
423d With First Day of Issue, Cambridge handstamp .... **£4.50** ☐
423e With First Day of Issue (N), Oxford handstamp .... **£4.50** ☐
423f With any one of some 25 additional relevant commemorative handstamps .... **£10.00** ☐
423g With Churchill, Crick, Shaw, or Goldings cds .... **£12.50** ☐
423h With Fleming Way, Fleming Road, Nobel Road, Quaker Road cds .... **£12.50** ☐
423i With Peacehaven, Science Museum, Oxford, Cambridge cds .... **£12.50** ☐

424. 2001, 22nd October
Flags and Ensigns. £1.08 Miniature Sheet
1st Union Flag, !st White Ensign, !st Jolly Roger, !st Chief of Defense Staff

424a Miniature Sheet on illustrated cover, any postmark .... **£1.50** ☐
424b With First Day of Issue, Royal Mail, Tallents House, Edinburgh handstamp .... **£4.00** ☐
424c With First Day of Issue, Rosyth, Dumfirmline handstamp (skull & crossbones) .... **£4.50** ☐
424d With First Day of Issue, Rosyth, Dumfirmline handstamp .... **£4.50** ☐
424e With any one of some 26 additional relevant commemorative handstamps .... **£8.50** ☐
424f With Chatham, Gosport, Drake, Barrow cds .... **£11.50** ☐
424g With St. Andrews cds, St. George's Cross cds, Union St. cds .... **£11.50** ☐
424h With Clyde Submarine Base cds, North Rosyth cds .... **£11.50** ☐

425. 2001, 22nd October
Flags & Ensigns. £1.62 Booklet. Self Adhesive
1st Jolly Roger, !st White Ensign + 4 x 1st Definitive
425a Complete Booklet on illustrated cover, with Self Adhesive Stamps, Barrow in Furness h/s. **£6.00** ☐
In addition all Flags and Ensigns handstamps (and cds) were available for use with this Booklet Catalogue values are the same as for the Flags and Ensigns Stamps, issued same day.

---

426. 2001, 22nd October
Unseen & Unheard, £6.76 Prestige Stamp Book. 4 Panes
(2 x 1st and 65p Submarine Stamps), (2 x 2nd and 45p Submarine Stamps), (All 4 Flags & Ensigns Stamps), (4 x 1st + 4 x E Scottish Stamps + label)

426a Four Complete Panes on illustrated covers, any postmark .... **£8.00** ☐
426b With Unseen & Unheard (submarine), Barrow-in-Furness handstamp .... **£24.00** ☐
426c With Unseen & Unheard (submarine), Birmingham handstamp .... **£24.00** ☐
426d With 1901-2001 (submarine service flag), Chatham handstamp .... **£24.00** ☐
426e With Royal Navy Submarine Museum...Centenary 1901-2001, Gosport h/s.. ...... **£24.00** ☐
426f With Submarines, 100th Anniversary, Gosport, Hampshire handstamp .... **£24.00** ☐
426g With R.N. Submarine Service Centenary, 1901-2001, Gosport, Hampshire h/s .... **£24.00** ☐
426h With R.N. Submarine Service Centenary, 1901-2001, Faslane, Helensburgh h/s . **£24.00** ☐

In addition all Flags and Ensigns handstamps and cds were available for use with this issue
Catalogue values for the 4 complete Panes, using Flags and Ensigns handstamps, are **£24** each.
cds catalogue values for the 4 complete Panes are **£30** each.

---

427. 2001, 6th November
Christmas Issue. Self-adhesive
2nd, 1st, E (Europe), 45p, 65p - Five Stamps Featuring Playful Robins

427a Set on illustrated cover, any postmark .... **£2.00** ☐
427b With First Day of Issue, Royal Mail, Tallents House, Edinburgh handstamp .... **£4.00** ☐
427c With First Day of Issue in English/Welsh text (snowflake), Bethlehem, Llandeilo h/s ... **£4.50** ☐
427d With First Day of Issue in English/Welsh text, Bethlehem, Llandeilo handstamp..... **£4.50** ☐
427e With any one of some 20 additional relevant commemorative handstamps .... **£10.00** ☐
427f With Nasareth cds, Holy Island cds, Angel Hill cds, or Noel Road cds .... **£12.50** ☐
427g With Jerusalem St cds, Godshill cds, St. Nicholas cds .... **£12.50** ☐
427h With Robins Lane cds, Birdholme cds, Branch End cds, or Robin Hood cds .... **£14.00** ☐
427i **Christmas Booklets** – 1st or 2nd x 2 on display cover, any postmark .... **£10.00** ☐

428. 2001, 18th December

Cartoons. £2.70 Customised Sheet

10 x 1st Cartoon Greetings Stamps with new labels. Stamps as issued in 1996.

428a	Complete Sheet on illustrated cover, any postmark	**£2.50** ☐
428b	With Seasons Greetings in English/Welsh text, Bethlehem, Llandeilo h/s (angel)	**£5.00** ☐
428c	With Merry Christmas, Mount Pleasant, London EC1 h/s (father christmas)	**£6.00** ☐
428d	With Merry Christmas from Royal Mail, Birmingham handstamp	**£6.00** ☐
428e	With Laughterton (postman), Lincoln handstamp	**£10.00** ☐
428f	With Cartoons, Nutts Corner, Crumlin handstamp	**£10.00** ☐
428g	With Cartoons, Money More, Magnerafelt handstamp	**£10.00** ☐
428h	With Cartoons, Letters, Lochbroom, Garve handstamp	**£10.00** ☐
428i	With Cartoons, Falstone, Hexham handstamp	**£10.00** ☐
428j	With Cartoons, Clock Face, St Helens handstamp	**£10.00** ☐
428k	With Cartoons, Lover, Salisbury handstamp	**£10.00** ☐
428l	With Cartoons, World's End, Waterlooville handstamp	**£10.00** ☐
428m	With Cartoons, Fetcham, Leatherhead handstamp	**£10.00** ☐
428n	With Cartoons, Braintree, Essex handstamp	**£10.00** ☐
428o	With Cartoons, Ringmore, Kingsbridge handstamp	**£10.00** ☐
428p	With Greet cds, Greetwell cds, Greetland cds	**£12.50** ☐
428q	With Laughterton cds, Laughton cds, Letters cds	**£12.50** ☐

429. 2002, 15th January 2002

Rudyard Kipling. Just So Stories Centenary. Self-adhesive

10 x 1st Stamps, Illustrating the Kipling Just So Stories

429a	Set of 10 stamps on illustrated cover, any postmark	**£2.50** ☐
429b	With First Day of Issue, Royal Mail, Tallents House, Edinburgh handstamp	**£5.00** ☐
429c	With First Day of Issue, Burwash, Etchingham handstamp (snake)	**£5.50** ☐
429d	With First Day of Issue, Burwash, Etchingham handstamp	**£5.50** ☐
429e	With any one of some 30 additional relevant commemorative handstamps	**£10.00** ☐
429f	With Burwash cds, Poets Field cds, Rottingdean cds, Westward Ho cds	**£12.50** ☐
429g	With Camels Head cds, Crabbs Cross cds, Crab Lane cds, Whale Hill cds	**£12.50** ☐

First Day Covers signed by the Stamp Designer

Covers, with one or more Stamps, signed by the designer are worth a 20% premium over catalogue prices.

430 2002, 6th February

The Queen's Golden Jubilee. 50th Anniversary of the Accession

Portraits of the Queen: 2nd Wilding,1st Beaton, E Snowdon, 45p Karsh, 65p Graham

430a	Set on illustrated cover, any postmark	£2.00 ☐
430b	With First Day of Issue, Royal Mail, Tallents House, Edinburgh handstamp	£4.50 ☐
430c	With First Day of Issue, Famous Have Been The Reigns Of Our Queens.Windsor h/s	£5.00 ☐
430d	With First Day of Issue, Windsor handstamp	£5.00 ☐
430e	With any one of some 41 additional relevant commemorative handstamps	£7.50 ☐
430f	With Jubilee Crescent cds, Jubilee Fields cds, Jubilee Oak cds	£12.00 ☐
430g	With Heathrow cds, Queen's Parade cds, Throne cds, Windsor cds	£12.00 ☐
430h	With Buckingham Palace cds, Windsor Castle cds **(£120)**, Sandringham cds	£110.00 ☐

431 2002, 5th March

Occasions Stamps

1st New Baby, 1st Love, 1st Hello, 1st Moving Home, 1st Best Wishes

431a	Set on illustrated cover, any postmark	£2.00 ☐
431b	With First Day of Issue, Royal Mail, Tallents House, Edinburgh handstamp	£3.50 ☐
431c	With First Day of Issue, Merry Hill, Wolverhampton handstamp (letters)	£4.00 ☐
431d	With First Day of Issue, Merry Hill, Wolverhampton handstamp	£4.00 ☐
431e	With any one of some 16 additional relevant commemorative handstamps	£7.50 ☐
431f	With Church cds, Greet cds, Lover cds, Weddington cds	£10.00 ☐
431g	With Bunny cds, Daisy cds, Newhaven cds, The Warren cds	£10.00 ☐

Modern Issues with a non relevant postmark are of little value, in today's market place.

QEII • Commemoratives 2002

432 2002, 19th March

Coastlines. UK Coastal Scenes

10 x 27p Se-tenant Block. Stamps Depict British Coastlines

432a	Set on illustrated cover, any postmark	**£2.50**	☐
432b	With First Day of Issue, Royal Mail, Tallents House, Edinburgh handstamp	**£4.50**	☐
432c	With First Day of Issue, Coast Poolewe, Achnasheen handstamp (crab)	**£5.00**	☐
432d	With First Day of Issue, Coast Poolewe, Achnasheen handstamp	**£5.00**	☐
432e	With any one of some 26 additional relevant commemorative handstamps	**£8.00**	☐
432f	With Broadstairs cds, Dover cds, Newquay cds, Padstow cds	**£12.50**	☐
432g	With Dunster cds, Portrush cds, Sandbanks cds, Studland cds	**£12.50**	☐
432h	With The Harbour cds, Harris cds, Seaview cds, The Rock cds	**£12.50**	☐

433 2002, 9th April

Circus (Europa Issue)

2nd Slack Wire Act, 1st Lion Tamer, E Trick Tri-cyclist, 45p Krazy Kar, 65p Equestrienne

433a	Set on illustrated cover, any postmark	**£2.00**	☐
433b	With First Day of Issue, Royal Mail, Tallents House, Edinburgh handstamp	**£4.00**	☐
433c	With First Day of Issue (Clown Head), Clowne, Chesterfield handstamp	**£4.50**	☐
433d	With First Day of Issue, Clowne, Chesterfield handstamp	**£4.50**	☐
433e	With any one of some 17 additional relevant commemorative handstamps	**£7.50**	☐
433f	With Big Top cds, Castle cds, Clowne cds, Laughterton cds	**£11.00**	☐
433g	With Addlestone cds, Chipperfield Road Tankerton cds	**£11.00**	☐

A checklist of pre-release covers is to be found on pages 458 - 459. Pre-release covers make a great addition to any first day cover collection.

434 2002, 23rd April

Occasions Reprint

5 x 1st (as issued March 5th) each with different label added

434a Set of Stamps with labels on illustrated cover, any postmark .... **£2.00** ☐
434b With Occasions, Greetwell, Gainsborough handstamp .... **£6.00** ☐
434c With Occasions Generic Issue, Gretna Green, Carlisle handstamp .... **£6.00** ☐
434d With United for Peace, St George's Day, Westminster, London handstamp .... **£6.00** ☐
434e With Alexander Dumas Bi-Centenary... Stories Rd, London SE5 handstamp .... **£6.00** ☐
434f With Bloody April, Arras, British Forces Postal Service 2663 .... **£6.00** ☐
434g With Lover cds, Greet cds, Bunny cds, Daisy Hill cds .... **£10.00** ☐

All prices in this catalogue are for clean covers, with undamaged stamps and clear postmarks.

435 2002, 25th April

HM The Queen Mother. In Memoriam

Four Portraits of The Queen Mother. Adaptation of Stamps Issued in 1990

1st - by Parkinson 1990. E - by Wilding 1948, 45p - by Park 1930, 65p - by Martin 1907

435a Set on illustrated cover, any postmark .... **£2.00** ☐
435b With First Day of Issue, Royal Mail, Tallents House, Edinburgh handstamp .... **£4.00** ☐
435c With First Day of Issue (St.James's Palace), London SW1 handstamp .... **£4.50** ☐
435d With First Day of Issue (non pictorial), London SW1 handstamp .... **£4.50** ☐
435e With any one of some 24 additional relevant commemorative handstamps .... **£7.50** ☐
435f With Balmoral cds, Glamis cds, Mey cds, Walmer cds .... **£11.00** ☐
435g With Bowes cds, Queen Elizabeth Ave cds, Throne cds, Windsor cds .... **£11.00** ☐
435h With House of Commons or House of Lords cds,any Forces PO cds (**£10**) .... **£15.00** ☐
435i With Buckingham Palace cds, Windsor Castle cds (**£120**) .... **£100.00** ☐

QEII • Commemoratives 2002

436 2002, 2nd May

Jet Aircraft. 50 Years of Passenger Jet Travel

2nd Airbus A340 2002, 1st Concorde 1976, E Trident 1964, 45p VC10 1964, 65p Comet 1952.

436a	Set on illustrated cover, any postmark	**£2.00** ☐
436b	With First Day of Issue, Royal Mail, Tallents House, Edinburgh handstamp	**£4.00** ☐
436c	With First Day of Issue (altimeter), Heathrow Airport, London handstamp	**£4.50** ☐
436d	With First Day of Issue, Heathrow Airport, London handstamp	**£4.50** ☐
436e	With any one of some 32 additional relevant commemorative handstamps	**£7.50** ☐
436f	With Heathrow Terminal 2 or 4 cds, Gatwick cds, Glasgow Airport cds, Stansted cds	**£11.00** ☐
436g	With Manchester Airport cds, Luton cds, Filton cds, Biggin Hill cds, Wing cds	**£11.00** ☐
436h	With Duxford cds, Farnborough cds, Hatfield cds, Hurn cds, Whittle le Woods cds	**£11.00** ☐

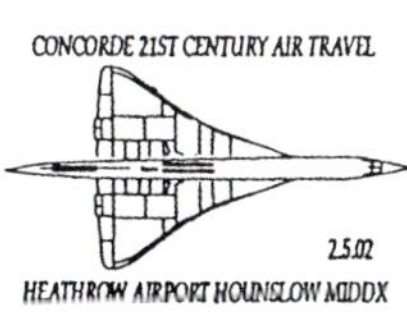

437 2002, 2nd May

Jet Aircraft. £1.93 Miniature Sheet.

The 5 Jet Aircraft Stamps - 2nd, 1st, E, 45p, 65p

All Jet Aircraft handstamps (and cds) were available for use with the Miniature Sheet

437a	Complete Miniature Sheet, with any postmark	**£2.00** ☐
437b	With any Jet Aircraft First Day of Issue handstamp, as above	**£4.50** ☐
437c	With any Jet Aircraft handstamp, as above	**£7.50** ☐
437d	With any Jet Aircraft cds, as above	**£11.00** ☐

438 2002, 2nd May

Jet Aircraft. £1.62 Booklet. Self-adhesive

2 x 1st Concorde Jet Aircraft Stamp + 4 x 1st Definitives

All Jet Aircraft handstamps (and cds) were available for use with the Booklet issue

438a	Complete Booklet, with any postmark	**£2.00** ☐
438b	With any Jet Aircraft First Day of Issue handstamp, as above	**£4.50** ☐
438c	With any Jet Aircraft handstamp, as above	**£7.50** ☐
438d	Self Adhesives, Heathrow Airport, Hounslow, Middx handstamp	**£7.50** ☐
438e	With any Jet Aircraft cds, as above	**£10.00** ☐

Jet Aircraft. 50 Years of Passenger Jet Travel

The jet engine was invented by Sir Frank Whittle and flew for the first time in 1941.
In 1952 the first commercial flight by a jet aircraft was achieved by a Comet - from Heathrow to Johannesburg.

439 2002, 21st May
Football World Cup. Sheet Format
1st Crowned Lion supporting Shield of St.George

439a	One 1st Stamp on illustrated cover, any postmark	**£0.50** ☐
439b	With First Day of Issue, Royal Mail, Tallents House, Edinburgh handstamp	**£2.50** ☐
439c	With First Day of Issue, Wembley handstamp (Goal, Goal)	**£3.00** ☐
439d	With First Day of Issue (non pictorial), Wembley handstamp	**£3.00** ☐
439e	With any one of some 28 additional relevant commemorative handstamps	**£4.50** ☐
439f	With The Ball cds, Ball Green cds, Lion Green cds, Moore cds, Haltwistle cds	**£6.50** ☐
439g	With New England cds, Wembley cds, Wembley Park cds,	**£6.50** ☐

440 2002, 21st May
Football World Cup. £1.35 Miniature Sheet
1st Crowned Lion + 4 x 1st Football on St.George Flag new Stamps
All Football World Cup handstamps (and cds) above were available for use with this issue

440a	Complete Miniature Sheet, with any postmark	**£2.00** ☐
440b	With any Football World Cup First Day of Issue handstamp, as above	**£3.50** ☐
440c	With any Football World Cup handstamp, as above	**£6.00** ☐
440d	With any Football World Cup cds, as above	**£9.00** ☐

441 2002, 21st May
Football World Cup. £1.62 Booklet. Self-adhesive
2 x 1st St. George Flag + 4 x 1st Definitives

441a	Complete Booklet, with any postmark	**£2.00** ☐
441b	With any Football World Cup First Day of Issue handstamp, as above	**£3.50** ☐
441c	With Self Adhesives Wembley, Home of Football handstamp	**£6.00** ☐
441d	With any Football World Cup handstamp, as above	**£6.00** ☐
441e	With any Football World Cup cds, as above	**£9.00** ☐

442 2002, 21st May
Football World Cup. Smilers Sheet
20 x 1st Football St.George Flag Stamp, each with a football fans/scenes label

442a	Single Stamp plus label on illustrated cover, with any postmark,	**£0.50** ☐
442b	With any Football World Cup First Day of Issue handstamp, as above	**£2.50** ☐
442c	With any Football World Cup handstamp, as above	**£4.00** ☐
442d	With any Football World Cup cds, as above	**£6.00** ☐
442e	Complete Sheet, any handstamp	**£16.00** ☐

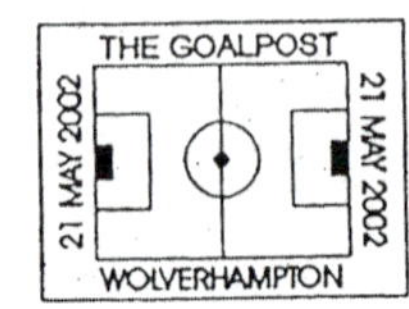

443 2002, 16th July

The XVII Commonwealth Games

2nd Swimming, 1st Running, E Cycling, 47p Long Jump, 68p Wheelchair Athletics

443a Set on illustrated cover, any postmark .... **£2.20** ☐
443b With First Day of Issue, Tallents House, Edinburgh handstamp .... **£4.00** ☐
443c With First Day of Issue, 25.07.02 Manchester handstamp .... **£4.50** ☐
443d With First Day of Issue (non pictorial), Manchester handstamp .... **£4.50** ☐
443e With any one of some 25 additional relevant commemorative handstamps .... **£7.50** ☐
443f With Fence cds, Jump cds, Bowling cds, Poole cds, Badminton cds .... **£11.00** ☐
443g With any Manchester cds, any Field PO cds, Manchester Airport cds .... **£11.00** ☐
443h With Stoke Mandeville cds, Bournville cds, The Chase cds .... **£11.00** ☐
443i With M2002 Games Village cds .... **£48.00** ☐

The Games were held in Manchester and opened by The Queen. 5,250 competitors and officials from 72 nations took part in 17 sports over a ten day period.

444 2002, 20th August

Peter Pan. 150th Anniversary Great Ormond Street Hospital

2nd Tinkerbell, 1st Darling Children, E Crocodile, 47p Hook, 68p Peter Pan

444a Set on illustrated cover, any postmark .... **£2.00** ☐
444b With First Day of Issue, Royal Mail, Tallents House Edinburgh handstamp .... **£4.00** ☐
444c With First Day of Issue, Hook handstamp .... **£4.50** ☐
444d With First Day of Issue (non pictorial), Hook handstamp .... **£4.50** ☐
444e With any one of some 21 additional relevant commemorative handstamps .... **£7.50** ☐
444f With Childs Hill cds, Kidsgrove cds, Farnham cds, Russell Square cds .... **£11.00** ☐
444g With Hook cds, Pan cds .... **£14.00** ☐

445 2002, 10th September

London Bridges

2nd Millennium Bridge, 1st Tower Bridge, E Westminster, 47p Blackfiars, 68p London

445a Set on illustrated cover, any postmark .... **£2.00** ☐

445b With First Day of Issue, Royal Mail,Tallents House, Edinburgh handstamp .... **£4.00** ☐

445c With First Day of Issue, London SEI handstamp .... **£4.50** ☐

445d With First Day of Issue (non pictorial), London SEI handstamp .... **£4.50** ☐

445e With any one of some 24 additional relevant commemorative handstamps .... **£7.50** ☐

445f With Blackfriars Road cds, Bridge cds, Ironbridge cds, London Bridge cds .... **£11.00** ☐

445g With Putney Bridge Rd cds, Vauxhall Bridge Rd cds, Westminster Bridge Road cds... **£11.00** ☐

445h With New Bridge cds, Rising Bridge cds, Longbridge cds .... **£12.00** ☐

446 2002, 10th September

London Bridges. £1.62 Booklet. Self-Adhesive

2 x 1st Tower Bridge + 4 x 1st Gold Definitives

446a Complete Booklet, on illustrated cover, with any postmark .... **£2.00** ☐

446b With any London Bridges First Day of Issue handstamp, as above .... **£4.00** ☐

446c With any London Bridges handstamp as above .... **£7.00** ☐

446d With Bridges Of London, NVI Booklet, Tower Hill, London EC3 handstamp .... **£7.50** ☐

446e With Bridges Of London, NVI Booklet, The Guildhall, London EC2 handstamp .... **£7.50** ☐

446f With Self Adhesives, Bridges of London handstamp .... **£7.50** ☐

446g With any London Bridges cds .... **£10.00** ☐

Most modern QEII covers with a non relevant postmark are of little value in today's market.

447 2002, 24th September
Astronomy. £1.08 Miniature Sheet. Block of 4 x 1st Stamps
Planetary Nebula in Aquila and Norma, Seyfert 2 Galaxy in Pegasus and Circinus

447a	Complete Sheet on illustrated cover, any postmark	**£2.00**	☐
447b	With First Day of Issue, Royal Mail, Tallents House, Edinburgh handstamp	**£3.50**	☐
447c	With First Day of Issue, Star, Glenrothes handstamp	**£4.00**	☐
447d	With First Day of Issue (non pictorial), Star, Glenrothes handstamp	**£4.00**	☐
447e	With any one of some 25 additional relevant commemorative handstamps	**£7.50**	☐
447f	With Greenwich cds, Herstmonceaux cds, Kennedy Centre cds, Seven Sisters cds.	**£10.00**	☐
447g	With Meridian Centre cds, Newton cds, The Science Museum cds, Shuttlewood cds..	**£10.00**	☐
447h	With Starcross cds, Starbeck Avenue cds, World's End cds	**£10.00**	☐

See Definitives section for pricing on the Astronomy Prestige Stamp Book

448 2002, 1st October
Generic Smilers Sheets (2). With New Labels Attached
10 x 1st Teddy Bear Stamps + 10 x 1st Dennis the Menace Stamps. With Joke Labels
20 x 1st Father Christmas (1997) Stamps. With Jingle Bells Labels

448a	Set of three Stamps with Label, any postmark	**£1.50**	☐
448b	With Smilers, Bearpark, Durham handstamp	**£6.00**	☐
448c	With Smilers, Bearstead, Maidstone handstamp	**£6.00**	☐
448d	With Smilers, Bean, Dartford handstamp	**£6.00**	☐
448e	With Smilers Issue, Bethlehem, Llandeilo handstamp	**£6.00**	☐
448f	With Bearpark cds, Laughterton cds, Laughton cds, Greetwell cds	**£10.00**	☐

QEII • Commemoratives 2002

449 2002, 8th October
Pillar to Post. 150th Anniversary First Roadside Pillar Box
2nd 1857 Box, 1st 1874 Box, E 1934 Box, 47p 1939 Box, 68p 1980 Box

449a Set on illustrated cover, any postmark .... **£2.00** ☐
449b With First Day of Issue, Royal Mail, Tallents House, Edinburgh handstamp .... **£4.00** ☐
449c With First Day of Issue, Bishops Caundle, Sherbourne handstamp .... **£4.50** ☐
449d With First Day of Issue (non pictorial), Bishops Caundle, Sherbourne handstamp .. **£4.50** ☐
449e With any one of some 25 additional relevant commemorative handstamps .... **£7.50** ☐
449f With Bishops Caundle cds, Botchergate cds, Box cds, Carronshore cds .... **£12.00** ☐
449g With Hythe cds, Mount Pleasant cds, Paris Avenue cds, Send cds .... **£12.00** ☐

450 2002, 5th November
Christmas Issue
2nd Spruce, 1st Holly, E Ivy, 47p Mistletoe, 68p Pine Cone

450a Set on illustrated cover, any postmark .... **£2.00** ☐
450b With First Day of Issue, Royal Mail, Tallents House, Edinburgh handstamp .... **£4.00** ☐
450c With First Day of Issue (English/Welsh text), Bethlehem, Llandeilo handstamp ...... **£4.50** ☐
450d With First Day of Issue (non pictorial, English/Welsh text), Bethlehem, Llandeilo h/s .... **£4.50** ☐
450e With any one of some 21 additional relevant commemorative handstamps .... **£7.50** ☐
450f With Berryhill cds, Botanic Gardens cds, Firtree cds, Ivy Bush cds, Ivybridge cds ... **£11.00** ☐
450g With Hollybank cds, Holly Lane cds, Holly Hedge cds,Hollybush cds, Holly Hall cds... **£11.00** ☐
450h Nasareth cds, Pinewoods cds, Thornberry cds, Woodlands cds, Kew Gardens cds .... **£11.00** ☐
450i With Buckingham Palace cds, Windsor Castle cds **(£46)** .... **£32.00** ☐
450j **Christmas Booklets** – 1st or 2nd x 2 on display cover, any postmark .... **£10.00** ☐

All prices in this catalogue are for clean covers, with undamaged Stamps and clear postmarks.

Anything less is worth less!

QEII • Commemoratives 2003

451. 2003, 14th January

Birds of Prey. Se-tenant

5 x 1st Barn Owl, 5 x 1st Kestrel

451a Set of 10 x 1st Class Se-tenant Stamps on illustrated cover, any postmark .... **£3.00** ☐
451b With First Day of Issue, Tallents House, Edinburgh handstamp .... **£4.50** ☐
451c With First Day of Issue, Hawkshead, Ambleside handstamp .... **£5.00** ☐
451d With First Day of Issue (non pictorial), Hawkshead, Ambleside handstamp .... **£5.00** ☐
451e With any one of some 28 additional relevant commemorative handstamps .... **£9.00** ☐
451f With Ashburton cds, Owlsmoor cds, Wingham cds, Barn Lane cds .... **£12.00** ☐
451g With Eagle cds, Hawkhurst cds, Hawkshead cds, Hawkswood cds .... **£12.00** ☐
451h With Falconwood cds, Falcon Lodge cds, Wing cds .... **£12.00** ☐

452. 2003, 21st January

Generic Greetings (Flowers). With New Labels Attached

10 x 1st Flowers Stamps (from 1997). Each with new label attached

452a Set with any one of 10 different Smilers handstamps .... **£9.00** ☐
(Ardingly, Chelsea, Harrogate, Kew, Llanarthney, Mevagissey, Rettendon Common, St.Austell, Torrington, Woking)
452b With Botanical Fine Arts, Kew Gardens handstamp .... **£9.00** ☐
452c With Bloomfield cds, Greet cds, Greetwell cds .... **£12.00** ☐
452d With Kew Gardens cds, Flowery Field cds, Chelsea cds .... **£12.00** ☐

A few other cds postmarks can be related to this issue - £10

Royal Mail did not treat this as a new issue, so no First Day of Issue handstamps available.

QEII • Commemoratives 2003

453. 2003, 4th February
Occasions Stamps. Third Series. Se-tenant
1st Gold Star, 1st I Love U, 1st Angel, 1st Yes, 1st Oops! 1st I did it!

453a	Set of Stamps on illustrated cover, any postmark	£2.00 ☐
453b	With First Day of Issue, Tallents House, Edinburgh handstamp	£4.00 ☐
453c	With First Day of Issue, Merry Hill, Wolverhampton handstamp	£4.50 ☐
453d	With First Day of Issue (non pictorial), Merry Hill, Wolverhampton handstamp	£4.50 ☐
453e	With any one of some 16 additional relevant commemorative handstamps	£7.50 ☐
453f	With Angel Hill cds, Lover cds, Gretna Green cds, Greet cds	£10.00 ☐
453g	With Greetwell cds, Tickenham cds, Tick Hill cds, Tickton cds	£10.00 ☐

454. 2003, 25th February
The Secret of Life. DNA and the Gnome
2nd End of the Beginning, 1st Comparative Genetics, E Cracking the Code,
47p Genetic Engineering, 68p Medical Futures

454a	Set of Stamps on illustrated cover, any postmark	£2.00 ☐
454b	With First Day of Issue, Tallents House, Edinburgh handstamp	£4.00 ☐
454c	With First Day of Issue, Cambridge handstamp	£4.50 ☐
454d	With First Day of Issue (non pictorial), Cambridge handstamp	£4.50 ☐
454e	With any one of some 24 additional relevant commemorative handstamps	£7.50 ☐
454f	With Cambridge cds, Crick cds, Watson Way cds, Weston Favell cds	£11.00 ☐
454g	With Cavendish cds, The Science Museum cds, Healing cds	£11.00 ☐
454h	With New Invention cds, Sheepy cds, Sandwich cds	£11.00 ☐

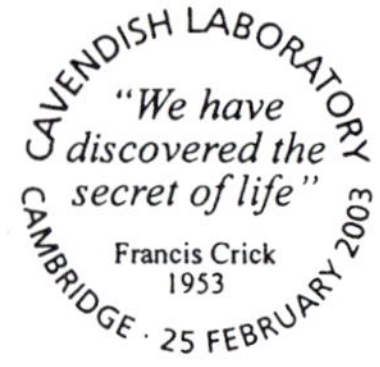

This is the 30th Edition of the Collect GB First Day Covers catalogue

QEII • Commemoratives 2003

455. 2003, 25th March

Fun Fruit & Veg. Self-adhesives

10 x 1st Class Stamps (Strawberry, Potato, Apple, Pepper, Pear, Orange, Tomato, Lemon, Sprout, Aubergine)

455a Set of 10 x 1st Class Stamps on illustrated cover, any postmark ....**£3.00** ☐
455b With First Day of Issue, Tallents House, Edinburgh handstamp ....**£4.50** ☐
455c With First Day of Issue, Pear Tree, Derby handstamp..**£5.00** ☐
455d With First Day of Issue (non pictorial), Pear Tree, Derby handstamp..........................**£5.00** ☐
455e With any one of some 24 additional relevant commemorative handstamps ....**£9.00** ☐
455f With Applecross cds, Orange Tree cds, Pear Tree cds, Strawberry Hill cds ....**£12.00** ☐
455g With The Allotments cds, The Orchards cds, Orchard Way cds, Ripe cds ....**£12.00** ☐
455h With Faversham cds, Jersey Farm cds, King Edward Road cds, Appledore cds....**£12.00** ☐

456. 2003, 29th April

Extreme Endeavours

2nd Amy Johnson, 1st Hillary/Tenzing, E Stark, 42p Shackleton, 47p Chichester, 68p Scott

456a Set of Stamps on illustrated cover, any postmark ....**£2.00** ☐
456b With First Day of Issue, Tallents House, Edinburgh handstamp ....**£4.00** ☐
456c With First Day of Issue, Plymouth handstamp ....**£4.50** ☐
456d With First Day of Issue (non pictorial), Plymouth handstamp ....**£4.50** ☐
456e With any one of some 32 additional relevant commemorative handstamps ....**£9.00** ☐
456f With North Pole Road cds, The Heights cds, Summit cds, The Camp cds ....**£10.00** ☐
456g With Chichester cds, Devonport cds, Plymouth cds, Hull cds ....**£10.00** ☐
456h With Edmund St cds, Gale Lane cds, Windwhistle cds, Freezywater cds..............**£10.00** ☐

JUST SO STORIES
CENTENARY
RUDYARD KIPLING
429

50TH ANNIVERSARY
QEII ACCESSION
TO THE THRONE
430

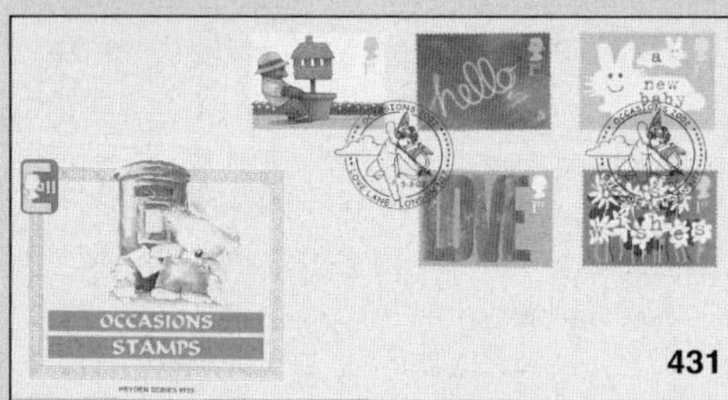
OCCASIONS
STAMPS
431

THE CIRCUS
EUROPA ISSUE
433

WORLD CUP 2002
21 - 5 - 2002
WEMBLEY
Football World Cup 2002
441

435

FOOTBALL
WORLD CUP
MINIATURE SHEET
440

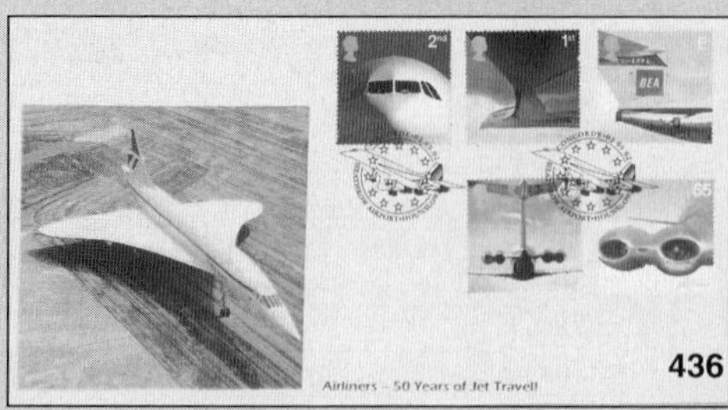
Airliners – 50 Years of Jet Travel
436

SEVENTEENTH
COMMONWEALTH
GAMES
443

QEII Issues - Selected Commemoratives 2002/03

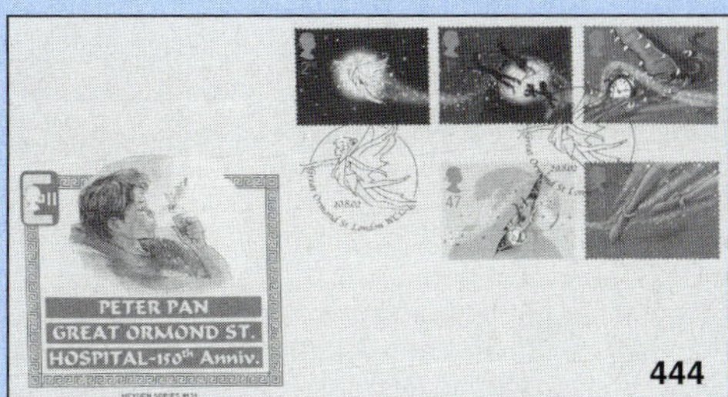

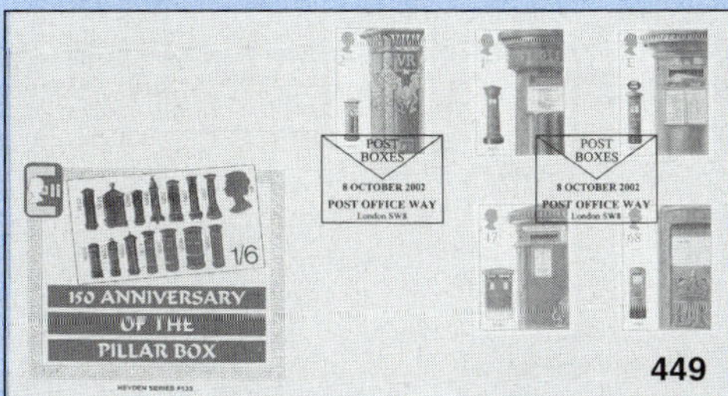

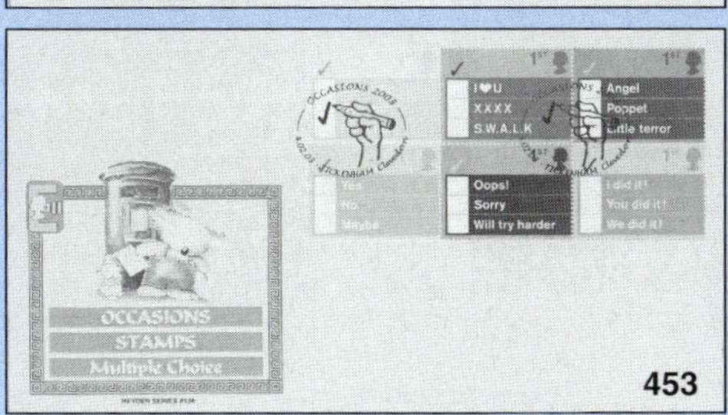

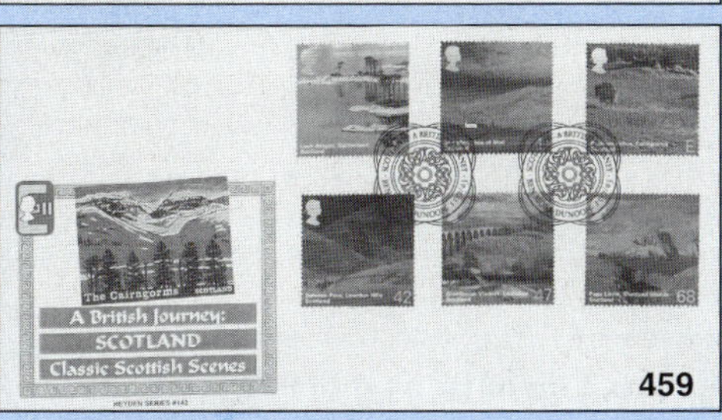

QEII • Commemoratives 2003

457. 2003, 2nd June

The Coronation. 50th Anniversary

10 x 1st Class Stamps. Se-tenant. Scenes from 1953 Coronation Events

457a Set of 10 x 1st Class Se-tenant Stamps on illustrated cover, any postmark .... **£3.00** ☐
457b With First Day of Issue, Tallents House, Edinburgh handstamp .... **£4.50** ☐
457c With First Day of Issue, London SW1 handstamp .... **£5.00** ☐
457d With First Day of Issue (non pictorial), London SW1 handstamp .... **£5.00** ☐
457e With any one of some 36 additional relevant commemorative handstamps .... **£9.00** ☐
457f With Queen's Drive cds, Queen's Parade cds, Queens Street cds, The Mall cds.. **£12.00** ☐
457g With Coronation Parade cds, Coronation Road cds, Coronation Sq. cds............... **£12.00** ☐
457h With Scone cds, Throne cds, Crown House cds, House of Commons cds .... **£12.00** ☐
457i With Windsor cds, Windsor Great Park cds, ... **£12.00** ☐
457j With Buckingham Palace cds, Windsor Castle cds **(£85)**, Balmoral cds .... **£80.00** ☐

458. 2003, 17th June

Prince William of Wales. 21st Birthday

28p, E, 47p, 68p. Contemporary Photographs of the Prince

458a Set of Stamps on illustrated cover, any postmark .... **£2.00** ☐
458b With First Day of Issue, Tallents House, Edinburgh handstamp .... **£4.00** ☐
458c With First Day of Issue, Caerdydd, Cardiff handstamp .... **£4.50** ☐
458d With First Day of Issue (non pictorial), Caerdydd, Cardiff handstamp .... **£4.50** ☐
458e With any one of some 18 additional relevant commemorative handstamps .... **£7.50** ☐
458f With William Street cds, Williamstown cds, St.Andrews cds, Wales cds .... **£9.50** ☐
458g With Princes Ave cds, Princes Parade cds, Princetown cds, Throne cds................. **£9.50** ☐
458h With Buckingham Palace cds, Windsor Castle cds **(£50)**, High Grove cds .... **£45.00** ☐

Any questions on Commemorative handstamps e-mail us at jhbfdc@gmail.com

QEII • Commemoratives 2003

459. 2003, 15th July

Scotland. A British Journey

2nd Loch Assynt, 1st Ben More, E Cairngorms, 42p Dalveen Pass,
47p Glenfinnan Viaduct, 68p Shetland Isles

459a Set of Stamps on illustrated cover, any postmark .... **£2.00** ☐
459b With First Day of Issue, Tallents House, Edinburgh handstamp .... **£4.00** ☐
459c With First Day of Issue, Baltasound, Unst handstamp .... **£4.50** ☐
459d With First Day of Issue (non pictorial), Baltasound, Unst handstamp .... **£4.50** ☐
459e With any one of some 27 additional relevant commemorative handstamps .... **£8.00** ☐
459f With Aros cds, Aith cds, Aviemore cds, Lochinver cds, Leadhills cds .... **£11.00** ☐
459g With The Scotlands cds, Glenfinnan cds, Lochside cds, Thistle Hill cds .... **£11.00** ☐

460. 2003, 12th August

Pub Signs

1st The Station, E Black Swan, 42p Cross Keys, 47p The Mayflower, 68p The Barley Sheaf

460a Set of Stamps on illustrated cover, any postmark .... **£2.00** ☐
460b With First Day of Issue, Tallents House, Edinburgh handstamp .... **£4.00** ☐
460c With First Day of Issue, Cross Keys, Hereford handstamp .... **£4.50** ☐
460d With First Day of Issue (non pictorial), Cross Keys, Hereford handstamp .... **£4.50** ☐
460e With any one of some 24 additional relevant commemorative handstamps .... **£8.00** ☐
460f With Old Swan cds, Cross Keys cds, Southsea cds, Thurnscoe cds .... **£11.00** ☐
460g With Barley Mow cds, The Station cds, Station Road cds, Red Lion cds .... **£11.00** ☐
460h With Beer cds, Brewery Road cds, Bar Road cds, The Bar cds, Brewood cds .... **£11.00** ☐
460i With Watney St cds, Worthington cds, Royal Oak cds, Black Bull cds .... **£11.00** ☐

The QEII Definitives Section starts on page 350

QEII • Commemoratives 2003

461. 2003, 18th September

Transports of Delight. The Golden Age of British Toy Making

1st Meccano, E Wells-Brimtoy, 42p Hornby. 47p Dinky Toys, 68p Mettoy

Miniature Sheet containing all five values issued same day. Same pricing.

461a	Set of Stamps on illustrated cover, any postmark	**£2.00** ☐
461b	With First Day of Issue, Tallents House, Edinburgh handstamp	**£4.00** ☐
461c	With First Day of Issue, Toye, Downpatrick handstamp	**£4.50** ☐
461d	With First Day of Issue (non pictorial), Toye, Downpatrick handstamp	**£4.50** ☐
461e	With First Day of Issue, Stampex, Autumn Exhibition, London handstamp	**£4.50** ☐
461f	With any one of some 31 additional relevant commemorative handstamps	**£8.00** ☐
461g	With Eagle cds, Ford cds, Hornby cds, Model Village cds, The Rocket cds	**£11.00** ☐
461h	With Epping cds, Margate cds, Pollock cds, Wells cds, Playing Place cds	**£11.00** ☐

462. 2003, 7th October

The British Museum. 250th Anniversary

2nd, 1st, E, 42p, 47p, 68p. Heads/Masks from the Museum

462a	Set of Stamps on illustrated cover, any postmark	**£2.50** ☐
462b	With First Day of Issue, Tallents House, Edinburgh handstamp	**£4.50** ☐
462c	With First Day of Issue, London WC1 handstamp	**£5.00** ☐
462d	With First Day of Issue (non pictorial), London WC1 handstamp	**£5.00** ☐
462e	With any one of some 21 additional relevant commemorative handstamps	**£9.00** ☐
462f	With Salt Hill cds, Sutton Woodbridge cds, Russel Square cds, Nile st cds	**£11.50** ☐
462g	With Elgin cds, The Galleries cds, Sloane Square cds Saxon Avenue cds	**£11.50** ☐

See Index on page 3 for full Catalogue Listings

463. 2003, 4th November

Christmas Issue

2nd Ice Spiral, 1st Icicle Star, E Frozen Snow, 53p Ice Ball, 68p Ice Hole, £1.12 Snow Pyramids

463a Set of Stamps on illustrated cover, any postmark .... **£2.50** ☐
463b With First Day of Issue, Tallents House, Edinburgh handstamp .... **£4.50** ☐
463c With First Day of Issue, Bethlehem, Llandeilo handstamp .... **£5.00** ☐
463d With First Day of Issue (non pictorial), Bethlehem, Llandeilo handstamp .... **£5.00** ☐
463e With any one of some 19 additional relevant commemorative handstamps .... **£9.00** ☐
463f With Freezywater cds, Frosterley cds, North Pole Rd cds, Winter Gardens cds..... **£12.00** ☐
463g With Crystal Peaks cds, Crystal Palace Rd cds, Holy Island cds, Holy Town cds.. **£12.00** ☐

464. 2003, 19th December

Rugby World Champions

Miniature Sheet. 2 x 1st + 2 x 68p Scenes from the Cup Final Match.

464a Sheet on illustrated cover, any postmark .... **£2.00** ☐
464b With First Day of Issue, Tallents House, Edinburgh handstamp .... **£4.00** ☐
464c With First Day of Issue, Twickenham handstamp .... **£4.50** ☐
464d With First Day of Issue (non pictorial), Twickenham handstamp .... **£4.50** ☐
464e With any one of some 20 additional relevant commemorative handstamps .... **£7.50** ☐
464f With Playing Place cds, Rugby cds, Twickenham cds, ... **£10.00** ☐
464g With New England cds, Sydney Road cds, The Ball, Widnes cds........ **£10.00** ☐

All prices in this catalogue are for clean covers with undamaged stamps and clear postmarks.

QEII • Commemoratives 2004

465. 2004, 13th January
Classic Locomotives
20p, 28p, E, 42p, 47p, 68p. Featuring six working Steam Locomotives
Miniature Sheet containing all six values issued same day. Same price as below

465a	Set of Stamps on illustrated cover, any postmark	**£2.00** ☐
465b	With First Day of Issue, Tallents House, Edinburgh handstamp	**£4.00** ☐
465c	With First Day of Issue, York handstamp	**£4.50** ☐
465d	With First Day of Issue (non pictorial), York handstamp	**£4.50** ☐
465e	With any one of some 35 additional relevant commemorative handstamps	**£8.00** ☐
465f	With Bewdley cds, Bo'ness cds, Keighley cds, Tywyn cds	**£11.00** ☐
465g	With Loughborough cds, Uckfield cds, Railway Rd cds, The Rocket cds	**£11.00** ☐

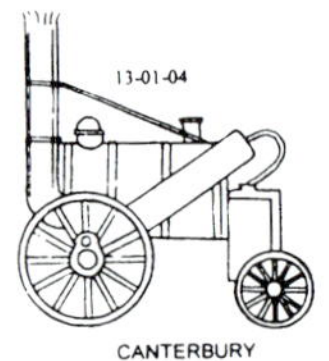

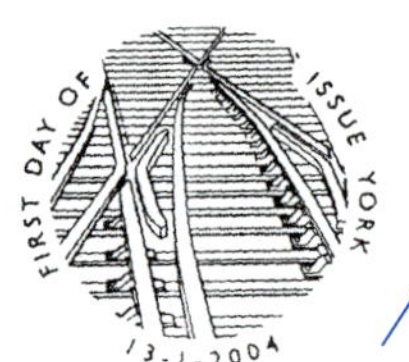

466. 2004, 3rd February
Occasions. Fourth Series. Entertaining Envelopes
5 x 1st Stamps. Featuring Humorous Drawings of an Envelope. Se-tenant

466a	Set of Stamps on illustrated cover, any postmark	**£2.00** ☐
466b	With First Day of Issue, Tallents House, Edinburgh handstamp	**£4.00** ☐
466c	With First Day of Issue, Merry Hill, Wolverhampton handstamp	**£4.50** ☐
466d	With First Day of Issue (non pictorial), Merry Hill, Wolverhampton handstamp	**£4.50** ☐
466e	With any one of some 12 additional relevant commemorative handstamps	**£7.50** ☐
466f	With Greet cds, Letterbreen cds, Letterhandoney cds, Send cds	**£10.00** ☐
466g	With Laughterton cds, Letter cds, Penn cds	**£10.00** ☐

Please refer to notes at the beginning of this catalogue for additional information

467. 2004, 26th February

The Lord of The Rings. Se-tenant

10 x 1st Stamps. Featuring Rare Drawings by J.R.R.Tolkien

467a Set of 10 x 1st Stamps on illustrated cover, any postmark .... **£2.50** ☐
467b With First Day of Issue, Tallents House, Edinburgh handstamp .... **£4.50** ☐
467c With First Day of Issue, Oxford handstamp .... **£5.00** ☐
467d With First Day of Issue (non pictorial), Oxford handstamp .... **£5.00** ☐
467e With First Day of Issue...Stampex, London NI handstamp .... **£5.00** ☐
467f With any one of some 26 additional relevant commemorative handstamps .... **£9.00** ☐
467g With Edgbaston cds, Oxford cds, The Shires cds, Wolvercote cds .... **£12.00** ☐
467h With High Holborn cds, Hurst Green cds, Ringwood cds, Ringmer cds .... **£12.00** ☐

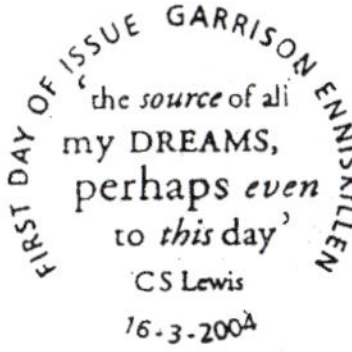

468. 2004, 16th March

Northern Ireland. A British Journey

2nd Ely Island, 1st Giant's Causeway, E Slemish, 42p Banns Road, 47p Glenelly, 68p Islandmore

468a Set of Stamps on illustrated cover, any postmark .... **£2.00** ☐
468b With First Day of Issue, Tallents House, Edinburgh handstamp .... **£4.00** ☐
468c With First Day of Issue, Garrison, Enniskillen handstamp .... **£4.50** ☐
468d With First Day of Issue (non pictorial), Garrison, Enniskillen handstamp .... **£4.50** ☐
468e With any one of some 17 additional relevant commemorative handstamps .... **£8.00** ☐
468f With Ballykeel cds, Bushmills cds, Monea cds, Strangford cds .... **£10.00** ☐
468g With Antrim cds, Draperstown cds, Strabane cds, Warrenpoint cds .... **£10.00** ☐

There are a few other cds that can be related to this issue. Prices from **£8**

469. 2004, 6th April
Entente Cordiale. A Joint English/French Issue
28p Lace 1. by Sir Terry Frost, 57p Coccinelle by Sonia Delaunay

469a	Set of 2 Stamps on illustrated cover, any postmark	**£1.00** ☐
469b	With First Day of Issue, Tallents House, Edinburgh handstamp	**£3.50** ☐
469c	With First Day of Issue, London SW1 handstamp	**£4.00** ☐
469d	With First Day of Issue (non pictorial), London SW1 handstamp	**£4.00** ☐
469e	With any one of some 16 additional relevant commemorative handstamps	**£6.00** ☐
469f	With Britannia cds, Calais Road cds, Dunkirk cds, Paris Avenue cds	**£9.00** ☐
469g	With Cheriton cds, Frogmore cds, Knightsbridge cds, Parliament St cds	**£9.00** ☐

Covers with UK + French Stamps and both UK and French Entente Cordiale handstamps £7.50

470. 2004, 13th April
Ocean Liners
1st RMS Queen Mary 2, E SS Canberra, 42p RMS Queen Mary, 47p RMS Mauretania, 57p SS City of New York, 68p PS Great Western
Miniature Sheet containing all six values issued same day. Same price as below.

470a	Set of Stamps on illustrated cover, any postmark	**£2.50** ☐
470b	With First Day of Issue, Tallents House, Edinburgh handstamp	**£4.50** ☐
470c	With First Day of Issue, Southampton handstamp	**£5.00** ☐
470d	With First Day of Issue (non pictorial), Southampton handstamp	**£5.00** ☐
470e	With any one of some 27 additional relevant commemorative handstamps	**£9.00** ☐
470f	With Belfast cds. Bristol cds, Glasgow cds, Southampton cds, Wallsend cds	**£11.00** ☐
470g	With Queen's Cross cds, Sea Lane cds, Sea Street cds, Seaview cds	**£11.00** ☐
470h	With Bottomboat cds, The Harbour cds, The Quarterdeck cds, Dover cds	**£11.00** ☐

Don't miss the Special Colour Feature, pages 160-176

QEII • Commemoratives 2004

471. 2004, 25th May

Royal Horticultural Society. 200th Anniversary

2nd Dianthus, 1st Dahlia, E Clematis, 42p Miltonia, 47p Lilium, 68p Delphinium

Miniature Sheet containing all six values issued same day. Same price as below.

471a Set of Stamps on illustrated cover, any postmark .... **£2.50** ☐
471b With First Day of Issue, Tallents House, Edinburgh handstamp .... **£4.50** ☐
471c With First Day of Issue, Wisley, Woking handstamp .... **£5.00** ☐
471d With First Day of Issue (non pictorial), Wisley, Woking handstamp .... **£5.00** ☐
471e With First Day of Issue, RHS...London SW1 handstamp .... **£5.00** ☐
471f With any one of some 25 additional relevant commemorative handstamps .... **£9.00** ☐
471g With Chelsea Royal Hospital cds, Ripley cds, Sissinghurst cds, Flore cds .... **£11.00** ☐
471h With Botanic Gardens cds, Bloomfield cds, Garden Village cds, Kew Rd cds .... **£11.00** ☐

472. 2004, 15th June

Wales. A British Journey (Europa Issue)

2nd Barmouth Bridge, 1st Hyddgen, 40p Brecon Beacons, 43p Pen-pych,
47p Rhewl, 68p Marloes Sands

472a Set of Stamps on illustrated cover, any postmark .... **£2.50** ☐
472b With First Day of Issue, Tallents House, Edinburgh handstamp .... **£4.50** ☐
472c With First Day of Issue, English and Welsh text handstamp .... **£5.00** ☐
472d With First Day of Issue (non pictorial), English and Welsh text handstamp .... **£5.00** ☐
472e With any one of some 19 additional relevant commemorative handstamps .... **£8.50** ☐
472f With Barmouth cds, Brecon cds, Marloes cds, Rhewl cds, Llangollen cds .... **£11.00** ☐
472g With Blaenrhondda cds, Machynlleth cds, Tregoran cds, Wales cds .... **£11.00** ☐

Please refer to notes at the beginning of this catalogue for additional information

473. 2004, 27th July
Generic Smilers. Rule Britannia!
20 x 1st Union Jack Flag Stamp with Label Attached (Stamp as issued in 2001)
473a Stamp with any one label attached and any of 4 commemorative handstamps.......**£4.50** □
473b With Britannia cds, St George's cds, St George's Cross cds, Windsor cds ....**£7.50** □
Royal Mail did not treat this as a new issue, so no First Day of Issue handstamps available.

---

474. 2004, 10th August
Royal Society of Arts. 250th Anniversary
1st Penny Black, 40p W. Shipley, 43p RSA Exams, 47p Chimney Sweeper,
57p Gill's Typeface, 68p Zero Waste
474a Set of Stamps on illustrated cover, any postmark..**£2.50** □
474b With First Day of Issue, Tallents House, Edinburgh handstamp ....**£4.50** □
474c With First Day of Issue, London WC2 handstamp ....**£5.00** □
474d With First Day of Issue (non pictorial), London WC2 handstamp ....**£5.00** □
474e With any one of some 20 additional relevant commemorative handstamps................**£8.50** □
474f With Hampstead Heath cds, Kidderminster cds, Trafalgar Square cds ....**£11.00** □
474g With Ditchling cds, New Covent Garden cds, Shipley cds.......................................**£11.00** □

All prices in this catalogue are for clean covers...

475. 2004, 16th September

Woodland Animals. Se-tenant

10 x 1st Class Stamps - Pine Martin, Roe Deer, Badger, Mouse, Wild Cat, Red Squirrel, Stoat, Bat, Mole, Fox

475a	Set of Stamps on illustrated cover, any postmark	£3.00 ☐
475b	With First Day of Issue, Tallents House, Edinburgh handstamp	£4.50 ☐
475c	With First Day of Issue, Woodland, Bishop Auckland handstamp	£5.00 ☐
475d	With First Day of Issue (non pictorial), Woodland, Bishop Auckland handstamp	£5.00 ☐
475e	With First Day of Issue...Stampex, London NI handstamp	£5.00 ☐
475f	With any one of some 25 additional relevant commemorative handstamps	£9.00 ☐
475g	With Beddgelert cds, Brockfield cds, Foxhole cds, Mole Hill Green cds	£12.00 ☐
475h	With Deerpark cds, Kinloch Rannoch cds, Mousehole cds, New Deer cds	£12.00 ☐
475i	With Catsfield cds, Nutgrove cds, Woodland cds	£12.00 ☐

476. 2004, 5th October

Scottish Parliament. Miniature Sheet

40p Thistle, 1st Lion, 2nd Saltire Flag, 1st Lion, 40p Thistle

476a	Complete Miniature Sheet on illustrated cover, any postmark	£2.50 ☐
476b	With Royal Mail, Tallents House, Edinburgh handstamp	£4.00 ☐
476c	With Royal Mail, Edinburgh, EH99 handstamp	£4.50 ☐
476d	With any one of some 8 additional relevant commemorative handstamps	£8.00 ☐
476e	With Edinburgh cds, Linlithgow cds, Parliament Street cds, The Scotlands cds	£10.00 ☐
476f	With The Scottish Parliament cds, St Andrew cds, Thistle Hill or Tollcross cds	£10.00 ☐

There were no Royal Mail handstamps this time that included the words 'First Day of Issue'

...with undamaged stamps and clear postmarks!

QEII • Commemoratives 2004

477. 2004, 12th October

The Crimean War 1854-1856. 150th Anniversary

2nd Pte McNamara, 1st Piper Muir, 40p SM Edwards, 57p Sgt Powell, 68p SM Poole, £1.12 Sgt Glasgow

477a	Set of Stamps on illustrated cover, any postmark	**£3.00**	☐
477b	With First Day of Issue, Tallents House, Edinburgh handstamp	**£4.50**	☐
477c	With First Day of Issue, London SW3 handstamp	**£5.00**	☐
477d	With First Day of Issue (non pictorial), London SW3 handstamp	**£5.00**	☐
477e	With any one of some 27 additional relevant commemorative handstamps	**£9.00**	☐
477f	With Battle cds, Chelsea Royal Hospital cds, Gun Hill cds, West Wellow cds	**£12.00**	☐
477g	With Alma Vale cds, Edward St cds, Muir of Ord cds, Poole cds, Raglan cds	**£12.00**	☐

478. 2004, 2nd November

Christmas Issue. Self-adhesive

2nd, 1st, 40p, 57p, 68p, £1.12. Scenes of Father Christmas on the Roof
Miniature Sheet with all six values (not self-adhesive) issued same day. Same pricing.

478a	Set of Stamps on illustrated cover, any postmark	**£3.00**	☐
478b	With First Day of Issue, Tallents House, Edinburgh handstamp	**£4.50**	☐
478c	With First Day of Issue, Bethlehem, Llandeilo handstamp	**£5.00**	☐
478d	With First Day of Issue (non pictorial), Bethlehem, Llandeilo handstamp	**£5.00**	☐
478e	With Father Christmas, Royal Mail, Tallents House, Edinburgh h/s	**£5.00**	☐
478f	With any one of some 22 additional relevant commemorative handstamps	**£9.00**	☐
478g	With Freezywater cds, Frosterley cds, North Pole Road cds, Holy Island cds	**£12.00**	☐
478h	With Holytown cds, Hutton Roof cds, Nasareth cds, St Nicholas or Noel Rd cds	**£12.00**	☐

See the Introduction for General Information

479. 2005, 11th January

Farm Animals. Se-tenant

10 x 1st Class Stamp. Featuring Pigs, Ducks, Horses, Cattle, Dog, Chicks, Sheep, Goat, Turkeys, Geese

479a	Set of 10 x 1st Se-tenant Stamps on illustrated cover, any postmark	£3.00 ☐
479b	With First Day of Issue, Tallents House, Edinburgh handstamp	£4.50 ☐
479c	With First Day of Issue, Paddock, Huddersfield handstamp	£5.00 ☐
479d	With First Day of Issue (non pictorial), Paddock, Huddersfield handstamp	£5.00 ☐
479e	With any one of some 21 additional relevant commemorative handstamps	£9.00 ☐
479f	With Bull Farm cds, Cowes cds, Fieldgate cds, Goose Green cds	£12.00 ☐
479g	With Jersey Farm cds, Malvern cds, Sheepwash cds, Tithe Farm cds	£12.00 ☐

480. 2005, 11th January

Generic Smilers. Farm Animals

20 x 1st Farm Animals Stamps, each with different Label (10) attached

480a	Any one Stamp with its Label and any relevant commemorative handstamp	£3.50 ☐
480b	Any one Stamp with its Label and any relevant cds	£4.50 ☐

Handstamps and cds as done for Farm Animals issue above.

---

481. 2005, 8th February

South West England. A British Journey

2nd Studland Bay, 1st Wheal Coates, 40p Start Point, 43p Horton Down, 57p Chiselcombe, 68p Lundy

481a	Set of Stamps on illustrated cover, any postmark	£2.50 ☐
481b	With First Day of Issue, Tallents House, Edinburgh handstamp	£4.00 ☐
481c	With First Day of Issue, The Lizard, Helston handstamp	£4.50 ☐
481d	With First Day of Issue (non pictorial), The Lizard, Helston handstamp	£4.50 ☐
481e	With any one of some 18 additional relevant commemorative handstamps	£8.00 ☐
481f	With Chedder cds, Penzance cds, St. Agnes cds	£9.50 ☐
481g	With Studland cds, The Lizard cds, White Rock cds	£9.50 ☐
481h	With Cornwall & Devon Mobile cds	£10.00 ☐

QEII • Commemoratives 2005

482. 2005, 24th February

Jane Eyre. Charlotte Bronte 150th Anniversary

2nd, 1st, 40p, 57p, 68p, £1.12. Featuring Characters from the Novel

Miniature Sheet containing all six values issued same day. Same pricing.

482a	Set of Stamps on illustrated cover, any postmark	**£3.00** ☐
482b	With First Day of Issue, Tallents House, Edinburgh handstamp	**£4.50** ☐
482c	With First Day of Issue, Haworth, Keighley handstamp	**£5.00** ☐
482d	With First Day of Issue (non pictorial), Haworth, Keighley handstamp	**£5.00** ☐
482e	With any one of some 23 additional relevant commemorative handstamps	**£9.00** ☐
482f	With Adel cds, Gateshead cds, Haworth cds, Rawdon cds	**£11.00** ☐
482g	With Ripon cds, Rochester cds, Thornton cds	**£11.00** ☐

483. 2005, 15th March

Magic! Centenary of The Magic Circle

1st, 40p, 47p, 68p, £1.12. Stamps Feature Different Magic Tricks

483a	Set of Stamps on illustrated cover, any postmark	**£3.00** ☐
483b	With First Day of Issue, Tallents House, Edinburgh handstamp	**£4.50** ☐
483c	With First Day of Issue, London NW1 handstamp	**£5.00** ☐
483d	With First Day of Issue (non pictorial), London NW1 handstamp	**£5.00** ☐
483e	With any one of some 21 additional relevant commemorative handstamps	**£8.50** ☐
483f	With Bunny cds, Hatt cds, Kings Cross cds, Poland St cds	**£10.00** ☐

Remember, from 1966 onwards, most hand addressed Commemorative covers are worth only 20% of catalogue prices.

484. 2005, 15th March

Generic Smilers Sheet. Magic!

20 x 1st Magic Stamp, with Labels showing four magic tricks

484a	Single Stamp with Label on illustrated cover, any postmark	**£1.00**	☐
484b	With First Day of Issue, Tallents House, Edinburgh handstamp	**£2.00**	☐
484c	With First Day of Issue, London NW1 handstamp	**£2.50**	☐
484d	With First Day of Issue (non pictorial), London NW1 handstamp	**£2.50**	☐
484e	With any one of some 18 additional relevant commemorative handstamps	**£4.50**	☐
484f	With Bunny cds, Hatt cds, Kings Cross cds, Poland St cds	**£6.00**	☐

485. 2005, 8th April

Royal Wedding. Charles and Camilla. Miniature Sheet

2 x 30p + 2 x 68p. Informal photos of the couple

485a	Miniature Sheet on illustrated cover, any postmark	**£2.00**	☐
485b	With First Day of Issue, Tallents House, Edinburgh handstamp	**£4.00**	☐
485c	With First Day of Issue, Windsor handstamp	**£4.50**	☐
485d	With First Day of Issue (non pictorial), Windsor handstamp	**£4.50**	☐
485e	With any one of some 14 additional relevant commemorative handstamps	**£8.00**	☐
485f	With Caernarfon cds, Prince Charles Ave cds, Wales cds	**£9.50**	☐
485g	With House of Commons or House of Lords cds	**£15.00**	☐
485h	With Buckingham Palace cds, Windsor Castle cds (**£40**)	**£28.00**	☐

The Royal Wedding Issue was delayed by one day because of the Pope's Funeral. Covers are available with both April 8th & 9th dates, adding 20% to the first day cover value.

Please refer to the Index on page 3 for a complete listing of all Reigns covered in the Catalogue.

486. 2005, 21st April
World Heritage Sites. Joint Issue with Australia
Four se-tenant Pairs, each showing a different British and Australian Site
2 x 2nd, 2 x 1st, 2 x 43p, 2 x 68p

486a Set of 8 Stamps on illustrated cover, any postmark .... **£3.00** □
486b With First Day of Issue, Tallents House, Edinburgh handstamp .... **£4.50** □
486c With First Day of Issue, Blenheim Palace, Woodstock handstamp .... **£5.00** □
486d With First Day of Issue (non pictorial), Blenheim Palace, Woodstock handstamp .... **£5.00** □
486e With any one of some 20 additional relevant commemorative handstamps .... **£10.00** □
486f With Amesbury cds, Canterbury cds, Druids Heath cds, Melbourne cds .... **£11.50** □
486g With Heddon On The Wall cds, Saltaire cds, Stromness cds, Woodstock cds .... **£11.50** □
486h With Windsor Castle cds .... **£25.00** □

487. 2005, 7th June
Trooping The Colour
2nd, 1st, 42p, 60p, 68p, £1.12. Scenes from Trooping The Colour

487a Set of Stamps on illustrated cover, any postmark .... **£3.00** □
487b With First Day of Issue, Tallents House, Edinburgh handstamp .... **£4.50** □
487c With First Day of Issue, London SW1 handstamp .... **£5.00** □
487d With First Day of Issue (non pictorial), London SW1 handstamp .... **£5.00** □
487e With any one of some 21 additional relevant commemorative handstamps .... **£9.00** □
487f With Coldstream cds, Queens Parade cds, Queens Square cds, Queens Way cds .... **£11.00** □
487g With The Parade cds, The Mall cds, March cds, any Field PO or Forces cds .... **£11.00** □
487h With House of Commons or House of Lords cds .... **£18.00** □
487i With Buckingham Palace cds, Windsor Castle cds **(£32)** .... **£28.00** □

488 2005, 7th June
Trooping The Colour. Miniature Sheet. Se-tenant Block
2nd, 1st, 42p, 60p, 68p, £1.12. Scenes from Trooping The Colour.
All pricing the same as for Trooping The Colour above.

QEII • Commemoratives 2005

489. 2005, 21st June

Generic Smilers Sheet. The White Ensign

20 x 1st White Ensign (2001) Stamp, with Labels featuring Signal Flags

489a	Single Stamp with Signal Flags Label attached, with any postmark	**£2.00** ☐
489b	With The White Ensign, Flagg, Buxton handstamp	**£3.50** ☐
489c	With Horatio Nelson, Burnham Thorpe, King's Lynn handstamp	**£3.50** ☐
489d	With Wimbledon, London SW19 handstamp	**£3.50** ☐
489e	With Fleet cds, Nelson cds, Admirals Way cds, Sea Street cds	**£5.00** ☐

490. 2005, 5th July

End of Second World War. 60th Anniversary. Miniature Sheet

1 x 1st Peace & Freedom (1995) Stamp + 5 x 1st Gold Definitive

490a	Miniature Sheet on illustrated cover, any postmark	**£2.00** ☐
490b	With First Day of Issue, Tallents House, Edinburgh handstamp	**£3.50** ☐
490c	With First Day of Issue, Peacehaven, Newhaven handstamp	**£4.00** ☐
490d	With First Day of Issue (non pictorial), Peacehaven, Newhaven handstamp	**£4.00** ☐
490e	With any one of some 19 additional relevant commemorative handstamps	**£7.50** ☐
490f	With Battlefield cds, Churchill cds, Dover cds, Peacehaven cds, any Field PO or Forces cds	**£9.00** ☐
490g	With House of Commons or House of Lords cds	**£20.00** ☐
490h	With Buckingham Palace cds	**£30.00** ☐

A number of fine first day cover Philatelic Gems
are illustrated throughout the catalogue.
See inside front cover, pages 40, 44, 78, 84, 93, 104, 184, 223, 231 and 363.

491. 2005, 19th July
British Motorcycles
1st Norton FI, 40p BSA Rocket, 42p Vincent, 47p Triumph, 60p Brough, 68p Royal Enfield

491a Set of Stamps on illustrated cover, any postmark .... **£3.00** ☐
491b With First Day of Issue, Tallents House, Edinburgh handstamp .... **£4.50** ☐
491c With First Day of Issue, Solihull handstamp .... **£5.00** ☐
491d With First Day of Issue (non pictorial), Solihull handstamp .... **£5.00** ☐
491e With any one of some 28 additional relevant commemorative handstamps .... **£9.00** ☐
491f With Brough cds, Enfield cds, Stevenage cds, The Rocket cds, Small Heath cds, Norton cds ... **£12.00** ☐
491g With Dunlop cds, Byker cds, Leathers Lane cds, Silverstone cds, Castle Donnington cds, RAC **£12.00** ☐

492. 2005, 5th August
London 2012, Host City. Miniature Sheet
6 x 1st Sport (1996) Stamps. New text and value

492a Miniature Sheet on illustrated cover, any postmark .... **£2.00** ☐
492b With First Day of Issue, Tallents House, Edinburgh handstamp .... **£3.50** ☐
492c With First Day of Issue, London E15 handstamp .... **£4.00** ☐
492d With First Day of Issue (non pictorial), London E15 handstamp .... **£4.00** ☐
492e With any one of some 17 additional relevant commemorative handstamps .... **£8.00** ☐
492f With City, London cds, Greenwich cds, Freemasons Road cds, Stratford cds, Weymouth cds **£8.50** ☐
492g With House of Commons or House of Lords cds .... **£25.00** ☐

In 2005 London was appointed to host the 2012 Olympic Games!

493. 2005, 23rd August

Changing Tastes in Britain. Europa Issue

2nd Rice, 1st Tea, 42p Sushi, 47p Pasta, 60p Chips, 68p Apples

493a Set of Stamps on illustrated cover, any postmark .... £3.00 ☐
493b With First Day of Issue, Tallents House, Edinburgh handstamp .... £4.50 ☐
493c With First Day of Issue, Cookstown handstamp .... £5.00 ☐
493d With First Day of Issue (non pictorial), Cookstown handstamp .... £5.00 ☐
493e With any one of some 19 additional relevant commemorative handstamps .... £9.00 ☐
493f With Bramley cds, Curry Rivel cds, Isle of Grain cds, New Covent Garden cds .... £12.00 ☐
493g With Rowelton cds, Saltwell Road cds, Strawberry Hill cds, Wheatley cds .... £12.00 ☐

494. 2005, 15th September

Classic ITV. Celebrating 50 Years

2nd, 1st, 42p, 47p, 60p, 68p.The Stamps feature six popular ITV programmes

494a Set of Stamps on illustrated cover, any postmark .... £3.00 ☐
494b With First Day of Issue, Tallents House, Edinburgh handstamp .... £4.50 ☐
494c With First Day of Issue, London SE19 handstamp .... £5.00 ☐
494d With First Day of Issue (non pictorial), London SE19 handstamp .... £5.00 ☐
494e With any one of some 20 additional relevant commemorative handstamps .... £9.00 ☐
494f With Box cds, Elstree cds, Harewood cds, Oxford cds, South Bank cds .... £12.00 ☐
494g With Teddington cds, Woodsley cds, Peel Park cds,Esholt cds .... £12.00 ☐

495. 2005, 15th September

Classic ITV 1955 - 2005. Generic Smilers Sheet

20 x 1st (Emmerdale) Stamp with Label

495a Stamp with Label attached, any postmark .... £1.50 ☐
495b Stamp with Label attached and any handstamp from Classic ITV Issue above .... £3.50 ☐
495c Stamp with Label attached and any Royal Mail fdi h/s from Classic ITV Issue .... £2.50 ☐
495d Stamp with Label attached and any cds postmark from Classic ITV Issue .... £4.50 ☐

QEII • Commemoratives 2005

496. 2005, 4th October

New Smilers Stamp Booklet. Self-adhesive

Six previously issued Smilers Stamps in 'definitive' format

6 x 1st (Flowers 1997, Hello 2002, Love 2002, Union Jack 2001, Teddy Bear 1990, Christmas 1996)

496a Set of Stamps on illustrated cover, any postmark .... **£2.00** ☐
496b With First Day of Issue, Tallents House, Edinburgh handstamp .... **£3.50** ☐
496c With First Day of Issue, Windsor handstamp .... **£4.00** ☐
496d With First Day of Issue (non pictorial), Windsor handstamp .... **£4.00** ☐
496e With any one of some 10 additional relevant commemorative handstamps .... **£7.00** ☐
496f Set with any cds relevant to one or more of the six Stamps .... **£9.00** ☐

497. 2005, 6th October

The Ashes. England Winners 2005. Miniature Sheet

2 x 1st + 2 x 68p.Scenes from the Test Series

497a Miniature Sheet on illustrated cover, any postmark .... **£2.00** ☐
497b With First Day of Issue, Tallents House, Edinburgh handstamp .... **£3.50** ☐
497c With First Day of Issue, London SE11 handstamp .... **£4.00** ☐
497d With First Day of Issue (non pictorial), London SE11 handstamp .... **£4.00** ☐
497e With any one of some 14 additional relevant commemorative handstamps .... **£7.00** ☐
497f With Edgbaston cds, Kennington cds, Old Trafford cds, St. John's Wood cds .... **£9.00** ☐
497g With Trent Bridge cds, The Oval cds, Over cds, Ash cds .... **£9.00** ☐

Write to us if you have questions on Commemorative handstamps for any QEII Stamp Issue.

498. 2005, 18th October

Trafalgar. 200th Anniversary. Se-tenant Pairs

2 x 1st + 2 x 42p + 2 x 68p. Six scenes from the 1805 Battle

498a	Set of Se-tenant Stamps on illustrated cover, any postmark	£3.00 ☐
498b	With First Day of Issue, Tallents House, Edinburgh handstamp	£4.50 ☐
498c	With First Day of Issue, Portsmouth handstamp	£5.00 ☐
498d	With First Day of Issue (non pictorial), Portsmouth handstamp	£5.00 ☐
498e	With any one of some 25 additional relevant commemorative handstamps	£9.00 ☐
498f	With Battle cds, Britannia cds, Burnham Market cds, Chatham cds, Deal cds, Fleet cds	£12.00 ☐
498g	With Cannons Walk cds, Greenwich cds, Hardy St cds, HMS Nelson, Portsmouth cds	£12.00 ☐
498h	With Nelson (Lancs/Treharris) cds, Portsmouth cds, Six Bells cds, The Harbour cds, Seaview cds	£12.00 ☐
498i	With The Quarterdeck cds, Trafalgar Place cds, Trafalgar Square cds, Trafalgar Road cds	£12.00 ☐
498j	With House of Commons or House of Lords cds	£20.00 ☐
498k	With Buckingham Palace cds	£30.00 ☐

499. 2005, 18th October

Trafalgar. Miniature Sheet

Block of six Stamps. Same as above

Miniature Sheet pricing as above for the Trafalgar Issue

Prestige Stamp Book - Battle of Trafalgar. Death of Nelson

This is listed in the Definitives Section of the catalogue

Try to only collect covers with relevant postmarks!

500. 2005, 1st November

Christmas Issue. Self-adhesive

Madonna and Child as seen through the eyes of different cultures

2nd Haiti, 1st Europe, 42p Europe, 60p India, 68p American Indian, £1.12 Aborigine

500a Set of Stamps on illustrated cover, any postmark .... **£3.50** □
500b With First Day of Issue, Tallents House, Edinburgh handstamp .... **£5.00** □
500c With First Day of Issue, Bethlehem, Llandeilo handstamp .... **£5.50** □
500d With First Day of Issue (non pictorial), Bethlehem, Llandeilo handstamp .... **£5.50** □
500e With any one of some 26 additional relevant commemorative handstamps .... **£9.50** □
500f With Bethlehem, Canterbury, Christchurch, Holy Island or Holyhead cds .... **£12.00** □
500g With Jerusalem Street, Noel Road, Wolverhampton, any Field PO or Forces cds.... **£12.00** □

501. 2005, 1st November

Christmas 2005. Miniature Sheet

Same six Stamps as the Christmas Issue - with gum

Miniature Sheet pricing as above for the Christmas Issue

---

502. 2006, 10th January

Animal Tales. Children's Book Illustrations. Joint Issue UK/US Postal Service

Se-tenant Pairs. One British book one US book in each pair

2 each 2nd Jeremy Fisher/Kipper,1st Crocodile/Paddington, 47p Boots/Alice, 68p Caterpillar/Maisey's ABC

502a Set of 4 Se-tenant Stamps on illustrated cover, any postmark .... **£3.50** □
502b With First Day of Issue, Tallents House, Edinburgh handstamp .... **£5.00** □
502c With First Day of Issue, Mousehole, Penzance handstamp .... **£5.50** □
502d With First Day of Issue (non pictorial), Mousehole, Penzance handstamp .... **£5.50** □
502e With any one of some 20 additional relevant commemorative handstamps .... **£10.00** □
502f With Paddington, Mousehole, Bunny, Catfield, Frogmore, Isle of Dogs or Bearsted cds.... **£12.00** □

QEII • Commemoratives 2006

503. 2006, 7th February

A British Journey. England

10 x 1st se-tenant Stamps, showing scenes of England ....

503a Set of 10 Se-tenant Stamps on illustrated cover, any postmark .... **£3.50** ☐
503b With First Day of Issue, Tallents House, Edinburgh handstamp .... **£5.00** ☐
503c With First Day of Issue, Tea Green, Luton handstamp .... **£5.50** ☐
503d With First Day of Issue (non pictorial), Tea Green, Luton handstamp .... **£5.50** ☐
503e With any one of some 21 additional relevant commemorative handstamps .... **£10.00** ☐
503f With Birmingham, Brancaster, Chipping Camden, Robin Hood's Bay or St.Paul's cds .. **£12.50** ☐

504. 2006, 23rd February

Brunel Bicentenary

1st Albert Bridge, 40p Box Tunnel, 42p Paddington Station, 47p Great Eastern, 60p Clifton Bridge, 68p Maidenhead Bridge

504a Set of Stamps on illustrated cover, any postmark .... **£3.00** ☐
504b With First Day of Issue, Tallents House, Edinburgh handstamp .... **£4.50** ☐
504c With First Day of Issue, Bristol handstamp .... **£5.00** ☐
504d With First Day of Issue (non pictorial), Bristol handstamp .... **£5.00** ☐
504e With First Day of Issue...Brunel, Stampex, London NI handstamp .... **£5.00** ☐
504f With any one of some 25 additional relevant commemorative handstamps .... **£9.00** ☐
504g With Box cds, Clifton, Bristol cds, Maidenhead cds, Paddington cds, Saltash cds... **£12.00** ☐

505. 2006, 23rd February

Brunel 1806 - 2006. Miniature Sheet

Same Stamps as above, block of six in Miniature Sheet format
Miniature Sheet pricing same as Brunel Bicentenary Issue above

2006, 23rd February

Isambard Kingdom Brunel Prestige Stamp Book

This is listed in the Definitives Section of the catalogue

506. 2006, 1st March
National Assembly for Wales. Miniature Sheet
Se-tenant Strip of five Welsh Country (2003) Pictorial Stamps.1 x 2nd + 2 x 1st + 2 x 68p

506a	Miniature Sheet on illustrated cover, any postmark	**£2.50** ☐
506b	With Royal Mail, Tallents House, Edinburgh handstamp	**£4.00** ☐
506c	With Caerdydd, Cardiff handstamp	**£4.50** ☐
506d	With any one of some 9 additional relevant commemorative handstamps	**£8.00** ☐
506e	With Cardiff cds, any other relevant cds	**£10.00** ☐

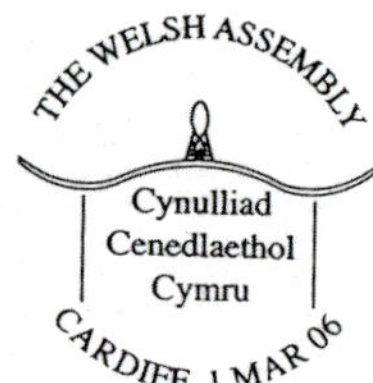

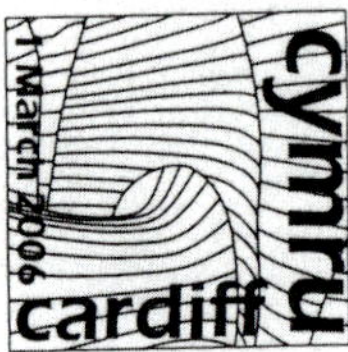

507. 2006, 7th March
Smilers Generic Sheet. Fun Fruit & Veg. Self-adhesive
20 x 1st Fun Fruit & Veg (2003) Stamps with speech bubble Labels

507a	Any Stamp with Label and one of 5 commemorative handstamps	**£3.50** ☐
507b	With any relevant cds	**£6.00** ☐

No Royal Mail handstamps were done for this Issue

508. 2006, 21st March
Ice Age Animals
1st Sabre-Tooth Cat, 42p Deer, 47p Rhino, 68p Mammoth, £1.12 Cave Bear

508a	Set of Stamps on illustrated cover, any postmark	**£3.00** ☐
508b	With First Day of Issue, Tallents House, Edinburgh handstamp	**£4.50** ☐
508c	With First Day of Issue, Freezywater, Enfield handstamp	**£5.00** ☐
508d	With First Day of Issue (non pictorial), Freezywater, Enfield handstamp	**£5.00** ☐
508e	With any one of some 14 additional relevant commemorative handstamps	**£9.00** ☐
508f	With Coldstream cds, Freezywater cds, Bearsden cds, Deerpark cds, any other relevant cds	**£12.00** ☐

QEII • Commemoratives 2006

509. 2006, 18th April

HM The Queen's 80th Birthday. 4 Se-tenant Pairs

2 x 2nd, 2 x 1st, 2 x 44p, 2 x 72p. Featuring Portraits of the Queen

509a Set of 4 Se-tenant Pairs on illustrated cover, any postmark .... **£3.50** ☐
509b With First Day of Issue, Tallents House, Edinburgh handstamp .... **£5.00** ☐
509c With First Day of Issue, Windsor handstamp .... **£5.50** ☐
509d With First Day of Issue (non pictorial), Windsor handstamp .... **£5.50** ☐
509e With any one of some 19 additional relevant commemorative handstamps .... **£10.00** ☐
509f With Queens Street cds, Queen Elizabeth Ave cds, Queens Rd cds, Queensway cds... **£11.50** ☐
509g With Throne cds, Windsor cds, Windsor Park cds .... **£12.00** ☐
509h With Buckingham Palace cds, Windsor Castle (**£60**) cds .... **£50.00** ☐

---

510. 2006, 25th May

Smilers Generic Sheet. Washington 2006 Exhibition.

20 x 1st Hello (2002) Stamps with US Mail Box Labels

510a Single Stamp with label on illustrated cover, any postmark .... **£2.50** ☐

No special handstamps were done for this release

---

511. 2006, 6th June

World Cup Winners

Six Stamps featuring footballers from Cup Winning Countries

1st - England, 42p - Italy, 44p - Argentina, 50p - Germany, 64p - France, 72p - Brazil

511a Set of Stamps on illustrated cover, any postmark .... **£3.00** ☐
511b With First Day of Issue, Tallents House, Edinburgh handstamp .... **£4.50** ☐
511c With First Day of Issue, Balls Park, Hertford handstamp .... **£5.00** ☐
511d With First Day of Issue (non pictorial), Balls Park, Hertford handstamp .... **£5.00** ☐
511e With any one of some 19 additional relevant commemorative handstamps .... **£9.00** ☐
511f With Wembley cds, Wembley Park cds, The Ball cds, any other relevant cds....... **£12.00** ☐

QEII • Commemoratives 2006

512. 2006, 6th June

England's Finest Hour...Wembley. World Cup Generic Sheet

20 x 1st World Cup Winners Stamp plus Label - Scenes from 1966 World Cup

512a Stamp with Label from Sheet, with any World Cup Winners handstamp from Issue **511** .....**£3.50** ☐
512b With any Royal Mail first day of issue (3) handstamp, from Issue **511**.....**£2.50** ☐
512c With any relevant cds, from Issue **511**.....**£5.50** ☐

---

513. 2006, 20th June

Modern Architecture. The Changing Skyline

1st - London, 42p - Dundee, 44p - Birmingham, 50p - Chichester, 64p - Isle of Tiree, 72p - Hull

513a Set of Stamps on illustrated cover, any postmark.....**£3.00** ☐
513b With First Day of Issue, Tallents House, Edinburgh handstamp.....**£4.50** ☐
513c With First Day of Issue, London EC3 handstamp.....**£5.00** ☐
513d With First Day of Issue (non pictorial), London EC3 handstamp.....**£5.00** ☐
513e With any one of some 12 additional relevant commemorative handstamps.....**£9.00** ☐
513f With Ascot cds, City of London cds, Chichester cds,.....**£12.00** ☐
513g With Hull or Birmingham or Dundee cds, any Isle of Tiree cds.....**£12.00** ☐
513h With New Buildings, Londonderry cds.....**£18.00** ☐

---

514. 2006, 4th July

Smilers Generic Sheet. For Life's Special Moments

20 x 1st Smilers Stamps in definitive size (as first issued in 2005), with Labels.
Sheet includes 4 x Love, 4 x Hello, 3 x Letter Box, 3 x Teddy Bear, 3 x Sun Flower, 3 x Union Jack

514a Stamp with Label, Generic Smilers Sheets, Giggleswick handstamp.....**£3.50** ☐
514b With Label and Pictorial Definitives, Generic Smilers, Buckingham Palace Rd, London SW1 h/s ...**£3.50** ☐
514c With Giggleswick cds, or any other relevant cds.....**£6.00** ☐

No Royal Mail handstamps were done for this issue

First Day Covers signed by the Stamp Designer

Covers, with one or more Stamps, signed by the designer are worth a 20% premium over catalogue prices

515. 2006, 18th July

The National Portrait Gallery. 150th Anniversary 1856 - 2006. Se-tenant

10 x 1st - Churchill, Reynolds, Eliot, Pankhurst, Woolf, Scott, Seacole, Shakespeare, Saunders, Darwin

515a	Set of Se-tenant Stamps on illustrated cover, any postmark	**£3.50**
515b	With First Day of Issue, Tallents House, Edinburgh handstamp	**£5.00**
515c	With First Day of Issue, London WC2 handstamp	**£5.50**
515d	With First Day of Issue (non pictorial), London WC2 handstamp	**£5.50**
515e	With any one of some 15 additional relevant commemorative handstamps	**£10.00**
515f	With Churchill cds, Statford-upon-Avon cds, Shakespeare St cds, or any other relevant cds	**£12.00**

2006, 31st August

1936 - Year of the Three Kings. Miniature Sheet

£3 Definitive Stamp. Details and pricing in the Definitives Section of the catalogue

---

516. 2006, 21st September

Victoria Cross. 150th Anniversary

2 x 1st, 2 x 64p, 2 x 72p. Featuring recipients of the Victoria Cross

516a	Set of Stamps on illustrated cover, any postmark	**£3.00**
516b	With First Day of Issue, Tallents House, Edinburgh handstamp	**£4.50**
516c	With First Day of Issue, Cuffley, Potters Bar handstamp	**£5.00**
516d	With First Day of Issue (non pictorial), Cuffley, Potters Bar handstamp	**£5.00**
516e	With First Day of Issue...Victoria Cross, Stampex, London NI handstamp	**£5.00**
516f	With any one of some 28 additional relevant commemorative handstamps	**£9.00**
516g	With Battle cds,Battle Hill cds,Battlefield Road cds,Bunkers Hill cds,Gun Hill cds	**£12.00**
516h	With Wargrave cds, Woolwich cds	**£12.00**
516i	With House of Commons or House of Lords cds, (Buckingham Palace cds **£35**)	**£20.00**

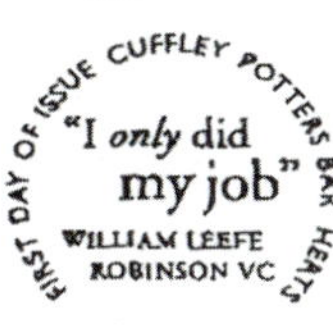

QEII • Commemoratives 2006

517. 2006, 21st September

Victoria Cross. Miniature Sheet

The Sheet includes the six Victoria Cross Stamps, plus Gallantry (1990) 20p Stamp

517a ...Miniature Sheet with any of the Victoria Cross commemorative h/s as **516** ....**£10.00** ☐

517b With any of the 4 Royal Mail first day of issue handstamps as **516** ....**£5.50** ☐

517c With any relevant cds as **516** ....**£12.50** ☐

2006, 21st September

Victoria Cross. Prestige Stamp Book

Details and pricing in Definitives Section of the catalogue

---

518. 2006, 3rd October

Sounds of Britain. Europa Issue

1st - Asian Sitar, 42p -Caribbean Bass, 50p - Irish Fiddle, 72p - American Blues, £1.19 - Latino Maracas

518a Set of Stamps on illustrated cover, any postmark...**£3.50** ☐

518b With First Day of Issue, Tallents House, Edinburgh handstamp ....**£4.50** ☐

518c With First Day of Issue, Rock, Kidderminster, Worcs handstamp............................**£5.00** ☐

518d With First Day of Issue (non pictorial), Rock, Kidderminster, Worcs handstamp.........**£5.00** ☐

518e With any one of some 14 additional relevant commemorative handstamps ....**£9.00** ☐

518f With Elton cds, Glastonbury cds, Knebworth cds, Rock cds, Wembley cds ....**£12.00** ☐

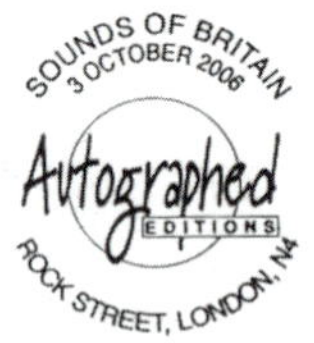

Don't forget that we now include sections on Overprints, Pre-releases, Missing Colours and Postal Stationery on fdc. These can all be found in the last part of the catalogue.

519. 2006, 17th October

New Smilers 'Special Moments' Stamp Book. Self-adhesive

6 x 1st Definitive Format Pictorial Stamps
(New Baby, Best Wishes, Thank you, Balloons, Fireworks, Champagne)

519a	Booklet Pane on illustrated cover, any postmark	**£2.00** ☐
519b	With First Day of Issue, Tallents House, Edinburgh handstamp	**£4.00** ☐
519c	With First Day of Issue, Grinshill, Shrewsbury handstamp	**£4.50** ☐
519d	With First Day of Issue (non pictorial), Grinshill, Shrewsbury handstamp	**£4.50** ☐
519e	With any one of some 7 additional relevant commemorative handstamps	**£8.00** ☐
519f	With any relevant cds	**£10.00** ☐

520. 2006, 7th November

Christmas Issue

2nd + 2nd Large - Snowman, 1st + 1st Large - Santa, 72p - Reindeer, £1.19 - Xmas Tree.

520a	Set of Stamps on illustrated cover, any postmark	**£3.00** ☐
520b	With First Day of Issue, Tallents House, Edinburgh handstamp	**£4.50** ☐
520c	With First Day of Issue, Bethlehem, Llandeilo handstamp	**£5.00** ☐
520d	With First Day of Issue (non pictorial), Bethlehem, Llandeilo handstamp	**£5.00** ☐
520e	With any one of some 21 additional relevant commemorative handstamps	**£9.00** ☐
520f	With Noel Road cds, Holy Island cds, Jerusalem cds, North Pole Road cds	**£12.00** ☐

521. 2006, 7th November

Christmas Miniature Sheet

Same six Stamps as the Christmas Issue above
All pricing as for the Christmas Issue.

QEII • Commemoratives 2006

522. 2006, 7th November

Christmas Generic Sheet

10 x 2nd, plus 10 x 1st Christmas Stamps with Labels (Snowflakes)

522a Either Stamp with Label and any Christmas Issue commemorative h/s as **521** .... **£4.50** ☐

522b Either Stamp with Label and any Royal Mail fdc (3) Christmas Issue h/s as **521** .... **£3.00** ☐

522c Either Stamp with Label and any relevant Christmas Issue cds .... **£6.00** ☐

523. 2006, 9th November

Lest We Forget. 90th Anniversary Battle of the Somme. Miniature Sheet

1st - Flanders Poppies, 4 x 72p - Regional Definitives (designs as issued previously)

523a Miniature Sheet on illustrated cover, any postmark .... **£3.00** ☐

523b With First Day of Issue, Tallents House, Edinburgh handstamp .... **£4.50** ☐

523c With First Day of Issue, London SW1 handstamp .... **£5.00** ☐

523d With First Day of Issue (non pictorial), London SW1 handstamp .... **£5.00** ☐

523e With any one of some 17 additional relevant commemorative handstamps .... **£9.00** ☐

523f With Brookwood,Battle,Battlefield,Dunkirk,Wargrave, any other relevant cds. .... **£12.00** ☐

Modern first day covers signed by a well known personality, with relevance to the Stamp Issue, are worth a premium over catalogue prices.

524. 2006, 9th November

We Will Remember Them. Generic Sheet

20 x 1st Flanders Poppies plus Memorial Label

524a	Stamp with Label and any Commemorative handstamp as **523**	**£3.50**	☐
524b	Stamp with Label and any Royal Mail first day of issue handstamp as **523**	**£2.50**	☐
524c	Stamp with Label and any relevant cds as **523**	**£6.00**	☐

525. 2006, 30th November

Celebrating Scotland. St. Andrew's Day. Miniature Sheet

1st - Lion Rampant, 1st - New Saltire Flag, 72p - St. Andrew, 72p - Edinburgh Castle

525a	Miniature Sheet on illustrated cover, any postmark	**£2.50**	☐
525b	With First Day of Issue, Tallents House, Edinburgh handstamp	**£4.00**	☐
525c	With First Day of Issue, St. Andrews, Fife handstamp	**£4.50**	☐
525d	With First Day of Issue (non pictorial), St. Andrews, Fife handstamp	**£4.50**	☐
525e	With any one of some 9 additional relevant commemorative handstamps	**£8.00**	☐
525f	With any Edinburgh cds, St.Andrews cds, The Scotlands cds, any Scottish cds	**£10.50**	☐
525g	With The Scottish Parliament cds	**£12.50**	☐

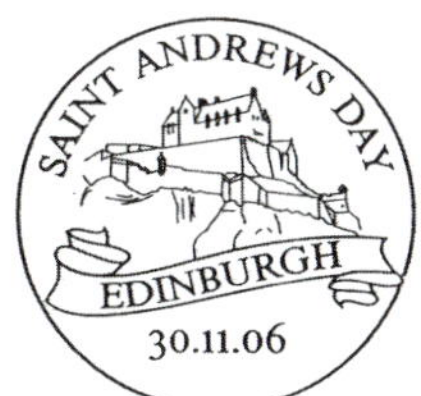

Remember, most modern hand addressed covers are worth only 20% of catalogue prices

QEII • Commemoratives 2007

526. 2007, 9th January

The Beatles. A Tribute to a Pop Phenomenon.

2 x 1st, 2 x 64p, 2 x 72p. Stamps Feature Beatles LP Sleeves. Self-adhesive

526a Set of Stamps on illustrated cover, any postmark .... **£3.50** ☐
526b With First Day of Issue, Tallents House, Edinburgh handstamp .... **£4.50** ☐
526c With First Day of Issue, Liverpool handstamp .... **£5.00** ☐
526d With First Day of Issue (non pictorial), Liverpool handstamp .... **£5.00** ☐
526e With any one of some 30 additional relevant commemorative handstamps .... **£9.00** ☐
526f With any Liverpool cds,Abbey road cds,Rock cds, Elstead cds, any relevant cds.**£10.00** ☐

527. 2007, 9th January

The Beatles. Miniature Sheet

4 x 1st. Stamps Feature Beatles Memorabilia. Not Self-adhesive

527a Miniature Sheet with any one of some 30 relevant commemorative h/s, as above..**£6.00** ☐
527b With any Royal Mail first day of issue (3) handstamp, same as above .... **£3.50** ☐
527c With any relevant cds, same as above .... **£8.00** ☐

All prices in this catalogue are for clean covers, with undamaged stamps and clear postmarks.

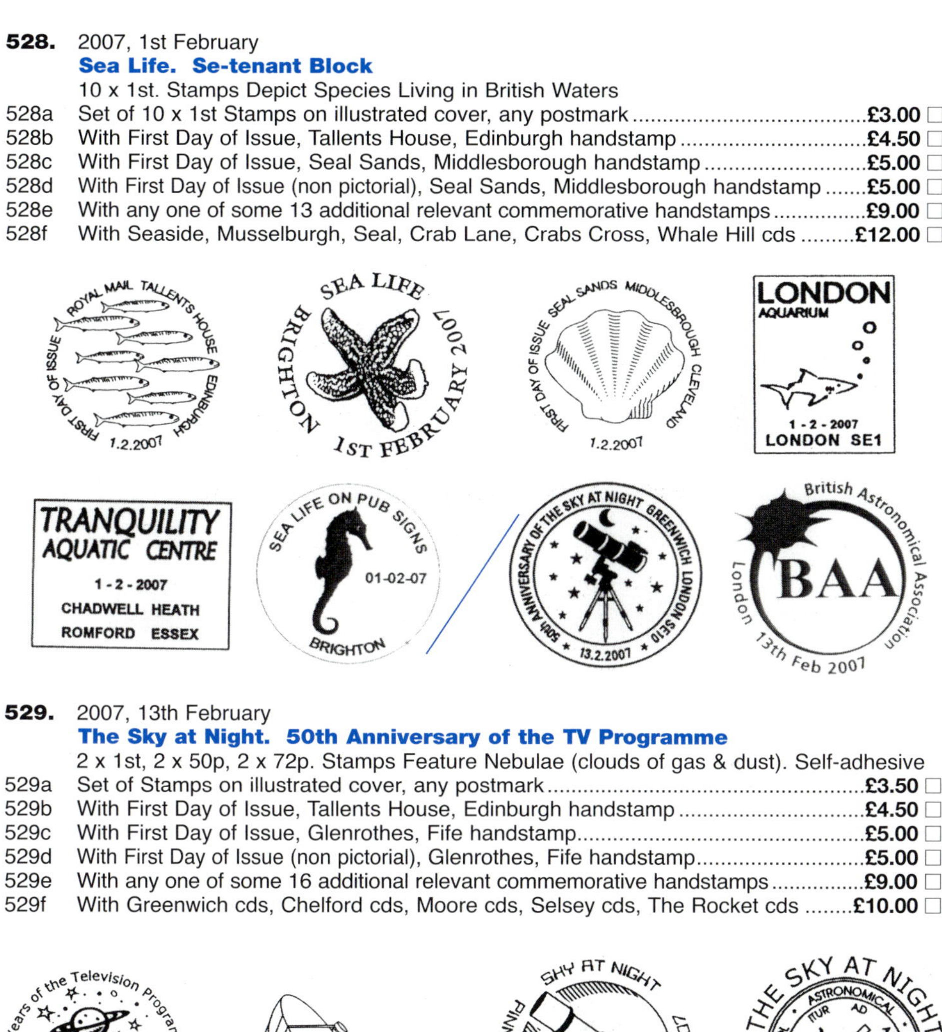

528. 2007, 1st February
Sea Life. Se-tenant Block
10 x 1st. Stamps Depict Species Living in British Waters

528a	Set of 10 x 1st Stamps on illustrated cover, any postmark	**£3.00** ☐
528b	With First Day of Issue, Tallents House, Edinburgh handstamp	**£4.50** ☐
528c	With First Day of Issue, Seal Sands, Middlesborough handstamp	**£5.00** ☐
528d	With First Day of Issue (non pictorial), Seal Sands, Middlesborough handstamp	**£5.00** ☐
528e	With any one of some 13 additional relevant commemorative handstamps	**£9.00** ☐
528f	With Seaside, Musselburgh, Seal, Crab Lane, Crabs Cross, Whale Hill cds	**£12.00** ☐

529. 2007, 13th February
The Sky at Night. 50th Anniversary of the TV Programme
2 x 1st, 2 x 50p, 2 x 72p. Stamps Feature Nebulae (clouds of gas & dust). Self-adhesive

529a	Set of Stamps on illustrated cover, any postmark	**£3.50** ☐
529b	With First Day of Issue, Tallents House, Edinburgh handstamp	**£4.50** ☐
529c	With First Day of Issue, Glenrothes, Fife handstamp	**£5.00** ☐
529d	With First Day of Issue (non pictorial), Glenrothes, Fife handstamp	**£5.00** ☐
529e	With any one of some 16 additional relevant commemorative handstamps	**£9.00** ☐
529f	With Greenwich cds, Chelford cds, Moore cds, Selsey cds, The Rocket cds	**£10.00** ☐

Write to us if you have questions on Commemorative handstamps for any QEII Stamp Issue.

QEII • Commemoratives 2007

530. 2007, 1st March

World of Invention. Technologies That Change Lives

2 x 1st - Bridge, Railway, 2 x 64p - Telephone, TV, 2 x 72p - Internet, Space Travel

530a Set of Stamps on illustrated cover, any postmark .... **£3.50** ☐
530b With First Day of Issue, Tallents House, Edinburgh handstamp .... **£4.50** ☐
530c With First Day of Issue, Pont Menai, Menai Bridge handstamp .... **£5.00** ☐
530d With First Day of Issue (non pictorial), Pont Menai, Menai Bridge handstamp .... **£5.00** ☐
530e With First Day of Issue...Invention, Stampex, London N1 handstamp .... **£5.00** ☐
530f With any one of some 19 additional relevant commemorative handstamps .... **£9.00** ☐
530g With Bridge, East Sheen, Helensburgh, Ironbridge, James Watt Dock cds .... **£10.00** ☐
530h With New Invention cds, The Science Museum cds .... **£12.00** ☐

1 MAR 07, WYLAM

1 MAR 07, EDINBURGH

1 MAR 07, LONDON SW14

1 MAR 07, LANGHOLM

1 MAR 07, HELENSBURGH

531. 2007, 1st March

World of Invention. Miniature Sheet

Same six Stamps as above. Not Self-adhesive

531a Miniature Sheet with any relevant commemorative handstamp, as above .... **£9.00** ☐
531b With any Royal Mail first day of issue (4) handstamp, as above .... **£4.50** ☐
531c With any relevant cds, as above .... **£10.00** ☐
531d Miniature Sheet plus the six Stamps, any cds .... **£16.00** ☐

2007, 1st March

World of Invention. Prestige Stamp Book

Details and pricing in Definitives Section of the Catalogue.

532. 2007, 1st March

Welsh Generic & Smilers Sheet

20 x Wales 1st Country Stamp, with Welsh scenes Label attached.
First Self-adhesive Country Stamp

532a Stamp with Welsh Label attached and any one of 3 relevant h/s featured below .... **£4.00** ☐

532b With any Welsh cds .... **£5.50** ☐

No Royal Mail handstamps done for this issue

Modern first day covers signed by a well known personality, with relevance to the Stamp Issue, are worth a premium over catalogue prices.

---

533. 2007, 22nd March

The Abolition of the Slave Trade. 200th Anniv. of 1807 Act of Parliament

Se-tenant Pairs. Featuring Leading Players in the Abolition of the Slave Trade
2 x 1st - Wilberforce/Equiano, 2 x 50p - Sharp/Clarkson, 2 x 72p - More/Sancho

533a Set of Se-tenant Pairs on illustrated cover, any postmark .... **£3.00** ☐

533b With First Day of Issue, Tallents House, Edinburgh handstamp .... **£4.50** ☐

533c With First Day of Issue, Hull handstamp .... **£5.00** ☐

533d With First Day of Issue (non pictorial), Hull handstamp .... **£5.00** ☐

533e With any one of some 15 additional relevant commemorative handstamps .... **£10.00** ☐

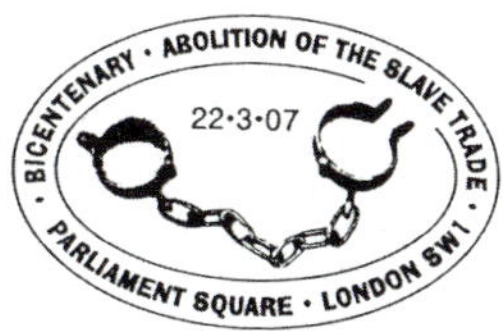

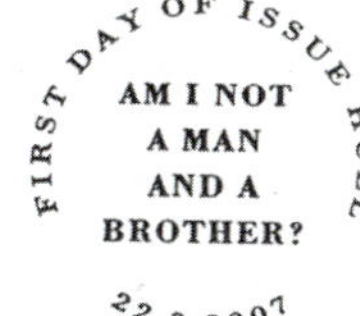

534. 2007, 23rd April
Celebrating England. Miniature Sheet
2 x 1st - Lion and St.George's Flag, 2 x 72p - St. George and Houses of Parliament

534a	Miniature Sheet on illustrated cover, any postmark	**£2.00** ☐
534b	With First Day of Issue, Tallents House, Edinburgh handstamp	**£4.00** ☐
534c	With First Day of Issue, St. Georges, Telford handstamp	**£4.50** ☐
534d	With First Day of Issue (non pictorial), St. Georges, Telford handstamp	**£4.50** ☐
534e	With any one of some 15 additional relevant commemorative handstamps	**£8.00** ☐
534f	With St.George's Cross, St.George, England's Lane, New England Road cds	**£10.00** ☐
534g	With House of Commons or House of Lords cds, Parliament Street cds	**£15.00** ☐
534h	With Buckingham Palace cds, (Windsor Castle cds **£28**)	**£22.00** ☐

535. 2007, 23rd April
Glorious England. Generic Sheet
20 x 1st Lion Stamp, with Labels showing English scenery attached

535a	Stamp with Label attached and any one of 15 relevant commemorative h/s,	**£4.00** ☐
535b	With any Royal Mail first day of issue (3) handstamp	**£2.50** ☐
535c	With any relevant cds	**£6.00** ☐

All postmarks same as previous Issue.

Improved Postal Stationery Coverage from 1972

Postal Stationery is covered in the body of the catalogue up to 1971.
From 1972 onwards we have added a detailed listing
in a separate section at the end of the catalogue.

QEII • Commemoratives 2007

536. 2007, 15th May
Beside the Seaside
1st - Ice-cream Cone, 46p - Sand Castle, 48p - Merry-go-round, 54p - Beach Huts, 68p - Deckchairs, 78p - Donkey Rides

536a	Set of Stamps on illustrated cover, any postmark	**£3.50** ☐
536b	With First Day of Issue, Tallents House, Edinburgh handstamp	**£4.50** ☐
536c	With First Day of Issue, Blackpool handstamp	**£5.00** ☐
536d	With First Day of Issue (non pictorial), Blackpool handstamp	**£5.00** ☐
536e	With any one of some 11 additional relevant commemorative handstamps	**£10.00** ☐
536f	With any seaside town cds, The Beach cds, Seaside cds, any other relevant cds	**£12.00** ☐

537. 2007, 17th May
Wembley Stadium 2007. Miniature Sheet
1st (World Cup Stamp 2002, minus inscription), 2 x 2nd + 2 x 78p Country Stamps

537a	Miniature Sheet on illustrated cover, any postmark	**£2.50** ☐
537b	With First Day of Issue, Tallents House, Edinburgh handstamp	**£4.00** ☐
537c	With First Day of Issue, Wembley handstamp	**£4.50** ☐
537d	With First Day of Issue (non pictorial), Wembley handstamp	**£4.50** ☐
537e	With any one of some 8 additional relevant commemorative handstamps	**£9.00** ☐
537f	With Moore, New England Road, Ramsey, The Ball, Wembley/Wembley Hill cds	**£11.00** ☐

THE NEW WEMBLEY STADIUM
| 17 | 05 | 07 |
WEMBLEY MIDDLESEX

Control Numbers and/or Cylinder Numbers
Covers showing these are worth a premium of 20% – 25%

QEII • Commemoratives 2007

538. 2007, 17th May
Memories of Wembley Stadium. Generic Sheet
20 x 1st (World Cup Stamp 2002, minus inscription), with Wembley Scenes Labels
538a Stamp with Label attached and any one of 9 relevant commemorative h/s, as **537** ......**£3.50** ☐
538b With any Royal Mail first day of issue (3) handstamp, as **537** ....**£2.50** ☐
538c With any relevant cds, as **537** ....**£6.00** ☐

---

539. 2007, 5th June
The Machin Definitives. 40th Anniversary. Miniature Sheet
2 x 1st - Machin portrait, Reproduction of 1967 4d, plus 2 x £1 - in old and new colours
539a Miniature Sheet on illustrated cover, any postmark ....**£3.00** ☐
539b With First Day of Issue, Tallents House, Edinburgh handstamp ....**£4.00** ☐
539c With First Day of Issue, Windsor handstamp ....**£4.50** ☐
539d With First Day of Issue (non pictorial), Windsor handstamp ....**£4.50** ☐
539e With First Day of Issue...Stoke-on-Trent handstamp ....**£4.50** ☐
539f With First Day of Issue (non pictorial), Stoke-on-Trent handstamp............................**£4.50** ☐
539g With any one of some 18 additional relevant commemorative handstamps ....**£9.00** ☐
539h With Barlaston cds, Eccleshall cds, Stoke-on-Trent cds, Windsor cds ....**£11.00** ☐
539i With House of Commons cds, House of Lords cds, (Buckingham Palace **£24**) .....**£15.00** ☐

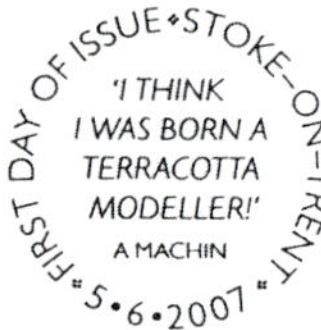

540. 2007, 5th June
40th Anniversary of the Machin Definitives. Generic Sheet
20 x 1st Machin Stamp with Labels attached showing 1967/69 Definitives
540a Stamp with Label attached with any one of 18 relevant commemorative h/s, as above **£3.50** ☐
540b With any Royal Mail first day of issue (4) handstamp, as above ....**£2.50** ☐
540c With any relevant cds, as above ....**£6.50** ☐

2007, 5th June
The Machin. The Making of a Masterpiece. Prestige Stamp Book
Details and pricing in the Definitives Section of the catalogue

---

See the Introduction for a comment on Generic Sheets

QEII • Commemoratives 2007

541. 2007, 3rd July

Grand Prix. 50th Anniversary

2 x 1st - BRM, Vanwall, 2 x 54p - Tyrrell, Lotus, 2 x 78p - Wiiliams, McLaren

541a Set of Stamps on illustrated cover, any postmark .... **£3.50** ☐
541b With First Day of Issue, Tallents House, Edinburgh handstamp .... **£4.50** ☐
541c With First Day of Issue, Silverstone, Towcester handstamp .... **£5.00** ☐
541d With First Day of Issue (non pictorial), Silverstone, Towcester handstamp .... **£5.00** ☐
541e With any one of some 19 additional relevant commemorative handstamps .... **£9.00** ☐
541f With Fawkham, Royal Automobile Club,The Drive, Silverstone, any relevant cds .**£12.00** ☐

542. 2007, 17th July

Harry Potter

7 x 1st. Se-tenant. Stamps feature cover designs from the original seven books

542a Set of Se-tenant Stamps on illustrated cover, any postmark .... **£2.50** ☐
542b With First Day of Issue, Tallents House, Edinburgh handstamp .... **£4.00** ☐
542c With First Day of Issue, Broom, Alcester handstamp .... **£4.50** ☐
542d With First Day of Issue (non pictorial), Broom, Alcester handstamp .... **£4.50** ☐
542e With any one of some 20 additional relevant commemorative handstamps .... **£8.00** ☐
542f With Broom cds, Potters Bar cds, Owlsmoor cds, Kings Cross cds .... **£10.50** ☐

543. 2007, 17th July

Harry Potter. Miniature Sheet

5 x 1st Stamps, featuring Hogwarts School Crest and its four Houses

543a Miniature Sheet on illustrated cover, any postmark .... **£2.00** ☐
543b With First Day of Issue, Tallents House, Edinburgh handstamp .... **£3.50** ☐
543c With First Day of Issue, Broom, Alcester handstamp .... **£4.00** ☐
543d With First Day of Issue (non pictorial), Broom, Alcester handstamp .... **£4.00** ☐
543e With any one of some 20 additional relevant commemorative handstamps .... **£7.00** ☐
543f With Broom cds, Potters Bar cds, Owlsmoor cds, Kings Cross cds .... **£9.50** ☐

544. 2007, 17th July

Harry Potter. Generic Smilers Sheet

4 x 5 Miniature Sheet 1st Stamps, with magic spells Labels attached

544a Single Stamp with Label attached, illustrated cover, any postmark .... **£1.00** ☐
544b With First Day of Issue, Tallents House, Edinburgh handstamp .... **£2.00** ☐
544c With First Day of Issue, Broom, Alcester handstamp .... **£2.50** ☐
544d With First Day of Issue (non pictorial), Broom, Alcester handstamp .... **£2.50** ☐
544e With any one of some 20 additional relevant commemorative handstamps .... **£4.00** ☐
544f With Broom cds, Potters Bar cds, Owlsmoor cds, Kings Cross cds .... **£5.50** ☐

QEII • Commemoratives 2007

545. 2007, 26th July
Scouting Centenary 2007
1st, 46p, 48p, 54p, 69p, 78p, featuring Scouts engaged in various activities

545a	Set of Stamps on illustrated cover, any postmark	£3.50 ☐
545b	With First Day of Issue, Tallents House, Edinburgh handstamp	£4.50 ☐
545c	With First Day of Issue, Brownsea Island, Poole handstamp	£5.00 ☐
545d	With First Day of Issue (non pictorial), Brownsea Island, Poole handstamp	£5.00 ☐
545e	With any one of some 14 additional relevant commemorative handstamps	£9.00 ☐
545f	With Chingford cds, Godalming cds, Sandbanks cds	£11.00 ☐

546. 2007, 4th September
Birds. UK Species in Recovery
10 x 1st se-tenant.Stamps feature Rare and Endangered Birds

546a	Set of Stamps on illustrated cover, any postmark	£3.50 ☐
546b	With First Day of Issue, Tallents House, Edinburgh handstamp	£4.50 ☐
546c	With First Day of Issue, Dartford handstamp	£5.00 ☐
546d	With First Day of Issue (non pictorial), Dartford handstamp	£5.00 ☐
546e	With any one of some 12 additional relevant commemorative handstamps	£9.00 ☐
546f	With Eagle cds, Hawkshead cds, Sandy cds, Wing cds	£12.00 ☐

The Birds featured in the September 4th Issue above are as follows:
White Tailed Eagle, Bearded Tit, Red Kite, Cirl Bunting,
Marsh Harrier, Avocet, Bittern, Dartford Warbler, Corncrake, Peregrine.
Each of these birds is now enjoying a recovery in numbers!

See Index on page 3 for full Catalogue Listings

547. 2007, 20th September

British Army Uniforms

3 x 1st, 3 x 78p. Two se-tenant triptychs, featuring uniformed working soldiers

547a	Set of Se-tenant Stamps on illustrated cover, any postmark	£3.00 ☐
547b	With First Day of Issue, Tallents House, Edinburgh handstamp	£4.50 ☐
547c	With First Day of Issue, Boot, Holmrook handstamp	£5.00 ☐
547d	With First Day of Issue (non pictorial), Boot, Holmrook handstamp	£5.00 ☐
547e	With First Day of Issue, Army Uniforms, Stampex, London N1 handstamp	£5.00 ☐
547f	With any one of some 19 additional relevant commemorative handstamps	£9.00 ☐
547g	With Aldershot cds, Bovington cds, Battle cds, Garrison cds	£11.00 ☐

2007, 20th September

British Army Uniforms. Prestige Stamp Book

Details and pricing in the Definitives Section of the catalogue

---

548. 2007, 16th October

Diamond Wedding Anniv. 60th Wedding Anniv.
The Queen and The Duke of Edinburgh

2 x 1st, 2 x 54p, 2 x 78p.Se-tenat pairs featuring photographs of the royal couple

548a	Set of Se-tenant Stamps on illustrated cover, any postmark	£3.00 ☐
548b	With First Day of Issue, Tallents House, Edinburgh handstamp	£4.50 ☐
548c	With First Day of Issue, Windsor, Berks handstamp	£5.00 ☐
548d	With First Day of Issue (non pictorial), Windsor, Berks handstamp	£5.00 ☐
548e	With any one of some 16 additional relevant commemorative handstamps	£9.50 ☐
548f	With Buckingham Palace cds (Windsor Castle **£25**)	£20.00 ☐
548g	With Edinburgh cds, Windsor cds, Throne cds, Queen St. cds,	£11.50 ☐

549. 2007, 16th October

Diamond Wedding Anniversary. First ever Self-adhesive Miniature Sheet

2 x 1st, 69p, 78p. Stamps feature further photographs of the Royal couple

549a	Miniature Sheet on illustrated cover, any postmark	£2.00 ☐
549b	With any Royal Mail First Day of Issue handstamp as above	£4.00 ☐
549c	With any one of some 16 additional relevant commemorative handstamps as above	£9.00 ☐
549d	With any relevant cds as above, or other	£11.00 ☐

550. 2007, 6th November

Christmas Issue Self-adhesive

2nd, 2nd Large, 1st, 1st Large, 78p, £1.24. Depicting Four Angels

550a Set of 6 Stamps on illustrated cover, any postmark .... **£3.50** ☐
550b With First Day of Issue, Tallents House, Edinburgh handstamp .... **£5.00** ☐
550c With First Day of Issue, Bethlehem, Llandeilo handstamp .... **£5.50** ☐
550d With First Day of Issue (non pictorial), Bethlehem, Llandeilo handstamp .... **£5.50** ☐
550e With any one of some 18 additional relevant commemorative handstamps .... **£11.00** ☐
550f With Nasareth cds, Noel Rd cds, Holy Island cds, any other relevant cds .... **£15.00** ☐

551. 2007, 6th November

Christmas Issue. Miniature Sheet

2nd, 2nd Large, 1st, 1st Large, 78p, £1.24. Depicting Four Angels

551a Miniature Sheet on illustrated cover, any postmark .... **£3.50** ☐
551b With First Day of Issue, Tallents House, Edinburgh handstamp .... **£5.00** ☐
551c With First Day of Issue, Bethlehem, Llandeilo handstamp .... **£5.50** ☐
551d With First Day of Issue (non pictorial), Bethlehem, Llandeilo handstamp .... **£5.50** ☐
551e With any one of some 18 additional relevant commemorative handstamps .... **£11.00** ☐
551f With Nasareth cds, Noel Rd cds, Holy Island cds, any other relevant cds .... **£15.00** ☐

552. 2007, 6th November

Christmas Extra Issue. Self-adhesive

2nd, Painting of Madonna and Child. 1st, Painting of The Madonna of Humility

552a Set of 2 Stamps on illustrated cover, any postmark .... **£1.00** ☐
552b With First Day of Issue, Tallents House, Edinburgh handstamp .... **£2.00** ☐
552c With First Day of Issue, Bethlehem, Llandeilo handstamp .... **£2.50** ☐
552d With First Day of Issue (non pictorial), Bethlehem, Llandeilo handstamp .... **£2.50** ☐
552e With any one of same 18 additional relevant commemorative handstamps, as above .... **£5.00** ☐
552f With Nasareth cds, Noel Rd cds, Holy Island cds, any other relevant cds .... **£7.50** ☐

553. 2007, 8th November
Lest We Forget. Battle of Passchendaele. Miniature Sheet
1st, New Poppy Stamp, 4 x 78p Country Definitives

553a Miniature Sheet on illustrated cover, any postmark .... **£3.50** ☐
553b With First Day of Issue, Tallents House, Edinburgh handstamp .... **£5.00** ☐
553c With First Day of Issue, Guns Fall Silent, London SW1 handstamp.......... **£5.50** ☐
553d With First Day of Issue (non pictorial), London SW1 handstamp .... **£5.50** ☐
553e With any one of some 14 additional relevant commemorative handstamps.......... **£11.00** ☐
553f With Battle cds, Wargrave cds, any other relevant cds.......... **£15.00** ☐

A Generic Sheet of 20 x 1st Poppy Stamp plus Labels issued same day. Not catalogued as such on fdc.

554. 2007, 30th November
Glorious Scotland. Generic Sheet
20 x 1st Lion Rampant Definitive, plus 10 x 2 Labels

554a Single Stamp plus Label on illustrated cover, any postmark.......... **£1.00** ☐
554b With Glorious Scotland, Fort William handstamp.......... **£5.00** ☐
554c With Glorious Scotland, Kyle of Lochalsh handstamp .... **£5.00** ☐
554d With Glorious Scotland, Edinburgh handstamp.......... **£5.00** ☐
554e With any Scottish town cds, or other relevant cds .... **£6.50** ☐

No Royal Mail fdi postmarks were done for this Issue

555. 2008, 8th January
James Bond. 100th Anniversary Ian Fleming
2 x 1st, 2 x 54p, 2 x 78p. Stamps Feature Bond Book Covers

555a Set of 6 Stamps on illustrated cover, any postmark.......... **£3.50** ☐
555b With First Day of Issue, Tallents House, Edinburgh handstamp .... **£4.50** ☐
555c With First Day of Issue, London SE1 handstamp .... **£5.00** ☐
555d With First Day of Issue (non pictorial), London SE1 handstamp .... **£5.00** ☐
555e With any one of some 22 additional relevant commemorative handstamps.......... **£10.00** ☐
555f With any relevant cds .... **£14.00** ☐

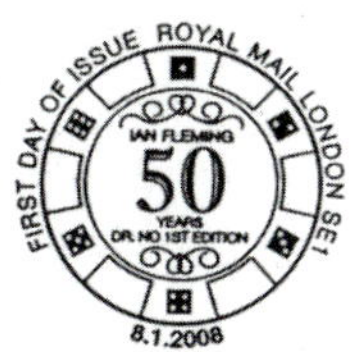

556. 2008, 8th January

James Bond. Miniature Sheet

2 x 1st, 2 x 54p, 2 x 78p. Stamps Feature Bond Book Covers

556a Miniature Sheet on illustrated cover, any postmark .... **£3.00** □
556b With any First Day of Issue postmark, as **555** .... **£5.00** □
556c With any one of 22 relevant commemorative handstamps, as **555** .... **£10.00** □
556d With any relevant cds .... **£14.00** □

James Bond - Prestige Stamp Book

This is listed in the Definitives Section of the catalogue.

---

557. 2008, 15th January

New Style Smilers Valentine Booklet. Self-adhesive

4 x 1st Defs, 2 x 1st Love Stamp + 2 Valentine Labels

557a Complete Pane on Illustrated cover, any postmark .... **£5.00** □
557b With Love Lane, Birmingham handstamp .... **£9.00** □
557c With Lover, Salisbury handstamp .... **£9.00** □
557d With Gretna Green, Gretna handstamp .... **£9.00** □
557e With River Cherwell, Oxford handstamp .... **£9.00** □
557f With any Valentine related cds .... **£12.00** □

---

558. 2008, 5th February

Working Dogs, Honouring Man's Best Friend

1st Assistance Dog, 46p Mountain Rescue Dog, 48p Police Dog, 54p Customs Dog 64p Sheepdog, 78p Guide Dog

558a Set of six Stamps on illustrated cover, any postmark .... **£3.50** ☐
558b With First Day of Issue, Tallents House, Edinburgh handstamp .... **£4.50** ☐
558c With First Day of Issue, Hound Green, Basingstoke handstamp .... **£5.00** ☐
558d With First Day of Issue, (non pictorial) Hound Green, Basingstoke handstamp .... **£5.00** ☐
558e With any one of some 14 additional relevant commemorative handstamps .... **£9.00** ☐
558f With Battersea, Dog & Gun, Dog Kennel Lane, Isle of Dogs cds .... **£12.00** ☐

---

559. 2008, 28th February

British Monarchs. The Houses of Lancaster and York

1st Henry IV, 1st Henry V, 54p Henry VI, 54p Edward IV, 69p Edward V, 69p Richard III

559a Set of six Stamps on illustrated cover, any postmark .... **£4.00** ☐
559b With First Day of Issue, Tallents House, Edinburgh handstamp .... **£5.00** ☐
559c With First Day of Issue, Tewkesbury, Glos handstamp .... **£5.50** ☐
559d With First Day of Issue, (non pictorial) Tewkesbury, Glos handstamp .... **£5.50** ☐
559e With First Day of Issue, Spring Stampex... London N1 handstamp .... **£5.50** ☐
559f With First Day of Issue ...Westminster, London SW1 handstamp .... **£5.50** ☐
559g With any one of some 15 additional relevant commemorative handstamps .... **£10.00** ☐
559h With Battle, Lancaster, York cds, or any other relevant cds .... **£13.50** ☐

560. 2008, 28th February

The Age of Lancaster and York. Miniature Sheet

1st Glyndwr, 1st Agincourt, 78p Tewkesbury, 78p Caxton

560a Miniature Sheet on illustrated cover, any postmark .... **£3.00** ☐
560b With First Day of Issue, Tallents House, Edinburgh handstamp .... **£4.00** ☐
560c With First Day of Issue, Tewkesbury, Glos handstamp .... **£4.50** ☐
560d With First Day of Issue, (non pictorial) Glos handstamp .... **£4.50** ☐
560e With any one of some 15 additional relevant commemorative handstamps .... **£9.00** ☐
560f With Battle, Lancaster, York, Caxton, Tenterden cds .... **£12.00** ☐

561. 2008, 28th February
New Smilers 'Add a Special Moment' Booklet. Self-adhesive
6 x 1st Definitive Format Pictorial Stamps. First issued 2005/6
(Hello, Flower, Union Flag, Balloons, Fireworks, Champagne)

561a Complete Pane on illustrated cover, any postmark .... **£6.00** ☐
561b With A Special Moment, Britannia, Bacup, Lancs Handstamp .... **£10.00** ☐
561c With A Special Moment, British, Talywain, Pontypool handstamp .... **£10.00** ☐
561d With any one of the British Monarchs handstamps, see previous page .... **£9.00** ☐
561e With any relevant cds .... **£12.50** ☐

562. 2008, 11th March
Celebrating Northern Ireland. Miniature Sheet. 4 Self-adhesive Stamps
2 x 1st Definitive size - Carrickfergus Castle, Giant's Causeway
2 x 78p Rectangular size - St. Patrick, Queen's Bridge Belfast

562a Miniature Sheet on illustrated cover, any postmark .... **£3.00** ☐
562b With First Day of Issue, Tallents House, Edinburgh handstamp .... **£4.00** ☐
562c With First Day of Issue, Downpatrick Co. Down handstamp .... **£4.50** ☐
562d With First Day of Issue (non pictorial), Downpatrick Co. Down handstamp .... **£4.50** ☐
562e With any one of some 9 additional relevant commemorative handstamps .... **£9.00** ☐
562f With any Northern Ireland cds .... **£10.00** ☐
562g With Belfast, Bushmills, Carrickfergus cds .... **£12.00** ☐

A generic sheet of 20 x 1st Country Stamp was also issued on March 11th. This was the first ever self-adhesive Country Stamp for Northern Ireland. Complete Sheet, with any postmark **£15.**

FIRST DAY OF ISSUE
11. 3. 2008
DOWNPATRICK CO DOWN

Control Numbers and/or Cylinder Numbers

Covers showing these are worth a premium of 20% – 25%

QEII • Commemoratives 2008

563. 2008, 13th March

Mayday: Rescue at Sea

1st Barra, 46p Appledore, 48p Portland, 54p St.Ives, 69p Selsey, 78p Tenby

563a Set of Stamps on illustrated cover, any postmark .... **£4.00** ☐
563b With First Day of Issue, Tallents House, Edinburgh handstamp .... **£5.00** ☐
563c With First Day of Issue, Poole, Dorset handstamp .... **£5.50** ☐
563d With First Day of Issue (non pictorial), Poole, Dorset handstamp .... **£5.50** ☐
563e With any one of some 17 additional relevant commemorative handstamps .... **£10.00** ☐
563f With Cromer, Lighthouse, Portland, or other relevant cds .... **£12.50** ☐

564. 2008, 1st April

Territorial Army Centenary. Commemorative Sheet

10 x 1st Class Union Flag + Label

564a Complete Sheet, with any postmark .... **£7.50** ☐
564b With 100 Years of the Territorial Army, Whitehall, London handstamp .... **£9.00** ☐
564c With Territorial Army Centenary 1908-2008, Wilton, Salisbury handstamp .... **£9.00** ☐
564d With any relevant cds .... **£12.50** ☐

565. 2008, 15th April

Insects. UK Species in Recovery. Se-tenant

10 x 1st Featuring ten of the UK's Rarest Insects

565a Set of Ten Se-tenant Stamps on illustrated cover, any postmark .... **£4.50** ☐
565b With First Day of Issue, Tallents House, Edinburgh handstamp .... **£5.50** ☐
565c With First Day of Issue, Crawley, W.Sussex handstamp .... **£6.00** ☐
565d With First Day of Issue (non pictorial), Crawley, W.Sussex handstamp .... **£6.00** ☐
565e With any one of some 11 additional relevant commemorative handstamps .... **£10.00** ☐
565f With Bugbrooke, Bugthorpe, Crawley, Selbourne, St. Bees cds .... **£12.50** ☐
565g With any other relevant cds .... **£12.50** ☐

566 2008, 13th May

Beside The Seaside Stamp Book. Self-Adhesive

2 x 1st Seaside Ice Cream + 4 x 1st Gold Definitive

566a Complete Booklet Pane on illustrated cover, any postmark .... **£3.00** ☐
566b With Summer Holidays, Brighton handstamp .... **£9.00** ☐
566c With Summer Holidays, Blackpool handstamp .... **£9.00** ☐
566d With any relevant cds .... **£12.00** ☐

---

567. 2008, 13th May

Cathedrals

1st Lichfield, 48p St Anne's Belfast, 50p Gloucester, 56p St Davids, 72p Westminster, 81p St Magnus Kirkwall

567a Set of Six Stamps on illustrated cover, any postmark .... **£4.00** ☐
567b With First Day of Issue, Tallents House, Edinburgh handstamp .... **£5.50** ☐
567c With First Day of Issue, London EC4 handstamp .... **£6.00** ☐
567d With First Day of Issue (non pictorial), London EC4 handstamp .... **£6.00** ☐
567e With any one of some 16 additional relevant commemorative handstamps .... **£10.00** ☐
567f With Belfast, Christchurch, Lichfield, Kirkwall cds (any London cds **£10**) .... **£13.00** ☐

568. 2008, 13 May

St Paul's Cathedral. 300th Annivesary. Miniature Sheet

2 x 1st, 2 x 81p - Interior Views of the Cathedral

568a Complete Miniature Sheet on illustrated cover, any postmark .... **£3.00** ☐
568b With First Day of Issue, Tallents House, Edinburgh handstamp .... **£4.50** ☐
568c With First Day of Issue, London EC4 handstamp .... **£5.00** ☐
568d With First Day of Issue (non pictorial), London EC4 handstamp .... **£5.00** ☐
568e With any one of the Cathedral Issue 567 commemorative handstamps .... **£9.00** ☐
568f With any cds, as for Cathedral Issue 567 .... **£12.00** ☐

569. 2008, 10th June

Classic Carry On and Hammer Films

1st Carry On Sergeant, 48p Dracula, 50p Carry On Cleo,
56p Curse of Frankenstein, 72p Carry On Screaming, 81p The Mummy

569a Set of Six Stamps on illustrated cover, any postmark .... **£4.00** ☐
569b With First Day of Issue, Tallents House, Edinburgh handstamp .... **£5.00** ☐
569c With First Day of Issue, Bray, Maidenhead handstamp .... **£5.50** ☐
569d With First Day of Issue (non pictorial), Bray, Maidenhead handstamp .... **£5.50** ☐
569e With any one of some 12 additional relevant commemorative handstamps .... **£10.50** ☐
569f With any Bray, Elstree, Denham, Ealing, Hollywood, Shepperton, Star cds .... **£14.00** ☐

CLASSIC FILMS - 10TH JUNE 2008 ELSTREE, HERTFORDSHIRE

FIRST DAY OF ISSUE ROYAL MAIL TALLENTS HOUSE EDINBURGH 10-06-2008

50th ANNIVERSARY · CLASSIC BRITISH CINEMA · STOUGHTON · GUILDFORD · SURREY · 10.6.08

CLASSIC FILMS - 10TH JUNE 2008 SHEPPERTON, SURREY

570. 2008, 10th June

Carry On Films Stamp Book

6 x 1st Gold Definitive + Advertisement Pane

570a Booklet, including Advertisement, on illustrated cover, any postmark .... **£2.00** ☐
570b With any Classic Films handstamp, Issue 569 .... **£6.00** ☐
570c With any relevant cds .... **£8.00** ☐

Royal Mail did not apply its First Day of Issue Classic Films handstamps to this Booklet, the Stamp having been issued previously.

---

571. 2008, 17th July

Air Displays. Celebrating 100 Years of Powered Flight

1st Red Arrows, 48p RAF Falcons, 50p Red Arrows, 56p Avro Flypast,
72p Parachuting, 81p Historic Air Race

571a Set of Six Stamps on illustrated cover, any postmark .... **£4.00** ☐
571b With First Day of Issue, Tallents House, Edinburgh handstamp .... **£5.00** ☐
571c With First Day of Issue, Farnborough, Hants. handstamp .... **£6.00** ☐
571d With First Day of Issue (non pictorial), Farnborough, Hants. handstamp .... **£6.00** ☐
571e With any one of some 16 additional relevant commemorative handstamps .... **£10.00** ☐
571f With Hendon, Farnborough, any relevant cds .... **£15.00** ☐
571g With any aerodrome cds, or RAF Post Office cds .... **£14.00** ☐

A Generic Sheet was also issued with 20 x 1st Red Arrows Stamp + Labels.
Complete Sheet, with any postmark is catalogued at **£15**.

FIRST DAY OF ISSUE FARNBOROUGH, HANTS 17.7.2008

17 07 2008 Air Displays Farnborough Hants

TRENCHARD HOUSE · FARNBOROUGH · HANTS · 17-7-08

AIRSHOWS RED ARROWS - LUTTERWORTH 17-07-08

See the Introduction for a comment on Commemorative Sheets

QEII • Commemoratives 2008

572. 2008, 24th July

1908 Olympic Games Centenary. Commemorative Sheet

10 x 1st Union Flag Stamp + Labels

572a Complete Sheet with any postmark.. **£7.50** ☐

572b With London 1908, White City, London W12 handstamp.. **£10.00** ☐

572c With London 1908 Olympic Games... White City W12 handstamp .... **£10.00** ☐

572d With London 1908, Windsor handstamp .... **£10.00** ☐

572e With any relevant cds.. **£12.50** ☐

No Royal Mail First Day of Issue handstamps, since this Stamp had been issued previously.

---

573. 2008, 5th August

Beijing 2008 Olympic Expo. Generic Sheet

10 x 1st Hello Stamp with Labels (Chinese Lanterns)

573a Complete Sheet with any postmark.. **£8.00** ☐

573b With any relevant cds.. **£12.50** ☐

No Royal Mail First Day of Issue handstamps, since the 1st Stamp has been issued previously.

No sponsored handstamps done.

---

574. 2008, 22nd August

Olympic Flag Handover. Miniature Sheet

4 x 1st Se-tenant Stamps - Beijing and London structures

574a Miniature Sheet on illustrated cover, any postmark.. **£2.50** ☐

574b With First Day of Issue, Tallents House, Edinburgh handstamp.. **£4.50** ☐

574c With First Day of Issue, London E15 handstamp .... **£5.50** ☐

574d With First Day of Issue (non pictorial), London E15 handstamp .... **£5.50** ☐

574e With any one of some 13 additional relevant commemorative handstamps.. **£9.00** ☐

574f With Croydon, London, Stratford, Wandsworth cds, any other relevant cds.. **£10.00** ☐

First Day Covers signed by the Stamp Designer

Covers with one or more Stamps signed by the designer, are worth a 20% premium over catalogue prices.

575. 2008, 18th September

RAF Uniforms. The History of Military Dress. Se-tenant Triplets

3 x 1st Drum Major 2007, Helicopter Winchman 1984, Hawker Hunter Pilot 1951,
3 x 81p Lancaster Gunner 1944, WAAF Plotter 1940, Pilot 1918

575a Both Se-Tenant Triplets on illustrated cover, any postmark .... **£4.00** ☐
575b With First Day of Issue, Tallents House, Edinburgh handstamp .... **£5.50** ☐
575c With First Day of Issue, Hendon, London NW9 handstamp .... **£6.50** ☐
575d With First Day of Issue (non pictorial), Hendon, London NW9 handstamp .... **£6.50** ☐
575e With First Day of Issue, Autumn Stampex...London N1 handstamp .... **£8.50** ☐
575f With any one of some 14 additional relevant commemorative handstamps.......... **£12.00** ☐
575g With any RAF Aerodrome cds, any other relevant cds .... **£15.00** ☐

2008, 18th September

Pilot to Plane: RAF Uniforms. Prestige Stamp Book

Details and pricing in the Definitives Section of the catalogue.

---

576. 2008, 14th October

Women of Distinction

1st Millicent Garrett Fawcett, 48p Elizabeth Garrett Anderson, 50p Marie Stopes
56p Eleanor Rathbone, 72p Claudia Jones, 81p Barbara Castle

576a Set of Six Stamps on illustrated cover, any postmark .... **£4.00** ☐
576b With First Day of Issue, Tallents House, Edinburgh handstamp .... **£5.50** ☐
576c With First Day of Issue, Aldeburgh, Suffolk handstamp .... **£6.50** ☐
576d With First Day of Issue (non pictorial), Aldeburgh, Suffolk handstamp .... **£6.50** ☐
576e With any one of some 11 additional relevant commemorative handstamps.......... **£12.00** ☐
576f With any relevant cds .... **£14.00** ☐

Distinction was achieved in the following fields (listed in order of Stamp value):
Votes for Women, Women's Health, Family Planning, Family Allowance, Civil Rights, Equal Pay

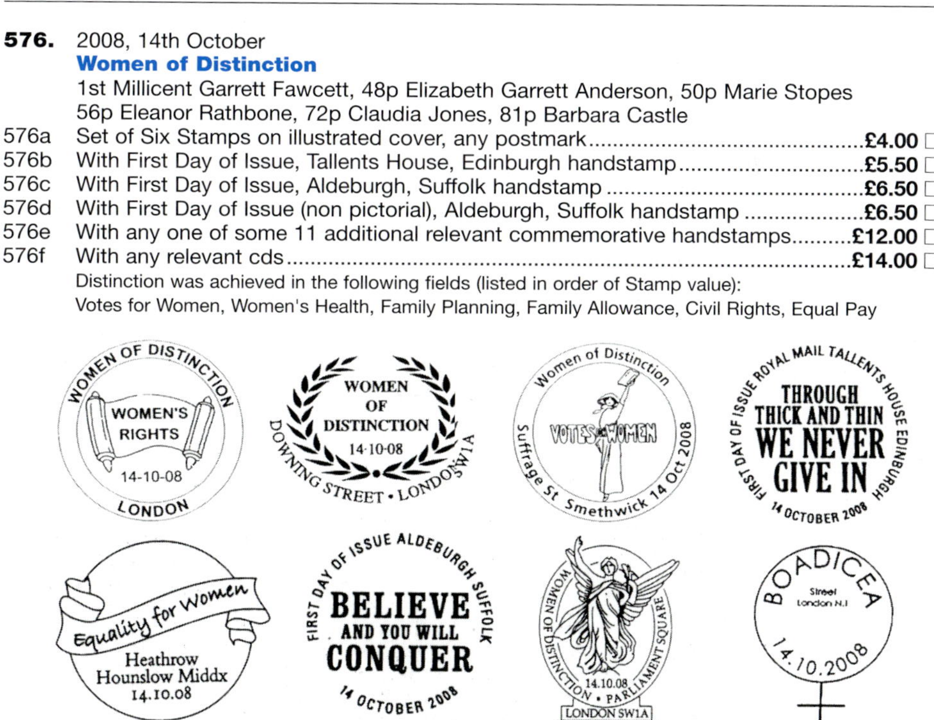

QEII • Commemoratives 2008

577. 2008, 4th November

Christmas Issue. British Pantomime

2nd, 2nd large, 1st, 1st Large, 50p, 81p, Pantomime Characters

577a	Set of Six Stamps on illustrated cover, any postmark	**£3.00** □
577b	With First Day of Issue, Tallents House, Edinburgh handstamp	**£4.50** □
577c	With First Day of Issue, Bethlehen Llandeilo handstamp	**£5.50** □
577d	With First Day of Issue (non pictorial), Bethlehen Llandeilo handstamp	**£5.50** □
577e	With any one of some 16 additional relevant commemorative handstamps	**£10.00** □
577f	With Bethlehem, Holy Island, Nasareth, Noel Rd, St Nicholas cds, any other relevant cds	**£12.00** □

A generic Smilers Sheet was issued on November 4, containing eight each 1st and 2nd Christmas Stamps plus four 81p Christmas Stamps, all with adjoining Labels.
The complete Sheet, with postmark is catalogued at **£14**.
The 1st and 2nd Madonna & Child Stamps from last Christmas (2007) were also re-issued on November 4th. No fdi services were offered for these previously issued Stamps.

578. 2008, 4th November

Christmas Issue. Miniature Sheet

Same set of Stamps as **577** above.
All pricing same as Christmas Issue **577** above.

---

579. 2008, 6th November

Lest We Forget. Armisitice 1918. Miniature Sheet

1st New Poppy Stamp, 4 x 81p Country Stamps

579a	Miniature Sheet on illustrated cover, any postmark	**£4.00** □
579b	With First Day of Issue, Tallents House, Edinburgh handstamp	**£5.50** □
579c	With First Day of Issue, London SW1 handstamp	**£6.50** □
579d	With First Day of Issue (non pictorial), London SW1 handstamp	**£6.50** □
579e	With any one of some 11 additional relevant commemorative handstamps	**£12.00** □
579f	With any relevant cds	**£14.00** □

A Generic Sheet with text and 20 x 1st New Poppy Stamp was also issued on November 6th.
The complete sheet, with any postmark, is catalogued at **£15**.

Write to us if you have questions on Commemorative handstamps for any QEII Stamp Issue.

---

580. 2009, 13th January
British Design Classics. Se-tenant
10 x 1st - Spitfire, Mini Skirt, Austin Mini, Anglepoise Lamp, Concorde, Telephone Kiosk, Polypropylene Chair, Penguin Books, London Underground Map, London Bus

580a Set of Ten Se-tenant Stamps on illustrated cover, any postmark .... **£4.00** ☐
580b With First Day of Issue, Tallents House, Edinburgh handstamp .... **£5.50** ☐
580c With First Day of Issue, Longbridge, Birmingham handstamp .... **£6.50** ☐
580d With First Day of Issue (non pictorial), Longbridge, Birmingham handstamp .... **£6.50** ☐
580e With any one of some 16 additional relevant commemorative handstamps .... **£12.00** ☐
580f With any relevant cds .... **£14.00** ☐

An Austin Mini Design Classics Generic Sheet was issued same day. It contained 20 x 1st Austin Mini Stamp + Labels. The complete Sheet, with any postmark, is catalogued at **£15.**

2009, 13th January
British Design Classics. Prestige Stamp Book
Details and pricing in the Definitive Section of the catalogue.

---

581. 2009, 22nd January
Robert Burns. 250th Anniversary. Miniature Sheet
2 x 1st New Burns Stamps + 1st, 2nd, 50p, 81p Existing Scottish Country Stamps

581a Miniature Sheet on illustrated cover, any postmark .... **£3.00** ☐
581b With First Day of Issue, Tallents House, Edinburgh handstamp .... **£4.50** ☐
581c With First Day of Issue, Alloway, Ayr handstamp .... **£5.50** ☐
581d With First Day of Issue (non pictorial), Alloway, Ayr handstamp .... **£5.50** ☐
581e With any one of some 13 additional relevant commemorative handstamps .... **£9.00** ☐
581f With any relevant cds .... **£12.50** ☐

582. 2009, 12th February
Charles Darwin. 200th Anniversary
1st Darwin, 48p Iguana, 50p Finches, 56p Atoll, 72p Bee Orchid, 81p Orang-utan.
All with 'jigsaw' perfs.

582a	Set of Six Stamps on illustrated cover, any postmark	**£4.00** ☐
582b	With First Day of Issue, Tallents House, Edinburgh handstamp	**£5.50** ☐
582c	With First Day of Issue, Shrewsbury handstamp	**£6.50** ☐
582d	With First Day of Issue (non pictorial), Shrewsbury handstamp	**£6.50** ☐
582e	With any one of some 17 additional relevant commemorative handstamps	**£10.00** ☐
582f	With Orpington, Shrewsbury and any other relevant cds	**£14.00** ☐

583. 2009, 12th February
Charles Darwin. Miniature Sheet
2 x 1st Cormorant, Tortoise + 2 x 81p Iguana, Mockingbird

583a	Miniature Sheet on illustrated cover, any postmark	**£3.00** ☐
583b	With First Day of Issue, Tallents House, Edinburgh handstamp	**£4.50** ☐
583c	With First Day of Issue, Shrewsbury handstamp	**£5.50** ☐
583d	With First Day of Issue (non pictorial), Shrewsbury handstamp	**£5.50** ☐
583e	With any one of some 17 additional relevant commemorative handstamps	**£9.00** ☐
583f	With Orpington, Shrewbury, or any other relevant cds	**£12.00** ☐

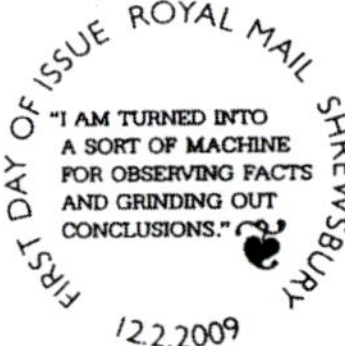

2009, 12th February
Charles Darwin. Prestige Stamp Book
Details and pricing in the Definitive Section of the catalogue.

Remember, from 1966 onwards, most hand addressed Commemorative covers are worth only 20% of catalogue prices.

QEII • Commemoratives 2009

584. 2009, 26th February

Celebrating Wales. Miniature Sheet

2 x 1st Welsh Dragon, Red Dragon + 2 x 81p St. David, National Assembly Building

584a Miniature Sheet on illustrated cover, any postmark.......... **£3.00** ☐
584b With First Day of Issue, Tallents House, Edinburgh handstamp.......... **£4.50** ☐
584c With First Day of Issue, Tyddewi, St. Davids handstamp.......... **£5.50** ☐
584d With First Day of Issue (non pictorial), Tyddewi, St. Davids handstamp.......... **£5.50** ☐
584e With First Day of Issue Spring Stampex, Celebrating Wales ... handstamp.......... **£5.50** ☐
584f With any one of some 10 additional relevant commemorative handstamps.......... **£9.00** ☐
584g With any relevant cds.......... **£12.00** ☐

A Generic Sheet entitled Glorious Wales was issued on March 1st. It contained 10 x 1st Welsh Dragon Stamp + Labels. Complete Sheet, with any postmark, is catalogued at **£10.**

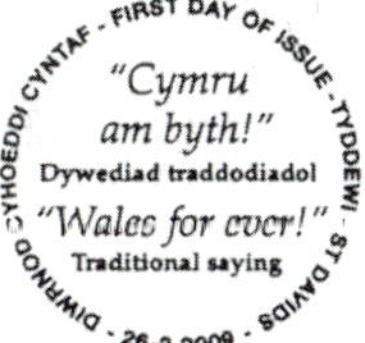

585. 2009, 10th March

Pioneers of the Industrial Revolution

4 x Se-tenant Pairs - 1st Matthew Bolton, James Watt, 50p Richard Arkwright, Josiah Wedgwood, 56p George Stevenson, Henry Maudslay, 72p James Brindley, John McAdam

585a Set of Four Se-tenant Pairs on illustrated cover, any postmark.......... **£5.00** ☐
585b With First Day of Issue, Tallents House, Edinburgh handstamp.......... **£6.50** ☐
585c With First Day of Issue, Steam Mills, Cinderford handstamp.......... **£7.50** ☐
585d With First Day of Issue (non pictorial), Steam Mills, Cinderford handstamp.......... **£7.50** ☐
585e With any one of some 12 additional relevant commemorative handstamps.......... **£12.50** ☐
585f With any relevant cds.......... **£15.00** ☐

586. 2009, 10th March

Design Classics Stamp Book

4 x 1st Definitive Stamp, 1st London Bus, 1st Telephone Kiosk

586a Complete Booklet on illustrated cover, any postmark .... **£3.00** ☐
586b With British Design Classics, Retail Book... London WC2 handstamp .... **£6.50** ☐
586c With British Design Classics, Retail Book... London W1 handstamp .... **£6.50** ☐
586d With any relevant cds .... **£9.00** ☐

No Royal Mail fdi postmarks since all Stamps had been issued previously.

A second Design Classics Generic Sheet was issued on March 2nd. It contained 20 x 1st Concorde Stamp + Labels. The complete Sheet, with any postmark, is catalogued at **£15.**

---

587. 2009, 21st April

Great British Monarchs. The House of Tudor

2 x 1st Henry VII, Henry VIII, 2 x 62p Edward VI, Jane Grey, 2 x 861p Mary 1, Elizabeth 1.

587a Set of Six Stamps on illustrated cover, any postmark .... **£4.00** ☐
587b With First Day of Issue, Tallents House, Edinburgh handstamp .... **£5.50** ☐
587c With First Day of Issue, London SE10 handstamp .... **£6.50** ☐
587d With First Day of Issue (non pictorial), London SE10 handstamp .... **£6.50** ☐
587e With any one of some 20 additional relevant commemorative handstamps .... **£11.00** ☐
587f With any relevant cds .... **£14.00** ☐

588. 2009, 21st April

The Age of the Tudors. Miniature Sheet

2 x 1st Mary Rose, The Field of Cloth of Gold 2 x 81p Royal Exchange, Francis Drake

588a Miniature Sheet on illustrated cover, any postmark .... **£3.00** ☐
588b With First Day of Issue, Tallents House, Edinburgh handstamp .... **£4.50** ☐
588c With First Day of Issue, London SE10 handstamp .... **£5.50** ☐
588d With First Day of Issue (non pictorial), London SE10 handstamp .... **£5.50** ☐
588e With any one of some 20 additional relevant commemorative handstamps .... **£9.00** ☐
588f With any relevant cds .... **£12.50** ☐

All postmarks same as for Great British Monarchs Issue **587.**

QEII • Commemoratives 2009

589. 2009, 21st April
Design Classics Second Stamp Book.
4 x 1st Definitive Stamp, 2 x 1st Austin Mini Stamp

589a Complete Booklet on illustrated cover, any postmark .... **£3.00** ☐
589b With British Design Classics Retail Book, Fawkham, Longfield DA3 handstamp .... **£6.50** ☐
589c With Design Classics Retail Book... Austin Rise, Longbridge handstamp .... **£6.50** ☐
589d With British Design Classics Retail Book, Longbridge, Birmingham 831 handstamp. **£6.50** ☐
589e With any relevant cds .... **£9.00** ☐

No Royal Mail fdi postmarks since all Stamps had been issued previously.

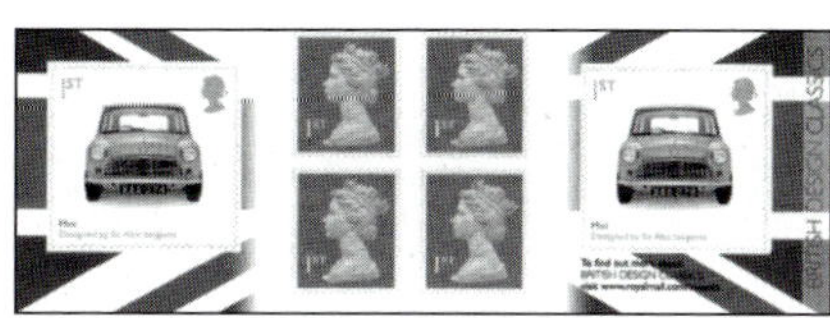

---

590. 2009, 30th April
Smilers for Kids. Four Self-adhesive Sheets
Big Ears, Wild Cherry, Little Miss Sunshine, Jeremy Fisher
Each Sheet contains 20 x 1st Stamps + Labels

590a Any Single Sheet, with any postmark .... **£15.00** ☐
590b With Smilers for Kids, Croydon handstamp .... **£16.50** ☐
590c With Smilers for Kids, London W8 handstamp .... **£16.50** ☐
590d With any relevant cds .... **£20.00** ☐

No Royal Mail fdi postmarks since all Stamps had been issued previously.

See the Introduction for General Information

See Index on page 3 for full Catalogue Listings

591. 2009, 19th May
Endangered Wild Plants. Se-tenant
10 x 1st Leek, Water-plantain, Lady's Slipper, Milkwort, Saxifrage, Woundwart, Spurge, Plymouth Pear, Sea Knotgrass, Deptford Pink

591a Set of Ten Se-tenant Stamps on illustrated cover, any postmark .... **£4.50** ☐
591b With First Day of Issue, Tallents House, Edinburgh handstamp .... **£6.00** ☐
591c With First Day of Issue, Kew, Richmond handstamp .... **£7.00** ☐
591d With First Day of Issue (non pictorial), Kew, Richmond handstamp .... **£7.00** ☐
591e With any one of some 15 additional relevant commemorative handstamps .... **£12.50** ☐
591f With any relevant cds .... **£15.00** ☐

592. 2009, 19th May
Endangered Wild Plants. Miniature Sheet
2 x 1st Palm House Kew Gardens, Seed Bank Wakehurst Place,
2 x 81p Pagoda Kew Gardens, Sacklet Crossing Kew Gardens

592a Complete Miniature Sheet on illustrated cover, any postmark .... **£3.00** ☐
592b With First Day of Issue, Tallents House, Edinburgh handstamp .... **£4.50** ☐
592c With First Day of Issue, Kew, Richmond handstamp .... **£5.50** ☐
592d With First Day of Issue (non pictorial), Kew, Richmond handstamp .... **£5.50** ☐
592e With any one of some 15 additional relevant commemorative handstamps .... **£9.00** ☐
592f With any relevant cds .... **£12.50** ☐

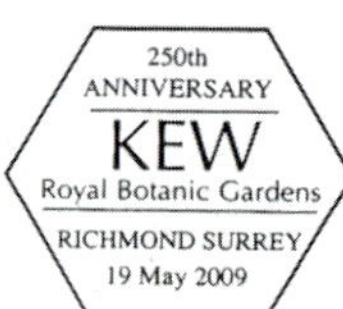

593. 2009, 21st May
National Association of Flower Arrangement Societies. Stamp Book
4 x 1st Definitive, 1st Iris, 1st Tulip

593a Complete Booklet on illustrated cover, any postmark .... **£3.00** ☐
593b With Flowers Retail Book, Kew Gardens, Birmingham handstamp .... **£6.00** ☐
593c With Flower Arrangement Society, 50th Anniversary, Halstead handstamp .... **£6.00** ☐
593d With Flower Arrangement Society, 50th Anniversary, London handstamp .... **£6.00** ☐
593e With any relevant cds .... **£9.00** ☐

No Royal Mail fdi postmarks since all Stamps had been issued previously.

QEII • Commemoratives 2009

594. 2009, 16th June
Mythical Creatures
2 x 1st Dragons, Unicorns, 2 x 62p Giants, Pixies, 2 x 90p Mermaids, Fairies
594a Set of Six Stamps on illustrated cover, any postmark.......................................**£4.50** □
594b With First Day of Issue, Tallents House, Edinburgh handstamp..............................**£6.00** □
594c With First Day of Issue, Dragonby, Scunthorpe handstamp...................................**£6.50** □
594d With First Day of Issue (non pictorial), Dragonby, Scunthorpe handstamp.............**£6.50** □
594e With any one of some 12 additional relevant commemorative handstamps..........**£12.00** □
594f With any relevant cds...**£15.00** □

---

595. 2009, 18th August
Post Boxes. 200th Year. Miniature Sheet
1st George V Box, 56p Edward VII Box, 81p Victoria Box, 90p QEII Box
595a Complete Miniature Sheet on illustrated cover, any postmark...............................**£3.00** □
595b With First Day of Issue, Tallents House, Edinburgh handstamp..............................**£4.50** □
595c With First Day of Issue, Wakefield, Yorkshire handstamp ....**£5.00** □
595d With First Day of Issue (non pictorial), Wakefield, Yorkshire handstamp..................**£5.00** □
595e With any one of some 16 additional relevant commemorative handstamps............**£9.00** □
595f With any relevant cds...**£12.50** □

A Generic Sheet was issued on the same date. With 20 x 1st George V Post Box Stamp + Labels. The Complete Sheet, with any postmark, is catalogued at **£15.**

2009, 18th August
Treasures of the Postal Museum. Prestige Stamp Book
Details and pricing in the Definitives Section of the catalogue.

All prices in this catalogue are for clean covers with undamaged stamps and clear postmarks.

QEII • Commemoratives 2009

596. 2009, 18th August
British Design Classics. Third Stamp Book
4 x 1st Definitive Stamp + 2 x 1st Concorde

596a	Complete Booklet on illustrated cover, any postmark	**£3.00** ☐
596b	With Concorde Stamp Book, Concorde Tower, Birmingham postmark	**£6.50** ☐
596c	With British Design Classics Retail Book, Heathrow, Hounslow handstamp	**£6.50** ☐
596d	With any relevant cds	**£9.00** ☐

No Royal Mail fdi postmarks since all Stamps had been issued previously.

---

597. 2009, 1st September
Fire and Rescue Services. 300th Anniversary
1st Firefighting, 54p Chemical Fire, 56p Emergency Rescue, 62p Flood Rescue
81p Search Rescue, 90p Fire Safety

597a	Set of Six Stamps on illustrated cover, any postmark	**£4.50** ☐
597b	With First Day of Issue, Tallents House, Edinburgh handstamp	**£5.50** ☐
597c	With First Day of Issue, Hose, Melton Mowbray handstamp	**£6.00** ☐
597d	With First Day of Issue (non pictorial), Hose, Melton Mowbray handstamp	**£6.00** ☐
597e	With any one of some 12 additional relevant commemorative handstamps	**£9.00** ☐
597f	With any relevant cds	**£12.50** ☐

Valuation Guide for GB Blocks of 4 on fdc

1840 to 1900 – three times the single fdc value

1902 to 1936 – two and a half times the single fdc value

1936 KEVIII – twice the single fdc value

1937 to 1951 – twice the single fdc value

1952 to date – one and a half times the single fdc value

598. 2009, 17th September
Royal Navy Uniforms
3 x 1st Se-tenant - Flight Deck Officer, Captain 1041, WRNS Officer
3 x 90p Se-tenant - Able Seaman 1880, Marine 1805, Admiral 1795

598a Pair of Tryptics on illustrated cover, any postmark .... **£4.00** □
598b With First Day of Issue, Tallents House, Edinburgh handstamp .... **£5.50** □
598c With First Day of Issue, Portsmouth handstamp .... **£6.00** □
598d With First Day of Issue (non pictorial), Portsmouth handstamp .... **£6.00** □
598e With First Day of Issue, Royal Navy Uniforms, Stampex, London N1 handstamp .. **£6.50** □
598f With any one of some 14 additional relevant commemorative handstamps.......... **£11.00** □
598g With any relevant cds .... **£14.00** □

2009, 17th September
Royal Navy Uniforms, Prestige Stamp Book
Details and pricing in the Definitives Section of the catalogue

---

599. 2009, 17th September
British Design Classics. Fourth Stamp Book
4 x 1st Definitive Stamp + 2 x 1st Mini Skirt

599a Complete Booklet on illustrated cover, any postmark .... **£3.00** □
599b With Mini Skirt Stamp Book...Knightsbridge Rd. Solihull handstamp .... **£6.50** □
599c With British Design Classics Retail Book, Blackheath, London SE3 handstamp .... **£6.50** □
599d With British Design Classics Retail Book, Chelsea, London SW1 handstamp .... **£6.50** □
599e With any relevant cds .... **£9.00** □

No Royal Mail fdi postmarks since all Stamps had been issued previously.

QEII Definitives in chronological order start on page 350

600. 2009, 8th October
Eminent Britons
2 x Five Se-tenant 1st Stamps
Fred Perry, Henry Purcell, Matt Busby, William Gladstone, Mary Wollstonecraft, Conan Doyle, Donald Campbell, Judy Fryd, Samuel Johnson, Martin Ryle

600a Set of Ten Se-tenant Stamps on illustrated cover, any postmark .... **£4.50** ☐
600b With First Day of Issue, Tallents House, Edinburgh handstamp .... **£5.50** ☐
600c With First Day of Issue, Bacup, Lancashire handstamp .... **£6.00** ☐
600d With First Day of Issue (non pictorial), Bacup, Lancashire handstamp .... **£6.00** ☐
600e With any relevant commemorative handstamp* .... **£10.00** ☐
600f With any relevant cds .... **£14.00** ☐

*Detail to be confirmed in the next catalogue.

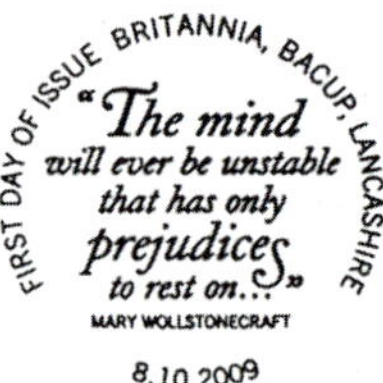

---

601. 2009, 22nd October
London 2012 Games
2 x Five Se-tenant 1st Stamps
Weightlifting, Badminton, Athletics, Dressage, Canoeing, Diving, Boccia, Basketball, Archery, Judo

601a Set of Ten Se-tenant Stamps on illustrated cover, any postmark .... **£4.50** ☐
601b With First Day of Issue, Tallents House, Edinburgh handstamp .... **£5.50** ☐
601c With First Day of Issue, Badminton, Glos handstamp .... **£6.00** ☐
601d With First Day of Issue (non pictorial), Badminton, Glos handstamp .... **£6.00** ☐
601e With any relevant commemorative handstamp* .... **£10.00** ☐
601f With any relevant cds .... **£14.00** ☐

*Detail to be confirmed in the next catalogue
A Commemorative Sheet was also issued on October 22nd.
The Complete Sheet, with any postmark, is catalogued at **£15.**

Don't forget that we now include sections on Overprints, Pre-release covers and Missing Colours on fdc. These can all be found in the last part of the catalogue.

QEII • Commemoratives 2009

602. 2009, 3rd November

Christmas Issue. Nativity in Stained Glass

2nd, 2nd Large, 1st, 1st Large, 56p, 90p, £1.35

602a Set of Seven Stamps on illustrated cover, any postmark .... **£5.00** ☐
602b With First Day of Issue, Tallents House, Edinburgh handstamp .... **£6.00** ☐
602c With First Day of Issue, Bethlehem, Llandeilo handstamp .... **£6.50** ☐
602d With First Day of Issue (non pictorial), Bethlehem, Llandeilo handstamp .... **£6.50** ☐
602e With any relevant commemorative handstamp* .... **£10.00** ☐
602f With any relevant cds .... **£15.00** ☐

*Detail to be confirmed in the next catalogue.

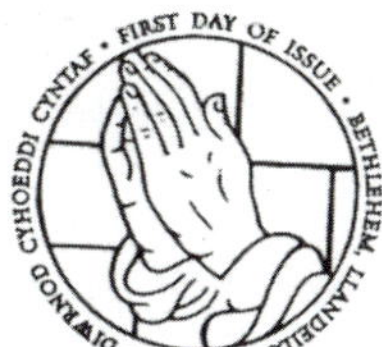

603. 2009, 3rd November

Christmas Issue. Miniature Sheet

Same Set of Seven Christmas Stamps as **602** above.
All pricing the same as the Christmas Issue **602** above.

A Christmas Generic Sheet was issued on November 3rd. 8 x 2nd, 8 x 1st, 2 x 56p, 2 x 90p Christmas Stamps. The Complete Sheet, with any postmark, is catalogued at **£18.**

The 2007 2nd and 1st Madonna & Child Stamps went back on sale from November 3rd for the 2009 Christmas period. No catalogue value since these were not new Stamps.

End of QEII Commemorative Issues

2010 NEW ISSUES

07 January .... **British Design**
02 February .... **Girl Guides Centenary**
25 February .... **Royal Society 250th Anniv.**
11 March...... **Battersea Dogs & Cats Home**
23 March........ **House of Stewart (Scotland)**
13 April......... **Action for Species: Mammals**
06 May........... **Accession of King George V**
08 May........................... **The King's Stamps**
13 May........................ **Britain Alone in 1940**
15 June.............................. **Children's Books**
19 August............................ **Stage Musicals**
16 September........... **Great British Railways**
12 October.. **House of Stuart (James/Anne)**
02 November....................... **Christmas Issue**

There will also be an Olympic and Paralympic Games Issue – date to be confirmed.
Please note dates are subject to change and more Issues could be added during the year!

QEII • Definitives, Regionals, Booklets, Coils, Dues, Gums, Perfs, Papers, etc. 1952-56

Catalogue prices are for clean illustrated or display covers, unless otherwise stated, with the full set of stamps as issued. Illustrated or display covers were readily available for all early and subsequent QEII Issues in this category.

Neat hand addressed covers are acceptable alternatives to printed, rubber stamped, or typed ones, up until the time of the Machin Head Issues, which started in 1967, for Definitives; from 1958 for Regionals, and from 1957 for Booklets, Coils, Dues, etc. Beyond these dates most hand addressed covers are worth only some 20% of the catalogue price. Exceptions are made in the case of rare cancellations, with a catalogue value of £85 or more. For all such cancellations a neat hand addressed cover is an acceptable alternative, without loss of catalogue value.

600. 1952-1954, 1959

Low Value Definitives

		Date	Plain	Illus.
600a	1½d Green, 2½d Red, any postmark	5.12.52	**£3.00**	**£12.50** ☐
600b	5d Brown, 8d Magenta, 1/- Bistre-Brown, any postmark	6.7.53	**£9.50**	**£40.00** ☐
600c	½d Orange, 1d Ultramarine, 2d Brown, any postmark	31.8.53	**£9.50**	**£40.00** ☐
600d	4d Lt. Blue, 1/3d Green, 1/6d Grey-Blue, any postmark	2.11.53	**£25.00**	**£128.00** ☐
600e	3d Lilac, 6d Claret, 7d Lt. Green, any postmark	18.1.54	**£25.00**	**£82.00** ☐
600f	9d Olive, 10d Blue, 11d Brown-Purple, any postmark	8.2.54	**£48.00**	**£165.00** ☐
600g	4½d Chestnut, any postmark	9.2.59	**£18.00**	**£150.00** ☐
600h	Post Card with QEII Portrait and any one of ½d, 1d, 1½d, 2d, 2½d, or 4d values			**£26.00** ☐
	Any cover with House of Commons/Lords cds	add **£50.00**		
	Any cover with Windsor cds	add **£60.00**		
	Any cover with Buckingham Palace cds	add **£150.00**		

601. 1955, 1st and 23rd September

Castles High Values

		Date	Plain	Illus.
601a	2/6d Brown, 5/- Red, on one or two covers, any pmk	23.9.55	**£75.00**	**£300.00** ☐
601b	2/6d Brown, Carrickfergus cds (Queens Rd cds plain **£215**)	23.9.55	**£80.00**	**£265.00** ☐
601c	10/- Ultramarine, £1 Black, on one or two covers, any pmk	1.9.55	**£200.00**	**£485.00** ☐
601d	10/- Ultramarine with Edinburgh cds	1.9.55	**£185.00**	**£240.00** ☐
601e	Set of 4 values with Windsor cds		**£425.00**	☐

602. 1953-1957

Postal Stationery

602a	2½d Red printed (square) envelope, any pmk	Issue Date 29.11.54	**£22.00** ☐
602b	2½d Red printed (rectangular) envelope, any pmk	Issue Date 29.11.54	**£27.50** ☐
602c	8½d Slate printed registered letter envelope, any pmk	Issue Date 29.11.54	**£50.00** ☐
602d	2d Brown printed post card, any pmk	Issue Date 6.4.55	**£60.00** ☐
602e	2½d Scarlet printed letter card, any pmk	Issue Date 16.5.55	**£60.00** ☐
602f	2½d Red printed (square) blue envelope, any pmk	Issue Date 11.6.56	**£35.00** ☐
602g	3d Violet printed envelope, any pmk	Issue Date 23.11.57	**£45.00** ☐
602h	6d Overseas Registered Letter, any pmk	Issue Date 1.6.56	**£62.00** ☐
602i	6d deep red airmail letter sheet, any pmk	Issue Date 3.6.53	**£10.00** ☐

603. 1955-1956

Watermark Change – St. Edward's Crown

Thirteen values were released between September and December 1955. Whilst the issue dates are known, no first day covers have been seen. A further five values were issued in 1956 and are known on display covers.

603a	2d Value, display cover, cds	Issue Date 17.10.56	**£150.00** ☐
603b	3d Value, display cover, cds	Issue Date 17.7.56	**£150.00** ☐
603c	7d Value, display cover, cds	Issue Date 23.4.56	**£175.00** ☐
603d	1/3d and 1/6d, on one display cover, cds	Issue Date 27.3.56	**£325.00** ☐

604. 1956, 12th June
Postage Due. 1d Violet-Blue
604a 1d Postage Due on plain cover, with any postmark .... **£600.00** ☐

604A. 1957, 1st October
604Aa Booklet Pane 6 x 3d, St Edwards crown, any postmark .... **£115.00** ☐

605. 1957, 19th November
Graphite Lines Issue – Naphthadag Experiment, Southampton
605a Set of six Wilding Defs, with graphite lines printed under the adhesive on the back of each stamp. Cachet or plain covers priced the same.
½d, 1d, 1½d, 2d, 2½d, 3d Southampton cds .... **£95.00** ☐

606. 1957, 27th November
The De Gruchy Perfins - Jersey
606a Set of 13 Perfins on one cover, Jersey cds .... **£260.00** ☐
606b Set of 10-12 Perfins as above, Jersey cds .... **£200.00** ☐

Although not strictly a regional issue, the De Gruchy Perfins are unique and they are from Jersey. They consist of Wilding Definitives up to the 1/- value, perforated by the firm of De Gruchy in Jersey. Prior to late 1957, these Perfins had never been made available mint, or in used sets, to collectors. The story goes that in November 1957 De Gruchy agreed to release five mint sets to a Mr. A. Steiner on the condition that they be posted the same day. The five covers had to be shown to the manager at De Gruchy the next day, to prove that all of the stamps had been used! Needless to say, Mr. Steiner did not post complete sets on all five covers!

607. 1957, 19th December
Introduction of First Automatic Letter Sorting Machine
607a Set of six Wilding Defs, with graphite lines, on one or two cachet covers.
½d, 1d, 1½d, 2d, 2½d, 3d Southampton 'S' machine cancel .... **£85.00** ☐

608. 1958, 18th August
3d Lilac, First Regional Stamp
Jersey, Guernsey, Isle of Man, Wales, Scotland, Northern Ireland
608a Jersey version, with any local postmark .... **£10.00** ☐
608b Guernsey version, with any local postmark .... **£10.00** ☐
608c Isle of Man version, with any local postmark .... **£15.00** ☐
608d Welsh version, with any Welsh postmark .... **£10.00** ☐
608e Scottish version, with any Scottish postmark .... **£10.00** ☐
608f Scottish version, with Balmoral Castle cds on plain cover .... **£60.00** ☐
608g Northern Ireland version, with any N. Ireland postmark .... **£10.00** ☐
608h All six stamps on one cover, any postmark .... **£60.00** ☐

609. 1958, 29th September
6d Claret, 1/3d Green – Wales, Scotland, Northern Ireland
609a Welsh stamp designs, any Welsh postmark .... **£15.00** ☐
609b Scottish stamp designs, any Scottish postmark .... **£15.00** ☐
609c Scottish stamp designs, with Balmoral Castle cds on plain cover .... **£65.00** ☐
609d Northern Ireland stamp designs, any N. Ireland postmark .... **£15.00** ☐
609e All three versions on one cover, any postmark .... **£35.00** ☐

610. 1959, 18th November
Phosphor–Graphite Issue - Wilding Definitives
610a Set of eight stamps, with graphite lines on the back and two phosphor bands on the front. Covers were processed through new sorting machine in Southampton.
½d, 1d, 1½d, 2d, 2½d, 3d, 4d, 4½d, with Southampton "S' machine cancel .... **£120.00** ☐
This set is usually on two cachet covers.

611. 1960, 6th July

Phosphor Lines Issue – New Letter Sorting Machine

611a Set of nine Wilding Definitives, with two phosphor bands on the front. Covers were processed through a new modified sorting machine in Southampton.
½d, 1d, 1½d, 2d, 2½d, 3d, 4d, 6d, 1/3d, with Southampton 'S' cancel........................**£140.00** ☐
This set is usually on two cachet covers.

612. 1960-1967

Phosphor Lined Issue – Wilding Definitives

612a	½d, 1d, 1½d, 2d, 2½d, 3d, 4d	Issue Date	22.6.60	Not known ☐
612b	4½d	Issue Date	13.9.61	Not known ☐
612c	5d on display cover, cds	Issue Date	9.6.67	**£130.00** ☐
612d	6d on display cover, cds	Issue Date	27.6.60	**£190.00** ☐
612e	7d on display cover, cds	Issue Date	15.2.67	**£170.00** ☐
612f	8d on display cover, cds	Issue Date	28.6.67	**£170.00** ☐
612g	9d	Issue Date	29.12.66	Not known ☐
612h	10d	Issue Date	30.12.66	Not known ☐
612i	1/- on illustrated or display cover, cds	Issue Date	28.6.67	**£300.00** ☐
612j	1/3d	Issue Date	5.6.61	Not known ☐
612k	1/6d	Issue Date	12.12.66	Not known ☐

The 8d and 1/- can also be found together on one cover and as such are worth **£375.00**

613. 1961, 1st February

Recorded Delivery - First Day of New Service

Envelope with Orange Brown Recorded Delivery label and 9 pence worth of postage. Stamp or stamps cancelled with first day postmark. Typed or hand written address.

613a Plain cover with label, correct postage, any postmark ....**£70.00** ☐
613b With Regional stamps and cancellation ....**£80.00** ☐
Not known on illustrated covers.

613A. 1961, 10th April

2d Light Red Brown

613Aa Single stamp from Booklet Pane with inverted watermark ....**£450.00** ☐

614. 1963, 29th January

3d Lilac, 6d Claret, 1/3d Green – Scotland (Phosphor)

614a Stamps as issued in 1958, but with two phosphor bands, machine cancel.............**£120.00** ☐
Most covers known are cacheted rather than illustrated. Plain covers are worth 20% of catalogue price.

615. 1963, 15th July

3d Lilac on Chalky Paper – Isle of Man

615a Stamp as issued in 1958, but printed on chalky paper, any local cancel.................**£310.00** ☐
615b On plain cover, any local postmark ....**£190.00** ☐

616. 1963, 15th July

2/- Holiday Booklet – First GB Se-tenant Stamps

616a Booklet Pane 3 x ½d plus 1 x 2½d,Se-tenant, any postmark ....**£97.50** ☐
616b Same, plus other two Panes (both 4 x 2½d) on one cover, any postmark ....**£115.00** ☐
Plain cover with all three Panes 90% of catalogue value.

617. 1963, 6th September

2/- Booklet _ Reprint Booklet Issued in Stratford-upon-Avon

617a Illustrated cover with reprint Pane 3 x ½d + 1 x 2½d Se-tenant, any postmark ....**£95.00** ☐
617b Illustrated cover with reprint Pane, plus 4 x 2½d Pane, any postmark.....................**£115.00** ☐

618. 1964, 8th June
2½d Red – Jersey, Guernsey, Isle of Man

618a Jersey issue, with local FDI or other local postmark .... **£17.50** ☐
618b Guernsey issue, with local FDI or other local postmark .... **£17.50** ☐
618c Isle of Man issue, with local FDI or other local postmark .... **£17.50** ☐
618d All three versions on one cover, any postmark .... **£40.00** ☐

619. 1964, 1st July
2/- Holiday Booklet – New Se-tenant Format

619a Illustrated cover with new Pane 2 x ½d plus 2 x 2½d Se-tenant, any pmk .... **£15.00** ☐
619b Set of five commemorative covers, each with different town name and matching postmark (Bournemouth, Rye, Salisbury, Stratford-upon-Avon and Winchester) .... **£42.00** ☐
619c With New Pane plus Geographic Set (Ord) both on one cover .... **£45.00** ☐

620. 1964, 1st July
2½d Wilding – Watermark Change (From 2/- Holiday Booklet)

620a New 2½d Type II with sideways watermark, illustrated/cachet cover, any pmk .... **£45.00** ☐

621. 1965, 17th May
3d Deep Lilac, 4d Deep Ultramarine – Phosphor Change

621a 3d one phos line, 4d two phos lines, any cover, any postmark .... **£135.00** ☐
621b 3d Value only on display cover, any postmark .... **£80.00** ☐
621c 4d Value only on display cover, any postmark .... **£75.00** ☐

622. 1965, 21st June
6/- Booklet – Three Panes of 6 x 4d

622a One Pane on illustrated cover, any postmark (non phos) .... **£170.00** ☐
622b One Pane on illustrated cover, any postmark (phosphor) .... **£185.00** ☐

623. 1965, 16th August
2/- Holiday Booklet – New Se-tenant Format

623a Se-tenant Pane 2 x 3d plus 2 x 1d, phosphor or plain on illustrated/cachet cover, any postmark .... **£85.00** ☐
623b Two Panes, with 1d stamps to the left on one Pane and to the right on the other .... **£170.00** ☐
623c Pane of 4 x 4d from the same Booklet, illustrated/cachet cover, phosphor or plain, any postmark .... **£75.00** ☐
623d Single 4d value, as above, phosphor or plain, any postmark .... **£48.00** ☐

624. 1965, 6th December
2/- Christmas Booklet – Two Panes of 4 x 3d

624a Pane of 4 x 3d on illustrated cover, any postmark .... **£275.00** ☐

625. 1966, 7th February
4d Blue – Jersey, Guernsey, Isle of Man, Wales, Scotland, N. Ireland

625a Set of six covers, with local FDI or other local postmark .... **£30.00** ☐
625b Additional 4d Blue Scottish issue with 2 phos bands .... **£10.00** ☐
625c All seven versions on one cover, any postmark .... **£35.00** ☐

Remember, most modern hand addressed covers are worth only 20% of catalogue prices

626. 1967, 1st March

9d Green, 1/6d Grey-Blue – Wales, Scotland, Northern Ireland

626a Set of three covers, each with appropriate stamps and local postmark .... **£28.00** ☐
626b Wales or N. Ireland stamps, with 'New Stamp Issue ...' slogan cancel .... **£36.00** ☐
626c All three versions on one cover, any postmark .... **£27.00** ☐

627. 1967-68

Castles High Values – No Watermark

627a £1 Black, unwatermarked paper, any cds ....Issue Date 6.12.67....... **£550.00** ☐
627b 10/- Ultramarine, unwatermarked paper, any cds ....Issue Date 16.4.68....... **£300.00** ☐
627c 5/- Red, unwatermarked paper, any cds ....Issue Date 16.4.68....... **£300.00** ☐
627d 2/6d Brown, unwatermarked paper, any cds ....Issue Date 3.7.68....... **£320.00** ☐

Prices are for plain covers. The 2/6d and £1 are also known on illustrated covers, and as such are worth a 30% premium.

628. 1967, 9th June

3d Lilac - Jersey. Phosphor Change. Wmk Crown

628a 3rd Lilac with phosphor centre band, George Town cds .... **£360.00** ☐

629. 1967, 5th September

4d Blue - Jersey. Phosphor Change. Wmk Crown

629a 4d Blue with 2 phosphor bands, George Town cds .... **£360.00** ☐

630. 1967, 21st September

6/- Booklet – First Machin Defs Booklet

630a Pane of 6 x 4d on illustrated cover, any postmark .... **£115.00** ☐

There were three Panes 6 x 4d in this Booklet.

631. 1968, 25th March

10/- Livingstone Booklet

631a All three Panes 6 x 1d, 6 x 3d, 6 x 4d illustrated cover, Stampex h/s .... **£120.00** ☐
631b Any one Pane on illustrated cover, any postmark .... **£45.00** ☐

632. 1968, 6th April

2/- Booklet

632a Two Panes 4 x 4d and 2 x 1d plus 2 x 3d Se-tenant, illustrated cover, any pmk .... **£125.00** ☐
632b Either Pane, illustrated/cachet cover, any postmark .... **£54.00** ☐

Philart has the issue date as April 17th, which we now believe to probably be correct.

633. 1968, 4th June

2/6d Castle High Value – Chalky Paper

633a 2/6d Brown, chalky paper, on illustrated cover, any cds .... **£360.00** ☐
633b Same on plain cover, any cds .... **£230.00** ☐

All QEII Definitives, Dues, Regionals, Booklets, Coils, Graphites and variations in Phosphors, Watermarks, Perfs, Gum Types, Papers, etc. are in this Section of the catalogue, starting on page 350.

634. 1967-68, 1969

Low Values - Machin Head Design

– 4d Brown Sepia, 1/- Violet, 1/9d Orange, Black	Issue Date	5.6.67
– 3d Violet, 9d Dark Green, 1/6d Indigo	Issue Date	8.8.67
– ½d Orange, 1d Olive, 2d Brown, 6d Claret	Issue Date	5.2.68
– 5d Blue, 7d Green, 8d Vermilion, 10d Grey	Issue Date	1.7.68
– 4d Vermilion, 8d Light Blue - (colour change)	Issue Date	6.1.69
– 9d Winchester Green	Issue Date	29.11.68

634a Set as above on five illustrated covers, any postmark .... **£10.00** ☐
634b With London FDI or Philatelic Bureau handstamp .... **£20.00** ☐
634c With Windsor FDI or Windsor, Berks handstamp .... **£25.00** ☐
634d 4d, 1/-, 1/9d with Buckingham Palace cds .... **£60.00** ☐
634e With Windsor Castle cds. Usually on plain cover .... **£65.00** ☐
634f With House of Commons cds .... **£45.00** ☐
634g With Coventry Cathedral, 5th Anniv. handstamp .... **£15.00** ☐
634h 3d, 9d, 1/6d with Buckingham Palace cds .... **£60.00** ☐
634i With Windsor Castle cds. Usually on plain cover .... **£68.00** ☐
634j With House of Commons cds .... **£45.00** ☐
634k ½d, 1d, 2d, 6d with Buckingham Palace cds .... **£60.00** ☐
634l With Sandringham, Norfolk cds .... **£75.00** ☐
634m With House of Commons cds .... **£45.00** ☐
634n 5d, 7d, 8d, 10d with Buckingham Palace cds .... **£60.00** ☐
634o With House of Commons cds .... **£45.00** ☐
634p With The Royal Tournament, BFPS 1068 h/s. Tournament cover .... **£32.50** ☐
634q 4d, 8d with Windsor, Berks large handstamp .... **£12.00** ☐
634r With House of Commons cds .... **£45.00** ☐
634s With Field Post Office 986 (BFPO 42) h/s. BFPS cover .... **£15.00** ☐
634t 9d Winchester Green with any cds .... **£115.00** ☐

635. 1968, 10th July

4/6d Cutty Sark Booklet

635a Two Panes 6 x 1d, 6 x 4d, illustrated cover, any postmark .... **£175.00** ☐
There were two Panes 6 x 4d and one Pane 6 x 1d in this Booklet.

636. 1968, 4th September

4d Brown, 5d Blue – Jersey, Guernsey, Isle of Man, Wales, Scotland, N. Ireland

636a Set of six covers, each with appropriate stamps and local postmark.......... **£25.00** ☐
636b 4d and 5d Wales, with 'For Sale ...New Stamps for Wales & Mon' slogan cancel .... **£40.00** ☐
636c 4d and 5d Scotland, with 'New Stamps for Scotland' slogan cancel.......... **£42.00** ☐
636d 4d and 5d Scotland, with Balmoral Castle cds.......... **£52.00** ☐
636e 4d and 5d Northern Ireland, with 'New 4d & 5d Stamps for N. Ireland' slogan cancel ... **£45.00** ☐

637. 1968, 16th September

2/-, 4/6d, and 10/- Booklets (The start of 1st and 2nd Class Post)

637a 2/- Booklet – Two Panes 4 x 4d, 2 x 4d plus 2 Se-tenant labels on illustrated/cachet cover, any postmark .... **£28.00** ☐
637b 2/- Booklet – Se-tenant Pane only, illustrated cover, any postmark .... **£17.50** ☐
637c 4/6d Booklet – Three Panes 2 x 6 x 4d, 6 x 1d on illustrated/cachet cover, any postmark. (Two Panes only, 6 x 4d and 6 x 1d cat. **£46**) .... **£65.00** ☐
637d 10/- Booklet – Set of three Panes 6 x 4d, 6 x 5d, 4 x 1d plus 2 x 4d Se-tenant, illustrated/cachet cover, any postmark .... **£87.50** ☐
637e 10/- Booklet – Se-tenant Pane only, illustrated cover, any postmark .... **£45.00** ☐
There were two each of the 4d and 5d Panes in the 10/- Booklet.

4d and 5d Postal Stationery

637f 4d Grey envelope, with any cds postmark .... **£18.00** ☐
637g 5d Dark Blue, printed Letter Card, with any cds postmark .... **£24.00** ☐

600a

600h

600j

600i

600e

600k

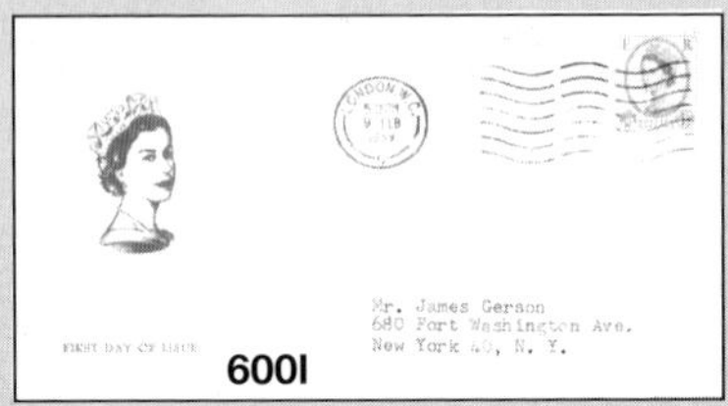

600l

601a

601c

600m

600m

600m

600m

QEII Issues - Selected Regionals 1958/69

608a

609a

614a

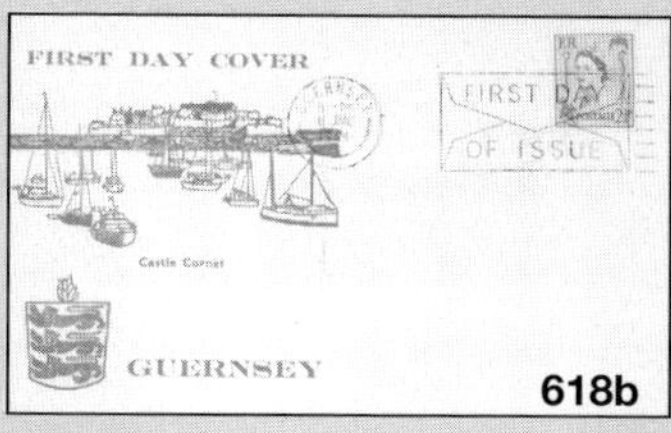

618b

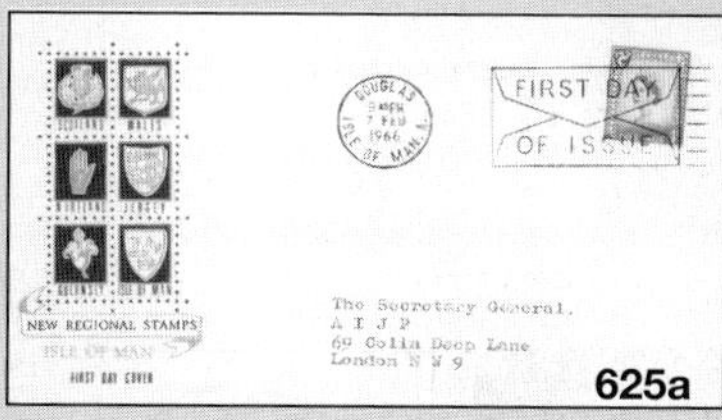

625a

626a

636b

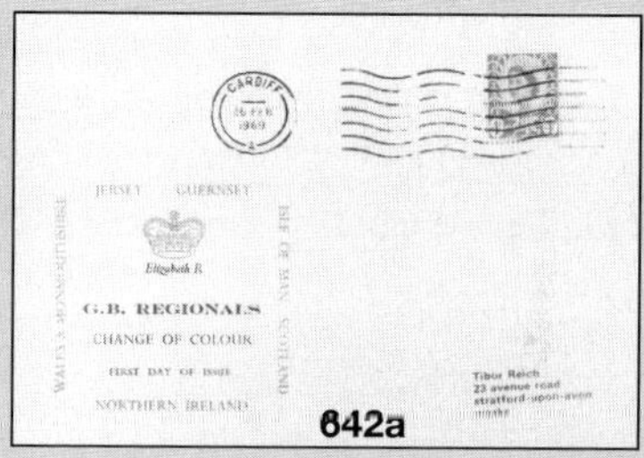

642a

652a

647a

647b

634a

634a

634a

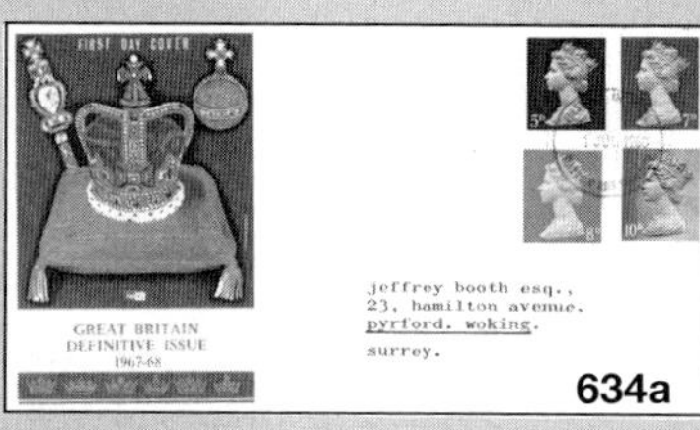

634a

634a

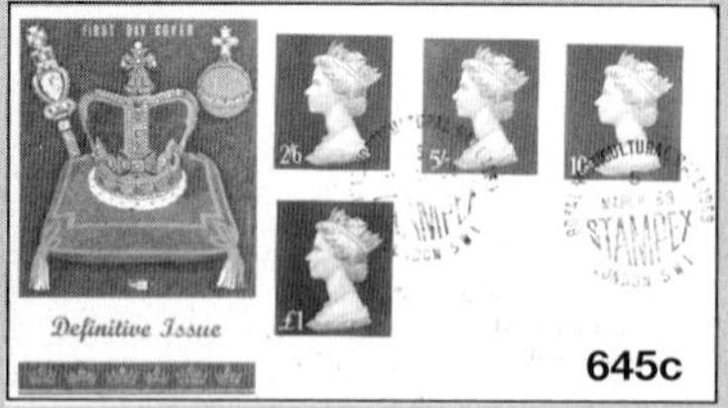

645c

646b

655e

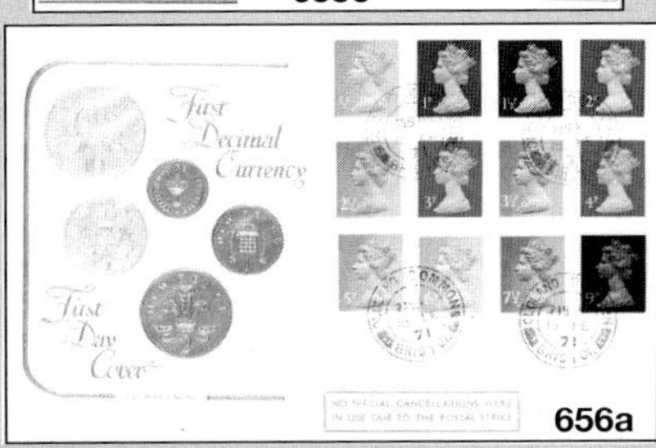

656a

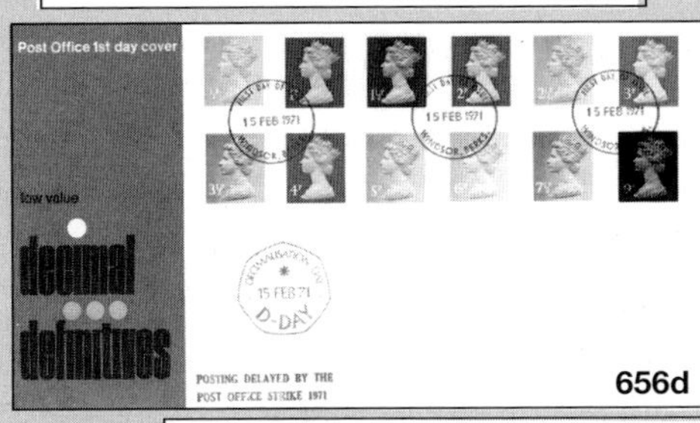

656d

658b

665d

QEII Issues - Selected Definitives 1972/92

674d

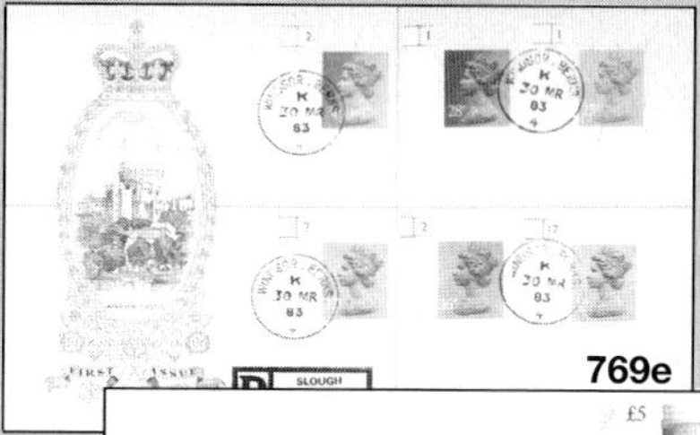

769e

841m

719d

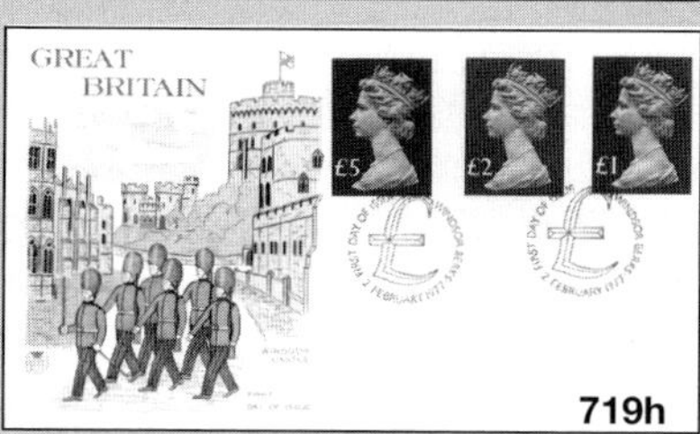

719h

281h

847e

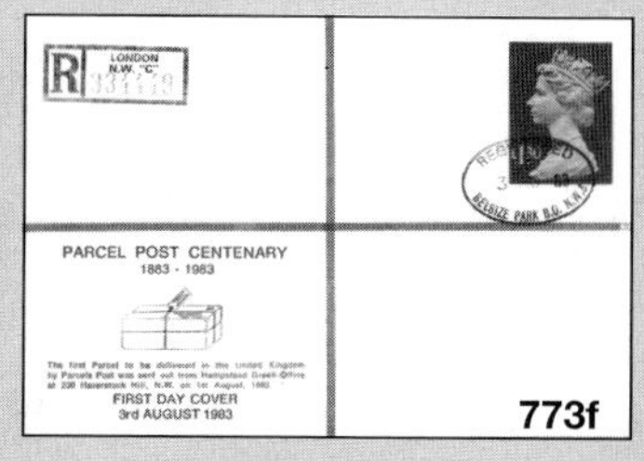

773f

862f

741e

882g

638. 1968, 16th October
6/- Woodpecker Booklet
638a Three Panes of 6 x 4d, illustrated/cachet cover, any postmark .... **£115.00** ☐
638b Single Pane of 6 x 4d, illustrated/cachet cover, any postmark .... **£68.00** ☐

639. 1968, 27th November
5/- Ightham Mote Booklet
639a Two Panes of 6 x 5d, illustrated/cachet cover, any postmark .... **£110.00** ☐
639b Single Pane of 6 x 5d, illustrated/cachet cover, any postmark .... **£86.00** ☐

640. 1969, 8th January
10/- Mary Kingsley Booklet – New Colour 4d Vermilion
640a 3 Panes only from the Booklet 6 x 5d, 6 x 4d, 4 x 1d plus 2 x 4d Se-tenant, illustrated cover, any postmark .... **£90.00** ☐
640b Se-tenant Pane only, illustrated cover, any postmark .... **£38.00** ☐
640c Se-tenant Pane only with January 6th postmark (pre-release), illustrated cover...... **£55.00** ☐
There were two each of the 4d and 5d Panes in this Booklet, plus the Se-tenant Pane.

641. 1969, 8th January
4/6d QEII Booklet
641a Two Panes only 6 x 4d, 6 x 1d, illustrated cover, any postmark .... **£85.00** ☐
There were two 6 x 4d Panes in this Booklet, plus one 6 x 1d Pane.

642. 1969, 26th February
4d Vermilion – Jersey, Guernsey, Isle of Man, Wales, Scotland, N. Ireland
642a Set of six covers, each with appropriate stamp and local postmark.......... **£25.00** ☐
642b All six versions on one cover, any postmark .... **£28.00** ☐

643. 1969, 28th February
6/- Barn Owl Booklet
643a One Pane 6 x 4d, illustrated cover, any postmark .... **£115.00** ☐
There were three Panes 6 x 4d in this Booklet.

644. 1969, 3rd March
2/- Booklet – New Colour 4d Vermilion
644a Two Panes 4 x 4d and 2 x 4d plus 2 labels Se-tenant, illustrated cover, any pmk... **£85.00** ☐
644b Se-tenant Pane only, illustrated cover, any postmark .... **£27.50** ☐

645. 1969, 5th March
Machin High Values
645a 2/6d Brown, 5/- Burgundy, 10/- Ultramarine, £1 Black, with any pmk. .... **£12.00** ☐
645b Set with London FDI or Philatelic Bureau handstamp .... **£15.00** ☐
645c Set with Stampex, London SW1, special handstamp .... **£32.00** ☐
645d Set with Windsor FDI handstamp .... **£28.00** ☐
645e Set with House of Commons SWI cds .... **£45.00** ☐
645f Set with Buckingham Palace cds .... **£140.00** ☐
645g Set on four QEII illustrated post cards, Windsor FDI handstamp .... **£58.00** ☐
Prices are for the set on one or more illustrated covers.

646. 1969, 27th August
1/- Stamp Vending Machine Multi-Value Coil
2 x 2d + 3d +1d + 4d, all Se-tenant. First ever strip of Se-tenant stamps.
646a Se-tenant strip, illustrated cover, any postmark .... **£4.50** ☐
646b With Windsor, Berks handstamp .... **£12.50** ☐
646c With National Postal Museum handstamp .... **£15.00** ☐
646d With House of Commons SWI cds .... **£30.00** ☐

647. 1969, 30th September
Last Day Cover – of British Postal Administration in Jersey and Guernsey
647a Last Day Cover, any Jersey stamp or stamps, local postmark....... **£15.00** ☐
647b Last Day Cover, any Guernsey stamp or stamps, local postmark....... **£15.00** ☐

648. 1968-70
Postal Stationery
648a 5d Dark Blue, printed envelope, any postmark.......Issue Date 7.10.69....... **£12.50** ☐
648b 4d Red, printed letter card, any postmark.......Issue Date 21.10.69....... **£11.00** ☐
648c 4d Red, printed letter card, National Postal Museum h/s .Issue Date 21.10.69....... **£13.00** ☐
648d 4d Red, printed envelope, any postmark.......Issue Date 5.1.70....... **£8.00** ☐
648e 3/5d Grey, printed registered letter, small size, any pmk..Issue Date 13.4.70....... **£12.50** ☐
648f 3/5d Grey, printed registered letter, large size, any pmk ..Issue Date 13.4.70....... **£12.50** ☐
648g 5d Dark Blue, printed letter card, any postmark.......Issue Date 20.4.70....... **£10.50** ☐
648h 4d Red, printed post card, any postmark.......Issue Date 8.6.70....... **£10.50** ☐
648i 4d Red, printed post card, National Postal Museum h/s ..Issue Date 8.6.70....... **£15.00** ☐
648j 9d Blue, airmail letter sheet, any postmark.......Issue Date 1.7.68....... **£14.00** ☐

649. 1969, 1st December
£1 Booklet – 'Stamps for Cooks'
649a Set of 4 Panes 15 x 4d twice, 15 x 5d, 3 joined Se-tenant strips 4d + 1d + 5d + 1d + 4d on matching covers with Milk Marketing Board special h/s....... **£68.00** ☐
649b Se-tenant strip from the Se-tenant Pane, MMB handstamp....... **£20.00** ☐
649c 15 x 4d uncoated paper, any postmark....... **£95.00** ☐

650. 1969, 10th December
1/6d All Over Phosphor
650a 1/6d on illustrated or cachet cover, any postmark....... **£6.50** ☐
650b Same with London or Southampton cds....... **£12.00** ☐

651. 1970, 3rd March
5/- Philympia Booklet
651a Two Panes both 6 x 5d, on illustrated cover with Stampex special handstamp....... **£65.00** ☐
651b Single Pane, illustrated or cachet cover, any postmark....... **£46.00** ☐

652. 1970, 28th September
9d Green – Scotland. Two Phosphor Bands, Chalky Paper, No Watermark
652a 9d Phos stamp, design as issued in 1967, black or purple local postmark....... **£25.00** ☐

653. 1970, 16th November
1/9d PVA Gum
653a 1/9d on illustrated or cachet cover, any postmark....... **£168.00** ☐

—— FROM NOW ON ALL ISSUES ARE IN DECIMAL CURRENCY ——

654. 1970, 17th June
Postage Due - Decimal To Pay Labels
10p, 20p, 50p, £1
654a Set on illustrated cover, any cds postmark....... **£515.00** ☐

655. 1970, 17th June
First Decimal High Values 10p Cerise, 20p Olive, 50p Ultramarine
655a Set on illustrated cover, any postmark....... **£3.00** ☐
655b With Philatelic Bureau handstamp....... **£5.50** ☐
655c With London FDI handstamp, or National Postal Museum ECI h/s....... **£12.50** ☐
655d With Windsor, Berks FDI handstamp....... **£18.00** ☐
655e With First Issue of British Decimal Stamps, Windsor handstamp....... **£24.00** ☐

655f With Becket Festival, Bramfield, Hertford handstamp .... £22.00 ☐
655g With House of Commons SW1 cds .... £48.00 ☐
655h With Buckingham Palace SW1 cds .... £85.00 ☐
655i With the 3 values, plus £1 recess printed, any postmark .... £600.00 ☐

656. 1971, 15th February
First Decimal Low Values
½p, 1p, 1½p, 2p, 2½p, 3p, 3½p, 4p, 5p, 6p, 7½p, 9p

656a Set on illustrated cover, any postmark, plus Post Office Strike cachet .... £2.50 ☐
656b With Philatelic Bureau handstamp and Post Office Strike cachet .... £5.00 ☐
656c With London FDI handstamp, and Post Office Strike cachet .... £6.50 ☐
656d With Windsor, Berks FDI handstamp, and Post Office Strike cachet .... £9.00 ☐
656e With any cds postmark and no P.O. Strike cachet .... £18.50 ☐
656f With Forces Post Office handstamp and no P.O. Strike cachet .... £18.50 ☐
656g With Field Post Office cds and no P.O. Strike cachet .... £18.50 ☐
656h With Windsor, Berks fdi handstamp and no P.O. Strike cachet .... £35.00 ☐
656i With Decimal Currency in the Post Office, Take a Leaflet, Hythe slogan .... £130.00 ☐
656j With 15th, Feb 1971 Decimal Day, Windsor, Berks. (Private Mail cancel) .... £50.00 ☐

The Post Office Strike cachet read as follows: "Posting Delayed by the Post Office Strike 1971". Some Post Offices as well as Forces and Field P.O.s were open on the first day, despite the strike, and cancelled stamps without applying the Strike cachet. Obviously these are worth a premium.

Royalty Post Cards

New Special GB Colour Feature!

Don't miss this wonderful fdc presentation on pages 160-176

Royalty Post Cards

Valuation Guide for GB Blocks of 4 on fdc

1840 to 1900 - three times the single fdc value
1902 to 1936 - two and a half times the single fdc value
1936 KEVIII - twice the single fdc value
1937 to 1951 - twice the single fdc value
1952 to date - one and a half times the single fdc value
(with a few 1952 to date issues at twice the single fdc value)

Gems • QEII First Decimal Issues

First Postage Due – To Pay Labels
Rare 1970 Set in Blocks of Four!

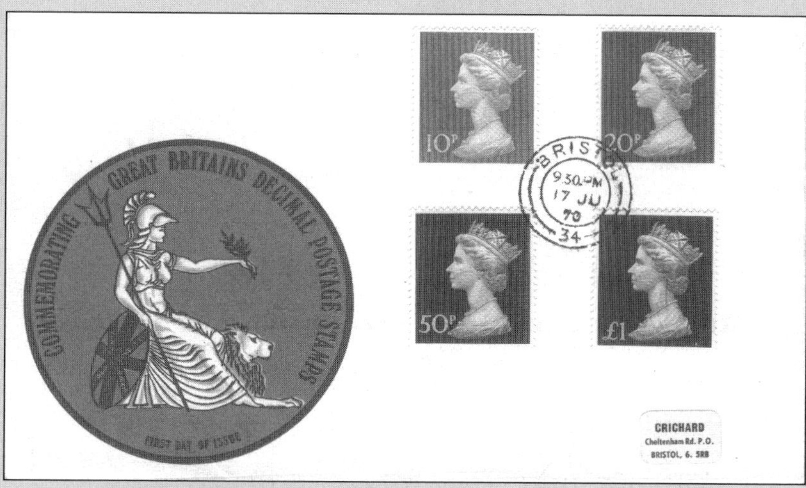

First Decimal High Value Definitives 1970
Together with the scarce Recess Printed £1!

657 1971, 15th February
Postage Due - To Pay Labels
½p, 1p, 2p, 3p, 4p, 5p
657a Set on illustrated cover, any cds postmark .... **£580.00** ☐
657b On set dated March 11th 1971 after Postal Strike .... **£130.00** ☐

658. 1971, 15th February
Multi-Value 5p Se-tenant Coil Strip
(2p + 2 x ½p + 2 x1p)
658a Se-tenant strip on illustrated cover, any postmark .... **£3.50** ☐
658b Same with Windsor, Berks FDI handstamp .... **£9.50** ☐
Nearly all covers have the Postal Strike cachet. Those few without the cachet are worth a 50% premium.

659. 1971, 15th February
2½p and 3p Coil Strips. Vertical & Horizontal Formats
659a Strip of 3 or more of each value from new Coils, any postmark .... **£750.00** ☐
These are very rare with day of issue postmarks. Single value on fdc **£450**.

660. 1971, 15th February
First Decimal Value Booklets
10p Booklet, 2 Panes
(2 x ½p + 2 x 2p)* and (2 x 1p + 2 x 1½p)*
25p Booklet, 3 Panes
(5 x ½p + label), (5 x 2½p + label), (4 x 2½p + 2 labels)
30p Booklet, 2 Identical Panes
(5 x 3p + label), (5 x 3p + label)
50p Booklet, 4 Panes
(5 x ½p + label), (5 x 2½p + label), (4 x 3p + 2 x 2½p)*, (6 x 3p)
660a Set of 10 different Panes with Strike cachets, FDI handstamp .... **£60.00** ☐
660b With Windsor, Berks FDI handstamp .... **£125.00** ☐
660c Without Strike cachet, cds postmark .... **£290.00** ☐
660d 10p Booklet Panes (2) any cover, no Strike cachet, with cds postmark .... **£50.00** ☐
660e 25p Booklet Panes (3) any cover, no Strike cachet, with cds postmark .... **£78.00** ☐
660f 30p Booklet Panes (2) any cover, no Strike cachet, with cds postmark .... **£45.00** ☐
660g 50p Booklet Panes (4) any cover, no Strike cachet, with cds postmark .... **£105.00** ☐
660h Set of 3 Se-tenant* Panes, Strike cachet, any FDI handstamp .... **£25.00** ☐
660i Set of 3 Se-tenant* Panes, Strike cachet, Windsor FDI handstamp .... **£50.00** ☐
The 10p Booklet was in a vertical format, whilst the other three Booklets were all in horizontal format.

---

661. 1971, 15th February
Postal Stationery

661a 2½p Dark Pink printed envelope (small size), Windsor FDI plus Strike cachet .... **£12.50** ☐
661b 2½p Dark Pink printed envelope (large size), Windsor FDI handstamp .... **£12.50** ☐
661c 2½p Dark Pink printed post card, Windsor FDI plus Strike cachet .... **£12.50** ☐
661d 2½p Dark Pink printed letter card, Windsor FDI plus Strike cachet .... **£12.50** ☐
661e 3p Ultramarine printed envelope (small size), Windsor FDI plus Strike cachet .... **£12.50** ☐
661f 3p Ultramarine printed envelope (large size), Windsor FDI handstamp.................... **£12.50** ☐
661g 3p Ultramarine printed letter card, Windsor FDI plus Strike cachet........................... **£12.50** ☐
661h 3p Ultramarine + 3p Light Ultramarine printed to order envelope, any cds............... **£25.00** ☐
661i 4p Light Brown + ½p Sky Blue printed to order envelope, any cds .... **£30.00** ☐

The large size envelopes and the printed to order envelopes do not usually have the "Posting Delayed..." cachet on them.

662. 1971, 7th July
2½p Magenta, 3p Ultramarine, 5p Violet, 7½p Chestnut
Isle of Man, Wales, Scotland, Northern Ireland

662a Set of four covers, each with appropriate stamps and regional FDI postmark .... **£11.50** ☐
662b All four Regions stamps on one cover, Bureau, Windsor or other cancel.................. **£10.00** ☐

663. 1971, 14th July
10p Booklet, 2 Se-tenant Panes, New Horizontal Format
(2 x ½p + 2 x 2p), and (2 x 1p + 2 x 1½p)

663a Both Panes on one cover, any postmark .... **£350.00** ☐
663b Same with Windsor, Berks postmark... **£475.00** ☐

664. 1971, 23rd July
30p Booklet, 2 Identical Panes, with New 'Blind' Imperforate
(5 x 3p + label), (5 x 3p + label)

664a Single Pane on cover, any postmark.. **£200.00** ☐
664a Same with Windsor, Berks postmark... **£325.00** ☐

To prevent blind people from confusing labels with stamps, the vertical perforations between the labels and the binding margin were removed.

665. 1971, 11th August
10p Orange-Brown. Change of Size and Colour

665a 10p on illustrated cover, any postmark .... **£2.00** ☐
665b With Philatelic Bureau handstamp.. **£3.50** ☐
665c With London FDI handstamp .... **£5.50** ☐
665d With Windsor FDI handstamp .... **£8.00** ☐

666. 1971, 17th September
25p Booklet, 3 Panes, with 'Blind' Imperforate
(5 x ½p + label), (5 x 2½p + label), (4 x 2½p + 2 labels)

666a Three Panes on one or more covers, any postmark.. **£180.00** ☐
666b With Windsor, Berks postmark.. **£210.00** ☐

Vertical perf. removed between labels and the binding margin.

667. 1971, 17th September
50p Booklet, 4 Panes, with 'Blind' Imperforate on 2 Panes only
(5 x ½p + label), (5 x 2½p + label)

667a Both 'Imperforate' Panes on one or two covers, any postmark .... **£160.00** ☐
667b With Windsor, Berks postmark.. **£210.00** ☐

Vertical perf. removed between labels and the binding margin. The 50p Booklet had 4 panes, all identical to the February 15th, 1971 50p Booklet, except for 'Blind' Imperf. on the two panes above.

668. 1971, 24th December
Christmas Booklets
25p Booklet, 3 Panes
(5 x ½p + label), (5 x 2½p + label), (4 x 2½p + 2 labels)
50p Booklet, 4 Panes
(3 Panes same as 25p Booklet), (5 x 2½p + label)

668a 25p (3 Panes), plus 50p (1 Pane) on 4 covers, any postmark ... **£112.00** ☐
668b Same with Windsor, Berks postmark ... **£185.00** ☐

Vertical perf. removed between labels and the binding margin, to avoid confusion by the Blind between labels and stamps. Most sets of these panes were done with a Southampton postmark.

669. 1972, 24th May
£1 Wedgwood Booklet, 4 Panes
(4 x ½p + 2 x 2½p), (3 x ½p + 9 x 2½p), (6 x 2½p + 6 x 3p), (12 x 3p)

669a Set of 4 complete Panes, with text, any postmark ... **£65.00** ☐
669b - With New £1 Stamp Book, Barlaston, Staffs FDI handstamp ... **£125.00** ☐
669c Set of 4 Panes, without text, Philatelic Bureau handstamp ... **£40.00** ☐
669d - With New £1 Stamp Book, Barlaston, Staffs FDI handstamp ... **£65.00** ☐
669e Complete Se-tenant Pane, plus 2 Se-tenant Strips, Bureau handstamp ... **£20.00** ☐
669f - With New £1 Stamp Book, Barlaston, Staffs FDI handstamp ... **£35.00** ☐
669g (4 x ½p + 2 x 2½p) miscut Pane, any postmark ... **£700.00** ☐

670. 1972, 23rd August
3p Ultramarine, Gum Arabic

670a 3p on illustrated cover, with bottom or right margin, cds postmark ... **£62.00** ☐
670b Same without margin, cds postmark ... **£45.00** ☐
670c Same with margin and National Postal Museum handstamp ... **£70.00** ☐

For the first time the perforation was continued through the bottom and right sheet margins.

671. 1972, 13th September

2½p Magenta, Gum Arabic

671a 2½p on illustrated cover, with any perf. margin, cds postmark .... **£60.00** ☐
671b Without margin, cds postmark .... **£35.00** ☐
671c With margin and National Postal Museum handstamp .... **£68.00** ☐

The perforation was continued through all margins with this issue.

672. 1972, 22nd September

½p Turquoise Gum Arabic

2½p Magenta, Gum Arabic - Scottish and Welsh Regionals

672a ½p on illustrated cover, with perf. margin, cds postmark .... **£60.00** ☐
672b 2½p Scottish Regional stamp .... **£35.00** ☐
672c 2½p Welsh Regional stamp .... **£35.00** ☐
672d All 3 stamps on one cover, any cds postmark .... **£100.00** ☐

Any of the above without the perforated margin are worth some £10 less per stamp.

673. 1972, 31st October

4p Ochre-Brown, Gum Arabic

673a 4p on illustrated cover, with perf. margin, cds postmark .... **£80.00** ☐
673b Without the perforated margin (selvedge), cds .... **£52.00** ☐

674. 1972, 6th December

£1 Black. Redrawn Value

674a £1 on illustrated cover, any postmark .... **£3.00** ☐
674b With Philatelic Bureau handstamp .... **£6.50** ☐
674c With London FDI handstamp .... **£9.50** ☐
674d With Windsor, Berks regular FDI handstamp .... **£16.50** ☐
674e With Windsor, Berks large FDI h/s (House of Commons cds **£30**) .... **£25.00** ☐
674f With National Postal Museum, London EC1 h/s (in brown) .... **£16.50** ☐
674g With Buckingham Palace cds .... **£125.00** ☐
674h With Windsor Castle cds .... **£180.00** ☐

675. 1972, 14th December

3p Ultramarine, Gum Arabic - Scottish Regional

675a 3p on illustrated cover, with perf. margin, cds postmark .... **£60.00** ☐
675b Without the perforated margin (selvedge), cds .... **£40.00** ☐

676. 1973, 1st February

50p All Over Phosphor

676a 50p Ultramarine on illustrated cover, any cds postmark .... **£95.00** ☐
676b With Southampton cds .... **£120.00** ☐
676c With National Postal Museum, London ECI handstamp .... **£132.00** ☐

677. 1973, 2nd April

£5 Postage Due - To Pay Label

677a £5 on plain cover, with any cds postmark .... **£600.00** ☐
677b On cachet or illustrated cover, any cds postmark .... **£650.00** ☐

678. 1973, 6th June

3p Ultramarine - Welsh Regional, 6p Light Emerald. Both Gum Arabic

678a 3p Welsh Regional, with perf. margin, any cds postmark .... **£62.00** ☐
678b 6p with perforated margin, any cds postmark .... **£125.00** ☐
678c Both stamps on one cover, any cds postmark .... **£155.00** ☐

Either of the above without the perforated margin is worth some £15 less.

679. 1973, 4th July
Isle of Man - Last Day of British Postal Services
679a Post Office Commemorative Cover with 1971 stamps, Douglas handstamp............**£12.00** ☐
679b Post Office Commemorative Cover with 1971 stamps, Whitehaven handstamp.......**£15.00** ☐
679c Any other cover with 1971 I.O.M. stamps and local postmark ....**£16.00** ☐
679d British Paintings stamps with I.O.M. FDI handstamp...**£32.00** ☐
In the early 19th century Douglas P.O. was a sub-office of Whitehaven Head Post Office in Cumberland. Hence the special Whitehaven handstamp used on the last day of British postal administration in the Isle of Man.

679A. 1973, 22nd August
3½p, Two Bands (PVAD gum)
679Aa With National Postal Museum handstamp (any other postmark **£60**) ....**£75.00** ☐

680. 1973, 10th September
3p Single Centre Phos Band
½p, 1p, 2p, 3p Dextrin added to standard PVA Gum
680a 3p Single Band on illustrated cover, any postmark ....**£10.00** ☐
680b With Windsor, Berks cds ....**£25.00** ☐
680c With National Postal Museum, London EC1 handstamp...**£24.00** ☐
680d With Remember to use the Post Code, Windsor slogan cancel...............................**£50.00** ☐
680e ½p with Dextrin, plus 3p Single Band Phos, Windsor cds...**£34.00** ☐
680f ½p with Dextrin, plus 3p with Dextrin, Windsor cds...**£76.00** ☐
680g 1p, 2p, 3p all with Dextrin, plus 3p Single Band, Windsor cds ....**£128.00** ☐
680h Same with any cds postmark...**£78.00** ☐

681. 1973, 27th September
£1 Printed on Contractors Paper
681a £1 Bluish Black on illustrated cover, any postmark...**£585.00** ☐
This is the official release date, but the earliest recorded use of this paper is October 1973!

681A. 1973, 9th October
½p Turquoise, Two Bands (PVAD gum)
681Aa With National Postal Museum handstamp (any other postmark **£60**) ....**£75.00** ☐

682. 1973, 24th October
4½p Slate, 5½p Violet, 8p Red. New Values
682a Three values on illustrated cover, any postmark..**£1.00** ☐
682b With Philatelic Bureau handstamp...**£3.50** ☐
682c With London FDI handstamp ....**£4.50** ☐
682d With Windsor, Berks regular FDI handstamp ....**£8.00** ☐
682e With Windsor, Berks large FDI (similar to Bureau handstamp) ....**£15.00** ☐
682f With Buckingham Palace SW1 cds ....**£65.00** ☐
682g With Windsor Castle cds..**£75.00** ☐

683. 1973, 30th October
6p with Dextrin added to standard PVA Gum
683a 6p on illustrated cover, any cds postmark ....**£178.00** ☐

684. 1973, 12th November
4p, 10p with Dextrin added to standard PVA Gum
684a 4p and 10p on one cover, any cds postmark ....**£165.00** ☐

685. 1973, 14th November
50p Booklet, 3 Panes
(5 x 3p + label) x 2, (5 x 3½p + label)
685a 2 Panes, one of each type, on illustrated cover, any postmark ....**£95.00** ☐
685b With Windsor, Berks postmark...**£160.00** ☐
685c With National Postal Museum, London EC1 handstamp...**£130.00** ☐

686. 1973, 30th November
20p Printed on Contractors Paper
686a 20p Olive-Green on any cover, any postmark .... **£375.00** ☐

687. 1973, 12th December
35p Booklet, 2 Identical Panes
(5 x 3½p + label) x 2
687a One or two Panes on illustrated cover, any postmark .... **£95.00** ☐
687b With Windsor, Berks postmark .... **£165.00** ☐

688. 1974, 23rd January
3½p Olive Grey, 5½p Violet, 8p Rosine. New Values
3p Ultramarine. Change to One Phos. Band
Wales, Scotland, Northern Ireland
688a Set of three covers, each with appropriate stamps and regional FDI handstamp .... **£8.50** ☐
688b All three Regions stamps on one cover, Bureau, Windsor, or other cancel .... **£15.00** ☐

689. 1974, 10th February
First Self Adhesive Labels
½p, 1p, 1½p, 5p + 3p, 5p + ½p
689a Set as printed by H.M. Stationery Office, any cover, any postmark .... **£280.00** ☐
This set is usually seen with a London WC or Wimbledon W20 cds.

690. 1974, 20th February
50p Printed on Contractors Paper
690a 50p Ultramarine on any cover, any postmark .... **£450.00** ☐

691. 1974, 22nd March
9p with Dextrin added to standard PVA Gum
691a 9p on illustrated cover, any cds postmark .... **£152.00** ☐

691A. 1974, 5th June
1½p Charcoal-Black, 5p Grey-Lilac, 2 Bands (PVAD gum)
691Aa With National Postal Museum handstamp (any other postmark **£110**) .... **£150.00** ☐

692. 1974, 19th June
Self Adhesive Labels
3p, 3½p
692a Both labels on cachet cover, any postmark .... **£58.00** ☐

693. 1974, 24th June
3½p Single Centre Phos Band
693a 3½p on illustrated cover, any postmark .... **£8.00** ☐
693b With National Postal Museum, London handstamp .... **£22.00** ☐
693c With Windsor, Berks postmark .... **£38.00** ☐

694. 1974, 21st August
7p Postage Due - To Pay Label
694a 7p Red-Brown on illustrated cover, any postmark .... **£52.00** ☐

695. 1974, 4th September
6½p Teal. New Value
695a 6½p on illustrated cover, any postmark .... **£1.50** ☐
695b With Philatelic Bureau handstamp .... **£3.00** ☐
695c With London FDI handstamp .... **£5.00** ☐
695d With Windsor, Berks regular FDI handstamp .... **£8.00** ☐
695e With Windsor, Berks large FDI (similar to Bureau handstamp) .... **£12.50** ☐

696. 1974, 9th October

45p Booklet, 2 Identical Panes

(5 x 4½p + blank label) x 2

696a One or two Panes on illustrated cover, any postmark .... **£82.00** ☐
696b With Windsor, Berks postmark........ **£145.00** ☐
696c Phosphor under Ink version, with Windsor, Berks cds........ **£200.00** ☐

697. 1974, 23rd October

35p Booklet, 2 Identical Panes

(5 x 3½p + blank label) x 2

697a One or two Panes on illustrated cover, any postmark .... **£78.00** ☐
697b With Windsor, Berks postmark........ **£130.00** ☐
697c With National Postal Museum, London EC1 handstamp........ **£115.00** ☐

698. 1974, 6th November

4½p Grey-Blue. New Value

3½p Olive-Grey. Change to One Phos Band

Wales, Scotland, Northern Ireland

698a Set of three covers, each with appropriate stamps and regional FDI handstamp .... **£5.00** ☐
698b All three Regions stamps on one cover, Bureau, Windsor or other cancel........ **£7.50** ☐

699. 1974, 13th November

4½p Experimental All Over Phosphor

699a 4½p Grey-Blue on illustrated cover, any postmark .... **£5.00** ☐
699b With Chief Office, London EC1 handstamp........ **£17.00** ☐
699c With National Postal Museum, London EC1 handstamp........ **£22.00** ☐
699d With Windsor, Berks postmark........ **£26.00** ☐
699e With Cambridge, Aberdeen, or Norwich cds .... **£32.00** ☐

This stamp was primarily distributed to Cambridge, Aberdeen and Norwich.

700. 1974/75

Postal Stationery

See special section at end of catalogue

701. 1975, 15th January

7p Brown. New Value

701a 7p on illustrated cover, any postmark .... **£1.50** ☐
701b With Philatelic Bureau handstamp........ **£3.00** ☐
701c With London FDI handstamp .... **£4.00** ☐
701d With Windsor, Berks regular FDI handstamp .... **£6.00** ☐
701e With Windsor, Berks large FDI (similar to Bureau handstamp) .... **£12.00** ☐
701f With Buckingham Palace SW1 cds .... **£65.00** ☐

Modern first day covers signed by a well known personality, with relevance to the Stamp Issue, are worth a premium over catalogue prices.

First Day Covers signed by the Stamp Designer

Covers, with one or more Stamps, signed by the designer are worth a 20% premium over catalogue prices.

702. 1975, 17th March
5½p Single Centre Phosphor Band
702a 5½p Violet on illustrated cover, any postmark .... **£2.00** ☐
702b With Windsor, Berks postmark .... **£6.50** ☐

703. 1975, 21st May
2½p Two Phos Bands. Dextrin added to Gum
703a 2½p Magenta on illustrated cover, any postmark .... **£5.00** ☐
703b With large Windsor Berks pictorial cancel .... **£12.50** ☐

704. 1975, 21st May
5½p Regional, Single Centre Phosphor Band
Wales, Scotland, Northern Ireland
704a 5½p Violet on illustrated cover, any Regional postmark .... **£3.50** ☐
704b With All Ulster Crusade - Arcadia, Portrush, Belfast slogan .... **£16.00** ☐
704c Set of 3 Regional 5½p stamps on one cover, Windsor, Berks handstamp .... **£16.00** ☐
The Regionals together on cover are usually with the 2½p magenta stamp added (**£17.50**).

705. 1975, 18th June
11p Postage Due - To Pay Label
705a 11p Slate-Green on illustrated cover, any postmark .... **£48.00** ☐

706. 1975, 24th September
6½p Teal, 8½p Yellow-Green (New Value)
706a Both stamps on illustrated cover, any postmark .... **£1.50** ☐
706b With Philatelic Bureau handstamp (8½p only) .... **£3.50** ☐
706c With London FDI handstamp, or Forces P.O. handstamp .... **£4.50** ☐
706d With Windsor, Berks, regular FDI handstamp .... **£8.00** ☐

707. 1975, 24th November
Speedpost - First Experimental Scheme
707a Speedpost red sticker on Brighton Area cover, Brighton cds .... **£32.00** ☐
707b On Brighton Area cover, Shoreham-by-Sea cds .... **£30.00** ☐
707c On Bexhill-on-Sea Area cover, Bexhill-on-Sea cds .... **£32.00** ☐
The Speedpost label is itself cancelled with an FDI handstamp (Bexhill) or a First Day of Service handstamp (Brighton), the cds postmark cancelled whatever stamps (min. 60p) were applied to the envelope.

708. 1975, 3rd December
10p Multi-Value Coil Strip
(6p + 2p + 1p + ½p + ½p)
708a 10p Strip on illustrated cover, any postmark .... **£3.00** ☐
708b With Windsor, Berks pictorial handstamp .... **£8.50** ☐

709. 1976, 14th January
6½p Green-Blue. 8½p Green-Yellow. New Values
Wales, Scotland, Northern Ireland
709a Set of three covers, each with appropriate stamps and regional FDI handstamp .... **£9.00** ☐
709b All three Regions stamps on one cover, Bureau, Windsor, or other cancel .... **£12.00** ☐

710. 1976, 28th January
6½p and 8½p Coil Strips. Vertical Format
710a Strip of 3 or more stamps of each value, from new coils, any postmark .... **£175.00** ☐
These are rare coils on first day and very few exist.

711. 1976, 25th February
9p Violet, 10p Lt. Orange-Brown. Colour Change
9½p Purple, 10½p Yellow, 11p Pinkish-Red. New Values
20p Slate. New Colour, Smaller Size

711a Set of six stamps on illustrated cover, any postmark .... £2.50 ☐
711b With Philatelic Bureau handstamp .... £4.50 ☐
711c With London FDI handstamp .... £6.50 ☐
711d With Windsor, Berks regular FDI handstamp .... £12.50 ☐
711e With Stampex, Years 200 U.S.A., London SW1 handstamp .... £18.00 ☐
711f With Forces Post Office handstamp, on BFPS cover .... £5.00 ☐
711g With House of Commons SW1 cds .... £38.00 ☐
711h With Buckingham Palace SW1 cds .... £62.00 ☐

712. 1976, 10th March
10p Experimental Folded Pane Booklet
(2 x ½p + 6p + 3 x 1p)

712a Complete Pane on illustrated cover, any postmark .... £2.00 ☐
712b With Windsor, Berks FDI handstamp .... £6.50 ☐
712c With P.O. Telecommunications Museum, Taunton handstamp .... £15.00 ☐

713. 1976, 24th March
8½p Experimental Phosphor Issue

713a 8½p Yellow-Green, on illustrated cover, any postmark .... £1.50 ☐
713b With Chief Office, London EC1 handstamp .... £5.00 ☐
713c With Windsor, Berks pictorial handstamp .... £6.50 ☐
713d With House of Commons or House of Lords SW1 cds .... £25.00 ☐

714. 1976, 14th July
65p, 85p Folded Booklets
65p Booklet, 1 Pane (10 x 6½p)
85p Booklet, 1 Pane (10 x 8½p)

714a Both Panes on 2 covers, any postmark .... £45.00 ☐
714b With Windsor, Berks pictorial handstamp .... £110.00 ☐

715. 1976, 13th October
6½p and 8½p Coil Strips. Horizontal Format

715a Strip of 4 or more of each value, from new Coils, any postmark .... £92.00 ☐
715b With Windsor, Berks pictorial handstamp .... £165.00 ☐

716. 1976, 20th October
10p Orange-Brown, 11p Scarlet. New Values
Wales, Scotland, Northern Ireland

716a Set of three covers, each with appropriate stamps and regional FDI handstamp .... £11.00 ☐
716b All three Regions stamps on one cover, Bureau, Windsor or other cancel .... £14.00 ☐

717. 1977, 26th January
50p Multi-Value Booklet, 1 Pane
(2 x ½p + 2 x 1p + 2 x 6½p + 4 x 8½p)

717a 50p Booklet left and right format Panes, illustrated cover, any postmark .... £6.00 ☐
717b With Chief Office, London EC1 handstamp .... £14.00 ☐
717c With Windsor, Berks pictorial handstamp .... £18.00 ☐

This booklet was printed in two formats, one with 6½p on the left of the Pane and the other with 6½p on the right of the Pane.

718. 1977, 26th January
6½p Single Phosphor Band - from 50p Booklet
718a 6½p Right Phos Band and 6½p Left Phos Band, together on one illustrated cover, any postmark .... **£3.50** ☐
718b With National Postal Museum, London EC1 handstamp .... **£11.50** ☐
718c With Windsor, Berks pictorial handstamp .... **£15.00** ☐

719. 1977, 2nd February
50p Ochre-Brown. New Colour, Smaller Size
£1 Blackish Olive, £2 Purple-Brown, £5 Salmon-Blue. All New Format
719a 50p on illustrated cover, any postmark .... **£1.75** ☐
719b With Philatelic Bureau handstamp .... **£3.50** ☐
719c With London FDI handstamp .... **£4.50** ☐
719d With First Day of Issue, Windsor, Berks special handstamp .... **£6.00** ☐
719e £1, £2 and £5 on illustrated cover, any postmark .... **£11.00** ☐
719f With Philatelic Bureau handstamp .... **£11.00** ☐
719g With London FDI handstamp .... **£12.50** ☐
719h With First Day of Issue, Windsor, Berks special handstamp .... **£25.00** ☐
719i With House of Commons SW1 cds .... **£48.00** ☐
Covers with all 4 values are worth a 20% premium.

720. 1977, 13th June
7p Single Centre Phos Band
720a 7p Purple-Brown on illustrated cover, any postmark .... **£1.00** ☐
720b With National Postal Museum, London EC1 handstamp .... **£4.50** ☐
720c With The Royal Image Exhibition... City of Bristol slogan .... **£4.50** ☐
720d With House of Commons SW1 cds .... **£12.00** ☐
720e With Windsor, Berks pictorial handstamp .... **£6.00** ☐

721. 1977, 13th June
50p Multi-Value Booklet, 1 Pane
(2 x 1d + 3 x 7p + 3 x 9p)
721a 50p Booklet left and right format Panes, illustrated cover, any postmark .... **£5.50** ☐
721b With Chief Office, London EC1 handstamp .... **£10.00** ☐
721c With Windsor Berks pictorial handstamp .... **£14.00** ☐
721d 7p with left Phos Band and 7p with right Phos Band (both from 50p Booklet), together on illustrated cover, any postmark .... **£4.00** ☐
721e With National Postal Museum, London EC1 handstamp .... **£6.50** ☐
721f With Windsor, Berks pictorial handstamp .... **£8.50** ☐
This booklet was printed in two formats, one with the 7p on the left of the Pane and one with the 7p on the right of the Pane.

722. 1977, 13th June
70p Booklet, 1 Pane (10 x 7p)
90p Booklet, 1 Pane (10 x 9p)
7p and 9p Coil Strips, Vertical Format
Scottish Experimental Packets, (7p and 9p Stamps)
722a 10 x 7p Pane and 10 x 9p Pane on 1 or 2 covers, any postmark .... **£10.50** ☐
722b With Windsor Berks pictorial handstamp .... **£25.00** ☐
722c 7p and 9p Strip of 3 or more of each value from new Coils, any postmark .... **£54.00** ☐
722d With Windsor Berks pictorial handstamp .... **£125.00** ☐
722e Scottish Experimental Packets, 7p and 9p Stamps, any postmark .... **£225.00** ☐

For a complete listing of all sections in this catalogue, see the Index on page 3.

723. 1977, 31st October
6p, 7p, 9p, 10p Halley Press Printings
723a Set of 4 stamps on one or more illustrated covers, any postmark .... **£200.00** ☐
723b With Windsor, Berks postmark .... **£265.00** ☐

724. 1977, 16th November
7p and 9p Coil Strips, Horizontal Format
724a Strip of 4 or more of each value, from new Coils, any postmark .... **£58.00** ☐
724b With Windsor, Berks pictorial handstamp .... **£145.00** ☐

725. 1977, 14th December
10p Multi-Value Coil Strip
(7p + 2 x 1d + 2 x ½p)
725a 10p Strip on illustrated cover, any postmark (½p and 1p only, **£2**) .... **£2.50** ☐
725b With Windsor, Berks new pictorial handstamp .... **£8.00** ☐
725c With House of Commons or House of Lords SW1 handstamp .... **£17.50** ☐

726. 1978, 18th January
7p Purple-Brown, 9p Violet, 10½p Steel-Blue. New Values
Wales, Scotland, Northern Ireland
726a Set of three covers, each with appropriate stamps and regional FDI handstamp .... **£8.00** ☐
726b All three Regions stamps on one cover, Bureau, Windsor, or other cancel .... **£10.00** ☐

727. 1978, 8th February
10p Booklet. 1 Multi-Value Pane
(2 x ½p + 2 x 1p + 7p + label)
727a 10p Pane on illustrated cover, any postmark .... **£2.50** ☐
727b With Windsor, Berks new pictorial handstamp .... **£5.50** ☐

728. 1978, 26th April
10½p Dull Blue. Colour Change
728a 10½p on illustrated cover, any postmark .... **£1.50** ☐
728b Same with Philatelic Bureau handstamp .... **£3.00** ☐
728c With London FDI handstamp .... **£4.50** ☐
728d With First Day of Issue, Windsor, Berks special handstamp .... **£7.50** ☐
728e With Chief Office, London EC1 handstamp .... **£8.00** ☐
728f With Caernarfon Gwynedd, Special Castle handstamp (2½" long!) .... **£10.00** ☐
728g With British Forces Post Office, Berlin1 handstamp. On BFPS cover .... **£13.50** ☐

729. 1978, 15th November
£1.60 Christmas Booklet, 1 Pane
(10 x 7p + 10 x 9p)
729a Se-tenant pair, on illustrated cover, Windsor postmark .... **£2.50** ☐
729b Complete Pane, on illustrated cover, any postmark .... **£5.00** ☐
729c With Windsor, Berks new pictorial postmark .... **£8.50** ☐

730. 1979, 5th February
70p, 90p 'Derby' Booklets. 1 Pane each
730a Both Panes (10 x 7p) and (10 x 9p) on illustrated covers, any postmark .... **£26.00** ☐
730b Both with Derby cds .... **£158.00** ☐
730c Both with Kedleston and Crich, Derbyshire cds .... **£135.00** ☐
Derby new P.O. opened same day. 70p cover Kedleston Hall, 90p cover Tram Museum, Crich.

731. 1979, 15th August

11½p Ochre-Brown, 13p Olive-Grey, 15p Ultramarine. New Values

731a Set on on illustrated cover, any postmark .... **£1.50** ☐
731b With Philatelic Bureau handstamp .... **£3.00** ☐
731c With London FDI handstamp .... **£5.00** ☐
731d With First Day of Issue, Windsor, Berks special handstamp .... **£10.00** ☐
731e With Sir Rowland Hill Centenary Exhibition, Kidderminster handstamp........ **£25.00** ☐
731f With Military Tattoo, Edinburgh special handstamp .... **£22.50** ☐
731g With Field Post Office 996 (or other) cds. On BFPS cover .... **£8.00** ☐
731h With Buckingham Palace SW1 cds .... **£68.00** ☐

732. 1979, 20th August

8p Single Centre Phos Band

10p Two Phos Bands on Phosphor Coated Stock

732a 8p Rosine and 10p Orange-Brown (Gutter Pair) any postmark........ **£2.00** ☐
732b With Windsor, Berks pictorial postmark........ **£5.00** ☐
732c With House of Commons, or House of Lords SW1 cds .... **£20.00** ☐
732d 8p Rosine only, Windsor, Berks postmark........ **£3.00** ☐
732e 10p Orange-Brown Gutter Pair, Windsor, Berks postmark .... **£4.50** ☐

733. 1979, 28th August

50p Multi-Value Booklet, 1 Pane

(2 x 2p + 2 x 8p + 3 x 10p + label)

733a 50p Booklet, left and right format Panes, illustrated cover, any postmark........ **£2.50** ☐
733b With Chief Office, London EC1 handstamp........ **£6.50** ☐
733c With Windsor, Berks pictorial handstamp........ **£8.50** ☐

This Booklet was printed in two formats, one with 8p on the left of the Pane, and the other with the 8p on the right of the Pane.

734. 1979, 28th August

8p Single Phosphor Band - from 50p Booklet

734a 8p Right and Left Phos Band, illustrated cover, Windsor, Berks pictorial pmk........ **£4.50** ☐

735. 1979, 3rd October

80p and £1 Booklets. 1 Pane each

735a Both Panes (10 x 8p) and (10 x 10p) on illustrated covers, any postmark .... **£5.00** ☐
735b With Windsor, Berks pictorial handstamp........ **£10.00** ☐
735c 10p All-over Phos from £1 Booklet, Windsor, Berks handstamp .... **£4.00** ☐

736. 1979, 10th October

1p, 2p All Over Phosphor

5p, 20p Phosphor Coated

736a All four stamps on one illustrated cover, any postmark........ **£2.50** ☐
736b With Windsor, Berks pictorial handstamp........ **£6.00** ☐

737. 1979, 17th October

10p London 1980 Booklet, 1 Pane

(8p + 2 x 1p + label)

737a Complete Pane on illustrated cover, London postmarks (other pmks **£1.50**)........ **£5.00** ☐
737b With Windsor, Berks pictorial handstamp........ **£4.50** ☐
737c With London 1980 International Stamp Exhibition slogan cancel........ **£25.00** ☐

738. 1979, 14th November
£1.80 Christmas Booklet, 1 Pane
8p and 10p Coils

738a Complete Pane (10 x 10p + 10 x 8p) illustrated cover, any postmark .... **£3.50** ☐
738b With First Day of Issue handstamp (Worthing, West Sussex) .... **£30.00** ☐
738c With Chief Office, London EC1 handstamp, or BPE Wembley h/s .... **£7.50** ☐
738d With Windsor, Berks pictorial handstamp .... **£7.50** ☐
738e 8p and 10p Strip of 3 or more of each value from new coils, any postmark .... **£55.00** ☐
738f With Windsor, Berks pictorial handstamp .... **£68.00** ☐

739. 1979, 12th December
8p Enschedé Printing. Single Centre Phos Band
1p, 2p, Phosphor Coated

739a All three stamps on one illustrated cover, any postmark .... **£2.50** ☐
739b Same with Chief Office, London EC1, or Windsor, Berks handstamp .... **£5.00** ☐

The Enschedé printing is the first time a British stamp was printed outside the UK!

740. 1980, 16th January
10p Multi-Value Coil Strip
(8p + 2 x 1p + 2 labels)

740a Complete Strip on illustrated cover, any postmark .... **£2.00** ☐
740b Same with Chief Office, London EC1, or Windsor, Berks handstamp .... **£6.50** ☐

741. 1980, 30th January
4p Greenish Blue. New Colour
12p Olive, 13½p Brown, 17p Emerald, 17½p Chestnut, 75p Black. New Values

741a Set on illustrated cover, any postmark .... **£2.00** ☐
741b With Philatelic Bureau handstamp .... **£4.00** ☐
741c With London FDI handstamp .... **£6.00** ☐
741d With First Day of Issue, Windsor, Berks special handstamp .... **£10.00** ☐
741e With House of Commons SW1 cds .... **£35.00** ☐

742. 1980, 4th February
10p Centre Phos Band. 10p Phos Coated

742a 10p Centre Phos Band on illustrated cover, any postmark inc. Windsor .... **£2.50** ☐
742b 10p Phos coated paper (used in error), any cover/pmk .... **£35.00** ☐
742c 10p Phos coated paper, Windsor, Berks pictorial handstamp .... **£82.00** ☐

743. 1980, 4th February
50p Multi-Value Booklet, 1 Pane
(3 x 2p + 2 x 10p + 2 x 12p + label)
£1 (10 x 10p) **and £1.20** (10 x 12p) **Booklets**

743a 50p Booklet, left and right format Panes, illustrated cover, any postmark .... **£3.50** ☐
743b With Chief Office, London EC1 handstamp .... **£7.50** ☐
743c With Windsor, Berks pictorial handstamp .... **£11.00** ☐
743d With National Postal Museum handstamp .... **£10.00** ☐
743e £1 and £1.20 Booklet Panes on one or two covers, any postmark .... **£6.00** ☐
743f With Chief Office, London EC1 handstamp .... **£12.00** ☐
743g With Windsor, Berks pictorial handstamp .... **£16.00** ☐
743h 10p Left and Right Phos Bands, from 50p Booklet, any postmark .... **£3.50** ☐
743i 12p with two Phos Bands, from 50p Booklet, any postmark .... **£3.50** ☐

744. 1980, 16th April
£3 Wedgwood Sponsored Booklet, 4 Panes
(6 x 2p), (9 x 10p), (9 x 12p), (2p + 4 x 10p + 4 x 12p)

744a Complete Set of 4 Entire Panes, Philatelic Bureau handstamp .... **£20.00** ☐
744b With First Day of Issue, Barlaston, Stoke-on-Trent, Staffs handstamp .... **£25.00** ☐
744c Multi-Value Pane only, Bureau or Barlaston handstamp .... **£4.50** ☐

Prices are for Panes with text. Panes of stamps only are worth 50% of above prices.

745. 1980, 21st May
2p, 5p House of Questa, 20p Waddington
50p Phosphor Coated

745a All four stamps on one illustrated cover, any postmark .... **£1.50** ☐
745b With Chief Office, London EC1 handstamp .... **£3.50** ☐
745c With Windsor, Berks pictorial handstamp .... **£5.50** ☐

746. 1980, 11th June
10p and 12p Coil Strips

746a 10p and 12p Strip of 3 or more of each value from new Coils, any postmark .... **£47.50** ☐
746b With Windsor, Berks pictorial handstamp .... **£62.50** ☐

747. 1980, 25th June
50p Chambon Press Booklet, 1 Pane
(2 x 10p + 2 x 12p + 3 x 2p + label)

747a 50p Booklet, left and right format Panes, illustrated cover, any postmark .... **£45.00** ☐
747b With Chief Office, London EC1 handstamp .... **£70.00** ☐
747c With Windsor, Berks pictorial handstamp .... **£82.00** ☐

748. 1980, 23rd July
12p Yellow-Green, 13½p Purple-Brown, 15p Ultramarine. New Values
Wales, Scotland, Northern Ireland

748a Set of three covers, each with appropriate stamps and regional FDI handstamp .... **£10.50** ☐
748b All three Regions stamps on one cover, Bureau, Windsor or other cancel .... **£14.00** ☐

The 10p of 1976 was re-issued on July 23rd, but with one Phos Band. It often appears with the above three values (with cds postmark) and as a set is valued at £15.00.

749. 1980, 27th August
10p London 1980 Booklet, 1 Pane
11p Phosphor Coated Paper

749a 10p Pane (2 x 1p + 8p + label) on illustrated cover, any postmark .... **£1.50** ☐
749b With Windsor, Berks pictorial handstamp, or London postmark .... **£3.50** ☐
749c 11p Phosphor coated, illustrated cover (any postmark £2), Windsor postmark .... **£5.00** ☐
749d 10p Pane and 11p Phos together on one cover, any postmark .... **£8.00** ☐

750. 1980, 22nd October
3p Magenta, New Colour. 22p Deep Blue. New Value

750a Both stamps on illustrated cover, any postmark .... **£2.00** ☐
750b With Philatelic Bureau handstamp .... **£4.00** ☐
750c With London FDI handstamp .... **£6.00** ☐
750d With First Day of Issue, Windsor, Berks special handstamp .... **£7.50** ☐
750e With House of Commons SW1 cds .... **£32.00** ☐

Remember, most modern hand addressed covers are worth only 20% of catalogue prices.

751. 1980, 12th November
£2.20 Christmas Booklet, 1 Pane
(10 x 12p + 10 x 10p)
751a Complete Pane on illustrated cover, any postmark .... **£4.50** ☐
751b With Windsor, Berks pictorial postmark .... **£10.00** ☐

752. 1980, 10th December
½p Phosphor Coated Paper
752a ½p on illustrated cover, any postmark (Windsor **£3**) .... **£1.50** ☐

753. 1981, 14th January
2½p Rose-Red, 11½p Drab Grey. New Colours
14p Grey-Blue, 15½p Pale Violet, 18p Deep Violet, 25p Purple. New Values
753a Set on illustrated cover, any postmark (matt or shiny) .... **£2.00** ☐
753b With Philatelic Bureau handstamp .... **£3.50** ☐
753c With London FDI handstamp .... **£5.50** ☐
753d With First Day of Issue, Windsor, Berks special handstamp .... **£10.00** ☐
753e With Field Post Office, or Forces Post Office cds .... **£5.00** ☐
753f With House of Commons SW1 cds .... **£37.50** ☐
753g With House of Lords SW1 cds .... **£40.00** ☐

754. 1981, 26th January
50p Booklet, 1 Pane
(½p + 1p + 14p + 3 x 11½p)
£1.15 (10 x 11½p), **£1.40** (10 x 14p) Booklets
754a 50p Booklet, left and right format Panes, illustrated cover, any postmark .... **£2.50** ☐
754b Same with Windsor, Berks pictorial handstamp .... **£6.00** ☐
754c £1.15 and £1.40 Booklet Panes on one or two covers, any postmark .... **£4.50** ☐
754d Same with Windsor, Berks pictorial postmark .... **£9.00** ☐
754e 11½p Left and Right Phos Bands, from 50p Booklet, any postmark .... **£2.00** ☐
754f Same with Windsor, Berks pictorial postmark .... **£5.00** ☐
754g 14p Two Phos Bands, from 50p Booklet, any postmark .... **£2.00** ☐
754h Same with Windsor, Berks pictorial postmark .... **£4.00** ☐

755. 1981, 11th March
11½p and 14p Coil Strips
755a Strip of 3 stamps or more of each value, illustrated cover, any postmark .... **£40.00** ☐
755b With Windsor, Berks pictorial handstamp .... **£62.00** ☐

756. 1981, 8th April
11½p Drab, 14p Grey-Blue, 18p Violet, 22p Cobalt-Blue. New Values
Wales, Scotland, Northern Ireland
756a Set of three covers, each with appropriate stamps and regional FDI handstamp .... **£9.00** ☐
756b All three Regions stamps on one cover, Bureau, Windsor or other cancel .... **£16.50** ☐

757. 1981, 6th May
£1.30 'Penny Black' Booklet, 1 Pane
(4 x 11½p + 6 x 14p)
757a Complete Pane on illustrated cover, Windsor, Berks handstamp .... **£7.50** ☐
757b With National Stamp Day 1981, London EC1 handstamp .... **£6.00** ☐
757c With National Stamp Day 1981, Cameo Stamp Centre handstamp .... **£6.00** ☐
757d With National Stamp Day 1981, British Library handstamp .... **£6.00** ☐
757e With National Stamp Day 1981, Birmingham handstamp .... **£6.00** ☐

758. 1981, 26th August
50p Booklet, 1 Pane (2 x 4p + 3 x 2½p + 3 x 11½p)
758a 50p Booklet, left and right format Panes, illustrated cover, any postmark .... **£3.50** ☐
758b Same with Windsor, Berks pictorial handstamp .... **£11.00** ☐
758c 2½p and 4p with two Phos Bands, from 50p Booklet, Windsor postmark .... **£3.00** ☐

759. 1981, 2nd September
11½p 'Readers Digest' Multi-Value Coil Strip
(2½p + 3 x 3p)
759a Complete Strip on illustrated cover, Windsor, Berks handstamp .... **£5.50** ☐
Specially produced for a Readers Digest promotion. Pre-release dates exist.

760. 1981, 11th November
£2.55 Christmas Booklet, 1 Pane
(10 x 14p + 10 x 11½p)
760a Complete Pane on illustrated cover, any postmark .... **£5.00** ☐
760b With Windsor, Berks pictorial handstamp .... **£12.00** ☐

761. 1981, 7th December
4p, 20p Phosphor Coated Paper - Waddington
761a Both stamps on one illustrated cover, any postmark .... **£6.50** ☐
761b With Windsor, Berks pictorial handstamp .... **£20.00** ☐

762. 1981, 30th December
12½p 'Readers Digest' Multi-Value Coil Strip (½p + 3 x 4p)
762a Complete Strip on illustrated cover, Windsor, Berks handstamp .... **£4.50** ☐

763. 1982, 27th January
5p Claret. New Colour
12½p Emerald, 16½p Pale Chestnut, 19½p Olive-Grey, 26p Rosine, 29p Ochre-Brown. New Values
763a Set on illustrated cover, any postmark .... **£1.50** ☐
763b With Philatelic Bureau handstamp .... **£3.50** ☐
763c With London FDI handstamp .... **£6.50** ☐
763d With First Day of Issue, Windsor, Berks special handstamp .... **£10.00** ☐
763e With Field Post Office, or Forces Post Office cds .... **£4.50** ☐
763f With House of Commons SW1 cds .... **£30.00** ☐
763g With House of Lords SW1 cds .... **£35.00** ☐

764. 1982, 1st February
50p Booklet, 1 Pane (½p + 3 x 12½p + 4 x 3p)
£1.25 Booklet, 1 Pane (10 x 12½p)
£1.55 Booklet, 1 Pane (10 x 15½p)
£1.43 Booklet, 1 Pane (4 x 12½p + 6 x 15½p)
12½p and 15½p Coil Strips
764a 50p Booklet, left and right format Panes, illustrated cover, any postmark .... **£2.00** ☐
764b Same with Windsor, Berks pictorial handstamp .... **£6.00** ☐
764c £1.25 and £1.55 Panes on illustrated cover, any postmark .... **£4.00** ☐
764d Same with Windsor, Berks pictorial handstamp .... **£9.00** ☐
764e £1.43 Pane on illustrated cover, any postmark .... **£3.00** ☐
764f Same with Windsor, Berks pictorial handstamp .... **£8.00** ☐
764g 12½p and 15½p Strip of 3 or more of each value from new Coils, any pmk .... **£32.00** ☐
764h Same with Windsor, Berks pictorial handstamp .... **£55.00** ☐

765. 1982, 24th February
12½p Light Emerald, 15½p Pale Violet, 19½p Grey, 26p Rosine. New Values
Wales, Scotland, Northern Ireland

765a Set of three covers, each with appropriate stamps and regional FDI handstamp .... **£12.00** ☐
765b With Stampex, London SW1 pictorial handstamp .... **£30.00** ☐
765c All three Regions stamps on one cover, Bureau, Windsor, or other cancel .... **£15.00** ☐

766. 1982, 19th May
£4 Stanley Gibbons Sponsored Booklet, 4 Panes
(7 x 12½p + 3p + 2p), (6 x 12½p), (6 x 15½p), (9 x 15½p)

766a Complete Set of 4 Entire Panes, Philatelic Bureau handstamp .... **£15.00** ☐
766b With SG Founded 1856, Plymouth handstamp .... **£20.00** ☐
766c With SG Founded 1856, London WC handstamp .... **£20.00** ☐
766d Se-tenant Pane only with any of the above 3 handstamps .... **£5.00** ☐

Panes without text (stamps only) are worth 50% of above prices.

767. 1982, 9th June
Postage Due - To Pay Labels
1p, 2p, 3p, 4p, 5p, 10p, 20p, 25p, 50p, £1, £2, £5. New Design

767a Complete Set on illustrated cover, Stratford-upon-Avon handstamp .... **£355.00** ☐
767b Set to 25p on 4 illustrated covers, Bath Sorting(B) Office handstamp .... **£130.00** ☐
767c Set to 25p in Gutter Pairs on illustrated covers, Bath handstamp and cachet .... **£195.00** ☐

768. 1982, 10th November
£2.80 Christmas Discount Booklet, 1 Pane
(10 x 12½p + 10 x 15½p)

768a £2.80 Booklet Pane, on illustrated cover, any postmark .... **£4.50** ☐
768b With Star, Glenrothes, Fife cds .... **£17.50** ☐
768c With Windsor, Berks pictorial handstamp .... **£14.00** ☐

This Booklet was discounted by the Post Office and sold at £2.50. This was the first time that the Post Office did this. All stamps have a star printed in the reverse side, under the gum.

769. 1983, 30th March
3½p Purple Brown, 17p Grey-Blue, New Colours
16p Drab-Olive, 20½p Ultramarine, 23p Red-Pink, 28p Violet,
31p Purple. New Values

769a Set on illustrated cover, any postmark .... **£2.00** ☐
769b With Philatelic Bureau handstamp .... **£4.00** ☐
769c With London FDI handstamp .... **£6.00** ☐
769d With First Day of Issue, Windsor, Berks special handstamp .... **£12.00** ☐
769e With Windsor, Berks cds .... **£32.00** ☐
769f With Forces Post Office cds .... **£8.00** ☐
769g With House of Commoms SW1 cds .... **£36.00** ☐

770. 1983, 5th April
50p Booklet, 1 Pane (2 x 1p + 3 x 3½p + 3 x 12½p)
£1.46 Booklet, 1 Pane (4 x 12½p + 6 x 16p)
£1.60 Booklet, 1 Pane (10 x 16p)

770a 50p Booklet Pane, on illustrated cover, any postmark .... **£1.75** ☐
770b With Gloucester Old Spot Pig, 10 Years of Breeding... handstamp .... **£12.00** ☐
770c With Windsor Philatelic Counter handstamp .... **£6.00** ☐
770d With London Chief Office EC1 Philatelic Counter handstamp .... **£5.00** ☐
770e £1.46 Booklet Pane, on illustrated cover, any postmark .... **£6.50** ☐

770f With Windsor Philatelic Counter handstamp .... **£10.00** ☐
770g With National Postal Museum, London EC1, red postmark .... **£7.50** ☐
770h £1.60 Booklet Pane, on illustrated cover, any postmark .... **£3.50** ☐
770i With Windsor Philatelic Counter handstamp .... **£10.00** ☐
770j With London Chief Office EC1, Philatelic Counter handstamp .... **£6.00** ☐
770k 1p Centre Band, 3½p Centre Band, 16p Two Phos Bands, any postmark .... **£3.50** ☐
The 50p Booklet features the Gloucester Old Spot Pig.

771. 1983, 20th April
16p Coil Strip. Vertical Format
771a 16p Strip of 3 stamps or more, illustrated cover, any postmark .... **£5.00** ☐
771b Same with Windsor (or London Chief Office) Philatelic Counter .... **£18.00** ☐

772. 1983, 27th April
16p Drab, 20½p Ultramarine, 28p Violet-Blue. New Values
Wales, Scotland, Northern Ireland
772a Set of three covers, each with appropriate stamps and regional FDI handstamp .... **£10.00** ☐
772b All three Regions stamps on one cover, Bureau, Windsor, or other cancel .... **£14.00** ☐

773. 1983, 3rd August
£1.30 Parcel Post Centenary Definitive Stamp
773a £1.30 on illustrated cover, any postmark .... **£2.50** ☐
773b With Philatelic Bureau handstamp .... **£6.00** ☐
773c With London E16 special handstamp .... **£10.50** ☐
773d With London NW FDI handstamp .... **£10.50** ☐
773e With Windsor, Berks FDI handstamp .... **£10.50** ☐
773f With Belsize Park B.O. NW3, registered Oval handstamp .... **£22.00** ☐
773g With Hampstead, S.D.O. NW3 registered cds .... **£25.00** ☐
773h With First Day of Sale, Parcel Centenary Postcard, Salisbury, Wilts h/s .... **£17.50** ☐
773i With Hampstead registered cds, 1 August 1983 Pre-Release (Centenary Day) .... **£60.00** ☐

774. 1983, 10th August
£1.60 Discount Booklet, 1 Pane (10 x 16p)
774a £1.60 Booklet Pane on illustrated cover, any postmark .... **£4.50** ☐
774b With Windsor, Berks Philatelic Counter handstamp .... **£12.00** ☐
774c 16p stamp with 'D' underprint, from £1.60 Booklet, any postmark .... **£4.00** ☐
The Booklet was sold for £1.45 by the Post Office. All stamps have a 'D' printed on the reverse side.

775. 1983, 14th September
£4 Royal Mint Sponsored Booklet, 4 Panes
(6 x 12½p) x 2, (6 x 16p + 2 x 3½p + 3p), (9 x 16p)
775a Complete Set of 4 Entire Panes, Philatelic Bureau handstamp .... **£12.00** ☐
775b With First Day of Issue, Llantrisant... Mid Glam. handstamp .... **£25.00** ☐
775c With London EC1, or Windsor Philatelic Counter handstamp .... **£20.00** ☐
775d Se-tenant Pane only with any postmark (Llantrisant pmk **£9**) .... **£4.00** ☐
Panes without text (stamps only) are worth only 50% of above prices.

776. 1983, 2nd November
16p Scottish Regional, Advanced Coated Stock
776a 16p on illustrated cover, Edinburgh Philatelic Counter (or other local) h/s .... **£3.50** ☐

Remember, most modern hand addressed covers
are worth only 20% of catalogue prices.

---

777. 1983, 9th November
£2.50 Christmas Discount Booklet, 1 Pane (20 x 12½p)
777a £2.50 Booklet Pane on illustrated cover, any postmark .... **£4.00** ☐
777b With Aladdin... Christmas '83 special handstamp .... **£15.00** ☐
777c With Windsor Philatelic Counter handstamp .... **£10.00** ☐
777d 12½p with Star underprint from the £2.50 Booklet, any postmark .... **£3.00** ☐
This Christmas Booklet was sold for £2.20 by the Post Office. All stamps with Star on reverse.

778. 1983, 14th December
10p Phosphor Coated Paper
778a 10p on illustrated cover, Windsor Philatelic Counter handstamp .... **£3.00** ☐

779. 1984, 10th January
12½p, 16p Welsh Regionals, Perforation Change
779a 12½p and 16p on illustrated cover, Cardiff Philatelic Counter handstamp .... **£4.50** ☐

780. 1984, 21st February
5p, 75p, Perforation Change
780a 5p and 75p on illustrated cover, Windsor Philatelic Counter handstamp .... **£5.00** ☐

781. 1984, 28th February
12½p, 16p Northern Ireland Regionals. Perforation Change
781a 12½p and 16p on illustrated cover, Belfast Philatelic Counter handstamp .... **£5.00** ☐

782. 1984, 1st May
Frama Postage Labels. ½p - 16p, Set of 32 Values
782a 32 values on 4 illustrated covers, Philatelic Bureau handstamp .... **£22.50** ☐
782b With Windsor, Cambridge, Southampton, or London handstamp .... **£30.00** ☐

783. 1984, 19th June
17p, 26p Advanced Coated Paper
783a 17p on illustrated cover, Windsor Philatelic Counter handstamp .... **£4.00** ☐
783b 26p on illustrated cover, Windsor (any other pmk **£60**) postmark .... **£82.00** ☐

784. 1984, 10th July
2p Perforation Change
784a 2p on illustrated cover, Windsor Philatelic Counter handstamp .... **£4.00** ☐

785. 1984, 14th August
13p Multi Value Coil Strip (1p + 3 x 4p)
785a Complete Coil Strip on illustrated cover, Windsor Philatelic Counter handstamp .... **£5.00** ☐

786. 1984, 28th August
13p Chestnut, 18p Olive-Grey, 22p Green. New Colours
24p Violet, 34p Ochre-Brown. New Values
786a Set on illustrated cover, any postmark .... **£2.00** ☐
786b With Philatelic Bureau handstamp .... **£3.50** ☐
786c With London FDI handstamp .... **£4.50** ☐
786d With First Day of Issue, Windsor, Berks special handstamp .... **£6.50** ☐
786e With Windsor Philatelic Counter handstamp .... **£9.00** ☐
786f With Windsor Castle, Windsor, Berks cds .... **£32.00** ☐
Set as above, plus £1.33 issued same day, on one cover. 150% premium.

787. 1984, 28th August
16½p, 17p Frama Postage Labels. New Values
787a Both values on illustrated cover, Windsor Philatelic Counter handstamp .... **£3.50** ☐

788. 1984, 28th August
£1.33 Parcel Post Definitive
788a £1.33 on illustrated cover, any postmark .... **£2.50** ☐
788b With Philatelic Bureau handstamp .... **£4.50** ☐
788c With London FDI handstamp .... **£7.50** ☐
788d With First Day of Issue, Windsor, Berks special handstamp .... **£15.00** ☐
788e With Hampstead S.D.O. NW3, Registered cds .... **£24.00** ☐
788f With North Eastern Parcel Centre, Washington, Tyne & Wear handstamp .... **£26.50** ☐
788g With National Postal Museum, London EC1 slogan cancel .... **£17.50** ☐

789. 1984, 3rd September
50p Orchid Booklet, 1 Pane (2 x 4p + 3 x 1p + 3 x 13p)
£1.30 Booklet, 1 Pane (10 x 13p) and **£1.70 Booklet, 1 Pane** (10 x 17p)
£1.54 Booklet, 1 Pane (4 x 13p + 6 x 17p)
789a 50p Booklet Pane on illustrated cover, any postmark .... **£2.50** ☐
789b Same with Windsor Philatelic Counter h/s (Garden Festival Liverpool **£6.50**) .... **£6.00** ☐
789c £1.30 Booklet Pane, plus £1.70 Booklet Pane, illustrated cover, any postmark .... **£10.00** ☐
789d Same with Windsor Philatelic Counter handstamp .... **£18.50** ☐
789e £1.54 Booklet, both left and right format Panes, illustrated cover, any pmk .... **£6.00** ☐
789f Same with Windsor Philatelic Counter handstamp .... **£10.00** ☐
789g 13p left and right Phos Bands, plus 17p two Phos Bands, (from £1.54 Booklet) .... **£4.50** ☐

790. 1984, 3rd September
13p and 17p Coil Strips
790a 13p and 17p Strip of 3 or more of each value, from new Coils, any postmark .... **£6.50** ☐
790b With Windsor Philatelic Counter handstamp .... **£30.00** ☐

791. 1984, 4th September
£4 Christian Heritage Sponsored Booklet, 4 Panes
(6 x 17p), (7 x 17p + 10p + 13p), (6 x 13p) x 2
791a Complete Set of 4 Entire Panes, Philatelic Bureau handstamp (other **£10**) .... **£18.50** ☐
791b With First Day of Issue, Canterbury handstamp .... **£22.00** ☐
791c With Celebration of Christian Heritage Year, London WC handstamp .... **£22.00** ☐
791d With Windsor Philatelic Counter handstamp .... **£22.00** ☐
791e With Christian Heritage slogan cancel .... **£52.50** ☐
791f Se-tenant Pane only, Christian Heritage slogan cancel .... **£18.00** ☐
791g Se-tenant Pane only, any of above postmarks (Windsor Castle cds **£50**) .... **£3.50** ☐

792. 1984, 23rd October
13p Chestnut, 17p Grey-Blue, 31p Purple. New Values
22p Yellow-Green. Colour Change
Wales, Scotland, Northern Ireland
792a Set of three covers, each with appropriate stamps and regional FDI handstamp .... **£12.00** ☐
792b All three Regions stamps on one cover, Bureau, Windsor, or other cancel .... **£15.00** ☐

Don't miss the Royalty Post Cards Feature!
See pages 160-176.

793. 1985, 8th January
£5 The Times Sponsored Booklet, 4 Panes
(9 x 17p), (9 x 13p), (6 x 17p), (4 x 13p + 2 x 17p + 2 x 4p + 34p)

793a Complete Set of 4 Entire Panes, Philatelic Bureau handstamp (or other) .... **£16.00** ☐
793b With First Day of Issue, London WC handstamp .... **£25.00** ☐
793c With Windsor Philatelic Counter handstamp .... **£27.50** ☐
793d With Fleet Street cds .... **£78.00** ☐
793e Se-tenant Pane only Windsor Philatelic Counter handstamp .... **£8.00** ☐
793f Se-tenant Pane only, with Bureau or London WC handstamp .... **£6.00** ☐
793g 4p left and right Phos Bands, plus 34p two Phos Bands from Times Booklet.. .... **£6.00** ☐
793h Any single Pane with The Times 1785 - 1985, London EC slogan .... **£20.00** ☐
793i Set of 4 Panes with The Times...slogan .... **£50.00** ☐

794. 1985, 19th February
75p Phosphor Coated Paper

794a 75p Phosphor paper change, Windsor Philatelic Counter handstamp .... **£125.00** ☐

795. 1985, 5th March
£1.55 Discounted (from £1.70) **Booklet,** (10 x 17p)

795a £1.55 Booklet Pane, on illustrated cover, any postmark .... **£4.50** ☐
795b Same with Windsor Philatelic Counter handstamp .... **£10.00** ☐
795c 17p single stamp only with 'D' underprint, any postmark .... **£2.50** ☐

This Booklet was printed with the discounted price, rather than the full price, on the cover for the first time. All stamps had a 'D' printed on the reverse side.

796. 1985, 25th June
17p Scottish Regional, on Phosphor Coated Stock

796a 17p on illustrated cover, Edinburgh Philatelic Counter .... **£4.00** ☐

797. 1985, 16th July
10p on Advanced Coated Stock

797a 10p on illustrated cover, with Windsor Philatelic Counter handstamp .... **£4.00** ☐

798. 1985, 17th September
£1.41 Parcel Post Definitive

798a £1.41 on illustrated cover, any postmark .... **£2.50** ☐
798b With Philatelic Bureau handstamp (new design), or London FDI .... **£5.00** ☐
798c With North Eastern Parcel Centre handstamp .... **£22.50** ☐
798d With First Day of Issue, Windsor, Berks special handstamp (new design) .... **£14.00** ☐
798e With Hampstead S.D.O. NW3, Registered cds .... **£22.00** ☐
798f With Field Post Office 330 or other cds .... **£6.50** ☐

799. 1985, 17th September
31p on Advanced Coated Stock

799a 31p on illustrated cover, with Windsor Philatelic Counter handstamp .... **£4.00** ☐

800. 1985, 29th October
7p Red-Brown, 12p Emerald-Green. New Colours

800a The pair on illustrated cover, any postmark .... **£1.50** ☐
800b With Philatelic Bureau handstamp .... **£3.50** ☐
800c With Special 'Italia' cachet and Bureau handstamp .... **£6.50** ☐
800d With London FDI handstamp .... **£5.50** ☐
800e With First Day of Issue, Windsor, Berks special handstamp .... **£8.00** ☐
800f With Field Post Office 330 or other cds .... **£3.50** ☐

The 12p was also released on the same day with a 'Star' underprint. This is catalogued together with the other two values at **£6.50** (Windsor pmk **£8.50**).

801. 1985, 29th October
12p Emerald Green, with 'Star' Underprint
801a 12p New Colour with 'Star' printed on reverse, any postmark .... **£3.50** ☐

802. 1985, 4th November
50p Discount Booklet, 1 Pane (3 x 17p + label)
802a 51p Booklet Pane on illustrated cover, Windsor postmark .... **£6.50** ☐
The Booklet was sold with a 1p discount at 50p instead of 51p.

803. 1985, 12th November
12p Coil Strip, Vertical Format
803a 12p Strip of 3 or more stamps from new Coil, any postmark .... **£4.50** ☐
803b With Windsor Philatelic Counter postmark .... **£12.00** ☐

804. 1985, 4th December
31p Scottish Regional. Redrawn Lion
804a 31p on illustrated cover, Edinburgh Philatelic Counter handstamp .... **£225.00** ☐

805. 1986, 7th January
12p Bright Green. New Colour
Wales, Scotland, Northern Ireland
805a Set of three covers, each with appropriate stamp and regional FDI handstamp .... **£8.00** ☐
805b All three Regions stamp on one cover, Bureau, Windsor, or other cancel .... **£12.50** ☐
The Philatelic Bureau applied two 12p stamps to their first day covers sent to overseas addresses.

806. 1986, 7th January
1p Advanced Coated Stock
806a 1p on illustrated cover (with other stamps), Windsor Philatelic Counter h/s .... **£3.50** ☐

807. 1986, 14th January
£1.20 Booklet, 1 Pane (10 x 12p Centre Band)
£1.50 Booklet, 1 Pane (4 x 12p + 6 x 17p)
807a £1.20 or £1.50 Booklet Pane, illustrated cover, any postmark .... **£5.00** ☐
807b Same, with Windsor Philatelic Counter handstamp .... **£12.50** ☐
807c 12p left and right Phos Bands, from £1.50 Booklet, Windsor handstamp .... **£4.00** ☐

808. 1986, 25th February
2p, 5p. Advanced Coated Stock
17p Wales and Northern Ireland Regionals, Advanced Coated Stock
808a 2p and 5p on illustrated cover, Windsor Philatelic Counter handstamp .... **£4.00** ☐
808b 17p Wales, illustrated cover, Cardiff Philatelic Counter handstamp .... **£5.50** ☐
808c 17p Northern Ireland, illustrated cover, Belfast Philatelic Counter handstamp .... **£6.00** ☐

809. 1986, 18th March
£5 British Rail Sponsored Booklet, 4 Panes
(6 x 17p), (9 x 17p), (9 x 12p), (6 x 12p + 2 x 17p + 31p)
809a Complete Set of 4 entire Panes. Philatelic Bureau handstamp .... **£26.00** ☐
809b With First Day of Issue, Crewe, Cheshire handstamp .... **£32.00** ☐
809c With any T.P.O. cds (Midland, Western, Northern, etc) .... **£52.00** ☐
809d Se-tenant Pane only, with Bureau or Crewe handstamp .... **£8.00** ☐
809e Se-tenant Pane only, with any T.P.O. cds .... **£12.50** ☐
809f 31p with two Phos Bands from the Railway Booklet, Windsor handstamp .... **£5.50** ☐
Panes without the photos (stamps only) are worth only 50% of above prices.

810. 1986, April-June
17p, 31p Scottish Regionals. Advanced Coated Stock - 29th April
12p Scottish Regional Perforation Change - 29th April
4p, 20p. Advanced Coated Stock, Questa Printing - 13th May
26p, 34p. Advanced Coated Stock - 24th June

810a 17p, 31p and 12p Scottish Regionals, Edinburgh Philatelic Counter .... **£5.50** ☐
810b 4p, 20p with Windsor Philatelic Counter handstamp .... **£5.00** ☐
810c 26p, 34p with Windsor Philatelic Counter handstamp .... **£5.00** ☐

811. 1986, 11th July
12p New Phosphor Ink

811a 12p on illustrated cover, with any postmark .... **£30.00** ☐
811b Same with Windsor Philatelic Counter handstamp .... **£52.00** ☐

812. 1986, July-August
50p Roman Booklet, 1 Pane (2 x 1p + 4 x 12p) **- 29th July**
£1 Discount Booklet, 1 Pane (6 x 17p) **- 29th July**
50p Discount Booklet, 1 Pane (3 x 17p + label) **- 12th August**

812a 50p Booklet Pane, illustrated cover, Windsor, or Bath Philatelic Counter h/s .... **£3.50** ☐
812b £1 Discount Booklet Pane, illustrated cover, any postmark .... **£6.00** ☐
812c Same with Windsor Philatelic Counter handstamp .... **£10.00** ☐
812d 50p Discount Booklet, illustrated cover, Windsor Philatelic Counter handstamp .... **£5.00** ☐

The £1 Booklet included stamps worth £1.02. The 50p Discount Booklet was actually worth 51p and had no 'Star' underprinting.

813. 1986, 2nd September
£1.50 Parcel Post Definitive

813a £1.50 on illustrated cover, any postmark .... **£2.50** ☐
813b With Philatelic Bureau handstamp .... **£5.00** ☐
813c With London FDI handstamp .... **£6.50** ☐
813d With First Day of Issue, Windsor, Berks special handstamp .... **£10.00** ☐
813e With Hampstead S.D.O. NW3 cds .... **£22.00** ☐

814. 1986, 23rd September
12p Coil Strip, Horizontal Format

814a 12p Strip of 3 or more stamps from new Coil, Windsor handstamp .... **£6.00** ☐

815. 1986, 7th October
28p Advanced Coated Stock
75 PVA Gum on New Paper (Stock)

815a Both stamps on illustrated cover, Windsor Philatelic Counter handstamp .... **£7.50** ☐
815b Single stamp on illustrated cover, Windsor Philatelic Counter handstamp .... **£4.00** ☐

816. 1986, 20th October
50p 'Roman Britain' Booklet, 1 Pane (1p + 13p + 2 x 18p)
50p 'Pond Life' Booklet, 1 Pane (1p + 2 x 5p + 3 x 13p)
£1 Discount Booklet, 1 Pane (1 x 13p + 5 x 18p)
£1.30 Booklet, 1 Pane (10 x 13p) **£1.80 Booklet, 1 Pane** (10 x 18p)

816a 50p 'Roman Britain' Booklet Pane, Windsor or St. Albans special handstamp .... **£5.00** ☐
816b 50p 'Pond Life' Booklet Pane, Windsor Philatelic Counter handstamp .... **£5.00** ☐
816c 50p 'Pond Life' Booklet Pane, Pond cds .... **£6.50** ☐
816d £1 Discount Booklet, Windsor Philatelic Counter handstamp .... **£5.00** ☐
816e £1.30 and £1.80 Booklet Panes, with any postmark .... **£12.00** ☐
816f Same with Windsor Philatelic Counter handstamp .... **£16.50** ☐
816g 5p Centre Band and 18p two Phos. Bands, any postmark .... **£4.00** ☐

817. 1986, 21st October
13p, 18p Coil Strips
817a 13p and 18p stamps in strips of 3 or more from new Coil, any postmark .... **£12.00** ☐
817b Same with Windsor Philatelic Counter handstamp .... **£30.00** ☐

818. 1986, 4th November
13p Scottish Regional, House of Questa Printing
818a 13p Scottish Regional Edinburgh handstamp .... **£3.50** ☐

819. 1986, 2nd December
£1.20 Christmas Discount Booklet, 1 Pane (10 x 13p)
819a £1.20 Booklet Pane, with 'Star' underprint, Windsor postmark .... **£7.00** ☐
819b Same with any Glastonbury handstamp (3 Versions) .... **£10.00** ☐
819c 13p stamp from the £1.20 Booklet, Windsor postmark .... **£4.00** ☐
819d Same with Christmas Greetings, BFPS handstamp .... **£6.00** ☐
The £1.20 Booklet contained stamps worth £1.30. Each stamp from the Pane was printed on the reverse with a 'Star'.

820. 1987, 6th January
18p Dark-Olive. New Colour
Wales, Scotland, Northern Ireland
820a Set of three covers, each with appropriate stamp and regional handstamp .... **£7.50** ☐
820b All three Regions stamp on one cover, Bureau, Windsor, or other cancel .... **£11.00** ☐

821. 1987, 27th January
22p, 26p, 28p Scottish Regionals. Advanced Coated Paper
26p, 28p, 31p Welsh Regionals. Advanced Coated Paper
26p, 28p, Northern Ireland Regionals. Advanced Coated Paper
821a Set of 3 illustrated covers, Scotland, Wales, N. Ireland handstamp .... **£10.00** ☐

822. 1987, 27th January
50p 'Porchester' Booklet, 1 Pane (1p + 13p + 2 x 18p)
50p 'Snail' Booklet, 1 Pane (1p + 2 x 5p + 3 x 13p)
£1 'Clarinet' Discount Booklet, 1 Pane (13p + 5 x 18p)
£1.30 'Keep in Touch' Booklet, 1 Pane (10 x 13p)
822a Any one of the above 4 Booklet Panes, with Windsor handstamp .... **£12.50** ☐
822b Complete Set of all 4 Booklet Panes, Windsor h/s .... **£44.00** ☐
All of these Panes were printed with a new Phosphor Ink.

823. 1987, 27th January
13p New Phosphor Ink
823a 13p on illustrated cover, with Windsor Philatelic Counter handstamp .... **£5.50** ☐

824. 1987, 3rd March
£5 P&O Sponsored Booklet, 4 Panes
(6 x 13p), (9 x 13p), (9 x 18p), (5 x 18p + 2 x 13p + 1p + 26p)
824a Complete Set of 4 entire Panes, illustrated cover, Bureau handstamp .... **£20.00** ☐
824b With First Day of Issue, Falmouth, Cornwall handstamp .... **£32.00** ☐
824c With Spring Stampex '87, London SW1 handstamp .... **£46.00** ☐
824d With Windsor Philatelic Counter handstamp .... **£25.00** ☐
824e With Maritime Mail cds .... **£72.00** ☐
824f Se-tenant Pane only, with Spring Stampex '87, London SW1 handstamp .... **£12.50** ☐
824g Same with either Windsor or Bureau handstamp (Falmouth **£9**) .... **£6.50** ☐
824h 1p One Phos band, 26p two Phos Bands from P&O Booklet, Windsor pmk .... **£4.50** ☐

825. 1987, 14th April
13p Regional. Coated Papers Ltd Stock. Wales, Scotland, N. Ireland
31p Regional. Advanced Coated Stock. North Ireland
13p Regional. Dextrin Gum. Wales
£1.80 Booklet, 1 Pane (10 x 18p). **Advanced Coated Stock**
3p Advanced Coated Stock. (Issued 5th May)

825a 13p Wales and Scotland plus 13p and 31p N. Ireland. 3 covers, local pmks ....**£9.50** ☐
825b 13p Wales with Dextrin Gum, Cardiff Philatelic Counter handstamp ....**£15.00** ☐
825c £1.80 Booklet Pane, with Windsor Philatelic Counter handstamp...............................**£7.50** ☐
825d 3p Advanced Coated Stock, Windsor Philatelic Counter handstamp..........................**£3.50** ☐

826. 1987, 23rd June
1p Coil Strip (1,000 stamps per complete coil!)

826a 1p Strip of 3 or more stamps from new Coil, Windsor Philatelic Counter h/s ....**£5.50** ☐

827. 1987, 4th August
52p 'Window' Booklet, 1 Pane (4 x 13p)
72p 'Window' Booklet, 1 Pane (4 x 18p)
£1.04 'Window' Booklet, 1 Pane (4 x 26p)
£1.30 'Window' Booklet, 1 Pane (10 x 13p)
£1.80 'Window' Booklet, 1 Pane (10 x 18p)

827a 52p Pane with Bristol, Nottingham, York, Preston, or Windsor postmark ....**£6.50** ☐
827b 72p Pane with Bristol, Nottingham, York, Preston, or Windsor postmark ....**£8.50** ☐
827c £1.04 Pane with Bristol, Nottingham, York, Preston, or Windsor postmark ....**£10.00** ☐
827d £1.30 Pane with Bristol, Nottingham, York, Preston, or Windsor postmark ....**£14.00** ☐
827e £1.80 Pane with Bristol, Nottingham, York, Preston, or Windsor postmark ....**£14.00** ☐
This was the first issue of Window style Booklet Panes. The Booklets were initially sold in Bristol, Nottingham, York, Preston and Windsor.
827f 26p Redrawn numeral, from £1.04 Booklet, any of above postmarks ....**£25.00** ☐

828. 1987, 15th September
£1.60 Parcel Post Definitive

828a £1.60 on illustrated cover, any postmark...**£2.50** ☐
828b With Philatelic Bureau handstamp.. **£4.00** ☐
828c With London FDI handstamp...**£6.50** ☐
828d With First Day of Issue, Windsor, Berks special handstamp ....**£10.50** ☐
828e With Field Post Office 850 or other cds..**£6.00** ☐
828f With Hampstead S.D.O. NW3 cds...**£22.00** ☐
828g North Eastern Parcel Service, Tyne & Wear h/s ....**£24.00** ☐

829. 1987, 29th September
50p Booklet, 1 Pane (1p + 2 x 5p + 3 x 13p)
£1.00 Discount Booklet, 1 Pane (5 x 18p + 13p)

829a 50p Booklet Pane, with Belfast or Windsor postmark...**£5.50** ☐
829b £1 Booklet Pane, with Baker Street cds...**£35.00** ☐
829c Same with Windsor Philatelic Counter handstamp ....**£8.00** ☐
The £1 Booklet contained stamps worth £1.03 and featured Sherlock Holmes.
829d 1p, 5p, 13p, 2 x 18p with straight edge from above Booklets, Windsor postmark.......**£6.00** ☐

830. 1988, 9th February
£5 Financial Times Sponsored Booklet, 4 Panes
(6 x 13p + 18p + 22p + 34p), (9 x 18p), (6 x 18p), (6 x 13p)

830a Complete Set of 4 entire Panes, with Philatelic Bureau handstamp ....**£20.00** ☐
830b Same with First Day of Issue, London EC4 handstamp ....**£30.00** ☐

830c With Fleet Street cds .... **£62.00** ☐
830d Se-tenant Pane only with Fleet Street cds .... **£22.50** ☐
830e Same with Philatelic Bureau, or London FDI handstamp .... **£7.00** ☐
830f 13p left, right and centre Phos Bands, 18p, 22p, 34p two Phos Bands, Windsor h/s .... **£8.00** ☐

831. 1988, 23rd February
2p, 75p Redrawn Numerals
831a Both stamps on illustrated cover, Windsor Philatelic Counter handstamp .... **£4.50** ☐

832. 1988, 18th March
13p Multi-Value Coil Strip (1p + 3 x 4p)
832a 13p Coil Strip on illustrated cover, any postmark .... **£12.00** ☐
832b With Windsor Philatelic Counter handstamp .... **£26.00** ☐

833. 1988, 29th March
18p Scottish, Welsh Regional. Printed on H & L Slater Paper
833a Pair of covers, with relevant Philatelic Counter handstamp .... **£5.00** ☐

834. 1988, 3rd May
18p Coil Strip
834a 18p Strip of 3 or more Stamps from new Coil, Windsor handstamp .... **£6.00** ☐

835. 1988, 26th July
2p, 4p, 5p, 75p Harrison Printing
1p Coil Strip
835a 2p, 4p, 5p, 75p on illustrated cover, Windsor Philatelic Counter handstamp .... **£6.00** ☐
835b 1p Strip of 3 or more stamps from new Coil, Windsor postmark .... **£8.50** ☐

836. 1988, 23rd August
20p Sky Blue, 28p Pale Brown. New Colours
14p Navy, 19p Orange, 23p Pale Green, 27p Brown, 32p Sepia, 35p Dark Brown. New Values
836a Set on illustrated cover, any postmark .... **£3.00** ☐
836b With Philatelic Bureau handstamp .... **£5.00** ☐
836c With London FDI handstamp .... **£6.50** ☐
836d With First Day of Issue, Windsor, Berks special handstamp .... **£10.00** ☐

837. 1988, 23rd August
56p 'Window' Booklet, 1 Pane (4 x 14p)
76p 'Window' Booklet, 1 Pane (4 x 19p)
£1.08 'Window' Booklet, 1 Pane (4 x 27p)
£1.40 'Window' Booklet, 1 Pane (10 x 14p)
£1.90 'Window' Booklet, 1 Pane (10 x 19p)
837a 56p Booklet Pane, Bristol, Nottingham, Preston, or York handstamp .... **£8.00** ☐
837b 76p Booklet Pane, Bristol, Nottingham, Preston, or York handstamp .... **£8.50** ☐
837c £1.08 Booklet Pane, Bristol, Nottingham, Preston, or York handstamp .... **£9.00** ☐
837d £1.40 Booklet Pane, Bristol, Nottingham, Preston, or York handstamp .... **£9.00** ☐
837e £1.90 Booklet Pane, Bristol, Nottingham, Preston, or York handstamp .... **£10.00** ☐
837f Any one of the above Panes with Windsor Philatelic Counter handstamp .... **£7.50** ☐

Remember, most modern hand addressed covers are worth only 20% of catalogue prices.

838. 1988, 5th September
50p Discount Booklet, 1 Pane (2 x 19p + 14p + label)
£1. Discount Booklet, 1 Pane (2 x 14p + 4 x 19p)
£1.40 Booklet, 1 Pane (10 x 14p)
£1.90 Booklet, 1 Pane (10 x 19p)

838a 50p Discount Pane, on illustrated cover, Windsor Philatelic Counter handstamp ....**£5.50** ☐
838b £1 Discount Pane, on illustrated cover, Windsor Philatelic Counter handstamp..........**£6.50** ☐
838c £1.40 Booklet Pane, on illustrated cover, Windsor Philatelic Counter handstamp ......**£8.00** ☐
838d £1.90 Booklet Pane, on illustrated cover, Windsor Philatelic Counter handstamp ....**£10.00** ☐

The 50p Booklet contained stamps worth 52p and the £1 Booklet contained stamps worth £1.04.

839. 1988, 5th September
14p Multi-Value Coil Strip (3 x 4p +2p)
19p and 14p Coil Strips (14p Horizontal and Vertical Format)

839a 14p Multi-Value Coil Strip, with Windsor Philatelic Counter handstamp.......................**£8.50** ☐
839b 19p plus 14p Strips (2) each with 3 or more stamps from new Coils, Windsor h/s ...**£14.00** ☐

840. 1988, 11th October
Window Booklets, Harrison Printing (straight edge Panes)
- 56p, 76p, £1.08, £1.40, £1.90 Booklets - content as Aug 23rd issue
Window Booklets, House of Questa Printing (in Litho)
- £1.40, £1.90 Booklets - content as Aug 23rd issue

840a Set of 5 straight edge Panes, any postmark (**£16**), Windsor postmark......................**£38.00** ☐
840b Pair of Questa Litho Panes, any postmark (**£10**), Windsor postmark ....**£18.50** ☐
840c 14p, 19p, 27p, all with one straight edge, any postmark (**£3**), Windsor postmark ....**£8.00** ☐
840d 14p, 19p, Questa Litho Printing, any postmark (**£1**), Windsor postmark......................**£4.50** ☐

The 56p and 76p Booklets were reprinted on Jan 24, 1989 with three straight edges per Booklet Pane. A pair of these complete Panes is catalogued at £2. (Windsor postmark £5).

841. 1988, 18th October
New High Value Castle Definitives
£1. Carrickfergus, £1.50 Caernarfon, £2 Edinburgh, £5 Windsor

841a Set on illustrated cover, any postmark..**£16.00** ☐
841b With Philatelic Bureau special handstamp ....**£22.50** ☐
841c With First Day of Issue, Windsor, Berks special handstamp ....**£30.00** ☐
841d All four Castle High Values, Carrickfergus, Co. Antrim handstamp ....**£40.00** ☐
841e All four Castle High Values, Caernarfon, Gwynedd handstamp ....**£40.00** ☐
841f All four Castle High Values, Edinburgh handstamp ....**£40.00** ☐
841g All four Castle High Values, Windsor, Berks handstamp ....**£40.00** ☐
841h With Carrickfergus cds ....**£275.00** ☐
841i With Caernarfon cds ....**£170.00** ☐
841j With Edinburgh cds ....**£170.00** ☐
841k With Windsor cds ....**£170.00** ☐
841l With Windsor Castle cds...**£230.00** ☐
841m With Buckingham Palace SW1 cds ....**£210.00** ☐
841n Set on 4 covers, each stamp with appropriate handstamp.....................................**£38.00** ☐
841o Set on 4 covers, each stamp with appropriate cds ....**£220.00** ☐

842. 1988, 8th November
19p Orange, 23p Pale Green, 32p Green-Blue. New Values
14p Navy Blue. New Colour
Wales, Scotland, Northern Ireland

842a Set of three covers, each with appropriate stamps and regional handstamp ....**£12.00** ☐
842b All three Regions stamps on one cover, Bureau, Windsor or other cancel................**£16.00** ☐

842A. 1989, 24th January
The First Booklets with 3 Imperforate Sides
- 56p Booklet (4 x 14p)
- 76p Booket (4 x 19p)
842Aa Both Panes with Windsor Philatelic Counter handstamp .... **£12.50** ☐

843. 1989, 21st March
£5. Scots Connection Prestige Booklet, 4 Panes of Regional Stamps
(6 x 14p), (6 x 19p), (9 x 19p), (5 x 14p + 2 x 19p + 23p + label)
843a Set of 4 entire Regional Panes, Philatelic Bureau handstamp .... **£16.00** ☐
843b With First Day of Issue, Inverness handstamp .... **£26.00** ☐
843c With Holyrood, Edinburgh cds .... **£34.00** ☐
843d Se-tenant Pane only, with Burns Statue, Ayr cds .... **£20.00** ☐
843e With Bureau or Inverness FDI handstamp .... **£7.50** ☐
843f With Melrose, or other Scottish cds .... **£14.00** ☐
843g 14p one Phos Band, plus 19p, 23p two Phos Bands, from Booklet, any pmk .... **£10.00** ☐

844. 1989, 25th April
£1. Discount Booklet, 1 Pane (2 x 14p + 4 x 19p), **Walsall Printing**
14p, 19p. One Straight Edge, from £1 Booklet
19p Scottish Regional. Questa Phosphor Coated Stock Printing
844a £1 Booklet Pane, any postmark (**£2**), Windsor Philatelic Counter handstamp .... **£5.00** ☐
844b Same with Walsall Security Printers handstamp (**£9**), or Walsall cds .... **£37.50** ☐
844c 14p and 19p from Booklet, any postmark (**£1.50**), Windsor Philatelic Counter .... **£5.50** ☐
844d 19p Scottish Regional Coated Phos, Edinburgh Philatelic Counter handstamp .... **£4.00** ☐
The £1 Booklet contained stamps worth £1.04.

845. 1989, 20th June
19p Welsh Regional, New Phosphor Coated Stock
845a 19p Regional, with Cardiff Philatelic Counter handstamp .... **£4.50** ☐

846. 1989, June - August
£1.90 'Window' Booklet (10 x 19p), **Jumelle Press Printing. 26th June**
£1.40 'Window' Booklet (10 x 14p), **Jumelle Press Printing. 10th July**
50p Discount Booklet (14p + 2 x 19p + label). **Chambon Press Printing. 8th August**
846a £1.90 Booklet Pane, any postmark (**£3**), Windsor Philatelic Counter .... **£8.00** ☐
846b £1.40 Booklet Pane, any postmark (**£2**), Windsor Philatelic Counter handstamp .... **£6.50** ☐
846c 50p Booklet Pane, any postmark (**£1.50**), Windsor Philatelic Counter handstamp .... **£3.50** ☐
The 50p Booklet contained stamps worth 52p.

847. 1989, 22nd August
NVI 'Window' Booklets. First Ever GB Non-Value 1st & 2nd Class Stamps
- 56p Booklet (4 x 2nd Class NVI Stamp). **Walsall Printing**
- 76p Booklet (4 x 1st Class NVI Stamp). **Walsall Printing**
- £1.40 Booklet (10 x 2nd Class NVI Stamp). **Harrison Printing**
- £1.90 Booklet (10 x 1st Class NVI Stamp). **Harrison Printing**
847a 56p Booklet Pane, Bureau postmark (**£3**), Windsor FDI handstamp .... **£5.00** ☐
847b 76p Booklet Pane, Bureau postmark (**£4**), Windsor FDI handstamp .... **£6.00** ☐
847c £1.40 Booklet Pane, Bureau postmark (**£8**), Windsor FDI handstamp .... **£10.00** ☐
847d £1.90 Booklet Pane, Bureau postmark (**£9**), Windsor FDI handstamp .... **£12.00** ☐
The Walsall Printing has 3 straight edges per Pane, whilst the Harrison Printing has only two (top and bottom). In August 1989 the First Class rate was 19p and the second class rate 14p.
847e 1st and 2nd NVI Stamps Walsall Printing, Bureau postmark (**£3**), Windsor FDI .... **£6.00** ☐
847f 1st and 2nd NVI Stamps Harrison Printing, Bureau postmark (**£3**), Windsor FDI .... **£6.00** ☐

848. 1989, 19th September
NVI 'Window' Booklets. Non-Value Indicator Stamps
- £1.40 Booklet (10 x 2nd Class NVI Stamp). **House of Questa Printing**
- £1.90 Booklet (10 x 1st Class NVI Stamp). **House of Questa Printing**
848a £1.40 Booklet Pane, with any postmark (**£4**), with Windsor Philatelic Counter h/s .....**£7.50** ☐
848b £1.90 Booklet Pane, with any postmark (**£5**), with Windsor Philatelic Counter h/s .....**£8.50** ☐
In September 1989 the First Class rate was 19p and the Second Class rate 14p.
848c 1st and 2nd NVI Stamps, House of Questa Printing, any pmk (**£2**), Windsor h/s ....**£5.00** ☐

849. 1989, 26th September
15p Lt. Blue, 20p Black, 24p Terracotta, 29p Purple, 34p Slate. New Colours
30p Sage, 37p Red. New Values
849a Set on illustrated cover, any postmark......**£3.00** ☐
849b With Philatelic Bureau special handstamp ......**£4.50** ☐
849c With London FDI handstamp......**£7.00** ☐
849d With First Day of Issue Windsor, Berks special handstamp ......**£10.00** ☐

850. 1989, 2nd October
New Postage Rate Booklets
- 50p Booklet, 1 Pane (2 x 15p + 20p + label)
- £1 'Window' Booklet, 1 Pane (5 x 20p + label)
- £1.16 Booklet, 1 Pane (4 x 29p)
850a 50p Booklet Pane, with any postmark (**£1**), Windsor Philatelic Counter h/s ......**£3.00** ☐
850b £1. Booklet Pane, with any postmark (**£2**), Windsor Philatelic Counter h/s ......**£5.00** ☐
850c £1.16 Booklet Pane, with any postmark (**£2**), Windsor Philatelic Counter h/s ......**£5.50** ☐

851. 1989, 10th October
15p Multi-Value Coil Strip (3 x 4p + 3p)
851a 15p Coil Strip, with any postmark (**£2**), Windsor Philatelic Counter handstamp..........**£6.00** ☐

852. 1989, 16th October
15p and 20p Coil Strips, Vertical and Horizontal Formats
852a 15p, 20p, Strips of 3 stamps or more from each Coil (any pmk **£6**), Windsor P.C. h/s...**£10.50** ☐

853. 1989, 28th November
20p Black, 24p Light Brown, 34p Slate-Blue. New Values
15p Sky Blue. New Colour
Wales, Scotland, Northern Ireland
853a Set of three covers, each with appropriate stamps and regional FDI handstamp .....**£13.50** ☐
853b All three Regions stamps on one cover, Bureau, Windsor or other cancel......**£18.00** ☐
The Bureau and Regional handstamps were in red, since one of the stamps (20p) was printed in black.

854. 1989, November - December
NVI 'Window' Booklets. Harrison Printing
- 60p Booklet (4 x 2nd Class NVI Stamp) **- 28th November**
- 80p Booklet (4 x 1st Class NVI Stamp) **- 5th December**
854a 60p Booklet Pane, with any pmk (**£8**), with Windsor handstamp ......**£18.00** ☐
854b 80p Booklet Pane, with any pmk (**£9**), with Windsor handstamp ......**£26.00** ☐
Both Booklet Panes have 3 straight edges.

1990, 10th January
Penny Black Anniversary Issue
15p, 20p, 29p, 34p, 37p, QEII/QV Profile Heads
This issue of five stamps is listed in the Commemoratives Section of the catalogue.

855. 1990, 30th January
'Window' Booklets. Penny Black Anniversary Stamps
- 60p Booklet, 1 Pane (4 x 15p) **- Walsall Printing**
- 80p Booklet, 1 Pane (4 x 20p) **- Walsall Printing**
- £1.50 Booklet, 1 Pane (10 x 15p) **- Harrison Printing**
- £2.00 Booklet, 1 Pane (10 x 20p) **- Harrison Printing**

855a Set of 4 complete Panes, with any pmk (**£14**), Windsor handstamp .... **£28.00** ☐

856. 1990, 30th January
Booklets. Penny Black Anniversary Stamps
- 50p Booklet, 1 Pane (2 x 15p + 20p + label) **- Harrison Printing**
- £1. Booklet, 1 Pane (5 x 20p + label) **- Harrison Printing**
- £1. Booklet, 1 Pane (5 x 20p + label) **- Walsall Printing**

856a Set of 3 complete Panes, with any pmk (**£10**), Windsor handstamp .... **£18.50** ☐

857. 1990, 13th March
50p Sand Shade. New Colour Variation

857a 50p on illustrated cover, any postmark .... **£3.00** ☐
857b With Windsor Philatelic Counter handstamp .... **£7.00** ☐

The Post Office did not consider this to be a true colour change, therefore no official first day postmarks were made available!

858. 1990, 20th March
£5 London Life Prestige Booklet, 4 Panes
(6 x 20p Penny Black Anniv.) x 2, (4 x 20p Europa 1990), (Multi-Value Pane*)

858a Complete Set of 4 entire Panes, Philatelic Bureau handstamp .... **£16.00** ☐
858b With Alexandra Palace, Victorian Heritage, London N22 handstamp .... **£26.00** ☐
858c With Europa...Stamp World London, Alexandra Palace, London N22 .... **£34.00** ☐
858d With First Day of Issue, Tower Hill, London EC3 handstamp .... **£22.00** ☐
858e Se-tenant Pane only, with Philatelic Bureau handstamp .... **£5.50** ☐
858f Se-tenant Pane only with Victorian Heritage, London N22 handstamp .... **£10.00** ☐
858g Se-tenant Pane only, with Europa... Stamp World London handstamp .... **£12.00** ☐
858h Se-tenant Pane only, with Tower Hill, London EC3 FDI handstamp .... **£10.00** ☐

*Multi Value Pane (50p + 20p +15p +1st NVI + 2nd NVI + label +15p, 20p, 29p Penny Black Anniv.)
Prices are for full Panes with illustrations. Panes of stamps only are worth 50% less.

859. 1990, 17th April
'Window' Booklets. Penny Black Anniversary Stamps
- 80p Booklet, 1 Pane (4 x 20p). **Harrison Printing**
- £1.50 Booklet, 1 Pane (10 x 15p). **House of Questa Printing**
- £2. Booklet, 1 Pane (10 x 20p). **House of Questa Printing**

859a 80p Booklet Pane, any postmark (**£3**), Windsor handstamp .... **£6.50** ☐
859b £1.50 Booklet Pane, any postmark (**£5**), Windsor handstamp .... **£9.00** ☐
859c £2. Booklet Pane, any postmark (**£8**), Windsor handstamp .... **£12.00** ☐

860. 1990, 17th April
£1.16 Booklet, 1 Pane (4 x 29p). **Walsall Printing**

860a £1.16 Booklet Pane, with any postmark (**£5**), Windsor handstamp .... **£7.50** ☐

861. 1990, 12th June
'Window' Booklets. Penny Black Anniversary Stamps
- £1.50 (10 x 15p). **Walsall Printing**
- £2 (10 x 20p). **Walsall Printing**

861a £1.50 Booklet Pane, any postmark (**£4**), Windsor handstamp .... **£8.00** ☐
861b £2.00 Booklet Pane, any postmark (**£6**), Windsor handstamp .... **£10.00** ☐

862. 1990, 7th August
NVI 'Window' Booklets. New NVI Stamp Colours
- 60p Booklet (4 x 2nd Class NVI Stamp). **Walsall Printing**
- 80p Booklet (4 x 1st Class NVI Stamp). **Walsall Printing**
- £1.50 Booklet (10 x 2nd Class NVI Stamp). **Walsall Printing**
- £2. Booklet (10 x 1st Class NVI Stamp). **Walsall Printing**
- £1.50 and £2 as above, but Harrison Printing
- £1.50 and £2 as above, but House of Questa Printing

862a 60p Booklet Pane, any postmark (**£2**), Windsor FDI handstamp .... **£5.50** ☐
862b 80p Booklet Pane, any postmark (**£2**), Windsor FDI handstamp .... **£6.50** ☐
862c £1.50 Booklet Pane, any printing any postmark (**£5**), Windsor FDI handstamp .... **£8.50** ☐
862d £2. Booklet Pane, any printing any postmark (**£6**), Windsor FDI handstamp .... **£10.00** ☐
862e Set of 8 Complete Panes any postmark (**£32**), Windsor FDI handstamp .... **£52.00** ☐
862f 1st and 2nd Class NVI Stamp from any Pane (**£3**), Windsor FDI handstamp .... **£5.00** ☐

863. 1990, 4th September
10p Lt. Tan, 17p Dark Blue, 22p Flame, 26p Stone, 27p Mauve, and 31p Ultramarine. New Colours
33p Emerald. New Value

863a Set on illustrated cover, any postmark .... **£2.50** ☐
863b With Philatelic Bureau handstamp .... **£4.50** ☐
863c With London FDI handstamp .... **£6.50** ☐
863d With First Day of Issue, Windsor, Berks special handstamp .... **£12.00** ☐

864. 1990, 4th September
50p Discount Booklet, 1 Pane (3 x 17p + label). Booklet Worth 51p
£1 Booklet, 1 Pane (2 x 17p + 3 x 22p + 3 labels)

864a 50p Booklet Pane, any postmark (**£1**), Windsor Philatelic Counter handstamp .... **£3.50** ☐
864b £1. Booklet Pane, any postmark (**£3**), Windsor Philatelic Counter handstamp .... **£6.00** ☐
864c 17p left and right Phos Bands, 22p two Phos Bands, Windsor handstamp .... **£4.00** ☐

865. 1990, 17th September
17p, 22p Coil Strips, Vertical Format

865a 17p, 22p Strips of 3 or more stamps, from new Coils, Windsor handstamp .... **£8.00** ☐

866. 1990, 17th September
£1.24 'Window' Booklet, 1 Pane (4 x 31p). **Walsall Printing**

866a £1.24 Booklet Pane, any postmark (**£3**), Windsor Philatelic Counter h/s .... **£6.50** ☐

867. 1990, 27th November
17p Multi-Value Coil Strip (5p + 3 x 4p)

867a 17p Coil Strip with any postmark (**£2**), Windsor Philatelic Counter handstamp .... **£5.00** ☐

868. 1990, 4th December
37p Magenta. New Value
17p Navy Blue, 22p Orange, 26p Drab. New Colours
Wales, Scotland, Northern Ireland

868a Set of three covers, each with appropriate stamps and regional FDI handstamp ..... **£12.50** ☐
868b All three Regions stamps on one cover, Bureau or other cancel (**£12**), Windsor ...... **£16.00** ☐

869. 1991, 19th March
£6 Agatha Christie Prestige Booklet. 4 Panes
(6 x 17p) x 2, (9 x 22p), (6 x 22p + 2 x 33p + label)

869a Complete Set of 4 entire Panes, Philatelic Bureau handstamp .... **£16.50** ☐
869b Same with First Day of Issue, Marple, Cheshire handstamp .... **£32.00** ☐
869c With Agatha Christie Centenary Year... Folkestone, Kent handstamp .... **£32.00** ☐
869d With Sunningdale, Berks handstamp .... **£32.00** ☐
869e With 'Take a Bite out of Crime' slogan .... **£36.00** ☐
869f Se-tenant Pane only, Philatelic Bureau handstamp .... **£6.00** ☐
869g Same with Marple, Cheshire, FDI handstamp .... **£10.00** ☐
869h With Folkestone, or Sunningdale handstamp .... **£10.00** ☐
869i With 'Take a Bite out of Crime' slogan .... **£22.00** ☐

Prices are for complete Panes with illustrations. Panes with stamps only are worth 50% less.

870. 1991, 14th May
22p Welsh Regional. Questa Printing. Coated Papers
22p, 26p, 37p, Scottish Regionals. Questa Printing. Coated Papers

870a 4 Stamps on 2 illustrated covers, Local Philatelic Counter handstamp .... **£10.00** ☐

871. 1991, 6th August
NVI 'Window' Booklets
- **68p Booklet** (4 x 2nd Class NVI stamp). **Walsall Printing**
- **£1.70 Booklet** (10 x 2nd Class NVI stamp). **Walsall Printing**
- **£2.20 Booklet** (10 x 1st Class NVI stamp). **House of Questa Printing**

871a 68p Booklet Pane, any postmark (**£2**), Windsor Philatelic Counter handstamp .... **£4.50** ☐
871b £1.70 Booklet Pane, any postmark (**£4**), Windsor Philatelic Counter handstamp .... **£9.00** ☐
871c £2.20 Booklet Pane, any postmark (**£6**), Windsor Philatelic Counter handstamp .... **£12.50** ☐

872. 1991, 10th September
6p Lime Green, 18p Lt. Green, 24p Rust, 28p Slate Blue, and
34p Purple, 35p Old Gold. New Colours
39p Rhododendron. New Value

872a Set on illustrated cover, any postmark .... **£2.50** ☐
872b With Philatelic Bureau handstamp .... **£4.00** ☐
872c With London FDI handstamp .... **£6.00** ☐
872d With First Day of Issue, Windsor, Berks special handstamp .... **£12.00** ☐
872e With 'New Postage Rates' slogan, various offices .... **£20.00** ☐

873. 1991, 10th September
50p Booklet, 1 Pane (2 x 1p + 2 x 24p)
£1 Booklet, 1 Pane (2 x 2p + 4 x 24p + 2 labels)

873a Both Panes any postmark (**£3**), Windsor FDI handstamp .... **£6.50** ☐
873b Same with 'New Postage Rates' slogan cancel .... **£14.00** ☐

874. 1991, 16th September
New Air Mail Rates 'Window' Booklets. Walsall Printing
- **£1.32 Booklet** (4 x 33p). Postcards air mail worldwide
- **£1.56 Booklet** (4 x 39p). Letters air mail worldwide

874a Both Booklet Panes any postmark (**£5**), Windsor Philatelic Counter handstamp .... **£10.00** ☐
874b With 'New Postage Rates' slogan cancel .... **£14.00** ☐
874c 33p, 39p from Booklets, with one straight edge, Windsor handstamp .... **£5.00** ☐

This is the 30th Edition of the Collect GB First Day Covers catalogue

875. 1991, 16th September
18p, 24p Coil Strips. Vertical Format
875a Both Strips of 3 stamps or more, from new Coils, Windsor handstamp....................... **£7.50** ☐
875b With 'New Postage rates' slogan cancel .... **£12.00** ☐

876. 1991, 1st October
18p, Multi-Value Coil Strip (2 x 5p + 2 x 4p)
876a 18p Coil Strip, any pmk (**£3**), Windsor Philatelic Counter handstamp.......................... **£5.00** ☐

877. 1991, 19th November
18p Enschedé Printing in Holland - One Phos Band, Coated Papers Stock
877a 18p Emerald Green, any postmark (**£1**), Windsor Philatelic Counter handstamp .... **£3.50** ☐

878. 1991, 3rd December
39p Purple. New Value
18p Yellow-Green, 24p Brown, 28p Slate-Blue. New Colours
Wales, Scotland, Northern Ireland
878a Set of three covers, each with appropriate stamps and regional FDI handstamp ..... **£12.00** ☐
878b All three Regions stamps on one cover, Bureau, Windsor, or other cancel .... **£16.50** ☐

879. 1992, 21st January
50p Phosphor Coated Stock. 3p Value Redrawn
879a Both stamps on illustrated cover, any postmark (**£2**), Windsor handstamp .... **£5.00** ☐

880. 1992, 11th February
33p, 39p Coil Strips. Vertical Format
880a 33p and 39p Strips of 3 stamps or more, from new Coils, Windsor handstamp.......... **£8.50** ☐

881. 1992, 25th February
£6 Wales Prestige Booklet, 4 Panes
(6 x 24p Regional), (6 x 18p Regional), (4 x 39p Wintertime Stamp), (Multi-Value Pane)*
881a Complete set of 4 entire Panes, Philatelic Bureau handstamp .... **£15.00** ☐
881b With First Day of Issue, Diwrnod... Cardiff handstamp .... **£17.50** ☐
881c With Cardiff Philatelic Counter handstamp.. **£17.50** ☐
881d With Stampex, London SW1 handstamp .... **£26.00** ☐
881e With Snowdon Mountain Railway, Caernarfon handstamp.. **£26.00** ☐
881f With assorted relevant Welsh cds postmarks .... **£36.00** ☐
881g Se-tenant Pane only, with Philatelic Bureau handstamp .... **£5.00** ☐
881h With Cardiff FDI handstamp.. **£6.50** ☐
881i With Cardiff Philatelic Counter handstamp.. **£6.50** ☐
881j With Stampex, London SW1 handstamp .... **£11.00** ☐
881k With Snowdon Mountain Railway handstamp.. **£11.00** ☐
881l With any relevant Welsh cds cancel.. **£12.50** ☐
*Multi-Value Pane (1st NVI + 2nd NVI + 2 x 33p + 2 x 18p Wales + 2 x 24p Wales + label).
Prices are for complete Panes with text. Panes with stamps only are worth 50% less.

Don't forget that we now include sections on Overprints,
Pre-release covers and Missing Colours on fdc.
These can all be found in the last part of the catalogue.

882. 1992, 24th March
Castle High Values - Security Printing
£1.00 Carrickfergus, £1.50 Caernarfon, £2.00 Edinburgh, £5.00 Windsor

882a Set on illustrated cover, any postmark .... **£12.00** ☐
882b With Philatelic Bureau special handstamp .... **£20.00** ☐
882c With First Day of Issue, Windsor, Berks special handstamp .... **£22.00** ☐
882d With Castle High Values, Carrickfergus, Co. Antrim handstamp .... **£26.00** ☐
882e With Castle High Values, Caernarfon, Gwynedd handstamp .... **£26.00** ☐
882f With Castle High Values, Edinburgh, Lothian handstamp .... **£26.00** ☐
882g With Castle High Values, Windsor, Berkshire handstamp .... **£26.00** ☐
882h With 'Castles' High Values, Security Printing, Windsor handstamp .... **£30.00** ☐
882i With Carrickfergus cds .... **£52.00** ☐
882j With Caernarfon cds .... **£52.00** ☐
882k With Edinburgh cds .... **£52.00** ☐
882l With Windsor cds .... **£52.00** ☐
882m With Windsor Castle cds .... **£165.00** ☐
882n With Buckingham Palace cds .... **£125.00** ☐
882o Set on 4 covers, each with appropriate handstamp (cds cancel **£42**) .... **£24.00** ☐
882p Set on 4 covers, each with Elephant & Castle B.O. SE1 cds .... **£40.00** ☐

The security printing incorporated optically variable ink on the Queens head and a special elongated central perforation on the left and right side of each stamp.

883. 1992, 28th July
78p 'Kelloggs' Booklet, 1 Pane, (2 x 39p + 4 air mail labels)

883a 78p Booklet Pane, on illustrated cover, any postmark .... **£5.00** ☐
883b With Windsor Philatelic Counter handstamp .... **£12.50** ☐

Booklet was featured on Kellogg's Bran Flakes packets.

884. 1992, 27th October
£6 Tolkien Centenary Prestige Booklet, 4 Panes
(6 x 24p)x 2, (6 x 18p), (2 x 18p + 2 x 24p + 2 x 39p + 1st & 2nd NVI Stamps + label)

884a Complete set of 4 entire Panes, Philatelic Bureau handstamp .... **£18.00** ☐
884b With First Day of Issue, Oxford handstamp .... **£20.00** ☐
884c With Centenary JRR Tolkien, Rings End, March, Cambs handstamp .... **£30.00** ☐
884d With Centenary of JRR Tolkien, Bagendon, Cirencester, Glos. h/s .... **£30.00** ☐
884e With JRR Tolkien Centenary, Meriden ... Coventry handstamp .... **£30.00** ☐
884f Se-tenant Pane only, Philatelic Bureau handstamp .... **£6.50** ☐
884g With, First Day of Issue, Oxford handstamp .... **£9.00** ☐
884h With Centenary JRR Tolkien, Rings End ... handstamp .... **£12.00** ☐
884i With, Centenary JRR Tolkien, Bagendon ... handstamp .... **£12.00** ☐
884j With J.R.R. Tolkien Centenary, Meriden ... handstamp .... **£14.50** ☐

Prices are for complete Panes with illustrations. Panes with stamps only are worth 50% less.

885. 1993, 9th February
£2.40 Greetings NVI Booklet, 1 Pane
(10 x 1st Class NVI stamps)

885a £2.40 Booklet Pane, any postmark (**£5**), with Windsor Philatelic Counter h/s .... **£8.50** ☐

886. 1993, 9th February
£1 Booklet, Litho printed by Walsall. 1 Pane
(4 x 24p + 2 x 2p + 2 labels)

886a £1 Booklet Pane, any postmark (**£3**), with Windsor Philatelic Counter handstamp ..... **£6.00** ☐

Four new stamp variations, 2p and 24p litho ACP, left and right straight edges.

887. 1993, 2nd March
£10 Britannia Stamp - Security Printing

887a £10 Stamp on illustrated cover, any postmark ..... **£12.00** ☐
887b With Philatelic Bureau special handstamp ..... **£18.00** ☐
887c With First Day of Issue, Windsor special handstamp ..... **£26.00** ☐
887d With First Day of Issue, London handstamp (Britannia) ..... **£26.00** ☐
887e With Windsor Philatelic Counter handstamp ..... **£24.00** ☐
887f With Britannia Way, London SW6 handstamp ..... **£28.00** ☐
887g With £10 High Value Definitive, Dover, Kent handstamp ..... **£28.00** ☐
887h With £10 High Value, Britannia, Porth Glamorgan handstamp ..... **£28.00** ☐
887i With Spring Stampex, London SW1 handstamp ..... **£32.00** ☐
887j With National Postal Museum, London EC1 handstamp ..... **£32.00** ☐
887k With 2.3. Windsor 93 handstamp ..... **£32.00** ☐
887l With Eur-Apex '93, London SW1 handstamp ..... **£32.00** ☐
887m With London SW1 permanent handstamp (picture of the Palace) ..... **£32.00** ☐
887n With Windsor cds ..... **£40.00** ☐
887o With Britannia cds (any office), or Pounds cds ..... **£45.00** ☐
887p With Windsor Castle cds ..... **£130.00** ☐
887q With Buckingham Palace cds ..... **£110.00** ☐

The security printing elements include two elliptical perforations at the top and bottom of the stamp, special security paper and inks, braille embossing of the word 'ten'.

888. 1993, 16th March
£1.80 NVI Booklet. New Value. Walsall
(10 x 2nd Class NVI Blue Stamps)

888a Complete Pane of new 2nd Class NVI Stamp, any postmark ..... **£5.00** ☐
888b With Windsor Philatelic Counter handstamp ..... **£10.50** ☐

Straight edges on top and bottom of stamp.

889. 1993, 6th April
NVI Booklets with Left and Right Elliptical Perforations
- 72p Booklet, Walsall Printing (4 x 2nd Class NVI Stamps)
- 96p Booklet, Harrison Printing (4 x 1st Class NVI Stamps)
- £1.80 Booklet, Questa Printing (10 x 2nd Class NVI Stamps)
- £2.40 Booklet, Harrison Printing (10 x 1st Class NVI Stamps)
- £2.40 Booklet, Walsall Printing (10 x 1st Class NVI Stamps)

889a Set of five complete Panes, any pmk (**£16**), Windsor Philatelic Counter ..... **£25.00** ☐

All stamps printed on Optical Brightening Agent free paper. Walsall and Questa litho printing and PVA gum. Harrison photogravure and PVA Dextrin gum.

890. 1993, 27th April
6p Light Olive-Green. Enschedé Printing. Elliptical Perfs
890a 6p Definitive Stamp, any pmk (**£1**), Windsor Philatelic Counter handstamp .... **£3.50** ☐
First time printed by Enschedé in Holland: Photogravure, two Phos bars.

891. 1993, 8th June
1p, 5p, 10p. Enschedé Printing, Elliptical Perfs
891a All 3 stamps with any pmk (**£1**), with Windsor Philatelic Counter handstamp .... **£3.50** ☐
First time printed by Enschedé in Holland: Photogravure, two Phos bands.

892. 1993, 27th July
30p, Enschedé Printing. Elliptical Perfs
892a 30p Definitive stamp, any pmk (**£1**), Windsor Philatelic Counter handstamp .... **£4.00** ☐
First time printed by Enschedé in Holland: Photogravure, two Phos bands.

893. 1993, 10th August
£6 Beatrix Potter Prestige Stamp Book, 4 Panes
(4 x 1st Class Peter Rabbit), (3 x 18p Regionals + 3 x 24p Regionals),
(3 x 1st Class NVI + 3 x 2nd Class NVI), (2 x 2nd Class NVI + 2 each 18p, 33p, 39p)
893a Complete set of 4 entire Panes, on illustrated covers, Philatelic Bureau h/s .... **£26.00** ☐
893b With First Day of Issue, Keswick handstamp .... **£28.00** ☐
893c With Beatrix Potter 1866-1943, Near Sawrey, Ambleside handstamp .... **£46.00** ☐
893d With Centenary of Beatrix Potter, Kensington, London W8 handstamp..................... **£46.00** ☐
893e With Centenary of Beatrix Potter, Gloucester handstamp .... **£46.00** ☐
893f With Beatrix Potter Anniversary, Catton, Hexham. handstamp .... **£46.00** ☐
893g With First Day of Issue, London handstamp (Dormouse)... **£28.00** ☐
893h With Any other relevant cds postmark (handstamp **£35**)... **£50.00** ☐
893i Multi Value Pane only, any relevant postmark.. **£11.00** ☐
The total value of the actual stamps in this Booklet is £5.64. Prices are for complete Panes with text. Panes with stamps only are worth 50% less.

894. 1993, 17th August
35p, Enschedé Printing. Elliptical Perfs
894a 35p Definitive Stamp, any pmk (**£1**) with Windsor Philatelic Counter handstamp ...... **£5.00** ☐
First time printed by Enschedé in Holland. Photogravure, two phos bands.

895. 1993, 7th September
72p Booklet, Harrison Printing. Elliptical Perforations
(4 x 2nd Class NVI Stamp)
895a 72p Booklet Pane, any **£2**), Windsor Philatelic Counter h/s .... **£5.50** ☐

896. 1993, 5th October
NVI Stamps Printed in Sheets. House of Questa
896a 1st and 2nd NVI Stamps, 3 or more joined vertically, any postmark .... **£2.50** ☐
896b With The First NVI Issued in Sheet Format, Windsor handstamp................................ **£5.00** ☐
896c With Windsor Philatelic Counter handstamp .... **£6.00** ☐
Printed in Sheets of 200 for the first time. Until now only available in Booklets.

897. 1993, 19th October
£4.80 NVI Booklet. First GB Self-adhesive Stamp!
(20 x 1st Class NVI Stamp)

897a	1st Class NVI Self-Adhesive Stamp on illustrated cover, any postmark	£2.00 ☐
897b	With Philatelic Bureau handstamp	£3.00 ☐
897c	With First Day of Issue, Newcastle upon Tyne handstamp	£5.00 ☐
897d	With First Day of Issue, London handstamp (1st NVI Stamp)	£5.00 ☐
897e	With Windsor 19.10.1993 handstamp	£8.00 ☐
897f	With First Non-Value Indicator 1st Self Adhesive Stamp, Windsor	£8.00 ☐
897g	With The First British Self-Adhesive Stamp, Newcastle-upon-Tyne h/s	£8.00 ☐
897h	With British Forces 2320 Postal Services handstamp	£6.50 ☐
897i	With Newcastle-upon-Tyne Philatelic Counter permanent h/s	£7.50 ☐
897j	With UK's First Self Adhesive Stamp... Walsall Security Printers h/s	£8.00 ☐
897k	With Lickey End, Bromsgrove handstamp	£8.50 ☐
897l	Complete Booklet Pane of 20 Stamps, any postmark	£18.00 ☐

Available for a six month trial period, primarily in the Tyne –Tees TV region

FIRST DAY OF ISSUE 19 OCT 1993 1ST LONDON · NEWCASTLE UPON TYNE PHILATELIC COUNTER · The FIRST Non-Value Indicator 1st Self Adhesive Stamp 19 OCT '93 WINDSOR · FIRST DAY OF ISSUE NEWCASTLE UPON TYNE 19 OCT 1993 PEEL & STICK

---

898. 1993, 26th October
19p Olive-Green, 25p Salmon-Pink, 29p Light Grey. New Colours
36p Ultramarine, 38p Red, 41p Stone. New Values

898a	Set on illustrated cover, any postmark	£2.50 ☐
898b	With Philatelic Bureau handstamp	£4.00 ☐
898c	With First Day of Issue, Windsor, Berks handstamp	£5.50 ☐
898d	With First Day of Issue, London handstamp (Lion)	£5.50 ☐
898e	With London SW1 permanent handstamp 2599 (The Palace)	£6.50 ☐
898f	With London Chief Office, Philatelic Counter permanent handstamp	£6.50 ☐
898g	With Windsor Philatelic Counter handstamp (Windsor Castle)	£6.50 ☐
898h	With London FDI handstamp	£4.50 ☐
898i	With Forces/Field Post Office handstamp or cds	£3.50 ☐
898j	With House of Commons, or House of Lords SW1 cds	£25.00 ☐
898k	With Buckingham Palace SW1 cds	£40.00 ☐
898l	With New Postage Rates, From 1 November slogan cancel	£12.00 ☐

LONDON SW1 · LONDON CHIEF OFFICE EC1 PHILATELIC COUNTER · WINDSOR PHILATELIC COUNTER · FIRST DAY OF ISSUE WINDSOR BERKS 26 OCT 1993

New postage rates came into force November 1st, 1993
2nd Class - 19p, 1st Class - 25p

899. 1993, 1st November
New Postage Rates Booklets
-50p Booklet, 1 Pane (2 x 25p + 2 x labels). **Harrison**
-£1 Booklet, 1 Pane (4 x 25p). **Walsall**
-£2 Booklet, 1 Pane (8 x 25p). **Harrison**
-£1.40 Booklet, 1 Pane (4 x 35p). **Walsall**
-£1.64 Booklet, 1 Pane (4 x 41p). **Walsall**

899a 50p Booklet Pane, with any postmark (**£2**), Windsor Philatelic Counter h/s ....**£3.50** ☐
899b £1 Booklet Pane, with any pmk (**£3**), Windsor Philatelic Counter h/s ....**£5.50** ☐
899c £2 Booklet Pane, with any pmk (**£5**), Windsor Philatelic Counter h/s ....**£9.50** ☐
899d £1.40 Booklet Pane, with any pmk (**£4**), Windsor Philatelic Counter h/s ....**£8.00** ☐
899e £1.64 Booklet Pane, with any pmk (**£4**), Windsor Philatelic Counter h/s ....**£8.00** ☐

900. 1993, 1st November
19p, 25p, 35p, 41p, Coil Strips. Vertical Format

900a All four values, Strips of 3 Stamps or more, from new Coils, Windsor P.C. h/s ....**£15.00** ☐

901. 1993, 7th December
25p Salmon-Pink, 30p Sage, 41p Stone. New Values
19p Olive-Green. New Colour
Wales, Scotland, Northern Ireland

901a Set of three covers, each with appropriate stamps and Regional FDI handstamp .....**£16.50** ☐
901b Same with First Day of Issue, London handstamp (National Emblems)....................**£13.50** ☐
901c All three Regions stamps on one cover, Bureau, Windsor, or other cancel...............**£19.50** ☐
901d Wales set with Happy Christmas Nadolig Llawen... handstamp centre, Cardiff ....**£6.50** ☐
901e Scotland set with Scotland and Northern Ireland First Day of Issue handstamp ....**£6.50** ☐
901f Northern Ireland set with Northern Ireland and Scotland First Day of Issue h/s ....**£6.50** ☐
901g Wales or N.Ireland set with Happy Christmas, Please Post Early slogan..................**£12.00** ☐

---

902. 1993, 14th December
4p, 20p, 50p, Enschedé Printing. Elliptical Perfs. 4mm Varnish Band

902a Set of 3 Definitive Stamps, any pmk (**£3**), Windsor Philatelic Counter h/s ....**£6.00** ☐

903 1994, 22nd February
NVI Window Booklets. Walsall. Elliptical Perfs
£1.90 (10 x 2nd NVI)
£2.50 (10 x 1st NVI)

903a Both Panes on illustrated cover, any postmark..**£7.50** ☐
903b With Windsor Philatelic Counter handstamp..**£12.00** ☐

904. 1994, 15th February
Postage Due - To Pay Labels. Elliptical Perfs
1p, 2p, 5p, 10p, 20p, 25p, £1, £1.20, £5. New Design

904a Set on one or more illustrated covers, any postmark .... **£12.00** ☐
904b With St. Edward's Crown Postage Dues... London EC3 handstamp .... **£25.00** ☐
904c With First Day of Issue, To Pay, London EC3 handstamp .... **£25.00** ☐
904d With To Pay Labels, 15th February 1994, Windsor handstamp .... **£30.00** ☐
904e With COD/Surcharges, Bedford handstamp .... **£125.00** ☐

---

905. 1994, 26th April
£1 Booklet, 1 Pane. Elliptical Perfs
(4 x 25p). **First time printed by Harrison**

905a £l Booklet Pane, any postmark (**£4**), Windsor Philatelic Counter h/s .... **£6.50** ☐

906. 1994, 19th July
19p Stamp, PVA Gum without Dextrin. Gum Trial
Printed in Sheet format with Elliptical Perfs by Harrison

906a 19p Stamp, illustrated cover, any pmk (**£3)** Windsor Philatelic Counter h/s .... **£5.00** ☐
This continues the gum trials started in January 1994 on the 35p Age of Steam Stamp.

906A. 1994 to 1996
Enschedé fdc's with Varnished Bands. (4mm or 2mm)

906Aa 29p Light Grey (4mm band) .... 24.05.1994 .... **£10.00** ☐
906Ab 38p Ultramarine (4mm band) .... 24.05.1994 .... **£10.00** ☐
906Ac 35p Old Gold (4mm band) .... 09.06.1994 .... **£15.00** ☐
906Ad 41p Stone (2mm band) .... 23.06.1994 .... **£15.00** ☐
906Ae 50p Sand (2mm band) .... 14.07.1994 .... **£15.00** ☐
906Af 20p Sea Green (2mm band) .... 28.07.1994 .... **£15.00** ☐
906Ag 4p Cobalt-Blue (2mm band) .... 13.09.1994 .... **£15.00** ☐
906Ah 1p Dark Maroon (2mm band) .... 23.11.1994 .... **£10.00** ☐
906Ai 30p Sage-Green (2mm band) .... 23.11.1994 .... **£10.00** ☐
906Aj 10p Light Tan (2mm band) .... 06.02.1995 .... **£15.00** ☐
906Ak 29p Lght Grey (2mm band) .... 31.03.1995 .... **£15.00** ☐
906Al 36p Ultramarine (2mm band) .... 12.05.1995 .... **£15.00** ☐
906Am 35p Old Gold (2mm band) .... 26.06.1995 .... **£15.00** ☐
906An 41p Stone (2mm band) .... 11.08.1995 .... **£15.00** ☐
906Ao 5p Ash-Pink (2mm band) .... 04.10.1996 .... **£7.50** ☐

All QEII Definitives, Dues, Regionals, Booklets, Coils, Graphites and variations in Phosphors, Watermarks, Perfs, Gum Types, Papers, etc. are listed in chronological order, **starting on page 350.**

907. 1994, 26th July
£6.04 Northern Ireland Prestige Stamp Book, 4 Panes. Elliptical Perfs
(4 x 30p Investiture Stamp), (4 x 25p + 6p + 19p Definitives),
(19p + 25p + 30p + 41p N.I. Regionals), (4 x 25p + 2 x 19p + 30p +41p N.I. Regionals)

907a Complete set of 4 entire Panes, on illustrated covers, Philatelic Bureau h/s .... **£16.00** ☐
907b Same with First Day of Issue, Belfast handstamp .... **£25.00** ☐
907c With First Day of Issue, London handstamp (Emblem) .... **£24.00** ☐
907d With Belfast, N. Ireland handstamp .... **£30.00** ☐
907e With The Mountains of Mourne, County Down, N. Ireland handstamp .... **£32.50** ☐
907f With the Giant's Causeway, Co. Antrim, N. Ireland handstamp .... **£32.50** ☐
907g With Northern Ireland permanent handstamp (No. 2636) .... **£27.50** ☐
907h With Northern Ireland Prestige Stamp Book, Belfast N.Ireland h/s .... **£35.00** ☐
907i With Belfast cds .... **£36.50** ☐
907j With Northern Ireland Prestige Stamp Book, On Sale 26 July slogan .... **£42.00** ☐

There are a few other cds postmarks that can be related to this issue. Set prices from **£15**.
Prices are for complete Panes with text. Panes with Stamps only are worth 50% less.

NORTHERN IRELAND
PRESTIGE STAMP
BOOK
ON SALE 26 JULY 1994

---

908. 1994, 27th July
£1 Bank of England Tercentenary Label. Elliptical Perfs
(4 x 1st Class NVI Stamp + Se-tenant Bank Label)

908a Booklet Pane on illustrated cover, any postmark .... **£3.00** ☐
908b With Three Hundred Years, Bank of England, London EC1 h/s .... **£9.50** ☐
908c With Bank of England, London EC2 handstamp .... **£9.50** ☐
908d With The Bank of England, 1664-1994, 300 Years, London EC2 h/s .... **£9.50** ☐
908e With Lombard St. or Britannia cds (Porth or other) .... **£30.00** ☐
908f With Stock Exchange, Pounds, or Moneymore cds .... **£35.00** ☐

The £1 Booklet also includes a 35p pre-printed postcard, this is catalogued at **£2** with any of the above h/s and **£4** with any of the above cds.

---

909. 1994, July
£2.50 WH Smith 'Win a Kite' Promotional Booklet. Walsall
(10 x 1st Class NVI Stamp). **Elliptical Perfs**
Sold from July through September by WH Smith. Actual first day of sale in July unconfirmed. Available in two versions: "You've Won!" (one out of every 50 Booklets printed) and "Better luck next time". Both versions sold by the Philatelic Bureau October 4th 1994.

909a Booklet Pane on (illustrated) cover, any early July postmark .... **£5.00** ☐
909b Same with any early July Swindon cds .... **£6.50** ☐

910. 1994, 9th August..

60p Slate-Blue. New Value. Wallsall

Sold only in £2.40 Booklet (4 x 60p). **Elliptical Perfs**

910a	60p Stamp on illustrated cover, any postmark	£2.00 ☐
910b	With Philatelic Bureau handstamp	£2.50 ☐
910c	With First Day of Issue, Windsor, Berks handstamp	£5.00 ☐
910d	With First Day of Issue, London handstamp (lion)	£5.00 ☐
910e	With London SW1 permanent handstamp 2599 (Buckingham Palace)	£5.00 ☐
910f	With London Chief Office, Philatelic Counter permanent handstamp	£5.00 ☐
910g	With Windsor Philatelic Counter handstamp	£5.50 ☐
910h	With London FDI handstamp (Heathrow Airport cds **£6**)	£3.50 ☐
910i	With Forces/Field Post Office handstamp or cds	£3.50 ☐
910j	With House of Commons, or House of Lords SW1 cds	£18.00 ☐
910k	With Buckingham Palace SW1 cds (Windsor Castle **£40**)	£30.00 ☐

Complete Pane of 4 x 60p adds 50% to above prices.

---

911. 1994, 17th August

Boots Miniature Sheet. Questa

(1st Class NVI Stamp + text). **Elliptical Perfs**

911a	Complete Miniature Sheet, any postmark	£2.00 ☐
911b	With Nottingham, 17th August 1994 handstamp	£5.00 ☐
911c	With Machin NVI... Miniature Sheet Format, Nottingham h/s	£5.00 ☐
911d	With Nottingham Philatelic Counter handstamp	£6.00 ☐
911e	With Nottingham cds, or Wellington cds	£9.00 ☐

Min.Sheet 'free' in Boots greeting card pre-packs. Was also available at 25p from Philatelic Bureau.

---

912. 1995, 31st January

19p 'Reader's Digest' Multi-Value Coil Strip

(3 x 5p + 4p)

912a	Complete Strip on illustrated cover, any postmark	£2.00 ☐
912b	With Windsor Philatelic Counter handstamp	£5.00 ☐
912c	With Reader's Digest Coil, Reader's Digest, Blagrove, Swindon handstamp	£6.50 ☐
912d	With Teamwork London 95, Royal Mail London South East handstamp	£4.50 ☐
912e	With Up Helly AA, Lerwick handstamp	£3.00 ☐

913. 1995, 11th April

2p Enschedé Printing. Elliptical Perfs. 2mm Varnish Band

913a	2p Stamp(s), any pmk (**£1**), Windsor Philatelic Counter handstamp	£3.50 ☐

914. 1995, 25th April

£6 National Trust Prestige Stamp Book, 4 Panes

(6 x 25p National Trust), (3 x 19p + 3 x 25p Regionals),
(10p + 2 x 19p + 2 x 25p + 30p + 31p + 41p Defs), (6 x 19p Defs)

914a Complete set of 4 entire Panes, on illustrated covers, British Philatelic Bureau h/s.. **£16.00** ☐
914b With First Day of Issue, Tintagel Old Post Office, Cornwall handstamp.................... **£18.50** ☐
914c With First Day of Issue, London handstamp (Oak Tree).................... **£24.00** ☐
914d With The National Trust Centenary... Erddig House, Wrexham, Clwyd h/s.................... **£30.00** ☐
914e With The National Trust Centenary... Biddulph Grange, Biddulph h/s.................... **£30.00** ☐
914f With The National Trust Centenary... Windermere, Cumbria handstamp.................... **£30.00** ☐
914g With The National Trust Centenary... Bodiam Castle, Bodiam handstamp.................... **£30.00** ☐
914h With This England, Oakham, Rutland handstamp.................... **£34.00** ☐
914i With Oaktree, Broad Oak, or Sevenoaks cds.................... **£40.00** ☐

Prices are for complete Panes. Stamps only are worth 50% less

---

915. 1995, 16th May

25p Coil Strip. Vertical Format
Printed by Harrison with 2 phos bands. Elliptical Perfs

915a 25p strip of 3 stamps or more, any pmk (**£2**), Windsor Philatelic Counter h/s.................... **£6.00** ☐

916. 1995, 16th May

£1 Vended Stamp Booklet. Harrison

(4 x 25p) 2 phos bands. **Elliptical Perfs**

916a Pane of 4 x 25p with Windsor Philatelic Counter handstamp.................... **£6.00** ☐
916b With Mitchell's Spitfire, Southampton handstamp.................... **£6.00** ☐
916c With R.J. Mitchell Centenary, Stoke-on-Trent handstamp.................... **£6.00** ☐
916d With Designer of Spitfire, BF 2465 PS handstamp.................... **£6.00** ☐
916e With Mitchell 1895-1937, Designer...Stoke-on-Trent handstamp.................... **£6.00** ☐

First machine vended stamp book with 2 band phos 25p stamp.

917. 1995, 16th May

£1 Mitchell Centenary. Commemorative Label (4 x 1st Class NVI + label)

917a Complete Label 4 x 1st Class NVI + Label, any pmk.................... **£2.50** ☐
917b With R.J. Mitchell... Designer of Spitfire, Stoke-on-Trent handstamp.................... **£6.00** ☐
917c With Centenary RJ Mitchell, Aircraft Designer, Stoke-on-Trent handstamp.................... **£6.00** ☐
917d With RJ Mitchell Centenary Year, 1895-1995, Southampton handstamp.................... **£6.00** ☐
917e With Centenary RJ Mitchell's Spitfire, Southampton handstamp.................... **£6.00** ☐
917f With Centenary RJ Mitchell, Designer Spitfire, BF 2465 PS handstamp.................... **£6.00** ☐
917g With VE Day 50th Anniv, BBMF Commemoration, London SWI handstamp.................... **£7.50** ☐
917h With Stoke-on-Trent, Hendon, Castle Bromwich, or Biggin Hill cds.................... **£10.50** ☐

A few other cds pmks can be related to this issue. Prices from £6.

---

918. 1995, 6th June
50p Vended Booklet, 1 Pane (2 x 25p + 2 labels) **2 Phos Bands**
£2. Vended Booklet, 1 Pane (8 x 25p) **2 Phos Bands**

918a Pane of 2 x 25p from 50p Booklet, with Windsor Philatelic Counter handstamp......... **£4.50**
918b Pane of 8 x 25p from £2 Booklet, with Windsor Philatelic Counter handstamp........... **£6.50**
918c Both Panes on one cover, Windsor Philatelic Counter handstamp............................ **£10.00**

919. 1995, 22nd August
£3. New Definitive High Value – Re-etched
£1. In Machin 'Low Values' Size – Enschedé, 2mm Varnish Band

919a Both values on 1 or 2 covers, any postmark.. **£6.00**
919b £1 and £3 Stamps on 2 covers with 2 British Philatelic Bureau handstamps.............. **£8.50**
919c £1 Stamp only with First Day of Issue, Windsor, Berks handstamp............................ **£5.50**
919d £3 Stamp only with First Day of Issue, Carrickfergus handstamp.............................. **£6.50**
919e Both values with First Day of Issue, London Handstamp (lion)................................. **£8.50**
919f Both values, Collect GB First Day Covers 1995... The Definitive Catalogue h/s....... **£14.50**
919g £1 Stamp with £3 High Value Definitive, Carrickfergus handstamp (animal)............... **£8.00**
919h £1 Stamp with £3 High Value Definitive, Carrickfergus handstamp (harp).................. **£8.00**
919i £3 Stamp with Newcastle cds.. **£12.00**
919j Both values with Carrickfergus or Windsor cds... **£20.00**
919k Both values with Queen Elizabeth Ave or Pounds cds.. **£20.00**
919l Both values with House of Commons, or House of Lords SWI cds.............................. **£27.50**
919m Both values with Buckingham Palace SWI cds.. **£35.00**
919n Both values with Windsor Castle cds.. **£42.00**

---

920. 1995, 11th September
Reprint of 'Boots' Min. Sheetlet
(1 x 1st Class NVI Stamp + text). Boots logo removed.

920a New Miniature Sheetlet, any postmark... **£2.00**
920b With Letter 'G' and Windsor, 11 Sep 95 handstamp.. **£5.00**

921. 1995, October - November
Phosphor (Fluor) Colour Change to Blue

921a 19p Scottish Regional, Edinburgh Philatelic Counter h/s, October 3rd........................ **£5.50**
921b 4 x 35p Walsall Booklet, Windsor Philatelic Counter h/s, October 5th......................... **£5.50**
921c 19p Welsh Regional, Cardiff Philatelic Counter h/s, October 19th.............................. **£5.50**
921d 4p Enschede Printing, Windsor Philatelic Counter h/s, October 24th (2mm Band)..... **£5.50**
921e 1st and 2nd Class NVI Stamps, Windsor Philatelic Counter h/s, November 14th....... **£8.00**
921f 2p Enschede Printing, Windsor Philatelic Counter h/s, November 16th (2mm Band). **£5.00**

The Fluor additive colour change is only visible under ultra-violet light.

We have added a new Section on Postal Stationery to the catalogue this year. See pages 462 - 463.

922. 1995, 12th December
£1.90 NVI Booklet, Harrison Printing. Elliptical Perfs
(10 x 2nd Class NVI Stamp)
76p NVI Booklet, Walsall Printing. Elliptical Perfs
(4 x 2nd Class NVI Stamp)

922a £1.90 Booklet Pane, any pmk **£4**. Windsor Philatelic Counter handstamp .... **£8.50** □
922b 72p Booklet Pane, any pmk **£3**. Windsor Philatelic Counter handstamp .... **£6.00** □
Stamps from both Booklets have blue Fluor additive in the Phosphor

923. 1996, 16th January
£1. Vended Booklet (4 x 25 p). **Elliptical Perfs. Questa**
£2. Vended Booklet (8 x 25 p). **Elliptical Perfs. Questa**

923a £1 Booklet Pane, any pmk **£3**. Windsor Philatelic Counter handstamp .... **£5.00** □
£2 Booklet Pane, any pmk **£4**. Windsor Philatelic Counter handstamp .... **£7.50** □
Stamps from both Booklets have blue Fluor additive in the Phosphor

924. 1996, January–February
Phosphor (Fluor) Colour Change to Blue

924a Both 10p and 35p Enschede Printing (2mm Band), Windsor Philatelic h/s. Jan 10th ...... **£5.50** □
924b 38p Enschede Printing, Windsor Philatelic Counter h/s. January 10th .... **£5.00** □
924c 19p N. Ireland Regional, Belfast Philatelic Counter h/s. February 1st .... **£5.00** □
924d Reprint 1995 Greetings Stamps Pane, Windsor Philatelic Counter h/s. February 13th ... **£14.00** □
924e 29p Enschede Printing (2mm Band), Windsor Philatelic Counter h/s. February 14th..... **£5.00** □
924f £2 Booklet Pane (8 x 25p), Elliptical Perf, Windsor Philatelic Counter h/s. Feb 20th.... **£7.50** □
The Fluor additive colour change is only visible under ultra-violet light

925. 1996, 6th February
25p Coil Strip, Horizontal Format
Non-Elliptical Perforation, Blue Fluor Additive in Phosphor

925a 25p Strip of 3 or more stamps from new Coil. Windsor handstamp .... **£5.50** □

926. 1996, 19th February
£2.50 Disney Promotional Booklet
(10 x 1st Class NVI Stamp) **Elliptical Perfs**

926a Booklet Pane on illustrated cover, any postmark **£3.00**. Windsor PC h/s .... **£7.50** □

927. 1996, 5th March
£1.50 High Value Definitive. Harrison Printing – Re-etched
Gum Change from PVA Dextrin to PVA

927a £1.50 Stamp on illustrated cover, any postmark **£4**. Cardiff or Windsor pmk .... **£8.00** □

928. 1996, March–April
Phosphor (Fluor) Colour Change to Blue

928a Both 1p and 50p, Windsor Philatelic Counter h/s. March 5th (2mm Band) .... **£5.00** □
928b 25p N. Ireland, Belfast Philatelic Counter h/s. March 5th .... **£5.00** □
928c Both 5p and 20p Enschede, with Windsor Philatelic Counter h/s. March 26th (2mm).. **£5.00** □
928d 6p Enschede, with Windsor Philatelic Counter h/s, March 26th (2mm Band) .... **£5.00** □
928e 30p Enschede, with Windsor Philatelic Counter h/s, March 26th (2mm Band) .... **£5.00** □
928f 41p Welsh Regional, Cardiff Philatelic Counter handstamp, April 30th.......... **£6.00** □
The Fluor additive colour change is only visible under ultra-violet light

929. 1996, 19th March
Olympic/Paralympic Airmail Booklets. Walsall
£1.64 (4 x 41p). **£2.40** (4 x 60p). **Elliptical Perfs.**
Phosphor (Fluor) Colour Change to Blue

929a £1.64 Booklet Pane, Heathrow Airport or Windsor handstamp .... **£7.00** ☐
929b £2.40 booklet Pane, Heathrow Airport or Windsor handstamp .... **£8.00** ☐

The Fluor additive colour change is only visible under ultra-violet light

930. 1996, 16th April
£1 HM The Queen's 70th Birthday Commemorative Label
(4 x 1st Class NVI Stamp + Special Label). **Walsall. Elliptical Perfs**

930a Booklet Pane on illustrated cover, any postmark .... **£2.50** ☐
930b With 70th Birthday Celebrations, Windsor handstamp .... **£5.50** ☐
930c With London or Windsor Philatelic Counter handstamp .... **£5.50** ☐
930d With 70th Birthday Celebrations, London SWI handstamp .... **£5.50** ☐
930e With 70th Birthday Celebrations, Balmoral, Crathie handstamp .... **£5.50** ☐
930f With 70th Birthday Celebrations, Westminster Abbey, London SWI h/s .... **£5.50** ☐
930g With QEII 70th Birthday Celebrations, Bruton Street, London WI h/s .... **£5.50** ☐
930h With Her Majesty The Queen 70th...Queen Street, London WI h/s .... **£5.50** ☐
930i With 70th Birthday Celebrations, HM Queen Elizabeth II, Windsor h/s .... **£5.50** ☐
930j With Queen Street, Queen Elizabeth Street, Queen Elizabeth Ave. cds .... **£12.00** ☐
930k With Buckingham Palace SWI cds .... **£35.00** ☐
930l With Windsor Castle cds (Windsor cds **£12**) .... **£45.00** ☐

WINDSOR PHILATELIC COUNTER

70th BIRTHDAY CELEBRATIONS WINDSOR 16 APR 96

70th Birthday Celebrations H.M. QUEEN ELIZABETH II 16·4·96 WINDSOR Berkshire

70th BIRTHDAY CELEBRATIONS 16 APRIL 96 BALMORAL CRATHIE

70th BIRTHDAY CELEBRATIONS 16 APRIL 1996 LONDON SW1

QUEEN ELIZABETH II 70th Birthday Celebrations 16·4·96 BRUTON STREET·LONDON W1

Westminster Abbey·London SW1 70th 16·4·96 BIRTHDAY CELEBRATIONS

LONDON SW1

930A. 1994, Aug - Dec
Re-etched High Value Definitives – Harrison Printing

930Aa £1.00, any postmark .... 02.12.1994 .... **£40.00** ☐
930Ab £1.50, any postmark .... 26.10.1994 .... **£40.00** ☐
930Ac £2.00, any postmark .... 15.11.1994 .... **£45.00** ☐
930Ad £5.00, any postmark .... 16.08.1994 .... **£180.00** ☐

All prices in this catalogue are for clean covers, with undamaged stamps and clear postmarks.

Anything less is worth less!

931. 1996, 14th May

£6.48 European Football Prestige Stamp Book, 4 Panes

(4 x 19p), (4 x 25p), (2 x 35p + 2 x 41p + 2 x 60p) New Football Stamps
(8 x 25p + Label) Two each England and Regional Definitive Stamps

931a	Complete Set of 4 Entire Panes on illustrated covers, Philatelic Bureau h/s	**£12.00** ☐
931b	With First Day of Issue, Manchester handstamp	**£16.00** ☐
931c	With First Day of Issue, Wembley handstamp	**£20.00** ☐
931d	With First Day of Issue, London (Footballer) handstamp	**£16.00** ☐
931e	With Dixie Dean, Everton FC . . . Liverpool handstamp	**£35.00** ☐
931f	With Duncan Edwards . . . Manchester United FC Museum, Manchester h/s	**£35.00** ☐
931g	With Billy Wright, Wolves, Wolverhampton handstamp	**£35.00** ☐
931h	With Bobby Moore, West Ham, London E13 handstamp	**£35.00** ☐
931i	With British Football Heroes, Manchester handstamp (2 versions, same text)	**£35.00** ☐
931j	With Wembley, May 14th handstamp (Football)	**£35.00** ☐
931k	With Danny Blanchflower, Tottenham, London N17 handstamp	**£38.50** ☐
931l	With British Football Heroes, Tottenham, London N17 handstamp	**£35.00** ☐
931m	With England World Cup Winners, 30th Anniversary, London E1 handstamp	**£35.00** ☐
931n	With British Football Heroes, Everton, Liverpool handstamp	**£35.00** ☐
931o	With British Football Heroes, Wembley, Middx handstamp	**£35.00** ☐
931p	With RNLI Official Postmark, Football Legends . . . Wembley handstamp	**£35.00** ☐
931q	With Collect GB First Day Covers Catalogue, Winning ..That's our goal, Wembley h/s	**£35.00** ☐
931r	With Evening Standard, Wembley handstamp	**£35.00** ☐
931s	With Arsenal FA Cup Winners, League Champions, Highbury, London N5 h/s	**£35.00** ☐
931t	With Brewers Fayre, Wembley, May 14 handstamp	**£35.00** ☐
931u	With Football Heroes, Wolverhampton handstamp	**£35.00** ☐
931v	With British Football Heroes, Wolverhampton handstamp	**£35.00** ☐
931w	With Football Heroes, The Mail on Sunday, Stoke-on-Trent, Staffs handstamp	**£35.00** ☐
931x	With Football Heroes, Stoke-on-Trent, Staffordshire handstamp	**£35.00** ☐
931y	With Wolverhampton Wanderers Football Club, Wolverhampton handstamp	**£35.00** ☐
931z	With A Celebration of Football, Wembley handstamp	**£35.00** ☐
931aa	With Celebration of Football, Autographed Editions, Wembley handstamp	**£35.00** ☐
931bb	With 1966 England Winners, Wembley handstamp	**£35.00** ☐
931cc	With Wembley 14th May, 1996, Middlesex handstamp	**£35.00** ☐
931dd	With Football Legends, Stoke-on-Trent, Staffs handstamp	**£35.00** ☐
931ee	With Football Legends, Bolton, Lancashire handstamp	**£35.00** ☐
931ff	With Preston North End FC, Preston, Lancs handstamp	**£35.00** ☐
931gg	With Jackie Milburn, Football Legend, Newcastle upon Tyne handstamp	**£35.00** ☐
931hh	With 60th Anniv. 1st FA Cup Semi-Final, Grimsby handstamp	**£35.00** ☐
931ii	With Hull City, 50 Years at Boothferry Park, Hull handstamp	**£35.00** ☐
931jj	With Wembley or Wembley Park cds	**£45.00** ☐
931kk	With any of the above Football towns cds	**£38.50** ☐

Many Sets of Booklet Panes were cancelled with a combination of the above postmarks (**£18**).
Prices are for complete Panes. Stamps only are worth 50% less

932. 1996, 25th June
20p Lt. Green, 26p Rust. Harrison. Colour Change
31p Purple, 37p Rhododendron, 39p Hot Pink,
43p Dark Brown, 63p Emerald Green. Enschede. Colour Change. 2mm Band
All Stamps have Blue fluor additive. Elliptical Perfs

932a Set on illustrated cover, any postmark .... **£3.50** ☐
932b With Philatelic Bureau handstamp.......... **£5.50** ☐
932c With First Day of Issue, Windsor handstamp.......... **£7.50** ☐
932d With First Day of Issue, London (lion) handstamp.......... **£7.50** ☐
932e With London or Windsor Philatelic Counter handstamp .... **£7.50** ☐
932f With Windsor cds **£15**. Buckingham Palace cds .... **£35.00** ☐
932g With House of Commons, or House of Lords cds .... **£25.00** ☐
932h With Windsor Castle cds.......... **£38.00** ☐
932i With Please Remember New Postage Rates... Slogan cancel.......... **£16.50** ☐

Postage rates were increased from July 8th, 1996.

933. 1996, 8th July
37p, 43p, Coil Strips. Vertical Format
Elliptical Perfs. Harrison. Blue Fluor Additive

933a Both Values, strips of 3 Stamps or more, Windsor Philatelic Counter handstamp .... **£6.00** ☐

934. 1996, 8th July
£1. Vended Booklet. Colour Change. Questa
(2 x 1p + 1 x 20p + 3 x 26p + 2 labels)
£2. Vended Booklet. Colour Change. Questa
(1 x 20p + 7 x 26p)
£1.48 Booklet. Colour Change. Walsall (4 x 37p)
£2.52 Booklet. Colour Change. Walsall (4 x 63p)
All Stamps have Blue Fluor Additive. Elliptical Perfs

934a £1 Booklet Pane, any postmark **£2** Windsor Philatelic Counter handstamp.......... **£3.50** ☐
934b £2 Booklet Pane, any postmark **£4**. Windsor Philatelic Counter handstamp.......... **£5.50** ☐
934c £1.48 Booklet Pane, any postmark **£4**. Windsor Philatelic Counter handstamp.......... **£6.50** ☐
934d £2.52 Booklet Pane, any postmark **£5**. Windsor Philatelic Counter handstamp.......... **£7.50** ☐
934e Any Pane with New Booklets for Postal Rate Change, Windsor handstamp .... **£14.00** ☐

935. 1996, 23rd July
20p Lt Green, 26p Rust, 31p Purple, 37p Rhododendron,
39p Hot Pink, 43p Dark Brown, 63p Emerald Green
New Regional Colour Changes. Wales, Scotland, N.Ireland
Questa Printing. Elliptical Perfs. Blue Fluor Additive

935a Set of three covers, with appropriate stamps and regional FDI handstamp .... **£22.50** ☐

A second FDI Scotland handstamp and a combined Scotland/N. Ireland handstamp were also available for this issue.

936. 1996, 17th September
£5 High Value. Gum Change to PVA only. Harrison. Re-etched

936a £5 on illustrated cover, any pmk **£9**. Windsor Philatelic Counter handstamp .... **£20.00** ☐

937. 1996, 12th December
63p Coil Strip
Elliptical Perfs. Harrison. Blue Fluor Additive

937a Strip of 3 Stamps or more, Windsor Philatelic Counter handstamp .... **£6.00** ☐
937b With Heathrow permanent handstamp.......... **£4.50** ☐

938. 1997, 12th February
£1.04 Hong Kong Commemorative Label
(4 x 1st Class NVI Stamp & Label)
938a Complete Commemorative Label, any postmark .... **£2.50** ☐
938b With Farewell to 99 Years in Hong Kong, Parliament Sq, London SW1 handstamp .... **£7.50** ☐
938c With Hong Kong Farewell, London SW1 handstamp .... **£7.50** ☐
938d With Hong Kong 1898-1997, Chinatown, London W1 handstamp .... **£7.50** ☐
938e With Hong Kong Farewell 1898-1997 Chinatown, London W1 handstamp .... **£7.50** ☐
938f With BFPO Hong Kong cds .... **£32.50** ☐
938g With Victoria Road cds, Queen Victoria Road cds, or Victoria Park cds .... **£25.00** ☐

939. 1997 18th March
Self-adhesive Stamps in Vertical Coils
(1st Class and 2nd Class NV1 Stamps)
939a Both Stamps on illustrated cover, any postmark .... **£2.00** ☐
939b With First Day of Issue, British Philatelic Bureau handstamp .... **£4.50** ☐
939c With First Day of Issue, Glasgow handstamp .... **£6.00** ☐
939d With First Day of Issue, London handstamp .... **£6.00** ☐
939e With Royal Mail Windsor handstamp .... **£7.00** ☐
939f With Self Adhesive Low Value Definitive Stamps, Windsor handstamp .... **£7.50** ☐
939g With Self Adhesive Stamps, 1st & 2nd NVI's, Windsor handstamp .... **£7.50** ☐

940. 1997, April-November
Gravure Printing by Harrison of Low Values
940a 1p, 6p, 43p, 50p, £1, Royal Mail Windsor handstamp .... April 1st .... **£7.50** ☐
940b 20p with Royal Mail Windsor handstamp .... April 29th .... **£4.00** ☐
940c 2p, 4p, 5p, 10p, 30p, 39p, with Royal Mail Windsor handstamp .... May 27th .... **£6.00** ☐
940d 31p, 37p, 63p, with Royal Mail Windsor handstamp .... Aug. 26th .... **£6.50** ☐
940e 26p with Royal Mail Windsor handstamp .... Nov. 18th .... **£4.50** ☐
940f All five covers above, any postmark (**£12**), Windsor handstamp .... **£28.00** ☐

941. 1997, 21st April
£2.60 NVI Booklet. Harrison, Gravure Printed
£2.60 NVI Booklet. Walsall, Gravure Printed
(10 x 1st Class NVI Stamp) **Elliptical Perfs. Gold Printing**
941a Complete Pane of Harrison or Walsall version, any postmark .... **£3.00** ☐
941b With First Day of Issue, British Philatelic Bureau handstamp .... **£6.50** ☐
941c With First Day of Issue, Windsor, Berks handstamp .... **£8.00** ☐
941d With any one of the special handstamps created for the Golden Wedding Issue and listed in the Commemoratives Section .... **£10.00** ☐
This Gold NVI Stamp was also issued in sheets of 200, together with a 26p Gold Stamp

942. 1997, 29th April
1st and 2nd Class NVI Coil Strips. Vertical Format. Harrison
942a Both Values, Strips of 3 Stamps or more, Royal Mail Windsor permanent h/s .... **£8.00** ☐

943. 1997, 29th April
£2.00 NVI Booklet. Harrison
(10 x 2nd Class NVI Stamp)
943a Complete Pane with any postmark .... **£3.50** ☐
943b Complete Pane with Royal Mail Windsor permanent handstamp .... **£8.50** ☐

944. 1997, 1st July
20p, 26p, 37p, 63p. Walsall Printing. Scotland, N. Ireland
20p, 26p, 37p, 63p. Walsall Printing. Wales (with 'p' dropped)

944a Set of three covers, each with appropriate stamps and regional postmark .... **£9.00** ☐

945. 1997, 29th July
£1.50, £2, £3, £5. New Enschede Printing. Re-etched

945a Set of 4 stamps with Royal Mail Windsor permanent handstamp.............................. **£16.50** ☐
945b With Windsor, Edinburgh, Caernarfon, or Carrickfergus h/s .... **£20.00** ☐

946. 1997, 26th August **37p, 43p Coil Strips. Vertical Format**

946a Both values, strips of 3 or more stamps, any pmk (**£4**), Windsor permanent h/s.......... **£8.50** ☐

947. 1997, 26th August
80p NVI Booklet (4 x 2nd Class NVI Stamp). **Walsall. Gravure**
£1.04 NVI Booklet (4 x 1st Class NVI Stamp). **Walsall. Gravure**
£1.48 Booklet (4 x 37p). **Air mail post card rate. Walsall. Gravure**
£2.52 booklet (4 x 63p). **Air mail letter rate. Walsall. Gravure**

947a Set of 4 Booklet Panes, any pmk (**£9**), Windsor permanent handstamp.................... **£17.50** ☐

948. 1997, 23rd September
£6.15 BBC 75th Anniversary Prestige Stamp Book
(3 x 20p + 3 x 26p), (3 x 26p Regionals + 3 x 37p Regional)
(4 x 1st NVI + 4 x 26p Gold + Label), (4 x 20p Childrens TV Issue)

948a Complete set of 4 entire Panes on illustrated covers, British Philatelic Bureau h/s .... **£16.00** ☐
948b With First Day of Issue, London W.I. handstamp, or London (microphone) h/s .... **£25.00** ☐
948c With First Day of Issue, Birmingham (radio) handstamp .... **£28.00** ☐
948d With BBC Birmingham, The Archers . . . handstamp .... **£35.00** ☐
948e With Celebrating 75 Years of the BBC, London W.I. handstamp .... **£30.00** ☐
948f With Celebrating 75 Years of the BBC, London W12 handstamp.............................. **£30.00** ☐
948g With Celebrating 75 Years of the BBC, Glasgow G12 handstamp .... **£30.00** ☐
948h With Celebrating 75 Years of the BBC, Cardiff CF5 handstamp .... **£30.00** ☐
948i With Celebrating 75 Years of the BBC, Belfast BT2 handstamp................................ **£30.00** ☐
948j With The Queens Stamps, National Postal Museum . . . handstamp .... **£30.00** ☐
948k With BBC Birmingham, BBC 75th Anniversary handstamp... **£30.00** ☐
948l With 75 Years of the BBC, BBC . . . House, London W12 handstamp .... **£38.00** ☐
948m With 75th Anniv. of the BBC, Autographed Editions, Shepherd's Bush h/s .... **£32.00** ☐

Prices are for complete Panes. Stamps only are worth 50% less

949. 1997, 21st October
Commonwealth Heads of Government Meeting. Commemorative Label
(4 x 1st Class NVI Stamp + Label). **Walsall. Printed Litho.**

949a Complete Label with Royal Mail Windsor permanent handstamp................................ **£6.00** ☐
949b With Commonwealth Edinburgh 97, Edinburgh EHI handstamp .... **£7.50** ☐
949c With Commonwealth Edinburgh 97, Edinburgh handstamp... **£7.50** ☐
949d With Commonwealth Heads of Government Meeting, Edinburgh handstamp .... **£7.50** ☐
949e With Commonwealth Heads of Government Meeting (building), Edinburgh h/s........... **£7.50** ☐

950. 1997, 18th November

£2.60 NVI Booklet. Walsall and Harrison printings

(10 x 1st Class NVI Stamp)

950a Both printings complete Panes with any pmk (**£4**), Windsor permanent handstamp..**£12.00** ☐

951. 1998, 10th March

£7.49 The Wilding Story Prestige Stamp Book

The Book contains 4 Panes of Wilding Decimal Stamps

(9 x 26p Wilding), (6 x 20p Wilding) (3 x 26p + 3 x 37p Wildings)

(4 x 20p + 2 x 26p + 2 x 37p Wildings)

951a Complete set of 4 entire Panes on illustrated covers, British Philatelic Bureau h/s ....**£16.00** ☐

951b With First Day of Issue, London SWI handstamp........**£22.00** ☐

951c With First Day of Issue, Stamp Show 2000, London handstamp........**£26.00** ☐

951d With The Definitive Portrait, Westminster Abbey, London SW1 handstamp........**£30.00** ☐

951e With The Definitive Portrait, Windsor handstamp........**£30.00** ☐

951f With The Definitive Portrait, HM QE11, London W1, Portman Square handstamp.....**£30.00** ☐

951g With The Definitive Portrait, HM QE11, London W5, Bond Street handstamp........**£30.00** ☐

951h With The Definitive Portrait, HM QE11, London W8, Earl's Court handstamp........**£30.00** ☐

951i With The Definitive Portrait, HM QE11, London ECI, King Edward St. handstamp.....**£30.00** ☐

951j With The Definitive Portrait, HM QE11, Longford, Gloucester handstamp........**£30.00** ☐

951k With Queen Alice, Lewis Carroll Centenary Year, Windsor handstamp........**£34.00** ☐

951l Cover with 20p, 26p, 37p, new Wildings, any of above handstamps........**£7.50** ☐

The new Wilding decimal values were previously issued as 5d, 6d and 7d Stamps in 1953/54

Prices are for complete Panes. Stamps only are worth 50% less

952. 1998, 6th April

1st and 2nd Class NVI Self-adhesive Stamps

Vertical Format. Elliptical Perfs. Enschede Printing

952a Both Stamps on illustrated cover, Royal Mail Windsor permanent handstamp........**£5.00** ☐

952b With Self-Adhesive Stamps, 1st & 2nd NVIs, Glasgow handstamp........**£6.50** ☐

952c With Self-Adhesive Stamps, 1st & 2nd NVIs, Windsor handstamp........**£6.50** ☐

952d With Self-Adhesive Stamps, Vertical format, Windsor handstamp........**£6.50** ☐

952e With 1st & 2nd NVI Self-Adhesive . . . HMS Watchman, Clydebank handstamp........**£6.50** ☐

See pages 454 - 457 for prices on GB fdc Overprints since 1893

953. 1998, 22nd June

1st and 2nd class NVI Self-adhesive Stamps

Vertical Format. Elliptical Perfs. Walsall Printing

953a Both Stamps on illustrated cover, Royal Mail Windsor permanent handstamp........**£6.00** ☐
953b With Self-Adhesive Stamps, Vertical format, Windsor handstamp..........................**£7.50** ☐
953c With 'dagger perfs', both Stamps on one cover, any postmark...........................**£375.00** ☐

954. 1998, 13th October

£6.16 Speed Prestige Stamp Book. 4 panes

954a Complete set of 4 entire Panes on illustrated covers, British Philatelic Bureau h/s ..**£18.50** ☐
954b With First Day of Issue, Chislehurst handstamp...**£25.00** ☐
954c With First Day of Issue, London handstamp...**£25.00** ☐
954d With Breaking Barriers (flags), Pendine, Carmarthen handstamp..........................**£30.00** ☐
954e With Breaking Barriers, Duxford, Cambridge handstamp..**£30.00** ☐
954f With Breaking Barriers, Beaulieu, Hampshire handstamp.......................................**£30.00** ☐
954g With Breaking Barriers, Coniston Water, Coniston handstamp ....**£30.00** ☐
954h With Breaking Barriers, Chislehurst handstamp ....**£30.00** ☐
954i With World Land Speed Records, Speed, Pendine handstamp.............................**£32.00** ☐

955. 1998, 14th November

£1.04 Prince of Wales Commemorative Label

(4 x 1st Class Stamp + Label)

955a Complete Commemorative Label, any postmark...**£2.00** ☐
955b With HRH The Prince of Wales, 50th Birthday, Tetbury handstamp.........................**£6.00** ☐
955c With 50th Birthday Tribute, HRH The Prince of Wales, Tetbury handstamp ....**£7.00** ☐
955d With 50th Birthday Tribute, HRH The Prince of Wales, Balmoral handstamp..........**£7.00** ☐
955e With 50th Birthday Tribute, HRH The Prince of Wales, Windsor handstamp...........**£7.00** ☐
955f With 50th Birthday Tribute, HRH Prince Charles ...Caernarfon handstamp ....**£7.00** ☐
955g With 50th Birthday, HRH The Prince of Wales, The Mall, London handstamp ....**£7.00** ☐
955h With 50th Birthday Tribute, The Prince of Wales, Balmoral, Crathie handstamp.....**£7.00** ☐
955i With 50th Birthday, HRH The Prince of Wales, St. Paul's, London handstamp......**£7.00** ☐
955j With HRH The Prince of Wales on his 50th Birthday...Dartmouth handstamp........**£7.00** ☐

HRH THE PRINCE OF WALES · TETBURY · 50TH BIRTHDAY · 14 NOV 1998

50th Birthday Tribute H.R.H. THE PRINCE OF WALES Windsor 14·11·98

BALMORAL·BALLATER·ABERDEENSHIRE 50th Birthday Tribute H.R.H. THE PRINCE OF WALES 14·11·98

H.R.H. THE PRINCE OF WALES 50th BIRTHDAY 14/11/98 ST PAULS, LONDON, EC4

956. 1998, 1st December

£1 NVI Booklet (10 x 2nd Class NVI Stamp). **Questa. Gravure**

£2.60 NVI Booklet (10 x 1st Class NVI Stamp). **Questa. Gravure**

£1.00 (3 x 26p + 1 x 20p + 2 x 1p + 2 labels) **Questa. Gravure**

£2.00 (7 x 26p + 1 x 20p) **Questa. Gravure**

956a Set of 4 Booklet Panes, any pmk (**£10**), Windsor permanent handstamp ....**£18.00** ☐

All prices in this catalogue are for clean covers,
with undamaged stamps and clear postmarks.

957. 1999, 19th January
£1.20 NVI Booklet (4 x 'E' Stamp)**. Walsall. Gravure**

957a Booklet Pane on illustrated cover, any postmark .... **£2.00** ☐
957b With First Day of Issue, British Philatelic Bureau handstamp .... **£4.00** ☐
957c With First Day of Issue (lions), Windsor, Berks handstamp .... **£6.50** ☐
957d With First Day of Issue, Windsor, Berks handstamp .... **£6.50** ☐
957e With First Day of Issue, Diwrnod Cyhoeddi Cyntaf, Windsor handstamp .... **£6.50** ☐
957f With First Day of Issue (lions), Diwrnod Cyhoeddi Cyntaf, Windsor, Berks h/s .... **£6.50** ☐
957g With European NVI, Waterloo Station, London handstamp .... **£7.50** ☐
957h With European NVI, Ashford, Kent handstamp .... **£7.50** ☐

958. 1999, 16th February
£7.54 Profile on Print Prestige Stamp Book
(8 x 1st NVI), (4 x 1st NVI), (4 x 1st NVI), (4 x 1st NVI), (9 x 1st NVI),

958a Complete Set of 5 entire Panes on illustrated covers, British Philatelic Bureau h/s.. **£20.00** ☐
958b With First Day of Issue, City of Westminster, London SW1 handstamp .... **£25.00** ☐
958c With First Day of Issue, London SW1 handstamp .... **£28.00** ☐
958d With First Day of Issue, Diwrnod Cyhoeddi Cyntaf, London SW1 handstamp .... **£35.00** ☐
958e With First Day of Issue, (palace) Diwrnod Cyhoeddi Cyntaf, London SW1 h/s .... **£35.00** ☐
958f With Profile on Print, HM Queen Elizabeth II, High Wycombe handstamp .... **£35.00** ☐
958g With Profile on Print, HM Queen Elizabeth II...Walsall handstamp .... **£35.00** ☐
958h With Profile on Print, HM Queen Elizabeth II, Stoke-on-Trent handstamp .... **£35.00** ☐
958i With Profile on Print, HM Queen Elizabeth II, Millbank, London handstamp .... **£35.00** ☐
958j With Profile on Print, HM Queen Elizabeth II, Piccadilly, London handstamp .... **£35.00** ☐
958k With Profile on Print, HM Queen Elizabeth II, Parkhouse St., London h/s..... .... **£35.00** ☐
958l With The Machin Portrait, Stoke-on-Trent, East Staffordshire handstamp .... **£35.00** ☐
958m With Profile on Print, Prestige Stamp Book, Windsor handstamp .... **£35.00** ☐

This Stamp Book included 1 Pane of large White 1st NVI self-adhesives, and 1 Pane of large size Black 1st NVI stamps. These are catalogued separately below.

959. 1999, 16th February
Large Size 1st NVI. From Profile on Print Prestige Stamp Book
Embossed in White on Self-adhesive Paper. Walsall

959a 1st NVI White Embossed Self-adhesive Stamp on illustrated cover, any postmark .... **£2.50** ☐
959b With any handstamp from Profile on Print Prestige Stamp Book .... **£7.50** ☐

960. 1999, 16th February
Large Size 1st NVI. From Profile on Print Prestige Stamp Book
Recess Printed in Black. Enschede

960a 1st NVI Black Stamp, on illustrated cover, with any postmark ....**£2.50** ☐
960b With any handstamp from Profile on Print Prestige Stamp Book ....**£7.00** ☐

961. 1999, 9th March
£1.50, £2, £3, £5. Small Format Definitives

961a All four values on illustrated cover, any postmark ....**£12.50** ☐
961b With First Day of Issue, British Philatelic Bureau handstamp ....**£15.50** ☐
961c With First Day of Issue, Windsor, Berks handstamp ....**£17.50** ☐
961d With First Day of Issue, Windsor, handstamp...**£17.50** ☐
961e With First Day of Issue, (lions), plus Welsh text, Windsor, Berks handstamp........**£20.00** ☐
961f With First Day of Issue, plus Welsh text, Windsor handstamp..............................**£20.00** ☐
961g With H.M. Queen Elizabeth II, High Value Definitve...London EC1 h/s.................**£20.00** ☐
961h With London SW1 (lions) handstamp ....**£20.00** ☐
961i With London W1 (lions) handstamp..**£20.00** ☐
961j With Edinburgh (lion) handstamp...**£20.00** ☐
961k With Cardiff (dragon) handstamp...**£20.00** ☐
961l With Belfast (hand) handstamp...**£20.00** ☐
961m With Balmoral (lion) Ballater, Aberdeenshire handstamp ....**£20.00** ☐
961n With Conwy (dragon) handstamp ....**£20.00** ☐
961o With Men of Letters, Dylan Thomas, Swansea handstamp...................................**£20.00** ☐
961p With Men of Letters, Robert Burns, Alloway, Ayr handstamp ....**£20.00** ☐
961q With Men of Letters, William Shakespeare, Stratford-upon-Avon handstamp ....**£20.00** ☐
961r With Men of Letters, Jonathan Swift, Kilroot, Carrickfergus handstamp ....**£20.00** ☐

962. 1999, 20th April
7p Lt.Grey, 38p Ultramarine, 44p Stone, 64p Sea Green. New Values

962a All four values on illustrated cover, any postmark ....**£2.50** ☐
962b With First Day of Issue, British Philatelic Bureau handstamp ....**£4.00** ☐
962c With First Day of Issue, Windsor, Berks handstamp ....**£6.00** ☐
962d With First Day of Issue, Windsor handstamp ....**£6.00** ☐
962e With First Day of Issue, (lions), plus Welsh text, Windsor, Berks handstamp..........**£6.00** ☐
962f With First Day of Issue, plus Welsh text, Windsor handstamp................................**£6.00** ☐
962g With Low Value Definitives, London SW1 handstamp...**£7.50** ☐

See page 45 onwards for all QEII Commemorative Issues

963. 1999, 26th April
£1 Booklet (1 x 1p + 1 x 2p + 1 x 19p + 3 x 26p + 2 labels). **Questa**
£2 Booklet (1 x 19p + 7 x 26p). **Questa**
£1.52 Booklet (4 x 38p). **Walsall**
£2.56 Booklet (4 x 64p). **Walsall**

963a Complete Set of all 4 Booklet Panes, with any postmark........ **£10.50** ☐
963b With Royal Mail Windsor permanent handstamp........ **£24.00** ☐

964. 1999, 12th May
Special Retail Booklet No.1. 2 Panes
(26p Pilgrim Fathers + 26p Mill Towns), (8 x 1st NVI)

964a Special Commemorative Stamps Pane only, with any postmark........ **£4.00** ☐
964b With Royal Mail Windsor permanent handstamp........ **£6.00** ☐
964c With Millennium Retail Book...Windsor, Berks handstamp........ **£6.00** ☐
964d With Millennium Booklet, A Tribute to the Pilgrim Fathers, Plymouth h/s........ **£6.00** ☐
964e With Millennium Booklet, Greenwich, London SE10 handstamp........ **£6.00** ☐
964f With Millennium Booklet...Bolton, Lancs handstamp........ **£6.00** ☐
964g With Millennium Booklet, Edinburgh handstamp........ **£6.00** ☐

965. 1999, 12th May
£1.04 Berlin Airlift Commemorative Label
(4 x 1st NVI Stamp + Label)

965a Complete Label, any postmark........ **£2.50** ☐
965b With 50th Anniversary, Ending of the Berlin Airlift, Oakington handstamp........ **£6.50** ☐
965c With 50th Anniversary, Ending of the Berlin Airlift, Brize Norton handstamp........ **£6.50** ☐
965d With 50th Anniversary, Ending of the Berlin Airlift, Watford handstamp........ **£6.50** ☐
965e With 50th Anniversary, Ending of the Berlin Airlift, Lyneham RAF Station h/s........ **£6.50** ☐
965f With 50th Anniversary Berlin Airlift, Brize Norton, Carterton handstamp........ **£6.50** ☐
965g With 50th Anniversary Berlin Airlift...RAF Abingdon handstamp........ **£6.50** ☐
965h With Berlin Airlift, A Tribute to the RAF, Oakington, Cambs handstamp........ **£6.50** ☐
965i With Berlin Airlift, RAF Lyneham Chippenham, Wiltshire handstamp........ **£6.50** ☐
965j With Berlin Airlift 48-49, Settle Road, London E13 handstamp........ **£6.50** ☐
965k With Berlin Airlift, RAF Museum, Grahame Parkway, London handstamp........ **£6.50** ☐

Try to collect covers with a relevant postmark.
Recent Issues, without this, are of little value in today's market place.

966. 1999, 8th June
19p Olive Green (re-issued value), 38p ultramarine, 64p Lt. Jade
Northern Ireland. Gravure. Walsall

966a	Set of 3 Regional Stamps, any Northern Ireland postmark	**£2.50** ☐
966b	With First Day of Issue, British Philatelic Bureau handstamp	**£4.50** ☐
966c	With First Day of Issue (hand), Belfast handstamp	**£6.00** ☐
966d	With First Day of Issue, Belfast handstamp	**£6.00** ☐
966e	With Walsall, West Midlands handstamp	**£7.50** ☐

967. 1999, 8th June
First Scottish Pictorial Stamps. Gravure. Walsall
2nd NVI (saltire), 1st NVI (lion), E Stamp (thistle), 64p (tartan)

967a	All 4 Stamps on illustrated cover, any Scottish postmark	**£2.50** ☐
967b	With First Day of Issue, British Philatelic Bureau handstamp	**£3.50** ☐
967c	With First Day of Issue, Edinburgh handstamp	**£4.50** ☐
967d	With First Day of Issue, The People of the Country...Edinburgh h/s	**£4.50** ☐
967e	With First Pictorial Issue, Lochawe, Dalmally handstamp	**£6.00** ☐
967f	With First Pictorial Issue, Glencoe, Ballachulish handstamp	**£6.00** ☐
967g	With First Pictorial Issue, Glasgow handstamp	**£6.00** ☐
967h	With First Pictorial Issue, Balmoral, Ballater, Aberdeenshire handstamp	**£6.00** ☐
967i	With First Pictorial Issue, Edinburgh, Scotland handstamp	**£6.00** ☐
967j	With First Pictorial Issue, Braemar, Ballater, handstamp	**£6.00** ☐
967k	With New Scottish Definitives (thistle), Edinburgh handstamp	**£6.00** ☐
967l	With The First Scottish Definitives (lion), Edinburgh handstamp	**£6.00** ☐
967m	With Walsall, West Midlands handstamp	**£7.50** ☐

968. 1999, 8th June
First Welsh Pictorial Stamps. Gravure. Walsall
2nd NVI (leek), 1st NVI (dragon), E Stamp (daffodil), 64p (feathers)

968a	All 4 Stamps on illustrated cover, any Welsh handstamp	**£2.50** ☐
968b	With First Day of Issue, British Philatelic Bureau handstamp	**£3.50** ☐
968c	With First Day of Issue, plus Welsh text, Cardiff handstamp	**£4.50** ☐
968d	With First Day of Issue, The Red Dragon…Cardiff handstamp	**£4.50** ☐
968e	With New Welsh Definitives (dragon), Cardiff handstamp	**£6.00** ☐
968f	With First Pictorial Issue, Cardiff handstamp	**£6.00** ☐
968g	With First Pictorial Issue, Caernarvon handstamp	**£6.00** ☐
968h	With First Pictorial Issue, Builth Wells handstamp	**£6.00** ☐
968i	With First Pictorial Issue, Caerphilly handstamp	**£6.00** ☐
968j	With First Pictorial Issue, Portmeirion, Minffordd, handstamp	**£6.00** ☐
968k	With The First Welsh Definitives, Cardiff handstamp	**£6.00** ☐
968l	With Walsall, West Midlands handstamp	**£7.50** ☐

969. 1999, 21st September

Special Retail Booklet No.2. 2 Panes

(2 x 26p Mechanical Farming), (8 x 1st NVI)

969a Special Commemorative Stamps Pane only, with any postmark .... **£4.00** ☐
969b With Royal Mail Windsor permanent handstamp.......... **£6.50** ☐
969c With Millennium Retail Book No.2....Windsor, Berks handstamp .... **£6.50** ☐
969d With Millennium Booklet, Detling , Maidstone handstamp.......... **£6.50** ☐
969e With Millenium Booklet, Cardiff handstamp .... **£6.50** ☐
969f With Millenium Booklet, Belfast handstamp.......... **£6.50** ☐
969g With Millenium Booklet, Stoneleigh, Coventry handstamp .... **£6.50** ☐

970. 1999, 21st September

£6.99 World Changers Prestige Stamp Book. 5 Panes

(4 Panes of Millennium Stamps, 1 Pane Mixed Value Defs)

970a Complete Set of 5 entire Panes on illustrated covers, any postmark.......... **£12.50** ☐
970b With First Day of Issue, British Philatelic Bureau handstamp .... **£20.00** ☐
970c With First Day of Issue (rays of light), Downe, Orpington handstamp .... **£22.00** ☐
970d With First Day of Issue, Downe, Orpington handstamp.......... **£24.00** ☐
970e With First Day of Issue (rays of light), plus Welsh text, Downe, Orpington h/s...... **£26.00** ☐
970f With First Day of issue, plus Welsh text, Downe, Orpington h/s .... **£26.00** ☐
970g With The Millenium Definitives, Windsor, Berks handstamp.......... **£30.00** ☐
970h With Science & Invention, Milestones of 20th Century, Moon Street, London h/s...... **£30.00** ☐
970i With Science & Invention, Exhibition Rd, London SW7 handstamp.......... **£30.00** ☐
970j With Science & Invention, Michael Faraday, Newington, London SE1 h/s .... **£30.00** ☐
970k With Science & Invention, Alan Turing, Paddington, London handstamp .... **£30.00** ☐
970l With Science & Invention, Charles Darwin, Downe, Orpington handstamp .... **£30.00** ☐
970m With Science And Invention, Dawn of a New Age, Birmingham handstamp.......... **£30.00** ☐
970n With Science And Invention, Edward Jenner, Berkeley, Glos handstamp.......... **£30.00** ☐

The Next Colour Feature!

What would you like to see? Why not write and let us know!

First Day Publishing Company, P.O. Box 11, Arundel, Sussex BN18 9SS

971. 1999, 1st October
£1.04 Rugby World Cup Commemorative Label
(4 x 1st NVI + Label)

971a Complete Commemorative Label, with any postmark .... **£3.00** ☐
971b With First Day of Issue, British Philatelic Bureau handstamp .... **£5.50** ☐
971c With Rugby World Cup, plus Welsh text, Cardiff handstamp .... **£6.50** ☐
971d With Cardiff (rugby ball), Wales handstamp .... **£6.50** ☐
971e With The Birthplace of Rugby Football, Rugby, Worcs. handstamp .... **£7.00** ☐
971f With Rugby 1999, Cardiff handstamp .... **£7.00** ☐
971g With Rugby 1999, Edinburgh handstamp .... **£7.00** ☐
971h With Rugby 1999, Belfast handstamp .... **£7.00** ☐
971i With Rugby 1999, Twickenham handstamp .... **£7.00** ☐
971j With Royal Navy Rugby, Devonport, Plymouth handstamp .... **£7.00** ☐
971k With Rugby - The Cup, Cardiff, Wales handstamp .... **£7.00** ☐
971l With 1999 Rugby Cup Finals, Cardiff, Wales handstamp .... **£7.00** ☐
971m With Rugby Street, London WC1 handstamp .... **£7.00** ☐
971n With Widnes Vikings RLFC, World Club Champions, Widnes handstamp .... **£7.50** ☐

---

972. 1999, 5th October
E' Stamp (30p letter rate to Europe). Issued in Sheets. De La Rue

972a E' Stamp on illustrated cover, Royal Mail Windsor (castle) permanent h/s .... **£3.50** ☐

973. 2000, 6th January
£2.60 Booklet (10 x 1st NVI). **1st NVI New Olive Colour. Gravure. Walsall**
£2.60 Booklet (10 x 1st NVI). **1st NVI New Olive Colour. Gravure. Questa**

973a Either complete 10 x 1st NVI Pane on illustrated cover, any postmark .... **£3.50** ☐
973b With First Day of Issue, British Philatelic Bureau handstamp .... **£5.00** ☐
973c With First Day of Issue, Windsor handstamp .... **£6.00** ☐
973d With First Day of Issue (lions), Windsor handstamp .... **£6.00** ☐
973e With Royal Mail Windsor permanent (castle) handstamp .... **£6.00** ☐
973f With The Millennium, Greeenwich, London SE10 handstamp .... **£8.00** ☐
973g With The Millennium Definitive (sundial), Greenwich, London SE10 handstamp .... **£8.00** ☐
973h With The Millennium Definitive (observatory), Greenwich, London SE10 h/s .... **£8.00** ☐
973i With The Millennium Definitive, Stonehenge, Salisbury handstamp .... **£8.00** ☐
973j With The Millennium Definitive, Royal Residences, Royal Mile, Edinburgh h/s .... **£8.00** ☐
973k With The Millennium Definitive, Royal Residences, Windsor, Berks handstamp .... **£8.00** ☐
973l With The Millennium Definitive, Royal Residences, Sandringham, Norfolk h/s .... **£8.00** ☐
973m With The Millennium Definitive, Royal Residences, Buckingham Palace Road h/s. **£8.00** ☐
973n With 150th Anniversary First French Stamp, Ceres Road, London SE18 h/s .... **£8.00** ☐
973o With HM The Queen Mother, Clarence House, London handstamp .... **£8.00** ☐
973p Both 10 x 1st NVI (Walsall and Questa) Panes, with any of above handstamps... **£14.00** ☐
973q Single 1st NVI Stamp (either Walsall or Questa), with any of above handstamps... **£2.50** ☐

974. 2000, 15th February
£7.50 Special by Design Prestige Stamp Book
(8 x 1st NVI), (9 x 1st NVI Country Stamps), (4 x 19p + 2 x 38p), (6 x 1st NVI Black)
New Stamps included were: 1st NVI Black, 1st NVI Scotland, Wales, N. Ireland

974a	Complete set of 4 entire Panes on illustrated covers, any postmark	£9.50 ☐
974b	With First Day of Issue, British Philatelic Bureau handstamp	£16.00 ☐
974c	With First Day of Issue (building), Earls Court, London SW5 handstamp	£17.50 ☐
974d	With First Day of Issue, Earls Court, London SW5 handstamp	£17.50 ☐
974e	With Special by Design, Buckingham Palace Rd, London SW1 handstamp	£25.00 ☐
974f	With Special by Design, Earl's Court, London SW5 handstamp	£25.00 ☐
974g	With Prestige Stamp Book, Special by Design, Earl's Court, London SW5 h/s	£25.00 ☐
974h	With Prestige Stamp Book, Special by Design, London EC4 handstamp	£25.00 ☐
974i	With Prestige Stamp Book, Special by Design, Cardiff handstamp	£25.00 ☐
974j	With Prestige Stamp Book, Special by Design, Belfast handstamp	£25.00 ☐
974k	With Prestige Stamp Book, Special by Design, Edinburgh handstamp	£25.00 ☐
974l	With ...National Postal Museum, Millennium Tribute...London E.C.1. handstamp	£25.00 ☐
974m	With Westminster Abbey, London SW1 handstamp	£25.00 ☐
974n	With Complete Set of 4 Panes, any combination of above handstamps	£25.00 ☐

975. 2000, 21st March
£1.04 Postman Pat Commemorative Label
(4 x 1st NVI + Label)

975a	Complete Commemorative Label, any postmark	£2.00 ☐
975b	With Postman Pat, Keswick handstamp	£6.00 ☐
975c	With Postman Pat, London SW13 handstamp	£6.00 ☐
975d	With Postman Pat, Colne handstamp	£6.00 ☐
975e	With Postman Pat, Leeds handstamp	£6.00 ☐
975f	With Onward to the 21st Century...Century Road, London E17 handstamp	£7.00 ☐
975g	With Year 2000 Definitives, Windsor Great Park, Windsor handstamp	£7.00 ☐
975h	With The Children's Favourite Postman, Earls Court, London handstamp	£7.00 ☐
975i	With The Millennium Definitives, Windsor, Berkshire handstamp	£7.00 ☐
975j	With Mawrth 21, 2000, Caerdydd, Cardiff handstamp	£6.00 ☐
975k	With Pattishall Post Office, Pattishall, Northampton handstamp	£7.50 ☐

Readers comments are always welcome!

976. 2000, 4th April

Opening of National Botanic Garden of Wales. £1.04 Commemorative Label

(4 x 1st NVI + Label)

976a Complete Pane 4 x 1st NVI + Label, World Famous Botanic Gardens, Kew h/s..... **£6.00** ☐
976b With Botanic Gardens, World Flora, Exotic Plants, Kew, Richmond h/s .... **£6.00** ☐
976c With Botanic Gardens, World Flora, Wales, (bee+3 buds)...Llanarthne h/s .... **£6.00** ☐
976d With Botanic Gardens, World Flora, Wales (bee+6 flowers)...Llanarthne h/s.......... **£6.00** ☐
976e With Botanic Gardens (flower), Sir Gaerfyrddin, Llanarthne handstamp.................. **£6.00** ☐
976f With Conservation, World Flora, Countryside, Westonbirt, Glos. handstamp .... **£6.00** ☐
976g With Llanarthne, Caerfyrddin, Llamarthney, Carmarthen handstamp....................... **£6.00** ☐
976h With any Welsh cds .... **£7.50** ☐

977. 2000, 11th April

£1.50, £2, £3, £5. New De La Rue Printing.
Small Format

977a Set of 4 stamps with Royal Mail Windsor permanent handstamp .... **£17.00** ☐
977b With De La Rue, High Values, London EC1 handstamp .... **£17.00** ☐
977c With De La Rue, High Values, Edinburgh handstamp.. **£17.00** ☐
977d With De La Rue, High Values, Belfast handstamp .... **£17.00** ☐
977e With De La Rue, High Values, Cardiff handstamp... **£17.00** ☐
977f With De La Rue, High Wycombe, Bucks handstamp .... **£17.00** ☐
977g With High Wycombe cds, or Windsor cds.. **£20.00** ☐

First Day Covers signed by the Stamp Designer

Covers, with one or more Stamps, signed by the designer are worth a 20% premium over catalogue prices.

Control Numbers and/or Cylinder Numbers

Covers showing these are worth a premium of 20% – 25%.

978. 2000, 25th April

8p Old Gold, 33p Slate-Blue, 40p Grey-Blue, 41p Red, 45p Lt. Purple, 65p Turquoise. New Low Values/Colours

978a Set of 6 Stamps on illustrated cover, any postmark .... **£3.00** ☐
978b With First Day of Issue, British Philatelic Bureau handstamp .... **£5.00** ☐
978c With First Day of Issue (lions), Windsor handstamp .... **£5.50** ☐
978d With First Day of Issue, Windsor handstamp .... **£5.50** ☐
978e With Royal Mail Windsor, permanent handstamp .... **£7.50** ☐
978f With New Definitive Stamp Issue, London handstamp .... **£7.50** ☐
978g With Stamp Show 2000, Earls Court, London handstamp .... **£7.50** ☐

979. 2000, 25th April

65p Purple. New Value Scottish Pictorial Definitive

979a With First Day of Issue, British Philatelic Bureau handstamp .... **£3.00** ☐
979b With First Day of Issue, The People Of The Country...Edinburgh, Scotland h/s .... **£4.00** ☐
979c With First Day of Issue, Edinburgh handstamp .... **£4.00** ☐
979d With New 65p Scottish Definitive, Edinburgh handstamp .... **£4.50** ☐
979e With any Scottish cds postmark .... **£6.00** ☐

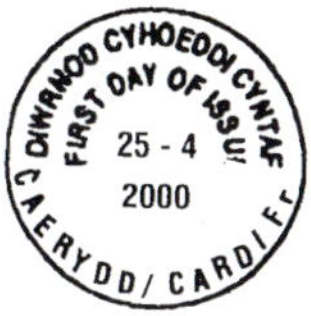

980. 2000, 25th April

65p Purple. New Value Welsh Pictorial Definitive

980a With First Day of Issue, British Philatelic Bureau handstamp .... **£3.00** ☐
980b With First Day of Issue (The Red Dragon...) English/Welsh text, Cardiff h/s .... **£4.00** ☐
980c With First Day of Issue, English/Welsh text, Cardiff handstamp .... **£4.00** ☐
980d With New 65p Welsh Definitive, Cardiff handstamp .... **£4.50** ☐
980e With any Welsh cds postmark .... **£6.00** ☐

981. 2000, 25th April

1st NVI, 40p, 65p. New Northern Ireland Non-Pictorial Definitives

981a All 3 Stamps with First Day of Issue, British Philatelic Bureau handstamp .... **£4.50** ☐
981b With First Day of Issue (hand), Belfast handstamp .... **£5.50** ☐
981c With First Day of Issue, Belfast handstamp .... **£5.50** ☐
981d With any Northern Ireland cds .... **£7.50** ☐

982. 2000, 27th April
New Definitive Booklets
£1 (3 x 1st NVI + 1 x 2nd NVI), **£2** (6 x 1st NVI + 2 x 2nd NVI) **Gravure. Questa**
£1.60 (4 x 40p)**, £2.60** (4 x 65p) **Gravure. Walsall**

982a Complete Set of 4 Panes, Royal Mail Windsor permanent handstamp.................. **£24.00** ☐
982b With 2 Panes £1, £2 Questa Printing, Windsor permanent handstamp .... **£9.50** ☐
982c With 2 Panes £1.60, £2.60 Walsall Printing, Windsor permanent handstamp .... **£15.00** ☐

983. 2000, 22nd May
Stamp Show 2000. Jeffery Matthews £2.59 Miniature Sheet
(4p, 5p, 6p, 10p, 31p, 39p, 64p, £1 + 2 labels)

983a Complete Miniature Sheet on illustrated cover, any postmark................................ **£3.00** ☐
983b With First Day of Issue, British Philatelic Bureau handstamp.................................. **£5.50** ☐
983c With First Day of Issue (crown), Earls Court, London SW5 handstamp.................... **£6.50** ☐
983d With First Day of Issue, Earls Court, London SW5 handstamp................................ **£6.50** ☐
983e With The Stamp Show 2000, Earls Court, London SW5 handstamp .... **£8.50** ☐
983f With The Stamp Show 2000, Art & Entertainment, Earls Court, London h/s............ **£8.50** ☐
983g With The Stamp Show 2000, Security Print Heritage, Earls Court, London SW5 h/s... **£8.50** ☐
983h With The Stamp Show 2000, The Artist's Palette, Earls Court, London SW5 h/s .... **£8.50** ☐
983i With The Stamp Show 2000, The Artist's Palette, Strand, London WC2 h/s............ **£8.50** ☐
983j With The Stamp Show 2000, The Artist's Palette, Piccadilly, London W1 h/s .... **£8.50** ☐
983k With The Stamp Show 2000, The Artist's Palette, Kidderminster handstamp .... **£8.50** ☐
983l With Stamp Show 2000 (stamp outline), Earls Court, London handstamp .... **£8.50** ☐
983m With Stamp Capital of the World, London handstamp.. **£8.50** ☐
983n With Coronation of Queen Elizabeth II, Westminster Abbey, London SW1 h/s........ **£8.50** ☐
983o With The Lyceum Post Office, Celebrates Stamp Show 2000, Liverpool h/s .... **£8.50** ☐
983p With London, Art Centre of the World, London W1 handstamp................................ **£8.50** ☐
983q With Dr Who Visits The Stamp Show 2000, Earls Court Road SW5 handstamp..... **£8.50** ☐
983r With Stamp Show 2000, Smilers, London SW5 (any one of series of 11 similar h/s)... **£8.50** ☐
983s With Earls Court cds, or Windsor cds .... **£16.00** ☐

---

984. 2000, 4th September
1st and 2nd NVI Stamps in 'Business Sheets' of 100. Self-adhesive

984a 1st NVI Orange plus 2nd NVI Blue on illustrated cover, Royal Mail Windsor h/s..... **£5.00** ☐
These were prviously available in rolls

2000, 26th May & 5th September Retail Booklets
These are listed in Commems Section because of content. See pages 293 and 298.

985. 2000, 18th September
£7.00 Treasury of Trees Prestige Stamp Book. 5 Panes
(2 x 65p) (4 x 45p) (4 x 2nd) Tree & Leaf, (2 x 65p) Stone & Soil, (1st+2nd+label) Defs

985a Complete set of 5 Panes on illustrated covers, any postmark................................. **£8.00** ☐
985b With First Day of Issue, British Philatelic Bureau handstamp................................ **£18.00** ☐

985c With First Day of Issue (tree), English/Welsh text, Llangernyw, Abergele h/s........**£19.00** ☐
985d With First Day of Issue, English/Welsh text, Llangernyw, Abergele handstamp.....**£19.00** ☐
985e With Prestige Stamp Book (badger), Treasury of Trees, London SW7 h/s ....**£25.00** ☐
985f With Prestige Stamp Book (branch), Treasury of Trees, London SW7 h/s.............**£25.00** ☐
985g With Prestige Stamp Book, Treasury of Trees, Birmingham handstamp................**£25.00** ☐
985h With Prestige Stamp Book, Treasury of Trees, Glasgow handstamp.....................**£25.00** ☐
985i With Prestige Stamp Book, Treasury of Trees, Ardingly handstamp......................**£25.00** ☐
985j With Prestige Stamp Book, Treasury of Trees, Cardiff handstamp ....**£25.00** ☐
985k With A Treasury of Trees, Kew Gardens, Richmond handstamp............................**£26.00** ☐
985l With Haywood Oaks, Sherwood Forest, Nottingham handstamp...........................**£25.00** ☐

Multi Value Definitives Pane only, with Bureau handstamp is worth **£3.00**

---

986. 2001, 29th January

£1.62 Queen Victoria Commemorative Label. Self-adhesive

(6 x 1st NVI + QV Label)

986a Complete Commemorative Label on illustrated cover, any postmark.......................**£2.50** ☐
986b With 1st Ever Self-adhesive Royal Mail Commemorative Label, Windsor h/s ....**£7.50** ☐
986c With Self-adhesive Stamp Books, London SW1 handstamp..................................**£7.50** ☐
986d With Queen Victoria Centenary 1901 - 2001, London SW1 handstamp ....**£7.50** ☐
986e With Queen Victoria 1901-2001, East Cowes, Isle of Wight handstamp.................**£7.50** ☐
986f With Queen Victoria, Autographed Editions, Kensington, London W8 handstamp ..**£7.50** ☐
986g With (QV head) The Strand, London WC2 handstamp...**£7.50** ☐
986h With (palace) Kensington, London W8 handstamp..**£7.50** ☐
986i With Centenary 1901-2001, Queen Victoria, East Cowes handstamp ....**£7.50** ☐
986j With Centenary, Death of Queen Victoria, East Cowes handstamp........................**£7.50** ☐
986k With Centenary, The Death of Queen Victoria, London SW1 handstamp ....**£7.50** ☐
986l With Centenary, Death of Queen Victoria, Windsor handstamp ....**£7.50** ☐
986m With Royal Mail Windsor permanent handstamp..**£7.50** ☐

987. 2001, 29th January

£2.70 NVI Vended Booklet. Self-adhesive. Questa. Gravure Printed

(10 x 1st NVI Stamp)

£1.90 NVI Vended Booklet. Self-adhesive. Questa. Gravure Printed

(10 x 2nd NVI Stamp)

All QV Commemorative Label handstamps were available for use with these Booklets

987a Set of 2 complete Booklet Panes, with any QV Commemorative Label h/s...........**£12.00** ☐

988. 2001, 29th January
£3.24 NVI Booklet. Self-adhesive. (12 x 1st NVI Stamp) **Questa. Gravure**
£2.28 NVI Booklet. Self-adhesive. (12 x 2nd NVI Stamp) **Questa. Gravure**
£3.24 NVI Booklet. Self-adhesive. (12 x 1st NVI Stamp) **Walsall. Gravure**
£1.62 NVI Booklet. Self-adhesive. (6 x 1st NVI Stamp) **Walsall. Gravure**
£1.14 NVI Booklet. Self-adhesive. (6 x 2nd NVI Stamp) **Walsall. Gravure**
All QV Commemorative Label handstamps were available for use with these Booklets
988a Set of 5 complete Booklet Panes, with any QV Label handstamp ....**£32.00** ☐

989 2001, 13th February
£3.24 Cats & Dogs Booklet. Self-adhesive
10 x 1st Cats & Dogs Stamps + 2 x 1st Defs
989a Complete Booklet Pane with any relevant handstamp* ....**£8.00** ☐
989b Complete Booklet Pane with any relevant cds* postmark ....**£12.50** ☐
*Please refer to Commeratives Issue no **410** of same date.

990. 2001, 6th March
Northern Ireland Pictorial Definitives
2nd Giant's Causeway, 1st Patchwork Fields, E Linen Design, 65p Parian China
990a Set on illustrated cover, any postmark ....**£2.00** ☐
990b With First Day of Issue, British Philatelic Bureau handstamp ....**£4.00** ☐
990c With First Day of Issue, At Dusk Horizons Drink...Belfast handstamp......................**£5.00** ☐
990d With First Day of Issue, Belfast handstamp ....**£5.00** ☐
990e With Northern Ireland Pictorial Stamps, Belfast handstamp ....**£6.00** ☐
990f With Pictorial Definitives, Giant's Causeway, Bushmills handstamp.........................**£6.00** ☐
990g With (cross), Belfast, Northern Ireland handstamp ....**£6.00** ☐
990h With Northern Ireland Pictorial Definitives, Lisburn, N. Ireland handstamp ....**£6.00** ☐
990i With Northern Ireland Pictorial Definitives, Newcastle, N. Ireland handstamp ....**£6.00** ☐
990j With Northern Ireland Pictorial Definitives, Belleek, Enniskillen handstamp ....**£6.00** ☐
990k With Northern Ireland Pictorial Definitives, Bushmills, N. Ireland handstamp ....**£6.00** ☐
990l With Northern Ireland Pictorial Definitives, Bushmills handstamp ....**£6.00** ☐
990m With Scotland & N. Ireland Royal Mail permanent handstamp.................................**£6.00** ☐
990n With any Northern Ireland cds..**£10.00** ☐

991. 2001, 17th April
£1 NVI Vended Booklet (3 x 1st + 1 x 2nd + 4 Labels)
991a Complete Booklet Pane with Labels, Royal Mail Windsor permanent handstamp...**£3.50** ☐
New Booklet includes amended Royal Mail website address.

Please refer to notes at the beginning of this catalogue for additional information

992. 2001, 23rd April

England Country Pictorial Definitives

2nd Lions, 1st Crowned Lion, E Oak Tree, 65p Tudor Rose

992a	Set on illustrated cover, any postmark	£2.00 ☐
992b	With First Day of Issue, British Philatelic Bureau, Edinburgh handstamp	£3.00 ☐
992c	With First Day of Issue, Cry God for Harry...Windsor handstamp	£4.00 ☐
992d	With First Day of Issue, Windsor handstamp	£4.00 ☐
992e	With English Pictorial Definitives, London handstamp	£6.00 ☐
992f	With English Pictorial Definitives, Windsor, Berkshire handstamp	£6.00 ☐
992g	With English Pictorial Definitives, Westminster, London SW1 handstamp	£6.00 ☐
992h	With English Pictorial Definitives, Lancaster handstamp	£6.00 ☐
993i	With English Pictorial Definitives, Bishopswood, Stafford handstamp	£6.00 ☐
992j	With First English Pictorial Definitives, St George's Day, London handstamp	£6.00 ☐
992k	With First Pictorial Definitives for England, Windsor handstamp	£6.00 ☐
992l	With Pictorial Country Definitives, London handstamp	£6.00 ☐
992m	With Pictorial Country Definitives, Belfast handstamp	£6.00 ☐
992n	With Pictorial Country Definitives, Edinburgh handstamp	£6.00 ☐
992o	With Pictorial Country Definitives, Cardiff handstamp	£6.00 ☐
992p	With St George's Day, Windsor, Berkshire handstamp	£6.00 ☐
992q	With St George & The Dragon, London EC1 handstamp	£6.00 ☐
992r	With St George & The Dragon, Windsor, Berkshire handstamp	£6.00 ☐
992s	With Shakespeare Country, St George's Day, Strafford upon Avon handstamp	£6.00 ☐
992t	With William Shakespeare, Stratford-upon-Avon handstamp	£6.00 ☐
992u	With The Heraldic Lion, Buckingham Palace Road, London SW1 handstamp	£6.00 ☐
992v	With There'll Always be an England, Bond St, London W1 handstamp	£6.00 ☐
992w	With Royal Mail Windsor permanent handstamp	£6.00 ☐

---

993. 2001, 4th July

1st and 2nd NVI Coils. Horizontal Format

993a	Both values, strips of 3 or more Stamps, Royal Mail Windsor permanent h/s	£5.00 ☐

2001, 22nd October

£6.76 Unseen & Unheard Prestige Stamp Book. 4 Panes

See details in Commemoratives Section.

994. Unassigned

All prices in this catalogue are for clean covers, with undamaged stamps and clear postmarks.

887k

911c

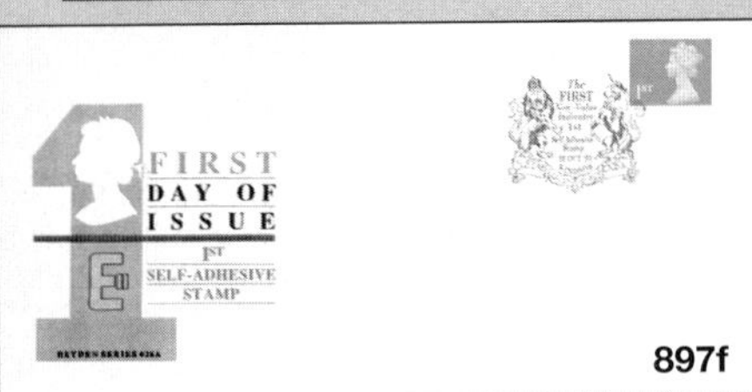

897f

917e

908c

919f

898c

930b

910c

932c

938d

948b

939c

949d

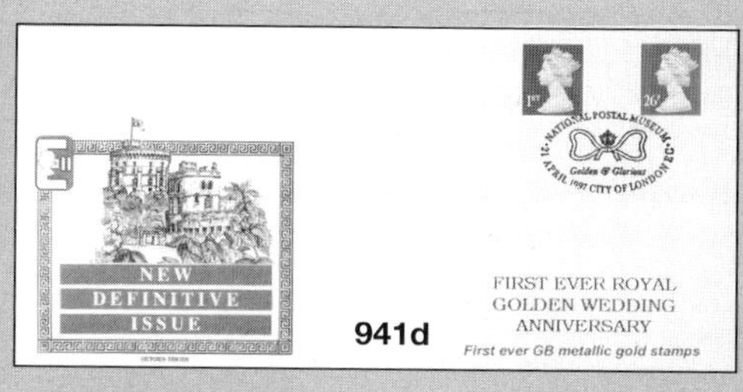

941d

951l

944a

951c

969g

974m

971d

975c

976b

983j

395c

422 (421x h/s)

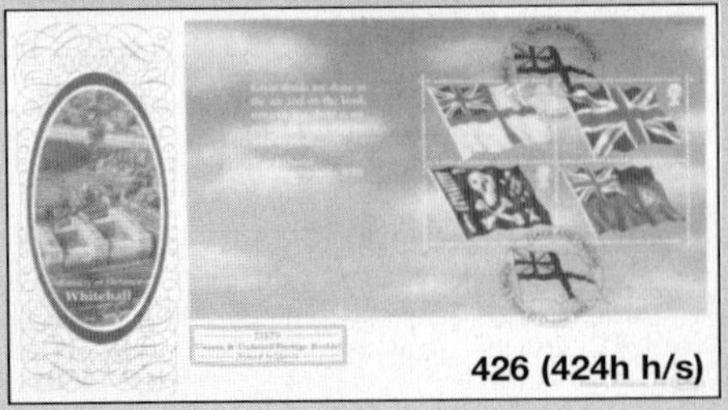

426 (424h h/s)

431 (430w h/s)

957c

961c

962c

968d

967e

973c

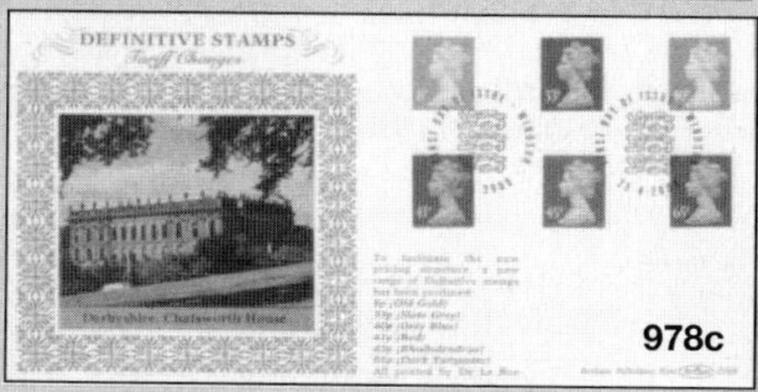

978c

981c

990e

992h

995. 2002, 6th February
£7.29 Gracious Accession Prestige Stamp Book. 4 Panes
All Panes Definitives (4 x 2nd + 4 x E + label), (2nd, 1st, E, 45p), (1st, E, 45p, 65p), (4 x Wilding design 1st + 5 x Wilding design 2nd + label)

995a Set of 4 Panes on illustrated covers, with any relevant commemorative* h/s .... **£16.00** ☐
995b With Britannia cds, Jubilee Fields cds, Kensington High Street cds .... **£25.00** ☐
995c With Buckingham Palace cds .... **£32.00** ☐
995d With Windsor Castle cds .... **£40.00** ☐
995e Panes 1 and 4 only as serviced by Royal Mail with fdi handstamp .... **£6.50** ☐
995f Wilding design 1st and 2nd Stamps with commemorative* handstamp .... **£4.50** ☐

*Please refer to Commemoratives Issue no **430** of same date.

996. 2002, 2nd May
Jet Aircraft £1.62 Booklet. Self-adhesive
2 x 1st Concorde Stamp + 4 x 1st Orange Definitive

996a Booklet with any relevant commemorative* handstamp .... **£4.00** ☐
996b With Filton Avenue, Bristol cds, and any other relevant* cds postmark .... **£7.50** ☐

*Please refer to Commemoratives Issue no **436** of same date.

997. 2002, 21st May
World Cup £1.62 Booklet. Self-adhesive
2 x 1st Lion Stamp + 4 x 1st Orange Definitive

997a Booklet with any relevant commemorative* handstamp .... **£4.00** ☐
997b With Self Adhesives, Wembley, Home of Football handstamp .... **£5.00** ☐
997c With any relevant cds* postmark .... **£7.50** ☐

*Please refer to Commemoratives Issue no **439** of same date.

998. 2002, 5th June
1st NVI Gold. Self-adhesive Booklets.
6 x 1st Questa and Walsall.
12 x 1st Walsall

998a 1st NVI Gold with 2002 Self Adhesives, London SW1 handstamp .... **£5.00** ☐
998b With HM The Queen's Golden Jubilee, Parliament Sq, London SW1 handstamp ... **£5.00** ☐
998c With HM The Queen's Golden Jubilee, Canterbury, Kent handstamp .... **£5.00** ☐
998d With HM The Queen's Golden Jubilee, Westminster, London SW1 handstamp ...... **£5.00** ☐
998e With HM The Queen's Golden Jubilee, Buckingham Palace Rd, London SW1 .... **£5.00** ☐
998f With Golden Jubilee, Pall Mall, London SW1 handstamp .... **£5.00** ☐
998g With Golden Jubilee, The Mall, London handstamp .... **£5.00** ☐
998h With Windsor permanent (castle) handstamp .... **£5.50** ☐

999. 2002, 4th July
New Definitive Values
37p Dark Grey, 42p Sage, 47p Sea Green, 68p Stone

999a Set with First Day of Issue, Tallents House (philatelic bureau) handstamp .... **£4.00** ☐
999b With First Day of Issue, London handstamp .... **£5.50** ☐
999c With First Day of Issue, Windsor (coat of arms) handstamp .... **£5.50** ☐
999d With New Definitives 37p, 42p, 47p, 68p, Windsor, Berkshire handstamp .... **£7.00** ☐
999e With Windsor permanent (castle) handstamp .... **£7.50** ☐

Remember, most modern hand addressed covers are worth only 20% of catalogue prices.

1000. 2002, 4th July
68p Pictorial Definitive
England, Ireland, Scotland, Wales

1000a Any one 68p Regional Pictorial Definitive with Tallents House first day of issue h/s...... **£2.50** ☐
1000b With appropriate (London/Windsor/Belfast/Edinburgh/Cardiff) fdi h/s .... **£4.00** ☐
1000c Set of four 68p Stamps with New Definitives...Windsor, Berks handstamp .... **£6.50** ☐
1000d With Windsor permanent (castle) handstamp .... **£6.50** ☐

1001. 2002, 4th July
New Self-adhesive Definitives. Walsall
42p Sage, 68p Stone. From New Booklets

1001a Both Self-adhesive Stamps with First Day of Issue, Tallents House handstamp...... **£3.00** ☐
1001b With First Day of Issue, London handstamp .... **£4.00** ☐
1001c With First Day of Issue, Windsor (arms) handstamp... **£4.50** ☐
1001d With Self Adhesive Stamps, Hampton, Middx handstamp .... **£6.00** ☐
1001e With New Definitives...Windsor, Berks handstamp.. **£6.00** ☐
1001f With Windsor permanent (castle) handstamp .... **£6.00** ☐

1002. 2002, 24th September
£6.83 Across the Universe Prestige Stamp Book. 4 Panes
(1st Scottish Def + 4 x 1st English Defs + 4 x 2nd English Defs), (4 x 1st Leicester NSC*), (4 x 1st Gold Def + 4 x E Def + label), (4 x 1st from 2002 Astronomy Miniature Sheet)

1002a Set of 4 Panes on illustrated covers with any relevant commemorative** h/s........ **£17.00** ☐
1002b With First Day of Issue, Tallents House (Philatelic Bureau) handstamp................. **£11.00** ☐
1002c With First Day of Issue, Star (galaxy) Glenrothes handstamp .... **£12.50** ☐
1002d With First Day of Issue, Star Glenrothes (plain) handstamp.................................. **£12.50** ☐
1002e With Greenwich cds, Kennedy Centre cds, Leicester cds, Seven Sisters cds .... **£22.00** ☐
1002f With Congleton cds, Skye Crescent cds, Starbeck Avenue cds, Worlds End cds . **£22.00** ☐

* Leicester National Space Centre Stamp from May 26, 2000 Commemorative Issue.
** Please refer to Commemorative Issue no **440** of same date.

In the September 2002 British Philatelic Bulletin Royal Mail stated that they had stopped cancelling Booklets/Panes because of postmarking difficulties with the new style (self-adhesive stamps) Booklets. All the Handstamp Centres were thus instructed to withdraw the first day cover service for Booklets. Next we hear that the ruling has been somewhat relaxed in 2003, only to be re-enforced in early 2004! The March 2004 Bulletin stated that no Booklets would be serviced after March 18. All somewhat confusing. Another problem has been that self-adhesive stamp Booklets & Booklet Panes need some form of glue to get them to stick to envelopes/covers.

1003. 2002, 15th October
1st Gold and 2nd Coils. Vertical Format. Enschede

1003a Both values, strips of 3 or more Stamps, with Windsor permanent (castle) handstamp... **£4.00** ☐

1004. 2002, 15th October
2nd, 1st, E. Wales Country Stamps. De La Rue
E. Northern Ireland Country Stamp. De La Rue

1004a All 4 Stamps on one or two covers with Windsor permanent (castle) handstamp ..... **£6.00** ☐

1005. 2002, 5th December
Wilding Design Definitives with Decimal Values. Miniature Sheet No.1
1p, 2p, 5p, 2nd, 1st, 33p, 37p, 47p, 50p. Original Wilding Colours

1005a Sheet with First Day of Issue, Tallents House (Philatelic Bureau) handstamp ....**£5.00** ☐
1005b With First Day of Issue, Windsor (watermarks) handstamp ....**£6.00** ☐
1005c With First Day of Issue, Windsor plain handstamp..**£6.00** ☐
1005d With Windsor permanent (castle) handstamp ....**£6.50** ☐
1005e With The Wilding Definitives Collection, Basingstoke, Hampshire handstamp.........**£8.50** ☐
1005f With The Wilding Definitives Collection, Buckingham Palace Rd handstamp ....**£8.50** ☐
1005g With The Wilding Definitives Collection, High Wycombe, Buckinghamshire h/s.......**£8.50** ☐
1005h With The Wilding Definitives Collection, King Edward St, London EC1A h/s............**£8.50** ☐
1005i With The Wilding Definitives Collection, Longford, Gloucester handstamp ....**£8.50** ☐
1005j With The Wilding Definitives Collection, Old Bond Street, London W1 handstamp ...**£8.50** ☐
1005k With The Wilding Definitives Collection, Portman Square, London W1 handstamp...**£8.50** ☐
1005l With The Wilding Definitives Collection, Regent St, London W1 handstamp ....**£8.50** ☐
1005m With The Wilding Definitives Collection, The Octagon, Milsom St. Bath handstamp...**£8.50** ☐
1005n With 50th Anniv...First QEII Wilding Definitive, Dorothy Wilding, Portman Sq. h/s.. **£8.50** ☐
1005o With Wilding Definitives, 1952-2002, George Street, London W1 handstamp ....**£8.50** ☐
1005p With 50th Anniversary of the first Elizabethan definitives, London SW1 handstamp ....**£8.50** ☐
1005q With Wilding Definitives, Autographed Editions, George Street, London W1 h/s .....**£8.50** ☐
1005r With Wilding Definitives (palette),George Street, London W1 handstamp................**£8.50** ☐
1005s With Wilding Definitives (camera), Bond Street, London W5 handstamp.................**£8.50** ☐
1005t With Westminster Abbey (throne), London SW1 handstamp...................................**£8.50** ☐
1005u With Wild About Wildings, Windsor handstamp ....**£8.50** ☐
1005v With Queen's Parade cds, Queen's Cross cds, Crown House cds, Throne cds ....**£12.50** ☐
1005w With Portman Square W1 cds, Innsworth cds, Windsor cds ....**£11.50** ☐

1006. 2003, 25th February
£6.99 Microcosmos Prestige Stamp Book. 4 Panes
(4 x 1st Defs + 4 x E Defs), (2 x 2nd DNA* + 2 x 1st DNA*),
(4 x E DNA Commemorative), (5 x 2nd N.I. Def + 4 x 1st N.I. Def)

1006a Set of 4 Panes on illustrated covers, with any relevant commemorative** h/s.......**£17.50** ☐
1006b With First Day of Issue, Tallents House (Philatelic Bureau) handstamp.................**£12.00** ☐
1006b With First Day of Issue, Cambridge (text) handstamp ....**£12.50** ☐
1006c With First Day of Issue, Cambridge (plain) handstamp...**£12.50** ☐
1006d With Crick, Northampton cds, Trinity St. Cambridge cds ....**£22.50** ☐
1006e With Watson Way cds, Weston Favell cds, Wilkins Road cds ....**£22.50** ☐

*Stamp from DNA Commemorative Issue of same date.
** See Issue no **454**.

1007. 2003, 4th March
1st NVI Wales Country Stamp. De La Rue

1007a 1st NVI Stamp with Windsor permanent (castle) handstamp ....**£3.50** ☐
1007b With any Welsh cds postmark ....**£4.50** ☐

1008. 2003, 27th March
Airmail Universal Rate NVI Stamps. Self-adhesive
52p (Europe up to 40 grams), £1.12 (Worldwide up to 40 grams)
1008a Both Stamps with First day of Issue, Tallents House (Philatelic Bureau) handstamp ... **£3.50** ☐
1008b With First Day of Issue, Windsor (arms) handstamp .... **£5.00** ☐
1008c With First Day of Issue, Windsor (plain) handstamp .... **£5.00** ☐
1008d With Windsor permanent (castle) handstamp .... **£6.50** ☐
1008e With New NVI Definitives, London SW1 handstamp .... **£6.50** ☐
1008f With Universal Airmail, Send, Woking handstamp .... **£6.50** ☐
1008g With Universal Rates, Birmingham handstamp .... **£6.50** ☐
1008h With Self Adhesives, Europe & Worldwide, London handstamp .... **£6.50** ☐
1008i With Across the English Channel, Dover, Kent handstamp .... **£6.50** ☐
1008j With Historic Moments in Aviation, Southampton handstamp .... **£6.50** ☐
1008k With any airport cds postmark ....
£10.00 ☐

1009. 2003, 6th May
34p Lime-Green. De La Rue
1009a 34p Stamp with First Day of Issue, Tallents House (Philatelic Bureau) handstamp .... **£2.50** ☐
1009b With First Day of Issue, Windsor (arms) handstamp .... **£3.50** ☐
1009c With First Day of Issue, Windsor (plain) handstamp .... **£3.50** ☐
1009d With Windsor permanent (castle) handstamp .... **£5.00** ☐
1009e With Machin Definitive, Stoke-on-Trent handstamp .... **£5.50** ☐

1010. 2003, 20th May
Wilding Design Definitives with Decimal Values. Miniature Sheet No.2
4p, 8p, 10p, 20p, 28p, 34p, E, 42p, 68p, Original Wilding Colours
1010a Sheet with First Day of Issue, Tallents House (Philatelic Bureau) handstamp .... **£4.50** ☐
1010b With First Day of Issue, Windsor (wmks) handstamp .... **£5.50** ☐
1010c With First Day of Issue, Windsor (plain) handstamp .... **£5.50** ☐
1010d With Windsor permanent (castle) handstamp .... **£6.50** ☐
1010e With Wilding Definitives 1953-59, Old Bond Street, London W1 handstamp .... **£8.50** ☐
1010f With The Wilding Definitives Collection, Basingstoke, Hampshire handstamp .... **£8.50** ☐
1010g With The Wilding Definitives Collection, Buckingham Palace Rd, London SW1 h/s.. **£8.50** ☐
1010h With The Wilding Definitives Collection, High Wycombe, Buckinghamshire h/s....... **£8.50** ☐
1010i With The Wilding Definitives Collection, King Edward St, London EC1A h/s.......... **£8.50** ☐
1010j With The Wilding Definitives Collection, Longford, Gloucester handstamp .... **£8.50** ☐
1010k With The Wilding Definitives Collection, Old Bond Street, London W1 handstamp.. **£8.50** ☐
1010l With The Wilding Definitives Collection, Portman Square, London W1 handstamp . **£8.50** ☐
1010m With The Wilding Definitives Collection, Regent St, London W1 handstamp .... **£8.50** ☐
1010n With The Wilding Definitives Collection, The Octagon, Milsom St. Bath h/s.......... **£8.50** ☐
1010o With Wilding Definitives II (palette), George Street, London W1 handstamp......... **£8.50** ☐
1010p With Wilding Definitives II, Autographed Editions, George Street, London W1 h/s .. **£8.50** ☐
1010q With Wilding Definitives II (Camera), George Street, London W1 handstamp .... **£8.50** ☐
1010r With Queen Elizabeth II, Wilding Definitives Collection II, Portman Sq. London h/s **£8.50** ☐
1010s With Wilding Revival Stamps Series II, Windsor handstamp .... **£8.50** ☐

1010t With Wilding Definitives 1953, Old Bond Street, London W1 handstamp.......... £8.50 ☐
1010u With 50th Anniversary first Elizabethan definitives, Edinburgh handstamp.......... £8.50 ☐
1010v With Portman Square cds, Innsworth cds, Windsor cds.......... £12.50 ☐
1010w With Crown Street cds, Crown House cds, Scone cds, Throne cds.......... £15.00 ☐
1010x With House of Commons cds.......... £25.00 ☐

1011. 2003, 28th May

1st NVI Gold Coil. Vertical. De La Rue Printing
2nd Wales Definitive. De La Rue Printing

1011a 1st NVI Definitive, strip of three or more Stamps, with Windsor permanent handstamp .. £4.00 ☐
1011b 2nd Wales Country Definitive with Windsor permanent (castle) handstamp.......... £3.50 ☐

1012. 2003, 2nd June

£7.46 A Perfect Coronation Prestige Stamp Book. 4 Panes

(4 x 2nd Def + 4 x 1st Def), (4 x 1st Coronation*), (4 x 1st Coronation*),
(2 x 47p + 2 x 68p + £1 Coronation Stamp*)

1012a Set of 4 Panes with First Day of Issue, Tallents House (Philatelic Bureau) handstamp . £12.50 ☐
1012b With First Day of Issue, London SW1 (text) handstamp.......... £14.00 ☐
1012c With First Day of Issue, London SW1 (plain) handstamp.......... £14.00 ☐
1012d With Windsor permanent (castle) handstamp.......... £18.00 ☐
1012e With any relevant Commemorative*(from Coronation Anniversary Issue)handstamp. £18.50 ☐
1012f With Canterbury cds, Kensington High Street cds, Windsor Great Park cds.......... £25.00 ☐
1012g With Queen's Parade cds, Scone cds, Throne cds.......... £25.00 ☐
1012h With Windsor cds, Balmoral cds.......... £35.00 ☐

*See Commemorative Issue no **457** of same date.

1013. 2003, 1st July

High Values. Gravure. Iridion Ink. De La Rue

£1.50 Terracotta, £2.00 Slate Blue, £3.00 Purple, £5.00 Grey-Blue

1013a Set with First Day of Issue, Tallents House (Philatelic Bureau) handstamp.......... £15.50 ☐
1013b With First Day of Issue, Windsor (arms) handstamp.......... £16.50 ☐
1013c With First Day of Issue, Windsor (plain) handstamp.......... £16.50 ☐
1013d With Windsor permanent (castle) handstamp.......... £19.00 ☐
1013e With High Value Definitives, Althorp, Northampton handstamp.......... £19.00 ☐
1013f With High Value Definitives, Blenheim, Woodstock, Oxon handtamp.......... £19.00 ☐
1013g With High Value Definitives, Downe, Orpington, Kent handstamp.......... £19.00 ☐
1013h With High Value Definitives, Hastings handstamp.......... £19.00 ☐
1013i With High Value Definitives, Portsmouth, Hampshire handstamp.......... £19.00 ☐
1013j With High Value Definitives, Stoke-on-Trent handstamp.......... £19.00 ☐
1013k With missing £ sign on £2.00 Slate Blue, any postmark.......... £250.00 ☐

1014. 2003, 14th October
2nd, 1st, E, 68p. White Borders.
England, N. Ireland, Scotland, Wales. Pictorial Country Definitives

1014a	England set of Stamps with any one of nine Royal Mail first day of issue h/s!	**£3.00** ☐
1014b	With Windsor permanent (castle) handstamp	**£4.50** ☐
1014c	With England Regional Definitives, Bakewell, Derbyshire handstamp	**£5.50** ☐
1014d	With England Regional Definitives, Castlerigg, Keswick handstamp	**£5.50** ☐
1014e	With England Regional Definitives, London handstamp	**£5.50** ☐
1014f	With England Regional Definitives, Newport, Isle of Wight handstamp	**£5.50** ☐
1014g	With Country Definitives (map), London, England handstamp	**£5.50** ☐
1014h	With Country Definitives (3 lions), London handstamp	**£5.50** ☐
1014i	Northern Ireland set of Stamps with any one of nine Royal Mail fdi handstamps!	**£3.50** ☐
1014j	With N. Ireland Regional Definitives, Belfast handstamp	**£5.50** ☐
1014k	With N. Ireland Regional Definitives, Cookstown handstamp	**£5.50** ☐
1014l	With N. Ireland Regional Definitives, Londonderry handstamp	**£5.50** ☐
1014m	With N. Ireland Regional Definitives, Portrush handstamp	**£5.50** ☐
1014n	With Country Definitives (map), Belfast, Northern Ireland handstamp	**£5.50** ☐
1014o	With Country Definitives (face), Belfast handstamp	**£5.50** ☐
1014p	Scotland set of Stamps with any one of nine Royal Mail first day of issue h/s!	**£3.50** ☐
1014q	With Scotland Regional Definitives, Callanish, Isle of Lewis handstamp	**£5.50** ☐
1014r	With Scotland Regional Definitives, Dunvegan, Isle of Skye handstamp	**£5.50** ☐
1014s	With Scotland Regional Definitives, Edinburgh handstamp	**£5.50** ☐
1014t	With Scotland Regional Definitives, Glencoe, Ballachulish handstamp	**£5.50** ☐
1014u	With Country Definitives (map), Edinburgh, Scotland	**£5.50** ☐
1014v	With Country Definitives (sporran), Edinburgh handstamp	**£5.50** ☐
1014w	Wales set of Stamps with any one of nine Royal Mail first day of issue h/s!	**£3.50** ☐
1014x	With Wales Regional Definitives, Cardiff handstamp	**£5.50** ☐
1014y	With Wales Regional Definitives, Cardigan handstamp	**£5.50** ☐
1014z	With Wales Regional Definitives, Llanberis, Caernarfon handstamp	**£5.50** ☐
1014aa	With Wales Regional Definitives, Llanrwst, Conway Valley handstamp	**£5.50** ☐
1014bb	With Country Definitives (map), Cardiff, Wales handstamp	**£5.50** ☐
1014cc	With Country Definitives (dragon), Caerdydd, Cardiff handstamp	**£5.50** ☐

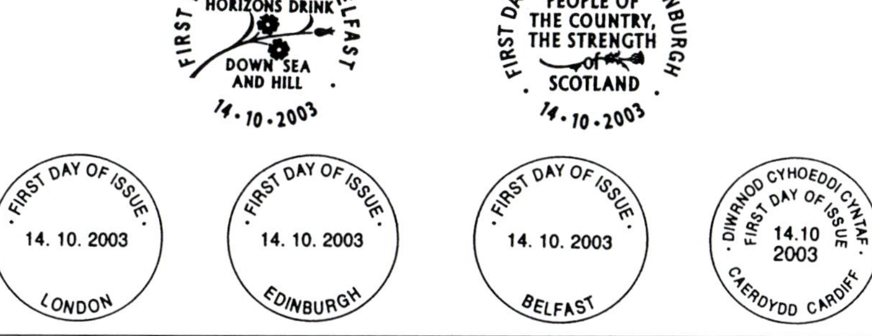

1015. 2004, 16th March

£7.44 Letters by Night Prestige Stamp Book. 4 Panes

(3 x 2nd Scottish Def + 3 x 1st English Def), (28p, E, 42p Trains* Commems), (4 x 1st Pub Signs** Commems), (4 x 1st Def + 4 x 37p Def + label)

1015a Set of 4 Panes with First Day of Issue, Stamp Book Centenary, Tallents House h/s ...... **£12.00** ☐
1015b With First Day of Issue, London NW10 (double ring) handstamp .... **£14.00** ☐
1015c With First Day of Issue, London NW10 (single ring) handstamp .... **£14.00** ☐
1015d With The Night Mail, Travelling Post Office, York handstamp .... **£20.00** ☐
1015e With Letters by Night, New Street, Birmingham handstamp .... **£20.00** ☐
1015f With Letters by Night, Final Journey of the TPO, Bristol handstamp .... **£20.00** ☐
1015g With Letters by Night, Bristol handstamp .... **£20.00** ☐
1015h With The Travelling Post Office, Letters by Night, Euston NW1 handstamp .... **£20.00** ☐
1015i With The Travelling Post Office, Letters by Night, Crewe handstamp .... **£20.00** ☐
1015j With The Travelling Post Office, Letters by Night, Carlisle handstamp .... **£20.00** ☐
1015k With The Travelling Post Office, Letters by Night, Newcastle handstamp .... **£20.00** ☐
1015l With The Travelling Post Office, Letters by Night, Edinburgh handstamp .... **£20.00** ☐
1015m With Royal Scot Class, LMS 6128 Meteor (locomotive), Glasgow handstamp ...... **£20.00** ☐
1015n With The Station cds, Railway Road cds, any famous train station cds .... **£25.00** ☐

*The three Trains Stamps were first issued on January 13, 2004.

**The 1st Pub Signs Stamp was first issued on 12th August, 2003.

1016. 2004, 1st April

New Definitives

7p Pink, 35p Dk. Brown, 39p Lt. Grey, 40p Blue, NVI (43p) Emerald-Green.

1016a Set of 5 New Defs on one or more covers, with First Day of Issue, Tallents House h/s... **£3.50** ☐
1016b With First Day of Issue, Windsor (arms) handstamp .... **£4.00** ☐
1016c With First Day of Issue, Windsor (plain) handstamp .... **£4.00** ☐
1016d With Windsor permanent (castle), handstamp .... **£6.50** ☐
1016e With Machin Definitives, Phil Stamp Collection, Stoke-on-Trent handstamp .... **£6.50** ☐

New Worldwide Postcard NVI Stamp (43p). Self-adhesive

1016f New Post Card rate NVI Stamp, with First Day of Issue, Tallents House handstamp... **£2.50** ☐
1016g With First Day of Issue, Windsor (arms) handstamp .... **£3.50** ☐
1016h With First Day of Issue, Windsor (plain) handstamp .... **£3.50** ☐
1016i With World of Postcards, Croydon handstamp .... **£5.50** ☐
1016j With World of Postcards, Falmouth handstamp .... **£5.50** ☐
1016k With World of Postcards, Southampton handstamp .... **£5.50** ☐
1016l With Universal Postcard Rate, Birmingham handstamp .... **£5.50** ☐
1016m With Self Adhesive, Universal Postcard Rate, London handstamp .... **£5.50** ☐
1016n With Universal Postcard, Phil Stamp Collection, Send, Woking handstamp .... **£5.50** ☐

For all QEII Commemorative Issues
please see pages 45 – 349

1017. 2004, 11th May

40p Country Definitive.
England, Northern Ireland, Scotland, Wales

1017a Any one of the 40p Stamps with any one of nine Royal Mail first day of issue h/s* .....**£3.00** ☐
1017b 40p England with Country Definitives, Phil Stamp Collection, London handstamp..**£4.50** ☐
1017c With Windsor permanent (castle) handstamp…(Windsor cds £8) ....**£4.50** ☐
1017c 40p N.Ireland with Country Definitives, Phil Stamp Collection, Belfast handstamp..**£4.50** ☐
1017d 40p Scotland with Country Definitives, Phil Stamp Collection, Edinburgh handstamp ...**£4.50** ☐
1017e 40p Wales with Country Definitives, Phil Stamp Collection, Caerdydd, Cardiff h/s....**£4.50** ☐

*The same nine handstamps were used on Definitives Issue no **1014**.

1018. 2004, 25th May

£7.23 Glory of the Garden Prestige Stamp Book. 4 Panes

(4 x 1st Def + 2 x 42p Def + 2 x 47p Def + label), (2nd + E + 42p + 68p RHS Commems*), (4 x 1st Flowers 1997 Commems), (2 x 1st + 2 x 47p RHS Commems*)

1018a Set of 4 Panes with First Day of Issue, Royal Mail, Tallents House handstamp ....**£12.50** ☐
1018b With First day of Issue, RHS Wisley (tapestry), Wisley, Woking handstamp..........**£14.00** ☐
1018c With First Day of Issue (plain), Wisley, Woking handstamp ....**£14.00** ☐
1018d With any relevant commemorative handstamp* from the RHS Issue of same date ...**£18.50** ☐
1018e With Bloomfield cds, Chelsea cds, Daisy Hill cds, Primrose Hill cds......................**£24.00** ☐
1018f With Botanic Gardens cds, Flore cds, Garden Village cds ....**£24.00** ☐

*Please refer to RHS Commemorative Issue of same date no **471**.

1019. 2004, 30th November

1st NVI Gold Coil. De La Rue

1019a Ist NVI Gold Stamp, strip of three or more, with Windsor permanent handstamp .....**£3.50** ☐

1020. 2005, 24th February

£7.44 The Bronte Sisters Prestige Stamp Book. 4 Panes

1020a Set of 4 Panes with First Day of Issue, Royal Mail, Tallents House handstamp ......**£12.50** ☐
1020b With First Day of Issue, Haworth (house), Keighley handstamp..............................**£14.00** ☐
1020c With First Day of Issue, Haworth (plain), Keighley handstamp ....**£14.00** ☐
1020d With any relevant commemorative handstamp* from the Jane Eyre Issue ....**£18.50** ☐
1020e With Ripon cds, Rawdon cds, Gateshead cds ....**£24.00** ☐
1020f With Haworth cds, Adel cds, Rochester cds, Thornton cds ....**£24.00** ☐

*Please refer to the Jane Eyre Issue no **482** of same date.

1021. 2005, 22nd March

The Castles Definitives 1955. 50th Anniversary. Miniature Sheet
2 x 50p - Carrickfergus, Windsor, 2 x £1 - Caernarfon, Edinburgh

1021a Miniature Sheet with any one of some 14 relevant commemorative handstamps...**£8.00** ☐
1021b With Royal Mail first day of issue (3) handstamp..**£5.00** ☐
1021c With Caernarfon cds, Carrickfergus cds, Edinburgh cds, Windsor cds ....**£12.00** ☐

1022. 2005, 5th April

9p Orange, 46p Old Gold. New Definitives
35p Lime-Green. Colour Change

1022a All 3 Values with any one of 11(!) Royal Mail first day of issue handstamps .... **£3.50** ☐
1022b With Machin Definitives, Stoke-on-Trent handstamp .... **£5.00** ☐
1022c With Windsor permanent (castle design) handstamp.. **£5.00** ☐

1023. 2005, 5th April

42p Country Pictorial Definitives. New Value. Walsall
England, N. Ireland, Scotland, Wales

1023a Any 42p Regional with First Day of Issue, Royal Mail,Tallents House handstamp... **£2.50** ☐
1023b England 42p with any one of 4 Royal Mail first day of issue, London/Windsor h/s .. **£3.50** ☐
1023c N. Ireland 42p with either of 2 Royal Mail first day of issue, Belfast handstamps .... **£3.50** ☐
1023d Scotland 42p with either of 2 Royal Mail first day of issue, Edinburgh handstamps **£3.50** ☐
1023e Wales 42p with either of 2 Royal Mail first day of issue, Cardiff handstamps.......... **£3.50** ☐

From May 10th the 42p Stamp was printed by De La Rue. No special pmks done
All eleven handstamps listed are illusrated above

1024. 2005, 18th October

£7.26 Battle of Trafalgar. Death of Nelson. Prestige Stamp Book. 4 Panes

(3 x 1st White Ensign Stamp), (4 x 1st + 2 x 50p + 2 x 68p all Defs + Label)
(1st + 42p + 68p Trafalgar left Stamps*), (1st + 42p + 68p Trafalgar right Stamps*)

1024a All 4 complete Panes with any one of 3 Royal Mail first day of issue handstamps **£12.50** ☐
1024b With any one of some 28 relevant commemorative handstamps .... **£18.00** ☐
1024c With any one of some 21 relevant cds .... **£22.00** ☐

* For stamp and postmark details see Trafalgar Issue of same date in Commemoratives section

1025. 2006, 23rd February
£7.40 Isambard Kingdom Brunel. Prestige Stamp Book. 4 Panes
(1st, 42p, 68p Brunel Stamps*), (40p, 47p, 60p Brunel Stamps*)
(47p Brunel Stamp, 2 x 68p Ocean Liners 2004 Stamp)
(4 x 1st, 2 x 35p, 2 x 40p Definitives, plus Label)

1025a All 4 complete Panes with any one of 3 Royal Mail first day of issue h/s .... **£12.50** ☐
1025b With any one of some 26 relevant commemorative handstamps .... **£18.00** ☐
1025c Box cds, Clifton cds, Bristol cds, Maidenhead cds, Paddington cds, Saltash cds.. **£22.00** ☐

*For Stamp details see Brunel Issue of same date in Commemoratives section

1026. 2006, 28th March
New Definitives. 37p Olive Green, 44p Ultramarine, 49p Rust, 72p Red

1026a Set of 4 Values with one of 11(!) Royal Mail first day of issue handstamps* .... **£3.50** ☐
1026b With Country Definitives, Phil Stamp Collection, Windsor handstamp...................... **£5.50** ☐
1026c With Machin Definitives, Phil Stamp Collection, Stoke-on-Trent handstamp .... **£5.50** ☐
1026d With New Definitives, Machin Road, Birmingham handstamp .... **£5.50** ☐

*To see these 11 postmarks, please refer to the April 5th, 2005 Definitives Issue

1027. 2006, 28th March
New Country Pictorial Stamps. 42p, 68p
England, Scotland, Wales, N. Ireland

1027a Set of any 2 Values with First Day of Issue, Royal Mail, Tallents House h/s .... **£3.00** ☐
1027b England 2 Values with either of 2 Royal Mail first day of issue, London h/s .... **£4.00** ☐
1027c England 2 Values with either of 2 Royal Mail first day of issue, Windsor h/s .... **£4.00** ☐
1027d N. Ireland 42p and 68p with either of 2 Royal Mail first day of issue, Belfast h/s..... **£4.00** ☐
1027e Scotland 42p and 68p with either of 2 Royal Mail first day of issue, Edinburgh h/s. **£4.00** ☐
1027f Wales 42p and 68p with either of 2 Royal Mail first day of issue, Cardiff h/s........... **£4.00** ☐
1027g Set of any 2 Values with Country Definitives, Phil Stamp Collection, Windsor h/s... **£5.50** ☐

The Royal Mail postmarks are as used for the April 5th, 2005 Definitives Issue

**Try to collect covers with a relevant postmark.
Recent Issues, without this, are of little value
in today's market place.**

1028. 2006, 1st August

New Definitives. Pricing in Proportion
1st, 2nd - Redesigned, 1st, 2nd - New Larger Design,
12p - Dark Turquoise, 14p - Salmon-Pink. New Machins

1028a Set of six Stamps with First day of Issue, Royal Mail, Tallents House handstamp...**£3.50** ☐
1028b With First day of Issue, Windsor handstamp....................**£4.50** ☐
1028c With any one of some 5 relevant commemorative handstamps ....**£6.50** ☐

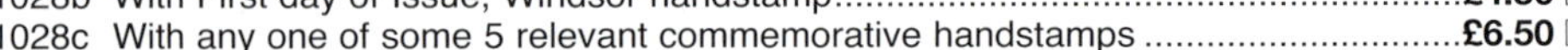

1029. 2006, 31st August

Year of the Three Kings. 70th Anniversary
Souvenir Sheetlet, £3 QEII Stamp and reproductions of 1d Kings Stamps

1029a Sheetlet with any Royal Mail first day of issue (3) handstamp ....**£5.00** ☐
1029b With any one of some 14 relevant commemorative handstamps ....**£7.50** ☐
1029c With any relevant cds ....**£10.50** ☐

1030. 2006, 21st September

£7.44 The Victoria Cross. Prestige Stamp Book. 4 Panes

(1st, 64p, 72p - VC Stamps), (1st, 64p, 72p - VC Stamps)
(4 x 1st new design Defs + 4 x 50p Defs + Label), (4 x 20p Gallantry Stamp)

1030a All 4 complete Panes with any Royal Mail first day of issue (4) handstamp..........**£12.50** ☐
1030b With any one of some 28 relevant commemorative handstamps ....**£18.00** ☐
1030c With any relevant cds ....**£22.00** ☐

A set of Commemorative Stamps and Miniature Sheet were also issued on this date.

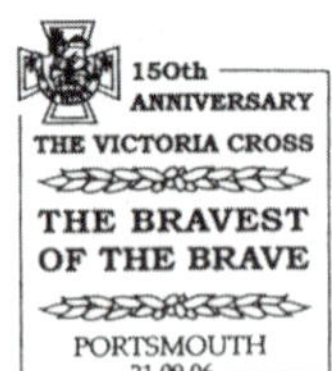

The Victoria Cross was instituted by Royal Warrant on January 29th, 1856. The first Investiture took place on June 26th, 1857.

1031. 2006, 17th October
New Smilers Definitives. Self-Adhesive
6 x 1st, Thank you, New Baby, Best Wishes, Balloons, Fireworks, Celebration

1031a Set of six Stamps, with First Day of Issue, Royal Mail, Tallents House handstamp . **£4.00** ☐
1031b With First Day of Issue, Grinshill, Shrewsbury handstamp ..... **£4.50** ☐
1031c With any one of some 7 relevant commemorative handstamps ..... **£7.00** ☐
1031d With any relevant cds ..... **£10.00** ☐

The six Stamps were issued in stamp book format

1032. 2007, 1st March
£7.49 World of Invention. Prestige Stamp Book. 4 Panes
(3 x 2nd Scotland + 3 x 44p Wales), (4 x 1st Defs + 4 x 5p Defs + Label)
(2 x 1st + 2 x 64p Invention Stamps), (2 x 1st + 2 x 72p Inventions Stamps)

1032a All 4 complete Panes with any Royal Mail first day of issue (4) handstamp ..... **£12.50** ☐
1032b With any one of some 19 relevant commemorative handstamps ..... **£18.00** ☐
1032c With any relevant cds ..... **£22.00** ☐

1033. 2007, 27th March
New Definitives. Postage Rate Increase
16p Pink, 48p Rhododendron, 50p Light Grey, 54p Rust, 78p Emerald-Green

1033a Set of five Stamps, with First Day of Issue, Royal Mail, Tallents House h/s ..... **£4.50** ☐
1033b With First Day of issue, Windsor (2) handstamp ..... **£5.50** ☐
1033c With First day of issue, London (2) handstamp ..... **£5.50** ☐
1033d With New Definitives, Queen Elizabeth Road, Birmingham handstamp ..... **£7.50** ☐
1033e With Royal Mail (castle) Windsor permanent handstamp ..... **£7.50** ☐

New postal rates came into force from April 2nd, 2007.
2nd - 24p, 1st - 34p, Europe - 48p, USA - 54p

1034. 2007, 27th March
New Country Pictorial Stamps. 48p, 78p. Postage Rate Increase
England, Northern Ireland, Scotland, Wales

1034a Any 48p and 78p version with First Day of Issue, Royal Mail,Tallents House h/s .... **£3.00** ☐
1034b England 48p, 78p with one of 4 Royal Mail first day of issue, London/Windsor h/s . **£4.00** ☐
1034c N. Ireland 48p, 78p with either of 2 Royal Mail first day of issue, Belfast h/s........... **£4.00** ☐
1034d Scotland 48p, 78p with either of 2 Royal Mail first day of issue, Edinburgh h/s .... **£4.00** ☐
1033e Wales 48p, 78p with either of 2 Royal Mail first day of issue, Cardiff handstamps .. **£4.00** ☐

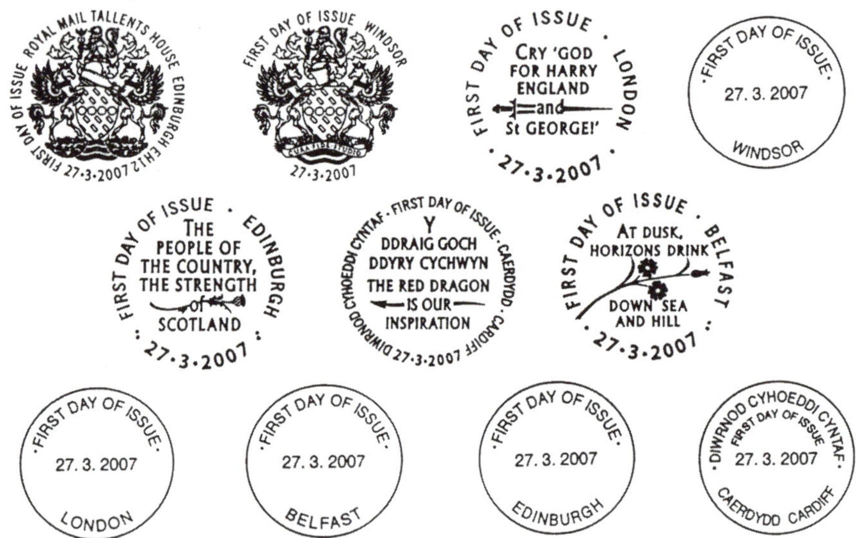

1035. 2007, 5th June
The Machin. 40th Anniversary
£1 Ruby. New Colour

1035a £1 Stamp on illustrated cover, any postmark .... **£2.50** ☐
1035b With First Day of Issue, Tallents House, Edinburgh handstamp .... **£4.00** ☐
1035c With First Day of Issue, Stoke-on-Trent handstamp .... **£4.50** ☐
1035d With First Day of Issue, Windsor handstamp .... **£4.50** ☐
1035e With First Day of Issue (non pictorial), Stoke-on-Trent handstamp .... **£4.50** ☐
1035f With First Day of Issue (non pictorial), Windsor handstamp .... **£4.50** ☐
1035g With any one of some 18 additional relevant commemorative handstamps .... **£7.00** ☐
1035h With Windsor cds (Buckingham Palace **£15**) .... **£12.00** ☐
1035i With House of Commons or House of Lords cds .... **£10.00** ☐
1035j With any relevant cds .... **£9.00** ☐

1036. 2007, 5th June
£7.66 The Machin. Prestige Stamp Book. 4 Panes
(4 x 2p, 2 x 46p, 2 x 48p Defs + Label), (2 x £1 Ruby, New Colour Definitive)
(2 x 1st Machin Commemorative, 2 x 1st 4d reproduction)
(2 x 1st Large, 2 x 1st Small, 2 x 2nd Large, 2 x 2nd Small Defs + Label)

1036a All 4 complete Panes with any Royal Mail first day of issue (5) handstamp* .... **£12.50** ☐
1036b With any one of some 18 relevant commemorative handstamps* .... **£18.00** ☐
1036c With any relevant cds* .... **£22.00** ☐

*See Issue 1035 of same date for details.

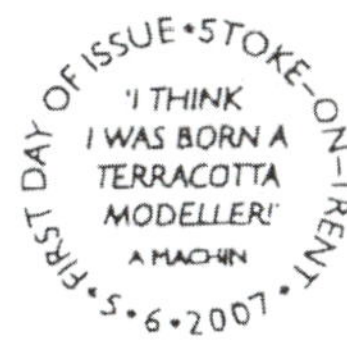

1037. 2007, 5th June
Machin Anniversary. Stamp Book
6 x 1st Definitive + 1st Machin Portrait

1037a Complete Booklet on illustrated cover, any postmark .... **£3.00** ☐
1037b With First Day of Issue - with any Royal Mail handstamp (5)* .... **£5.00** ☐
1037c With any one of some 18 additional relevant commemorative handstamps* .... **£8.00** ☐
1037d With Windsor cds, or any other relevant cds* .... **£10.00** ☐

*See Issue 1035 for details.

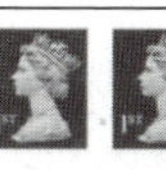

1038. 2007, 20th September
£7.66 Army Uniforms. Prestige Stamp Book. 4 Panes
(3 x 1st Army Uniform), (3 x 78p Army Uniform), (2 x 1p + 4 x 46p + 2 x 54p Definitives + Label), (4 x 1st Country Defs.* + 5 Labels)

1038a Complete Set of 4 entire Panes on illustrated covers, any postmark .... **£9.00** ☐
1038b With First Day of Issue, Tallents House, Edinburgh handstamp .... **£12.00** ☐
1038c With First Day of Issue, Boot, Holmrook handstamp .... **£13.00** ☐
1038d With First Day of Issue (non pictorial), Boot, Holmrook handstamp....................... **£13.00** ☐
1038e With any one of some 20 additional relevant commemorative handstamps.......... **£18.00** ☐
1038f With Battle, Bovington, Garrison, or any other relevant cds .... **£21.00** ☐

*England, Scotland, Northern Ireland, Wales

1039. 2008, 8th January

£7.40 James Bond. Prestige Stamp Book. 4 Panes

(8 x 1st Definitive + Label), (1st Casino Royal, 54p Goldfinger, 78p Your Eyes Only), (1st Dr. No, 54p Diamonds Forever, 78p Russia with Love), (2 x 1st White Ensign Flag + 2 x 1st Union Flag of 2001)

1039a Complete Set of 4 entire Panes on illustrated covers, any postmark .... **£9.00** ☐
1039b With First Day of Issue, Tallents House, Edinburgh handstamp .... **£12.00** ☐
1039c With First Day of Issue, London SE1 handstamp .... **£13.00** ☐
1039d With First Day of Issue (non pictorial), London SE1 handstamp .... **£13.00** ☐
1039e With any one of some 22 additional relevant commemorative handstamps .... **£18.00** ☐
1039f With any relevant cds .... **£21.00** ☐

1040. 2008, 1st April

New Definitive Values. De La Rue. Gravure

15p Shocking Pink, 56p Lime-Green, 81p Sea Green

1040a Set of Three Stamps on illustrated cover, any postmark .... **£2.00** ☐
1040b With First Day of Issue, Tallents House, Edinburgh handstamp .... **£3.00** ☐
1040c With First Day of Issue, Windsor handstamp .... **£3.50** ☐
1040d With First Day of Issue (non pictorial), Windsor handstamp .... **£3.50** ☐
1040e With First Day of Issue (non pictorial), London handstamp .... **£3.50** ☐
1040f With New Definitives, Queen Elizabeth Rd. Birmingham handstamp .... **£6.50** ☐
1040g With any relevant cds .... **£8.00** ☐

All prices in this catalogue are for clean covers, with undamaged stamps and clear postmarks.

Anything less is worth less!

1041. 2008, 1st April
New Country Definitives. De La Rue. Gravure
50p, 81p - England, N. Ireland, Scotland, Wales

1041a Set of Two Stamps for England, N. Ireland, Scotland, or Wales on illus. cover, any pmk ... **£2.00** ☐
1041b With First Day of Issue - any one of 4 handstamps as illustrated below .... **£3.00** ☐
1041c With First Day of Issue (non pictorial) - any one of 4 h/s as illustrated below .... **£3.00** ☐
1041d With any relevant cds .... **£7.50** ☐

All postmarks from Issue 1040 above were also available for the Country Stamps. Price **£3** each.

1042. 2008, 18th September
£7.15 Pilot to Plane: RAF Uniforms. Prestige Stamp Book, 4 Panes
(3 x 81p RAF Uniforms), (3 x 1st RAF Uniforms),
(2 x 20p Spitfire from 1997 + 2 x 1st Air Display from 2008),
(4 x 2nd + 4 x 1st Definitives + Label)

1042a Complete Set of 4 entire Panes on illustrated covers, any postmark .... **£8.50** ☐
1042b With First Day of Issue, Tallents House, Edinburgh handstamp............................ **£11.00** ☐
1042c With First Day of Issue, Hendon, London NW9 handstamp................................ **£12.00** ☐
1042d With First Day of Issue (non pictorial), Hendon, London NW9 handstamp .... **£12.00** ☐
1042e With First Day of Issue, Autumn Stampex...London N1 handstamp .... **£13.00** ☐
1042f With any one of some 14 additional relevant commemorative handstamps.......... **£17.50** ☐
1042g With any RAF Aerodrome cds, any other relevant cds .... **£20.00** ☐

Readers comments are always welcome

1043. 2008, 29th September

Celebrating 50 Years of Country Stamps. Miniature Sheet

9 x 1st Country Stamps - 3 each Scotland, Wales, Northern Ireland

1043a Miniature Sheet on illustrated cover, any postmark .... **£4.00** ☐
1043b With First Day of Issue, Tallents House, Edinburgh handstamp .... **£5.50** ☐
1043c With First Day of Issue, Gloucester handstamp .... **£6.00** ☐
1043d With First Day of Issue (non pictorial), Gloucester handstamp .... **£6.00** ☐
1043e With any one of some 12 additional relevant commemorative handstamps .... **£9.50** ☐
1043f With any relevant cds .... **£12.50** ☐

All stamps are previously issued designs (in 1958) with values changed to 1st.

1044. 2008, 29th September

£7.56 The Regional Definitives. Prestige Stamp Book. 4 Panes

(3 x 1st each for Scotland, N.Ireland, Wales), (6 x 1st Scotland*), (6 x 1st N.Ireland*), (6 x 1st Wales*)

1044a Complete Set of 4 Stamps, on illustrated cover, any postmark .... **£9.50** ☐
1044b With First Day of Issue, Tallents House, Edinburgh handstamp .... **£14.00** ☐
1044c With First Day of Issue, Gloucester handstamp .... **£15.00** ☐
1044d With First Day of Issue (non pictorial), Gloucester handstamp .... **£15.00** ☐
1044e With any one of some 12 additional relevant commemorative handstamps .... **£20.00** ☐
1044f With any relevant cds .... **£24.00** ☐

*Each of these three Panes have 3 x current Country 1st Stamps + 3 x 1958 design 1st Stamps.

This is the 30th Edition of the Collect GB First Day Covers catalogue.
We hope that you are enjoying it and find it useful
in developing your own collection.

1045. 2009, 13th January

£7.68 British Design Classics. Prestige Stamp Book. 4 Panes

(4 x 16p + 4 x 50p Definitives + Label), (2 x 1st Austin Mini + 2 x 1st Routemaster Bus), (6 x 1st Underground Map, Telephone Kiosk, Penguin Books, Anglepoise Lamp, Chair, Mini Skirt), (2 x 1st Concorde + 2 x 1st 2002 Concorde Stamp)

1045a Complete Set of 4 entire Panes, on illustrated covers, any postmark .... **£9.00** ☐
1045b With First Day of Issue, Tallents House, Edinburgh handstamp .... **£12.00** ☐
1045c With First Day of Issue, Longbridge, Birmingham handstamp .... **£13.00** ☐
1045d With First Day of Issue (non pictorial), Longbridge, Birmingham handstamp .... **£13.00** ☐
1045e With any one of some 16 additional relevant commemorative handstamps.......... **£18.00** ☐
1045f With any relevant cds .... **£21.00** ☐

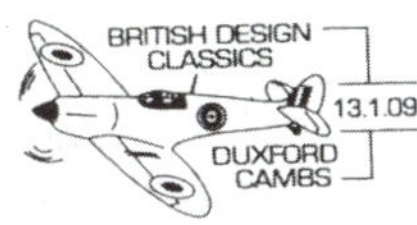

1046. 2009, 12th February

£7.75 Charles Darwin 1809-1882. Prestige Stamp Book. 4 Panes

(48p, 50p, 56p Darwin Stamps), (Darwin Miniature Sheet*), (1st, 72p, 81p Darwin Stamps), (2 x 5p + 2 x 10p + 2 x 48p Definitives + 2 x 1st Definitive + Label)

1046a Complete Set of 4 entire Panes on illustrated covers, any postmark .... **£9.00** ☐
1046b With First Day of Issue, Tallents House, Edinburgh handstamp .... **£12.00** ☐
1046c With First Day of Issue, Shrewsbury handstamp .... **£13.00** ☐
1046d With First Day of Issue (non pictorial), Shrewsbury handstamp .... **£13.00** ☐
1046e With any one of some 17 additional relevant commemorative handstamps.......... **£18.00** ☐
1046f With any relevant cds .... **£21.00** ☐

*See Darwin Commemorative Issue 583 for detail.

Please refer to the **Introduction** for additional comment on:

Generic Sheets, Commemorative Sheets, Modern Smilers Sheets, Signed First Day Covers – by the Designer or a Personality, Control Numbers/Cylinder Numbers, Postal Stationery.

Don't forget that we now include sections on Overprints, Pre-release covers, Missing Colours and Postal Stationery on fdc. These can found in the last part of the catalogue.

1047. 2009, 17th February

New Security Definitives. Gravure. Self-adhesive

Iridescent Ink. Four Semi-circular Slits on each Stamp

(i) 2nd, 1st, 50p, £1 (ii) £1.50, £2, £3, £5

1047a	(i) 2nd, 1st, 50p, £1 on illustrated cover, any postmark	**£3.00** ☐
1047b	With First Day of Issue, Tallents House, Edinburgh handstamp	**£4.50** ☐
1047c	With First Day of Issue, Windsor handstamp	**£5.00** ☐
1047d	With First Day of Issue (non pictorial), Windsor handstamp	**£5.00** ☐
1047e	With Machin Definitives, Security Features, London SE1 handstamp	**£8.50** ☐
1047f	With Machin Definitives, Security Features, London SW1 handstamp	**£8.50** ☐
1047g	With Machin Definitives, Security Features, Windsor handstamp	**£8.50** ☐
1047h	With New Definitives, Queen Elizabeth Rd, Birmingham handstamp	**£8.50** ☐
1047i	With Windsor cds (Buckingham Palace cds £20)	**£16.50** ☐
1047j	With House of Commons cds or House of Lords cds	**£15.00** ☐
1047k	With any other relevant cds	**£12.50** ☐
1047l	(ii) £1.50, £2, £3, £5 on illustrated cover, any postmark	**£12.50** ☐
1047m	With First Day of Issue, Tallents House, Edinburgh handstamp	**£14.00** ☐
1047n	With First Day of Issue, Windsor handstamp	**£14.50** ☐
1047o	With New Definitives, Queen Elizabeth Rd, Birmingham handstamp	**£14.50** ☐
1047p	With First Day of Issue (non pictorial), Windsor handstamp	**£14.50** ☐
1047q	With Machin Definitives, Security Features, London SE1 handstamp	**£18.00** ☐
1047r	With Machin Definitives, Security Features, London SW1 handstamp	**£18.00** ☐
1047s	With Machin Definitives, Security Features, Windsor handstamp	**£18.00** ☐
1047t	With New Definitives, Queen Elizabeth Rd, Birmingham handstamp	**£18.00** ☐
1047u	With Windsor cds (Buckingham Palace cds £30)	**£26.00** ☐
1047v	With House of Commons cds or House of Lords cds	**£25.00** ☐
1047w	With any other relevant cds	**£22.00** ☐
1047x	All stamps (i) + (ii) on one cover, any postmark	**£15.00** ☐
1047y	Any Royal Mail handstamp	**£18.50** ☐
1047z	With any one of the 4 Commemorative handstamps	**£24.00** ☐
1047aa	With Windsor cds (Buckingham Palace cds £40)	**£32.00** ☐
1047bb	With House of Commons cds or House of Lords cds	**£30.00** ☐
1047cc	With any other relevant cds	**£27.50** ☐

1048. 2009, 31st March
New Definitives
17p Olive-green, 22p Stone, 62p Red, 90p Ultramarine

1048a Set of Four Stamps on illustrated cover, any postmark .... **£2.50** ☐
1048b With First Day of Issue, Tallents House, Edinburgh handstamp .... **£3.50** ☐
1048c With First Day of Issue, Windsor handstamp .... **£4.00** ☐
1048d With First Day of Issue (non pictorial), Windsor handstamp .... **£4.00** ☐
1048e With New Machin Definitives, Windsor, Berks handstamp .... **£7.50** ☐
1048f With New Definitives, Queen Elizabeth Rd, Birmingham handstamp .... **£7.50** ☐
1048g With Windsor cds (Buckingham Palace cds £15) .... **£11.00** ☐
1048h With House of Commons cds or House of Lords cds .... **£12.00** ☐
1048i With any other relevant cds .... **£8.50** ☐

Any one of a further 8 First Day of Issue handstamps, prepared for the new Country Stamps, could also be used on these New Definitives. Catalogue price for the Set of Four Stamps with any of these handstamps **£4**.

1049. 2009, 31st March
New Country Stamps. England, Scotland, Northern Ireland, Wales
56p, 90p (New values on old 50p and 81p designs)

1049a 56p + 90p Stamps for any one of England, Scotland, N. Ireland or Wales, on illus. cover, any pmk **£2.00** ☐
1049b With any one of the 11 First Day of Issue handstamps illustrated below .... **£3.50** ☐
1049c With New Machin Definitives, Windsor, Berks handstamp .... **£6.00** ☐
1049d With New Definitives, Queen Elizabeth Rd, Birmingham handstamp .... **£6.00** ☐
1049e With any relevant regional cds .... **£8.50** ☐

1050. 2009, 18th August

£8.18 Treasures of the BPMA*. Prestige Stamp Book. 4 Panes

(4 x 20p Defs from 1990 + 4 x 1st Defs from 2000 + Label), (4 x 20p Royal Mail Coach Stamp from 1988), (1st + 56p + 81p + 90p Post Boxes Commemorative Miniature Sheet Stamps, issued 18 August 2009), (4 x 17p + 2 x 22p + 2 x 62p Definitives + Label)

1050a Complete Set of Four entire Panes on illustrated covers, any postmark................**£9.00** ☐
1050b With First Day of Issue, Tallents House, Edinburgh handstamp............................**£12.00** ☐
1050c With First Day of Issue, London EC1 handstamp..**£13.00** ☐
1050d With First Day of Issue (non pictorial), London EC1 handstamp...........................**£13.00** ☐
1050e With any one of some 16 additional relevant commemorative handstamps..........**£18.00** ☐
1050f With any relevant cds...**£21.00** ☐

*British Postal Museum Archives

See also Commemorative Issue **595** of the same date.

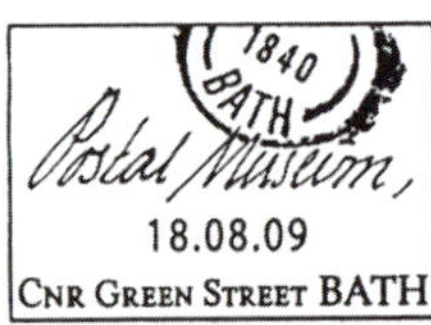

1051. 2009, 17th September

£7.93 Royal Navy Uniforms. Prestige Stamp Book

(3 x 1st Navy Uniforms), (3 x 90p Navy Uniforms), (2 x 1st White Ensign 2001 Stamp + 2 x 1st Jolly Roger 2001 Stamp) , (2 x 1p + 4 x 17p + 2 x 90p Definitives) ..

1051a Complete Set of Four entire Panes on illustrated covers, any postmark£9.00
1051b With First Day of Issue, Tallents House, Edinburgh handstamp............................**£12.00** ☐
1051c With First Day of Issue, Portsmouth handstamp..**£13.00** ☐
1051d With First Day of Issue (non pictorial), Portsmouth handstamp.............................**£13.00** ☐
1051e With First Day of Issue, Autumn Stampex... handstamp...**£18.00** ☐
1051f With any one of some 14 additional relevant commemorative handstamps..........**£14.00** ☐
1051g With any relevant cds...**£21.00** ☐

See also Commemorative Issue **598** of the same date.

End of QEII Definitives, Regionals, Prestige Stamp Books, Booklets, Coils, Dues, Gums, Perfs, Papers, etc.

1052. 2008, 8th October
Post & Go Stamps
1st Class Up to 100g, 1st Class Large Up to 100g, Europe Up to 20g, Worldwide Up to 10g, Worldwide Up to 20g
1052a Set of Five Stamps on illustrated cover(s), with Bristol postmark ....**£6.50** ☐

1053. 2009, 31st March
Post & Go Stamps
Reproductions of the Five Stamps issued on 8th October 2008
These are separate Stamps, not Se-tenant
1053a Set of Five Stamps on illustrated cover, with Post & Go, Bristol handstamp ....**£5.00** ☐
1053b With Post & Go, Windsor handstamp ....**£5.00** ☐

More information on these new type of Stamps in the next catalogue.

2010 NEW ISSUES

07 January.............................**British Design**
02 February...............**Girl Guides Centenary**
25 February.......**Royal Society 250th Anniv.**
11 March......**Battersea Dogs & Cats Home**
23 March........**House of Stewart (Scotland)**
13 April.........**Action for Species: Mammals**
06 May........... **Accession of King George V**
08 May...........................**The King's Stamps**
13 May........................ **Britain Alone in 1940**
15 June.............................**Children's Books**
19 August............................**Stage Musicals**
16 September...........**Great British Railways**
12 October..**House of Stuart (James/Anne)**
02 November.......................**Christmas Issue**

There will also be an Olympic and Paralympic Games Issue – date to be confirmed.
Please note dates are subject to change and more Issues could be added during the year!

GB Overprints - From 1893 to 1963

Queen Victoria – Queen Elizabeth II

The market for GB Overprints on First Day Cover is still a relatively small one - perhaps because no new stamps have been issued since the mid-1960's! GB Overprints started in the late 1800's and finished basically when the last GB Overseas Postal Administrations were closed in the 1960's. During this period of time many GB Stamp Issues were overprinted and there is certainly a wide selection of good fdc material for Collectors to study.

In general GB Overprints on fdc continue to be an overlooked and an under valued aspect of stamp collecting. Clearly fewer covers were produced on fdc of every overprinted issue, compared to the non overprinted stamps, hence catalogue values should be generally higher for overprinted fdc's. The study of GB Overprints on fdc offers a wealth of really fascinating historical and geographical information on Britain's overseas postal involvement over a seventy or more year period of time. If you are looking for a different aspect of GB First Day Covers to start collecting, then GB Overprints should be considered a strong candidate and one which surely will give hours of pleasure and worthwhile study.

001. 1893, 25th February. Constantinople

001a QV ½d Vermillion, 40 Paras Overprint, clear BPO backstamp .... **£465.00** ☐
A unique group of 18 on piece exists. Value **£2,500+**.

002. 1906, 2nd July. KEVII Definitive

002a 2d Green and Carmine, Levant 1 Piastre Overprint, Beyrout pmk .... **£2,900.00** ☐

003. 1922, 17th February. KGV First Irish Overprint Definitives

003a KGV Profile Head Defs. Set on 2 covers with Dollard and Thom 5 line Overprint.. **£1,750.00** ☐
Single values up to 2d (**£100**), up to 6d (**£250**), up to 1/- (**£350**)

004. 1937, 16th February. KGV Gravure Definitives

004a 9d Olive, Morocco Agencies (French) Overprint. BPO pmk...................................... **£120.00** ☐
004b 1d +1½d Tangier Overprint, 11th Feb.1935. BPO Tangier pmk .... **£65.00** ☐

005/8 1935, 8th May. KGV Silver Jubilee Issue

005/8a Complete on 4 fdc's, Tangier, Morocco Agencies (British/French/Spanish) Overprints. **£280.00** ☐
005/8b Single cover set of any of the 4 Overprint versions... **£65.00** ☐
005/8c Tangier Set (3) in Blocks of 4 .... **£150.00** ☐
005/8d French Morocco Set (4) in Blocks of 4.. **£175.00** ☐

009. 1936, 26th October, KEVIII Definitives

009a Cover with 11 Overprints of Tangier, Morocco Agencies (British/French/Spanish) .... **£46.00** ☐
009b Single cover set of any of the 4 Overprint versions.. **£12.00** ☐

010. 1937, 13th May. KGVI Coronation

010a 1½d brown, cover with 3 Overprints Tangier, Morocco Agencies (French/Spanish)..... **£16.00** ☐
010b 1½d Block of 4, any Overprint version (larger Blocks from **£20**) .... **£12.50** ☐

011. 1940, 6th May. KGVI Penny Black Centenary

011a ½d, 1d, 1½d, 2½d Morocco Agenicies (Spanish), BPO Tetuan pmk .... **£150.00** ☐
011b ½d, 1d, 1½d Tangier Overprint pairs, BPO Tangier pmk .... **£185.00** ☐
011c Same three values, Tangier Overprint, known in Blocks (**£280**) and singles......... **£150.00** ☐
Only these three values available (very few) in Tangier on the first day of issue.

GB Overprints - From 1893 to 1963

012. **1946, 11th June. KGVI Victory issue**
012a 2½d and 3d set, Tangier Overprint, BPO Tangier pmk .... **£18.00** □
012b Also known in Blocks of 4, BPO Tangier registered pmk .... **£45.00** □

013/14. **1948, 26th April. KGVI Silver Wedding**
013a 2½d, £1 set, Morocco Agencies (Spanish) Overprint .... **£225.00** □
013b £1 in block of 4, Morocro Agencies (Spanish) overprint, local pmk .... **£275.00** □
014a Set with Tangier Overprint on illustrated cover .... **£300.00** □
014b 2½d known in Block of 4, BPO Tangier pmk .... **£35.00** □

015/18. **1948, 29th July. KGVI Olympic Games**
015a 2½, 3d, 6d, 1/- Set, Bahrain Overprint .... **£35.00** □
016a Set with Tangier Overprint, illustrated cover .... **£27.50** □
017a Set with Morocco Agencies (Spanish) Overprint, illustrated cover .... **£27.50** □
018a Set with Kuwait Overprint, illustrated cover .... **£38.00** □

019/22. **1949, 10th October. KGVI Universal Postal Union**
019a 2½d, 3d, 6d, 1/- Set, Muscat Overprint, illustrated cover .... **£45.00** □
020a Set with Tangier Overprint, illustrated cover, local pmk .... **£35.00** □
021a Set with Bahrain Overprint, illustrated cover, local pmk .... **£45.00** □
022a Set with Kuwait Overprint, illustrated cover, local pmk .... **£45.00** □

023. **1937, 11th June. KGVI First Definitives**
023a ½d, 1d, 2½d M.A. Overprint (Spanish) + ½d, 1d Tangier + ½d M.A. (French) .... **£12.00** □
023b ½d, 1d Tangier known in blocks (**£20**), also ½d M.A. (French) in Block .... **£10.00** □

024. **1937, 4th August. KGVI First Definitives**
024a 1½d Tangier Overprint plus 1½d Morocco Agencies (Spanish) Overprint .... **£25.00** □
024b 1½d with either Tangier or Morocco Agencies Overprint (in Blocks **£25**) .... **£17.50** □

025. **1942, 2nd March. KGVI First Definitives**
025a Set of 5 values with first M.E.F. Overprint. Asmara or Eritrea pmk .... **£60.00** □
025b Set with M.E.F. Overprint, but Somalia April 13, 1942 fdc pmk .... **£70.00** □

026. **1943, 1st January. KGVI Definitives**
026a Set of 9 values with M.E.F. Overprint, Asmara pmk .... **£185.00** □

027. **1943, 15th January. KGVI Definitives**
027a Set of 8 Low Values with E.A.F. Overprint, Mogadiscio pmk .... **£275.00** □

028. **1944, 2nd December. KGVI Definitive (Colour Change)**
028a ½d Light Green, with Tangier Overprint, Tangier pmk (in Blocks **£40**) .... **£30.00** □

029. **1946, 14th January. KGVI High Values**
029a 2/6d Green with E.A.F. Overprint, Somalia pmk .... **£265.00** □

030 **1948, 1st July. KGVI Definitives**
030a Set of 13 values with B.M.A. Tripolitania Overprint, Tripoli pmk .... **£350.00** □

031. **1948, 1st April. KGVI Definitives**
031a Set of 10 values with Kuwait Overprint, pmk (misspelt Kuwatt **£425**) .... **£325.00** □
031b 5/- Red, Kuwait Overprint, pmk misspelt Kuwatt .... **£165.00** □

032. **1948, 27th May. KGVI Definitives**
032a Set of 11 values with B.M.A. Somalia Overprint, Somalia pmk .... **£295.00** □

GB Overprints - From 1893 to 1963

033.	**1948/49, KGVI Definitives**		
033a	First 7 values up to 6d, 1 April 1948, with Bahrain Overprint, Bahrain pmk	**£60.00**	☐
033b	10/- Lt Blue, 4 July 1949, with Bahrain Overprint, Bahrain pmk	**£160.00**	☐
033c	2/6, 5/-, 10/- with 1st January 1949 Tangier Overprint	**£325.00**	☐
034.	**1949, 19th January. KGVI Definitives**		
034a	12 values with B.M.A. Eritrea Overprint, Asmara pmk	**£350.00**	☐
034b	8d, with 1st February 1949, B.M.A. Eritrea Overprint	**£30.00**	☐
035.	**1949, 16th August. KGVI Definitives**		
035a	Set of 17 with Morocco Agencies Overprint, BPO pmk	**£365.00**	☐
036.	**1950, 2nd January. KGVI Definitives**		
036a	Set of 11 with B.A. Somalia Overprint, Somalia pmk	**£260.00**	☐
037.	**1950, 6th February. KGVI Definitives**		
037a	Set of 13 with B.A. Eritrea Overprint, Eritrea pmk	**£275.00**	☐
038.	**1950, 6th February. KGVI Definitives**		
038a	Set of 13 with B.A. Tripolitania Overprint, Tripoli pmk	**£265.00**	☐
039.	**1950, 6th February. KGVI Postage Due Stamps**		
039a	Set of 5 with B.A. Tripolitania Overprint, Tripoli pmk	**£325.00**	☐
040	**1950/51, October/May. KGVI Definitives**		
040a	4d, Oct. 2nd 1950 Bahrain Overprint (in Blocks **£25**)	**£18.00**	☐
040b	Set of 6 up to 2/6d, May 3rd 1951, Bahrain Overprint	**£75.00**	☐
	First three Low values known in blocks of 4. Valued at **£16** each		
041.	**1951, 3rd May. KGVI Festival Definitives**		
041a	2/6d Green, new design with B.A. Tripolitania Overprint, Tripoli pmk	**£50.00**	☐
041b	Set of 13 values, B.A. Tripolitania Overprint, Tripoli pmk	**£260.00**	☐
042.	**1951, 3rd May. KGVI Festival Definitives**		
042a	Set of 7 values with Morocco Agencies Overprint, BPO pmk	**£130.00**	☐
042b	Set of 8 values with Tangier Overprint, BPO pmk	**£150.00**	☐
042c	Set of 5 low values Tangier Overprint, Festival May 4th pmk	**£50.00**	☐
042d	Set of 8 values with Kuwait Overprint, Kuwait pmk	**£165.00**	☐
042e	Set of 6 values with Bahrain Overprint, Bahrain pmk	**£155.00**	☐
043.	**1951, 1st October. KGVI Post Due Stamps**		
043a	Set of 6 values with Southern Rhodesia Overprint	**£380.00**	☐
044.	**1953, 3rd June. QEII Coronation Issue**		
044a	Set of 4 values with Bahrain Overprint, Bahrain pmk	**£28.00**	☐
044b	Set of 4 values with Kuwait Overprint, Kuwait pmk	**£28.00**	☐
044c	Set of 4 values with Muscat Overprint, Muscat pmk (June 10th)	**£28.00**	☐
044d	Set of 4 values with Tangier Overprint, BPO pmk	**£26.00**	☐
044e	Coronation 6d Air Letter, Bahrain, Muscat, or Kuwait Overprint	**£22.00**	☐
045.	**1957, 1st August. QEII World Scout Jubilee Jamboree**		
045a	Set of 3 values with Muscat NP Overprint, any local pmk	**£60.00**	☐
045b	Set of 3 values with Bahrain NP Overprint, pmk	**£60.00**	☐
045c	Set of 3 values with Qatar NP Overprint, any local pmk	**£60.00**	☐

Illustrations of most GB Overprint covers listed can be seen in the 1998/99 catalogue

GB Overprints - From 1893 to 1963

046. 1952/55, QEII Morocco Definitives. Set of 10 Values
046a 1952, 5th December. 1½d, 2½d Morocco Agencies Overprint .... £20.00 ☐
046b 1953, 31st August. ½d, 1d, 2d Morocco Agencies Overprint .... £16.00 ☐
046c 1955, 1st March. 4d, 6d Morocco Agencies Overprint .... £25.00 ☐
046d 1953, 6th July. 5d, 8d, 1/- Morocco Agencies Overprint .... £18.00 ☐

047. 1952/54, QEII Tangier Definitives. Set of 17 Values
047a 1952, 5th December. 1½d, 2½d Tangier Overprint, BPO pmk .... £22.50 ☐
047b 1953, 31st August. ½d, 1d, 2d Tangier Overprint, BPO pmk .... £16.00 ☐
047c 1954, 18th January. 3d, 6d, 7d Tangier Overprint, BPO pmk .... £22.50 ☐
047d 1953, 6th July. 5d, 8d, 1/-Tangier Overprint, BPo pmk .... £16.00 ☐
047e 1954, 8th February. 9d, 10d, 11d Tangier Overprint, BPO pmk .... £35.00 ☐
047f 1953, 2nd November 4d, 1/3d, 1/6d Tangier Overprint, BPO pmk .... £30.00 ☐

048. 1952/54, QEII Bahrain Definitives. Set of 10 Values
048a 1952, 5th December. 1½d, 2½d Bahrain Overprint, local pmk .... £25.00 ☐
048b 1953, 31st August. ½d, 1d, 2d Bahrain Overprint, local pmk .... £20.00 ☐
048c 1954, 18th January. 3d, 6d Bahrain Overprint, local pmk .... £28.00 ☐
048d 1953, 2nd November. 4d, 1/3d, 1/6d Bahrain Overprint, local pmk .... £30.00 ☐

049. 1953/55, QEII Definitives
049a 1953, 2nd September. ½d, 1d, 2d Muscat Annas Overprint .... £20.00 ☐
049b 1955, 23rd September. 2/6d High Value Muscat Rupees Overprint .... £75.00 ☐
049c 1953, 31st August. ½d, 1d, 2d, Kuwait Overprint .... £25.00 ☐

050. 1955, 23rd September. QEII Castle High Values
050a Set of 3 values, 2/6d, 5/-,10/- Tangier Overprint, BPO pmk .... £225.00 ☐
050b Set of 3 values, 2/6d, 5/-,10/- Bahrain Overprint, local pmk .... £250.00 ☐
050c Set of 3 values, 2/6d, 5/-,10/- Kuwait Overprint, local pmk .... £260.00 ☐

051. 1954/56, QEII Morocco Agencies Definitives
051a 1954, 1st September. ½d Morocco Agencies (Spanish) Overprint .... £18.00 ☐
051b 1955, 1st March. 1d Morocco Agencies (Spanish) Overprint .... £18.00 ☐
051c 1956, 15th August. 4d Morocco Agencies (Spanish) Overprint .... £20.00 ☐

052. 1956, 1st February. QEII Qatar Definitives. Set of 11
052a Umm Said (Qatar) Overprint (currency only) fdc set .... £225.00 ☐
Umm Said Post Office opened Feb. 1st, 1956.

053. 1957, 1st March. QEII Qatar Castle High Value
053a 5/- Red, 1st March. 5 Rupees Qatar Overprint, local pmk .... £135.00 ☐

054 1957, QEII Wilding Definitives. Set of 11
054a April 1st Bahrain NP Overprint Set, Bahrain pmk .... £130.00 ☐
054b June 1st Kuwait NP Overprint Set, Kuwait pmk .... £130.00 ☐
054c April 1st Qatar Overprint Set (15 Values), Qatar pmk .... £250.00 ☐

055. 1957, 1st April. QEII Tangier Centenary Definitives. Set of 20
055a Centenary of British Post Office in Tangier, 1857 - 1957, Tangier Overprint .... £80.00 ☐
055b Same but last day of issue, 30th April 1957 .... £65.00 ☐
055c 1-4 values with special machine slogan cancellation (first or last day) .... £16.00 ☐

056. 1963, 30th March. QEII Abu Dhabi Definitives. Set of 11
056a Introduction of Abu Dhabi Postal Services. Value only Overprint .... £240.00 ☐
This cover is the rare Das Island pmk. Also known with Abu Dhabi pmk (**£180**)

The Value Only Overprints (both KGVI and QEII) were first used in Muscat. However, they were later used in Dubai, Qatar, Umm Said, Abu Dhabi and Das Island.

GB Pre-Release Covers Checklist

This is the third time that we offer a checklist of GB Pre-Release Covers for Commemorative Issues. For some Issues there is more than one pre-release date, however we have only recorded the ones that we have actually seen. If you have other dates or pre-release covers in your Collection, please do send/email details, together with clear copies of the actual covers and we will then add them to our list.

Commemorative Issue		Known Pre-Release	Valuation	
1900	QV Halfpenny Green	15.04.00	**£850.00**	☐
1911	KGV Coronation Halfpenny	21.06.11	**£750.00**	☐
1929	KGV Postal Union Congress, 1d only	01/03/09.05.29	**£160.00**	☐
1935	KGV Silver Jubilee	04.05.35, 06.05.35	**£100.00**	☐
1935	KGV Silver Jubilee, Morocco Agencies O/P	10.03.35	**£120.00**	☐
1937	KGVI Coronation	10/11/12.05.37	**£25.00**	☐
1937	KGVI Coronation, Buckingham Palace cds	12.05.37	**£2,100.00**	☐
1937	KGVI Coronation, Morocco Agencies Fr. O/P..	13 04.37	**£50.00**	☐
1940	KGVI Stamp Centenary, 1d only	04.05.40	**£40.00**	☐
1940	KGVI Stamp Centenary	04.05.40, 05.05.40	**£65.00**	☐
1946	KGVI Victory Issue	10.06.46	**£30.00**	☐
1948	KGVI Silver Wedding	25.04.48	**£260.00**	☐
1948	KGV Olympic Games	28.07.48	**£50.00**	☐
1951	KGVI Festival of Britain	02.05.51	**£50.00**	☐
1953	QEII Coronation Set, any pmk	02.06.53	**£200.00**	☐
1953	QEII Coronation Set, Buckingham Palace cds	02.06.53	**£2,250.00**	☐
1953	QEII Coronation 2$^{1}/_{2}$d, Tangier Overprint	01.06.53	**£55.00**	☐
1953	QEII Coronation Air Letter	02.06.53	**£45.00**	☐
1960	QEII General Letter Office	06.07.60	**£45.00**	☐
1960	QEII Europa Issue	18.09.60	**£45.00**	☐
1961	QEII POSB	21.08.61	**£80.00**	☐
1961	QEII Parliament Conference	22.09.61, 23.09.61	**£40.00**	☐
1962	QEII National Productivity Year, 3d only	17.10.62	**£30.00**	☐
1962	QEII National Productivity Year	13.11.62	**£60.00**	☐
1963	QEII Paris Postal Conference	06.05.63	**£40.00**	☐
1963	QEII Nature Week	15.05.63	**£45.00**	☐
1963	QEII Lifeboat Conference	30.05.63	**£45.00**	☐
1964	QEII Botanical Conference	31.07.64	**£75.00**	☐
1964	QEII Botanical Conference	2/3/4.08.64	**£50.00**	☐
1965	QEII Churchill	06.07.65	**£45.00**	☐
1965	QEII Parliament 6d only	17.07.65	**£30.00**	☐
1965	QEII Parliament	08/10/12/17.07.65	**£45.00**	☐
1965	QEII Salvation Army, 3d only	07.08.65	**£30.00**	☐
1965	QEII Salvation Army	06.08.65	**£45.00**	☐
1965	QEII ITU Centenary	18.05.65	**£50.00**	☐
1965	QEII ITU Centenary	11.07.65	**£40.00**	☐
1966	QEII Burns	24.01.66	**£35.00**	☐

GB Pre-Release Covers Checklist

Commemorative Issue		Known Pre-Release	Valuation
1966	QEII Landscapes	26.04.66	**£40.00** ☐
1966	QEII British Birds, any one of 4	18/19/21/23/25.07.66	**£25.00** ☐
1966	QEII World Cup Winners	30.07.66, 16.08.66	**£38.00** ☐
1966	QEII Christmas Issue	30.11.66	**£45.00** ☐
1967	QEII EFTA	16.02.67	**£45.00** ☐
1968	QEII Bridges, 4d only	28.04.68	**£30.00** ☐
1968	QEII Christmas Issue, Philatelic Bureau fdi!	04.09.68	**£65.00** ☐
1969	QEII British Ships, 5d only	13.01.69	**£30.00** ☐
1969	QEII Concorde	02.03.69	**£45.00** ☐
1969	QEII Anniversaries	01.04.69	**£40.00** ☐
1969	QEII Gandhi	13.07.69	**£40.00** ☐
1970	QEII Literary Anniversaries, 4 x 5d	01.01.70	**£40.00** ☐
1970	QEII Rural Architecture	11.01.70	**£40.00** ☐
1970	QEII Commonwealth Games	15.06.70	**£45.00** ☐
1971	QEII General Anniversaries, Phil Bureau fdi	28.07.71	**£50.00** ☐
1975	QEII Charity Stamp	15.01.75	**£30.00** ☐
1977	QEII Silver Jubilee	01/10/11/14.05.77	**£50.00** ☐
1977	QEII Silver Jubilee, 9d Added Value	14.06.77	**£20.00** ☐
1978	QEII Horses, Horsington cds	03.07.78	**£60.00** ☐
1978	QEII Christmas Issue	18.11.78, 21.11.78	**£40.00** ☐
1981	QEII National Trust	16.06.81, 23.06.81	**£35.00** ☐
1981	QEII Royal Wedding	15.07.81	**£35.00** ☐
1981	QEII Duke of Edinburgh Awards	06.08.81	**£30.00** ☐
1981	QEII Fishing	11.09.81, 12.09.81	**£30.00** ☐
1982	QEII Maritime Heritage	16.05.82	**£30.00** ☐
1984	QEII Economic Summit	30.05.84	**£30.00** ☐
1984	QEII British Council	21.09.84	**£30.00** ☐
1986	QEII Domesday Book	20.05.86	**£30.00** ☐
1986	QEII Royal Wedding	15.07.86	**£30.00** ☐
1988	QEII Edward Lear Miniature Sheet	06.09.88	**£30.00** ☐
1989	QEII Greetings Booklet	17.01.89	**£35.00** ☐
1990	QEII Gallantry	09.09.90	**£30.00** ☐
1991	QEII Sport	06.06.91, 10.06.91	**£30.00** ☐
1992	QEII Tennyson, 39p only	28.02.92	**£20.00** ☐
1993	QEII Christmas Issue	1.11.93	**£30.00** ☐
1994	QEII Summertime	28.07.94	**£30.00** ☐
1994	QEII Medical Discoveries	24.09.94	**£30.00** ☐
1998	QEII Diana Princess of Wales	02.02.98	**£65.00** ☐
1998	QEII Carnival	24.08.98	**£30.00** ☐
2002	QEII Circus	03.04.02	**£30.00** ☐
2002	QEII Christmas Issue	23.10.02	**£35.00** ☐
2003	QEII Extreme Endeavours	28.04.03	**£30.00** ☐
2003	QEII Pub Signs, 42p only	28.07.03	**£20.00** ☐
2004	QEII Occasions	31.01.04	**£30.00** ☐
2005	QEII Trafalgar Miniature Sheet	17.10.05	**£35.00** ☐

GB QEII Missing Colours Checklist

Since we first introduced a QEII Missing Colours check list, there has been considerable interest in this area of first day cover collecting. Prices have risen noticeably and this is reflected in our latest listing below. There have always been plenty of missing colours on mint GB Stamps, but clearly nowhere near as much on first day covers.

We are looking to expand the listing next time and invite Collectors to send in details of any first day cover Missing Colour items, in their collection, that we have not listed – a colour scan or colour photo is essential in order to see clearly the missing colour(s) concerned.

Commorative Issue		Value	Missing Colour	Valuation
1961	QEII Post Office Savings Bank	1/6d	orange-brown	**£600.00** ☐
1964	QEII Geographical	1/6d	violet (face value)	**£950.00** ☐
1964	QEII Botanical Congress	9d	green (leaves)	**£8,000.00** ☐
1964	QEII Opening of Forth Bridge	6d	light blue	**£3,000.00** ☐
1965	QEII Joseph Lister	4d	indigo	**£3,500.00** ☐
1965	QEII Post Office Tower	3d	olive-yellow (Tower!)	**£5,000.00** ☐
1965	QEII I.T.U Centenary	1/6d	light pink	**£2,500.00** ☐
1966	QEII World Football Cup	6d	black	**£350.00** ☐
1966	QEII World Football Cup (phosphor)	6d	black	**£400.00** ☐
1966	QEII British Birds	4 x 4d	green	**£350.00** ☐
1966	QEII British Birds	4 x 4d	brown (legs)	**£600.00** ☐
1966	QEII British Birds (phopsphor)	4 x 4d	brown (legs)	**£600.00** ☐
1966	QEII Battle of Hastings	6 x 4d	deep blue	**£600.00** ☐
1966	QEII Battle of Hastings	6 x 4d	blue	**£1,200.00** ☐
1966	QEII Battle of Hastings	6 x 4d	orange	**£500.00** ☐
1966	QEII Battle of Hastings (phosphor)	6 x 4d	grey	**£650.00** ☐
1966	QEII Battle of Hastings	6 x 4d	olive-green	**£900.00** ☐
1967	QEII EFTA (phosphor)	9d	lilac	**£350.00** ☐
1968	QEII EFTA (phosphor)	1/6d	brown	**£600.00** ☐
1967	QEII Wild Flowers (Hawthorn)	4d	slate-purple	**£1,200.00** ☐
1967	QEII British Paintings	1/6d	gold (head)	**£7,500.00** ☐
1968	QEII Bridge	9d	ultramarine	**£6,000.00** ☐
1969	QEII Notable Anniversaries	1/6d	black	**£225.00** ☐
1969	QEII Notable Anniversaries	1/6d	green	**£465.00** ☐
1969	QEII Notable Anniversaries	1/6d	lemon	**£6,500.00** ☐
1969	QEII British Cathedrals	5d	green	**£150.00** ☐
1969	QEII British Cathedrals	9d	black	**£250.00** ☐
1969	QEII Investiture Prince of Wales	3 x 5d	red	**£2,750.00** ☐
1970	QEII Rural Architecture	1s	new blue	**£225.00** ☐
1970	QEII Anniversaries	5d	gold (head)	**£1,250.00** ☐
1970	QEII Anniversaries	1s	green & embossing	**£200.00** ☐

GB QEII Missing Colours Checklist

Commorative Issue		Value	Missing Colour	Valuation
1970	QEII Anniversaries	1/9d	lemon (trousers)	**£5,750.00** ☐
1970	QEII Literary Anniversaries	1/6d	silver (Grasmere)	**£150.00** ☐
1971	QEII Literary Anniversaries	5p	gold (head)	**£700.00** ☐
1971	QEII British Anniversaries	9p	myrtle-green	**£2,750.00** ☐
1971	QEII British Anniversaries	9p	olive-brown	**£275.00** ☐
1971	QEII British Anniversaries	9p	lemon	**£5,500.00** ☐
1971	QEII Christmas	7½p	emerald	**£1,250.00** ☐
1972	QEII General Anniversaries	9p	black	**£750.00** ☐
1972	QEII British Polar Explorers	5p	gold (head)	**£250.00** ☐
1972	QEII Village Churches	3p	gold (head)	**£250.00** ☐
1972	QEII Broadcasting Anniversaries	7½p	brownish-slate (head)	**£4,000.00** ☐
1973	QEII British Explorers (pair)	3p	gold (head)	**£250.00** ☐
1973	QEII British Explorers	9p	gold (head)	**£250.00** ☐
1975	QEII Sailing	8p	black	**£175.00** ☐
1979	QEII Min. Sheet: Sir Rowland Hill	4 values	gold (head)	**£600.00** ☐
1979	QEII Min. Sheet: Sir Rowland Hill	4 values	pale greenish-yellow	**£600.00** ☐
1979	QEII Min. Sheet: Sir Rowland Hill	11½p	rosine	**£1,000.00** ☐
1995	QEII Greetings (in Art)	10 x 1st	silver	**£5,500.00** ☐
2003	QEII Birds of Prey	10 x 1st	grey	**£2,750.00** ☐

Towering above any cover in the Missing Colours Section, comes this wonderful Post Office Tower fdc.
Whilst a few copies are known mint/used of the 1965 error, this is believed to be the only one on first day cover.

GB Postal Stationery Supplement 1972-1982

Postal Stationery is covered in the body of the Catalogue up to the end of 1971.
This detailed listing covers all Postal Stationery from 1972 onwards.
Postal Stationery was discontinued by Royal Mail in 1982.

Issue		Date	Valuaton
PS01	5p Air Mail Letter sheet (Christmas)	18.10.1972	**£2.50** ☐
PS02	3p +½p blue, small or large envelope	02.10.1973	**£5.00** ☐
PS03	3p blue, letter card	14.11.1973	**£7.50** ☐
PS04	3d blue, postcard	20.02.1974	**£7.50** ☐
PS05	3d blue, small envelope	20.02.1974	**£7.50** ☐
PS06	3d blue, large envelope	27.02.1974	**£7.50** ☐
PS07	3½p olive-green, letter card	14.11.1973	**£7.50** ☐
PS08	3½p olive-green, postcard	01.05.1974	**£7.50** ☐
PS09	3½p olive-green, small or large envelope	24.06.1974	**£7.50** ☐
PS10	4½p light blue, letter card	28.08.1974	**£8.00** ☐
PS11	4½p light blue, postcard	11.09.1974	**£8.00** ☐
PS12	4½p light blue, small or large envelope	31.07.1974	**£8.00** ☐
PS13	5½p purple, letter card	17.03.1975	**£8.00** ☐
PS14	5½p purple, small or large envelope	17.03.1975	**£8.00** ☐
PS15	6p Air Mail Letter sheet (Christmas)	29.10.1974	**£2.50** ☐
PS16	6½p light blue, letter card	29.09.1975	**£8.00** ☐
PS17	6½p light blue, small or large envelope	29.09.1975	**£9.50** ☐
PS18	7p red-brown, letter card	14.04.1975	**£11.00** ☐
PS19	7p red-brown, postcard	14.04.1975	**£11.00** ☐
PS20	7p red-brown, small or large envelope	17.03.1975	**£11.00** ☐
PS21	8½p light green, letter card	29.09.1975	**£11.00** ☐
PS22	8½p light green, postcard	29.09.1975	**£11.00** ☐
PS23	8½p light green, small or large envelope	29.09.1975	**£11.00** ☐
PS24	35p, 43½p, 44p, 46p registered envelopes	17.03.1975	**£15.00** ☐
PS25	10½p Air Mail Letter sheet (Scotland)	14.07.1976	**£2.50** ☐
PS26	10½p Air Mail Letter sheet (Wales)	29.09.1976	**£2.50** ☐
PS27	10½p Air Mail Letter sheet (Christmas)	17.11.1976	**£2.50** ☐
PS28	7p purple-brown, letter card	13.06.1977	**£10.00** ☐
PS29	7p purple-brown, small or large envelope	13.06.1977	**£10.00** ☐
PS30	9p deep blue, letter card (one band)	13.06.1977	**£10.00** ☐
PS31	9p deep blue, postcard (one band)	13.06.1977	**£10.00** ☐
PS32	9p deep blue, small or large envelope (one band)	13.06.1977	**£10.00** ☐
PS33	9p deep blue, small or large envelope (two bands)	09.07.1979	**£10.00** ☐
PS34	10½p Air Mail Letter sheet (Christmas)	22.11.1978	**£2.50** ☐
PS34	8p crimson, letter card	15.08.1979	**£9.00** ☐
PS35	8p crimson, small or large envelope	15.08.1979	**£9.00** ☐
PS35	10p orange, letter card (two bands)	15.08.1979	**£9.00** ☐
PS36	10p orange, small or large envelope (two bands)	15.08.1979	**£9.00** ☐
PS37	10p orange, large envelope – revised size (two bands)	14.11.1979	**£9.00** ☐
PS38	12p Air Mail Letter sheet (Christmas)	21.11.1979	**£2.50** ☐

GB Postal Stationery Supplement 1972-1982

Issue		Date	Valuaton
PS39	10p orange, letter card (one bands)	04.02.1980	**£9.00** ☐
PS39	10p orange, small or large envelope (one band)	04.02.1980	**£9.00** ☐
PS40	12p light green, letter card	04.02.1980	**£8.00** ☐
PS41	12p light green, postcard	04.02.1980	**£8.00** ☐
PS42	12p light green, small or large envelope	04.02.1980	**£8.00** ☐
PS43	14½p Air Mail Letter sheet (Christmas)	19.11.1980	**£2.50** ☐
PS44	11½p grey, letter card	26.01.1981	**£8.00** ☐
PS45	11½p grey, small or large envelope	26.01.1981	**£8.00** ☐
PS46	14p light blue, letter card	26.01.1981	**£8.00** ☐
PS47	14p light blue, small or large envelope	26.01.1981	**£8.00** ☐
PS48	12½p light green, small or large envelope	01.02.1982	**£8.00** ☐
PS49	15½p bright violet, small or large envelope	01.02.1982	**£8.00** ☐
PS50	1st brown and gold post note	21.04.1982	**£12.50** ☐

List of Advertisers

The Publisher wishes to thank all of the above Advertisers for their support in the 30th edition of the

Collect GB First Day Covers Catalogue.

This page is for notes

VOLUME FIVE HUNDRED AND FORTY NINE

METHODS IN ENZYMOLOGY

Riboswitch Discovery, Structure and Function

METHODS IN ENZYMOLOGY

VOLUME FIVE HUNDRED AND FORTY NINE

METHODS IN ENZYMOLOGY

Riboswitch Discovery, Structure and Function

Edited by

DONALD H. BURKE-AGUERO

Department of Molecular Microbiology & Immunology and Department of Biochemistry, University of Missouri, USA

AMSTERDAM • BOSTON • HEIDELBERG • LONDON
NEW YORK • OXFORD • PARIS • SAN DIEGO
SAN FRANCISCO • SINGAPORE • SYDNEY • TOKYO
Academic Press is an imprint of Elsevier

Academic Press is an imprint of Elsevier
225 Wyman Street, Waltham, MA 02451, USA
525 B Street, Suite 1800, San Diego, CA 92101-4495, USA
32 Jamestown Road, London NW1 7BY, UK
The Boulevard, Langford Lane, Kidlington, Oxford OX5 1GB, UK

First edition 2014

Notices

Knowledge and best practice in this field are constantly changing. As new research and experience broaden our understanding, changes in research methods, professional practices, or medical treatment may become necessary.

Practitioners and researchers must always rely on their own experience and knowledge in evaluating and using any information, methods, compounds, or experiments described herein. In using such information or methods they should be mindful of their own safety and the safety of others, including parties for whom they have a professional responsibility.

To the fullest extent of the law, neither the Publisher nor the authors, contributors, or editors, assume any liability for any injury and/or damage to persons or property as a matter of products liability, negligence or otherwise, or from any use or operation of any methods, products, instructions, or ideas contained in the material herein.

ISBN: 978-0-12-801122-5
ISSN: 0076-6879

For information on all Academic Press publications visit our website at store.elsevier.com

CONTENTS

CONTRIBUTORS

Luigi J. Alvarado
Department of Chemistry and Biochemistry, Center for Biomolecular Structure & Organization, University of Maryland, College Park, Maryland, USA

Clemens Anklin
Bruker BioSpin Corp., Billerica MA, USA

Philip C. Bevilacqua
Department of Chemistry and Center for RNA Molecular Biology, The Pennsylvania State University, University Park, Pennsylvania, USA

Jarrod T. Bogue
Department of Biochemistry & Biophysics, and Center for RNA Biology, University of Rochester School of Medicine and Dentistry, Rochester, New York, USA

Jonathan Bouvette
Département de Biochimie et Médecine Moléculaire, Université de Montréal, Montreal, Quebec, Canada

Steven Busan
Department of Chemistry, University of North Carolina, Chapel Hill, North Carolina, USA

J. Carlos Penedo
SUPA School of Physics and Astronomy, and Biomedical Sciences Research Complex, University of St. Andrews, St. Andrews, Fife, United Kingdom

Andrew L. Chang
Department of Chemistry, Stanford University, Stanford, California, USA

Bin Chen
Department of Chemistry and Biochemistry, Center for Biomolecular Structure & Organization, University of Maryland, College Park, Maryland, USA

Pallavi K. Choudhary
Department of Chemistry, University of Zurich, Zürich, Switzerland

Peter V. Cornish
Department of Biochemistry, University of Missouri, Columbia, Missouri, USA

T. Kwaku Dayie
Department of Chemistry and Biochemistry, Center for Biomolecular Structure & Organization, University of Maryland, College Park, Maryland, USA

Geneviève Di Tomasso
Département de Biochimie et Médecine Moléculaire, Université de Montréal, Montreal, Quebec, Canada

Jackie M. Esquiaqui
Department of Chemistry, University of Florida, Gainesville, Florida, USA

Gail E. Fanucci
Department of Chemistry, University of Florida, Gainesville, Florida, USA

Oleg V. Favorov
Department of Biomedical Engineering, University of North Carolina, Chapel Hill, North Carolina, USA

Adrian R. Ferré-D'Amaré
National Heart, Lung and Blood Institute, Bethesda, Maryland, USA

Margo P. Gebbie
Department of Chemistry and Biochemistry, and Maryland Pathogen Research Institute, University of Maryland, College Park, MD, USA

Nancy L. Greenbaum
Hunter College and The Graduate Center of The City University of New York, New York, USA

Claudia Höbartner
Research Group Nucleic Acid Chemistry, Max Planck Institute for Biophysical Chemistry, and Institute for Organic and Biomolecular Chemistry, Georg August University Göttingen, Göttingen, Germany

Bao Ho
Department of Pharmaceutical Sciences; Department of Molecular Biology and Biochemistry, and Department of Chemistry, University of California, Irvine, California, USA

Charles G. Hoogstraten
Department of Biochemistry and Molecular Biology, Michigan State University, East Lansing, Michigan, USA

Jermaine L. Jenkins
Department of Biochemistry & Biophysics; Center for RNA Biology, and Structural Biology & Biophysics Facility, University of Rochester School of Medicine and Dentistry, Rochester, New York, USA

Randi Jimenez
Department of Pharmaceutical Sciences; Department of Molecular Biology and Biochemistry, and Department of Chemistry, University of California, Irvine, California, USA

Fethullah Karabiber
Department of Computer Engineering, Yildiz Technical University, Istanbul, Turkey

Christoph Kreutz
Institute of Organic Chemistry and Center for Molecular Biosciences (CMBI), University of Innsbruck, Innrain, Innsbruck, Austria

Daniel A. Lafontaine
RNA Group, Department of Biology, Faculty of Science, Université de Sherbrooke, Sherbrooke, Québec, Canada

Regan M. LeBlanc
Department of Chemistry and Biochemistry, Center for Biomolecular Structure & Organization, University of Maryland, College Park, Maryland, USA

Vincent T. Lee
Department of Cell Biology and Molecular Genetics, and Maryland Pathogen Research Institute, University of Maryland, College Park, MD, USA

Pascale Legault
Département de Biochimie et Médecine Moléculaire, Université de Montréal, Montreal, Quebec, Canada

Joseph A. Liberman
Department of Biochemistry & Biophysics, and Center for RNA Biology, University of Rochester School of Medicine and Dentistry, Rochester, New York, USA

Andrew P. Longhini
Department of Chemistry and Biochemistry, Center for Biomolecular Structure & Organization, University of Maryland, College Park, Maryland, USA

Yiling Luo
Department of Chemistry and Biochemistry, University of Maryland, College Park, Maryland, USA

Andrej Lupták
Department of Pharmaceutical Sciences; Department of Molecular Biology and Biochemistry, and Department of Chemistry, University of California, Irvine, California, USA

Isabelle Martin-Verstraete
Laboratoire Pathogenèse des Bactéries Anaérobies, Institut Pasteur, and University of Paris Diderot, Sorbonne Paris Cité, Cellule Pasteur, Paris, France

Kaley McCluskey
SUPA School of Physics and Astronomy, University of St. Andrews, St. Andrews, Fife, United Kingdom

Maureen McKeague
Department of Bioengineering, Stanford University, Stanford, California, USA

Zenia Norman
Department of Biochemistry, University of Missouri, Columbia, Missouri, USA

James G. Omichinski
Département de Biochimie et Médecine Moléculaire, Université de Montréal, Montreal, Quebec, Canada

Darshan K. Patel
Department of Cell Biology and Molecular Genetics, University of Maryland, College Park, MD, USA

Julio Polanco
Department of Pharmaceutical Sciences; Department of Molecular Biology and Biochemistry, and Department of Chemistry, University of California, Irvine, California, USA

Robert P. Rambo*
Physical Bioscience Division Lawrence Berkeley National Lab, Berkeley, California, USA

*Current address: Diamond Light Source Ltd, Harwell Science & Innovation Campus, Didcot, United Kingdom

Francis E. Reyes†
Physical Bioscience Division Lawrence Berkeley National Lab, Berkeley, California, USA

Greggory M. Rice
Department of Chemistry, University of North Carolina, Chapel Hill, North Carolina, USA

Isabelle Rosinski-Chupin
Unité de Biologie des Bactéries à Gram-Positif, Institut Pasteur, and CNRS UMR 3525, Paris, France

Mohammad Salim
Department of Biochemistry & Biophysics, and Center for RNA Biology, University of Rochester School of Medicine and Dentistry, Rochester, New York, USA

Alix Salvail-Lacoste
Département de Biochimie et Médecine Moléculaire, Université de Montréal, Montreal, Quebec, Canada

Michelle F. Schaffer
Department of Chemistry, University of Zurich, Zürich, Switzerland

Camille R. Schwartz
Physical Bioscience Division Lawrence Berkeley National Lab, Berkeley, California, USA

Euan Shaw
SUPA School of Physics and Astronomy, University of St. Andrews, St. Andrews, Fife, United Kingdom

Bassem Shebl
Department of Biochemistry, University of Missouri, Columbia, Missouri, USA

Eileen M. Sherman
Department of Chemistry, University of Central Florida, Orlando, Florida, USA

Roland K.O. Sigel
Department of Chemistry, University of Zurich, Zürich, Switzerland

Herman O. Sintim
Department of Chemistry and Biochemistry, University of Maryland, College Park, Maryland, USA

Christina D. Smolke
Department of Bioengineering, Stanford University, Stanford, California, USA

Olga Soutourina
Laboratoire Pathogenèse des Bactéries Anaérobies, Institut Pasteur, and University of Paris Diderot, Sorbonne Paris Cité, Cellule Pasteur, Paris, France

Patrick St-Pierre
RNA Group, Department of Biology, Faculty of Science, Université de Sherbrooke, Sherbrooke, Québec, Canada

† Current address: Janelia Farm Research Campus, Howard Hughes Medical Institute, Ashburn, Virginia, USA

Krishna C. Suddala
Biophysics, and Single Molecule Analysis Group, Department of Chemistry, University of Michigan, Ann Arbor, Michigan, USA

Minako Sumita[‡]
Department of Biochemistry and Molecular Biology, Michigan State University, East Lansing, Michigan, USA

John A. Tainer
Life Sciences Division, Lawrence Berkeley National Laboratory, Berkeley, and The Scripps Research Institute, La Jolla, California, USA

Pallavi Thaplyal
Department of Chemistry and Center for RNA Molecular Biology, The Pennsylvania State University, University Park, Pennsylvania, USA

Nils G. Walter
Single Molecule Analysis Group, Department of Chemistry, University of Michigan, Ann Arbor, Michigan, USA

Katherine Deigan Warner
National Heart, Lung and Blood Institute, Bethesda, Maryland, USA, and Department of Chemistry, University of Cambridge, Cambridge, United Kingdom

Katarzyna Wawrzyniak-Turek
Research Group Nucleic Acid Chemistry, Max Planck Institute for Biophysical Chemistry, and Institute for Organic and Biomolecular Chemistry, Georg August University Göttingen, Göttingen, Germany

Joseph E. Wedekind
Department of Biochemistry & Biophysics; Center for RNA Biology, and Structural Biology & Biophysics Facility, University of Rochester School of Medicine and Dentistry, Rochester, New York, USA

Kevin M. Weeks
Department of Chemistry, University of North Carolina, Chapel Hill, North Carolina, USA

Neil A. White
Department of Biochemistry and Molecular Biology, Michigan State University, East Lansing, Michigan, USA

Jing-Dong Ye
Department of Chemistry, University of Central Florida, Orlando, Florida, USA

Jinwei Zhang
National Heart, Lung and Blood Institute, Bethesda, Maryland, USA

Caijie Zhao
Hunter College and The Graduate Center of The City University of New York, New York, USA

[‡] Current address: Chemistry and Physics Department, California University of Pennsylvania, 250 University Avenue, California, PA 15419, USA

PREFACE

The early years of the twenty-first century have seen an explosion of interest in the diverse capabilities of RNA. Riboswitches capture the excitement and promise of this field. They are structurally dynamic, they sense and respond to specific molecular partners, their occupancy states governs gene regulatory decisions, and they can be engineered to reprogram gene regulatory circuitry. Importantly, many of the experimental and theoretical tools that have been used to study riboswitches can also be applied to other RNAs, and tools developed for studies of other RNAs can be applied to riboswitches.

These two volumes (*Methods in Enzymology* 549 and 550) include 40 contributions that outline cutting-edge methods representing a wide spectrum of research questions and scientific themes. The first volume emphasizes natural riboswitches, from their discovery to assessment of their structures and functions. The second volume shifts the focus to applying riboswitches as tools for a variety of applications and as targets for inhibition by potential new antibacterial compounds. A third volume (*Methods in Enzymology* 553) will appear shortly after these two focusing on computational methods for predicting and evaluating dynamic RNA structures. Although the chapters are organized into discrete themes, many cut across thematic boundaries by weaving together diverse methodological solutions and several of the chapters could fit comfortably into more than one section.

VOLUME 1

Riboswitch discovery. In the early days of the riboswitch field, new riboswitches were discovered at a frenetic pace, often by comparing large sets of bacterial genomes. While that approach continues to identify new members of known riboswitch families, the pace has slowed, and new discovery methods are needed. The series begins with two chapters outlining new methods that utilize informatics approaches in combination either with RNASeq and genome-wide methods (Rosinski-Chupin) or with *in vitro* selection (Ho) to discover new natural riboswitches.

Sample preparation. Any effort to characterize purified, functional RNAs will only be as good as the corresponding sample preparations. Therefore, the next five chapters are dedicated to methods for the synthesis and preparation of large RNAs. Three groups exploit specialty nucleic acids with functionalities of their own. The first chapter in this set describes the use of cotranscribed aptamer affinity tags that are removed by activatable self-cleavage (Di Tomasso). This is followed by methods for using catalytic deoxyribozyme ligases to assemble large RNAs from synthetic fragments, some of which carry site-specific spin labels for electron paired resonance studies (Wawrzyniak-Turek). The third chapter in this set describes the combined use of aminoacyl transferase ribozymes and chemical protection to generate charged tRNAs on a large scale (Zhang). These are followed by two chapters that integrate organic chemical methods with improved enzymology to produce photocleavable biotinylated guanosine that incorporates at the $5'$ end of *in vitro* transcripts (Luo) and large quantities of selectively $^{13}C/^{15}N$-labeled RNA in previously unattainable labeling patterns for improved spectroscopic analysis (Alvarado).

Structure and function. The biochemical functions of riboswitches are inextricably linked with their three-dimensional structures. The next several chapters, therefore, provide methods for evaluating riboswitch structure and function. Updated protocols are provided for the widely utilized SHAPE method of structural probing, along with details of how to implement new software for data interpretation (Rice). It is well recognized that structural context can perturb pK_a values within RNA and DNA; hence, the next chapter details how to measure them without falling into traps of oversimplifying the underlying molecular processes (Taplyal). The next chapter provides methods for obtaining appropriate crystals for ligand–RNA complexes, with emphasis on fragment-bound TPP riboswitches (Warner). This section ends with a detailed description of experimental and analytical methods for using small-angle X-ray scattering to define RNA conformations in solution (Reyes).

Conformational dynamics. Spectroscopic methods are ideal for following riboswitch conformational dynamics in real time. The first two chapters of this section describe site-specific incorporation of spectroscopic labels and their use in addressing specific question, first with ^{19}F NMR to probe conformational exchange (Zhao) and then with spin-label probes for electron paramagnetic resonance spectroscopy of large RNAs (Esquiaqui). Single-molecule methods such as smFRET have become a staple of modern biophysical analysis. Three chapters provide detailed guidance on many facets of smFRET, from sample preparation, data acquisition, and analysis to explorations of folding landscapes (Shaw, Suddala, and Shebl). The last chapter of this section describes how to integrate surface plasmon resonance

(SPR), isothermal titration calorimetry, and circular dichroism to examine tertiary docking (Hoogstraten).

Ligand interactions. One of the most important characteristics of riboswitches is their ability to sense the presence of specific metabolites by forming bound molecular complexes. Isothermal titration calorimetry is one of the most powerful methods for evaluating the energetics of RNA–small molecule complexes (Wedekind). SPR is another powerful tool for characterizing aptamer kinetic and equilibrium binding properties and is detailed in two chapters (Chang and Schaffer). Finally, an innovative and relatively new technique known as DRaCALA is described in the last chapter of the first volume (Patel).

VOLUME 2

The second volume in this series takes a different perspective on riboswitches. Specifically, now that nature has shown us that RNA modules can sense metabolites and report on them, how can we take advantage of that ability to engineer new properties into cells and biochemical systems? Necessarily, this volume takes a much broader view of riboswitches than those found in nature, encompassing ligand-responsive transcriptional and translational modules, ribozymes, sensors, and modules that induce fluorescence in a fluorophore upon formation of the bound complex. It encompasses Synthetic Biology applications as tools to understand normal biological processes, and as tools to reprogram metabolite flux in workhorse organisms. Finally, it comes full circle by screening small-molecule libraries for inhibitors of natural riboswitches.

In short, this second volume details methods at the cutting edge of the translational science of riboswitches.

Artificial riboswitches. The first six chapters of the second volume provide methods for several approaches to construct and optimize artificial riboswitches. There has been substantial progress toward designing artificial riboswitches from scratch, especially when guided by experimental validation (Moerl). A contrasting approach uses *in vitro* selection/evolution to obtain ligand-responsive ligase ribozymes from highly diverse starting populations (Olea), or to reshape and reprogram the ligand-binding and expression platforms of natural riboswitches (Batey). The next chapter presents methods for optimizing signal transduction, since regulation sometimes benefits from maximizing suppression of basal expression in the OFF state and sometimes from maximizing expression in the ON state

(Goodson). The next two chapters address optimization in two very different cell-free systems, first using coupled transcription–translation to optimize a ligand-responsive self-cleaving ribozyme, or "aptazyme" (Ichihashi), and then taking advantage of a eukaryotic mechanism by which ribosomes "shunt" past certain secondary structures, which can be stabilized to increase shunting efficiency by binding to the analyte ligand (Ogawa).

Ligand-responsive fluorescent sensors. There has been longstanding interest in coupling the binding of ligands to RNA with the emission of light. One such system is that of the recently described Spinach (and Spinach2) aptamer mimics of green fluorescent protein, which are the focus of the next five chapters, each in a different system. The first chapter in this section, from the lab that discovered and first described the Spinach system, presents methods for using it to image intracellular RNA in mammalian cells (Strack). The next two chapters describe how to use these modules in bacterial cells, first as intracellular sensors of intracellular cyclic dinucleotide levels (Kellenberger) and then for simultaneous and independent monitoring of mRNA and protein levels (Pothoulakis). The next chapter takes this same question into solution and into vesicle-based artificial cells (van Nies). The fifth chapter in this section couples sensing of oligonucleotide "ligands" with Spinach2 output in real time for sequence-specific target quantitation and potential point-of-care applications (Bhadra).

Synthetic biology: Conditional control of gene expression. The third section of this volume lays out several methods for using artificial or natural riboswitches to study gene function. This has proven to be a powerful tool in organisms for which limited genetic tools are available, such as the intracellular pathogen Mycobacteria (Van Vlack), as well as in more readily manipulated, nonpathogenic bacteria such as *Streptomyces coelicolor* (Rudolph). Eukaryotes can be similarly studied. A clever variation on this approach is to make the expression of query genes to be dependent upon a regulatory protein whose expression is controlled by a natural riboswitch, as demonstrated here for the unicellular alga *Chlamydomonas reinhardtii* vitamin-repressible riboswitch (Ramundo). An alternative approach is presented in the next chapter, which describes utilization of self-cleaving aptazyme to identify sequence variants that respond to various ligands to regulate gene expression in the yeast *Saccharomyces cerevisiae* (Klauser).

Synthetic biology: Pathway optimization. The fourth section provides methods that illustrate two examples of using riboswitches as tools to optimize metabolic pathways for Synthetic Biology applications. The first chapter details a computational approach focused on kinetic folding with experimental validation to build aptazymes that respond cotranscriptionally to the presence of metabolites, and the experimental validation of those devices (Sparkman-Yager). The second chapter describes a method for using riboswitches to impose selective growth advantages on cells that optimally channel their metabolic output into production of a desired compound (Jang).

Antiriboswitches drug screens. The final section reverses the perspective, treating riboswitches as targets for antibacterial drug development and ligand-binding specificity as the basis for identifying antibiotic candidates. The first chapter lays out a sensitive, fluorescence-based screening cascade for identifying compounds that target the T-box riboswitch antiterminator element (Liu). The second chapter describes screening platform that uses cell-free lysates to monitor translational read-through of a mammalian frameshift signal that is under the control of the preQ1-I riboswitch (Yu).

I first encountered riboswitches in a conference on RNA-Based Life in November, 2001 in separate presentations from Miranda-Ríos and Breaker. At the time of this writing (November, 2014), a PubMed search turns up 771 hits for the term "riboswitch," and it will be well over 800 by the time of the publication of these volumes. The field is moving fast and in many directions. A great number of talented people with diverse expertise have contributed to these volumes, and all of us hope that they will serve as a useful resource to advance RNA research both within the riboswitch field and beyond.

Donald H. Burke-Aguero

PART I

Riboswitch Discovery

CHAPTER ONE

Riboswitch Discovery by Combining RNA-Seq and Genome-Wide Identification of Transcriptional Start Sites

Isabelle Rosinski-Chupin[*,†,1], **Olga Soutourina**[‡,§,1], **Isabelle Martin-Verstraete**[‡,§,2]

[*]Unité de Biologie des Bactéries à Gram-Positif, Institut Pasteur, Paris, France
[†]CNRS UMR 3525, Paris, France
[‡]Laboratoire Pathogenèse des Bactéries Anaérobies, Institut Pasteur, Paris, France
[§]University of Paris Diderot, Sorbonne Paris Cité, Cellule Pasteur, Paris, France
[1]These two authors contribute equally to this chapter
[2]Corresponding author: e-mail address: isabelle.martin-verstraete@pasteur.fr

Contents

Methods in Enzymology, Volume 549
ISSN 0076-6879
http://dx.doi.org/10.1016/B978-0-12-801122-5.00001-5

Abstract

Deep-sequencing technologies applied to RNA have tremendous potential to identify novel transcripts with single-nucleotide resolution. By combining whole-transcript cDNA sequencing (RNA-seq) and genome-wide identification of transcription start sites (dRNA-seq), it is possible to characterize long 5′-untranslated regions potentially endowed with regulatory capacities and to detect premature termination of transcription. This can be used to identify new potential riboswitches. In this chapter, we provide a detailed protocol of the dRNA-seq method based on differential pretreatment of RNAs with tobacco acid pyrophosphatase to differentiate between 5′-ends of primary and processed RNAs. We also give a briefer protocol of the preparation of RNA-seq libraries and of how to go through data bioinformatics analysis and data visualization using genome browsers. This approach is powerful to identify novel riboswitches and to demonstrate the functionality of riboswitches predicted *in silico*.

1. INTRODUCTION

In recent years, the importance of regulatory mechanisms based on the action of RNA molecules became widely appreciated. In bacteria, regulatory RNAs play a critical role in adaptive responses and in various physiological, metabolic, and pathogenic processes. In particular, small noncoding RNAs (sRNAs) have been recently identified in many bacteria including major pathogens (Gripenland et al., 2010; Papenfort & Vogel, 2010; Romby & Charpentier, 2010). Such sRNAs rely on a variety of mechanisms to control their targets, including direct binding to low-molecular weight effector molecules (riboswitches), binding to proteins, interaction with double-stranded DNA, or RNA/RNA duplex formation with mRNA targets (Brantl, 2012; Waters & Storz, 2009). Riboswitches, which affect gene expression in *cis*, are known to sense inorganic ligands like metal ions, purines and their derivatives, coenzymes and related compounds, amino acids, and phosphorylated sugars (Serganov & Nudler, 2013). These systems are composed of two modular domains consisting of an aptamer, involved in the specific recognition of the metabolite, and an expression platform controlling gene expression by altering the structure of mRNA. Upon interaction with the effector, which is usually the product transported or synthesized by the operon they control, riboswitches undergo a conformational change leading to positive or negative effects on transcription termination or translation (Nudler & Mironov, 2004). These regulatory switches are based on the ligand-dependent formation of mutually exclusive RNA conformations. In the case of a transcriptional control, the structures serve as terminator and antiterminator hairpins; while in control at the translational level, the structures sequester or release ribosome-binding sites.

The recent use of deep-sequencing technologies with Roche 454, Illumina Genome Analyzer, or Applied Biosystems SOLiD platforms revealed an unexpected bacterial transcriptome complexity and identified a large number of new regulatory RNAs (Croucher & Thomson, 2010; Sorek & Cossart, 2010). In general, the RNA-seq is a powerful technique of next-generation sequencing (NGS) to explore the transcriptome in great depth. Such high-throughput sequencing of cDNA allows strand-specific identification of novel transcripts with single-nucleotide resolution and leads to accurate operon definition, correction of gene annotation, and discovery of regulatory RNAs. Two independent sequencing approaches can be combined: a whole-transcript cDNA sequencing (RNA-seq) and a differential 5′-end sequencing (dRNA-seq), which allows the identification of transcriptional start sites (TSSs) at genomic scale (Sahr et al., 2012; Soutourina et al., 2013; Wurtzel et al., 2010). In general, the size of 5′-untranslated regions (UTRs) in bacteria is rather small. As a consequence, the detection of a relatively long 5′-UTR could indicate the possibility of regulatory capacities for this region. Such combined genome-wide transcriptome analyses are powerful for identification of long UTR of prokaryotic mRNAs that may contain important regulatory elements such as riboswitches. In the absence of sequence and structural similarity to known riboswitches, these regulatory elements might be difficult to detect *in silico*. Thus, deep-sequencing whole-transcript analysis would map 5′- or 3′-UTR as contiguous expression extending into the flanking intergenic region of genes. In theory, the presence of a riboswitch associated with a given TSS could be suggested when such contiguous expression is interrupted in a particular growth condition, indicating premature termination of transcription and/or self cleavage. Using this approach, a number of predicted riboswitches have been detected in bacteria and several candidates for novel riboswitches have been proposed (Soutourina et al., 2013; Toledo-Arana et al., 2009).

The overview of the described method for genome-wide riboswitch detection is shown in Fig. 1.1. The procedure begins with total RNA extraction and enrichment for the mRNAs by the depletion of rRNAs. These depleted RNAs are then used for cDNA library preparations according to the specific protocols for TSS mapping and whole-transcript sequencing (Figs. 1.2 and 1.3). The resulting cDNA libraries are then

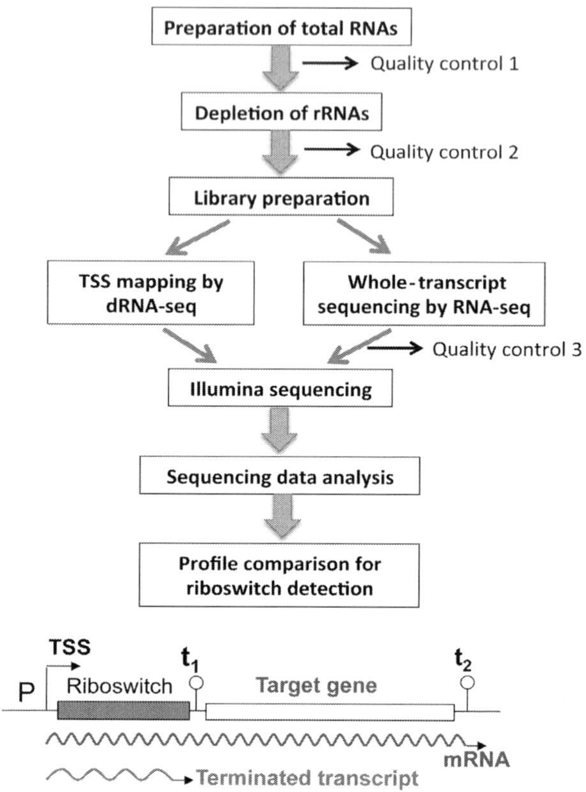

Figure 1.1 Schematic overview of the method.

subjected to Illumina sequencing followed by the sequencing data analysis. The quality control steps using Agilent Bioanalyzer 2100 (Figs. 1.1 and 1.4) are important to check the integrity of total RNAs, the extent of rRNA depletion, and the quality of cDNA library before sequencing. The output of RNA-seq is composed of millions of short sequence reads that are computationally mapped to the reference genome, and expressed regions are determined based on their coverage by RNA-seq reads (Fig. 1.5). For genome-wide identification of TSS, the sequencing data are compared between a sample treated with tobacco acid pyrophosphatase (TAP enzyme) (TAP^+) and another one without this treatment (TAP^-). TAP converts 5′-triphosphates (5′-PPP) into 5′-monophosphates (5′-P) allowing 5′-adapter ligation required for sequencing and thus the enrichment with primary transcript reads (Fig. 1.2). In this approach, the discrimination between primary transcripts and transcripts processed by cleavage or degradation is achieved

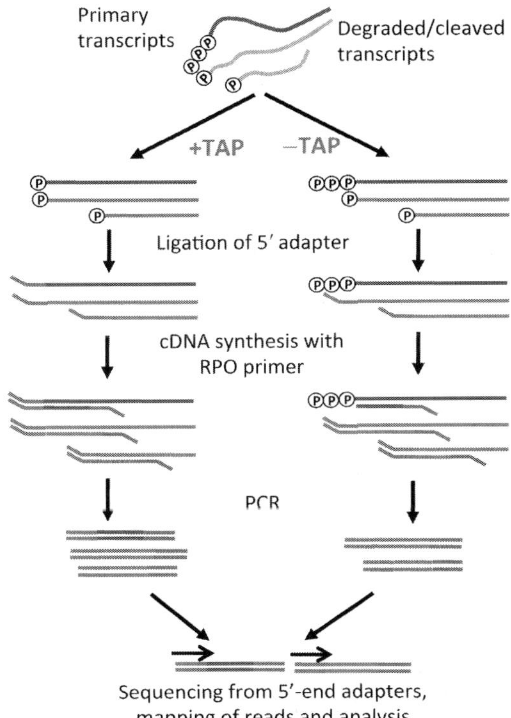

Figure 1.2 TSS mapping by dRNA-seq. (See the color plate.)

by the nature of their 5′-end. Primary transcripts carry a 5′-PPP group, while processed transcripts have 5′-P. The TSS would correspond to position with significantly greater number of reads in TAP^+ sample, and potential cleavage site would correspond to position with large number of reads in both TAP^+ and TAP^- samples. dRNA-seq leads to a list of potential TSS throughout the genome sequence. The manual inspection of sequencing read distribution using available visualization tools would be needed to compare the patterns obtained by dRNA-seq for 5′-end sequencing and RNA-seq analysis for whole-transcript coverage to identify riboswitches as potential regulatory elements (Figs. 1.6 and 1.7).

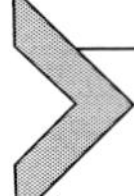

2. RNA ISOLATION AND mRNA ENRICHMENT

2.1. Equipment and materials

- FastPrep FP120 homogenizer
- Nanodrop spectrophotometer

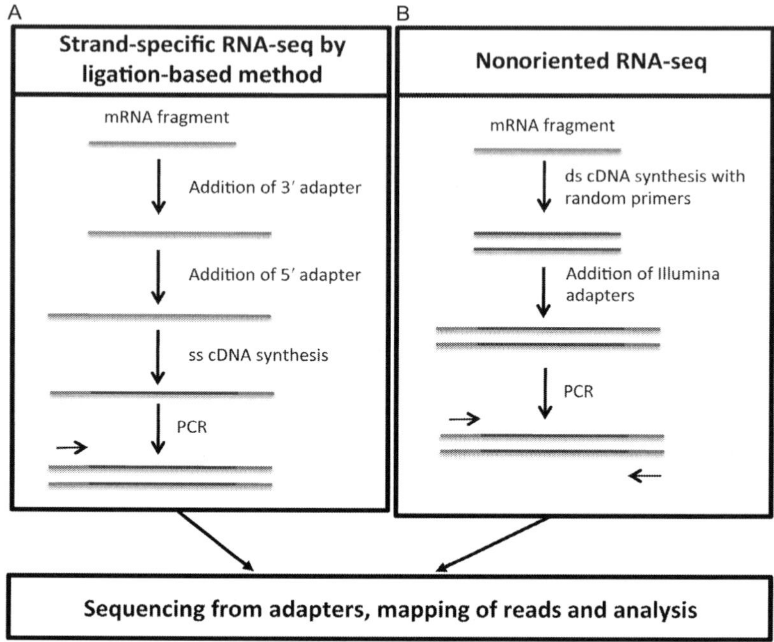

Figure 1.3 Whole-transcript sequencing by (A) strand-specific RNA-seq and (B) non-oriented RNA-seq. (See the color plate.)

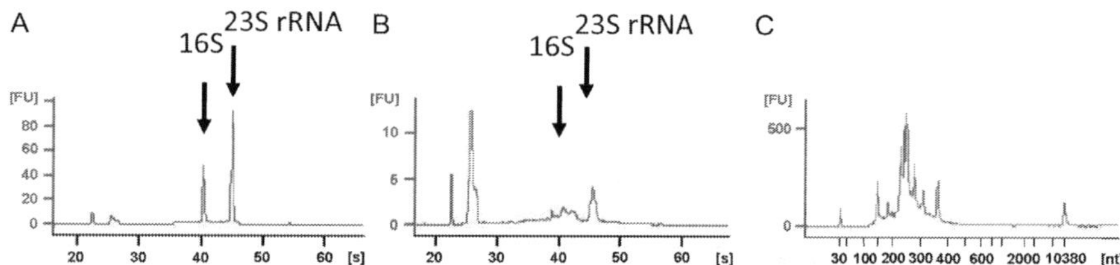

Figure 1.4 Quality controls at the different steps of the library preparation using Agilent 2100 Bioanalyzer. Typical profiles obtained for (A) total RNA; (B) RNA depleted for 23S and 16S rRNAs; (C) cDNA library ready for sequencing.

- Agilent 2100 Bioanalyzer for RNA and DNA quality control
- RNA 6000 Nano Total RNA kit
- Life Technologies Turbo DNA-free kit
- Life Technologies MICROBExpress bacterial mRNA enrichment kit
- Resuspension solution* (10% glucose, 60 m*M* EDTA, 12.5 m*M* Tris pH 7.6)
- Trizol

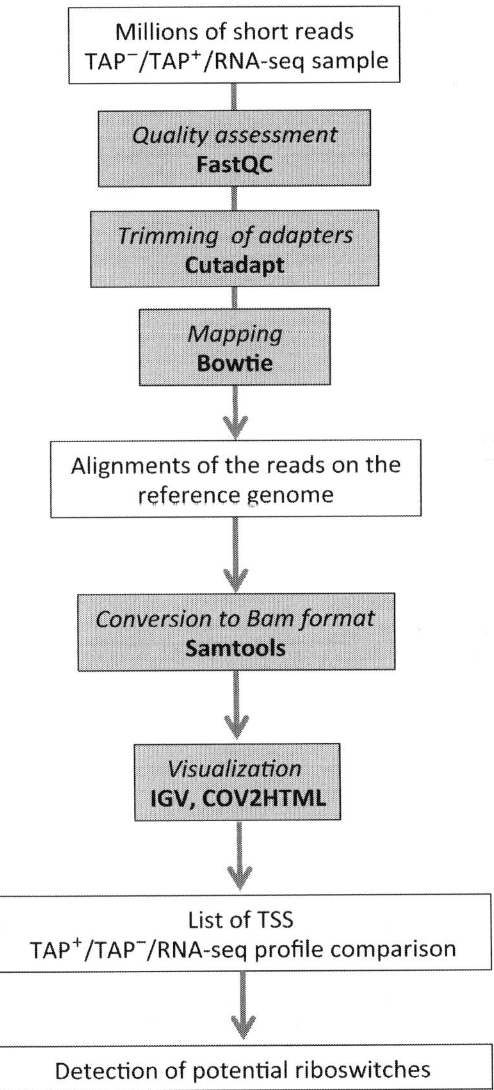

Figure 1.5 Strategy of bioinformatics analysis.

- Acid phenol pH 4.5 (Sigma P4682)
- Chloroform/isoamyl alcohol (24/1) (v/v)
- Isopropanol
- 3 *M* Sodium acetate, pH 5.2*
- 5 mg/ml Glycogen
- Ice-cold 100% Ethanol

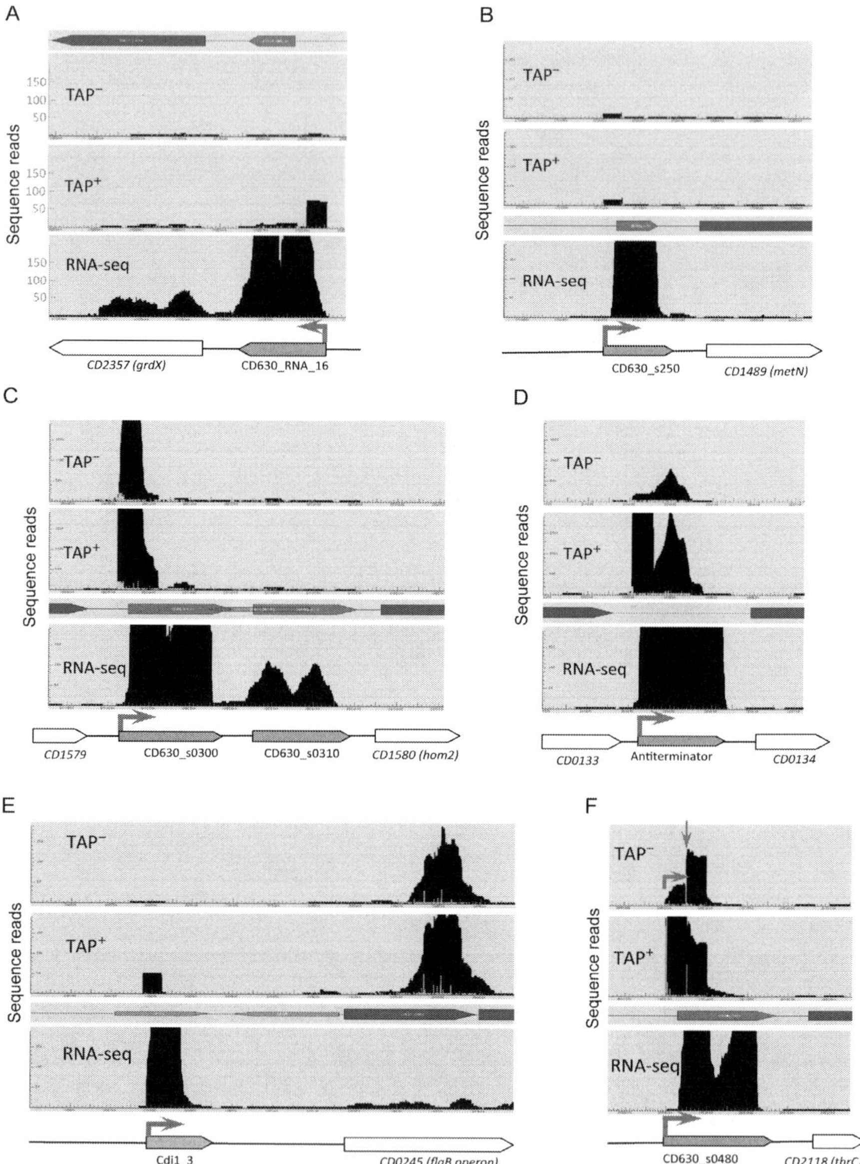

Figure 1.6 Characteristic riboswitch patterns in *C. difficile*. (A) Glycine-responsive riboswitch; (B) S-box; (C) two T-boxes in tandem; (D) PTS antiterminator; (E) c-di-GMP-responsive riboswitch; (F) cleavage site of T-box (Thr). The riboswitches are indicated by gray arrows. The TSS and processing sites are pointed out by red broken arrows and vertical arrows, respectively. (See the color plate.)

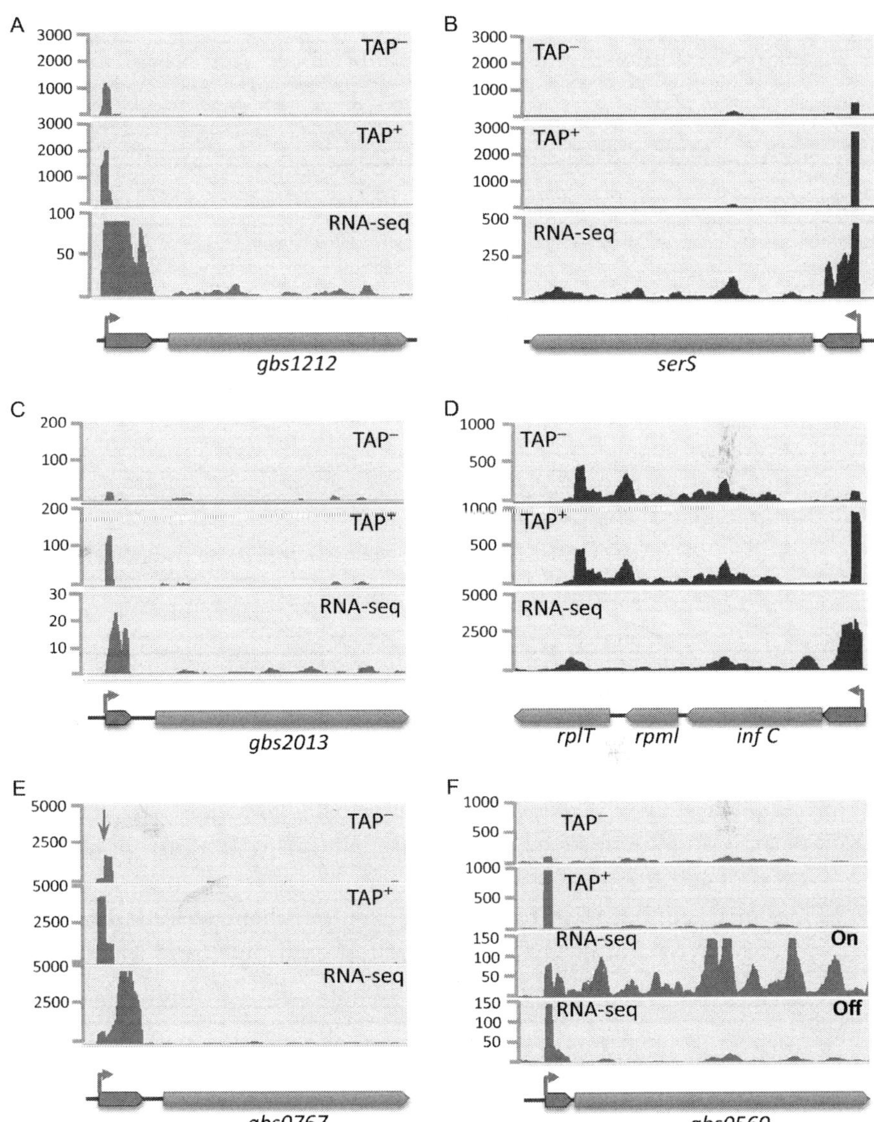

Figure 1.7 Riboswitch profiles in *S. agalactiae*. (A) Glycine-responsive riboswitch; (B) T-box; (C) PyrR-binding site; (D) L20 leader; (E) FMN riboswitch with internal cleavage; (F) *yybP–ykoY* leader in on/off state. (See the color plate.)

- Ice-cold 70% Ethanol
- RNase-free water
- Sarstedt screw cap 2 ml tubes (Sarstedt 72693)
- Glass beads 200–300 μm, acid-washed (Sigma-Aldrich G1277)

– Magnetic stand (Invitrogen Magna-Sep)

*All aqueous solutions should be prepared in RNase-free water.

2.2. RNA isolation and quality control

High-quality bacterial RNA is crucial for these protocols and RNA integrity must be carefully controlled. For Gram-positive bacteria, we recommend the following protocol:

1. Rapidly centrifuge 15–40 ml of bacterial culture and use fresh pellet. Alternatively, the pellet can be frozen in dry ice/ethanol and stored at −80 °C. With this protocol, we successfully prepared RNA from mid-log but also late exponential and stationary phase cultures.
2. Resuspend the pellet in 400 μl of resuspension buffer and quickly transfer the suspension into a screw cap 2-ml microtube containing 500 μl acid phenol and 0.4 g of glass beads.
3. Break bacterial cell walls using two cycles in FastPrep (speed: 6, time: 30 s) at 4 °C, separated by 1 min. Centrifuge for 5 min at 13,000 × *g* at 4 °C.
4. Transfer the upper layer to a new collection tube. Be careful not to aspirate from the middle layer.
5. Add 1 ml trizol and thoroughly mix by repeated pipetting. Incubate at room temperature for 5 min. Add 100 μl acid phenol:chloroform: isoamyl alcohol (25:24:1 volume ratio). Mix thoroughly by repeated pipetting and incubate at room temperature for 3 min. Centrifuge for 5 min at 13,000 × *g* at 4 °C.
6. Transfer the upper layer to a new collection tube, add 200 μl chloroform:isoamyl alcohol. Gently mix by repeated pipetting. Incubate at room temperature for 5 min and centrifuge at 13,000 × *g* for 5 min at 4 °C.
7. Transfer the upper layer into a new collection tube and proceed to RNA precipitation by adding 500 μl isopropanol. Mix by inversion and keep on ice for at least 15 min. Centrifuge for 15 min at 13,000 × *g* at 4 °C. Rinse the pellet with 1 ml 70% ethanol, centrifuge for 5 min, eliminate the ethanol, and dry the pellet.
8. Resuspend the pellet in 50 μl RNase-free water. Incubate at 55 °C for 10 min to help for pellet dissolution and keep on ice.
9. As traces of DNA may still be present, we recommend performing a DNA removal treatment. Life Technologies' Turbo DNA-free kit permits efficient digestion of DNA contamination followed by

complete removal of the enzyme and divalent cations. In particular, it avoids DNase heat inactivation, which could lead to RNA chemical degradation in the presence of divalent cations. Add 5 μl 10× DNase buffer to the 50 μl RNA solution and 2 μl DNase and incubate for 20–60 min at 37 °C. Add 10 μl DNase inactivation reagent, mix well, and incubate for 5 min at room temperature, mixing occasionally. Centrifuge for 1 min at room temperature. Carefully transfer the supernatant, which contains the RNA, into a fresh tube, avoiding transferring the DNase inactivation reagent. Additional centrifugation steps could help to eliminate the rest of the DNase inactivation reagent, which otherwise could inhibit further applications.

10. Control the RNA quality on Agilent 2100 Bioanalyzer with RNA 6000 nanochip. The RNA Integrity Number (RIN) must be higher than 9 (see profile in Fig. 1.4A).
11. Keep aliquots of the RNA at −80 °C.

2.3. mRNA enrichment and quality control

The preparation of the dRNA-seq libraries is RNA consuming, and you will need to deplete at least 15 μg of total RNA. Use MICROBExpress bacterial mRNA enrichment kit to deplete RNA preparation in ribosomal RNA. This kit was found to work well with most Gram-positive and -negative bacteria; however, there are some cases of partial or total incompatibility depending on the organism. We recommend having a look on Life Technologies Web site before utilization. Since rRNA depletion relies on 16S and 23S rRNA capture probes, it is important not to saturate the capacity of the column. Therefore, we generally use 8 μl of Capture Oligo Mix and 100 μl of Oligo MagBeads for 15 μg of total RNA. Carefully follow manufacturer's instructions. If the final RNA solution has a brownish color, put the tube on the magnetic stand for 3 min to eliminate the small amounts of Oligo Magbeads remaining in the solution. Transfer the mRNA solution (50 μl for 15 μg starting material) to a new RNase-free tube. Put aside 5 μl of this solution to control for rRNA depletion on Agilent 2100 Bioanalyzer. The depleted mRNA can be kept at −80 °C. Typical profiles for RNA preparation before and after rRNA depletion are shown in Fig. 1.4A and B. Note that after rRNA depletion, the RIN is no longer a good indicator of RNA quality, since the RIN value is based on the ratio between the two rRNA peaks.

3. GENOME-WIDE MAPPING OF TRANSCRIPTION START SITES BY dRNA-SEQ

dRNA-seq relies on the comparison between two libraries, prepared with or without pretreatment by tobacco acid phosphatase (TAP). Therefore, it is important to keep the other sources of differences at a minimum. The two libraries will be prepared from the same pool of depleted RNA and reactions will be run in parallel (Fig. 1.2).

3.1. Equipment and materials

- Microcentrifuge
- PCR machine
- Qubit fluorometer (Invitrogen)
- Agilent 2100 Bioanalyzer
- Tobacco Acid Pyrophosphatase Epicentre (Tebu-bio), 10 U/μl
- Acid Phenol pH 4.5
- Chloroform:isoamyl alcohol (24:1 volume ratio)
- 3 *M* Sodium acetate pH 5.2
- 5 mg/ml Glycogen
- Ice-cold Ethanol 100% or 70%
- RNase-free water
- Certified low-range Agarose (Bio-Rad)
- T4 RNA ligase
- True Seq Small RNA kit (Illumina)
- Superscript II reverse transcriptase (Invitrogen)
- RNase out (Invitrogen)
- 25 m*M* dNTP
- 100 μ*M* SRA 5′ adapter: 5′-GUUCAGAGUUCUACAGUCCGACG AUC. Kept at −80 °C.
- 100 μ*M* RPO Random-primer 5′-CCTTGGCACCCGAGAATTCC ANNNNNN-3′, HPLC purified.
- RP1: 5′-AATGATACGGCGACCACCGACAGGTTCAGAGTTCT ACAGTCCGA
- Phusion DNA Polymerase (Finnzymes)
- Agencourt AMPure beads XP (Beckman)
- QIAquick gel purification kit (Qiagen)
- Agilent Bioanalyzer DNA 1000 kit
- TAE 50×
- Low-molecular weight DNA ladder

3.2. Hydrolysis of triphosphate groups at mRNA 5′-ends by TAP

1. Prepare two PCR tubes each containing 22 µl of the depleted mRNA and complete to 44 µl with RNase-free water. Melt RNA structures by heating for 10 min at 65 °C in a PCR machine and transfer to ice for at least 2 min.
2. Add 5 µl of 10× TAP buffer.
3. In only one of the two tubes, add 1 µl TAP (10 units) ("TAP$^+$" sample). TAP will be replaced by 1 µl water in the other tube ("TAP$^-$" sample). Incubate at 37 °C for 1 h in a PCR machine.
4. Transfer to Eppendorf tubes and inactivate TAP by phenol/chloroform extraction: to each tube, add 300 µl RNase-free water, 200 µl acid phenol, 200 µl chloroform/isoamyl alcohol 24/1. Mix well for 1 min and centrifuge for 2 min at 13,000 × *g*.
5. Transfer the aqueous phases into clean tubes and proceed to ethanol precipitation. To each tube, add 40 µl 3 *M* sodium acetate, 7 µl glycogen (5 mg/ml), and 1 ml 100% ethanol. Place to −20 °C for at least 1 h.
6. Centrifuge for 30 min at 13,000 × *g* at 4 °C.
7. Rinse the pellets with 200 µl cold 70% ethanol and centrifuge for 10 min.
8. Carefully remove all traces of ethanol and air dry the pellets.
9. Resuspend each pellet in 7 µl RNase-free water and continue with ligation of 5′-adapter.

3.3. Ligation of adapter on 5′-end of mRNAs

1. For TAP$^+$ and TAP$^-$ samples, mix 6.2 µl RNA and 1.1 µl SRA 5′ adapter (100 µ*M*) in a PCR tube.
2. Incubate at 65 °C for 10 min in a PCR machine to denature secondary structures and quickly put on ice.
3. In each tube, add:

10× T4 RNA ligase buffer	1.1 µl
10 m*M* ATP	1.1 µl
RNaseOUT	0.5 µl
T4 RNA ligase	1 µl

and incubate at 20 °C for 6 h. This incubation can be pursued by an overnight step at 4 °C if needed.

3.4. cDNA first strand synthesis by random priming

1. For TAP^+ and TAP^- samples, mix 11 μl of the RNA-5′-adapter ligation products with 2.5 μl of random primer RPO (100 μ*M*).
2. Heat denature at 65 °C for 10 min and place on ice.
3. To each tube, add:

5 × first strand buffer	5 μl
12.5 m*M* dNTP mix	1.25 μl
100 m*M* DTT	2.5 μl
RNase OUT	1 μl
RNase-free water	1.75 μl
Superscript II Reverse Transcriptase	1 μl

4. In a PCR machine, incubate for 10 min at 20 °C and then 1 h at 42 °C.

3.5. cDNA sizing on agarose gels

The sizing on agarose gel will select for cDNA/RNA hybrids of appropriate sizes for Illumina sequencing and remove adapters. However, since we wish to obtain information on the 5′-ends of sRNAs, the lower limit of the sizing will stand at around 130 nt, which is less than usually for Illumina sequencing samples. The electrophoretic migration must be sufficient to separate cDNAs from primers and primer dimers but not too long in order to get a relatively small gel slice corresponding to 130–250 nt cDNAs.

1. Choose a gel comb that accommodates 30 μl sample per well.
2. Soak the electrophoresis apparatus and the comb in 3% hydrogen peroxide for 30 min to inactivate RNases. Remove peroxide by extensively rinsing with RNase-free water prior to use.
3. Prepare 50 ml of 2% agarose gel using Certified Low Range Agarose in 1 × TAE buffer. Be careful when melting the agarose gel because a gel that is not enough concentrated due to incomplete dissolution will melt during electrophoresis and you will lose your sample. Let it cool to about 50 °C and add ethidium bromide to the gel before pouring.
4. Add 5 μl of 5 × loading dye provided with the QIAquick gel purification kit to each TAP^+ and TAP^- reverse-transcribed sample.
5. Cover the gel with a minimal amount of 1 × TAE buffer.
6. Load 5 μl low-molecular weight DNA ladder to outside wells.

7. Load entire samples (30 μl) on gel leaving an empty lane between samples to avoid cross-contamination.
8. Run for 1 h 30 min at 7 V/cm.
9. Place the gel on a clean UV-transparent plastic film and rapidly take a photograph of the gel, keeping exposure of the gel to UV light at minimum.
10. Using a clean scalpel for each lane, excise a region of gel corresponding to a 130–250 nt range for the TAP^+ and TAP^- samples. The two gel slices must be as similar as possible. When possible, a full-size photograph of the gel that will be placed under the gel is the best way to visualize the position of the ladder without reexposing the gel to UV light. The mass of the gel slice must be lower than 400 mg in order to use one QIAquick column per sample.
11. Proceed to cDNA extraction using the QIAquick gel extraction kit according to manufacturer's instructions. Use 300 μl of QG buffer for 100 mg of gel and incubate for 10 min at room temperature with frequent vortexing to dissolve the gel. The optional washing step with QG buffer will be performed. For elution, add 30 μl of RNase-free water to the center of the QIAquick membrane and let stand for 4 min before centrifugation.

3.6. PCR amplification

The PCR amplification step will allow synthesizing the second strand of the cDNA, to enrich for fragments that contain both 5′- and 3′-adapters and to increase the quantity of material. The two primers will therefore be able to hybridize to the 5′- and 3′-adapters sequences. In addition, they will introduce sequences required for the hybridization to the flow cell. The capacity of an Illumina sequencing flow cell generally greatly exceeds the sequencing depth requirements of a bacterial RNA-seq experiment. Sample multiplexing is a useful technique to reduce sequencing costs by increasing the number of samples analyzed in a single run. To accomplish that, individual "barcode" sequences, also called "indexes," are added to each sample by means of one of the PCR primers. This allows each sample to be distinguished and sorted during the analysis ("demultiplexing" step). Here, the index is carried by the primer hybridizing to the 3′-adapter. Different versions of the primer ("indexed primers") sharing the sequence necessary for hybridization to the 3′-adapter but differing by their index are available. With a HighSeq Illumina platform, we generally load up to six samples (three TAP^+ and three TAP^- samples or a combination of samples from

RNA-seq and dRNA-seq) in a same lane of the flow cell. Carefully choose the combination of indexed primers so that they are compatible. Be aware that not all combinations can be used for successful demultiplexing step. For two samples, it is recommended to use Illumina indexes 6 and 12, for three samples: indexes 4, 6, and 12, and for six samples, indexes 2, 4, 5, 6, 7, and 12.

Prepare the PCR reactions by mixing:

PCR grade water	18 μl
5× Phusion HF buffer	10 μl
25 μ*M* RP1 Primer	0.5 μl
25 μ*M* Indexed Primer	0.5 μl
dNTP (12.5 m*M* each)	1 μl
TAP^+ or TAP^- sample	20 μl
Phusion DNA polymerase	0.5 μl

Amplify using:

a.	30 s at 98 °C
b.	*13–15 cycles of:*
	10 s at 98 °C
	30 s at 60 °C
	15 s at 72 °C
c.	10 min at 72 °C
d.	Hold at 4 °C

3.7. Purification of the PCR products on Agencourt AMPure beads

Purify the PCR products to eliminate the primers using Agencourt AMPure XP Beads. Make sure that beads came to room temperature before proceeding.

1. Vortex the beads until they are well dispersed.
2. Add 90 μl of AMPure XP beads for 50 μl PCR and mix by pipetting at least 10 times.

3. Incubate at room temperature for 10 min.
4. Place tubes on magnetic stand and let sit for 5 min or until the liquid appears clear.
5. Remove and discard the majority of the supernatant from each tube. Add 200 µl of 75% ethanol and let it incubate on the stand for 30 s and then discard ethanol.
6. Repeat ethanol wash one more time. At the end, completely remove all traces of ethanol.
7. Let stand at room temperature for 15 min to dry.
8. Remove from magnetic stand and resuspend the dried beads in 40 µl water. Mix by pipetting up and down 10 times and incubate at room temperature for 2 min.
9. Place tubes on magnetic stand and let stand for 2 min or until the liquid appears clear.
10. Transfer 37.5 µl of the supernatant to a new tube.

3.8. Quality control of the libraries

Appropriate quantification of libraries is recommended when using NGS technologies. We recommend using Invitrogen's Qubit Fluorometer as it utilizes a fluorescent dye that binds to nucleic acids for quantification. We also recommend checking the size of your library using Agilent 2100 BioAnalyzer and DNA 1000 kit (see profile in Fig. 1.4C). A bad library would have adapter junk at 100–120 bp. Note that the profiles of the libraries obtained with this protocol are somewhat unusual with a multitude of small peaks, instead of a broad and smooth peak. This is due to the enrichment in 5′-ends of abundant RNA species, such as 16S and 23S RNAs (which still constitute a large fraction of the sample), 5S, tRNAs, and some small abundant ncRNAs.

Send to an Illumina sequencing platform. Sequencing only 50 nucleotides using sequencing primers for TruSeq will be sufficient. Under these conditions, the cDNA will be sequenced from the extremity corresponding to 5′-end of the mRNA.

3.9. Data analysis

Sequencing will provide millions of short reads. If you proceed to the analysis of the run quality, with FastQC software for instance, note that several indicators of quality may have bad scores (per base GC content, Sequence Duplication Levels, Overrepresented sequences, and *K*-mer content in particular). This has two main reasons: (i) selection for low-molecular range cDNA fragments, some of them might be smaller than 50 nt and consequently you will also sequence parts of the 3′ adapter; (ii) 5′-ends of rRNAs or tRNAs will be enriched distorting the GC content to GC content of these sequences and creating overrepresented sequences and *K*-mers. Nevertheless proceed to bioinformatics analysis as described later (Fig. 1.5 and Section 5).

4. GENOME-WIDE ANALYSIS OF TRANSCRIPT LENGTH BY RNA-SEQ

Information on ncRNA length can be obtained using RNA-seq. At present, you will have the choice between nondirectional RNA-seq or strand-specific RNA-seq. Both have advantages and drawbacks. Nondirectional RNA-seq does not provide information on transcription orientation. However, this information can be easily recovered from TSS mapping with dRNA-seq. In contrast, strand-specific RNA-seq maintains this information but has the disadvantage to lead to less regular coverage along the transcripts. Although more tedious than the dUTP-based methodology for which commercial kits are now available, the ligation-based strand-specific RNA-seq provides better results for mapping the 3′-ends of small ncRNAs. Here, we will give only a short overview of library preparation for nondirectional RNA-seq and for ligation-based strand-specific RNA-seq (Fig. 1.3).

4.1. Strand-specific RNA-Seq library construction

Strand-specific RNA-seq libraries using primer ligation method can be generated essentially as described (Levin et al., 2010) with the following modifications. Adapters and primers are from the TruSeq Small RNA Prep kit (Illumina). Start with 1 μg total RNA, deplete ribosomal RNA as previously described, and incubate with 5 U of TAP for 1 h at 37 °C. After chloroform/acid phenol (1/1) extraction and ethanol precipitation, fragment the RNAs using one of the RNA fragmentation reagents. We generally use the RNA Fragmentation Reagent kit (Ambion) and an incubation time of 3 min at 70 °C. However, we recommend to adjust the fragmentation time for your own RNA to obtain a maximum of RNA fragments in the 100–300 nt range. After fragmentation, we use RNeasy MinElute Cleanup (Qiagen) columns to purify the RNA. As chemical fragmentation mainly results in 5′-OH and a mixture of 3′-, 2′- and 2′,3′ cyclic phosphate ends, you will need to polish 3′-ends and phosphorylate 5′-ends before proceeding to ligation of adapters. Dephosphorylate the fragmented RNA by treating with 5 U of antarctic Phosphatase (Biolabs) for 30 min at 37 °C followed by 5 min at 65 °C. RNA are thereafter rephosphorylated with 20 U T4 polynucleotide kinase (Biolabs) 60 min at 37 °C and purified through RNeasy MinElute Cleanup (Qiagen) columns. Elute with 14 μl RNase-free water and use 6 μl of the eluted RNA for ligation to 1 μl RNA 3′-adapter in a final volume of 10 μl in the presence of 200 U Truncated T4 RNA Ligase 2 (Biolabs). After 1 h incubation at 28 °C, the reaction is stopped with 1 μl of stop solution (Illumina) and incubated for 15 min at 28 °C. RNA ligated with 3′-adapter is ligated on its 5′-end using 1.1 μl 5′-RNA adapter in the presence of ATP 1 m*M* and 11 U T4 RNA ligase (Biolabs) and incubated at 28 °C for 1 h. Reverse transcription of the double-ligated RNA will be performed using Superscript II Reverse transcriptase and 1 μl RNA reverse transcription primer from 1 h at 50 °C. We amplify the whole sample in a 50-μl PCR reaction in the presence of Phusion Taq polymerase, a 2 μl of RP1 PCR primer, and a 2 μl of indexed PCR primer with the following thermocycling conditions: 30 s at 98 °C, 14 cycles of 98 °C for 10 s, 60 °C for 30 s, 72 °C for 15 s followed by 10 min at 72 °C. Finally, the PCR products are purified twice with 1.3 volumes of AMPure beads (Agencourt), DNA concentration is measured using Qubit quantification, and size of the PCR products is estimated on DNA 1000 Bioanalyzer chip (Agilent) before sequencing using the Illumina HiSeq 2000 machine.

4.2. Nonoriented whole-transcript RNA-Seq library preparation

For nonoriented RNA-seq library construction, the TruSeq RNA Sample Prep kit (RS-930-2001) from Illumina can be used according to manufacturer's instructions with few adjustments. Briefly, the enriched mRNAs are fragmented by chemical treatment at 94 °C for 8 min and then converted into cDNA using Superscript II Reverse transcriptase and random primers. Purification is performed on Qiaquick columns (Qiagen). After end repair and adenylation of the 3′-ends, specific adapters are ligated. The products are purified on E-Gel (Life Technologies) and amplified by 15 cycles of PCR. After purification on Qiaquick columns (Qiagen), the libraries are checked for quality on DNA 1000 Bioanalyzer chip (Agilent) before sequencing using the Illumina HiSeq 2000 machine.

5. PROCESSING AND ANALYSIS OF dRNA-SEQ AND RNA-SEQ DATA

Typically, sequencing will provide tens of millions of short sequences ("reads"). Figure 1.5 gives the overall steps, from read sequences to the discovery of potential new riboswitches using a genome browser such as COV2HTML (Monot, Orgeur, Camiade, Brehier, & Dupuy, 2014) or the Integrated Genome Viewer (IGV) (Robinson et al., 2011). After initial checks on sequence quality (for instance with FastQC), reads are trimmed from adapter sequences with cutadapt and mapped to a reference genome. The mapping step may be done using one of many aligners that have been developed (Hatem, Bozdag, Toland, & Catalyurek, 2013). We currently use Bowtie 1, which works well with bacterial genomes and is ultrafast for reads shorter than 50 nt. The files generated by the aligner, in SAM format, are then transformed with the Samtools into a sorted and indexed BAM format, which is generally required by the genome browser.

We will only give the main command lines necessary to go through read alignments and conversion of the SAM format. For more detailed information on how to use the different programs, please consult the documentation associated with each program. This protocol assumes users having a Unix-like operating system (i.e., Linux or MacOS X), with a bash shell or similar. All commands given here are meant to be run in a terminal window.

5.1. Softwares and supplementary files required for the analysis

Here is a list of sites from which you can easily download the programs:

- FastQC : http://www.bioinformatics.babraham.ac.uk/projects/download.html
- cutadapt: https://code.google.com/p/cutadapt/
- Bowtie 1: http://bowtie-bio.sourceforge.net/index.shtml
- Samtools: http://samtools.sourceforge.net/
- COV2HTML: https://mmonot.eu/COV2HTML/connexion.php
- IGV: http://www.broadinstitute.org/software/igv/

Several additional files are also needed:

- The reference genome sequence under fasta format
- The gene model annotation for the reference genome under a GTF or GFF format.

If the reference genome sequence has been published, these files are available from the ftp sites of NCBI or ENSEMBL databases (ftp://ftp.ncbi.nlm.nih.gov/genomes/Bacteria/ or http://bacteria.ensembl.org/info/data/ftp/index.html).

Supplementary remarks

- As a reference genome, choose the bacterial strain that is phylogenetically the closest to the strain you are working on and for which a complete genome sequence is available.
- Make sure that the gene annotation uses the same coordinate system and the same sequence name as the reference FASTA file, otherwise you will be unable to successfully use the genome browser.

5.2. Protocol

In the following protocol, Unix commands will appear in Courier font, prefaced by a dollar sign ($): `$ unix_command`

Seq.fastq and seqref.fna will refer to the read sequence file under fastq format, as generated by Illumina sequencing and to the fasta file for the reference genome sequence, respectively.

5.2.1 Trimming of the adapter sequences

As previously mentioned, a substantial proportion of the cDNA fragments generated during the preparation of dRNA-seq libraries may be shorter than 50 nt, leading to hybrid reads from which the adapter sequence must be trimmed with cutadapt. Use the following command:

```
$ cutadapt -a TGGAATTCTCGGGTGCCAAGG -m 25 Seq.fastq -o reads_after_trimming.fastq
```

where the sequence defined with –a corresponds to the adapter sequence. Reads shorter than 25 nt after trimming will be eliminated with the –m option.

5.2.2 Creation of a reference index for bowtie 1

Before reads can be aligned, the reference FASTA files need to be preprocessed into an index that allows the aligner easy computing. To create the index, use the command:

```
$ bowtie-build seqref.fna seqrefind
```

A set of .ebwt files will be created. This procedure needs to be run only once for each reference genome.

5.2.3 Alignment of the reads to the reference genome

```
$ bowtie -S -n 2 -l 25 -k 1 --best -p 1 -m 1 seqrefind reads_after_trimming.fastq alignment_output.sam
```

Using these options, only the best alignment will be reported for each read (–k 1 ––best) and alignments to sequences present more than once in the genome will be discarded (–m 1). Up to two mismatches (–n 2) in the 25 first nucleotides will be allowed in order to accommodate sequencing errors and sequence polymorphisms between the reference strain and the strain under study. Depending on your computer, you can choose to utilize more than one processor (–p option) in parallel to accelerate computation process.

5.2.4 Conversion of the SAM file to a sorted BAM file and creation of an index

Run the samtools with the following commands, successively:

```
$ samtools view -bS alignment_output.sam > alignment_output.bam
$ samtools sort alignment_output.bam alignment_output_sorted
$ samtools index alignment_output_sorted.bam
```

5.2.5 Visualization of the alignments on a genome browser

For visualization of the data, we use IGV (Robinson et al., 2011) or COV2HTML (Monot et al., 2014). Import the reference genome sequence, the annotation information and the sorted bam files as described in the documentations of the browser. With the two browsers, you will be able to load the two files corresponding to the dRNA-seq (TAP^+ and TAP^-) and the file corresponding to the RNA-seq experiments.

6. CHARACTERIZATION OF NEW POTENTIAL RIBOSWITCHES USING dRNA-SEQ AND RNA-SEQ ANALYSES

Several criteria could be considered for the search for potential riboswitches, in particular, acting by a premature termination of transcription mechanism:

- Characteristic profiles revealed by RNA-seq (Figs. 1.6 and 1.7) show a great number of sequence reads mapping to a short portion upstream of the gene that might correspond to a terminated transcript; under inducing conditions, the contiguous expression extending from the 5′-flanking intergenic region to a protein-coding gene could be observed (Figs. 1.6A and 1.7F);

- Identification of a TSS upstream of this RNA-seq peak associated with the absence of an additional TSS just upstream of the coding gene (a possibility of sRNA remains at this step if the absence of TSS upstream of the gene is related to the low level of expression or technical difficulties);
- Presence of a rho-independent terminator between the identified TSS and the coding part of the potential target gene;
- Nature of potential riboswitch-regulated genes that may encode various metabolic functions;
- Rfam search for the conserved regulatory RNAs that allows distinguishing between conserved riboswitches and other regulatory RNA elements. In the absence of Rfam match the possibility of identification of a novel regulatory RNA should be considered; the nature and the mechanism of control would need further experimental validations;
- Detection of a long 5′-UTR indicating the possibility of regulatory capacities for this region, Rfam search could be useful in this case for identification of potential regulatory elements in this 5′-UTR.

Based on general Rfam search data for potential regulatory RNAs the possibility for riboswitch identification could be raised by reexamining the RNA-seq data. Further Northern blot and qRT-PCR analysis under conditions depending on the nature of the regulatory element and on the controlled gene would confirm the type of regulatory RNA detected.

By this approach, we have identified about 66 potential riboswitches in *Clostridium difficile* including 20 T-boxes, 5 SAM-riboswitches, 4 L-boxes, 16 c-di-GMP-responsive riboswitches, and 8 ribozymes of group I introns (Soutourina et al., 2013). In *Streptococcus agalactiae*, this combined strategy allowed identification of 24 potential riboswitches (I. Rosinski-Chupin, personal communication).

Characteristic patterns corresponding to riboswitches detected in *C. difficile* and *S. agalactiae* are presented in Figs. 1.6 and 1.7. Figures 1.6A and 1.7A show the TSS detection by TAP^{+}/TAP^{-} profile comparison upstream of *CD2357* (*grdX*) gene and *gbs1212* gene, respectively, associated with the presence of a characteristic peak in RNA-seq corresponding to glycine-responsive riboswitches. Figure 1.6B presents an S-box riboswitch detected upstream of *CD1489* (*metN*) gene encoding a methionine transporter. Characteristic T-box profile upstream of *gbs0343* (*serS*) gene encoding a seryl-tRNA synthetase was detected in *S. agalactiae* (Fig. 1.7B). Interestingly, deep sequencing also revealed the two T-box elements in tandem located upstream of the *C. difficile CD1580* gene encoding a homoserine dehydrogenase (Fig. 1.6C). Deep-sequencing analysis led to the detection of an antiterminator element upstream of the *CD0134* gene encoding a PTS component (Fig. 1.6D) in *C. difficile* and PyrR-binding site or L20 leader region for transcriptional attenuation within an UTR of *S. agalactiae gbs2013* gene encoding major facilitator protein and *gbs1454* (*infC*) gene encoding translation initiation factor IF3, respectively (Fig. 1.7C and D). An example of a particular class of riboswitches responsive to c-di-GMP located upstream of the large *C. difficile* flagella *flgB* operon is shown in Fig. 1.6E. In addition to TSS mapping, the comparison of TAP^+ and TAP^- profiles allows identification of specific ribonucleolytic cleavage sites within regulatory regions. Indeed, specific ribonucleases have been shown to cleave riboswitches or T-box motifs to initiate their ligand-dependent turnover in several bacteria (Altman, Wesolowski, Guerrier-Takada, & Li, 2005; Even et al., 2005; Shahbabian, Jamalli, Zig, & Putzer, 2009). Examples of such internal cleavage sites (pointed out by vertical arrow) within a Thr-specific T-box upstream of *CD2118* (*thrC*) gene encoding the threonine synthase of *C. difficile* (Fig. 1.6F) and within an FMN riboswitch upstream of *gbs0767* gene encoding the riboflavin deaminase of *S. agalactiae* (Fig. 1.7E) are shown. Finally, Fig. 1.7F illustrates the RNA-seq profiles for the *yybP–ykoY* leader region upstream of *gbs0560* gene encoding cation transporting ATPase in *S. agalactiae* in "ON" and "OFF" states under two different experimental conditions.

In conclusion, the combination of two deep-sequencing approaches—RNA-seq for whole-transcript analysis and dRNA-seq for global TSS identification—together with *in silico* analysis represents a powerful approach to search for regulatory RNAs in general and to identify the riboswitches in a given bacterial species. The experimental evidence for functional known riboswitches could be obtained, and the possibility of new riboswitches could be suggested by this global approach, leading to the interesting perspectives for discovery of new unexpected mechanisms of gene regulation based on regulatory RNAs in bacteria.

REFERENCES

Altman, S., Wesolowski, D., Guerrier-Takada, C., & Li, Y. (2005). RNase P cleaves transient structures in some riboswitches. *Proceedings of the National Academy of Sciences of the United States of America*, *102*(32), 11284–11289.

Brantl, S. (2012). Acting antisense: Plasmid- and chromosome-encoded sRNAs from Gram-positive bacteria. *Future Microbiology*, 7(7), 853–871.

Croucher, N. J., & Thomson, N. R. (2010). Studying bacterial transcriptomes using RNA-seq. *Current Opinion in Microbiology*, *13*(5), 619–624.

Even, S., Pellegrini, O., Zig, L., Labas, V., Vinh, J., Brechemmier-Baey, D., et al. (2005). Ribonucleases J1 and J2: Two novel endoribonucleases in *B.subtilis* with functional homology to *E.coli* RNase E. *Nucleic Acids Research*, *33*(7), 2141–2152.

Gripenland, J., Netterling, S., Loh, E., Tiensuu, T., Toledo-Arana, A., & Johansson, J. (2010). RNAs: Regulators of bacterial virulence. *Nature Reviews. Microbiology*, *8*(12), 857–866.

Hatem, A., Bozdag, D., Toland, A. E., & Catalyurek, U. V. (2013). Benchmarking short sequence mapping tools. *BMC Bioinformatics*, *14*, 184.

Levin, J. Z., Yassour, M., Adiconis, X., Nusbaum, C., Thompson, D. A., Friedman, N., et al. (2010). Comprehensive comparative analysis of strand-specific RNA sequencing methods. *Nature Methods*, 7(9), 709–715.

Monot, M., Orgeur, M., Camiade, E., Brehier, C., & Dupuy, B. (2014). COV2HTML: A visualization and analysis tool of bacterial next generation sequencing (NGS) data for postgenomics life scientists. *OMICS*, *18*(3), 184–195.

Nudler, E., & Mironov, A. S. (2004). The riboswitch control of bacterial metabolism. *Trends in Biochemical Sciences*, *29*(1), 11–17.

Papenfort, K., & Vogel, J. (2010). Regulatory RNA in bacterial pathogens. *Cell Host and Microbe*, *8*(1), 116–127.

Robinson, J. T., Thorvaldsdottir, H., Winckler, W., Guttman, M., Lander, E. S., Getz, G., et al. (2011). Integrative genomics viewer. *Nature Biotechnology*, *29*(1), 24–26.

Romby, P., & Charpentier, E. (2010). An overview of RNAs with regulatory functions in Gram-positive bacteria. *Cellular and Molecular Life Sciences*, *67*(2), 217–237.

Sahr, T., Rusniok, C., Dervins-Ravault, D., Sismeiro, O., Coppee, J. Y., & Buchrieser, C. (2012). Deep sequencing defines the transcriptional map of *L. pneumophila* and identifies growth phase-dependent regulated ncRNAs implicated in virulence. *RNA Biology*, *9*(4), 503–519.

Serganov, A., & Nudler, E. (2013). A decade of riboswitches. *Cell*, *152*(1–2), 17–24.

Shahbabian, K., Jamalli, A., Zig, L., & Putzer, H. (2009). RNase Y, a novel endoribonuclease, initiates riboswitch turnover in *Bacillus subtilis*. *The EMBO Journal*, *28*(22), 3523–3533.

Sorek, R., & Cossart, P. (2010). Prokaryotic transcriptomics: A new view on regulation, physiology and pathogenicity. *Nature Reviews. Genetics*, *11*(1), 9–16.

Soutourina, O. A., Monot, M., Boudry, P., Saujet, L., Pichon, C., Sismeiro, O., et al. (2013). Genome-wide identification of regulatory RNAs in the human pathogen *clostridium difficile*. *PLoS Genetics*, *9*(5), e1003493.

Toledo-Arana, A., Dussurget, O., Nikitas, G., Sesto, N., Guet-Revillet, H., Balestrino, D., et al. (2009). The Listeria transcriptional landscape from saprophytism to virulence. *Nature*, *459*(7249), 950–956.

Waters, L. S., & Storz, G. (2009). Regulatory RNAs in bacteria. *Cell*, *136*(4), 615–628.

Wurtzel, O., Sapra, R., Chen, F., Zhu, Y., Simmons, B. A., & Sorek, R. (2010). A single-base resolution map of an archaeal transcriptome. *Genome Research*, *20*(1), 133–141.

CHAPTER TWO

Discovering Human RNA Aptamers by Structure-Based Bioinformatics and Genome-Based *In Vitro* Selection

Bao Ho[*,†,‡], **Julio Polanco**[*,†,‡], **Randi Jimenez**[*,†,‡], **Andrej Lupták**[*,†,‡,1]
[*]Department of Pharmaceutical Sciences, University of California, Irvine, California, USA
[†]Department of Molecular Biology and Biochemistry, University of California, Irvine, California, USA
[‡]Department of Chemistry, University of California, Irvine, California, USA
[1]Corresponding author: e-mail address: aluptak@uci.edu

Contents

Abstract

In vitro selection and structure-based searches have emerged as useful techniques for the discoveries of structurally complex RNAs with high affinity and specificity toward metabolites. Here, we focus on the design of a human genomic library that serves as the DNA template for *in vitro* selection of RNA aptamers. In addition, the structural solutions obtained from the *in vitro* selection can be used for structure-based searches for discovery of analogous aptamers in various genomic databases.

1. INTRODUCTION

Over the past two decades, *in vitro* selection (also known as SELEX) has served as a powerful tool for the discovery of novel DNA and RNA

Methods in Enzymology, Volume 549
ISSN 0076-6879
http://dx.doi.org/10.1016/B978-0-12-801122-5.00002-7

aptamers. Since then, extensive selection and structural studies have highlighted the structural diversity within a given random pool of DNA or RNA sequences (Stoltenburg, Reinemann, & Strehlitz, 2007). Initial *in vitro* selection studies utilized pools of synthetic random DNAs flanked by fixed, primer-binding sequences that were transcribed into amplifiable RNAs of similar diversity to determine the frequency of aptamers capable of binding a target molecule (Ellington & Szostak, 1990; Tuerk & Gold, 1990). More recently, modifications to the *in vitro* selection procedure have aimed to identify naturally occurring aptamers and other functional nucleic acids by using genome-derived DNA pools as templates for selections. In the case of adenosine, but not GTP, both synthetic and genomic DNA selections revealed a number of structurally conserved aptamer sequences (Burke & Gold, 1997; Curtis & Liu, 2013; Davis & Szostak, 2002; Sassanfar & Szostak, 1993; Vu et al., 2012). These adenosine-binding motifs are sequence-independent and represent a rare example of convergent molecular evolution spanning both genomic and synthetic sequence space.

Genomic SELEX was introduced by Singer and Gold using a genomic library for *in vitro* selection studies using a set of primers consisting of a fixed 5′ end sequence and a randomized 3′ tail. This allowed for amplification of fragmented human, yeast, and *Escherichia coli* genomic DNA *in vitro*, followed by size selection and primer extension to allow for transcription (Singer, Shtatland, Brown, & Gold, 1997). On the other hand, Salehi-Ashtiani et al. designed a genomic pool by partial digestion of human genomic DNA using DNase I. After digestion, hairpin sequences of known composition were ligated onto the genomic DNA, subjected to single-stranded digestion and then amplified by primer extension (Salehi-Ashtiani, Lupták, Litovchick, & Szostak, 2006).

Among the best-characterized aptamer structures is the adenosine-binding motif. Both synthetic and genomic selections reveal a conserved binding pocket consisting of an 11-nucleotide loop and a bulged G formed by two flanking helical motifs (Fig. 2.1). Nuclear magnetic resonance and mutation studies have shown that these conserved nucleotides and flanking helices are required for the formation of a binding pocket to allow base stacking and hydrogen-bonding interactions with the ligand (Dieckmann, Butcher, Sassanfar, Szostak, & Feigon, 1997; Dieckmann, Suzuki, Nakamura, & Feigon, 1996; Jiang, Kumar, Jones, & Patel, 1996; Vu et al., 2012). Although the sequence compositions of the flanking helical motifs vary, the adenosine-binding loop is largely sequence conserved, and both of these properties are exploited with structure-based search algorithms.

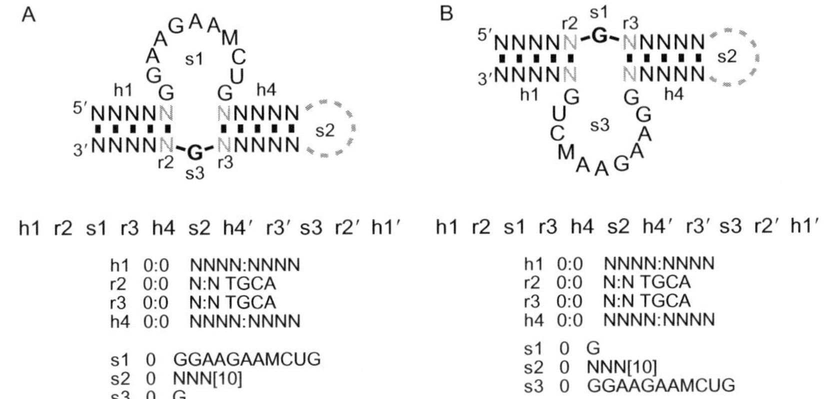

Figure 2.1 Secondary structure descriptors for an adenosine aptamer. The aptamer has been found to exist in both the 5′ (A) and 3′ (B) strands (Burgstaller & Famulok, 1994; Sassanfar & Szostak, 1993; Vu et al., 2012). The bulged guanosine nucleotide necessary for ligand binding is in bold.

Structure-based search algorithms are powerful tools in the discovery of functional RNAs. Their success comes from the ability to find sequences in unrelated, unprocessed sequence data that match complex motifs (Gautheret, Major, & Cedergren, 1990). Their appeal lies in the user accessibility: the ease of use, the flexibility in descriptor design, and the efficiency and speed of searches. Structure-based search programs are used to identify sequences capable of fitting into a given secondary structure. These programs match the patterns of base-paired and single-stranded regions as defined by the user in a descriptor file. Furthermore, the descriptor allows the user to specify regions of strict Watson-Crick base pairing, wobble pairs, mismatches, and single-nucleotide insertions in helices. Two user-friendly programs with similar syntax are RNABOB (ftp://selab.janelia.org/pub/software/rnabob/) and RNArobo (Jimenez, Rampasek, Brejova, Vinar, & Lupták, 2012); the implementation of neither of these programs requires extensive programming skills. The implementation of RNABOB is as previously described (Riccitelli & Lupták, 2010) and will be outlined briefly below.

Our approach here focuses on the design of a genomic DNA pool for use in *in vitro* selection. In principle, the pool can sample the entire genome of the target organism at single-nucleotide resolution (in both directions, with respect to the engineered RNA polymerase promoter), independent of expression of individual genes, but lacks sequences corresponding to spliced and otherwise processed transcripts. Structural characterization of the resulting aptamers can be used to generate structure descriptors for mapping sequences against a genome database.

2. PRECAUTIONS

As ribonucleic acids are highly sensitive to degradation, it is advisable that the following procedures are conducted in an RNase-free laboratory environment. RNase-free reagents, consumables, and equipment are required. Proper handling of RNA includes, but is not limited to, frequent disinfection of gloves, benches, and instruments with ethanol or weak oxidizers (diluted bleach or hydrogen peroxide), regular change of gloves, and maintenance of RNA over ice while preparations of experiments take place. In addition, laboratory personnel should be properly equipped and trained for utilizing ^{32}P. Material safety data sheets of reagents included within these procedures are provided by their distributors and should be followed to minimize hazardous occurrences.

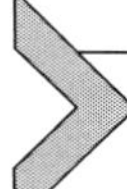

3. GENERATING A HUMAN GENOMIC DNA POOL

3.1. Materials

3.1.1 High molecular weight human genomic DNA

High molecular weight human genomic DNA isolated from whole blood cells is commercially available and can be purchased from suppliers such as Clontech or Promega. For the procedure outlined below, it is critical that the source DNA be of high molecular weight since the DNA will be subjected to sonication for fragmentation.

3.1.2 Adapter oligonucleotide sequences

The sequences of known composition consist of two pairs of synthetic oligonucleotides. The forward adapter contains a T7 promoter to allow for transcription, a 3′ dT overhang, and a 5′ phosphate modification on the complementary strand (Fig. 2.2). The reverse adapter contains a 5′ phosphate modification and a 3′ dT overhang on the complementary strand (Fig. 2.2). With regards to adapter design, the following requirements must be considered: oligonucleotide sequences should not form any interactions that may interfere with directional ligation of DNA, the melting temperature of each adapter set is within range of 55–70 °C for polymerase chain reaction (PCR) amplification and primers should not anneal to form primer dimers or nonspecific amplification byproducts. The sequences are chosen

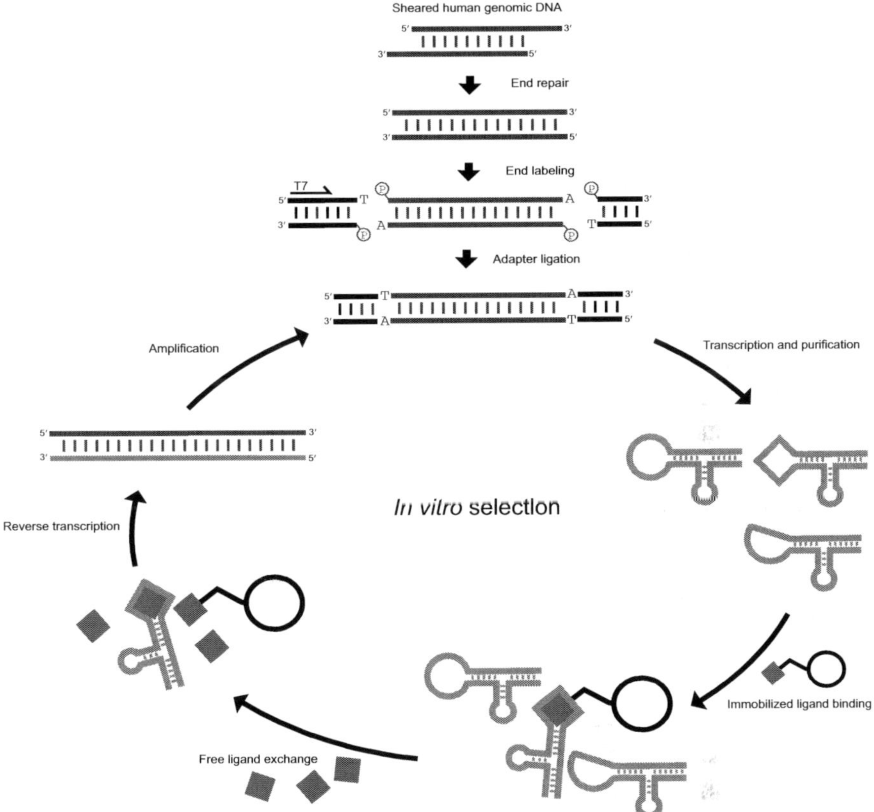

Figure 2.2 Overview of the design of a human genomic pool and *in vitro* selection. The library construction begins with sheared human genomic DNA, modified to allow ligation of sequences of known compositions. The library serves as a template for subsequent selection of RNA sequences with affinity and specificity toward a target molecule.

to promote efficient transcription and amplification, and if one of the goals of the *in vitro* selection is high-throughput sequencing (HTS), then the sequence is also matched to primer sequences used by the HTS platform of choice.

3.1.3 Enzymes

The following enzymes are used to prepare the genomic DNA for adapter ligation and PCR amplification: T4 DNA polymerase, T4 polynucleotide kinase (PNK), *E. coli* Klenow fragment (exo-), T4 DNA ligase, *Pfu* DNA Polymerase. All enzymes are commercially available from New England Biolabs and other suppliers.

3.1.4 Buffers

A solution 10 m*M* Tris·HCl, pH 8.0 can be used for the dilution, elution, or resuspension of the DNA throughout each step. For gel electrophoresis a 44.5 m*M* Tris·borate, pH 8.3, 1 m*M* EDTA solution is used as a running buffer. All gels are poststained in an ethidium bromide-water bath prior to imaging.

3.1.4.1 Tris/borate/EDTA buffer (10 ×)

Tris/borate/EDTA (TBE) buffer is widely utilized as the buffer for electrophoresis. The running concentration is typically 1 × or 0.5 ×. The following buffer is at 10 × and can be diluted with water to the appropriate concentration. Stock and running buffers can be stored at room temperature.

890 m*M* Tris·HCl, 890 m*M* boric acid, 20 m*M* EDTA

3.1.5 Instruments and miscellaneous

Covaris S2 focused acoustic shearer

Agarose and polyacrylamide gel electrophoresis (PAGE) loading equipment

PCR thermocycler (Eppendorf, BioRad)

Spectrophotometer (Nanodrop from Thermo scientific)

DNA purification kit (Qiagen)

UV light, short wavelength, with a camera mount

Image density analysis software (ImageJ)

3.2. Procedures

3.2.1 Preparation of genomic DNA

In a 0.5-mL microcentrifuge tube, aliquot 3 μg of high molecular weight human genomic DNA for a final volume of 130 μL in 10 m*M* Tris·HCl pH 8.0. Using the Covaris S2 acoustic shearer, tune the instrument to shear the genomic DNA to the size of interest. Note that shorter high frequency bursts correspond to larger fragment sizes. Verify the efficiency of fragmentation by running a small amount of the sheared DNA product on a 2% agarose gel along with a molecular weight standards. Sheared genomic DNA usually runs as a smeared band with the highest intensity corresponding to the median target size.

3.2.2 Repairing genomic DNA ends

Due to nonspecific physical shearing, the single-stranded overhangs generated by sonication are processed to generate double-stranded blunt ends.

To generate blunt-ended DNA products, a nucleotide polymerization reaction is performed using 500 μ*M* deoxynucleotide triphosphates, 50 m*M* NaCl, 10 m*M* Tris·HCl pH 8.0, 10 m*M* $MgCl_2$, 1 m*M* dithiotreitol (DTT), 3 units of T4 DNA polymerase, or other DNA polymerase with 3′ exonuclease activity, and 3 μg of sheared genomic DNA. The reaction is incubated at 12 °C for 15–30 min and subsequently purified using a DNA purification kit.

3.2.3 Addition of 5′ phosphate group onto genomic DNA

To prepare the genomic DNA for ligation, a 5′ phosphate is added enzymatically using T4 PNK. The following reagents are combined in a PCR tube and incubated at 37 °C overnight: 200 μ*M* adenosine triphosphate (ATP), 70 m*M* Tris·HCl pH 7.6, 10 m*M* $MgCl_2$, 5 m*M* DTT, 5% polyethylene glycol 8000, 2 m*M* spermidine, 10 units of T4 PNK, 3 μg of end-repaired genomic DNA product, and deionized water. Overnight incubation is significantly longer than is typically used for phosphorylation of oligonucleotides and is used here to ensure phosphorylation of long, blunt-ended DNAs. Once completed, the phosphorylated DNA product is purified using a silica membrane (Qiagen spin column) and quantified by spectrophotometry.

3.2.4 Addition of 3′ dA overhangs

To generate complementary cohesive ends to aid in adapter ligation, deoxyadenosine overhangs are introduced to the 3′ ends of the genomic DNA (Fig. 2.1). This reaction uses 100 μ*M* dATP, 10 m*M* Tris·HCl pH 8.0, 50 m*M* NaCl, 10 m*M* $MgCl_2$, 1 m*M* DTT, 5 units of Klenow fragment (3′-5′ exo-), 3 μg of phosphorylated genomic DNA product, and deionized water. The reaction is incubated at 37 °C for 30 min. The DNA product is then purified using a Qiagen DNA purification spin column and quantified by spectrophotometry.

3.2.5 Adapter ligation

To prepare for adapter ligation, a master stock is generated by dilution of each adapter oligonucleotide to a final concentration of 25 μ*M*. The adapter ligation reaction is set up in a PCR tube with 1 m*M* ATP, 10 m*M* DTT, 50 m*M* Tris·HCl pH 7.5, 10 m*M* $MgCl_2$, 30 units of T4 DNA ligase, 3 μL of 25 μ*M* stock adapter solution, ~2 μg of genomic DNA from Section 3.2.4, and deionized water. The reaction is then incubated at 16 °C for 30 min and prepared for PCR using a DNA purification kit.

3.2.6 PCR amplification

To ensure successful ligation of the adapters, the final DNA product is amplified by PCR using a set of two adapter sequences corresponding to the forward and reverse primers. The PCR reaction is set up with the entire adapter-ligated DNA product in 200 μ*M* dNTPs, 10 m*M* Tris·HCl, pH 8.3, 50 m*M* KCl, 1.5 m*M* $MgCl_2$, and 2 μ*M* of both forward and reverse primers. During PCR, aliquots are taken out every four cycles for a total of 24 PCR cycles. These PCR fractions are purified using a 2% agarose gel and density analysis to determine sequence diversity.

4. *IN VITRO* SELECTION OF RNA APTAMERS

4.1. Materials

4.1.1 Selection buffers

These buffers should provide physiological-like conditions to promote RNA structures similar to cellular ones. Binding buffer should facilitate binding of aptamers onto immobilized ligands. Elution buffer, in addition to being similar to its binding counterpart, contains elevated concentration of magnesium chloride to accommodate chelating by negatively-charged ligands (e.g., adenosine triphosphate; Vu et al., 2012), to maintain sufficient amount of Mg^{2+} to allow RNA to fold into a stable tertiary structure. In addition, the concentration of the free ligand should mimic its physiological concentration within the cell or exceed the approximate concentration of the ligand on the beads. Harsh elution buffer should contain denaturing condition in order to completely remove bound RNAs from the selection matrix. Storage of these buffers should adhere to appropriate conditions of their components. For example, where the ligand is a nucleotide triphosphate, the elution buffer should be frozen in multiple small aliquots to prevent hydrolysis.

4.1.1a Binding buffer: 140 m*M* KCl, 10 m*M* NaCl, 20 m*M* Tris·HCl, 5 m*M* $MgCl_2$.

4.1.1b Elution buffer: 140 m*M* KCl, 10 m*M* NaCl, 20 m*M* Tris·HCl, 5 m*M* $MgCl_2$, desired concentration of free ligand (in case of di- or triphosphorylated ligand, such as ATP, Mg^{2+} concentration needs to be increased by the ligand concentration to avoid changing the free Mg^{2+} concentration in the solution; e.g., we supplemented 5 m*M* ATP with an additional 5 m*M* $MgCl_2$; Vu et al., 2012).

4.1.1c Harsh elution buffer: 8 *M* urea and 5 m*M* EDTA.

4.1.2 Polyacrylamide gel electrophoresis

A stock of 15% can be prepared starting from the commercially available 40% acrylamide:bisacrylamide (19:1) solution. The 15% acrylamide stock should be preserved away from light and stored at 4 °C. Ammoniumpersulphate (APS) and tetramethylethylenediamine (TEMED) should be kept at 4 °C. The ^{32}P marker is for isolation of radiolabeled product once electrophoresis is completed.

4.1.2a 15% denaturing polyacrylamide stock: acrylamide:bisacrylamide (19:1) solution 40% w/v (CalBiochem), 1 × TBE buffer, 7 *M* urea, water.

4.1.2b Gel polymerization agents: 10% APS in water and TEMED.

4.1.2c 2 × RNA loading dye: 0.01% bromophenol blue, 0.005% xylene cyanol, and 8 *M* urea in 1 × TBE buffer.

4.1.2d ^{32}P marker: [α-^{32}P] ATP, water, paper, scotch tape.

4.1.2e Ethanol precipitation: 300 m*M* KCl, GlycoBlue (Life Technologies), ethanol.

4.1.3 Agarose gel electrophoresis

4.1.3a 2% agarose gel: electrophoresis grade agarose, 0.5 × TBE buffer, 1 × ethidium bromide.

4.1.3b 2 × DNA loading dye: 0.01% bromophenol blue, 0.005% xylene cyanol, and 8 *M* urea in 1 × TBE buffer.

4.1.4 Transcription

The following reaction buffers should accommodate radiolabeled and nonlabeled transcripts, respectively. Albeit similar, the concentration of ATP included in the buffer for radioactive transcription is one order of magnitude less than that of the other nucleotides. This is designed to promote the incorporation of [α-^{32}P] ATP into the backbone of transcribed products, resulting in radiolabeled RNAs.

4.1.4a Buffer for radioactive transcription (2 × stock): 4 m*M* Spermidine, 80 m*M* Tris·HCl pH 7.5, 20% DMSO, 20 m*M* DTT, 0.1% Triton X-100, 50 m*M* $MgCl_2$, 2 m*M* GTP, 2 m*M* CTP, 2 m*M* UTP, 0.2 m*M* ATP.

4.1.4b Buffer for nonradioactive transcription (2 × stock): 4 m*M* Spermidine, 80 m*M* Tris·HCl pH 7.5, 20% DMSO, 20 m*M* DTT, 0.1% Triton X-100, 50 m*M* $MgCl_2$, 2 m*M* GTP, 2 m*M* CTP, 2 m*M* UTP, 2 m*M* ATP.

4.1.4c DNA template: approximately 0.1 μ*M* of genomic library or previous round's PCR product (∼0.1 μ*M*) final concentration.

4.1.5 Reverse transcription

50 m*M* Tris·HCl (pH 8.3 at 25 °C), 75 m*M* KCl, 3 m*M* $MgCl_2$, 10 m*M* DTT, 0.5 m*M* dGTP, 0.5 m*M* dCTP, 0.5 m*M* dTTP, 0.5 m*M* dATP, 0.5 μ*M* reverse primer, RNA, 1 unit of reverse transcriptase.

4.1.6 Polymerase chain reaction

1 × *Taq* buffer (New England BioLabs), 0.5 m*M* dGTP, 0.5 m*M* dCTP, 0.5 m*M* TTP, 0.5 m*M* dATP, 2 μ*M* reverse primer, 2 μ*M* forward primer, cDNA, 1 unit of thermophillic DNA polymerase.

4.1.7 Enzymes

4.1.7a Transcription: T7 RNA Polymerase (New England Biolabs).
4.1.7b Reverse Transcription: ThermoScript Reverse Transcriptase (Life Technologies).
4.1.7c PCR: *Taq* DNA Polymerase (New England Biolabs).

4.1.8 Affinity column for in vitro *selection*

The selection matrix should have the target ligand immobilized onto it. Most experiments utilize commercially available sepharose matrix, e.g., ATP agarose (gamma phosphate-linked, Innova BioSciences; C8-linked; Sigma–Aldrich; Vu et al., 2012), or synthesized them via different linker with activated matrix, such as thiol sepharose (Davis & Szostak, 2002) or *N*-hydroxysuccinimide (NHS) sepharose (GE Healthcare Life Sciences). The concentration of immobilized ligand is often available form the manufacturer or should be measured by spectrophotometry (for example, using a UV–vis spectrophotometer with an integrating sphere or by fluorescence intensity if the ligand is fluorescent), and matched with the concentration of the free ligand within the elution buffer.

4.2. Procedure

4.2.1 Transcription

The protocols for radiolabeled and nonlabeled transcription are near identical, save for the addition of [α-^{32}P] ATP. Upon completion, the following reactions should be kept at −20 °C and should be used in the next experiment within the next few days to prevent RNA degradation and excessive decay of ^{32}P incorporated into the backbone. The transcription utilizes T7 RNA polymerase because the construct incorporates the T7 promoter.

The polymerase can be matched to a promoter of choice, depending on the design of the genomic pool.

4.2.1a Radioactive labeling of RNA via *in vitro* transcription: Mix 10 μL buffer for radioactive transcription, 2 μL DNA template, 0.5 μL T7 RNA polymerase, 0.5 μL [α-^{32}P] ATP (PerkinElmer), and deionized water to a total reaction volume of 20 μL in a small vial. Incubate at 37 °C for 3 h.

4.2.1b *In vitro* transcription: Mix 10 μL buffer for nonradioactive transcription, 2 μL DNA template, 0.5 μL T7 RNA polymerase, and deionized water to a total reaction volume of 20 μL in a small vial. Incubate at 37 °C for 3 h.

4.2.2 Purification of transcribed product

Transcribed RNAs can be purified by PAGE, as the reaction might contain side products, aborted constructs, and unreacted starting materials. In both radioactive and nonradioactive transcriptions, loading dye provides an approximate tracking of running samples, as well as increases the density of running samples to ensure that the RNAs stay within the wells. Visualization by UV shadowing (see step 4.2.2d) can identify nonradiolabeled RNAs on the polyacrylamide matrix, whereas the location of radiolabeled RNAs must be determined using ^{32}P markers and phosphor screen or photographic film. The markers help aligning the print-out onto the actual gel.

4.2.2a Polyacrylamide gel electrophoresis

1. Ensure that glass plates are clean and sterilized.
2. Prepare a 7.5% polyacrylamide solution by diluting polyacrylamide stock (15%) with equal volume of 8 *M* urea in 0.5 × TBE buffer.
3. For a gel cast of 16.5 cm by 22 cm dimension and 0.75 m*M* spacer, pour a plug at the end by mixing 5 mL 15% polyacrylamide, 50 μL 10% APS, and 5 μL TEMED. Wait until solidified.
4. Mix the rest of 15% polyacrylamide (20 mL) with 200 μL 10% APS and 20 μL TEMED. Pour into cast and apply comb.
5. Once gel is solidified, install onto electrophoresis apparatus. Overflow running wells with 0.5 × TBE.
6. Run gel at constant power of 20 W for 30 min.
7. Prepare running RNA solution by mixing *in vitro* transcription reaction and RNA loading dye (1:1 volume ratio).
8. Load solution onto wells. Run sample at 20 W. Duration is dependent upon the size of the transcription product.

4.2.2b Preparation of ^{32}P marker

1. Mix 5 μL 2× RNA loading dye, 5 μL water, and 0.5 μL [α-^{32}P] ATP
2. Pipette solution onto multiple spots of a small rectangular piece of paper
3. Once the liquid has evaporated, cover both side of the marker with tapes to prevent contamination. Now the dyed spots on the markers are radioactive.

4.2.2c Visualization of radioactively-labeled RNA

1. Remove gel plates from box once run is completed. Detach plates and cover gel with plastic wrap.
2. Secure two ^{32}P markers onto plastic-wrapped polyacrylamide gel with scotch tapes. Put a phosphor screen (GE Healthcare Life Sciences) on top of gel. Expose for at least 15 min.
3. Remove phosphor screen. Scan via Typhoon scanner under radioactive mode.
4. Obtain print-out of scanned image without scaling. Align image to gel based on location of ^{32}P markers.

4.2.2d Visualization of nonradioactive RNA

1. Remove gel plates from box once run is completed. Detach plates and cover gel with plastic wrap.
2. Visualize nonradioactive RNA with 254 nm UV light by placing the gel on a fluorescent thin layer chromatography plate. RNA absorbs the UV light, casting a shadow on the plate. Caution: prolonged exposure of RNA to UV light causes cross-linking.

4.2.2e Elution and precipitation of RNA from acrylamide matrix

1. Remove gel pieces containing visualized transcribed products.
2. Suspend gel pieces in 300 m*M* KCl. Elute at room temperature with shaking for at least 3 h. Add 0.5 μL GlycoBlue into the solution, mix well.
3. Transfer solution of eluted RNA onto a vial. Take care not to pipet out small bits of polyacrylamide. Add 95% ethanol at twice the volume of eluted solution. Let RNA precipitate in ethanol solution at −20 °C for at least 1 h.
4. Centrifuge at 20,000 × *g* for 30 min. Discard supernatant. Repeat at lower duration if necessary.
5. Let pellet dry at room temperature for 15 min. Resuspend evaporated RNA pellet in 20 μL physiological buffer.

4.2.3 In vitro *selection of RNA aptamers*

The selection strategy for aptamers is designed to enrich the pool for molecules that display high affinity and specificity toward the target ligand. The starting RNA library should exhibit a sufficiently high diversity to cover the whole genome at single-nucleotide resolution in both directions. The desired RNAs bind to the immobilized ligands on the selection agarose matrix, whereas the unbound RNAs are eliminated from the column by washing. Bound RNAs are then eluted through exchange with free ligand. Once the elutions are combined, free ligands and ions within the fraction can be removed using a desalting step (e.g., using Sephadex G25 column). It is critical that the presence of the free ligand be reduced prior to ethanol precipitation, as high concentration of free ligand can coprecipitate with selected RNA and inhibit subsequent reverse transcription. The progress of an *in vitro* selection is monitored by comparing the percentage of eluted RNAs across the rounds. In theory, the binding of the pool should increase with each round of selection, although it is often not measurable in the first few rounds of the selection. A counter-selection step can be included to increase stringency of the experiment, by incubating the RNA pool with beads containing a compound related to, but distinct from, the target molecule. A less stringent counter-selection step involves just the beads and the linker, and these are used to subtract molecules that have affinity for these components of the target system. A competitive elution with a ligand analog before the elution with the target ligand can be utilized to further increase selectivity of the aptamers (e.g., for ATP selection, a pre-elution step with dATP or ADP may be desirable to enrich for ATP-specific aptamers).

4.2.3a *In vitro* selection through affinity binding to targeted ligand

1. Withdraw desired volume of selection matrix onto a spin-filter or a disposable column. In principle, any amount of beads that results in correct effective concentration of the target molecule can be used, if the beads are agitated to ensure mixing of the RNA pool with the targets. The beads should ideally cover the filter surface, so that the solution is exposed to them during each step. Wash the beads with the same volume of binding buffer. Repeat at least three times. Incubate resuspended radioactive RNA solution at 70 °C for 3 min to unfold.
2. Transfer unfolded RNA onto beads and let incubate with shaking for 30 min at room temperature. Centrifuge column at 3000 × *g* for 1 min. Collect flow-through.

3. Wash the beads with the same volume of selection buffer. Centrifuge at 3000 × *g* for 1 min. Collect wash. Repeat three times.
4. Incubate the beads with the same volume of elution buffer. Incubate at room temperature with shaking for 30 min. The free ligand within the elution buffer and increased duration help promote ligand exchange. Centrifuge column at 3000 × *g* for 1 min. Collect elution. Repeat three times.
5. Transfer the same reaction volume of harsh (see step 4.1.1c) elution buffer onto the beads. Agitate the reaction at room temperature for 15 min by rocking or shaking. Centrifuge at 3000 × *g* for 1 min. Collect harsh elution. Add physiological buffer to dried beads.
6. Measure radioactivity of each fraction by Cherenkov counting on a liquid scintillation counter. This value will help quantify the percentage of eluted RNAs within the purified transcription.

4.2.3b Desalting of selected RNA

1. Combine eluted fractions and transfer to a Microcon centrifugal filter of appropriate size (YM-10).
2. Centrifuge at 14,000 × *g* for 12 min. Invert the filter onto another collection vial, centrifuge at 1000 × *g* for 3 min. Wash the filter with small volume (20–30 μL) of 300 m*M* KCl.
3. Collect filtered RNA, add 1 μL of GlycoBlue (or glycogen) and precipitate with ethanol.

4.2.4 Reverse transcription of selected RNAs

1. Prepare a 20 μL solution of reverse transcription buffer.
2. Dissolve RNA pellet in transcription buffer.
3. Place the reaction vial in a thermocycler.
4. Set the thermocyler at 45 °C for 30 min.
5. Store cDNA at −20 °C or continue on to PCR.

4.2.5 Polymerase chain reaction

The concentration of selected sequences after each round of *in vitro* selection is often not sufficient to move onto the next round. As such, these sequences need to be reverse transcribed and amplified to an appropriate concentration for the next transcription. When analyzing aliquots of the PCR, the aliquot with the fewest PCR cycles yielding a full-length band should be used for the subsequent selection.

4.2.5a Amplification of cDNA

1. Prepare a reaction mixture by mixing 5 μL 10 × *Taq* buffer, 1.25 μL of 20 μ*M* forward primer, 1.25 μL of 20 μ*M* reverse primer, 2 μL of each dNTP at 5 m*M*, 1.5 unit of *Taq* enzyme (or other PCR-competent DNA polymerase), 10 μL of cDNA from the reserve transcription, and 39 μL of distilled deionized water to a total of 50 μL reaction volume.
2. Run the following steps on a thermocyler
   - **a.** 95 °C for 3 min
   - **b.** 95 °C for 30 s
   - **c.** 55 °C for 30 s
   - **d.** 72 °C for 1 min
   - **e.** Repeat steps *b* to *d* for 32 cycles, withdrawing aliquots of 9 μL every 4 cycles, starting at cycle 8.

4.2.5b Agarose gel casting

1. Ensure that the plastic cast for agarose gel is clean and sterilized
2. Assemble the agarose casting apparatus. Install plastic comb with desired number of wells.
3. In a flask, combined 50 mL 0.5 × TBE buffer with 1 g agarose.
4. Heat up the mixture in a microwave until all agarose is dissolved. Caution: overboiling of agarose might create spilling and burning hazard.
5. Add 0.5 μL ethidium bromide into 2% agarose in 0.5 × TBE solution.
6. Pour the above solution onto agarose casting apparatus.
7. Let the agarose gel solidify at room temperature.

4.2.5c Agarose Gel Electrophoresis

1. Prepare running samples by mixing 2 μL of each aliquot with 2 μL of 2 × DNA loading dye.
2. Remove the plastic comb and place the solidified 2% agarose gel into the electrophoresis box.
3. Fill the box with 0.5 × TBE buffer until the buffer level is high enough to cover the agarose gel.
4. Load 2 μL of running samples into each well, and a DNA ladder for reference.
5. Collect the electric cables with a direct current power supply so that the samples run from cathode to anode.
6. Run electrophoresis at a constant potential of 200 V for 15 min.

4.2.5d Visualization of DNA on agarose gel

1. Remove agarose gel from the electrophoresis box.
2. Visualize DNA via UV light. Caution: prolonged exposure of DNA to UV light causes cross-linking.

5. STRUCTURE-BASED SEARCHES FOR NATURALLY OCCURRING APTAMERS

5.1. Materials

5.1.1 Unix compliant operating system

Any computer with a Unix platform can implement the RNABOB program. Our searches were run on iMac with Mac OS X 2.8 GHz Intel Core 2 Duo Processor and 2 GB 667 MHz DDR2 SDRAM.

5.1.2 RNABOB

The program can be downloaded from: ftp://selab.janelia.org/pub/software/rnabob/. Information regarding implementation can be found in the accompanying files (rnabob.man, rnabob.ps).

5.1.3 RNArobo

The program can be downloaded from http://compbio.fmph.uniba.sk/rnarobo/. Information regarding implementation is found on the same webpage.

5.2. Procedures

5.2.1 Descriptor

The descriptors (Fig. 2.2) used to find adenosine aptamers in the human genome are based on *in vitro* selected RNAs that bind adenosine containing molecules (Burgstaller & Famulok, 1994; Burke & Gold, 1997; Sassanfar & Szostak, 1993).

5.2.1a The motif of interest should be defined as a pattern using the following code: h for helical elements (allows G–U wobble pairs), r for relational elements or user-defined stringency of Watson-Crick base pairing for each residue, and s for single-stranded elements. The first line of the descriptor is the order of these elements beginning at the 5′ end of the motif. Each strand of helical and relational elements must be represented. For example, h1 and h1′ represent each side of helix 1.

5.2.1b The next lines of the descriptor define the nucleotide content of each individual element and each line contains three or four fields:

1. The name of the element from the motif topology given in the first line of the descriptor.
2. The number of nucleotide mismatches allowed. For each side of helical and relational elements, mismatches are specified separately. For example, "0:1" means the 5′ side of the helix may not contain any sequence mismatches (mutations), but the 3′ side can contain up to one base-pairing mismatch (mis-pair).
3. Sequence specificity written in IUPAC nucleotide code.
4. The list of strict base pairs required (T, C, G, or A). Only relational elements contain this field.

Note that the length of helices is intended to limit the size of output from structure-based searches and therefore also limit false positives returned. In general, more stringent descriptors yield a group of sequences with higher confidence to display *in vitro* activity. For adenosine aptamers, as long as the sequence and correct folding of the binding pocket are maintained, the length of helices and the structure of the peripheral domain (Fig. 2.2, s2) are arbitrary. Loosening the length requirement of helices can be written as "h1 0:0 NNNN[*x*]:NNNN[*x*]" which defines helix 1 as being at least four base pairs in length but it can be up to $4+x$ base pairs. In addition, loosening s2 can be accomplished by increasing the number in the square brackets.

5.2.2 Sequence data

This file must contain DNA or RNA sequences in common database formats. Any sequence information can be searched, including whole genomes, metagenomic data, genes, ESTs, etc. Searches can focus on 5′ UTRs, intergenic regions, introns, 3′ UTRs, or noncoding regions.

REFERENCES

Burgstaller, P., & Famulok, M. (1994). Isolation of RNA aptamers for biological cofactors by in-vitro selection. *Angewandte Chemie International Edition in English*, *33*(10), 1084–1087.

Burke, D. H., & Gold, L. (1997). RNA aptamers to the adenosine moiety of S-adenosyl methionine: Structural inferences from variations on a theme and the reproducibility of SELEX. *Nucleic Acids Research*, *25*(10), 2020–2024. http://dx.doi.org/10.1093/nar/25.10.2020.

Curtis, E. A., & Liu, D. R. (2013). Discovery of widespread GTP-binding motifs in genomic DNA and RNA. *Chemistry & Biology*, *20*(4), 521–532. http://dx.doi.org/10.1016/j.chembiol.2013.02.015.

Davis, J. H., & Szostak, J. W. (2002). Isolation of high-affinity GTP aptamers from partially structured RNA libraries. *Proceedings of the National Academy of Sciences of the United States of America*, *99*(18), 11616–11621.

Dieckmann, T., Butcher, S. E., Sassanfar, M., Szostak, J. W., & Feigon, J. (1997). Mutant ATP-binding RNA aptamers reveal the structural basis for ligand binding. *Journal of Molecular Biology*, *273*(2), 467–478.

Dieckmann, T., Suzuki, E., Nakamura, G. K., & Feigon, J. (1996). Solution structure of an ATP-binding RNA aptamer reveals a novel fold. *RNA*, *2*(7), 628–640.

Ellington, A. D., & Szostak, J. W. (1990). In vitro selection of RNA molecules that bind specific ligands. *Nature*, *346*(6287), 818–822.

Gautheret, D., Major, F., & Cedergren, R. (1990). Pattern searching/alignment with RNA primary and secondary structures: An effective descriptor for tRNA. *Computer Applications in the Biosciences*, *6*(4), 325–331.

Jiang, F., Kumar, R. A., Jones, R. A., & Patel, D. J. (1996). Structural basis of RNA folding and recognition in an AMP-RNA aptamer complex. *Nature*, *382*(6587), 183–186.

Jimenez, R. M., Rampasek, L., Brejova, B., Vinar, T., & Lupták, A. (2012). Discovery of RNA motifs using a computational pipeline that allows insertions in paired regions and filtering of candidate sequences. *Methods in Molecular Biology*, *848*, 145–158. http://dx.doi.org/10.1007/978-1-61779-545-9_10.

Riccitelli, N. J., & Lupták, A. (2010). Computational discovery of folded RNA domains in genomes and in vitro selected libraries. *Methods*, *52*(2), 133–140. http://dx.doi.org/10.1016/j.ymeth.2010.06.005.

Salehi-Ashtiani, K., Lupták, A., Litovchick, A., & Szostak, J. W. (2006). A genomewide search for ribozymes reveals an HDV-like sequence in the human CPEB3 gene. *Science*, *313*(5794), 1788–1792.

Sassanfar, M., & Szostak, J. W. (1993). An RNA motif that binds ATP. *Nature*, *364*(6437), 550–553.

Singer, B. S., Shtatland, T., Brown, D., & Gold, L. (1997). Libraries for genomic SELEX. *Nucleic Acids Research*, *25*(4), 781–786.

Stoltenburg, R., Reinemann, C., & Strehlitz, B. (2007). SELEX—A (r)evolutionary method to generate high-affinity nucleic acid ligands. *Biomolecular Engineering*, *24*(4), 381–403. http://dx.doi.org/10.1016/j.bioeng.2007.06.001.

Tuerk, C., & Gold, L. (1990). Systematic evolution of ligands by exponential enrichment: RNA ligands to bacteriophage T4 DNA polymerase. *Science*, *249*(4968), 505–510.

Vu, M. M., Jameson, N. E., Masuda, S. J., Lin, D., Larralde-Ridaura, R., & Luptak, A. (2012). Convergent evolution of adenosine aptamers spanning bacterial, human, and random sequences revealed by structure-based bioinformatics and genomic SELEX. *Chemistry & Biology*, *19*(10), 1247–1254. http://dx.doi.org/10.1016/j.chembiol.2012.08.010.

PART II

Synthesis and Sample Prep Methods for Large RNAs

CHAPTER THREE

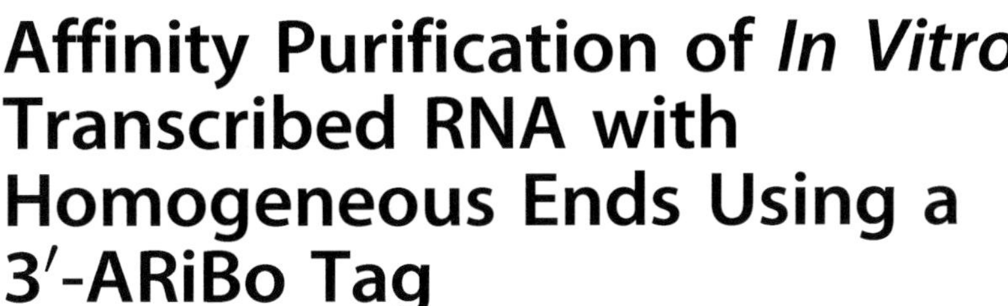

Affinity Purification of *In Vitro* Transcribed RNA with Homogeneous Ends Using a 3′-ARiBo Tag

Geneviève Di Tomasso, Alix Salvail-Lacoste, Jonathan Bouvette, James G. Omichinski, Pascale Legault[1]

Département de Biochimie et Médecine Moléculaire, Université de Montréal, Montreal, Quebec, Canada

[1]Corresponding author: e-mail address: pascale.legault@umontreal.ca

Contents

Abstract

Common approaches for purification of RNAs synthesized *in vitro* by the T7 RNA polymerase often denature the RNA and produce RNAs with chemically heterogeneous 5′- and 3′-ends. Thus, native affinity purification strategies that incorporate 5′ and 3′ trimming technologies provide a solution to two main disadvantages that arise from standard approaches for RNA purification. This chapter describes procedures for non-denaturing affinity purification of *in vitro* transcribed RNA using a 3′-ARiBo tag, which

Methods in Enzymology, Volume 549
ISSN 0076-6879
http://dx.doi.org/10.1016/B978-0-12-801122-5.00003-9

yield RNAs with a homogeneous 3′-end. The applicability of the method to RNAs of different sequences, secondary structures, and sizes (29–614 nucleotides) is described, including suggestions for troubleshooting common problems. In addition, this chapter presents three complementary approaches to producing 5′-homogeneity of the affinity-purified RNA: (1) selection of the starting sequence; (2) Cse3 endoribonuclease cleavage of a 5′-CRISPR tag; or (3) self-cleavage of a 5′-hammerhead ribozyme tag. The additional steps to express and purify the Cse3 endonuclease are detailed. In light of recent results, the advantages and limitations of current approaches to achieve 5′-homogeneity of affinity-purified RNA are discussed, such that one can select a suitable strategy to purify the RNA of interest.

1. INTRODUCTION

In vitro synthesis and purification of RNA represent essential tools for the functional and structural characterization of RNA. One of the most widely used approaches for preparation of RNA involves *in vitro* transcription with the T7 RNA polymerase (T7 RNAP) followed by purification using denaturing gel electrophoresis. The T7 RNAP can generally produce any RNA sequence starting with a purine that is strictly complementary to its DNA template, but often produces faulty RNA sequences due to transcription errors that yield transcripts with 5′- and/or 3′-end sequence heterogeneity. Nevertheless, the standard approach for RNA preparation has several advantages particularly for generating small quantities (<1 mg) of short RNAs (45 nt or less), since the RNA can be conveniently transcribed from synthetic templates and purified at nucleotide resolution (Milligan, Groebe, Witherell, & Uhlenbeck, 1987; Wyatt, Chastain, & Puglisi, 1991). For longer RNA sequences, it becomes more difficult to achieve separation of transcription products that differ by a few nucleotides using denaturing gel electrophoresis, making it challenging to obtain RNA samples with 5′- and/or 3′-end homogeneity. Furthermore, denaturing gel electrophoresis has several limitations for purification of RNA; it denatures the RNA (Uhlenbeck, 1995), leads to contamination with acrylamide oligomers (Lukavsky & Puglisi, 2004), and is a very time consuming and tedious method for large-scale purification of mg quantities of RNA. Given the pitfalls associated with the standard approach for *in vitro* preparation of RNA, several methods have been developed to generate RNA with 5′- and/or 3′-end homogeneity, including endonuclease processing of an RNA precursor with ribozymes (Batey, Gilbert, & Montange, 2004; Batey & Kieft, 2007; Dzianott & Bujarski, 1988; Ferré-D'Amaré & Doudna,

1996; Grosshans & Cech, 1991; Price, Ito, Oubridge, Avis, & Nagai, 1995; Schürer, Lang, Schuster, & Mörl, 2002; Taira, Nakagawa, Nishikawa, & Furukawa, 1991; Walker, Avis, & Conn, 2003) and the CRISPR-specific nucleases (Lee et al., 2013; Salvail-Lacoste, Di Tomasso, Piette, & Legault, 2013). In addition, novel methods have been developed to purify RNA under nondenaturing conditions in a time-efficient manner by size-exclusion and ion-exchange chromatography as well as by affinity methods (for recent reviews, see Ahmed & Ficner, 2014; Batey, 2014; Edelmann, Niedner, & Niessing, 2014).

Affinity purification has revolutionized protein purification and has a broad range of applications in biochemical, structural, and proteomic studies. Interestingly, it is currently gaining increasing importance for RNA applications since a number of RNA-specific strategies have emerged over the past 10 years. We recently optimized a batch affinity method that relies on a 3′-ARiBo tag to purify *in vitro* transcribed RNA under native conditions with a high level of purity and high yields (Di Tomasso, Dagenais, et al., 2012; Di Tomasso, Lampron, Dagenais, Omichinski, & Legault, 2011). This ARiBo tag contains an **A**ctivatable *glmS* **Ri**bozyme (Cochrane, Lipchock, & Strobel, 2007; Wilkinson & Been, 2005; Winkler, Nahvi, Roth, Collins, & Breaker, 2004) and the ***Bo**xB* RNA from bacteriophage λ. The λ*boxB* RNA allows immobilization on glutathione-Sepharose (GSH-Sepharose) resin via a λN-glutathione-*S*-transferase (GST) fusion protein, whereas the activatable *glmS* ribozyme is used to liberate the RNA of interest and concomitantly produce a homogeneous 3′-end.

So far, the ARiBo technology is the only RNA affinity purification approach that has been tailored to generate RNA products with both 5′- and 3′-sequence homogeneity. In the simplest approach, 5′-sequence homogeneity of affinity-purified RNAs can result from careful selection of the starting nucleotides (Salvail-Lacoste et al., 2013). Alternatively, 5′-sequence homogeneity of affinity-purified RNAs can be achieved with the use of cleavable 5′-tags, which also allows production of RNAs starting with any nucleotide. This was previously accomplished by incorporating a small CRISPR tag at the 5′-end of several ARiBo-fusion RNAs that were subsequently cleaved by the *Thermus thermophilus* Cse3 endoribonuclease (Salvail-Lacoste et al., 2013). More recently, we also incorporated a small self-cleavable hammerhead (HH) ribozyme at the 5′-end of ARiBo-fusion RNAs to provide an alternative approach to purifying RNA with 5′-homogeneity.

This chapter describes detailed procedures for the basic affinity purification of RNA using a 3′-ARiBo tag, along with three different complementary approaches for producing 5′-homogeneity of the purified RNA: (1) selection of the starting sequence; (2) Cse3 endoribonuclease cleavage of a 5′-CRISPR tag; or (3) self-cleavage of a 5′-HH ribozyme tag. Several examples of RNAs that have been successfully affinity purified using a 3′-ARiBo tag, either with or without a cleavable 5′-tag, are provided. Combining either the 5′-HH ribozyme tag or the 5′-CRISPR tag with affinity purification of RNA using a 3′-ARiBo tag presents specific advantages and limitations that will be discussed. Suggestions for troubleshooting common problems are described based on the authors' experience. Affinity purification methods that incorporate 5′- and 3′-trimming technologies provide a solution to several key problems that arise with common approaches for RNA preparation, suggesting that the ARiBo-based method will have a broad range of utility for nondenaturing preparation of RNAs with homogeneous ends for numerous applications.

2. BATCH AFFINITY PURIFICATION OF RNA USING A 3′-ARiBo TAG

2.1. General scheme

Affinity purification with the ARiBo method is a simple stepwise procedure for purification of RNA under nondenaturing conditions (Fig. 3.1A). The RNA is first transcribed *in vitro* with an ARiBo tag at its 3′-end. In our laboratory, several ARiBo tags have been tested that contain the activatable *glmS* ribozyme from *Bacillus anthracis* (Cochrane et al., 2007; Wilkinson & Been, 2005; Winkler et al., 2004) and the *boxB* RNA from bacteriophage λ (Di Tomasso et al., 2011; Salvail-Lacoste et al., 2013). The most commonly used ones are the ARiBo1 and ARiBo4 tags (Fig. 3.1B), in which the λ*boxB* RNA is integrated in the P1 stem of the *glmS* ribozyme.

Following transcription, the ARiBo-fusion protein is incubated with a λN-GST fusion protein. Among the several λN-GST fusion proteins that were tested in our laboratory, the λN^+-L^+-GST (Fig. 3.1C) was found to be optimal for affinity purification (Di Tomasso et al., 2011). In this chimeric protein, a variant of the wild-type λN peptide that binds the λ*boxB* RNA with an affinity of 10 p*M* (λN^+; Austin, Xia, Ren, Takahashi, & Roberts, 2002) is fused to the amino terminus of GST through a $(Gly\text{-}Ala)_{10}$ linker. Following the incubation of the λN^+-L^+-GST fusion protein with the ARiBo-fusion RNA, the resulting complex is immobilized on GSH-Sepharose resin in batch mode. After several washes to remove nonspecifically bound impurities from the transcription reaction, the

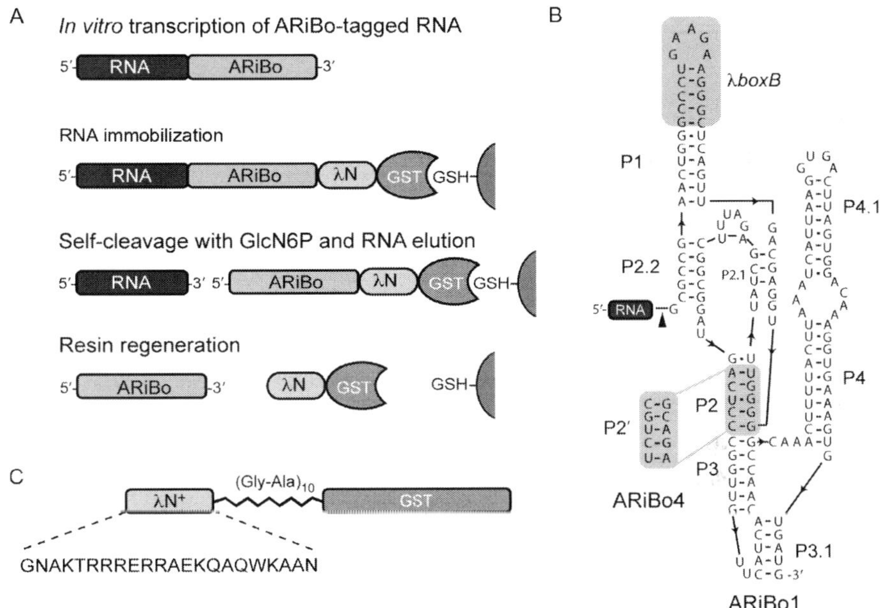

Figure 3.1 Affinity purification of RNA using a 3′-ARiBo tag. (A) Schematic of the basic procedure. (B) The ARiBo-fusion RNA, showing the ARiBo1-tag sequence that corresponds to the *B. anthracis glmS* ribozyme sequence in which the P1 stem has been modified to include the *boxB* RNA from bacteriophage λ. The ARiBo4 tag was obtained by modifying the P2 stem of the ARiBo1 tag. (C) Diagram of the λN$^+$-L$^+$-GST fusion protein. (See the color plate.)

RNA is eluted by incubation with glucosamine-6-phosphate (GlcN6P), which activates the *glmS* ribozyme. An important feature of the *glmS* ribozyme is that it has very low background activity in the absence of GlcN6P. However, one needs to keep in mind that Tris and related compounds (Cochrane et al., 2007; McCarthy et al., 2005; Roth, Nahvi, Lee, Jona, & Breaker, 2006; Winkler et al., 2004) can activate the ribozyme; thus, these compounds need to be eliminated from any solutions that are used along the purification process. If needed, the resin can be regenerated by stepwise incubations with 2.5 *M* NaCl and 20 m*M* GSH.

2.2. Designing the ARiBo-fusion RNA

To obtain high yield of affinity-purified RNA, the ARiBo-fusion RNA must be properly folded to ensure that the λ*boxB* RNA is able to bind to the λN-GST fusion protein and the *glmS* ribozyme can be efficiently cleaved in the presence of GlcN6P. To help ensure proper folding of the RNA, we routinely perform secondary structure predictions (e.g., mFold, Zuker, 2003 or Sfold, Ding, Chan, & Lawrence, 2004) on the ARiBo-fusion RNA from which we examine the possibility of undesirable secondary structure formation between the RNA and the ARiBo tag. These simulations help guide either the initial choice of a specific ARiBo tag (e.g., ARiBo1 or ARiBo4, Fig. 3.1B) for purification of a specific RNA or the design of alternative ARiBo-tag sequences if initial results of affinity purifications are not optimal. In particular, the G-rich strand within the P2 stem of ARiBo1 may induce misfolding of some ARiBo-fusion RNAs. The ARiBo4 tag, with an altered P2 stem, was found to allow more efficient *glmS* cleavage than the ARiBo1 tag in certain cases, likely because it reduces misfolding of ARiBo-fusion RNAs (Salvail-Lacoste et al., 2013).

In designing the ARiBo-fusion RNA, it is important to remember that at least 1 nt upstream of the *glmS* ribozyme cleavage site must be unpaired. Although efficient *glmS* cleavage (>98%) can be achieved regardless of the type of nucleotide at the 3′-end of the RNA (A, G, C, or U), it is generally completed faster and at lower concentration of GlcN6P when this nucleotide is an adenine, typically in 15 min at 1 m*M* GlcN6P. Thus, if the identity of the 3′-end nucleotide(s) is not critical, one is advised to incorporate an adenine residue at this position and possibly one or two additional unpaired residues to facilitate self-cleavage of the *glmS* ribozyme, and thereby prevent long-elution time that could lead to RNA degradation and lower purification yields.

2.3. Cloning of the plasmid DNA template

Several types of template can be used for *in vitro* transcription, including synthetic oligonucleotides, polymerase chain reaction (PCR) products, and linearized DNA plasmids; however, the latter two are preferred for transcription of longer RNAs (>50 nt) such as ARiBo-fusion RNAs. The use of DNA plasmids is particularly valuable because once its sequence is validated, it can be produced repeatedly and reliably at scales up to several milligrams. The basic ARiBo vector is a high-copy number plasmid derived from pTZ19R that can be modified to code for the ARiBo-fusion RNA of interest (Di Tomasso et al., 2011). For cloning purposes, the pARiBo vectors contain three unique restriction sites: *Hin*dIII upstream of the T7 promoter, *Apa*I within the λ*boxB* sequence of the ARiBo tag, and *Eco*RI downstream of the ARiBo tag. For purification of small RNAs (<30 nt), it is straightforward to use the modified QuickChange site-directed procedure (Agilent Technologies) with the basic pARiBo plasmid to generate the plasmid template, as previously described (Di Tomasso, Dagenais, et al., 2012). For longer RNA sequences, a dsDNA template is first generated that codes for the T7 promotor, the RNA sequence, and part of the ARiBo tag up to the *Apa*I site. This dsDNA template is then digested with *Hin*dIII and *Apa*I, and subsequently ligated in the pARiBo plasmid previously digested with the same restriction enzymes and dephosphorylated. It is important to extend the restriction sites by at least 4 nt on each end of the dsDNA template to ensure efficient cleavage by the two restrictions enzymes. This dsDNA template can be prepared using standard PCR or recursive PCR, which is particularly convenient for cloning DNA sequences of 90 bases to several kilobases in length (Bowman, Azizi, Lenz, Roy, & Williams, 2012; Prodromou & Pearl, 1992; Sandhu, Aleff, & Kline, 1992). The resulting plasmids are then transformed into competent DH5α cells. Individual colonies should be used for glycerol stocks, which we typically prepare by mixing 600 μL of a fresh overnight culture with 400 μL of 50% glycerol and then store at −80 °C. Plasmids from individual colonies should be sequenced to ensure that it allows transcription of the expected ARiBo-fusion RNA prior to producing larger quantities of plasmid for *in vitro* transcription.

2.4. Bacterial cell culture and plasmid preparation

The instructions provided below are given for a medium-scale preparation, which uses 150 mL of cell culture to provide purified plasmids (0.3–1 mg) sufficient for ~4–12 mL of transcription reactions. For larger transcription reactions (60–200 mL), large-scale preparations can be performed, which use 2.5 L of cell culture to provide 5–17 mg of purified plasmid.

1. Inoculate 5 mL culture of LB-Amp medium [Luria–Bertani (LB) medium with 100 μg/mL ampicillin] with 25 μL of a glycerol stock and grow 6–8 h at 37 °C with vigorous shaking (~220 rpm).
2. Inoculate 150 mL LB-Amp in a 500-mL flask with 150 μL of the preculture and grow overnight at 37 °C with shaking (~220 rpm).
3. Pellet the cells by centrifugation at 6000 × *g* for 15 min and discard the supernatant. Store the cell-containing pellet at −80 °C until needed or continue with the next step.
4. Extract the plasmid from the cell pellet using a plasmid Maxi kit (e.g., Qiafilter Plasmid Maxi Kit from Qiagen) according to the supplier's protocol. Resuspend the purified plasmid in water (purified water with an electrical resistivity of 18 MΩ cm at 21 °C is used throughout). Determine the DNA concentration by UV absorbance at 260 nm.

5. Linearize the plasmid with *Eco*RI. For 300 μg of plasmid, use 300 U of *Eco*RI, 40 μL of 5 × *Eco*RI/HEPES Buffer (0.5 *M* HEPES pH 7.5, 50 m*M* $MgCl_2$, 250 m*M* NaCl, 0.125% Triton X-100) and complete the volume to 200 μL with water. Incubate overnight at 37 °C. Although plasmid cleavage with *Eco*RI is generally complete under these conditions, it is important to verify for full plasmid linearization using an agarose gel, since uncut plasmids will reduce the transcription yield of the desired RNA.
6. Inactivate the restriction enzyme by heating at 65 °C for 5 min and transferring on ice. Store the linearized DNA plasmid at 4 °C. No additional purification is required.

2.5. *In vitro* transcription of RNA and optimization of *glmS* cleavage conditions

Transcription reactions are performed at various scales, typically ranging from 50 μL up to 50 mL. Although several small-scale transcriptions are usually performed to optimize transcription yields, we generally find that yields of ARiBo-fusion RNAs transcribed from linearized plasmids are satisfactory when using the standard conditions. The optimized small-scale reaction is used to test different *glmS* cleavage conditions and can then be simply scaled up to prepare larger amounts of RNA. The *glmS* cleavage conditions should be optimized to obtain maximum cleavage using the lowest possible GlcN6P concentration and the shortest time period to help reduce both the cost and the potential for RNA degradation.

1. Set up a small-scale transcription reaction of 100 μL using standard conditions: 10 μL of 400 m*M* HEPES pH 8.0, 5 μL of 1 *M* freshly prepared DTT, 10 μL of 1% Triton X-100, 4 μL of 25 m*M* spermidine, 5 μL of 0.5 *M* $MgCl_2$, 4 μL of 100 m*M* stocks of each NTP (ATP, UTP, GTP, and CTP) previously adjusted to pH 8.0 with NaOH, 8 μg of linearized plasmid DNA, 1 μL of a 0.3 U/μL dilution of RNAsin Ribonuclease inhibitor (Promega) prepared in RNasin Buffer (20 m*M* HEPES pH 7.6, 50 m*M* KCl, 8 m*M* DTT and 50% (v/v) glycerol) and 1 μL of in-house purified His-tagged T7 RNAP (6 mg/mL). The exact amount of T7 RNAP will depend on the enzyme source. For optimization purposes, five other transcription reactions can also be set up using standard conditions in which one component is changed: the concentration of $MgCl_2$ (20 and 30 m*M* instead of 25 m*M*), the template concentration (12 μg/100 μL instead of 8 μg/100 μL), the nucleotide concentration (4 m*M* GMP is added), or the enzyme concentration

(increase the initial amount by twofold). If needed, 5–10 m*M* glucose-6-phosphate can be added to inhibit ARiBo-tag cleavage that may occur during transcription if *glmS* activators are present (Cochrane et al., 2007; McCarthy et al., 2005; Roth et al., 2006; Watson & Fedor, 2011; Winkler et al., 2004).

2. Incubate transcription reactions for 3 h at 37 °C. It is normal to observe formation of a white precipitate during the transcription reaction due to production of insoluble Mg^{2+}-pyrophosphate complexes. Inorganic phosphatase can be added to the reaction to reduce the precipitate, and this may increase the yield of transcription (Cunningham & Ofengand, 1990).
3. Stop the transcription reaction by adding the necessary volume of 0.5 *M* EDTA pH 8.0 such that the EDTA concentration is equal to the $MgCl_2$ concentration. Store at −20 °C.
4. Analyze samples on a denaturing polyacrylamide gel to select the transcription condition that produces the highest yield of ARiBo-fusion RNA (Section 2.7.2).
5. Set up 100-μL cleavage reactions using a 3-μL aliquot of the transcription reaction, 4 μL of 0.5 *M* Tris pH 7.6, 2 μL of 0.5 *M* $MgCl_2$ and varying amounts of 40 m*M* GlcN6P pH 7.6 (typically 2.5, 5, and 10 μL to achieve concentrations of 1, 2, and 4 m*M*).
6. Incubate the *glmS* cleavage reactions at 37 °C for 1 h, removing 5-μL aliquots at different times (e.g., 0, 15, 30, and 60 min). To stop the reaction, each aliquot is mixed with 95 μL of Gel Loading Buffer (GLB: 20 mg bromophenol blue, 5 mL EDTA 0.5 *M* pH 8.0, and 95 mL formamide) and quickly cooled on ice.
7. Analyze aliquots of the stopped cleavage reaction in parallel with control samples containing known amounts of a purified RNA on a denaturing polyacrylamide gel to estimate the percentage of *glmS* cleavage and the maximum expected yield of the RNA of interest for each cleavage condition (Section 2.7.3). Determine the condition that provides the highest yield. It is best to use the same RNA as the control for quantification, but if not available, a purified RNA of similar size could be used.

2.6. Batch affinity purification

Batch affinity purification from an ARiBo-fusion precursor is achieved using the λN^{+}-L^{+}-GST fusion protein and GSH-Sepharose resin. A detailed protocol for expression and purification of the λN^{+}-L^{+}-GST fusion protein has been previously reported (Di Tomasso, Lampron, et al., 2012). Batch affinity purifications are usually performed using spin cups (Pierce) to recover the GSH-Sepharose resin. Typically, one spin cup is used for purification of 3.5 nmol of input ARiBo-fusion RNA in a total incubation volume of 400 μL. As described below, the procedure can be easily adapted for 1–7 nmol of input RNA. Although the use of spin cups is not essential, it eliminates the delicate step of decanting the supernatant that would be used otherwise to recover the resin (Di Tomasso et al., 2011), and thus improves recovery of the GSH-Sepharose resin during the purification. As a result, the overall procedure is performed in a more time-efficient manner, and high RNA purity and yield can be achieved with better reproducibility. Alternatively, GSH-linked magnetic resin (e.g., MagneGST from Promega) can be used to perform batch purification and for easy recovery of the resin without centrifugation. The use of magnetic beads can be particularly useful for purification of small amounts of RNA ($\leq$1 nmol), but can become very expensive for purification of larger RNA quantities. Typically, 20 μL of MagneGST resin (or 80 μL resin slurry) is used to purify 1 nmol of input ARiBo-fusion RNA in a total incubation volume of 120 μL using a small tube that allows for good mixing of the resin with the incubation buffers (e.g., 0.5 mL PCR tube). For large-scale applications, the spin cups are replaced by disposable filter units (50-mL Steriflip filter units from Millipore) and the centrifugation steps are replaced by aspirations. Typically, each Steriflip is used for purifying 250 nmol of input ARiBo-fusion RNA in a total incubation volume of 25 mL, but the procedure can be adapted to purify 25–500 nmol of input ARiBo-fusion RNA by adjusting the RNA concentration and reducing the total incubation volume by no more than 2.5-fold to maintain adequate mixing.

The procedure provided below is for the purification of 3.5 nmol of input ARiBo-fusion RNA using spin cups, but can be scaled up or down when using GSH-linked magnetic resin or Steriflip filter units. All resin incubations are performed at room temperature with gentle rotation of the spin cup. To pellet the resin, all centrifugation steps are performed for 1 min at 5000 × *g*.

1. In a 1.5-mL Eppendorf tube, add 17.5 nmol of λN^{+}-L^{+}-GST fusion protein to a transcription volume that corresponds to 3.5 nmol of RNA to be purified. A 5:1 molar ratio of protein:RNA is typically used to provide high RNA yield and purity; ratios as low as 3:1 can be used to provide similar purities, but may result in lower yields (Di Tomasso et al., 2011). Adjust the total volume to 400 μL with Equilibration Buffer

(50 mM HEPES pH 7.5) and incubate 15 min. Longer incubation times may improve yields, particularly for larger RNAs. For different amounts of RNA (0.25–2 ×), the amount of fusion protein should be scaled up or down accordingly, but the total volume of Equilibration Buffer should remain the same.

2. During the incubation, prepare the GSH-Sepharose resin in a spin cup. Add 125 μL of GSH-Sepharose resin (163 μL of the 77% slurry) to the spin cup. Wash twice by adding 400 μL of PBS (10 mM Na_2HPO_4, 2 mM KH_2PO_4, 2.7 mM KCl, and 140 mM NaCl at pH 7.4) and centrifuge immediately. Discard the eluate. For different amounts of RNA (0.25–2 ×), the amount of GSH-Sepharose resin should be correspondingly scaled up or down, but the total incubation volume should remain the same.
3. Add the RNA–protein mix to the spin cup containing the washed resin. Incubate 15 min and centrifuge. Keep the load eluate (LE) on ice for quantitative analysis. Longer incubation times may improve yields, particularly for larger RNAs.
4. To wash the resin, add 400 μL of Equilibration Buffer, incubate 5 min and centrifuge. Repeat twice. Keep the wash eluates (W1, W2, and W3) on ice for quantitative analysis. If needed, an alkaline phosphatase step can be inserted between the first and second washes to remove 5′-phosphates (Di Tomasso, Dagenais, et al., 2012; Di Tomasso et al., 2011), but make sure to replace the standard Tris Buffer by HEPES during this incubation to avoid premature activation of the *glmS* ribozyme.
5. To elute the RNA, add 400 μL of optimized Elution Buffer and incubate at 37 °C for the selected time period (Section 2.5) with periodic inversion of the tube, then at room temperature for 5 min and centrifuge. In parallel, a control reaction in which 3 μL of the transcription reaction is added to 97 μL of Elution Buffer is incubated under the same conditions for quantitative analysis (Section 2.7.2). Keep the RNA elution sample (E1) on ice for quantitative analysis and further processing. After elution with GlcN6P, wash the resin as follows: add 400 μL of Equilibration Buffer, incubate 5 min and centrifuge. Keep the RNA elution sample (E2) on ice for quantitative analysis and further processing. An additional wash of the resin with the Equilibration Buffer could be performed, but does not usually help recover a significant amount of RNA. To remove residual RNA on the resin, add 400 μL of 2.5 M NaCl, incubate for 5 min, and then centrifuge. Keep the eluate (NaCl) on ice for quantitative analysis. Resuspend the resin in 125 μL of PBS.

6. To completely regenerate the resin, the used resin is generally collected in a 50-mL screw-cap conical tube until a significant amount of resin is available (≥5 mL). The resin is then washed using a single Steriflip filter unit and 4 × resin volume of solutions: twice with PBS (incubate 5 min and aspirate), three times with 20 m*M* L-glutathione in PBS (incubate 15 min and aspirate), and once with 20% ethanol (incubate 5 min and aspirate). To keep the L-glutathione in its active reduced form, it should be added to the PBS Buffer just before use and the buffer should be adjusted to pH 8.0 with NaOH. Store the regenerated resin in 20% ethanol at 4 °C.
7. Once the affinity purification is completed, monitor the purification on a denaturing polyacrylamide gel (Section 2.7 and Fig. 3.2).
8. Combine the RNA elution samples (E1 and E2), concentrate them using an ultracentrifugation device (e.g., Amicon Ultra-15 from Millipore), and exchange them into an appropriate storage buffer. Several buffers can be used for RNA applications, although we recommend storing the RNA at neutral pH (between 5 and 8) in the absence of divalent cations to prevent its degradation.
9. The RNA concentration can be estimated by UV absorbance at 260 nm (A_{260}) using a conversion factor of 1 $OD_{260}=40$ µg/mL. To obtain a more accurate concentration, one should use extinction coefficients (ε_{260}) determined by taking the sum of ε_{260} values for each nucleotide (Cavaluzzi & Borer, 2004) within the RNA sequence and multiplying this sum by a hyperchromicity factor corresponding to the ratio of A_{260} values before and after nuclease P1 digestion (Legault, 1995; Zaug, Grosshans, & Cech, 1988).

2.7. Quantitative analyses for batch affinity purification using a 3′-ARiBo tag

Although a semiquantitative analysis may be sufficient for cases where RNA yield and purity is not critical, we strongly advise performing quantitative analysis by gel electrophoresis to monitor the various steps of batch affinity purification. In particular, it is critical to determine the amount of RNA produced after *glmS* cleavage in the transcription reaction such that the batch affinity purification can be performed under optimal conditions. In addition, quantitative analysis is useful for optimizing the conditions of *in vitro* transcription and *glmS* cleavage and for monitoring the various steps of the batch affinity purification.

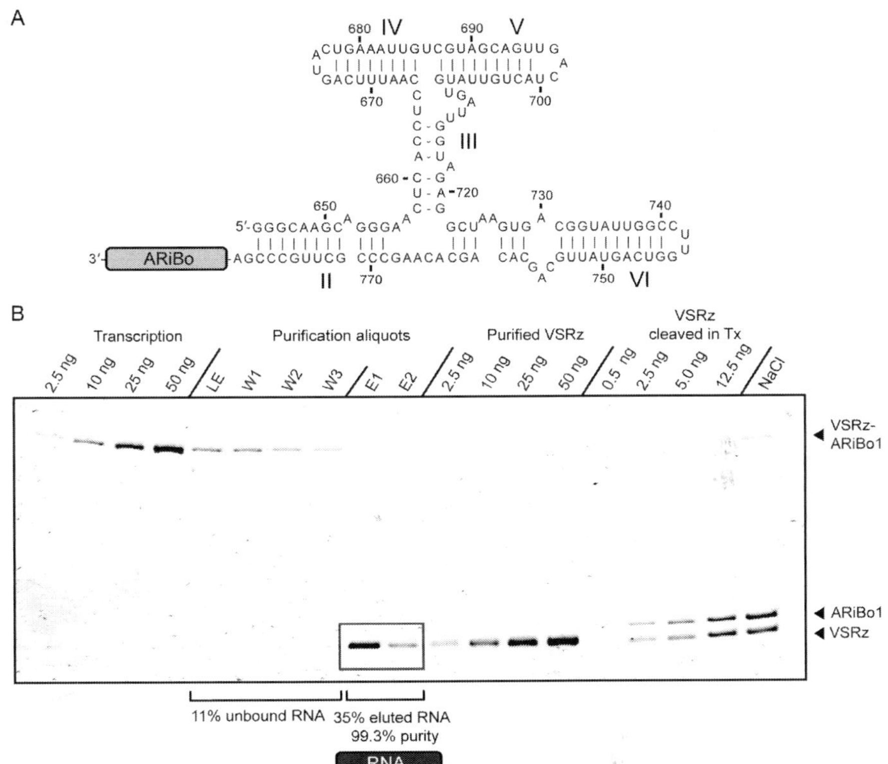

Figure 3.2 Typical results of affinity purification of RNA using a 3′-ARiBo tag. (A) Primary and proposed secondary structures of the 138-nt *Neurospora* VS ribozyme (VSRz) fused to the ARiBo tag. (B) Small-scale batch affinity purification of VSRz analyzed on a 7.5% denaturing polyacrylamide gel stained with SYBR Gold. The RNA was affinity purified using standard procedures, except that 250 m*M* NaCl and 50 m*M* EDTA were added for E1 and 100 m*M* NaCl and 50 m*M* EDTA were added for E2 (Section 2.8). Aliquots from each purification steps were loaded on the gel as described in Section 2.7.4. Bands are annotated on the right side of the gel.

2.7.1 Denaturing gel electrophoresis

All solutions used for denaturing gel electrophoresis are passed through a 0.22-μm filter to minimize detection of undesirable fluorescent speckles on the SYBR Gold-stained gel.

1. Prepare an analytical denaturing polyacrylamide gel in 1 × TBE Buffer (50 m*M* Tris-base, 50 m*M* boric acid, and 1 m*M* EDTA) using a ratio of 19:1 acrylamide:bisacrylamide and 7 *M* urea. The percentage of polyacrylamide, typically between 7.5% and 20%, depends on the size of the RNA to be purified. Prerun the gel in 1 × TBE at 400–600 V for 20 min.

2. Prepare samples to be analyzed in volumes ≤10 μL (Sections 2.7.2–2.7.4) and add 10 μL of GLB.
3. Load samples and run the gel at 400–600 V for 2–4 h, depending on the gel concentration, typically until the bromophenol blue is at the bottom of the gel.
4. Stain the gel 5 min with 200 mL of fresh SYBR Gold staining solution (e.g., 1:10,000 dilution of Invitrogen SYBR Gold nucleic acid gel stain in TBE Buffer).
5. Scan on a Molecular Imager and quantify band intensities using reliable analysis software. We currently use a ChemiDoc MP Imaging system (Bio-Rad) and quantify band intensities using the ImageLab software version 4.0.1 (Bio-Rad).

2.7.2 Quantitative analysis of ARiBo-fusion RNA produced by in vitro *transcription*

1. Prepare a 1:200 dilution in water of the transcription reaction and mix 1.5 μL of this dilution with 10 μL of GLB for gel analysis.
2. Quantify the intensity of the high-molecular weight band on the gel to select the transcription condition that produces the highest yield of ARiBo-fusion RNA.

2.7.3 Quantitative analysis of glmS *cleavage in the transcription reaction*

Gel-based analysis of *glmS* cleavage in the transcription reaction allows quantification of both the percentage of *glmS* cleavage and the maximum expected yield of RNA from batch affinity purification.

1. Load 10 μL of the stopped cleavage reaction in each well, which should correspond to ~5–20 ng of cleaved RNA. Also load control samples containing varying amounts of purified RNA (2.5, 10, 25, and 50 ng RNA).
2. The percentage of *glmS* cleavage in the solution is determined using Eq. (3.1), where BI_{ARiBo} and BI_{Fusion} are the band intensities of the ARiBo tag and ARiBo-fusion RNA, respectively, whereas nt_{ARiBo} and nt_{Fusion} are the number of nucleotides in these RNAs:

$$\left[\frac{BI_{ARiBo}/nt_{ARiBo}}{(BI_{ARiBo}/nt_{ARiBo}) + (BI_{Fusion}/nt_{Fusion})}\right] \times 100\% \tag{3.1}$$

3. The maximum expected yield of RNA (in μg/μL transcription and nmol/μL transcription) is obtained from quantitative analysis of the

optimized cleavage condition as follows. First, the data in the control lanes are used to derive a standard curve relating band intensity to the quantity of control RNA, and regression analysis is used to define a linear equation that relates these two parameters. The linear equation is then used to determine the quantity (in ng) of RNA (N_{RNA}) corresponding to the amount of transcription volume loaded on the gel. For accurate quantification, the regression analysis should be consistent with a linear model and the quantity of RNA determined should fall within the range used to generate the standard curve.

2.7.4 Quantitative analysis of batch affinity purification

The quantitative analysis of batch affinity purifications is performed on a single denaturing gel to monitor the purification, ensure reproducibility of the results and for troubleshooting. Several samples are typically loaded on the gel (Fig. 3.2B): (1) control samples containing different volumes of the transcription reaction corresponding to specific amounts of ARiBo-fusion RNA (2.5, 10, 25, and 50 ng RNA; lanes 1–4 in Fig. 3.2B); (2) aliquots from LE and wash eluates (W1, W2, and W3) corresponding to 250 ng of ARiBo-fusion RNA assuming that 100% of the input RNA is present in each eluate (lanes 5–8 in Fig. 3.2B); (3) aliquots from the RNA elutions (E1 and E2) corresponding to 100 ng of the RNA assuming a 100% purification yield at each step (lanes 9 and 10 in Fig. 3.2B); (4) control samples containing a range of known amounts of purified RNA derived from OD_{260} measurements (2.5, 10, 25, and 50 ng RNA; lanes 11–14 in Fig. 3.2B); (5) control samples containing different volumes of the transcription reaction cleaved with GlcN6P and corresponding to specific amounts of purified RNA (0.5, 2.5, 5.0, and 12.5 ng RNA; lanes 15–18 in Fig. 3.2B); and (6) aliquot from the NaCl wash (lane 19 in Fig. 3.2B) corresponding to 50 ng of the RNA of interest assuming 100% RNA recovery at this step.

1. From gel lanes loaded with specific amounts of ARiBo-fusion RNA, derive a standard curve relating band intensity to the quantity of ARiBo-fusion RNA (N_{Fusion}).
2. From gel lanes loaded with a range of known amounts of purified RNA, derive a standard curve relating band intensity to the quantity of purified RNA (N_{RNA}).
3. From gel lanes loaded with different volumes of the transcription reaction cleaved with GlcN6P, calculate the exact quantity of RNA (N_{RNA}) detected in these lanes using the standard curve that relates band intensity to N_{RNA}. Subsequently, determine the exact quantity of ARiBo tag

(N_{ARiBo}) detected in these same lanes from Eq. (3.2), in which $\mathrm{nt}_{\mathrm{RNA}}$ and $\mathrm{nt}_{\mathrm{ARiBo}}$ represent the number of nucleotides in the purified RNA and the ARiBo tag, respectively:

$$N_{\mathrm{ARiBo}} = \left(\frac{N_{\mathrm{RNA}}}{\mathrm{nt}_{\mathrm{RNA}}}\right) \times \mathrm{nt}_{\mathrm{ARiBo}} \qquad (3.2)$$

Finally, use these same gel lanes to derive a standard curve relating band intensity to the quantity of ARiBo tag (N_{ARiBo}).

4. Determine the percentage *of glmS cleavage in solution* from one of the gel lanes in which the transcription reaction is cleaved with GlcN6P using Eq. (3.1).
5. Determine the *percentage of glmS cleavage on the resin* from the NaCl lane using Eq. (3.1).
6. Determine the *percentage of unbound RNA* using Eq. (3.3), in which $\Sigma N_{\mathrm{Fusion}}$ represents the total amount of ARiBo-fusion RNA (ng) detected in lanes LE, W1, W2, and W3, and I_{Fusion} represents the input of the same RNA at equivalent volumes of batch affinity purification (250 ng).

$$\left[\frac{\Sigma N_{\mathrm{Fusion}}}{I_{\mathrm{Fusion}}}\right] \times 100\% \qquad (3.3)$$

7. Determine the *percentage of RNA eluted* using Eq. (3.4), in which ΣN_{RNA} represents the total amount of purified RNA detected in the elution lanes and I_{RNA} represents the maximum amount of purified RNA that could be present in these elution lanes (100 ng):

$$\left[\frac{\Sigma N_{\mathrm{RNA}}}{I_{\mathrm{RNA}}}\right] \times 100\% \qquad (3.4)$$

8. Determine the *percentage of RNA purity* with respect to the residual ARiBo tag from the E1 lane using Eq. (3.5):

$$\left[\frac{N_{\mathrm{RNA}}}{N_{\mathrm{RNA}} + N_{\mathrm{ARiBo}}}\right] \times 100\% \qquad (3.5)$$

2.8. Troubleshooting

As shown in Fig. 3.3, several RNAs have been purified with high yield and purity using the ARiBo-tag method, and these RNAs have different sequences, secondary structures, and sizes (29–342 nt). However, for some

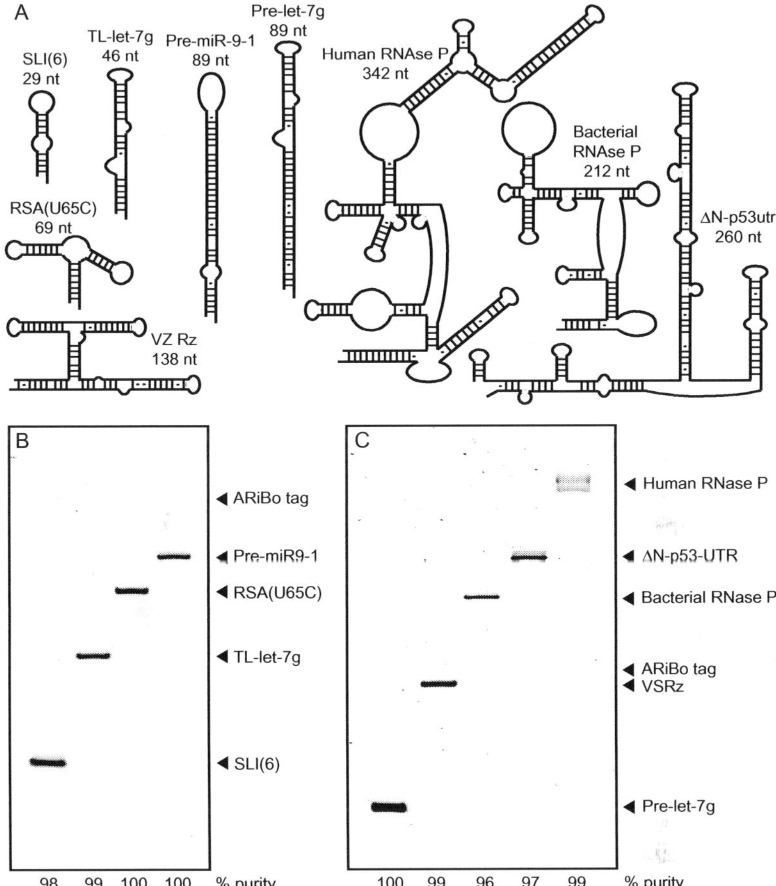

Figure 3.3 RNA affinity purification using an ARiBo tag is applicable to a diverse set of RNAs. (A) Schematic representation of several RNAs that have been affinity purified: SLI(6) derived from the *Neurospora* VS ribozyme substrate (Salvail-Lacoste et al., 2013); TL-let-7g derived from the terminal loop of the human let-7g precursor (Desjardins, Yang, Bouvette, Omichinski, & Legault, 2012); pre-miR-9-1, a stem-loop that encompasses the human miR-9-1 precursor (Griffiths-Jones, 2004); pre-let-7g, a stem-loop that encompasses the human let-7g precursor (Desjardins et al., 2012); RSA(U65C), a mutant of the adenine riboswitch aptamer form *Bacillus subtilis* (Delfosse et al., 2010); a *Neurospora* VS ribozyme (Fig. 3.2A); a minimized bacterial RNase P RNA (Esakova & Krasilnikov, 2010; Siegel, Banta, Haas, Brown, & Pace, 1996); the extended 5′-UTR of human p53 mRNA (ΔNp53utr; Blaszczyk & Ciesiolka, 2011); and human RNase P RNA (Esakova & Krasilnikov, 2010). (B and C) Small-scale batch affinity purifications of several RNAs using a 3′-ARiBo tag analyzed on (B) 15% and (C) 7.5% denaturing polyacrylamide gels stained with SYBR Gold. Aliquots of the E1 elution fractions were loaded on the gel. Bands corresponding to the different RNAs are annotated on the right side of the gel. The two larger RNAs do not migrate uniformly, most likely because they are not completely denatured under these conditions. In (C), the RNAs larger than 200 nt were purified using longer incubation times for RNA binding to the λN-GST fusion protein (1 h) and for RNA immobilization on the GSH-Sepharose resin (1 h) as well as using 0.25 *M* NaCl after the E1 incubation to increase yields.

RNAs, lower yields and purity may be observed. Low yields may be due to poor cleavage of the *glmS* ribozyme. Typically, >95% cleavage is obtained with a 15-min incubation in 1 m*M* GlcN6P. However, efficient cleavage of some ARiBo-fusion RNA may require a higher concentration of GlcN6P and/or a longer incubation time, particularly when the nucleotide at the 3′-end of the desired RNA is not an unpaired adenine (Di Tomasso et al., 2011). If increasing incubation time or GlcN6P concentration does not improve *glmS* cleavage, this may indicate misfolding of the ARiBo-fusion RNA. Such behavior is typical with RNAs that fail to adopt a stable secondary structure since this can interfere with the folding of the *glmS* ribozyme within the ARiBo-fusion RNA. In such cases, the following approaches can be easily tested to possibly improve *glmS* cleavage: (1) refold the ARiBo-fusion RNA by heating and subsequently cooling; (2) increase the *glmS* cleavage temperature (e.g., 42 °C); and (3) store the transcription reaction at 4 °C (instead of −20 °C) or perform the purification immediately after the transcription is completed. Of note, incubations at higher temperatures and for longer periods of time may lead to degradation of the RNA. If none of these options represent a viable solution, using an alternative ARiBo tag that prevents misfolding of the ARiBo-fusion RNA may help improve cleavage of the *glmS* ribozyme.

In some cases, complete *glmS* cleavage of the ARiBo-fusion RNA is achieved, but only a small fraction of the RNA population is recovered at the elution steps, whereas a sizeable fraction is detected in the subsequent wash with 2.5 *M* NaCl. In this high-salt wash, one would expect to mainly elute the ARiBo-tag RNA, as previously observed for purification of the 29-nt SLI RNA, the 46-nt TL-let-7g and the 69-nt RSA(U65C) RNAs (Di Tomasso, Dagenais, et al., 2012; Di Tomasso et al., 2011; Salvail-Lacoste et al., 2013). However, with larger RNAs, such as the 138-nt *Neurospora* VS ribozyme (VSRz), variable amounts of purified RNA may coelute with the ARiBo tag at this step (Fig. 3.2B), possibly due to nonspecific binding. In such cases, a better recovery of the desired RNA at the elution step can often be attained by adding NaCl to the buffers used for RNA elution and subsequent washes, but at a concentration (i.e., <0.5 *M*) that minimizes coelution of the ARiBo tag. The elution steps can be modified as follows: (1) after the E1 incubations, add 0.25–0.5 *M* NaCl and 50 m*M* EDTA, incubate 5 min, and centrifuge; (2) after the E2 incubation, add 0.1–0.25 *M* NaCl, incubate 5 min, and centrifuge.

Although most RNAs are purified with high purity (>99%) with respect to the potential ARiBo-tag contaminants, lower purity levels have been observed in situations where suboptimal conditions were used for affinity purification. In such cases, it is important to verify that the λN-GST fusion protein is RNAse free (Di Tomasso, Lampron, et al., 2012) and that Tris is not present in the transcription reaction or at any stage of the purification, even in trace amounts. However, most often, lower purity of the eluted RNA originates from inaccurate quantification of the estimated maximum yield of RNA. In such cases, the optimum purification conditions are not met, in particular the recommended ratios of λN-GST fusion protein and GSH-Sepharose resin.

Further optimization of the ARiBo method will involve defining optimal conditions for purification of larger RNAs. At the current time, we have shown that three RNAs containing more than 200 nt can be purified at high yield using a 3′-ARiBo tag: a 212-nt minimal bacterial RNaseP RNA, the 260-nt 5′-UTR of the human p53 mRNA, and the 342-nt human RNAseP RNA (Fig. 3.3). These larger RNAs were obtained with purity of ~96–99% with respect to the residual ARiBo tag. Interestingly, we also recently affinity purified a 614-nt RNA derived from the human miR-106b-25 cluster with greater than 95% purity (results not shown). If needed, purity levels ≥99% could be obtained by further optimizing purification conditions and/or by incubating the E1 and E2 eluates with GSH-Sepharose resin preloaded with the λN-GST fusion protein. Alternatively, the eluted RNA can be further purified with a different method to remove the residual ARiBo tag. For example, we previously used affinity-purified RNA for ^{32}P-labeling of RNAs that were subsequently purified by denaturing gel electrophoresis (Desjardins, Bouvette, & Legault, 2014). Alternatively, a first step of affinity purification could be easily followed by size-exclusion (Kim, McKenna, Puglisi, & Puglisi, 2007; Lukavsky & Puglisi, 2004; McKenna et al., 2007) or ion-exchange chromatography (Easton, Shibata, & Lukavsky, 2010; Keel, Easton, Lukavsky, & Kieft, 2009). These chromatographic methods are usually performed under native conditions. In addition, they allow for separation of the native RNA conformer from misfolded species, such as multimers and aggregates, to allow subsequent characterization of a homogeneous population of folded RNA molecules.

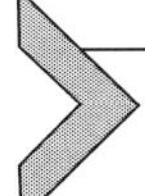

3. ENSURING 5′-HOMOGENEITY OF AFFINITY-PURIFIED RNA

Several avenues have been explored to achieve 5′-sequence homogeneity of affinity-purify T7 transcripts using ARiBo tags. The simplest approach is to select a 5′-sequence that yields a negligible amount of 5′-sequence heterogeneity. However, this is only possible when the 5′-sequence composition of the RNA of interest is optimal or is not strictly restricted. In other cases, it is possible to add a 5′-tag that can be processed prior to affinity purification of the ARiBo-fusion RNA. For 5′-tags to be compatible with affinity purification, it is crucial that they are completely cleaved to avoid contamination of the purified RNA with residual 5′-tags, either covalently bound or not. At this time, two types of 5′-tag have been shown to be compatible with the ARiBo affinity purification method, either a HH ribozyme tag that self-cleaves in the transcription reaction or a CRISPR tag that is cleaved by the addition of the Cse3 endonuclease (Figs. 3.4 and 3.5; Salvail-Lacoste et al., 2013). As described below, they both present advantages and limitations for affinity purification, and thus it is best to have both options available.

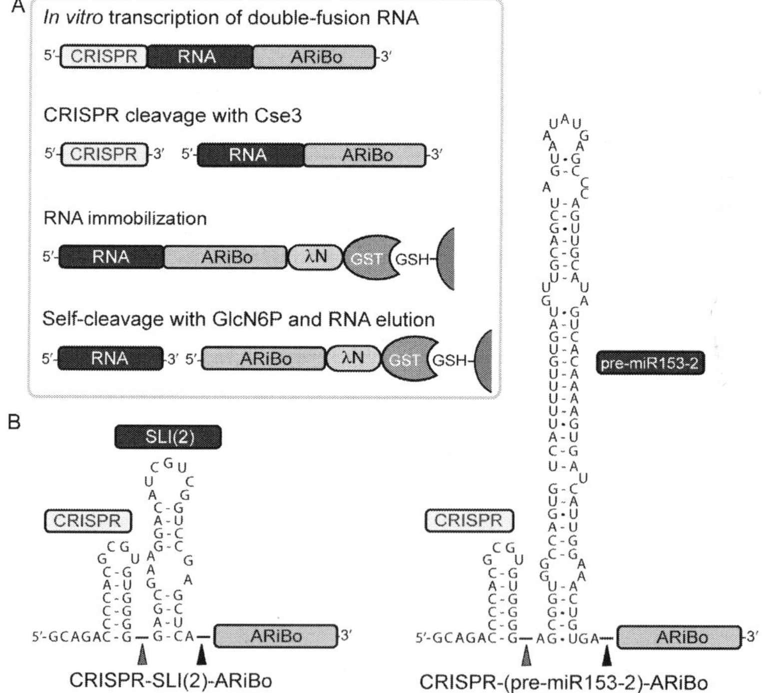

Figure 3.4 Affinity purification of RNA using a 5′-CRISPR tag and a 3′-ARiBo tag. (A) Schematic of the procedure. (B) Partial sequence and proposed secondary structures of CRISPR-RNA-ARiBo precursors for affinity purification of SLI(2) and pre-miR153-2. (See the color plate.)

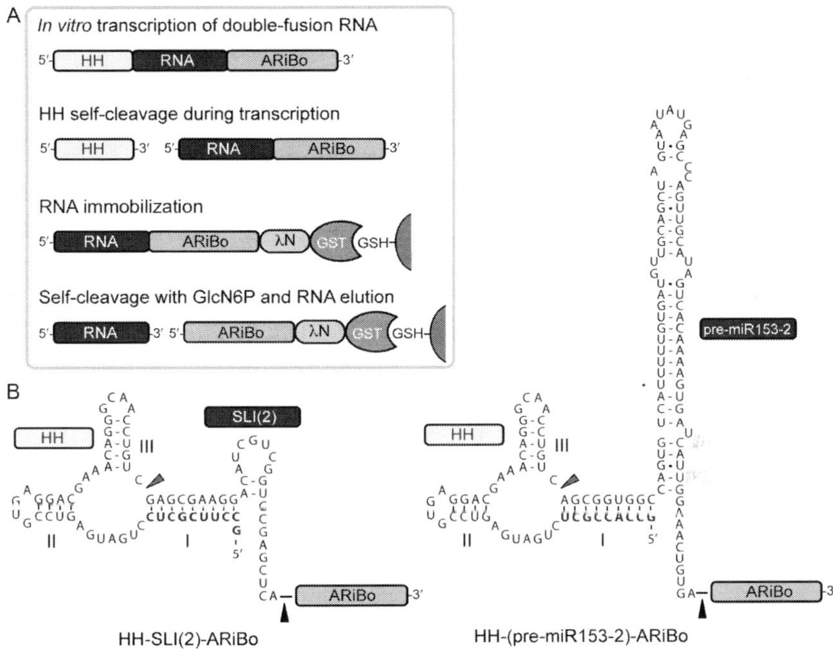

Figure 3.5 Affinity purification of RNA using a 5′-HH tag and a 3′-ARiBo tag. (A) Schematic of the procedure. (B) Partial sequence and proposed secondary structures of HH-RNA-ARiBo precursors for affinity purification of SLI(2) and pre-miR153-2. The 5′-HH tag contains three helical domains (numbered in roman numerals) and its variable 5′-sequence (burgundy) needs to be tailored to the RNA sequence of interest. (See the color plate.)

3.1. General considerations in the selection of 5′-sequences

It has been well established that transcription from the G-initiating class III promoter can yield 5′-sequence heterogeneity, particularly for sequences starting with GGG (Cunningham, Weitzmann, & Ofengand, 1991; Imburgio, Rong, Ma, & McAllister, 2000; Martin, Muller, & Coleman, 1988; Pleiss, Derrick, & Uhlenbeck, 1998; Sherlin et al., 2001) and GAG (Ferré-D'Amaré & Doudna, 1996). However, several other starting sequences can yield 5′-sequence heterogeneity, as recently reported in a systematic study of the effect of starting sequences on 5′-sequence heterogeneity (Salvail-Lacoste et al., 2013). In this study, batch affinity purifications were performed on 32 small SLI RNA hairpins (29 nt) that are substrates of the *Neurospora* VSRz. These sequences share a common core sequence, but contain all possible sequence combinations within the first 3 nt: an A or a G at the first position, and one of all four common nucleotides at the second and third positions. The SLI sequences starting with a G were transcribed from the class III consensus promoter and those starting with an A were transcribed from the class II ϕ2.5 promoter. All RNAs were transcribed as ARiBo-fusion precursors with the wild-type T7 RNAP as well as with the P266L variant known to facilitate promoter clearance (Guillerez, Lopez, Proux, Launay, & Dreyfus, 2005; Ramírez-Tapia & Martin, 2012; Tang et al., 2014). From this study, it was concluded that this P266L variant helps decrease 5′-heterogeneity in several cases (Salvail-Lacoste et al., 2013). In addition, it was possible to define a list of 5′-GNN and 5′-ANN sequences that yield negligible amount of 5′-sequence heterogeneity ($\leq$1%) for SLI RNA hairpins (Table 3.1) and are likely to yield similar results for other

Table 3.1 Suggested 5′-sequences to obtain 5′-sequence homogeneity of affinity-purified RNA[a]

5′ Sequences	5′-Sequence heterogeneity ≤1%	5′ Sequences	5′-Sequence heterogeneity ≤1%
GGG	No	AGG	No
GAG	No	AAG	Yes
GCG	No	ACG	Yes
GUG	Yes	AUG	Yes[b]
GGA	Yes	AGA	No
GAA	Yes	AAA	No
GCA	Yes[b]	ACA	No
GUA	Yes	AUA	No
GGC	No	AGC	Yes
GAC	Yes	AAC	No
GCC	No	ACC	No
GUC	Yes	AUC	No
GGU	No	AGU	Yes[b]
GAU	Yes	AAU	No
GCU	Yes	ACU	Yes
GUU	Yes	AUU	Yes

[a]Using either the wild-type T7 RNA polymerase or the P266L T7 RNA polymerase, both purified with a C-terminal His_6 tag. The sequences starting with a G were synthesized from the T7 class III promoter, whereas the sequences starting with an A were synthesized from the T7 class II ϕ2.5 promoter.
[b]Using the P266L T7 RNA polymerase only.
Adapted from Salvail-Lacoste et al. (2013).

RNAs. This list of sequences can now serve as a guide to achieve 5′-homogeneity in future RNA synthesis with the T7 RNAP.

3.2. Affinity purification of RNA using a 5′-CRISPR tag and a 3′-ARiBo tag

In contrast to the self-cleaving HH ribozyme, the Cse3 endonuclease cleavage of a CRISPR tag does not require formation of a stable structure with the RNA of interest, and this presents a distinct advantage for trimming the 5′-end of T7 transcripts. For example, the *T. thermophilus* Cse3 endonuclease binds a 21-nt hairpin and cleaves directly after G21 (Fig. 3.4B; Gesner, Schellenberg, Garside, George, & Macmillan, 2011). To be compatible with the ARiBo-based affinity purification, the Cse3 endonuclease conditions must provide complete cleavage of the 5′-CRISPR tag. Compliance with this requirement is crucial as it prevents coelution of CRISPR contaminants with the RNA of interest. To evaluate the general applicability of the CRISPR/Cse3 system, Cse3 cleavage of a CRISPR tag was previously tested using RNAs starting with different 5′-ends (Salvail-Lacoste et al., 2013). For RNAs starting with a paired adenine or a single stranded AUG, AU, AC, or AG sequence, complete cleavage (≥99%) with Cse3 was obtained within 30 min at 37 °C. Since CRISPR cleavage is generally more efficient at 70 °C with this thermophile endonuclease, complete cleavage of the 5′-CRISPR tag for RNAs starting with several other sequences required an incubation time between 15 and 90 min at 70 °C. Importantly, this study established that complete cleavage of a 5′-CRISPR tag with Cse3 can be achieved for RNAs starting with any of the four standard nucleotides. However, since long incubations at 70 °C can denature the RNA and cause undesirable RNA degradation, it is preferable to use starting sequences that allow complete cleavage of the CRISPR tag by Cse3 at 37 °C in 30 min or less.

The compatibility of the Cse3/CRISPR system with the affinity purification of RNA was also investigated. The standard ARiBo-based procedure was modified to incorporate a Cse3 cleavage step after the transcription reaction but prior to affinity immobilization (Fig. 3.4A). This procedure relies on bacterial overexpression and subsequent purification of the Cse3 endonuclease (Salvail-Lacoste et al., 2013). The purified Cse3 endonuclease can subsequently be used to cleave the 5′-CRISPR tag of the CRISPR-RNA-ARiBo double-fusion RNAs directly in the transcription reaction.

3.2.1 Bacterial expression of the Cse3 endonuclease

The *T. thermophilus* Cse3 endonuclease is expressed with an N-terminal His_6 tag from a pET-30a(+) vector (Gesner et al., 2011; Salvail-Lacoste et al., 2013). For bacterial expression, this vector is transformed into competent Rosetta (DE3) cells (Novagen) using standard procedures. Individual colonies should be used to prepare a glycerol stock. If this is a new clone in the laboratory, one should sequence the vector and evaluate protein expression from a small-scale culture (e.g., 5 mL) prior to expressing the protein from a large-scale culture (8 L).

1. Inoculate 5 mL of LB-Kan-Chl medium (LB broth supplemented with both 50 μg/mL kanamycin and 35 μg/mL chloramphenicol) with 25 μL of a glycerol stock of the Cse3-expressing pET-30a(+) vector cloned into Rosetta (DE3) cells (Gesner et al., 2011; Salvail-Lacoste et al., 2013). Grow overnight (~16 h) at 37 °C with vigorous shaking (~220 rpm).
2. In the morning, use 1 mL of the preculture to inoculate 1 L of LB-Kan-Chl medium in a 4-L flask. Repeat to prepare a total of 2 L of culture. Grow 6–8 h at 37 °C with shaking (~220 rpm).
3. Dilute the cultures by mixing each 1-L culture with 3 L of LB-Kan-Chl medium and distributing equally in three 4-L flasks (1.33 L of culture per flask in a total of six flasks). Grow for 15 min at 25 °C with shaking.
4. Collect a 500-μL preinduction aliquot of the culture.
5. Induce protein expression by adding to each flask 4 mL of Isopropyl β-D-1-thiogalactopyranoside (2 g/24 mL) and grow overnight (~16 h) at 25 °C with shaking.
6. Collect a 500-μL postinduction aliquot of the culture.
7. Pellet the cells by centrifugation at 6000 × *g* for 10 min and discard the supernatant. Store pellets at −80 °C until purification.
8. Verify for efficient induction on a 15% SDS–polyacrylamide gel, which is apparent from the increased intensity of the 30-kDa band in the postinduction aliquot lane versus the preinduction aliquot lane.

3.2.2 Purification of the Cse3 endonuclease

Protein purification should be performed as quickly as possible to prevent degradation. In addition, all solutions and protein-containing samples should be kept at 4 °C or on ice. If possible, the FPLC purification should be conducted in a cold room. Starting at Step 11, it is important to employ RNase-free methods. We typically remove aliquots at several steps of the protocol to monitor the success of the purification by SDS-PAGE.

1. Resuspend the bacterial culture pellets from an 8-L preparation into 80 mL of Cse3 Buffer (20 m*M* Tris pH 7.4, 1 *M* NaCl, 1 m*M* DTT, and 20 m*M* imidazole) supplemented with 150 mg of protease inhibitor cocktail (Sigma-Aldrich).
2. Process the resuspended cells with a mechanical homogenizer [e.g., Ultra Turrax T25 Basic cell disrupter (IKA)] until all clumps are disrupted.
3. Lyse cells by passing the cell slurry through a French Press at 800–1000 psi and collect lysate on ice. Sonicate 10 s. Pass the cell slurry through the French Press a second time. The cell lysate should become clear and take on a darker color.
4. Transfer the cell lysate to four 30-mL centrifuge tubes and centrifuge for 15 min at 12,000 × *g* and 4 °C to pellet unbroken cells and insoluble material. When the centrifugation is completed, take a 30-μL aliquot of the supernatant.
5. Heat the remainder of the supernatant for 30 min at 55 °C. Transfer the supernatant to four 30-mL ultracentrifuge tubes and centrifuge for 60 min at 138,000 × *g* and 4 °C. When the centrifugation is completed, take a 30-μL aliquot of the supernatant.
6. During the centrifugation, prepare the Ni^{2+}-charged IMAC Sepharose 6 Fast Flow resin as follows. Resuspend the IMAC Sepharose 6 Fast Flow resin (GE Healthcare) in the supplier bottle by vigorous mixing. Transfer 10 mL of the resin slurry to a 50-mL screw-cap conical tube and wash with 40 mL of water. To wash, resuspend in water, centrifuge 3 min at 1150 × *g* in a swinging bucket rotor, and decant supernatant. Then, charge the resin with nickel (Ni^{2+}) by washing with 10 mL of 200 m*M* $NiSO_4$ and then twice with 40 mL Cse3 Buffer.
7. Add supernatant from the high-speed spin of cell lysate to the Ni^{2+}-charged IMAC Sepharose 6 Fast Flow resin and transfer all supernatants and resin to a 250-mL plastic bottle.
8. Incubate for 1 h on a rotator at 4 °C.
9. After incubation, transfer the resin with cell lysate back to a 50-mL screw-cap conical tube, 50 mL at a time. After each addition, centrifuge the resin 3 min at 1150 × *g* and decant supernatant. Repeat until all the resin and lysate is transferred from the 250- to the 50-mL tube.
10. Wash the resin in the 50-mL tube twice with 40 mL Cse3 Buffer.
11. Elute the His-tagged Cse3 protein as follows. Resuspend in 40 mL of Cse3 Elution Buffer (Cse3 Buffer supplemented with 180 m*M* imidazole and pH adjusted to pH 7.4). Incubate on the rotator for 10 min at

room temperature. Centrifuge the resin for 3 min at 1150 × *g* and decant supernatant. Take a 30-μL aliquot of the first elution supernatant. Repeat the elution process twice, with 40 mL and then 20 mL of Cse3 Elution Buffer, and take 30-μL aliquots of each elution supernatant. Pool the elution supernatants (~100 mL) and pass through a 0.22-μm filter.

12. Resuspend the resin in PBS and take a 30-μL aliquot. Centrifuge 3 min at 1150 × *g* and take a 30-μL aliquot of the supernatant.
13. Transfer the pooled elution supernatant to dialysis tubing (MWCO of 12–14 kDa and 29 mm in diameter) and dialyze against 4 L of FPLC-A Buffer (20 m*M* sodium phosphate at pH 7.4, 1 m*M* EDTA and 1 m*M* DTT) overnight at 4 °C with slow stirring.
14. Monitor the batch affinity purification on IMAC Sepharose 6 Fast Flow resin using a 15% SDS- polyacrylamide gel.
15. Carefully remove the sample from the dialysis tubing with a 10-mL serological pipette and transfer to a 250-mL flask.
16. Prepare an SP-Sepharose High-Performance column (26 mm inner diameter and 200 mm tube height) with 75 mL of SP-Sepharose High-Performance resin (GE Healthcare). Wash the column for 25 min with 100% FPLC-A Buffer at 3 mL/min.
17. Load sample on the column through an FPLC pump or using a 50-mL superloop at 3 mL/min. Elute protein using a gradient from 0% to 100% FPLC-B Buffer (FPLC-A with 2 *M* NaCl) over 600 mL at 3 mL/min with UV detection at 280 nm. Collect 9-mL fractions.
18. Run a 15% SDS–polyacrylamide gel to select the fractions (~9) containing the purified protein, minimizing contamination with other proteins.
19. Pool selected fractions, transfer to dialysis tubing (MWCO of 12–14 kDa), and dialyze against 2 L of Cse3 storage buffer (50 m*M* HEPES at pH 8.0, 100 m*M* NaCl, 2 m*M* DTT, and 20% glycerol) overnight at 4 °C with slow stirring.
20. The following day, carefully transfer the dialyzed sample with a 10-mL serological pipette to a 50-mL screw-cap conical tube. Determine the sample volume.
21. Determine the protein concentration by UV spectroscopy at 280 nm using an extinction coefficient of 31,970 cm^{-1} M^{-1}. Using this procedure, we typically obtain a yield of ~400 mg of purified protein from an 8-L culture at a final storage concentration of ~8 mg/mL (0.25–0.3 m*M*).

22. Distribute in 1–10 mL aliquots and store at −20 °C.
23. The Cse3 endonuclease should be ready to use, although one may want to verify the final purity by SDS-PAGE. To ensure compatibility with batch affinity purification, it is important to verify that the purified protein is RNase free, as previously described for the λN-GST fusion protein (Di Tomasso, Lampron, et al., 2012).

3.2.3 Cse3 endonuclease cleavage of the CRISPR-RNA-ARiBo precursor

Cse3 cleavage of the CRISPR-RNA-ARiBo precursor is first optimized to identify conditions that provide complete cleavage of the CRISPR tag prior to performing the Cse3 cleavage reaction on a larger scale.

1. For optimization purposes, four 25 μL Cse3 cleavage reactions are generally set up using a volume of transcription corresponding to 1 μ*M* of CRISPR-RNA-ARiBo precursor. The reaction is incubated with either 2 or 4 μ*M* of purified Cse3 endonuclease at either 37 or 70 °C in Cse3 Cleavage Buffer (20 m*M* HEPES pH 7.5 and 150 m*M* KCl) supplemented with 0.2 U of RNAsin (Promega). Aliquots (0.75 μL) are typically removed at 5, 15, and 30 min, mixed with 10 μL of GLB and stored on ice.
2. Samples are analyzed on a denaturing polyacrylamide gel to select the cleavage condition that produces the highest yield of ARiBo-fusion RNA (Section 3.4.1).
3. For affinity purification, a volume of transcription corresponding to 1.86 nmol of CRISPR-RNA-ARiBo is typically incubated with 3.72 nmol (or more if needed) of purified Cse3 endonuclease under optimized conditions of temperature and incubation time (e.g., 15 min at 70 °C) in Cse3 Cleavage Buffer supplemented with 1.67 U of RNAsin in a total reaction volume of 200 μL. A 2-μL aliquot is taken for quantitative analysis.
4. Optionally, a Cse3 endonuclease inactivation step can be added to improve sample migration on the denaturing polyacrylamide gels. Heat sample for 2 min at 95 °C and cool on ice for 5 min. This step should not affect the performance of the method.
5. After Cse3 cleavage, the standard batch affinity purification is resumed as described in Section 2.6, but starting with 1.75 nmol of ARiBo-fusion RNA. To minimize the amount of CRISPR-tag impurity in the elution step, it is preferable to supplement the Equilibration Buffer with 10 m*M* of $MgCl_2$.

The success of the method depends on the RNA of interest, as shown for the purification of SLI(2) and human pre-miR153-2 RNAs from CRISPR-RNA-ARiBo precursors (Fig. 3.6A and B). Affinity purification of the small SLI(2) hairpin without the CRISPR tag yields a purified SLI(2) RNA that contains ~15% RNA contaminants due to 5′-heterogeneity (Salvail-Lacoste et al., 2013). However, when using a 5′-CRISPR tag, the SLI(2) RNA can be purified with both 5′- and 3′-homogeneity and very low levels of CRISPR tag and ARiBo-tag contaminants (≤1%; Fig. 3.6A; Salvail-Lacoste et al., 2013). Similarly, affinity purification of the human pre-miR153-2 RNA using both a 5′-CRISPR tag and a 3′-ARiBo tag helps remove both 5′- and 3′-heterogeneity (Fig. 3.6B). However, this purification produced a nonnegligible amount of contaminants, resulting from off-target cleavage during the Cse3 cleavage step. The presence of off-target cleavage products is also observed during purification of another pre-miRNA, pre-let-7g, that was affinity purified with the same tags (not shown). It appears that off-target RNA cleavage during the Cse3 cleavage step at 70 °C is linked to the high concentration of Cse3 endonuclease needed to achieve complete CRISPR cleavage, since control incubations with lower concentrations of the Cse3 endonuclease did not produce off-target RNA cleavage. Thus, it may be difficult for some RNAs to optimize conditions that allow complete cleavage of the CRISPR tag without producing off-target cleavage. Nevertheless, the CRISPR/Cse3 system provides a novel tool for affinity purification of several RNAs that is highly efficient to eliminate 5′-sequence heterogeneity of T7 transcripts.

3.3. Affinity purification of RNA using a 5′-HH and a 3′-ARiBo tag

The well-characterized HH ribozyme is likely the most convenient enzymatic tool currently employed to achieve 5′-homogeneity of T7 transcripts because its cleavage occurs spontaneously during transcription without the need for either additional reagents or purification steps. Although a HH tag can be directly attached at the 5′-end of the RNA without any restriction on the 5′-sequence of the RNA, its cleavage requires formation of a stable stem between ribozyme residues and the RNA target. Therefore, the HH sequence must be tailored to the 5′-end of the RNA of interest, and general guidelines have been reported for designing 5′-HH tags that are efficiently cleaved during transcription (Avis, Conn, & Walker, 2012; Walker et al., 2003). Nevertheless, it can be challenging to identify an ideal ribozyme sequence and cleavage conditions compatible with affinity purification of

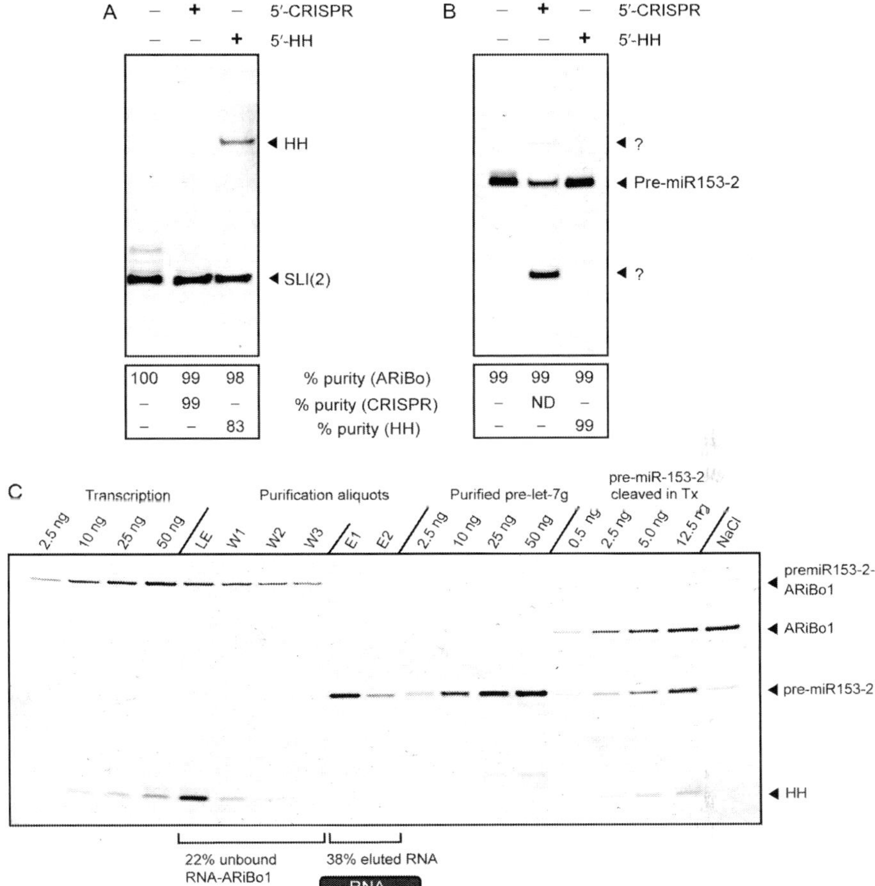

Figure 3.6 Small-scale affinity purification of RNAs from CRISPR-RNA-ARiBo and HH-RNA-ARiBo precursors. Purifications of (A) SLI(2) and (B) pre-miR153-2 from RNA-ARiBo precursors without a 5′-tag or with either a 5′-CRISPR or a 5′-HH tag. Aliquots of the E1 elution fractions were analyzed on (A) 15% and (B) 10% denaturing polyacrylamide gels stained with SYBR Gold. Bands corresponding to different RNAs are annotated on the right side of the gel. The percentages of purity of the eluted RNAs are provided with respect to the residual tags (ND: not determined). (C) Small-scale affinity purification of pre-miR153-2 from a HH-RNA-ARiBo precursor analyzed on a 10% denaturing polyacrylamide gel stained with SYBR Gold. The RNA was affinity purified with standard procedures and aliquots from each purification steps were loaded on the gel as described in Section 3.4.2.

any RNA of interest. In particular, cleavage may be incomplete if the formation of the functional HH ribozyme structure is inhibited due to the structural stability of the RNA of interest (Grosshans & Cech, 1991; Price et al., 1995; Walker et al., 2003). On the other hand, a highly stable HH ribozyme could help facilitate complete cleavage, but may be difficult to dissociate from the RNA of interest under native conditions.

The general procedure of RNA affinity purification from a HH-RNA-ARiBo double-fusion RNA (Fig. 3.5A) is essentially the same as described for purification from an RNA-ARiBo precursor (Fig. 3.1A), because HH self-cleavage yields the RNA-ARiBo precursor directly in the transcription reaction. For a 5′-HH tag to be compatible with affinity purification, it is important that it is completely cleaved to avoid contamination of the purified RNA with a residual 5′-tag. Thus, it is important to design a HH ribozyme that forms a stable stem with the RNA of interest. For example, for purification of SLI(2) and human pre-miR153-2, specific 5′-HH tags were designed to form a stable stem I with the 5′-sequence of the RNA (Fig. 3.5B). As shown in Fig. 3.6A, this design is not compatible with affinity purification of SLI(2), since substantial amount of 5′-HH tag contaminant ($\geq$17%) is present in the RNA elution, even when 10 mM $MgCl_2$ is added to the Equilibration Buffer to reduce the amount of 5′-HH tag contaminant. Since the 5′-HH tag was almost completely cleaved in the transcription reaction ($\geq$98%), these results indicate that the tag remains tethered to the RNA after cleavage. In contrast, affinity purification of the pre-miR153-2 RNA from a HH-RNA-ARiBo precursor yields pure RNA with negligible amount of HH tag and ARiBo-tag contamination ($\leq$1%; Fig. 3.6B). Thus, for certain RNAs, affinity purification using a 5′-HH tag and a 3′-ARiBo tag is straightforward and allows for rapid purification of RNA with both 5′- and 3′-sequence homogeneity. However, other RNAs, like SLI(2), may require additional optimization. In some cases, the extent of 5′-HH tag cleavage and release of its 3′-product can be improved by thermal cycling (i.e., several cycles of heating and cooling) that allows for folding and unfolding of the RNA (Avis et al., 2012). Alternatively, one could test different stem I sequences using the minimal HH sequence employed here, or incorporate a HH ribozyme sequence that is stabilized by a tertiary interaction (Khvorova, Lescoute, Westhof, & Jayasena, 2003; Martick & Scott, 2006; Saksmerprome, Roychowdhury-Saha, Jayasena, Khvorova, & Burke, 2004). Such tertiary interaction can enable more efficient cleavage of a 5′-HH tag by the HH ribozyme, particularly in highly structured RNAs (Burke & Rhee, 2010; Meyer & Masquida, 2014) and may also help with purification of RNAs from HH-RNA-ARiBo precursors.

3.4. Quantitative analyses when using a 5′-tag

The quantitative analysis of affinity-purified RNA using a 5′-tag and a 3′-ARiBo tag is similar to that using only a 3′-ARiBo tag (Section 2.7). The quantity of ARiBo-fusion RNA produced by *in vitro* transcription and the percentage of *glmS* cleavage in the transcription reaction can be obtained from aliquots of transcription reactions in which the 5′-tag has been cleaved. However, additional analyses are performed to quantify cleavage of the 5′-tag prior to purification and for quantitative analysis of batch affinity purification, as described below.

3.4.1 Quantitative analysis of 5′-tag cleavage in the transcription reaction

For the 5′-HH tag, prepare a 1:200 dilution of the transcription reaction and mix ~1.5 μL of this dilution with 10 μL of GLB for gel analysis. For the 5′-CRISPR tag, use the stopped Cse3 cleavage reaction (~0.75 μL in 10 μL of GLB) for gel analysis. The percentage *of 5′-tag cleavage in solution* is determined using Eq. (3.6), where BI_{Fusion} and BI_{Double} are the band intensities of ARiBo-fusion RNA and double-fusion RNA (CRISPR-RNA-ARiBo or HH-RNA-ARiBo), respectively, whereas nt_{Fusion} and nt_{Double} are the number of nucleotides of the ARiBo-fusion and double-fusion RNAs, respectively:

$$\left[\frac{BI_{Fusion}/nt_{Fusion}}{(BI_{Fusion}/nt_{Fusion}) + (BI_{Double}/nt_{Double})}\right] \times 100\% \qquad (3.6)$$

3.4.2 Quantitative analysis of batch affinity purification

Several samples are typically loaded on the gel (Fig. 3.6C): (1) a control sample containing a volume of the transcription reaction corresponding to 25 ng of double-fusion RNA (for 5′-CRISPR tags only); (2) control samples containing different volumes of either the transcription reaction in which the 5′-HH tag is cleaved or the Cse3 cleavage reaction corresponding to specific amounts of ARiBo-fusion RNA (2.5, 10, 25, and 50 ng RNA; lanes 1–4 in Fig. 3.6C); (3) aliquots from LE and wash eluate corresponding to 250 ng of ARiBo-fusion RNA assuming that 100% of the input RNA is present in each eluate (lanes 5–8 in Fig. 3.6C); (4) aliquots from the RNA elution corresponding to 100 ng of the RNA assuming a 100% purification yield at each step (lanes 9 and 10 in Fig. 3.6C); (5) control samples containing known amounts of purified RNA (2.5, 10, 2, and 50 ng; lanes 11–14 in Fig. 3.6C). For purifications from a CRISPR-RNA-ARiBo precursor, combine these control samples with known amounts of purified CRISPR tag (1, 2.5, 5, and 10 ng); (6) control samples containing different volumes of either the transcription reaction after cleavage with GlcN6P (for 5′-HH tags) or the Cse3 cleavage reaction after cleavage with GlcN6P (for 5′-CRISPR tags). These control samples correspond to specific amounts of purified RNA (0.5, 2.5, 5.0, and 12.5 ng RNA; lanes 15–18 in Fig. 3.6C); and (7) aliquot from the NaCl wash corresponding to 50 ng of the RNA of interest assuming 100% RNA recovery at this step (lane 19 in Fig. 3.6C).

General quantifications are performed as described in Section 2.7. In addition, for purifications with a 5′-CRISPR tag, a standard curve is derived from gel lanes loaded with known amounts of CRISPR tag to relate band intensity to the quantity of purified CRISPR (N_{CRISPR}). For purification with a 5′-HH tag, a standard curve is derived from gel lanes of the transcription reaction cleaved with GlcN6P, as described for the ARiBo tag in Section 2.7.2, to relate band intensity to the quantity of 5′-HH tag (N_{HH}). One can then calculate the *percentage of 5′-tag cleavage in solution* from the control lanes showing 5′-tag cleavage using Eq. (3.1), and the *percentage of RNA purity* with respect to the residual CRISPR tag and the residual HH tag from the E1 lane using Eqs. (3.7) and (3.8), respectively:

$$\left[\frac{N_{\mathrm{RNA}}}{N_{\mathrm{RNA}} + N_{\mathrm{CRISPR}}}\right] \times 100\% \qquad (3.7)$$

$$\left[\frac{N_{\mathrm{RNA}}}{N_{\mathrm{RNA}} + N_{\mathrm{HH}}}\right] \times 100\% \qquad (3.8)$$

4. SUMMARY

At this time, several RNAs ranging from 29 to 614 nt in length have been affinity purified from RNA-ARiBo precursors transcribed *in vitro* by the T7 RNAP. The 3′-homogeneity of the purified RNA is ensured by specific self-cleavage of the ARiBo tag; however, 5′-homogeneity requires additional considerations. The percentage of 5′-heterogeneity is negligible for T7 RNA transcripts starting with specific nucleotides, including 10/16 sequences starting with GNN and 7/16 sequences starting ANN. For other starting sequences, it is preferable to incorporate a cleavable 5′-tag, and both 5′-CRISPR and 5′-HH tags have been tested for affinity purification. These tags are useful because they do not restrict the sequence of the RNA interest. An important advantage of the CRISPR/Cse3 system is that it does not require interaction of the tag with the RNA of interest. However, efficient CRISPR cleavage requires high concentrations of Cse3 that may render this procedure impractical for large-scale applications. In addition, for several RNA sequences, Cse3 cleavage may require a long incubation of the CRISPR-RNA-ARiBo precursor (up to 45–90 min) at 70 °C, which could denature the RNA and promote its degradation. Furthermore, incubation with the Cse3 endonuclease at high concentration can produce off-target cleavages that limit the general applicability of using a 5′-CRISPR tag for RNA purification. Given that they self-cleave directly in the transcription, 5′-HH tags represent a good alternative. One known shortcoming of the 5′-HH tag is the limited extent of cleavage observed with some very stable RNAs, but it may be possible to circumvent this by designing 5′-HH tags and using cleavage conditions that favor folding of the active HH ribozyme structure. For affinity purification using a 5′-HH tag, one must obtain complete cleavage of the 5′-HH tag, and the 5′-HH tag must completely dissociate from the RNA of interest to prevent contamination of the purified sample. Evidently, neither the 5′-HH tag nor the 5′-CRISPR tag provides a general solution to RNA purification, but hopefully one of the approaches presented here will allow for purification of the RNA of interest with both 5′- and 3′-end homogeneity.

ACKNOWLEDGMENTS

We thank coworkers that have contributed to the development of the ARiBo method, including Philipe Lampron, Alexandre Desjardins, Alexis Rompré-Brodeur, Pierre Dagenais, Benjamin L. Piette, and Vanessa Delfosse. This work was supported by grants from the Canadian Institutes for Health Research to P. L. (MOP-86502 and PPP-122895) and J. G. O. (MOP-74739), the Natural Sciences and Engineering Council of Canada and the Parkinson Society of Canada. P. L. holds a Canada Research Chair in Structural Biology and Engineering of RNA.

REFERENCES

Ahmed, Y. L., & Ficner, R. (2014). RNA synthesis and purification for structural studies. *RNA Biology, 11*, 427–432.

Austin, R. J., Xia, T., Ren, J., Takahashi, T. T., & Roberts, R. W. (2002). Designed arginine-rich RNA-binding peptides with picomolar affinity. *Journal of the American Chemical Society, 124*, 10966–10967.

Avis, J. M., Conn, G. L., & Walker, S. C. (2012). Cis-acting ribozymes for the production of RNA in vitro transcripts with defined 5′ and 3′ ends. *Methods in Molecular Biology, 941*, 83–98.

Batey, R. T. (2014). Advances in methods for native expression and purification of RNA for structural studies. *Current Opinion in Structural Biology, 26C*, 1–8.

Batey, R. T., Gilbert, S. D., & Montange, R. K. (2004). Structure of a natural guanine-responsive riboswitch complexed with the metabolite hypoxanthine. *Nature*, *432*, 411–415.

Batey, R. T., & Kieft, J. S. (2007). Improved native affinity purification of RNA. *RNA*, *13*, 1384–1389.

Blaszczyk, L., & Ciesiolka, J. (2011). Secondary structure and the role in translation initiation of the 5′-terminal region of p53 mRNA. *Biochemistry*, *50*, 7080–7092.

Bowman, J. C., Azizi, B., Lenz, T. K., Roy, P., & Williams, L. D. (2012). Preparation of long templates for RNA in vitro transcription by recursive PCR. *Methods in Molecular Biology*, *941*, 19–41.

Burke, D. H., & Rhee, S. S. (2010). Assembly and activation of a kinase ribozyme. *RNA*, *16*, 2349–2359.

Cavaluzzi, M. J., & Borer, P. N. (2004). Revised UV extinction coefficients for nucleoside-5′-monophosphates and unpaired DNA and RNA. *Nucleic Acids Research*, *32*, e13.

Cochrane, J. C., Lipchock, S. V., & Strobel, S. A. (2007). Structural investigation of the GlmS ribozyme bound to its catalytic cofactor. *Chemistry and Biology*, *14*, 97–105.

Cunningham, P. R., & Ofengand, J. (1990). Use of inorganic pyrophosphatase to improve the yield of in vitro transcription reactions catalyzed by T7 RNA polymerase. *Biotechniques*, *9*, 713–714.

Cunningham, P. R., Weitzmann, C. J., & Ofengand, J. (1991). SP6 RNA polymerase stutters when initiating from an AAA... sequence. *Nucleic Acids Research*, *19*, 4669–4673.

Delfosse, V., Bouchard, P., Bonneau, E., Dagenais, P., Lemay, J. F., Lafontaine, D. A., et al. (2010). Riboswitch structure: An internal residue mimicking the purine ligand. *Nucleic Acids Research*, *38*, 2057–2068.

Desjardins, A., Bouvette, J., & Legault, P. (2014). Stepwise assembly of multiple Lin28 proteins on the terminal loop of let-7 miRNA precursors. *Nucleic Acids Research*, *42*, 4615–4628.

Desjardins, A., Yang, A., Bouvette, J., Omichinski, J. G., & Legault, P. (2012). Importance of the NCp7-like domain in the recognition of pre-let-7g by the pluripotency factor Lin28. *Nucleic Acids Research*, *40*, 1767–1777.

Ding, Y., Chan, C. Y., & Lawrence, C. E. (2004). Sfold web server for statistical folding and rational design of nucleic acids. *Nucleic Acids Research*, *32*, W135–W141.

Di Tomasso, G., Dagenais, P., Desjardins, A., Rompré-Brodeur, A., Delfosse, V., & Legault, P. (2012). Affinity purification of RNA using an ARiBo tag. In G. L. Conn (Ed.), *Recombinant and in vitro RNA synthesis: Methods and protocols*: *Vol. 941* (p. 306). New York: Humana Press.

Di Tomasso, G., Lampron, P., Dagenais, P., Omichinski, J. G., & Legault, P. (2011). The ARiBo tag: A reliable tool for affinity purification of RNAs under native conditions. *Nucleic Acids Research*, *39*, e18.

Di Tomasso, G., Lampron, P., Omichinski, J. G., & Legault, P. (2012). Preparation of λN-GST fusion protein for affinity immobilization of RNA. In G. L. Conn (Ed.), *Recombinant and in vitro RNA synthesis: Methods and protocols*: *Vol. 941* (p. 306). New York: Humana Press.

Dzianott, A. M., & Bujarski, J. J. (1988). An in vitro transcription vector which generates nearly correctly ended RNAs by self-cleavage of longer transcripts. *Nucleic Acids Research*, *16*, 10940.

Easton, L. E., Shibata, Y., & Lukavsky, P. J. (2010). Rapid, nondenaturing RNA purification using weak anion-exchange fast performance liquid chromatography. *RNA*, *16*, 647–653.

Edelmann, F. T., Niedner, A., & Niessing, D. (2014). Production of pure and functional RNA for in vitro reconstitution experiments. *Methods*, *65*, 333–341.

Esakova, O., & Krasilnikov, A. S. (2010). Of proteins and RNA: The RNase P/MRP family. *RNA*, *16*, 1725–1747.

Ferré-D'Amaré, A. R., & Doudna, J. A. (1996). Use of cis- and trans-ribozymes to remove 5′ and 3′ heterogeneities from milligrams of in vitro transcribed RNA. *Nucleic Acids Research, 24*, 977–978.

Gesner, E. M., Schellenberg, M. J., Garside, E. L., George, M. M., & Macmillan, A. M. (2011). Recognition and maturation of effector RNAs in a CRISPR interference pathway. *Nature Structural and Molecular Biology, 18*, 688–692.

Griffiths-Jones, S. (2004). The microRNA registry. *Nucleic Acids Research, 32*, D109–D111.

Grosshans, C. A., & Cech, T. R. (1991). A hammerhead ribozyme allows synthesis of a new form of the Tetrahymena ribozyme homogeneous in length with a 3′ end blocked for transesterification. *Nucleic Acids Research, 19*, 3875–3880.

Guillerez, J., Lopez, P. J., Proux, F., Launay, H., & Dreyfus, M. (2005). A mutation in T7 RNA polymerase that facilitates promoter clearance. *Proceedings of the National Academy of Sciences of the United States of America, 102*, 5958–5963.

Imburgio, D., Rong, M. Q., Ma, K. Y., & McAllister, W. T. (2000). Studies of promoter recognition and start site selection by T7 RNA polymerase using a comprehensive collection of promoter variants. *Biochemistry, 39*, 10419–10430.

Keel, A. Y., Easton, L. E., Lukavsky, P. J., & Kieft, J. S. (2009). Large-scale native preparation of in vitro transcribed RNA. *Methods in Enzymology, 469*, 3–25.

Khvorova, A., Lescoute, A., Westhof, E., & Jayasena, S. D. (2003). Sequence elements outside the hammerhead ribozyme catalytic core enable intracellular activity. *Nature Structural Biology, 10*, 708–712.

Kim, I., McKenna, S. A., Puglisi, E. V., & Puglisi, J. D. (2007). Rapid purification of RNAs using fast performance liquid chromatography (FPLC). *RNA, 13*, 289–294.

Lee, H. Y., Haurwitz, R. E., Apffel, A., Zhou, K., Smart, B., Wenger, C. D., et al. (2013). RNA–protein analysis using a conditional CRISPR nuclease. *Proceedings of the National Academy of Sciences of the United States of America, 110*, 5416–5421.

Legault, P. (1995). *Structural studies of ribozymes by heteronuclear NMR spectroscopy*. Boulder, CO: University of Colorado at Boulder.

Lukavsky, P. J., & Puglisi, J. D. (2004). Large-scale preparation and purification of polyacrylamide-free RNA oligonucleotides. *RNA, 10*, 889–893.

Martick, M., & Scott, W. G. (2006). Tertiary contacts distant from the active site prime a ribozyme for catalysis. *Cell, 126*, 309–320.

Martin, C. T., Muller, D. K., & Coleman, J. E. (1988). Processivity in early stages of transcription by T7 RNA polymerase. *Biochemistry, 27*, 3966–3974.

McCarthy, T. J., Plog, M. A., Floy, S. A., Jansen, J. A., Soukup, J. K., & Soukup, G. A. (2005). Ligand requirements for glmS ribozyme self-cleavage. *Chemical Biology, 12*, 1221–1226.

McKenna, S. A., Kim, I., Puglisi, E. V., Lindhout, D. A., Aitken, C. E., Marshall, R. A., et al. (2007). Purification and characterization of transcribed RNAs using gel filtration chromatography. *Nature Protocols, 2*, 3270–3277.

Meyer, M., & Masquida, B. (2014). cis-Acting 5′ hammerhead ribozyme optimization for in vitro transcription of highly structured RNAs. *Methods in Molecular Biology, 1086*, 21–40.

Milligan, J. F., Groebe, D. R., Witherell, G. W., & Uhlenbeck, O. C. (1987). Oligoribonucleotide synthesis using T7 RNA polymerase and synthetic DNA templates. *Nucleic Acids Research, 15*, 8783–8798.

Pleiss, J. A., Derrick, M. L., & Uhlenbeck, O. C. (1998). T7 RNA polymerase produces 5′ end heterogeneity during in vitro transcription from certain templates. *RNA, 4*, 1313–1317.

Price, S. R., Ito, N., Oubridge, C., Avis, J. M., & Nagai, K. (1995). Crystallization of RNA–protein complexes. I. Methods for the large-scale preparation of RNA suitable for crystallographic studies. *Journal of Molecular Biology, 249*, 398–408.

Prodromou, C., & Pearl, L. H. (1992). Recursive PCR: A novel technique for total gene synthesis. *Protein Engineering*, *5*, 827–829.
Ramírez-Tapia, L. E., & Martin, C. T. (2012). New insights into the mechanism of initial transcription: The T7 RNA polymerase mutant P266L transitions to elongation at longer RNA lengths than wild type. *The Journal of Biological Chemistry*, *287*, 37352–37361.
Roth, A., Nahvi, A., Lee, M., Jona, I., & Breaker, R. R. (2006). Characteristics of the *glmS* ribozyme suggest only structural roles for divalent metal ions. *RNA*, *12*, 607–619.
Saksmerprome, V., Roychowdhury-Saha, M., Jayasena, S., Khvorova, A., & Burke, D. H. (2004). Artificial tertiary motifs stabilize trans-cleaving hammerhead ribozymes under conditions of submillimolar divalent ions and high temperatures. *RNA*, *10*, 1916–1924.
Salvail-Lacoste, A., Di Tomasso, G., Piette, B. L., & Legault, P. (2013). Affinity purification of T7 RNA transcripts with homogeneous ends using ARiBo and CRISPR tags. *RNA*, *19*, 1003–1014.
Sandhu, G. S., Aleff, R. A., & Kline, B. C. (1992). Dual asymmetric PCR: One-step construction of synthetic genes. *Biotechniques*, *12*, 14–16.
Schürer, H., Lang, K., Schuster, J., & Mörl, M. (2002). A universal method to produce in vitro transcripts with homogeneous 3′ ends. *Nucleic Acids Research*, *30*, e56.
Sherlin, L. D., Bullock, T. L., Nissan, T. A., Perona, J. J., Lariviere, F. J., Uhlenbeck, O. C., et al. (2001). Chemical and enzymatic synthesis of tRNAs for high-throughput crystallization. *RNA*, *7*, 1671–1678.
Siegel, R. W., Banta, A. B., Haas, E. S., Brown, J. W., & Pace, N. R. (1996). Mycoplasma fermentans simplifies our view of the catalytic core of ribonuclease P RNA. *RNA*, *2*, 452–462.
Taira, K., Nakagawa, K., Nishikawa, S., & Furukawa, K. (1991). Construction of a novel RNA-transcript-trimming plasmid which can be used both in vitro in place of run-off and (G)-free transcriptions and in vivo as multi-sequences transcription vectors. *Nucleic Acids Research*, *19*, 5125–5130.
Tang, G. Q., Nandakumar, D., Bandwar, R. P., Lee, K. S., Roy, R., Ha, T., et al. (2014). Relaxed rotational and scrunching changes in P266L mutant of T7 RNA polymerase reduce short abortive RNAs while delaying transition into elongation. *PLoS One*, *9*, e91859.
Uhlenbeck, O. C. (1995). Keeping RNA happy. *RNA*, *1*, 4–6.
Walker, S. C., Avis, J. M., & Conn, G. L. (2003). General plasmids for producing RNA in vitro transcripts with homogeneous ends. *Nucleic Acids Research*, *31*, 1–6.
Watson, P. Y., & Fedor, M. J. (2011). The glmS riboswitch integrates signals from activating and inhibitory metabolites in vivo. *Nature Structural and Molecular Biology*, *18*, 359–363.
Wilkinson, S. R., & Been, M. D. (2005). A pseudoknot in the 3′ non-core region of the glmS ribozyme enhances self-cleavage activity. *RNA*, *11*, 1788–1794.
Winkler, W. C., Nahvi, A., Roth, A., Collins, J. A., & Breaker, R. R. (2004). Control of gene expression by a natural metabolite-responsive ribozyme. *Nature*, *428*, 281–286.
Wyatt, J. R., Chastain, M., & Puglisi, J. D. (1991). Synthesis and purification of large amounts of RNA oligonucleotides. *Biotechniques*, *11*, 764–769.
Zaug, A. J., Grosshans, C. A., & Cech, T. R. (1988). Sequence-specific endoribonuclease activity of the Tetrahymena ribozyme: Enhanced cleavage of certain oligonucleotide substrates that form mismatched ribozyme-substrate complexes. *Biochemistry*, *27*, 8924–8931.
Zuker, M. (2003). Mfold web server for nucleic acid folding and hybridization prediction. *Nucleic Acids Research*, *31*, 3406–3415.

CHAPTER FOUR

Deoxyribozyme-Mediated Ligation for Incorporating EPR Spin Labels and Reporter Groups into RNA

Katarzyna Wawrzyniak-Turek[*,†], **Claudia Höbartner**[*,†,1]
[*]Research Group Nucleic Acid Chemistry, Max Planck Institute for Biophysical Chemistry, Göttingen, Germany
[†]Institute for Organic and Biomolecular Chemistry, Georg August University Göttingen, Göttingen, Germany
[1]Corresponding author: e-mail address: claudia.hoebartner@mpibpc.mpg.de

Contents

Abstract

Preparation of site-specifically labeled RNA for spectroscopic studies is a multistep process and requires handling of delicate samples. This chapter is focused on the synthesis of spin-labeled RNA using convertible nucleosides and the application of the deoxyribozyme 9DB1* for the ligation of RNA fragments. The convertible nucleoside approach enables the attachment of nitroxyls as paramagnetic reporters at the exocyclic amino groups of cytidine, adenosine, and guanosine nucleobases in synthetic RNA. The deoxyribozyme 9DB1* is a synthetic single-stranded DNA with RNA ligase activity that can be used as an alternative to protein enzymes (T4 RNA/DNA ligases) for covalently joining RNA fragments via native 3′–5′ phosphodiester bonds. The combination of solid-phase synthesis and DNA-catalyzed RNA ligation provides reliable access to site-

Methods in Enzymology, Volume 549
ISSN 0076-6879
http://dx.doi.org/10.1016/B978-0-12-801122-5.00004-0

specifically labeled functional RNAs for spectroscopic studies. A particular advantage of using deoxyribozymes for RNA ligation lies in the mild reaction conditions that prevent chemical damage to sensitive labels. As an example, we describe a detailed protocol for the synthesis of TEMPO-labeled SAM-I riboswitch RNA.

1. INTRODUCTION

The biological functions of RNA are tightly connected to hierarchical folding into diverse and complex three-dimensional structures. The site-specific installation of reporter groups benefits spectroscopic methods for elucidating structure and dynamics of folded RNA. Electron paramagnetic resonance (EPR) spectroscopy of nucleic acids has advanced into a powerful technique that reveals details on local and global structural aspects (Krstic, Endeward, Margraf, Marko, & Prisner, 2012). In combination with high-resolution data (e.g., from nuclear magnetic resonance (NMR)) and global shape analysis (e.g., obtained from small angle X-ray scattering (SAXS)), EPR data can substantially improve the overall understanding of functional RNA and RNA–protein complexes (Carlomagno, 2014). In addition, fluorescence-based methods provide valuable details and offer the possibility for multiplexing of several fluorophores and real-time detection (St-Pierre, McCluskey, Shaw, Penedo, & Lafontaine, 2014).

Paramagnetic or fluorescent reporter groups can be site-specifically installed in RNA by solid-phase synthesis, a general approach that is compatible with a wide variety of functional moieties. In addition, solid-phase synthesis provides access to prefunctionalized RNA that contains functional groups for further bioorthogonal conjugation reactions. Well-known examples include 2′-amino- and 5-aminoallyl-pyrimidine nucleosides for coupling with N-hydroxysuccinimide (NHS) esters or isocyanates (Edwards & Sigurdsson, 2007), or various types of alkynes (e.g., 5-ethinyl-pyrimidine, 2′-propargyl nucleosides, or 7-alkynyl-7-deazapurines) amenable to Cu-catalyzed 1,3-dipolar cycloadditions (CuAAC, a common type of click reaction; Ding, Wunnicke, Steinhoff, & Seela, 2010; Jakobsen, Shelke, Vogel, & Sigurdsson, 2010), or Pd-catalyzed cross-coupling reactions (Piton et al., 2007; Schiemann et al., 2007). Convertible nucleosides (Allerson, Chen, & Verdine, 1997) represent an additional class of prefunctionalized moieties installed by solid-phase synthesis. They can be further derivatized with various desired probes, including spin labels.

Because solid-phase synthesis of RNA is limited in length to ca. 50 nt, studying larger RNAs of functional interest demands the combination of chemical and enzymatic approaches. The ligation of short RNA fragments to longer constructs can be achieved by traditional enzymatic ligation methods, using T4 DNA or T4 RNA ligases (Frilander & Turunen, 2008; Persson, Willkomm, & Hartmann, 2005). While T4 RNA ligase joins single-stranded fragments with free 3′-hydroxyl acceptor and 5′-phosphate donor termini; T4 DNA ligase requires the RNA fragments to be base-paired with a fully complementary splint made of DNA, RNA, or 2′-*O*-methyl RNA (also known as template; Lang & Micura, 2008). RNA ligase II is a newer addition to the enzyme repertoire for splinted RNA ligations (Viollet, Fuchs, Munafo, Zhuang, & Robb, 2011). These biochemical methods are well established and continue to serve the research community, but they often require substantial optimization and can lead to undesired side-products that limit the yield of desired product.

An increasingly popular alternative to RNA ligase proteins is the use of catalytically active single-stranded DNA (DNA catalysts, DNA enzymes, or DNAzymes), known as RNA-ligating deoxyribozymes (Silverman, 2009). DNA catalysts identified by *in vitro* selection from random DNA libraries can catalyze the formation of a native 3′-5′-phosphodiester bond between two defined RNA fragments (Höbartner & Silverman, 2007; Purtha, Coppins, Smalley, & Silverman, 2005). Currently, the best deoxyribozyme for this purpose is called 9DB1*, which is in the focus of the present protocol. The specificity for ligation of the target RNA fragments is ensured by Watson–Crick base-pairing to the binding arms that are part of the deoxyribozyme. The mild reaction conditions used in DNA-catalyzed ligations prevent chemical damage to sensitive labels or reporters in either of the RNA fragments to be joined.

In this chapter, we provide a general description for the synthesis of spin-labeled RNA with convertible nucleosides and general RNA ligation using the DNA enzyme 9DB1*. Finally, as an applied example, we give a detailed protocol for the synthesis of spin-labeled SAM-I riboswitch RNA.

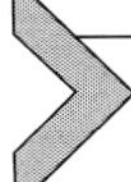

2. SYNTHESIS OF SPIN-LABELED RNA USING CONVERTIBLE NUCLEOSIDES

Paramagnetic labels for EPR spectroscopy can be introduced into RNA by various synthetic strategies. In general, three types of labeling schemes can be distinguished (Shelke & Sigurdsson, 2012). First, spin-labeled nucleosides can be directly incorporated during solid-phase synthesis, which has been successfully employed for various DNA oligonucleotides, but is more challenging for the synthesis of RNA (so far there is only one example; Höbartner, Wachowius, Gophane, & Sigurdsson, 2012). The second approach includes postsynthetic labeling schemes of prefunctionalized nucleosides, involving bioorthogonal reactions such as amide bond formation, disulfide or thioether formation, or dipolar cycloadditions (Shelke & Sigurdsson, 2012). The third strategy uses noncovalent binding of spin-labeled moieties at defined sites in structured DNA or RNA (Shelke, Sandholt, & Sigurdsson, 2014; Shelke & Sigurdsson, 2010). Several excellent recent reviews summarize the diverse approaches to install spin labels at the nucleobase, at the ribose or at the phosphate backbone of DNA or RNA (Krstic et al., 2012; Shelke & Sigurdsson, 2012). Here, we describe the postsynthetic substitution of convertible nucleosides. This reliable and generally applicable method has been used for the synthesis of spin-labeled SAM-I riboswitch RNA, which is in the focus of this protocol.

Convertible nucleoside phosphoramidite building blocks that contain activated substituents at either position 4 of uridine, or positions 2 or 6 of purine nucleosides, enable the synthesis of spin-labeled N^4-substituted cytidines, N^6-subsituted adenosines, or N^2-substituted guanosines (Fig. 4.1;

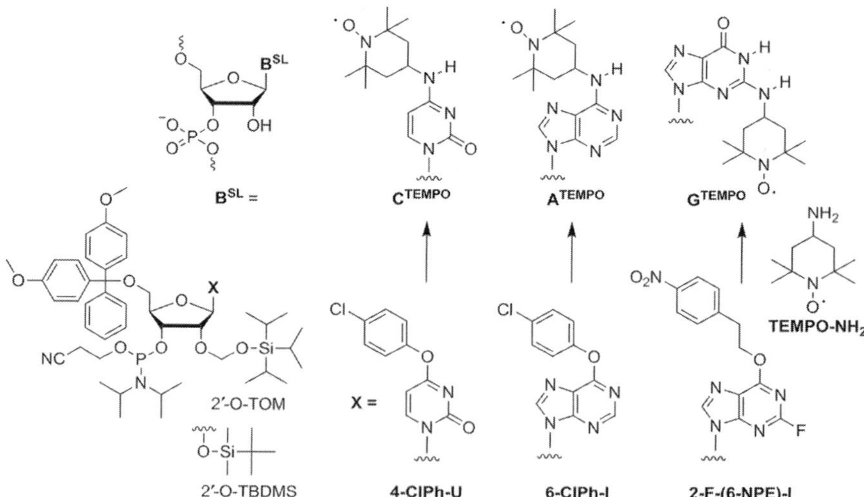

Figure 4.1 Spin-labeled nucleosides N^4-TEMPO-cytidine, N^6-TEMPO-adenosine, and N^2-TEMPO-guanosine in synthetic RNA, generated upon substitution of the convertible nucleosides O^4-(4-chlorphenyl)uridine, O^6-(4-chlorophenyl)inosine, or 2-fluoroinosine with 4-amino-TEMPO.

Allerson et al., 1997). The most common convertible nucleoside is O^4-(4-chlorophenyl)uridine, which yields N^4-TEMPO-cytidine upon substitution with TEMPO-amine in RNA (Sicoli, Wachowius, Bennati, & Höbartner, 2010). Alternatively, the five-membered ring nitroxide analog TPA-amine has also been used (Büttner, Seikowski, Wawrzyniak, Ochmann, & Höbartner, 2013). The substitution reaction is carried out during the deprotection of the nucleobase and phosphate-protecting groups under alkaline conditions. The amine of interest (here 4-amino-TEMPO) is provided as a concentrated methanolic solution, and substitution reactions are performed at elevated temperatures (45–55 °C) for at least 24 h. Alternative leaving groups on position 4 of pyrimidine nucleosides are triazole or tetrazole moieties, which can also be substituted with primary amines. Analogously, O^6-(4-chlorophenyl)inosine leads to N^6-TEMPO-adenosine upon reaction with TEMPO-NH_2 (Sicoli et al., 2010). It should be noted that the substitution reaction to adenosine proceeds more slowly and requires prolonged incubation times. The synthesis of N^2-TEMPO-labeled guanosine is best achieved using 2-fluoroinosine as the convertible nucleoside, a strategy that has been described for labeling of DNA and of RNA (Sicoli et al., 2008, 2010).

An important advantage of postsynthetic labeling is the fact that the paramagnetic group is not exposed to any reaction conditions that could potentially lead to degradation of the label (loss of radical), such as during standard detritylation and/or oxidation conditions encountered in solid-phase synthesis. The 2′-TBDMS-protected convertible nucleoside phosphoramidites and TEMPO-NH_2 are commercially available, which make the synthesis of TEMPO-labeled RNA easily accessible. Alternatively, 2′-TOM-protected convertible uridine phosphoramidite can be readily prepared in five steps from uridine (Büttner et al., 2013).

In contrast to DNA, there is an important practical consideration for the synthesis of TEMPO-labeled RNA with the convertible nucleoside approach. While DNA can be treated repeatedly with TEMPO-NH_2, in case the substitution was not complete in the first step, repeated incubation is not possible for RNA oligonucleotides. Analysis is difficult when the 2′-protecting groups (TOM or TBDMS) are still on, and a fully deprotected RNA cannot be treated with the methanolic amine solutions, as the alkaline conditions will lead to transesterification and cleavage of the phosphodiester backbone. It is therefore important to choose the substitution conditions such that the reaction is complete before proceeding to cleavage of the 2′-protecting groups. For short RNA (<25 nt), it is possible to separate minor amounts of unlabeled byproducts by gel electrophoresis or anion exchange chromatography. In contrast, obtaining fully labeled longer RNAs in high quality is challenging by direct chemical synthesis. Ligation methods are, therefore, needed to join purified spin-labeled short fragments into larger RNAs of interest.

3. DNA-CATALYZED LIGATION OF RNA USING 9DB1*

Deoxyribozymes are synthetic, single-stranded DNAs with the ability to catalyze chemical reactions (Schlosser & Li, 2009). Most practically useful DNA enzymes catalyze reactions of other nucleic acid substrates, such as cleavage or formation of phosphodiester bonds (Silverman & Baum, 2009). The general architecture of a deoxyribozyme includes a catalytic core sequence of 15–60 nt flanked by two binding arms for hybridization with the nucleic acid substrate(s). Several DNA catalysts that can efficiently catalyze the covalent ligation of RNA fragments have been identified by *in vitro* selection in the Silverman Laboratory (Silverman, 2009). The 9DB1 deoxyribozyme (Purtha et al., 2005), catalyzes the formation of a native 3′–5′ phosphodiester bond between two RNA fragments, namely a 5′-triphosphorylated donor RNA and the 3′-OH group of an acceptor RNA. Our recent studies by combinatorial mutation interference analysis resulted in the minimized version called 9DB1* (Fig. 4.2; Wachowius & Höbartner, 2011; Wachowius, Javadi-Zarnaghi, & Höbartner, 2010), which is a general catalyst for the ligation of various labeled and unmodified RNA substrates.

The 9DB1* (and the original 9DB1) deoxyribozyme joins two RNA sequences that match the D|RA sequence motif at the ligation site (D = A, G, or U; R = A or G; Purtha et al., 2005). The choice of the ligation site in a target RNA, therefore, requires identification of such a motif within the sequence. In case a D | RA motif is not present, in many cases it is possible to generate an appropriate ligation junction by functionally silent mutations, such as in unpaired regions that are not expected to be involved in tertiary interactions, or by introducing compensatory base-pair mutations in a stem. In all cases where mutations are introduced, it is important to check the functionality of the RNA variant in appropriate biochemical assays. The binding arms of the deoxyribozyme are then designed as complementary to at least 10-nt upstream and downstream of the ligation junction. In addition, it may be advisable that the ligation junction is chosen at least 3 nt downstream of the spin-labeled nucleotide. (We have not tested any ligation

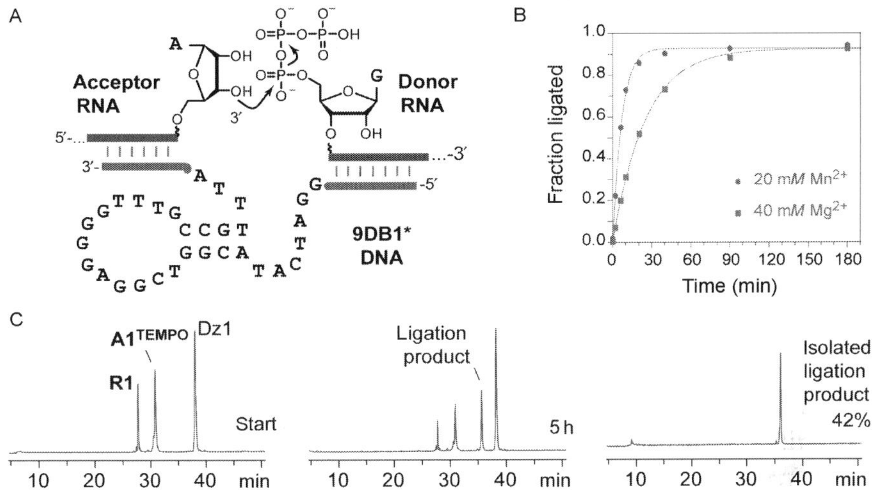

Figure 4.2 DNA-catalyzed RNA ligation by deoxyribozyme 9DB1*. (A) Acceptor and donor RNA hybridize to the binding arms via Watson–Crick base pairing. The 3′-terminal acceptor nucleotide and the 5′-terminal triphosphorylated donor nucleotide remain unpaired. The DNA sequence of the catalytic core is given. (B) Example of ligation kinetic analysis of unmodified acceptor and donor RNA under single-turnover conditions in the presence of 20 m*M* Mn^{2+} at pH 7.5 ($k_{obs}=0.15$ min^{-1}) and 40 m*M* Mg^{2+} at pH 9.0 ($k_{obs}=0.04$ min^{-1}). (C) Anion exchange HPLC traces for the analysis of preparative ligation of spin-labeled acceptor RNA A1 with donor R1 using 9DB1* (Dz1) before ligation (left), after 5 h incubation (middle), and analysis of isolated spin-labeled ligation product (right). Sequences (5′–3′ direction): R1 pppGACCUCGCAUCGUG, A1 GACGUC^{TEMPO}GGAA GACGUCAGUA, Dz1 *CACGATGCGA GGT*GGATCAT ACGGTCGGAG GGGTTTGCCG TTTA*ACTGAC GTCTTCCGAC* (binding arms in italics). *Figure adapted from data reported in Büttner et al. (2013).*

junction directly adjacent to spin-labeled nucleotides, but reduced ligation efficiency can be expected if the spin-label interferes with productive orientation of the RNA termini in the active site of the deoxyribozyme). In general, we recommend that analytical-scale screening of ligation conditions be performed (according to the protocol given below) to determine the optimal ligation site for the RNA of interest.

Especially for long RNA substrates that might be susceptible to degradation at higher pH, it is advantageous to perform RNA ligation reactions at pH 7.5. The original ligation conditions for the 9DB1 deoxyribozyme used 40 m*M* Mg^{2+} at pH 9.0 and 37 °C. During characterization and minimization of 9DB1, we demonstrated that the ligation is equally efficient and slightly faster when the Mg^{2+} cofactor is replaced by Mn^{2+} and the pH reduced to 7.5 (Fig. 4.2B). Besides the smaller size of the minimized deoxyribozyme, and therefore better folding properties, the optimized reaction conditions are key benefits of using 9DB1*. Furthermore, a major advantage of deoxyribozymes compared to protein enzymes for the ligation of spin-labeled substrates is the sole requirement for divalent metal ions as cofactors and the complete absence of a reducing agent, such as DTT. We recently compared the ligation of spin-labeled RNAs with T4 DNA ligase and deoxyribozyme 9DB1* (Büttner et al., 2013). Reactions catalyzed by the protein enzyme generated a number of undesired byproducts, including a reduced tetramethylpiperidine substituent (degradation product of TEMPO). We note that T4 DNA ligase can, in principle, also be used in a DTT-free reaction buffer; nevertheless, the concentration of DTT that is used in the storage buffer of the enzyme was sufficient to complicate the purification of high-quality spin-labeled RNA. In contrast, the ligation reaction with 9DB1* proceeded very cleanly and produced spin-labeled ligation products in high quality and good yield. Figure 4.2C shows an example for anion exchange HPLC analysis of a preparative DNA-catalyzed ligation reaction. TEMPO-labeled acceptor RNA A1 was ligated to 5′-triphosphorylated donor RNA R1 using the 9DB1* deoxyribozyme Dz1. The RNA fragments and the deoxyribozyme were annealed in equimolar ratio at a concentration of 20 μ*M*. Upon addition of 20 m*M* $MnCl_2$, the reaction solution was incubated at pH 7.5 (50 m*M* HEPES, 150 m*M* NaCl, 2 m*M* KCl) at 37 °C for 5 h. The spin-labeled ligation product was isolated by denaturing PAGE in 42% yield, and analyzed by anion exchange chromatography, mass spectrometry (MS), and continuous-wave EPR spectroscopy.

3.1. General protocol for DNA-catalyzed RNA ligation on analytical scale for testing ligation sites and screening of ligation conditions

Analytical assays of 9DB1*-catalyzed ligation kinetics are performed under single-turnover conditions with 5′-^{32}P-labeled acceptor RNA, *in vitro*-transcribed donor RNA and corresponding deoxyribozyme in a ratio of 1:10:5 with 1 μ*M* deoxyribozyme. Reactions are performed individually in the presence of 20 m*M* Mn^{2+} (pH 7.5) and 40 m*M* Mg^{2+} (pH 9.0) to determine optimal ligation conditions for a particular set of RNA substrates.

3.1.1 Reagents

- 5′-^{32}P-labeled acceptor RNA,
- *In vitro*-transcribed donor RNA,

- 9DB1* deoxyribozyme with binding arms complementary to the RNA substrates,
- 10 × Annealing buffer (50 m*M* HEPES, pH 7.5, 150 m*M* NaCl, 1 m*M* EDTA),
- 5 × Ligation buffer A (250 m*M* HEPES, pH 7.5, 750 m*M* NaCl, 10 m*M* KCl),
- 5 × Ligation buffer B (250 m*M* CHES, pH 9.0, 750 m*M* NaCl, 10 m*M* KCl),
- 10 × Mn^{2+} solution (200 m*M* $MnCl_2$),
- 10 × Mg^{2+} solution (400 m*M* $MgCl_2$),
- Stop solution (80% formamide, 1 × TB (89 m*M* each Tris and boric acid, pH 8.3), 50 m*M* EDTA and 0.025% bromophenol blue and xylene cyanol).

3.1.2 Procedure

2 pmol of 5′-^{32}P-labeled acceptor RNA, 10 pmol of 9DB1* deoxyribozyme, and 20 pmol of *in vitro*-transcribed donor RNA are annealed in 5 m*M* HEPES, pH 7.5, 15 m*M* NaCl, and 0.1 m*M* EDTA (final volume 7 μl) by heating at 95 °C for 2 min and incubation at room temperature for 15 min after removing the tubes from the heat block. Ligation reactions are initiated by the addition of 2 μl of ligation buffer A and 1 μl of 10 × Mn^{2+} solution or 2 μl of ligation buffer B and 1 μl of 10 × Mg^{2+}. Reaction mixtures are incubated at 37 °C for 5 h. At selected time points (0, 2, 10, 30, 60, 120, 180, 300 [min]), 1 μl aliquots are withdrawn and quenched in 3 μl stop solution. Samples are resolved by denaturing PAGE (10–20% acrylamide, depending on length of RNA). The gel is dried under vacuum (at 80 °C for 30 min), exposed to a Phosphor storage screen and the scanned image is analyzed by ImageQuant (Molecular Dynamics). The ligation yield is determined by volume integration, and the yield versus time data are fitted to the first-order kinetics equation: ligation yield $= Y(1 - e^{-kt})$, where $k = k_{obs}$ and $Y =$ final yield.

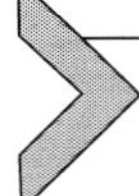

4. PROTOCOLS FOR SYNTHESIS OF SPIN-LABELED SAM-I RIBOSWITCH

DNA-catalyzed ligation is a general approach that can be applied for the preparation of any spin-labeled target RNA. This section provides a detailed protocol for the preparation of TEMPO-labeled riboswitch RNA. We chose the 118-mer *yitJ* SAM-I riboswitch domain of *Bacillus subtilis* as an example (Fig. 4.3; Heppell et al., 2011). This long, spin-labeled

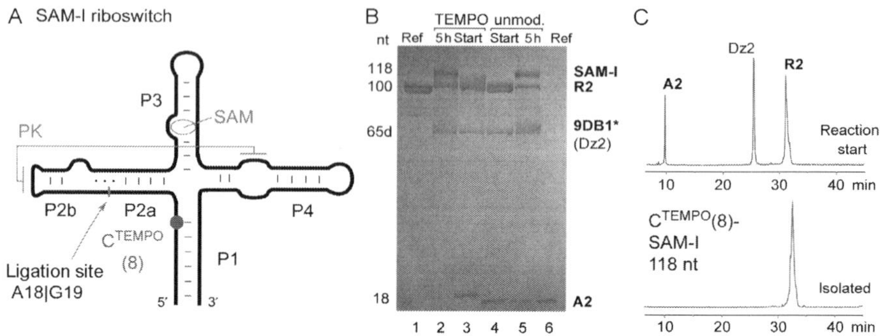

Figure 4.3 Synthesis of spin-labeled riboswitch RNA. (A) Schematic depiction of spin-labeled SAM-I riboswitch with C^{TEMPO} at position 8, generated via ligation between A18 and G19. (B) Gel image of ligation reaction: lane 1, reference of donor substrate R2 (100 nt); lanes 2 and 3, ligation of spin-labeled A2 and 5′-triphosphorylated R2 (5 h and start); lanes 4 and 5, unmodified comparison (start and 5 h); lane 6, reference of acceptor substrate A2 (18 nt). Full-length ligated SAM-I riboswitch (118 nt) is visible as a top band in lanes 2 and 5. (C) Anion exchange HPLC analysis of ligation reaction, monitored at 260 nm: initial reaction mixture containing A2, R2, and Dz2 (top), purified C^{TEMPO}-labeled SAM-I riboswitch (bottom). *Figure adapted from data reported in Büttner et al. (2013).*

RNA was prepared via 9DB1*-DNA-catalyzed ligation of a TEMPO-labeled 18-nt synthetic RNA fragment and a 5′-triphosphorylated 100-nt donor substrate at pH 7.5 in the presence of Mn^{2+}. The TEMPO label was introduced at position C8 of the 18-nt 5′-terminal fragment (A2) using a convertible uridine phosphoramidite during solid-phase synthesis. The ligation site resided within helix P2, between nucleotides A18 and G19. The 5′-triphosphorylated donor substrate (R2) spans nt 19–118 and was generated by *in vitro* transcription from a double-stranded DNA template produced by polymerase extension of overlapping primers.

4.1. Synthesis of spin-labeled RNA (acceptor substrate)

The RNA strand A2 comprising the convertible nucleoside was prepared by oligonucleotide solid-phase synthesis on polystyrene support using 2′-O-TOM-protected, standard RNA phosphoramidites and 4-(4-chlorophenyl)uridine phosphoramidite. Standard RNA coupling conditions were employed with *S*-benzylthiotetrazole as an activator. The final 5′-dimethoxytrityl group was cleaved off. After complete assembly of the oligonucleotide sequence, the solid support was incubated with 4-amino-TEMPO for installation of the spin label. The modified RNA was then further deprotected, purified, and analyzed by HPLC and ESI-MS.

A detailed procedure for TEMPO spin-label installation and RNA oligonucleotide deprotection is provided.

4.1.1 Reagents

- O^4-(4-chlorophenyl)-5′-*O*-(4,4′-dimethoxytrityl (DMT))-2′-*O*-triisopropylsilyloxymethyl (TOM) uridine 3′-cyanoethyl diisopropylphosphoramidite and 5′-*O*-DMT-2′-*O*-TOM-protected 3′-cyanoethyl diisopropylphosphoramidites of N^6-acetyladenosine, N^4-acetylcytidine, N^2-acetylguanosine, and uridine (each as fresh 100 m*M* solution in acetonitrile, dried over molecular sieves),
- 0.25 *M S*-benzylthiotetrazol in acetonitrile,
- Standard solid-phase synthesis reagents: Deblock solution (3% dichloroacetic acid in 1,2-dichloroethane), Cap A (0.5 *M N,N*-dimethylaminopyridine in acetonitrile), Cap B (acetic anhydride/sym-collidine/acetonitrile = 3:2:5), oxidation (10 m*M* iodine in acetonitrile/sym-collidine/water = 10/1/5),
- 2 *M* 4-Amino-TEMPO in methanol,
- NH_4OH (25% aq),
- 1 *M* TBAF in THF,
- 1 *M* Tris–HCl, pH 8.0,
- 20% Polyacrylamide gel (acrylamide:bisacrylamide 19:1), 0.07 × 20 × 30 cm,
- TBE buffer (89 m*M* Tris, 89 m*M* boric acid, 2 m*M* EDTA, pH 8.0),
- Gel-loading buffer (80% formamide, 1 × TB (89 m*M* each Tris and boric acid, pH 8.3), 50 m*M* EDTA, and 0.025% bromophenol blue and xylene cyanol),
- TEN extraction buffer (10 m*M* Tris–HCl, pH 8.0, 300 m*M* NaCl, 1 m*M* EDTA),
- Ethanol abs.,
- HPLC buffers: A (25 m*M* Tris–HCl, pH 8.0, 6 *M* urea) and B (25 m*M* Tris–HCl, pH 8.0, 6 *M* urea, 0.5 *M* $NaClO_4$),
- Dionex DNAPAc PA200 column, 4 × 250 mm.

4.1.2 Procedure

The oligonucleotide 5′-UUCUUAUXAAGAGAAGCA (X = 4-chlorophenyl-U) is assembled on rA-containing polystyrene solid support using 2′-*O*-TOM-protected RNA phosphoramidites at 100 m*M* in dry acetonitrile and standard solid-phase synthesis conditions, according to the available instrument. We use a Pharmacia Gene Assembler Plus or an ABI 394 synthesizer and prefer 4 min coupling time for RNA building blocks.

After completion of the synthesis, the solid support containing the fully protected RNA (ca. 0.3 μmol) is incubated with 120 μl of 2 *M* 4-amino-TEMPO in methanol at 45 °C for 24 h. After centrifugation, the supernatant is removed and the solid support is washed with ethanol. 500 μl of NH_4OH (25% aq) is added and the mixture is incubated in a tightly closed vial at 55 °C for 5 h. The solid support is subsequently removed by filtration and the solution is evaporated to dryness. The residue is dissolved in 500 μl of 1 *M* TBAF in THF and incubated at room temperature for 16 h to cleave the 2′-*O*-TOM groups. The reaction is quenched by the addition of 500 μl of aqueous buffer (1 *M* Tris–HCl, pH 8.0), and THF is removed under reduced pressure. The sample is applied on a Sephadex G10 size-exclusion column (HiTrap desalting column, 3 × 5 ml in series) and eluted with water. The desalting process is monitored by recording UV absorbance at 280 nm and conductivity. The collected eluate is concentrated to provide the crude product, which can be stored at −20 °C.

Oligonucleotide purification is performed by PAGE on 20% polyacrylamide gel (acrylamide:bisacrylamide 19:1) containing 7 *M* urea in 1 × TBE buffer. The RNA sample is mixed with gel-loading buffer, loaded into the well, and the gel is run at 35 W. Bands are detected by UV shadowing, extracted by the "crush and soak" method using TEN buffer and recovered by ethanol precipitation as described previously (Sicoli et al., 2010). The quality of the spin-labeled RNA product is analyzed by anion exchange HPLC (with 6 *M* urea at 70 °C) and by ESI-MS.

4.2. *In vitro* transcription of donor substrate

In vitro transcription is performed with T7 RNA polymerase and double-stranded DNA template containing T7 RNA polymerase promoter, according to the standard protocol (Milligan, Groebe, Witherell, & Uhlenbeck, 1987). Double-stranded DNA used as a template is produced by polymerase extension of overlapping primers. Synthetic single-stranded DNA template comprising T7 RNA promoter complement and synthetic T7 RNA promoter can be employed for the preparation of shorter RNA targets.

4.2.1 Reagents

- Double-stranded DNA template comprising T7 RNA polymerase promoter (sequence of template strand is 5′-TTCTTATCTT

CCAAGCTGTT CGAGCTTGCT GGATTTAGCA CCTTGGTCAT GGCTGATCGC CATTACACCG GTTGCTGAAG CTTCGTCGGG CCAGTCCCTC *TATAGTGAGT CGTATTACAG*-3′, T7 RNA polymerase promoter in italics),

- Buffers and reagents (1 *M* Tris–HCl, pH 8.0, 1 *M* $MgCl_2$, 250 m*M* DTT, and 100 m*M* spermidine),
- Transcription annealing buffer 10× (40 m*M* Tris–HCl, pH 8.0, 150 m*M* NaCl, 1 m*M* EDTA),
- 100 m*M* each ATP, CTP, GTP, and UTP,
- T7 RNA polymerase,
- 0.5 *M* EDTA pH 8.0,
- 10% PAGE for purification.

4.2.2 Procedure

100 pmol of double-stranded DNA template, or 100 pmol of single-stranded DNA template and 100 pmol of synthetic T7 RNA promoter strand, is annealed in the presence of 4 m*M* Tris–HCl pH 8.0, 15 m*M* NaCl, and 0.1 m*M* EDTA in a final volume of 50 μl by heating at 95 °C for 2 min and incubation at room temperature for at least 15 min after removing the tube from the heat block. Following addition of buffer and NTPs to a final concentration of 40 m*M* Tris–HCl pH 8.0, 30 m*M* $MgCl_2$, 10 m*M* DTT, 2 m*M* spermidine, and 4 m*M* of each NTP in 100 μl final volume, 2 μl of T7 RNA polymerase (we use home-made enzyme, but T7 RNAP is also commercially available) is added and the reaction is incubated at 37 °C for 5 h. Afterwards the reaction is quenched by the addition of 20 μl EDTA (0.5 *M*) and 50 μl of gel loading buffer. The product is purified by 10% denaturing PAGE.

4.3. Preparative DNA-catalyzed ligation of SAM-I RNA fragments

The ligation of spin-labeled acceptor RNA and *in vitro*-transcribed donor RNA is performed on a 1.5 nmol scale using equimolar ratio of RNA substrates and deoxyribozyme. The reaction is incubated for 5 h in the presence of Mn^{2+} cofactor at pH 7.5. The ligation progress is monitored by anion exchange HPLC or denaturing PAGE (Fig. 4.3B). The ligation product is purified by gel electrophoresis, and the deoxyribozyme can also be isolated and re-used.

4.3.1 Reagents

- Spin-labeled acceptor RNA A2 (5′-UUCUUAU**C**$^{\mathbf{TEMPO}}$AAGAGAAGCA-3′),
- *In vitro*-transcribed donor RNA R2 (5′ppp-GAGGGACUGG CCCGACGAAG CUUCAGCAAC CGGUGUAAUG GCGAUCAGCC AUGACCAAGG UGCUAAAUCC AGCAAGCUCG AACAGCUUGG AAGAUAAGAA-3′),
- 9DB1 mini deoxyribozyme Dz2 (5′-*GCTTCGTCGG CCAGTCCCT*G GATCATACGG TCGGAGGGGT TTGCCGTTTA *GCTTCTCTTG ATAAG*-3′, binding arms in italics),
- 10 × Annealing buffer (50 m*M* HEPES, pH 7.5, 150 m*M* NaCl, 1 m*M* EDTA),
- 5 × Ligation buffer A (250 m*M* HEPES, pH 7.5, 750 m*M* NaCl, 10 m*M* KCl),
- 10 × Mn^{2+} solution (200 m*M* $MnCl_2$).

4.3.2 Procedure

1.5 nmol of spin-labeled acceptor RNA A2, *in vitro*-transcribed donor RNA R2, and 9DB1* DNA Dz2 are annealed in a volume of 70 μl in the presence of 5 m*M* HEPES, pH 7.5, 15 m*M* NaCl, and 0.1 m*M* EDTA by heating at 95 °C for 2 min and incubation at room temperature for 15 min as above. The ligation reaction buffer and divalent metal ion are added from 10 × and 5 × concentrated stock solutions, respectively. Following the addition of 20 μl of 5 × concentrated ligation buffer and 10 μl of 200 m*M* $MnCl_2$, the reaction mixture is incubated at 37 °C for 5 h. The reaction is then quenched by 10 μl 0.5 *M* EDTA and ethanol precipitated by the addition of cold ethanol (3 vol). The ligated product is purified on 15% denaturing polyacrylamide gel.

The ligation progress can be monitored by HPLC analysis or gel electrophoresis. In either case, an aliquot containing 100 pmol of the target RNA is withdrawn from the reaction mixture before ligation initiation and after 5 h. The full-length, ligated, spin-labeled RNA product will appear as a top band on a gel or as a peak with the longest retention time on HPLC profile. The ligation yield can be calculated from the peak area monitored by UV absorbance at 260 nm (taking into account the different extinction coefficients of fragments and ligation product). Typically 60–80% conversion is obtained under preparative conditions. The isolated yields are generally lower due to incomplete recovery of long RNAs from gel slices. Under the above described conditions, the full-length spin-labeled SAM-I riboswitch

RNA was isolated in 30% yield, analyzed, and further characterized by anion exchange HPLC and EPR spectroscopy.

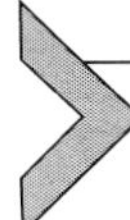

5. GENERAL CONSIDERATIONS AND FUTURE DEVELOPMENTS

This section lists some critical parameters for successful synthesis of long-labeled RNA and meaningful biophysical studies and discusses further efforts needed for the development of spin labels and deoxyribozymes for RNA ligation.

5.1. Choice of label position

Any label or reporter group that is bulkier or has different functional groups than natural nucleosides can cause variations of structure, dynamics, or function of the target RNA. It is, therefore, imperative that RNA folding is checked by more than one method for any synthetic RNA that is used for biophysical or structural studies (Ahmed & Ficner, 2014). Various labeling sites along the RNA sequence should be considered, and spectroscopic data should be obtained and analyzed from labels/reporter groups installed at different positions (Esquiaqui, Sherman, Ionescu, Ye, & Fanucci, 2014).

5.2. Number and type of labels

EPR spectroscopy of single-labeled RNA samples provides information on RNA dynamics in the vicinity of the label and can be used to monitor alterations upon environmental changes due to factors such as ligand binding or interaction with metal ions. Conformational changes that lead to larger rearrangements or domain reorganization can be detected by measuring distances or distance changes between two nitroxide labels by pulsed EPR experiments (pulsed electron double resonance (PELDOR), double electron–electron resonance (DEER); Reginsson & Schiemann, 2011b). It is worth noting that EPR can provide accurate distance distributions using the same label twice within the RNA of interest. For example, two (same or different) convertible nucleosides can be incorporated during solid-phase synthesis and subsequently be substituted in a single step with one type of nitroxide. In contrast, fluorescence resonance energy transfer (FRET) experiments (which can yield information on intramolecular distances of comparable range as PELDOR (~2–8 nm)) require two different reporter groups, namely a fluorescence donor and an acceptor dye or quencher.

In addition to distance information, modern EPR techniques can reveal relative orientations of nitroxides within a molecule or macromolecular complex (Reginsson & Schiemann, 2011a; Tkach et al., 2013). These experiments require the spin labels to be rigidly attached to the labeling site without any rotational freedom around single bonds. Rigid spin labels for nucleic acids have so far only been reported for cytidine (Barhate, Cekan, Massey, & Sigurdsson, 2007; Höbartner et al., 2012), but are also desirable for purine nucleosides. Other important developments target the synthesis of new spin labels with longer half-lives in cellular environment, which will be highly advantageous for in-cell EPR studies (Azarkh et al., 2013; Hänsel, Luh, Corbeski, Trantirek, & Dötsch, 2014).

5.3. Position and sequence context of ligation junction

The choice of ligation sites is constrained by the nucleotide preferences of 9DB1* (for ligation at D|RA as discussed earlier, Section 3). In practice, the donor RNA will preferably be initiated with 5′-GA for high transcription yields (initiation with 5′-AA is possible with an alternative T7 promoter, Coleman, Wang, & Huang, 2004, but in our hands transcription yields are often not as high as with 5′-GA).

If more than one reporter group is introduced, the ligation junction needs to be chosen downstream of all modifications. In other words, site-specific labels can only be introduced into the acceptor RNA, because the donor RNA has to provide a 5′-triphosphate as electrophile. Although chemical methods for 5′-triphosphate synthesis have been described (Burgess & Cook, 2000; Zlatev et al., 2010), the synthesis of spin-labeled RNA with 5′-triphosphate has not yet been demonstrated. Combination of spin labeling via convertible nucleoside and solid-phase synthesis of triphosphates is expected to be challenging.

To overcome this limitation, deoxyribozymes are required that can use alternative, chemically activated donor substrates for the formation of native 3′–5′ phosphodiester bonds. Such DNA catalysts are yet to be developed. *In vitro* selection experiments along these lines are currently in progress in our laboratory. Attractive substrates include 5′,5′-linked adenylates or 5′-phosphorimidazolides as electrophiles, which have been used by other deoxyribozymes for the synthesis of 2′,5′-branched nucleic acids or RNA-peptide conjugates (Brandsen, Velez, Sachdeva, Ibrahim, & Silverman, 2014; Lee, Mui, & Silverman, 2011). A set of new deoxyribozymes is expected to enable ligation at even more diverse junctions than currently accessible, including pyrimidines as 5′-terminal donor nucleosides.

5.4. Alternative DNA-catalyzed approaches for site-specific labeling of RNA

Besides catalyzing linear RNA ligations, deoxyribozymes can also activate internal 2′-OH groups of ribonucleotides for reaction with 5′-triphosphates, resulting in the formation of 2′,5′-branched RNA. The binding arms are designed to guide the deoxyribozyme to the desired labeling position by hybridization directly upstream and downstream of the target nucleoside. In an approach termed DNA-catalyzed labeling of RNA, 17-nt-long tagging RNAs were ligated to the RNA of interest (Baum & Silverman, 2007). Recently, a general and versatile, DNA-catalyzed labeling strategy was described that allows ribose-labeled mononucleotides to be site-specifically attached at desired adenosine nucleotides within *in vitro*-transcribed RNA. Fluorescent, spin-labeled, biotinylated, or crosslinker-modified guanosine triphosphates were efficiently installed in up to 160-nt-long functional RNAs (Büttner, Javadi-Zarnaghi, & Höbartner, 2014). Because long, native, or *in vitro*-transcribed RNA can be directly used for this labeling approach, preparation and ligation of RNA fragments can be avoided. So far, adenosines are the only type of internal nucleotides that can be targeted with this strategy, but deoxyribozymes for analogous labeling reactions at other internal nucleotides (guanosines, cytidines, or uridines) are expected from ongoing and future *in vitro* selection experiments. This will further broaden the general applicability of deoxyribozymes for post-transcriptional labeling of RNAs.

ACKNOWLEDGMENTS

This work was supported by the International Research Training Grant (IRTG1422) Metal Sites in Biomolecules, the Cluster of Excellence and DFG Research Centre for Nanoscale Microscopy and Molecular Physiology of the Brain, and the Max Planck Society.

REFERENCES

Ahmed, Y. L., & Ficner, R. (2014). RNA synthesis and purification for structural studies. *RNA Biology*, *11*, 427–432.

Allerson, C. R., Chen, S. L., & Verdine, G. L. (1997). a chemical method for site-specific modification of RNA: The convertible nucleoside approach. *Journal of the American Chemical Society*, *119*, 7423–7433.

Azarkh, M., Singh, V., Okle, O., Seemann, I. T., Dietrich, D. R., Hartig, J. S., et al. (2013). Site-directed spin-labeling of nucleotides and the use of in-cell EPR to determine long-range distances in a biologically relevant environment. *Nature Protocols*, *8*, 131–147.

Barhate, N., Cekan, P., Massey, A. P., & Sigurdsson, S. T. (2007). A nucleoside that contains a rigid nitroxide spin label: A fluorophore in disguise. *Angewandte Chemie, International Edition*, *46*, 2655–2658.

Baum, D. A., & Silverman, S. K. (2007). Deoxyribozyme-catalyzed labeling of RNA. *Angewandte Chemie, International Edition*, *46*, 3502–3504.

Brandsen, B. M., Velez, T. E., Sachdeva, A., Ibrahim, N. A., & Silverman, S. K. (2014). DNA-catalyzed lysine side chain modification. *Angewandte Chemie, International Edition*, *53*, 9045–9050.

Burgess, K., & Cook, D. (2000). Syntheses of nucleoside triphosphates. *Chemical Reviews*, *100*, 2047–2060.

Büttner, L., Javadi-Zarnaghi, F., & Höbartner, C. (2014). Site-specific labeling of RNA at internal ribose hydroxyl groups: Terbium-assisted deoxyribozymes at work. *Journal of the American Chemical Society*, *136*, 8131–8137.

Büttner, L., Seikowski, J., Wawrzyniak, K., Ochmann, A., & Höbartner, C. (2013). Synthesis of spin-labeled riboswitch RNAs using convertible nucleosides and DNA-catalyzed RNA ligation. *Bioorganic and Medicinal Chemistry*, *21*, 6171–6180.

Carlomagno, T. (2014). Present and future of NMR for RNA–protein complexes: A perspective of integrated structural biology. *Journal of Magnetic Resonance*, *241*, 126–136.

Coleman, T. M., Wang, G., & Huang, F. (2004). Superior 5′ homogeneity of RNA from ATP-initiated transcription under the T7 phi 2.5 promoter. *Nucleic Acids Research*, *32*, e14.

Ding, P., Wunnicke, D., Steinhoff, H. J., & Seela, F. (2010). Site-directed spin-labeling of DNA by the azide-alkyne 'click' reaction: Nanometer distance measurements on 7-deaza-2′-deoxyadenosine and 2′-deoxyuridine nitroxide conjugates spatially separated or linked to a 'dA–dT' base pair. *Chemistry*, *16*, 14385–14396.

Edwards, T. E., & Sigurdsson, S. T. (2007). Site-specific incorporation of nitroxide spin-labels into 2′-positions of nucleic acids. *Nature Protocols*, *2*, 1954–1962.

Esquiaqui, J. M., Sherman, E. M., Ionescu, S. A., Ye, J. D., & Fanucci, G. E. (2014). Characterizing the dynamics of the leader–linker interaction in the glycine riboswitch with site-directed spin labeling. *Biochemistry*, *53*, 3526–3528.

Frilander, M. J., & Turunen, J. J. (2008). RNA ligation using T4 DNA ligase. In R. K. Hartmann, A. Bindereif, A. Schön, & E. Westhof (Eds.), *Handbook of RNA biochemistry* (pp. 36–52). Weinheim, Germany: Wiley-VCH Verlag GmbH.

Hänsel, R., Luh, L. M., Corbeski, I., Trantirek, L., & Dötsch, V. (2014). In-cell NMR and EPR spectroscopy of biomacromolecules. *Angewandte Chemie, International Edition*, *53*, 10300–10314.

Heppell, B., Blouin, S., Dussault, A. M., Mulhbacher, J., Ennifar, E., Penedo, J. C., et al. (2011). Molecular insights into the ligand-controlled organization of the SAM-I riboswitch. *Nature Chemical Biology*, 7, 384–392.

Höbartner, C., Sicoli, G., Wachowius, F., Gophane, D. B., & Sigurdsson, S. T. (2012). Synthesis and characterization of RNA containing a rigid and non-perturbing cytidine-derived spin label. *Journal of Organic Chemistry*, 77, 7749–7754.

Höbartner, C., & Silverman, S. K. (2007). Recent advances in DNA catalysis. *Biopolymers*, *87*, 279–292.

Jakobsen, U., Shelke, S. A., Vogel, S., & Sigurdsson, S. T. (2010). Site-directed spin-labeling of nucleic acids by click chemistry: Detection of a basic sites in duplex DNA by EPR spectroscopy. *Journal of the American Chemical Society*, *132*, 10424–10428.

Krstic, I., Endeward, B., Margraf, D., Marko, A., & Prisner, T. F. (2012). Structure and dynamics of nucleic acids. *Topics in Current Chemistry*, *321*, 159–198.

Lang, K., & Micura, R. (2008). The preparation of site-specifically modified riboswitch domains as an example for enzymatic ligation of chemically synthesized RNA fragments. *Nature Protocols*, *3*, 1457–1466.

Lee, C. S., Mui, T. P., & Silverman, S. K. (2011). Improved deoxyribozymes for synthesis of covalently branched DNA and RNA. *Nucleic Acids Research*, *39*, 269–279.

Milligan, J. F., Groebe, D. R., Witherell, G. W., & Uhlenbeck, O. C. (1987). Oligoribonucleotide synthesis using T7 RNA polymerase and synthetic DNA templates. *Nucleic Acids Research*, *15*, 8783–8798.

Persson, T., Willkomm, D. K., & Hartmann, R. K. (2005). *T4 RNA ligase* (pp. 53–74). Weinheim, Germany: Wiley-VCH.

Piton, N., Mu, Y., Stock, G., Prisner, T. F., Schiemann, O., & Engels, J. W. (2007). Base-specific spin-labeling of RNA for structure determination. *Nucleic Acids Research*, *35*, 3128–3143.

Purtha, W. E., Coppins, R. L., Smalley, M. K., & Silverman, S. K. (2005). General deoxyribozyme-catalyzed synthesis of native 3′–5′ RNA linkages. *Journal of the American Chemical Society*, *127*, 13124–13125.

Reginsson, G. W., & Schiemann, O. (2011a). Pulsed electron–electron double resonance: Beyond nanometre distance measurements on biomacromolecules. *The Biochemical Journal*, *434*, 353–363.

Reginsson, G. W., & Schiemann, O. (2011b). Studying biomolecular complexes with pulsed electron–electron double resonance spectroscopy. *Biochemical Society Transactions*, *39*, 128–139.

Schiemann, O., Piton, N., Plackmeyer, J., Bode, B. E., Prisner, T. F., & Engels, J. W. (2007). Spin labeling of oligonucleotides with the nitroxide TPA and use of PELDOR, a pulse EPR method, to measure intramolecular distances. *Nature Protocols*, *2*, 904–923.

Schlosser, K., & Li, Y. (2009). Biologically inspired synthetic enzymes made from DNA. *Chemistry and Biology*, *16*, 311–322.

Shelke, S. A., Sandholt, G. B., & Sigurdsson, S. T. (2014). Nitroxide-labeled pyrimidines for non-covalent spin-labeling of abasic sites in DNA and RNA duplexes. *Organic and Biomolecular Chemistry*, *12*, 7366–7774.

Shelke, S. A., & Sigurdsson, S. T. (2010). Noncovalent and site-directed spin labeling of nucleic acids. *Angewandte Chemie, International Edition*, *49*, 7984–7986.

Shelke, S. A., & Sigurdsson, S. T. (2012). Site-directed spin labelling of nucleic acids. *European Journal of Organic Chemistry*, *2012*, 2291–2301.

Sicoli, G., Mathis, G., Delalande, O., Boulard, Y., Gasparutto, D., & Gambarelli, S. (2008). Double electron–electron resonance (DEER): A convenient method to probe DNA conformational changes. *Angewandte Chemie, International Edition*, *47*, 735–737.

Sicoli, G., Wachowius, F., Bennati, M., & Höbartner, C. (2010). Probing secondary structures of spin-labeled RNA by pulsed EPR spectroscopy. *Angewandte Chemie, International Edition*, *49*, 6443–6447.

Silverman, S. K. (2009). Deoxyribozymes: Selection design and serendipity in the development of DNA catalysts. *Accounts of Chemical Research*, *42*, 1521–1531.

Silverman, S. K., & Baum, D. A. (2009). Use of deoxyribozymes in RNA research. *Methods in Enzymology*, *469*, 95–117.

St-Pierre, P., McCluskey, K., Shaw, E., Penedo, J. C., & Lafontaine, D. A. (2014). Fluorescence tools to investigate riboswitch structural dynamics. *Biochimica et Biophysica Acta*, *1839*, 1005–1019.

Tkach, I., Pornsuwan, S., Höbartner, C., Wachowius, F., Sigurdsson, S. T., Baranova, T. Y., et al. (2013). Orientation selection in distance measurements between nitroxide spin labels at 94 GHz EPR with variable dual frequency irradiation. *Physical Chemistry Chemical Physics*, *15*, 3433–3437.

Viollet, S., Fuchs, R. T., Munafo, D. B., Zhuang, F., & Robb, G. B. (2011). T4 RNA ligase 2 truncated active site mutants: Improved tools for RNA analysis. *BMC Biotechnology*, *11*, 72.

Wachowius, F., & Höbartner, C. (2011). Probing essential nucleobase functional groups in aptamers and deoxyribozymes by nucleotide analogue interference mapping of DNA. *Journal of the American Chemical Society*, *133*, 14888–14891.

Wachowius, F., Javadi-Zarnaghi, F., & Höbartner, C. (2010). Combinatorial mutation interference analysis reveals functional nucleotides required for DNA catalysis. *Angewandte Chemie, International Edition*, *49*, 8504–8508.

Zlatev, I., Lavergne, T., Debart, F., Vasseur, J. J., Manoharan, M., & Morvan, F. (2010). Efficient solid-phase chemical synthesis of 5′-triphosphates of DNA, RNA, and their analogues. *Organic Letters*, *12*, 2190–2193.

CHAPTER FIVE

A Flexible, Scalable Method for Preparation of Homogeneous Aminoacylated tRNAs

Jinwei Zhang, Adrian R. Ferré-D'Amaré[1]
National Heart, Lung and Blood Institute, Bethesda, Maryland, USA
[1]Corresponding author: e-mail address: adrian.ferre@nih.gov

Contents

Abstract

Transfer RNAs (tRNAs) are cellular courier molecules that decipher the genetic code in messenger RNAs and enable the transfer of appropriate esterified amino acids to the growing peptide chain. The preparation of biophysical quantities of homogeneous aminoacylated tRNAs has remained a significant technical challenge. This is primarily due to the difficulty in removing contaminating nonaminoacylated tRNAs that are have very similar properties overall, as well as the hydrolytic instability of the aminoacyl linkage. We describe a flexible, scalable method to prepare homogeneous aminoacylated tRNAs that is also broadly compatible with mutant, misacylated, or otherwise aberrant tRNAs and other RNAs. This method combines ribozyme-mediated aminoacylation with reversible N-pentenoylation of the esterified amino acid, which not only protects against spontaneous deacylation but also provides a hydrophobic purification handle. This protocol makes it straightforward to produce biophysical quantities of natural and unnatural aminoacylated tRNAs and has proven essential for mechanistic investigations of the T-box riboswitches.

1. INTRODUCTION

Transfer RNAs (tRNAs) are cellular noncoding RNAs that carry out essential adaptor functions during protein synthesis. Working in

Methods in Enzymology, Volume 549
ISSN 0076-6879
http://dx.doi.org/10.1016/B978-0-12-801122-5.00005-2

conjunction with aminoacyl-tRNA synthetases (aaRSs) that covalently attach appropriate amino acids to their 3′ termini, tRNAs serve as an information conduit and structural medium that converts the genetic information in trinucleotide units (or codons) into amino acid sequences, which prescribe the structure and function of cellular proteins (Banerjee et al., 2010). Beside their canonical roles in translation, it is increasingly apparent that tRNAs have evolved to execute a wide range of noncanonical cellular functions in transcriptional regulation, posttranslational protein modification, cellular signal transduction, stress response, etc., (Geslain & Pan, 2011; Phizicky & Hopper, 2010).

The availability of highly purified components is a prerequisite for quantitative biochemical and biophysical analyses in many *in vitro* systems. The preparation of various aminoacylated tRNAs (aa-tRNAs) have traditionally required laborious cloning, expression, and purification of individual cognate aaRSs, as these enzymes are highly specific toward their tRNA substrates (Walker & Fredrick, 2008). Aminoacylation reactions using aaRSs almost invariably produce a heterogeneous mixture of aa-tRNAs and (uncharged) non-aa-tRNAs. Such mixtures can adequately support protein synthesis, albeit the kinetics, and thermodynamics of aa-tRNA utilization may be difficult to establish. Importantly, in the study of other systems that discriminate between charged and uncharged tRNAs, such as the bacterial T-box riboswitches (Grundy & Henkin, 1993; Zhang & Ferré-D'Amaré, 2013) and the eukaryotic Gcn2 kinase (Dong, Qiu, Garcia-Barrio, Anderson, & Hinnebusch, 2000), it is necessary to separate aa-tRNAs from non-aa-tRNAs. The small differences in size, charge, and composition between these tRNAs make it a significant technical challenge to achieve satisfactory separation, in particular for tRNAs charged with small amino acids such as glycine and alanine. Significantly, the aminoacyl bond between tRNA 3′ termini and esterified amino acids are prone to rapid hydrolysis at even slightly alkaline conditions (Hentzen, Mandel, & Garel, 1972). The resulting unavailability of homogeneous aa-tRNAs has hampered, for instance, the functional studies of T-box riboswitches for two decades. Thus far, the method of choice to isolate aa-tRNAs took advantage of selective binding of aa-tRNAs to immobilized translation factor EF-Tu, but suffered from generally low efficiency (5–30%) of EF-Tu activation by GTP as well as tRNA deacylation during purification (Asahara & Uhlenbeck, 2005; Louie, Masuda, Yoder, & Jurnak, 1984; Nissen et al., 1995; Ohtsuki, Yamamoto, Doi, & Sisido, 2010).

In this chapter, we describe a simple, broadly applicable protocol to prepare biophysical quantities of highly purified (>95%) aa-tRNAs.

This flexible method does not require proteins, such as aaRS or EF-Tu, and is compatible with mutant or misacylated tRNAs and tRNAs charged with unnatural or modified amino acids. Application of this method has enabled detailed mechanistic investigations of the T-box riboswitches (Zhang & Ferré-D'Amaré, 2014). Further, this procedure can also be used for preparation of aminoacylated RNAs other than tRNAs as long as the RNA has a single-stranded 3′ terminus.

2. METHODS

2.1. tRNA aminoacylation using the flexizyme

To achieve broad compatibility with mutant or misacylated tRNAs and other RNAs, aminoacylation is performed using an *in vitro* selected ribozyme termed flexizyme (Fx, 46 nucleotides, Fig. 5.1A) instead of proteinaceous aaRS enzymes (Goto, Katoh, & Suga, 2011; Lee, Bessho, Wei, Szostak, & Suga, 2000; Xiao, Murakami, Suga, & Ferré-D'Amaré, 2008). Unlike aaRSs, flexizyme requires preactivated amino acids as donors for RNA aminoacylation. All natural amino acids and many nonnatural amino acids and hydroxy acids can be accepted by flexizyme. Depending on the chemical nature of the amino acid, an appropriate leaving group (cyanomethyl ester, 3,5-dinitrobenzyl ester, 4-chlorobenzyl thioester, or

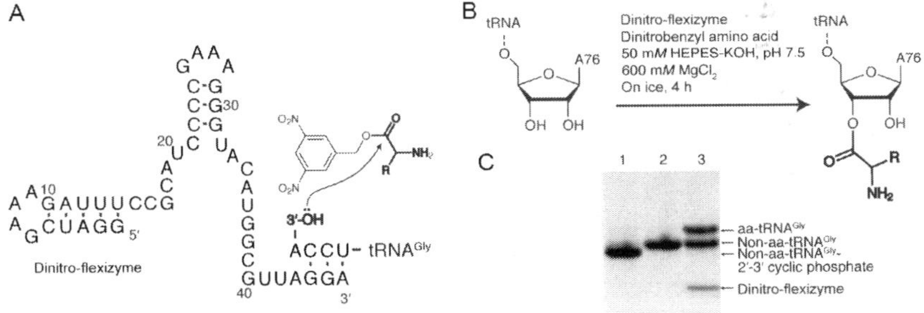

Figure 5.1 RNA aminoacylation by flexizyme. (A) Sequence and secondary structure of dinitroflexizyme (dFx) is depicted bound to $tRNA^{Gly}$ through base pairing. The 3′ terminal region of dFx (residues 44–46) and tRNA (residues 73–75) form three base pairs, positioning the tRNA terminal 3′OH to initiate nucleophilic attack on the carbonyl carbon of the dinitrobenzyl glycine ester (arrow). (B) Reaction conditions and chemical changes to the tRNA after aminoacylation. (C) Acid gel analysis showing the gel-mobility change caused by aminoacylation. tRNA aminoacylation and protonation of the α-amine near neutral pH partially neutralizes the negative charge of the tRNA, reducing the gel mobility of aa-tRNA. In contrast, the same non-aa $tRNA^{Gly}$ that carries a terminal 2′,3′-cyclic phosphate adds to the overall negative charge and thus exhibits increased gel mobility.

4-[(2-aminoethyl)carbamoyl]benzyl thioester) and a matching flexizyme variant (aFx, dFx, or eFx) are used (Goto et al., 2011). Generally, for aromatic amino acids, the enhanced flexizyme (eFx) and cyanomethyl ester substrates are used. For nonaromatic amino acids, the dinitroflexizyme (dFx) and 3,5-dinitrobenzyl ester is the most versatile combination.

To illustrate the use of the flexizyme as a broadly applicable aminoacylation system, we describe a representative protocol using *in vitro* transcribed *Bacillus subtilis* $tRNA^{Gly}$, dFx, and dinitrobenzyl glycine as the acceptor, catalyst, and substrate for glycylation, respectively (Fig. 5.1).

1. Synthesis of dinitrobenzyl glycine. Chemical synthesis of glycine dinitrobenzyl ester is performed essentially as described with minor modifications (Murakami, Ohta, Ashigai, & Suga, 2006). Briefly, 1.05 g of α-*N*-Boc-Glycine (6 mmol) and 1.08 g of 3,5-dinitrobenzyl chloride (5 mmol) are dissolved in 1.4 mL triethylamine (10 mmol) and 1.0 mL dimethylformamide, and stirred for 16 h at 21 °C. Subsequently, 90 mL diethylether is added and the mixture is washed 3 × with 30 mL 0.5 *M* HCl, 3 × with 30 mL 4% $NaHCO_3$, and once with 50 mL brine (saturated NaCl solution in water). The organic layer is extracted and mixed with anhydrous $MgSO_4$ powder for drying and subsequently concentrated under reduced pressure using a rotary evaporator, before being incubated with 20 mL 4 *M* HCl/ethyl acetate for 20 min at 21 °C. The mixture is concentrated, washed 3 × with 30 mL of diethylether and dried. The residue is then dissolved in 1:3 (v/v) methanol-ethyl acetate and crystallized by slow addition of hexanes and mixing by manual shaking. The product is verified by mass spectrometry and NMR.
2. *In vitro* transcription of $tRNA^{Gly}$ and dFx. *B. subtilis* $tRNA^{Gly}$ (75 nt) and dFx (46 nt) are transcribed *in vitro* using DNA templates produced by PCR and recombinant T7 RNA polymerase as described (Milligan, Groebe, Witherell, & Uhlenbeck, 1987), purified by electrophoresis on 8% polyacrylamide, 8 *M* urea TBE gels (29:1 acrylamide: bisacrylamide), electroeluted using a Whatman Elutrap system, concentrated using Amicon Ultra centrifugal filters (10 kD molecular weight cut off), washed once with 1 *M* KCl, desalted 4 × with DEPC-treated water, and stored at −20 °C before use.
3. Ribozyme-mediated aminoacylation. Aminoacylation using flexizyme is performed as previously described (Murakami et al., 2006). Briefly, to 200 μL buffer containing 5 m*M* HEPES-KOH (pH 7.5) in diethylpyrocarbonate (DEPC)-treated water, $tRNA^{Gly}$, and dFx are added

to 40 μ*M* and 60 μ*M*, respectively. Using a thermocycler, the mixture is heated to 90 °C for 2 min and slowly cooled to 21 °C over a course of 8 min. A stock solution of 2 *M* $MgCl_2$ is then added to this RNA mixture to produce 600 m*M* $MgCl_2$. This mixture is kept at 21 °C for 5 min and then on ice for 3 min. To initiate the aminoacylation reaction, 25 m*M* dinitrobenzylglycine dissolved in 100% DMSO is added to produce a final concentration of 5 m*M* and the reaction is allowed to proceed on ice for 2–6 h (Fig. 5.1B). NaOAc pH 5.5 and ethanol are added to 100 m*M* and 70%, respectively, to quench the reaction and precipitate the RNAs. The RNAs are subsequently washed with 70% ethanol, dried in a centrifugal vacuum concentrator, dissolved in 10 m*M* NaOAc pH 5.5, and stored at −80 °C.

4. Analysis of aminoacylation efficiency using acid PAGE. The efficiency of aminoacylation (typically 50–60%) is evaluated using acid gel electrophoresis (6.5% polyacrylamide; 29:1 acrylamide:bisacrylamide, Fig. 5.1C). The gels are cast and run in 100 m*M* NaOAc pH 5.5 as described (Varshney et al., 1991).

2.2. Chemical protection of the aminoacyl bond

The hydrolytic instability of the aminoacyl bond partly stems from the protonation of the free α-amine group of the esterified amino acid near neutral pH. The resulting α-ammonium is more positively charged and has a higher propensity to draw electrons from the neighboring carbonyl group, making it a better eletrophile for hydrolysis (Walker & Fredrick, 2008). To stabilize the labile aminoacyl bond against spontaneous hydrolysis, the aminoacylation mixture is reacted with *N*-pentenoyl succinimide (Fig. 5.2A). N-pentenoylation of the alpha-amino group of esterified amino acid significantly stabilizes the aminoacyl bond (Lodder, Wang, & Hecht, 2005). Similarly, peptidyl-tRNAs that carry substituted α-amines are much more hydrolytically stable (Strickland & Jacobson, 1972; Walker & Fredrick, 2008). Although N-pentenoylation requires alkaline pH under which the aminoacyl bond is rapidly hydrolyzed, under the following experimental conditions, N-pentenoylation occurs faster than deacylation, thus converting most aa-tRNAs into protected aa-tRNAs that are stable at alkaline pH (Fig. 5.2C). In addition, N-pentenoylation adds five hydrophobic carbons to the aa-tRNA, which can serve as an effective purification handle using reversed-phase high-performance liquid chromatography (RP-HPLC).

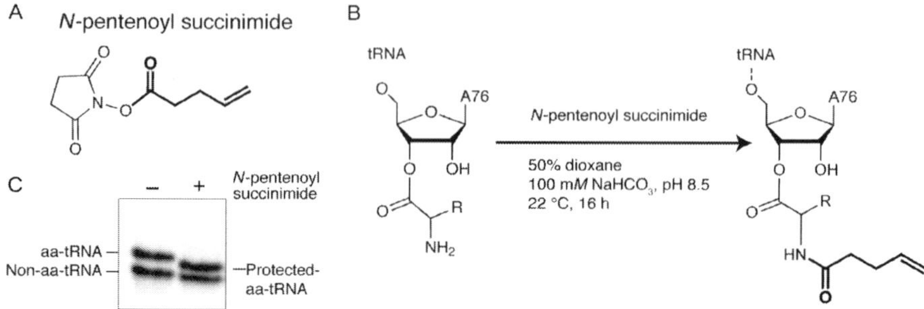

Figure 5.2 Pentenoylation of the aminoacylated tRNA. (A) Chemical structure of *N*-pentenoyl succinimide. (B) Reaction conditions and chemical changes to the aa-tRNA. (C) Acid gel analysis showing the gel-mobility change caused by *N*-pentenoylation of aa-tRNA. Pentenoylation of the α-amine of the esterified amino acid prevents its protonation near neutral pH, thus increasing its overall negative charge whilst adding 82 Da in molecular weight. This results in an intermediate mobility between aa-tRNA and non-aa-tRNA.

1. Chemical synthesis of *N*-pentenoyl succinimide. *N*-pentenoyl succinimide is synthesized essentially as described with minor modifications (Lodder, Golovine, Laikhter, Karginov, & Hecht, 1998; Lodder et al., 2005). Briefly, 5.0 mL pentenoic acid and 5.6 g *N*-hydroxysuccinimide are dissolved in 95 mL dichloromethane (CH_2Cl_2), to which 10.3 g of *N,N'*-dicyclohexylcarbodiimide is added. The reaction mixture is stirred at 21 °C for 90 min, filtered to remove *N,N'*-dicyclohexylurea, and concentrated under reduced pressure (~380 mBar) at 40 °C using a rotary evaporator. The concentrated oily mixture is then loaded onto a silica gel column and eluted isocratically with 7:3 hexane–ethyl acetate (v/v) using an Isolera One purification system. The fractions containing *N*-pentenoyl succinimide are pooled, dried under reduced pressure (100 mBar), dissolved in ethyl acetate, and crystallized by gradual addition of hexanes and mixing by manual shaking. The product (6.6 g, 68% yield) is verified by mass spectrometry and NMR.
2. N-pentenoylation of aa-tRNA. The aminoacylation mixture containing 100 μ*M* tRNA is mixed 1:1 (v/v) with 100 m*M* *N*-pentenoyl succinimide previously dissolved in 100% dioxane. Next, 1/10 volume of 1 *M* $NaHCO_3$ is added to raise the pH to ~8.5 to initiate the reaction, which is allowed to proceed for 16 h at room temperature with gentle stirring (Fig. 5.2B). The reaction is quenched by adding NaOAc pH 5.5 to a final concentration of 300 m*M*, precipitated by adjusting to 70% (v/v) ethanol, dried, and stored at −80 °C. The N-pentenoylation is

typically near-quantitative, converting essentially all aa-tRNAs to protected-aa-tRNAs (Fig. 5.2C).

2.3. Purification of protected aminoacylated tRNA and deprotection

For tRNAs esterified with aromatic or other highly hydrophobic side chains, aa-tRNAs and non-aa-tRNAs can be directly separated using RP-HPLC, based on their difference in hydrophobicity (Cayama et al., 2000; Zhang et al., 2008). For tRNAs esterified with other amino acids, in particular those with small or polar side chains (e.g., glycine, alanine), chromatographic methods are generally unable to achieve satisfactory separation. In these cases, N-pentenoylation of the esterified amino acid adds significantly to the overall hydrophobicity of the aa-tRNA, thus providing a means to effectively separate aa-tRNAs from non-aa-tRNAs.

1. RP-HPLC separation of protected aa-tRNA from non-aa-tRNA. The pentenoylation reaction mixture is diluted into RP-HPLC buffer A [20 m*M* NH_4OAc pH 5.5, 10 m*M* $MgOAc_2$, 400 m*M* NaCl, and

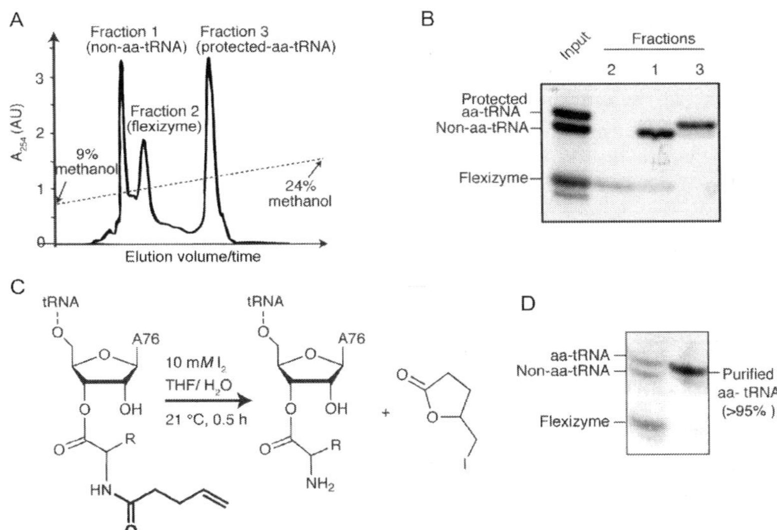

Figure 5.3 Purification of protected aa-tRNA and deprotection. (A) RP-HPLC separation of non-aa-tRNA (fraction 1), dFx (fraction 2), and pentenoyl-aa-tRNA (fraction 3) using a linear gradient of methanol (9–24%). Pentenoyl-glycyl-$tRNA^{Gly}$ elutes at approximately 16% methanol. (B) Acid gel analysis of the fractions from the chromatogram in (A). (C) Chemical changes during deprotection by aqueous iodine. (D) Final product of purified, deprotected aa-tRNA assayed by acid PAGE.

5% (v/v) methanol] and fractionated at 0.5 mL/min on a C18 column (Waters Symmetry Shield RP18 3.5 μm, 4.6 × 150 mm) previously equilibrated in the same buffer. A linear gradient of methanol from 9% (v/v) to 24% (v/v) over 10 column volumes is used to fractionate the RNA mixture into non-aa-tRNA (fraction 1), flexizyme (fraction 2), and pentenoylated-aa-tRNA (fraction 3; Fig. 5.3A and B). Fractions containing N-protected aa-tRNA are pooled, precipitated with 70% ethanol, dried, and resuspended in 10 mM NaOAc pH 5.5 before deprotection.

2. Deprotection of N-pentenoylated aa-tRNA. For deprotection, N-protected aa-tRNA is mixed with 1/4 volume of 50 m*M* iodine previously dissolved in 1:1 (v/v) tetrahydrofuran:H_2O and allowed to react for 0.5 h at room temperature (Lodder et al., 1998, 2005). Deprotected aa-tRNA is brought up to 0.3 *M* NaOAc pH 5.5, precipitated by adjusting to 70% (v/v) ethanol, washed, dried, and stored at −80 °C. Typical final purity of glycyl-$tRNA^{Gly}$ is better than 95% based on acid gel PAGE and RP-HPLC analysis (Fig. 5.3D). The very mild condition under which N-pentenoylated aa-tRNA is deprotected safeguards the aminoacyl linkage.

ACKNOWLEDGMENTS

We thank J. Posakony for assistance with chemical synthesis and NMR analysis, Y. Goto and H. Suga for a gift of dinitrobenzylglycine and suggestions on flexizyme use, S. Hecht for suggesting the use of the pentenoyl protecting group, N. Tjandra for access to NMR, R. Levine and D.-Y. Lee for help with mass spectrometry, G. Piszczek for biophysical analytical support, and N. Baird, K. Fredrick, M. Ibba, M. Lau, P. Nissen, C. Jones, O. Uhlenbeck, A. Roll-Mecak, and K. Warner for discussions. This work employed the Biochemistry and Biophysics core facilities of the National Heart, Lung and Blood Institute (NHLBI) and was supported in part by the intramural program of the NHLBI, NIH.

REFERENCES

Asahara, H., & Uhlenbeck, O. C. (2005). Predicting the binding affinities of misacylated tRNAs for Thermus thermophilus EF-Tu.GTP. *Biochemistry, 44*, 11254–11261.

Banerjee, R., Chen, S., Dare, K., Gilreath, M., Praetorius-Ibba, M., Raina, M., et al. (2010). tRNAs: Cellular barcodes for amino acids. *FEBS Letters, 584*, 387–395.

Cayama, E., Yepez, A., Rotondo, F., Bandeira, E., Ferreras, A. C., & Triana-Alonso, F. J. (2000). New chromatographic and biochemical strategies for quick preparative isolation of tRNA. *Nucleic Acids Research, 28*, E64.

Dong, J., Qiu, H., Garcia-Barrio, M., Anderson, J., & Hinnebusch, A. G. (2000). Uncharged tRNA activates GCN2 by displacing the protein kinase moiety from a bipartite tRNA-binding domain. *Molecular Cell, 6*, 269–279.

Geslain, R., & Pan, T. (2011). tRNA: Vast reservoir of RNA molecules with unexpected regulatory function. *Proceedings of the National Academy of Sciences of the United States of America, 108*, 16489–16490.

Goto, Y., Katoh, T., & Suga, H. (2011). Flexizymes for genetic code reprogramming. *Nature Protocols*, *6*, 779–790.

Grundy, F. J., & Henkin, T. M. (1993). tRNA as a positive regulator of transcription antitermination in *B. subtilis*. *Cell*, *74*, 475–482.

Hentzen, D., Mandel, P., & Garel, J. P. (1972). Relation between aminoacyl-tRNA stability and the fixed amino acid. *Biochimica et Biophysica Acta*, *281*, 228–232.

Lee, N., Bessho, Y., Wei, K., Szostak, J. W., & Suga, H. (2000). Ribozyme-catalyzed tRNA aminoacylation. *Nature Structural Biology*, 7, 28–33.

Lodder, M., Golovine, S., Laikhter, A. L., Karginov, V. A., & Hecht, S. M. (1998). Misacylated transfer RNAs having a chemically removable protecting group. *Journal of Organic Chemistry*, *63*, 794–803.

Lodder, M., Wang, B., & Hecht, S. M. (2005). The N-pentenoyl protecting group for aminoacyl-tRNAs. *Methods*, *36*, 245–251.

Louie, A., Masuda, E., Yoder, M., & Jurnak, F. (1984). Affinity purification of aminoacyl-tRNA. *Analytical Biochemistry*, *141*, 402–408.

Milligan, J. F., Groebe, D. R., Witherell, G. W., & Uhlenbeck, O. C. (1987). Oligoribonucleotide synthesis using T7 RNA polymerase and synthetic DNA templates. *Nucleic Acids Research*, *15*, 8783–8798.

Murakami, H., Ohta, A., Ashigai, H., & Suga, H. (2006). A highly flexible tRNA acylation method for non natural polypeptide synthesis. *Nature Methods*, *3*, 357–359.

Nissen, P., Kjeldgaard, M., Thirup, S., Polekhina, G., Reshetnikova, L., Clark, B. F., et al. (1995). Crystal structure of the ternary complex of Phe-tRNAPhe, EF-Tu, and a GTP analog. *Science*, *270*, 1464–1472.

Ohtsuki, T., Yamamoto, H., Doi, Y., & Sisido, M. (2010). Use of EF-Tu mutants for determining and improving aminoacylation efficiency and for purifying aminoacyl tRNAs with non-natural amino acids. *Journal of Biochemistry*, *148*, 239–246.

Phizicky, E. M., & Hopper, A. K. (2010). tRNA biology charges to the front. *Genes and Development*, *24*, 1832–1860.

Strickland, J. E., & Jacobson, K. B. (1972). Effects of amino acid structure, ionic strength, and magnesium ion concentration on rates of nonenzymic hydrolysis of aminoacyl transfer ribonucleic acid. *Biochemistry*, *11*, 2321–2323.

Varshney, U., Lee, C. P., & RajBhandary, U. L. (1991). Direct analysis of aminoacylation levels of tRNAs *in vivo*. Application to studying recognition of Escherichia coli initiator tRNA mutants by glutaminyl-tRNA synthetase. *The Journal of Biological Chemistry*, *266*, 24712–24718.

Walker, S. E., & Fredrick, K. (2008). Preparation and evaluation of acylated tRNAs. *Methods*, *44*, 81–86.

Xiao, H., Murakami, H., Suga, H., & Ferré-D'Amaré, A. R. (2008). Structural basis of specific tRNA aminoacylation by a small *in vitro* selected ribozyme. *Nature*, *454*, 358–361.

Zhang, J., & Ferré-D'Amaré, A. R. (2013). Co-crystal structure of a T-box riboswitch stem I domain in complex with its cognate tRNA. *Nature*, *500*, 363–366.

Zhang, J., & Ferré-D'Amaré, A. R. (2014). Direct evaluation of tRNA aminoacylation status by the T-box riboswitch using intermolecular stacking and steric readout. *Molecular Cell*, *55*, 148–155.

Zhang, C. M., Liu, C., Christian, T., Gamper, H., Rozenski, J., Pan, D., et al. (2008). Pyrrolo-C as a molecular probe for monitoring conformations of the tRNA 3′ end. *RNA*, *14*, 2245–2253.

CHAPTER SIX

Synthesis of a Biotinylated Photocleavable Nucleotide Monophosphate for the Preparation of Natively Folded RNAs

Yiling Luo*, Herman O. Sintim*,[1], T. Kwaku Dayie*,†,[1]

*Department of Chemistry and Biochemistry, University of Maryland, College Park, Maryland, USA

†Center for Biomolecular Structure and Organization, University of Maryland, College Park, Maryland, USA

[1]Corresponding authors: e-mail address: hsintim@umd.edu; dayie@umd.edu

Contents

Methods in Enzymology, Volume 549
ISSN 0076-6879
http://dx.doi.org/10.1016/B978-0-12-801122-5.00006-4

Abstract

RNAs are involved in many functional roles in the cell, and this functional diversity is predicated on RNAs adopting requisite three-dimensional architectures. Preparing such "natively folded" RNAs with a homogeneous population is sometimes problematic for structural or enzymatic studies. Yet, standard methods for RNA preparations denature the RNA and create a heterogeneous population of conformers. Therefore, preparation of "natively folded" RNAs without going through the process of denaturing and refolding is important to obtain maximal biological function. Here, we present a simple strategy using "click" chemistry to couple biotin to a "caged" photocleavable (PC) guanosine monophosphate (GMP) in high yield. This biotin-PC-GMP is readily accepted by T7 RNA polymerase to transcribe "natively folded" RNAs ranging in size from 27 to 493 nucleotides. This facile strategy allows efficient biotinylation of RNA and provides a traceless means to remove the biotin after the purification. Such preparation of natively folded RNAs should benefit biophysical and therapeutic applications.

1. THEORY

The incorporation of affinity labels into biomolecules has great promise in biotechnology for isolation of molecules such as riboswitches via attachment of an affinity tag followed by separation using an affinity media. However, traditional methods were limited by the difficulty of releasing the affinity label from the target biomolecule without leaving a scar or irreversibly modifying or denaturing the RNA. Herein, we describe a solution to this problem by using a reagent that facilitates the synthesis of a biotinylated RNA, which can be immobilized on a streptavidin or an avidin column and then released as a natively folded RNA without the biotin tag using photocleavage. Phage T7 RNA polymerase (T7 RNAP) is known to initiate transcription with nucleotide monophosphate (Milligan, Groebe, Witherell, & Uhlenbeck, 1987). We therefore rationalized that a guanosine monophosphate that is modified with a biotin affinity tag linked via a spacer arm to a photoreactive nitrophenyl group (Olejnik, Krzymanska-Olejnik, & Rothschild, 1998) would be readily accepted by T7 RNAP to synthesize RNAs. The synthesized biotinylated and phototagged RNAs could then be readily purified after immobilization on a NeutrAvidin (or streptavidin or avidin) column followed by photorelease using UV light to produce natively folded RNAs. This modified guanosine monophosphate (referred to as biotin-PC GMP) was synthesized using Click

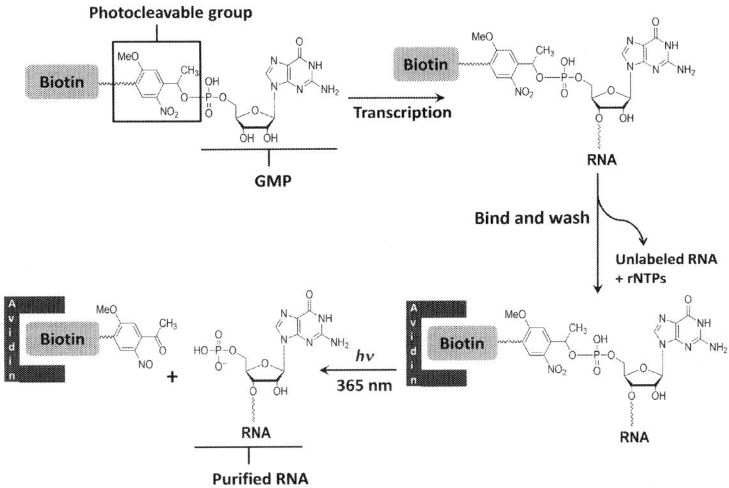

Scheme 6.1 Preparation of native RNA using biotin-PC GMP as an initiator.

chemistry to couple an alkyne-bearing nitrophenyl guanosine monophosphate with a biotin azide, using copper catalysis. Earlier, we demonstrated that T7 RNAP can accept this "caged" biotin-PC GMP (Luo, Eldho, Sintim, & Dayie, 2011). RNAs with biotin-PC GMP attached to their 5′ ends can be readily prepared by transcription priming (Sampson & Uhlenbeck, 1988). During transcription with the T7 RNAP, nucleotides lacking a 5′-triphosphate cannot be incorporated into an elongating RNA chain, but they can be used to initiate a transcript. Transcription priming with biotin-PC GMP, however, produces a mixed population of modified and unmodified RNAs. Nonetheless, only the RNA with biotin-PC GMP tag binds to the streptavidin or avidin column, and all the enzymes, NTPs, and unlabeled RNA are washed away. Long-wavelength UV (365 nm), which does not damage RNA, can then be used to release the photocleavable (PC) biotin affinity tags (Scheme 6.1). Since the RNA is not subjected to unfolding and refolding steps during PC affinity purification, the purified RNA maintains its native fold. This nondenaturing RNA preparation method should prove valuable in obtaining RNAs with homogeneous populations that are functionally more active than those prepared by denaturing methods and with obligatory refolding steps, and should be more suited for making RNAs such as riboswitches that require switching their structures for function.

2. EQUIPMENT

Bruker 400 MHz spectrometer
Empty gravity flow columns
Heating block
High vacuum
HPLC fitted with a reverse phase C18 column (4.6 mm × 250 mm, 5 μm particle size)
Mass spectrometer (ESI-MS)
Microcentrifuge
1.5-mL Microcentrifuge tubes
Micropipettors
Micropipettor tips
Nitrogen gas
PCR machine
Platform rotator/mixer
Polyacrylamide gel electrophoresis equipment
PureSolv™ solvent purification system
Rotary evaporator
Silica gel (40–63 μm silica gel) column chromatography
TLC plate
0.5-mL Ultra spin filter (MWCO of 3 and 10 kDa)
UV source (long wavelength and short wavelength)
UV/vis spectrophotometer
Water bath

3. MATERIALS

40% Acrylamide/bisacrylamide (19:1) (EMD)
Acetonitrile [CH_3CN] (Fisher)
p-Anisaldehyde (TCI)
O-Benzotriazole-*N*, *N*′ *N*′-tetramethyl-uronium-hexafluorophosphate [HBTU] (Nova Biochem)
Biotin-dPEG™ 3+4-azide (QuantaBiodesign)
Bromophenol blue (BP) (EMD)
Boric acid (Sigma–Aldrich)
Chloroform [$CHCl_3$] (VWR)

Copper (II) sulfate [$CuSO_4$] (Alfa Aesar)
2′,3′-Diacetyl guanosine (*n*-*i*Bu) 5′-CED phosphoramidite (ChemGenes)
Dibasic potassium phosphate [K_2HPO_4] (JT Baker)
Dichloromethane [DCM] (VWR)
Dimethylformamide [DMF] (Sigma–Aldrich)
Dithiothreitol [DTT] (Sigma–Aldrich)
DNA template (IDT, see Procedure section)
Ethidium bromide (EMD)
Ethylenediaminetetracetic acid [EDTA] (JT Baker)
Ethyl-thiol-tetrazol [ETT] (GlenResearch)
Guanosine monophosphate [GMP] (Amresco)
1-Hydroxybenzotriazole [HOBt] (Chem-Impex International)
4-[4-(1-Hydroxyethyl)-2-methoxy-5-nitrophenoxyl]butyric acid (Sigma–Aldrich)
Inorganic pyrophosphatase (New England Biolabs)
Iodine solution [0.02 *M* in THF/pyridine/H_2O 70:20:10]
Isoascorbic acid (Sigma–Aldrich)
Magnesium chloride [$MgCl_2$] (Sigma–Aldrich)
Methanol [MeOH] (VWR)
Monobasic potassium phosphate [KH_2PO_4] (JT Baker)
NeutrAvidin Agarose Resin solution (Thermo Scientific)
28–30% $NH_3{\cdot}H_2O$ (Sigma–Aldrich)
rNTPs: rATP, rGTP, rCTP, rUTP (Invitrogen)
PEG 8000 (CalBiochem)
Potassium chloride [KCl] (Sigma–Aldrich)
Propargylamine (Sigma–Aldrich)
RNase inhibitor (New England Biolabs)
Sodium thiosulfate [$Na_2S_2O_3$] (J. T. Baker)
Spermidine (Alfa Aesar)
Streptavidin (Promega)
Tetrahydrofuran [THF] (Fisher Scientific)
Triethylamine [Et_3N] (Sigma–Aldrich)
T7 RNA polymerase (P226L mutant T7 is used in all experiments here; Guillerez, Lopez, Proux, Launay, & Dreyfus, 2005)
Tris base (Fisher Scientific)
Triton X-100 (Sigma–Aldrich)
Urea (EMD)
Xylene cyanol (XC) (Sigma–Aldrich)

3.1. Stock solutions and buffers

10× Transcription buffer

Component	Final concentration	Stock	Amount
Tris–HCl, pH 8.0	400 m*M*	1 *M*	4 mL
DTT	100 m*M*	1 *M*	1 mL
Triton X-100	0.1% (v/v)	1%	1 mL
Spermidine, pH 7.0	10 m*M*	500 m*M*	0.2 mL

Add sterilized water to 10 mL

100 m*M* Nucleotide 5′-triphosphate mix (ATP/CTP/UTP mix) stock

Component	Final concentration	Stock	Amount
rATP	33 m*M*	100 m*M*	0.25 mL
rCTP	33 m*M*	100 m*M*	0.25 mL
rUTP	33 m*M*	100 m*M*	0.25 mL

2× Urea gel loading buffer

Component	Final concentration	Stock	Amount
Tris–HCl, pH 8.0	50 m*M*	1 *M*	0.5 mL
Urea	12 *M*	–	7.2 g
EDTA, pH 8.0	1.5 m*M*	50 m*M*	0.3 mL
BP	0.05% (w/v)	–	5 mg
XC	0.05% (w/v)	–	5 mg

Add sterilized water to 10 mL

10× Tris Borate EDTA (TBE) buffer

Component	Final concentration	Stock	Amount
Tris–HCl, pH 8.0	0.9 *M*	–	108 g
Boric acid	0.9 *M*	–	55 g
EDTA, pH 8.0	10 mm	500 m*M*	20 mL

Add sterilized water to 10 mL

12% Denaturing polyacrylamide gel (PAGE) solution

Component	Final concentration	Stock	Amount
Acrylamide/bis-acrylamide (29:1)	12%	40%	30 mL
Urea	8 *M*	–	48 g
TBE buffer	1×	10×	10 mL

Add sterilized water to 100 mL

Potassium phosphate buffer (0.1 *M*, pH 6.4)

Component	Final concentration	Stock	Amount
K_2HPO_4	–	1 *M*	27.8 mL
KH_2PO_4	–	1 *M*	72.2 mL

PEG 8000 (80 mg/mL)

Dissolve 800 mg of PEG 8000 to a final volume of 10 mL with sterilized water

Heat at 40 °C until completely dissolved.

$MgCl_2$ (100 m*M*)

Dissolve 953.2 mg of $MgCl_2$ to a final volume of 100 mL with sterilized water

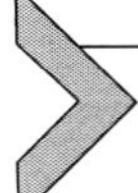

4. PROTOCOL

4.1. Duration

Preparation	
Biotin-PC GMP synthesis	About 1 week[a]
In vitro transcription optimization with biotin-PC GMP	2 days
Purification of transcribed biotin-PC RNA	Half day

[a]The yield of biotin-PC GMP from the following synthesis scale is ~80 mg, which is equivalent to ~570 μL of 100 m*M* biotin-PC GMP stock. It is enough for 1–2 mL scale transcription based on transcription efficiency.

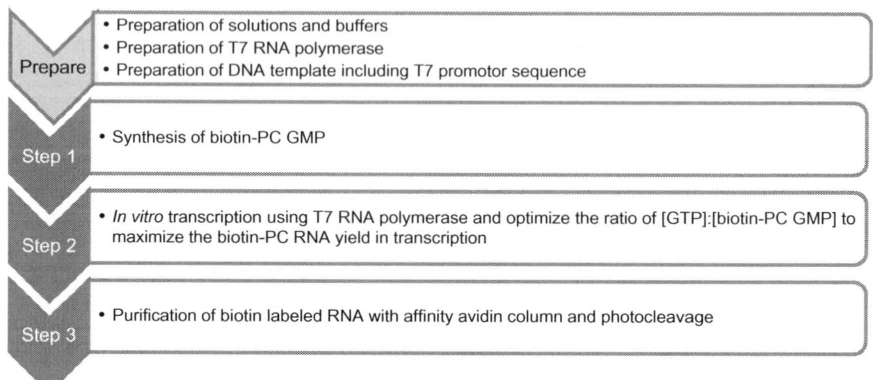

Figure 6.1 Flowchart of complete protocol, including preparation.

4.2. Preparation

Obtain from commercial sources or by solid-phase synthesis the T7 RNAP promoter sequence (5′-*C*<u>TA ATA CGA CTC ACT ATA</u> G-3′, the extra G at 3′-end is for transcription initiation efficiency and the extra C italicized at the 5′-end of the promoter improves transcription yield; Baklanov, Golikova, & Malgin, 1996) and a DNA template carrying the complementary T7 promoter sequence upstream of the desired RNA for *in vitro* transcription; the core promoter sequence is underlined (Fig. 6.1). Here we use the template strand of ribosomal A-site (Fourmy, Recht, Blanchard, & Puglisi, 1996; 5′-GmGmC GAC TTC ACC CGA AGG TGT GAC GCC TAT AGT GAG TCG TAT TAG-3′) and the template strand of D5 RNA (Gumbs, Padgett, & Dayie, 2006; Michel, Costa, & Westhof, 2009; 5′-g AAC CGT ACG TGC GAC TTT CAT CGC ATA CGG CTC c TAT AGT GAG TCG TAT TAG-3′), for example, where two terminal 2′-*O*-methyl modifications in the template strand indicated by "m" is introduced to substantially reduce the amount of transcripts with extra nucleotides at the 3′-end (Kao, Zheng, & Rudisser, 1999).

4.3. Caution

RNase-free conditions are important for maintaining the integrity of the RNA. All pipette tips, tubes, and water used should be autoclaved in advance. Disposable gloves should be worn at all times. The purification step is better conducted at 4 °C, and the purified RNA (especially >60 nts) sample is preferably placed on ice at all times to minimize inherent spontaneous cleavage of the RNA.

5. STEP 1: SYNTHESIS OF BIOTIN-PC GMP

5.1. Overview

See Scheme 6.2.

5.2. Duration

One week.

5.2.1 Synthesis of PC alkyne

Step a in Scheme 6.2, 12–14 h.

1.1 Add distilled propargylamine (0.26 mL, 4 mmol, 4 eq.), HBTU (758 mg, 2 mmol, 2 eq.), HOBt (67.5 mg, 0.5 mmol, 0.5 eq.), and Et_3N (280 μL, 2 mmol, 2 eq.) to a solution of 4-[4-(1-hydroxyethyl)-2-methoxy-5-nitrophenoxyl] butyric acid (**1**) (300 mg, 1 mmol, 1 eq.) in dry DMF (6 mL).

1.2 Stir the mixture under nitrogen at room temperature overnight.

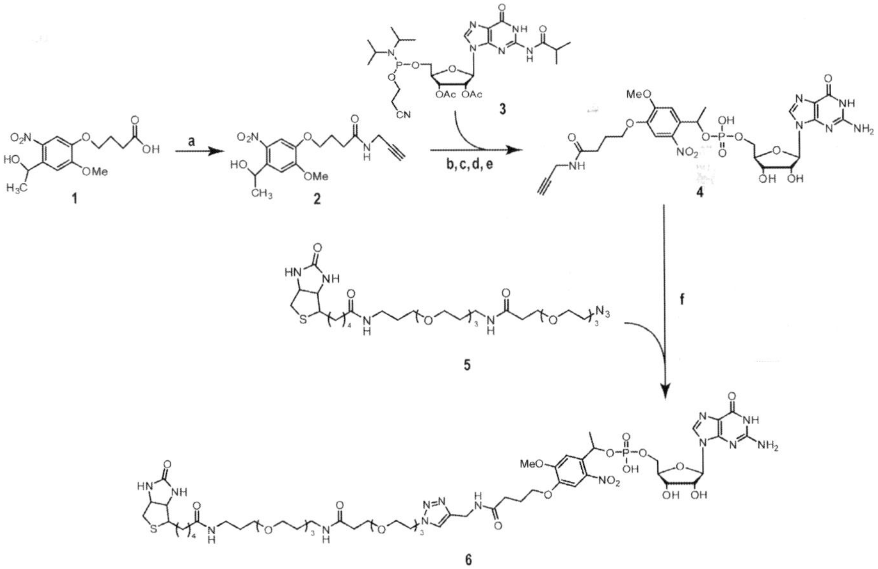

Scheme 6.2 Procedures for the chemical synthesis of biotin-PC GMP (Luo et al., 2011). Reagents and conditions: (a) 1-Hydroxybenzotriazole (HOBt), *O*-Benzotriazole-*N*, *N*′, *N*′-tetramethyl-uronium-hexafluorophosphate (HBTU), triethylamine [Et_3N], dimethylformamide [DMF] (s); (b) Ethyl-thiol-tetrazol (ETT), MeCN (s); (c) I_2 (Tetrahydrofuran [THF]/pyridine/H_2O 7:2:1); (d) $Na_2S_2O_3$; (e) 28–30% $NH_3{\cdot}H_2O$; and (f) $CuSO_4$, isoascorbic acid, THF/water (s).

1.3 Next morning, remove the solvent using rotary evaporator under vacuum.

1.4 Purify the mixture by silica gel column chromatography with a step gradient of MeOH (0.5–2.5%) in $CHCl_3$. Check the product on silica TLC plate (R_f of product is at ~0.6).

1.5 Evaporate the solvent of the flow-through from the silica column using rotary evaporator under vacuum.

1.6 Dry the residue under vacuum to obtain product **2** as a yellow solid (235 mg, 70%).

1.7 Check the purity of compound **2** by ^{1}H NMR, ^{13}C NMR, and ESI-MS (Luo et al., 2011).

5.2.1.1 Tip

Please refer to compound characterization data for each step reaction (Luo et al., 2011).

5.2.1.2 Tip

The reaction should be performed in an oven-dried glassware under N_2 atmosphere.

5.2.1.3 Tip

Dry DMF could be commercially purchased or dried using the PureSolv™ solvent purification system (Innovative Technology Inc.).

5.2.2 Synthesis of PC alkyne GMP

Steps b–e in Scheme 6.2, 3 days.

Step b, 12 h.

2.1 Mix compound **2** (198 mg, 0.59 mmol, 1.5 eq.) and ETT (153 mg, 1.18 mmol, 3 eq.) and dry the mixture under high vacuum for 1 h.

2.2 Add the solution of 2′,3′-diacetyl guanosine (*n*-*i*Bu) CED phosphoramide (**3**) (250 mg, 0.39 mmol, 1 eq.) in anhydrous CH_3CN (3 mL) dropwise to the mixture above, under nitrogen.

2.3 Stir the reaction mixture at room temperature overnight.

2.4 Next morning, evaporate the CH_3CN solvent using rotary evaporator under vacuum and obtain the phosphite derivative as yellow oil. Steps c and d, 30 min.

2.5 Dissolve 2 eq. of the crude phosphite derivative obtained from step b without purification in an "oxidation" solvent (27 mL, 0.02 *M* I_2 in 7:2:1 of THF:pyridine: H_2O, 3 eq.).

2.6 Stir the mixture at room temperature for 10 min.
2.7 Quench the reaction by adding $Na_2S_2O_3$ (86 mg, 0.54 mmol, 3 eq.) in H_2O (1 mL).
2.8 Continue stirring the mixture at room temperature for another 10 min until the mixture turns from brown to yellow.
2.9 Evaporate the solvent of the mixture using rotary evaporator under vacuum and obtain the oxidized product (phosphate derivative) as a yellow solid. Step e (deprotection), 24 h.
2.10 Add a solution of 28–30% aqueous ammonia (35 mL) directly to the crude product obtained in step 2.9.
2.11 Stir this reaction mixture at 65 °C for 8 h.
2.12 Then open the tube to evaporate away the aqueous ammonia at room temperature in the fume hood for another 3 h.
2.13 Purify the reaction mixture using a Varian HPLC fitted with a reverse phase C18 column (4.6 mm × 250 mm, 5 μm particle size).
- Elute the reaction mixture using linear gradients of solvent A (water) and B (100% acetonitrile) as follow: 5–15% B for 15 min, 15–40% B for 5 min, 40–90% for 4 min, 90% B hold for 4 min.
- Monitor UV–vis absorption of the eluent at 254 nm (compound **5** should elute at ~18–20 min).

2.14 Collect the HPLC fractions with maximal absorbance at 254 nm and evaporate the solvent using rotary evaporator under vacuum to obtain compound **5** (66.39 mg, overall yield of 25% from compound **2**).
2.15 Check the purity of compound **5** by ^{1}H NMR, ^{13}C NMR, and ESI-MS (Luo et al., 2011).

5.2.2.1 Tip

CH_3CN should be distilled from CaH_2 and used immediately to improve the yield.

5.2.3 Synthesis of biotin-PC GMP

Step f in Scheme 6.2, 12–14 h

3.1 Add biotin-dPEG™ 3+4-azide (48.6 mg, 0.0675 mmol, 1 eq.), $CuSO_4 \cdot 5H_2O$ (3.37 mg, 0.0135 mmol, 0.2 eq.), and isoascorbic acid (23.8 mg, 0.135 mmol, 2 eq.) to a solution of PC alkyne GMP (**5**) (46 mg, 0.0675 mmol, 1 eq.) from step 2.14 in THF/water (1:1 (v/v), 3.5 mL)
3.2 Stir the reaction mixture at room temperature for 5 h.

3.3 Evaporate the solvent using rotary evaporator under vacuum.

3.4 Redissolve the mixture into a small amount of water (~1 mL).

3.5 Purify the reaction mixture using a Varian HPLC fitted with a reverse phase C18 column (4.6 mm × 250 mm, 5 μm particle size).

- Elute the reaction mixture using linear gradients of solvent A (water) and B (100% acetonitrile) as follow: 5–20% B for 8 min, 20–40% B for 12 min, 40–90% B for 2 min, 90% B hold for 2 min.
- Monitor the UV–vis absorption of the eluent at 254 nm (compound **6** elutes at ~16–17 min).

3.6 Collect the HPLC fractions and evaporate the solvent using rotary evaporator under vacuum to obtain product **6** (80.32 mg, 85%).

3.7 Check the purity of **6** by ^{1}H NMR, ^{13}C NMR, and ESI-MS (Luo et al., 2011).

5.2.3.1 Tip

Before each purification step, it is necessary to spot the starting material and product on the TLC plate to trace the reaction and confirm that the reaction works.

5.2.3.2 Tip

Biotin-PC GMP is stable at −20 °C for long-term storage (~6 months).

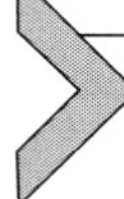

6. STEP 2: TRANSCRIPTION OF D5 AND RIBOSOMAL A-SITE RNAs USING UNMODIFIED GTP AND BIOTIN-PC GMP

6.1. Overview

Transcribe the RNA using T7 RNA polymerase and optimize the ratio of [GTP]:[biotin-PC GMP] to maximize the biotin-PC-labeled RNA.

6.2. Duration and transcription optimization

Two days.

2.1 In a 1.5-mL microcentrifuge tube with final volume of 10 μL, combine 150 n*M* of DNA template and 150 n*M* of T7 RNAP promoter sequence. Heat at 90 °C for 2 min and cool down to room temperature before adding the following:

1 μL of 10 × transcription buffer;

2 μL of 80 mg/mL PEG 8000;

2 units of RNase inhibitor (New England Biolabs);

2 units of inorganic pyrophosphatase;

1.5 μL of 100 m*M* $MgCl_2$;

NTPs (ATP, CTP, and UTP), GTP, and biotin-PC GMP at different ratio combinations as below, and 0.5 μL of T7 RNA polymerase (4 mg/mL).

For the NTP conditions, add varying amount of 100 m*M* NTPs (ATP/CTP/UTP) stock mixture without GTP/biotin-PC GMP as 0.35, 0.5, or 1 μL for each individual condition to give final [NTP] of 3.5, 5, or 10 m*M*. Then supplement with varying amounts of [GTP]/[biotin-PC GMP] mix to obtain the requisite ratio needed for efficient priming and elongation. For example at a final [NTP] = 3.5 m*M* (0.35 μL of [ATP/CTP/UTP] added), supplement with these *four different* combinations:

1. 3.5 μL of 10 m*M* GTP and no biotin-PC GMP;
2. 1.4 μL of 10 m*M* GTP and 2.1 μL of 10 m*M* biotin-PC GMP;
3. 0.7 μL of 10 m*M* GTP and 2.8 μL of 10 m*M* biotin-PC GMP;
4. 0.175 μL of 10 m*M* GTP and 3.325 μL of 10 m*M* biotin-PC GMP.

Similarly for a final [NTP] = 5 m*M* (0.5 μL of [ATP/CTP/UTP] added), supplement with these *four different* combinations:

1. 5 μL of 10 m*M* GTP and no biotin-PC GMP;
2. 2 μL of 10 m*M* GTP and 3 μL of 10 m*M* biotin-PC GMP;
3. 1 μL of 10 m*M* GTP and 4 μL of 10 m*M* biotin-PC GMP;
4. 0.5 μL of 10 m*M* GTP and 4.5 μL of 10 m*M* biotin-PC GMP.

Again for a final [NTP] = 10 m*M* (1 μL of [NTP] added), supplement with these *four different* combinations:

1. 5 μL of 20 m*M* GTP and no biotin-PC GMP;
2. 2 μL of 20 m*M* GTP and 3 μL of 20 m*M* biotin-PC GMP;
3. 1 μL of 20 m*M* GTP and 4 μL of 20 m*M* biotin-PC GMP;
4. 0.5 μL of 20 m*M* GTP and 4.5 μL of 20 m*M* biotin-PC GMP.

4.1 Incubate each reaction condition at 37 °C for 4 h.

4.2 Stop the reaction by adding 10 μL 2 × urea gel loading buffer to each reaction.

4.3 Run 5 μL of each condition on a 12%, 0.75-mm denaturing PAGE gel. Using the BP and XC dyes as markers, run the gel till the XC dye has migrated three quarters to the bottom of the gel at 120 V.

4.4 Remove gel from apparatus and stain the gel with 50 mL of 0.5 μg/mL ethidium bromide (EtBr) for 10 min.

4.5 Scan the gel with gel scanner and quantify the RNA product band using software such as Bio-Rad Quantity One and plot the yield of GTP-RNA and Biotin-PC RNA for each condition.
4.6 Choose the optimized transcription condition and scale-up the transcription, if necessary.
4.7 Load the transcription mixture into a tube fitted with a 0.5-mL ultraspin filter with a MWCO of 3 kDa (the MWCO is chosen to be at least 2.5 times smaller than the MW of the RNA of interest) and add potassium phosphate buffer (0.1 *M*, pH 6.4) to 500 μL volume.
4.8. Spin the tube at 12,000 rpm for 20 min and remove the filtrate.
4.9. Wash the transcription mixture three more times with potassium phosphate buffer (pH 6.4) to completely remove unincorporated free biotin-PC GMP from the transcription reaction.
4.10. Reverse the filter device by turning it upside down in a clean microcentrifuge tube, spin for 2 min at 1000 × *g* to transfer the transcription mixture from the device to the tube.
4.11. Incubate the filtered biotin-PC RNA transcription mixture with NeutrAvidin affinity beads (see Section 7, step 3).

6.3. Tip

For each RNA studied, the amount of NTP (ATP/CTP/UTP), GTP, and biotin-PC GMP needs to be optimized.

6.4. Tip

For longer RNA (>60 nts), it is preferable to generate a DNA template carrying the T7 promoter sequence upstream of the desired RNA by standard PCR for *in vitro* transcription.

7. STEP 3: PURIFICATION OF BIOTIN-LABELED RNA WITH AFFINITY AVIDIN COLUMN AND PHOTOCLEAVAGE

7.1. Overview

The biotin-PC RNA mixture is purified with avidin affinity column to remove unincorporated biotin-labeled RNA from the transcription reaction mixture. The biotin-PC RNA bound to the resin is then irradiated with UV light at 365 nm for 1 h for photocleavage and subsequently recovered by elution.

7.2. Duration

1.5–2 h.

5.1 Take 3 eq. of NeutrAvidin Agarose Resin based on its binding capacity (the binding capacity used here is 1–2 mg of biotinylated BSA per mL of resin).

5.2 Pre-equilibrate the NeutrAvidin resin using 0.1 *M* potassium phosphate buffer (pH 6.4).

5.3 Discard the pre-equilibrated buffer and add the filtered transcription mixture (step 4.11) to the pre-equilibrated NeutrAvidin resin.

5.4 Incubate the transcription mixture with the NeutrAvidin resin at room temperature for 1 h.

5.5 Transfer the resin to an empty gravity flow column.

5.6 Wash the column with 9–10 column volumes of potassium phosphate buffer to remove all unbound molecules.

5.7 Directly irradiate the resin with long-wavelength UV light (365 nm) from top of the open column (<5 cm) for 1 h.

5.8 After irradiation, elute the bound RNA from the resin with 8–10 column volumes of 0.1 *M* potassium phosphate buffer (pH 6.4).

5.9 Concentrate the eluted RNA using a spin filter with a MWCO of 3 kDa.

7.3. Tip

The purification step is best conducted at 4 °C.

7.4. Tip

Save small aliquots of the sample at each step of purification (transcription mixture before purification, the flow-through from the wash step, flow-through following photocleavage) and run the samples on a denaturing PAGE to compare with the same treated GTP-transcribed RNA. The biotin-PC RNA formed can be confirmed by streptavidin biotin-PC RNA gel shift experiment.

An example of denaturing PAGE shift assay for biotin-PC RNA and RNA biotinylation assay with streptavidin is shown in Fig. 6.2.

8. CONCLUSIONS

Herein, we have described the design, synthesis, and evaluation of a nitrophenyl PC biotin GMP derivative (biotin-PC GMP) that can be used as a reagent to label RNA molecules at the 5′-terminus. Some of the

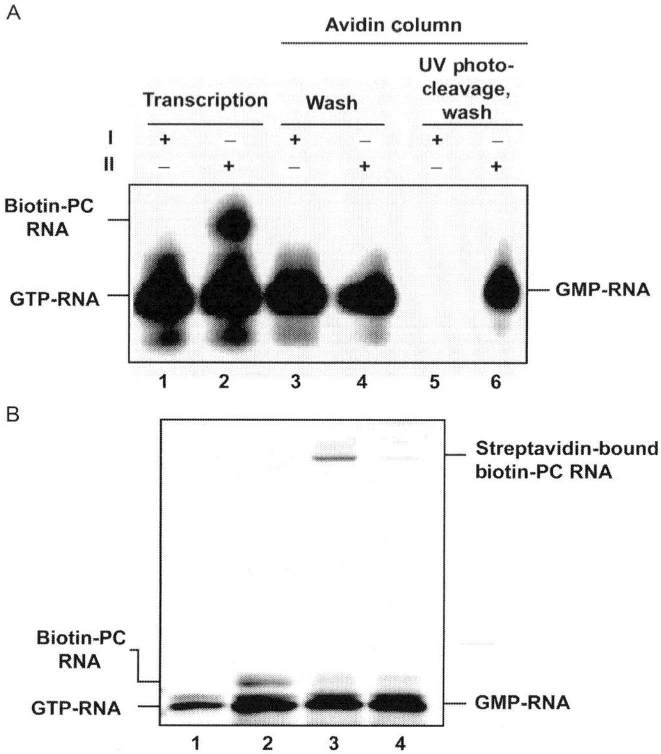

Figure 6.2 Denaturing PAGE assay for biotin-PC modified D5 RNA. (A) Transcription of D5 RNA with (+) or without biotin-PC GMP (–) followed by purification of the D5 RNA (GTP-D5 or biotin-PC GMP-D5 RNA) with a NeutrAvidin column after photocleavage. Lane 1: Transcription of D5 with unmodified GTP (I); Lane 2: Transcription of D5 with biotin-PC GMP/GTP mixture (II); Lane 3: NeutrAvidin column flow-through of unlabeled GTP-D5 RNA; Lane 4: NeutrAvidin flow-through of biotin-PC-labeled D5 RNA. As expected, unlabeled GTP-D5 is washed off the column. Lane 5: Elution of the RNA on the NeutrAvidin column following photo cleavage of unlabeled D5 RNA. As expected, there is no unmodified D5 RNA left on the NeutrAvidin column following the initial wash shown in Lane 3. Lane 6: Elution of the RNA on the NeutrAvidin column following photocleavage of biotin-PC-labeled D5 RNA. Note that as expected photocleavage releases biotin-PC-modified D5 RNA as GMP-D5 RNA that now runs at almost the same position as the unmodified GTP-D5 RNA. The RNAs are depicted as: GTP-transcribed RNA (I), biotin-PC-transcribed RNA (II). (B) RNA biotinylation assay with NeutrAvidin. Lane 1: Unlabeled D5 RNA; Lane 2: Biotin-PC-labeled D5 RNA; Lane 3: Biotin-PC-labeled D5 RNA incubated with excess NeutrAvidin (three times number of moles to RNA) for 1 h. Lane 4: GMP-RNA, flow-through using 10-K MWCO spin filter after photocleavage of NeutrAvidin-biotin-PC RNA.

properties that are important for this biotin-PC GMP tag to be useful in the purification of RNAs include the following: selective and average (~25%) incorporation by T7 RNAP under standard transcription reaction conditions; high affinity toward the streptavidin or avidin-modified capture bead for purification; and efficient photorelease on illumination with near-UV light. The resulting 5′-phosphorylated RNA is "scarless," remains unaltered, and retains full activity (Luo et al., 2011). Having a 5′-phosphorylated RNA through photocleavage is also advantageous for other biophysical applications that require phosphorylation on the 5′ end, such as ligation reaction, without going through cumbersome intermediate steps of dephosphorylation and rephosphorylation. Additionally, a biotin-PC GMP-RNA could enable facile isolation of RNA macromolecular complexes, controlled photorelease of RNAs for triggering or monitoring RNA–ligand interactions, and for therapeutic applications.

ACKNOWLEDGMENTS

Supported by NIH (GM077326 to T. K. D.), and National Science Foundation (CHE1213668 to T. K. D. and H. O. S.).

REFERENCES

Baklanov, M. M., Golikova, L. N., & Malgin, E. G. (1996). Effect on DNA transcription of nucleotide sequences upstream to T7 promoter. *Nucleic Acids Research, 24*, 3659–3660.

Fourmy, D., Recht, M. I., Blanchard, S. C., & Puglisi, J. D. (1996). Structure of the A site of *Escherichia coli* 16S ribosomal RNA complexed with an aminoglycoside antibiotic. *Science, 274*, 1367–1371.

Guillerez, J., Lopez, P. J., Proux, F., Launay, H., & Dreyfus, M. (2005). A mutation in T7 RNA polymerase that facilitates promoter clearance. *Proceedings of the National Academy of Sciences of the United States of America, 102*, 5958–5963.

Gumbs, O. H., Padgett, R. A., & Dayie, K. T. (2006). Fluorescence and solution NMR study of the active site of a 160-kDa group II intron ribozyme. *RNA, 12*, 1693–1707.

Kao, C., Zheng, M., & Rudisser, S. (1999). A simple and efficient method to reduce nontemplated nucleotide addition at the 3 terminus of RNAs transcribed by T7 RNA polymerase. *RNA, 5*, 1268–1272.

Luo, Y., Eldho, N. V., Sintim, H. O., & Dayie, T. K. (2011). RNAs synthesized using photocleavable biotinylated nucleotides have dramatically improved catalytic efficiency. *Nucleic Acids Research, 39*, 8559–8571.

Michel, F., Costa, M., & Westhof, E. (2009). The ribozyme core of group II introns: A structure in want of partners. *Trends in Biochemical Sciences, 34*, 189–199.

Milligan, J. F., Groebe, D. R., Witherell, G. W., & Uhlenbeck, O. C. (1987). Oligoribonucleotide synthesis using T7 RNA polymerase and synthetic DNA templates. *Nucleic Acids Research, 15*, 8783–8798.

Olejnik, J., Krzymanska-Olejnik, E., & Rothschild, K. J. (1998). Photocleavable affinity tags for isolation and detection of biomolecules. *Methods in Enzymology, 291*, 135–154.

Sampson, J. R., & Uhlenbeck, O. C. (1988). Biochemical and physical characterization of an unmodified yeast phenylalanine transfer RNA transcribed in vitro. *Proceedings of the National Academy of Sciences of the United States of America, 85*, 1033–1037.

CHAPTER SEVEN

Chemo-Enzymatic Synthesis of Selectively $^{13}C/^{15}N$-Labeled RNA for NMR Structural and Dynamics Studies

Luigi J. Alvarado*, Andrew P. Longhini*, Regan M. LeBlanc*, Bin Chen*, Christoph Kreutz†, T. Kwaku Dayie*,[1]

*Department of Chemistry and Biochemistry, Center for Biomolecular Structure & Organization, University of Maryland, College Park, Maryland, USA
†Institute of Organic Chemistry and Center for Molecular Biosciences (CMBI), University of Innsbruck, Innrain, Innsbruck, Austria
[1]Corresponding author: e-mail address: dayie@umd.edu

Contents

Methods in Enzymology, Volume 549
ISSN 0076-6879
http://dx.doi.org/10.1016/B978-0-12-801122-5.00007-6

Abstract

RNAs are an important class of cellular regulatory elements, and they are well characterized by X-ray crystallography and nuclear magnetic resonance (NMR) spectroscopy in their folded or bound states. However, the apo or unfolded states are more difficult to characterize by either method. Particularly, effective NMR spectroscopy studies of RNAs in the past were hampered by chemical shift overlap of resonances and associated rapid signal loss due to line broadening for RNAs larger than the median size found in the PDB (~25 nt); most functional riboswitches are bigger than this median size. Incorporation of selective site-specific $^{13}C/^{15}N$-labeled nucleotides into RNAs promises to overcome this NMR size limitation. Unlike previous isotopic enrichment methods such as phosphoramidite, *de novo*, uniform-labeling, and selective-biomass approaches, this newer chemical-enzymatic selective method presents a number of advantages for producing labeled nucleotides over these other methods. For example, total chemical synthesis of nucleotides, followed by solid-phase synthesis of RNA using phosphoramidite chemistry, while versatile in incorporating isotope labels into RNA at any desired position, faces problems of low yields (<10%) that drop precipitously for oligonucleotides larger than 50 nt. The alternative method of *de novo* pyrimidine biosynthesis of NTPs is also a robust technique, with modest yields of up to 45%, but it comes at the cost of using

16 enzymes, expensive substrates, and difficulty in making some needed labeling patterns such as selective labeling of the ribose C1′ and C5′ and the pyrimidine nucleobase C2, C4, C5, or C6. Biomass-produced, uniformly or selectively labeled NTPs offer a third method, but suffer from low overall yield per labeled input metabolite and isotopic scrambling with only modest suppression of ^{13}C–^{13}C couplings. In contrast to these four methods, our current chemo-enzymatic approach overcomes most of these shortcomings and allows for the synthesis of gram quantities of nucleotides with >80% yields while using a limited number of enzymes, six at most. The unavailability of selectively labeled ribose and base precursors had prevented the effective use of this versatile method until now. Recently, we combined an improved organic synthetic approach that selectively places $^{13}C/^{15}N$ labels in the pyrimidine nucleobase (either $^{15}N_1$, $^{15}N_3$, $^{13}C_2$, $^{13}C_4$, $^{13}C_5$, or $^{13}C_6$ or any combination) with a very efficient enzymatic method to couple ribose with uracil to produce previously unattainable labeling patterns (Alvarado et al., 2014). Herein we provide detailed steps of both our chemo-enzymatic synthesis of custom nucleotides and their incorporation into RNAs with sizes ranging from 29 to 155 nt and showcase the dramatic improvement in spectral quality of reduced crowding and narrow linewidths. Applications of this selective labeling technology should prove valuable in overcoming two major obstacles, chemical shift overlap of resonances and associated rapid signal loss due to line broadening, that have impeded studying the structure and dynamics of large RNAs such as full-length riboswitches larger than the ~25 nt median size of RNA NMR structures found in the PDB.

1. THEORY

Ribonucleic acid (RNA) is central to key biological processes such as signaling, gene regulation, catalysis, and viral infectivity (Breaker, 2009; Lu et al., 2011; Mattick, 2007; Newman & Nagai, 2010; Serganov & Nudler, 2013; Steitz, 2008). This functional diversity is due in part to the elaborate and pliable three-dimensional structures RNAs can adopt. Nuclear magnetic resonance (NMR) spectroscopy is one of the major methods utilized for RNA structure elucidation. However, for RNAs longer than 25 nucleotides, this technique suffers from conformational heterogeneity, extensive chemical shift overlap, and rapid signal decay (Dayie, 2008).

Four approaches were previously proposed to address these limitations: (i) total chemical synthesis of RNA using phosphoramidite chemistry; (ii) *de novo* biosynthesis of NTPs; (iii) biomass synthesis of NTPs; or (iv) selective-biomass synthesis of NTPs (Batey, Inada, Kujawinski, Puglisi, & Williamson, 1992; Hoffman & Holland, 1995; Johnson, Julien, & Hoogstraten, 2006; Lemaster & Kushlan, 2001; Milecki, 2002; Nikonowicz et al., 1992; Quant et al., 1994; Schultheisz, Szymczyna,

Scott, & Williamson, 2011; Thakur & Dayie, 2012; Thakur, Sama, Jackson, Chen, & Dayie, 2010; Wunderlich et al., 2012). NTPs obtained from methods (ii)–(iv) are then used in T7 RNA polymerase based RNA transcription. The biggest advantage of method (i) is the maximum flexibility it affords in positioning the label simply by varying the phosphoramidites used; however, the solid-phase synthesis methodology is extremely inefficient for making RNAs greater than 50 nucleotides as the yield drops significantly with increasing size of the polynucleotide (Wunderlich et al., 2012). Method (ii) proceeds with modest yields of ~45% for pyrimidine biosysnthesis (Schultheisz et al., 2011), and requires ~16 enzymes, expensive precursor glucose and aspartic acid substrates, and inaccessibility to some pyrimidine labels. Traditionally large quantities of uniformly labeled nucleotides were cost-effectively produced using biomass growth of bacteria on labeled media containing $^{15}NH_4Cl$ and a variety of uniformly labeled carbon sources such as ^{13}C-acetate, ^{13}C-glucose, ^{13}C-glycerol, ^{13}C-methanol, or ^{13}C-pyruvate (Batey et al., 1992; Hoffman & Holland, 1995; Johnson et al., 2006; Lemaster & Kushlan, 2001; Nikonowicz et al., 1992; Thakur & Dayie, 2012; Thakur et al., 2010). However, by using site-specifically labeled forms of these carbons sources and metabolically modified bacteria, ^{13}C isotopes could be readily incorporated at designated locations (Hoffman & Holland, 1995; Johnson et al., 2006; Lemaster & Kushlan, 2001; Thakur & Dayie, 2012; Thakur et al., 2010). Nonetheless, both of these methods (iii and iv) suffer from low overall yield per labeled input metabolite, and residual isotopic scrambling invariably leads to inadequate suppression of ^{13}C–^{13}C coupling (Alvarado et al., 2014; Thakur & Dayie, 2012).

A fifth approach, the chemo-enzymatic synthesis of NTPs followed by *in vitro* RNA transcription is potentially the most versatile method available. Until recently, lack of commercially available selectively labeled ribose and base precursors, unfortunately, prevented the realization of its full potential (Alvarado et al., 2014). We recently made an important technological advance in combining chemical synthesis of selective ^{13}C/^{15}N-labeled pyrimidine nucleobases with enzymatic synthesis to achieve site-specific labeling that overcomes most of these earlier deficiencies (Alvarado et al., 2014).

Here, we outline this robust approach that efficiently couples chemically synthesized ribose and nucleobase using enzymes from the pentose phosphate pathway to synthesize NTPs, followed by *in vitro* RNA transcription (Figs. 7.1, 7.2) (Alvarado et al., 2014; Tolbert & Williamson, 1996).

This approach enables labeling pyrimidine nucleobases selectively with any combination of the following: $^{15}N_1$, $^{15}N_3$, and $^{13}C_2$ from ^{13}C–^{15}N-labeled urea; $^{13}C_4$ and $^{13}C_5$ from ^{13}C-labeled bromoacetic acid; and $^{13}C_6$ from $K^{13}CN$. Additionally, it enables labeling ribose at any carbon position to produce previously unattainable labeled NTP patterns on a gram scale with >80% yields (based on input nucleobase). These labels contain isolated two-spin systems in both the ribose and the nucleobase and, thus, are ideal for both structural and dynamic studies for large RNAs such as riboswitches.

As an example, the starting materials $1',5'$-$^{13}C_2$-D-ribose and 6-^{13}C-1,3-$^{15}N_2$-uracil can be enzymatically coupled to synthesize $1',5',6$-$^{13}C_3$-1,3-$^{15}N_2$-uridine $5'$-triphosphate (UTP, Fig. 7.1), as showcased in our recent work (Alvarado et al., 2014). Importantly, any labeled combination of either ribose or uracil moieties can be used in our method. In the first step,

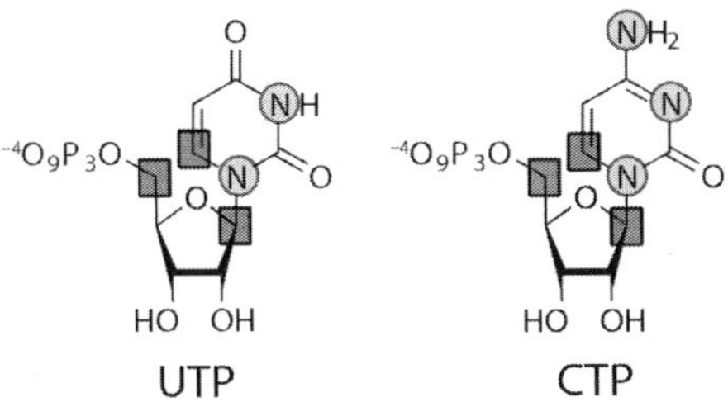

Figure 7.1 Selective site-specifically $^{13}C/^{15}N$-labeled uridine (left) and cytidine (right) $5'$-triphosphates. This is one of the potential labeling combinations to be synthesized using our methodology. Squares, ^{13}C; circles, ^{15}N.

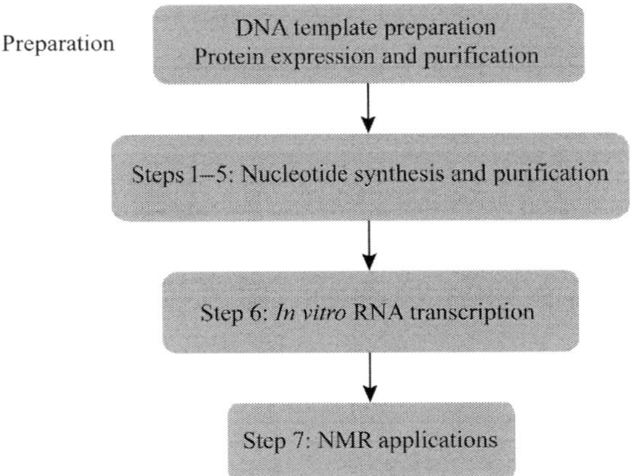

Figure 7.2 Flowchart of the complete protocol, including preparation.

UTP is synthesized in a one-pot reaction, followed by affinity purification. Cytidine 5′-triphosphate (CTP) is then synthesized in a one-pot reaction from UTP, followed by affinity purification. These newly synthesized nucleotides are then used directly for *in vitro* RNA transcription (Brunelle & Green, 2013). The labeled RNA is then purified to homogeneity by denaturing purification as detailed by Petrov, Wu, Puglisi, and Puglisi (2013). Herein, we detail the methodology to synthesize these nucleotides.

Finally, we demonstrate the versatility of these labels for obtaining structural and dynamic data for small (~20 nt) to large (>150 nt) RNAs. We show representative examples of how NMR spectral resolution and signal-to-noise ratios are enhanced with the incorporated specific isotopic labels in three RNAs of interest: iron-responsive element (IRE) RNA (29 nt), a riboswitch (63 nt), and HIV-1 core encapsidation signal (155 nt). It is anticipated that this methodology should find wide application in probing hitherto "difficult" to characterize RNAs such as full-length riboswitches that include both aptamer and expression platform regions.

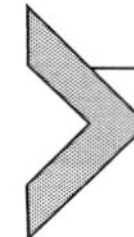

2. EQUIPMENT

0.22-μm cellulose acetate filters (GE Healthcare)
0.5-mL 3K molecular weight cutoff (MWCO) microcentrifuge spin columns (Millipore, RNase, DNase, pyrogen free)
0.5-mL microcentrifuge tubes (RNase, DNase, pyrogen free)
100-mL round-bottom flask
100-mL three-necked round-bottom flask
2-mL Pasteur pipet, long neck
50-mL conical tubes (RNase, DNase, pyrogen free)
50-mL round-bottom flask
600/800 MHz NMR instrument equipped with at least $^{1}H/^{13}C/^{15}N$ probes
Balloons with a wall thickness of at least 0.3 mm
Bent adapters with NS-stopcocks
C18 reverse-phase Vydac analytical column
Freeze dryer
Freezer (−20 and −80 °C)
High vacuum rotary vane pump
Liquid chromatography system

Low-speed tabletop centrifuge
Low-volume Shigemi tubes
Magnetic stirrer with heating and an oil bath or heat block
Magnetic stirring bar
Microcentrifuge
Micropipettor tips (RNase, DNase, pyrogen free)
Micropipettors
pH meter and electrode
Polyacrylamide gel electrophoresis (PAGE) equipment, preparative size
Razor
Reflux condenser
Refrigerator (4 °C)
Rotary evaporator with a diaphragm pump
Sorbtech® solvent-resistant column
Speedvac
Suction filter
Syringe
UV/Vis spectrophotometer
Water bath

3. MATERIALS

Unless stated otherwise, our chemicals were obtained from Sigma-Aldrich.

^{13}C-potassium cyanide (K^{13}CN)
$^{15}N_2$-urea
2′-Deoxy-adenosine 5′-triphosphate (dATP)
2-Bromoacetic acid
4,4-Dimethyl-4-silapentane-1-sulfonic acid (DSS)
40% Acrylamide/bis-acrylamide (19:1)
5% Palladium on barium sulfate (5% $Pd/BaSO_4$)
50% Aqueous acetic acid
Acetic anhydride
Acid phenol:chloroform 5:1, pH 4.5 (Ambion)
Affi-Gel Boronate Gel (BioRad)
Ammonium persulfate
Ampicillin
Boric acid (H_3BO_3)
Bovine serum albumin (BSA)

Table 7.1 Enzymes utilized in the synthesis of UTP and CTP

Enzyme	Abbreviation	E.C.	Source	Vendor
Ribokinase	RK	2.7.1.15	*Escherichia coli*[a]	–[a]
Phosphoribosyl pyrophosphate synthetase	PRPPS	2.7.6.1	Human[a]	–[a]
Uridine phosphoribosyl transferase	UPRT	2.4.2.9	*E. coli*[a]	–[a]
Cytidine triphosphate synthetase	CTPS	6.3.4.2	*E. coli*[a]	–[a]
Nucleoside monophosphate kinase	NMPK	2.7.4.4	Bovine liver	Roche
Creatine kinase	CK	2.7.3.2	Rabbit muscle	Sigma
Myokinase (adenylate kinase)	MK	2.7.4.3	Rabbit muscle	Sigma
Thermostable inorganic pyrophosphatase	TIPP	3.6.1.1	*Thermococcus litoralis*	NEB

[a]Arthur, Alvarado, and Dayie (2011).

Bromophenol blue
Celite
Concentrated hydrochloric acid (HCl)
Creatine kinase (CK) (see Table 7.1)
Creatine phosphate
Cytidine triphosphate synthetase (CTPS) (recombinantly expressed)
Diethylether
Dithiothreitol (DTT)
Dry ice
Ethanol, 100%
Ethylenediaminetetraacetic acid (EDTA)
Formamide
Hydrochloric acid (HCl)
Hydrogen gas
Magnesium chloride ($MgCl_2$)
Methanol, >98% (HPLC grade)
Myokinase (MK)
N,*N*,*N*′,*N*′-Tetramethylethylenediamine
Nucleoside monophosphate kinase (NMPK) (Roche)
pH indicator paper

Phosphoribosyl pyrophosphate synthetase (PRPPS) (recombinantly expressed)
Polyethylene glycol, MW 8000
Potassium chloride (KCl)
Ribokinase (RK) (recombinantly expressed)
Ribose (unlabeled and in various labeled forms)
RNase/DNase-free water
rNTPs: rATP, rUTP, rCTP, rGTP
Sodium acetate (NaOAc)
Sodium carbonate (Na_2CO_3)
Sodium phosphate dibasic heptahydrate ($Na_2HPO_4 \cdot 7H_2O$)
Sodium phosphate monobasic monohydrate ($NaH_2PO_4 \cdot H_2O$)
Spermidine
T7 RNA polymerase (processive P266L mutant, recombinantly expressed)
Thermostable inorganic pyrophosphatase (TIPP) (New England Biolabs)
Triethylamine bicarbonate (TEABC)
Tris base
Triton X-100
Uracil (unlabeled and in various labeled forms by chemical synthesis, *vide infra*)
Urea
Uridine phosphoribosyl transferase (UPRT) (recombinantly expressed)
Xylene cyanol

3.1. Solutions and buffers

Step 1: 50% aqueous acetic acid
Slowly add 100 mL glacial acetic acid to 100 mL distilled water

Steps 2–5: 1 *M* Triethylammonium bicarbonate, pH 9.4
Dissolve 121 mL triethylamine in 1 L water (final volume)
Bubble CO_2 into the solution until pH 9.4

Acidified water, pH 4.6
Bubble CO_2 into autoclaved water until pH 4.6

Vydac column buffer A

Component	Final concentration	Stock	Amount
$NaH_2PO_4 \cdot H_2O$	12.5 m*M*	1 *M*	12.5 mL
$Na_2HPO_4 \cdot 7H_2O$	12.5 m*M*	0.5 *M*	25 mL

Adjust to pH 2.8 with glacial acetic acid. Add water to 1 L. Filter through 0.22-μm hydrophilic membrane.

Vydac column buffer B

Component	Final concentration	Stock	Amount
$NaH_2PO_4 \cdot H_2O$	62.5 m*M*	1 *M*	62.5 mL
$Na_2HPO_4 \cdot 7H_2O$	62.5 m*M*	0.5 *M*	125 mL

Adjust to pH 2.8 with glacial acetic acid. Add water to 1 L. Filter through 0.22-μm hydrophilic membrane.

NMPK solution

Component	Final concentration	Stock	Amount
NMPK	–	–	60 mg
Tris–HCl, pH 6.5	50 m*M*	1 *M*	50 μL
Glycerol	50% (v/v)	100% (v/v)	0.5 mL

Add water to 1 mL.

Creatine kinase (CK) solution

Component	Final concentration	Stock	Amount
Creatine kinase	–	–	1 mg
Tris–HCl, pH 7.5	50 m*M*	1 *M*	50 μL
Glycerol	50% (v/v)	100% (v/v)	0.5 mL

Add water to 1 mL.

Step 6: 10× transcription buffer

Component	Final concentration	Stock	Amount
Tris–HCl, pH 8.0	400 m*M*	1 *M*	4 mL

DTT	100 m*M*	1 *M*	1 mL
Triton X-100	0.1% (v/v)	10%	0.1 mL
Spermidine, pH 7.0	10 m*M*	500 m*M*	0.2 mL

Add water to 10 mL.

2× formamide RNA loading buffer

Component	Final concentration	Stock	Amount
Formamide	95% (v/v)	100% (v/v)	9.5 mL
SDS	0.025% (w/v)	10% (w/v)	25 μL
EDTA, pH 8.0	0.5 m*M*	50 m*M*	0.1 mL
Bromophenol blue	0.05% (w/v)	–	5 mg
Xylene cyanol	0.05% (w/v)	–	5 mg

Add water to 10 mL.

10× Tris–Borate–EDTA buffer

Component	Final concentration	Stock	Amount
Tris	0.9 *M*	–	108 g
Boric acid	0.9 *M*	–	240 g
EDTA, pH 8.0	10 m*M*	500 m*M*	20 mL

Add water to 1 L.

13% denaturing PAGE solution

Component	Final concentration	Stock	Amount
Acrylamide/bis-acrylamide (19:1)	13%	40%	162.5 mL
Urea	8 *M*	–	240 g
TBE buffer	1×	10×	50 mL

Add water to 500 mL. Protect from light.

3 *M* Sodium acetate, pH 5.2

Dissolve 24.6 g NaOAc in 100 mL water (final volume)

4. PROTOCOL

1. Duration

Preparation	About 1 week
Step 1	4–5 days
Steps 2–5	About 2 weeks
Step 6	1 week

2. Preparation (See Fig. 7.2)

If the desired RNA is >70 nt, generate a DNA template for *in vitro* transcription carrying the T7 promoter sequence (5′-TAATACGAC TCACTATAGGG) upstream of the desired RNA by standard PCR techniques. Alternately, if desired RNA is <70 nt, you may utilize a synthetic DNA template overhang carrying the sequence of interest. Approximately 10–50 pmol of DNA is needed for each transcription reaction.

Express and purify RK, PRPPS, UPRT, and CTPS as described previously by Arthur et al. (2011). Preferably, stock enzyme solutions concentrations will be ~10 mg/mL.

Purchase the corresponding nucleotide building blocks, e.g., ribose and nucleobase, from commercial sources (Isotec, Cambridge Isotope Laboratories). Alternately, synthesize the nucleobases as described in Step 1 below, or by Kreutz and coworkers (Wunderlich et al., 2012).

3. Caution

The homogeneity of the DNA templates is of utmost importance in RNA preparation. It is critical that all synthetic DNA templates used to produce RNAs <70 nt are purified by denaturing gel electrophoresis to minimize resulting heterogeneous RNA populations after *in vitro* transcription. Additionally, including two final 2′-OCH_3 nucleotides on the 5′-end of the template strand will reduce $N+1$ transcript heterogeneity.

The activity of RK, PRPPS, UPRT, and CTPS may decrease >50% after 6 months of storage at −20 °C. Therefore, if possible, store the minimum amount needed at −20 °C, and the rest at −80 °C.

RNase-free conditions are of utmost importance to maintaining the integrity of RNA. All reagents, buffers, and solutions should be

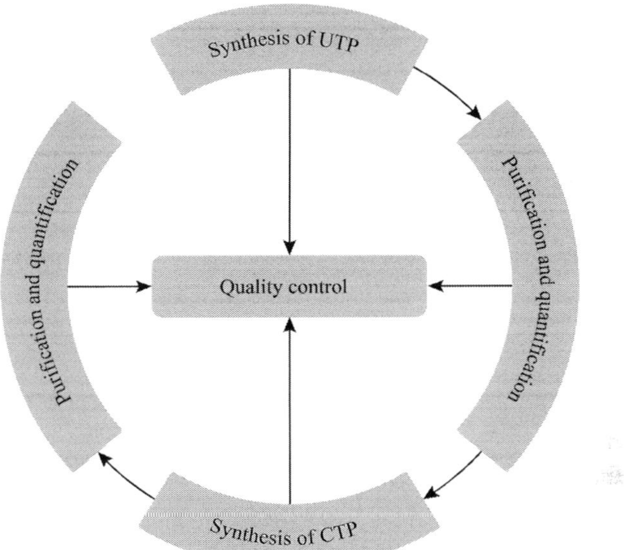

Figure 7.3 Flowchart of nucleotide synthesis. Notice that it is recommended to perform quality control at all stages to ensure maximal yield.

autoclaved (except for urea-containing solutions). Alternatively, they can be sterile filtered. All materials, such as glass plates, should be thoroughly washed and oven-dried before use. Wear gloves at all times.

Some of the buffers used in the protocol are highly volatile. Please prepare these buffers under a chemical fume hood (Fig. 7.3).

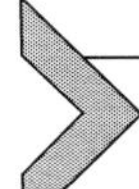

5. STEP 1: SYNTHESIS OF URACIL

5.1. Overview

Uracils with various stable isotope labeling patterns are accessible via chemical synthesis. Starting from potassium cyanide and 2-bromoacetic acid, the cyano acetylurea precursor is obtained in good yields. In the final step, uracil is formed under reductive reaction conditions using palladium on barium sulfate under a hydrogen atmosphere. Various $^{13}C/^{15}N$-labeling patterns are amenable using this approach. Here, we exemplify the uracil synthesis for the 6-^{13}C–$^{15}N_2$-uracil derivative.

5.2. Duration

4–5 days

1.1 Synthesis of 3-^{13}C-cyanoacetic acid: Dissolve 2-bromoacetic acid (6.99 g, 50.3 mmol) in 20 mL of water in a 100-mL round-bottom flask equipped with a reflux condenser and a magnetic stirring bar.

1.2 Add sodium carbonate (Na_2CO_3, 3.4 g, 32.1 mmol) predissolved in 10 mL of water until pH 9 is reached. Check the pH with a pH indicator paper.

1.3 Dissolve K^{13}CN (3.24 g, 49 mmol) in 10 mL of water and add to the 100-mL round-bottom flask. Heat the reaction mixture using an oil bath or a heat block to 80 °C for 3 h while stirring.

1.4 Remove the heating source and continue stirring at room temperature for 20 h.

1.5 Next, add concentrated HCl stepwise until pH 1 is reached. Check the pH after every addition.

1.6 Remove the solvent by evaporation using a rotary evaporator. The residue is then dried in high vacuum for 30 min. A yellow-white semisolid salt cake is obtained.

1.7 Extract the 3-^{13}C-cyanoacetic acid from the semisolid mass by suspending the salt cake in diethylether (five 100-mL portions). The ether extract is filtered through a suction filter and the yellow ethereal solution is evaporated to dryness. The oily residue solidifies upon cooling on ice.

1.8 The solidified yellowish to orange 3-^{13}C-cyanoacetic acid is then dried in high vacuum for 2 h.

1.9 Synthesis of 3-^{13}C–$^{15}N_2$-cyanoacetyl urea: The 3-^{13}C-cyanoacetic acid from the previous step (2.0 g, 23.3 mmol) is placed in a 50-mL round-bottom flask equipped with a reflux condenser and a magnetic stirring bar.

1.10 Add $^{15}N_2$-urea (1.5 g, 25 mmol) and 5 mL of acetic anhydride. Heat this reaction mixture to 90 °C for 30 min. After about 5 min a white precipitate can be observed.

1.11 Add 1–2 mL water and let the mixture cool to room temperature. The 3-^{13}C–$^{15}N_2$-cyanoacetyl urea can then be isolated by filtration and is then dried in high vacuum for 5 h.

1.12 Synthesis of 6-^{13}C–$^{15}N_2$-Uracil: Add 5% Pd/$BaSO_4$ (800 mg) and 10 mL 50% aqueous acetic to a 100-mL three-necked round-bottom flask equipped with a magnetic stirring bar and bent adapters with NS-stopcocks. The adapters are used to either evaporate the flask or spill the evacuated flask with hydrogen gas using a balloon.

1.13 The evacuation hydrogen spill procedure is repeated three times. The brown suspension then turns black.

1.14 Simultaneously, 3-^{13}C–$^{15}N_2$-cyanoacetyl urea (1.6 g, 12.5 mmol) is dissolved in 40 mL of boiling aqueous 50% acetic acid and then added to the reduced palladium catalyst.

1.15 The reaction is stirred at room temperature under a hydrogen atmosphere. Refill the hydrogen balloon if necessary.

1.16 Before filtering through a celite pad on a suction filter, the mixture is heated to 70 °C for 1 h.

1.17 The filtrate is concentrated until a white precipitate is observed. Then, 6-^{13}C–$^{15}N_2$-uracil is precipitated by storing the suspension at 4 °C overnight.

1.18 Uracil is obtained by filtration over a suction filter and the white solid is dried in high vacuum. The expected yield is 1.15 g (82%).

5.3. Tip

As the labeled compounds are rather expensive, it is advisable to carry out the reactions using unlabeled compounds first to gain familiarity with the procedure.

5.4. Tip

Add the sodium carbonate solution in step 1.2 slowly to avoid frothing due to CO_2 evolution. In step 1.5, add the HCl again slowly to avoid frothing due to CO_2 evolution.

5.5. Tip

The 1–2 mL of water added in step 1.11 is needed to resuspend the precipitated product to facilitate isolation by filtration.

5.6. Tip

The reaction progress starting at step 1.12 should be monitored every 12 h. For that purpose, take a small aliquot (500 μL) of the reaction suspension and centrifuge to clear the suspension. Remove the supernatant and transfer to a 10-mL round-bottom flask. Then, the solvent is removed by evaporation and the remaining white solid is dried in high vacuum for 1 h. Then, dissolve the residue in 500 μL deuterated dimethylsulfoxide (DMSO-d_6) and acquire a 1D ^{13}C spectrum. The conversion yield to uracil can be qualitatively estimated by comparing the starting material ^{13}C peak at 116 ppm and the product ^{13}C peak at 142 ppm.

6. STEP 2: SYNTHESIS OF UTP

6.1. Overview

Site-specifically labeled uracil and ribose are combined to produce uridine monophosphate using enzymes from the nucleotide salvage pathway. Uridine monophosphate is then phosphorylated, taking advantage of NMPK and creatine kinase. All aliquots taken at various reaction time points are analyzed on a C18 reverse-phase Vydac analytical column as described in step 4 to track the progress of the reaction.

6.2. Duration

11 h

2.1 Prepare the reaction mixture for the synthesis of UMP by adding the following reagents in the order shown (with UPRT added last) to a 50-mL conical tube.

Component	Final concentration	Stock	Amount
Sodium phosphate monobasic	9.4 m*M*	1 *M*	94 μL
Sodium phosphate dibasic	40.6 m*M*	500 m*M*	812 μL
$MgCl_2$	10 m*M*	1 *M*	100 μL
Ampicillin	2 mg/mL	100 mg/mL	200 μL
DTT	10 m*M*	1 *M*	100 μL
dATP	0.5 mL	100 m*M*	50 μL
Creatine phosphate	100 m*M*	500 m*M*	2000 μL
Uracil	8 m*M*	50 m*M*	1600 μL
Bovine serum albumin	0.1 mg/mL	10 mg/mL	100 μL
Creatine kinase	0.005 mg/mL	1 mg/mL	50 μL
Myokinase	0.010 U/μL	5 U/μL	20 μL
Pyrophosphatase	0.004 U/μL	2 U/μL	20 μL
RK	0.005 U/μL	0.5 U/μL	100 μL
PRPPS	0.0003 U/μL	0.01 U/μL	300 μL
UPRT	0.005 U/μL	0.4 U/μL	125 μL

Add 4.23 mL water to 9.9 mL final volume.

2.2 Incubate at 37 °C for 10 min to equilibrate temperature.

2.3 Start reaction by adding 100 μL of 1 *M* ribose to bring the final concentration of ribose to 10 m*M*.

2.4 Remove a 50 μL aliquot of the reaction (Time 0).

2.5 Place the reaction in a 37 °C water bath and incubate for 5 h.

2.6 Collect aliquots at 2 h (Time 2) and 5 h (Time 5).

2.7 Once uracil is completely depleted, as determined by FPLC, add the following components to the reaction mixture.

Component	Final concentration	Stock	Amount
KCl	10 m*M*	1 *M*	10 μL
dATP	0.1 m*M*	100 m*M*	10 μL
Creatine phosphate	10 m*M*	500 m*M*	200 μL
NMPK	0.05 mg/mL	10 mg/mL	50 μL

2.8 Incubate at 37 °C for 4 h. Alternately, the reaction may run overnight.

2.9 Remove a final aliquot of the reaction (Time Final).

2.10 At this stage, the reaction can either be immediately purified or, alternatively, frozen and purified later.

6.3. Tip

If possible, use a magnetic stirrer. This is to ensure a homogeneous enzymatic reaction throughout the allotted time.

6.4. Tip

In the past we have observed white precipitate. This does not affect the outcome or yield of the reaction.

6.5. Tip

The final concentrations of RK, PRPPS, and UPRT can be decreased or increased if needed without adversely affecting the yield of the reaction. It only affects the completion time.

6.6. Tip

The phosphorylation state of dATP is of utmost importance for the ATP-regeneration system. If possible, aliquot stock dATP solution in small amounts to minimize freeze–thaw cycles that may promote dATP hydrolysis.

6.7. Tip

Commercial myokinase is stored as an ammonium sulfate precipitate. However, due to the low volume needed and the large final reaction volume, it can be used directly without centrifuging it and using the pellet. Thoroughly mix the resuspension before taking the corresponding aliquot.

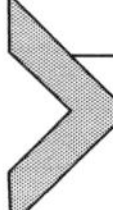

7. STEP 3: SYNTHESIS OF CTP

7.1. Overview

UTP is converted into CTP in a single-step reaction catalyzed by CTP synthetase. The progress of the reaction is monitored by C18 reverse-phase Vydac analytical chromatography as described in step 4 (Section 8) to track the progress of the reaction.

7.2. Duration

8 h

3.1 Add the following reagents in the order shown (with CTPS added last).

Component	Final concentration	Stock	Amount
Tris–HCl, pH 8.0	50 m*M*	1 *M*	500 μL
$MgCl_2$	10 m*M*	1 *M*	100 μL
Ampicillin	2 mg/mL	100 mg/mL	200 μL
dATP	4 m*M*	100 m*M*	400 μL
UTP	2 m*M*	50 m*M*	400 μL
CTPS	0.10 mg/mL	17.8 mg/mL	56.2 μL

Add 7.94 mL water to 9.6 mL final volume.

3.2 Incubate at 37 °C for 10 min.

3.3 Add 400 μL of 500 m*M* $^{15}NH_4Cl$ to bring the final concentration to 20 m*M*.

3.4 Take a 50-μL aliquot (Time 0).

3.5 Incubate at 37 °C for 6 h.

3.6 Take 50-μL aliquots at 3 and 6 h (Time 3 and Final).

3.7 At this stage, the reaction can either be immediately purified or, alternatively, frozen at −20 °C and purified later.

7.3. Tip

If possible, use a magnetic stirrer. This is to ensure a homogeneous enzymatic reaction throughout the allotted time.

7.4. Tip

The final concentration of CTPS can be decreased or increased if needed without majorly affecting the yield of the reaction. It would only affect the completion time.

7.5. Tip

The phosphorylation state of dATP is of utmost importance for the ATP-regeneration system. If possible, aliquot stock dATP solution in small amounts to minimize freeze–thaw cycles that may promote dATP hydrolysis.

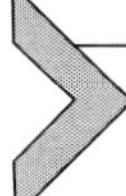

8. STEP 4: PURIFICATION AND QUANTIFICATION

8.1. Overview

Synthesized UTP and CTP are purified on a Sorbtech solvent-resistant column packed with approximately 10 g of Affi-Gel Boronate Gel. Purified nucleotides are lyophilized and redissolved at high concentrations for use in *in vitro* transcription reactions.

8.2. Duration

3 days

4.1 Thaw the UTP or CTP reaction on ice.

4.2 Add 10 mL 1 *M* TEABC pH 9.4 to the reaction and let sit at room temperature for 15 min.

4.3 Centrifuge at 12,800 × *g* for 10 min to pellet all precipitated proteins.

4.4 Sterile filter the reaction mixture by passing it through a 0.22-μm syringe filter.

4.5 The reaction is slowly loaded manually onto a Sorbtech column packed with 10 g Affi-Gel Boronate Gel kept at 4 °C.

4.6 The column is washed, at 4 mL/min, with four column volumes (CV) of 1 *M* TEABC to wash-off dATP and any remaining proteins.

4.7 Acidified water pH 4.3 is then used to elute the UTP or CTP off the column until the UV trace has returned to baseline (Fig. 7.4).

4.8 The elution fractions are transferred directly to a lyophilization vessel when the absorbance measured at 254 nm begins to rise.

4.9 The collected flow through is frozen with constant spinning in a dry ice–ethanol bath, ca. −78 °C.

4.10 The sample is lyophilized *in vacuo* for one and a half days to remove all water and residual TEABC. This step is performed with a large-scale freeze-dryer.

4.11 At the end of the lyophilization, add 2 mL of ddH_2O to redissolve the ribonucleotides. Transfer to two 1.5-mL Eppendorf tubes and wash the lyophilization vessel twice with 2 mL of ddH_2O, transferring to Eppendorf tubes as before.

4.12 Reduce the sample volume into dryness (or near dryness) for 2 h, transfer the contents to two tubes, and reduce sample volume for 2 more hours. This step is performed with a Speedvac.

4.13 Finally, consolidate the sample into one tube each for UTP and CTP and calculate the nucleotide concentration by measuring absorbance at 260 nm for UTP (molar extinction coefficient 10,000 M^{-1} cm^{-1}) or 271 nm for CTP (molar extinction coefficient 9,000 M^{-1} cm^{-1}). The final yield can be calculated based on a theoretical yield of 80 μmol of UTP or 20 μmol of CTP. Adjust the nucleotide

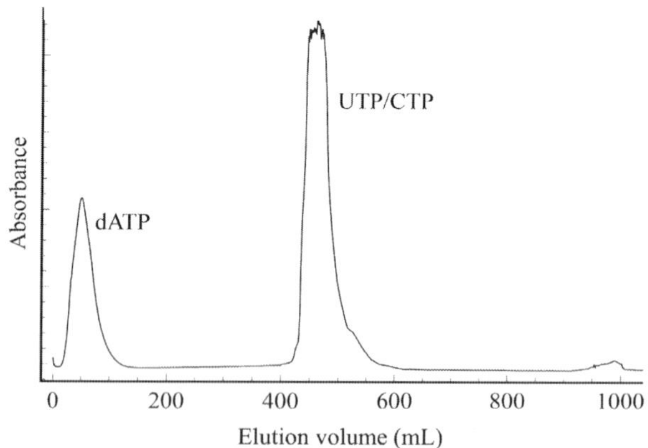

Figure 7.4 FPLC chromatogram of boronate purification of UTP or CTP monitored at 254 nm. When purifying CTP, which has an absorbance maximum at 270 nm, the peak will be significantly less intense.

concentrations to 50–100 m*M* and store at −20 °C in 10 m*M* Tris–HCl pH 7.5 and 0.5 m*M* EDTA.

8.3. Tip

The binding capacity of Affi-Gel Boronate gel is 50 mg of ligand (e.g., ribonucleotides) per 1 g of resin.

8.4. Tip

The packing of the boronate beads in the column is crucial. Before running any samples through, test the column with commercial standards. Boronate beads double or triple their size in 1 *M* TEABC. Conversely, they shrink when in acidified water. If the user notes a decrease in purification yields, the column should be repacked, and washed thoroughly. A stringent regenerating protocol is suggested by the manufacturer in which the beads are washed with 0.1 *M* glacial acetic acid, rinsed extensively with water, and finally reequilibrated with 1 *M* TEABC.

8.5. Tip

The pH for both 1 *M* TEABC and acidified water may drift over time. Thus, it is recommended that these solutions be made fresh prior to the purification.

8.6. Tip

Sample must be manually loaded onto the boronate column due to the high back pressure caused by the volatility of 1 *M* TEABC.

8.7. Tip

To avoid sample loss during sample concentration, transfers should be made from samples with lowest concentrations to highest concentration.

8.8. Tip

Most FPLC UV detectors are limited to a 254 nm detection wavelength. The molar extinction coefficient for CTP is rather low at such wavelength; thus, the purification chromatogram may appear lower than it actually is; always check the final product on a spectrophotometer. In our experience purification yields are >90%.

9. STEP 5: QUALITY CONTROL

9.1. Overview

During the course of the reaction, aliquots are analyzed to ensure that reactions proceed to completion. The final quality control is performed using a combination of NMR and liquid chromatography.

9.2. Duration

4 h

5.1. Vydac analysis of aliquots

5.1.1 Spin each 50-μL aliquot for 15 min at 8000 × *g* in a 0.5 mL, 3K MWCO centrifugal filtration column to remove protein contaminants.

5.1.2 With a syringe, load 10 μL of the filtrate into a 100-μL sample loop.

5.1.3 Run the following protocol to separate the nucleotide components in each aliquot. Representative traces for the UTP and CTP reaction are shown in Fig. 7.5: 0% Vydac buffer A for 4 CV, linear gradient from 0% to 100% Vydac buffer B for 4 CV, 100% Vydac buffer B for 2 CV, and 0% Vydac buffer B for 4 CV (reequilibration) (Fig. 7.5).

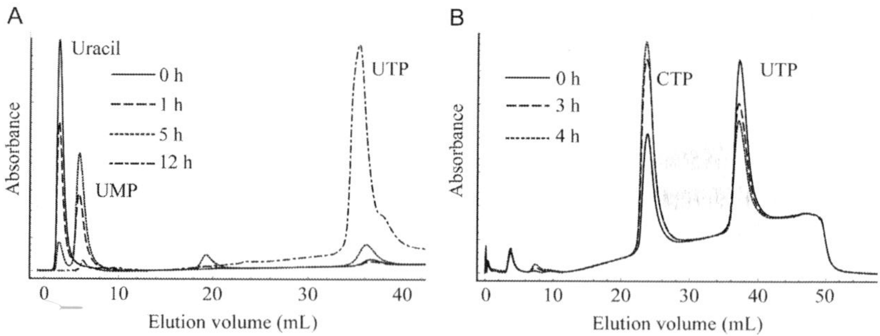

Figure 7.5 FPLC chromatograms of the one-pot syntheses of UTP and CTP. (A) The synthesis of UMP is nearly complete at 5 h. At this point, the components to synthesize UTP are added, completing its synthesis at 12 h. (B) The synthesis of CTP is nearly complete at 4 h. Both UTP/dATP and CTP/dADP have identical elution volumes, hence the peaks do not appear to be completely depleted, as dATP and dADP are both in large excess in the reaction mixture.

5.2. NMR verification

5.2.1. Prepare purified UTP or CTP in the following mixture:

Component	Final concentration	Stock	Amount (μL)
UTP/CTP	1 m*M*	50 m*M*	13
D_2O	10% (v/v)	100% (v/v)	65
DSS	0.1 m*M*	1 m*M*	65

Add ddH_2O to 650 μL and transfer to a regular-volume NMR tube.

5.2.2. For both UTP and CTP, run a 2D heteronuclear single quantum coherence (HSQC) experiment of the C1′ region to verify complete conversion of ribose to UTP. Run other experiments such as 1D ^{31}P and 1D ^{13}C to further validate phosphorylation state and coupling patterns, respectively.

9.3. Tip

Thorough cleaning of the injection syringe is recommended to avoid cross-sample contamination. Otherwise, sample carryover from prior time points may appear as incomplete reactions.

9.4. Tip

Typical acquisition parameters for 2D HSQC experiments of the ribose region are 4.7 ppm ^{1}H carrier, 80 ppm ^{13}C carrier, 13 ppm ^{1}H spectral width, and 50 ppm ^{13}C spectral width.

Typical acquisition parameters for 2D HSQC experiments of the base region are 4.7 ppm ^{1}H carrier, 130 ppm ^{13}C carrier, 13 ppm ^{1}H spectral width, and 94 ppm ^{13}C spectral width.

Typical acquisition parameters for 1D ^{31}P experiments of the phosphate region are 0 ppm for the ^{31}P carrier and 60 ppm spectral width.

Typical acquisition parameters for 1D ^{13}C experiments of both the ribose and base regions are 110 ppm for the ^{13}C carrier and 120 ppm spectral width.

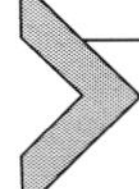

10. STEP 6: *IN VITRO* RNA TRANSCRIPTION

10.1. Overview

Site-specifically labeled UTP and/or CTP are used to transcribe RNA *in vitro* using T7 RNA polymerase. Optimization of NTP and Mg^{2+}

concentrations at small and mid-scales is extremely important to maximize yields before scaling up to larger volumes. This optimization has been described elsewhere (Milligan, Groebe, Witherell, & Uhlenbeck, 1987). Synthesized RNA is purified by denaturing gel electrophoresis and subsequently electroeluted. Labeled RNA is finally exchanged into an appropriate buffer and used for NMR spectroscopy.

10.2. Duration

3 days

6.1 The following reaction is assembled in the order shown (with T7 RNA polymerase added last):

Component	Final concentration	Stock	Amount
Transcription buffer	1×	10×	1000 μL
$MgCl_2$	Varies	1 *M*	Varies
PEG	80 mg/mL	400 mg/mL	2000 μL
DNA template	0.3 μ*M*	10 μ*M*	300 μL
DTT	0.01 *M*	1 *M*	100 μL
TIPP	2 U/mL	2000 U/mL	10 μL
ATP	Varies	100 m*M*	Varies
GTP	Varies	100 m*M*	Varies
Specifically labeled UTP	Varies	100 m*M*	Varies
Specifically labeled CTP	Varies	100 m*M*	Varies
T7 RNA polymerase	0.10 mg/mL	10 mg/mL	100 μL

Add water to 10 mL.

6.2 Incubate reaction at 37 °C for 3 h.
6.3 Add 10 mL of acid phenol:chloroform to reaction and vortex for 10 s.
6.4 Spin reaction at 3200 × *g* for 10 min in a tabletop centrifuge to separate aqueous and organic layers.
6.5 Transfer aqueous layer to two fresh 50-mL falcon tubes.
6.6 Add 5 mL water to the remaining organic layer and vortex for 10 s.
6.7 Spin reaction at 3200 × *g* for 10 min in a tabletop centrifuge to separate aqueous and organic layers.
6.8 Pool together all aqueous layers.

6.9 Add 1/10 volumes of 3 *M* sodium acetate pH 5.3 and 3 volumes of cold 100% ethanol to precipitate RNA.
6.10 Store at −20 °C overnight.
6.11 Spin down precipitate at 12,800 × *g* for 45 min.
6.12 Remove excess ethanol.
6.13 Wash pellets with 2 mL of cold 70% ethanol.
6.14 Spin down precipitate at 12,800 × *g* for 45 min.
6.15 Carefully remove excess ethanol.
6.16 Air dry pellet for 30 min.
6.17 Redissolve pellet in minimal volume of 8 *M* urea, 1 × TBE.
6.18 Purify RNA by denaturing gel electrophoresis as described by Puglisi and coworkers (Petrov et al., 2013).

10.3. Tip

The homogeneity of the purified RNA is of utmost importance for the subsequent steps. Ensure that the sample is of uniform length and conformation by using denaturing and native PAGE analysis.

10.4. Tip

Optimization of both NTP and Mg^{2+} concentrations is essential for *in vitro* RNA transcriptions. In our experience, we have had success in optimizing individual NTP concentrations ranging from 1.25 to 5 m*M* and Mg^{2+} concentrations ranging from 5 to 25 m*M*. Additionally, T7 RNA polymerase concentration should also be optimized. In our experience, we have utilized 0.05–1 mg/mL of enzyme.

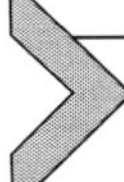

11. STEP 7: NMR APPLICATIONS

11.1. Overview

With increasing RNA size (>35 nt), the utility of traditional RNA labeling and NMR methodologies becomes more limited (Alvarado et al., 2014). However, RNAs transcribed with our site-specific $^{13}C/^{15}N$ isotopic labeling patterns can be exploited in NMR spectroscopy to obtain structural and dynamics information hitherto unavailable. Extensive protocols for resonance assignment, structure determination, and dynamics characterization have been published elsewhere (Bothe et al., 2011; Dayie, 2005, 2011; Pardi, 1995). Here, we present some examples of heteronuclear NMR experiments that show the increased resolution and signal-to-noise ratio of both the IRE (29 nt), a riboswitch (63 nt), and HIV-1 core encapsidation signal (155 nt) when transcribed with our custom labels.

11.2. Heteronuclear single quantum coherence (HSQC)

Several resonance assignment experiments utilize HSQC, a through-bond experiment that correlates two active nuclei via their *J*-coupling constant ($^1J_{CH}$), usually ranging from 147 to 216 Hz in RNA. Unfortunately, resonances in both ribose and nucleobases exhibit narrow chemical shift dispersion, and such a narrow dispersion leads to significant overlap in the two-dimensional correlation map. Here, we show how our site-specifically labeled IRE RNA, a 63-nt riboswitch, and HIV-1 RNAs reduce the degree of spectral overlap in two-dimensional HSQC experiments (Fig. 7.6) without the need of constant-time experiments. Even though these constant-time experiments remove carbon–carbon couplings in uniformly labeled samples, their implementation leads to rapid signal decay and decreased signal-to-noise levels. With our specific isolated two-spin labels, we do not need to compromise on sensitivity or resolution.

11.3. Transverse relaxation optimized spectroscopy (TROSY)

RNAs synthesized with our selective site-specifically labeled NTPs (prepared using chemo-enzymatic methodology) benefit from transverse relaxation optimized spectroscopy (TROSY) techniques that mitigate problems of crowding, rapid relaxation, low resolution, and sensitivity (Miclet et al., 2004; Thakur et al., 2010). Compared to a regular HSQC, TROSY experiments select the slowest relaxing multiplet component of each resonance, leading to enhanced resolution and sensitivity. This approach is particularly important for larger RNAs, such as the HIV-1 RNA used here, in order to observe resonances inaccessible by traditional HSQC experiments (Fig. 7.7). Using a C6 methine-optimized TROSY, we obtained a twofold improvement in signal-to-noise ratio for the HIV-1 RNA (155 nt). A C5′-optimized TROSY showed only marginal improvement for the IRE RNA (29 nt). This highlights the importance of utilizing TROSY-based experiments for structural and dynamics analysis of large RNAs.

12. CONCLUSION

We have outlined a fast, efficient, and economical chemo-enzymatic synthetic approach to incorporate site-selectively $^{13}C/^{15}N$-labeled pyrimidine

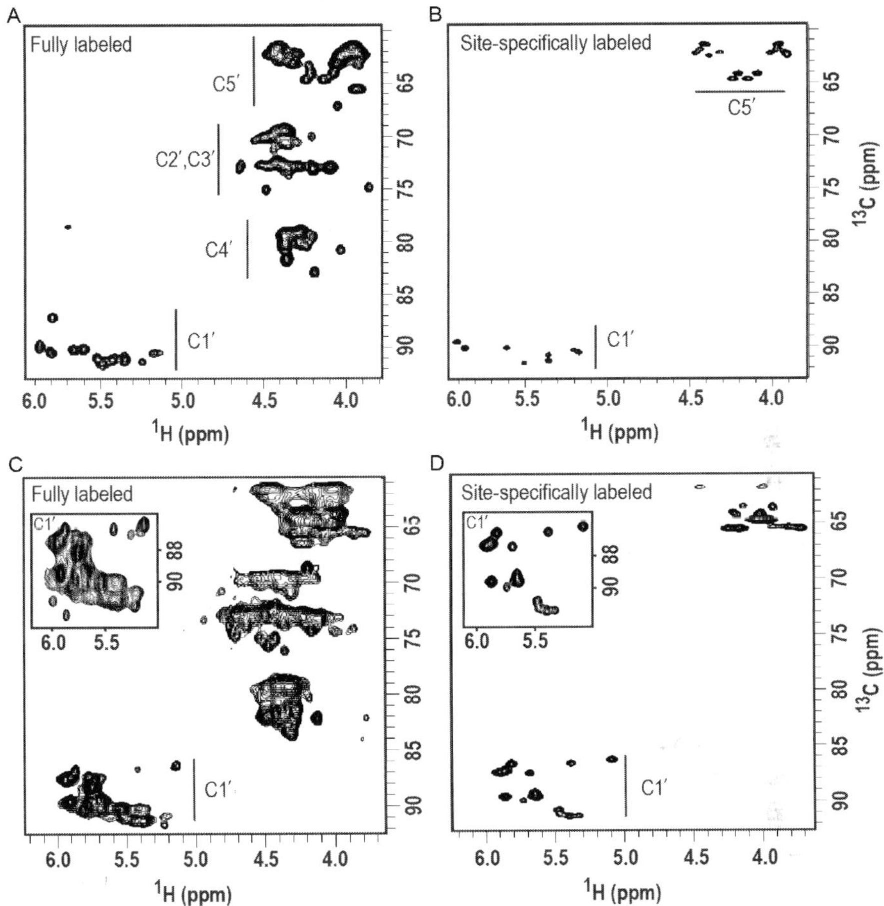

Figure 7.6 Site-specific labels produced by chemo-enzymatic synthesis provide HSQC spectra with improved resolution and reduced spectral crowding. Two-dimensional HSQC of the ribose region of (A) fully $^{13}C/^{15}N$-labeled and (B) 1′,5′,6-$^{13}C_3$-1,3,4-$^{15}N_3$-CTP-labeled IRE RNA; (C) fully $^{13}C/^{15}N$-labeled and (D) 1′,5′,6-$^{13}C_3$-1,3-$^{15}N_2$-UTP-labeled 63-nt riboswitch. All experiments were run with identical parameters and without constant-time intervals. Spectral width: 6009 and 7247 Hz in the ^1H and ^{13}C dimensions, respectively. 1024 and 256 complex points were acquired in t_2 and t_1, respectively, with 64 scans per slice. Insets: Expanded C1′ regions show the degree of resonance overlap in uniform $^{13}C/^{15}N$-labeled RNA. Note that the insets are shown at lower levels.

nucleotides into any RNA sequence of interest to facilitate structure and dynamics characterization of functional RNAs typically larger than 30 nt. This chemo-enzymatic approach provides not only better yields with less labor but also new patterns of rNTP labels that are not available with current approaches. Three RNAs—IRE (29 nt), a riboswitch (63 nt), and HIV-1

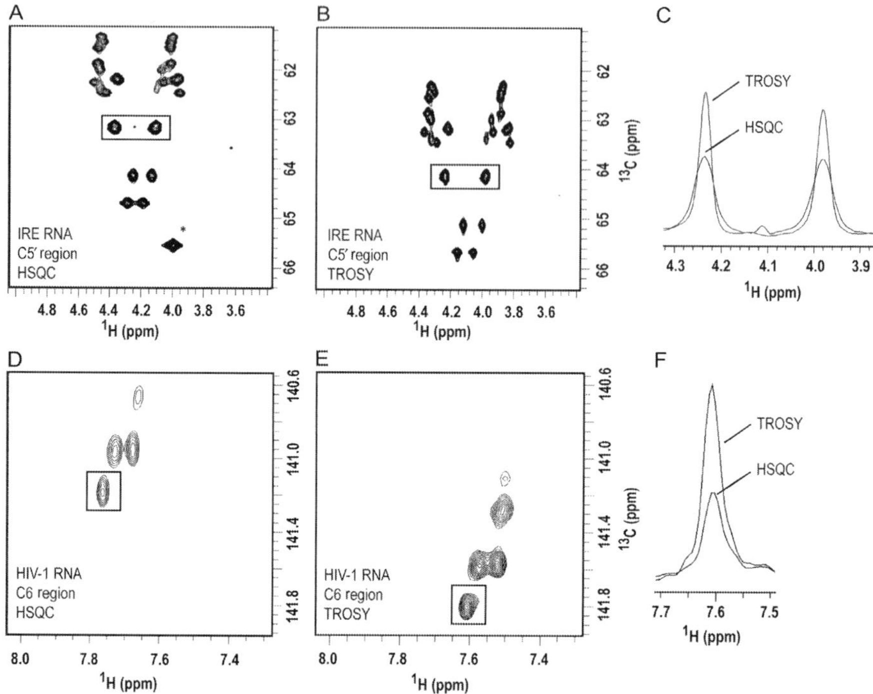

Figure 7.7 TROSY spectra acquired with RNA samples labeled with site-specific labels produced by chemo-enzymatic synthesis exhibit enhanced resolution and sensitivity than HSQC experiments. Two-dimensional (A) HSQC versus (B) methylene-optimized TROSY spectra of $1',5',6\text{-}^{13}C_3\text{-}1,3\text{-}^{15}N_2$-UTP/$1',5',6\text{-}^{13}C_3\text{-}1,3,4\text{-}^{15}N_3$-CTP-labeled IRE RNA. (C) One-dimensional slice overlay of the boxed peaks in both (A) and (B), notice the spectral quality enhancement due to the TROSY effect. Two-dimensional (D) HSQC versus (E) methine-optimized TROSY spectra of $1',5',6\text{-}^{13}C_3\text{-}1,3\text{-}^{15}N_2$-UTP-labeled HIV-1 RNA. (F) Overlay of one-dimensional slice of the boxed peak in both (D) and (E), notice the spectral quality enhancement due to the TROSY effect. For IRE RNA, the spectral widths used were 3597 and 905 Hz in the ^1H and ^{13}C dimensions, respectively. 1024 and 256 complex points were acquired in t_2 and t_1, respectively, with eight scans per slice. For HIV-1 RNA, the spectral widths used were 3597 and 754 Hz in the ^1H and ^{13}C dimensions, respectively. 512 and 128 complex points were acquired in t_2 and t_1, respectively, with 128 scans per slice. *Peak is not shown in (B) due to the resonance offset in TROSY experiments.

RNA (155 nt)—were used to illustrate the usefulness of this approach. We hope that this methodology will open up new avenues for multidimensional heteronuclear and homonuclear solution and solid-state NMR methods to study the structure and dynamics of large RNA, such as full-length riboswitches, which have till now remain unexplored (Cherepanov, Glaubitz, & Schwalbe, 2010; Marchanka, Simon, & Carlomagno, 2013).

ACKNOWLEDGMENTS

We thank Dr. Michael F. Summers (University of Maryland, Baltimore County) for providing the HIV-1 RNA construct and Dr. Sarah C. Keane (University of Maryland, Baltimore County) for making the HIV-1 core encapsidation signal RNA. Supported partially by NIH P50 GM103297 (T. K. D.), NMR instrumentation by NSF DBI1040158 (T. K. D.), and the Austrian Sciences Fund (I844 and P26550 to C. K.).

REFERENCES

Alvarado, L. J., LeBlanc, R. M., Longhini, A. P., Keane, S. C., Jain, N., Yildiz, Z. F., et al. (2014). Regio-selective chemical-enzymatic synthesis of pyrimidine nucleotides facilitates RNA structure and dynamics studies. *ChemBioChem*, *15*(11), 1573–1577.

Arthur, P. K., Alvarado, L. J., & Dayie, T. K. (2011). Expression, purification and analysis of the activity of enzymes from the pentose phosphate pathway. *Protein Expression and Purification*, *76*(2), 229–237.

Batey, R. T., Inada, M., Kujawinski, E., Puglisi, J. D., & Williamson, J. R. (1992). Preparation of isotopically labeled ribonucleotides for multidimensional NMR spectroscopy of RNA. *Nucleic Acids Research*, *20*(17), 4515–4523.

Bothe, J. R., Nikolova, E. N., Eichhorn, C. D., Chugh, J., Hansen, A. L., & Al-Hashimi, H. M. (2011). Characterizing RNA dynamics at atomic resolution using solution-state NMR spectroscopy. *Nature Methods*, *8*(11), 919–931.

Breaker, R. R. (2009). Riboswitches: From ancient gene-control systems to modern drug targets. *Future Microbiology*, *4*(7), 771–773.

Brunelle, J. L., & Green, R. (2013). In vitro transcription from plasmid or PCR-amplified DNA. *Methods in Enzymology*, *530*, 101–114.

Cherepanov, A. V., Glaubitz, C., & Schwalbe, H. (2010). High-resolution studies of uniformly $^{13}C,^{15}N$-labeled RNA by solid-state NMR spectroscopy. *Angewandte Chemie*, *49*(28), 4747–4750.

Dayie, K. T. (2005). Resolution enhanced homonuclear carbon decoupled triple resonance experiments for unambiguous RNA structural characterization. *Journal of Biomolecular NMR*, *32*(2), 129–139.

Dayie, K. T. (2008). Key labeling technologies to tackle sizeable problems in RNA structural biology. *International Journal of Molecular Sciences*, *9*(7), 1214–1240.

Dayie, T. K. (2011). Nucleic acids: Dynamics studies by solution NMR. In R. K. Harris (Ed.), *eMagRes*. Chichester, UK: John Wiley & Sons, Ltd.

Hoffman, D. W., & Holland, J. A. (1995). Preparation of carbon-13 labeled ribonucleotides using acetate as an isotope source. *Nucleic Acids Research*, *23*(16), 3361–3362.

Johnson, J. E., Julien, K. R., & Hoogstraten, C. G. (2006). Alternate-site isotopic labeling of ribonucleotides for NMR studies of ribose conformational dynamics in RNA. *Journal of Biomolecular NMR*, *35*(4), 261–274.

Lemaster, D. M., & Kushlan, D. M. (2001). Dynamical mapping of *E. coli* thioredoxin via ^{13}C NMR relaxation analysis. *Journal of the American Chemical Society*, *118*, 9255–9264.

Lu, K., Heng, X., Garyu, L., Monti, S., Garcia, E. L., Kharytonchyk, S., et al. (2011). NMR detection of structures in the HIV-1 5′-leader RNA that regulate genome packaging. *Science*, *334*(6053), 242–245.

Marchanka, A., Simon, B., & Carlomagno, T. (2013). A suite of solid-state NMR experiments for RNA intranucleotide resonance assignment in a 21 kDa protein–RNA complex. *Angewandte Chemie*, *52*(38), 9996–10001.

Mattick, J. S. (2007). A new paradigm for developmental biology. *The Journal of Experimental Biology*, *210*, 1526–1547.

Miclet, E., Williams, D. C., Jr., Clore, G. M., Bryce, D. L., Boisbouvier, J., & Bax, A. (2004). Relaxation-optimized NMR spectroscopy of methylene groups in proteins and nucleic acids. *Journal of the American Chemical Society, 126*(34), 10560–10570.

Milecki, J. (2002). Specific labelling of nucleosides and nucleotides with ^{13}C and ^{15}N. *Journal of Labelled Compounds and Radiopharmaceuticals, 45*(4), 307–337.

Milligan, J. F., Groebe, D. R., Witherell, G. W., & Uhlenbeck, O. C. (1987). Oligoribonucleotide synthesis using T7 RNA polymerase and synthetic DNA templates. *Nucleic Acids Research, 15*(21), 8783–8798.

Newman, A. J., & Nagai, K. (2010). Structural studies of the spliceosome: Blind men and an elephant. *Current Opinion in Structural Biology, 20*(1), 82–89.

Nikonowicz, E. P., Sirr, A., Legault, P., Jucker, F. M., Baer, L. M., & Pardi, A. (1992). Preparation of ^{13}C and ^{15}N labelled RNAs for heteronuclear multi-dimensional NMR studies. *Nucleic Acids Research, 20*(17), 4507–4513.

Pardi, A. (1995). Multidimensional heteronuclear NMR experiments for structure determination of isotopically labeled RNA. *Methods in Enzymology, 261*(1991), 350–380.

Petrov, A., Wu, T., Puglisi, E. V., & Puglisi, J. D. (2013). RNA purification by preparative polyacrylamide gel electrophoresis. *Methods in Enzymology, 530*, 315–330.

Quant, S., Wechselberger, R. W., Wolter, M. A., Wörner, K.-H., Schell, P., Engels, J. W., et al. (1994). Chemical synthesis of 13C-labelled monomers for the solid-phase and template controlled enzymatic synthesis of DNA and RNA oligomers. *Tetrahedron Letters, 35*(36), 6649–6651.

Schultheisz, H. L., Szymczyna, B. R., Scott, L. G., & Williamson, J. R. (2011). Enzymatic de novo pyrimidine nucleotide synthesis. *Journal of the American Chemical Society, 133*(2), 297–304.

Serganov, A., & Nudler, E. (2013). A decade of riboswitches. *Cell, 152*(1–2), 17–24.

Steitz, T. A. (2008). A structural understanding of the dynamic ribosome machine. *Nature Reviews. Molecular Cell Biology, 9*(3), 242–253.

Thakur, C. S., & Dayie, T. K. (2012). Asymmetry of 13C labeled 3-pyruvate affords improved site specific labeling of RNA for NMR spectroscopy. *Journal of Biomolecular NMR, 52*(1), 65–77.

Thakur, C. S., Sama, J. N., Jackson, M. E., Chen, B., & Dayie, T. K. (2010). Selective 13C labeling of nucleotides for large RNA NMR spectroscopy using an *E. coli* strain disabled in the TCA cycle. *Journal of Biomolecular NMR, 48*(4), 179–192.

Tolbert, T. J., & Williamson, J. R. (1996). Preparation of specifically deuterated RNA for NMR studies using a combination of chemical and enzymatic synthesis. *Journal of the American Chemical Society, 118*, 7929–7940.

Wunderlich, C. H., Spitzer, R., Santner, T., Fauster, K., Tollinger, M., & Kreutz, C. (2012). Synthesis of (6-(13)C)pyrimidine nucleotides as spin-labels for RNA dynamics. *Journal of the American Chemical Society, 134*(17), 7558–7569.

PART III

Structure and Folding

SHAPE Analysis of Small RNAs and Riboswitches

Greggory M. Rice*[,1], Steven Busan*[,1], Fethullah Karabiber[†], Oleg V. Favorov[‡,2], Kevin M. Weeks*[,2]

*Department of Chemistry, University of North Carolina, Chapel Hill, North Carolina, USA
[†]Department of Computer Engineering, Yildiz Technical University, Istanbul, Turkey
[‡]Department of Biomedical Engineering, University of North Carolina, Chapel Hill, North Carolina, USA
[1]Contributed equally.
[2]Corresponding authors: e-mail address: favorov@bme.unc.edu; weeks@unc.edu

Contents

Methods in Enzymology, Volume 549
ISSN 0076-6879
http://dx.doi.org/10.1016/B978-0-12-801122-5.00008-8

Abstract

We describe structural analysis of small RNAs by SHAPE chemical probing. RNAs are treated with 1-methyl-7-nitroisatoic anhydride, a reagent that detects local nucleotide flexibility; and *N*-methylisatoic anhydride and 1-methyl-6-nitroisatoic anhydride, reagents which together detect higher-order and noncanonical interactions. Chemical adducts are quantified as stops during reverse transcriptase-mediated primer extension. Probing information can be used to infer conformational changes and ligand binding and to develop highly accurate models of RNA secondary structures.

1. THEORY

The biological activities of many RNAs, including ribozymes, riboswitches, and viral packaging elements, are mediated by their structures. SHAPE reagents probe the flexibility of the RNA backbone; can detect higher-order or noncanonical interactions; and are widely used to validate existing structure models, generate new models, and test RNA structure–function hypotheses (Merino, Wilkinson, Coughlan, & Weeks, 2005; Weeks & Mauger, 2011). Structural modeling that incorporates data from three SHAPE reagents [1M7 and the "differential" reagents 1M6 (1-methyl-6-nitroisatoic anhydride) and NMIA (*N*-methylisatoic anhydride)] is the current gold standard for RNA structure modeling, with greater than 90% base pair accuracy in nearly all RNAs tested. Structurally diverse riboswitches have been accurately modeled using SHAPE, including the M-Box, SAM-I, fluoride, lysine, glycine, adenine, Pre-Q1, cyclic-di-GMP, and thiamine-pyrophosphate (TPP) riboswitches (Hajdin et al.,

2013; Rice, Leonard, & Weeks, 2014). SHAPE has also provided new insights into the effects of ligand binding (Steen, Siegfried, & Weeks, 2011; Warner et al., 2014) and the cellular environment (Tyrrell, McGinnis, Weeks, & Pielak, 2013) on riboswitch folding and structure.

This workflow outlines the strategy for probing the structure of an RNA using a three-reagent SHAPE experiment (Rice et al., 2014), reverse transcription-mediated primer extension, and capillary electrophoresis, processed using the *QuShape* software (Karabiber, McGinnis, Favorov, & Weeks, 2013). Structure modeling using differential SHAPE and thermodynamic constraints is demonstrated using the *RNAstructure* program (Reuter & Mathews, 2010). We focus on the 5S ribosomal RNA and the TPP riboswitch as examples. This strategy produces SHAPE reactivity profiles and secondary structure models. The SHAPE modification and analysis can be completed in approximately two half-days. This approach can be applied to RNAs (or regions of an RNA) up to several hundred nucleotides in length, limited only by reverse transcriptase processivity and capillary electrophoresis read lengths.

2. EQUIPMENT

Capillary electrophoresis instrument (and associated buffers and reagents)
Microcentrifuge (at least 10,000 × *g*)
Thermocycler or at least two heat blocks or water baths
Ice bucket
Syringe, 27 gauge (for removing dimethyl sulfoxide (DMSO) from storage bottle)
0.65- and 1.5-mL RNase-free microcentrifuge tubes
Micropipettor and RNase-free tips
Clean, dust-free bench surface

3. MATERIALS

RNA of interest
HEPES, pH 8, 1 *M* solution
NaCl, 5 *M* solution
$MgCl_2$, 1 *M* solution

TPP or other ligand of interest
RNase-free water (*not* DEPC-treated)
SHAPE reagents

- 1-Methyl-7-nitroisatoic anhydride (1M7) (synthesis protocol from 4-nitroisatoic anhydride (Mortimer & Weeks, 2007; Turner, Shefer, & Ares, 2013.))
- NMIA (Aldrich 129887)
- 1M6 (Aldrich S888079)

DMSO, neat, stored in a desiccator
Glycogen, molecular biology grade, 20 mg/mL
Absolute ethanol, ≥98%
SUPERase-In RNase inhibitor (optional; Life Technologies AM2694)
Fluorescently labeled reverse-transcription primers (available from Life Technologies, Integrated DNA Technologies, and others)
Superscript III reverse transcriptase (Invitrogen 18080-044) kit containing:

- SuperScript III Reverse Transcriptase (200 U/μL)
- Superscript First-Strand buffer, 5×
- Dithiothreitol (DTT), 0.1 *M*

dNTP mix, 10 m*M* each dATP, dTTP, dGTP, dCTP in water, stored at −20 °C
ddNTP for sequencing
Highly deionized (hi-di) formamide, 100 μL aliquots, stored at −20 °C

3.1. Solutions and buffers

Step 1

3.3× folding buffer

Component	Final concentration (m*M*)	Stock (*M*)	Amount (μL)
HEPES, pH 8.0	333	1	333
NaCl	333	5	66.6
$MgCl_2$	33	1	33.3

Add RNase-free water to 1 mL

50 m*M* TPP

Dissolve 23 mg TPP in 1 mL RNase-free water

80 m*M* 1M7

Dissolve 1 mg 1M7 in 56 μL DMSO

80 m*M* 1M6

Dissolve 1 mg 1M6 in 56 µL DMSO

80 m*M* NMIA

Dissolve 1 mg NMIA in 71 µL DMSO

Step 2

411 Master Mix

Component	Final concentration	Stock	Amount (µL)
First-strand buffer (from SSIII kit)	3.3 ×	5 ×	400
DTT (from SSIII kit)	17 m*M*	0.1 *M*	100
dNTP mix	1.7 m*M*	10 m*M*	100

This buffer may be stored at −20 °C in 100 µL aliquots for up to a year. An aliquot should be discarded after three freeze–thaw cycles.

80% ethanol

Mix 40 mL absolute ethanol with 10 mL RNase-free water

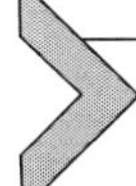

4. PROTOCOL

4.1. Preparation

This protocol assumes that the RNA of interest has been synthesized and purified. For most applications, we recommend that a template for the RNA motif of interest be generated by PCR such that it will ultimately encode sequences that will add RNA structure cassette sequences to the 5′- and 3′-ends of the RNA, and add the T7 promoter sequences (Fig. 8.1). This PCR template can then be transcribed *in vitro* using T7 RNA polymerase. The standardized structure cassette allows the same labeled reverse-transcription primers to be used on every targeted RNA. At least two reverse-transcription primers complementary to the primer-binding site of the structure cassette, each one 5′-labeled with a different fluorophore (see Tip 6.3), should be obtained and diluted to 1.25 µ*M*. We recommend that the RNA be gel or column purified. The RNA should be dissolved in RNase-free water or 0.5 × TE buffer pH 8.0 at 5 µ*M* and stored at −20 °C in aliquots.

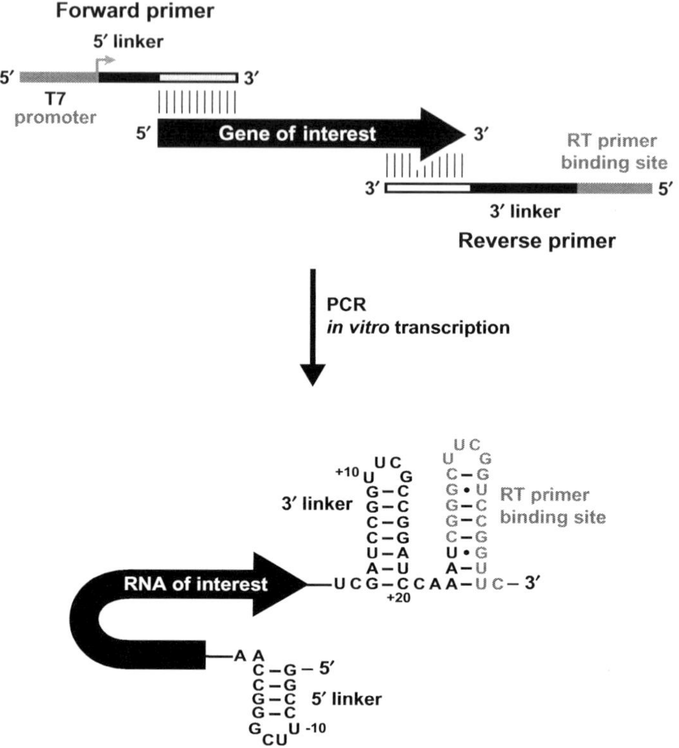

Figure 8.1 Structure cassette design for *in vitro* RNA synthesis. *Adapted from figure 7 in Merino et al. (2005).*

4.2. Duration

Preparation	1 h
Protocol	2 days

See Fig. 8.2 for a flowchart overview of the protocol.

5. STEP 1: RNA FOLDING AND SHAPE PROBING

5.1. Overview

Fold the RNA in a SHAPE-compatible buffer (here we use a HEPES buffer, a Tris–EDTA buffer may also be used) in the presence of ligand (if required), and add SHAPE reagent.

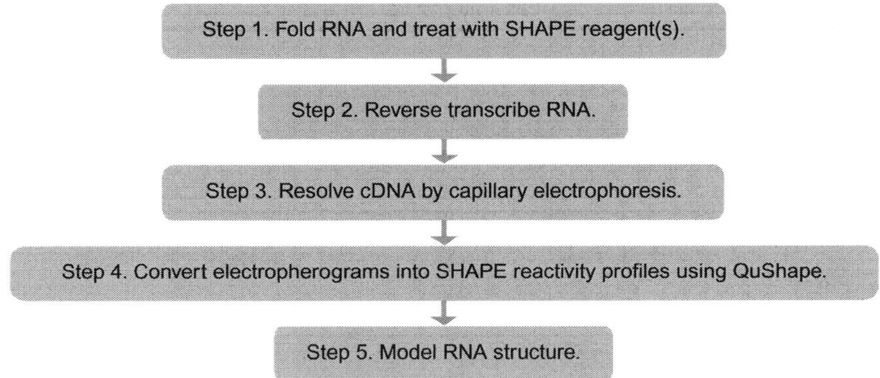

Figure 8.2 Flowchart overview of the entire strategy for modeling RNA secondary structure, based on SHAPE experimental information.

5.2. Duration

1.5–2.5 h.

1.1. Add 2 μL of 5 μ*M* RNA (10 pmol) to 10 μL of RNase-free water to a 0.65-mL microcentrifuge tube.

1.2. Heat mixture at 95 °C for 2 min then immediately place on ice for 2 min.

1.3. Add 6 μL of 3.3 × folding buffer and mix well.

1.4. Incubate at 37 °C for 20 min to allow RNA to refold.

1.5. To a fresh 0.65-mL tube, add 2 μL of water or ligand (for example, 50 m*M* TPP) (see Tip 5.4).

1.6. Add 18 μL of folded RNA from step 1.4 to this tube and mix well.

1.7. Incubate at 37 °C for 10 min to allow ligand binding.

1.8. Make a fresh stock of 80 m*M* SHAPE reagent (1M7, 1M6, or NMIA).

1.9. To a 0.65-mL tube, add 1 μL of 80 m*M* SHAPE reagent; label (+). To another 0.65-mL tube, add 1 μL of neat DMSO; label (−).

1.10. Add 9 μL of folded RNA to the (+) tube. Mix quickly by pipetting and incubate at 37 °C. Incubate 3 min for 1M6 or 1M7 reagents or 22 min for NMIA (see Tip 5.5).

1.11. Add 9 μL of folded RNA to the (−) tube for the no reagent control. Mix quickly and incubate for the same amount of time as the (+) sample.

1.12. Perform an ethanol precipitation. To each reaction, add 90 μL RNase-free water, 4 μL 5 *M* NaCl, 1 μL glycogen (20 mg/mL), and 240 μL ethanol. Mix well. Incubate at −80 °C for 30 min followed by centrifugation in a microfuge at 4 °C for 30 min at maximum speed.

5.3. Tip

Following the modification, the 1M7 treated sample will change color from yellow to orange. 1M6 and NMIA reactions do not change color.

5.4. Tip

If studying ligand effects on RNA structure, perform the steps in Section 5.2 multiple times in parallel, varying the ligand concentration in step 1.5.

5.5. Tip

The SHAPE reagent incubation time is dependent on temperature and pH of the system studied. Incubation times will be longer at lower temperatures and more acidic pH. At 5 half-lives the SHAPE reagent will be mostly consumed by the competing hydrolysis reaction. Depending on buffer conditions and temperature, incubation time may need to be optimized. Reagent kinetics can be readily determined by monitoring hydrolysis product formation (Merino et al., 2005; Mortimer & Weeks, 2007).

6. STEP 2: PRIMER EXTENSION

6.1. Overview

Perform reverse transcription to detect sites of SHAPE modification, and sequencing to enable electropherogram peak alignment.

6.2. Duration

2 h

1.1. Prepare 411 Master Mix.

1.2. In two 0.65-μL tubes from the last step in Section 5, resuspend the pelleted RNA (about 2.5 pmol each) from the (+) and (−) SHAPE samples in 11 μL water or 10 μL water and 1 μL Superase-In RNase inhibitor (optional).

1.3. In a new 0.65-μL tube, combine 5 pmol RNA and water to 10 μL; label "Sequencing."

1.4. To each of the (+), (−), and sequencing tubes, add 2 μL fluorescently labeled reverse-transcription primer, 1.25 μ*M* (2.5 pmol), and mix by pipetting (see Tips 6.3 and 6.4).

1.5. Incubate 5 min at 65 °C.

1.6. Incubate 3 min at 45 °C.

1.7. Place on ice 2 min.

1.8. Add 6 μL 411 Master Mix to each of the (+) reagent, (−) reagent, and sequencing tubes.

1.9. Add 1 μL SuperScript III to each tube and mix well.

1.10. Sequencing tube only: Add 1 μL ddC, ddA, or ddT, 10 m*M*, or 1 μL ddG, 0.25 m*M*. (Concentration of dideoxynucleotide may need to be adjusted empirically, see Tip 7.5.)

1.11. Incubate 1 min at 45 °C.

1.12. Incubate 40 min at 52 °C.

1.13. Incubate 10 min at 65 °C, then hold at 4 °C.

1.14. Optional: Add 1 μL glycogen to sequencing tube only, 20 mg/mL (may facilitate recovery of small nucleic acids).

1.15. Add 120 μL absolute ethanol to each tube and mix well. Incubate at −80 °C for 30 min (see Tip 6.5).

1.16. Centrifuge for 30 min at >10,000 × *g* (at 4 °C if possible).

1.17. Carefully discard supernatant.

Optional steps to reduce salt carryover (*recommended*):

1.17a. Rinse pellet with 500 μL 80% ethanol and do not disturb the pellet.

1.17b. Centrifuge for 5 min at >10,000 × *g*.

1.17c. Discard supernatant.

Repeat steps 1.17a–c twice.

1.18. Let pellets dry 5 min at room temperature.

1.19. Resuspend each pellet in 10 μL hi-di formamide.

1.20. Denature at 95 °C for 2 min.

6.3. Tip

Select fluorophores that are supported by the specific capillary electrophoresis instrument to be used, and consider which pairs of samples will ultimately be analyzed in the same capillary. For example, in the widely supported G5 dye set, use the fluorophore VIC to produce (+) or (−) SHAPE cDNA and the fluorophore NED for sequencing. 5-FAM and 6-JOE are also commonly used as a compatible dye pair. *QuShape* supports mobility shift correction for the following fluorescein-derived dyes: 5-FAM, 6-FAM, TET, HEX, 6-JOE, NED, and VIC.

6.4. Tip

Two sequencing reactions can be used for RNAs whose SHAPE reactivity peaks are difficult to align to a reference sequence. Use a different fluorophore for each type of dideoxynucleotide being used so that both sequencing reactions can be analyzed in the same capillary.

6.5. Tip

The salt remaining from the primer extension reaction is sufficient for the ethanol precipitation. No extra NaCl is required.

6.6. Tip

For the ethanol precipitation of the (+) and (−) SHAPE reactions following primer extension, additional glycogen is not needed since it will carry through from the first precipitation.

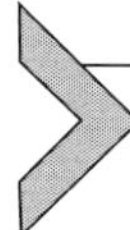

7. STEP 3: CAPILLARY ELECTROPHORESIS

7.1. Overview

Resolve products of primer extension reactions by capillary gel electrophoresis.

7.2. Duration

1.5 h

2.1. For each sample, load ~1.5 pmol cDNA and ~0.5 pmol sequencing cDNA in 8–12 μL hi-di formamide in a single plate well. These concentrations may require adjustment for different CE instruments (see tips below).

2.2. Electrophorese samples according to instrument protocol. This step is typically automated.

7.3. Tip

The dynamic range of CE fluorescence detectors is typically rather small, and oversaturation of the signal can easily occur. This artifact manifests as high, flat, "clipped" peaks in the electropherogram. Some clipping on the 5′- and 3′-ends of the trace is normal and tolerable, but clipping in the center of the trace is undesirable. If this occurs, fill the capillaries with new polymer to flush out any residual cDNA molecules, load a lower concentration of cDNA in each well, and rerun. *Do not* use oversaturated electropherograms for SHAPE analysis or structure modeling.

7.4. Tip

Sequencing reactions may be performed on a larger scale (20–50 ×) and the products stored for reanalysis by freezing in formamide at 4 °C or −20 °C in the dark.

7.5. Tip

Sequencing reactions are very sensitive to the ratio of ddNTP terminator to dNTPs and may not be successful without optimization. Run 0.5 pmol of the sequencing products alone on the CE instrument to ensure success before mixing with experimental samples.

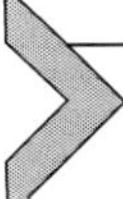

8. STEP 4: DATA PROCESSING USING QuShape

8.1. Overview

The *QuShape* analytical computer program performs a series of data processing operations to calculate SHAPE reactivities based on the CE-generated data that have been recorded in ABIF files (see http://www.chem.unc.edu/rna/qushape/). The user controls *QuShape* via a graphical interface. This interface includes the main *Data View* window, the *Tool Inspector* window, and the *Script Inspector* window (Fig. 8.3). Results of every operation are plotted in the *Data View* window, allowing the user to monitor the quality of each data processing step. As a default, selection of each successive data processing step is automatic. The standard procedure is for the user to execute each tool as it appears in the *Tool Inspector* window (by clicking the *Apply* button), inspect the result in the *Data View* window, and proceed to the next tool in the default sequence (by clicking the *Done* button). However, if the user is not satisfied with the results of the automatic procedure, the *Tool Inspector* window offers the user additional analytical tools and parameter controls that can be employed by clicking on them.

8.2. Duration

5–20 min depending on RNA length

See Fig. 8.4 for a flowchart overview of the protocol.

1.1 Create a new project by clicking *New Project* in the *File* menu. Enter the name of the project and select the directory that contains the raw CE data files. Select the project type. If there is just one sequencing lane in each capillary in the files obtained from electrophoresis, select

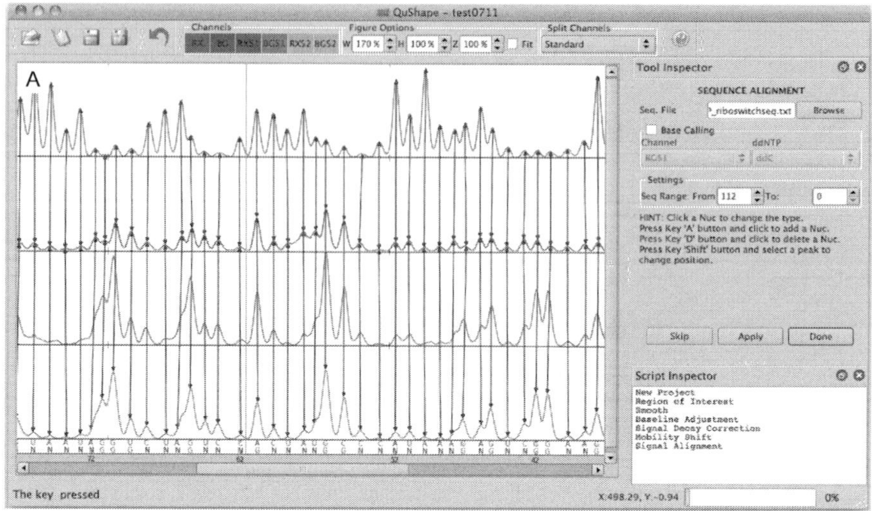

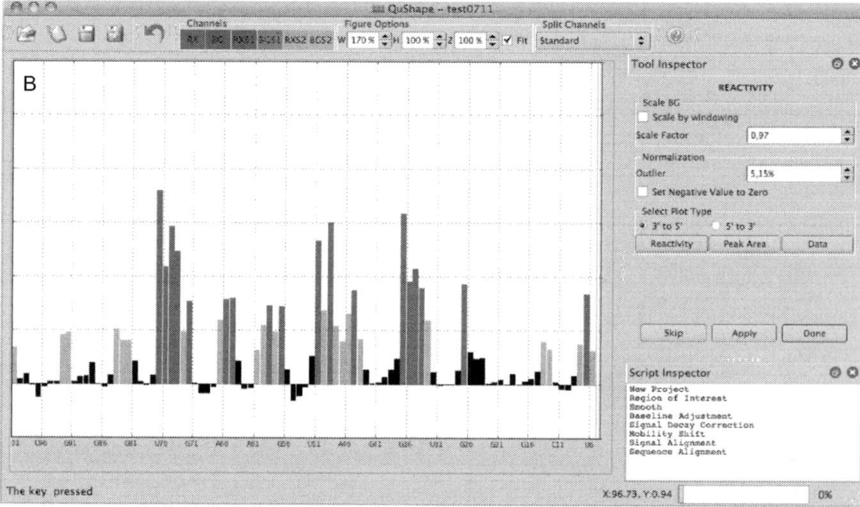

Figure 8.3 *QuShape* graphical user interface. The main *Data View* window (center) displays the results of the most recently performed operation. The *Tool Inspector* window (upper right) displays user-controllable parameters and options for the selected tool, which allow manual control over each algorithmic step in instances where the default execution is not satisfactory. The *Script Inspector* window (lower right) lists the sequence of tools applied thus far to the data. (A) Screenshot of the *QuShape* display at the completion of the Sequence Alignment step. The main window displays four electropherograms traces: (+) SHAPE reaction signal (RX); (−) SHAPE reaction signal (BG); ddNTP sequencing signal in the (+) reaction capillary (RXS1); and ddNTP sequencing signal in the (−) reaction capillary (BGS1). The matched peaks in the four traces are indicated by vertical lines. Peaks classified as *specific* are labeled G at the bottom of the window, while peaks classified as *nonspecific* are labeled N. The optimally aligned RNA nucleotide sequence is also displayed at the bottom of the window. (B) Screenshot of the *QuShape* display at the completion of the *Reactivity* step. The main window displays the normalized reactivities of the nucleotides.

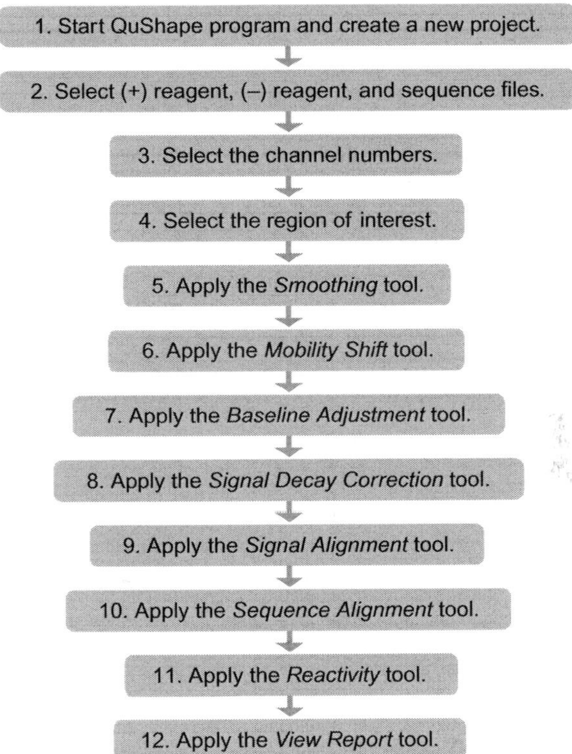

Figure 8.4 Flowchart for automated processing of SHAPE data, quantified by capillary electrophoresis, using *QuShape*.

One Sequencing Channel. Otherwise select the second option, *Two Sequencing Channels*. Press the *Next* button to go to next step.

1.2 Select CE data files using the *Browse* button. Text- or ABIF-formatted (+) *Reaction* and (−) *Reaction* files are both acceptable. The RNA *Sequence* file (.txt, .seq, .fasta) or a Reference Project (*Ref. Proj.*) file (.qushape) is selected in the same way. Click the *Next* button to go to the last step of creating a new project.

1.3 Select the channel numbers. Select channels in the (+) *Reaction Channels* panel to specify *RX* and *RXS1* (RX and RXS refer to the SHAPE reaction signal and the sequencing signal, respectively, in the presence of reagent). For the sequencing ladder, the ddNTP type (ddC, ddG, ddT, ddA) must be selected. Repeat the same for *BG* and *BGS1* in the (−) *Reaction Channels* panel (BG and BGS refer to the SHAPE reaction signal and the sequencing signal, respectively, in the absence of reagent). If there is another sequencing lane, *RXS2* and *BGS2* should be selected in the (+) and (−) Reaction Channels panels, respectively. After specifying all the channels, press the *Apply* button to view the data display in the *Data View* window. If all selections are correct, press the *Done* button to proceed to the analysis. If there is a problem with specified options, use the *Back* button to go to the previous dialog to change the parameters.

1.4 Select the region of interest (ROI) along the elution time axis using the *Region of Interest* tool: Either type the elution time values of the start and end points directly in the boxes in the *Tool Inspector* window or, more conveniently, select the start point of the ROI by pressing and holding down the "F" (*from*) key on the keyboard and then placing the mouse arrow at the desired elution time position in the plot in the *Data View* window and clicking the left mouse button. The end point of the ROI is selected similarly by pressing and holding down the "T" (*to*) key, and then placing the mouse arrow at the desired elution time position in the *Data View* window and clicking the left mouse button. Once the start and end points of the ROI are entered, the user-chosen ROI will be displayed in the *Data View* window on a gray background.

1.5 Apply the *Smoothing* tool to filter out high-frequency noise in the data and correct saturated data points. If not satisfied with the default results, the user can select a different smoothing method and/or change the width of the smoothing filter in the *Window Size* box. Unchecking *Saturation Correction* option disables correction of saturated points in the trace.

1.6 Apply the *Mobility Shift* tool to align pairs of signals within each capillary. Use the selection boxes to change dye type of each trace if the automatically shown dye type, determined during the project creation step, is incorrect.

1.7 Apply the *Baseline Adjustment* tool to remove baseline offset by specifying the baseline window. Baseline is defined by the minima of a set of consecutive elution time intervals whose length is specified in the *Baseline Window* (default value is 60). If smoothing of the baseline drift is desired, the *Smooth the Baseline Drift* box should be checked.

1.8 Apply the *Signal Decay Correction* tool. *Automatic Summation* is the default method to correct gradual signal decay. If not satisfied, select either *Exponential* method or *Summation* method. The *Summation* method is the same method as the automatic approach, but the user can specify the value of the key parameter, *Factor*.

1.9 Apply the *Signal Alignment* tool to align pairs of signals across two capillaries. After this alignment procedure is finished, the aligned RX and BG signals will be plotted superimposed in one panel in the *Data View* window and the aligned RXS and BGS signals will be plotted superimposed in the other panel, so that the accuracy of the alignment can be checked visually. If misalignment is found, it can be corrected manually after clicking the *Modify Matched Peaks* button.

1.10 Apply the *Sequence Alignment* tool to assign each peak in the (+) SHAPE reaction and (−) SHAPE reaction signals to their corresponding RNA position. Once this operation is finished, the display in the *Data View* window will change to a view in which corresponding peaks in RX, BG, and BGS traces are linked by vertical arrows (Fig. 8.3A). The results of base calling and sequence alignment will be shown at the bottom of the BGS panel; the top row shows the RNA sequence and the bottom row shows the results of base calling. If the alignment is not accurate, the errors can be corrected manually.

1.11 Apply the *Reactivity* tool to calculate SHAPE reactivities for all nucleotides in the selected ROI based on their peaks in the (+) SHAPE reaction and (−) SHAPE reaction signals. This tool performs three operations. First, a whole-signal Gaussian integration is performed for all peaks in the (+) and (−) reaction signals, fitting each peak with a Gaussian function individually optimized for position, height, and width. Next, the scaling operation scales the BG signal relative to the RX signal. This scaling is necessary because the (+) and (−) reaction primer extension reactions were performed separately and not necessarily under fully identical conditions. When the *Reactivity* tool is open, the scaling factor is computed automatically and is displayed in the *Scale Factor* window (Fig. 8.3B). When the *Reactivity* tool is executed, by clicking the *Apply* button, the BG signal will be scaled by this factor. If not satisfied, other scaling factor values can be tested by entering them in the *Scale Factor* window. Finally, the normalization operation subtracts the integrated values for the (−) reaction peaks from the (+) reaction peaks, and normalizes the difference to obtain the normalized nucleotide-resolution reactivity for every RNA position.

A box normalization-based algorithm is used to normalize data. This normalization scales reactivities to a scale spanning 0 to ~2, where zero indicates no reactivity and 1.0 is the average intensity for highly reactive RNA positions. Nucleotides with normalized

SHAPE reactivities 0–0.40, 0.40–0.85, and >0.85 correspond qualitatively to unreactive, moderately reactive, and highly reactive positions, respectively, and are plotted in different colors. As a part of the normalization procedure, the percentage of outliers is determined automatically and is displayed in the *Outlier* window. A different percentage can be selected. There are three alternative displays of the output of the *Reactivity* tool: (1) "*Reactivity*" button plots the normalized reactivities of all nucleotides; (2) "*Peak Area*" button plots the areas of RX and BG peaks; (3) "*Data*" button draws the same plot as provided through the *Sequence Alignment* tool (linked RX, BG, RXS, and BGS traces, as well as the nucleotide sequence); in addition, it overlays each peak in RX and BG traces with its Gaussian estimation.

1.12 Apply the *View Report* tool to output the computed nucleotide SHAPE reactivities. The final report of *QuShape* data processing is displayed as a table in the *Tool Inspector* window. This table contains the following information about each nucleotide: *SeqNum*—nucleotide number; *seqRNA*—nucleotide base type; *posSeq*—position of the nucleotide in the sequence ladder; *posRX*—position of the RX peak; *areaRX*—area of the RX peak; *posBG*—position of the BG peak; *areaBG*—area of the BG peak; *areaDiff*—difference between RX and BG areas; *normDiff*—normalized difference (the normalized reactivity of the nucleotide). This table can be saved as a tab-delimited text file by clicking the "*Save as Text*" button.

8.3. Tip

QuShape runs under Windows, MacOS/X, and Linux and uses open-source software. Its downloading and installation instructions can be found in the Installation Guide section at http://www.chem.unc.edu/rna/qushape/.

8.4. Tip

Some of the tools are computationally intensive, and their execution can take tens of seconds. During their execution (after pressing the *Apply* button), the left-bottom corner of the screen will display the "*Applying...*" message. Once the operation is finished, this message will change to "*Applied*," and the *Done* button in the *Tool Inspector* window will become enabled (its appearance will change from dim to sharp contrast).

8.5. Tip

The start and the end segments of electropherogram traces typically have stretches of excessive and undifferentiated fluorescence that obscure peaks corresponding to the nucleotides at the either end of the studied RNA. The ROI must be selected, using the *Region of Interest* tool, along the elution time axis to avoid these unusable segments.

8.6. Tip

After the signal alignment procedure is finished, the accuracy of the alignment can be checked visually. If misalignment is found, it can be corrected manually after clicking the *Modify Matched Peaks* button. This will change the display: RXS signal will be plotted above BGS signal and vertical lines will be drawn linking a subset of the matched peaks in the two signals. An incorrect link between two peaks in the two signals can be changed by pressing and holding the "*Shift*" key while placing the mouse arrow on the wrong peak, clicking and holding the left mouse button, and dragging the link to the desired peak. If a new link is desired, press and hold the "*A*" key while clicking with the mouse on the two peaks that should be linked. If a link must be removed, press and hold the "*D*" key while clicking on that link with the mouse. Once all the desired link changes are made, click the *Apply* button to realign the two signals according to the newly imposed constraints.

8.7. Tip

In the sequence alignment step, the *Base-Calling* box should be used if the user wants to come back to the sequence alignment after pressing the "*Done*" button and moving to other tools. In that case, the *Sequence Alignment* tool can be called from the *Sequence* menu with the base-calling operation enabled, so that upon execution of this tool the previous manually corrected base assignments will be discarded. Therefore, the *Base-Calling* box should be unchecked if you want to use previously obtained base-calling results.

8.8. Tip

If the sequence alignment is not accurate, the errors can be corrected manually. Four different manual correction operations are available:

(1) The base label of a peak in the BGS trace can be changed. For example, suppose that ddC was used for sequencing. Consequently, the bottom row consists of "N" and "G" labels. Clicking on "N" with the mouse will turn it to "G." Clicking on "G" will turn it to "N."

(2) An extra base can be added to the bottom row. By pressing and holding the "*A*" key while clicking at a particular location in the bottom row with the mouse, an "N" will be inserted at that location and this added nucleotide will be linked to RX and BG.

(3) A base and corresponding links can be deleted by pressing and holding the "*D*" key while clicking at a base.

(4) Computed locations of the peak centers in BG and RX can be moved by pressing the "*Shift*" key and dragging the arrow to the desired location.

After modifying the sequences, press *Apply* to see the new alignment with nucleotides matched to the peaks in RX and BG. Note that at this time the base-calling operation will be disabled. If this operation needs to be performed again, check the *Base-Calling* box.

8.9. Tip

In the reactivity step, the scaling factor is automatically determined for the entire BG data set, and all BG signals are scaled by this factor. When working with very long sequences, it may be more accurate to scale BG locally, rather than globally. To use local scaling, check the "*Scale by Windowing*" box (Fig. 8.3B).

9. STEP 5: DATA PROCESSING AND RNA MODELING

9.1. Overview

Prepare files needed for RNA secondary structure modeling and then use the software package *RNAstructure* (Reuter & Mathews, 2010) to generate models. All python scripts indicated below are freely available from the Weeks lab Web site: http://www.chem.unc.edu/rna/qushape.

9.2. Duration

20 min hands-on time

0–6 h computer time (depending on sequence length)

1.1 Using a spreadsheet editor or text editor, format the report file obtained at the end of *QuShape* data processing into two columns consisting of nucleotide number and SHAPE reactivity value. Positions where data quality is poor, such as those with high background in the DMSO control, or where SHAPE reactivity could not be determined should be entered as "–999." Save this file as a ".txt" file or "windows formatted text" from Excel. Numbering should start at 1 and the file should contain as many nucleotides as the RNA being modeled. Each experiment (e.g., 1M7, 1M6, NMIA) should have its own file.

1.2 Use the python script "simple2boxplot.py" to normalize the 1M7 SHAPE reactivities with the boxplot method. With the normalization script in the same folder, type: "python simple2boxplot.py fileIN.txt fileOUT.txt," where "fileIN" is the formatted 1M7 file from the previous step. Change "fileOUT" to a unique name for the outputted file. The output of this script will be boxplot normalized 1M7 SHAPE reactivities suitable for folding.

1.3 Use the python script "boxplot2simple.py" to normalize the 1M6 SHAPE reactivities using the "simple" normalization method. With the normalization script in the same folder, type: "python boxplot2simple.py fileIN.txt fileOUT1M6.txt," where "fileIN" is the formatted 1M6 file from step 1.1. Change "fileOUT1M6.txt" to a memorable and unique name that will contain the outputted simple normalized 1M6 reactivities.

1.4 Repeat step 1.3 for the NMIA SHAPE reactivities.

1.5 Use the python script "differenceByWindow.py" to subtract the normalized 1M6 SHAPE reactivities from the NMIA reactivities.

1.5a At the command prompt type "python differenceByWindow.py nmia.txt 1m6.txt differenceOUT.txt 25." The input files for the difference calculating script (nmia.txt and 1m6.txt) are the resulting files from steps 1.4 and 1.3, respectively. The last argument of the command, "25," defines the window size for the sliding baseline.

1.5b When the command is finished running, a graph will appear showing the result of the difference calculation before and after using a sliding window difference. The differential SHAPE reactivities should occur sparsely throughout the length of the RNA and be roughly evenly distributed across positive and negative amplitudes (Fig. 8.5, bottom). In rare cases, alternative window sizes may need to be tried until suitable parameters are found.

1.6 Using a Web browser, go the *RNAstructure* online structure prediction server at: http://rna.urmc.rochester.edu/RNAstructureWeb/Servers/Predict1/Predict1.html

1.7 Fill out the fields on the Web form. Make sure to include a sequence title, the RNA sequence, and an e-mail address.

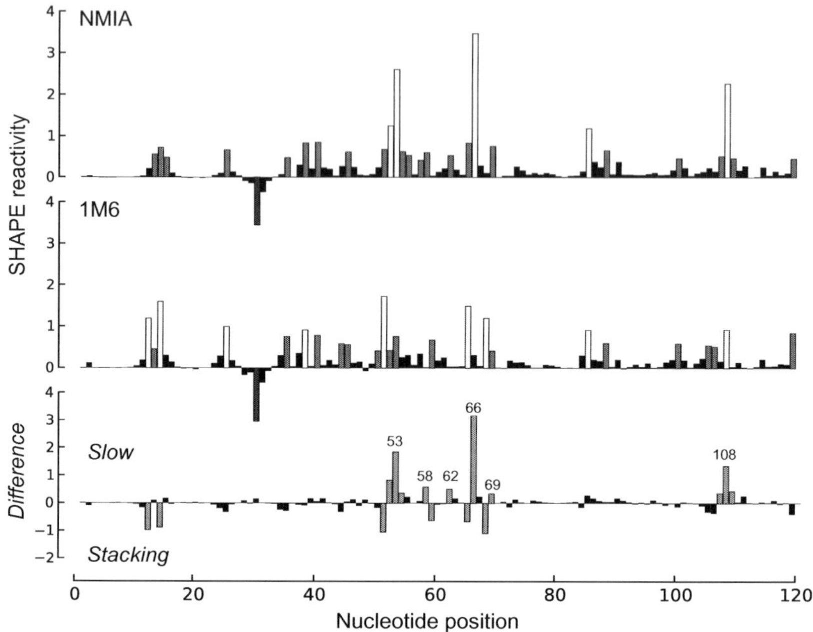

Figure 8.5 Differential SHAPE analysis of the *Escherichia coli* 5S rRNA. Normalized SHAPE reactivities from reactions with NMIA (top) and 1M6 (middle) are highlighted by nucleotide reactivity. Differential SHAPE reactivities (bottom) were calculated by first scaling 1M6 to NMIA reactivities over a moving window and then subtracting 1M6 from NMIA reactivities. Strong differential reactivity enhancements (>|0.3| SHAPE-units) are colored gray. Nucleotide positions showing strong positive-amplitude (favoring NMIA) differential reactivities are labeled. *Adapted from figure 2 (in color) in Rice et al. (2014).*

1.8 Under the optional data heading, choose to upload a SHAPE constraints file. Select the boxplot normalized 1M7 file (step 1.2).

1.9 Also under the optional data heading, choose to upload the calculated difference file. Select the file from step 1.5.

1.10 Enjoy a cup of coffee while your RNA folds. You will receive an e-mail when the secondary structure modeling is complete. The effect of including differential SHAPE reactivity information is illustrated in Fig. 8.6. The complete procedure is outlined in Fig. 8.7.

9.3. Tip

Step 1.5, the script "differenceByWindow.py," will crash if there is a stretch of no data larger than the window size given. It may be necessary to perform this step in two parts (where there are data present) and then recombine the separate files.

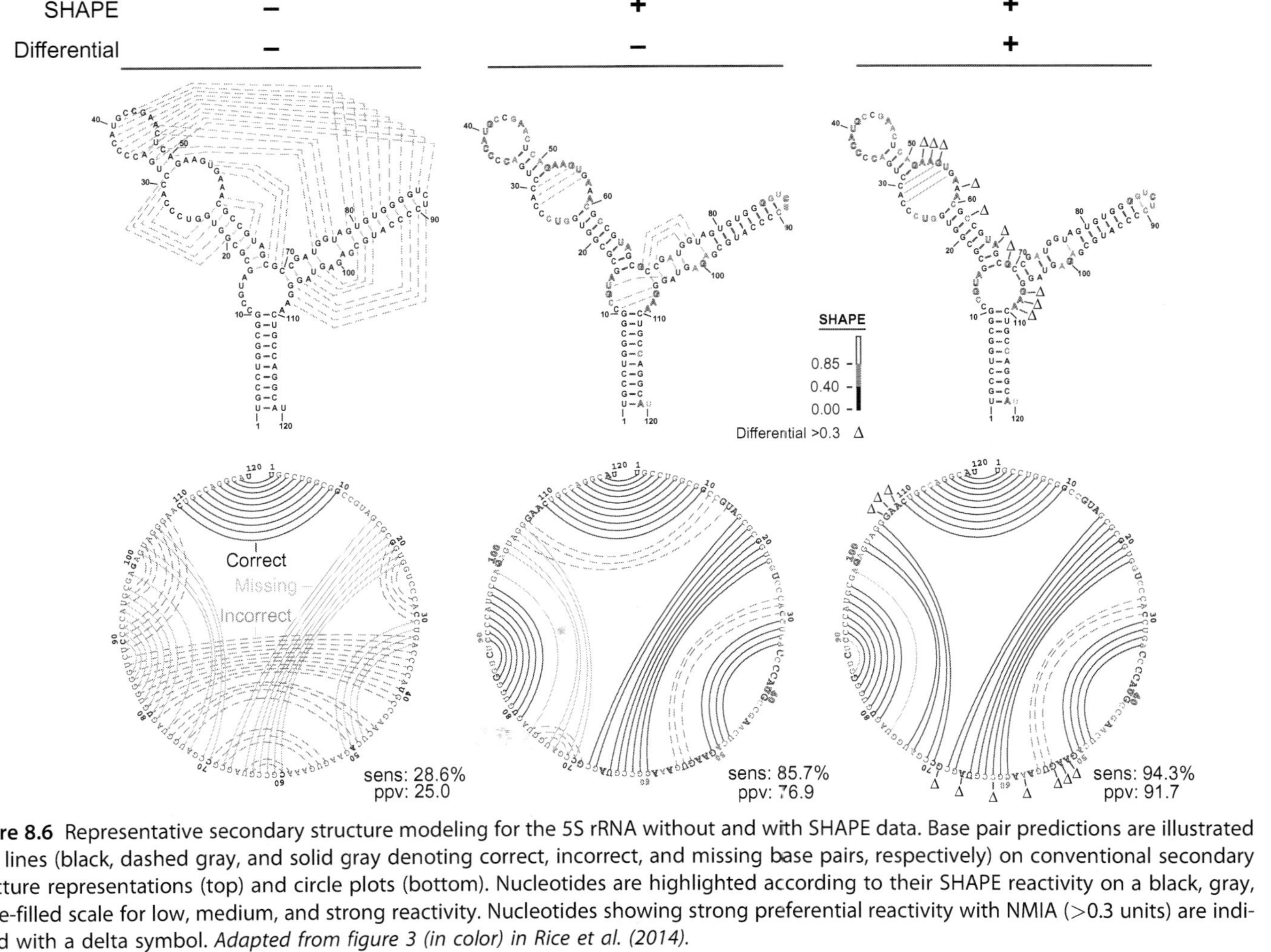

Figure 8.6 Representative secondary structure modeling for the 5S rRNA without and with SHAPE data. Base pair predictions are illustrated with lines (black, dashed gray, and solid gray denoting correct, incorrect, and missing base pairs, respectively) on conventional secondary structure representations (top) and circle plots (bottom). Nucleotides are highlighted according to their SHAPE reactivity on a black, gray, white-filled scale for low, medium, and strong reactivity. Nucleotides showing strong preferential reactivity with NMIA (>0.3 units) are indicated with a delta symbol. *Adapted from figure 3 (in color) in Rice et al. (2014).*

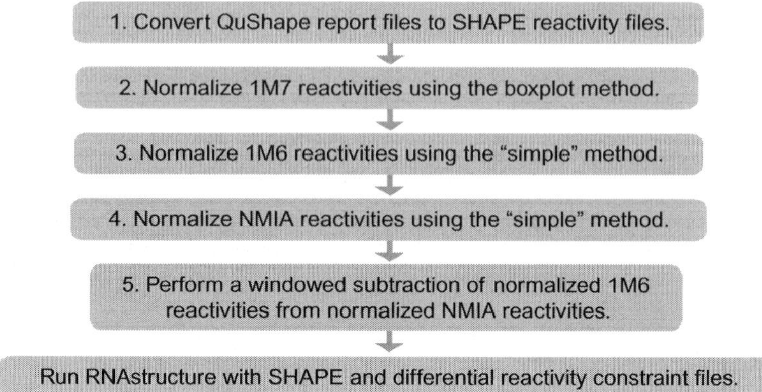

Figure 8.7 Flowchart for RNA secondary structure modeling using the full three-reagent SHAPE experiment, analyzed using *RNAstructure*.

9.4. Tip

For step 1.5b, windows sizes between 15 and 50 are reasonable. Selection of lower numbers results in more aggressive reactivity matching. This parameter can usually be left at 25. The real window size is calculated as $2n+1$. Setting this parameter to 25 thus results in a 51 nucleotide centered sliding window.

9.5. Tip

For step 1.5b, a slight bias toward positive-amplitude differential SHAPE signals is fine.

ACKNOWLEDGMENTS

Work in our labs, focused on creating concise and accurate approaches for analyzing RNA structure, is supported by the NIH and NSF.

REFERENCES

Hajdin, C. E., Bellaousov, S., Huggins, W., Leonard, C. W., Mathews, D. H., & Weeks, K. M. (2013). Accurate SHAPE-directed RNA secondary structure modeling, including pseudoknots. *Proceedings of the National Academy of Sciences of the United States of America*, *110*(14), 5498–5503. http://dx.doi.org/10.1073/pnas.1219988110.

Karabiber, F., McGinnis, J. L., Favorov, O. V., & Weeks, K. M. (2013). QuShape: Rapid, accurate, and best-practices quantification of nucleic acid probing information, resolved by capillary electrophoresis. *RNA*, *19*(1), 63–73. http://dx.doi.org/10.1261/rna.036327.112.

Merino, E. J., Wilkinson, K. A., Coughlan, J. L., & Weeks, K. M. (2005). RNA structure analysis at single nucleotide resolution by selective 2′-hydroxyl acylation and primer extension (SHAPE). *Journal of the American Chemical Society*, *127*(12), 4223–4231. http://dx.doi.org/10.1021/ja043822v.

Mortimer, S. A., & Weeks, K. M. (2007). A fast-acting reagent for accurate analysis of RNA secondary and tertiary structure by SHAPE chemistry. *Journal of the American Chemical Society*, *129*(14), 4144–4145. http://dx.doi.org/10.1021/ja0704028.

Reuter, J. S., & Mathews, D. H. (2010). RNA structure: Software for RNA secondary structure prediction and analysis. *BMC Bioinformatics*, *11*, 129. http://dx.doi.org/10.1186/1471-2105-11-129.

Rice, G. M., Leonard, C. W., & Weeks, K. M. (2014). RNA secondary structure modeling at consistent high accuracy using differential SHAPE. *RNA*, *20*(6), 846–854. http://dx.doi.org/10.1261/rna.043323.113.

Steen, K. A., Siegfried, N. A., & Weeks, K. M. (2011). Selective 2′-hydroxyl acylation analyzed by protection from exoribonuclease (RNase-detected SHAPE) for direct analysis of covalent adducts and of nucleotide flexibility in RNA. *Nature Protocols*, *6*(11), 1683–1694. http://dx.doi.org/10.1038/nprot.2011.373.

Turner, R., Shefer, K., & Ares, M. (2013). Safer one-pot synthesis of the "SHAPE" reagent 1-methyl-7-nitroisatoic anhydride (1m7). *RNA*, *19*(12), 1857–1863. http://dx.doi.org/10.1261/rna.042374.113.

Tyrrell, J., McGinnis, J. L., Weeks, K. M., & Pielak, G. J. (2013). The cellular environment stabilizes adenine riboswitch RNA structure. *Biochemistry*, *52*(48), 8777–8785. http://dx.doi.org/10.1021/bi401207q.

Warner, K. D., Homan, P., Weeks, K. M., Smith, A. G., Abell, C., & Ferré-D'Amaré, A. R. (2014). Validating fragment-based drug discovery for biological RNAs: Lead fragments bind and remodel the TPP riboswitch specifically. *Chemical Biology*, *21*(5), 591–595. http://dx.doi.org/10.1016/j.chembiol.2014.03.007.

Weeks, K. M., & Mauger, D. M. (2011). Exploring RNA structural codes with SHAPE chemistry. *Accounts of Chemical Research*, *44*(12), 1280–1291. http://dx.doi.org/10.1021/ar200051h.

CHAPTER NINE

Experimental Approaches for Measuring pK_a's in RNA and DNA

Pallavi Thaplyal, Philip C. Bevilacqua[1]

Department of Chemistry and Center for RNA Molecular Biology, The Pennsylvania State University, University Park, Pennsylvania, USA

[1]Corresponding author: e-mail address: pcb5@psu.edu

Contents

Abstract

RNA and DNA carry out diverse functions in biology including catalysis, splicing, gene regulation, and storage of genetic information. Interest has grown in understanding how nucleic acids perform such sophisticated functions given their limited molecular repertoire. RNA can fold into diverse shapes that often perturb pK_a values and allow it to ionize appreciably under biological conditions, thereby extending its molecular diversity. The goal of this chapter is to enable experimental measurement of pK_a's in RNA and DNA. A number of experimental methods for measuring pK_a values in RNA and DNA have been developed over the last 10 years, including RNA cleavage kinetics; UV-, fluorescence-, and NMR-detected pH titrations; and Raman crystallography. We

Methods in Enzymology, Volume 549
ISSN 0076-6879
http://dx.doi.org/10.1016/B978-0-12-801122-5.00009-X

begin with general considerations for choosing a pK_a assay and then describe experimental conditions, advantages, and disadvantages for these assays. Potential pitfalls in measuring a pK_a are provided including the presence of apparent pK_a's due to a kinetic pK_a or coupled acid- and alkali-promoted RNA unfolding, as well as degradation of RNA, precipitation of metal hydroxides and poor baselines. Use of multiple data fitting procedures and the study of appropriate mutants are described as ways to avoid some of these pitfalls. Application of these experimental methods to RNA and DNA will increase the number of available nucleic acid pK_a values in the literature, which should deepen insight into biology and provide benchmarks for pKa calculations. Future directions for measuring pK_a's in nucleic acids are discussed.

1. INTRODUCTION

Nucleic acids perform complex chemical functions such as catalysis, molecular recognition, and folding. The building blocks of RNA are rather simple, consisting of the ribose sugar–phosphate backbone and four similar nucleobases. One way RNA achieves additional functionality is through ionization of its nucleobases and sugar–phosphate backbone. To motivate experimental measurement of RNA pK_a values, we provide a brief background on RNA ionization and roles for charged bases in the Introduction; in-depth discussion of these issues is available elsewhere (Bevilacqua, Brown, Nakano, & Yajima, 2004; Wilcox, Ahluwalia, & Bevilacqua, 2011). The remainder of the chapter provides practical descriptions of various approaches available for measuring RNA pK_a's as well as potential problems.

Sites of ionization and unperturbed pK_a values in RNA are provided in Fig. 9.1. Typically, all four nucleobases are uncharged at biological pH: A and C are unprotonated on their imino nitrogens, while G and U are protonated. Under acidic pH conditions, the imino nitrogens of A and C protonate and become cationic with unperturbed pK_a values between ~3.6 and 4.3 (Izatt, Christensen, & Rytting, 1971), while under basic pH conditions, the imino nitrogens on G and U deprotonate and become anionic with unperturbed pK_a values near ~9.2–9.6 (Izatt et al., 1971). Each phosphodiester in the backbone has a low pK_a, near 1, and so is negatively charged. Any terminal phosphate monoester has the potential for being dianionic, with the higher pK_a being near neutrality. Biological importance of a phosphate monoester is unclear, however, given that most eukaryotic mRNAs have a 5′ cap. The 2′OH of the ribose sugar has a high pK_a, between ~12 and 14, and so is neutral at biological pH. Ionization of the

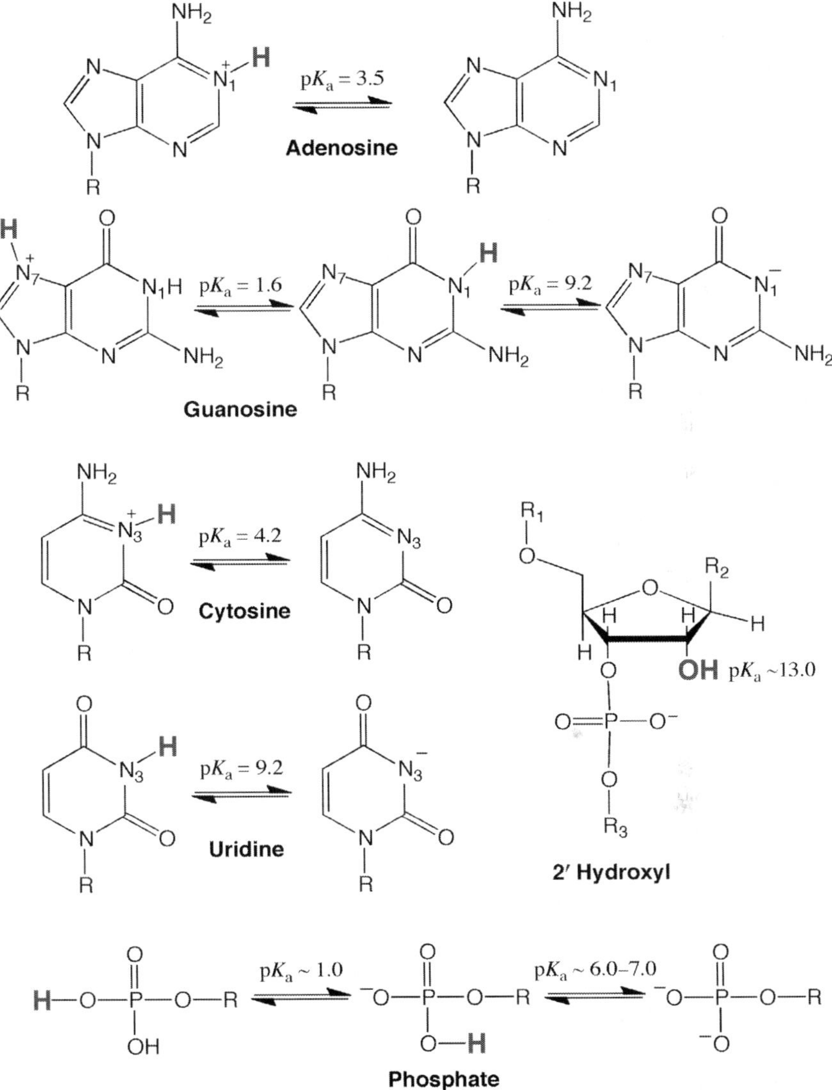

Figure 9.1 Sites of protonation and pK_a's of the four nucleobases and the ribose–phosphate backbone. Note that all unperturbed nucleobases are primarily in their neutral form at biological pH (~7.2). All nucleobase ionizations are on the Watson–Crick imino nitrogens, except for the left-hand ionization of guanosine, which is on the Hoogsteen face.

2′OH is important for ribozyme catalysis and RNA degradation (Izatt et al., 1971; Li & Breaker, 1999; Velikyan, Acharya, Trifonova, Földesi, & Chattopadhyaya, 2001).

Individual pK_a's in an RNA molecule are often perturbed from the above values, making experimental measurement very important. Secondary and tertiary structure elements, including hydrogen bonding, stacking, phosphate positioning, and metal ion coordination, can perturb pK_a values. For instance, hydrogen bonding[1] of the neutral nucleobases shifts the pK_a of the imino nitrogen further away from neutrality owing to coupling of ionization and folding (Legault & Pardi, 1997; Moody, Lecomte, & Bevilacqua, 2005). The imino nitrogen pK_a's for A and C thus shift even lower than 3.5, while those on G and U shift even higher than 9.5. In other words, hydrogen bonding of neutral bases generally disfavors nucleobase ionization. Hydrogen bonding of positively or negatively ionized nucleobases, on the other hand, typically shifts a pK_a toward neutrality; additionally, a high local electrostatic potential can favor protonation (Bevilacqua et al., 2004; Moody et al., 2005; Tang, Alexov, Pyle, & Honig, 2007; Wilcox et al., 2011). Such pK_a shifting may enable RNA to perform specialized catalytic and molecular recognition functions under biological conditions. Additionally, certain organelles (Tang et al., 2007) and disease states have altered pH gradient (both intra- and extracellular) (Gerweck & Seetharaman, 1996; Griffiths, 1991), which could generally facilitate ionization.

Prior experimental studies on a number of ribozymes have uncovered shifting of putative general acid adenine and cytosine pK_a's *toward neutrality* including the HDV (Gong et al., 2007; Nakano & Bevilacqua, 2007; Nakano, Chadalavada, & Bevilacqua, 2000), hairpin (Cottrell, Scott, & Fedor, 2011; Guo et al., 2009), and lead-dependent ribozymes (Legault & Pardi, 1994), arguing for a role as a cationic protonated nucleobase in the reactant state. Additionally, studies have revealed importance of pK_a shifting in ligand/cofactor binding to riboswitches as well. For example, the *glmS* riboswitch–ribozyme has a pK_a for the exocyclic amine of the GlcN6P shifted downward toward neutrality, while it has a pK_a for the phosphate of GlcN6P shifted upward toward neutrality (Gong, Klein, Ferré-D'Amaré, & Carey, 2011). In addition, the purine riboswitch binds xanthine strongly at low pH but not at high pH, consistent with xanthine's pK_a near

[1] Hydrogen bonding that leads to such pK_a shifting can be canonical base pairing of the Watson–Crick face, or it can be noncanonical base pairing of the Watson–Crick face, which often occurs in complex RNAs.

neutrality (Gilbert, Reyes, Edwards, & Batey, 2009). Experimental pK_a approaches applied in these instances include kinetics, fluorescence, NMR, and Raman crystallography—all described herein. At the same time, fluorescence and kinetics experiments have indicated that putative general base guanine pK_a's are shifted *away from neutrality* in the hairpin and *glmS* ribozymes, arguing for a role as a neutral protonated nucleobase in the reactant state (Liu, Cottrell, Scott, & Fedor, 2009; Viladoms, Scott, & Fedor, 2011).

Lastly, the methods described herein apply equally to DNA in its single-stranded and double-stranded form and should apply to complex DNAs such as deoxyribozymes. In fact, we have already applied these methods to dsDNA in several instances to reveal effects of helix position, temperature, and ionic strength on DNA pK_a's using NMR and fluorescence (Moody, Brown, & Bevilacqua, 2004; Siegfried, O'Hare, & Bevilacqua, 2010; Wilcox & Bevilacqua, 2013).

Theory has potential to identify shifted pK_a's and reveal molecular driving forces. Theoretical advances have been made in the area of pK_a prediction (Lee, Salsbury, & Brooks, 2004; Moser, Range, & York, 2010; Tang et al., 2007). It is our hope that the experimental approaches described herein will lead to more RNA and DNA pK_a measurements, which will benchmark and thus help advance theoretical nucleic acid pK_a calculations.

2. EXPERIMENTAL PARAMETERS FOR pH TITRATIONS

In this section, we outline key experimental considerations for choosing, designing, and interpreting a pK_a experiment. Potential pitfalls in pK_a determination are indicated, with emphasis placed on data fitting procedures and pK_a assignments through appropriate mutants as ways to avoid these pitfalls. We also discuss general effects of pH on RNA conformation and configuration.

2.1. Potential pitfalls: pH-promoted RNA unfolding, RNA degradation, and poor baselines

In this chapter, we describe obtaining pK_a's on both *folded* and *unfolded* nucleic acids. The interest in *folded* RNA and DNA is that these species often have the pK_a's closest to neutrality due to hydrogen bonding with ionized bases and due to electrostatic potentials, and they serve interesting biological roles. For instance, dsRNA is important for miRNA regulation of gene expression, ribozymes regulate viral replication and gene expression, and mutations in dsDNA are important for fidelity of DNA replication. The interest in *unfolded* RNA and DNA is that these provide pK_a's for the functional groups that are furthest from neutrality, such as the 2′OH, and also serve to complete thermodynamic cycles linking pK_a values and RNA folding (Moody et al., 2005).

The most difficult part of conducting a pK_a experiment on a folded RNA or DNA is isolating the two-state ionization of interest from interfering processes. Ideally, the pH range in a pK_a experiment should go from 2 units below the pK_a to 2 units above. This range allows the fraction of protonated RNA to vary from ~99% to ~1% to provide good baselines over the first and last ~0.5 pH units. Optimally, 12–25 evenly spaced data points should be collected over this pH range. Achieving this four-unit pH range often poses a problem, however, as RNA unfolds at strongly acidic or alkaline pH. Acid- and alkali-promoted denaturation of RNA structure occurs because of competition for hydrogen bonding (Fig. 9.2).

Acid or alkaline denaturation interferes strongly with pK_a measurement, as its dependence on pH is often steep (Moody et al., 2005). We have provided a formalism for handling linkage between proton binding and folding in RNA (Moody et al., 2005) and recently applied it to NMR-detected pH titrations (Fig. 9.3A; Siegfried et al., 2010). While this treatment is beyond the scope of this paper, it is important to be mindful of the detrimental effects extreme pH can have on RNA folding. The experimental range should be limited in the pH 5–9 region, and if pH 4 or 10 is needed, GC base pairing can be engineered to help avoid denaturation. If denaturation does occur, which should be obvious from steep outer transitions, we suggest showing the denaturation data but not including it in the fit (Fig. 9.3B). Additionally, apparent pK_a's (data that can be fit to a pK_a equation but are not due to an ionization) that creep toward neutrality occur when multiple unperturbed ionizations independently affect RNA stability (Fig. 9.3C; Knitt & Herschlag, 1996). In this case, there is no ionization near neutrality and the data should not be reported as such.

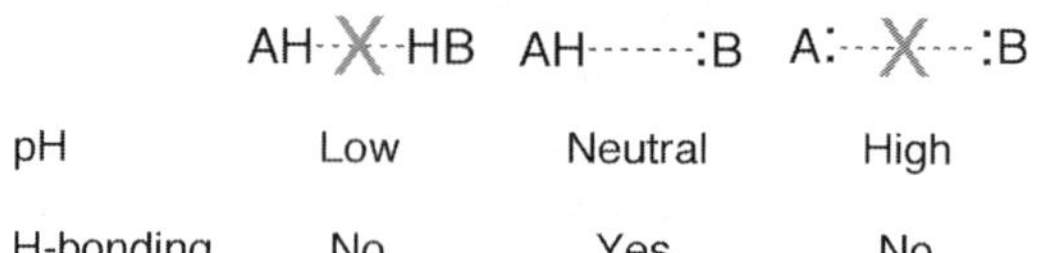

Figure 9.2 Schematic representing the loss of hydrogen bonding under acidic and alkaline pH conditions. Note that neutral pH is optimum for hydrogen bonding. At very low and high values (<~5 and >~9), the observed pK_a may become complicated due to the competition of solvent ions with hydrogen bonding.

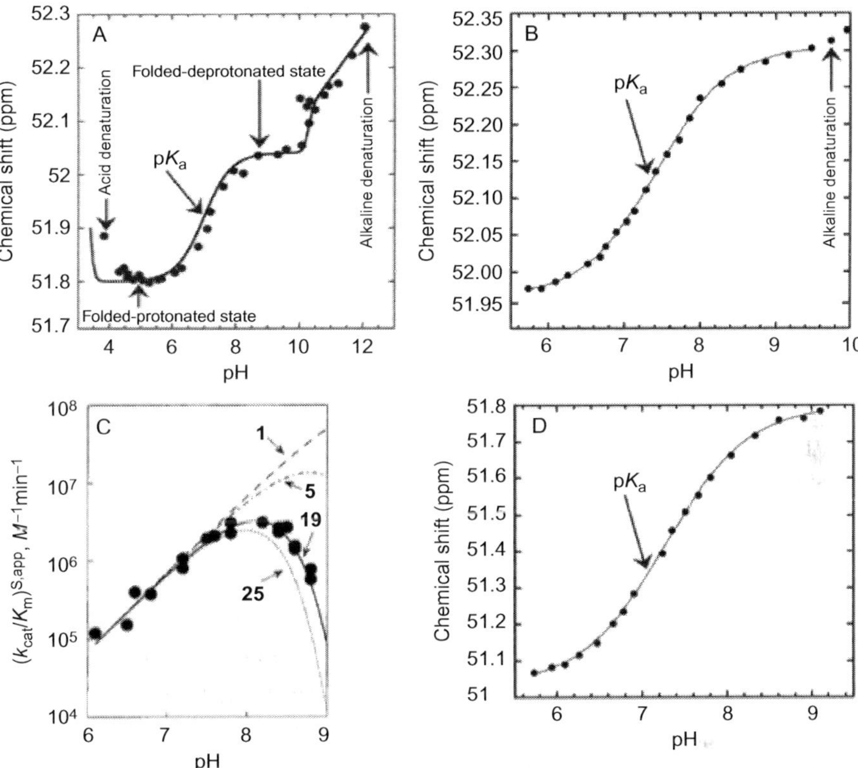

Figure 9.3 Different factors affecting observed pK_a. (A) ^{31}P NMR-based pH titration over a wide pH range (4.0–12.0) of a 19 mer dsDNA containing an $A^+ \cdot C$ wobble base pair. The plot shows five regions: acid denaturation (negative slope between pH ~3.8 and 4.5), protonated folded state (flat slope between pH ~4.5 and 6.0), ionization of the wobble base pair (positive slope between pH~6.0 and 8.0), deprotonated folded state (flat slope between pH ~8.0 and 10.0), and alkaline dentaturation (positive slope between pH ~10.0 and 12.0). (B) ^{31}P NMR-based pH titration of DNA with interference from alkaline denaturation. The data above pH 9.4 were not included in the fit to Eq. (9.4) to obtain the pK_a. (C) The pH-dependent cleavage of RNA under constant Na^+ concentration. The different lines represent the number of independent ionizations affecting the observed pK_a. The solid line represents 19 independent ionization events each with a microscopic pK_a ~9.4, which gives rise to an apparent pK_a of ~7.6. (D) ^{31}P NMR-based pH titration of DNA with no interference from unfolding. The observed pK_a is close to neutrality and is easily determined with the ideal baselines. *Panel (A) Adapted with permission from Siegfried et al. (2010). Copyright (2010) American Chemical Society. Panel (B) Adapted with permission from Wilcox and Bevilacqua (2013). Copyright (2013) American Chemical Society. Panel (C) Adapted with permission from Knitt and Herschlag (1996). Copyright (1996) American Chemical Society. Panel (D) Adapted with permission from Wilcox and Bevilacqua (2013). Copyright (2013) American Chemical Society.*

Considering the above issues of pH-promoted RNA unfolding and degradation, the easiest pK_a's to measure experimentally in a folded RNA are those closest to neutrality. This is a nice coincidence since such pK_a values are often the ones of greatest functional interest. Figure 9.3D provides an NMR-detected pH titration with a pK_a near 7 that has ideal behavior—full baselines and no interference from RNA unfolding. Most experiments on folded RNAs do not show such ideal behavior, however; (Fig. 9.3A–C), RNA functional groups either do not have pK_a values in the neutral pH range, or the signal change is not as strong. In these instances, a lower or upper limit to the pK_a value may be all that one can obtain.

The most difficult part of conducting a pK_a experiment on an unfolded RNA or DNA is obtaining quality data at high pH. Difficulties include precipitation of divalent metals as metal hydroxides and carbonates, and the high ionic strength that occurs at high pH (and thus at all pH if ionic strength is kept constant). These issues are described in Section 3.2, and procedures to estimate baselines for these cases are described in Section 4.1. Additionally, bear in mind that RNA can readily degrade at pH values greater than 10 in single-stranded regions (Soukup & Breaker, 1999) and other hot spots (Kierzek, 1992a, 1992b). Such degradation is exacerbated at elevated temperatures and in the presence of divalent ions, especially transition metals. At the end of any titration, but especially one that extends above pH 10, the RNA should thus be checked for degradation by denaturing PAGE with Sybr Gold or 5′-kinase detection.

2.2. Choosing the pH probe and meter

When carrying out pH titrations, it is essential that the pH probe provide an accurate reading. The probe should be calibrated with pH standards within the range of the pH titration and at the temperature of the reaction. In general, we titrate from high to low pH through the introduction of small volumes of HCl (~1 μL additions of a pH ~1 solution). This approach avoids adding metal ions via a metal hydroxide. We aim for 12–25 evenly spaced pH data points and adjust the concentration of HCl empirically to accomplish this with additions of just a 1–2 μL per data point; note that we do not attempt to get certain exact pH values. We therefore first calibrate the meter with pH 7 and 10 standards. For fluorescence experiments, we use colorless calibration standards (BDH General–VWR) to avoid potential contamination of the probe with fluorophores. Also, fresh pH standards are used for pH meter calibration to avoid any problems with breakdown of the standards, dissolved CO_2 (g), or cross-contamination. *Note*: The use of buffers is reserved for Section 2.3.

The pH of the solution should be measured before and after each data point is acquired to ensure that pH is maintained throughout the course of the measurement. Good mixing of the sample and the acid is critical and can be obtained either by multiple inversions or multiple mixings with a Pipetman set to 1 mL. In general, the two pH meter readings should agree within 0.05 units, and their average is used in the pK_a fitting. If the two meter readings differ by more than this, then the probe should be recalibrated and the measurement repeated. While the spectrum of interest is being collected, we submerge the probe in the pH 7 standard. During the course of the titration, once the pH nears ~7, the probe should be recalibrated in the pH 4 and 7 standards.

Our lab has used an Accumet 3-mm microcombination electrode with a calomel reference or a Mettler Toledo 3-mm diameter AgCl reference measured on a Corning 430 or Accument AB15 basic pH meter (Moody et al., 2004). More recently, we have employed a stainless steel ISFET micro pH probe (IQ Scientific Instruments) with a Hach IQ150 or IQ160 pH meter (Ganguly, Thaplyal, Rosta, Bevilacqua, & Hammes-Schiffer, 2014; Siegfried et al., 2010; Wilcox & Bevilacqua, 2013). This probe, which is inert to RNA and DNA and considerably more durable than the glass probe, fits inside tubes of >3 mm diameter. It can thus be used to measure pH directly in 4-mm NMR tubes (see Section 4.4); in these cases, only ~200 μL of sample is need to obtain a reading.

2.3. Whether to use a buffer

For assays where the RNA concentration is very low (e.g., n*M*) such as ribozyme kinetics, conventional buffers such as HEPES or MES are utilized to maintain pH. In Raman crystallography, conventional buffers are also utilized so that a constant-pH solution can permeate the crystals. Not all pH titrations require addition of a conventional buffer, however. When the RNA concentration is relatively high (e.g., μ*M* to m*M*) such as in UV-, fluorescence, and NMR-detected pH titrations, the RNA can effectively buffer itself near the pKa. In these cases, a conventional buffer is not used; instead, small amounts of a dilute solution of HCl are added directly to the RNA sample to change the pH. The new pH is then read out with a pH meter (see Section 2.2). For measurements of the 2′OH pK_a, metal hydroxide is utilized to achieve the desired high pH value, with each pH data point prepared separately. In these cases, the ionic strength is adjusted to a desired constant value with metal chloride. Experiments conducted in the absence of a conventional buffer have the advantage that data collection is generally rapid. It is also possible to prepare a series of buffers at fixed pH values for fluorescence titrations by a fluorescence plate reader, which can also facilitate high-throughput (Liu et al., 2009).

2.4. Corrections to the pH meter reading and the use of pH paper

The meter reading from a conventional pH electrode can be perturbed by moderate to high ionic strength, especially if cations are small monovalents such as Na^+ or Li^+. In such instances, the pH meter reading should be corrected. We do so by preparing standard solutions of a strong acid (e.g., HCl) and a strong base (e.g., NaOH) between 10^{-2} and 10^{-4} M (Chadalavada, Cerrone-Szakal, Wilcox, Siegfried, & Bevilacqua, 2012). A calibration curve of actual pH ($=-\log a_{H+}$) versus measured meter reading is made for these standards, in a background of constant ionic strength of interest. The calibration curve is then used to obtain the actual pH from a pH meter reading of the sample at the same ionic strength. Lastly, a simple but powerful technique useful in any of the experiments below is to spot a very small volume (<1 μL) of the reaction on pH paper and make a reading. There is a large assortment of pH paper available, including some that give readings with an accuracy of 0.2 units or better. This simple process, which requires extremely little sample and is convenient for radioactive samples, gives the experimentalist confidence that pH is where he/she expects and is not being affected by addition of salts, gases, or any other additives.

2.5. Choosing an experimental method and assigning the pK_a

A major consideration is choosing the experimental method for pK_a determination. This choice is closely linked to assigning the observed pK_a to a specific residue. For instance, the pH dependence of reaction kinetics (Section 3) provides just an overall observed pK_a for the RNA. It then becomes necessary to decide whether the dependence of rate on pH reflects a true ionization event or a change in the rate-limiting step, which may not be associated with an ionization event. Even when the pK_a reflects a true ionization event, assigning the pK_a to a specific residue requires mutagenesis and remeasuring of the rate-pH profile (Nakano et al., 2000). One can also make mutants that shift the pK_a by substitution of related bases, for example, substituting A for C (see Section 3.1). Methods employing UV, fluorescence, NMR, and Raman detection also require mutagenesis to assign the pK_a to a specific residue, typically by making base pair changes that prevent ionization by base pairing up the motif (see Sections 4.2–4.5).

At the other end of the spectrum, NMR can inform on the specific atom ionizing, either through assignment of the spectrum or by installation of a functional group that shifts a resonance to an isolated region of the spectrum (Section 4.4) (Moody et al., 2004; Siegfried et al., 2010). Fluorescence, likewise, can hone in on an ionizing base through judicious incorporation of a stacking-sensitive base such as 2-aminopurine (2AP) (Wilcox & Bevilacqua, 2013) or incorporation of a modified purine such as 8-azaguanine or 8-azaadenine (Section 4.3) (Cottrell et al., 2011; DaCosta, Fedor, & Scott, 2007; Liu et al., 2009; Viladoms et al., 2011). Some pH titration detection methods can be used without any labeling of the RNA at all, which is advantageous, as the potential for perturbation by the label is removed. Nonlabeling methods for pK_a determination include detection by UV spectroscopy (Section 4.2); ^{1}H, ^{13}C, and ^{15}N NMR (Section 4.4); and Raman microscopy (Section 4.5).

3. RNA CLEAVAGE KINETICS

Kinetics assays are often utilized to obtain a pK_a in RNA systems and can be used in naturally occurring ribozymes as well as selected ones such as kinase ribozymes (Bevilacqua, 2008; Biondi et al., 2013). The rate of self-cleavage of a ribozyme or a chimeric oligonucleotide containing a single ribose linkage is monitored as a function of pH to obtain an observed pK_a. The former is a folded RNA, while the latter is typically an unfolded RNA. In these cases, it is important to determine whether the observed pK_a is due to ionization of a residue or to a change in the rate-limiting step, and to assign the pK_a to an appropriate residue.

3.1. Ribozyme cleavage

Previous work from our lab has focused on the reaction mechanism of the HDV ribozyme (Cerrone-Szakal, Siegfried, & Bevilacqua, 2008; Nakano, Cerrone, & Bevilacqua, 2003; Nakano et al., 2000). Both *cis-* and *trans-*acting versions of the ribozyme have been used to determine pK_a's. For each of the methods described below, the 5′ or 3′ terminal nucleotide is radiolabeled. General procedures for radiolabeling RNA are available elsewhere (Bevilacqua, Brown, Chadalavada, & Parente, 2003). ^{32}P-labeling enables high sensitivity and we typically work with very low RNA concentrations, near a few nanomolar. Alternatively, the RNA can be end-labeled with a fluorophore (Qin & Pyle, 1999).

In *trans*-acting ribozymes, experiments are typically conducted under single-turnover conditions in which the enzyme is in excess over the substrate. To ensure that the enzyme concentration is saturating, control experiments with several concentrations of enzyme are carried out and similar rates should be obtained. Typically, the enzyme and the substrate strand are annealed at 95 °C, followed by cooling at room temperature for 10 min. The pH is maintained by the addition of 25–50 m*M* buffer. We typically use the Good buffers as these are largely nonreactive and do not bind most metal ions (Good et al., 1966): MES for pH 4.5–6.5, HEPES for pH 6.5–8.5, and CAPS for pH 9.0–11.0. Controls include using different buffers at the same pH in the pH overlap region, as well as several different concentrations of the same buffer to test whether buffer contributes to the reaction. The reaction is usually initiated by the addition of metal ion, and time points are removed as small volume aliquots, quenched in excess EDTA, and placed on powdered dry ice. The reactant and the product are fractionated by PAGE and the gels are dried and quantified using a Typhoon PhosphoImager (MolecularDynamics). The fraction of the substrate cleaved is fit to a single-exponential equation using nonlinear curve program with a Levenberg–Marquadt algorithm such as Kaleidagraph (Synergy Software):

$$f_{\text{cleaved}} = A + Be^{-k_{\text{obs}}t} \tag{9.1}$$

where f_{cleaved} is the fraction of the cleaved substrate, A is the fraction of the substrate cleaved at completion, $-B$ is the amplitude of the reaction, $(A + B)$ is the burst phase, $(1 - A)$ is the fraction that never cleaves, and k_{obs} is the observed first-order rate constant. The observed rate constant k_{obs} is then plotted versus the pH, and fit to the Henderson–Hasselbach equation for a one-channel mechanism[2] to obtain the pK_a of the reaction:

$$k_{\text{obs}} = \frac{k_{\text{max}}}{1 + 10^{n(\text{p}K_a - \text{pH})}} \tag{9.2a}$$

where k_{max} is the maximal observed rate constant and n is the Hill coefficient, which may be related to the number of ionization events.

[2] "One channel" refers to only one of the two species, protonated or deprotonated, contributing to the mechanism. If both species contribute, then more complex data are obtained with an apparent pK_a as described below and in Fig. 9.4D.

There are two typical ways to plot rate constant-pH data and both are provided in Fig. 9.4. The sample data shown here are for chimeric oligonucleotides, which contain a single ribose linkage, but apply equally well to ribozymes.

In the first method, k_{obs} is plotted versus pH, and y is fit directly to Eq. (9.2a) (Fig. 9.4A). This method has the advantage that k_{max} can be read

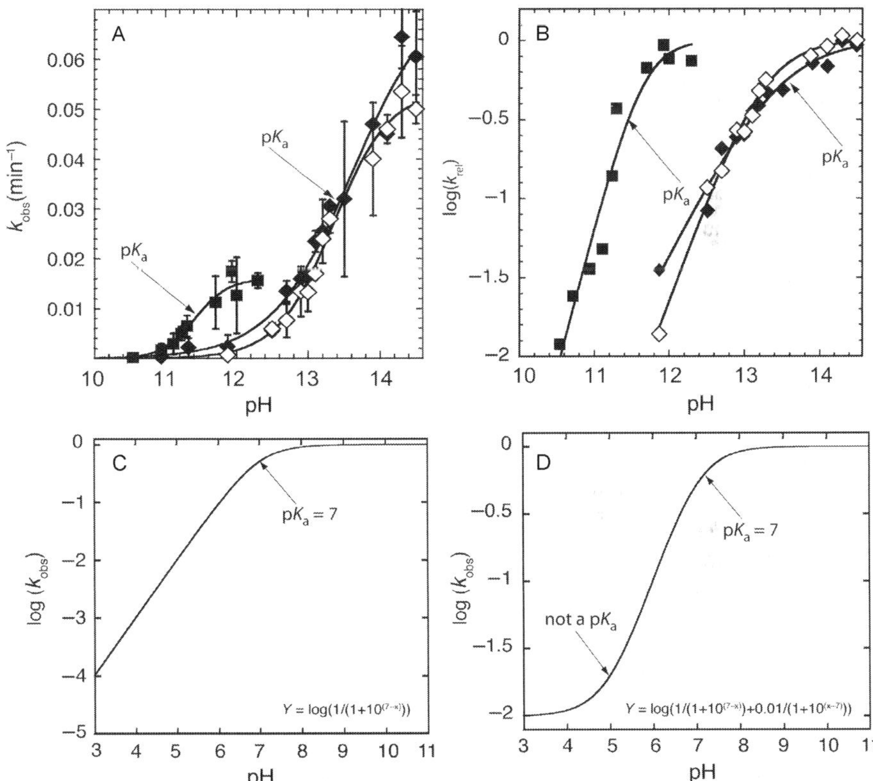

Figure 9.4 RNA cleavage kinetics-based determination of pK_a. (A) Plot of k_{obs} versus pH. The pK_a is determined by fitting the plot to Eq. (9.2a) and (9.2b). The pK_a can be visually identified by the inflection point, which is the point at which k_{obs} is equal to half of the k_{max}. (B) Plot of log (k_{obs}) versus pH. The pK_a is determined by fitting the plot to Eq. (9.2b). The rounding or "flex" point and the slope of the line in the log linear region can be utilized to visually determine the pK_a and the Hill coefficient, respectively. (C) and (D) Simulated plot of log (k_{obs}) versus pH, in which (C) the rate increases log linearly (slope ~1) with pH, and (D) the rate decreases log linearly and then levels off at low pH without a low pK_a. *Panel (A) Adapted with permission from Ganguly et al. (2014). Copyright (2014) American Chemical Society. Panel (B) Adapted with permission from Ganguly et al. (2014). Copyright (2014) American Chemical Society. Panel (D) Adapted from Bevilacqua et al. (2003).*

graphically from the maximum y-value, and the pK_a can be found at the inflection point, which is the pH where k_{obs} is half k_{max}. In the second method, log k_{obs} is plotted versus pH and y is fit to the right-hand side of Eq. (9.2b) (Fig. 9.4B).

$$\log k_{obs} = \log\left(\frac{k_{max}}{1+10^{n(pK_a-pH)}}\right) \tag{9.2b}$$

This method has the advantage that n can be read graphically from the slope in the linear portion of the plot; in this plot, the pK_a is near the rounding or "flex" point of the curve. A subtle but important point is that rate data can contribute meaningfully to such a logarithmic plot even at pH values far below the pK_a. This is because one can usually collect longer time points. This property of logarithmic plots is useful for detecting poorly populated species that may be important for a reaction, something not afforded by the spectroscopic approaches described in Section 4.

Poor fitting of data to Eq. (9.2b) can happen for one of several reasons. If the rate does not decrease log linearly with decreasing pH but instead levels off in a sigmoid-like fashion, it can be due to a second reaction channel that opens at low pH in which the other ionization state contributed to the reaction. This is essentially a pH-dependent change in the rate-limiting step and can give rise to an apparent pK_a, as labeled in Fig. 9.4D. Furthermore, if the rate changes more steeply with increasing pH than expected, it could be due to an apparent pK_a arising from multiple independent ionizations; e.g., Knitt & Herschlag (1996) showed that 19 independent ionizations of unperturbed value 9.4 give rise to an apparent pK_a of 7.6 (Fig. 9.3C). This can be spotted by failure of Eq. (9.2b) but success of the logarithm of Eq. (9.3) in fitting the data.

$$k_{obs} = \frac{k_{cat}}{K_M} = \frac{k_{max}/[H^+]}{(1+10^{pH-pK_a})^n} \tag{9.3}$$

As mentioned, these are not true microscopic ionizations near neutrality and should not be reported as such.

The pK_a obtained from kinetics experiments could also be due to a change in the rate-limiting step from chemistry to some other process, which is, often referred to as a "kinetic pK_a" (Fersht, 1985). To test whether chemistry is rate limiting in the plateau region, one should conduct a solvent isotope effect test or measure a phosphorothioate effect in this region (Frederiksen & Piccirilli, 2009; Nakano et al., 2000). Typically, solvent isotope effects on proton transfer processes are three- to sevenfold if chemistry is rate limiting (Fersht, 1985), while thio effects can range from ~5 to more than 1000 (Dahm & Uhlenbeck, 1991; DeRose, 2003; Frederiksen & Piccirilli, 2009; Kraut, Carroll, & Herschlag, 2003). Although these tests are not foolproof, they provide support that chemistry is rate-limiting in the plateau region. Additionally, the putative ionizing base can be mutated to a related base with a different pK_a. For example, in the HDV ribozyme the C75A mutant helped assign the observed pK_a to C75 by observation of a shift in the ribozyme-measured pK_a similar to the shift in the pK_a between CMP and AMP (Nakano et al., 2000). Ultimately, it is best to also pursue a complementary method of pK_a determination in which population is directly measured through a spectroscopic technique as a function of pH, such as described in Section 4. In sum, ribozyme cleavage kinetics provide a way to attain a pK_a of any RNA or DNA enzyme, naturally occurring or selected. The equations for extracting a pK_a are provided, but one has to be wary of pitfalls as described above.

3.2. Chimeric oligonucleotide cleavage

As mentioned above, there is keen interest in measuring the pK_a of the 2′OH since it is a common nucleophile in ribozymes and mRNA degradation. A convenient approach to measure the pK_a of the 2′OH, which is typically between ~12 and 14, has been developed by Li and Breaker (1999). This assay relies on the pH-dependent cleavage of an unfolded chimeric oligonucleotide containing a single ribose linkage; it can be used to compare the effect of metal ions and RNA sequence on the pK_a of the 2′OH (Ganguly et al., 2014; Li & Breaker, 1999). The chimeric oligonucleotide is labeled on its 5′-end as described above, renatured at 90 °C, and its cleavage is monitored as a function of pH. Samples are neutralized with 100 mM Tris pH 7.0, fractionated by PAGE, and analyzed on the PhosphorImager. Data are fit to the same equations as in Section 3.1, namely, Eqs. (9.1)–(9.2b). It is important to maintain constant ionic strength throughout the pH range of the experiment, which is pH ~10.0–14.0 for monovalent ions, and pH ~9.0–12.0 for divalent ions. This is achieved by adding specific volumes of metal hydroxide solutions (e.g., NaOH or KOH) in the presence of appropriate volumes of metal chloride solutions (e.g., NaCl or KCl).

Unfortunately, the same chimeric oligonucleotide cleavage experiment cannot be carried out in the presence of divalent metal ions such as Mg^{2+} owing to the precipitation of magnesium hydroxide above pH ~9. The reaction can, however, be performed in the presence of Ca^{2+}; e.g., pH 12.2 can be achieved in 10 mM Ca^{2+} without formation of calcium hydroxide solid (Fig. 9.4A and B; Ganguly et al., 2014). Calcium does pose a new experimental problem, though, which is the formation of $CaCO_3$ precipitates in the presence of CO_2 (aq.). Solutions must therefore be degassed to remove dissolved CO_2 and the reactions carried out under an inert gas atmosphere (preferably argon). One limitation of this method is that metal-bound hydroxide could contribute to the observed pK_a, intended to come from the 2'OH. To assure measurement of the pK_a on the 2′OH itself, we used an RNA-centric proxy of ionization, namely, chemical shift of the H1′ sugar proton on a model system (3'AMP) (see Section 4.4). To summarize, pK_a values for the 2′OH can be attained in model oligonucleotides using many of the same methods and equations as used for ribozymes.

4. SPECTROSCOPIC-DETECTED METHODS

4.1. General considerations for spectroscopic-detected pH titrations

The next four subsections (4.2–4.5) describe experimental approaches for measuring pK_a's that rely on readout through a spectroscopic approach. Absorbance and NMR are label-free methods and so least likely to perturb the pK_a on the RNA. In these, a given observed spectroscopic signal S_{obs} (e.g., absorbance A, fluorescence F, chemical shift δ, or Raman intensity I) is plotted versus pH and fit to Eq. (9.4) to obtain the pK_a:

$$S_{obs} = S_{AH} + \frac{S_A - S_{AH}}{1 + 10^{n(pK_a - pH)}} \tag{9.4}$$

where S_{obs} is the observed signal at a given pH, S_{AH} is the signal at low pH, S_A is the signal at high pH, and n is the Hill coefficient, which may be related to the number of ionization events. If the data warrant, S_{AH} and S_A can be set equal to sloping lines, which gives rise to two more variables that can be fixed to constants if long enough baselines can be measured. Additionally, if n is found to be $\sim$1, some researchers will fix the value at unity. We prefer to report the value of n to see its range, but this is really a matter of style and has little effect on final free energy values if consistency in usage of n is maintained. Equation 9.4 is similar to Eqs. (9.2a) and (9.2b), but differs in that both the protonated and unprotonated states contribute in Eq. (9.4), while only one of the two states (the reactive state) contributes in the one-channel model in Eqs. (9.2a) and (9.2b). Furthermore, unlike Eqs. (9.2a) and (9.2b), the logarithm of Eq. (9.4) is generally not taken because data cannot be extended past ~5–95% of the maximum signal due to poor signal-to-noise, which generally requires plotting over ~4 pH units centered at the pK_a. If the data do not fit well to Eq. (9.4), it could be because of acid or alkaline denaturation or perhaps due to apparent pK_a's from multiple ionizations (Fig. 9.3A–C).

In some cases, one of the baselines cannot be obtained, which could be due to pH denaturation of folded RNA or precipitation of metal hydroxides. In these cases, it may be possible to estimate the missing baseline through an approximation such as shown in Eq. (9.5) (Ganguly et al., 2014; Velikyan et al., 2001):

$$S_{\text{obs}} = S_{\text{A}} + (S_{\text{AH}} - S_{\text{obs}})(a_{\text{H}^+}/K_{\text{a}}) \tag{9.5}$$

As mentioned in Section 2.3, a conventional buffer is not added for UV-, fluorescence-, and NMR-detected pH titrations and instead the RNA buffers itself.

4.2. UV absorbance-detected pH titrations

The four nucleobases absorb UV light quite strongly and ionization of the nucleobases generally leads to a change in extinction coefficient (Bock, Ling, Morell, & Lipton, 1956). This makes changes in UV absorbance a convenient and label-free (i.e., nonperturbing) method for determining a pK_a (Moody et al., 2005). The extent of change in the UV spectrum upon ionization is different for each of the four bases. For CTP, GTP, and UTP, there are striking differences in the absorbance spectra upon ionization, with absorbance increasing at some wavelengths and decreasing at others (Bock et al., 1956). For ATP, there are also differences in the spectra upon ionization, but the effects are more subtle. This means that one can estimate which of the four bases is ionizing by comparing the pH difference UV spectrum (i.e., difference of the high and low pH baseline spectra) of the sample of interest to the pH difference UV spectrum of the four bases. As the ionizing RNA gets larger, the contribution of the ionizing base diminishes on a percentage basis but still can be detectable for reasonably size RNAs, especially if the ionizing base is C, G, or U; as described below, we have applied this to a 19 mer. Figure 9.5A and B shows that the ionization of C in an *unfolded* oligonucleotide is readily detectable in the background of UC and UUCUU.

Hyperchromicity in the 260–280 nm region arising from unstacking in a *folded* hairpin upon deprotonation can be used to monitor a pK_a as well. Even as little as a 4% change in hyperchromicity provides ample signal

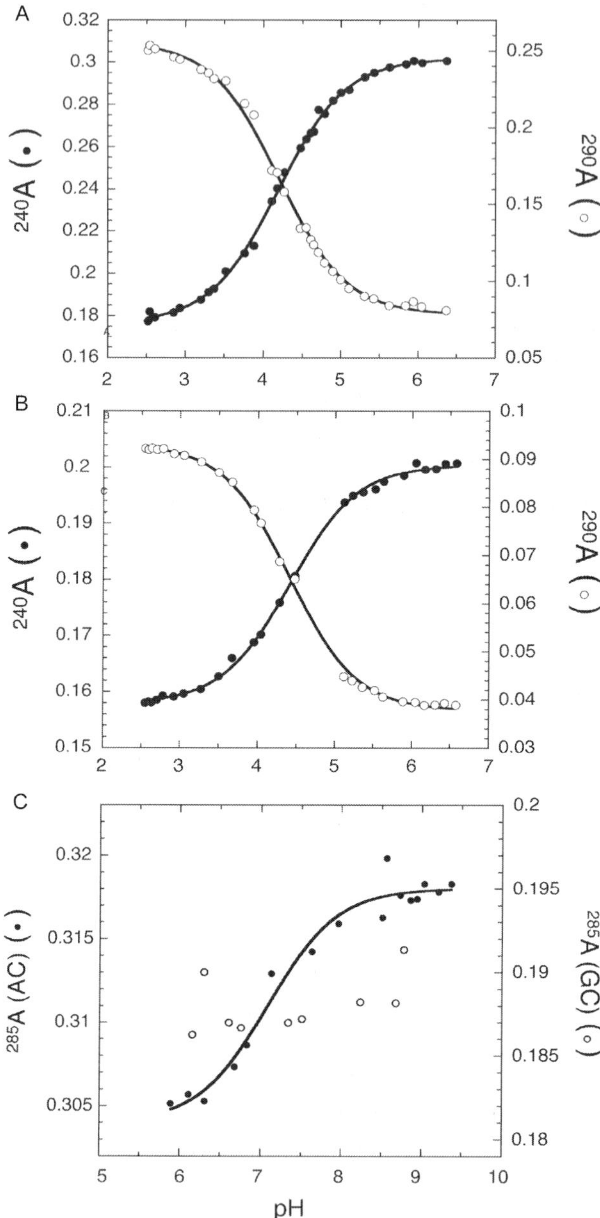

Figure 9.5 UV absorbance-based determination of pK_a. (A) and (B) Plot of absorbance at 240 nm (solid circles) and 290 nm (open circles) versus pH to determine pK_a of cytosine in two unstructured oligonucleotides (A) UC and (B) UUCUU. (C) Plot of absorbance at 285 nm for a 19 mer oligonucleotide folded hairpin containing A^+·C wobble pair (solid circles), and a control oligonucleotide containing an GC base pair substitution (hollow circles). *Note*: The shifted pK_a due to the formation of the protonated A^+·C wobble pair could be detected even though the magnitude of hyperchromicity is only 4%. The pK_a was determined by fitting the data to Eq. (9.4). *Adapted with permission from Moody et al. (2005). Copyright (2005) RNA.*

change to measure a pK_a in a 19 mer hairpin with a single A^+·C wobble pair (Fig. 9.5C, closed symbols). In principle, even larger RNAs could be studied if the ionizing base were other than A, given the greater spectral change (Bock et al., 1956). A control in which the wobble pair is replaced by a Watson–Crick base pair leads to loss of signal and helps assign the pK_a (Fig. 9.5C, open symbols).

To obtain a pK_a in a UV absorbance-detected pH titration, absorbance is measured at different pH values according to the general principles provided in Section 2. Briefly, experiments are usually carried out in 100 m*M* KCl to mimic biological conditions and to offset small changes in salt concentration during the pH titration. Before the start of the experiment, the spectrophotometer is zeroed in the presence of 100 m*M* KCl. The oligonucleotide is heated at a temperature greater than the denaturing temperature to ensure unfolding (usually 90 °C) and added to the cuvette with the buffer containing 100 m*M* KCl. Because the percentage signal change in UV absorbance-detected titrations can be small, the cuvette should not be removed throughout the titration. Instead, use a ring stand to lower the pH meter into the cuvette and mix the small volume acid into the sample with a Pipetman set to 1 mL. Data are fit to Eq. (9.4) to obtain the pK_a and the Hill coefficient. In sum, UV-detected pH titrations provide a very general and label-free manner to attain a pK_a in any functional RNA or DNA and should work with RNAs of 20 or more bases, including small riboswitches and ribozymes.

4.3. Fluorescence-detected pH titrations

A limitation of absorbance detection is that absorbance changes throughout the titration can be relatively small since changes in base pairing and stacking upon ionization can be modest. One way to overcome this is to install a fluorescent base at a unique location in the RNA or DNA that is sensitive to either local unfolding/folding or an overall conformational change. Fluorescence-detected methods generally offer several advantages over absorbance. Fluorescence is much more sensitive than absorbance, allowing more dilute samples to be used; the change in signal is localized to a specific region of the RNA or DNA; and the change in signal tends to be larger than with absorbance.

Recently, our lab utilized fluorescence changes in 2AP, a fluorescent isomer of A (Fig. 9.6A), to measure pK_a values in RNA and DNA oligonucleotides (Wilcox & Bevilacqua, 2013).

Here, we describe how changes in fluorescence of 2AP with pH can be used to determine pK_a's in the secondary and tertiary structure of RNA and DNAs. The first step in using 2AP-detected pH titrations is to design a

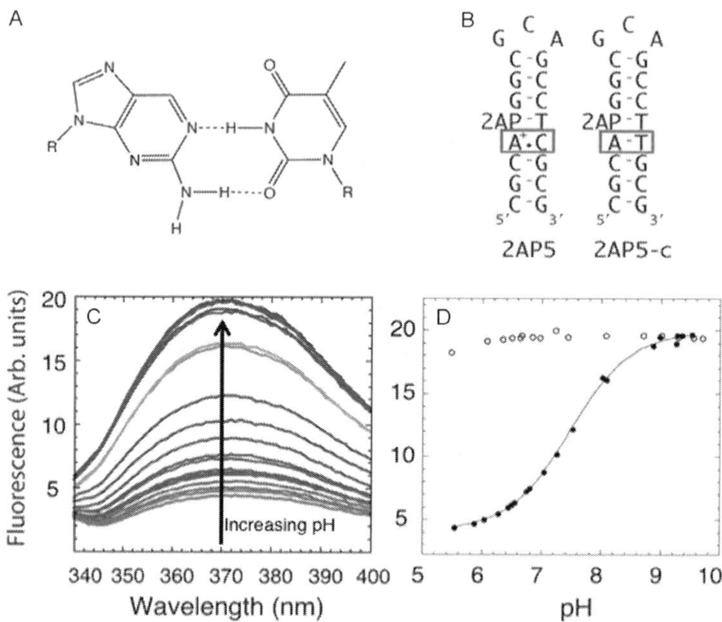

Figure 9.6 Fluorescence-based determination of pK_a using 2AP-substituted oligonucleotides. (A) 2AP is structurally similar to adenine and is able to form a two-hydrogen bond base pair with thymine. (B) DNA constructs containing the $A^+ \cdot C$ wobble (2AP5) and the control construct containing an AT Watson–Crick (2AP5-c) base pair. The signal change for the 2AP substitution was optimal when 2AP was positioned directly above the wobble base pair. (C) Fluorescence spectra at different pH for 2AP5 construct, with pink corresponding to low pH and blue to high pH. (D) Plot of observed fluorescence as a function of pH for 2AP5 (solid circles) and 2AP5-c (hollow circles). 2AP5-c shows no change in fluorescence with pH, whereas the 2AP5 shows a fourfold change in fluorescence. *Adapted with permission from Wlicox and Bevilacqua (2013). Copyright (2013) American Chemical Society.* (See the color plate.)

2AP-containing RNA or DNA. It is well known that the fluorescence of 2AP decreases approximately twofold upon stacking (Jean & Hall, 2001). We thus design oligonucleotides wherein the 2AP is adjacent to a nucleobase that is likely to undergo a change in stacking upon ionization (Fig. 9.6B). Care should be taken to ensure that the substitution of 2AP does not perturb the secondary or tertiary structure of the oligonucleotide. One way to accomplish this is by comparing the pK_a measured by fluorescence to a pK_a measured by another method such as NMR, while another is to conduct an activity assay on the fluorescent RNA or DNA such as binding or kinetics, if a functional assay is available. Ideally, little or no change in activity should be observed.

DNA and RNA oligonucleotides containing 2AP can be purchased commercially from IDT and Dharmacon. At the start of the experiment, the oligonucleotide is denatured at 90 °C for 2 min and cooled at room temperature for 10 min. The pH of the oligonucleotide is brought to pH ~10 by the addition of a small amount of KOH. As per Section 2.3, these experiments are done in the absence of any buffer. Our lab uses a 1-cm pathlength quartz cuvette. Spectra are collected on Horiba Jobin Yvon Fluoromax-4 and analyzed using FluorEssence and KaleidaGraph software. The concentration of oligonucleotide used is ~10 μ*M*.[3] For 2AP-substituted transcripts, the samples are excited at 304 nm, and emission spectra are collected from 325 to 400 nm. Slit widths are adjusted according to the sample's fluorescence to ensure ample signal-to-noise ratio and should remain constant throughout the titration and between titrations on different constructs to allow direct comparisons of data. The fluorescence data as a function of pH are fit to Eq. (9.4).

Fluorescence-detected determination of pK_a values in DNA monitors secondary structure formation. In this assay, the pK_a shifting in DNA hairpins was examined by placing a 2AP adjacent to an d(A^+)·dC wobble (Fig. 9.6B). At pH values below the pK_a, the protonated base pair is formed, resulting in the quenching of the fluorescence from 2AP (Fig. 9.6C and D closed symbols). At pH above the pK_a, an increase in fluorescence is observed. Different positioning of the 2AP within the hairpin showed that 2AP adjacent to the wobble base pair and just downstream of the ionizing A gave optimal pH–titration curves (Fig. 9.6B and D). A control in which the d(A^+)·dC was changed to an AT base pair gave no change in fluorescence and thus helped assign the pK_a (Fig. 9.6B and D, open symbols). The pK_a's obtained using this method have been corroborated with NMR experiments (Wilcox & Bevilacqua, 2013).

Fluorescence-detected determination of pK_a values in RNA can also detect tertiary structure formation (Wilcox & Bevilacqua, 2013). The functional structure of beet western yellows virus RNA depends upon the formation of a pseudoknot that is formed as a result of protonation of C8 at neutral pH. Mutational studies have shown that a base quartet that C8 forms in conjunction with G12, A25, and C26 is essential for the RNA to perform its functional features. In an effort to measure the pK_a of C8, 2AP was incorporated at position 9, which is in close stacking proximity to C8. Following the same trend as that described for 2AP-labeled

[3] A lower concentration might be possible, but this one gives excellent signal to noise and is high enough to buffer itself throughout the titration.

DNA, an increase in pH resulted in an increase in fluorescence, in this case due to loss of stacking from breaking of tertiary interactions. (Data not shown but similar to Fig. 9.6C and D.) The pH–titration curves were then used to determine the pK_a and Hill coefficient of 8.15 and 0.94, respectively (Wilcox & Bevilacqua, 2013). The results agreed with a pK_a extrapolated from a thermodynamic linkage study (Cornish & Giedroc, 2006). Control experiments on a double mutant oligonucleotide that forms a non-ionized quartet showed no change in fluorescence with pH, and gave the same fluorescence as the wild type at low pH, which helped assign the pK_a to C8.

Recently, Fedor and coworkers have applied 8-azaguanine and 8-azaadenine to measure pK_a's in RNA. Briefly, they synthesized 8aza-modified purine mono and triphosphates through an enzymatic synthesis procedure (DaCosta et al., 2007). These bases were then installed into a large RNA through transcription, in some cases onto the 5′-end of a ribozyme through NMP-primed transcription. In general, after such a procedure, the ribozyme (or RNA) can be constructed through T4 RNA ligation. Remarkably, the fluorescence of the modified RNA increased 10- to 100-fold upon deprotonation of the purine. The authors have used this method to conclude that the guanine positioned to be the general base in the hairpin and *glmS* ribozymes has an upward-perturbed pK_a and thus seems to function in the neutral protonated form at biological pH (Liu et al., 2009; Viladoms et al., 2011). In contrast, the adenine positioned to be the general acid in the hairpin ribozyme has a pK_a shifted toward neutrality (Cottrell et al., 2011). These authors made measurements in a SpectraMax plate reader using buffers at different pH and fit the data to an equation equivalent to Eq. (9.4). To conclude, insertion of a fluorescent base that is in proximity to a base pairing, stacking, or refolding event provides a way to monitor a pH-dependent event and determine a local pK_a in any functional RNA of interest.

4.4. NMR-detected pH titrations

NMR has been extensively utilized to determine pK_a's in DNA and RNA. The sensitivity of the chemical shift to local RNA structure makes NMR especially useful for pK_a measurement. An NMR assay can be performed by indirect labeling or no labeling at all and so is unlikely to perturb the pK_a. Depending upon the assay, the pK_a's can be assigned to a nucleobase or to the 2′hydroxyl.

^{31}P, ^{1}H, and ^{13}C are the most widely used nuclei for nucleic acids. ^{31}P (100% of natural phosphorus) and ^{1}H (99.98% of natural hydrogen) are abundant in nature, whereas ^{13}C (~1% of natural carbon) has low natural abundance. The hydrogen and carbon nuclei occur at various positions within an RNA molecule, in contrast to phosphorus, which is only found at the phosphate bonds. The high occurrence of hydrogen and carbon nuclei within an RNA molecule can be advantageous in terms of providing many possible positions for detection but can also lead to convolution of data and difficulty in interpretation of an NMR spectrum.

Phosphorus (^{31}P) NMR spectroscopy provides a potentially simple way to measure pK_a shifting, as each residue has one phosphorus atom and phosphorus is a spin ½ nucleus, giving rise to one singlet in a proton-decoupled experiment. However, most phosphorus atoms resonate in a congested region of the spectrum, precluding monitoring of chemical shift with pH. Substitution of a specific phosphate with a phosphorothioate results in a large downfield shift of the sulfur-linked phosphorus resonance by ~50 ppm in ^{31}P NMR (Moody et al., 2004), providing an uncluttered spectrum (Fig. 9.7A).

We have applied phosphorothioate-substituted oligonucleotide ^{31}P NMR spectroscopy to pK_a determination in both single-strand and double-strand DNA and RNA (Moody et al., 2004; Siegfried et al., 2010; Wilcox & Bevilacqua, 2013) in which the substituted phosphate is placed adjacent to an ionizing base pair. These phosphorus atoms have a pH-dependent change in chemical shift, caused by local structure changing upon base pair formation (Fig. 9.7B). This substitution, which is available commercially in DNA and RNA, gives rise to two diastereomers (R_P and S_P). Although it is possible to separate the two diastereomers using HPLC, we typically use the mixture, which gives rise to two peaks in the proton-decoupled ^{31}P NMR (Fig. 9.7A). Often both peaks can be followed uniquely, thereby allowing the measurement of a pK_a from two different substitutions in a single experiment (e.g., Fig. 9.7B, circles). Typically, a control oligonucleotide in which the ionizing base is mutated to form a Watson–Crick base pair with its pairing partner is studied to confirm the pK_a assignment (Fig. 9.7B, diamonds). The protonated and unprotonated states can be in a rapid exchange on the chemical shift timescale, corresponding to single Lorentzian peaks at low and high pH (Fig. 9.7A). In such cases, the data can be fit to Eq. (9.4) (Fig. 9.7B).

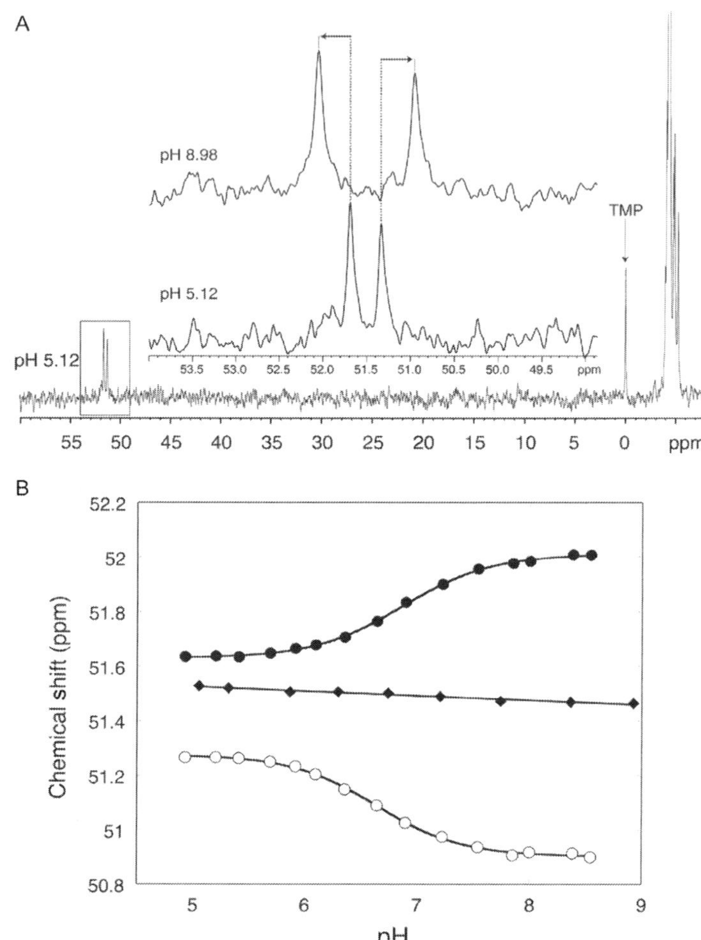

Figure 9.7 ^{31}P NMR-based determination of pK_a. (A) The downfield shift of the phosphorus peak with a phosphorothioate substitution. The inset is an expansion of the boxed region at the lowest (5.12) and highest (8.98) pH. (B) Plot of chemical shift of the phosphorus peaks versus pH for oligonucleotides containing a protonated A^+·C wobble pair (solid and hollow circles) and a control oligonucleotide where the A^+·C wobble pair is replaced with a Watson–Crick base pair. The pK_a can be determined by fitting the plot to Eq. (9.4). *Adapted with permission from Moody et al. (2004). Copyright (2004) American Chemical Society.*

Similar to the fluorescence assays, the titration is conducted without a conventional buffer. Oligonucleotide concentrations vary from 0.5 to 5 m*M*, and pH is varied through the addition of small amounts of HCl. Typically, the experiments are carried out in the background of 100 m*M* KCl and 5–10% D_2O as a deuterium lock to correct drift of the NMR magnetic field. An internal standard (1% trimethyl phosphate in 5% D_2O in a coaxial tube) is used as a reference and set to 0 ppm. The oligonucleotide is renatured before the start of the experiment, and the pH is determined before and after each measurement by inserting a microprobe into the NMR tube (see Section 2.2). Our lab has used Bruker AMX2-500 MHz (Moody et al., 2004), Bruker Advance III-500 MHz (Siegfried et al., 2010), and Bruker AV-3-600 (Wilcox & Bevilacqua, 2013) spectrophotometers for obtaining ^{31}P spectra.

Proton (^1H) NMR spectroscopy provides the ability to measure pK_a values in RNA, especially those values that are far removed from neutrality. For the purpose of determining the pK_a of the 2′OH, Chattopadhyaya et al. utilized ^1H NMR on ribonucleosides and derivatives (Velikyan et al., 2001). Samples were prepared in 100% D_2O at ~5 mM and contained 3-(trimethylsilyl)-1-propane-sulfonic acid as an internal standard. For pDs (the equivalent of pH in a D_2O solvent) between 7.0 and 13.0 buffers were used, while for pD between 13.0 and 14.0, 0.158 to 1 M NaOD was added. Experiments were performed at 25 °C on a 500 MHz spectrometer, and chemical shifts of nonexchanging protons (H1′, H2′ and H3′) near 2′OH were monitored as a function of pH, which acted as a proxy for the pK_a of the exchangeable 2′OH. The pK_a of the 2′OH was inferred using Eq. (9.4), and pK_a values determined from monitoring each of the three nonexchanging protons agreed. The high pH baseline value (pD > 14.0) could not be determined well because of tuning issues at high salt and was instead extrapolated using Eq. (9.5). The pK_a's for the ribonucleosides and their derivatives, which were corrected using the meter correction of pD = pH + 0.40, were found to be between 12.2 and 13.6 (Velikyan et al., 2001).

Recent studies from our lab extended this method to assess pK_a shifting of the 2′OH resulting from mono- and divalent metal ions (Ganguly et al., 2014). We studied 3′AMP as a model compound and prepared 1–2 mM solutions in 10% D_2O and 90% H_2O. We used mostly water because D_2O shifts pK_a values of N-linked protons higher by ~0.4–0.6 units, even after the meter correction (Nakano et al., 2000; Schowen & Schowen, 1982). Water suppression was thus necessary in our studies and was accomplished through presaturation using the general noesygppr1d pulse sequence. The solution contained 4,4-dimethyl-4-silapentance-1-sulfonic acid (DSS) as an internal standard in a 4-mm tube with 250 μL of sample. Each data point was prepared independently in a total volume of 500 μL. The desired pH was obtained by addition of NaOH or $Ca(OH)_2$, while ionic strength was maintained through addition of NaCl or $CaCl_2$. After the spectrum was collected, the 250 μL was added back to the centrifuge tube, the sample was mixed well, and the pH was checked again.

The highest attainable pH with NaOH is 13.7 (=0.5 *M* NaOH) due to tuning issues with the instruments, while the highest pH obtained with $Ca(OH)_2$ was 12.2 due to precipitation at higher pH (see Section 3.2 for handling in argon). Data were collected on a Bruker AV 3–600 MHz spectrophotometer at 25 °C. The chemical shift of H1′ peak was monitored as a function of pH because this peak is isolated from the water peak, still present despite suppression. Determination of the pK_a and Hill coefficient was the same as described above for Velikyan et al. (2001).

A third good method for pK_a determination is ^{13}C NMR spectroscopy. Legault and Pardi monitored the aromatic C2–H2 cross peaks of all seven adenines in the lead-dependent ribozyme using HMQC spectra (Legault & Pardi, 1994, 1997). Good spectral dispersion was found, and it was possible to determine the pK_a of each residue. One adenine in particular, A25, gave a pK_a of 6.5, which was associated with formation of a protonated A^+·C wobble. The authors also provide tables of which carbon atoms have chemical shifts that are most sensitive to pH in all four nucleobases. In sum, NMR is exceptionally powerful for pK_a determination, and a variety of RNA nuclei (^{31}P, ^{1}H, ^{13}C) have been monitored in pK_a studies. Labeling of the RNA is typically necessary for ^{13}C, but not ^{31}P or ^{1}H, which are naturally high abundance. The method of pK_a determination by NMR spectroscopy is applicable to nucleotides, oligonucleotides, and full length functional RNAs.

4.5. Raman crystallography pH titrations

Raman spectroscopy can be conducted on crystals of proteins and RNA. It has been used to probe mechanisms of protein enzymes, in which reactions are carried out in the crystals (Carey & Dong, 2004) and to examine the fold of functional RNAs including tRNAs (Chen, Giegé, Lord, & Rich, 1975). We applied Raman crystallography to crystals of the precleaved HDV ribozyme because previous attempts at using ^{13}C NMR to obtain pK_a values on the precleaved ribozyme had been met with experimental difficulties of line shifting, broadening, and splitting (Lupták, Ferré-D'Amaré, Zhou, Zilm, & Doudna, 2001). It turned out that specific Raman spectral features could be assigned to protonated cytosines and that these could be further linked to specific cytosines through mutagenesis (Gong et al., 2007).

Here, we provide a brief summary of the Raman crystallography pK_a method developed by the Carey, Golden, and Bevilacqua labs. We have provided a full methods paper on pK_a determination of RNAs by Raman earlier and refer the interested reader to this (Gong et al., 2009). Crystals of the precleaved ribozyme were grown in the presence of a modification of the nucleophilic 2′OH to methoxy, deoxy, or fluoro to prevent ribozyme reactivity in the crystal. Additionally, crystals of a control ribozyme in which the putative ionizing base is mutated, here C75U, were grown and also crystallized to allow assignment of the pK_a. Raman spectra were obtained via a HoloLab Series 5000 Raman microscope at ambient temperature in which the crystals were in the hanging drop. The crystals were soaked for 15–20 min in a stabilization buffer containing 50% 2-methyl-2,4-pentanediol and acetate or cacodylate buffers (50 m*M*) differing by 0.2 pH units. Data were fit to an equation equivalent to Eq. (9.4). In this approach, we were able to measure a pK_a for C75 that couples anticooperatively with Mg^{2+}, with pK_a values of 6.15 and 6.40 in 20 and 2 m*M* Mg^{2+}, respectively (Gong et al., 2007). These pK_a values agree quite well with those determined by kinetics measurements (Nakano et al., 2000).

It is worth noting that the Raman crystallographic method has since proven valuable for pK_a determination in several other functional RNAs including the hairpin (Guo et al., 2009) and *glmS* (Gong et al., 2011) ribozymes, where pK_a values of 5.46 for A38 (6.26 for a pretransition state analogue, Liberman et al., 2012) and 7.26 for the glcN6P cofactor were measured, respectively. One reason that Raman crystallography may be generally useful for pK_a determination in large RNA is that multiple diverse folds of the RNA in the starting state are discouraged by the crystal lattice while local structural accommodations necessary for ionization are allowed, as the experiments are at ambient temperature. It is important to note that most RNA crystals are ~70% solvent, making the experimental conditions somewhat analogous to the inside of the cell (Minton, 2001). The method of Raman crystallography for pK_a determination is relatively new but has potential to be applicable to any functional RNA or DNA. Moreover, diffraction quality crystals are not needed; we have obtained quality Raman spectra from crystals that diffract to only 5 Å (Gong et al., 2009).

5. PERSPECTIVE

In this chapter, we provided five experimental methods for determining pK_a's in RNA. These include reaction cleavage kinetics and spectroscopic-detected pH titrations by UV, fluorescence, NMR, and

Raman crystallography. We showed that while it is possible to obtain ideal two-state behavior when pK_a's are at neutrality, more often additional complexities are found in the data such as pH-induced RNA unfolding, poor upper baselines, kinetic pK_a's, and RNA degradation, which have to be identified and dealt with. Assigning an observed pK_a to a particular residue often requires controls in which the ionizing base is mutated to create a base pair, which should eliminate the signal change, or is mutated to another ionizing base, which should shift the pK_a by a known amount. In addition, testing the ability of different equations to fit the data can help spot apparent pK_a's, either due to a change in rate-limiting step or to multiple independent ionizations, which are not assignable to a single ionization event. Ultimately, measuring the pK_a by more than one technique can give greater confidence in the result. This is illustrated in the case of C75 in the HDV ribozyme, whereby convergent results were obtained from cleavage kinetics and spectroscopic signal changes.

Moving forward, it will be important to develop methods to test pK_a values of all atoms in an RNA at one time, and to do so in a genome-wide fashion. Strobel and coworkers have applied pH-dependent DMS mapping to the ribosome and identified a pH-dependent conformational change (Muth, Chen, Kosek, & Strobel, 2001; Muth, Ortoleva-Donnelly, & Strobel, 2000), as well as NAIM to entire ribozymes (Jones & Strobel, 2003; Oyelere & Strobel, 2000; Suydam & Strobel, 2008), which are important efforts in this direction. Applying such broadly informing techniques will yield a better sense of the prevalence and importance of pK_a shifting in RNA biology. Identification and measurement of such pK_a values should also prove valuable as benchmarks to theorists as they seek to identify shifted pK_a's in RNAs and to understand molecular driving forces for shifting.

ACKNOWLEDGMENTS

We thank Jamie Bingaman, Donald Burke, and Joe Wedekind for providing insightful comments on the manuscript. Support was provided by NIH Grant R01GM095923 and NSF Grant CHE-1213667.

REFERENCES

Bevilacqua, P. C. (2008). Proton transfer in ribozyme catalysis. In D. M. J. Lilley, & F. Eckstein (Eds.), *Ribozymes and RNA catalysis* (pp. 11–36). Cambridge: Royal Society of Chemistry.

Bevilacqua, P. C., Brown, T. S., Chadalavada, D. M., & Parente, A. D. (2003). Kinetic analysis of ribozyme cleavage. In K. Johnson (Ed.), *Kinetic analysis of macromolecules* (pp. 49–74). Oxford: Oxford University Press.

Bevilacqua, P. C., Brown, T. S., Nakano, S., & Yajima, R. (2004). Catalytic roles for proton transfer and protonation in ribozymes. *Biopolymers*, *73*(1), 90–109.

Biondi, E., Poudyal, R. R., Forgy, J. C., Sawyer, A. W., Maxwell, A. W. R., & Burke, D. H. (2013). Lewis acid catalysis of phosphoryl transfer from a copper(II)-NTP complex in a kinase ribozyme. *Nucleic Acids Research*, *41*, 3327–3338.

Bock, R. M., Ling, N. S., Morell, S. A., & Lipton, S. H. (1956). Ultraviolet absorption spectra of adenosine-5′-triphosphate and related 5′-ribonucleotides. *Archives of Biochemistry and Biophysics*, *62*, 253–264.

Carey, P. R., & Dong, J. (2004). Following ligand binding and ligand reactions in proteins via Raman crystallography. *Biochemistry*, *43*, 8885–8893.

Cerrone-Szakal, A. L., Siegfried, N. A., & Bevilacqua, P. C. (2008). Mechanistic characterization of the HDV genomic ribozyme: Solvent isotope effects and proton inventories in the absence of divalent metal ions support C75 as the general acid. *Journal of the American Chemical Society*, *130*(44), 14504–14520.

Chadalavada, D. M., Cerrone-Szakal, A. L., Wilcox, J. L., Siegfried, N. A., & Bevilacqua, P. C. (2012). Mechanistic analysis of the Hepatitis Delta Virus (HDV) ribozyme: Methods for RNA preparation, structure mapping, solvent isotope effects, and co-transcriptional cleavage. *Methods Molecular Biology*, *848*, 21–40.

Chen, M. C., Giegé, R., Lord, R. C., & Rich, A. (1975). Raman spectra and structure of yeast phenylalanine transfer RNA in the crystalline state and in solution. *Biochemistry*, *14*, 4385–4391.

Cornish, P. V., & Giedroc, D. P. (2006). Pairwise coupling analysis of helical junction hydrogen bonding interactions in luteoviral RNA pseudoknots. *Biochemistry*, *45*, 11162–11171.

Cottrell, J. W., Scott, L. G., & Fedor, M. J. (2011). The pH dependence of hairpin ribozyme catalysis reflects ionization of an active site adenine. *The Journal of Biological Chemistry*, *286*, 17658–17664.

DaCosta, C. P., Fedor, M. J., & Scott, L. G. (2007). 8-Azaguanine reporter of purine ionization state in structured RNA. *Journal of the American Chemical Society*, *129*, 3426–3432.

Dahm, S. C., & Uhlenbeck, O. C. (1991). Role of divalent metal ions in the hammerhead RNA cleavage reaction. *Biochemistry*, *30*(39), 9464–9469.

DeRose, V. J. (2003). Metal ion binding to catalytic RNA molecules. *Current Opinion in Structural Biology*, *13*(3), 317–324.

Fersht, A. (1985). *Enzyme structure and mechanism* (2nd ed.). New York: Freeman.

Frederiksen, J. K., & Piccirilli, J. A. (2009). Identification of catalytic metal ion ligands in ribozymes. *Methods*, *49*(2), 148–166.

Ganguly, A., Thaplyal, P., Rosta, E., Bevilacqua, P. C., & Hammes-Schiffer, S. (2014). Quantum mechanical/molecular mechanical free energy simulations of the self-cleavage reaction in the hepatitis delta virus ribozyme. *Journal of the American Chemical Society*, *136*(4), 1483–1496.

Gerweck, L. E., & Seetharaman, K. (1996). Cellular pH gradient in tumor versus normal tissue: Potential exploitation for the treatment of cancer. *Cancer Research*, *56*, 1194–1198.

Gilbert, S. D., Reyes, F. E., Edwards, A. L., & Batey, R. T. (2009). Adaptive ligand binding by the purine riboswitch in the recognition of guanine and adenine analogs. *Structure*, *17*(6), 857–868.

Gong, B., Chen, J.-H., Chase, E., Chadalavada, D. M., Yajima, R., Golden, B. L., et al. (2007). Direct measurement of a pK(a) near neutrality for the catalytic cytosine in the genomic HDV ribozyme using Raman crystallography. *Journal of the American Chemical Society*, *129*(43), 13335–13342.

Gong, B., Chen, J.-H., Yajima, R., Chen, Y., Chase, E., Chadalavada, D. M., et al. (2009). Raman crystallography of RNA. *Methods*, *49*(2), 101–111.

Gong, B., Klein, D. J., Ferré-D'Amaré, A. R., & Carey, P. R. (2011). The glmS ribozyme tunes the catalytically critical pK(a) of its coenzyme glucosamine-6-phosphate. *Journal of the American Chemical Society*, *133*, 14188–14191.

Good, N. E., Winget, G. D., Winter, W., Connolly, T. N., Izawa, S., & Sing, R. M. M. (1966). Hydrogen ion buffers for biological research. *Biochemistry*, *5*, 467–477.

Griffiths, J. R. (1991). Are cancer cells acidic? *British Journal of Cancer*, *64*, 425–427.

Guo, M., Spitale, R. C., Volpini, R., Krucinska, J., Cristalli, G., Carey, P. R., et al. (2009). Direct Raman measurement of an elevated base pKa in the active site of a small ribozyme in a precatalytic conformation. *Journal of the American Chemical Society*, *131*, 12908–12909.

Izatt, R. M., Christensen, J. J., & Rytting, J. H. (1971). Sites and thermodynamic quantities associated with proton and metal ion interaction with ribonucleic acid, deoxyribonucleic acid, and their constituent bases, nucleosides, and nucleotides. *Chemical Reviews*, *71*, 439–481.

Jean, J. M., & Hall, K. B. (2001). 2-Aminopurine fluorescence quenching and lifetimes: Role of base stacking. *Proceedings of the National Academy of Sciences of the United States of America*, *1998*, 37–41.

Jones, F. D., & Strobel, S. A. (2003). Ionization of a critical adenosine residue in the neurospora Varkud Satellite ribozyme active site. *Biochemistry*, *42*, 4265–4276.

Kierzek, R. (1992a). Hydrolysis of oligoribonucleotides: Influence of sequence and length. *Nucleic Acids Research*, *20*, 5073–5077.

Kierzek, R. (1992b). Nonenzymatic hydrolysis of oligoribonucleotides. *Nucleic Acids Research*, *20*, 5079–5084.

Knitt, D. S., & Herschlag, D. (1996). pH dependencies of the Tetrahymena ribozyme reveal an unconventional origin of an apparent pKa. *Biochemistry*, *35*, 1560–1570.

Kraut, D. A., Carroll, K. S., & Herschlag, D. (2003). Challenges in enzyme mechanism and energetics. *Annual Review of Biochemistry*, *72*, 517–571.

Lee, M. S., Salsbury, F. R., & Brooks, C. L. (2004). Constant-pH molecular dynamics using continuous titration coordinates. *Proteins*, *56*, 738–752.

Legault, P., & Pardi, A. (1994). In situ probing of adenine protonation in RNA by 13C NMR. *Journal of the American Chemical Society*, *116*, 8390–8391.

Legault, P., & Pardi, A. (1997). Unusual dynamics and pKa shift at the active site of a lead-dependent ribozyme. *Journal of the American Chemical Society*, *119*, 6621–6628.

Li, Y., & Breaker, R. R. (1999). Kinetics of RNA degradation by specific base catalysis of transesterification involving the 2′-hydroxyl group. *Journal of the American Chemical Society*, *121*(4), 5364–5372.

Liberman, J. A., Guo, M., Jenkins, J. L., Krucinska, J., Chen, Y., Carey, P. R., et al. (2012). A transition-state interaction shifts nucleobase ionization toward neutrality to facilitate small ribozyme catalysis. *Journal of the American Chemical Society*, *134*(41), 16933–16936.

Liu, L., Cottrell, J. W., Scott, L. G., & Fedor, M. J. (2009). Direct measurement of the ionization state of an essential guanine in the hairpin ribozyme. *Nature Chemical Biology*, *5*, 351–357.

Lupták, A., Ferré-D'Amaré, A. R., Zhou, K., Zilm, K. W., & Doudna, J. A. (2001). Direct pKa measurement of the active-site cytosine in a genomic hepatitis delta virus ribozyme. *Journal of the American Chemical Society*, *123*, 8447–8452.

Minton, A. P. (2001). The influence of macromolecular crowding and macromolecular confinement on biochemical reactions in physiological media. *The Journal of Biological Chemistry*, *276*, 10577–10580.

Moody, E. M., Brown, T. S., & Bevilacqua, P. C. (2004). Simple method for determining nucleobase pKa values by indirect labeling and demonstration of a pKa of neutrality in dsDNA. *Journal of the American Chemical Society*, *126*(33), 10200–10201.

Moody, E. M., Lecomte, J. T. J., & Bevilacqua, P. C. (2005). Linkage between proton binding and folding in RNA: A thermodynamic framework and its experimental application for investigating pKa shifting. *RNA*, *11*, 157–172.

Moser, A., Range, K., & York, D. M. (2010). Accurate proton affinity and gas-phase basicity values for molecules important in biocatalysis. *The Journal of Physical Chemistry B*, *114*(43), 13911–13921. http://dx.doi.org/10.1021/jp107450n.

Muth, G. W., Chen, L., Kosek, A. B., & Strobel, S. A. (2001). pH-dependent conformational flexibility within the ribosomal peptidyl transferase center. *RNA*, 7, 1403–1415.

Muth, G. W., Ortoleva-Donnelly, L., & Strobel, S. A. (2000). A single adenosine with a neutral pKa in the ribosomal peptidyl transferase center. *Science*, *289*, 947–950.

Nakano, S., & Bevilacqua, P. C. (2007). Mechanistic characterization of the HDV genomic ribozyme: A mutant of the C41 motif provides insight into the positioning and thermodynamic linkage of metal ions and protons. *Biochemistry*, *46*(11), 3001–3012.

Nakano, S., Cerrone, A. L., & Bevilacqua, P. C. (2003). Mechanistic characterization of the HDV genomic ribozyme: Classifying the catalytic and structural metal ion sites within a multichannel reaction mechanism. *Biochemistry*, *42*(10), 2982–2994.

Nakano, S., Chadalavada, D. M., & Bevilacqua, P. C. (2000). General acid-base catalysis in the mechanism of a hepatitis delta virus ribozyme. *Science*, *287*(5457), 1493–1497.

Oyelere, A. K., & Strobel, S. A. (2000). Biochemical detection of cytidine protonation within RNA. *Journal of the American Chemical Society*, *122*, 10259–10267.

Qin, P. Z., & Pyle, A. M. (1999). Site-specific labeling of RNA with fluorophores and other structural probes. *Methods*, *18*, 60–70.

Schowen, B. K., & Schowen, R. L. (1982). Solvent isotope effects on enzyme-systems. *Methods in Enzymology*, *87*, 551–606.

Siegfried, N. A., O'Hare, B., & Bevilacqua, P. C. (2010). Driving forces for nucleic acid pKa shifting in an A(+).C wobble: Effects of helix position, temperature, and ionic strength. *Biochemistry*, *49*(15), 3225–3236.

Soukup, G. A., & Breaker, R. R. (1999). Relationship between internucleotide linkage geometry and the stability of RNA. *RNA*, *5*(10), 1308–1325.

Suydam, I. T., & Strobel, S. A. (2008). Fluorine substituted adenosines as probes of nucleobase protonation in functional RNAs. *Journal of the American Chemical Society*, *130*, 13639–13648.

Tang, C. L., Alexov, E., Pyle, A. M., & Honig, B. (2007). Calculation of pKas in RNA: On the structural origins and functional roles of protonated nucleotides. *Journal of Molecular Biology*, *366*(5), 1475–1496.

Velikyan, I., Acharya, S., Trifonova, A., Földesi, A., & Chattopadhyaya, J. (2001). The pKa's of 2′-hydroxyl group in nucleosides and nucleotides. *Journal of the American Chemical Society*, *123*(12), 2893–2894.

Viladoms, J., Scott, L. G., & Fedor, M. J. (2011). An active-site guanine participates in glmS ribozyme catalysis in its protonated state. *Journal of the American Chemical Society*, *133*, 18388–18396.

Wilcox, J. L., Ahluwalia, A. K., & Bevilacqua, P. C. (2011). Charged nucleobases and their potential for RNA catalysis. *Accounts of Chemical Research*, *44*(12), 1270–1279.

Wilcox, J. L., & Bevilacqua, P. C. (2013). A simple fluorescence method for pKa determination in RNA. *Journal of the American Chemical Society*, *135*, 7390–7393.

CHAPTER TEN

Crystallographic Analysis of TPP Riboswitch Binding by Small-Molecule Ligands Discovered Through Fragment-Based Drug Discovery Approaches

Katherine Deigan Warner[*,†], **Adrian R. Ferré-D'Amaré**[*,1]

[*]National Heart, Lung and Blood Institute, Bethesda, Maryland, USA

[†]Department of Chemistry, University of Cambridge, Cambridge, United Kingdom

[1]Corresponding author: e-mail address: adrian.ferre@nih.gov

Contents

Abstract

Riboswitches are structured mRNA elements that regulate gene expression in response to metabolite or second-messenger binding and are promising targets for drug discovery. Fragment-based drug discovery methods have identified weakly binding small molecule "fragments" that bind a thiamine pyrophosphate (TPP) riboswitch. However, these fragments require substantial chemical elaboration into more potent, drug-like molecules. Structure determination of the fragments bound to the riboswitch is the necessary next step. In this chapter, we describe the methods for co-crystallization and structure determination of fragment-bound TPP riboswitch structures. We focus on considerations for screening crystallization conditions across multiple crystal forms and provide guidance for building the fragment into the refined crystallographic model. These methods are broadly applicable for crystallographic analyses of any small molecules that bind structured RNAs.

Methods in Enzymology, Volume 549
ISSN 0076-6879
http://dx.doi.org/10.1016/B978-0-12-801122-5.00010-6

1. INTRODUCTION

Riboswitches are *cis*-acting mRNA elements that specifically bind cellular metabolites or second messengers and modulate expression of genes in *cis*, typically those involved in the metabolism of their cognate ligand (Roth & Breaker, 2009; Serganov & Nudler, 2013; Zhang, Lau, & Ferré-D'Amaré, 2010). Riboswitches are promising targets for the development of novel antibiotics, due to their specific recognition of small molecules, prevalence in bacteria, and control of genes necessary for survival or virulence in pathogens (Deigan & Ferré-D'Amaré, 2011).

Fragment-based approaches have emerged as promising methods in drug discovery (Scott, Coyne, Hudson, & Abell, 2012). In a fragment-based screen, small molecules (~300 Da) with modest affinity for a target macromolecule are identified and then chemically elaborated into more potent compounds. Recently, application of the fragment-based method against an RNA target led to the discovery of several fragments that bind the *Escherichia coli thiM* thiamine pyrophosphate (TPP) riboswitch aptamer domain with K_d between 20 and 700 μM (Cressina, Chen, Abell, Leeper, & Smith, 2011). With further development, such fragments have the potential to be elaborated into ligands specific for a riboswitch from a particular organism, for use as antimicrobial compounds or chemical tools. However, rational elaboration requires structural information describing the interactions between the fragment and the riboswitch.

The method of choice to obtain high-resolution structural information on fragment binding to macromolecules is X-ray crystallography (Blow, 2002; Drenth, 2007; Rupp, 2010). The process for solving a crystal structure of a riboswitch bound to a fragment is conceptually straightforward when the structure of either the riboswitch bound to its cognate ligand or an empty riboswitch with a preformed ligand-binding site has been determined previously. A prerequisite is the growth of well-ordered co-crystals of the riboswitch-fragment complex of interest. Fragment co-crystals can be obtained in one of two ways. First, if the empty structure has been solved and is believed to contain a preorganized ligand-binding site, the small molecules can be soaked into these empty crystals (Klein & Ferré-D'Amaré, 2006). This requires that the ligand-binding site be accessible to the outside of the crystal through solvent channels. Second, if the structure of the riboswitch bound to its cognate ligand has been solved, or if the empty structure is thought to be different than the folded structure (Baird & Ferré-D'Amaré, 2010), crystals of the RNA-fragment complex, formed in solution prior to crystallization, can be grown. Generally, RNA-fragment co-crystallization conditions must be optimized, but can be guided by the co-crystallization conditions used for the cognate complex.

In this chapter, we describe the co-crystallization approach to solving structures of the *E. coli thiM* TPP riboswitch bound to different fragments. Application of this method has yielded structural insight into the binding mode of fragments to the *E. coli thiM* TPP riboswitch and visualization of fragment-induced reorganization of the ligand-binding site (Warner et al., 2014). While the method is described for fragments that bind the TPP riboswitch, it is broadly applicable to any small molecules that bind structured RNAs when pertinent crystal forms have been described.

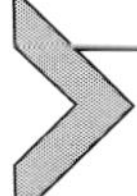

2. METHODS

2.1. Growth of riboswitch-fragment co-crystals

To increase the chance of successful fragment co-crystal growth, multiple crystal forms should be examined, if available. Starting with a known crystal form eliminates RNA sequence as a variable and allows the screening and optimization to focus on crystallization conditions.

Although crystallization conditions are generally reported in the literature as a single set or narrow range of conditions, optimization of crystallization conditions is almost always required for the growth of crystals of sufficient quality for structure determination, even when attempts are made to reproduce cognate complex co-crystals from literature conditions. Generally, single, well-ordered crystals of sufficient size are required for useful resolution, and variations in conditions may impact the presence of parasitic crystals, size, and crystalline order.

When working to employ published crystals unfamiliar to the experimenter, initial screens of crystallization conditions for growing co-crystals of the RNA bound to its cognate ligand are useful to ensure that the RNA and the particular crystal form being reproduced are "well behaved" and can offer insight into the development of efficient screens for co-crystallization of fragment complexes. The selection of a tractable number of well-behaved fragments also increases the likelihood of success. If information is available on the selectivity of the fragments, this can be used, in conjunction with practical considerations such as solubility, to define a subset of candidate fragments to initially attempt to co-crystallize. Once candidate crystal forms and fragments have been evaluated, fragment co-crystallization conditions can be screened.

2.1.1 Considerations in transcription template and RNA construct design

If available, multiple crystal forms should be screened to increase the chances of success. Four crystal forms of the TPP riboswitch have been described: three of the *E. coli thiM* TPP riboswitch (Edwards & Ferré-D'Amaré, 2006; Kulshina, Edwards, & Ferré-D'Amaré, 2010; Serganov, Polonskaia, Phan, Breaker, & Patel, 2006) and one of the *Arabidopsis thaliana thiC* TPP riboswitch (Thore, 2006). For the TPP riboswitch-binding fragments, three crystal forms were examined, and fragment structures were solved using two of these (crystal forms I and II, Fig. 10.1). We found that certain fragments only grew crystals of acceptable quality in certain crystal forms.

When using a previously described crystal form, it is key to replicate exactly the RNA sequence described in the original conditions. In addition, it is good practice to pay special care to other tricks that may have been employed to facilitate crystallization, such as a bimolecular construct or the use of ribozymes to produce homogenous 5′- and 3′-ends (Ferré-D'Amaré & Doudna, 1996).

If 5′- or 3′-ribozymes are employed, and the ribozyme is close in length to that of the desired riboswitch RNA (within ~10 nt for ~100 nt RNA), additional nucleotides can be added to the end of the ribozyme to allow for more efficient purification of the riboswitch RNA by polyacrylamide gel electrophoresis (PAGE). These additional nucleotides can be incorporated into the DNA template.

For crystal form I (Edwards & Ferré-D'Amaré, 2006), a hammerhead ribozyme was encoded 5′ of the *thiM* TPP riboswitch sequence, and a Varkund Satellite ribozyme substrate stem loop was encoded 3′ of the sequence. The resultant riboswitch RNA has a 5′-OH and a 2′,3′-cyclic phosphate.

For crystal form II (Serganov et al., 2006), a hepatitis delta virus (HDV) ribozyme was encoded 3′ of the *thiM* TPP riboswitch sequence to yield an RNA with a 5′-triphosphate and a 2′,3′-cyclic phosphate. Additional nucleotides were added to the 3′-end of the HDV ribozyme to allow for more efficient separation of the riboswitch from the ribozyme during gel electrophoresis.

2.1.2 Considerations in fragment selection

Fragments should first be evaluated by selectivity information, if available. In this study, only fragments selective for a TPP riboswitch over a lysine

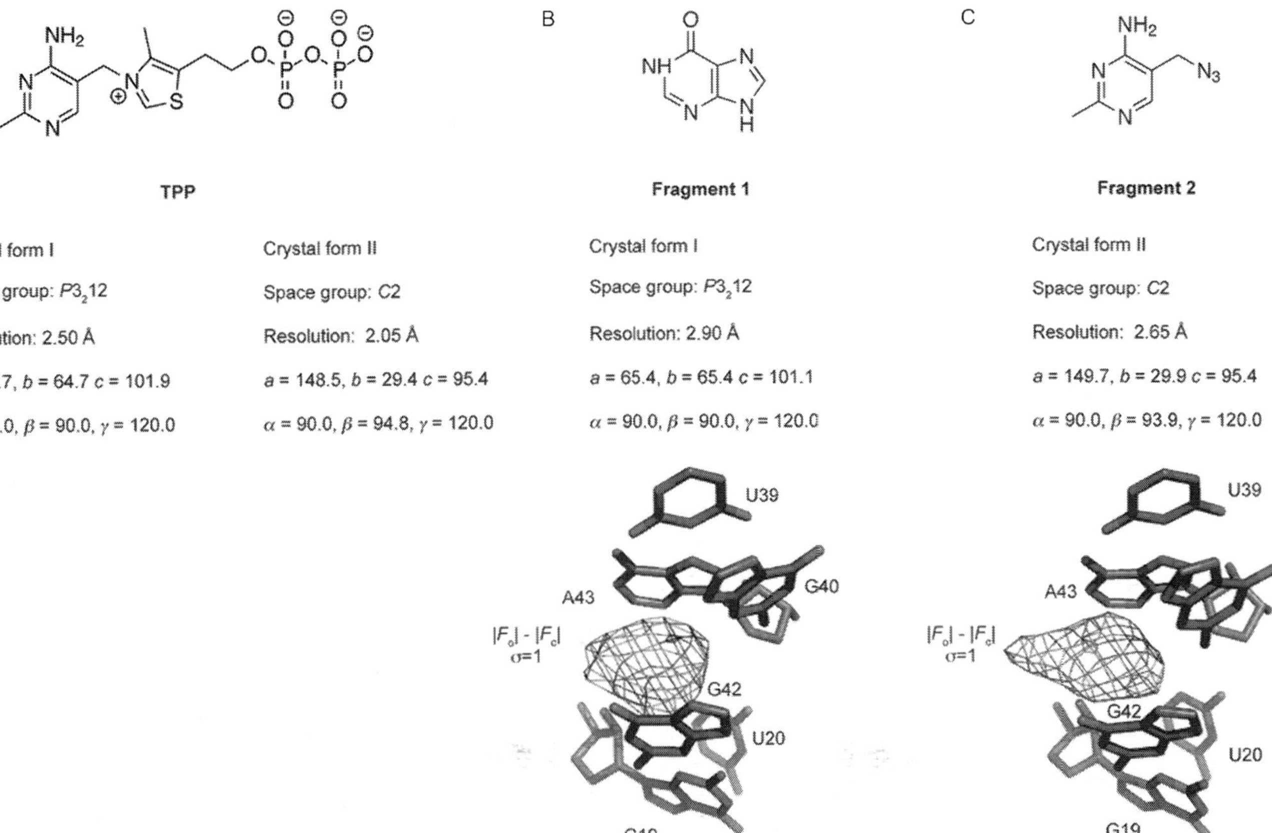

Figure 10.1 Two crystal forms were used for growth of fragment co-crystal structures. (A) Two crystal forms of the riboswitch in complex with its cognate ligand, TPP, were used to grow fragment crystals. (B) Fragment **1** co-crystals were grown in crystal form I. Preligand unbiased residual $|F_o| - |F_c|$ electron density at 3.0 s.d. contoured around the final refined ligand is shown (bottom). (C) Fragment **2** co-crystals were grown in crystal from II. $|Fo| - |Fc|$ electron is as in (B).

riboswitch (Cressina et al., 2011) were considered. Solubility is also a factor. If fragments are only soluble in solvents other than water, the effect of that solvent on crystal growth should be considered. Fragments that were not soluble in water and were not soluble in DMSO to at least $\sim 25 \times K_d$ were not considered for crystallization trials, to prevent high levels of DMSO in crystallization, which may adversely affect crystal growth.

2.1.3 In vitro *transcription of TPP riboswitch RNA*

TPP riboswitch RNA (Edwards & Ferré-D'Amaré, 2006; Serganov et al., 2006; Thore, 2006) was transcribed *in vitro* using DNA templates, which encoded the appropriate ribozymes and were produced either by restriction digestion of a plasmid or by PCR, and recombinant T7 RNA polymerase as described (Milligan, Groebe, Witherell, & Uhlenbeck, 1987) and purified by electrophoresis on polyacrylamide, 8 *M* urea, 1 × TBE gels (29:1 acrylamide:bisacrylamide), where the percentage of polyacrylamide was selected to give sufficient separation between the TPP riboswitch RNA and any ribozymes used, typically 8–12%. RNA was electroeluted from gel slices using a Whatman Elutrap system, concentrated, washed once with 1 *M* KCl, and desalted extensively through serial dilution with water by ultrafiltration using Amicon Ultra centrifugal filters (10 kDa molecular weight cutoff), and stored at 4 °C in water or in 0.1 m*M* EDTA prior to use. We find that if proper care is taken to avoid RNase contamination, RNA stored in this manner lasts for at least 6 months.

2.1.4 Initial screens of crystallization conditions with the cognate ligand

In general, crystallization involves the simultaneous optimization of a number of solution variables, in order to achieve the appropriate level of supersaturation for nucleation and crystal growth (McPherson, 1999). While optimization can be carried out employing large-scale screening and powerful analytical methods (e.g., Carter, 1997), in the majority of cases, small-scale, qualitative screens are constructed to evaluate the effect and interdependence of a handful of variables at a time.

To evaluate the behavior of a specific crystal form in the presence of the cognate ligand, initial screens are performed, typically consisting of a small sparse matrix in which a limited number of conditions are varied. For crystal form I (Edwards & Ferré-D'Amaré, 2006), the conditions described for the cognate co-crystals indicate incubation of 150 μ*M* RNA with 0.5 m*M* TPP in 5 m*M* Tris–HCl (pH 8.1), 3 m*M* $MgCl_2$, 10 m*M* NaCl, 100 m*M* KCl, and 0.5 m*M* spermine at 37 °C for 30 min, with co-crystals grown by vapor diffusion of 3 μL drops by mixing the RNA solution 1:1 with a reservoir solution of 26–30% polyethyleneglycol (PEG) 2000, 0.2 *M* NH_4Cl, 10 m*M* $CaCl_2$ (or $MnCl_2$), and 50 m*M* Na cacodylate (pH 6.0). Patterns of behavior in crystal growth were observed while varying the percentage of the precipitant (20–30% PEG 2000), identity of the precipitant (PEG 2000 vs. PEG 3350), concentration of NH_4Cl (0.05–0.5 *M*), and the ratio of RNA solution to reservoir solution. The RNA folding conditions were not varied (although this might be essential in some cases), and drops were set up as described earlier, except with a final drop volume of 1 μL. In crystal form I, higher concentrations of PEG 2000 were found to yield larger and more single cognate ligand co-crystals, while crystals were tolerant of variation in NH_4Cl concentration. Equivalent trials were carried out for crystal form II. For a third crystal form, poor growth of the cognate ligand co-crystals was observed in trials, and the crystal form was abandoned.

2.1.5 *Initial screens for fragment co-crystals*

For growth of fragment co-crystals, initial crystal screens are guided by patterns observed in the cognate ligand screens. For screens with fragment **1** and crystal form I, the percentage of PEG 2000 was kept constant at 30%, the concentration of NH_4Cl was either 0.2 *M* or 0.5 *M*, and the buffer identity, buffer pH, divalent cation identity, and ratio of RNA solution to reservoir solution were varied. Figure 10.2 shows the initial screen that resulted in good fragment co-crystal growth under a range of conditions and eventual structure solution for fragment **1** in crystal form I. While the co-crystal structure of fragment **1** was solved from a condition in the initial screen, other fragments required more extensive variation of conditions. In our study, we found that crystal growth for different RNA-fragment complexes varied substantially, without correlating with binding affinity of the fragment for the RNA.

2.1.6 *Development of cryoprotectant solutions for vitrification of fragment co-crystals*

Once co-crystals are obtained, cryoprotection conditions must be determined. Ideally, cryoprotection of a crystal should allow for vitrification of the water surrounding and inside the crystal, without damaging the crystal (Garman, 2003; Rodgers, 1997). Screens for optimal cryoprotectant conditions can begin with the reported cryoprotection conditions from the cognate ligand co-crystals, and trial and error on cognate ligand co-crystals is helpful.

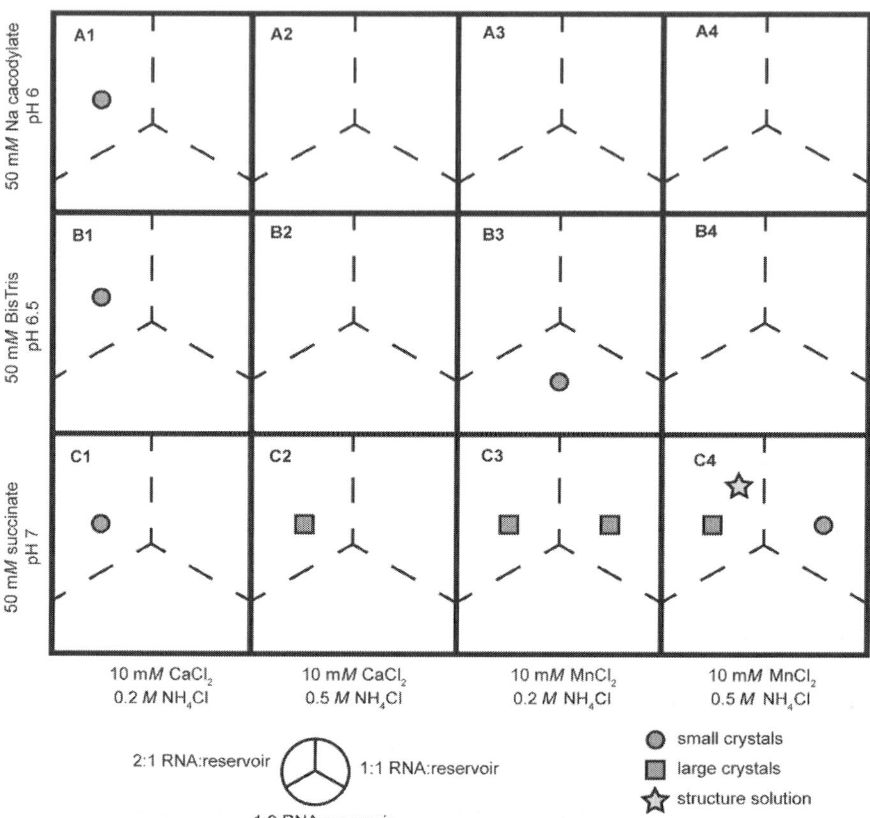

Figure 10.2 A representation of a screen of co-crystallization conditions for fragment **1** co-crystals. Each cell in the matrix represents a well on a crystal screening plate. Buffer identity, pH, divalent cation identity, and NH_4Cl concentration are varied while the precipitant concentration (30% PEG 2000) and RNA folding conditions are held constant. Each well contained three drops, in which the ratio of RNA solution to reservoir solution was varied, represented by the three dashed line divisions in each cell. Circles represent conditions that yielded crystals of small size or poor quality. Squares represent conditions that yielded large crystals (greater than 100 μm in at least two dimensions). A star indicates the crystal growth condition for the crystal from which the fragment co-crystal structure was solved.

Conditions can initially be screened for ability to vitrify, by screening mother liquor supplemented with ~15% cryoprotection candidate. Upon cooling, a successful cryoprotectant will yield a transparent drop and an X-ray diffraction pattern free from ice rings (water powder diffraction).

Additionally, various methods of cryoprotection schemes should be considered. Robust crystals may survive a quick dip in neat cryoprotectant.

Crystals can be transferred to an artificial mother liquor, supplemented with cryoprotectant. Crystals that are sensitive to large changes in mother liquor can be serially transferred through drops of increased cryoprotection concentration. Some crystals can survive cryoprotectant addition directly to the original drop. Alternatively, particularly fragile crystals may require growth in mother liquor that contains sufficient levels of cryoprotectant for direct freezing from the crystal growth drop.

Regardless of the cryoprotection scheme employed, crystals vitrified in various cryoprotectants must be screened to assay for effects on crystal quality. Cryoprotection schemes that reproducibly yield X-ray data of poorer quality should be discarded. More extensive discussion of cryoprotection methods can be found elsewhere (Alcorn & Juers, 2010; Berejnov, Husseini, Alsaied, & Thorne, 2006).

Fragment co-crystals in crystal form I were initially vitrified in mother liquor supplemented with 15% Ficoll or sucrose and 1 m*M* fragment. For fragment-TPP riboswitch co-crystals, $\sim$10–20% glycerol, ethylene glycol, and sucrose were found to be the most useful cryoprotectants. Co-crystals were transferred to drops containing artificial mother liquor supplemented with cryoprotectant, either directly or through a series of drops containing increasing cryoprotectant concentration, in two to four increments of 2.5–5.0% cryoprotectant per step. Equilibration time in cryoprotectant-supplemented drops was less than 1 min.

It should be noted that the concentration of ligand in the cryoprotection solution can be an important experimental variable. Moreover, the precise composition of the solution may have an important impact on whether fragments bind the RNA with sufficient occupancy to allow crystallographic visualization. For instance, for crystals of the *glmS* ribozyme-riboswitch, we have found that the pH of the cryoprotection conditions determines whether the cognate ligand yields detectable electron density in its binding site (Klein, Wilkinson, Been, & Ferré-D'Amaré, 2007).

2.2. Structure solution by molecular replacement

After data collection and reduction, assuming fragments do not promote complete rearrangement of the RNA, fragment co-crystal structures can be solved either by molecular replacement with the structure of an empty or cognate ligand co-crystal or, if fragment co-crystals are isomorphous with the known crystal form, by inspection of a difference Fourier map, possibly after refinement of the RNA model. Here, we will discuss the molecular replacement method. After molecular replacement, strong positive density in the difference ($|F_o|-|F_c|$) map should indicate fragment position even in the early stages of refinement. The ligand-binding site and the ligand itself should only be built after all other regions of the model have been rebuilt as appropriate and refined.

2.2.1 Structure solution by molecular replacement

Fragments co-crystal structures can be solved by molecular replacement using structures of the crystal form employed for fragment co-crystal growth. Ions, ligand, and water molecules should first be removed from the search model. In this study, molecular replacement was carried out with PHASER (McCoy et al., 2007); various molecular replacement strategies are described elsewhere (Scapin, 2013). PHASER yielded results with high log-likelihood gain (LLG) values (the difference between the model and a random solution) and translation function Z (TFZ)-scores (the number of standard deviations above the mean of translation function search solutions): for fragment **1**, LLG=1092, TFZ=29.8; for fragment **2**, LLG=2270, TFZ=12.1.

2.2.2 Model building and refinement

Refinement of the fragment co-crystal structures is initially focused on all regions of the RNA except for the binding site. After all other major issues (such as significant peaks in the $|F_o|-|F_c|$ map) outside of the binding site are accounted for, the binding site can be solved.

At this stage, a region of strong positive density in the difference ($|F_o|-|F_c|$) map indicates the location and, provided the resolution is sufficient, the binding orientation of the fragment (Fig. 10.1). For the TPP riboswitch-fragment co-crystals, the electron density corresponding to the fragments was the most significant peak in the difference map, even in the first rounds of refinement. Careful inspection of the ligand-binding site is necessary to account for any fragment-induced reorganization of the binding site. The fragments in this study promoted a previously unobserved rotation of a guanine (G72) into a region of the binding pocket previously occupied by a pyrophosphate of the cognate ligand TPP (Warner et al., 2014).

2.2.3 Building the fragment into the model

Before a fragment can be built into a purported fragment-binding site, a series of energetic and geometric parameters for the ligand must be defined.

A range of utilities exist that define these parameters for various refinement programs (Lebedev et al., 2012; Moriarty, Grosse-Kunstleve, & Adams, 2009; Schüttelkopf & van Aalten, 2004; Winn et al., 2011). Once the ligand is built into the model, care should be taken to ensure that the correct orientation of the fragment is chosen. Factors such as geometry, real-space R factor, postrefinement $|F_o| - |F_c|$ peak size, and anomalous signal can be used to guide ligand orientation, but in structures solved to modest resolution, ambiguity in fragment orientation may persist. In this case, it is helpful to report multiple possible fragment orientations.

3. CONCLUSIONS

Crystallographic analysis of fragment binding to the TPP riboswitch has delineated the binding location of fragments, as well as unexpected fragment-induced rearrangement of the ligand-binding site (Warner et al., 2014). The growth of co-crystals and subsequent structure solution by molecular replacement described here is conceptually straightforward and is broadly applicable for any small molecule ligands that bind in a well-formed binding site in an RNA. However, in practice the process can range from trivial, given a well-behaved crystal form and small molecule co-crystals that grow in very similar conditions, to as difficult as solving a novel crystal structure (Ferré-D'Amaré & Doudna, 2001; Ferré-D'Amaré, 2010), if small molecule co-crystals are found to require the development of a new crystal form.

ACKNOWLEDGMENTS

We thank the staff at beamlines 24-ID-C of APS and 5.0.1 and 5.0.2 of ALS for crystallographic data collection support and N. Baird, M. Chen, C. Jones, M. Lau, A. Serganov, M. Warner, and J. Zhang for discussions. This work is partly based on research conducted at ALS on the BCSB beamlines and at APS on the NE-CAT beamlines, all of which are supported by the National Institute for General Medical Sciences, NIH. The use of ALS and APS was supported by the US Department of Energy. This work was supported in part by the NIH-Oxford/Cambridge Research Scholars program and the intramural program of the National Heart, Lung and Blood Institute (NHLBI), NIH.

REFERENCES

Alcorn, T., & Juers, D. H. (2010). Progress in rational methods of cryoprotection in macromolecular crystallography. *Acta Crystallographica. Section D: Biological Crystallography*, *66*, 366–373.

Baird, N. J., & Ferré-D'Amaré, A. R. (2010). Idiosyncratically tuned switching behavior of riboswitch aptamer domains revealed by comparative small-angle X-ray scattering analysis. *RNA*, *16*, 598–609.

Berejnov, V., Husseini, N. S., Alsaied, O. A., & Thorne, R. E. (2006). Effects of cryoprotectant concentration and cooling rate on vitrification of aqueous solutions. *Journal of Applied Crystallography, 39*, 244–251.

Blow, D. (2002). *Outline of crystallography for biologists*. Oxford: Oxford University Press.

Carter, C. W. (1997). Response surface methods for optimizing and improving reproducibility of crystal growth. *Methods in Enzymology, 276*, 74–99.

Cressina, E., Chen, L., Abell, C., Leeper, F. J., & Smith, A. G. (2011). Fragment screening against the thiamine pyrophosphate riboswitch thiM. *Chemical Science, 2*, 157–165.

Deigan, K. E., & Ferré-D'Amaré, A. R. (2011). Riboswitches: Discovery of drugs that target bacterial gene-regulatory RNAs. *Accounts of Chemical Research, 44*, 1329–1338.

Drenth, J. (2007). *Principles of protein X-ray crystallography*. New York: Springer.

Edwards, T. E., & Ferré-D'Amaré, A. R. (2006). Crystal structures of the Thi-Box Riboswitch bound to Thiamine Pyrophosphate analogs reveal adaptive RNA-small molecule recognition. *Structure, 14*, 1459–1468.

Ferré-D'Amaré, A. R. (2010). Use of the spliceosomal protein U1A to facilitate crystallization and structure determination of complex RNAs. *Methods, 52*, 159–167.

Ferré-D'Amaré, A. R., & Doudna, J. A. (1996). Use of cis- and trans-ribozymes to remove 5′ and 3′ heterogeneities from milligrams of in vitro transcribed RNA. *Nucleic Acids Research, 24*, 977–978.

Ferré-D'Amaré, A. R., & Doudna, J. A. (2001). Methods to crystallize RNA. In S. L. Beaucage, D. E. Bergstrom, G. D. Glick, & R. A. Jones (Eds.), *Current protocols in nucleic acid chemistry* (pp. 7.6.1–7.6.10). New York: John Wiley & Sons.

Garman, E. (2003). "Cool" crystals: Macromolecular cryocrystallography and radiation damage. *Current Opinion in Structural Biology, 13*, 545–551.

Klein, D. J., & Ferré-D'Amaré, A. R. (2006). Structural basis of glmS ribozyme activation by glucosamine-6-phosphate. *Science, 313*, 1752–1756.

Klein, D. J., Wilkinson, S. R., Been, M. D., & Ferré-D'Amaré, A. R. (2007). Requirement of helix P2.2 and nucleotide G1 for positioning the cleavage site and cofactor of the glmS ribozyme. *Journal of Molecular Biology, 373*, 178–189.

Kulshina, N., Edwards, T. E., & Ferré-D'Amaré, A. R. (2010). Thermodynamic analysis of ligand binding and ligand binding-induced tertiary structure formation by the thiamine pyrophosphate riboswitch. *RNA, 16*, 186–196.

Lebedev, A. A., Young, P., Isupov, M. N., Moroz, O. V., Vagin, A. A., & Murshudov, G. N. (2012). JLigand: A graphical tool for the CCP4 template-restraint library. *Acta Crystallographica. Section D: Biological Crystallography, 68*, 431–440.

McCoy, A. J., Grosse-Kunstleve, R. W., Adams, P. D., Winn, M. D., Storoni, L. C., & Read, R. J. (2007). Phaser crystallographic software. *Journal of Applied Crystallography, 40*, 658–674.

McPherson, A. (1999). *Crystallization of biological macromolecules*. Cold Spring Harbor, New York: Cold Spring Harbor Laboratory Press.

Milligan, J. F., Groebe, D. R., Witherell, G. W., & Uhlenbeck, O. C. (1987). Oligoribonucleotide synthesis using T7 RNA polymerase and synthetic DNA templates. *Nucleic Acids Research, 15*, 8783–8798.

Moriarty, N. W., Grosse-Kunstleve, R. W., & Adams, P. D. (2009). electronic Ligand Builder and Optimization Workbench (eLBOW): A tool for ligand coordinate and restraint generation. *Acta Crystallographica. Section D: Biological Crystallography, 65*, 1074–1080.

Rodgers, D. W. (1997). Practical cryocrystallography. *Methods in Enzymology, 276*, 183–203.

Roth, A., & Breaker, R. R. (2009). The structural and functional diversity of metabolite-binding riboswitches. *Annual Review of Biochemistry, 78*, 305–334.

Rupp, B. (2010). *Biomolecular crystallography*. New York: Garland Science.

Scapin, G. (2013). Molecular replacement then and now. *Acta Crystallographica. Section D: Biological Crystallography*, *69*, 2266–2275.

Schüttelkopf, A. W., & van Aalten, D. M. F. (2004). PRODRG: A tool for high-throughput crystallography of protein–ligand complexes. *Acta Crystallographica. Section D: Biological Crystallography*, *60*, 1355–1363.

Scott, D. E., Coyne, A. G., Hudson, S. A., & Abell, C. (2012). Fragment-based approaches in drug discovery and chemical biology. *Biochemistry*, *51*, 4990–5003.

Serganov, A., & Nudler, E. (2013). A decade of riboswitches. *Cell*, *152*, 17–24.

Serganov, A., Polonskaia, A., Phan, A. T., Breaker, R. R., & Patel, D. J. (2006). Structural basis for gene regulation by a thiamine pyrophosphate-sensing riboswitch. *Nature*, *441*, 1167–1171.

Thore, S. (2006). Structure of the eukaryotic thiamine pyrophosphate riboswitch with its regulatory ligand. *Science*, *312*, 1208–1211.

Warner, K. D., Homan, P., Weeks, K. M., Smith, A. G., Abell, C., & Ferré-D'Amaré, A. R. (2014). Validating fragment-based drug discovery for biological RNAs: Lead fragments bind and remodel the TPP Riboswitch specifically. *Chemistry & Biology*, *21*, 591–595.

Winn, M. D., Ballard, C. C., Cowtan, K. D., Dodson, E. J., Emsley, P., Evans, P. R., et al. (2011). Overview of the CCP4 suite and current developments. *Acta Crystallographica. Section D: Biological Crystallography*, *67*, 235–242.

Zhang, J., Lau, M. W., & Ferré-D'Amaré, A. R. (2010). Ribozymes and riboswitches: Modulation of RNA function by small molecules. *Biochemistry*, *49*, 9123–9131.

CHAPTER ELEVEN

Methods for Using New Conceptual Tools and Parameters to Assess RNA Structure by Small-Angle X-Ray Scattering

Francis E. Reyes*[,1], Camille R. Schwartz*, John A. Tainer[†,‡], Robert P. Rambo*[,2,3]

*Physical Bioscience Division Lawrence Berkeley National Lab, Berkeley, California, USA
[†]Life Sciences Division, Lawrence Berkeley National Laboratory, Berkeley, California, USA
[‡]The Scripps Research Institute, La Jolla, California, USA
[1]Current address: Janelia Farm Research Campus, Howard Hughes Medical Institute, Ashburn, Virginia, USA
[2]Current address: Diamond Light Source Ltd, Harwell Science & Innovation Campus, Didcot, United Kingdom
[3]Corresponding author: e-mail address: robert_p_rambo@hotmail.com

Contents

Abstract

Understanding the biological activities of riboswitches and of RNA in general requires a thorough analysis of both the spatial arrangement of the residues and the dynamics of

Methods in Enzymology, Volume 549
ISSN 0076-6879
http://dx.doi.org/10.1016/B978-0-12-801122-5.00011-8

the structural ensemble. Specifically, evaluating the structural basis for riboswitch function requires analyses of many relevant states that include ligand-bound and -free, high Mg^{2+}, and quite possibly, the active transcription state, which is challenging to achieve by most methods. Small angle X-ray scattering (SAXS) is an enabling technique for comprehensive analyses of RNA structures in solution. Here, we describe recent SAXS tools and technologies that substantially improve the potential for accurate and comprehensive analyses of flexibility, unstructured elements, conformational selection, and induced fit in RNA function. We note equipment needed plus appropriate annealing and purification procedures. We describe key model-independent parameters (SAXS invariants) which can be used to monitor changes in a particle's thermodynamic state: the Guinier-based R_g, the volume-of-correlation (V_c), the Porod–Debye exponent (P_E), and the power-law parameter, Q_R, that determines mass directly from the SAXS data. We also consider the value of real-space parameters and of multiphase modeling with MONSA to locate secondary structure elements within SAXS volumetric envelopes. For conformation changes, experiments with nanogold-labeled RNA analyzed using the SAXS structural comparison map and volatility ratio difference metric enable high-throughput evaluation of solution-state conformations. Collectively, the described tools and procedures enable quantitative and comprehensive measures of riboswitch structures with general implications for our views and strategies of RNA structural analysis.

1. INTRODUCTION

X-ray crystallographic studies of riboswitch aptamer domains with their cognate ligands have yielded tremendous insight into how RNA can be harnessed to recognize small molecule ligands specifically. The current repertoire of small molecule ligands includes amino acids, nucleobases, nucleotides, metals, and cofactors (Peselis & Serganov, 2014). Naturally, these studies have been extended to understand how riboswitches discriminate among related molecules in a complex cellular environment (Gilbert & Batey, 2009; Johnson, Reyes, Polaski, & Batey, 2012; Serganov, Huang, & Patel, 2008; Trausch et al., 2014). While "equilibrium" studies of riboswitches are easy to perform and are useful for guiding virtual screening of alternative ligands (Daldrop et al., 2011), a number of studies have suggested that such conditions are far from physiological.

Biochemical and structural investigations of full-length riboswitches, as opposed to solely their aptamer domains, have reinforced the notion that a complete understanding of riboswitch function requires a consideration of its behavior in the context of its free state or active transcription. For instance, the add riboswitch from *Vibrio vulnificus* displays a three-state behavior in limiting amounts of adenine (Reining et al., 2013). Several studies have observed multiple conformations in ligand-free aptamers (Chen, Zuo, Wang, & Dayie, 2012; Stoddard et al., 2010; Vicens, Mondragon, & Batey, 2011), suggesting that some riboswitch aptamer domains are preorganized in the absence of ligand, sampling a number of binding-competent states that may be different than the bound state, otherwise known as "conformational selection" (Zhang, Jones, & Ferre-D'Amare, 2014). Strikingly, transcriptional pausing by the *Escherichia coli* btuB riboswitch can have profound effects on RNA folding (Perdrizet, Artsimovitch, Furman, Sosnick, & Pan, 2012). Conceivably, a balancing act among speed of transcription, RNA folding, and ligand is carefully maintained for efficient regulation (Frieda & Block, 2012; Garst & Batey, 2009). Taken together, these studies reveal the importance of ligand-free studies of riboswitches toward understanding their structure and function.

Conformational heterogeneity of riboswitches in the free state precludes the use of X ray crystallography for structural studies. Instead, solution-state experiments such as nuclear magnetic resonance, hydroxyl-radical probing, selective 2′-hydroxyl acylation analyzed by primer extension (John, Merino, & Weeks, 2004) and small angle X-ray scattering (SAXS) (Perry & Tainer, 2013; Petoukhov & Svergun, 2013; Rambo & Tainer, 2010a, 2013b; Sibille & Bernado, 2012) can be used for comprehensive structural analyses. SAXS is a solution-state measurement that requires minimal sample (<17 μL) and time (Hura et al., 2009). An entire experiment can be performed in less than 4 minute making the experiment highly efficient and economical. SAXS is a robust technique that can be performed on a wide range of RNA masses and solution conditions (Baird & Ferre-D'Amare, 2010; Gopal, Zhou, Knobler, & Gelbart, 2012; Rambo & Tainer, 2010b). The development of modern SAXS synchrotron beamlines, as typified by SIBYLS at the Advanced Light Source (Classen et al., 2013) and of commercial laboratory SAXS instruments, has made SAXS measurements readily available for routine structural investigations. However, SAXS is limited by sample quality and requires extensive evaluations of sample heterogeneity for reliable interpretation (Perez & Nishino, 2012; Rambo & Tainer, 2010b). We present general considerations for the robust application of SAXS to RNA and riboswitches in particular. In this chapter, we present specific recommendations when considering a structural study of RNAs by SAXS and, using the SAM-I, adenosylcobalamin, and lysine riboswitches illustrate the role SAXS can play in elucidating new mechanistic and structural insights These riboswitch systems exemplify general issues in structural biology regarding unstructured components, flexibility, and interactions, in addition to conformational switching, selection, and induced fit. The equipment, procedures, parameters, and modeling described here provide the means to enable efficient quantitative and comprehensive measures of RNA structures.

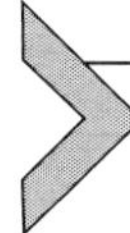

2. SPECIALIZED EQUIPMENT

We refer the reader to the review on *in vitro* transcription (Beckert & Masquida, 2011). All analysis was performed with the JAVA-based program ScÅtter available at www.bioisis.net. We suggest the following equipment for performing the analysis discussed in this chapter (Tables 11.1–11.3).

3. PREPARATION OF THE RNA FOR A SAXS STUDY

3.1. Assessing the folded state of the RNA

SAXS offers the opportunity to perform a structural analysis of a wide variety of macromolecular RNA types (Gajda, Martinez Zapien, Uchikawa, & Dock-Bregeon, 2013; Rambo & Tainer, 2010b; Yang, Parisien, Major, & Roux, 2010) that not only includes the canonical classes of structured RNA (e.g., introns, riboswitches, ribozymes) but also the classes of seemingly unstructured RNA described as either noncoding or single stranded (Gopal et al., 2012; Ribitsch et al., 1985). However, as SAXS is a solution-scattering technique, care must be used to ensure homogenous samples. In most cases, the RNA of interest is *in vitro* transcribed, followed by a denaturing purification and then renatured through an annealing procedure (Fig. 11.1). The denaturing purification typically leads to chemically homogenous RNA (Fig. 11.1B) observed as a single migrating band on an 8 *M* urea denaturing polyacrylamide gel electrophoresis (PAGE).

Table 11.1 Silica hydrophilic polymer-based size exclusion column (SEC) withstand high operating pressures at high flow rates without sacrificing column efficiency

Shodex SEC column	Exclusion limit (kDa)	Column volume (mL)
KW402.5-4F	150	4.8
KW403-4F	600	4.8
KW404-4F	1000	4.8

The columns are ideal for screening and for the KW series, a typical SEC run will take 16 minutes Columns are not stable to 1 *M* NaOH washes.

Table 11.2 High-performance liquid chromatography (HPLC) instruments for analytical scale preparation of RNA samples for SAXS

HPLC	Note
AKTA Ettan microLC[a]	Can equilibrate and perform several runs with 50-mL of running buffer, ideal for including ligands in buffer during SEC separations
Agilent Infinity 1260[a]	Operates in continuous flow mode with an autoinjector. Ideal for inline light scattering and SAXS instrumentation
BioRad BioLogic	Can be used with larger (15 mL) KW 800 series Shodex columns for processing larger sample quantities. Required flow rates are 1–1.5 mL/min

[a]These HPLCs are specific to ultrasmall flow rates such as 50 μL/min and must be able to withstand tubing diameters of 100–150 μm. Large tubing diameters should be avoided to reduce sample dilution during purification. The instruments are analytical scale and need to be restricted to nonpreparative workloads in order to maintain a clean system for RNA studies. To reduce background from buffer contaminants, we recommend installation of an inline 0.1-μm filter after the HPLC pump but prior to the sample loading valve.

Table 11.3 Thorough characterization of the hydrodynamic state of an RNA sample can be reliably achieved using light scattering analysis during SEC purification

Accessories	Source	Note
Multiangle light scattering (MALS) instrument	Wyatt	18-angle detector is preferred for studies of large macromolecular assemblies
Quasi-elastic light scattering (QELS) detector	Wyatt	Time-resolved light scattering measurements that can determine radius-of-hydration
Refractive index detector	Wyatt	Conformation-independent assessment of RNA or protein concentration
Inline buffer filter (<0.1 μm)	Millipore	Reduces baseline noise in light scattering detectors
Inline buffer vacuum degasser	Rheodyne	Reduces baseline noise in light scattering and refractive index detector

MALS provides absolute mass measurements across the SEC elution peak assessing mass heterogeneity, whereas QELS provides relative estimates of the radius-of-hydration assessing conformational heterogeneity. Unlike fixed wavelength absorbance-based concentration detectors that typically monitor proteins or nucleic acids, refractive index (rI) detectors monitor optical differences between a reference buffer and sample. rI detectors can reveal small differences between a sample and buffer background due to salts and dissolved gases.

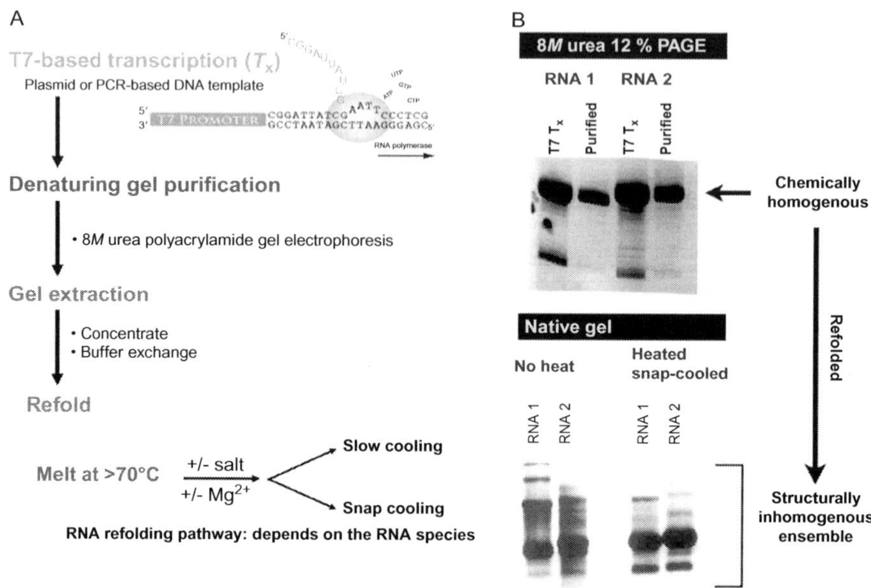

Figure 11.1 General outline for purification of *in vitro* synthesized RNA for structural purposes. (A) T7 RNA polymerase-based methods for synthesizing large amounts of template-directed RNA using either plasmid or PCR amplified DNA templates. Following enzymatic synthesis, RNA is purified by electrophoresis through an 8 *M* urea polyacrylamide denaturing gel (slab) to remove truncated transcription products and enzyme. The RNA of interest (ROI) is visualized by UV shadowing and physically excised as a gel slice. The ROI is extracted from the gel, exchanged into an appropriate storage buffer, and concentrated. Since the RNA was purified by denaturing methods, an annealing step is taken to refold the RNA. (B) Denaturing purification of SAM-I riboswitch (94 nucleotides). Ethidium bromide staining clearly demonstrates product heterogeneity before gel extraction (T7 T_x lanes), whereas gel extraction and purification produces a single mass species (purified lanes). Native gel purification of refolded, purified RNA leads to a polydisperse sample and ambiguity regarding mass of each band. Snap cooling of the RNA (annealing) reduces higher mass species (no heat) but not completely. *Denaturing and native PAGE of SAM-I courtesy of Robert Batey, University of Colorado at Boulder.*

Subsequently, the chemically homogenous RNA is renatured and analyzed using native PAGE (Fig. 11.1B).

Native PAGE has been tremendously useful for understanding RNA structure and folding (Woodson & Koculi, 2009); however, the method is inadequate for evaluating the quality of the RNA sample for SAXS studies due to the inability to assess the mass of the RNA reliably or to detect the presence (<5%) of misfolded species (Rambo & Tainer, 2010b). The presence of misfolded species can confound SAXS interpretation and limit the usefulness of the SAXS data. As an alternative method for accessing RNA sample quality, we suggest using size exclusion chromatography (SEC) coupled inline with a multiangle light scattering (MALS) instrument (Rambo & Tainer, 2010b). We direct the reader to an excellent review on the theory and application of MALS (Wyatt, 1993). Furthermore, entire SEC runs can be performed in less than 15 minute using modern high precision silica-based size exclusion columns. These columns can withstand high pressures without sacrificing column resolution (Table 11.1).

The MALS instrument is used principally for determining the molecular mass (MM) of the eluting peaks during an SEC separation. Since the scattering process depends only on the square of the particle mass, the MALS instrument can observe non-RNA or -protein species such as residual polyacrylamide during the SEC separation. Residual polyacrylamide carried over from the denaturing purification step is invisible at wavelengths between 260 and 280 nm but is readily visible by MALS and the associated refractive index (rI) detector. Ideally, the MALS instrument will have greater than 16 detectors with an integrated quasi-elastic light scattering (QELS) detector. The additional MALS detectors provide angular scattering information for an independent determination of a particle's radius-of-gyration, R_g, whereas the QELS information will determine the radius-of-hydration, R_h. In the absence of SAXS information, knowing the mass, R_h, and R_g can immediately suggest the shape of the RNA. Furthermore, changes in RNA compaction can be monitored directly by following R_h.

Mass determination from SEC-MALS requires an accurate concentration measurement across the profile of the elution peak. This is reliably achieved by simultaneous monitoring of the rI during the chromatographic separation. In the solution state, the RNA rI increment (the change in rI per change in RNA concentration) is independent of particle size, shape or level-of-compactness and can be used to determine RNA concentration. However, rI does depend on buffer composition: therefore, the experimental rI must be determined from a standard such as the P4–P6 domain (Rambo & Doudna, 2004; Rambo & Tainer, 2010b). Figure 11.2A illustrates information obtained from an SEC-MALS run. Based on the concentration detector alone (i.e., rI or UV monitor), the SEC profile would be described by two major peaks between 14 and 22 minutes. However, inspection of the light scattering signal during the SEC separation shows three peaks. Since the light scattering intensity is proportional to particle mass, we can conclude that peak 1 is a massive aggregate at exceptionally low concentration that would contribute a scattering signal nearly equal

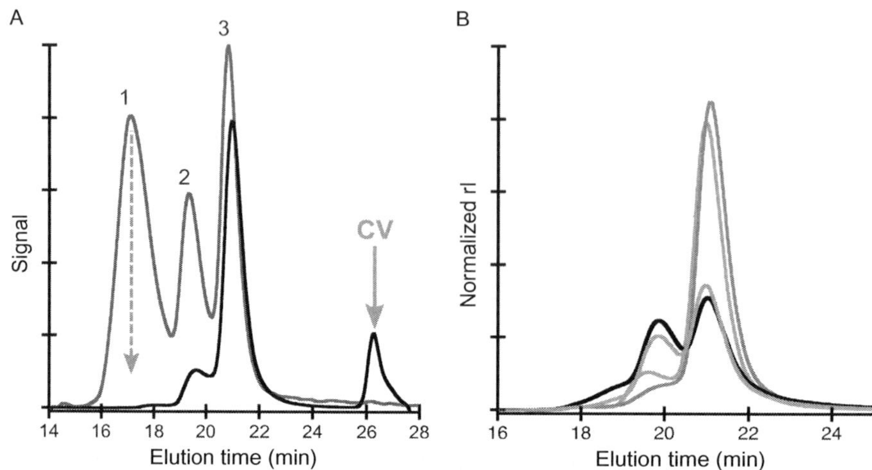

Figure 11.2 Size exclusion chromatographic (SEC) separation of SAM-I riboswitch under varying annealing conditions. (A) Elution profile of SAM-I riboswitch monitored by refractive index (concentration detector, black) and light scattering (mass detector, red). Cyan and gray arrows mark the void and column volumes, respectively. Peak 1 is an aggregate peak given by the high light scattering at very low concentration. Peak 2 is an RNA dimer. Peak 3 corresponds to the RNA monomer. (B) Elution profile (refractive index) of SAM-I riboswitch annealed using four different refolding strategies. RNA was heated (85 °C) and either snap- or slow cooled in the presence and absence of Mg^{2+} under dilute conditions (~0.1 mg/mL). In the absence of Mg^{2+}, snap cooled using prechilled buffer (cyan) performed better than slow cooling (orange) which performed better than snap cooling (green) and slow cooling (black) in the presence of Mg^{2+}. Annealing in the presence of Mg^{2+}, results in severe material loss of monomeric RNA. RNA was concentrated to 5 mg/mL using a 5-kDa cut-off spin concentrator at 18 °C. (See the color plate.)

to peak 3. The aggregate peak would corrupt the observed SAXS profile, thereby limiting the scope and interpretation of the experiment.

Based on the SEC profile and analysis of the MALS data in Fig. 11.2A, an optimal SAXS sample can be obtained by sampling the eluting peak directly. In this case, peak 3 is monodisperse (symmetric elution peak containing a single mass species) and corresponds to the monomeric form of the RNA. If the SAXS instrument cannot be directly connected inline to the SEC instrument, then a sample must be taken manually by attaching a small (<1 μL) outlet tube directly to the UV cell. It can be anticipated that injecting a 25–50 μL sample will distribute the sample elution peak over a volume of ~500 μL. For a sample with ~10% heterogenous contamination, we observe a five- to sixfold dilution based on the UV absorbance at peak elution. Therefore, a sample injected at 5–10 mg/mL will yield ~1 mg/mL

SAXS sample at peak elution, which is an ideal concentration for modern SAXS instruments. However, if the sample contains significant heterogenous contamination, then there will be a significant material loss of the RNA of interest due to the RNA being distributed over the heterogenous state (Fig. 11.2B). In these situations, it may be best to optimize the refolding strategy of the RNA or seek a native purification method (Batey & Kieft, 2007; Gopal et al., 2012; Kazantsev et al., 2011).

Through our many collaborations with RNA crystallography research groups, we have examined a wide range of RNAs that include the SAM-I, lysine, and B_{12} riboswitches, P4–P6 RNA domain, HDV and CPEB3 ribozyme, tRNA, tRNA-like RNAs, RNase P, and pre-Q1 (Costantino, Pfingsten, Rambo, & Kieft, 2008; Garst, Heroux, Rambo, & Batey, 2008; Hammond, Rambo, Filbin, & Kieft, 2009; Hammond, Rambo, & Kieft, 2010; Johnson et al., 2012; Kazantsev et al., 2011; Rambo & Tainer, 2010b; Stoddard et al., 2010; Strulson, Yennawar, Rambo, & Bevilacqua, 2013). In each case, after refolding, the RNA sample always contained contaminating species that required optimization of the refolding protocol and SEC purification. From our experience, we suggest a refolding strategy outlined in Fig. 11.3. We have found that annealing the RNA under dilute conditions (~0.1 mg/mL) in the absence of Mg^{2+} has been critical to minimizing intermolecular multimerization. As demonstrated by the SAM-I riboswitch in Fig. 11.2B, the optimal refolding strategy is characterized by the absence of Mg^{2+} during annealing, with snap cooling (using prechilled buffer) performing better than slow cooling (judged by the larger leading elution peak). Annealing the RNA in the presence of Mg^{2+}, under dilute conditions produced a heterogenous sample with nearly 50% of the RNA lost to a heterogenous state. In some cases (e.g., B_{12} riboswitch and RNase P), a refolding strategy that adequately promoted the RNA into a monodisperse, homogenous state could not be determined. For RNase P, a native purification method that optimized monodispersity and catalytic activity was developed. Here, both A- and B-type RNase P were transcribed in a high-salt condition that was optimal for RNA-only catalyzed activity. Interestingly, this RNA was more compact than either the refolded or low salt (Kazantsev et al., 2011), suggesting that cotranscriptional folding yields greater natively folded RNA.

For RNAs in the unstructured class, purification methods will need to be developed that maintain native-like conditions. It can be anticipated that these RNAs will have local structures that form during transcription, and attempts to refold the RNA will likely create a heterogenous kinetically

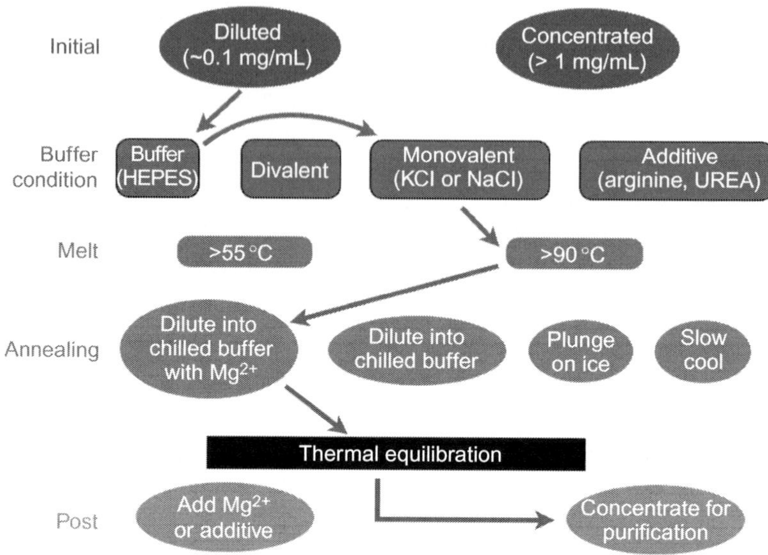

Figure 11.3 Template for generating and testing annealing strategies. A good annealing strategy should minimize material loss of the RNA, i.e., minimize formation of dimer or aggregated forms of the RNA. For "buffer condition" select one or more followed by choosing a melting temperature. The annealing step can be performed using prechilled buffer with or without Mg^{2+} followed by a thermal equilibration at room temperature. The RNA will be dilute and will require concentration step prior to SEC separation.

trapped state. Gopal et al. (2012) examined three single-stranded RNAs from 1000 to 2800 nucleotides (nt) by SAXS and used a mild treatment (phenol–chloroform extraction) to remove transcription-related proteins followed by an ethanol precipitation.

3.2. Importance of buffer subtraction

A solution-state biological SAXS curve is a difference measurement taken as the difference in scattering intensities between the sample and corresponding buffer. Here, buffer refers to the mixture of salts, additives (e.g., glycerol, sucrose, etc.) and weak acid or base used to suspend the biological molecule in a water environment and sample refers to the RNA of interest suspended in the buffer. The observed intensity differences between the sample and buffer are small (<1%); therefore, to minimize systematic errors in the difference, it is necessary that the buffer be as closely matched as possible to the sample buffer. Buffer matching can be readily accomplished using (1) spin concentrator, (2) microdialysis, or (3) SEC. Spin concentrators are effective but must be washed with buffer at least three times prior to buffer exchanging the sample. Here, the flow through buffer can be used as the matching buffer for SAXS. Dialysis is also effective for concentrated samples but requires much longer equilibration times and may not be suitable for samples that are unstable at high concentrations. The prior two methods are suitable for sample concentrations >1 mg/mL; however, for RNA samples <0.5 mg/mL, exact matching of the buffer is critical to the accuracy of the intensity difference. For such dilute samples, it is recommended to use SEC purified samples and the corresponding buffer. As seen in Fig. 11.2A, the rI detector shows a small peak occurring at the column volume and corresponds to the differences in small molecules between the injected sample and buffer (e.g., salts, dissolved gases, glycerol). Therefore, to ensure a closely matched buffer, it is recommended the SAXS buffer be taken after 1.2 column volumes.

4. INTERPRETATION OF THE X-RAY SCATTERING CURVE

X-rays are scattered by electrons and the excess intensity that gives the observed SAXS difference will be due to the collection of electrons comprising the RNA and associated bound waters. The three-dimensional collection of electrons forming the RNA structure defines the molecular form factor, $A(q)$, and we assume the RNAs are noninteracting (negligible interparticle interference) forming a monodisperse sample.

There are many methods for calculating a SAXS profile from a set of atomic coordinates. These methods can be divided into two classes based on their explicit use of atomic scattering form factors. Algorithms such as SASTBX (Liu, Morris, Hexemer, Grandison, & Zwart, 2012), CRYSOL (Svergun, Barberato, & Koch, 1995), Aqua-SAXS (Poitevin, Orland, Doniach, Koehl, & Delarue, 2011), and AXES (Grishaev, Guo, Irving, & Bax, 2010) use atomic scattering form factors directly, whereas FOXS (Schneidman-Duhovny, Hammel, Tainer, & Sali, 2013) and DALAI-GA (Chacon, Diaz, Moran, & Andreu, 2000) use the $P(r)$-distribution (histogram of the set of interatomic distance vectors) scaled by an approximation function. The $P(r)$-distribution is a resolution-limited distribution that fully describes the structural state of the RNA. Since we are examining the solution state of the RNA, a SAXS measurement will scatter from ~10,000 billion RNAs during a single exposure. Therefore, the $P(r)$-distribution will be the sum of each of the RNAs and is a description of the thermodynamic state. In general, SAXS intensity calculations from $P(r)$-distributions is given by Eq. (11.1):

$$I_{\text{molecule}}(q) = \int P(r) \cdot \frac{\sin(q.r)}{q.r} \mathrm{d}r \tag{11.1}$$

where q is the scattering momentum vector with units of Å^{-1}, r is the interatomic distance vector (Å), and $I(q)$ is the scattered intensity at the specified q. The integration is limited to the maximum dimension, $d_{\max}$, of the RNA. A more detailed explanation of scattering theory and applications can be found in several comprehensive reviews (Glatter & Kratky, 1982; Rambo & Tainer, 2013b; Svergun, Feĭgin, & Taylor, 1987).

4.1. Quantitating compactness

Approximations to the $P(r)$-distribution can be used to provide resolution-limited information regarding macroscopic properties of the RNA. For a polymer exhibiting a Gaussian distribution between all intersegmental distances, Debye (Glatter & Kratky, 1982) derived an analytical expression (Eq. 11.2) showing that $I(q)$ is dependent on the product $(q \cdot R_g)^2$.

$$I(q) = \frac{2\left(\mathrm{e}^{-R_g^2 \cdot q^2} + R_g^2 \cdot q^2 - 1\right)}{\left(R_g^2 \cdot q^2\right)^2} \tag{11.2}$$

For RNA, intersegmental units refer to the smallest rigid units (nucleotides or small base-paired regions) displaying the aforementioned Gaussian distribution. The expression in Eq. (11.2) shows that within a limited q-range, the intensity approaches an asymptotic limit.

$$\lim_{q \to \infty} I(q) \cdot q^2 = \frac{2}{R_g^2}\left(1 - \frac{1}{q^2 \cdot \mathrm{R}_g^2}\right)$$

The asymptotic limit is readily evident as a plateau (Rambo & Tainer, 2011) in a $q^2 \cdot I(q)$ versus q^2 plot (Debye–Kratky plot).

In contrast, both Porod and Debye (Debye, Anderson, & Brumberger, 1957; Glatter & Kratky, 1982) showed for particles with a discrete surface and electron density contrast with the surrounding buffer, $I(q)$ is directly proportional to q^{-4} scaled by a constant k (Eq. 11.3).

$$I(q) = k \cdot \frac{1}{q^4} \tag{11.3}$$

Similar to the Debye approximation from above, the q^{-4} relationship is valid within a limited q-range and is evident by a plateau (Rambo & Tainer, 2011) in a $q^4 \cdot I(q)$ versus q^4 plot (Porod–Debye plot).

The Debye and Porod–Debye approximations define a q-limited power-law relationship (Fig. 11.4) that can be used to characterize the thermodynamic state of the RNA. The approximations are low resolution where in the case of the Gaussian-like coil, $I(q)$ depends only on the macroscopic property R_g. Likewise, for the Porod–Debye approximation, the scattering will depend on the particle's surface area, a well-defined quantity for a compact particle. Transitions of the RNA from a compact particle with a well-defined surface area to a Gaussian-like chain can be visually assessed by creating three types of plots (Fig. 11.5): Debye–Kratky plot, $q^3 \cdot I(q)$ versus q^3 (SIBYLS) plot and Porod–Debye plot. Here, the plot that demonstrates the most hyperbolic-like asymptotic plateau in the low q-range data suggests the power of the exponent. The asymptotic plateau occurs immediately after the Guinier region ($q \cdot R_g > 1.3$) and is observed after the major inflection point in one of the aforementioned plot types. It should be noted that particles can have more than one Porod–Debye region (Ciccariello,

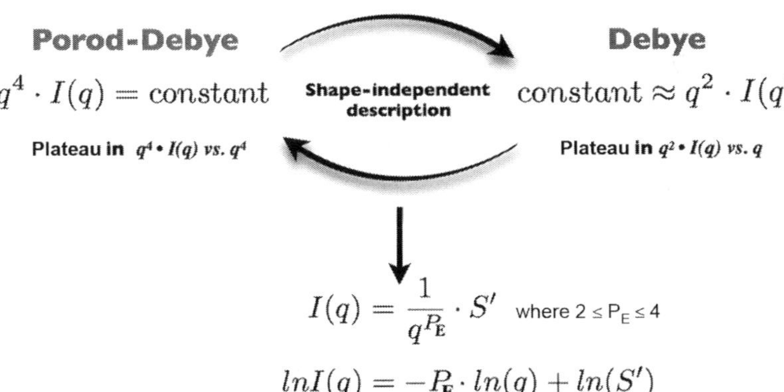

Figure 11.4 SAXS power-law relationships as indicators of RNA compactness. At low resolution, the SAXS profile of an RNA can be approximated by either its surface area (Porod–Debye approximation) or its R_g (Debye approximation). For the Porod–Debye approximation, the SAXS curve will decay as q^{-4}, whereas for the Debye approximation of a Gaussian chain, the SAXS curve will decay as q^{-2}. The exponential decay (Porod–Debye exponent, P_E) can be determined directly by fitting a line to the appropriate scattering range in a log–log plot. P_E will be bounded between 2 and 4 and can be determined using the program ScÅtter available at www.bioisis.net.

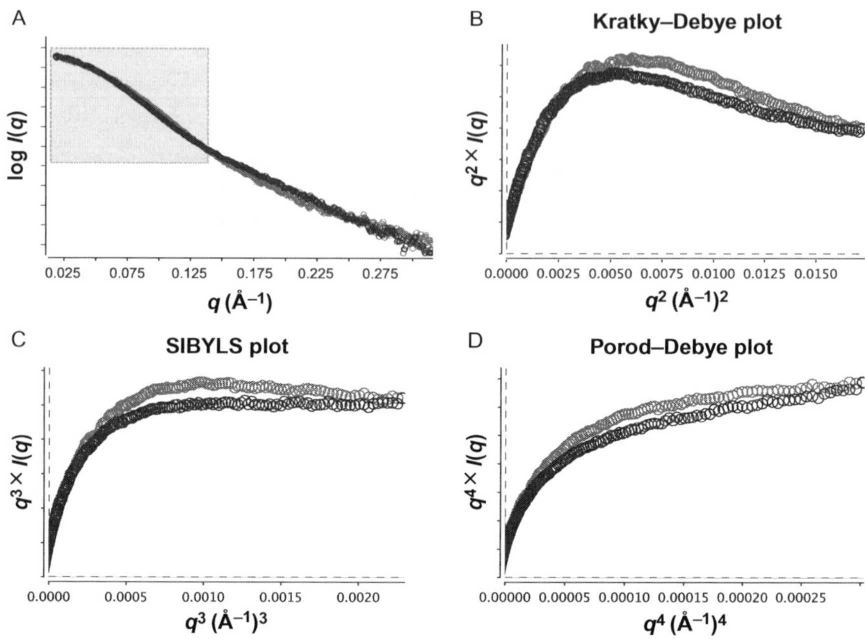

Figure 11.5 Flexibility plots for the SAM-I riboswitch in the presence (red) and absence (black) of ligand. (A) SAXS data plot as log $I(q)$ versus q. Boxed region defines limits for the plots in B–D. (B) Kratky–Debye plot ($q^2 \cdot I(q)$ vs. q^2). A plateau would indicate the data could be approximated using the Debye approximation for a Gaussian chain with a P_E near 2. (C) SIBYLS plot ($q^3 \cdot I(q)$ vs. q^3). A plateau would indicate a P_E near 3. (D) Porod–Debye plot ($q^4 \cdot I(q)$ vs. q^4). A plateau would indicate a P_E near 4 and that the data could be approximated using the Porod–Debye approximation for particles with a defined surface and contrast. For the SAM-I riboswitch, the (+) ligand state has a P_E near 4, whereas the (−) ligand state would be near 3. These plots clearly demonstrate a change in state of the riboswitch in the presence of ligand. Figures were prepared using the program ScÅtter available at www.bioisis.net. (See the color plate.)

Goodisman, & Brumberger, 1988) and the above discussion refers to the primary Porod–Debye region occurring immediately after the Guinier region.

Alternatively, a log–log transform of the SAXS data and subsequent fitting of the best line within the Porod–Debye region will determine the power-law Porod–Debye exponent, P_E. The exponent is bounded between 2 and 4 and we can expect for an RNA that undergoes a transition from a compact-folded state to a multiconformer, less compact state, P_E will decrease. The Porod–Debye exponent is a unique, quantitative descriptor of the thermodynamic ensemble that can be used for following gross changes in the folded state of the RNA.

4.2. SAXS invariants

The Porod–Debye exponent is an example of a model-independent parameter that can be derived directly from the SAXS data. Additional model-independent parameters (Glatter & Kratky, 1982; Svergun et al., 1987) are the Guinier-based R_g, volume (V_P), and correlation length (l_c). If the SAXS intensities are calibrated to an absolute scale (Orthaber, Bergmann, & Glatter, 2000), then the MM of the particle can be determined. The Guinier R_g is determined from a linear approximation of the low q data ($q \cdot R_g < 1.3$), whereas V_P and l_c are determined using the Porod invariant, Q. The Porod invariant is readily defined for compact particles but is undefined (Rambo & Tainer, 2013a) for particles behaving as Gaussian-like chains (flexible). Instead, we can examine the ratio of V_P to l_c, a term known as the volume-of-correlation (V_c) (Rambo & Tainer, 2013a). V_c is defined for both compact and flexible particles and can be used to monitor changes in a particle's thermodynamic state. Furthermore, the ratio of V_c and R_g^2 defines a power-law parameter (Rambo & Tainer, 2013a), Q_R, that determines the mass of a particle directly from a SAXS curve.

4.3. Real-space parameters

The $P(r)$-distribution is a resolution-limited histogram of all electron pair distances within the RNA. The shape of the distribution can be determined using indirect Fourier transform (IFT) methods where an orthogonal set of basis functions is used to parameterize the empirical SAXS dataset (Glatter & Kratky, 1982; Liu & Zwart, 2012; Moore, 1980; Svergun, 1992).

In practice, determining the $P(r)$-distribution by IFT is an iterative process that requires several trial d_{max} values to be evaluated by the experimenter. The goal is to find the smallest d_{max} that supports the following: (1) the $P(r)$ is greater than zero for $0 < r < d_{max}$, and (2) maximally smooth (minimize the sum of the second derivative $P(r)$ commensurate with the given SAXS resolution). In addition, the lowest and highest q-values defining the useable range of the SAXS dataset should be adjusted to test the robustness of the chosen d_{max} to the aforementioned criteria.

The first and second moments of $P(r)$-distribution define the average distance ($r_{average}$) and real space R_g. It should be noted, the Guinier R_g is a low-resolution approximation of the SAXS intensities that uses a small subset of the data ($q \cdot R_g < 1.3$), whereas the real space R_g is determined from all the available SAXS data but depends on the choice of d_{max}. The chosen d_{max} should produce real space values for R_g and $I(0)$ that are in close agreement to the Guinier determined values. Difficult IFT solutions and large differences between real and reciprocal space values (>5%) can be indicative of poor data and sample quality (Putnam, Hammel, Hura, & Tainer, 2007) (e.g., aggregation or poor buffer subtraction).

Comparing SAXS data in real space as normalized $P(r)$-distributions is an excellent and recommended method for detecting conformational changes. It can be expected that small structural differences will not produce significant observable differences in $I(q)$ for $q < 2||d_{\mathrm{max}}{}^{-1}$ unless SAXS data are collected to sufficiently high resolution. In addition, for small changes where intensities can be corrupted by poor buffer subtractions and parasitic scattering near the beam stop, IFT methods can mitigate minor scattering issues thereby better demonstrating small differences in real space.

4.4. Dimensionless Kratky plot

The Kratky plot ($q^2 \cdot I(q)$ vs. q) is a standard qualitative method for asserting the compact (flexible) state of the RNA. The Kratky plot visualizes the Debye formalism for a Gaussian-like chain and should demonstrate a hyperbolic plateau within a limited q-range of the SAXS data (Rambo & Tainer, 2011; Receveur-Brechot & Durand, 2012). In the case of a compact particle, the Kratky plot will converge to baseline at higher q-values with a single maximum occurring after the Guinier region ($q \cdot R_g > 1.3$). Furthermore, the magnitude and location of the maximum (plateau) will vary depending on the concentration, MM and degree of compactness of the particle (Durand et al., 2010). This can make comparisons of the same RNA under different conditions problematic. The Kratky plot can be normalized by using $(q \cdot R_g)^2 \cdot I(q)/I(0)$ instead of $q^2 \cdot I(q)$ and plotting the data against $q \cdot R_g$ (Durand et al., 2010). Dividing by $I(0)$ normalizes the data for particle concentration and V_P, whereas plotting against $q \cdot R_g$ scales the q-axis to particle size. The plot is dimensionless and for globular particles, the plot will show a peak value at $q \cdot R_g = \sqrt{3}$ with a maximum of 1.104 (Fig. 11.6A) (Durand et al., 2010). In contrast, a Gaussian-like chain will have a peak maximum of 2 that is shifted right of $\sqrt{3}$. For nonglobular but compact particles, the peak will shift slightly right and upward. The use of a R_g-based dimensionless Kratky plot provides a semi-quantitative method for asserting changes in the compact state of the RNA by noting the location and height of the maximum.

Alternatively, a dimensionless Kratky plot can be made using V_c (Fig. 11.6B) by plotting $(q^2 \cdot V_c) \cdot I(q)/I(0)$ against $q^2 \cdot V_c$. Here, peak (plateau)

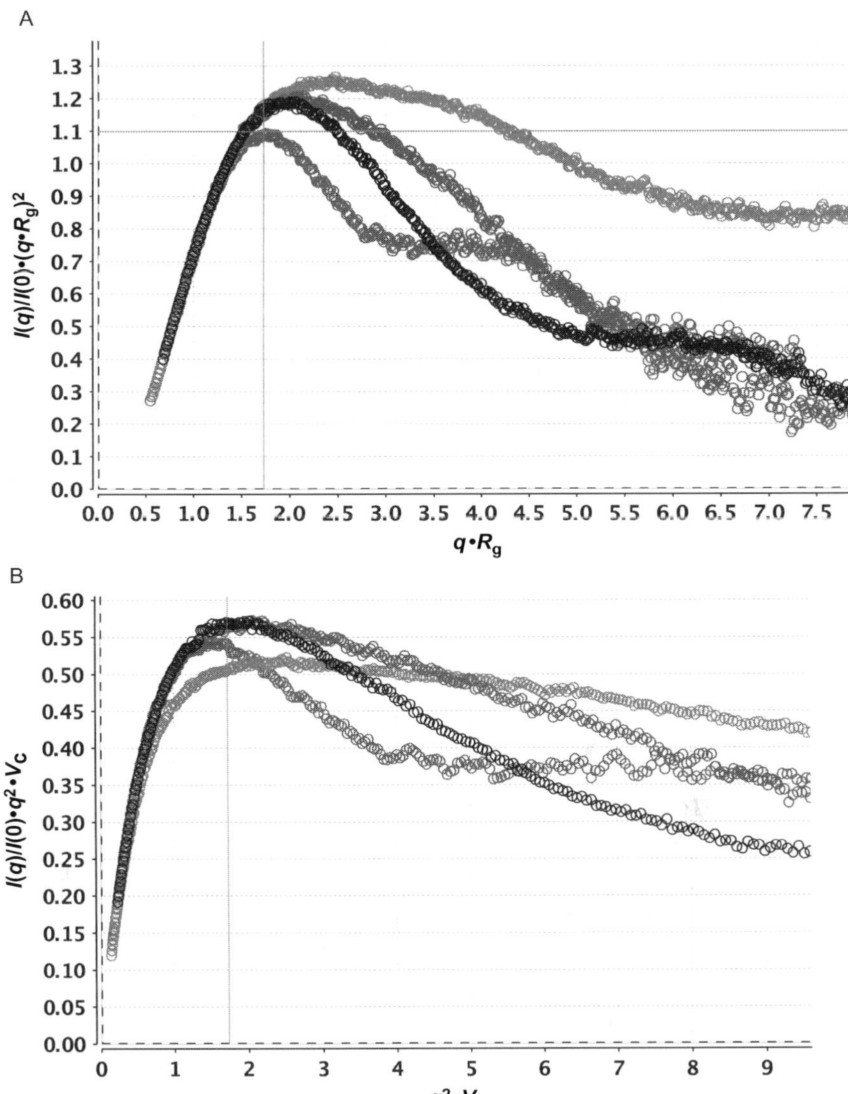

Figure 11.6 Dimensionless Kratky plots. P4–P6 domain (black), tRNA^{phe} + Mg^{2+} (red), tRNA^{phe} − Mg^{2+} (cyan), and TyMV UDP (purple). (A) R_g-based plot, cross hair (gray) marks the position of the peak for an ideal, compact, globular particle at $q{\cdot}R_g = \sqrt{3}$. Less compact or nonglobular particles will have a peak shifted upward and to the right. (B) V_c-based plot, vertical line represents $\sqrt{3}$. Peak height is inversely proportional to the particle's surface-to-volume ratio with the maximum occurring for a sphere at 0.85. Changes in peak height reflect changes to the particles surface to volume ratio. Similar peak heights for P4–P6 domain and tRNA^{phe} + Mg^{2+} V_c-based plots suggest similar surface-to-volume ratios. Dimensionless plots will be sensitive to the accuracy of the Guinier region or real space transforms. Figures were prepared using the program ScÅtter available at www.bioisis.net. (See the color plate.)

height will be inversely proportional to the particle surface–volume ratio. The plot will have a maximum of 0.85 (perfect sphere) and can readily illustrate condition specific changes in the surface-to-volume ratio of an RNA (Fig. 11.6B). We suggest a comprehensive analysis using both dimensionless Kratky plots. In Fig. 11.6A, SAXS data for $tRNA^{phe}$ (76 nt), TyMV-UDP (109 nt), and P4-P6 RNA domain (160 nt) are plotted using both dimensionless Kratky plots. First, comparison of folded $tRNA^{phe}$ with P4–P6 RNA domain in the R_g-based plot show the tRNA peak is shifted to the right, suggesting tRNA is less globular than P4–P6. However, the peak heights are nearly coincident in the V_c-based plot, suggesting the two RNAs have similar surface-to-volume ratios. It has been firmly established that the P4–P6 domain from the Group I intron is a compact, folded domain in solution (Murphy & Cech, 1993), whereas tRNA are multiconformer displaying a wide range of rigid and nonrigid body motions (Wang & Jernigan, 2005). In a Mg^{2+}-free state, the $tRNA^{phe}$ peak height increases in the R_g-based plot, suggesting a less compact state. It can be expected that a less compact state will have a comparatively greater surface-to-volume ratio, and in the V_c-based Kratky plot for the Mg^{2+}-free $tRNA^{phe}$, we observe the expected decrease in peak height. Finally, TyMV-UDP RNA is considered a tRNA-like structure from Turnip yellow mosaic virus. The R_g-based plot shows the peak for TyMV-UDP occurs at $\sqrt{3}$ with a peak height ~1.1 implying the RNA is globular in solution unlike $tRNA^{phe}$. However, the V_c-based plot shows TyMV-UDP has a greater surface-to-volume ratio than $tRNA^{phe}$. This can be reconciled by noting the P_E for TyMV-UDP is less than $tRNA^{phe}$ ($3 < 3.5$) suggesting TyMV-UDP exists as a globular multiconformer state in solution.

5. CASE STUDIES

The SAXS-derived parameters (R_g, V_c, V_P, P_E, d_{max}, and $r_{average}$) can be used to provide a comprehensive evaluation of the state of an RNA in solution. Furthermore, these parameters, including the dimensionless Kratky plots and $P(r)$-distribution, can be used to comparatively uncover mechanisms in folding or binding (e.g., conformational capture) by an RNA. Here, we will use reported SAXS data of the SAM-I (Stoddard et al., 2010) and LYS riboswitches (Garst et al., 2008) from the SAXS database Bioisis.net to examine two different riboswitch mechanisms.

5.1. SAM-I riboswitch

The SAM-I riboswitch is a 94 nt RNA aptamer that binds the small molecule *S*-adenosylmethionine (SAM). X-ray crystallographic studies of the riboswitch in the presence (+) and absence (−) of SAM revealed nearly identical riboswitch structures, suggesting that the unbound state of the RNA has a preformed binding site that is blocked by an internal adenosine. SAM (+) SAXS data showed an excellent agreement with the bound X-ray crystal structure. However, the apo-structure implies the solution state would be occupied by a single distinct conformation but paradoxically poses the problem of how substrate recognition could proceed when the binding pocket is blocked. Fitting the apo-structure to SAM (−) SAXS data immediately showed that the apo-structure from the crystal could not explain the solution state. The SAXS invariants R_g, V_c, and V_P (Table 11.4) all increased in the absence of SAM, suggesting that the riboswitch is becoming less compact. Does this apo solution state represent a conformational change to a single distinct species or a change in state of the riboswitch? Examining the Porod–Debye exponent, P_E, and apparent volume, V_P, shows a significant decrease in P_E (3.6–3.0) with a 36% increase in V_P. The drop in P_E is consistent with the riboswitch adopting a multiconformer, flexible state. The

Table 11.4 SAXS-derived parameters describing the solution (thermodynamic) state of RNA

	SAM(−)	SAM(+)	SAM(EDTA)	LYS(−)	LYS(+)	LYS(EDTA)
R_g^{Guinier} (Å)	23.45	22.58	32.08	30.10	31.35	41.35
$R_g^{\mathrm{realspace}}$ (Å)	24.77	22.59	34.60	30.72	30.27	43.86
V_c^{Guinier} (Å^2)	295	277	354	399	423	454
$V_c^{\mathrm{realspace}}$ (Å^2)	294	264	n/a	373	394	n/a
Volume[a] (Å^3)	75,900	56,300	162,000	105,000	106,000	269,000
P_E	3.0	3.6	2.1	3.4	3.4	1.9
d_{max} (Å)	79	74	118	101	99	163
$r_{average}$ (Å)	31.8	29.2	41	39.1	38.6	54.5

[a]Volume calculations are based on Guinier $I(0)$.
The set of parameters can be used comparatively to suggest changes in RNA compaction or flexibility. Compaction is readily identified by simultaneous decreases in R_g, V_c, d_{max}, $r_{average}$ and particle volume, whereas changes in the flexible state of the RNA can be implied by changes in the Porod–Debye exponent, P_E.

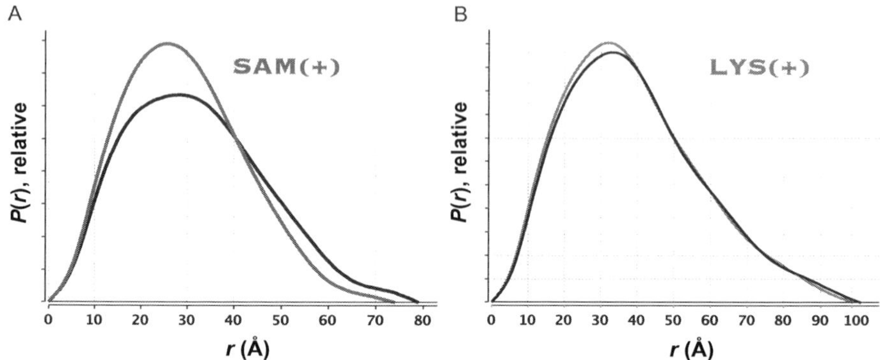

Figure 11.7 Normalized *P*(*r*)-distributions demonstrating conformational differences. Each distribution is scaled by $I(0)^{-1}$ and normalizes for RNA concentration and volume. (A) SAM-I riboswitch in the presence (red) and absence (black) of ligand. Large increase in peak height and narrowing of the distribution suggests significant compaction of the RNA in the presence of ligand. (B) LYS riboswitch in the presence (blue) and absence (black) of ligand. Overlay shows small but significant differences suggesting a small conformational change occurs upon binding. (See the color plate.)

multiconformer state will occupy a larger apparent volume suggesting the riboswitch goes from a collapsed single species to a multiconformer state. In fact, the SAXS data of the free state could not be modeled without using an ensemble of structures (Stoddard et al., 2010). The ensemble illustrated an opening of the SAM binding site akin to a conformational capture mechanism. Furthermore, the delocalization of the SAM-riboswitch in the free state is also apparent in the *P*(*r*) distribution (Fig. 11.7A). Overlaying and normalizing the *P*(*r*) distributions of the (+) and (−) states to their respective *I*(0) values shows a large decrease in peak height and spreading of the SAM (−) *P*(*r*) distribution.

5.2. LYS riboswitch

In contrast, the LYS riboswitch SAXS experiments detail a much different binding mechanism. The X-ray crystal structure of the (+) lysine state showed the ligand to be completely buried within the RNA. Furthermore, crystallization in the (−) lysine state illustrated a nearly identical arrangement of nucleotides comprising the binding pocket, suggesting a conformational change must be necessary to promote substrate recognition before encapsulation. Solution-state experiments using chemical probing showed the (−) and (+) lysine states to be nearly identical, thus arguing that the recognition and binding of the substrate occurs as a small perturbation to the RNA structure. As mentioned above, the most reliable method for detecting small differences by SAXS will be through a direct comparison of the normalized *P*(*r*) distributions (Fig. 11.7A). Here, comparison of the *P*(*r*) distributions (q_{max} = 0.31 Å^{-1}) shows a small (~2 Å) decrease in d_{max} as the riboswitch transitions to the (+) state with slight but significant changes throughout the *P*(*r*) distribution. Illustrated by the transition to the (+) lysine state, compaction of objects of the same mass and composition will show an increase in the *P*(*r*) peak height with a corresponding decrease (1.5%) in R_g (Table 11.4). However, comparing the Guinier R_g values show an opposite effect, a 4% increase during the transition to the (+) state. The inconsistencies between real and reciprocal space R_g highlights the sensitivity and reliability of the Guinier region for detecting small differences. Nonetheless, we see no change in P_E between the two states (Table 11.4), suggesting the riboswitch maintains the same thermodynamic state of compactness and conclude that switching occurs through a small lysine stabilized conformational change.

6. MULTIPHASE VOLUMETRIC MODELING

Volumetric modeling of RNA SAXS data using DAMMIN/F (Svergun, 1999) provides a low-resolution three-dimensional shape of the thermodynamic state. Since this shape will be the average of the thermodynamic ensemble, the structural interpretation of the shape must be informed by the SAXS parameters mentioned above. Unrealistic particle volumes (V_P), low P_E values or significant differences between real and reciprocal space values suggest aggregation or a flexible unfolded state. Volumetric models in these cases of aggregation or flexible particles will contain artifacts and loose details in the averaged model. Regardless, volumetric models will be difficult to interpret at the secondary structure level without performing additional SAXS experiments using derivatives of the RNA. For the VS ribozyme (Lipfert, Ouellet, Norman, Doniach, & Lilley, 2008) and HIV REV response element (Fang et al., 2013), comparative DAMMIN/F modeling of various helical deletion or extension constructs inferred the location of secondary structure elements such that an all atom model of the RNA could be constructed. This inferred approach required significant structural features to exist in the base model to facilitate the alignment of the various constructs.

A more reliable method for locating secondary structure elements within SAXS volumetric models can be achieved with the program MONSA (Svergun & Nierhaus, 2000; Svergun, Petoukhov, & Koch, 2001). MONSA is a multiphase modeling algorithm that can integrate all the input SAXS information during a single modeling run. Helical extensions or deletions are modeled as separate volume elements (phases) with their relative arrangements in three-dimensional space unambiguously determined notwithstanding mirror symmetry or severe changes to the base structure. Consider a SAXS experiment on a structured RNA with a 12-bp extension. MONSA would require two separate SAXS curves (wild-type and wild-type plus extension) with estimates of the volume elements specifying the wild-type RNA and the extension. The volumes can be determined from V_P with V_P (extension) taken as the difference from the two curves. As with DAMMIN/F, 15–20 independent modeling runs should be performed and averaged.

6.1. B_{12} riboswitch

To test MONSA in RNA modeling, we performed modeling on synthetic data created from the *E. coli* B_{12} riboswitch (PDB 4GMA). Here, a deletion of the P1,3 regulatory stem-loop was made (Fig. 11.8), and simulated SAXS data for the full-length and deletion constructs were used in modeling. In this example, we only specified the volume of the (−) P1,3 (117,000 Å^3) construct, leaving the volume for the P1,3 stem-loop constrained by the SAXS data. MONSA produced two volumetric models (Fig. 11.8E) in their relative arrangement clearly identifying the location of P1,3. Though the P1,3 volume was unconstrained, the averaged volume shows a density consistent with the P1,3 stem-loop (Fig. 11.8F). The P1,3 stem-loop is 27 nucleotides representing 12.8% of the riboswitch; in our experience, we have used MONSA to identify differences as small as 6 kDa in the volumetric models. In practice, the volume for each phase should be specified but multirounds of MONSA can be performed where one of the phases is left unconstrained. Leaving a phase unconstrained is a useful strategy to evaluate the quality of the samples as the final volume should be consistent with expectations. In addition, each MONSA run must be initiated with a different random number seed to insure independence for the final model averaging step by DAMAVER.

7. GOLD LABELS AND COMPREHENSIVE CONFORMATIONS

A major strength of SAXS is the ability to be high-throughput and therefore to provide comprehensive analysis of macromolecules under many biologically relevant conditions. Although not yet utilized for RNA, the sample preparations and analytical tools have been developed for DNA using nanogold labels (5-nm gold balls) (Hura, Tsai, et al., 2013). This technique

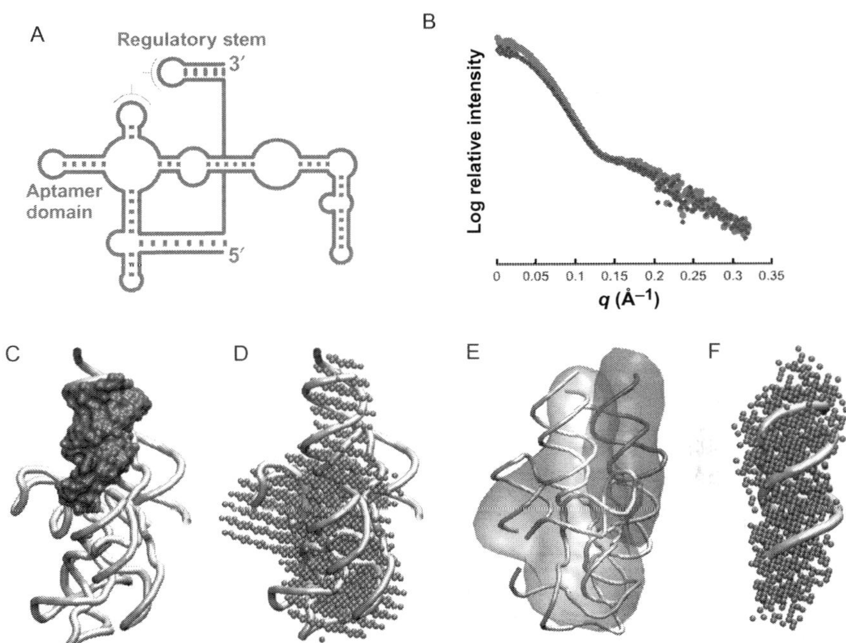

Figure 11.8 Secondary structure identification within volumetric model using MONSA. (A) Secondary structure of B_{12} riboswitch (Johnson et al., 2012). Full-length RNA (WT) is divided into two independent domains: (1) aptamer domain (APT, gray) and (2) regulatory P1,3 stem. (B) Simulated SAXS data with noise for WT (purple) and APT (gray). Data were simulated with CRYSOL (Svergun et al., 1995) using default parameters. Noise was transposed onto the simulated datasets from real SAXS data using a Gaussian sampling algorithm. (C) Atomistic model (PDB 4GMA) showing orientation of regulatory stem (purple) and APT (gray). (D) Averaged volumetric model (beads) of the APT volume calculated using MONSA from the SAXS data in B. (E) Averaged volumetric model of the APT domain (gray) and regulatory stem (purple). Relative orientation of the two volumes was determined by MONSA during the *ab initio* modeling using the SAXS data in B. (F) Alignment of the regulatory stem within the MONSA volume. In this example, only the APT volume (V_P^{APT}) was constrained during the MONSA modeling. V_P^{APT} was determined as the Porod volume using the program ScÅtter available at www.bioisis.net. In practice, the final model will be an average of 15–20 MONSA runs with the volume of each phase (APT domain and P13 stem) constrained during the MONSA modeling. All atomistic models were superimposed using SUPCOMB (Kozin & Svergun, 2001). (See the color plate.)

can examine short or long sequences of nucleic acids in most solution conditions, including those closest to cellular environments. Gold atoms have an electron (e^-) density greater than protein and RNA ($4.6e^-/Å^3$ for gold nanocrystals vs. 0.43 and $0.55e^-/Å^3$ for protein or nucleic acid, respectively). In water, the measured scattering of a gold nanocrystal with 50 Å diameter was 5400-fold higher than that of 31-bp dsDNA (Hura, Tsai, et al., 2013). Thus, measured scattering in mixed systems containing gold nanocrystals, nucleic acids, and proteins is dominated by the gold signal. Selective labeling methods can be used to identity specific secondary structure elements or follow small conformational changes. In practice, the gold is in the form of a nanocrystal coated with a neutral PEG ligand. Experiments with the protein ATPase MutS and dsDNA labeled at both ends provided end-to-end distance measurements under a variety of salt concentrations (0–200 m*M* NaCl). The nanogold labels did not precipitate protein, are stable, and may be useful in designing experiments to understand RNA and RNA–protein mechanisms.

Other developments relevant to detecting conformation changes, are the SAXS structural comparison map (SCM) and volatility of ratio (V_R) difference metric (Hura, Budworth, et al., 2013), which together provide quantitative and superposition-independent evaluation of solution-state conformations. SCMs are diagonally symmetric matrices that contain the set of pairwise agreements from a collection of SAXS curves. SCMs can be color mapped to illustrate the degree of similarity among multiple conformations. V_R, which is visually displayed in an SCM, is given by the ratio between two experimental SAXS profiles. This ratio is normalized such that the average across a specified resolution range is 1 and V_R is determined from a binned partition of the ratio. For $d_{max} < 400$ Å and $q < 0.2$ Å^{-1}, we suggest using 25 bins.

SAXS experiments on human MSH2-MSH3 ATPase in complex with mismatch or normal DNA in the presence of various nucleotide ligands resulted in a large number of curves to analyze. V_R calculations and creation of an SCM efficiently revealed multiple unique conformational states showing how the different nucleotide ligands drive the sculpting of the DNA conformation (Hura, Budworth, et al., 2013). Furthermore, V_R-based SCM approaches were successful at resolving various discrete translation states of the ribosome (Fig. 11.9). It will be interesting to see V_R applied to riboswitches and to RNA in general where high-throughput SAXS experiments that explore condition space together with SCMs can help uncover novel functional states.

8. CONSIDERATIONS

Macromolecular crystallography provides unmatched precision in the analysis of specific RNA riboswitch structural states. However, the methods and results presented here show that flexibility, disorder, conformational

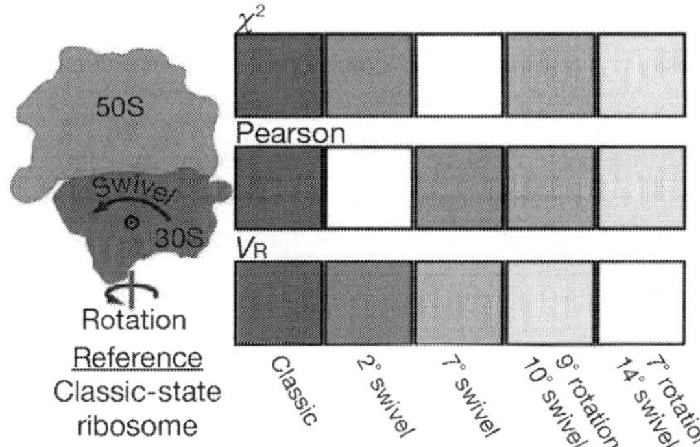

Figure 11.9 SAXS applied to measure structural similarity. χ^2, Pearson correlation coefficient and V_R scores were assigned a gradient color from red (high similarity) to white (low similarity). Comparison of ribosomal structures solved with the 30S subunit rotated about two axes (annotated by rotation and swivel degree) relative to the 50S subunit. Left to right: Protein Data Bank reference structures 3R8T:4GD2, 3I21:3I22, 3I1O:3I1P, 3R8S:4GD1, and 3UOQ:3UOS. *Adapted from Hura, Budworth, et al. (2013).* (See the color plate.)

variation, and other aspects of dynamic states, defined by biological SAXS experiments, are critical to an accurate description of RNA biology, activity, and mechanisms. Fortunately, SAXS data interpretation tools and technologies are evolving at a rapid pace due to the involvement of a growing group of developers and users (Gajda et al., 2013; Kofinger & Hummer, 2013; Moore, 2014; Pollack, 2011; Rambo & Tainer, 2013a; Schneidman-Duhovny, Hammel, & Sali, 2011; Schneidman-Duhovny et al., 2013; Yang et al., 2010). A critical component for these developments has been the accessibility of SAXS experimental data for both for structural validation and for software development.

As we outlined here, SAXS is a multidimensional structural technique that can both inform on sample quality and mechanisms of activity and therefore should be considered in any structural analyses of RNA. Besides complementing X-ray crystallography, electron microscopy, and NMR, SAXS provides fundamental information about macromolecular interfaces and their solvent interactions. This information can be used to drive biological research into areas previously unavailable and to suggest improvements in the analysis of data from other methods, such as NMR and crystallography. New and updated SAXS beamlines and laboratory equipment are expanding the user community and the types of biological problems amendable to SAXS (Perez & Nishino, 2012). The growth of SAXS is stimulating experts to develop improved experimental and computational methods.

Yet, despite many seminal SAXS advances, the information in the comprehensive set of electron pair distances that is specified by the *P*(*r*)-distribution remains greatly underappreciated and underutilized. Therefore, there exists great scope for continued advances of SAXS over the next decade. Ultimately, a more complete description of the thermodynamic ensemble from SAXS experiments may help reduce the increasing complexity of macromolecular structural biology by contributing to general principles of interaction, conformation, and mechanism.

ACKNOWLEDGMENTS

We are grateful to Michal Hammel, Greg Hura, and Robert T. Batey for insightful discussions. This work is supported in part by funding to foster collaboration with Bruker and Lawrence Berkeley National Laboratory on Novel Technology for Structural Biology. The SIBYLS beamline (BL12.3.1) facility and team at the ALS is supported by United States Department of Energy program Integrated Diffraction Analysis Technologies DEAC02-05CH11231 and by the National Institute of Health Grant R01GM105404.

REFERENCES

Baird, N. J., & Ferre-D'Amare, A. R. (2010). Idiosyncratically tuned switching behavior of riboswitch aptamer domains revealed by comparative small-angle X-ray scattering analysis. *RNA*, *16*, 598–609.

Batey, R. T., & Kieft, J. S. (2007). Improved native affinity purification of RNA. *RNA*, *13*, 1384–1389.

Beckert, B., & Masquida, B. (2011). Synthesis of RNA by in vitro transcription. *Methods in Molecular Biology*, *703*, 29–41.

Chacon, P., Diaz, J. F., Moran, F., & Andreu, J. M. (2000). Reconstruction of protein form with X-ray solution scattering and a genetic algorithm. *Journal of Molecular Biology*, *299*, 1289–1302.

Chen, B., Zuo, X., Wang, Y. X., & Dayie, T. K. (2012). Multiple conformations of SAM-II riboswitch detected with SAXS and NMR spectroscopy. *Nucleic Acids Research*, *40*, 3117–3130.

Ciccariello, S., Goodisman, J., & Brumberger, H. (1988). On the Porod law. *Journal of Applied Crystallography*, *21*, 117–128.

Classen, S., Hura, G. L., Holton, J. M., Rambo, R. P., Rodic, I., McGuire, P. J., et al. (2013). Implementation and performance of SIBYLS: A dual endstation small-angle X-ray scattering and macromolecular crystallography beamline at the Advanced Light Source. *Journal of Applied Crystallography*, *46*, 1–13.

Costantino, D. A., Pfingsten, J. S., Rambo, R. P., & Kieft, J. S. (2008). tRNA-mRNA mimicry drives translation initiation from a viral IRES. *Nature Structural & Molecular Biology*, *15*, 57–64.

Daldrop, P., Reyes, F. E., Robinson, D. A., Hammond, C. M., Lilley, D. M., Batey, R. T., et al. (2011). Novel ligands for a purine riboswitch discovered by RNA-ligand docking. *Chemistry & Biology*, *18*, 324–335.

Debye, P., Anderson, H. R., & Brumberger, H. (1957). Scattering by an inhomogeneous solid. II. The correlation function and its application. *Journal of Applied Physics*, *28*, 5.

Durand, D., Vives, C., Cannella, D., Perez, J., Pebay-Peyroula, E., Vachette, P., et al. (2010). NADPH oxidase activator p67(phox) behaves in solution as a multidomain protein with semi-flexible linkers. *Journal of Structural Biology*, *169*, 45–53.

Fang, X., Wang, J., O'Carroll, I. P., Mitchell, M., Zuo, X., Wang, Y., et al. (2013). An unusual topological structure of the HIV-1 Rev response element. *Cell, 155*, 594–605.

Frieda, K. L., & Block, S. M. (2012). Direct observation of cotranscriptional folding in an adenine riboswitch. *Science, 338*, 397–400.

Gajda, M. J., Martinez Zapien, D., Uchikawa, E., & Dock-Bregeon, A. C. (2013). Modeling the structure of RNA molecules with small-angle X-ray scattering data. *PloS One, 8*, e78007.

Garst, A. D., & Batey, R. T. (2009). A switch in time: Detailing the life of a riboswitch. *Biochimica et Biophysica Acta, 1789*, 584–591.

Garst, A. D., Heroux, A., Rambo, R. P., & Batey, R. T. (2008). Crystal structure of the lysine riboswitch regulatory mRNA element. *The Journal of Biological Chemistry, 283*, 22347–22351.

Gilbert, S. D., & Batey, R. T. (2009). Monitoring RNA-ligand interactions using isothermal titration calorimetry. *Methods in Molecular Biology, 540*, 97–114.

Glatter, O., & Kratky, O. (1982). *Small angle X-ray scattering*. London; New York: Academic Press.

Gopal, A., Zhou, Z. H., Knobler, C. M., & Gelbart, W. M. (2012). Visualizing large RNA molecules in solution. *RNA, 18*, 284–299.

Grishaev, A., Guo, L., Irving, T., & Bax, A. (2010). Improved fitting of solution X-ray scattering data to macromolecular structures and structural ensembles by explicit water modeling. *Journal of the American Chemical Society, 132*, 15484–15486.

Hammond, J. A., Rambo, R. P., Filbin, M. E., & Kieft, J. S. (2009). Comparison and functional implications of the 3D architectures of viral tRNA-like structures. *RNA, 15*, 294–307.

Hammond, J. A., Rambo, R. P., & Kieft, J. S. (2010). Multi-domain packing in the aminoacylatable 3′ end of a plant viral RNA. *Journal of Molecular Biology, 399*, 450–463.

Hura, G. L., Budworth, H., Dyer, K. N., Rambo, R. P., Hammel, M., McMurray, C. T., et al. (2013). Comprehensive macromolecular conformations mapped by quantitative SAXS analyses. *Nature Methods, 10*, 453–454.

Hura, G. L., Menon, A. L., Hammel, M., Rambo, R. P., Poole, F. L., II, Tsutakawa, S. E., et al. (2009). Robust, high-throughput solution structural analyses by small angle X-ray scattering (SAXS). *Nature Methods, 6*, 606–612.

Hura, G. L., Tsai, C. L., Claridge, S. A., Mendillo, M. L., Smith, J. M., Williams, G. J., et al. (2013). DNA conformations in mismatch repair probed in solution by X-ray scattering from gold nanocrystals. *Proceedings of the National Academy of Sciences of the United States of America, 110*, 17308–17313.

John, D. M., Merino, E. J., & Weeks, K. M. (2004). Mechanics of DNA flexibility visualized by selective 2′-amine acylation at nucleotide bulges. *Journal of Molecular Biology, 337*, 611–619.

Johnson, J. E., Jr., Reyes, F. E., Polaski, J. T., & Batey, R. T. (2012). B12 cofactors directly stabilize an mRNA regulatory switch. *Nature, 492*, 133–137.

Kazantsev, A. V., Rambo, R. P., Karimpour, S., Santalucia, J., Jr., Tainer, J. A., & Pace, N. R. (2011). Solution structure of RNase P RNA. *RNA, 17*, 1159–1171.

Kofinger, J., & Hummer, G. (2013). Atomic-resolution structural information from scattering experiments on macromolecules in solution. *Physical Review. E, Statistical, Nonlinear, and Soft Matter Physics, 87*, 052712.

Kozin, M. B., & Svergun, D. I. (2001). Automated matching of high- and low-resolution structural models. *Journal of Applied Crystallography, 34*, 33–41.

Lipfert, J., Ouellet, J., Norman, D. G., Doniach, S., & Lilley, D. M. (2008). The complete VS ribozyme in solution studied by small-angle X-ray scattering. *Structure, 16*, 1357–1367.

Liu, H., Morris, R. J., Hexemer, A., Grandison, S., & Zwart, P. H. (2012). Computation of small-angle scattering profiles with three-dimensional Zernike polynomials. *Acta Crystallographica. Section A, 68*, 278–285.

Liu, H., & Zwart, P. H. (2012). Determining pair distance distribution function from SAXS data using parametric functionals. *Journal of Structural Biology, 180*, 226–234.

Moore, P. (1980). Small-angle scattering. Information content and error analysis. *Journal of Applied Crystallography, 13*, 168–175.

Moore, P. B. (2014). The effects of thermal disorder on the solution-scattering profiles of macromolecules. *Biophysical Journal, 106*, 1489–1496.

Murphy, F. L., & Cech, T. R. (1993). An independently folding domain of RNA tertiary structure within the Tetrahymena ribozyme. *Biochemistry, 32*, 5291–5300.

Orthaber, D., Bergmann, A., & Glatter, O. (2000). SAXS experiments on absolute scale with Kratky systems using water as a secondary standard. *Journal of Applied Crystallography, 33*, 218–225.

Perdrizet, G. A., II, Artsimovitch, I., Furman, R., Sosnick, T. R., & Pan, T. (2012). Transcriptional pausing coordinates folding of the aptamer domain and the expression platform of a riboswitch. *Proceedings of the National Academy of Sciences of the United States of America, 109*, 3323–3328.

Perez, J., & Nishino, Y. (2012). Advances in X-ray scattering: From solution SAXS to achievements with coherent beams. *Current Opinion in Structural Biology, 22*, 670–678.

Perry, J. J., & Tainer, J. A. (2013). Developing advanced X-ray scattering methods combined with crystallography and computation. *Methods, 59*, 363–371.

Peselis, A., & Serganov, A. (2014). Themes and variations in riboswitch structure and function. *Biochimica et Biophysica Acta, 1839*, 908–918.

Petoukhov, M. V., & Svergun, D. I. (2013). Applications of small-angle X-ray scattering to biomacromolecular solutions. *The International Journal of Biochemistry & Cell Biology, 45*, 429–437.

Poitevin, F., Orland, H., Doniach, S., Koehl, P., & Delarue, M. (2011). AquaSAXS: A web server for computation and fitting of SAXS profiles with non-uniformally hydrated atomic models. *Nucleic Acids Research, 39*, W184–W189.

Pollack, L. (2011). Time resolved SAXS and RNA folding. *Biopolymers, 95*, 543–549.

Putnam, C. D., Hammel, M., Hura, G. L., & Tainer, J. A. (2007). X-ray solution scattering (SAXS) combined with crystallography and computation: Defining accurate macromolecular structures, conformations and assemblies in solution. *Quarterly Reviews of Biophysics, 40*, 191–285.

Rambo, R. P., & Doudna, J. A. (2004). Assembly of an active group II intron-maturase complex by protein dimerization. *Biochemistry, 43*, 6486–6497.

Rambo, R. P., & Tainer, J. A. (2010a). Bridging the solution divide: Comprehensive structural analyses of dynamic RNA, DNA, and protein assemblies by small-angle X-ray scattering. *Current Opinion in Structural Biology, 20*, 128–137.

Rambo, R. P., & Tainer, J. A. (2010b). Improving small-angle X-ray scattering data for structural analyses of the RNA world. *RNA, 16*, 638–646.

Rambo, R. P., & Tainer, J. A. (2011). Characterizing flexible and intrinsically unstructured biological macromolecules by SAS using the Porod-Debye law. *Biopolymers, 95*, 559–571.

Rambo, R. P., & Tainer, J. A. (2013a). Accurate assessment of mass, models and resolution by small-angle scattering. *Nature, 496*, 477–481.

Rambo, R. P., & Tainer, J. A. (2013b). Super-resolution in solution X-ray scattering and its applications to structural systems biology. *Annual Review of Biophysics, 42*, 415–441.

Receveur-Brechot, V., & Durand, D. (2012). How random are intrinsically disordered proteins? A small angle scattering perspective. *Current Protein & Peptide Science, 13*, 55–75.

Reining, A., Nozinovic, S., Schlepckow, K., Buhr, F., Furtig, B., & Schwalbe, H. (2013). Three-state mechanism couples ligand and temperature sensing in riboswitches. *Nature, 499*, 355–359.

Ribitsch, G., De Clercq, R., Folkhard, W., Zipper, P., Schurz, J., & Clauwaert, J. (1985). Small-angle X-ray and light scattering studies on the influence of Mg^{2+} ions on the structure of the RNA from bacteriophage MS2. *Zeitschrift für Naturforschung. Section C, 40*, 234–241.

Schneidman-Duhovny, D., Hammel, M., & Sali, A. (2011). Macromolecular docking restrained by a small angle X-ray scattering profile. *Journal of Structural Biology, 173*, 461–471.

Schneidman-Duhovny, D., Hammel, M., Tainer, J. A., & Sali, A. (2013). Accurate SAXS profile computation and its assessment by contrast variation experiments. *Biophysical Journal, 105*, 962–974.

Serganov, A., Huang, L., & Patel, D. J. (2008). Structural insights into amino acid binding and gene control by a lysine riboswitch. *Nature, 455*, 1263–1267.

Sibille, N., & Bernado, P. (2012). Structural characterization of intrinsically disordered proteins by the combined use of NMR and SAXS. *Biochemical Society Transactions, 40*, 955–962.

Stoddard, C. D., Montange, R. K., Hennelly, S. P., Rambo, R. P., Sanbonmatsu, K. Y., & Batey, R. T. (2010). Free state conformational sampling of the SAM-I riboswitch aptamer domain. *Structure, 18*, 787–797.

Strulson, C. A., Yennawar, N. H., Rambo, R. P., & Bevilacqua, P. C. (2013). Molecular crowding favors reactivity of a human ribozyme under physiological ionic conditions. *Biochemistry, 52*, 8187–8197.

Svergun, D. (1992). Determination of the regularization parameter in indirect-transform methods using perceptual criteria. *Journal of Applied Crystallography, 25*, 495–503.

Svergun, D. I. (1999). Restoring low resolution structure of biological macromolecules from solution scattering using simulated annealing. *Biophysical Journal, 76*, 2879–2886.

Svergun, D., Barberato, C., & Koch, M. H. J. (1995). CRYSOL—a program to evaluate X-ray solution scattering of biological macromolecules from atomic coordinates. *Journal of Applied Crystallography, 28*, 768–773.

Svergun, D. I., Feĭgin, L. A., & Taylor, G. W. (1987). *Structure analysis by small-angle X-ray and neutron scattering*. New York: Plenum Press.

Svergun, D. I., & Nierhaus, K. H. (2000). A map of protein-rRNA distribution in the 70 S *Escherichia coli* ribosome. *The Journal of Biological Chemistry, 275*, 14432–14439.

Svergun, D. I., Petoukhov, M. V., & Koch, M. H. (2001). Determination of domain structure of proteins from X-ray solution scattering. *Biophysical Journal, 80*, 2946–2953.

Trausch, J. J., Xu, Z., Edwards, A. L., Reyes, F. E., Ross, P. E., Knight, R., et al. (2014). Structural basis for diversity in the SAM clan of riboswitches. *Proceedings of the National Academy of Sciences of the United States of America, 111*, 6624–6629.

Vicens, Q., Mondragon, E., & Batey, R. T. (2011). Molecular sensing by the aptamer domain of the FMN riboswitch: A general model for ligand binding by conformational selection. *Nucleic Acids Research, 39*, 8586–8598.

Wang, Y., & Jernigan, R. L. (2005). Comparison of tRNA motions in the free and ribosomal bound structures. *Biophysical Journal, 89*, 3399–3409.

Woodson, S. A., & Koculi, E. (2009). Analysis of RNA folding by native polyacrylamide gel electrophoresis. *Methods in Enzymology, 469*, 189–208.

Wyatt, P. (1993). Light scattering and the absolute characterization of macromolecules. *Analytica Chimica Acta, 272*, 1–40.

Yang, S., Parisien, M., Major, F., & Roux, B. (2010). RNA structure determination using SAXS data. *The Journal of Physical Chemistry. B, 114*, 10039–10048.

Zhang, J., Jones, C. P., & Ferre-D'Amare, A. R. (2014). Global analysis of riboswitches by small-angle X-ray scattering and calorimetry. *Biochimica et Biophysica Acta, 1839*, 1020–1029.

PART IV

Dynamics

CHAPTER TWELVE

Use of ^{19}F NMR Methods to Probe Conformational Heterogeneity and Dynamics of Exchange in Functional RNA Molecules

Caijie Zhao*, Clemens Anklin†, Nancy L. Greenbaum*,[1]

*Hunter College and The Graduate Center of The City University of New York, New York, USA
†Bruker BioSpin Corp., Billerica MA, USA
[1]Corresponding author: e-mail address: nancy.greenbaum@hunter.cuny.edu

Contents

Abstract

Functional RNA molecules are often very plastic and often undergo changes in base-pairing patterns to achieve alternative secondary and tertiary conformations associated with their roles in multiple events in gene expression. Solution NMR techniques are an excellent tool for the analysis of conformational heterogeneity and dynamic exchange. In this work, we measure the rates associated with spontaneous interconversion between major conformers in folded RNA sequences by use of a ^{19}F–^{19}F EXSY NMR experiment, taking advantage of RNA samples carrying a single 5-^{19}F-pyrimidine label. We first utilize this approach to determine kinetic exchange rates between conformers in a model RNA stem loop capable of adopting two conformations. We then probe the dynamics of conformational rearrangements in a larger RNA construct, the U2–U6 snRNA complex of the human spliceosome. In the case of the U2–U6 snRNA complex,

Methods in Enzymology, Volume 549
ISSN 0076-6879
http://dx.doi.org/10.1016/B978-0-12-801122-5.00012-X

such a rearrangement in the context of the intact spliceosome may have critical implications in splicing activity.

1. INTRODUCTION

Biomolecular structures are dynamic, exhibiting motions on many timescales ranging from sub-pico- or nanoseconds to seconds or minutes (Bothe et al., 2011). The most rapid motions are associated with stretching of bonds, bending of bond angles and rotation; slower motions correspond to biomolecular folding and global conformational change. For biologically active, noncoding RNA molecules, such as ribozymes, snRNA, and riboswitches, biological activity is often accompanied by such conformational change involving altered base-pairing patterns. Elucidation of the biological activity of these functional RNA molecules requires an understanding of these motions. Thus, it is essential to characterize the distribution of folds and the dynamics of conformational interconversion.

Structural heterogeneity of RNA, i.e., the distribution of alternative folds, can be measured through a number of approaches, including gel electrophoretic mobility (Zarrinkar & Williamson, 1994), enzymatic, or chemical probing (Biondi & Burke, 2014; Low et al., 2014), fluorescence resonance energy transfer (FRET) spectroscopy (Guo, Karunatilaka, & Rueda, 2009; Haller, Altman, Souliere, Blanchard, & Micura, 2013), solution-state NMR spectroscopy (D'Souza & Summers, 2004; Gonzalez & Tinoco, 1999), and computational simulation (Xu & Chen, 2012). Information obtained from different methods has made it possible to map the RNA free-energy landscape, which contains useful information about steady-state distribution and dynamic interconversion between conformers. Because of an incomplete understanding of RNA structural features, it is not yet possible to predict full details in the free-energy landscape; however, measurements of dynamic exchange among populated RNA conformers by solution-state NMR contributes valuable information about biologically important conformations.

Solution-state NMR has unique advantages in measuring the dynamics of biological molecules such as protein and nucleic acids. Nuclei typically observed in NMR studies of RNA include ^{1}H, ^{13}C, ^{15}N, and ^{31}P, which are either naturally present in high abundance (^{1}H and ^{31}P) or can be enriched in RNA oligomers by transcription with labeled nucleotide triphosphates (^{13}C and ^{15}N). NMR approaches monitoring ^{1}H, ^{13}C, or ^{15}N

address a broad range of detection timescales spanning picoseconds to seconds, which enables probing of a many dynamic processes such as base flipping (Reiter, Blad, Abildgaard, & Butcher, 2004), interhelical motions in the interhelical twist (Zhang, Stelzer, Fisher, & Al-Hashimi, 2007), sugar puckering transitions (Johnson & Hoogstraten, 2008), and conformational rearrangement between conformers (Kloiber, Spitzer, Tollinger, Konrat, & Kreutz, 2011; Lee, Dethoff, & Al-Hashimi, 2014). In addition, specific NMR techniques have been developed that can focus on the entire structure and on the particular sites within a molecule. The recent development of the nonuniform sampling technique, which enables rapid detection of multidimensional experiments, provides an excellent way for measuring structural rearrangements induced by binding of ligands dynamically (Schmieder, Stern, Wagner, & Hoch, 1993; Tugarinov, Kay, Ibraghimov, & Orekhov, 2005).

The application of heteronuclear NMR experiments significantly improves the spectra overlap that is generally encountered in ^{1}H NMR spectra, but it may still be difficult to monitor individual nucleotides, particularly in the case of conformational heterogeneity. One way around this complication is observation of a molecule into which a single ^{13}C- or ^{15}N-labeled nucleotide has been incorporated by chemical synthesis (Kloiber et al., 2011). An unfortunate limitation of this approach is that the isotopically labeled phosphoramidites are not commercially available and thus require specialized chemical synthesis expertise.

Thus, the introduction of an additional NMR active heteronucleus, such as ^{19}F, enhances the opportunities for structural analysis without the technical difficulty associated with incorporation of a single ^{13}C or ^{15}N nucleus. ^{19}F-labeled nucleotides, while not naturally appearing in RNA molecules, can be incorporated in oligomers by solid-phase synthesis (including commercial syntheses). Common locations for ^{19}F substitution include the 5-position of pyrimidine bases and the 2′-position in a purine ribose. Previous research revealed that incorporation of ^{19}F in these positions was a useful method for identifying distribution between two conformers of a bistable RNA stem loop (i.e., a sequence capable of adopting two fold; Kreutz, Kahlig, Konrat, & Micura, 2005; Puffer et al., 2009) and did not alter the thermal stability of the folded RNA molecules (although incorporation of ^{19}F-substituted ribose in a pyrimidine increased thermal stability; Kreutz et al., 2005). If more than one structural context, or environment, of the ^{19}F-labeled nucleotide is present in the population of folded RNA molecules, resonance peaks representing each of these environments will appear in the resulting spectrum with peak area corresponding to fractional representation. These observations provide the basis for utilizing ^{19}F NMR for measurement of RNA dynamics.

By comparison with the complexity associated with the analysis of ^{1}H, ^{13}C, and ^{15}N spectra containing large numbers of resonance peaks, ^{19}F NMR spectra of oligomers into which a single ^{19}F nucleus has been introduced greatly simplify the analysis of the behavior of that site. An additional advantage of the ^{19}F nucleus is its high NMR sensitivity (0.83 times the sensitivity of ^{1}H, 52.4 and 228.2 times that of ^{13}C and ^{15}N, respectively). Moreover, the sensitivity of the fluorine chemical shift to its environment is considerably greater than that of ^{1}H because of the larger number of electrons surrounding the ^{19}F nucleus. In particular, there is a marked difference in chemical shift of ^{19}F localized in a double-stranded versus single-stranded region, thus providing an excellent reporter for base-pairing status. Finally, exchange between conformations on multiple timescales can be readily observed for ^{19}F-labeled samples. These advantages contribute to making ^{19}F NMR, a valuable approach for monitoring the environment of a specific site in an RNA oligomer. Here, we illustrate the application of ^{19}F NMR to probe the RNA conformational heterogeneity and dynamics in both a model molecule and a biological functioning complex.

2. METHODS

2.1. Sample design

NMR spectroscopy experiments designed to monitor the structural context of a ^{19}F nucleus take advantages of the distinct chemical shift differences of a fluorine nucleus when located in different chemical environments, in this case between double- and single-stranded regions. Thus, the key aspect of applying this method is to design the sample with the fluorine label in a useful position, i.e., one that will reflect a change in base-pairing status associated with a conformational change. Chemical shift values for ^{19}F-labeled pyrimidines in double-stranded regions flanked by a specific nucleotide sequence are observed to be upfield of those for single-stranded regions surrounded by the same sequence. However, precise chemical shift values depend upon the substituted nucleotide position and the sequence context should be verified in control oligomers of the same sequence constrained to form either double- or single-stranded conformations (see below).

2.2. Sample preparation

RNA oligomers with ^{19}F-labeled nucleotides in specific positions can be made by solid-phase synthesis and obtained commercially. We obtained our samples of oligomers containing a single ^{19}F-labeled cytidine (C) or uracil (U) from ThermoFisher. As always with chemical synthesis, the yield of full-length oligomers primarily depends on the length of sequence and the substitution of ^{19}F generally does not affect the yield. To obtain an optimal yield of a long-RNA sequence, it may be helpful to consider truncating the full-length sequence into a shorter (unlabeled) oligomer containing an extensive sequence that can be annealed with another strand after the purification of each strand separately. Unlabeled pairing partners can be synthesized chemically or by *in vitro* transcription methods. Individual oligomers are then deprotected and purified by PAGE or HPLC to obtain the desired product. Finally, samples are exchanged into the desired NMR buffer and annealed before NMR experiments. Each of these steps is described in detail in other chapters of this volume.

In the case of a sample containing more than one strand (typically one labeled, one or more unlabeled), it is necessary to assay for essentially complete pairing of the labeled strand. For this reason, it is advisable to include a small excess of the unlabeled strand.

2.3. One-dimensional ^{19}F experiments to identify the distribution of folds

To identify the conformational distribution of the sample, one-dimensional NMR experiments are performed on the ^{19}F-labeled sample using a dedicated ^{19}F NMR probe or a broadband probe tuned to the ^{19}F frequency (94% that of ^{1}H for any field strength). Because of the high sensitivity of the ^{19}F nucleus and large chemical shift dispersion, high-field strength is not necessary for good signal in small oligomers; in fact, chemical shift anisotropy at high-field strength (600 MHz and greater) may contribute to line broadening. If a single site is labeled, all resonance peaks visible in the resulting spectrum reflect the distribution of environments in which the ^{19}F nucleotide is located. If more than one site is labeled, there will be multiple resonance peaks corresponding to the different environments experienced by each ^{19}F nucleus.

Unambiguous assignments are required before further analysis. To establish precise chemical shift values for any system, it is important to obtain accurate assignments in control samples with the same nucleotide sequence as the sample under examination constrained to form either double- or single-stranded conformations. Having obtained unambiguous assignments, one can then analyze the distribution of each conformer by calculating the areas of the peaks corresponding with each conformer.

Once peaks in the sample spectrum are unequivocally assigned, the distribution among conformers can be analyzed from the ratio of the integrated areas under each of the two (or more) peak(s) (example shown in Fig. 12.1B). Several peaks or shoulders falling within the regions of the spectrum corresponding to single- or double-stranded RNA imply the presence of alternative environments or intermediates in folding. Any change in the ratio under different conditions (e.g., variation in temperature, ionic strength, and Mg^{2+} concentration) provides information about the effect of these conditions on the equilibrium population of different folds.

2.4. Two-dimensional ^{19}F–^{19}F EXSY experiments to measure conformational exchange

Two-dimensional ^{19}F–^{19}F EXSY (EXchange SpectroscopY) experiments performed on ^{19}F-labeled RNA molecules, when acquired at different mixing times, provide information about the dynamics of RNA

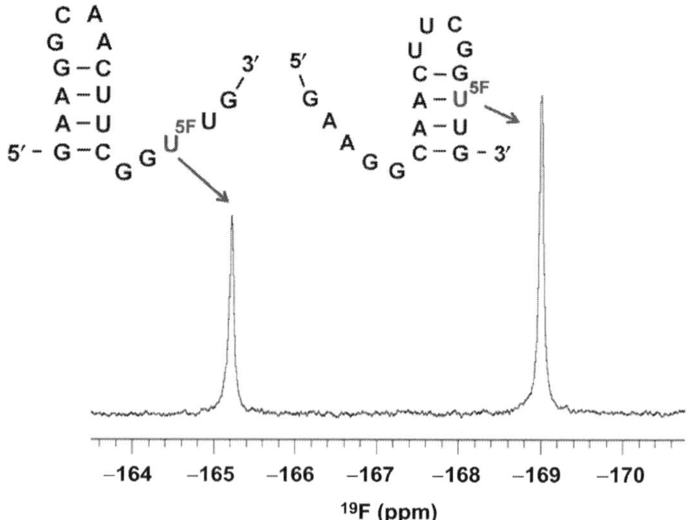

Figure 12.1 Proposed secondary structures of the bistable sample and the one-dimensional ^{19}F spectrum of it. The 5-^{19}F-labeled uridine, marked in the figure, was in either a single- or double-stranded environment, depending upon the fold. The corresponding NMR peaks to each fold were labeled in the figure.

conformational interconversion that occurs on the timescales of milliseconds (Kloiber et al., 2011; Latham, Zimmermann, & Pardi, 2009). Analogous to NOESY experiments, the range of mixing times in EXSY experiments is chosen to overlap with the anticipated timescale of the interconversion process. For example, at a very short mixing time (say, 1 ms), only the auto peaks would be visible, but at longer mixing times (maybe 2–100 ms) the intensity of the cross peaks increases and that of the auto peaks decreases. At even longer mixing times, the cross peaks will decrease (Fig. 12.2).

For each mixing time, the intensities (volumes) of the diagonal (auto) and the exchange (cross) peaks are quantified. The intensity (I) of the auto peaks for the two states and the exchange peaks between them are expressed by the following equations derived by Kay and coworkers (Farrow, Zhang, Forman-Kay, & Kay, 1994):

$$I_{AA}(T) = I_A(0)\left\{-(\lambda_2 - a_{11})e^{-\lambda_1 T} + (\lambda_1 - a_{11})e^{-\lambda_2 T}\right\}/(\lambda_1 - \lambda_2) \quad (12.1)$$

$$I_{BB}(T) = I_B(0)\left\{-(\lambda_2 - a_{22})e^{-\lambda_1 T} + (\lambda_1 - a_{22})e^{-\lambda_2 T}\right\}/(\lambda_1 - \lambda_2) \quad (12.2)$$

$$I_{AB}(T) = I_A(0)\left(a_{21}e^{-\lambda_1 T} - a_{21}e^{-\lambda_2 T}\right)/(\lambda_1 - \lambda_2) \quad (12.3)$$

$$I_{BA}(T) = I_B(0)\left(a_{12}e^{-\lambda_1 T} - a_{12}e^{-\lambda_2 T}\right)/(\lambda_1 - \lambda_2) \quad (12.4)$$

where $a_{11} = R_A + k_{AB}$, $a_{12} = -k_{BA}$, $a_{21} = -k_{AB}$, $a_{22} = R_B + k_{BA}$, $\lambda_1 = {}^1/_2\left\{(a_{11} + a_{22}) + \left[(a_{11} - a_{22})^2 + 4k_{AB}k_{BA}\right]^{1/2}\right\}$, and $\lambda_2 = {}^1/_2\left\{(a_{11} + a_{22}) - \left[(a_{11} - a_{22})^2 + 4k_{AB}k_{BA}\right]^{1/2}\right\}$. T represents the mixing time, R_A and R_B represent the relaxation rates of conformers in states A and B, respectively, and k_{AB} and k_{BA} are kinetic rate constants of the exchange between the states.

From the equations above, one can observe that as the mixing time increases, the intensity of the diagonal peaks I_{AA} and I_{BB} decrease as relative intensity of the cross peaks I_{AB} and I_{BA} builds up until $T = \ln \lambda_1 - \ln \lambda_2$ and then starts to decay. R_A, R_B, k_{AB}, and k_{BA} can then be extracted from simulations of Eqs. (12.1)–(12.4) simultaneously with softwares such as Matlab or Mathematica. Plots of the data generated from these equations for the bistable stem loop are shown in Fig. 12.2B.

Below are two examples illustrating the use of these one-dimensional ^{19}F NMR spectra to analyze conformational distribution of RNA conformers and of two-dimensional ^{19}F–^{19}F EXSY NMR spectra to evaluate the dynamics of conformational interconversion.

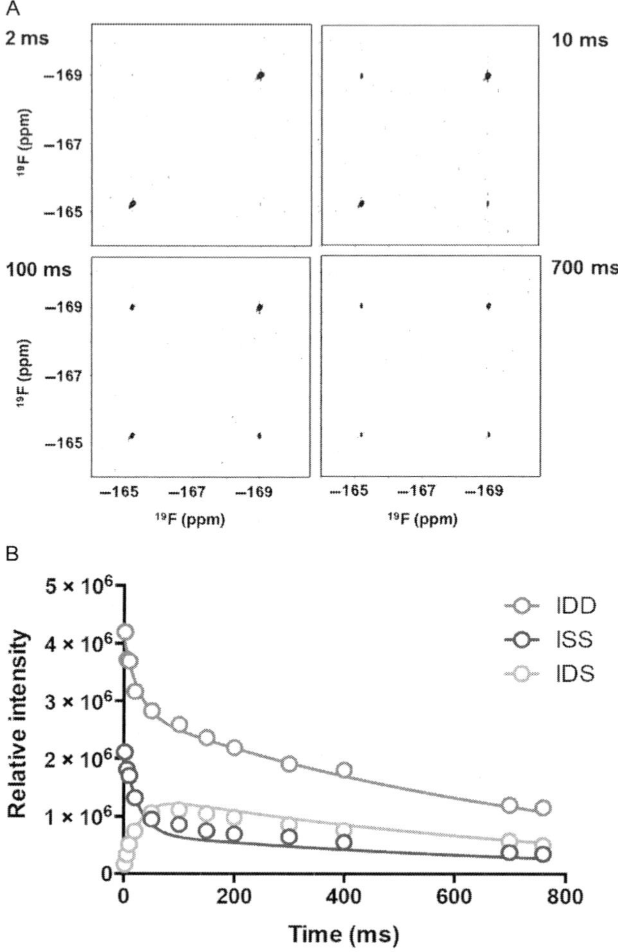

Figure 12.2 (A) Regions of two-dimensional ^{19}F–^{19}F EXSY spectra at mixing times of 2, 10, 100, and 700 ms, as marked. Spectra were acquired at 470.22 MHz. The ^{19}F excitation pulse was 15 μs and relaxation delay was 2.5 s. 4096 × 200 points and 10,527.7 Hz spectral width were used in acquisition. (B) Plot of the intensities of exchange peaks versus the mixing times (2–760 ms) from which exchange values were calculated. In this figure, I_{DD} represents the intensity of the auto peak for double-stranded 5-^{19}F-U, I_{SS} represents the intensity of the auto peak for single-stranded 5-^{19}F-U, I_{SD} and I_{DS} represent the intensities of exchange peaks from "*S*" to "*D*" and vice versa. The curves fit to the data points for I_{SD} and I_{DS} are essentially identical and overlap fully; therefore, only the curve for I_{DS} is shown. Fitting of the curve was achieved using Prism 6 software suite (GraphPad Software Inc.) with in-house written scripts. (See the color plate.)

2.5. Application to analysis of distribution and exchange in a bistable RNA stem loop

A model RNA sequence, 5′-GAAGGCAACUUCGG**^{5F}U**UG-3′, is proposed to adopt two conformations (Fig. 12.1A) in which the 5-F-labeled U resides in single- or double-stranded environments, respectively. A sample of this oligomer was generated by solid-phase synthesis (ThermoFisher) and prepared as described (Section 2.2) to test the feasibility of the method. A similar sequence was used previously to analyze the distribution of two conformers (Kloiber et al., 2011; Puffer et al., 2009); however, the sequence examined by those investigators differs from the sequence used here by having longer base-paired stems and thus considerably slower exchange kinetics.

The one-dimensional ^{19}F NMR spectrum of this model molecule exhibits two ^{19}F peaks with chemical shifts at −165.2 and −169.0 ppm, which were assigned according to values in the literature and attributed to ^{19}F–U in a double- and single-stranded region, respectively (Puffer et al., 2009). The ratio of the areas of the two peaks in a fully relaxed state was calculated to be 0.57:1 (single:double, respectively), corresponding to the distribution of the two conformers (Zhao, Devany, & Greenbaum, 2014).

The distribution of conformers was also evaluated from spectra of exchangeable protons acquired for the same samples under the same conditions with the exception of different temperature. Specifically, we monitored the relative peak areas of characteristic imino proton peaks of guanosines participating in G·A and U·G pairs at the base of the two proposed tetraloops. The presence of these imino proton peaks is consistent with formation of each of these two conformations. However, because the peaks involving exchangeable protons form non-Watson–Crick interactions within a loop, which are likely to engage in different exchange rates with solvent, there is no accurate way to assess the ratio of conformers from the areas of these imino peaks.

To investigate the exchange rate between the two conformers, ^{19}F–^{19}F EXSY experiments were performed at mixing times between 2 and 760 ms. The fact that the two peaks are well separated and relatively sharp based on the size of the molecule suggests that there is very little exchange broadening, implying that the interconversion occurs on a slow dynamic timescale, and the timescale was considered when setting up the mixing time. Representative ^{19}F–^{19}F EXSY spectra acquired with mixing times of 2, 10, 100, and 700 ms are shown in Fig. 12.2. The experiments were repeated at various mixing times. As an illustration of the build up and decay of cross peaks, data showing the changes in intensity for each of the auto- and exchange cross peaks are shown in Fig. 12.2B. The intensity of each diagonal and cross peak was calculated after processing the data with NMR Pipe and fit to Eqs. (12.1)–(12.4) to extract the kinetic parameters. We found that the exchange rate between the two conformers in this case is $37.3 \pm 2.8\,s^{-1}$ (Zhao, Devany, & Greenbaum, 2014).

In principle, it is possible that there is a structural intermediate involved in any exchange process, which would be visible by the appearance of additional resonance peaks. However, we have observed no evidence for presence of intermediates between the two conformers in either ^{19}F or ^{1}H NMR spectra, and have thus applied a two-state model during the calculations of kinetic rates in this case. If more than two conformers present at the same time, a more careful procedure is required to evaluate the kinetics of the system correctly.

Although the example presented above focused on a single model RNA sequence, we note that this same approach can be applied to a wide range of RNA sequences in order to gain further insight into the dynamics and thermodynamics associated with RNA folding and function.

2.6. Application to analysis of distribution and exchange in a biologically significant system

This approach was also applied to a far more complex and biologically important system, that of the protein-free human spliceosomal U2–U6 snRNA complex, which is implicated in mediating catalysis in pre-mRNA splicing (Fabrizio & Abelson, 1990; Madhani & Guthrie, 1992; McPheeters & Abelson, 1992). Previous research reveals that the human U2–U6 snRNA complex binds several catalytically important metal ions at distant sites, implying precise folding (Huppler, Nikstad, Allmann, Brow, & Butcher, 2002; Sontheimer, Sun, & Piccirilli, 1997; Valadkhan & Manley, 2002; Yean, Wuenschell, Termini, & Lin, 2000; Yuan et al., 2007). Moreover, evidence suggesting the likelihood of different active sites for each of the two cleavage reactions (Hilliker, Mefford, & Staley, 2007; Madhani & Guthrie, 1992; Mefford & Staley, 2009; Sun & Manley, 1995) supports a model involving conformational rearrangement during the course of the overall reaction. Data indicating that multiple conformations for the human U2–U6 snRNA complex in the protein-free state (schematic models in Fig. 12.3A) have been obtained from FRET (Karunatilaka & Rueda, 2014) and NMR (Zhao et al., 2013) studies. In particular, one-dimensional ^{19}F NMR spectra from our group of the human U2–U6 snRNA complex labeled with a single 5-^{19}F cytosine in

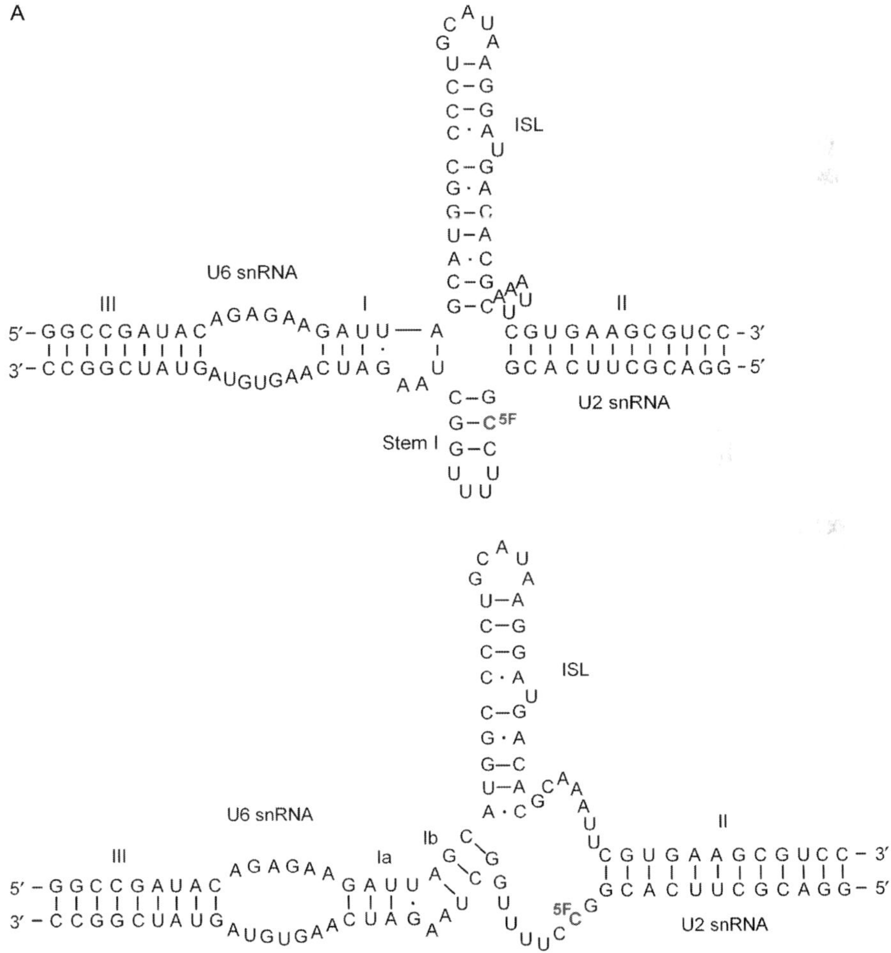

Figure 12.3 (A) Proposed secondary structures of human U2–U6 snRNA complex. (upper) The four-helix conformation and (lower) the three-helix conformation. In each model, the location of the 5-^{19}F-cytidine substitution is noted.

(Continued)

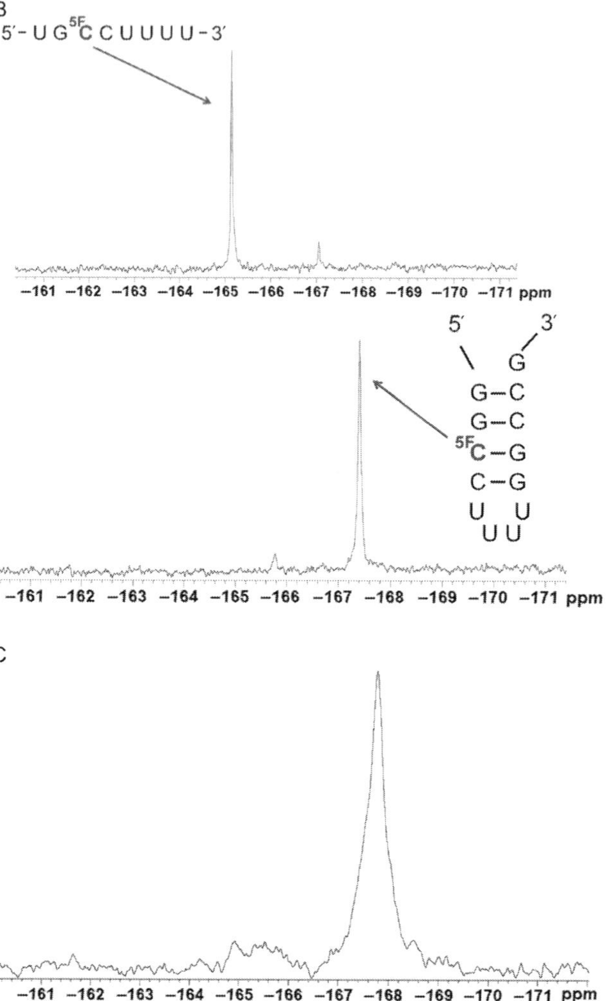

Figure 12.3—Cont'd (B) One-dimensional ^{19}F NMR spectra of control RNA oligomers acquired; (upper) single-stranded control oligomer; and (lower) double-stranded control oligomer. The sequences were indicated by each spectrum and the position of 5-^{19}F-C substitution is shown in the figure. (C) One-dimensional ^{19}F NMR spectra of the human U2–U6 snRNA.

a region that would be double- or single-stranded in each of the two proposed models (Fig. 12.3A, modified nucleotide is identified indicated a relatively sharp ^{19}F peak at −167.8 ppm (with a small "shoulder") and a very broad (and likely multi-component) peak centered around −165.4 ppm (Fig. 12.3C). These peaks overlapped with those observed in ^{19}F spectra of

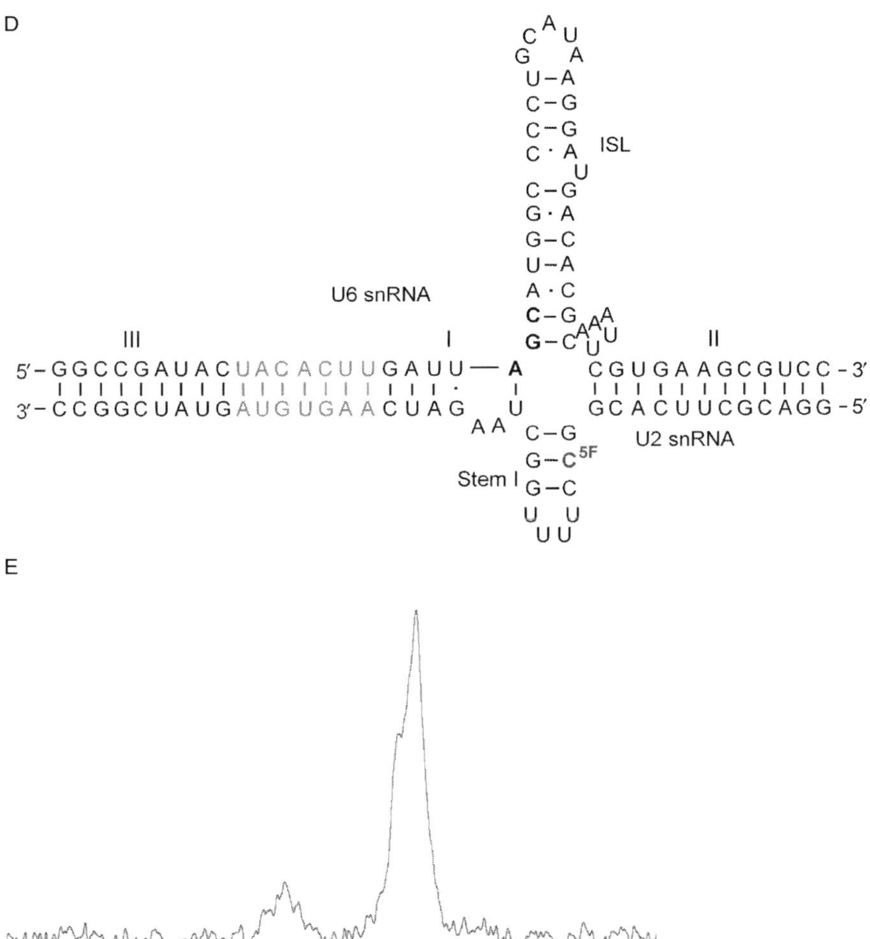

Figure 12.3—Cont'd (D) Proposed secondary structures of human U2–U6 snRNA complex with mutated ACAGAGA loop. The mutated base pairs are labeled in light gray and the substituted 5-^{19}F-cytidine is noted in the figure. (E) One-dimensional ^{19}F NMR spectra of the human U2–U6 snRNA with mutated ACAGAGA loop. All spectra were acquired on a Varian INOVA 500MHz spectrometer equipped with a broadband probe (spectrometer frequency of ^{19}F is 470.220 MHz) at 25 °C, spectral width was 61,633.3 Hz, ^{19}F excitation pulse length was 15 μs, number of scans was 12,000–24,000 depending on different samples, acquisition time was 1.063 s, and relaxation delay was 1.5 s. Spectra were referenced by external neat trifluoroacetic acid (−78.5 ppm).

control oligomers in which the ^{19}F-labeled cytosine was in the identical sequence context as the U2–U6 snRNA complex but constrained to be within a double-stranded (−167.8 ppm) or single-stranded (−165.4 ppm) segment (Fig. 12.3B). The ratio of the peak areas in the spectrum of the U2–U6 snRNA complex is consistent with approximately 86% of the complex forming a four-helix fold, with ~14% in one of several three-helix conformers (Zhao et al., 2013). However, we note that the very broad peak corresponding to the single-stranded environment is likely to represent multiple alternative conformations or intermediates, whereas the sharper peak corresponding to the double-stranded environment has a single "shoulder" (also representing an alternative double-stranded conformer or intermediate).

In agreement with the results above (Zhao et al., 2013), NMR studies of the lowest energy conformation of the U2–U6 snRNA complex of the yeast *Saccharomyces cerevisiae* were found to be stabilized in a four-helix junction (Fig. 12.3A, upper) (Sashital, Cornilescu, McManus, Brow, & Butcher, 2004); however, more recent and comprehensive studies of the yeast sequence with an elongated Stem II employing SAXS, NMR, and modeling techniques support a predominant three-helix structure (Fig. 12.3A, lower; Burke, Sashital, Zuo, Wang, & Butcher, 2012). There are a number of sequence differences between the junction region of the human and yeast sequences; therefore, it is not yet clear whether the difference in preferred folds of the protein-free human and yeast complexes are related to these sequence differences or to differences in experimental conditions or techniques used.

Monitoring spectral changes of RNA with a single ^{19}F-substituted nucleotide under different experimental conditions or in the presence of selected sequence mutations makes it possible to identify changes or perturbations in the distribution of conformers. As an illustration, we wanted to test whether the conformation surrounding the central junction of the human U2–U6 snRNA complex was dependent on the presence of the large and phylogenetically conserved internal ACAGAGA loop formed between U2- and U6-snRNA strands. To evaluate the role of the loop, we transcribed a sample of a mutant U6-snRNA strand in which the ACAGAGA sequence was replaced by a sequence that would be fully complementary to the opposing U2-snRNA sequence, resulting in a fully paired U2–U6 stem (Fig. 12.3D). A one-dimensional ^{19}F spectrum of the mutant complex in the absence of the loop was essentially identical to that of the original complex containing the loop; i.e., a large and relatively sharp peak associated with the double-stranded region and a lesser and very broad peak (or combination of peaks) corresponding to single-stranded environments, implying that the two complexes have similar overall folds and distribution of folds (and intermediates) and that the presence or absence of the loop does not bias junction structure (Fig. 12.3E).

Similarly, we analyzed the effect of temperature and Mg^{2+} on the distribution of the two major conformers. FRET studies have suggested that binding of Mg^{2+} has a marked impact on the conformational distribution of the yeast complex (Guo et al., 2009). To evaluate this effect on the human complex, we repeated the one-dimensional ^{19}F NMR experiment in the presence of 5 m*M* $MgCl_2$. The comparison of the spectra in the absence and presence of Mg^{2+} ion exhibited a slight increase of the fraction of single-stranded peak from ~14% to ~17% at 25 °C (Zhao et al., 2013), suggesting only a small degree of shift in the human complex induced by Mg^{2+}.

The fact that the single-stranded peak is distinct from the double-stranded peak and that the location of each overlaps with the control resonance chemical shifts suggests that any exchange between the conformations is in slow chemical exchange (with respect to the timescale as detected by NMR). In contrast, the "breathing" of base pairs is anticipated to reside within the rapid chemical exchange timescale; therefore, we expect that the presence of the different peaks does not correspond with simple opening and closing of Stem I.

However, it is still unknown whether the majority four-helix conformation and the conformation represented by the single-stranded peak are in dynamic exchange with each other or simply represent two stable alternative folds. We thus performed the two-dimensional ^{19}F–^{19}F EXSY experiments on the U2–U6 snRNA complex (acquisition parameters specified in the legend of Fig. 12.4). Analogous to the studies with the bistable stem loop, we observed the build up and decay of the exchange cross peaks, suggesting the dynamic exchange between different conformations. However, in contrast with the study of the smaller model system, we noted multiple cross peaks displaying exchange between the major and "shoulder" components of the peak associated with the double-stranded environment and at least four components associated with the single-stranded region. Moreover, different exchange cross peaks appeared to build up and decay with somewhat different timescales, suggesting that these are independent events. Due to the complexity of the spectra and the poor signal-to-noise ratio in this large system, we are not yet able to make a convincing quantitative analysis of the built up and decay of the diagonal and cross peaks as we did for the simpler

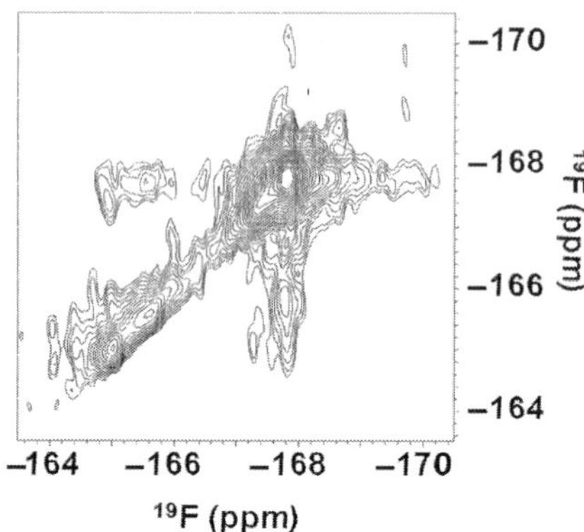

Figure 12.4 Representative two-dimensional ^{19}F–^{19}F EXSY spectrum of human U2–U6 snRNA complex acquired at 600 MHz with mixing time of 100 ms. The appearance of exchange NOEs is consistent with interconversion between the two models shown in Fig. 12.3A, likely including multiple alternative or intermediate folds, on a subsecond timescale. Spectrum was acquired on a Bruker 600-MHz spectrometer equipped with a dedicated ^{19}F CyroProbe (spectrometer frequency of ^{19}F is 564.603 MHz) at 25 °C. ^{19}F excitation pulse length was 10.42 μs, spectral width was 14,115.1 Hz, acquisition time was 0.036 s, and relaxation delay was 1.8 s. The number of points was 1024 × 64, and the number of scans was 256.

bistable stem loop sample. However, significantly, our data demonstrate dynamic exchange between different conformations in U2–U6 snRNA complex, which fully supports the possibility of facile conformational interconversion under conditions that may be experienced with different stages of spliceosome activity.

3. CONCLUSION AND REMARKS

Solution NMR techniques based on observations of ^{1}H, ^{13}C, ^{15}N, and ^{31}P have long been valuable tools in structural biology. Application to the study of dynamics on multiple timescales ranges from rapid local motions in the nanosecond range to global rearrangements in the millisecond to second range. As an extension of traditional NMR experiments, experiments using ^{19}F offer several advantages for identification and measurements of distribution and exchange rates for multiple RNA conformations with very little ambiguity: (1) ability to label at a single site during chemical synthesis; (2) high sensitivity of the ^{19}F nucleus that is similar to ^{1}H and far greater than ^{13}C or ^{15}N; and (3) significant and well-documented differences between chemical shifts of ^{19}F in a single- or double-stranded environment. The

^{19}F nucleus is also suitable for the measurement of exchange processes in the range of microsecond to millisecond timescales. Therefore, it should also be possible to gain information about higher-energy transient states via Car-Purcel-Meiboom-Gill (CPMG) experiments, as has been done in proteins (Larda, Simonetti, Al-Abdul-Wahid, Sharpe, & Prosser, 2013).

The method described here should be widely applicable to conformational changes in other folded RNA molecules, RNA-small molecule complexes, and RNA–protein complexes. Of particular interest are the changes occurring in riboswitches, both in the absence and presence of their metabolite ligands.

ACKNOWLEDGMENTS

This work was supported by NSF Grant MCB 0929394 and PSC-CUNY Grant ENHC-43-98 to N. L. G. The project described was also supported by Grant Number RR003037 from the National Center for Research Resources (NCRR), a component of the National Institutes of Health (NIH); its contents are solely the responsibility of the authors and do not necessarily represent the official views of NCRR or NIH. The authors thank Ranajeet Ghose (City College of CUNY) for assistance with calculations and providing Fig. 12.2B, and Matthew Devany (Hunter College of CUNY) for assistance with optimizing the ^{19}F–^{19}F EXSY of the model sequence. The authors acknowledge the facilities of the Chemistry NMR Facility at the Hunter College of CUNY.

REFERENCES

Biondi, E., & Burke, D. H. (2014). RNA structural analysis by enzymatic digestion. *Methods in Molecular Biology*, *1086*, 41–52.

Bothe, J. R., Nikolova, E. N., Eichhorn, C. D., Chugh, J., Hansen, A. L., & Al-Hashimi, H. M. (2011). Characterizing RNA dynamics at atomic resolution using solution-state NMR spectroscopy. *Nature Methods*, *8*, 919–931.

Burke, J. E., Sashital, D. G., Zuo, X., Wang, Y. X., & Butcher, S. E. (2012). Structure of the yeast U2/U6 snRNA complex. *RNA*, *18*, 673–683.

D'Souza, V., & Summers, M. F. (2004). Structural basis for packaging the dimeric genome of Moloney murine leukaemia virus. *Nature*, *431*, 586–590.

Fabrizio, P., & Abelson, J. (1990). Two domains of yeast U6 small nuclear RNA required for both steps of nuclear precursor messenger RNA splicing. *Science*, *250*, 404–409.

Farrow, N. A., Zhang, O., Forman-Kay, J. D., & Kay, L. E. (1994). A heteronuclear correlation experiment for simultaneous determination of ^{15}N longitudinal decay and chemical exchange rates of systems in slow equilibrium. *Journal of Biomolecular NMR*, *4*, 727–734.

Gonzalez, R. L., Jr., & Tinoco, I., Jr. (1999). Solution structure and thermodynamics of a divalent metal ion binding site in an RNA pseudoknot. *Journal of Molecular Biology*, *289*, 1267–1282.

Guo, Z., Karunatilaka, K. S., & Rueda, D. (2009). Single-molecule analysis of protein-free U2-U6 snRNAs. *Nature Structural & Molecular Biology*, *16*, 1154–1159.

Haller, A., Altman, R. B., Souliere, M. F., Blanchard, S. C., & Micura, R. (2013). Folding and ligand recognition of the TPP riboswitch aptamer at single-molecule resolution. *Proceedings of the National Academy of Sciences of the United States of America*, *110*, 4188–4193.

Hilliker, A. K., Mefford, M. A., & Staley, J. P. (2007). U2 toggles iteratively between the stem IIa and stem IIc conformations to promote pre-mRNA splicing. *Genes & Development, 21*, 821–834.

Huppler, A., Nikstad, L. J., Allmann, A. M., Brow, D. A., & Butcher, S. E. (2002). Metal binding and base ionization in the U6 RNA intramolecular stem-loop structure. *Nature Structural Biology, 9*, 431–435.

Johnson, J. E., Jr., & Hoogstraten, C. G. (2008). Extensive backbone dynamics in the GCAA RNA tetraloop analyzed using 13C NMR spin relaxation and specific isotope labeling. *Journal of the American Chemical Society, 130*, 16757–16769.

Karunatilaka, K. S., & Rueda, D. (2014). Post-transcriptional modifications modulate conformational dynamics in human U2-U6 snRNA complex. *RNA, 20*, 16–23.

Kloiber, K., Spitzer, R., Tollinger, M., Konrat, R., & Kreutz, C. (2011). Probing RNA dynamics via longitudinal exchange and CPMG relaxation dispersion NMR spectroscopy using a sensitive ^{13}C-methyl label. *Nucleic Acids Research, 39*, 4340–4351.

Kreutz, C., Kahlig, H., Konrat, R., & Micura, R. (2005). Ribose 2′-F labeling: A simple tool for the characterization of RNA secondary structure equilibria by ^{19}F NMR spectroscopy. *Journal of the American Chemical Society, 127*, 11558–11559.

Larda, S. T., Simonetti, K., Al-Abdul-Wahid, M. S., Sharpe, S., & Prosser, R. S. (2013). Dynamic equilibria between monomeric and oligomeric misfolded states of the mammalian prion protein measured by ^{19}F NMR. *Journal of the American Chemical Society, 135*, 10533–10541.

Latham, M. P., Zimmermann, G. R., & Pardi, A. (2009). NMR chemical exchange as a probe for ligand-binding kinetics in a theophylline-binding RNA aptamer. *Journal of the American Chemical Society, 131*, 5052–5053.

Lee, J., Dethoff, E. A., & Al-Hashimi, H. M. (2014). Invisible RNA state dynamically couples distant motifs. *Proceedings of the National Academy of Sciences of the United States of America, 111*, 9485–9490.

Low, J. T., Garcia-Miranda, P., Mouzakis, K. D., Gorelick, R. J., Butcher, S. E., & Weeks, K. M. (2014). Structure and dynamics of the HIV-1 frameshift element RNA. *Biochemistry, 53*, 4282–4291.

Madhani, H. D., & Guthrie, C. (1992). A novel base-pairing interaction between U2 and U6 snRNAs suggests a mechanism for the catalytic activation of the spliceosome. *Cell, 71*, 803–817.

McPheeters, D. S., & Abelson, J. (1992). Mutational analysis of the yeast U2 snRNA suggests a structural similarity to the catalytic core of group I introns. *Cell, 71*, 819–831.

Mefford, M. A., & Staley, J. P. (2009). Evidence that U2/U6 helix I promotes both catalytic steps of pre-mRNA splicing and rearranges in between these steps. *RNA, 15*, 1386–1397.

Puffer, B., Kreutz, C., Rieder, U., Ebert, M. O., Konrat, R., & Micura, R. (2009). 5-Fluoro pyrimidines: Labels to probe DNA and RNA secondary structures by ^{1}D ^{19}F NMR spectroscopy. *Nucleic Acids Research, 37*, 7728–7740.

Reiter, N. J., Blad, H., Abildgaard, F., & Butcher, S. E. (2004). Dynamics in the U6 RNA intramolecular stem-loop: A base flipping conformational change. *Biochemistry, 43*, 13739–13747.

Sashital, D. G., Cornilescu, G., McManus, C. J., Brow, D. A., & Butcher, S. E. (2004). U2-U6 RNA folding reveals a group II intron-like domain and a four-helix junction. *Nature Structural & Molecular Biology, 11*, 1237–1242.

Schmieder, P., Stern, A. S., Wagner, G., & Hoch, J. C. (1993). Application of nonlinear sampling schemes to COSY-type spectra. *Journal of Biomolecular NMR, 3*, 569–576.

Sontheimer, E. J., Sun, S., & Piccirilli, J. A. (1997). Metal ion catalysis during splicing of premessenger RNA. *Nature, 388*, 801–805.

Sun, J. S., & Manley, J. L. (1995). A novel U2-U6 snRNA structure is necessary for mammalian mRNA splicing. *Genes & Development*, *9*, 843–854.

Tugarinov, V., Kay, L. E., Ibraghimov, I., & Orekhov, V. Y. (2005). High-resolution four-dimensional ^{1}H-^{13}C NOE spectroscopy using methyl-TROSY, sparse data acquisition, and multidimensional decomposition. *Journal of the American Chemical Society*, *127*, 2767–2775.

Valadkhan, S., & Manley, J. L. (2002). Intrinsic metal binding by a spliceosomal RNA. *Nature Structural Biology*, *9*, 498–499.

Xu, X., & Chen, S. J. (2012). Kinetic mechanism of conformational switch between bistable RNA hairpins. *Journal of the American Chemical Society*, *134*, 12499–12507.

Yean, S. L., Wuenschell, G., Termini, J., & Lin, R. J. (2000). Metal-ion coordination by U6 small nuclear RNA contributes to catalysis in the spliceosome. *Nature*, *408*, 881–884.

Yuan, F., Griffin, L., Phelps, L., Buschmann, V., Weston, K., & Greenbaum, N. L. (2007). Use of a novel Forster resonance energy transfer method to identify locations of site-bound metal ions in the U2-U6 snRNA complex. *Nucleic Acids Research*, *35*, 2833–2845.

Zarrinkar, P. P., & Williamson, J. R. (1994). Kinetic intermediates in RNA folding. *Science*, *265*, 918–924.

Zhang, Q., Stelzer, A. C., Fisher, C. K., & Al-Hashimi, H. M. (2007). Visualizing spatially correlated dynamics that directs RNA conformational transitions. *Nature*, *450*, 1263–1267.

Zhao, C., Bachu, R., Popovic, M., Devany, M., Brenowitz, M., Schlatterer, J. C., et al. (2013). Conformational heterogeneity of the protein-free human spliceosomal U2-U6 snRNA complex. *RNA*, *19*, 561–573.

Zhao, C., Devany, M., & Greenbaum, N. L. (2014). Measurement of chemical exchange between RNA conformers by ^{19}F NMR. in press, http://dx.doi.org/10.1016/j.bbrc.2014.09.075.

CHAPTER THIRTEEN

Site-Directed Spin-Labeling Strategies and Electron Paramagnetic Resonance Spectroscopy for Large Riboswitches

Jackie M. Esquiaqui*, Eileen M. Sherman†, Jing-Dong Ye†,[1], Gail E. Fanucci*,[1]

*Department of Chemistry, University of Florida, Gainesville, Florida, USA
†Department of Chemistry, University of Central Florida, Orlando, Florida, USA
[1]Corresponding authors: e-mail address: yejingdong@gmail.com; gefanucci@gmail.com

Contents

Abstract

Genetic regulation effected by RNA riboswitches is governed by ligand-induced structural reorganization with modulation of RNA conformation and dynamics. Characterization of the conformational states of riboswitches in the presence or absence of salts and ligands is important for understanding how interconversion of riboswitch RNA folding states influences function. The methodology of site-directed spin labeling (SDSL) coupled with electron paramagnetic resonance (EPR) spectroscopy is suitable for such studies, wherein site-specific incorporation of a nitroxide radical spin probe allows for local dynamics and conformational changes to be investigated. This chapter reviews a strategy for SDSL-EPR studies of large riboswitches and uses the full length 232 nucleotide (nt) kink-turn motif-containing *Vibrio cholerae* (*VC*) glycine riboswitch as an example. Spin-labeling strategies and the challenges of incorporating spin labels into large riboswitches are reviewed and the approach to overcome these challenges is

Methods in Enzymology, Volume 549
ISSN 0076-6879
http://dx.doi.org/10.1016/B978-0-12-801122-5.00013-1

described. Results are subsequently presented illustrating changes in dynamics within the labeled region of the *VC* glycine riboswitch as observed using SDSL-EPR.

The discovery of riboswitches revealed a unique class of RNA molecules exhibiting the ability to independently and selectively bind cognate metabolite ligands that induce genetic regulation without the obligate aid of any protein counterpart (Breaker, 2011; Serganov & Patel, 2012a, 2012b). Many investigations, each utilizing a diverse array of biochemical and biophysical techniques, have been aimed at elucidating structural and dynamic processes governing ligand binding in riboswitches (Dalgarno et al., 2013; Regulski & Breaker, 2008; Reining et al., 2013; Wunnicke et al., 2011). In particular, biophysical methods, such as fluorescence spectroscopy, nuclear magnetic resonances (NMRs) spectroscopy, infrared spectroscopy, and electron paramagnetic resonance (EPR) spectroscopy, are well suited for answering structural and dynamic questions regarding biological macromolecular function, but often require incorporation of external probes.

EPR spectroscopy, coupled with site-specific incorporation of nitroxide radicals, known as site-directed spin labeling (SDSL), has emerged as a powerful tool for the study of dynamics and conformational sampling of biological macromolecules, particularly of proteins (Klare, 2013; Klug & Feix, 2008). Recent advances have also been made in SDSL approaches in nucleic acids, which encompass DNAs and RNAs, including riboswitches. When compared to NMR spectroscopy, an advantage of SDSL-EPR spectroscopy is that this methodology does not restrict the molecular size of the biomolecule of interest, which is advantageous for the study of riboswitches or other large RNAs, many of which exceed the size limitation imposed by relaxation effects in NMR (Fanucci & Cafiso, 2006; Tolbert et al., 2010). In fact, many current SDSL applications of proteins are targeted at characterization of membrane-protein structure, dynamics and conformational changes. Additionally, the sensitivity of EPR is in general 10–100 × greater for SDSL investigations over traditional NMR applications, allowing for smaller sample sizes to be investigated.

A necessary requirement of the SDSL-EPR approach is the site-specific incorporation of a persistent unpaired electron for detection. Usually, nitroxide-based radicals are chosen for SDSL-EPR. In the last two decades, SDSL-EPR applications in protein science have expanded remarkably, most likely due to developments in molecular biology and chemical biology aimed at facile protein sequence manipulation. The reader is pointed to other recent reviews for more information on general recent advances in SDSL-EPR (Hubbell, Lopez, Altenbach, & Yang, 2013; Jeschke, 2013).

A variety of labeling strategies have also been developed for site-specific incorporation of nitroxide-based probes into nucleic acids. These can involve, for example, modification of the phosphate backbone, specific labeling of thiouridine bases, and 2′ modifications of the ribose sugar (Zhang, Cekan, Sigurdsson, & Qin, 2009). These synthetic strategies can be equally applied to DNA or RNA constructs. A limitation to this approach is that it commonly makes use of synthetic nucleic acid strategies that inherently limit the size of RNA that can be cost-efficiently produced to fewer than 40 nt (El-Sagheer & Brown, 2010). Consequently, SDSL of larger RNAs and riboswitches has been limited. As an alternative, in-trans SDSL methods have been utilized in the study of packing RNA and ribozymes (Grant, Boyd, Herschlag, & Qin, 2009; Zhang et al., 2012). The combination of synthetic and enzymatic procedures for site-specific incorporation of nucleotide analogs into large RNA molecules has been described (Solomatin & Herschlag, 2009), but few have been reported for SDSL of riboswitches over 100 nt in length. Spin labeling of the 118 nt SAM-I riboswitch was recently described using a unique DNA-catalyzed RNA ligation scheme (Buttner, Seikowski, Wawrzyniak, Ochmann, & Hobartner, 2013). Results provided a promising and novel way to incorporate spin labels into larger riboswitches. Convertible nucleosides were used for SDSL of this riboswitch and entailed sophisticated synthetic skills as well as investment in an expensive RNA solid-phase synthesizer.

This chapter focuses on a facile method for incorporating nitroxide spin labels into the large, full length (232 nt) *Vibrio cholerae* glycine riboswitch for the study of backbone dynamics using continuous-wave (CW)-EPR spectroscopy. The designed methodology adapts from the reported protocols of splinted ligation of commercially available synthetic RNA fragments that have been postsynthetically spin labeled to *in vitro*-transcribed larger fragments, thus requiring minimal synthetic effort while providing sample quantities in yields satisfactory for multiple CW-EPR experiments. For the detailed study of the *VC* glycine riboswitch and characterization of backbone dynamics using SDSL-EPR, the reader is pointed to our recent publication (Esquiaqui, Sherman, Ionescu, Ye, & Fanucci, 2014).

Briefly described, selected biochemical and biophysical techniques used to study riboswitches are reviewed including a more detailed review of RNA spin-labeling strategies for EPR spectroscopy of riboswitches. Ligation schemes for the preparation of large-labeled RNAs are reviewed followed by experimental details for the preparation of the spin-labeled 232 nt *VC* glycine riboswitch including details regarding potential pitfalls and yield optimization. The preparation of riboswitch samples for EPR experiments and subsequent analysis of EPR data to obtain information regarding dynamics will then be described.

1. TECHNIQUES USED FOR RIBOSWITCH STUDIES

Riboswitches function to modulate genetic expression through precise ligand binding events that result in RNA structural rearrangement (Serganov & Patel, 2012b). Typically located in the 5′-untranslated region of mRNA transcripts, riboswitches are composed of two distinct domains referred to as the aptamer domain and expression platform domain, regulating the expression of genes that are often involved in the metabolism of the bound ligand. Aptamers are highly conserved and function to recognize and bind cognate metabolite at threshold cellular concentrations (Roth & Breaker, 2009). The less conserved expression platform domain is located downstream of aptamers and functions to mediate ligand binding to genetic regulation by its own conformational reorganization (Mandal & Breaker, 2004). Interest in understanding riboswitch function has led to a diversity of investigations utilizing both biochemical and biophysical techniques. In recent years, a growing number of spectroscopic methods have become amenable to the study of riboswitches, offering yet another powerful tool for elucidating relationships among structure, dynamics, and function.

1.1. Biochemical

Many questions have been addressed using a diversity of biochemical methods (Karns et al., 2013; Kwon & Strobel, 2008; Tyrrell, McGinnis, Weeks, & Pielak, 2013). One of the most widely used assays for studying riboswitches is in-line probing which was developed by the Breaker lab (Soukup & Breaker, 1999) and has been extensively used to probe secondary structural modulation of riboswitches upon ligand binding. The assay is based upon nucleophilic attack of the 2′-hydroxyl oxygen on the adjacent backbone phosphorus center which occurs when in-line geometry is exhibited and thus results in RNA cleavage (Regulski & Breaker, 2008). In-line geometry is influenced by RNA structural flexibility, and cleavage patterns can be used to characterize structural changes upon ligand

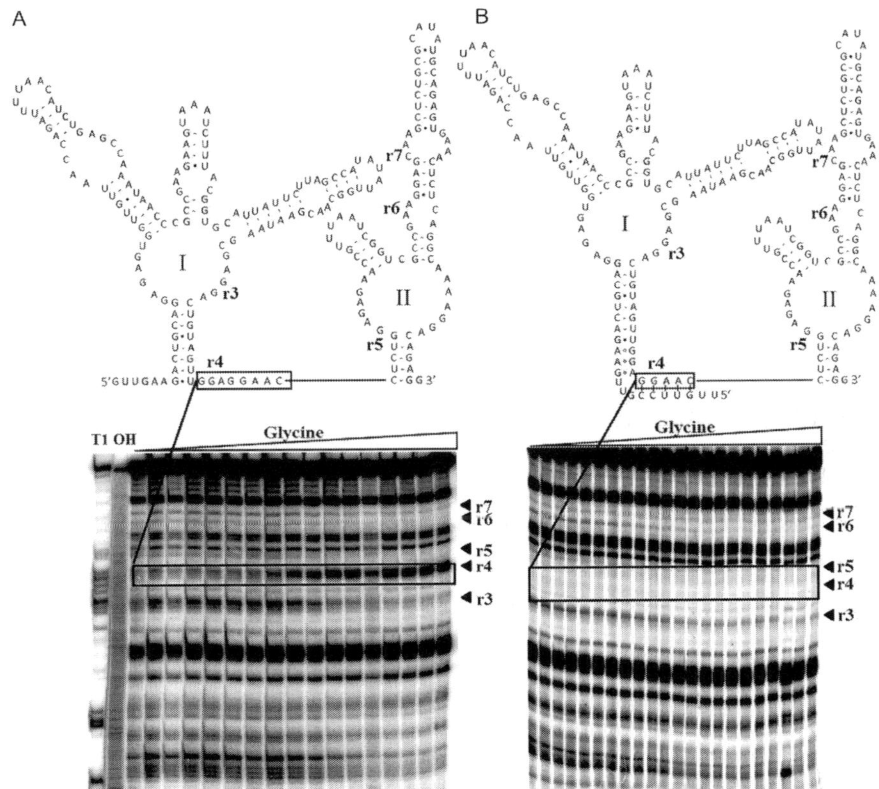

Figure 13.1 (A) Top panel shows the secondary structure for the *VC* glycine riboswitch lacking the leader sequence, and the corresponding in-line probing gel results is shown in the bottom panel. (B) Top panel shows the secondary structure for the construct containing the leader sequence, and the bottom panel shows the corresponding in-line probing gel results. For the gel results and secondary structures shown, region 4 is boxed to indicate the interaction that was identified due to the protection pattern observed (Sherman, Esquiaqui, Elsayed, & Ye, 2012).

binding-induced riboswitch folding. One example of in-line probing results that led to the identification of the leader–linker interaction in the 232 nt *VC* glycine riboswitch is shown in Fig. 13.1 (Sherman et al., 2012).

In-line probing studies have provided a wealth of riboswitch information, most at the level of secondary structure. When used in combination with spectroscopy, further details can be elucidated regarding conformational sampling between riboswitch states, local dynamics, and even structure determination.

1.2. Spectroscopy and labeling

For many riboswitches, knowledge of the molecular level details associated with ligand binding and induced conformational change is desired. This requires obtaining information regarding, for example, both the ligand-free state and the ligand-bound state, and characterization of the transitions between these states. All of these questions are readily suited for spectroscopic studies. Many spectroscopic methods often require that an external probe be introduced into the biomolecule of interest. Advancements in solid-phase RNA synthesis have allowed for production of RNAs that contain modifications to incorporate site-specific probes, but this strategy imposes limitations upon the length of RNA that can be synthesized (El-Sagheer & Brown, 2010). Consequently, for large riboswitches, feasible, efficient, and cost-effective labeling strategies remain a primary challenge. To study changes in dynamics, EPR and RNA-SDSL are briefly reviewed followed by the applied protocol for the *VC* glycine riboswitch.

1.2.1 EPR

Electron paramagnetic resonance (EPR) spectroscopy is a powerful tool for probing differential dynamics of motion of biological macromolecules that are described with correlation times ranging from picoseconds (ps) to nanoseconds (ns); CW-EPR line shape analysis and simulation is often employed for this purpose (Zhang et al., 2009). CW-EPR relies upon the sensitivity of EPR line shapes to reflect nitroxide motion whereby it becomes possible to extract information regarding local dynamics. Furthermore, conformational sampling of biomolecule states can be investigated using pulsed EPR approaches such as double electron–electron resonance, also known as PELDOR (Fanucci & Cafiso, 2006; Hubbell et al., 2013). Pulsed EPR experiments utilize two or more spin labels to determine distances and distance distributions within a biomolecule of interest. Distance measurements provide information regarding the conformational ensemble with the breadths of the distance profiles sometimes reflective of conformational dynamics. Both approaches are amenable to the study of riboswitches and are useful for probing differential dynamics among various conformational folded states of riboswitches. The application of EPR spectroscopy to the study of RNA is rapidly growing, but fewer studies have been reported for EPR of riboswitches, perhaps due to the large size of many natural riboswitches, which presents a challenge for SDSL as will be discussed in Section 1.3.

1.3. Site-directed spin labeling

SDSL is a technique that allows for site-specific incorporation of non-native spin probes into a biomolecule of interest. When used in conjunction with EPR spectroscopy, site-specific labeling with nitroxide radical spin probes is often utilized to study changes in local dynamics or to determine distances between two labeled sites. Strategies for SDSL of proteins are well established (Columbus & Hubbell, 2002; Hubbell, Cafiso, & Altenbach, 2000) and in recent years, many successful and diverse methods for SDSL of nucleic acids, specifically RNA, have emerged, and many protocols and reviews have been published on this subject (Edwards & Sigurdsson, 2007; Piton et al., 2007; Schiemann et al., 2007; Shelke & Sigurdsson, 2012; Sicoli, Wachowius, Bennati, & Hobartner, 2010; Sigurdsson, 2011; Sowa & Qin, 2008; Zhang et al., 2009). As reviewed by Sigurdsson (2011), two primary methods can be used to achieve SDSL of RNA: the phosphoramidite strategy and the postsynthesis spin-labeling method. In the phosphoramidite approach, RNAs are generated on a solid-phase RNA synthesizer and synthetically produced phosphoramidites that contain a nitroxide radical moiety are site specifically incorporated during the synthesis process. Alternatively, in the postsynthesis method, modified functional groups are incorporated into the RNA during solid-phase synthesis, and these functional groups are reacted with a desired spin label subsequent to synthesis. In both schemes, RNA solid-phase synthesis is utilized and is suitable for production of small RNAs; however, a primary challenge for SDSL of RNA remains site-specific incorporation of spin probes into large RNAs such as many natural riboswitches. A brief review of RNA-SDSL and important considerations will be discussed before presentation of strategies for spin labeling of large riboswitch RNAs.

1.3.1 Labeling positions

Advancements in RNA-SDSL have made it feasible to study local RNA dynamics at various and specific structural elements including the nucleobases, the ribose sugar, and the phosphate backbone (Cai et al., 2006; Edwards & Sigurdsson, 2007; Grant et al., 2009; Popova, Kalai, Hideg, & Qin, 2009; Shelke & Sigurdsson, 2012; Sigurdsson, 2011; Sowa & Qin, 2008; Zhang et al., 2009, 2012). Examples of spin-labeled RNAs are shown in Fig. 13.2A–C. These positions involve covalent labeling through a number of varying chemistries. An important consideration for nucleic acid labeling positions is minimizing perturbation of nucleic acid

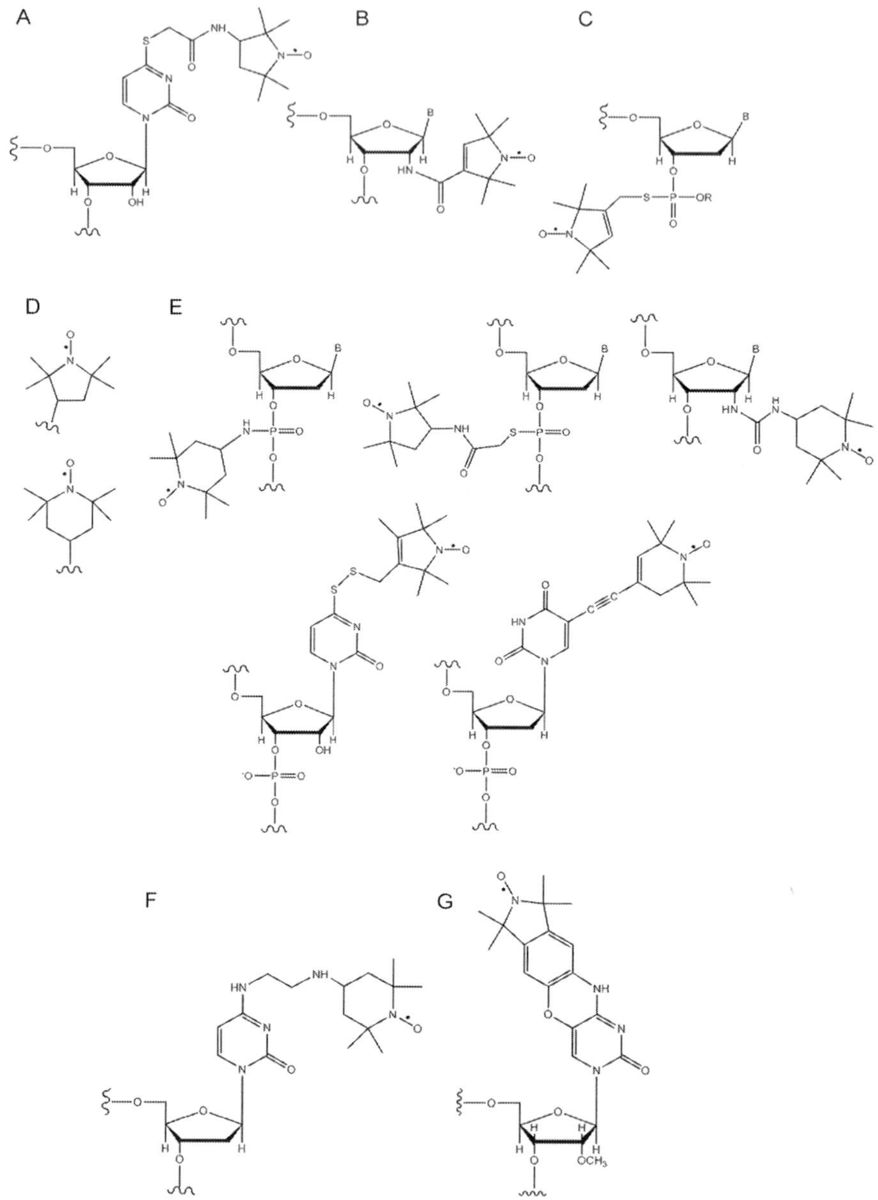

Figure 13.2 Select examples of spin-labeled RNA structures. (A) Nucleobase labeling, (B) ribose labeling, and (C) phosphate backbone labeling. (D) General structure for five- and six-membered nitroxide spin labels (E) Select examples of more structurally diverse spin labels. Comparison of a (F) flexible versus (G) rigid spin label that can be used in nucleic acid SDSL.

structure and function due to the presence of the modified sites and/or the corresponding spin-labeled site. Consequently, careful review in the structural context of the labeled sites and in the overall function of the specific RNA is essential, and appropriate control experiments must be performed to validate the use of SDSL-EPR. Control experiments often used include UV thermal denaturation, isothermal titration calorimetry, NMR if amenable, and functional assays such as in-line probing for RNA riboswitches (Baird & Ferre-D'Amare, 2013; Esquiaqui et al., 2014; Qin, Hideg, Feigon, & Hubbell, 2003).

1.3.2 Choice of spin label

Nitroxide spin labels are persistent radicals with a general structure that consists of a nitroxide radical contained within a five- or six-membered heterocyclic ring that is protected by bulky neighboring methyl groups as shown in Fig. 13.2D. The diversity of nitroxide spin labels is based upon the size of the heterocyclic ring, the saturation and modifications of the heterocyclic ring, and the method of chemical connectivity of the nitroxide moiety to the biomolecule of interest as illustrated in Fig. 13.2E (Schiemann et al., 2007; Shelke & Sigurdsson, 2012; Sigurdsson, 2011; Zhang et al., 2009).

There are various chemistries to connect the spin label to the RNA that can be employed, and this is an important factor that influences the motion and flexibility of the spin label. Spin labels that are attached to the RNA via multiple single bonds will exhibit more motion due to torsional oscillations around the connecting bonds. Conversely, a nitroxide moiety that is fused to additional ring structures will be restricted in motion and, hence, are termed rigid spin labels. Examples of flexible versus rigid spin labels are shown in Fig. 13.2F and G.

When utilizing flexible spin labels, it is imperative that the additional motion of the probe be accounted for, particularly if distance measurements between two labels are to be determined. For example, published work for the flexible R5 spin label utilizes the NASNOX software to account for rotameric states of the probe (Price, Sutch, Cai, Qin, & Haworth, 2007). Motionally flexible spin labels can complicate the analysis of distance distributions in pulsed EPR experiments. The use of motionally restrained labels minimizes this challenge (Tkach et al., 2007). Therefore, choosing the appropriate spin label is also largely dependent upon the method of RNA-SDSL chosen (phosphoramidite vs. postsynthesis methods). The phosphoramidite approach allows for more diverse spin labels, such as rigid spin labels, to be incorporated into the RNA and allows one to design the location and structure of the spin probe. The advantage of producing unique spin labels, such as the rigid spin label shown in Fig. 13.2G, is the application to more sophisticated experiments such as high-frequency PELDOR for orientation selection in distance measurements (Hobartner, Sicoli, Wachowius, Gophane, & Sigurdsson, 2012; Tkach et al., 2007).

1.3.3 SDSL for CW and pulsed EPR

SDSL of RNA for the purpose of investigating local dynamics differs from SDSL for the purpose of determining distance measurements in the number of labeled sites required for each method. In the former, only one site is specifically labeled, and CW-EPR is employed. To probe conformational sampling through determination of distance distributions, two labeled sites are required and either CW-EPR or pulsed EPR can be applied. In larger RNAs, such as many riboswitches, optimal locations for placement of two spin labels pose an additional challenge and often require production of larger modified/spin-labeled RNAs beyond the capability of solid-phase synthesis. The development and advancement of ligation strategies can circumvent this obstacle and will be further discussed.

1.3.4 Advantages/disadvantages

SDSL-EPR offers the benefit of requiring minimal quantities of sample and is sensitive to as little as 1 nmol of spin-labeled RNA (Zhang et al., 2009). This is particularly advantageous for SDSL of RNA that relies upon solid-phase synthesis, where yields are limited by efficiency. Furthermore, both phosphoramidite and postsynthetic RNA labeling have their advantages and disadvantages. The phosphoramidite strategy involves construction and synthesis of custom phosphoramidite building blocks that can be directly used during in-house RNA solid-phase synthesis and allows for unique design of spin label moieties and varying connections to the RNA. However, knowledge of synthetic techniques is required in addition to an RNA synthesizer. In contrast, postsynthetic labeling involves purchase of commercially available modified synthetic RNA and commercially available spin labels or spin label precursors hence restricting the variety of spin-labeling locations and spin-label moieties that can be chosen for SDSL of the RNA. However, no synthesis of phosphoramidites or RNA is required, and minimal synthetic effort is needed to attach the purchased spin probe to the purchased RNA. In both schemes, reactivity and chemical oxidation/reduction of the radical is a potential disadvantage, and conditions during either solid-phase synthesis or postsynthetic labeling must be considered to avoid loss of the radical. Conditions during solid-phase synthesis can cause oxidation/reduction of the nitroxide-containing phosphoramidites and appropriate measures should be implemented to avoid loss of the radical. Similarly, in postsynthetic labeling, reagents used during SDSL must not interfere or react with the spin label or its chemistry of attachment. One such example is use of the *S*-(2,2,5,5-tetramethyl-2,5-dihydro-1H-pyrrol-3-yl) methyl methanesulfonothioate (MTSL) spin label with 4-thiouridine-modified RNA that results in a labile thiol linkage that can be reduced by reagents such as dithiothreitol (DTT).

The recent advancements in RNA-SDSL are applicable to the study of riboswitches; however, the dependence of RNA-SDSL upon solid-phase RNA synthesis poses a limit to the size of RNA that can be spin labeled or modified. Consequently, continued effort toward developing efficient methods to label larger riboswitches is of importance and is the focus of succeeding sections.

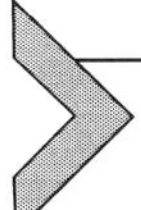

2. LIGATION METHODS FOR SDSL OF LARGE RIBOSWITCHES

RNA ligation methodologies to incorporate site-specific modifications or probes into large constructs are well established in the literature and have been successfully used for a variety of experimental techniques (Moore & Query, 2000; Rieder, Hobartner, & Micura, 2009; Solomatin & Herschlag, 2009). The general scheme for ligation reactions involves generation of a small fragment of modified RNA, often synthetically produced, that is then joined to a large RNA fragment that has been obtained using *in vitro* transcription with T7 RNA polymerase (Solomatin & Herschlag, 2009). Methods for covalent joining of the two RNA fragments include both enzymatic reactions and DNA-catalyzed reactions. Many ligations using enzymes have been reported for production of large (>100 nt) labeled RNAs (Akiyama & Stone, 2009; Rieder et al., 2009; Solomatin & Herschlag, 2009); however, until recently, to our knowledge, the only report of a spin-labeled riboswitch greater than 100 nt was achieved through a novel approach by using convertible nucleosides and an RNA ligation reaction catalyzed by a deoxyribozyme (Buttner et al., 2013). In our recently published work, we have utilized enzymatic ligation with T4 DNA ligase to incorporate spin labels into the large *VC* glycine riboswitch (Esquiaqui et al., 2014). It is the goal of remaining sections of this chapter to present successful employment of T4 DNA ligase-mediated RNA ligation for the production of the 232 nt spin-labeled *VC* glycine riboswitch. An overview of the method, potential difficulties, advantages, and experimental details for using this strategy will be described. The presentation of this methodology provides an additional tool available for the study of dynamics of large riboswitches.

2.1. T4 DNA ligase

Protocols for RNA ligations using T4 DNA ligase have been reported (Akiyama & Stone, 2009; Solomatin & Herschlag, 2009). T4 DNA ligase recognizes nicked double-stranded substrates and can catalyze the formation of a phosphodiester bond between a 3′-OH group of one RNA and 5′-monophosphate group of a different RNA. Joining of the two RNAs is achieved in an annealing step using a DNA splint that is partly complementary to each RNA fragment. Conditions that optimize formation of this DNA/RNA–RNA ternary complex allow for efficient ligation of the RNAs and influence the yield of full length product obtained (Kurschat, Muller, Wombacher, & Helm, 2005). The enzyme requires that the 5′-end contains a monophosphate, and therefore, if the RNA fragment providing the 5′-end is obtained using *in vitro* transcription, it can be produced using GMP-initiated transcription or, alternatively, it must first be dephosphorylated and subsequently monophosphorylated which can easily be achieved using alkaline phosphatases followed by reaction with a kinase. Figure 13.3 depicts a generalized example for the annealing step described.

Ligation is then performed by addition of T4 DNA ligase in stoichiometric amounts. T4 DNA ligase is commercially available, or it can be expressed

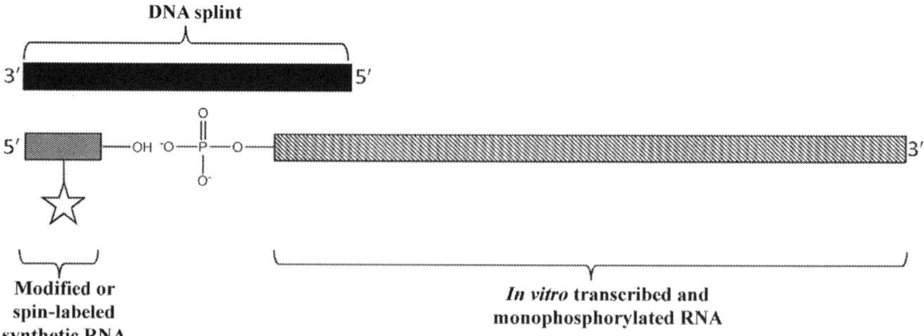

Figure 13.3 Generalized schematic for the annealing step of T4 DNA ligase-mediated splinted ligation. The optimized DNA splint length used was 40 nt forming 20 base pairs with the *in vitro*-transcribed RNA and 20 base pairs with the synthetic RNA fragment.

and purified in high yields suitable for large-scale ligation reactions (Solomatin & Herschlag, 2009; Strobel & Cech, 1995).

For SDSL of large riboswitches, the advantage of using this methodology is realized in the minimal synthetic effort required to incorporate a modified site within the RNA. The site-specific modification is chosen based on selective reactivity to a desired spin label that can be introduced post-synthetically, pre- or postligation. Spin labels such as R5 and MTSL are commercially available. Facile spin-labeling procedures of the synthetic RNA often require straightforward addition of the label, allowing for the labeling reaction to occur over a few to several hours under appropriate conditions, which may vary in temperature, pH, agitation, and amount of ambient light.

2.2. Considerations for SDSL and T4 DNA-mediated ligation of large riboswitches

Two crucial steps in the initial design for successful ligation using T4 DNA ligase are to decide upon the location of the ligation junction and to select the specific site(s) for placement of the spin label. Determination of the site to be spin labeled should involve avoiding potential interference with riboswitch function; therefore, specific nucleotides or structural regions important for function should be reviewed to avoid selection of a problematic site for SDSL. It is also advisable to avoid spin label placement near (between 1 and 10 nt) the ligation junction as this may diminish ligation efficiency. Formation of the DNA/RNA–RNA ternary complex is vital to obtaining high ligation efficiencies. The ligation junction should be chosen to minimize the formation of intramolecular structures that can inhibit efficient hybridization. This is important for large riboswitches which often contain more diversified and complex structural features.

The design for ligation with T4 DNA ligase of the 232 nt *VC* glycine riboswitch is shown in Fig. 13.4 and was chosen to probe the backbone dynamics of the leader–linker interaction (Esquiaqui et al., 2014). The R5 spin label was utilized, and Fig. 13.4B and C shows the chosen locations for SDSL, as well as, the R5 spin-labeling reaction which has been previously reported (Qin et al., 2007).

The 20 nt synthetic-modified RNA provides the 3′-hydroxyl and the 5′-monophosphate is supplied by the 212 nt *in vitro*-transcribed RNA that contains the remaining riboswitch sequence that was dephosphorylated and then monophosphorylated prior to ligation.

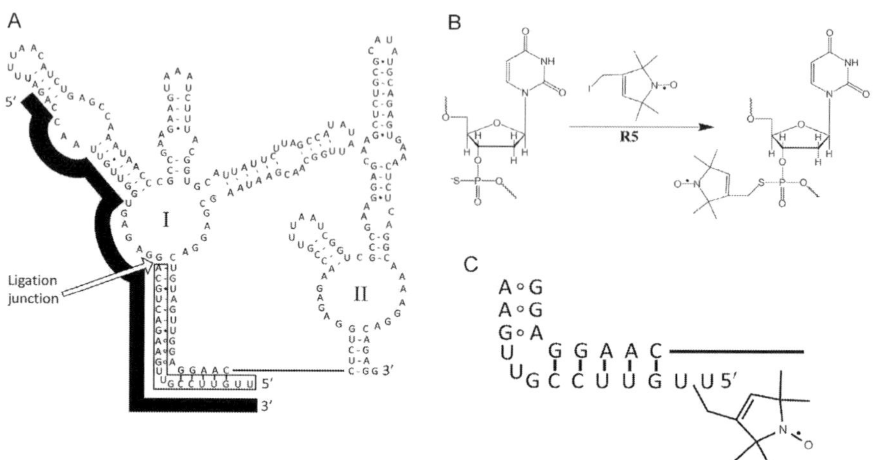

Figure 13.4 (A) Ligation design for the VC glycine riboswitch. The 40 nt DNA splint is indicated in solid black, and the synthetic RNA containing a modified site is boxed. The remaining sequence corresponds to *in vitro*-transcribed RNA. The ligation junction between RNA fragments is also indicated by the arrow. (B) R5 SDSL reaction scheme. (C) Location of R5 in the VC glycine riboswitch.

2.2.1 Optimizing conditions

The natural substrate for T4 DNA ligase is duplex DNA. One well-known challenge and disadvantage associated with using T4 DNA ligase is low ligation efficiency for the unnatural DNA/RNA–RNA hybrid substrate, hence requiring stoichiometric amounts of the enzyme. A number of reports have addressed this issue with recommendations for how to improve yield of product RNA, and many are aimed at optimizing formation of the ternary complex during the annealing step (Kurschat et al., 2005; Moore & Query, 2000). Many protocols use equimolar amounts of DNA splint relative to the two RNA fragments to be ligated; however, our best yields have resulted from altering the ratio of DNA splint to synthetic RNA to *in vitro*-transcribed RNA (Crary, Kurz, & Fierke, 2002). For ligation of the 232 nt *VC* glycine riboswitch, *in vitro*-transcribed RNA was the limiting reagent, and the large scale used was 10 nmol. Following the protocol outlined later, including purification with denaturing (8 *M* urea) polyacrylamide gel electrophoresis (dPAGE), we have been able to achieve 64% yield of the full length (232 nt), ligated, spin-labeled *VC* glycine riboswitch. For CW-EPR experiments, this quantity is more than ample for several experiments, including control studies, and can be easily scaled up further to obtain larger quantities for other techniques. The optimized ratio used in the protocol below for synthetic RNA to *in vitro*-transcribed RNA to DNA splint is 4:1:3.5. This ratio was determined by systematically performing several ligations at small sub-nmol (0.1 nmol) scales with conditions varied for both the annealing and ligation steps and should be performed for each new or varied construct.

If the *in vitro*-transcribed RNA is to be monophosphorylated prior to ligation, it can be prepared either using GMP transcription or dephosphorylated and monophosphorylated using enzymatic reactions with a phosphatase followed by a kinase. The latter is the approach used in the following protocol. Importantly, dephosphorylation and monophosphorylation conditions should first be optimized. Inefficient production of monophosphorylated RNA will undoubtedly result in poor ligation. As a general note, it is advised that optimization of dephosphorylation and monophosphorylation reactions also be performed first at small (sub-nmol) scales.

To optimize ligation efficiency, systematic variation of the following conditions should be performed: ratio of splint DNA and RNAs, length of DNA splint, annealing temperature and time, salt concentration, ATP concentration, and ligation temperature and time. Scaled up reactions can be performed after optimized conditions have been determined for the annealing and ligation steps. It is highly recommended that each large-scale stock of freshly prepared monophosphorylated *in vitro* RNA is tested using a small-scale ligation prior to proceeding to large-scale ligation reactions as a positive control for any potential issues during the monophosphorylation procedures.

Purification of the ligated product can result in large loss of product depending upon the chosen procedures implemented. The protocol described in proceeding sections utilizes dPAGE to purify and separate unligated from ligated product. Substantial increases in yield were obtained by using large-scale ethanol precipitations as opposed to centrifugal concentrating devices.

2.2.2 Protocol

2.2.2.1 Synthetic RNA preparations

Custom synthetic RNAs can be purchased from Dharmacon (Pittsburgh, PA) or integrated DNA Technologies (Commercial Park, IA) with the desired site-specific modifications. For SDSL of the *VC* glycine riboswitch with the R5 spin label, RNA oligomers were purchased with phosphorothioate modifications at select locations. Purchased synthetic RNAs from Dharmacon are delivered with the 2′-hydroxyl protected by

2′-O-bis(2-acetoxyethoxy)methyl, also known as ACE, and should be removed through incubation in the supplied deprotection buffer following the vendor's instruction.

2.2.2.1.1 Deprotection of synthetic RNA Synthetic RNA pellets should be briefly spun down to collect dislodged pellet followed by addition of 400 μL of the provided acetic acid deprotection buffer at pH 3.8. Dissolve the RNA pellet via pipetting, vortex for 10 s, and spin down contents again for 10 s. Incubate the RNA for 30 min at 60 °C.

The deprotected RNA can be directly dried using a lyophilizer or a SpeedVac. Alternatively, the RNA can first be extracted with phenol: chloroform:isoamyl alcohol (25:24:1) (PCA) (Fisher Scientific, Pittsburgh, PA), ethanol precipitated, and then dried prior to dissolving in water and determining the concentration using UV absorbance at 260 nm. It is preferable that the stock concentration of deprotected synthetic RNA be approximately 0.5 m*M* for SDSL.

2.2.2.1.2 Spin labeling of synthetic RNA Procedures for chemical modification of RNA with the R5 spin label have been previously published and should be referred to accordingly (Qin et al., 2007). The R5 spin label or R5 spin label precursor can be obtained from Toronto Research Chemicals, Inc. (Toronto, Ontario).

Dissolve the appropriate amount of purchased or prepared R5 spin label in 20 μL of acetonitrile (Fisher Scientific, Pittsburgh, PA) such that the final concentration of R5 spin label is 60 m*M* or greater. The appropriate amount of R5 used is based on the scale of synthetic RNA that will be used in the ligation, which is in turn dependent on the determined optimized ratio discussed previously. SDSL reactions are generally performed using 10-fold molar excess of spin label to RNA; however, the published protocol for R5 labeling (Qin et al., 2007) recommends that the R5 concentration be maintained greater than 60 m*M*. To the R5 spin label, add the ~0.5 m*M*-modified synthetic RNA and 10 μL of 1 *M* MES (Fisher Scientific, Pittsburgh, PA) at pH 5.8. Add RNase-free water so that the final volume is 100 μL. Cover the reaction tube with foil and incubate in the dark for 16–24 h with gentle, constant shaking.

Extract the spin-labeled RNA oligomer using PCA followed by ethanol precipitation and dissolution in 200 μL of Tris-EDTA (TE) buffer (Fisher Scientific, Pittsburgh, PA). Determine the concentration using UV absorbance at 260 nm prior to proceeding to splinted ligation.

2.2.2.2 Transcribed RNA preparations

The *in vitro*-transcribed RNA was produced using standard T7 RNA polymerase procedures. Many protocols have been published using this general procedure, and details for production of the *VC* glycine riboswitch RNA can be found in Esquiaqui et al. (2014) and Sherman, Holmes, and Ye (2014).

2.2.2.2.1 Dephosphorylation and monophosphorylation For the protocol below, the scale of *in vitro* RNA is 15 nmol, although this can be further scaled up if larger quantities are needed. Fast Alkaline Phosphatase (FASTAP) (Thermo Scientific, Waltham, MA) was used in the following optimized procedures to remove the triphosphate from the RNA. Other phosphatases are commercially available that may differ in activity compared to FASTAP and, therefore, may require differing optimized conditions. In our experience, using freshly purchased FASTAP is preferred. In our hands, successful dephosphorylation of the RNA has been best achieved when utilizing smaller reaction volumes. Therefore, in three separate tubes, prepare 500 μL reaction volumes. Add the *in vitro*-transcribed RNA to a final concentration of 10 μM, RNase-free water, 10 × FASTAP buffer (Thermo Scientific, Waltham, MA), and 1 unit FASTAP enzyme per 13 pmol RNA and incubate for 3 h at 37 °C. FASTAP is inactivated by heating for 5 min at 75 °C. To ensure rapid and uniform heat exchange during the inactivation step, we recommend dividing the total reaction volume (1.5 mL) into 100 μL aliquots and then recombining these into three 500 μL aliquots before proceeding to the monophosphorylation step with T4 Polynucleotide kinase at 1 mL reaction volume (T4 PNK, New England Biolabs, Ipswich, MA).

To each tube, add water, 100 μL of the provided 10 × T4 PNK buffer, ATP to a final concentration of 130 μ*M*, and 20 units of T4 PNK per 1 nmol RNA and incubate for 1 h at 37 °C. Perform PCA extraction and ethanol precipitation before re-dissolving in TE buffer and determining the final concentration.

2.2.2.3 Small- and large-scale ligations

Small-scale ligations with as little at 0.1 nmol of RNA can be used to systematically perform many trials with varying conditions to determine optimized annealing and ligation parameters. For the VC glycine riboswitch, the determinant factor for a good ligation was the ratio of synthetic RNA to *in vitro*-transcribed RNA to DNA splint. A ratio of 4:1:3.5

was determined to be optimal and is used in the following protocol for setup of small-scale ligation using 0.1 nmol *in vitro*-transcribed RNA and for the subsequent scaled up ligation of 10 nmol *in vitro*-transcribed RNA. During trials where optimized conditions are being determined, an unmodified RNA can be used to reduce the cost of synthetic RNA purchased. However, after conditions are optimized, the modified, spin-labeled synthetic RNA should be tested to ensure that the spin-labeled location does not perturb enzymatic ligation with T4 ligase.

2.2.2.3.1 Annealing The reaction volume for the small-scale annealing step is 10 μL. Add the deprotected spin-labeled synthetic RNA, monophosphorylated RNA transcript, and DNA splint to the reaction tube in a 4:1:3.5 nmol ratio. From a prepared stock solution, add the appropriate volume of NaCl to a final concentration of 0.5 *M* and RNase-free water up to 10 μL and mix the reaction volume by pipetting. Heat the sample at 95 °C in a heat block for 2 min. Remove the heat block from the heating source and with the sample still in the heating block allow it to equilibrate to room temperature for 2–3 h.

Note: The 4:1:3.5 ratio was optimized for the designed ligation of the *VC* glycine riboswitch and may need to be optimized for other RNA systems.

2.2.2.3.2 Ligation The final reaction volume for ligation is 100 μL. To the 10-μL annealed complex, add water, 10 μL of 10× T4 DNA ligase buffer (New England Biolabs, Ipswich, MA), and stoichiometric amounts of T4 DNA ligase (New England Biolabs, Ipswich, MA, or in-house expressed/purified, Strobel & Cech, 1995). Mix by gently pipetting and incubate at 30 °C for 3 h.

Note: T4 DNA ligase buffer provided by New England Biolabs contains 10 m*M* $MgCl_2$, 1 m*M* ATP, and 10 m*M* DTT. During trials to vary conditions, this buffer can be prepared with differing concentrations of $MgCl_2$ and ATP.

Note: For synthetic RNAs that are spin labeled with moieties sensitive to reduction by DTT, such as MTSL, preparation of T4 DNA ligase buffer without DTT can be used. In our experience, this has not altered ligation efficiency.

Note: If using T4 DNA ligase that has been expressed and purified, it is recommended that 0.2 units of RNase inhibitor (RNasin Plus RNase Inhibitor, Promega, Madison, WI) per 1 μL reaction volume also be added to the ligation.

To asses ligation results qualitatively, a small dPAGE can be used. Cast the correct percentage gel according to the size of synthetic RNA, *in vitro* RNA, and full length ligated RNA. For the VC glycine riboswitch, an 8% dPAGE gel was used to visualize the unligated and ligated RNAs as shown in Fig. 13.5. Also shown in Fig. 13.5 are results for a few initial trials prior to optimization.

Mix 10 μL of the ligation reaction with 10 μL of RNA loading dye and also prepare samples of *in vitro*-transcribed and synthetic RNA. Load samples onto the gel and run for the appropriate time. StainsAll (Sigma-Aldrich, St. Lois, MO) can be used to visualize RNAs on the gel and should be prepared according to vendor's instruction.

2.2.2.3.3 Scaling up ligation reactions Optimized annealing and ligation conditions can be scaled up linearly. For the small-scale 0.1 nmol ligation described earlier, a 10-fold volume scale up with concentrations held constant per reaction tube was found to be optimal where 1 nmol per tube × 10 tubes is used. Prior to proceeding to the full large-scale ligation

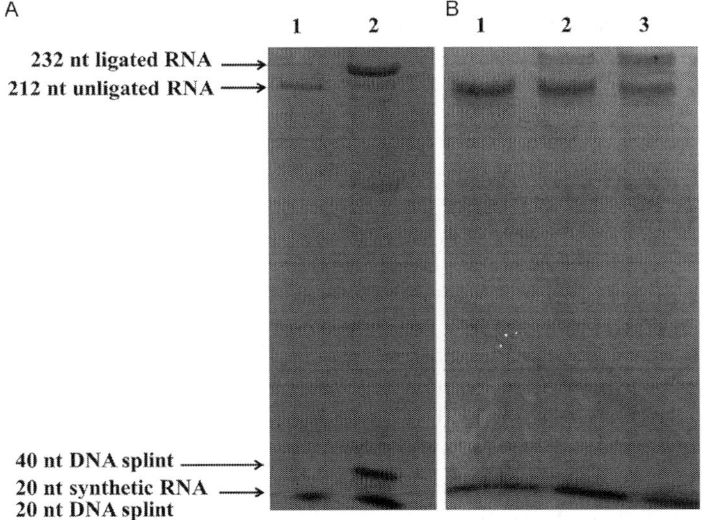

Figure 13.5 (A) Image of an 8% denaturing PAGE gel showing product results for a ligation using optimized conditions with a 40-nt DNA splint. Lane 1 contains unligated *in vitro* RNA and lane 2 contains a scaled up 1 nmol reaction as described in the text. The unlabeled band in lane 2 is assumed to be a side product due to unspecific ligation but is removed during purification. (B) Image of an 8% denaturing PAGE gel showing results from initial failed trials of splinted ligation using a 20-nt DNA splint. Lanes 1, 2, and 3 contain varying concentrations of $MgCl_2$ (30, 20, and 10 μ*M*, respectively), and each contains a ratio of 1:1.2:1.1 of *in vitro* RNA to synthetic RNA to DNA splint.

of several nmols of RNA, a 1-nmol scale ligation should be tested. Large-scale ligations of the *VC* glycine riboswitch were prepared at the 10 nmol scale.

2.2.2.4 Large-scale purification of ligation product

To purify the 212 nt unligated RNA from the 232 nt ligated product and all other species in the ligation reaction, dPAGE is utilized and provides good resolution between the two RNAs. The large-scale ligation described will yield 10 mL of reaction volume and must first be concentrated prior to purification by dPAGE. Amicon centrifugal concentrators are commonly used for this purpose. However, we have found that RNA losses tend to be large; therefore, we used large-scale PCA extraction and ethanol precipitation to concentrate the ligation reaction.

2.2.2.4.1 Large-scale PCA extraction PCA extraction of the 10-mL ligation volume should be performed as would normally be done with an equal volume of PCA added to the RNA in a 50-mL falcon tube followed by thorough vortexing and centrifugation at 3500 rpm using an Eppendorf 5810 R centrifuge with an A4-81 rotor, or equivalent g-force, at 4 °C, for 5 min. The top phase can then be transferred as two equivalent volume aliquots into separate 50-mL Falcon tubes and subsequent large-scale ethanol precipitation can be performed.

2.2.2.4.2 Large-scale ethanol precipitation To each volume of extracted RNA add 1/10th the volume of 3 *M* sodium acetate (Fisher Scientific, Pittsburgh, PA) at pH 5.2 and three times the volume of cold 100% ethanol (Fisher Scientific, Pittsburgh, PA). Vortex for 20 s and incubate at −80 °C for 30–45 min. To pellet the RNA, centrifuge at 3500 rpm, 4 °C using an Eppendorf 5810 R centrifuge with an A4-81 rotor, or equivalent g-force, for 1 h. Decant the supernatant and dissolve the RNA pellet in 200 μL TE buffer. Add an equal volume of RNA loading dye and load onto the dPAGE for purification.

Critical Step: In our experience, the time of centrifugation for the large-scale ethanol precipitation is important for avoiding RNA loss. The 1-h centrifugation time was our optimized parameter. To ensure minimal loss of RNA, the collected supernatant should be centrifuged again using the same conditions to verify that no further RNA is pelleted.

2.2.2.4.3 Purification by dPAGE Adequate resolution of the large, 232 nt, 10 nmol scale-ligated riboswitch RNA from the unligated 212 nt *in vitro* RNA required use of ~23 mm plates, 3 mm spacers/combs, and preparation of a 6% gel which was run for 3–4 h at 4 °C using 15 W power. These conditions may differ for other ligation reactions involving RNAs of different lengths. Visualize the correct band corresponding to the ligated RNA using a hand-held UV (minimizing the UV exposure of the RNA) and excise the band using sterile and nuclease-free techniques into dialysis tubing of the appropriate molecular weight cut-off (MWCO). Electroelute the RNA in 10–20 mL TE buffer at 4 °C, using 120 V, for 12–16 h in a horizontal electroelution chamber (Fisher Scientific, Pittsburgh, PA).

Using sterile and nuclease-free techniques, recover the 10–20 mL solution containing the electroeluted ligation product and concentrate the RNA using large-scale PCA extraction and large-scale ethanol precipitation as previously described. The obtained RNA pellet can be dried using a rotary evaporator such as a SpeedVac or by lyophilization. It can then be re-dissolved in 10–20 μL nuclease-free water or desired nuclease-free buffer before determining the final concentration.

2.2.2.4.4 Sample preparation for CW-EPR Samples for X-band (9.5 GHz) CW-EPR using loop gap or dielectric resonators require as little as 5 μL of 100 μ*M*-labeled RNA. For the VC glycine riboswitch, EPR samples were prepared by loading 0.6 mm I.D. × 0.85 mm O.D. glass capillary tubes (Fiber Optic Center, New Bedford, MA) with 5 μL of approximately 100 μ*M* spin-labeled riboswitch. Flame seal the capillary tubes at one end and load samples using a syringe needle (Hamilton, Reno, NV). To prepare ligand-bound riboswitch samples, add the appropriate concentration of respective ligand to aliquotted fractions of RNA and load each into its own capillary tube for EPR investigation.

3. CW-EPR SPECTRAL ANALYSIS OF RIBOSWITCHES

CW-EPR is often used for site-specific interrogation of local dynamics, and the utility of SDSL-EPR for RNA structure and dynamics studies has been nicely reviewed by Sowa and Qin (2008). CW-EPR spectral analysis can be performed by utilizing simulations to quantitate the nitroxide rotational correlation time and order parameter, and examples of such RNA studies have been reported (Grant et al., 2009). Additionally, empirical line shape analyses can be used to characterize dynamics. Here, we describe CW-EPR for a single-labeled site within the VC glycine riboswitch at the 5′-end and emphasize use of line shape analysis that can be used to extract information regarding local dynamics. Several parameters describe nitroxide motion as reported by the sensitivity of CW-EPR line shapes and these include both the rate and amplitude of motion (Sowa & Qin, 2008). One such example is the intensity of the high (h_{-1}), central (h_0), and low-field (h_{+1}) resonance lines as labeled in Fig. 13.6A.

Integral area normalized intensities of the central and high-field transitions, for example, can be used to compare spectra and changes in dynamics. Larger intensity values are representative of greater motion compared to smaller intensity values. Figure 13.6B exemplifies the usefulness of this parameter through comparison of a 20-nt R5 spin-labeled synthetic RNA fragment before and after ligation. Prior to ligation, the rotational correlation time is governed by the fast isotropic motion of the small (~6 kDa) RNA tumbling in solution. After ligation to the large full length (~75 kDa) *VC* glycine riboswitch, incomplete anisotropic averaging occurs and the intensity of each transition decreases. The ability to compare spectra in this capacity is of particular application to the study of riboswitches where spectra can be collected and compared for varying conditions and in the ligand-free versus ligand-bound states. Figure 13.6C shows spectra comparing the 232 nt VC glycine riboswitch in the absence and presence of glycine ligand and demonstrates how changes in local dynamics can be compared. For R5 labeling, both the R_p and S_p diastereomers are present; however, differences in backbone dynamics can still be differentiated (Esquiaqui et al., 2014). Quantifying h_0 intensity changes using integral area normalized spectra can be performed using free software such as Easyspin (Stoll & Schweiger, 2006).

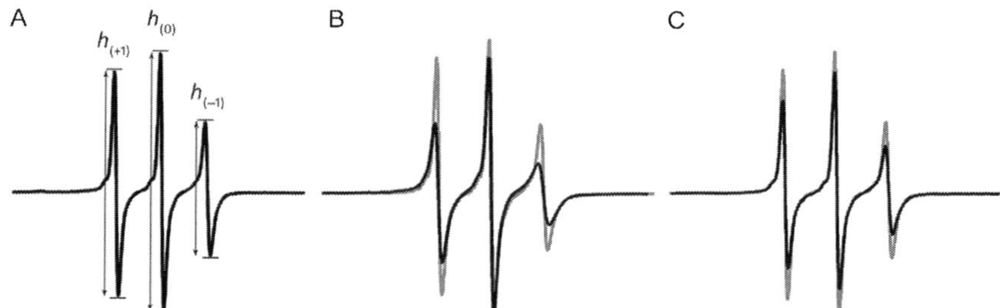

Figure 13.6 Integral area normalized CW-EPR spectra. (A) X-band nitroxide spectrum with high (h_{-1}), central (h_0), and low-field (h_{+1}) transitions labeled. (B) Comparison of an R5 spin-labeled 20 nt synthetic RNA fragment before (gray) and after (black) ligation. (C) Comparison of the R5 spin-labeled 232 nt VC glycine riboswitch in the absence (gray) and presence (black) of glycine ligand.

Additional empirical parameters can be used to further describe changes in dynamics, such as the second moment $\langle H_2 \rangle$ and central line width ΔH_{pp}, reviewed elsewhere (Fanucci & Cafiso, 2006; Sowa & Qin, 2008). Both quantitative and empirical methods for analyzing CW-EPR data provide a powerful tool for the study of riboswitches. The ability to utilize EPR spectroscopy for the study of large riboswitches relies upon feasible and efficient incorporation of spin labels. Here, we have reviewed strategies that can be applied for this purpose. Specifically, we have provided details for a facile ligation method using T4 DNA ligase to spin label the *VC* glycine riboswitch that is 232 nt in length.

REFERENCES

Akiyama, B. M., & Stone, M. D. (2009). Assembly of complex RNAs by splinted ligation. *Methods in Enzymology*, *469*, 27–46.

Baird, N. J., & Ferre-D'Amare, A. R. (2013). Modulation of quaternary structure and enhancement of ligand binding by the K-turn of tandem glycine riboswitches. *RNA*, *19*(2), 167–176.

Breaker, R. R. (2011). Prospects for riboswitch discovery and analysis. *Molecular Cell*, *43*(6), 867–879.

Buttner, L., Seikowski, J., Wawrzyniak, K., Ochmann, A., & Hobartner, C. (2013). Synthesis of spin-labeled riboswitch RNAs using convertible nucleosides and DNA-catalyzed RNA ligation. *Bioorganic and Medicinal Chemistry*, *21*(20), 6171–6180.

Cai, Q., Kusnetzow, A. K., Hubbell, W. L., Haworth, I. S., Gacho, G. P., Van Eps, N., et al. (2006). Site-directed spin labeling measurements of nanometer distances in nucleic acids using a sequence-independent nitroxide probe. *Nucleic Acids Research*, *34*(17), 4722–4730.

Columbus, L., & Hubbell, W. L. (2002). A new spin on protein dynamics. *Trends in Biochemical Sciences*, *27*(6), 288–295.

Crary, S. M., Kurz, J. C., & Fierke, C. A. (2002). Specific phosphorothioate substitutions probe the active site of Bacillus subtilis ribonuclease P. *RNA*, *8*(7), 933–947.

Dalgarno, P. A., Bordello, J., Morris, R., St-Pierre, P., Dube, A., Samuel, I. D., et al. (2013). Single-molecule chemical denaturation of riboswitches. *Nucleic Acids Research*, *41*(7), 4253–4265.

Edwards, T. E., & Sigurdsson, S. T. (2007). Site-specific incorporation of nitroxide spin-labels into 2'-positions of nucleic acids. *Nature Protocols*, *2*(8), 1954–1962.

El-Sagheer, A. H., & Brown, T. (2010). New strategy for the synthesis of chemically modified RNA constructs exemplified by hairpin and hammerhead ribozymes. *Proceedings of the National Academy of Sciences of the United States of America*, *107*(35), 15329–15334.

Esquiaqui, J. M., Sherman, E. M., Ionescu, S. A., Ye, J., & Fanucci, G. E. (2014). Characterizing the dynamics of the leader-linker interaction in the glycine riboswitch with site-directed spin labeling. *Biochemistry*, *53*, 3526–3528.

Fanucci, G. E., & Cafiso, D. S. (2006). Recent advances and applications of site-directed spin labeling. *Current Opinion in Structural Biology*, *16*(5), 644–653.

Grant, G. P., Boyd, N., Herschlag, D., & Qin, P. Z. (2009). Motions of the substrate recognition duplex in a group I intron assessed by site-directed spin labeling. *Journal of the American Chemical Society*, *131*(9), 3136–3137.

Hobartner, C., Sicoli, G., Wachowius, F., Gophane, D. B., & Sigurdsson, S. T. (2012). Synthesis and characterization of RNA containing a rigid and nonperturbing cytidine-derived spin label. *The Journal of Organic Chemistry*, 77(17), 7749–7754.

Hubbell, W. L., Cafiso, D. S., & Altenbach, C. (2000). Identifying conformational changes with site-directed spin labeling. *Natural Structural Biology*, *7*(9), 735–739.

Hubbell, W. L., Lopez, C. J., Altenbach, C., & Yang, Z. (2013). Technological advances in site-directed spin labeling of proteins. *Current Opinion in Structural Biology*, *23*(5), 725–733.

Jeschke, G. (2013). Conformational dynamics and distribution of nitroxide spin labels. *Progress in Nuclear Magnetic Resonance Spectroscopy*, *72*, 42–60.

Karns, K., Vogan, J. M., Qin, Q., Hickey, S. F., Wilson, S. C., Hammond, M. C., et al. (2013). Microfluidic screening of electrophoretic mobility shifts elucidates riboswitch binding function. *Journal of the American Chemical Society*, *135*(8), 3136–3143.

Klare, J. P. (2013). Site-directed spin labeling EPR spectroscopy in protein research. *Biological Chemistry*, *394*(10), 1281–1300.

Klug, C. S., & Feix, J. B. (2008). Methods and applications of site-directed spin labeling EPR spectroscopy. *Methods in Cell Biology*, *84*, 617–658.

Kurschat, W. C., Muller, J., Wombacher, R., & Helm, M. (2005). Optimizing splinted ligation of highly structured small RNAs. *RNA*, *11*(12), 1909–1914.

Kwon, M., & Strobel, S. A. (2008). Chemical basis of glycine riboswitch cooperativity. *RNA*, *14*(1), 25–34.

Mandal, M., & Breaker, R. R. (2004). Gene regulation by riboswitches. *Nature Reviews Molecular Cell Biology*, *5*(6), 451–463.

Moore, M. J., & Query, C. C. (2000). Joining of RNAs by splinted ligation. *Methods in Enzymology*, *317*, 109–123.

Piton, N., Mu, Y., Stock, G., Prisner, T. F., Schiemann, O., & Engels, J. W. (2007). Base-specific spin-labeling of RNA for structure determination. *Nucleic Acids Research*, *35*(9), 3128–3143.

Popova, A. M., Kalai, T., Hideg, K., & Qin, P. Z. (2009). Site-specific DNA structural and dynamic features revealed by nucleotide-independent nitroxide probes. *Biochemistry*, *48*(36), 8540–8550.

Price, E. A., Sutch, B. T., Cai, Q., Qin, P. Z., & Haworth, I. S. (2007). Computation of nitroxide-nitroxide distances in spin-labeled DNA duplexes. *Biopolymers*, *87*(40), 40–50.

Qin, P. Z., Haworth, I. S., Cai, Q., Kusnetzow, A. K., Grant, G. P., Price, E. A., et al. (2007). Measuring nanometer distances in nucleic acids using a sequence-independent nitroxide probe. *Nature Protocols*, *2*(10), 2354–2365.

Qin, P. Z., Hideg, K., Feigon, J., & Hubbell, W. L. (2003). Monitoring RNA base structure and dynamics using site-directed spin labeling. *Biochemistry*, *42*(22), 6772–6783.

Regulski, E. E., & Breaker, R. R. (2008). In-line probing analysis of riboswitches. *Methods in Molecular Biology*, *419*, 53–67.

Reining, A., Nozinovic, S., Schlepckow, K., Buhr, F., Furtig, B., & Schwalbe, H. (2013). Three-state mechanism couples ligand and temperature sensing in riboswitches. *Nature*, *499*(7458), 355–359.

Rieder, R., Hobartner, C., & Micura, R. (2009). Enzymatic ligation strategies for the preparation of purine riboswitches with site-specific chemical modifications. *Methods in Molecular Biology*, *540*, 15–24.

Roth, A., & Breaker, R. R. (2009). The structural and functional diversity of metabolite-binding riboswitches. *Annual Review of Biochemistry*, *78*, 305–334.

Schiemann, O., Piton, N., Plackmeyer, J., Bode, B. E., Prisner, T. F., & Engels, J. W. (2007). Spin labeling of oligonucleotides with the nitroxide TPA and use of PELDOR, a pulse EPR method, to measure intramolecular distances. *Nature Protocols*, *2*(4), 904–923.

Serganov, A., & Patel, D. J. (2012a). Metabolite recognition principles and molecular mechanisms underlying riboswitch function. *Annual Review of Biophysics*, *41*, 343–370.

Serganov, A., & Patel, D. J. (2012b). Molecular recognition and function of riboswitches. *Current Opinion in Structural Biology*, *22*(3), 279–286.

Shelke, S. A., & Sigurdsson, S. T. (2012). Site-directed spin labelling of nucleic acids. *European Journal of Organic Chemistry*, *2012*(12), 2291–2301.

Sherman, E. M., Esquiaqui, J., Elsayed, G., & Ye, J. D. (2012). An energetically beneficial leader-linker interaction abolishes ligand-binding cooperativity in glycine riboswitches. *RNA*, *18*(3), 496–507.

Sherman, E. M., Holmes, S., & Ye, J. D. (2014). Specific RNA-binding antibodies with a four-amino-acid code. *Journal of Molecular Biology*, *426*, 2145–2157.

Sicoli, G., Wachowius, F., Bennati, M., & Hobartner, C. (2010). Probing secondary structures of spin-labeled RNA by pulsed EPR spectroscopy. *Angewandte Chemie International Edition in English*, *49*(36), 6443–6447.

Sigurdsson, S. T. (2011). Nitroxides and nucleic acids: Chemistry and electron paramagnetic resonance (EPR) spectroscopy. *Pure and Applied Chemistry*, *83*(3), 677–686.

Solomatin, S., & Herschlag, D. (2009). Methods of site-specific labeling of RNA with fluorescent dyes. *Methods in Enzymology*, *469*, 47–68.

Soukup, G. A., & Breaker, R. R. (1999). Relationship between internucleotide linkage geometry and the stability of RNA. *RNA*, *5*(10), 1308–1325.

Sowa, G. Z., & Qin, P. Z. (2008). Site-directed spin labeling studies on nucleic acid structure and dynamics. *Progress in Nucleic Acid Research and Molecular Biology*, *82*, 147–197.

Stoll, S., & Schweiger, A. (2006). EasySpin, a comprehensive software package for spectral simulation and analysis in EPR. *Journal of Magnetic Resonance*, *178*(1), 42–55.

Strobel, S. A., & Cech, T. R. (1995). Minor groove recognition of the conserved G.U. pair at the Tetrahymena ribozyme reaction site. *Science*, *267*(5198), 675–679.

Tolbert, B. S., Miyazaki, Y., Barton, S., Kinde, B., Starck, P., Singh, R., et al. (2010). Major groove width variations in RNA structures determined by NMR and impact of 13C residual chemical shift anisotropy and 1H-13C residual dipolar coupling on refinement. *Journal of Biomolecular NMR*, *47*(3), 205–219.

Tkach, I., Pornsuwan, S., Hobartner, C., Wachowius, F., Sigurdsson, S. T., Baranova, T. Y., et al. (2007). Orientation selection in distance measurements between nitroxide spin labels at 94 GHz EPR with variable dual frequency irradiation. *Physical Chemistry Chemical Physics*, *15*(10), 3433–3437.

Tyrrell, J., McGinnis, J. L., Weeks, K. M., & Pielak, G. J. (2013). The cellular environment stabilizes adenine riboswitch RNA structure. *Biochemistry*, *52*(48), 8777–8785.

Wunnicke, D., Strohbach, D., Weigand, J. E., Appel, B., Feresin, E., Suess, B., et al. (2011). Ligand-induced conformational capture of a synthetic tetracycline riboswitch revealed by pulse EPR. *RNA*, *17*(1), 182–188.

Zhang, X., Cekan, P., Sigurdsson, S. T., & Qin, P. Z. (2009). Studying RNA using site-directed spin-labeling and continuous-wave electron paramagnetic resonance spectroscopy. *Methods in Enzymology*, *469*, 303–328.

Zhang, X., Tung, C. S., Sowa, G. Z., Hatmal, M. M., Haworth, I. S., & Qin, P. Z. (2012). Global structure of a three-way junction in a phi29 packaging RNA dimer determined using site-directed spin labeling. *Journal of the American Chemical Society*, *134*(5), 2644–2652.

CHAPTER FOURTEEN

Using sm-FRET and Denaturants to Reveal Folding Landscapes

Euan Shaw*, Patrick St-Pierre†, Kaley McCluskey*, Daniel A. Lafontaine†,[1], J. Carlos Penedo*,‡,[1]

*SUPA School of Physics and Astronomy, University of St. Andrews, St. Andrews, Fife, United Kingdom
†RNA Group, Department of Biology, Faculty of Science, Université de Sherbrooke, Sherbrooke, Québec, Canada
‡Biomedical Sciences Research Complex, University of St. Andrews, St. Andrews, Fife, United Kingdom
[1]Corresponding authors: e-mail address: daniel.lafontaine@usherbrooke.ca; jcp10@st-andrews.ac.uk

Contents

Abstract

RNA folding studies aim to clarify the relationship among sequence, tridimensional structure, and biological function. In the last decade, the application of single-molecule fluorescence resonance energy transfer (sm-FRET) techniques to investigate RNA structure and folding has revealed the details of conformational changes and timescale of the process leading to the formation of biologically active RNA structures with subnanometer resolution on millisecond timescales. In this review, we initially summarize the first wave of single-molecule FRET-based RNA techniques that focused on analyzing the influence of mono- and divalent metal ions on RNA function, and how these studies have provided

Methods in Enzymology, Volume 549
ISSN 0076-6879
http://dx.doi.org/10.1016/B978-0-12-801122-5.00014-3

very valuable information about folding pathways and the presence of intermediate and low-populated states. Next, we describe a second generation of single-molecule techniques that combine sm-FRET with the use of chemical denaturants as an emerging powerful approach to reveal information about the dynamics and energetics of RNA folding that remains hidden using conventional sm-FRET approaches. The main advantages of using the competing interplay between folding agents such as metal ions and denaturants to observe and manipulate the dynamics of RNA folding and RNA–ligand interactions is discussed in the context of the adenine riboswitch aptamer.

1. INTRODUCTION

The formation of secondary and tertiary interactions between different domains of an RNA sequence is essential to yield the compact structure that is responsible for the range of catalytic and regulatory functions observed in many noncoding RNAs (Li, Vieregg, & Tinoco, 2008). This RNA folding process from a random coiled chain of nucleic acids to a functional tridimensional structure is understood to take place hierarchically and to be assisted by mono- and divalent metal ions (Fig. 14.1; Woodson, 2005). First,

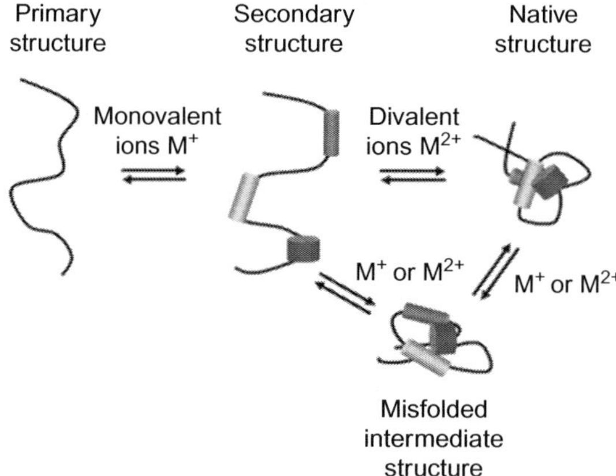

Figure 14.1 Folding of RNA induced by monovalent (M^+) and divalent metal ions (M^{2+}). Interaction of the RNA chain with positive monovalent ions neutralizes most of the phosphate charge and induced its collapse into a more compact conformation where self-recognition processes between nucleobases promote base-pairing and secondary RNA structure formation. With assistance from divalent metal ions, RNA folding can further progress to native-like conformations that undergo additional conformational rearrangements leading to native structures. In certain cases, nonspecific contacts leading to a set of nonnative intermediate states can be formed along the folding pathway that need to be resolved to allow the formation of the native structure.

the linear RNA polymer adopts its secondary structure through a self-recognition process involving the formation of stable base-pairs with help from monovalent metal ions, such as K^+ and Na^+. Subsequently, tertiary interactions can be established between RNA domains to yield the native structure (Fig. 14.1). From a biophysical perspective, the RNA folding process relates to the search for the global energy minimum along the conformational landscape and can be divided into early- and late-stage events (Sosnick & Pan, 2003). When an unfolded RNA structure initially interacts with added ions, the RNA rapidly collapses (often <1 ms), either nonspecifically into a species similar to the molten globules observed during protein folding, or into RNA structures containing some tertiary interactions that may or may not correspond to specific contacts present in the native structure (Woodson, 2010). In those cases where nonnative interactions have been formed, the RNA can remain kinetically trapped in this local minimum for long periods of time compared to the average lifetime of the RNA in the cell (Sosnick & Pan, 2003). For instance, kinetic traps have been observed for the P3–P7 catalytic domain of the *Tetrahymena* group I ribozyme (Treiber, Rook, Zarrinkar, & Williamson, 1998) and the *Bacillus subtilis* RNase P (Woodson, 2010).

While predicting the RNA secondary structure is possible using thermodynamic models (Andersen, 2010; Mathews, 2006), no equivalent theoretical framework has been developed to model the network of contacts that constitute the tertiary structure and how this is influenced by metal ions. Fortunately, during the last decade, improvements in fluorescence detection have allowed the development of single-molecule techniques that enabled us to investigate the RNA tertiary structure and the folding pathway with an unprecedented level of detail (Al-Hashimi & Walter, 2008; Bokinsky & Zhuang, 2005; Li et al., 2008; Tinoco, Chen, & Qu, 2010). The majority of these single-molecule studies have utilized fluorescence resonance energy transfer (FRET) as a molecular ruler to monitor the distance between dye-labeled nucleotides (Fig. 14.2A) and how this varies during real-time folding (Fernandez-Luna, 2008; Ha, 2004; Joo, Balci, Ishitsuka, Buranachai, & Ha, 2008; McKinney et al., 2004; Roy, Hohng, & Ha, 2008; Tinoco & Gonzalez, 2011). In a FRET assay, the RNA under investigation is labeled with a pair of fluorescent molecules, one acting as a FRET donor and the other acting as a FRET acceptor. The dipole–dipole interaction between them causes energy transfer from the initially excited donor to the acceptor, leading to a decrease in the donor emission and a concomitant increase in the acceptor emission (Clegg, 1995; Clegg, Murchie, Zechel, & Lilley, 1993).

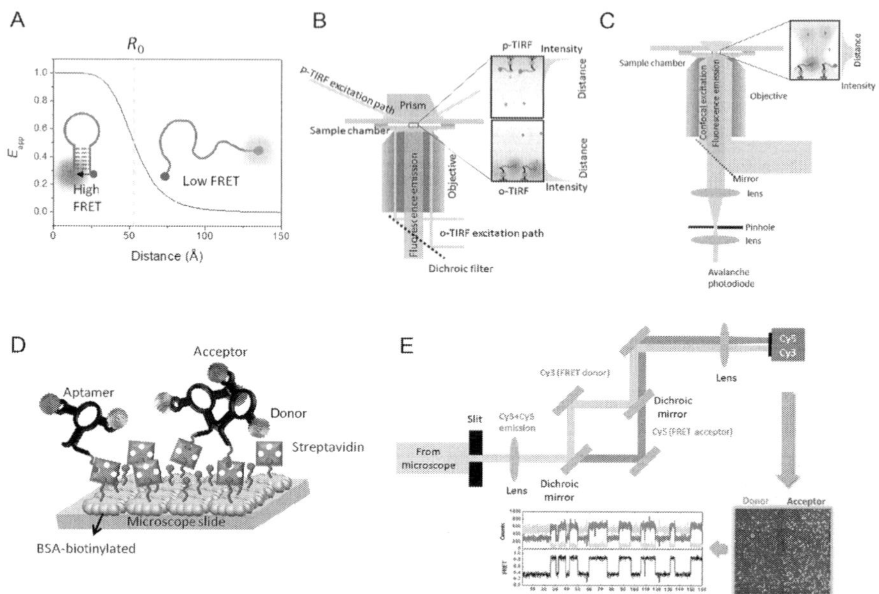

Figure 14.2 Principle of single-molecule FRET (sm-FRET). (A) Efficiency of FRET as a function of interdye separation, *R*. E_{FRET} depends on the inverse of the sixth-power of the distance, making changes in FRET-sensitive indicators of conformational changes in fluorescently labeled RNA molecules. (B) Schematic of the excitation pathway for prism-type total-internal reflection fluorescence (p-TIRF) and objective-type TIRF (o-TIRF). In p-TIRF, the excitation laser is focused onto the upper face of the sample chamber through a quartz prism, while in o-TIRF, it is coupled onto the lower face through the extreme edge of the microscope objective using a dichroic mirror. In confocal microscopy (C), the objective focuses the excitation beam as in ordinary confocal microscopy. In all cases, dye fluorescence is collected by a high numerical aperture microscope objective (water-immersion for p-TIRF and oil-immersion for o-TIRF). Residual excitation light is filtered or directed away from the detection optics. The intensity of the evanescent wave generated at the quartz microscope slide/water interface (p-TIRF) or at the glass coverslip/water interface decays exponentially with the distance from the surface. This allows excitation of a very thin layer within the sample chamber, immediately adjacent to the surface where the RNA is immobilized. (D) Schematics of sample immobilization using the noncovalent interactions between biotinylated bovine serum albumin (BSA) and streptavidin or neutravidin. Sixty microliters of a 1 mg/mL solution of biotinylated BSA (bi-BSA) is injected into the sample chamber and incubated for 10 min to allow nonspecific binding to the slide. After washing the unbound bi-BSA another 60 μL of a 0.2 mg/mL solution of streptavidin is injected into the chamber and allowed to incubate for 10 min. After washing the unbound streptavidin, a 100–200 p*M* solution of biotinylated RNA is injected into the sample chamber and allowed to incubate for 5 min. (E) Schematic of the optical emission pathway common to p-TIRF and o-TIRF. The fluorescence emission from the sample is collected by the objective and directed onto a slit to select an appropriate image size that fills half of the EMCCD chip. The fluorescent signal containing Cy3 (FRET donor, green) and Cy5 (FRET acceptor, red) is

The efficiency of the energy transfer process is given by $E = 1/(1 + (R/R_0)^6)$, where R represents the donor–acceptor distance and R_0 represents the distance at which the FRET efficiency is 50% (Förster distance). The dependence of the efficiency of the FRET process on the inverse of the sixth-power of the distance makes FRET very sensitive to distance changes in the interval from ~2 to 8 nm, which is relevant for many biological processes including RNA folding (Clegg, 1995; Clegg et al., 1993; Joo et al., 2008).

2. SINGLE-MOLECULE FRET: TECHNICAL ASPECTS

In the last decade, the development of single-molecule fluorescence microscopy has allowed FRET to be measured in individual molecules either freely diffusing or immobilized on a microscope slide (Blouin, Craggs, Lafontaine, & Penedo, 2009; Cornish & Ha, 2007; McCluskey, Shaw, Lafontaine, & Penedo, 2014; Roy et al., 2008). In this chapter, we will focus on its application to investigate riboswitch conformational changes. Readers are referred to a number of review articles for other applications (Blouin, Mulhbacher, Penedo, & Lafontaine, 2009; Rothenberg & Ha, 2010; Schuler & Hofmann, 2013). Single-molecule fluorescence resonance energy transfer (sm-FRET) offers a number of advantages over conventional ensemble-averaging methods. The possibility of following conformational changes taking place in individual molecules allows us to divide the RNA population into its constituent species, discard molecules with partial labeling, study kinetic processes that cannot be synchronized, and reveal heterogeneity in folding and kinetic pathways (Cornish & Ha, 2007; Tinoco & Gonzalez, 2011).

RNA folding typically occurs on a millisecond to minute timescale which allows the use of microscopy techniques that employ prism-based or objective-based total-internal reflection fluorescence (p-TIRF or o-TIRF, respectively) as the excitation method and CCD camera detection

separated into its two components using a dichroic mirror and then recombined using a second dichroic mirror to allow simultaneous imaging of each signal into each half of the camera. A representative image and single-molecule trace showing donor and acceptor variations in fluorescence intensity as a function of time for a nucleic acid sample exhibiting two-state dynamics are shown. FRET efficiency can be calculated from the Cy3 (green) and Cy5 (red) intensities (see main text), resulting in a single-molecule trajectory of E_{app} versus time, as shown in the bottom panel (black). (See the color plate.)

with on-chip amplification (Fig. 14.2B; Joo et al., 2008; Roy et al., 2008). Temporal resolutions in the submillisecond range are also possible using confocal microscopes and point detectors such as avalanche photodiodes (Fig. 14.2C). However, because confocal geometries record only one molecule at a time, these faster acquisition rates intrinsically limit the statistics to a lower number of molecules compared to wide-field approaches and are incompatible with irreversible processes. Single-molecule TIR microscopy methods combined with surface-immobilization of the RNA sequence allows the simultaneous monitoring of hundred of single molecules for long periods of time (Fig. 14.2D). There are a number of ways in which the nucleic acid structure can be tethered to the microscope slide (McCluskey et al., 2014). The most widely used method requires one strand of the RNA structure to carry a biotin moiety that can be incorporated during solid-phase synthesis from commercial sources (Integrated DNA Technologies (IDT), USA; Thermo Fisher Scientific, USA) or added post-synthetically using RNA sequences carrying a primary amino group and *N*-hydroxysuccinimidobiotin (NHS-Biotin; Piercenet, USA). A brief description of the immobilization protocol of biotin-functionalized RNA structures includes the following steps: (i) initial incubation of 60 μL of a 1 mg/mL biotinylated bovine serum albumin (BSA; Sigma) for 15 min, (ii) washing of unbound bi-BSA with 100 μL of buffer solution (50 m*M* Tris–HCl, pH 8), (iii) 15 min incubation with 60 μL of 0.2 mg/mL neutravidin (Sigma), (iv) repeat step (ii) to remove unbound streptavidin, and (v) addition of ~60 μL of a 50–100 p*M* solution of the fluorescently labeled RNA construct carrying the biotin moiety. After 10 min incubation, wash with imaging buffer (see details below) to remove unbound constructs and check for sample density in the TIR microscope (200–300 spots are considered an appropriate density).

For a single FRET pair, the ratio $I_{acc}/(I_{acc}+I_{don})$, where I_{acc} and I_{don} are the acceptor and donor fluorescence intensities, yields the apparent FRET efficiency which directly reflects the relative changes in the RNA structure as a function of time (Roy et al., 2008). The details of the emission pathway, which is common to p-TIRF and o-TIRF, are shown in Fig. 14.2E. The combination of Cy3 as donor and Cy5 as acceptor is the most commonly used FRET pair in single-molecule folding studies of surface-immobilized RNA (Förster distance (R_0) of ~53 Å). Importantly, the photostability of the Cy5 acceptor dye is much lower than that of Cy3, but the addition imaging buffers containing oxygen scavenging systems (i.e., glucose oxidase/catalase or the more recent protocatechuic acid/protocatechuate-3,4-dioxygenase system) and triplet-state quenchers such as Trolox (6-hydroxy-2,5,7,8-tetramethylchroman-2-carboxylic acid) or β-mercaptoethanol is enough to improve the optical performance of both dyes (Cornish & Ha, 2007; McCluskey et al., 2014; Roy et al., 2008). Trolox powder is usually dissolved in methanol (0.1 g per 430 μL). After the addition of 3.2 mL of water, a precipitate is formed that can be redissolved by adding ~350 μL of 1 *M* NaOH and adjusting the final pH of the solution to ~9.0–9.5. Aliquots should be stored at −20 °C to improve long-term stability.

One of the main limitations in the early days of sm-FRET techniques was to extract reliably all the information available from a noisy time-dependent FRET trajectory and to obtain a kinetic scheme to model the functional pathway. The need to analyze single-molecule traces obtained from systems of increasing complexity prompted the development of user-independent methods based on hidden Markov modeling (HMM) to determine in a probabilistic way the number of conformations and the rates of transition between them (McKinney, Joo, & Ha, 2006). Over the last few years, HMM methods have been extensively used to analyze sm-FRET trajectories. The detailed description of the different algorithms is beyond the scope of this chapter and we refer the reader to excellent reports regarding the application of HMM to sm-FRET data (Chodera et al., 2011; Keller, Kobitski, Jäschke, Nienhaus, & Noé, 2014; van de Meent, Bronson, Wood, Gonzalez, & Wiggins, 2013).

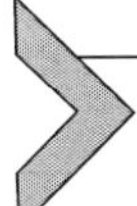

3. RIBOSWITCH STRUCTURE AND BIOLOGICAL FUNCTION

Riboswitches are highly structured noncoding RNAs found in the untranslated region of certain messenger RNAs (mRNAs). Riboswitches control gene expression by sensing the cellular concentration of a particular metabolite to which they bind with high affinity and specificity (Blouin, Craggs, et al., 2009; Blouin, Mulhbacher, et al., 2009; Vitreschak, Rodionov, Mironov, & Gelfand, 2004). They are mostly found in bacterial and fungal genomes, with only one example, the thiamine pyrophosphate (TPP) riboswitch found in plants. Riboswitches are composed of two modular domains: a metabolite-sensing domain, called the aptamer domain, and the expression platform (Fig. 14.3) The aptamer domains are highly conserved, whereas the expression platforms vary widely in sequence and structure to allow the control of gene regulation by different mechanisms, such as modulating the formation of Rho-independent transcriptional terminators,

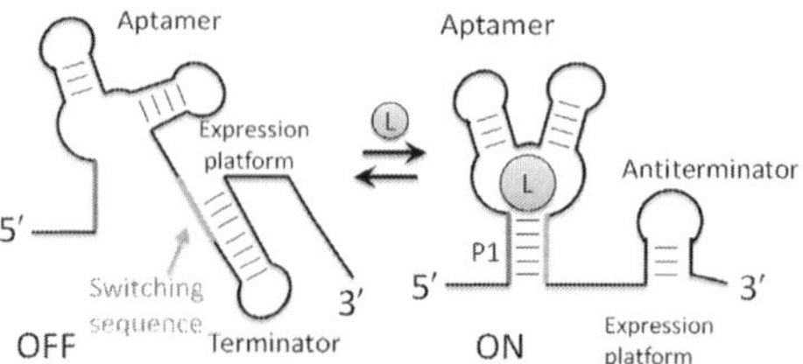

Figure 14.3 Schematic of a riboswitch regulating gene expression by transcription termination. In the ligand-free state, the "switching sequence" (green (light gray in the print version)) participates in the formation of a terminator stem in the expression platform that dictates transcription termination. In the presence of ligand (L), the aptamer domain undergoes a conformational change and the "switching sequence" becomes an integral part of the aptamer domain allowing the formation of an antiterminator stem that allows transcription to continue.

sequestering the Shine–Dalgarno sequences required for translation initiation or controlling mRNA splicing and mRNA stability (Bastet, Dubé, Massé, & Lafontaine, 2011; Lemay et al., 2011). Riboswitches modulate the expression of genes located downstream of the riboswitch sequence and normally associated with the biosynthesis or transport of their cognate metabolite. The control of the regulation mechanism can be triggered by a variety of small molecules including nucleotides, amino acids, and cofactors (Serganov, 2009; Winkler & Breaker, 2003). Riboswitches have attracted considerable interest since their discovery a decade ago because of their potential as targets for antibacterial drug development (Blount & Breaker, 2006; Deigan & Ferré-D'Amaré, 2011; Mulhbacher, St-Pierre, & Lafontaine, 2010; Winkler & Breaker, 2005). A simplified model of the regulatory mechanism in riboswitches is described in Fig. 14.3, and several recent reviews have summarized the architectures and regulatory pathways for many riboswitch structures (Montange & Batey, 2008; Serganov & Nudler, 2013).

Since the first sm-FRET study reporting the folding pathway of the adenine riboswitch aptamer domain (Lemay, Penedo, Tremblay, Lilley, & Lafontaine, 2006), sm-FRET studies have now been reported for the S-adenosylmethionine (SAM-I) (Eschbach, St-Pierre, Penedo, & Lafontaine, 2012; Heppell et al., 2011); SAM-II (Haller, Rieder, Aigner, Blanchard, & Micura, 2011), lysine (Fiegland, Garst, Batey, & Nesbitt, 2012), TPP (Haller, Altman, Soulière, Blanchard, & Micura, 2013), preQ1 (Suddala et al., 2013), and c-di-GMP riboswitches (Wood, Ferré-D'Amaré, & Rueda, 2012). In this chapter, we will describe the combination of sm-FRET and chemical denaturants to investigate the folding landscape and ligand-binding mechanism on the adenine aptamer. For additional information regarding other riboswitches, the reader is referred to several excellent reviews summarizing current sm-FRET studies (Haller, Soulière & Micura, 2011; Heppell, Mulhbacher, Penedo, & Lafontaine, 2009; Karunatilaka & Rueda, 2009; Savinov, Perez, & Block, 2014).

3.1. sm-FRET studies of the adenine aptamer under nondenaturing conditions

Purine-sensing aptamer domains are organized around a three-way junction connecting three helical domains (P1, P2, and P3, Fig. 14.4A; Delfosse et al., 2010; Kim & Breaker, 2008; Wickiser, Cheah, Breaker, & Crothers, 2005). The crystal structures available for these aptamers in the bound state have shown that the ligand is completely buried inside the RNA-binding pocket and also indicate the presence of a tertiary interaction occurring between the loops at the end of stems P2 and P3 (Allner, Nilsson, & Villa, 2013; Serganov et al., 2004). The interaction between both loops of the adenine-binding add riboswitch aptamer from *Vibrio vulnificus* in the presence of adenine ligand and metal ions was investigated by sm-FRET (Lemay et al., 2006; Tremblay et al., 2011). In this study, a Cy3 and Cy5 FRET pair was incorporated at positions U27 (P2 loop) and U53 (P3 loop) because of their high accessibility to the solvent, as shown in the crystal structure (Serganov et al., 2004). The influence of divalent metal ions in the structure of the adenine aptamer revealed a Mg^{2+}-induced transition from a low-FRET state (E_{app} ~0.25) to a high-FRET state (E_{app} ~0.9). Such shortening of the interdye distance induced by the addition of Mg^{2+} ions with a $[Mg^{2+}]_{1/2}$ of ~20 μM was in agreement with ensemble FRET measurements and suggested that surface-immobilization did not affect the folding pathway. The state with the high-FRET efficiency, which was predominant at high Mg^{2+} concentrations, was assigned to the formation of the loop–loop interaction in the absence of adenine ligand (ligand-free docked state, $\mathbf{D_{LF}}$). The low-FRET state clearly corresponded to an undocked tertiary structure (**UD**). Addition of adenine ligand only increased the relative population of molecules showing a high-FRET state but did not alter the FRET value. Because the loop–loop docked state bound to the ligand ($\mathbf{D_{LB}}$) showed an identical inter-dye distance value to that of the ligand-free ($\mathbf{D_{LF}}$) state, it was not possible, based on differences in FRET efficiency, to differentiate docked states with and without ligand bound. A dwell-time analysis of the effect of the ligand on the interconversion between **UD** and docked states revealed a approximately twofold stabilization of the loop–loop interaction when the RNA–ligand complex was formed. The analysis of the dwell times at 0.5 mM concentration of Mg^{2+} ions revealed a marked heterogeneity (~100-fold)

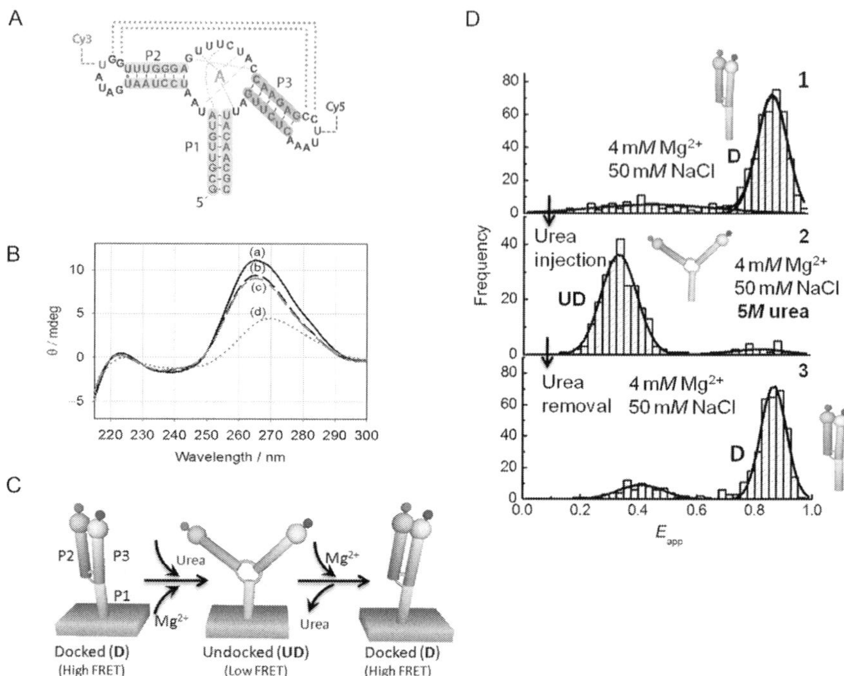

Figure 14.4 (A) Secondary structure of the add adenine riboswitch showing the network of interactions within the aptamer core that are involved in ligand sensing (orange) and in the stabilization of the tertiary structure. The G–C base pairs responsible for the formation of the loop–loop interaction are also shown. The locations of the donor (Cy3) and the acceptor (Cy5) dyes used as FRET pair in single-molecule studies are also displayed. (B) Urea-induced denaturation is specific to the tertiary structure. Circular dichroism (CD) spectra of the adenine aptamer plotted as ellipticity (millidegrees) versus wavelength (nm). [RNA] = 12 μ*M*. (a) 50 m*M* Tris–HCl, pH 7.8, 50 m*M* NaCl, 4 m*M* Mg^{2+}, (b) 50 m*M* Tris–HCl, pH 7.8, No NaCl, No Mg^{2+}, (c) 50 m*M* Tris–HCl, pH 7.8, 50 m*M* NaCl, 4 m*M* Mg^{2+}, 5 *M* urea, (d) 50 m*M* Tris–HCl, pH 7.8, No NaCl, No m*M* Mg^{2+}, 7 *M* urea. (C) Schematic of the folding/unfolding/refolding cycles performed on the add adenine aptamer from *Vibrio vulnificus* to test the reversibility of single-molecule denaturation processes. Surface-immobilized adenine aptamers labeled with an FRET pair as indicated in (A) are placed in an initial docked state characterized by the formation of the loop–loop interaction (high-FRET state). In a first denaturing cycle, the loop–loop interaction is disrupted by the addition of urea (undocked state, low FRET). Subsequent replacement of urea by Mg^{2+} restores the docked state. (D) Single-molecule FRET histograms corresponding to the cycles described in (C). (1) In a background of 4 m*M* Mg^{2+} and 50 m*M* Na^+ most of the aptamer molecules are in the docked conformation as indicated by the histogram centered at E_{app} ~0.9. (2) Addition of 5 *M* urea while maintaining the concentrations of mono- and divalent ions shifts the sm-FRET histogram completely to the undocked conformation (E_{app} ~0.3). (3) An additional refolding cycle removing urea restores the aptamer molecules to the high-FRET docked state and confirms the reversibility of the denaturation process. *Adapted from Dalgarno et al. (2013).* (See the color plate.)

in the docking and undocking rates, which was reduced by one order of magnitude after the addition of 50 μ*M* adenine ligand.

Importantly, in addition to a relative increase in the population of the $\mathbf{D_{LF}}$ state, a significant shift from E_{app} ~0.25, with no added Mg^{2+} ions, to a value of E_{app} ~0.5 at 0.5 m*M* Mg^{2+} ions was observed in the single-molecule histograms corresponding to the low-FRET state. These single-molecule experiments were obtained with a 50-ms integration and suggested the presence of an additional intermediate state (**I**, E_{app} ~0.5) on going from **U** to $\mathbf{D_{LF}}$. The presence of this intermediate state was confirmed using the shortest integration time available on the camera (16 ms, acquiring only half chip of the camera). Although the authors did not speculate about the exact structure of this intermediate state, a plausible structure based on sm-FRET and other biochemical evidence was put forward by Batey and coworkers (Gilbert & Batey, 2006) in which the **I** state may be related to the coaxial stacking of helices P1 and P3. In this state, the loops will be brought to a closer distance leading to a detectable increase in FRET efficiency.

4. COMBINATION OF sm-FRET AND DENATURANTS TO INVESTIGATE RIBOSWITCH FOLDING

The majority of sm-FRET studies on RNA folding have been developed almost exclusively around the effect of mono- and divalent metal ions promoting the transition from the unfolded to the native state (Al-Hashimi & Walter, 2008; Lemay, Penedo, Mulhbacher, & Lafontaine, 2009; Savinov et al., 2014). In contrast, the application of sm-FRET to investigate protein folding has followed a different route, based on the application of denaturant agents (i.e., urea, guanidium chloride) to reveal the unfolding pathway and the rate-limiting steps for several proteins (Schuler & Hofmann, 2013). This is a striking difference if we take into account that the applicability of denaturant agents, mostly urea, to investigate RNA folding had already been demonstrated at the ensemble level (Pan & Sosnick, 1997; Treiber et al., 1998).

A recent sm-FRET study has revisited our understanding of the folding pathway of the ligand-free and ligand-bound states of the adenine aptamer providing an example of how, using the competing interplay between folding and unfolding agents, it is possible to extract information that remained previously hidden using conventional sm-FRET (Dalgarno et al., 2013). Although the authors used the adenine riboswitch as a model due to the amount of preexisting structural knowledge, this hybrid technique holds the potential to provide a much higher level of detail about other similar RNA–ligand interactions and complementary information to that obtained by other single-molecule techniques such as optical tweezers (Greenleaf, Frieda, Foster, Woodside, & Block, 2008). In section 4.1, we briefly describe several aspects related to the application of urea to investigate RNA folding at the ensemble level, and then in sections 4.2 to 4.8, at single-molecule level in the context of the adenine riboswitch.

4.1. Urea-induced perturbation of RNA folding: Ensemble studies

The ability of urea to denature folded states in proteins has been known and used for some time to investigate their thermodynamic stability (Bennion & Daggett, 2003). In contrast, urea-induced denaturation of nucleic acids has been much less explored, and how urea alters RNA folding remains poorly understood (Lambert & Draper, 2007; Priyakumar, Hyeon, Thirumalai, & MacKerell, 2009). Recent molecular dynamics (MD) simulations performed on the 22 nt RNA hairpin P5GA (Koculi, Cho, Desai, Thirumalai, & Woodson, 2012) and the PreQ1-riboswitch (Yoon, Thirumalai, & Hyeon, 2013) have provided some insights into the mechanism of RNA denaturation by urea. Both all-atom MD studies suggest a two-step mechanism for urea-induced unfolding, which is mainly driven by hydrogen-bonding and stacking interactions with the nucleobases. Interestingly, no significant interaction between urea and the phosphodiester backbone was observed. In this two-stage process, the initial step requires the infiltration of water molecules into the hydrophobic pocket between the RNA bases. This increases the accessibility of urea to displace interbase hydrogen bonds. In a second step, urea solvates the disrupted bases by establishing multiple hydrogen-bonding and stacking interactions.

The applicability of urea to investigate RNA folding has already been demonstrated at the ensemble level in a number of studies (Shelton, Sosnick, & Pan, 1999; Sosnick, 2001; Sosnick & Pan, 2003). Since then, several ensemble level studies have employed urea to characterize the folding mechanism of large RNAs and the nature of the rate-limiting folding step. For instance, the addition of urea accelerated the folding of the P3–P7 catalytic domain of the *Tetrahymena* ribozyme (Treiber et al., 1998) and the ribozyme from *Bacillus subtilis* RNase P (Woodson, 2010), suggesting that slow folding of large RNAs might arise from the need to resolve a significant number of interactions in the trapped state to progress further to the native state (Woodson, 2010). The use of urea-induced denaturation has emerged as an experimental method to determine the presence of kinetic traps along the folding pathway (Sosnick & Pan, 2003). Because disruption of the trapped structure should facilitate folding, the observation of an acceleration of the folding rate in the presence of urea is usually taken as evidence that the rate-limiting step involves a kinetic trap. On the contrary, addition of urea to an RNA structure that folds without kinetic traps may decelerate folding because urea affects the RNA–Mg^{2+} interaction at low concentrations of Mg^{2+} ions (Sosnick & Pan, 2003).

4.2. Urea-induced perturbation of RNA folding: Single-molecule studies

Although the potential of using chemical denaturation in RNA folding has already been demonstrated at the ensemble level, only a handful of studies had reported its application in single-molecule studies. An early study by Bokinsky and coworkers on the minimal form of the hairpin ribozyme used urea-induced denaturation to probe whether stacking between both helical stems in the undocked state could constitute a kinetic barrier (Bokinsky et al., 2003). They observed a urea-induced decrease in the loop–loop docking rate, indicating that unstacking was not a major contributor to the folding barrier. This was further confirmed by the observation that a ribozyme variant where helical stacking was disfavored did not accelerate the docking rate. Recently, a very elegant single-molecule study using alternating laser excitation and confocal microscopy has reported the application of urea to investigate the hairpin-pseudoknot structural equilibrium of the human telomerase RNA pseudoknot and compared it with a 2 nt non-complementary variant involved in dyskeratosis congenita (Holmstrom & Nesbitt, 2014). By combining the information obtained from urea-induced denaturation with temperature measurements on both constructs, the authors concluded that the mutant pseudoknot is unable to form a functionally relevant triple-helix form known to exist in the wild-type structure. Moreover, in contrast to the accepted model of urea destabilizing the RNA structure mostly by establishing a network of hydrogen bonds with the RNA, it was found that urea altered the WT pseudoknot structure conformation by making unfolding more entropically favorable, thus providing new mechanistic insights into how chemical denaturants destabilize RNA structures.

In section 4.3, we describe in detail the technical considerations that need to be taken into account to investigate riboswitch function by combining sm-FRET with urea-induced denaturation in a single experiment using a total-internal reflection (TIR) microscope. Although we focus on the use of urea as a chemical denaturant, our lab has used similar protocols and methods in the context of other denaturants such as formamide and betaine (Penedo, J. C and Lafontaine, D. A, unpublished data).

4.3. Technical considerations when combining sm-FRET and chemical denaturants

Single-molecule studies of riboswitch folding and ligand recognition mechanisms by FRET using wide-field TIR techniques rely on the immobilization of the RNA structure on the quartz slide to observe the folding dynamics for sufficiently long periods of time (Karunatilaka & Rueda, 2009, McCluskey et al., 2014, Roy et al., 2008). For this, the conventional biotin–streptavidin interaction using a biotinylated RNA is normally the method of choice because of its simplicity. However, several considerations need to be taken into account when using chemical denaturants. As reported by Kurzban and coworkers, streptavidin does not unfold in 6 *M* urea, thereby establishing a threshold to the urea concentration that can be used (Kurzban, Bayer, Wilchek, & Horowitz, 1991). In fact, streptavidin seems to unfold very slowly even in a similar concentration of a stronger denaturant such as guanidinium chloride. Using an intrinsic fluorescence assay, the authors also reported that urea can weakly bind streptavidin within the biotin-binding site with an association constant around $\sim 1.3\ M^{-1}$. In our studies on the urea-induced unfolding of adenine aptamers (Dalgarno et al., 2013), no effect on the number of immobilized aptamers was observed for concentrations of denaturant below 5 *M* when using imaging buffers commonly employed in single-molecule microscopy (50 m*M* Tris, pH 7.8, 50 m*M* NaCl, 0.4–6% glucose (w/w), 0.02 mg/mL glucose catalase (Roche), 0.1 mg/mL glucose oxidase (Sigma). However, a progressive decrease in the number of surface-immobilized aptamers was clearly observed when using concentrations of urea above 7 *M*. This effect was significantly more pronounced in the absence of monovalent ions, with almost 90% of the immobilized aptamers being released into the solution. Whether this effect could be due to urea affecting the nonspecific binding of biotinylated BSA to the quartz surface, or indeed by affecting the biotin–streptavidin interaction, remains to be clarified. Based on our experience, we recommend the use of imaging buffers with a minimum of 10 m*M* concentration of monovalent ions (Na^+ or K^+). At this concentration of monovalent ions, urea concentrations up to 5 *M* can be used safely without disrupting the biotin–streptavidin interaction. Importantly, we have recently observed a significantly higher resistance to urea at lower concentrations of monovalent ions (~1 m*M*) when replacing streptavidin by its deglycosylated version, neutravidin (Penedo, J. C, unpublished data). Neutravidin also offers the additional advantage of a substantially lower non-specific interaction with the negatively charged quartz surface due to its lower pI (6.3) and it is increasingly being used in single-molecule microscopy.

Another aspect to take into account when using TIR as the excitation method to combine sm-FRET with chemical denaturation is related to the variation in refractive index of solutions containing increasing concentrations of urea. Early studies quantified the variation of the refractive index for aqueous solutions, at room temperature, containing up to 9 *M* urea (Warren & Gordon, 1966). In the visible region (~540 nm), the refractive index was found to change from 1.33 in pure water to ~1.408 in 9 *M* urea. TIR-based illumination methods rely on the optical propagation properties of an excitation laser beam traveling from a medium of higher to a medium of lower refractive index to determine the value of the critical angle that ensures the formation of an evanescent wave at the liquid–quartz interface (Fig. 14.2B; Walter, 2008). The exponential decay of the intensity of this evanescent wave within ~100 nm from the surface is used to achieve selective illumination of immobilized RNAs labeled with the FRET pair and to obtain an appropriate signal-to-noise ratio (Fig. 14.2B). Thus, the critical angle for a laser beam traveling from a quartz medium (n_D ~1.46) to an aqueous solution (n_D ~1.33) exhibits TIR at a critical angle given by: $\Theta_c = \sin^{-1}(1.33/1.46) = 66°$. For comparison, a 4 *M* solution of urea with a refractive index of 1.366 changes the critical angle by a moderate 3° (Θ_c ~69°), whereas a 9 *M* concentration of urea (n_D ~1.408) changes this value by almost 9° to a value of ~75°. We have observed that small variations in the critical angle corresponding to urea concentrations of ~4–5 *M* are well tolerated in a TIR microscope optimized to work in aqueous solution, retaining a good signal-to-noise with no need for additional changes in the beam propagation angle. However, for higher concentrations of urea, we recommend either to change the propagation angle accordingly or to carry out the sm-FRET experiments using a confocal configuration (Fig. 14.2C).

When using chemical denaturants to investigate the tertiary folding of riboswitches, it is also critical to ensure that the secondary structure remains unaffected by performing control experiments using, for example, spectroscopic techniques based on circular dichroism (CD). In CD spectroscopy, the differential absorption of right- and left-handed circularly polarized light by a chiral molecule is defined in terms of the ellipticity parameter (Θ) which is expressed in degrees (Sosnick, 2001). However, a more convenient way of characterizing the CD information is the difference in the molar extinction coefficients: $\Delta\varepsilon = \varepsilon_L - \varepsilon_R$ [M^{-1} cm^{-1}]. Absorbance values in the region between 0.3 and 0.8 absorbance units are optimal. A 10–20 μg/mL sample of RNA with an A_{260} ~0.5 in a 1-cm path length cuvette is normally sufficient to take a reasonably good signal, although this might depend on the particular spectrometer settings. Useful spectral information is between 200 and 320 nm and the maximal absorbance of the nucleotide bases is in the region around 260 nm. The application of CD spectroscopy to investigate nucleic acids has been reviewed by Sosnick, Fang, and Shelton (1999)) and more recently by Kypr, Kejnovská, Renčiuk, and Vorlíčková (2009). In the context of the adenine aptamer from *V. vulnificus*, the CD spectra obtained at 7 *M* urea in the absence of metal ions showed a 57% decrease in the intensity of the band at 265 nm and a slight shift to higher wavelength, similar to those obtained under thermal denaturing conditions (Fig. 14.4B). These changes are indicative of substantial reductions in base stacking and major disruptions in the secondary structure of the RNA. In contrast, the CD spectra at the highest urea concentration used in the sm-FRET studies (5 *M*) in the presence of background of Na^+ ions displayed only minor (>10%) changes in the 265 nm region and no shift in its maximum was observed. The differences between both spectra were taken as evidence for urea-induced denaturation being specific to elements of the tertiary structure.

4.4. Urea-induced effects on the single-molecule dynamics of adenine aptamers

To analyze the influence of urea on the dynamics of the add adenine aptamer by sm-FRET, Dalgarno et al. (2013) used a construct with identical labels and located at exactly the same positions on the RNA sequence as those previously employed by Lemay et al. to monitor the loop–loop interaction (Fig. 14.4A; Lemay et al., 2006). The single-molecule procedures and analysis protocols described in the next sections, although specifically discussed in the context of this aptamer, should be broadly applicable to other metabolite-sensing mRNAs just by adapting them to the particular ion and ligand-binding requirements of each regulatory element. Given the intrinsic complexity of the riboswitch dynamics and its dependence on many variables (Mg^{2+}, ligand and urea concentrations), we have divided the next sections according to how chemical denaturation can be used to extract information about different aspects of riboswitch function: reversibility of RNA–urea interaction (Section 4.5), folding pathway of ligand-free and ligand-bound aptamers (Section 4.6), ligand-induced stabilization of the aptamer domain (Section 4.7), and rate-limiting folding step for ligand-free and ligand-bound docked states (Section 4.8).

4.5. *In situ* cycling between Mg^{2+} and urea: A method to quantify the reversibility of chemical denaturation

Prior to a detailed study using urea titrations, it is important to confirm that urea-induced unfolding is a reversible process. Because the RNA is immobilized on the quartz slide, a reversibility test can be carried out by performing several cycles of urea-induced unfolding and Mg^{2+}-assisted refolding while maintaining constant the concentration of monovalent ions (Fig. 14.4C). For the adenine aptamer, the single-molecule histogram obtained in a background of Mg^{2+} ions (~4 m*M*), sufficient to place the aptamer in the ligand-free docked state $\mathbf{D_{LF}}$ (E_{app} ~0.9), was completely shifted to a value of E_{app} ~0.3 upon addition of 5 *M* urea (Fig. 14.4D). This E_{app} value agrees with that obtained in the absence of Mg^{2+} ions that was assigned to a conformation where the loop–loop interaction is not formed (undocked state, **UD**). The same sample was efficiently refolded on the slide by replacing in a single washing step the urea-containing buffer (50 m*M* Tris, pH 7.8, 50 m*M* Na^{+}, 4 m*M* Mg^{2+}, 5 *M* urea) with an identical buffer lacking urea (Fig. 14.4D). This confirmed that urea-induced denaturation of the adenine aptamer is a reversible process and it can be detected at the single-molecule level. The observation that the tertiary structure of a single aptamer can undergo repetitive cycles of folding and unfolding suggests that future studies aiming to manipulate the folding landscape in a controlled manner using the interplay between folding agents (i.e., Mg^{2+}) and unfolding agents (i.e., urea) should be possible. Such studies should pave the way to monitor folding under nonequilibrium conditions, and importantly, to place the riboswitch structure at virtually any point of its conformational space. For instance, by controlling the magnitudes of the folding and unfolding rates using an appropriately balanced concentration of Mg^{2+} and urea, it could be feasible to shift the equilibrium toward low-populated and transient intermediate species, thus allowing their structural characterization in further detail.

4.6. Methods for comparing Mg^{2+}-assisted folding and urea-induced unfolding

It is important to determine whether urea-induced unfolding of the RNA structure takes place through similar conformational states as those observed along the Mg^{2+}-induced folding pathway. The number of states induced by urea and their FRET values can be quantified by extracting the single-molecule histograms at increasing concentrations of urea in a constant background of Mg^{2+} ions. For the adenine aptamer, a concentration of 4 mM Mg^{2+} was chosen to ensure that all aptamers are in the docked state before the addition of urea. As the concentration of urea was progressively increased up to 5 M, a shift in the major population of the sm-FRET histograms was observed from a value of E_{app} of ~0.9 to a value of ~0.3 (Fig. 14.5A), the latter becoming the major population at urea concentrations higher than ~2.5 M. The similarity between these values and those observed during folding in Mg^{2+} (Lemay et al., 2006) clearly indicates that both folding (promoted by Mg^{2+} ions) and unfolding (promoted by urea) take place through identical conformational states. An additional shift was also detected in the FRET efficiency value of the low-FRET histogram from E_{app} ~0.45 with no urea to E_{app} ~0.3 at 5 M urea. This result suggested the presence of an intermediate state in the urea-induced unfolding pathway (Fig. 14.5A). Whether this intermediate state matches that detected in the Mg^{2+}-assisted folding route remains to be proved. However, because the FRET efficiency obtained at 5 M urea (E_{app} ~0.3) is similar to that observed for the undocked state in the absence of Mg^{2+} ions, it seems plausible to suggest that both intermediates could indeed represent the same on-path structural state of the aptamer domain.

4.7. Influence of urea on the undocking rates: A method to quantify the ligand-induced stabilization of the aptamer domain

The ligand-free and ligand-bound states represent the two possible outcomes of the gene regulation process. Therefore, establishing their structure and dynamics is equally important from a functional perspective. Moreover, the ligand-induced stabilization of the aptamer domain determines the riboswitch regulatory state and is at the heart of the gene regulation mechanism. However, despite their functional relevance, experimentally quantifying such stabilization at physiologically relevant concentrations of metal ions and ligand has always been a challenge using sm-FRET. First, the ability to measure the single-molecule dynamics of relatively long-lived ligand-bound states with sufficient statistical counting is limited by the photobleaching lifetime of the fluorophores (<1 min depending on excitation conditions). Second, in certain cases, such as the adenine aptamer, the ligand-free (**D_{LF}**) and ligand-bound (**D_{LB}**) states exhibit identical peripheral

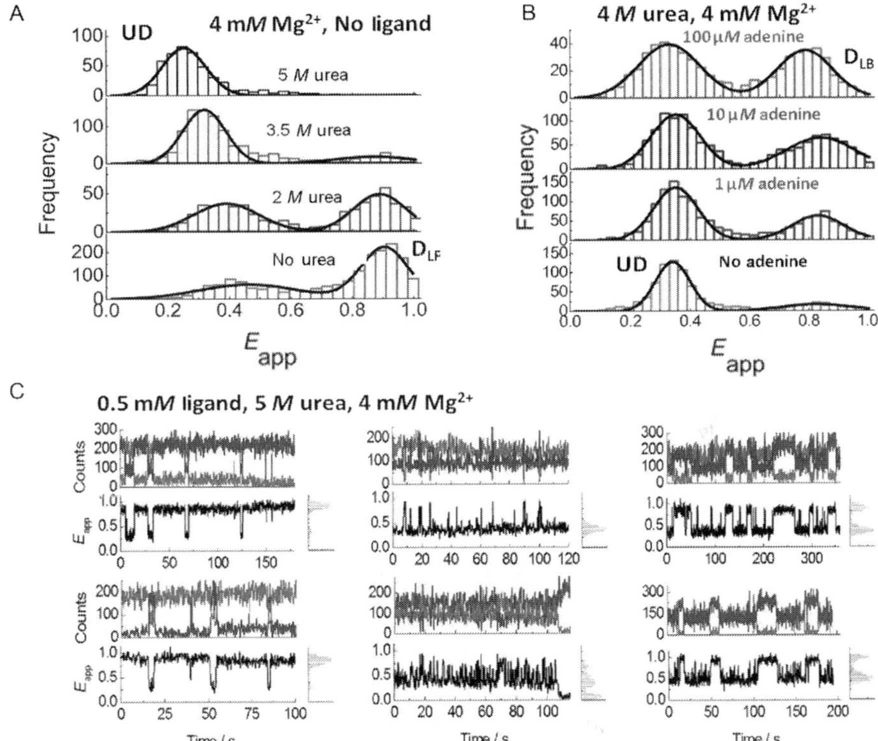

Figure 14.5 Dynamic heterogeneity in the presence of ligand. (A) Single-molecule histograms of FRET efficiency as a function of the indicated urea concentrations obtained in the absence of ligand. (B) Single-molecule FRET histograms obtained as a function of adenine concentration in the presence of 4 *M* urea and 4 m*M* Mg^{2+} showing the relative variation in the population of docked ($E \sim 0.9$) and undocked states ($E \sim 0.3$). (C) Single-molecule trajectories obtained for adenine aptamers in the presence of 500 μ*M* adenine ligand, 4 m*M* Mg^{2+} and 5 *M* urea grouped according to the dynamic pattern observed for the fluctuation between the **D** and **UD** states. Left panel: long-lived docked state ($\mathbf{D_{LB}}$) with occasional fluctuations to a short-lived undocked (**UD**) conformation. Mid-panel: rapid fluctuations between short-lived ligand-free docked states ($\mathbf{D_{LF}}$) and undocked states (**UD**). Right panel: combination of transitions between short-lived ($\mathbf{D_{LF}}$) and long-lived ($\mathbf{D_{LB}}$) docked states to short-lived **UD** states. *Adapted from Dalgarno et al. (2013).* (See the color plate.)

structure and therefore are indistinguishable by FRET measurements. The work by Dalgarno et al. demonstrates how the potential of chemical denaturants acting as a driving force to disrupt the RNA–ligand interaction can be harnessed to overcome these challenges (Dalgarno et al., 2013). The ability to differentiate $\mathbf{D_{LF}}$ and $\mathbf{D_{LB}}$ states, and from this to quantify the ligand-induced stabilization of the aptamer domain, is based on the fact that the formation of the RNA–ligand complex strongly protects the $\mathbf{D_{LB}}$ state compared to $\mathbf{D_{LF}}$ against urea-induced undocking.

In the context of the adenine riboswitch, quantifying the stabilization of the aptamer domain due to ligand binding was performed in a background of divalent metal ions that was enough to stabilize most of the molecules in the ligand-free docked state ($\mathbf{D_{LF}}$) (i.e., 4 mM Mg^{2+} for the adenine aptamer). Subsequently, a sufficiently high concentration of urea was added to revert the molecules to the undocked conformation (**UD**) (i.e., ~4 M urea for the adenine aptamer). Increasing the concentration of ligand at these conditions progressively shifted the single-molecule FRET histograms toward the ligand-bound docked state ($\mathbf{D_{LB}}$) (Fig. 14.5B). Due to the limitations explained previously regarding the maximum amount of urea that can be used in a wide-field TIR microscope (~5 M), increasing the concentration of ligand is the recommended method, although its applicability may be limited by the solubility of each particular ligand. Importantly, single-molecule trajectories obtained in the presence of ligand showed a heterogeneous dynamic behavior regarding the dwell time of the docked state (Fig. 14.5C). Within the same trace, it was possible to observe coexisting docked states with dwell times differing by more than an order of magnitude (Fig. 14.5C). The frequency of long-lived docked states became higher by increasing the ligand concentration. By plotting the 2D contour plot of docking and undocking dwell times at each ligand concentration (Fig. 14.6A) and fitting the undocking dwell times, a biexponential distribution of undocking rates was found. The fast-decay component was identical to that obtained in the absence of ligand (~1.2 ± 0.01 s^{-1}), whereas the slow-decay component showed a 10-fold slower rate constant (~0.14 ± 0.01 s^{-1}). The authors assigned this slow component to urea-induced undocking events taking place from the ligand-bound state ($\mathbf{D_{LB}}$) based on the increase in its relative contribution to the biexponential decay as a function of ligand added. This observation provided the first experimental evidence for the use of denaturants in single-molecule FRET studies as a method to differentiate otherwise identical states in terms of FRET efficiency. As an example of the potential of characterizing riboswitch properties by dynamic sorting without the intrinsic requirement for a variation in interdye distance, Dalgarno et al. quantified the difference in stability between the $\mathbf{D_{LB}}$ and $\mathbf{D_{LF}}$ states using information from the urea-induced undocking rates (Fig. 14.6B; Dalgarno et al., 2013). A 50-fold stabilization was found by comparing the undocking rates in the presence (0.045 ± 0.003 s^{-1}) and the absence of ligand (2.1 ± 0.1 s^{-1}) (Fig. 14.6C),

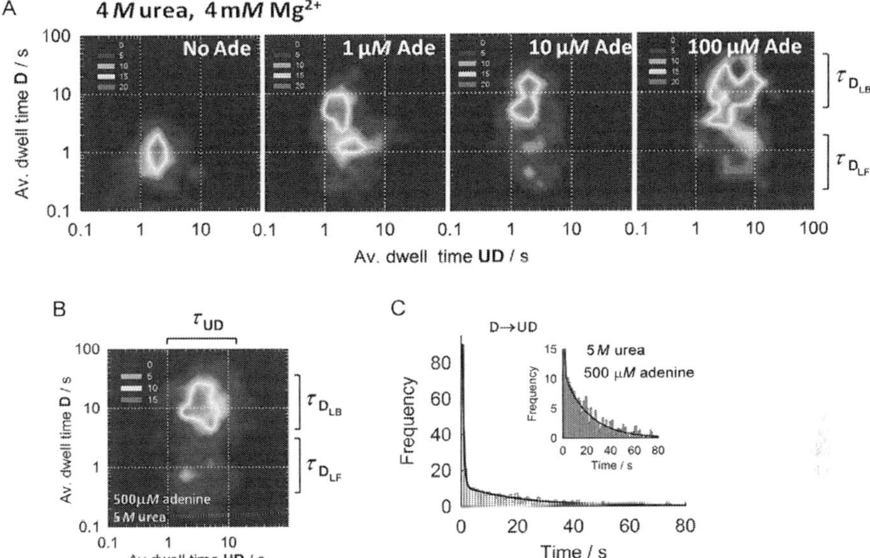

Figure 14.6 Differentiating ligand-free (A) and ligand-bound docked states (B, C) based on their stability against urea-induced denaturation. (A) 2D contour plots of average dwell times on the docked (**D**) and undocked state (**UD**) obtained at the indicated concentrations of adenine ligand in a background of 4 *M* urea and 4 m*M* Mg^{2+}. The stabilization of the docked state can be clearly seen from the shift in the contour map without ligand (short $\tau_{D_{LF}}$) and with ligand (long $\tau_{D_{LB}}$). (B) Contour map showing the distribution of average dwell times of the docked and undocked states at 5 *M* urea, 500 μ*M* ligand, and 4 m*M* Mg^{2+}. (C) Exponential distribution of dwell times for the undocking transition at the conditions indicated in (B). The decay was fitted to a biexponential function (solid line) with a fast component with a value of 2.1 ± 0.1 s^{-1} (minor contribution) and a slow component with a value of 0.045 ± 0.003 s^{-1} (major component), corresponding to undocking events taking place from ligand-free and ligand-bound states, respectively. *Adapted from Dalgarno et al. (2013).* (See the color plate.)

which is in very good agreement with the two orders of magnitude found using optical tweezers (Greenleaf et al., 2008).

4.8. Influence of urea on the docking rates: A method to evaluate the rate-limiting step for folding

As demonstrated by Dalgarno and coworkers, a comparative analysis of the influence of ligand-binding on the folding of the aptamer domain as a function of urea and Mg^{2+} ion concentration provides some insights into whether ligand-binding at an early stage of the folding process may alter the rate-limiting step for docking (Dalgarno et al., 2013). Urea titrations were performed in the presence and absence of adenine ligand at two different concentrations of Mg^{2+} ions: 100 μ*M* and 1 m*M*. A 100 μ*M* concentration of Mg^{2+} ions represents subsaturating folding conditions near the $[Mg^{2+}]_{1/2}$, which is ~10 and 22 μ*M* with and without ligand, respectively. As previously demonstrated by ensemble and single-molecule FRET, at this concentration of Mg^{2+} ions, docking between the two loop domains happens only transiently, and NMR techniques suggest that the aptamer core is mostly disorganized (Kim & Breaker, 2008; Serganov et al., 2004). In contrast, at 1 m*M* Mg^{2+} the loop–loop interaction is completely established and the aptamer is stable in this conformation for long periods of time, even in the absence of ligand (Fig. 14.5A). From urea titrations at different concentrations of Mg^{2+} ions, with and without ligand, it was found that increasing the urea concentration decreases the rate for loop–loop docking (Fig. 14.7A), and this was taken as evidence of a trap-free folding pathway. The authors reasoned that if a misfolded state, such as P1-P2 stacking or the formation of nonnative interactions within the aptamer core was part of the tertiary folding pathway of the adenine aptamer, the ability of urea to disrupt these nonnative states should increase the docking rate. Interestingly, the relative decrease in k_{dock} in the absence of ligand showed a very similar value approximately two- to threefold) independently of the concentration of Mg^{2+} ions (Fig. 14.7B). In contrast, in the presence of adenine, the decrease in k_{dock} was strongly dependent on the concentration of Mg^{2+} ions. At a 100 μ*M* concentration of Mg^{2+} ions, the single-molecule trajectories

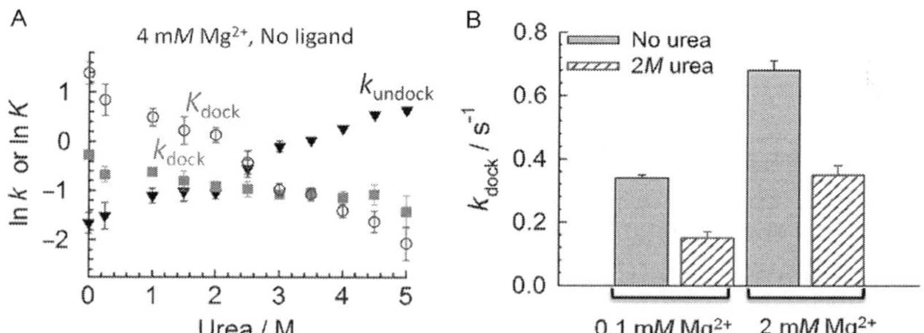

Figure 14.7 Influence of urea on the folding kinetics of ligand-free adenine aptamers. (A) Variation of the equilibrium constant (K_{dock}), docking rate (k_{dock}), and undocking rate (k_{undock}) as a function of urea concentration in a background of 4 m*M* Mg^{2+} ions. (B) Comparison of k_{dock} values (s^{-1}) obtained for ligand-free docking with (2 *M*) and without urea at the subsaturating (0.1 m*M*) and saturating (2 m*M*) concentrations of Mg^{2+} ions. In the absence of ligand, the magnitude of the urea-induced deceleration of k_{dock} is similar (~two- to threefold) at both concentrations of Mg^{2+} suggesting a rate-limiting step in the absence of ligand being dominated by a conformational search mechanism (see main text). *From Dalgarno et al. (2013).*

showed a much slower docking process, lasting for several tens of seconds in the presence of urea (2 *M*) and adenine (100 μ*M*) (Fig. 14.8A), compared to those recorded in the absence of urea (Fig. 14.8B). By plotting the dwell times for the docked state in the presence of 100 μ*M* adenine, at two limiting Mg^{2+} concentrations (0.1 m*M* and 4 m*M* Mg^{2+}), the authors calculated an eightfold deceleration of k_{dock} in the presence of urea and only a twofold decrease with no urea (Fig. 14.9A). Similar results were obtained by exploring the deceleration of the docking process at 100 μ*M* Mg^{2+} as a function of adenine concentration between conditions with no urea and 2 *M* urea (Dalgarno et al., 2013). A decrease of ~1.6-fold was obtained with no adenine, which increased to approximately eightfold in the presence of 250 μ*M* adenine (Fig. 14.9B). Because the influence of ligand binding on the

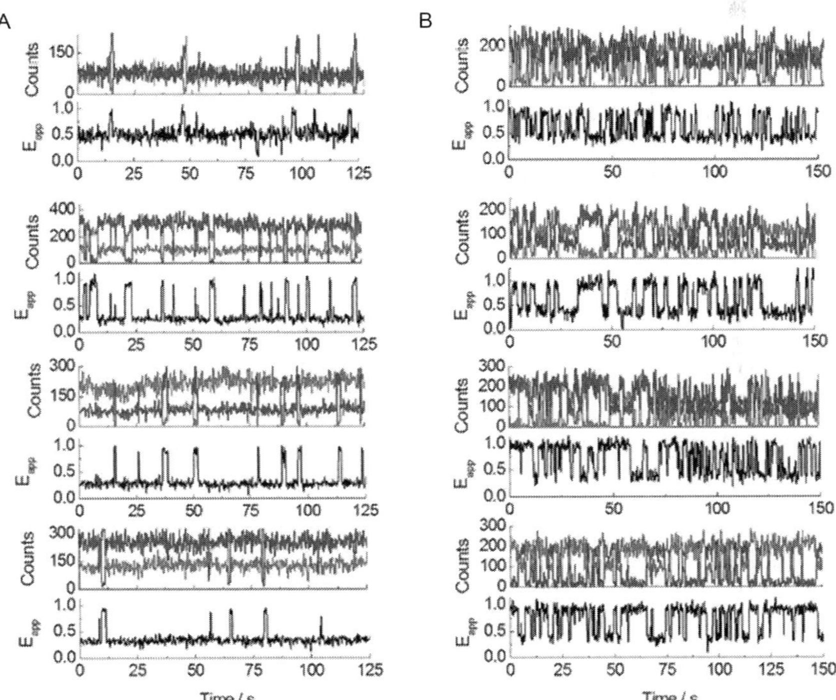

Figure 14.8 Representative single-molecule intensity trajectories (top panels) and FRET traces (bottom panels) obtained in the presence of 100 μ*M* adenine ligand, 100 μ*M* Mg^{2+}, and 2 *M* urea concentration (A) and in the absence of urea (B). A comparison between both groups of trajectories clearly reveals a pronounced urea-induced deceleration of the docking process in the presence of adenine ligand. The dwell time of the docked state reflects the **UD** → **D** transition, which becomes much longer lived in the presence of adenine and urea (A). *Adapted from Dalgarno et al. (2013).* (See the color plate.)

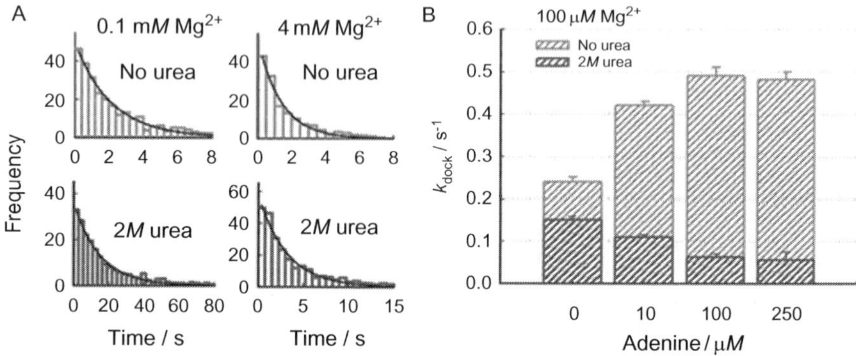

Figure 14.9 (A) Single-molecule dwell time histograms obtained for the docking process in a background concentration of 100 μ*M* adenine at the indicated concentrations of Mg^{2+} ions in the absence (top panels) and in the presence of 2 *M* urea (bottom panels). At 0.1 m*M* xMg^{2+} ions, the presence of urea induces a much longer-lived docked state (bottom left panel) compared to saturating concentrations of Mg^{2+} (bottom right panel). (B) Comparison of k_{dock} values in s^{-1} as a function of ligand concentration with and without urea. All rate constants have been obtained in a similar 100 μ*M* background of Mg^{2+}. As previously reported by Lemay et al. (2006), in the absence of urea, increasing the concentration of adenine ligand accelerates folding by approximately twofold at saturating ligand concentrations. In contrast, in the presence of moderate concentrations of urea (2 *M*), addition of ligand inhibits docking at subsaturating concentrations of Mg^{2+} ions. This has been interpreted as evidence for a rate-limiting step dominated by Mg^{2+} trapping (see main text). *Adapted from Dalgarno et al. (2013).*

docking dynamics was dependent on the concentration of Mg^{2+} ions, Dalgarno and coworkers proposed a ligand-induced switching in the rate-limiting step for docking (Dalgarno et al., 2013). According to this model, at saturating concentrations of Mg^{2+} ions (>1 m*M*), the rate-limiting step is similar for ligand-free and ligand-bound aptamers and involves the formation of native tertiary contacts between both loops. Such conformational search models have been previously proposed for the docking of the hairpin ribozyme, which also carries two interacting loops in adjacent arms (Bokinsky et al., 2003) and suggests that productive encounters between peripheral folding elements may be a common feature contributing to the folding barrier of other functional RNAs. In contrast, when docking is compromised, for instance at low concentrations of Mg^{2+} ions, ligand binding to a partially docked aptamer requires the interaction with specific Mg^{2+} ions to progress to the native structure. Importantly, the requirement for ion trapping within the aptamer structure agrees with crystal structures of the ligand-bound aptamer domain, where up to five Mg^{2+} ions have been detected at specific positions (Serganov et al., 2004). It is worth noting that without the information extracted from the chemical denaturation data, the influence of ligand binding at early stages of aptamer folding would remain hidden using conventional sm-FRET techniques. In summary, the work on the adenine aptamer exemplifies how combining sm-FRET with chemical denaturation is a useful and easy-to-implement method to investigate RNA folding landscapes at a much higher level of detail.

5. SUMMARY AND PROSPECTS

During the last decade, single-molecule FRET studies of RNA folding induced by mono- and divalent metal ions have been widely used and have yielded important insights into RNA function. However, in general, these well-established sm-FRET techniques imply a rather passive approach, where stochastic reversible unfolding of the RNA structure can be, depending on the RNA stability, a process much slower than the time window for dye photobleaching. As described in this chapter, balancing the competing effect of folding (i.e., Mg^{2+}, small molecules) and unfolding agents (i.e., urea) constitutes a more attractive approach that allows to manipulate the folding landscape of the RNA itself and to alter the stability of RNA–ligand complexes. While the progress has been significant, further advances on the application of sm-FRET techniques and chemical denaturation will surely help to solve many of the remaining questions in catalytic and regulatory RNA, and perhaps, pave the way to kinetically isolate on-path intermediate states for further analysis.

REFERENCES

Al-Hashimi, H. M., & Walter, N. G. (2008). RNA dynamics: It is about time. *Current Opinion in Structural Biology*, *18*, 321–329.

Allner, O., Nilsson, L., & Villa, A. (2013). Loop-loop interaction in an adenine-sensing riboswitch: A molecular dynamics study. *RNA*, *19*, 916–926.

Andersen, E. S. (2010). Prediction and design of DNA and RNA structures. *New Biotechnology*, *27*, 184–193.

Bastet, L., Dubé, A., Massé, E., & Lafontaine, D. A. (2011). New insights into riboswitch regulation mechanisms. *Molecular Microbiology*, *80*, 1148–1154.

Bennion, B. J., & Daggett, V. (2003). The molecular basis for the chemical denaturation of proteins by urea. *Proceedings of the National Academy of Sciences of the United States of America*, *100*, 5142–5147.

Blouin, S., Craggs, T. D., Lafontaine, D. A., & Penedo, J. C. (2009). Functional studies of DNA-protein interactions using FRET techniques. *Methods in Molecular Biology*, *543*, 475–502.

Blouin, S., Mulhbacher, J., Penedo, J. C., & Lafontaine, D. A. (2009). Riboswitches: Ancient and promising genetic regulators. *Chembiochem*, *10*, 400–416.

Blount, K. F., & Breaker, R. R. (2006). Riboswitches as antibacterial drug targets. *Nature Biotechnology*, *24*, 1558–1564.

Bokinsky, G., Rueda, D., Misra, V. K., Rhodes, M. M., Gordus, A., Babcock, H. P., et al. (2003). Single-molecule transition-state analysis of RNA folding. *Proceedings of the National Academy of Sciences of the United States of America*, *100*, 9302–9307.

Bokinsky, G., & Zhuang, X. (2005). Single-molecule RNA folding. *Accounts of Chemical Research*, *38*, 566–573.

Chodera, J. D., Elms, P., Noé, F., Keller, B., Kaiser, C. M., Ewall-Wice, A., et al. (2011). Bayesian hidden Markov model analysis of single-molecule force spectroscopy: Characterizing kinetics under measurement uncertainty. *arXiv:1108.1430 [cond-mat.stat-mech]*.

Clegg, R. M. (1995). Fluorescence resonance energy transfer. *Current Opinion in Biotechnology*, *6*, 103–110.

Clegg, R. M., Murchie, A., Zechel, A., & Lilley, D. (1993). Observing the helical geometry of double-stranded DNA in solution by fluorescence resonance energy transfer. *Proceedings of the National Academy of Sciences of the United States of America*, *90*, 2994–2998.

Cornish, P. V., & Ha, T. (2007). A survey of single-molecule techniques in chemical biology. *ACS Chemical Biology*, *2*, 53–61.

Dalgarno, P. A., Bordello, J., Morris, R., St-Pierre, P., Dubé, A., Samuel, I. D. W., et al. (2013). Single-molecule chemical denaturation of riboswitches. *Nucleic Acids Research*, *41*, 4253–4265.

Deigan, K. E., & Ferré-D'Amaré, A. R. (2011). Riboswitches: Discovery of drugs that target bacterial gene-regulatory RNAs. *Accounts of Chemical Research*, *44*, 1329–1338.

Delfosse, V., Bouchard, P., Bonneau, E., Dagenais, P., Lemay, J. F., Lafontaine, D. A., et al. (2010). Riboswitch structure: An internal residue mimicking the purine ligand. *Nucleic Acids Research*, *38*, 2057–2068.

Eschbach, S. H., St-Pierre, P., Penedo, J. C., & Lafontaine, D. A. (2012). Folding of the SAM-I riboswitch: A tale with a twist. *RNA Biology*, *9*, 535–541.

Fernandez-Luna, M. T. (2008). Riboswitch folding one at a time and step by step. *RNA Biology*, *5*, 20–23.

Fiegland, L. R., Garst, A. D., Batey, R. T., & Nesbitt, D. J. (2012). Single-molecule studies of the lysine riboswitch reveal effector-dependent conformational dynamics of the aptamer domain. *Biochemistry*, *51*, 9223–9233.

Gilbert, S. D., & Batey, R. T. (2006). Riboswitches: Fold and function. *Chemical Biology*, *13*, 805–807.

Greenleaf, W. J., Frieda, K. L., Foster, D. A. N., Woodside, M. T., & Block, S. M. (2008). Direct observation of hierarchical folding in single riboswitch aptamers. *Science*, *319*, 630–633.

Ha, T. (2004). Structural dynamics and processing of nucleic acids revealed by single-molecule spectroscopy. *Biochemistry*, *43*, 4055–4063.

Haller, A., Altman, R. B., Soulière, M. F., Blanchard, S. C., & Micura, R. (2013). Folding and ligand recognition of the TPP riboswitch aptamer at single-molecule resolution. *Proceedings of the National Academy of Sciences of the United States of America*, *110*, 4188–4193.

Haller, A., Rieder, U., Aigner, M., Blanchard, S. C., & Micura, R. (2011). Conformational capture of the SAM-II riboswitch. *Nature Chemical Biology*, 7, 393–400.

Haller, A., Soulière, M. F., & Micura, R. (2011). The dynamic nature of RNA as key to understanding riboswitch mechanisms. *Accounts of Chemical Research*, *44*, 1339–1348.

Heppell, B., Blouin, S., Dussault, A. M., Mulhbacher, J., Ennifar, E., Penedo, J. C., et al. (2011). Molecular insights into the ligand-controlled and organization of the Sam-i riboswitch. *Nature Chemical Biology*, 7, 384–392.

Heppell, B., Mulhbacher, J., Penedo, J. C., & Lafontaine, D. A. (2009). Application of fluorescent measurements for characterization of riboswitch-ligand interactions. *Methods in Molecular Biology*, *540*, 25–37.

Holmstrom, E. D., & Nesbitt, D. J. (2014). Single molecule FRET studies of the human telomerase RNA pseudoknot: Temperature/urea dependent folding kinetics and thermodynamics. *Journal of Physical Chemistry B, 118*, 3853–3863.

Joo, C., Balci, H., Ishitsuka, Y., Buranachai, C., & Ha, T. (2008). Advances in single-molecule fluorescence methods for molecular biology. *Annual Review of Biochemistry, 77*, 51–76.

Karunatilaka, K. S., & Rueda, D. (2009). Single-molecule fluorescence studies of RNA: A decade's progress. *Chemical Physics Letters, 476*, 1–10.

Keller, B. G., Kobitski, A., Jäschke, A., Nienhaus, G. U., & Noé, F. (2014). Complex RNA folding kinetics revealed by single-molecule FRET and hidden Markov models. *Journal of the American Chemical Society, 136*, 4534–4543.

Kim, J. N., & Breaker, R. R. (2008). Purine sensing by riboswitches. *Biology of the Cell, 100*, 1–11.

Koculi, E., Cho, S. S., Desai, R., Thirumalai, D., & Woodson, S. A. (2012). Folding path of P5abc RNA involves direct coupling of secondary and tertiary structures. *Nucleic Acids Research, 40*, 8011–8020.

Kurzban, G., Bayer, E., Wilchek, M., & Horowitz, P. (1991). The quaternary structure of streptavidin in urea. *The Journal of Biological Chemistry, 266*, 14470–14477.

Kypr, J., Kejnovská, I., Renčiuk, D., & Vorlíčková, M. (2009). Circular dichroism and conformational polymorphism of DNA. *Nucleic Acids Research, 37*, 1713–1725.

Lambert, D., & Draper, D. E. (2007). Effects of osmolytes on RNA secondary and tertiary structure stabilities and RNA-Mg^{2+} interactions. *Journal of Molecular Biology, 370*, 993–1005.

Lemay, J.-F., Desnoyers, G., Blouin, S., Heppell, B., Bastet, L., St-Pierre, P., et al. (2011). Comparative study between transcriptionally-and translationally-acting adenine riboswitches reveals key differences in riboswitch regulatory mechanisms. *PLoS Genetics*, 7, e1001278.

Lemay, J.-F., Penedo, J. C., Mulhbacher, J., & Lafontaine, D. A. (2009). Molecular basis of RNA-mediated and gene regulation and on the adenine riboswitch by single-molecule and approaches. *Methods in Molecular Biology, 540*, 65–76.

Lemay, J.-F., Penedo, J. C., Tremblay, R., Lilley, D. M. J., & Lafontaine, D. A. (2006). Folding of the adenine riboswitch. *Chemical Biology, 13*, 857–8968.

Li, P. T., Vieregg, J., & Tinoco, I., Jr. (2008). How RNA unfolds and refolds. *Annual Review of Biochemistry*, 77, 77–100.

Mathews, D. H. (2006). Revolutions in RNA secondary structure prediction. *Journal of Molecular Biology, 359*, 526–532.

McCluskey, K., Shaw, E., Lafontaine, D. A., & Penedo, J. C. (2014). Single-molecule fluorescence of nucleic acids. *Methods in Molecular Biology, 11*, 287–292.

McKinney, S. A., Joo, C., & Ha, T. (2006). Analysis of single-molecule FRET trajectories using hidden Markov modeling. *Biophysical Journal, 91*, 1941–1951.

McKinney, S., Tan, E., Wilson, T., Nahas, M., Declais, A., Clegg, R., et al. (2004). Single-molecule studies of DNA and RNA four-way junctions. *Biochemical Society Transactions, 32*, 41–45.

Montange, R. K., & Batey, R. T. (2008). Riboswitches: Emerging themes in RNA structure and function. *Annual Review of Biophysics, 37*, 117–133.

Mulhbacher, J., St-Pierre, P., & Lafontaine, D. A. (2010). Therapeutic applications of ribozymes and riboswitches. *Current Opinion in Pharmacology, 10*, 551–556.

Pan, T., & Sosnick, T. R. (1997). Intermediates and kinetic traps in the folding of a large ribozyme revealed by circular dichroism and UV absorbance spectroscopies and catalytic activity. *Nature Structural and Molecular Biology, 4*, 931–938.

Priyakumar, U. D., Hyeon, C., Thirumalai, D., & MacKerell, A. D., Jr. (2009). Urea destabilizes RNA by forming stacking interactions and multiple hydrogen bonds with nucleic acid bases. *Journal of the American Chemical Society, 131*, 17759–17761.

Rothenberg, E., & Ha, T. (2010). Single-molecule FRET analysis of helicase functions. *Methods in Molecular Biology*, *587*, 29–43.

Roy, R., Hohng, S., & Ha, T. (2008). A practical guide to single-molecule FRET. *Nature Methods*, *5*, 507–516.

Savinov, A., Perez, C. F., & Block, S. M. (2014). Single-molecule studies of riboswitch folding. *Biochimica et Biophysica Acta*, *1839*, 1030–1045.

Schuler, B., & Hofmann, H. (2013). Single-molecule spectroscopy of protein folding dynamics—Expanding scope and timescales. *Current Opinion in Structural Biology*, *23*, 36–47.

Serganov, A. (2009). The long and the short of riboswitches. *Current Opinion in Structural Biology*, *19*, 251–259.

Serganov, A., & Nudler, E. (2013). A decade of riboswitches. *Cell*, *152*, 17–24.

Serganov, A., Yuan, Y.-R., Pikovskaya, O., Polonskaia, A., Malinina, L., Phan, A. T., et al. (2004). Structural basis for discriminative regulation of gene expression by adenine-and guanine-sensing mRNAs. *Chemical Biology*, *11*, 1729–1741.

Shelton, V. M., Sosnick, T. R., & Pan, T. (1999). Applicability of urea in the thermodynamic analysis of secondary and tertiary RNA folding. *Biochemistry*, *38*, 16831–16839.

Sosnick, T. R. (2001). Characterization of tertiary folding of RNA by circular dichroism and urea. *Current Protocols in Nucleic Acid Chemistry*, *11–5*.

Sosnick, T. R., Fang, X., & Shelton, V. M. (1999). Application of circular dichroism to study RNA folding transitions. *Methods in Enzymology*, *317*, 393–409.

Sosnick, T. R., & Pan, T. (2003). RNA folding: Models and perspectives. *Current Opinion in Structural Biology*, *13*, 309–316.

Suddala, K. C., Rinaldi, A. J., Feng, J., Mustoe, A. M., Eichhorn, C. D., Liberman, J. A., et al. (2013). Single transcriptional and translational preQ1 riboswitches adopt similar pre-folded ensembles that follow distinct folding pathways into the same ligand-bound structure. *Nucleic Acids Research*, *41*, 10462–10475.

Tinoco, I., Chen, G., & Qu, X. (2010). RNA reactions one molecule at a time. *Cold Spring Harbor Perspectives in Biology*, *2*, a003624.

Tinoco, I., & Gonzalez, R. L. (2011). Biological mechanisms, one molecule at a time. *Genes and Development*, *25*, 1205–1231.

Treiber, D. K., Rook, M. S., Zarrinkar, P. P., & Williamson, J. R. (1998). Kinetic intermediates trapped by native interactions in RNA folding. *Science*, *279*, 1943–1946.

Tremblay, R., Lemay, J.-F., Blouin, S., Mulhbacher, J., Bonneau, É., Legault, P., et al. (2011). Constitutive regulatory activity of an evolutionarily excluded riboswitch variant. *Journal of Biological Chemistry*, *286*, 27406–27415.

van de Meent, J.-W., Bronson, J. E., Wood, F., Gonzalez Jr., R. L., & Wiggins, C. H. (2013). Hierarchically-coupled hidden Markov models for learning kinetic rates from single-molecule data. arXiv:1305.3640 [stat.ML].

Vitreschak, A. G., Rodionov, D. A., Mironov, A. A., & Gelfand, M. S. (2004). Riboswitches: The oldest mechanism for the regulation of gene expression? *Trends in Genetics*, *20*, 44–50.

Walter, N. G. (2008). Single molecule detection, analysis, and manipulation. In R. A. Meyers (Ed.), *Encyclopedia of Analytical Chemistry*.

Warren, J. R., & Gordon, J. A. (1966). On the refractive indices of aqueous solutions of urea. *The Journal of Physical Chemistry*, *70*, 297–300.

Wickiser, J. K., Cheah, M. T., Breaker, R. R., & Crothers, D. M. (2005). The kinetics of ligand binding by an adenine-sensing riboswitch. *Biochemistry*, *44*, 13404–13414.

Winkler, W. C., & Breaker, R. R. (2003). Genetic control by metabolite-binding riboswitches. *Chembiochem*, *4*, 1024–1032.

Winkler, W. C., & Breaker, R. R. (2005). Regulation of bacterial gene expression by riboswitches. *Annual Review of Microbiology*, *59*, 487–517.

Wood, S., Ferré-D'Amaré, A. R., & Rueda, D. (2012). Allosteric tertiary interactions preorganize the c-di-GMP riboswitch and accelerate ligand binding. *ACS Chemical Biology, 7*, 920–927.

Woodson, S. A. (2005). Metal ions and RNA folding: A highly charged topic with a dynamic future. *Current Opinion in Chemical Biology, 9*, 104–109.

Woodson, S. A. (2010). Compact intermediates in RNA folding. *Annual Review of Biophysics, 39*, 61–77.

Yoon, J., Thirumalai, D., & Hyeon, C. (2013). Urea-induced denaturation of preQ1-riboswitch. *Journal of the American Chemical Society, 135*, 12112–12121.

CHAPTER FIFTEEN

Riboswitch Structure and Dynamics by smFRET Microscopy

Krishna C. Suddala*[,†], Nils G. Walter[†,1]
*Biophysics, University of Michigan, Ann Arbor, Michigan, USA
[†]Single Molecule Analysis Group, Department of Chemistry, University of Michigan, Ann Arbor, Michigan, USA
[1]Corresponding author: e-mail address: nwalter@umich.edu

Contents

Abstract

Riboswitches are structured noncoding RNA elements that control the expression of their embedding messenger RNAs by sensing the intracellular concentration of diverse metabolites. As the name suggests, riboswitches are dynamic in nature so that studying their inherent conformational dynamics and ligand-mediated folding is important for understanding their mechanism of action. Single-molecule fluorescence energy transfer (smFRET) microscopy is a powerful and versatile technique for studying the folding pathways and intra- and intermolecular dynamics of biological macromolecules, especially RNA. The ability of smFRET to monitor intramolecular distances and their temporal evolution make it a particularly insightful tool for probing the structure and dynamics of

Methods in Enzymology, Volume 549
ISSN 0076-6879
http://dx.doi.org/10.1016/B978-0-12-801122-5.00015-5

riboswitches. Here, we detail the general steps for using prism-based total internal reflection fluorescence microscopy for smFRET studies of the structure, dynamics, and ligand-binding mechanisms of riboswitches.

1. INTRODUCTION

Riboswitches are present in up to 4% of all bacterial mRNAs, usually in the 5′-untranslated regions (Breaker, 2011, 2012; Serganov & Nudler, 2013; Winkler & Breaker, 2005). They are structured domains that regulate gene expression in response to a physiological signal. This physiological signal is most commonly a change in the concentration of a metabolite, but riboswitches that sense temperature, pH, and metal ions have also been discovered (Bastet, Dube, Masse, & Lafontaine, 2011; Peselis & Serganov, 2014). Many different classes of riboswitches have been identified that bind metabolites—such as nucleobases and their derivatives, amino acids, coenzymes, second messengers, and specific metal ions—to control the expression of proteins involved in essential cellular pathways (Barrick & Breaker, 2007; Peselis & Serganov, 2014; Serganov & Nudler, 2013). Riboswitches control gene expression largely through intrinsic transcription termination or inhibition of translation initiation, although some that modulate mRNA splicing, mRNA degradation, and Rho protein-mediated termination have also been discovered (Bastet et al., 2011). Riboswitches consist of a highly conserved aptamer domain that is involved in ligand sensing, followed by a variable expression platform (or gene regulatory element) that undergoes a structural change in response to ligand binding by the aptamer. Both domains share a common sequence referred to as the "switching" sequence that communicates the ligand bound state of the aptamer domain to the expression platform (Garst & Batey, 2009; Serganov & Nudler, 2013). Currently, more than 20 classes of riboswitches are known that bind chemically diverse ligands (Peselis & Serganov, 2014; Serganov & Nudler, 2013). In certain cases, multiple classes of riboswitches, with distinct secondary and tertiary structures, have been identified that recognize a common ligand. Examples include the more than five classes of riboswitches recognizing the coenzyme SAM and three classes of $preQ_1$-binding riboswitches (McCown, Liang, Weinberg, & Breaker, 2014; Serganov & Nudler, 2013).

Over the past decade, high-resolution crystal and nuclear magnetic resonance (NMR) structures of various classes of ligand-bound riboswitch aptamer domains have been solved that provide insight into the molecular recognition principles used by RNA (Fig. 15.1) (Peselis & Serganov, 2014; Serganov & Nudler, 2013). Structures range from simple pseudoknots to large RNAs with multihelix junctions. These structures highlight the diversity in architecture and the size of riboswitch aptamer domains and show how RNAs can utilize a limited repertoire of functional groups to achieve high specificity and affinity for their typically small cognate ligands. For RNA, like all other biological macromolecules, structural dynamics are crucial for proper biological function (Al-Hashimi & Walter, 2008; Dethoff, Chugh, Mustoe, & Al-Hashimi, 2012). Due to a rugged free energy landscape and inherent flexibility, RNA structures can adopt multiple conformations that interconvert on a range of timescales (Al-Hashimi & Walter, 2008; Marek, Johnson-Buck, & Walter, 2011; Mustoe, Brooks, & Al-Hashimi, 2014; Solomatin, Greenfeld, Chu, & Herschlag, 2010; Zhuang et al., 2002). Riboswitch RNAs are intrinsically dynamic in nature, and their structural dynamics play a critical role in the ligand-mediated folding process (Haller, Souliere, et al., 2011. Riboswitches couple changes in the conformational ensemble caused by ligand binding to effect gene regulation. Although the large number of crystal structures (Fig. 15.1) show atomic details of the ligand recognition mode, these static models do not provide information on the dynamics or the ligand-mediated folding pathways that are critical for riboswitch function. In addition, ligand-free riboswitches sample multiple closely related and, in some instances, transient conformations, which are nontrivial to detect using methods that average across ensembles and often across time. Due to the challenges in studying ligand-free riboswitch structure and dynamics, our understanding of the ligand-mediated folding process that forms the basis of gene regulation by riboswitches is far from complete (Liberman & Wedekind, 2012).

In recent years, a number of biophysical studies using NMR spectroscopy, molecular dynamics simulations, small-angle X-ray scattering (SAXS), and single molecule approaches have provided details of the conformation, and dynamics and effect of ligand on the folding kinetics of different riboswitch classes (Brenner et al., 2010; Chen, Zuo, Wang, & Dayie, 2012; Feng, Walter, & Brooks, 2011; Fiegland et al., 2012; Frieda & Block, 2012; Haller et al., 2013; Haller, Rieder, et al., 2011; Lemay et al., 2006; Noeske et al, 2007; Reining et al., 2013; Rieder, Kreutz, & Micura, 2010; Souliere et al., 2013; Suddala et al., 2013; Whitford et al., 2009). These studies point to a general mechanism where in the presence of Mg^{2+}, the ligand-free riboswitch exists in multiple

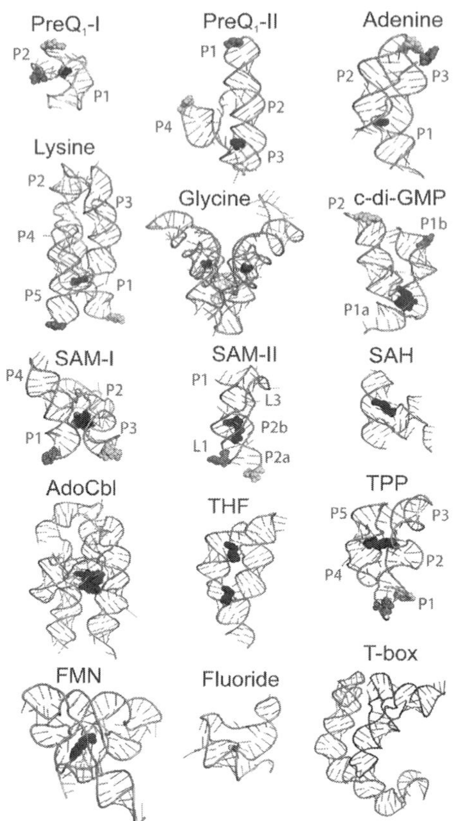

Figure 15.1 Structures of different riboswitch classes. Structures of the preQ$_1$-I (PDB: 2L1V;Kang, Peterson, & Feigon, 2009), preQ$_1$-II (PDB: 4JF2; Liberman, Salim, Krucinska, & Wedekind, 2013), adenine (PDB: 1Y26; Serganov et al., 2004)), lysine (PDB: 3D0U; Garst, Heroux, Rambo, & Batey, 2008), glycine (PDB: 3P49; Butler, Xiong, Wang, & Strobel, 2011), c-di-GMP (PDB: 3IWN; Kulshina, Baird, & Ferre-D'Amare, 2009), SAM-I (PDB: 3IQR; Stoddard et al., 2010), SAM-II (PDB: 2QWY; Gilbert, Rambo, Van Tyne, & Batey, 2008), SAH (PDB: 3NPQ; Edwards, Reyes, Heroux, & Batey, 2010), AdoCbl (PDB: 4GMA; Johnson, Reyes, Polaski, & Batey, 2012), THF (PDB: 4LVV; Trausch & Batey, 2014)), TPP (PDB: 2GDI; Serganov, Polonskaia, Phan, Breaker, & Patel, 2006), FMN (PDB: 2YIE; Vicens, Mondragon, & Batey, 2011), Fluoride (PDB: 4ENC; Ren, Rajashankar, & Patel, 2012), and the T-box (PDB: 4LCK; Zhang & Ferre-D'Amare, 2013) riboswitches are shown. Riboswitch RNAs are shown in cartoon representation in gray with their ligands in blue. Green and red spheres indicate nucleotides labeled with Cy3 and Cy5 fluorophores, respectively, in the preQ$_1$-I (Suddala et al., 2013), preQ$_1$-II (Souliere et al., 2013), adenine (Lemay, Penedo, Tremblay, Lilley, & Lafontaine, 2006), lysine (Fiegland, Garst, Batey, & Nesbitt, 2012), c-di-GMP (Wood, Ferre-D'Amare, & Rueda, 2012), SAM-I (Heppell et al., 2011), SAM-II (Haller, Rieder, Aigner, Blanchard, & Micura, 2011; Haller, Souliere, & Micura, 2011), and TPP (Haller, Altman, Souliere, Blanchard, & Micura, 2013) riboswitches that were studied using smFRET microscopy. The *xpt* guanine riboswitch (Brenner, Scanlan, Nahas, Ha, & Silverman, 2010, not shown) is very similar to the adenine riboswitch. In smFRET studies of riboswitches where multiple constructs were used, only one of them is shown here for clarity. Structures are not drawn to scale. (See the color plate.)

interconverting conformations including "folded-like" states that become stabilized upon ligand binding. Divalent metal ions (mainly Mg^{2+}) are known to be crucial for RNA folding by stabilizing tertiary interactions (Johnson-Buck, McDowell, & Walter, 2011; Misra & Draper, 1998). In the case of many riboswitches, Mg^{2+} was shown to be essential for the RNA to sample "folded"-like conformations in the absence of ligand. Although Mg^{2+} is not required for ligand binding, it was shown to generally accelerate ligand-dependent folding and slow down the unfolding rate (Brenner et al., 2010; Haller, Rieder, et al., 2011; Haller, Souliere, et al., 2011; Lemay et al., 2006; Santner, Rieder, Kreutz, & Micura, 2012). However, despite a wealth of structural knowledge on ligand-bound conformations, there is a scarcity of information on ligand-free riboswitch conformations. Crystal structures of a few classes of ligand-free riboswitches are available, and they resemble the ligand-bound ones with only local conformational differences around the ligand-binding site (Peselis & Serganov, 2014). However, when studied in solution under ambient conditions, ligand-free conformations are generally observed to be more extended than in the (frozen) crystal. Biophysical methods such as SAXS and NMR spectroscopy have been used to interrogate the ligand-free conformations of riboswitches (Baird & Ferre-D'Amare, 2010; Chen et al., 2012; Haller, Rieder, et al., 2011; Haller, Souliere, et al., 2011; Reining et al., 2013; Santner et al., 2012). However, due to the difficulties in probing dynamic and lowly populated conformations using such ensemble methods, ligand-free conformations are often recalcitrant to structural inquiry. Consequently, single-molecule fluorescence resonance energy transfer (smFRET) has become an increasingly popular tool to avoid ensemble averaging and study ligand-free riboswitch conformations in solution, as well as their dynamics and ligand-dependent folding pathways (Liberman & Wedekind, 2012; Savinov, Perez, & Block, 2014; St-Pierre, McCluskey, Shaw, Penedo, & Lafontaine, 2014; Suddala et al., 2013).

1.1. Single-molecule fluorescence resonance energy transfer

1.1.1 Advantages of single-molecule methods

Conventional experiments on biological macromolecules are performed in bulk, where a large number of molecules (typically $\sim10^{10}$–10^{15}) provide an average signal for an observable parameter of interest, such as the catalytic rate constant k_{cat} for enzymes, the size dimensions, or the diffusion constant of a molecular species. While such bulk methods are valuable in providing information on the general behavior of a molecule and will continue to be useful, they suffer from an important problem—ensemble and time averaging. Ensemble methods provide only limited information on the distribution of the observable parameter across molecules in the sample but typically only a single-average value, thus leading to a loss of valuable information (Deniz, Mukhopadhyay, & Lemke, 2008; Tinoco & Gonzalez, 2011; Walter & Bustamante, 2014; Walter, Huang, Manzo, & Sobhy, 2008). For example, when ensemble methods are used to study a biomolecule (such as a riboswitch) that exists in equal populations of two distinct states, they often report an average state that is not a real conformation. The only exceptions are cases where the timescale of the measurement is significantly shorter than the interconversion speed of the states such that two distinct state signals are detected, for example, using certain NMR and ensemble fluorescence or Förster resonance energy transfer (FRET) techniques (Bothe et al., 2011; Walter, Burke, & Millar, 1999). When more than two states are involved, even this possibility becomes remote. In addition, the presence of any lowly populated, transient states (sometimes—ambiguously—referred to as "excited" states) is extremely challenging to detect using ensemble methods (Dethoff, Petzold, Chugh, Casiano-Negroni, & Al-Hashimi, 2012; Tinoco & Gonzalez, 2011; Walter & Bustamante, 2014; Walter et al., 2008). Therefore, single-molecule methods are ideally suited for studying dynamic biomolecular systems, such as riboswitch RNAs that generally exist in multiple distinct conformations (Brenner et al., 2010; Fiegland et al., 2012; Haller et al., 2013; Haller, Rieder, et al., 2011; Haller, Souliere, et al., 2011; Heppell et al., 2011; Lemay et al., 2006; Suddala et al., 2013; Wood et al., 2012; Zhuang, 2005; Zhuang et al., 2000). In addition, the ability to observe a single molecule for a long period of time using smFRET enables studies of dynamic and static heterogeneity (where molecules do and do not interconvert in their behavior, Marek et al., 2011, respectively, over the available observation time window). Systems can be studied both under equilibrium and nonequilibrium conditions, and the rate constants for conversion between different conformations can be obtained (Paudel & Rueda, 2014; Roy, Hohng, & Ha, 2008; Tinoco & Gonzalez, 2011; Zhao & Rueda, 2009; Zhuang et al., 2002). Furthermore, single-molecule methods are usually performed at very low (~p*M*) concentrations and, therefore, require little material to work with. This is especially advantageous for studying systems that aggregate or form multimers at higher concentrations. Due to many advantages, over the past two decades, smFRET has been applied to study the structure, folding, and dynamics of biomolecules such as DNA, RNA, and proteins, as well as for investigating large macromolecular assemblies

(Deniz et al., 2008; Krishnan et al., 2013; Marshall, Aitken, Dorywalska, & Puglisi, 2008; Savinov et al., 2014; Schuler & Eaton, 2008; Tinoco & Gonzalez, 2011; Vafabakhsh & Ha, 2012; Zhuang, 2005).

1.1.2 Fluorescence resonance energy transfer

FRET refers to the nonradiative energy transfer between donor and acceptor fluorophores that are spatially proximal to each other (Roy et al., 2008; Stryer, 1978). To be suitable as a FRET pair, the emission spectrum of the donor needs to overlap with the excitation spectrum of the acceptor. Energy transfer via FRET occurs only when the fluorophores are present within a certain distance that depends on the identity of the FRET pair and is generally <100 Å. Therefore, FRET can be used as a sensitive spectroscopic ruler to measure intra- or intermolecular distances in the nm range (~3–7 nm) (Fig. 15.2A) (Ditzler, Aleman, Rueda, & Walter, 2007; Roy et al., 2008; Schuler, Lipman, Steinbach, Kumke, & Eaton, 2005).

The excitation energy of the donor is transferred to the acceptor through a dipole–dipole coupling interaction that is distance dependent. The FRET efficiency, E, is given by the equation:

$$E = \frac{1}{1 + (R/R_0)^6}. \tag{15.1}$$

where R is the distance between the donor and the acceptor fluorophores. R_0, known as the Förster radius, refers to the distance between the fluorophores where the energy transfer efficiency is 50% (Fig. 15.2A). The value of R_0 depends on the spectroscopic properties of the donor and acceptor fluorophores and the local environment. Generally, R_0 is constant for a given FRET pair under similar buffer conditions. The R_0 values for commonly used FRET pairs range from 40 to 60 Å. For example, the R_0 value for the Cy3 (donor)–Cy5 (acceptor) pair of fluorophores is ~54 Å, with a roughly linear dependency of the FRET efficiency from ~30 to 70 Å (Roy et al., 2008). Therefore, distance changes below 30 Å and above 75 Å cannot be easily distinguished and will yield FRET values close to 1 and 0, respectively (Fig. 15.2A).

FRET results in a decrease in the intensity of the donor fluorophore with a simultaneous increase in the acceptor fluorophore intensity. Combining FRET with single-molecule detection results in a powerful technique known as smFRET, which has been used to probe the conformational dynamics of a variety of biomolecules and large complexes (Haller et al.,

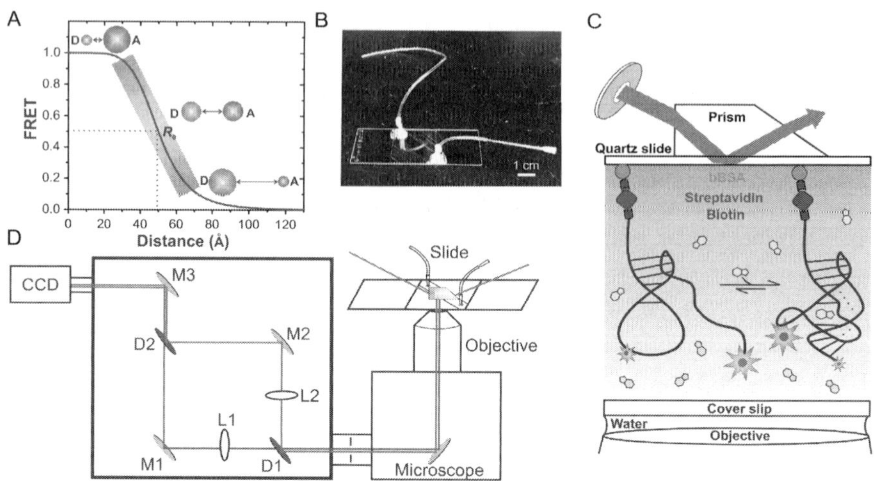

Figure 15.2 Prism-based TIRF microscopy setup for smFRET studies of riboswitches, as previously described (Suddala et al., 2013). (A) FRET efficiency dependence on inter-fluorophore distance. Donor (D) and acceptor (A) fluorophores are shown in green (dark gray in print version) and red (light gray in print version), respectively. R_0 refers to the Förster radius. The linear range of the FRET measurements is shown in gray. (B) Photograph of the quartz slide with microfluidic channel for smFRET experiments. (C) Schematic of the smFRET experiment for studying dynamics of the *Bsu* preQ_1-I riboswitch (Suddala et al., 2013). The secondary structure of the riboswitch is shown in black and the ligand (preQ_1) is shown in yellow (light gray in print version). (D) Prism-based TIRF microscopy setup. M1, M2, M3, mirrors; D1, D2, dichroic mirrors; L1, L2, lenses; CCD, ICCD camera.

2013; Krishnan et al., 2013; Marshall et al., 2008; Roy et al., 2008; Savinov et al., 2014; Schuler & Eaton, 2008; Suddala et al., 2013; Vafabakhsh & Ha, 2012; Zhuang, 2005). In smFRET experiments, one generally monitors the donor and acceptor fluorophore intensities of individual molecules as the apparent FRET efficiency (E), calculated as:

$$E = \frac{I_A}{I_A + I_D} \tag{15.2}$$

where I_D and I_A are the background corrected donor and acceptor intensities, respectively. For molecules that are judiciously labeled with a FRET pair, structural dynamics manifest as anticorrelated changes in the intensities of the donor and acceptor fluorophores. Immobilizing molecules permits long observation times of their FRET changes, which in turn make it possible to study their conformational dynamics and folding (Fig. 15.2C). smFRET investigation of riboswitches is sometimes performed using confocal microscopy, but more commonly employing total internal reflection fluorescence (TIRF) microscopy (Fiegland et al., 2012; Haller et al., 2013; Haller, Rieder, et al., 2011; Haller, Souliere, et al., 2011; Savinov et al., 2014; Suddala et al., 2013). Here, we limit our discussion to the general steps in smFRET studies of riboswitches using prism-based TIRF microscopy, due to its simplicity and wide applicability. For detailed protocols of the different sections discussed here, the reader is encouraged to also consult some of the previously published reviews (Joo & Ha, 2012a, 2012b; Rinaldi, Suddala, & Walter, 2015; Roy et al., 2008; Zhao & Rueda, 2009).

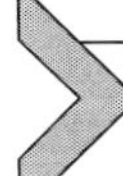

2. METHODS

2.1. Labeling and purification of riboswitches

For studying riboswitch structure and dynamics using smFRET, molecules have to be labeled with both donor and acceptor fluorophores (Roy et al., 2008; Solomatin & Herschlag, 2009; Walter, 2003; Walter & Burke, 2000). In addition, typically a biotin moiety needs to be present on the molecule for immobilization onto the quartz slide surface using biotin–streptavidin chemistry (Fig. 15.2C). A key aspect of obtaining a doubly fluorophore-labeled RNA is the judicious selection of nucleotide positions for labeling (Fig. 15.1). Depending on the structure of the aptamer, the fluorophores should be positioned such that they report large-scale distance changes between functionally important regions forming the key tertiary interactions involved in "switching." For example, in the adenine- and guanine-binding riboswitches, fluorophores were placed adjacent to the hairpin loops P2 and P3 that form a critical tertiary interaction stabilized by ligand binding (Brenner et al., 2010; Lemay et al., 2006) (Fig. 15.1). Similarly, for riboswitches adopting a pseudoknot fold, such as the preQ$_1$-I and SAM-II classes, the fluorophores should be attached to report formation of the thermodynamically less stable helix (generally P2 or P3, closest to the 3′-end) that is stabilized by the ligand (Haller, Rieder, et al., 2011; Haller, Souliere, et al., 2011; Souliere et al., 2013; Suddala et al., 2013) (Figs. 15.1 and 15.2C). In this regard, the availability of a high-resolution crystal or NMR structure will significantly aid in choosing which nucleotides to label. Structural knowledge is especially valuable for labeling riboswitches with complex architectures. For simpler riboswitches, RNA secondary structure along with nucleotide conservation data may suffice for the selection of suitable labeling positions. In the absence of a high-resolution structure for the riboswitch, chemical structure probing data using methods such as selective 2′-hydroxyl acylation analyzed by primer extension (Wilkinson, Merino, & Weeks, 2006) or in-line probing (Regulski & Breaker, 2008) can reveal the identity of nucleotides that form intramolecular interactions (or intermolecular interactions with the ligand), as well as those exposed to solvent. As a rule of thumb, nucleotides that are evolutionarily less conserved, solvent exposed, and not involved in any intramolecular interactions should be chosen for fluorophores labeling. This strategy will ensure that the presence of the bulky fluorophores (molecular weight approximately equivalent to the size of one to two nucleotides) is unlikely to affect the structure, folding, and/or ligand binding by the riboswitch. Furthermore, the labeling sites should be positioned such that they report distance changes within the linear FRET range of the fluorophores for maximum sensitivity (Fig. 15.2A). The larger the change in the FRET values, the easier it will be to distinguish them, aiding in the subsequent data analysis. Ideally, the labeling sites should be chosen such that a minimum difference of 0.2 (as defined by Eq. 15.2) is obtained between any two FRET states.

There are many ways of achieving site-specific labeling of RNA with fluorophores for smFRET experiments (Rinaldi et al., 2015; Solomatin & Herschlag, 2009; Walter, 2003; Walter & Burke, 2000). However, the most common and easy way of internally labeling riboswitch RNAs is to conjugate *N*-hydroxysuccinimide (NHS) ester derivatives of fluorophores to free primary amine functional groups of modified nucleotides. Aminoallyl uridine is incorporated into the sequence in the place of uridine during chemical synthesis of oligoribonucleotide (RNA) and labeled using an NHS ester fluorophore. In recent years, due to an increase in the efficiency of RNA chemical synthesis, ordering custom designed singly or doubly fluorophore-labeled RNAs with additional modifications, such as 3′ or 5′ biotin, has become affordable. Currently, this is feasible for RNAs that are <70 nt in length, such as the small preQ$_1$-I riboswitches (Suddala et al., 2013). Internal labeling of large riboswitch RNAs, however, is more challenging and often involves multiple steps (Rinaldi et al., 2015; Solomatin & Herschlag, 2009). One commonly used method involves chemically synthesizing two or more short RNAs that are labeled independently and covalently linked by T4 DNA/RNA ligase-mediated splinted ligation (Lang & Micura, 2008). This method was used to generate a doubly labeled construct for smFRET study of the SAM-II and the preQ$_1$-II riboswitches (Haller, Rieder, et al., 2011; Haller, Souliere, et al., 2011; Souliere et al., 2013). A similar strategy was used for the *pbuE* adenine, the TPP, and the c-di-GMP riboswitches, where two RNA oligonucleotides with internally labeled fluorophores and a 5′-biotin were simply heat annealed and then ligated using T4 RNA/DNA ligase (Haller et al., 2013; Lemay et al., 2006; Wood et al., 2012). Alternatively, for even larger riboswitches, site-specific labeling is difficult but a doubly labeled construct can be obtained by annealing fluorescently labeled oligonucleotides to *in vitro* transcribed RNA. For the large lysine riboswitch, a strategy was successfully used where a biotin-labeled DNA oligonucleotide and a Cy3–Cy5 doubly labeled RNA oligonucleotide were both annealed to a 179-nt *in vitro* transcribed *lysC* RNA to generate the smFRET construct (Fiegland et al., 2012). Sequences can be added to the riboswitch for the purpose of annealing oligonucleotides, but structural interference has to be carefully avoided.

For labeling of RNA at the 3′ or 5′ end, a free amine group can be introduced during chemical synthesis, which can then be reacted with a fluorophore NHS ester (Qin & Pyle, 1999; Rinaldi et al., 2015). Another means of 3′-end labeling of RNA is oxidization with sodium periodate followed by labeling with a hydrazide-derivatized fluorophore or biotin. In addition, the 5′-end with a phosphate group can be activated with EDC (1-ethyl-3-[3-dimethylaminopropyl] carbodiimide hydrochloride). The product can be reacted with imidazole and ethylene diamine to generate a primary amine that can be subsequently labeled with any NHS-ester conjugated fluorophore or biotin. Alternatively, after reaction with EDC, the 5′-end of the RNA can be directly labeled with a hydrazide derivative of the fluorophore (Qin & Pyle, 1999; Rinaldi et al., 2015). However, it is important to note that the labeling of RNA using EDC or periodate oxidation involves multiple steps and may result in limited yields. Nevertheless, these methods can be useful to end-label *in vitro* transcribed large riboswitch RNAs. Labeling is often nontrivial and requires multiple steps of purification to remove unlabeled and singly labeled RNAs. Following labeling, excess unreacted dye can be removed by gel filtration and ethanol precipitation. The labeling efficiency can be assessed by measuring the concentrations of RNA and the two fluorophores using a UV–vis spectrophotometer. If the labeling efficiency is high enough (>80%), the RNA can be directly used for smFRET experiments without further purification. However, purification of the doubly labeled RNA using denaturing gel electrophoresis or reverse-phase HPLC is recommended when the labeling yield is lower. This enrichment of doubly labeled riboswitch will enable imaging of hundreds of molecules during subsequent smFRET experiments, resulting in the faster acquisition of statistically significant data.

A variety of chemically diverse fluorophores can be used for smFRET studies of riboswitches (Roy et al., 2008). In general, the cyanine family of dyes is widely used due to their good photostability and quantum yield. The Cy3–Cy5 FRET pair has been most widely used for studying dynamics of RNA by smFRET. Improved derivatives of these dyes such as Cy3B and Dy547, which are known to exhibit higher quantum yield and better photostability, may be used in place of Cy3 (Cooper et al., 2004; Roy et al., 2008). Furthermore, a new class of reportedly more stable "self-healing" cyanine fluorophore-triplet quencher conjugates is now available in which the presence of a proximal protective agent suppresses the formation of triplet and radical states, leading to higher photostability of the fluorophore (Zheng et al., 2014). These self-healing dyes can also be used for smFRET studies of riboswitches. It is important to note that some of the fluorophores, such as the cyanine family dyes, are known to stack on the ends of DNA and RNA helices, which can lead to mild orientation dependence of the FRET value (Ouellet, Schorr, Iqbal, Wilson, & Lilley, 2011). The interactions of dyes with RNA potentially may also alter the rates of structural transitions. Furthermore, some fluorophores, such as those of the Alexa family, are known to be quenched by neighboring bases, which will result in a reduced signal and also photophysical effects such as intensity fluctuations due to spectral shift and triplet state blinking (Stennett, Ciuba, & Levitus, 2014). Although the cyanine dyes are less prone to such effects, it is wise to avoid labeling RNAs near a stretch of particularly guanine nucleotides that have redox potentials suitable to exchange electrons with the excited state of a fluorophore (Walter & Burke, 1997). Naturally, it is important to consider all these factors when selecting fluorophore-labeling positions.

2.2. Preparation of quartz slides

smFRET experiments on riboswitches are routinely performed on immobilized molecules in a microfluidic channel made using quartz slides (1″ × 3″ × 1 mm thick, G. Finkenbeiner, Inc.) and glass cover slips (24 × 30 mm, VWR Micro Cover Glasses) (Fig. 15.2B) (Michelotti, de Silva, Johnson-Buck, Manzo, & Walter, 2010; Roy et al., 2008; Suddala et al., 2013). To this end, the slide surface needs to be thoroughly cleaned using a multistep protocol to remove any organic impurities (Krishnan et al., 2013; Zhao & Rueda, 2009). Any fluorescent impurities will impede observation of true single molecules and contribute false background signals. Impurities may also affect the local environment of molecules, which may result in heterogeneities in their behavior. The cleaning process first involves boiling the used slides in deionized water to soften the epoxy for removing the cover slips used to make the microfluid channel. Any remaining debris on the slides should be scrapped off using a razor blade. This is followed by scrubbing the slide surface thoroughly with a thick paste of detergent (Alconox, Inc.) or alternatively, by sonicating them in a-10% (w/v) detergent solution for 30 min. After this, the slides are rinsed thoroughly with double-distilled water and sonicated in it for 10 min. Next, slides are sonicated sequentially in a series of four organic and inorganic solvents: (a) acetone, (b) methanol, (c) 5:1:1 (v/v) mixture of double-deionized water:28% (w/v) ammonium hydroxide:30% (w/v) hydrogen peroxide, and finally (d) 1 M potassium hydroxide. Each sonication step in solvent is performed for at least 30 min, and after every step the slides are rinsed and sonicated in double-deionized water for 10 min. In the end, the slide surface is flamed thoroughly using a propane torch to destroy any remaining organic impurities. A microfluidic channel is made on the clean slides by sandwiching two strips of double-sided sticky tape ~4–6 mm apart between the quartz slide and a clean rectangular glass coverslip (Michelotti et al., 2010; Roy et al., 2008). The edges of the channel are sealed with epoxy (for example, Hardman DOUBLE/BUBBLE Fast-Setting Epoxy) to prevent leakage of the buffer. The microfluidic channel thus made has a low volume of ~30–50 μL that helps decrease background fluorescence from buffer contaminants. A pair of 1 mm holes drilled into the quartz slide will act as inlet and outlet ports for the flow into the channel of buffers containing different molecules. Pipette tips (2–200 μL; epTIPS, Eppendorf) are cut to a length of ~1 cm from the tip and snugly inserted into the two holes of the quartz slide. Into the open ends of the tips, a long ~10- to 15-cm plastic tube (0.02″ thick, Tygon Tubing) is inserted, followed by sealing the tips and tubing with epoxy. The slides are left at RT for ~30 min for the epoxy to harden. The tubing can be cut to an appropriate length to create an inlet and outlet channel before using the quartz slide for smFRET experiments and flowing buffers containing different solutes (such as ligands, ions, osmolytes, and crowding agents) into the channel using a clean syringe (Fig. 15.2B). Buffer exchange enables the convenient study of riboswitch structure and folding under different conditions on a single slide.

2.3. Surface attachment and oxygen scavenging systems

Due to their negative backbone charge, nucleic acids generally do not adsorb significantly even to a bare slide surface. For riboswitches, surface tethering for smFRET is therefore most easily achieved using biotinylated bovine serum albumin (bBSA) and streptavidin on plain quartz slides. By contrast, for studies involving proteins, polyethylene glycol (PEG)-passivated slides should be used, and both types of slides have been utilized for smFRET studies of riboswitches (Haller et al., 2013; Haller, Rieder, et al., 2011; Haller, Souliere, et al., 2011; Suddala et al., 2013). For PEG-passivated slides, the surface should be treated with PEG (molecular weight: 5000) before making the microfluidic channel to reduce nonspecific binding of molecules, especially proteins to the surface. In this method, the clean slide surface is treated with aminosilane, followed by reaction with an NHS-ester-modified PEG containing a fraction (5%) of biotin-PEG. For surface immobilization via bBSA, the microfluidic channel is first coated by flowing 80 μL of 1 mg/mL solution of bBSA and incubating (let sit at room temperature) for 5 min to allow nonspecific adsorption onto the slide surface. The excess unbound bBSA is washed out with 100 μL of a 1 × smFRET buffer of choice (based on experimental requirements), followed by flowing 80 μL of 0.2 mg/mL streptavidin into the channel. After incubation for 5 min, the unbound streptavidin is washed off with 100 μL of 1 × buffer. Next, 20–100 p*M* of doubly labeled RNA is flowed onto the slide until an optimal density is obtained (~300–400 molecules per field of view), and the unbound molecules are washed away with the 1 × buffer.

For imaging the immobilized molecules, a suitable 1 × smFRET buffer supplemented with an enzymatic oxygen scavenging system (OSS) should be used that will increase the longevity of the fluorophores before photobleaching, permitting long observation times. A widely used OSS consists of protocatechuic acid protocatechuate-3,4-dioxygenase enzyme, and a triplet-state quencher such as Trolox (6-hydroxy-2,5,7,8-tetramethylchroman-2-carboxylic acid) to slow down fluorophore photobleaching and reduce dye blinking, respectively (Aitken, Marshall, & Puglisi, 2008; Krishnan et al., 2013). Alternatively, a glucose oxidase/catalase-based enzymatic system is also widely used (Roy et al., 2008). However, it is important to note that, due to the production of carboxylic acids in both of these systems, the pH of the buffer may decrease over time and needs to be carefully checked (Shi, Lim, & Ha, 2010). Therefore, a sufficient strength of buffering species ($\geq$50 m*M*) should be used when studying riboswitch RNAs, particularly if any putative pH-sensitive elements such as noncanonical base pairs are present. Recently, a pyranose oxidase/catalase system was proposed as a better alternative for the smFRET study of such pH-sensitive systems (Swoboda et al., 2012). In addition, degassing the buffers will aid in decreasing the free molecular oxygen, thereby further prolonging the fluorescence signal.

2.4. smFRET using prism-based TIRF microscopy

smFRET microscopy for studying riboswitch structure and dynamics is generally done using wide-field illumination (Brenner et al., 2010; Haller et al., 2013; Haller, Rieder, et al., 2011; Haller, Souliere, et al., 2011; Lemay et al., 2006; Souliere et al., 2013; Suddala et al., 2013; Wood et al., 2012). In this method, fluorescence signal from hundreds of molecules can be recorded simultaneously using a sensitive CCD camera. The molecules are generally immobilized onto the surface of a microfluidic channel for enabling the long observation times (on the order of tens of seconds to minutes) needed for studying the often slow conformational dynamics and folding of riboswitches and/or to record significant numbers of conformational transitions for accurate rate determination (Fig. 15.2C). The immobilized molecules can be excited either by direct illumination as in confocal microscopy or by using an evanescent field in TIRF microscopy (Roy et al., 2008; Walter et al., 2008). The evanescent field is generated using total internal reflection (TIR) of the excitation laser at the quartz–water interface. The TIR of the incident laser can be achieved by using an objective (objective-TIRF microscopy), but more easily by using a prism (prism-based TIRF microscopy, Fig. 15.2C and D). The intensity of the evanescent field decays exponentially with distance from the reflecting surface and therefore only excites immobilized molecules that are within ~100 nm of the surface. The advantage of using TIR microscopy is that it eliminates the background fluorescence from solvent and any labeled molecules free in solution, resulting in a high signal-to-noise (S/N) ratio that is critical for single-molecule detection. The prism-based TIRF microscope (Fig. 15.2D) is relatively simple to assemble and, therefore, has been widely used for studying the conformational dynamics of various riboswitch classes (Haller et al., 2013; Haller, Rieder, et al., 2011; Haller, Souliere, et al., 2011; Joo & Ha, 2012a, 2012b; Roy et al., 2008; Savinov et al., 2014; Suddala et al., 2013).

Figure 15.2D shows a general schematic for the prism-based TIRF microscopy setup. The quartz slide rests on top of a 1.2-numerical aperture 60 × water immersion objective (e.g., Olympus UplanApo) of an inverted microscope (IX 71; Olympus). The quartz prism is placed on top of the slide containing the microfluidic channel, where it is used to achieve TIR of the excitation laser to generate an evanescent field that excites the surface-tethered molecules in the channel. A 532-nm (diode-pumped Nd:YAG, CW) laser is used to excite Cy3 (donor) for FRET measurements and intermittent excitation with a 638-nm red diode laser can be used to check for the presence of Cy5 (acceptor), which helps differentiate donor-only molecules from those showing large-distance zero-FRET states. Mineral oil with a refractive index that matches the quartz slide is placed between the prism and the slide surface to fill any optical gaps. The oil also enables smooth movement of the slide for imaging different regions in the microfluidic channel and prevents scratching the prism surface. The fluorescent emission from the molecules is collected through the objective, and the scattered excitation light is removed using a dichroic mirror. Additionally, the image of the surface-tethered molecules is split into donor and acceptor emissions using a pair of dichroic mirrors (D1, D2, Fig. 15.2D) and two mirrors (M1, M2) to project both colors side-by-side onto two halves of a CCD camera. More details of the prism-based TIRF microscope we use can be found in several references (Michelotti et al., 2010; Roy et al., 2008; Zhao & Rueda, 2009).

2.5. Heat-annealing of riboswitch RNAs

Before immobilization onto the slide, riboswitch RNAs need to be folded into their native conformations. RNA is generally stored at low temperatures (−20 or −80 °C) in autoclaved double-distilled water or in near-neutral pH buffers without any divalent cations to prevent its degradation over time. However, under such low-temperature, low-ionic strength conditions and due to repeated freeze-thawing, RNA molecules may misfold or form nonspecific aggregates. Heating will break the aggregates and unfold misfolded RNA molecules, allowing them to fold into their native conformations. There is no standard procedure for folding of RNAs, and diverse heat-annealing protocols are used. Commonly, RNA is heated in a buffer with monovalent ions such as Na^+ or K^+ but without Mg^{2+} to 60–80 °C for 2–5 min. The RNA is then cooled either rapidly by placing on ice or slowly by allowing to equilibrate to room temperature to fold into its secondary structure. This is followed by the addition of Mg^{2+} to the required concentration to facilitate the formation of tertiary interactions. For smFRET experiments, heat annealing after diluting the RNA to the required low concentrations of 20–100 p*M* will prevent the formation of dimers/aggregates, which can be easily identified by multistep photobleaching in the smFRET experiment. Higher temperatures such as 90 °C should be tried in cases where heating at 75 °C is not effective in breaking the aggregates. As a control, a few different temperature and time regimes should be tried to optimize the folding protocol and to test if the folding protocol has any significant effect on the smFRET results.

3. PRACTICAL EXPERIMENTAL CONSIDERATIONS

Before starting to image single molecules, the slide needs to be coated with bBSA and streptavidin for immobilizing the RNA. For PEG-passivated slides, only streptavidin has to be flowed onto the slide as it binds to the biotin–PEG. It is important to visualize the slide surface after flowing the bBSA and/or streptavidin to make sure that it is clean with minimal impurities before immobilizing doubly labeled riboswitch molecules. Organic fluorescent impurities often look similar to the donor-labeled molecules and, therefore, cannot be distinguished easily. Even minor contamination of any stock solution will render the surface dirty; therefore, all the buffers and solutions for smFRET should be passed through a 0.2-μm filter. For immobilization of riboswitch molecules using a newly labeled stock, start with a low concentration (~20 p*M*) of the labeled RNA. Optimize the concentration needed to achieve an ideal density of ~300–400 molecules per field of view (256 × 12 pixels, or half of a typical CCD chip). Higher densities will lead to overlap of signals from neighboring spots that makes the identification of single molecules difficult. By contrast, a low density will require more movies to be taken to collect sufficient data. The laser power should be optimized both to maximize the S/N ratio and to prolong the lifetime of the dyes. Higher power will give better signal but will also lead to faster photobleaching. The laser intensity can be controlled using neutral density filters to reach a compromise between high S/N ratio and slow photobleaching. Different kinds of CCD cameras such as an intensified CCD (ICCD) and the newer electron multiplying CCD (EMCCD) are used for TIRF-based smFRET studies of riboswitches. EMCCD cameras, in particular, can be cooled to very low temperatures and may have better sensitivity at faster time resolution (currently ~33 ms for full frame) (Roy et al., 2008; Zhao &

Rueda, 2009). The time resolution can be further increased by reading out only part of the chip or by using pixel binning. Choosing the right frame rate for imaging is important and, if possible, molecules should be imaged at multiple time resolutions to capture a range of dwell times. A faster time resolution generally requires using high laser intensities to increase the signal. This will lead to increased photobleaching and, therefore, slower transitions (with longer dwell times) will be missed. Similarly, faster dynamics will be missed when imaging at a slower camera frame rate. Therefore, for riboswitches with heterogeneous kinetics, the rates of structural dynamics calculated could depend on the choice of the camera frame rate. In addition, when imaging riboswitches by smFRET, it is important to excite at the end with the red laser to check for emission of the acceptor fluorophore. This will help distinguish low-FRET states from donor-only species. Although such low-FRET states may be caused by blinking of the acceptor fluorophore, observation of long-lived states in the presence of a triplet state quencher such as Trolox likely indicates genuine conformations with distances >75 Å. Use of alternative FRET pairs with larger R_0 can help in resolving these conformations (Roy et al., 2008). For kinetic measurements, titrations can be performed sequentially on the same slide to minimize variability between experiments. Ligand titrations should sample a few concentrations below the dissociation equilibrium constant (K_d) and a few above it up to saturating conditions (>10 K_d).

4. DATA ANALYSIS

Using wide-field TIRF microscopy, a large number of immobilized molecules are imaged simultaneously and analyzed using custom written Matlab or Visual C++ code, or other programs such as Micro-Manager (plugin for ImageJ, open source) or Metamorph (Molecular Devices, Inc., commercial imaging software) to obtain the raw FRET movies (Blanco & Walter, 2010). Individual smFRET time traces are extracted from the movies using image analysis programs written in IDL (Research Systems, Boulder) or Matlab (MathWorks, Inc.). This is done by taking an average image of the first 30 frames for each movie to identify individual spots in both halves of the image (Cy3 and Cy5 spots). After identification of individual spots in one channel, their corresponding spots in the other channel are located and intensities recorded over time. For accurate colocalization of the donor and acceptor spots in both channels, a slide made with surface immobilized red-fluorescent beads is used to calibrate the correspondence of the donor and the acceptor images (Churchman, Okten, Rock, Dawson, & Spudich, 2005;

Roy et al., 2008). Generally, depending on the labeling efficiency and the density of spots on the surface, at least 40–100 smFRET traces can be obtained from each movie. Ergodic behavior is observed when the long-time average of one molecule represents the ensemble average of snapshots from many molecules. In most cases, nonergodic behavior is observed instead, and significant numbers of smFRET traces are needed to characterize the equilibrium properties of a riboswitch, and for direct comparison with ensemble-averaged benchmark measurements (Marek et al., 2011).

4.1. FRET histograms

The smFRET time traces from multiple movies taken under a given condition are combined to generate a dataset containing ideally several hundred molecules. These traces provide direct information on the conformational states sampled by individual molecules and the dwell times spent in each of the FRET states before transitioning to other FRET states (Fig. 15.3A). smFRET traces can be analyzed using a number of methods to yield information on the structure and dynamics of the RNA (Blanco & Walter, 2010). One straightforward way of analyzing the data is to generate a population FRET histogram by binning the first 50 or 100 frames of each time trace (to ensure that the dataset is not biased toward a few long-lived molecules). Such a histogram directly shows the ensemble FRET distribution of all riboswitch molecules included (Fig. 15.3B). By fitting the histogram with a sum of Gaussian functions, the minimum number of distinct conformations sampled by the riboswitch and their equilibrium distribution can be obtained under a given condition. In addition, the mean value and the width of each Gaussian function can yield more information about the corresponding conformations sampled. Rough distance estimates between the fluorophores in each conformation are estimated from the mean apparent FRET value of the Gaussian curve using Eq. (15.1). Depending on the labeling strategy, generally the shortest distance (corresponding to the highest FRET state) should be similar to the distance observed in the ligand-bound crystal structure of the riboswitch. Distances for the other FRET states will provide information on the extent of compactness (degree of foldedness) of those conformations. In general, most riboswitches studied using smFRET have displayed two-state behavior, corresponding to ligand-bound and ligand-free conformations with different properties (Savinov et al., 2014). However, a few riboswitches with more than two states have also been documented (Lemay et al., 2006; Reining et al., 2013).

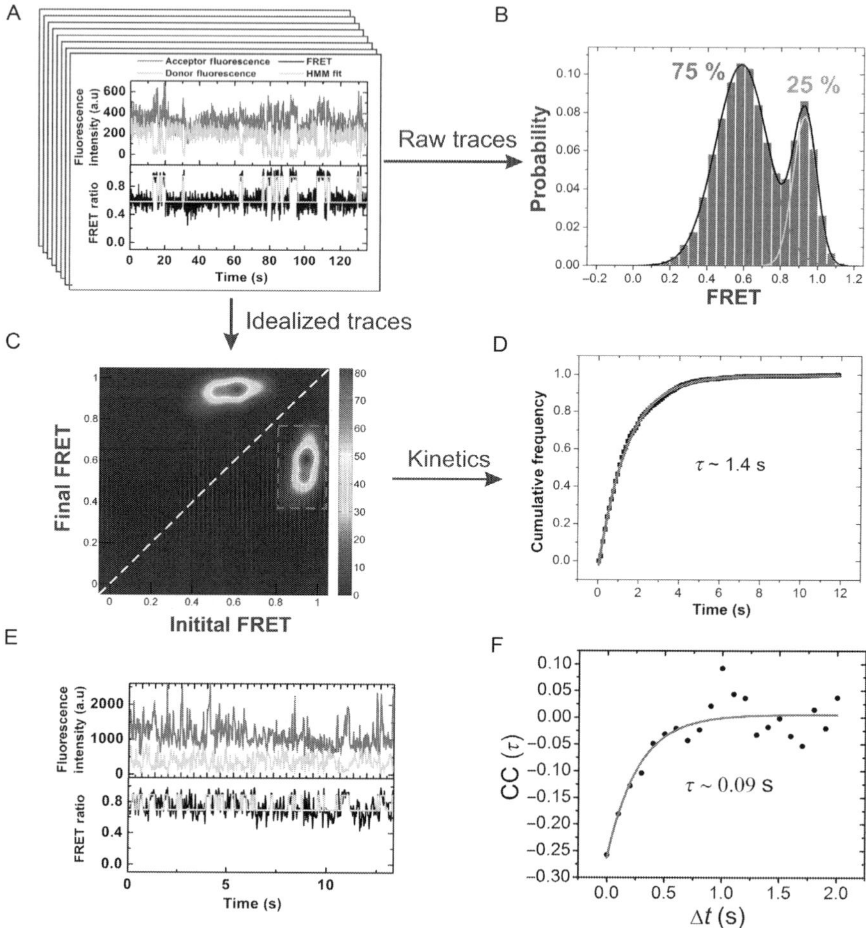

Figure 15.3 Analysis of smFRET data. (A) Raw single-molecule time trace showing anti-correlated donor (green) and acceptor (red) intensities for the *Bsu* $preQ_1$-I riboswitch in the presence of 100 n*M* $preQ_1$ and no Mg^{2+} (60 ms time resolution, unpublished data). The FRET trace (black) idealized with a two-state HMM fit (cyan) is shown in the lower plot. (B) FRET histogram showing two major populations and their equilibrium distribution. (C) Transition density plot (TDP) showing as heat maps the transitions from initial to final FRET states and their frequency. The dwell times of all the molecules in a given FRET state (~0.9 in this example, red broken box) can be extracted from this plot. (D) Cumulative dwell time distribution of the dwell times in the ~0.9 FRET state fit with a single-exponential function. (E) An smFRET trace of the ligand-free *Bsu* $preQ_1$-I riboswitch with very fast dynamics (33 ms time resolution, unpublished data). (F) Cross-correlation curve of the trace shown in panel E fit with a single exponential to obtain the combined rate of transitions ($k_{1,2}+k_{2,1}=1/\tau$, for a two-state process). (See the color plate.)

Folding studies on riboswitches using smFRET routinely probe the effects of ligand and different ions on the FRET distribution and dynamics (Brenner et al., 2010; Fiegland et al., 2012; Haller et al., 2013; Haller, Rieder, et al., 2011; Haller, Souliere, et al., 2011; Lemay et al., 2006; Souliere et al., 2013; Suddala et al., 2013; Wood et al., 2012). As a first step, the FRET histogram of the riboswitch is obtained in the absence of both ligand and Mg^{2+}, but in the presence of monovalent cations. Later, the folding of the riboswitch can be probed in the presence of ligand and/or Mg^{2+} to delineate their effect(s), either individually or together, on the conformational dynamics of the riboswitch. Titrations of Mg^{2+} or ligand can be performed on the same slide by adjusting the composition of the input solution of the microfluidic flow cell. Such experiments can be used to monitor the effects of increasing ligand or Mg^{2+} concentrations on the FRET distributions and conformational dynamics of the riboswitch. The occupancy (as seen from the FRET histograms) of one of the conformations, corresponding to the ligand-bound folded state, is expected to increase as a function of ligand concentration. The increasing fraction of the ligand-bound state (typically of high FRET) can be fit with a standard Hill equation (with $n=1$) from which a half-saturation value ($K_{1/2}$) value can be estimated that relates to the K_d obtained from biochemical methods. Any large discrepancies (>10-fold) between these two values could indicate misfolding of the RNA or fluorophore interference with proper ligand binding and needs to be investigated.

The mean and width of the individual Gaussian peaks can provide additional information on the compactness and dynamic nature of the underlying conformations. The width of individual peaks depends on the instrument noise (shot noise) but also on the conformational behavior of the corresponding structural ensembles (Suddala et al., 2013). A larger width indicates a broad and dynamic conformational ensemble, while a smaller width suggests a stable structure. Following the changes in the mean FRET value and width of the different Gaussian peaks at varying ligand and/or Mg^{2+} concentrations can also provide additional details on the conformational ensemble and folding of the riboswitch (Suddala et al., 2013).

4.2. Kinetic analysis

The more interesting data from smFRET experiments are the dwell times of individual molecules in different FRET states that can be used to kinetically characterize the ligand-dependent folding pathways of riboswitches (Savinov et al., 2014). For riboswitches exhibiting two distinct states with slow interconversion dynamics, the smFRET traces can be idealized using a defined FRET threshold to obtain the transition kinetics (Blanco & Walter, 2010). More often, the smFRET traces may be noisy and/or display rapid fluctuations between closely spaced states that need advanced methods to analyze. Statistical methods such as Hidden Markov Modeling (HMM) are used to idealize such smFRET traces in an unbiased manner, to detect transitions between FRET states, and to extract dwell times of individual molecules in the different states (Fig. 15.3A) (Blanco & Walter, 2010; Qin & Li, 2004). Freely available programs such as QuB, vbFRET, and HaMMy, along with custom Matlab scripts are generally used for HMM analysis of smFRET data (Bronson, Fei, Hofman, Gonzalez, & Wiggins, 2009; McKinney, Joo, & Ha, 2006; Qin & Li, 2004). Recently, an extensive data analysis package with a graphical interface named SMART has been described for the objective analysis of complex smFRET data and can be freely downloaded at https://simtk.org/home/smart (Greenfeld, Pavlichin, Mabuchi, & Herschlag, 2012).

Using the idealized traces (Fig. 15.3A), a transition density plot (TDP) can be generated that shows the different kinds of transitions and their frequency in all molecules as heat maps (Fig. 15.3C) (Blanco & Walter, 2010). Dwell times of all molecules in each FRET state before transitioning to a different state can be extracted from the TDP. The dwell times are then plotted as a cumulative distribution plot and fit with an exponential function to extract the rate constants of conformational dynamics between the different states (Fig. 15.3D) (Blanco & Walter, 2010). For a simple two-state process, the dwell time distributions can be fit with a single-exponential function. However, heterogeneity is often observed in single-molecule measurements so that the dwell time distributions are best fit with a sum of exponential functions that suggests the presence of multiple similar structures with different kinetic properties. Careful investigation of the heterogeneities can provide more information about the conformational and dynamic properties of the different FRET states. The heterogeneities in conformational dynamics can also be visualized using a scatter plot of average dwell times in different FRET states for every time trace, and the effect of ligand on this distribution can be studied (Lemay et al., 2006). For a detailed review on the analysis of complex multistate smFRET data, the reader is referred to a reference (Blanco & Walter, 2010).

4.3. Cross-correlation analysis

HMM analysis of smFRET traces will fail to detect all transitions in cases where the conformational dynamics of a riboswitch are very fast (Fig. 15.3E) and close to the time resolution of the camera (typically 10–100 ms) (Roy et al., 2008; Suddala et al., 2013). This will result in an underestimation of the rates of structural changes. Imaging the molecules at the fastest achievable frame rate of the camera can help resolve the faster dynamics, but will also lead to a decrease in the S/N ratio. Alternatively, one may switch to a confocal system that uses a point detector to achieve higher time resolution, but only one molecule can be investigated at a time, limiting throughput. In such situations, cross-correlation (CC) analysis can be performed on the wide-field smFRET traces to quantify the anticorrelation between the donor and acceptor intensities (Kim et al., 2002; Ragunathan, Liu, & Ha, 2012; Suddala et al., 2013). CC analysis measures the decay in the extent of anticorrelation between the donor and acceptor intensities (autocorrelation of the FRET trace yields the same information) as a function of increasing time-lag between the two traces. In essence, one of the intensity traces is kept fixed while the other trace is moved in the calculation at small time (Δt) increments, and the CC value at each step is calculated. The CC value plotted against the time lag is fit with a single-exponential function to obtain the lifetime of the decay (τ, Fig. 15.3F). The inverse of the lifetime yields the sum of rates for transitions between different FRET states (Kim et al., 2002; Ragunathan et al., 2012; Suddala et al., 2013). For individual traces, the rate of transition to a given FRET state can then be obtained by multiplying the fraction of time spent in that state with the sum of rate constants ($k_{1,2}+k_{2,1}=1/\tau$), effectively averaging over any molecular heterogeneity. Multiple smFRET traces with fast dynamics can be analyzed this way to obtain a distribution of rates for riboswitch folding and unfolding. Analyzing how increasing concentrations of ligand affect the rates of conformational dynamics between different FRET states can potentially reveal the mechanism of ligand binding, which is extremely difficult to investigate using ensemble methods (Kim et al., 2013).

5. INDUCED-FIT VERSUS CONFORMATIONAL SELECTION

Kinetic analysis of ligand-dependent conformational dynamics using smFRET can reveal the major folding mechanism of a riboswitch

(Hatzakis, 2014; Savinov et al., 2014; Suddala et al., 2013). Traditionally, the ligand-mediated folding pathways for biomolecules such as riboswitches have been classified into two contrasting mechanisms—induced-fit and conformational selection (Fig. 15.4A) (Hammes, Chang, & Oas, 2009; Kim et al., 2013). In the classical definition of induced-fit mechanism, the riboswitch (or receptor) exists predominantly in an "open" ligand-free state and does not sample ligand-bound-like or "closed" conformations in the absence of ligand. Ligand binding to the apo (or open) conformation induces the riboswitch into the folded conformation, which is generally similar to the ligand-bound crystal structure. In conformational selection (also referred to as conformational capture or population shift), the ligand-free ensemble samples a small, but significant population of folded-like (or closed) conformations, albeit transiently. Ligand specifically recognizes such conformations and stabilizes them upon binding. Therefore, induced-fit and conformational selection mechanisms are also sometimes referred to as "binding first" and "folding first" processes, respectively (Hammes et al., 2009; Suddala et al., 2013). However, studies on proteins have shown that the two mechanisms are not mutually exclusive, but rather co-exist to different extents depending

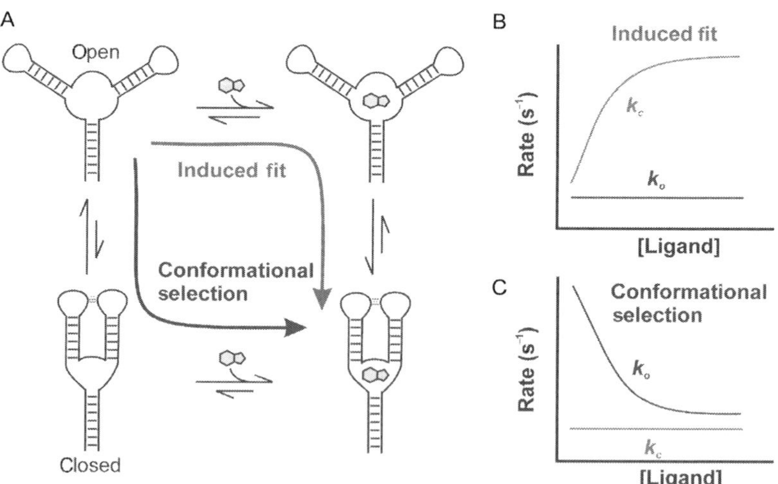

Figure 15.4 Schematic for the kinetic analysis of ligand-mediated folding mechanism of a riboswitch. (A) Induced-fit (red (light gray in print version)) and conformational selection (blue (black in print version)) models of ligand-mediated riboswitch folding. Expected rate constant dependence on ligand concentration for riboswitches folding via (B) induced-fit and (C) conformational selection mechanisms. Idealized curves depict the net forward folding, or closing, reaction (k_C, green (light gray in print version)), and the net reverse unfolding, or opening, reaction (k_O, blue (black in print version)).

on the buffer conditions and the relative concentrations of the receptor and ligand (Daniels et al., 2014; Kim et al., 2013). Therefore, kinetic assays (either ensemble or single molecule) only reveal the major pathway under a chosen set of experimental conditions (Hammes et al., 2009). Calculation of relative flux through each pathway may offer quantitative insight into how ligand concentrations and buffer conditions affect the partitioning of folding through either mechanisms (Daniels et al., 2014). Recently, the process of ligand binding to an open conformation of a receptor that can sample ligand-free, folded-like conformations has been referred to as adaptive induced-fit mechanism, to distinguish it from the classical definition. In addition, binding of ligand to folded-like states followed by local adjustments in the structure has been classified as extended conformational selection mechanism (Csermely, Palotai, & Nussinov, 2010).

While the absence of any ligand-free closed conformations suggests that folding should proceed via an induced-fit like mechanism, the converse is not true. That is, the presence of ligand-free closed conformations does not rule out the possibility that an induced-fit mechanism is in action (Hammes et al., 2009). The differentiating step for both the mechanisms is the conformation to which the ligand preferentially binds. Induced-fit and conformational selection can be differentiated by ligand binding to the open and closed conformations, respectively, which generate distinct signatures of ligand-dependent kinetics of conformational dynamics (Fig. 15.4) (Hammes et al., 2009; Kim et al., 2013; Suddala et al., 2013). In the induced-fit mechanism, the rate of closing or folding (k_c) increases with ligand concentration and the opening rate (k_o) may be slowed or remain unaffected (Fig. 15.4B). In contrast, in conformational selection, the ligand binding has no effect on the closing rate while the opening rate decreases (Fig. 15.4C). This distinction is based on the assumption of a two-state model of riboswitch folding, which is mostly true for many riboswitches (Savinov et al., 2014). For some riboswitches that display more than two conformations, such as the *pbuE* adenine riboswitch, the kinetic data may be still more heterogeneous and complex and hard to interpret (Lemay et al., 2006; Reining et al., 2013). Taken together, probing riboswitch structure and dynamics using smFRET provides valuable information not only on the conformations sampled but also on the ligand-mediated folding mechanism, which is difficult to probe with other methods (Savinov et al., 2014). Therefore, following the methods described in this article, especially the kinetic analysis of smFRET data (Section 4.2 and Fig. 15.4), will enable a detailed investigation of the ligand-mediated folding mechanisms of riboswitches.

6. SUMMARY AND CONCLUSIONS

Understanding gene regulation by riboswitches requires characterizing their structural and dynamic properties. Here, we have provided details of investigating riboswitch conformation and dynamics using smFRET based on TIRF microscopy. The steps described apply to current state-of-the-art studies of dual fluorophore-labeled riboswitch RNAs and the effect of ligand on them using two-color smFRET experiments. In the near future, we anticipate that more complex riboswitches and folding mechanisms will be studied, and increasingly advanced techniques such as three-color smFRET (Hohng, Joo, & Ha, 2004; Kim et al., 2013) will be applied to correlate ligand binding and riboswitch folding in real time. In addition, ligand-dependent cotranscriptional riboswitch folding, for which smFRET studies are decidedly nontrivial, may be pursued to gain insight into the increasingly complex nature of cellular folding landscapes of riboswitches (Dangkulwanich, Ishibashi, Bintu, & Bustamante, 2014).

ACKNOWLEDGMENTS

This work was supported by NIH Grant GM062357 and a sub-award on GM063162 (PI Joseph E. Wedekind) to N. G. W.

REFERENCES

Aitken, C. E., Marshall, R. A., & Puglisi, J. D. (2008). An oxygen scavenging system for improvement of dye stability in single-molecule fluorescence experiments. *Biophysical Journal*, *94*(5), 1826–1835.

Al-Hashimi, H. M., & Walter, N. G. (2008). RNA dynamics: It is about time. *Current Opinion in Structural Biology*, *18*(3), 321–329.

Baird, N. J., & Ferre-D'Amare, A. R. (2010). Idiosyncratically tuned switching behavior of riboswitch aptamer domains revealed by comparative small-angle X-ray scattering analysis (vol 16, pg 598, 2010). *RNA*, *16*(7), 1447.

Barrick, J. E., & Breaker, R. R. (2007). The distributions, mechanisms, and structures of metabolite-binding riboswitches. *Genome Biology*, *8*(11), R239.

Bastet, L., Dube, A., Masse, E., & Lafontaine, D. A. (2011). New insights into riboswitch regulation mechanisms. *Molecular Microbiology*, *80*(5), 1148–1154.

Blanco, M., & Walter, N. G. (2010). Analysis of complex single-molecule FRET time trajectories. *Methods in Enzymology*, *472*, 153–178.

Bothe, J. R., Nikolova, E. N., Eichhorn, C. D., Chugh, J., Hansen, A. L., & Al-Hashimi, H. M. (2011). Characterizing RNA dynamics at atomic resolution using solution-state NMR spectroscopy. *Nature Methods*, *8*(11), 919–931.

Breaker, R. R. (2011). Prospects for riboswitch discovery and analysis. *Molecular Cell*, *43*(6), 867–879.

Breaker, R. R. (2012). Riboswitches and the RNA world. *Cold Spring Harbor Perspectives in Biology*, *4*(2), a003566.

Brenner, M. D., Scanlan, M. S., Nahas, M. K., Ha, T., & Silverman, S. K. (2010). Multivector fluorescence analysis of the xpt guanine riboswitch aptamer domain and the conformational role of guanine. *Biochemistry, 49*(8), 1596–1605.

Bronson, J. E., Fei, J. Y., Hofman, J. M., Gonzalez, R. L., & Wiggins, C. H. (2009). Learning rates and states from biophysical time series: A Bayesian approach to model selection and single-molecule FRET data. *Biophysical Journal, 97*(12), 3196–3205.

Butler, E. B., Xiong, Y., Wang, J., & Strobel, S. A. (2011). Structural basis of cooperative ligand binding by the glycine riboswitch. *Chemistry & Biology, 18*(3), 293–298.

Chen, B., Zuo, X., Wang, Y. X., & Dayie, T. K. (2012). Multiple conformations of SAM-II riboswitch detected with SAXS and NMR spectroscopy. *Nucleic Acids Research, 40*(7), 3117–3130.

Churchman, L. S., Okten, Z., Rock, R. S., Dawson, J. F., & Spudich, J. A. (2005). Single molecule high-resolution colocalization of Cy3 and Cy5 attached to macromolecules measures intramolecular distances through time. *Proceedings of the National Academy of Sciences of the United States of America, 102*(5), 1419–1423.

Cooper, M., Ebner, A., Briggs, M., Burrows, M., Gardner, N., Richardson, R., et al. (2004). Cy3B (TM): Improving the performance of cyanine dyes. *Journal of Fluorescence, 14*(2), 145–150.

Csermely, P., Palotai, R., & Nussinov, R. (2010). Induced fit, conformational selection and independent dynamic segments: An extended view of binding events. *Trends in Biochemical Sciences, 35*(10), 539–546.

Dangkulwanich, M., Ishibashi, T., Bintu, L., & Bustamante, C. (2014). Molecular mechanisms of transcription through single-molecule experiments. *Chemical Reviews, 114*(6), 3203–3223.

Daniels, K. G., Tonthat, N. K., McClure, D. R., Chang, Y. C., Liu, X., Schumacher, M. A., et al. (2014). Ligand concentration regulates the pathways of coupled protein folding and binding. *Journal of the American Chemical Society, 136*(3), 822–825.

Deniz, A. A., Mukhopadhyay, S., & Lemke, E. A. (2008). Single-molecule biophysics: At the interface of biology, physics and chemistry. *Journal of the Royal Society Interface, 5*(18), 15–45.

Dethoff, E. A., Chugh, J., Mustoe, A. M., & Al-Hashimi, H. M. (2012). Functional complexity and regulation through RNA dynamics. *Nature, 482*(7385), 322–330.

Dethoff, E. A., Petzold, K., Chugh, J., Casiano-Negroni, A., & Al-Hashimi, H. M. (2012). Visualizing transient low-populated structures of RNA. *Nature, 491*(7426), 724–728.

Ditzler, M. A., Aleman, E. A., Rueda, D., & Walter, N. G. (2007). Focus on function: Single molecule RNA enzymology. *Biopolymers, 87*(5–6), 302–316.

Edwards, A. L., Reyes, F. E., Heroux, A., & Batey, R. T. (2010). Structural basis for recognition of S-adenosylhomocysteine by riboswitches. *RNA, 16*(11), 2144–2155.

Feng, J., Walter, N. G., & Brooks, C. L., III. (2011). Cooperative and directional folding of the preQ1 riboswitch aptamer domain. *Journal of the American Chemical Society, 133*(12), 4196–4199.

Fiegland, L. R., Garst, A. D., Batey, R. T., & Nesbitt, D. J. (2012). Single-molecule studies of the lysine riboswitch reveal effector-dependent conformational dynamics of the aptamer domain. *Biochemistry, 51*(45), 9223–9233.

Frieda, K. L., & Block, S. M. (2012). Direct observation of cotranscriptional folding in an adenine riboswitch. *Science, 338*(6105), 397–400.

Garst, A. D., & Batey, R. T. (2009). A switch in time: Detailing the life of a riboswitch. *Biochimica et Biophysica Acta, 1789*(9–10), 584–591.

Garst, A. D., Heroux, A., Rambo, R. P., & Batey, R. T. (2008). Crystal structure of the lysine riboswitch regulatory mRNA element. *Journal of Biological Chemistry, 283*(33), 22347–22351.

Gilbert, S. D., Rambo, R. P., Van Tyne, D., & Batey, R. T. (2008). Structure of the SAM-II riboswitch bound to S-adenosylmethionine. *Nature Structural & Molecular Biology*, *15*(2), 177–182.

Greenfeld, M., Pavlichin, D. S., Mabuchi, H., & Herschlag, D. (2012). Single molecule analysis research tool (SMART): An integrated approach for analyzing single molecule data. *PLoS One*, 7(2), e30024.

Haller, A., Altman, R. B., Souliere, M. F., Blanchard, S. C., & Micura, R. (2013). Folding and ligand recognition of the TPP riboswitch aptamer at single-molecule resolution. *Proceedings of the National Academy of Sciences of the United States of America*, *110*(11), 4188–4193.

Haller, A., Rieder, U., Aigner, M., Blanchard, S. C., & Micura, R. (2011). Conformational capture of the SAM-II riboswitch. *Nature Chemical Biology*, 7(6), 393–400.

Haller, A., Souliere, M. F., & Micura, R. (2011). The dynamic nature of RNA as key to understanding riboswitch mechanisms. *Accounts of Chemical Research*, *44*(12), 1339–1348.

Hammes, G. G., Chang, Y. C., & Oas, T. G. (2009). Conformational selection or induced fit: A flux description of reaction mechanism. *Proceedings of the National Academy of Sciences of the United States of America*, *106*(33), 13737–13741.

Hatzakis, N. S. (2014). Single molecule insights on conformational selection and induced fit mechanism. *Biophysical Chemistry*, *186*, 46–54.

Heppell, B., Blouin, S., Dussault, A. M., Mulhbacher, J., Ennifar, E., Penedo, J. C., et al. (2011). Molecular insights into the ligand-controlled organization of the SAM-I riboswitch. *Nature Chemical Biology*, 7(6), 384–392.

Hohng, S., Joo, C., & Ha, T. (2004). Single-molecule three-color FRET. *Biophysical Journal*, *87*(2), 1328–1337.

Johnson, J. E., Jr., Reyes, F. E., Polaski, J. T., & Batey, R. T. (2012). B12 cofactors directly stabilize an mRNA regulatory switch. *Nature*, *492*(7427), 133–137.

Johnson-Buck, A. E., McDowell, S. E., & Walter, N. G. (2011). Metal ions: Supporting actors in the playbook of small ribozymes. *Metal Ions in Life Sciences*, *9*, 175–196.

Joo, C., & Ha, T. (2012a). Preparing sample chambers for single-molecule FRET. *Cold Spring Harbor Protocols*, *2012*(10), 1104–1108.

Joo, C., & Ha, T. (2012b). Prism-type total internal reflection microscopy for single-molecule FRET. *Cold Spring Harbor Protocols*, *2012*(12).

Kang, M., Peterson, R., & Feigon, J. (2009). Structural insights into riboswitch control of the biosynthesis of queuosine, a modified nucleotide found in the anticodon of tRNA. *Molecular Cell*, *33*(6), 784–790.

Kim, E., Lee, S., Jeon, A., Choi, J. M., Lee, H. S., Hohng, S., et al. (2013). A single-molecule dissection of ligand binding to a protein with intrinsic dynamics. *Nature Chemical Biology*, *9*(5), 313–318.

Kim, H. D., Nienhaus, G. U., Ha, T., Orr, J. W., Williamson, J. R., & Chu, S. (2002). Mg2+−dependent conformational change of RNA studied by fluorescence correlation and FRET on immobilized single molecules. *Proceedings of the National Academy of Sciences of the United States of America*, *99*(7), 4284–4289.

Krishnan, R., Blanco, M. R., Kahlscheuer, M. L., Abelson, J., Guthrie, C., & Walter, N. G. (2013). Biased Brownian ratcheting leads to pre-mRNA remodeling and capture prior to first-step splicing. *Nature Structural & Molecular Biology*, *20*(12), 1450–1457.

Kulshina, N., Baird, N. J., & Ferre-D'Amare, A. R. (2009). Recognition of the bacterial second messenger cyclic diguanylate by its cognate riboswitch. *Nature Structural & Molecular Biology*, *16*(12), 1212–1217.

Lang, K., & Micura, R. (2008). The preparation of site-specifically modified riboswitch domains as an example for enzymatic ligation of chemically synthesized RNA fragments. *Nature Protocols*, *3*(9), 1457–1466.

Lemay, J. F., Penedo, J. C., Tremblay, R., Lilley, D. M., & Lafontaine, D. A. (2006). Folding of the adenine riboswitch. *Chemistry & Biology*, *13*(8), 857–868.

Liberman, J. A., Salim, M., Krucinska, J., & Wedekind, J. E. (2013). Structure of a class II preQ1 riboswitch reveals ligand recognition by a new fold. *Nature Chemical Biology*, *9*(6), 353–355.

Liberman, J. A., & Wedekind, J. E. (2012). Riboswitch structure in the ligand-free state. *Wiley Interdisciplinary Reviews. RNA*, *3*(3), 369–384.

Marek, M. S., Johnson-Buck, A., & Walter, N. G. (2011). The shape-shifting quasispecies of RNA: One sequence, many functional folds. *Physical Chemistry Chemical Physics*, *13*(24), 11524–11537.

Marshall, R. A., Aitken, C. E., Dorywalska, M., & Puglisi, J. D. (2008). Translation at the single-molecule level. *Annual Review of Biochemistry*, *77*, 177–203.

McCown, P. J., Liang, J. J., Weinberg, Z., & Breaker, R. R. (2014). Structural, functional, and taxonomic diversity of three PreQ1 riboswitch classes. *Chemistry & Biology*, *21*(7), 880–889.

McKinney, S. A., Joo, C., & Ha, T. (2006). Analysis of single-molecule FRET trajectories using hidden Markov modeling. *Biophysical Journal*, *91*(5), 1941–1951.

Michelotti, N., de Silva, C., Johnson-Buck, A. E., Manzo, A. J., & Walter, N. G. (2010). A bird's eye view tracking slow nanometer-scale movements of single molecular nano-assemblies. *Methods in Enzymology*, *475*, 121–148.

Misra, V. K., & Draper, D. E. (1998). On the role of magnesium ions in RNA stability. *Biopolymers*, *48*(2–3), 113–135.

Mustoe, A. M., Brooks, C. L., & Al-Hashimi, H. M. (2014). Hierarchy of RNA functional dynamics. *Annual Review of Biochemistry*, *83*, 441–466.

Noeske, J., Buck, J., Furtig, B., Nasiri, H. R., Schwalbe, H., & Wohnert, J. (2007). Interplay of 'induced fit' and preorganization in the ligand induced folding of the aptamer domain of the guanine binding riboswitch. *Nucleic Acids Research*, *35*(2), 572–583.

Ouellet, J., Schorr, S., Iqbal, A., Wilson, T. J., & Lilley, D. M. (2011). Orientation of cyanine fluorophores terminally attached to DNA via long, flexible tethers. *Biophysical Journal*, *101*(5), 1148–1154.

Paudel, B., & Rueda, D. (2014). RNA folding dynamics using laser-assisted single-molecule refolding. *Methods in Molecular Biology*, *1086*, 289–307.

Peselis, A., & Serganov, A. (2014). Themes and variations in riboswitch structure and function. *Biochimica et Biophysica Acta*, *1839*(10), 908–918.

Qin, F., & Li, L. (2004). Model-based fitting of single-channel dwell-time distributions. *Biophysical Journal*, *87*(3), 1657–1671.

Qin, P. Z., & Pyle, A. M. (1999). Site-specific labeling of RNA with fluorophores and other structural probes. *Methods*, *18*(1), 60–70.

Ragunathan, K., Liu, C., & Ha, T. (2012). RecA filament sliding on DNA facilitates homology search. *eLife*, *1*, e00067.

Regulski, E. E., & Breaker, R. R. (2008). In-line probing analysis of riboswitches. *Methods in Molecular Biology*, *419*, 53–67.

Reining, A., Nozinovic, S., Schlepckow, K., Buhr, F., Furtig, B., & Schwalbe, H. (2013). Three-state mechanism couples ligand and temperature sensing in riboswitches. *Nature*, *499*(7458), 355–359.

Ren, A., Rajashankar, K. R., & Patel, D. J. (2012). Fluoride ion encapsulation by Mg2+ ions and phosphates in a fluoride riboswitch. *Nature*, *486*(7401), 85–89.

Rieder, U., Kreutz, C., & Micura, R. (2010). Folding of a transcriptionally acting preQ1 riboswitch. *Proceedings of the National Academy of Sciences of the United States of America*, *107*(24), 10804–10809.

Rinaldi, A. J., Suddala, K. C., & Walter, N. G. (2015). Native purification and labeling of RNA for single molecule fluorescence studies. *Methods in Molecular Biology*, *1240*.

Roy, R., Hohng, S., & Ha, T. (2008). A practical guide to single-molecule FRET. *Nature Methods*, *5*(6), 507–516.

Santner, T., Rieder, U., Kreutz, C., & Micura, R. (2012). Pseudoknot preorganization of the preQ1 class I riboswitch. *Journal of the American Chemical Society*, *134*(29), 11928–11931.

Savinov, A., Perez, C. F., & Block, S. M. (2014). Single-molecule studies of riboswitch folding. *Biochimica et Biophysica Acta*, *1839*(10), 1030–1045.

Schuler, B., & Eaton, W. A. (2008). Protein folding studied by single-molecule FRET. *Current Opinion in Structural Biology*, *18*(1), 16–26.

Schuler, B., Lipman, E. A., Steinbach, P. J., Kumke, M., & Eaton, W. A. (2005). Polyproline and the "spectroscopic ruler" revisited with single-molecule fluorescence. *Proceedings of the National Academy of Sciences of the United States of America*, *102*(8), 2754–2759.

Serganov, A., & Nudler, E. (2013). A decade of riboswitches. *Cell*, *152*(1–2), 17–24.

Serganov, A., Polonskaia, A., Phan, A. T., Breaker, R. R., & Patel, D. J. (2006). Structural basis for gene regulation by a thiamine pyrophosphate-sensing riboswitch. *Nature*, *441*(7097), 1167–1171.

Serganov, A., Yuan, Y. R., Pikovskaya, O., Polonskaia, A., Malinina, L., Phan, A. T., et al. (2004). Structural basis for discriminative regulation of gene expression by adenine- and guanine-sensing mRNAs. *Chemistry & Biology*, *11*(12), 1729–1741.

Shi, X., Lim, J., & Ha, T. (2010). Acidification of the oxygen scavenging system in single-molecule fluorescence studies: In situ sensing with a ratiometric dual-emission probe. *Analytical Chemistry*, *82*(14), 6132–6138.

Solomatin, S. V., Greenfeld, M., Chu, S., & Herschlag, D. (2010). Multiple native states reveal persistent ruggedness of an RNA folding landscape. *Nature*, *463*(7281), 681–684.

Solomatin, S., & Herschlag, D. (2009). Methods of site-specific labeling of RNA with fluorescent dyes. *Methods in Enzymology*, *469*, 47–68.

Souliere, M. F., Altman, R. B., Schwarz, V., Haller, A., Blanchard, S. C., & Micura, R. (2013). Tuning a riboswitch response through structural extension of a pseudoknot. *Proceedings of the National Academy of Sciences of the United States of America*, *110*(35), E3256–E3264.

Stennett, E. M. S., Ciuba, M. A., & Levitus, M. (2014). Photophysical processes in single molecule organic fluorescent probes. *Chemical Society Reviews*, *43*(4), 1057–1075.

Stoddard, C. D., Montange, R. K., Hennelly, S. P., Rambo, R. P., Sanbonmatsu, K. Y., & Batey, R. T. (2010). Free state conformational sampling of the SAM-I riboswitch aptamer domain. *Structure*, *18*(7), 787–797.

St-Pierre, P., McCluskey, K., Shaw, E., Penedo, J. C., & Lafontaine, D. A. (2014). Fluorescence tools to investigate riboswitch structural dynamics. *Biochimica et Biophysica Acta*, *1839*(10), 1005–1019.

Stryer, L. (1978). Fluorescence energy transfer as a spectroscopic ruler. *Annual Review of Biochemistry*, *47*, 819–846.

Suddala, K. C., Rinaldi, A. J., Feng, J., Mustoe, A. M., Eichhorn, C. D., Liberman, J. A., et al. (2013). Single transcriptional and translational preQ1 riboswitches adopt similar pre-folded ensembles that follow distinct folding pathways into the same ligand-bound structure. *Nucleic Acids Research*, *41*(22), 10462–10475.

Swoboda, M., Henig, J., Cheng, H. M., Brugger, D., Haltrich, D., Plumere, N., et al. (2012). Enzymatic oxygen scavenging for photostability without pH drop in single-molecule experiments. *ACS Nano*, *6*(7), 6364–6369.

Tinoco, I., Jr., & Gonzalez, R. L., Jr. (2011). Biological mechanisms, one molecule at a time. *Genes & Development*, *25*(12), 1205–1231.

Trausch, J. J., & Batey, R. T. (2014). A disconnect between high-affinity binding and efficient regulation by antifolates and purines in the tetrahydrofolate riboswitch. *Chemistry & Biology*, *21*(2), 205–216.

Vafabakhsh, R., & Ha, T. (2012). Extreme bendability of DNA less than 100 base pairs long revealed by single-molecule cyclization. *Science*, *337*(6098), 1097–1101.

Vicens, Q., Mondragon, E., & Batey, R. T. (2011). Molecular sensing by the aptamer domain of the FMN riboswitch: A general model for ligand binding by conformational selection. *Nucleic Acids Research*, *39*(19), 8586–8598.

Walter, N. G. (2003). Probing RNA structural dynamics and function by fluorescence resonance energy transfer (FRET). *Current Protocols in Nucleic Acid Chemistry*, (Chapter 11, Unit 11.10).

Walter, N. G., & Burke, J. M. (1997). Real-time monitoring of hairpin ribozyme kinetics through base-specific quenching of fluorescein-labeled substrates. *RNA*, *3*(4), 392–404.

Walter, N. G., & Burke, J. M. (2000). Fluorescence assays to study structure, dynamics, and function of RNA and RNA-ligand complexes. *Methods in Enzymology*, *317*, 409–440.

Walter, N. G., Burke, J. M., & Millar, D. P. (1999). Stability of hairpin ribozyme tertiary structure is governed by the interdomain junction. *Nature Structural Biology*, *6*(6), 544–549.

Walter, N. G., & Bustamante, C. (2014). Introduction to single molecule imaging and mechanics: Seeing and touching molecules one at a time. *Chemical Reviews*, *114*(6), 3069–3071.

Walter, N. G., Huang, C. Y., Manzo, A. J., & Sobhy, M. A. (2008). Do-it-yourself guide: How to use the modern single-molecule toolkit. *Nature Methods*, *5*(6), 475–489.

Whitford, P. C., Schug, A., Saunders, J., Hennelly, S. P., Onuchic, J. N., & Sanbonmatsu, K. Y. (2009). Nonlocal helix formation is key to understanding S-adenosylmethionine-1 riboswitch function. *Biophysical Journal*, *96*(2), L7–L9.

Wilkinson, K. A., Merino, E. J., & Weeks, K. M. (2006). Selective 2′-hydroxyl acylation analyzed by primer extension (SHAPE): Quantitative RNA structure analysis at single nucleotide resolution. *Nature Protocols*, *1*(3), 1610–1616.

Winkler, W. C., & Breaker, R. R. (2005). Regulation of bacterial gene expression by riboswitches. *Annual Review of Microbiology*, *59*, 487–517.

Wood, S., Ferre-D'Amare, A. R., & Rueda, D. (2012). Allosteric tertiary interactions preorganize the c-di-GMP riboswitch and accelerate ligand binding. *ACS Chemical Biology*, 7(5), 920–927.

Zhang, J., & Ferre-D'Amare, A. R. (2013). Co-crystal structure of a T-box riboswitch stem I domain in complex with its cognate tRNA. *Nature*, *500*(7462), 363–366.

Zhao, R., & Rueda, D. (2009). RNA folding dynamics by single-molecule fluorescence resonance energy transfer. *Methods*, *49*(2), 112–117.

Zheng, Q., Juette, M. F., Jockusch, S., Wasserman, M. R., Zhou, Z., Altman, R. B., et al. (2014). Ultra-stable organic fluorophores for single-molecule research. *Chemical Society Reviews*, *43*(4), 1044–1056.

Zhuang, X. (2005). Single-molecule RNA science. *Annual Review of Biophysics and Biomolecular Structure*, *34*, 399–414.

Zhuang, X., Bartley, L. E., Babcock, H. P., Russell, R., Ha, T., Herschlag, D., et al. (2000). A single-molecule study of RNA catalysis and folding. *Science*, *288*(5473), 2048–2051.

Zhuang, X., Kim, H., Pereira, M. J., Babcock, H. P., Walter, N. G., & Chu, S. (2002). Correlating structural dynamics and function in single ribozyme molecules. *Science*, *296*(5572), 1473–1476.

CHAPTER SIXTEEN

Ribosome Structure and Dynamics by smFRET Microscopy

Bassem Shebl, Zenia Norman, Peter V. Cornish[1]
Department of Biochemistry, University of Missouri, Columbia, Missouri, USA
[1]Corresponding author: e-mail address: cornishp@missouri.edu

Contents

Abstract

Composed of both RNA and protein components, the ribosome is one of the largest macromolecular machines in life responsible for the production of all protein. Interestingly, the major catalytic center of the ribosome (the peptidyl transferase center) and much of the binding regions for both mRNA and tRNA are composed of RNA making the ribosome one of the most complex and widely studied ribozymes. Further, large-scale conformational rearrangements throughout the ribosome are required for

Methods in Enzymology, Volume 549
ISSN 0076-6879
http://dx.doi.org/10.1016/B978-0-12-801122-5.00016-7

proper function making the ribosome a riboswitch as well. Recent advances in single-molecule biophysics have significantly augmented our understanding of ribosome function as both a ribozyme and riboswitch. Here, we discuss single-molecule Förster resonance energy transfer and its application to the study of the ribosome. Also, we describe how these experiments are designed from sample preparation to data acquisition and analysis. The general approach and methods described here can be generally applied to many other biological systems.

1. INTRODUCTION

The ribosome is a highly dynamic molecular machine fundamental for cellular protein production. The mega-Dalton scale (~2.5) biomolecular machine incorporates ribosomal ribonucleic acid (rRNA) sequences interwoven with protein components. The highly structured rRNAs carry out the major catalytic functions within the ribosome. In addition, rRNA acts as a regulatory platform for translation via interacting with small molecules such as antibiotics. Thus, ribosomes provide a stand-alone platform for studying a wide range of RNA interactions. The insights gained from such a platform can highlight possible corresponding mechanisms for relevant structured RNA sequences such as ribozymes and riboswitches. Accordingly, the experimental approaches developed for investigating one field can be readily extrapolated and adapted to other dynamic RNA molecules.

Through various approaches, single-molecule (sm) biophysics has provided a unique and dynamic view of numerous biochemical processes. Notably, structural and mechanistic investigations of protein synthesis have gained a renewed interest. Early investigations using single-molecule Förster resonance energy transfer (smFRET) focused on the pathways of tRNA selection and accommodation in the A-site (Blanchard, Gonzalez, Kim, Chu, & Puglisi, 2004; Blanchard, Kim, Gonzalez, Puglisi, & Chu, 2004). These studies also revealed the fluctuation of P- and A-site tRNAs between classical and hybrid states (Kim, Puglisi, & Chu, 2007). Since then, sm approaches have expanded to shed light on virtually every stage of translation (Aitken, Petrov, & Puglisi, 2010; Marshall, Aitken, Dorywalska, & Puglisi, 2008; Petrov et al., 2011).

While research groups have successfully employed various sm techniques, this chapter will primarily focus on smFRET-based interrogation of the ribosome. To perform smFRET experiments successfully, there are several considerations that should be addressed. In particular, the investigator should determine which aspect of translation will be investigated. Following this, one needs to choose the appropriate labeling scheme and target specific sites for conjugation of fluorescent dyes. The potential likelihood of perturbing ribosome function requires extensive characterization of the activity of the ribosome in translation. This search is guided by the now extensive structural investigations available in the literature as well as other smFRET studies. Lastly, there are several critical aspects related to data acquisition and interpretation to accurately evaluate the final model. Here, we will discuss each of these areas in detail and refer the reader to other papers where further guidance is provided (Ermolenko et al., 2007; Fei et al., 2010; Hickerson, Majumdar, Baucom, Clegg, & Noller, 2005; Majumdar, Hickerson, Noller, & Clegg, 2005; Roy, Hohng, & Ha, 2008).

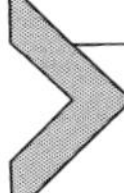

2. OVERVIEW OF RIBOSOME STRUCTURE AND FUNCTION

The general structural and mechanistic features of the ribosome are highly conserved across species. As such, the ribosome is engineered to synthesize proteins accurately and to respond quickly to changes in environmental factors. With such a stringent processivity, the ribosome has a relatively low misincorporation rate *in vivo* during protein synthesis (6×10^{-4} to 5×10^{-3} per amino acid) (Zaher & Green, 2009). In addition to the ribosome, a host of accessory factors are involved in the highly regulated process of translation. Many of the most abundant proteins in the cell are involved in some way with protein synthesis, and the ribosome constitutes some 25% of the dry weight of *Escherichia coli*, clearly indicating that much of the energy of the cell is dedicated to ensuring that the process of translation is maintained (Nierhaus, 1982).

Structurally. The bacterial ribosome is composed of two asymmetric subunits (50S and 30S in bacteria) each of which is formed from RNA and protein components. rRNA in both subunits is folded into many complex secondary and tertiary folds. Ribosomal proteins primarily facilitate the proper folding of the ribosome and are located on the periphery, with a few exceptions. Thus, a series of RNA–RNA, RNA–protein, and protein–protein interactions are prevalent and essential for both the structure and function of the ribosome. rRNA predominantly forms the major catalytic centers of the ribosome, while proteins have a rather supportive role. In fact, proteins fortify the underlying RNA network and undergo mechanistically supportive conformational changes during translation.

The small subunit (30S) is subdivided into two major domains: a head and a body (Yusupov, 2001). The mRNA entrance and exit tunnels allow the mRNA to pass through the 30S subunit, where the ribosome encloses about 30 nucleotides (Culver, 2001). The 50S subunit consists of a central protuberance with a few extensions protruding at both sides of the subunit. In addition, the 50S subunit bears the catalytic centers of the ribosome (Gao et al., 2009; Yusupov, 2001). The growing polypeptide chain exits the ribosome via an exit tunnel embedded in the 50S subunit. The two subunits come together to form 70S with three tRNA binding sites: an aminoacyl-tRNA (A) site, a peptidyl-tRNA (P) site, and an exit (E) site (Fig. 16.1).

Functionally. In bacteria, translation is divided into three major steps: initiation, elongation, and termination. Initiation involves assembling the ribosomal subunits along with the mRNA, and an initiator tRNA forming the 70S initiation complex. Henceforth, the ribosome is prepared for the next stage, elongation (Schmeing & Ramakrishnan, 2009).

Elongation involves a recurring cycle of sequential additions of amino acid monomers to a growing polypeptide chain. Toward that, the ribosome undergoes a repetitive set of conformational changes (Cornish, Ermolenko, Noller, & Ha, 2008; Cornish et al., 2009; Ratje et al., 2010; Valle et al., 2003). Each cycle starts with a P-site tRNA bearing the nascent polypeptide chain. The mRNA decoding process dictates the next amino acid in the sequence. Elongation factor-Tu (EF-Tu) delivers the aminoacyl-tRNA (aa-tRNA) to the ribosome in a ternary complex with GTP. After an accommodation step that ensures the fidelity of tRNA selection, aa-tRNA fits in the A-site. Next, peptide bond formation transfers the

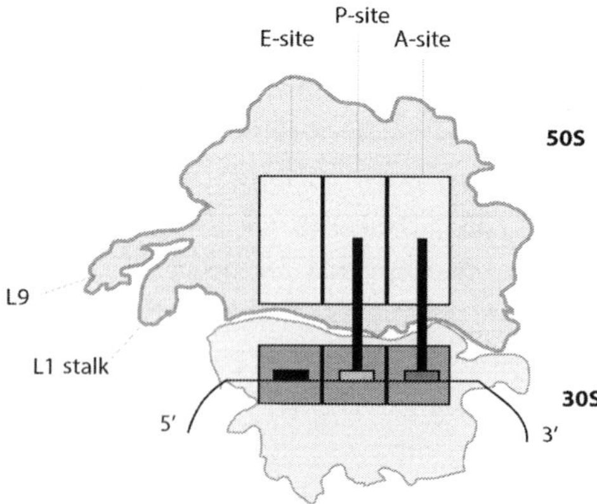

Figure 16.1 Schematic of ribosome structure.

growing chain to the A-site tRNA, leaving a deacylated tRNA in the P-site. The P- and A-site tRNAs alternate repetitively between classical and hybrid states (Blanchard, Kim, et al., 2004; Moazed & Noller, 1989) In the hybrid state, only the acceptor ends move to the next site, while their respective anticodon stem loop stay attached to the same site on the 30S subunit. Accompanying that movement, intersubunit ratcheting takes place (Cornish et al., 2008; Frank & Agrawal, 2000). Subunit ratcheting is required for translation to occur (Horan & Noller, 2007). Binding of elongation factor-G (EF-G) stabilizes the rotated state of the ribosome (Cornish et al., 2008). GTP hydrolyses follows, the tRNAs translocate fully along the mRNA to the classical state. The now-deacylated E-site tRNA leaves the ribosome and the P-site holds the peptidyl-tRNA. In addition, the ribosome returns back to the nonrotated state and EF-G-GDP leaves the ribosomal complex, at which point the ribosome is ready for the next cycle of elongation.

This process continues until a stop codon is recognized in the A-site. This recruits release factors, RF1/2, RF3, and RRF, which catalyze the release of the completed polypeptide chain and the subsequent dissociation of the ribosomal subunits releasing bound deacylated tRNA and mRNA (Schmeing & Ramakrishnan, 2009).

3. METHODOLOGY

3.1. What is out there?

For over half a century, the structure of the ribosome and the mechanism of translation have been extensively studied via a wide range of techniques (Blanchard, 2009; Moore, 2012). However, the golden era of ribosomal structural studies started with the release of the first high-resolution crystal structure of the ribosome in 2000 and included the Nobel prize in Chemistry in 2009 (Ban, 2000; Schluenzen et al., 2000; Wimberly et al., 2000).

X-ray crystallography. has been an invaluable contributor and a major technique to producing high-resolution structures of the ribosome (Jin, Kelley, & Ramakrishnan, 2011; Korostelev, Trakhanov, Laurberg, & Noller, 2006; Yusupov, 2001). However, producing high-quality structures is dependent on the quality of the crystal tested (Blanchard, 2009; Moore, 2012). This requires compositional and structural homogeneity of the sample, which is hard to obtain. In addition, many of the current structures are for relatively stable complexes rather than transient intermediate states. In many cases, these complexes are stabilized by employing non-hydrolysable substrate analogues or antibiotics that can perturb the natural energy landscape (Moore, 2012). Consequently, the captured states might be displaced as compared to the naturally occurring local minima.

Cryogenic Electron Microscopy (Cryo-EM), on the other hand, samples a wider range of states of the dynamic ribosome (Diaconu et al., 2005; Fischer, Konevega, Wintermeyer, Rodnina, & Stark, 2010; Frank & Agrawal, 2000; Ratje et al., 2010; Valle et al., 2003). Comparatively, sample preparation is easier. In addition, the continually developing toolbox of particle-sorting algorithms might help overcome the homogeneity problem in crystallography by separating distinctive states and conformations (Blanchard, 2009). The resolution that can be obtained from cryo-EM has generally lagged behind that of X-ray crystallography. However, with the recent advances in direct electron detection, high-resolution structures have been obtained for large biomolecular complexes. Furthermore, cryo-EM requires smaller quantities and works for flexible complexes or heterogeneous samples. Nevertheless, proteins smaller than 100 kDa and resolutions better than 2 Å are out of range for cryo-EM. Yet, X-ray crystallography still holds the key to this domain (Amunts et al., 2014; Kuhlbrandt, 2014). Another limitation to cryo-EM is the reliability of particle-sorting algorithms used, and the nature of the investigated sample, i.e., frozen (Moore, 2012).

For the most part, X-ray crystallography and cryo-EM have contributed immensely to the field albeit with several challenges. For one, molecular machines usually have highly dynamic regions within their structure. Dynamic regions blur the collected data, interfering heavily with reconstruction and interpretation of the affected region. In addition, structural studies are not performed at equilibrium. Thus, a snapshot of a highly dynamic system will give insights into the structural aspects of translation but lacks the animated kinetic perspective. On the contrary, bulk kinetic experiments provide an overview of kinetic data of the ensemble system. However, the intricacies of individual molecules are lost. Hence, a growing need of sm approaches evolved.

3.2. Why single-molecule approaches?

Structural and bulk kinetic techniques, although indispensable, suffer from limitations. Structurally, only conformational states pertaining to local minima are stable enough to be detected, but the intermediate states are not detectable. In addition, ensemble averaging of the signal obscures rare species, unstable intermediates, and minor parallel kinetic pathways. Thus, for a stochastic kinetic process, a large amount of insightful data is lost.

Thus, not surprisingly, there is an increased interest in using sm approaches over the past decade or so for many different systems (Fig. 16.2). sm techniques overcome most of the shortcomings of bulk methods. smFRET is one technique out of a wide rainbow that exploits the ability to measure distances between two fluorescent dyes. Labeling a biological molecule with a dye pair (donor–acceptor) allows the determination of conformational changes within the molecule via smFRET, given that they exist within the special proximity of one another (20–80 Å) (Fig. 16.3). smFRET exploits the non-radiative transfer of energy between the dye pair through their coupled dipoles. The extent to which energy is transferred is inversely proportional to the sixth power of distance between the two dyes.

smFRET allows a dynamic observation of the process under investigation, out of which kinetic rates, conformational changes, and interactions; among other parameters, can be probed directly. Equally important is the capability of monitoring the entire reaction co-ordinate, depending on the fluorophore photobleaching lifetime, for a sm. Moreover, one can identify rare species, parallel kinetic pathways, sporadic events, and stochastic kinetics of thermodynamic biological complexes. Furthermore, synchronization of complex biochemical reactions is straightforward. Notably, detecting unstable and short lived intermediates and transition rates across states allows mapping of energy landscape for complex biological systems (Ha, 2001; Joo & Ha, 2008; Roy et al., 2008).

3.3. Why is the ribosome an ideal system for smFRET?

Despite the complexity of the ribosome, there is a growing number of high-resolution crystal structures at different states offering good starting points for choosing labeling sites (Fernández et al., 2014; Pulk & Cate, 2013; Tourigny, Fernandez, Kelley, & Ramakrishnan, 2013; Zhou, Lancaster, Donohue, & Noller, 2013). The advances in labeling schemes facilitate ribosome specific labeling either through directly labeling proteins (Cornish et al., 2008, 2009; Fei et al., 2009)or tRNA (Blanchard, Kim, et al., 2004) or via hybridization to complementary oligonucleotides bearing a fluorophore (Aitken & Puglisi, 2010; Marshall, Dorywalska, & Puglisi, 2008; Fig. 16.4). In addition, a few discrete stable conformational states of the ribosome have relatively high activation barriers separating neighboring states (Blanchard, 2009). However, manipulating the energy landscape

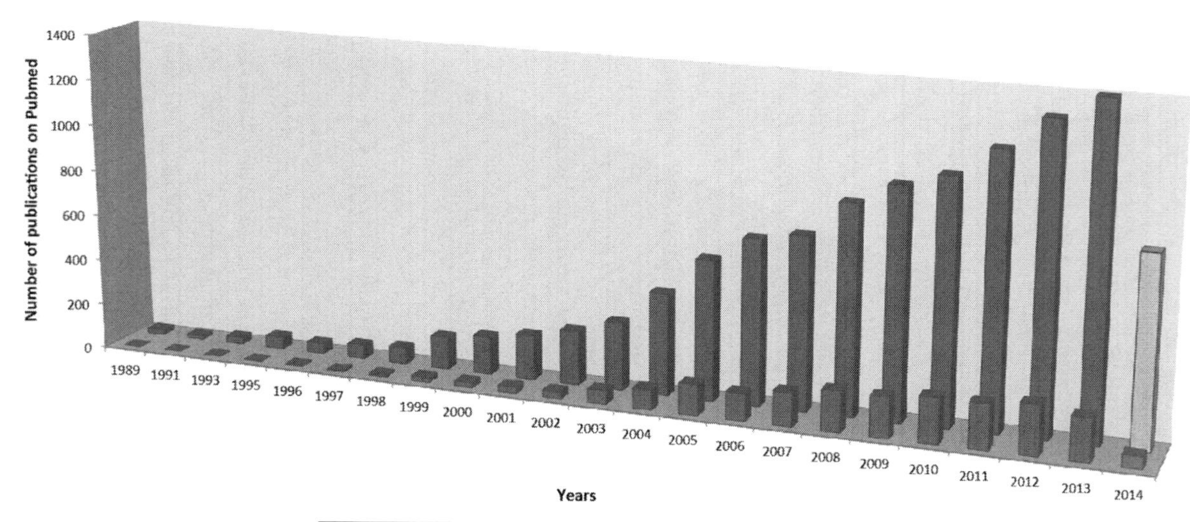

Figure 16.2 Trend in single-molecule research by year.

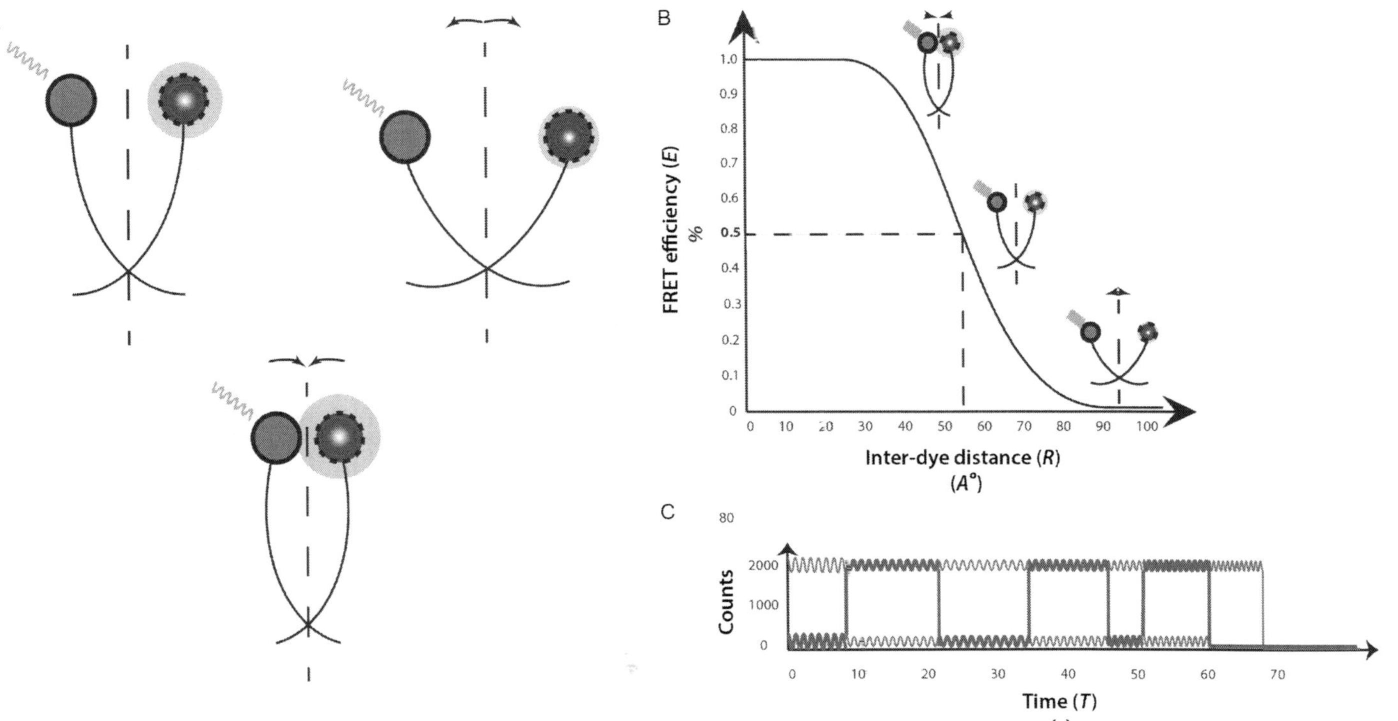

Figure 16.3 FRET. (A) Schematic of a conformational change of dual labeled molecule with both donor and acceptor dyes. (B) The energy transfer efficiency is inversely related to the sixth power of the distance separating the two dyes. R_0 is separating distance of the two dyes at which energy transfer is 50% efficient. Designing experiments around this value ensures the highest sensitivity. (C) A schematic of an anti-correlated FRET trace. Green (left gray circle in the print version) (A and B) or thinner trace in (C): donor dye, and red (right gray circle in the print version) (A and B) or thicker trace in (C): acceptor dye.

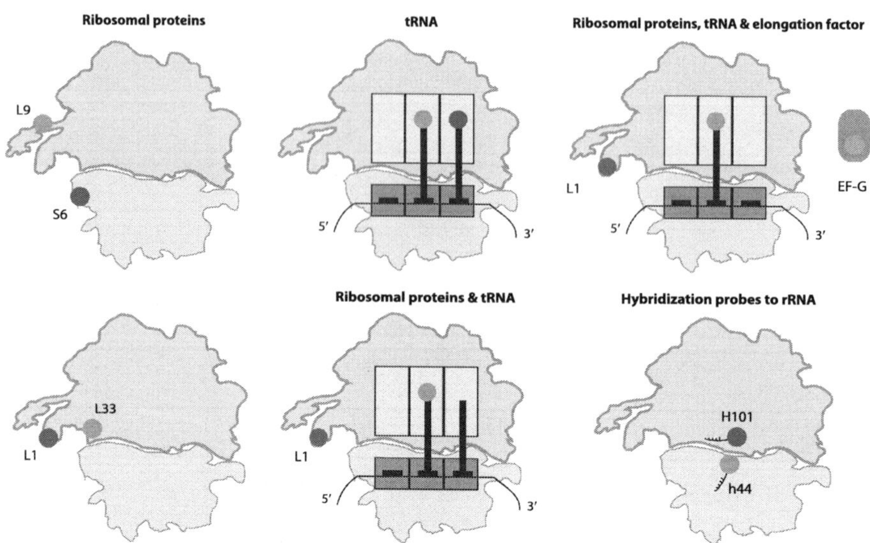

Figure 16.4 Labeling schemes. A schematic of the different labeling schemes that have been used in investigating sm dynamics. Green (light gray circle in the print version): Cy3, red (dark gray circle in the print version): Cy5/Cy5.5, and cyan (light gray circle on EF-G in the print version): AttoA674N.

by lowering those barriers within an experimentally reasonable limit is possible via changing Mg^{2+} concentration (Blanchard, Kim, et al., 2004; Kim et al., 2007).Temporally, the lifetime of the substeps of translation ranges between milliseconds to few minutes. Furthermore, spatially, the dynamic range (DR) of motion of the ribosome especially during translocation ranges between 5 and 40 Å. Hence, both spatial and temporal aspects of translation are within the detection limits of smFRET and the current capabilities of modern detection hardware (Blanchard, 2009; Munro, Vaiana, Sanbonmatsu, & Blanchard, 2008). For instance, Munro, Altman, O'Connor, and Blanchard (2007) used smFRET with a 2.5-fold enhanced temporal resolution over a previous paper. The improved resolution unraveled a new distinct tRNA hybrid intermediate state that was obscured previously (Blanchard, Kim, et al., 2004).

4. RIBOSOME DYNAMICS

The ribosome is highly dynamic especially during tRNA and mRNA translocation, which is counterintuitive since safeguarding the reading frame entails a stable ribosome (Korostelev, Ermolenko, & Noller, 2008).

However, the ribosome shows a highly dynamic nature with both large-scale (global) and localized changes. Both play a role in various steps during translation: recognition, translocation, and fidelity.

4.1. Choosing a question

The very first approach to ribosome dynamics is to determine which aspect of the translation process is to be investigated, e.g., intersubunit rotation, tRNA dynamics, L1 stalk movement, or even intermolecular interactions between the various elements of translation such as EF-G accommodation and its role during translocation.

Quantitative and precise distance measurements are challenging with standard smFRET experiments mainly due to inaccurate estimation of the orientational freedom and the quantum yield of the dyes (Lakowicz, 2007; Roy et al., 2008). Thus, the accuracy of distance measurements is limited. Because of the hydrophobic nature of most of the commonly used dyes, dye–complex interactions may limit the rotational freedom of the attached dyes, for example, through a stacking effect on nucleic acid bases and hydrophobic interactions with exposed hydrophobic protein patches (Michaelis, 2010). Thus, all of these factors should be investigated experimentally for all samples used in smFRET experiments. Also, the step to be investigated should involve a measurable FRET change. Comparing high-resolution structures of different complexes along the reaction path will give an indication of the predicted movement changes.

Despite the above-mentioned limitations, smFRET is a highly sensitive technique due to the ideally suited temporal and spatial resolution of the measurements for many biological systems. While not always quantitative in the distance measurements, the qualitative changes in distance changes at the sm level can provide very powerful and clear indications of what molecules are up to in real time. Thus, smFRET can detect conformational changes, binding, and dissociation events among a wide spectrum of other parameters within 2–8 nm distance limit.

4.2. Choosing a dye

An ideal fluorescent dye does exhibit a few favorable properties. First, it is photostable, thus resisting photobleaching at least at the timescale of the dynamic motion under investigation. Second, a dye with minimal intensity fluctuations is required. In addition, one picks bright dyes, i.e., choosing the highest possible extinction coefficient and quantum yield. Equally important, the excitation and emission ranges of the dye lie within the attainable visible region of the spectrum. Also, the dye is small enough not to perturb the structural integrity of the investigated biocomplex nor affect its activity. Finally, the dye needs to be available in a chemically usable form allowing specific attachment to the molecule of interest. Few dyes provide good examples of the aforementioned properties: Alexa, Atto, cyanine, and tetramethylrhodamine (TMR). Alexa and Atto have been used for diffusing molecules (Munro, Altman, Tung, Sanbonmatsu, & Blanchard, 2010). Cyanine dyes and TMR have been used for immobilized molecules.

However, smFRET deals with donor–acceptor dye pairs rather than a single dye. Correspondingly, an ideal FRET dye-pair has compatible features. For example, the quantum yields of both dyes are comparable to one another to facilitate data analysis. Furthermore, the dyes show a good spectral overlap between the donor dye emission and the acceptor dye absorption. At the same time, a large separation between the emission spectra of the dyes is desirable to minimize crosstalk between donor and acceptor dye channels on the detector. With that in mind, Cy3 and Cy5 are the most commonly used FRET pair since they have good spectral separation and comparable quantum yields (Joo & Ha, 2008). In addition, Cy3 and Cy5 are commercially available with a wide range of derivatives, such as: NHS-esters, maleimides, and azides (Lumiprobe Life Science Solutions and GE Healthcare). Figure 16.4 and Table 16.1 show several labeling schemes used in studying ribosome dynamics, which can be extrapolated to comparable biological platforms.

4.3. Using phylogenetic analysis and structural modeling to guide choice of labeling sites

Choosing labeling sites is a critical step that is applicable to any biological molecule. A careful phylogenetic analysis is usually necessary beforehand to minimize perturbing highly conserved sequences. One can perform a multiple sequence alignment comparing the sequence of interest, whether a protein or an mRNA, across species. BLAST (Altschul, Gish, Miller, Myers, & Lipman, 1990) and CLUSTAL-W (Thompson, Higgins, & Gibson, 1994) are useful and simple tools to perform phylogenetic analysis. Highly conserved regions that emerge from the alignment are not be pursued for labeling. Further, labeling sites are chosen to be surface-accessible to enhance accessibility when labeling with the dye. A high-resolution crystal structure is preferred in this instance. The availability of high-resolution structures of the biocomplex in question facilitates picking labeling positions

Table 16.1 Selected examples of several labeling schemes used in studying ribosome dynamics

Paper	Aim	Imaging buffer used	Fluorescent constructs used
Spontaneous intersubunit rotation in single ribosomes(Cornish et al., 2008)	Investigating *intersubunit dynamics*	Polyamine buffer B[a]	• Doubly labeled ribosomal constructs ○ 70S:S6 (Cy5)/L9 (Cy3) ○ 70S:S11 (Cy5)/L9 (Cy3)
Irreversible chemical steps control intersubunit dynamics during translation (Marshall, Dorywalska, & Puglisi, 2008b)	Investigating *intersubunit dynamics*	Tris–polymix buffer[b] *at 5 mM Mg^{2+} without reducing agent—Oxygen scavenging system used 1 mM Trolox, 2.5 mM 3,4-dihydroxybenzoic acid (PCA), and 250 nM protocatechuate dioxygenase (PCD)*	• Doubly labeled ribosomal construct ○ 70S:h44 (Cy3)/H101 (Cy5) • Doubly labeled ribosomal construct and labeled tRNA ○ 70S:h44 (Cy3)/H101 (Cy5) and Phe-tRNA^{Phe} (Cy2)
Following movement of the L1 stalk between three functional states in single ribosomes (Cornish et al., 2009)	Investigating *L1 stalk dynamics*	Polyamine buffer B[a]	• Doubly labeled ribosomal construct ○ 70S:L1 (Cy5)/L33 (Cy3)
Coupling of ribosomal L1 stalk and tRNA dynamics during translation elongation (Fei, Kosuri, MacDougall, & Gonzalez, 2008)	Investigating *L1 stalk dynamics*	Tris–polymix buffer[b]	• Singly labeled ribosomal construct and labeled tRNA ○ 70S:L1 (Cy5) and Phe-tRNA^{Phe} (Cy3)
tRNA dynamics on the ribosome during translation** (Blanchard, Kim, Gonzalez, Puglisi, & Chu, 2004b)	Investigating *tRNA dynamics*	Tris–polymix buffer[b]	• Nonspecifically labeled 70S:50S (Cy3) • Labeled Methionine Cy3-Met-tRNA^{fMet} • Labeled tRNAs ○ fMet-tRNA^{fMet} (Cy3) and Phe-tRNA^{Phe} (Cy5)

Continued

Table 16.1 Selected examples of several labeling schemes used in studying ribosome dynamics—cont'd

Paper	Aim	Imaging buffer used	Fluorescent constructs used
Spontaneous formation of the unlocked state of the ribosome is a multistep process (Munro et al., 2009)	Investigating *correlational dynamics of L1 stalk and tRNA*	Tris–polymix buffer[b]	• Singly labeled ribosomal construct and labeled tRNA ○ 70S:L1 (Cy5) and $tRNA^{fMet}$ (Cy3) ○ $tRNA^{fMet}$ (Cy3) and fMet-Phe-$tRNA^{Phe}$ (Cy5) ○ 70S:L1 (Cy5.5), $tRNA^{fMet}$ (Cy3), and fMet-Phe-$tRNA^{Phe}$ (Cy5) ○ 70S:L1 (Cy5.5), $tRNA^{Phe}$ (Cy3), and NAc-Phe-Lys-$tRNA^{Lys}$ (Cy5)
A fast dynamic mode of the EF-G-bound ribosome (Munro et al., 2010)	Investigating *correlational dynamics of L1 stalk, tRNA, and EF-G*	Tris–polymix buffer[b]	• Singly labeled ribosomal construct, labeled tRNA, and labeled EF-G ○ 70S:L1 (Cy5) and $tRNA^{fMet}$ (Cy3) ○ EF-G (A647N) and $tRNA^{fMet}$ (Cy3) ○ 70S:L1 (Cy5) and $tRNA^{fMet}$ (Cy3) ○ EF-G (A647N) and $tRNA^{Phe}$ (Cy3) ○ 70S:L1 (Cy5.5), $tRNA^{fMet}$ (Cy3), and EF-G (A647N) ○ 70S:L1 (Cy5.5), $tRNA^{Phe}$ (Cy3), and EF-G (A647N)

[a]Polyamine buffer B (20 m*M* Hepes.KOH (pH 7.5), 6 m*M* $MgCl_2$, 150 m*M* NH_4Cl, 6 m*M* β-mercaptoethanol, 2 m*M* spermidine, 0.1 m*M* spermine, 0.8 mg/ml glucose oxidase, 0.625% glucose, 1.5 m*M* 6-hydroxy-2,5,7,8-tetramethyl-chromane-2-carboxylic acid (Trolox), and 0.03 mg/ml catalase).
[b]Tris–polymix buffer (50 m*M* Tris–OAc, 100 m*M* KCl, 5 m*M* NH_4OAc, 0.5 m*M* $Ca[OAc]_2$, 6 m*M* 2-mercaptoethanol, 5 m*M* putrescine, and 1 m*M* spermidine) at 15 m*M* $Mg(OAc)_2$, and pH 25C 7.5, supplemented with an oxygen-scavenging system (25 units/ml glucose oxidase, 250 units/ml catalase, and 1% β-D-glucose).

with high specificity. We compare structures using online available software packages such as VMD (Humphrey, Dalke, & Schulten, 1996), PYmol (DeLano, 2002), or Swiss-PDB (Guex & Peitsch, 1997). However, if one is not available for the molecule of interest, but is for a similar molecule, a combination of sequence alignment and the alternate structure may facilitate choosing an appropriate labeling site. Also, the sites need to be away from active sites, for instance an enzyme pocket, to minimize perturbing the biological activity of the molecule. Furthermore, the distances between the chosen sites are near the R_0 of the used dye-pair to achieve maximum sensitivity. In case of proteins, naturally occurring cysteines are mutated to alternative amino acids found to exist at the same position in a phylogenetic sequence alignment. Next, we introduce single cysteine residues at the required sites. Now with candidate positions picked, structural modeling facilitates the identification of matching candidates. In other words, labeling sites are matched to identify pairs where distance changes are expected to achieve the highest FRET sensitivity.

4.4. Fluorescently labeling various translation components

4.4.1 tRNA labeling

Generally speaking, nucleic acid can be labeled internally or on the 5′ or 3′ end (Marshall, Aitken, et al., 2008). Despite being a viable option for other RNA sequences such as riboswitches, end-labeling is not an option for tRNA, since both 5′ and 3′ are functionally important in binding amino acids. However, internal labeling can be used for tRNA. One approach involves inserting a fluorescently tagged nucleotide during oligonucleotide synthesis using phosphoramidite chemistry. Again, this can be problematic as it might introduce perturbations in the backbone of the tRNA. A successful tRNA labeling scheme tends to exploit the naturally occurring modified nucleotides in the tRNA backbone (Blanchard, Kim, et al., 2004). For instance, you can label $tRNA^{fMet}$ at the 4-thiouridine at nucleotide position 8 (s4U8) with Cy3/5-maleimide and/or $tRNA^{Phe}$ at the primary aliphatic amino group of the 3-(3-amino-3-carboxypropyl)-uridine at position 47 (acp3U47) with Cy3/5-NHS-esters (Fei et al., 2010).

4.4.2 Ribosome labeling

Specific labeling of the rRNA is challenging because of the high degree of conservation of ribosomal components and the importance of keeping the structural integrity of the ribosomes. However, two approaches are available to label specific sites on the ribosome.

Labeling ribosomal proteins. Choosing the appropriate approach is based on the lethality of a chromosomal deletion of the candidate protein. If the bacterial cell can survive its absence, then a knockout (KO) mutant is generated using one-step gene deletion of the chromosomal copy of the gene via recombination (Datsenko & Wanner, 2000). Preparing more complicated constructs with several KO mutants is feasible using phage transduction (Fei et al., 2010). Gene deletions are confirmed via PCR and sequencing. The mutants can be purified as tight-coupled ribosomes or as separate subunits and reassociated (Ermolenko et al., 2007; Hickerson et al., 2005). Based on the phylogenetic analysis performed earlier, a mutated clone of the protein is purified and labeled with the corresponding donor/acceptor dye (Fei et al., 2010; Guo & Noller, 2012; Hickerson et al., 2005). The mutated labeled protein is reassociated with the KO mutant subunit/ribosome via partial *in vitro* reconstitution. However, in the case of a lethal KO, the whole subunit requires full *in vitro* reconstitution from purified components (rRNA and r-proteins) (Culver & Noller, 1999). The major *advantage of this approach is that* mutating r-proteins provides a wider range of possible sites exploiting different dynamics on the ribosome. *On the negative side,* reconstituted ribosomes are less active than the wild-type controls (Dorywalska, 2005; Marshall, Aitken, et al., 2008). Also, the population of purified ribosomes shows some labeling heterogeneity. However, in smFRET such heterogeneities do not weigh in significantly. For example, a construct missing the donor dye will not be detected, while a construct missing the acceptor dye will not show any FRET (Joo & Ha, 2008).

Labeling ribosomal RNA. Another approach targets rRNA via hybridizing fluorescently labeled synthetic oligonucleotides to surface-accessible helical extensions engineered into the rRNA via PCR at specific sites (Dorywalska, 2005; Marshall, Dorywalska, et al., 2008). Again, the sites are chosen based on a phylogenetic analysis. Ribosomal mutants can be purified as tight-coupled homogeneous preparations. After that, the fluorescently tagged oligonucleotides are hybridized to the helical extensions. Since no *in vitro* assembly is required, i.e., ribosomes are purified as tight-coupled constructs, ribosomes maintain higher activity and functionality compared to the first approach. In addition, the purified preparation is more homogeneous (Marshall, Aitken, et al., 2008). However, rRNAs show a higher degree of conservation compared to r-proteins. Thus, it is less flexible to choose labeling sites which limits the range of exploitable dynamic motions on the ribosome using this approach (Marshall, Aitken, et al., 2008). Moreover, even minor extensions to the rRNA raise the activation barrier required for the ribosome to sample the conformational space and hinder processes like intersubunit ratcheting (5 kJ/mol for 1–2 base pairs added) (Blanchard, 2009). Thus, it can misguide thermodynamic and kinetic interpretations.

4.4.3 Translation factors labeling

Translation factors such as EF-G and EF-Tu can also be labeled for smFRET experiments. Considering EF-G as an example, two methods have been used to introduce labeling sites. The first method involves introducing a nonnatural amino acid, p-acetyl-L-phenylalanine, into a specific position on EF-G *in vivo* through suppression of an amber stop codon. The purified EF-G is then labeled with A647N hydroxylamine (Munro et al., 2010). A second method involves a similar approach to r-proteins mentioned previously. Following a phylogenetic analysis, naturally occurring cysteines are replaced with alternative amino acids. Then, we can introduce unique single, or double, cysteine mutations at the required site for labeling with Cy3- and Cy5-maleimide dyes (Ermolenko, Salsi, & Farah, 2014).

4.5. Testing activity of purified translation components

After purifying and labeling the different elements and prior to acquiring data, the functional activity of the entire translation system needs to be assessed. There are different approaches to assess different elements of the system. We refer the reader to Fei et al. (2010) and Ermolenko et al. (2007) for detailed protocols and further guidance. Here, we briefly describe one method, filter binding. This assay assesses tRNA binding efficiency and the peptidyl transferase activity of the purified ribosomes compared to their wild-type counterpart (Ermolenko et al., 2007; Hickerson et al., 2005). Aside from being a fast assay, filter binding requires lesser sample than toe-printing for instance, which is an advantage in case of utilizing expensive dyes

4.5.1 Filter binding and puromycin reactivity assay

Adapted with minor modification from Ermolenko et al. (2007):

Buffer A: *20 mM Hepes–KOH (pH 7.5), 6 mM* $Mg(CH_3COO)_2$, *150 mM* NH_4Cl, *6 mM β-mercaptoethanol, 0.1% (v/v) octaethylene glycol monododecyl ether (Nikkol), 2 mM spermidine, 0.1 mM spermine.*

Buffer B: *50 mM Hepes–KOH (pH 7.5), 20 mM* $MgCl_2$, *100 mM* NH_4Cl, *6 mM β-mercaptoethanol.*

1. *Priming the P-site:* Ribosomes (0.2 μ*M*) are incubated for 20 min at 37 °C with m291, which is a derivative of T4 gene 32 (0.4 μ*M*), and $tRNA^{fMet}$ (0.4 μ*M*) in buffer A.
2. *Priming the A-site*: Next, incubate the sample with N-Ac-[^{3}H] Phe-$tRNA^{Phe}$ (0.4 μ*M*) for 30 min at 37 °C. Keep the reaction volume small (≈10 μl).
3. *Testing tRNA binding*: Divide the sample in half and dilute with 5 μl of buffer A. Apply the first half to a nitrocellulose HA filter, wash with ice-cold buffer B. Dry the filters and count in scintillation cocktail (Bio-Safe II, RPI).
4. *Testing peptidyl transferase activity*:
   - **a.** To the other half of the reaction, add EF-G to a final concentration of 1 μ*M* and GTP to a final concentration of 0.5 m*M*. Incubate for 10 min at 37 °C.
   - **b.** Next, add 1.1 μl of 10 m*M* puromycin and incubate for 15 min at 37 °C.
   - **c.** Add 30 μl of water and 40 μl of magnesium sulfate saturated with 0.3 *M* sodium acetate (pH 5.5) to release puromycin and the attached peptidyl chain.
   - **d.** Extract N-Ac-[^{3}H]Phe-puromycin with 1 ml ethyl acetate. Mix 0.8 ml of the reaction with scintillation cocktail and count.

Puromycin, an antibiotic, mimics the aminoacyl-terminus of aminoacylated-tRNA. Puromycin has a high specificity toward acylated-tRNA in the P-site rather than tRNA occupying the A-site (Marshall, Aitken, et al., 2008). Thus, peptidyl chain attached to P-site tRNA is transferred to puromycin through peptidyl transfer. This tests for tRNA translocation and peptidyl transferase activity of the ribosome. Another version of the puromycin test is fluorescence-dependent and can be used to test the construct under smFRET settings. A fluorescently labeled amino acid is incorporated via translation to a ribosome-attached peptide chain. Disappearance of the fluorescent signal on the addition of puromycin indicates peptidyl-puromycin release (Blanchard, Kim, et al., 2004).

4.6. Assessing the spectroscopic properties of the labeled components

An equally important test is assessing the spectroscopic properties of the attached dyes in the biological context of the experiment. Several factors can affect fluorescence intensity and/or FRET. For instance, non-stoichiometric labeling and dye environment can misguide and complicate data interpretation. Thus, it is of importance to assess and account for changes in extinction coefficients, quantum yield, triplet state formation, quenching, labeling stoichiometry. We refer the reader to the following resources for further guidance (Blanchard, Kim, et al., 2004; Ermolenko et al., 2007; Lakowicz, 2007; Majumdar et al., 2005; Michaelis, 2010; Qin, Yu, Zuo, & Cornish, 2014; Roy et al., 2008; Zheng et al., 2014).

4.7. Ribosomal complex assembly

Two methods are used to assemble ribosomal complexes for smFRET experiments:

Factor-free initiation. Incubate 70S ribosomes, target mRNA sequence and P-site tRNA together for 20 min at 37 °C. Subsequently, add A-site tRNA and incubate for another 20 min at 37 °C (Cornish et al., 2008; Ermolenko et al., 2007; Hickerson et al., 2005). The sample is ready for use. The protocol is easily expandable to include various translation factors such as EF-G-GTP or EF-Tu or even small molecules like antibiotic. *An advantage to this approach is the ease of assembly as it is time saving.*

Factor-aided initiation. Immobilize a 30S preinitiation complex containing fMet-tRNA^{fMet} to the slide surface via biotinylated mRNA. The mRNA template needs to have an upstream 5′ untranslated region and a Shine-Dalgarno sequence. Next, deliver 50S subunit, along with initiation (IF2) and elongation factors (EF-G and aa-tRNA-EF-Tu-GTP), to the assembly chamber. The presence of IF2 guides the *in vitro* assembly of 70S complex (Aitken & Puglisi, 2010; Chen, Petrov, et al., 2014). *An advantage to this approach is that only functionally active subunits will join together to form a complex.*

4.8. Immobilization schemes

Slide preparation and assembly (Joo & Ha, 2008; Roy et al., 2008). The ribosome complex formed above needs to be injected and immobilized into the prepared slide chamber. By immobilizing complexes, the system can be investigated for a longer time scale compared to freely diffusing molecules. By exploiting the binding affinity of Neutravidin–Biotin complexes, the entire translation complex is efficiently immobilized on the slide/coverslip surface. To minimize nonspecific binding to slide surface, especially with a protein sample, passivate the slide surface using a mixture of polyethylene glycol (PEG) and biotin-attached PEG. Prime the biotinylated-PEG with Neutravidin. This provides a platform for subsequent immobilizations.

We can immobilize different biocomplexes by incubating the slide with biotinylated molecules. For instance, the ribosomal biocomplex can be stably immobilized using a biotin end-labeled mRNA template. A variation of this theme is to hybridize the mRNA sequence to a biotinylated single-stranded DNA (Qin et al., 2014). Attaching handles to the ribosome instead of immobilizing mRNA templates has been used previously in the context of single-molecule techniques. The immobilized ribosomes were used to measure the stability of SD sequence–16S rRNA interaction using optical tweezers (Uemura et al., 2007). However, this immobilization scheme has not been employed in smFRET experiments.

4.9. Imaging

Imaging buffer. After immobilizing the sample, the assembly buffer is exchanged with an imaging buffer. To reduces photobleaching and enhance imaging lifetime of the dyes, molecular oxygen has to be eliminated. Thus, an oxygen-scavenging system is usually added. One efficient system is a mixture of glucose oxidase, catalase, and β-D-glucose. A better alternative is a mixture of protocatechuic acid and protocatechuate-3,4-dioxygenase (Dave, Terry, Munro, & Blanchard, 2009; Roy et al., 2008). However, removing molecular oxygen prolongs the residence time of the dye in the nonfluorescent triplet state. To counter that effect, the imaging buffer contains a triplet state quencher such as Trolox (Roy et al., 2008).

Quality assessment and controls. Appropriate controls are required to assure the quality and cleanliness of the assembled slides and materials used, which is crucial to minimize the randomly acquired fluorescent spots. After that, eliminating Neutravidin allows assessment of non-specific binding to slide surface. A slide chamber is deemed good if the imaged fluorescent spot density is $<10\%$ of the specifically tethered ribosomal complexes (Joo & Ha, 2008; Roy et al., 2008).

Imaging samples. Various translation factors can be introduced via mixing with the imaging buffer. Buffer mixtures can be introduced to the slide chamber either manually or, preferably, using a controlled syringe pump. Whether a full translation system is added (Chen, Petrov, et al., 2014) or sequential addition of factors such as EF-G and EF-Tu-GTP–tRNA ternary complexes (Cornish et al., 2008) is based on the experimental objective. To clarify, stepwise addition of translation factors and tRNA is the method of choice to monitor the system at equilibrium. On the other hand, adding a full translation mixture to the slide allows real-time observation of sequential cycles of translocation and translation.

As has been noted above, sample preparation and appropriate controls are crucial. However, proper settings of the FRET instrument are also critical to assuring precise and accurate measurements of FRET efficiency. Therefore, a thorough understanding of the imaging instrumentation and parameters are critical for obtaining meaningful FRET data.

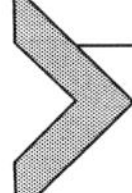

5. DATA ACQUISITION

5.1. Selecting a camera

Quantitative measurements in FRET are obtained through digital images that are reconstructed by silicon imaging cameras. The two common types of cameras used in biological experiments are the CCD (charged coupled device) and the CMOS (complementary metal oxide semiconductor). The CCD is an analog detector composed of pixels and is sensitive to photons. Electron multiplication (EM) CCDs generally work as CCDs, but are equipped with EM technology and have higher quantum efficiency (QE). The CMOS camera offers lower cost systems at smaller sizes compared to the more expensive CCD cameras. CMOS cameras also have capabilities to avoid smearing and fast imaging response, which are recommended in biological experiments that require high temporal resolution. The disadvantages to the CMOS camera are lower QE and DR; therefore, CCD technology offers greater sensitivity to light over CMOS cameras.

Each camera is equipped with silicon detectors that are divided into a large number of light-sensitive areas, known as pixels, arranged in a two-dimensional array on a silicon substrate. The semiconductor properties allow for each pixel on the detector to function as a potential well to store the charge from the photons during acquisition measurements. In CCD cameras, the photons are detected by each pixel and are converted to a digital signal or digital number which represents intensity values through an analog-to-digital converter (ADC). Conversely, CMOS cameras use transistors that allow pixels to be read individually (Faramarzpour et al., 2008).

5.2. Signal to noise

5.2.1 Dark noise, readout noise, Poisson noise

Cameras are prone to noise that contribute to the FRET fluctuations, which can affect accuracy and precisions of FRET measurements. The key to decreasing uncertainties in fluctuations in FRET measurements is to increase the signal-to-noise ratio (SNR). The SNR is a measure that determines the clarity of the signal from the background noise. The most common types of camera noise are dark charge (dark noise) and readout noise. Dark charge is caused by dark current that is detected by pixels, typically while there is no illumination, and is thermally related. Dark noise is substantially reduced by cooling the camera. Once the camera is cooled, the remaining instrumental noise is readout noise. Readout noise comes from the preamplifier on the chip and is a factor in CCD cameras; however, readout noise is not a critical factor in EM CCDs due to the multiplication of the signal during detection of photons. Furthermore, noise is present in the fluorescence signal. Poisson noise (also known as signal or shot noise) is the noise found in the signal that causes a statistical uncertainty called the Poisson distribution. Poisson noise cannot be eliminated from a signal (Waters, 2007, 2009).

5.2.2 Exposure time, QE, DR, gain

One of the simplest ways to increase SNR is to use longer exposure times. Longer exposure times allow for the photons to accumulate in the detector increasing the signal. The percentages of photons that are detected and collected by the camera depend on the QE. For example, a camera can have a specific QE of 60–90% (depending on the wavelength emission light). This measurement means that 60–90% of photons are detected, but 10–40% of photons are not detected. Detectors are also limited to a certain DR. For example, an 8-bit camera is limited to intensity values of 0–255; if the capacity is reached, the pixels will become saturated, thereby decreasing the DR. It is recommended to use the full DR ($\sim$90) for very low intensity areas of a sample. An increased gain will allow you to use the full DR. Gray-level steps represent the intensity or the brightness of a pixel in the image. For example, an 8-bit ADC will have gray levels ranging from 0 to 255. Increasing the gain divides the signal into several gray-level steps. However, excessive use of gain can appear very noisy and grainy due to inaccurate digitization (Waters, 2007, 2009).

5.2.3 Binning

Another method to overcome dim areas of a sample is binning. Binning allows an increase in SNR by increasing the intensity of the pixels without increasing read out noise. When an image is binned, the signal from the adjacent pixel is summed together creating a "super pixel." For smaller pixels, the 2×2 binning will result in a pixel that is four times brighter and is twice as fast as a single pixel (Waters, 2007). Therefore, if you have a 512×512 image, which is binned at 2×2, 4×4, and 8×8, the image resolution readouts will be 256×256, 128×128, and 64×64, respectively. However, the tradeoff for binning is a loss in spatial resolution (Pawley, 2010).

5.2.4 Nyquist theorem: Undersampling, oversampling

Aliasing arises when the signal is acquired at a sampling frequency that is inadequate to capture the changes in the signal. Aliasing can be avoided by following the Nyquist theorem, which states that a pixel must be sampled at two times smaller than the resolution limit of the microscope. Undersampling of a signal will cause the detector to miss critical moments in a signal. However, oversampling offers several benefits, such as increase in resolution, decrease of Poisson noise, and antialiasing (Pawley, 2010). Figure 16.5 shows an example of undersampling a signal versus sampling at the Nyquist sampling rate. Similar to binning, the tradeoff to the Nyquist theorem is also spatial resolution due to the magnification of the image (Pawley, 2010; Waters, 2009).

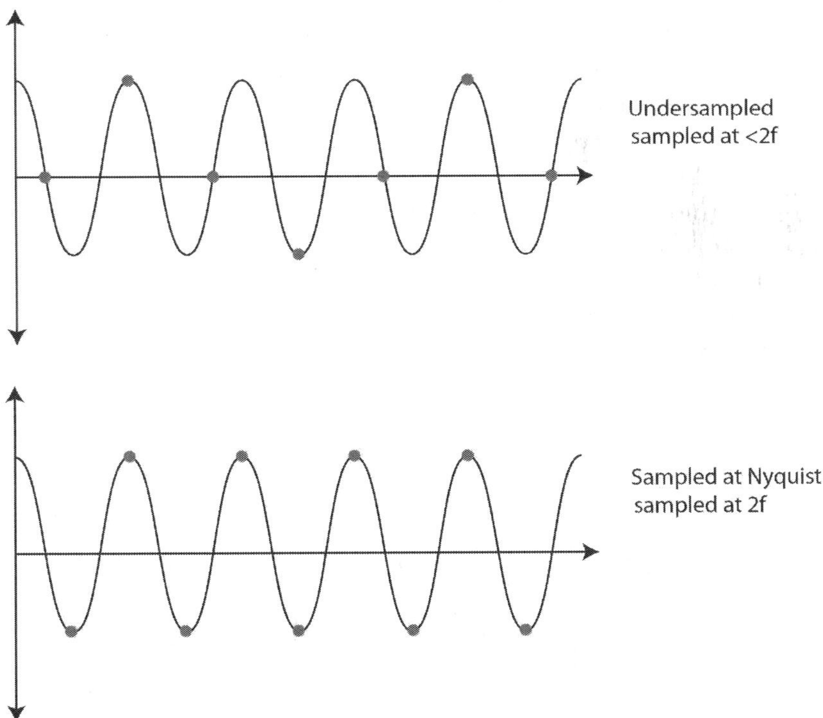

Figure 16.5 Nyquist sampling frequency. The top image shows a signal that is sampled at Nyquist theorem. The instrument is able to capture critical moments in the signal—the crest and trough of the peak. The lower image shows how an instrument can miss critical moments in your signal—if the signal is undersampled.

5.2.5 Bit depth

Bit depth also plays an important role in the accuracy of the FRET efficiency. The greater the bit depth, the greater the digitization resolution is of an image. As the bit depth increases, the variance of errors decreases, allowing an increase in accuracy of FRET measurements. For example, an 8-bit camera and 16-bit camera will have a FRET efficiency measurement varied at 10% and 1% error, respectively (Vogel, Thaler, & Koushik, 2006).

5.2.6 Improving temporal resolution

Maximum frame rates are achieved by overclocking the horizontal and vertical clock speed. Overclocking is the method by optimizing instrument parameters to operate faster than the clock frequency specified by the manufacturer. Overclocking of the pixels allows rapid increases of charges that are horizontally and vertically shifted through the readouts of the sensor. Overclocking may be used in combination with "Crop mode." Typically, acquisition is taken in the image mode, which allows the readout of the complete 512 × 512 sensor of the CCD. However, using the complete sensor is not ideal for fast acquisition; the crop mode focuses on a selected region of interest (ROI) on the CCD chip. The ROI is smaller and allows for a smaller array size of your image. Avoid light on the rest of the sensor, as it will cause problems during cropping. If crop mode is not ideal for your experiment, binning can also improve temporal resolution. Binning may increase acquisition times, because fewer pixels are read out from the camera. For example, 2 × 2 binning will allow your acquisition to be twice as fast (4 × 4 binning is four times faster, etc.).

5.3. Acquisition

During acquisition, the signal is recorded in real time using homemade software (e.g., LabView, micromanager, C++, or Image J) to obtain 16-bit images from a 512 × 512 CCD camera (other camera sizes are available: e.g. 1024 × 1024 and 128 × 128). Donor and acceptor channels are split using a series of optics and imaged onto the CCD camera, each at 512 × 256 (Joo & Ha, 2008). The software obtains a spool of the images and saves the raw images to a movie or image file (i.e., 16-bit tiff file, .sif, etc.). After acquisition, the images are analyzed by MatLab or IDL scripts. We average the first 10 frames to identify isolated peaks from a composite image of the donor and acceptor (Roy et al., 2008). Next, we subtract the background from the peaks. We use postimaging methods to remove unwanted spectral bleed through and photobleaching. Spectral bleed through is caused when the FRET signal is contaminated by the overlap of donor emission into the acceptor channel, which may artificially increases the observed FRET signal.

Since the donor and acceptor fluorescent spots are on different halves of the EMCCD camera, these signals need to be mapped with respect to each other. To begin the image mapping, we select three fluorescence peaks from the donor image and then select the corresponding peaks in the acceptor image through LabView. Once peaks are selected, the x and y positions are saved from each chosen peak. Positions are used to calculate a linear transformation between the acceptor and donor images. Next, the image threshold is selected for the image and the image is converted to binary by a MatLab function to find peaks and FRET pairs. We calculate FRET efficiency using the following equation: $E = I_A/(I_A + I_D)$, where I_A and I_D are acceptor and donor intensities, respectively (Roy et al., 2008).

5.3.1 Analysis algorithms

The most common analysis algorithms provide dwell time analysis, cross-correlation, and hidden Markov modeling (HMM). Cross-correlation or dwell time analysis is used to determine FRET values from two states. To use dwell time analysis, a threshold is either automatically or manually selected. The transition rates are determined from exponential decay fits to the dwell distributions of each state. Next, each dwell time is fitted to a histogram constructed by choosing bins on the logarithmic time axis (Joo & Ha, 2008; Sigworth & Sine, 1987). Cross-correlation analysis is used to observe faster transitions that dwell time analysis is too slow to detect. Cross-correlation determines whether the donor and acceptor transitions are moving in an anticorrelated manner. Time scales are determined by $CC(\tau) = \int I_D(t) I_A(t-\tau)dt$, where t is the time and τ is the lag time. Then, the function is fitted to a single exponential curve by $-Ae^{-(k_{A\to B} + k_{B\to A})\tau}$, where k represents the transition rates between states A and B, or B and A (Joo & Ha, 2008). We use HMM to analyze more complex time trajectories with two states or more that are indistinguishable due to noise. Once HMM yields ideal trajectories, the discrete FRET states are evaluated using transition density plot using dynamic algorithms, such as Viterbi, which provides the transition probabilities of the most likely sequence of states. The logarithm values of the transition probabilities yields symmetry and relates Gibbs free energy of activation to the kinetic rates $\Delta G_{A\to B}{}^{\ddagger} \propto \ln k_{A\to B}$ (Joo & Ha, 2008; McKinney, Joo, & Ha, 2006). Blanco et al. provides a review of the available HMM software, such as HaMMy and QuB (Blanco & Walter, 2010).

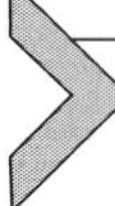

6. BUILDING AND VERIFYING HISTOGRAMS, NORMALIZATION, GAUSSIAN FITTING

FRET efficiency histograms are constructed and calculated by binning FRET efficiencies (Gopich & Szabo, 2010). FRET histograms are typically built from the first 10 frames for each molecule. Structural information and dynamics of a molecule are retrieved from the shape of the histogram by fitting to Gaussian curves. Fitting of the Gaussian curves is implemented in software such as Microcal Origin (McKinney et al., 2006). The number of Gaussian curves that are fitted to a histogram typically depends on what type of information and the number of parameters or states that you are attempting. Variations in the shape of the histogram, such as width, can typically come from Poisson noise, conformational dynamics, and fluctuations of residence time (Dahan et al., 1999). Also, if the times are binned inaccurately by selecting the wrong bin size, the shape of the histogram can be affected. Binning sizes are verified by calculating chi-squared $x^2 = \sum_{k=1}^{n} \frac{(O_k - E_k)^2}{E_k}$ where E_k is the expected number of measurements and O_k is the observed number (Taylor, 1997). Another way to ensure accuracy in FRET histograms is to use long time trajectories of donor and acceptor photons. Shorter time trajectories may provide less accurate FRET measurements; therefore, using longer traces will give better results. A decrease in laser intensity during experiments can help yield longer traces (observation time is limited by photobleaching).

FRET signal normalization is considered when the samples vary in concentration (i.e., FRET experiments on two different proteins), stoichiometry, fluorophores (i.e., quantum yield), and instrument settings. Also, normalization is considered when some of the donors and acceptors do not participate in FRET. Elder et al. give a review over the different normalizations that are used for FRET measurements (Elder et al., 2009).

7. FUTURE DIRECTIONS

Despite our advancing knowledge on translation and ribosome dynamics, many questions still need to be answered. Nevertheless, we are in the time of collaborative interdisciplinary approaches. Ribosome dynamics has been explored by a wide array of techniques. The collective technological and biochemical knowledge gained can be extrapolated to different research areas.

Bearing in mind the concurrent advances in high-throughput sm data acquisition introduced to the field via ZMWs, scanning thousands of molecules during a single run is now doable (Chen, Dalal, et al., 2014; Moran-Mirabal & Craighead, 2008). Accordingly, from a ribosome-dynamics perspective, the next focus is how molecules function and interact rather than simple structural glimpses. Multicolor FRET(Hohng, Joo, & Ha, 2004; Lee et al., 2010; Munro et al., 2010), multiparameter FRET (Widengren et al., 2006), combined Tweezers-smFRET setups (Comstock, Ha, & Chemla, 2011; Hohng et al., 2007; Lang, Fordyce, & Block, 2003), and advances in labeling schemes (Joo, Balci, Ishitsuka, Buranachai, & Ha, 2008; Zheng et al., 2014) or more stable dyes will open new horizons and support more comprehensive studies.

REFERENCES

Aitken, C. E., Petrov, A., & Puglisi, J. D. (2010). Single ribosome dynamics and the mechanism of translation. *Annual Review of Biophysics*, *39*(1), 491–513. http://dx.doi.org/10.1146/annurev.biophys.093008.131427.

Aitken, C. E., & Puglisi, J. D. (2010). Following the intersubunit conformation of the ribosome during translation in real time. *Nature Structural & Molecular Biology*, *17*(7), 793–800. http://dx.doi.org/10.1038/nsmb.1828.

Altschul, S. F., Gish, W., Miller, W., Myers, E. W., & Lipman, D. J. (1990). Basic local alignment search tool. *Journal of Molecular Biology*, *215*(3), 403–410. http://dx.doi.org/10.1016/S0022-2836(05)80360-2.

Amunts, A., Brown, A., Bai, X. C., Llacer, J. L., Hussain, T., Emsley, P., et al. (2014). Structure of the yeast mitochondrial large ribosomal subunit. *Science*, *343*(6178), 1485–1489. http://dx.doi.org/10.1126/science.1249410.

Ban, N. (2000). The complete atomic structure of the large ribosomal subunit at 2.4 A resolution. *Science*, *289*(5481), 905–920. http://dx.doi.org/10.1126/science.289.5481.905.

Blanchard, S. C. (2009). Single-molecule observations of ribosome function. *Current Opinion in Structural Biology*, *19*(1), 103–109. http://dx.doi.org/10.1016/j.sbi.2009.01.002.

Blanchard, S. C., Gonzalez, R. L., Kim, H. D., Chu, S., & Puglisi, J. D. (2004). tRNA selection and kinetic proofreading in translation. *Nature Structural & Molecular Biology*, *11*(10), 1008–1014. http://dx.doi.org/10.1038/nsmb831.

Blanchard, S. C., Kim, H. D., Gonzalez, R. L., Puglisi, J. D., & Chu, S. (2004). tRNA dynamics on the ribosome during translation. *Proceedings of the National Academy of Sciences of the United States of America*, *101*(35), 12893–12898. http://dx.doi.org/10.1073/pnas.0403884101.

Blanco, M., & Walter, N. G. (2010). Analysis of complex single-molecule FRET time trajectories. *Methods in Enzymology*, *472*, 153–178. http://dx.doi.org/10.1016/S0076-6879(10)72011-5.

Chen, J., Dalal, R. V., Petrov, A. N., Tsai, A., O'Leary, S. E., Chapin, K., et al. (2014). High-throughput platform for real-time monitoring of biological processes by multicolor single-molecule fluorescence. *Proceedings of the National Academy of Sciences*, *111*(2), 664–669. http://dx.doi.org/10.1073/pnas.1315735111.

Chen, J., Petrov, A., Johansson, M., Tsai, A., O'Leary, S. E., & Puglisi, J. D. (2014). Dynamic pathways of −1 translational frameshifting. *Nature*, *512*, 328–332. http://dx.doi.org/10.1038/nature13428.

Comstock, M. J., Ha, T., & Chemla, Y. R. (2011). Ultrahigh-resolution optical trap with single-fluorophore sensitivity. *Nature Publishing Group, 8*(4), 335–340. http://dx.doi.org/10.1038/nmeth.1574.

Cornish, P. V., Ermolenko, D. N., Noller, H. F., & Ha, T. (2008). Spontaneous intersubunit rotation in single ribosomes. *Molecular Cell, 30*(5), 578–588. http://dx.doi.org/10.1016/j.molcel.2008.05.004.

Cornish, P. V., Ermolenko, D. N., Staple, D. W., Hoang, L., Hickerson, R. P., Noller, H. F., et al. (2009). Following movement of the L1 stalk between three functional states in single ribosomes. *Proceedings of the National Academy of Sciences, 106*(8), 2571–2576. http://dx.doi.org/10.1073/pnas.0813180106.

Culver, G. M. (2001). Meanderings of the mRNA through the ribosome. *Structure with Folding & Design, 9*(9), 751–758.

Culver, G. M., & Noller, H. F. (1999). Efficient reconstitution of functional Escherichia coli 30S ribosomal subunits from a complete set of recombinant small subunit ribosomal proteins. *RNA, 5*(6), 832–843.

Dahan, M., Deniz, A. A., Ha, T., Chemla, D. S., Schultz, P. G., & Weiss, S. (1999). Ratiometric measurement and identification of single diffusing molecules. *Chemical Physics, 247*(1), 85–106.

Datsenko, K., & Wanner, B. L. (2000). One-step inactivation of chromosomal genes in Escherichia coli K-12 using PCR products. *Proceedings of the National Academy of Sciences of the United States of America, 97*(12), 6640–6645.

Dave, R., Terry, D. S., Munro, J. B., & Blanchard, S. C. (2009). Mitigating unwanted photophysical processes for improved single-molecule fluorescence imaging. *Biophysical Journal, 96*(6), 2371–2381. http://dx.doi.org/10.1016/j.bpj.2008.11.061.

DeLano, W. L. (2002). *The PyMOL molecular graphics, system.* Palo Alto, CA, USA: DeLano Scientific.

Diaconu, M., Kothe, U., Schlünzen, F., Fischer, N., Harms, J. M., Tonevitsky, A. G., et al. (2005). Structural basis for the function of the ribosomal L7/12 stalk in factor binding and GTPase activation. *Cell, 121*(7), 991–1004. http://dx.doi.org/10.1016/j.cell.2005.04.015.

Dorywalska, M. (2005). Site-specific labeling of the ribosome for single-molecule spectroscopy. *Nucleic Acids Research, 33*(1), 182–189. http://dx.doi.org/10.1093/nar/gki151.

Elder, A. D., Domin, A., Kaminski Schierle, G. S., Lindon, C., Pines, J., Esposito, A., et al. (2009). A quantitative protocol for dynamic measurements of protein interactions by Forster resonance energy transfer-sensitized fluorescence emission. *Journal of the Royal Society, Interface, 6*(Suppl. 1), S59–S81. http://dx.doi.org/10.1529/biophysj.103.022087.

Ermolenko, D. N., Majumdar, Z. K., Hickerson, R. P., Spiegel, P. C., Clegg, R. M., & Noller, H. F. (2007). Observation of intersubunit movement of the ribosome in solution using FRET. *Journal of Molecular Biology, 370*(3), 530–540. http://dx.doi.org/10.1016/j.jmb.2007.04.042.

Ermolenko, D. N., Salsi, E., & Farah, E. (2014). Elongation factor G undergoes an extensive structural rearrangement during ribosomal translocation. *The FASEB Journal, 28*(752.3) http://www.fasebj.org/content/28/1_Supplement/752.3.

Faramarzpour, N., El-Desouki, M., Deen, M., Fang, Q., Shirani, S., & Liu, L. W. C. (2008). CMOS imaging for biomedical applications. *IEEE Potentials, 27*(3), 31–36. http://dx.doi.org/10.1109/MPOT.2008.916105.

Fei, J., Bronson, J. E., Hofman, J. M., Srinivas, R. L., Wiggins, C. H., & Gonzalez, R. L., Jr. (2009). Allosteric collaboration between elongation factor G and the ribosomal L1 stalk directs tRNA movements during translation. *Proceedings of the National Academy of Sciences of the United States of America, 106*(37), 15702–15707.

Fei, J., Kosuri, P., MacDougall, D. D., & Gonzalez, R. L., Jr. (2008). Coupling of ribosomal L1 stalk and tRNA dynamics during translation elongation. *Molecular Cell, 30*(3), 348–359. http://dx.doi.org/10.1016/j.molcel.2008.03.012.

Fei, J., Wang, J., Sternberg, S. H., MacDougall, D. D., Elvekrog, M. M., Pulukkunat, D. K., et al. (2014). A highly purified, fluorescently labeled *in vitro* translation system for single-molecule studies of protein synthesis. *Methods Enzymololgy*, *472*, 221–259. http://dx.doi.org/10.1016/S0076-6879(10)72008-5.

Fernández, I. S., Ng, C. L., Kelley, A. C., Wu, G., Yu, Y.-T., & Ramakrishnan, V. (2014). Unusual base pairing during the decoding of a stop codon by the ribosome. *Nature*, *500*(7460), 107–110. http://dx.doi.org/10.1038/nature12302.

Fischer, N., Konevega, A. L., Wintermeyer, W., Rodnina, M. V., & Stark, H. (2010). Ribosome dynamics and tRNA movement by time-resolved electron cryomicroscopy. *Nature*, *466*(7304), 329–333. http://dx.doi.org/10.1038/nature09206.

Frank, J., & Agrawal, R. K. (2000). A ratchet-like inter-subunit reorganization of the ribosome during translocation. *Nature*, *406*(6793), 318–322. http://dx.doi.org/10.1038/35018597.

Gao, Y. G., Selmer, M., Dunham, C. M., Weixlbaumer, A., Kelley, A. C., & Ramakrishnan, V. (2009). The structure of the ribosome with elongation factor G trapped in the posttranslocational state. *Science*, *326*(5953), 694–699. http://dx.doi.org/10.1126/science.1179709.

Gopich, I. V., & Szabo, A. (2010). FRET efficiency distributions of multistate single molecules. *The Journal of Physical Chemistry B*, *114*(46), 15221–15226. http://dx.doi.org/10.1021/jp105359z.

Guex, N., & Peitsch, M. C. (1997). SWISS-MODEL and the swiss-PdbViewer: An environment for comparative protein modeling. *Electrophoresis*, *18*(15), 2714–2723. http://dx.doi.org/10.1002/elps.1150181505.

Guo, Z., & Noller, H. F. (2012). Rotation of the head of the 30S ribosomal subunit during mRNA translocation. *Proceedings of the National Academy of Sciences of the United States of America*, *109*(50), 20391–20394. http://dx.doi.org/10.1073/pnas.1218999109/-/DCSupplemental.

Ha, T. (2001). Single-molecule fluorescence resonance energy transfer. *Methods*, *25*(1), 78–86. http://dx.doi.org/10.1006/meth.2001.1217.

Hickerson, R., Majumdar, Z. K., Baucom, A., Clegg, R. M., & Noller, H. F. (2005). Measurement of internal movements within the 30S ribosomal subunit using Förster resonance energy transfer. *Journal of Molecular Biology*, *354*(2), 459–472. http://dx.doi.org/10.1016/j.jmb.2005.09.010.

Hohng, S., Joo, C., & Ha, T. (2004). Single-molecule three-color FRET. *Biophysical Journal*, *87*(2), 1328–1337. http://dx.doi.org/10.1529/biophysj.104.043935.

Hohng, S., Zhou, R., Nahas, M. K., Yu, J., Schulten, K., Lilley, D. M. J., et al. (2007). Fluorescence-force spectroscopy maps two-dimensional reaction landscape of the Holliday junction. *Science*, *318*(5848), 279–283. http://dx.doi.org/10.1126/science.1146113.

Horan, L. H., & Noller, H. F. (2007). Intersubunit movement is required for ribosomal translocation. *Proceedings of the National Academy of Sciences of the United States of America*, *104*(12), 4881–4885. http://dx.doi.org/10.1073/pnas.0700762104.

Humphrey, W., Dalke, A., & Schulten, K. (1996). VMD: Visual molecular dynamics. *Journal of Molecular Graphics*, *14*(1), 33–38. http://dx.doi.org/10.1016/0263-7855(96)00018-5.

Jin, H., Kelley, A. C., & Ramakrishnan, V. (2011). Crystal structure of the hybrid state of ribosome in complex with the guanosine triphosphatase release factor 3. *Proceedings of the National Academy of Sciences*, *108*(38), 15798–15803. http://dx.doi.org/10.1073/pnas.1112185108.

Joo, C., Balci, H., Ishitsuka, Y., Buranachai, C., & Ha, T. (2008). Advances in single-molecule fluorescence methods for molecular biology. *Annual Review of Biochemistry*, 77(1), 51–76. http://dx.doi.org/10.1146/annurev.biochem.77.070606.101543.

Joo, C., & Ha, T. (2008). Single-molecule FRET with total internal reflection microscopy. *Single-molecule techniques: A laboratory manual* (pp. 3–36). Long Island, New York: Cold Spring Laboratory Press.

Kim, H. D., Puglisi, J. D., & Chu, S. (2007). Fluctuations of transfer RNAs between classical and hybrid states. *Biophysical Journal, 93*(10), 3575–3582. http://dx.doi.org/10.1529/biophysj.107.109884.

Korostelev, A., Ermolenko, D. N., & Noller, H. F. (2008). Structural dynamics of the ribosome. *Current Opinion in Chemical Biology, 12*(6), 674–683. http://dx.doi.org/10.1016/j.cbpa.2008.08.037.

Korostelev, A., Trakhanov, S., Laurberg, M., & Noller, H. F. (2006). Crystal structure of a 70S ribosome-tRNA complex reveals functional interactions and rearrangements. *Cell, 126*(6), 1065–1077. http://dx.doi.org/10.1016/j.cell.2006.08.032.

Kuhlbrandt, W. (2014). The resolution revolution. *Science, 343*(6178), 1443–1444. http://dx.doi.org/10.1126/science.1251652.

Lakowicz, J. R. (2007). *Principles of fluorescence spectroscopy*. New York: Springer Science & Business Media.

Lang, M. J., Fordyce, P. M., & Block, S. M. (2003). Combined optical trapping and single-molecule fluorescence. *Journal of Biology, 2*(1), 6.

Lee, J., Lee, S., Ragunathan, K., Joo, C., Ha, T., & Hohng, S. (2010). Single-molecule four-color FRET. *Angewandte Chemie, International Edition, 49*(51), 9922–9925. http://dx.doi.org/10.1002/anie.201005402.

Majumdar, Z. K., Hickerson, R., Noller, H. F., & Clegg, R. M. (2005). Measurements of internal distance changes of the 30S ribosome using FRET with multiple donor–acceptor pairs: Quantitative spectroscopic methods. *Journal of Molecular Biology, 351*(5), 1123–1145. http://dx.doi.org/10.1016/j.jmb.2005.06.027.

Marshall, R. A., Aitken, C. E., Dorywalska, M., & Puglisi, J. D. (2008). Translation at the single-molecule level. *Annual Review of Biochemistry*, 77(1), 177–203. http://dx.doi.org/10.1146/annurev.biochem.77.070606.101431.

Marshall, R. A., Dorywalska, M., & Puglisi, J. D. (2008). Irreversible chemical steps control intersubunit dynamics during translation. *Proceedings of the National Academy of Sciences, 105*(40), 15364–15369. http://dx.doi.org/10.1073/pnas.0805299105.

McKinney, S. A., Joo, C., & Ha, T. (2006). Analysis of single-molecule FRET trajectories using hidden Markov modeling. *Biophysical Journal, 91*(5), 1941–1951. http://dx.doi.org/10.1529/biophysj.106.082487.

Michaelis, J. (2010). Quantitative distance and position measurement using single-molecule FRET. In C. Bräuchle, D. C. Lamb and J. Michaelis (Eds.) *Single Particle Tracking and Single Molecule Energy Transfer* (pp. 191–214). Wiley-VCH Verlag GmbH & Co.

Moazed, D., & Noller, H. F. (1989). Intermediate states in the movement of transfer RNA in the ribosome. *Nature, 342*(6246), 142–148. http://dx.doi.org/10.1038/342142a0.

Moore, P. B. (2012). How should We think about the ribosome? *Annual Review of Biophysics, 41*(1), 1–19. http://dx.doi.org/10.1146/annurev-biophys-050511-102314.

Moran-Mirabal, J. M., & Craighead, H. G. (2008). Zero-mode waveguides: Sub-wavelength nanostructures for single molecule studies at high concentrations. *Methods, 46*(1), 11–17. http://dx.doi.org/10.1016/j.ymeth.2008.05.010.

Munro, J. B., Altman, R. B., O'Connor, N., & Blanchard, S. C. (2007). Identification of Two distinct hybrid state intermediates on the ribosome. *Molecular Cell, 25*(4), 505–517. http://dx.doi.org/10.1016/j.molcel.2007.01.022.

Munro, J. B., Altman, R. B., Tung, C. S., Cate, J. H. D., Sanbonmatsu, K. Y., & Blanchard, S. C. (2009). Spontaneous formation of the unlocked state of the ribosome is a multistep process. *Proceedings of the National Academy of Sciences, 107*(2), 709–714. http://dx.doi.org/10.1073/pnas.0908597107.

Munro, J. B., Altman, R. B., Tung, C.-S., Sanbonmatsu, K. Y., & Blanchard, S. C. (2010). A fast dynamic mode of the EF-G-bound ribosome. *The EMBO Journal, 29*(4), 770–781. http://dx.doi.org/10.1038/emboj.2009.384.

Munro, J. B., Vaiana, A., Sanbonmatsu, K. Y., & Blanchard, S. C. (2008). A new view of protein synthesis: Mapping the free energy landscape of the ribosome using single-molecule FRET. *Biopolymers*, *89*(7), 565–577. http://dx.doi.org/10.1002/bip.20961.

Nierhaus, K. H. (1982). Structure, assembly, and function of ribosomes. *Current topics in microbiology and immunology*: *Vol. 97* (pp. 81–155). Berlin, Heidelberg: Springer Berlin Heidelberg. http://dx.doi.org/10.1007/978-3-642-68318-3_3.

Pawley, J. (2010). *Handbook of biological confocal microscopy*. New York: Springer Science & Business Media.

Petrov, A., Kornberg, G., O'Leary, S., Tsai, A., Uemura, S., & Puglisi, J. D. (2011). Dynamics of the translational machinery. *Current Opinion in Structural Biology*, *21*(1), 137–145. http://dx.doi.org/10.1016/j.sbi.2010.11.007.

Pulk, A., & Cate, J. H. D. (2013). Control of ribosomal subunit rotation by elongation factor G. *Science*, *340*(6140), 1235970. http://dx.doi.org/10.1126/science.1235970.

Qin, P., Yu, D., Zuo, X., & Cornish, P. V. (2014). Structured mRNA induces the ribosome into a hyper-rotated state. *EMBO Reports*, *15*, 185–190. http://dx.doi.org/10.1002/embr.201337762.

Ratje, A. H., Loerke, J., Mikolajka, A., Brünner, M., Hildebrand, P. W., Starosta, A. L., et al. (2010). Head swivel on the ribosome facilitates translocation by means of intra-subunit tRNA hybrid sites. *Nature*, *468*(7324), 713–716. http://dx.doi.org/10.1038/nature09547.

Roy, R., Hohng, S., & Ha, T. (2008). A practical guide to single-molecule FRET. *Nature Publishing Group*, *5*(6), 507–516. http://dx.doi.org/10.1038/nmeth.1208.

Schluenzen, F., Tocilj, A., Zarivach, R., Harms, J., Gluehmann, M., Janell, D., et al. (2000). Structure of functionally activated small ribosomal subunit at 3.3 angstroms resolution. *Cell*, *102*(5), 615–623.

Schmeing, T. M., & Ramakrishnan, V. (2009). What recent ribosome structures have revealed about the mechanism of translation. *Nature*, *461*(7268), 1234–1242. http://dx.doi.org/10.1038/nature08403.

Sigworth, F. J., & Sine, S. M. (1987). Data transformations for improved display and fitting of single-channel dwell time histograms. *Biophysical Journal*, *52*(6), 1047–1054. http://dx.doi.org/10.1016/S0006-3495(87)83298-8.

Taylor, J. (1997). *Introduction to error analysis, the study of uncertainties in physical measurements*. Sausalito, California: University Science Books.

Thompson, J. D., Higgins, D. G., & Gibson, T. J. (1994). CLUSTAL W: Improving the sensitivity of progressive multiple sequence alignment through sequence weighting, position-specific gap penalties and weight matrix choice. *Nucleic Acids Research*, *22*(22), 4673–4680.

Tourigny, D. S., Fernandez, I. S., Kelley, A. C., & Ramakrishnan, V. (2013). Elongation factor G bound to the ribosome in an intermediate state of translocation. *Science*, *340*(6140), 1235490. http://dx.doi.org/10.1126/science.1235490.

Uemura, S., Dorywalska, M., Lee, T.-H., Kim, H. D., Puglisi, J. D., & Chu, S. (2007). Peptide bond formation destabilizes Shine–Dalgarno interaction on the ribosome. *Nature*, *446*(7134), 454–457. http://dx.doi.org/10.1038/nature05625.

Valle, M., Zavialov, A., Sengupta, J., Rawat, U., Ehrenberg, M., & Frank, J. (2003). Locking and unlocking of ribosomal motions. *Cell*, *114*(1), 123–134. http://dx.doi.org/10.1016/S0092-8674(03)00476-8.

Vogel, S. S., Thaler, C., & Koushik, S. V. (2006). Fanciful FRET. *Science Signaling*, *2006*(331), re2. http://dx.doi.org/10.1126/stke.3312006re2.

Waters, J. C. (2007). Live-cell fluorescence imaging. *Methods Enzymololgy*, *81*, 115–140. http://dx.doi.org/10.1016/S0091-679X(06)81007-1.

Waters, J. C. (2009). Accuracy and precision in quantitative fluorescence microscopy. *The Journal of Cell Biology*, *185*(7), 1135–1148. http://dx.doi.org/10.1021/ar040136s.

Widengren, J., Kudryavtsev, V., Antonik, M., Berger, S., Gerken, M., & Seidel, C. A. M. (2006). Single-molecule detection and identification of multiple species by multiparameter fluorescence detection. *Analytical Chemistry*, *78*(6), 2039–2050. http://dx.doi.org/10.1021/ac0522759.

Wimberly, B. T., Brodersen, D. E., Clemons, W. M., Morgan-Warren, R. J., Carter, A. P., Vonrhein, C., et al. (2000). Structure of the 30S ribosomal subunit. *Nature*, *407*(6802), 327–339. http://dx.doi.org/10.1038/35030006.

Yusupov, M. M. (2001). Crystal structure of the ribosome at 5.5 A resolution. *Science*, *292*(5518), 883–896. http://dx.doi.org/10.1126/science.1060089.

Zaher, H. S., & Green, R. (2009). Fidelity at the molecular level: Lessons from protein synthesis. *Cell*, *136*(4), 746–762. http://dx.doi.org/10.1016/j.cell.2009.01.036.

Zheng, Q., Juette, M. F., Jockusch, S., Wasserman, M. R., Zhou, Z., Altman, R. B., et al. (2014). Ultra-stable organic fluorophores for single-molecule research. *Chemical Society Reviews*, *43*(4), 1044. http://dx.doi.org/10.1039/c3cs60237k.

Zhou, J., Lancaster, L., Donohue, J. P., & Noller, H. F. (2013). Crystal structures of EF-G-ribosome complexes trapped in intermediate states of translocation. *Science*, *340*(6140), 1236086. http://dx.doi.org/10.1126/science.1236086.

CHAPTER SEVENTEEN

Unraveling the Thermodynamics and Kinetics of RNA Assembly: Surface Plasmon Resonance, Isothermal Titration Calorimetry, and Circular Dichroism

Charles G. Hoogstraten[2], Minako Sumita[1], Neil A. White

Department of Biochemistry and Molecular Biology, Michigan State University, East Lansing, Michigan, USA
[1]Current address: Chemistry and Physics Department, California University of Pennsylvania, 250 University Avenue, California, PA 15419, USA
[2]Corresponding author: e-mail address: hoogstr3@msu.edu

Contents

Abstract

The mechanisms and driving forces of the assembly of RNA tertiary structure are a topic of much current interest. In several systems, including our own work in the docking transition of the hairpin ribozyme, intramolecular RNA tertiary folding has been converted into an intermolecular binding event, allowing the full power of contemporary biophysical techniques to be brought to bear on the analysis. We review the use of three such methods: circular dichroism to isolate the binding of multivalent cations coupled to tertiary assembly, surface plasmon resonance to determine the rates of association and dissociation, and isothermal titration calorimetry to dissect the thermodynamic contributions to RNA assembly events. We pay particular attention to practical aspects of these studies, such as careful preparation of samples with fixed free concentrations

Methods in Enzymology, Volume 549
ISSN 0076-6879
http://dx.doi.org/10.1016/B978-0-12-801122-5.00017-9

of cations in order to avoid errors due to ion depletion effects that are common in RNA systems. Examples of applications from our own work with the hairpin ribozyme are shown. Distinctions among the data handling procedures for the various techniques used and solution conditions encountered are also discussed.

1. THE RNA FOLDING PROBLEM AND ASSEMBLY OF RNA TERTIARY STRUCTURE

From the 1970s to the mid-1990s, classic crystallographic and biophysical studies of tRNA structure and folding provided essentially the sole example of globular structure in RNA (Saenger, 1984). These studies gave rise to the well-established paradigm of the formation of helical segments in monovalent salts and the requirement of multivalent cations such as Mg^{2+} for the assembly of those segments into folded tertiary structure (Leroy & Guéron, 1977). With the renaissance in RNA structural studies in the last 20 years, it has become clear that riboswitches, ribozymes, untranslated region protein-binding sites from mRNAs, and other functional RNA molecules can take up a wide variety of tertiary structures that rival those of protein domains for architectural complexity (Conn & Draper, 1998; Doherty & Doudna, 2001; Ferré-D'Amaré & Doudna, 1999; Garst, Edwards, & Batey, 2011; Hoogstraten & Sumita, 2007; Noller, 2005; Vicens & Cech, 2006), reviving interest in the energetics and mechanisms of RNA tertiary structure formation. In particular, there is as yet no widely accepted general description of the driving force for the assembly of helices and other secondary structure elements into globular tertiary structures, in contrast with the textbook picture of protein folding driven by the burial of nonpolar amino acid side chains (Baldwin, 2007). Early RNA structural analyses emphasized the importance of the formation of a core of partially dehydrated metal ions that is analogous in some ways to the hydrophobic core of a globular protein (Cate et al., 1996; Correll, Freeborn, Moore, & Steitz, 1997). Although such site-bound metal ions certainly play a critical role in neutralizing unfavorable interactions formed by the close juxtaposition of phosphate groups, their role in providing an overall negative free energy change for folding has been questioned (Draper, 2008; Misra & Draper, 1998; Misra, Shiman, & Draper, 2003). In addition, the relatively simple picture of assembly of rigid secondary elements into larger structures, originally derived from studies of the tRNA cloverleaf, has been complicated by the observation of significant rearrangements in secondary elements upon tertiary structure formation in several other RNA systems (DeAbreu, Olive, & Collins, 2011; Rupert & Ferré-D'Amaré, 2001; Rupert, Massey,

Sigurdsson, & Ferré-D'Amaré, 2002; Wu & Tinoco, 1998), implicating conformational heterogeneity and dynamics in the assembly process (Leulliot & Varani, 2001; Treiber & Williamson, 2001; Williamson, 2000). Thus, detailed structural, biophysical, and thermodynamic analyses of tertiary structure formation in riboswitches and other folded RNAs remain a topic of strong interest from experimentalists and theoreticians.

Many biophysical technologies, including those discussed in this chapter, rely on the physical separation of the system into two molecular components that can be mixed or titrated into each other. In this way, the complicated process of structure formation is operationally reduced to an experimentally tractable process of the binding of one component to another, with the results reflective of the structural interface between the components. Thus, one barrier to the detailed experimental analysis of RNA folding is that most intermolecular RNA–RNA interactions consist either of pure secondary structure assembly (i.e., hybridization), not considered herein, or of an inherent coupling of helix formation with simultaneous tertiary assembly. In some cases, careful dissection of these phenomena has been possible, as in the Feig group's detailed calorimetric study of core folding in the hammerhead ribozyme via subtraction of measured contributions from helix formation (Mikulecky, Takach, & Feig, 2004). The most important contributions to the limited database of RNA tertiary thermodynamic studies, however, have come from a small number of systems in which tertiary interactions can form independently of hybridization. Examples include the tetraloop–tetraloop receptor interaction (Vander Meulen & Butcher, 2012; Vander Meulen, Davis, Foster, Record, & Butcher, 2008), the kissing interaction of two stem loops in the VS ribozyme (Bouchard & Legault, 2014), and the loop A–loop B docking interaction in the hairpin ribozyme (Sumita, White, Julien, & Hoogstraten, 2013; Fig. 17.1).

In the following sections, we discuss practical aspects of our group's use of difference circular dichroism (CD) and surface plasmon resonance (SPR) analyses to dissect the ion dependence, kinetics, and thermodynamics of tertiary structure formation in the hairpin system (Sumita et al., 2013). We use these biophysical techniques as an important complement to NMR spectroscopic studies of structure and dynamics (Johnson & Hoogstraten, 2008). One key advantage of the hairpin ribozyme is the extensive biochemical and structural literature in the system (Esteban, Banerjee, & Burke, 1997; Fedor, 2000; Ferré-D'Amaré & Rupert, 2002; Lilley, 2011; Walter & Burke, 1998; Wilson, Nahas, Ha, & Lilley, 2005). For example, loop A residue G+1 is known to form a key component of the docking interface by intercalating into the stacked structure of loop B (Fig. 17.1, right). A point

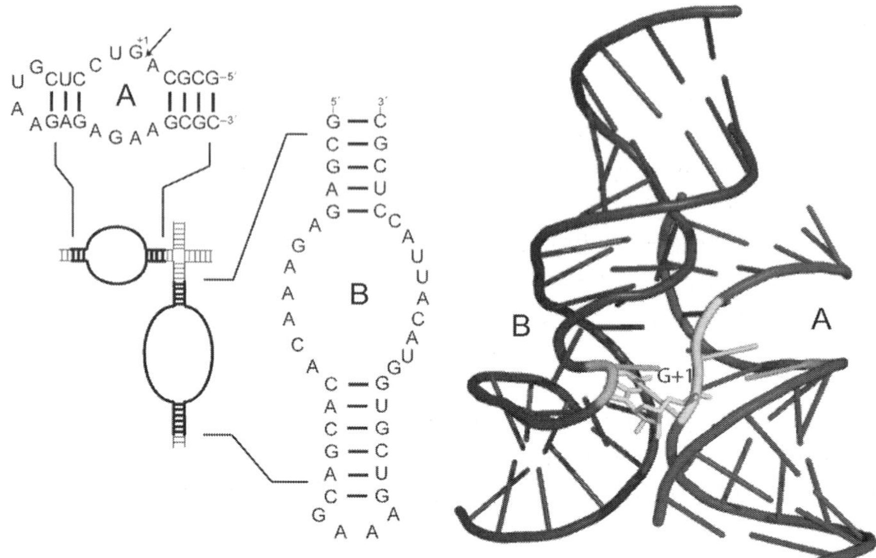

Figure 17.1 Left: Schematic secondary structure of the native four-way junction form of the hairpin ribozyme with the constructs used to represent loop A and loop B in our binding work in the system shown. In three dimensions, the two internal loops interact ("dock") to form an intricately structured interface. The arrow indicates the site of self-cleavage. Right: Three-dimensional structure of the docked form (Salter, Krucinska, Alam, Grum-Tokars, & Wedekind, 2006) (PDB: 2OUE), with the G+1 residue that forms a key part of the tertiary interface highlighted. *Figure prepared with PyMol (Delano, 2002).* (See the color plate.)

mutation to adenosine at this site, G+1A, completely eliminates docking and has been used extensively in our studies as a nondockable control molecule that differs only slightly from wild type. As discussed below, the unusually slow kinetics of this system make the important technique of isothermal titration calorimetry (ITC) problematic, but we discuss this technology also in the context of the tetraloop–receptor and VS systems, where it has played an important role in biophysical analysis.

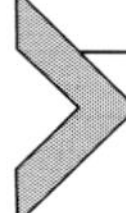

2. PRACTICAL ASPECTS OF BIOPHYSICAL STUDIES OF RNA ASSEMBLY

2.1. RNA assembly: Specification and control of ionic conditions

For essentially all physical analyses of RNA, it is critical to specify whether the listed ionic conditions comprise "total" or "free" ion concentrations, since the presence of a polyanionic nucleic acid will tend to deplete monovalent and multivalent cations from bulk solution. This effect is strongest at high RNA concentration, low ion concentration, and (for multivalent ions) low background concentrations of monovalent ions. For example, if a 100-nucleotide RNA construct is dissolved at 50 μ*M* concentration in a buffer containing 5 m*M* Mg^{2+}, simple mass action considerations would predict the removal of up to 50 ions from bulk solution to neutralize the charge on each RNA molecule, decreasing the net concentration of free Mg^{2+} in bulk solution by half, to 2.5 m*M*. In practice, some of the RNA charge will be screened by monovalent ions (usually Na^+ or K^+) supplied by the buffer, and free ions will behave according to a non-mass-action driven electrostatic distribution (Misra & Draper, 1999), reducing these effects somewhat. At appropriate conditions, however, such ion depletion effects can indeed significantly affect the solution conditions and significantly perturb various assays. Controlling depletion of free ion is particularly critical when the binding constant (K_d) for ions is itself the parameter of interest. These effects can be alleviated by the preparation of all RNA samples using dialysis techniques (see below), which fix the *free* ion concentration, rather than simply dissolving purified nucleic acid in the desired buffer, which fixes the *total* ion concentrations. In our laboratory, we routinely perform a back-of-the-envelope calculation of potential ion depletion effects based on mass action prior to sample preparation; although this calculation will often overstate the quantitative magnitude of ion depletion, it provides a fast and useful assessment of whether incorporating a dialysis step into sample preparation is prudent. For ITC measurements, dialysis is performed in essentially every case to avoid buffer mismatch artifacts (see below). By contrast, prior dialysis is unnecessary for the component to be immobilized in SPR and other surface-based measurements, since buffer rinse steps after immobilization effectively equilibrate the free ion concentration.

For some buffer components, dialysis may be problematic. In our hands, for example, commercial centrifugal dialysis units such as Centricon (EMD Millipore), which we routinely use for their combination of convenience and high sample recovery, tend to retain a substantial fraction of hexammine cobalt ions above the membrane during each spin, leading to sharply increased concentrations of $Co(NH_3)_6^{3+}$ and consequent precipitation of RNA upon repeated addition of buffer (K. Julien & C. G. H., data not shown). A sample preparation method incorporating careful stepwise dialysis that effectively fixes free concentrations of $Co(NH_3)_6^{3+}$ without undue levels of RNA loss is given in Protocol 1.

2.1.1 Protocol 1: Large-scale RNA purification and buffer exchange via dialysis

We routinely purify *in vitro*-transcribed RNA samples using an adaptation of the size exclusion chromatography method of Puglisi and coworkers (Kim, McKenna, Viani, & Puglisi, 2007), which has the major advantages of maintaining the RNA in its native state and avoiding the introduction of acrylamide contamination. For the 26- and 42-nucleotide hairpin ribozyme constructs used in our work, Superdex 75 was used. Above about 60 nucleotides, Superdex 200 is likely to give better results.

Procedures

1. Transcribed RNAs are purified on an ÄKTA chromatography system (GE Healthcare) using a Superdex 75 (26/60) column according to Kim et al. (2007) with an eluent of 10 m*M* phosphate buffer (pH 6.5) with 100 m*M* NaCl at a flow rate of 3.0 mL min^{-1}.
2. The fractions containing desired RNAs are combined, concentrated, and desalted against RNAse-free, double-deionized water using Amicon Ultra 15 centrifugal filtration units (Millipore).
3. RNA are diluted to approximately 98% of the desired final volume in cobalt-free buffer (20 m*M* HEPES, 20 μ*M* Na_2EDTA, pH 7.5) and then dialyzed against the same buffer in a Spectra/Por microdialysis apparatus with a regenerated cellulose membrane, approximate molecular weight cutoff 2000 Da.
4. Concentrated stock $Co(NH_3)_6^{3+}$ is added to the sample to the desired final concentration, and the dialysate is simultaneously switched to $Co(NH_3)_6^{3+}$-containing buffer. To prevent excessive time under dialysis with consequent RNA aggregation in the specific case of $Co(NH_3)_6^{3+}$, the dialysis should be halted after 1–2 h. A control experiment in which the transfer of ions was monitored using the 475 nm absorbance band of $Co(NH_3)_6^{3+}$ indicated that this time was sufficient for $Co(NH_3)_6^{3+}$ concentrations to equilibrate on the two sides of the membrane.
5. Final RNA concentrations are determined from UV absorbance values at 260 nm. We recommend that accurate extinction coefficients be obtained using complete RNA digestion followed by spectrophotometric analysis (Gray, Hung, & Johnson, 1995), as relatively small inaccuracies in concentration can seriously perturb the CD difference analysis. In the case of the hairpin ribozyme, the obtained values were 214,000 M^{-1} cm^{-1} for loop A, 354,000 M^{-1} cm^{-1} for loop B, and 232,000 M^{-1} cm^{-1} for the G+1A mutant of loop A (Sumita et al., 2013).

6. Immediately prior to spectroscopy or binding measurements, RNAs are renatured by heating to 65 °C for 2–5 min, followed by quickly cooling on ice for 5 min.

2.2. RNA assembly: Binding parameters and choice of methodology

Essentially all biophysical methods for the study of intermolecular interactions, whether large molecule–large molecule, large molecule–small molecule, or biomolecule–ion, revolve around the measurement of the equilibrium dissociation constant K_d for the reaction

$$AB \leftrightarrow A + B \tag{17.1}$$

where A and B are the two components of the complex. In addition to experimental convenience and appropriateness for the particular system under study (for example, the availability of an endogenous or added fluorophore, the ability to immobilize one binding component for SPR easily and reproducibly, or the availability of large amounts of pure material for ITC), the choice of technique for binding measurements is often dictated by the additional information desired. As a valid equilibrium constant, a binding constant may be mathematically dissected in several ways, often corresponding to different classes of measurement. For example, separation of the dissociation (equilibrium) constant into individual rate constants yields:

$$K_d = \frac{k_{off}}{k_{on}} \tag{17.2}$$

where k_{on} and k_{off} are the association and dissociation rate constants, respectively. SPR techniques, by observing the accumulation of mobile component on the reaction surface in real time, provide direct access to these k_{on} and k_{off} values, which may hold implications for the role of conformational sampling and structural transitions in RNA recognition. By contrast, if the thermodynamic properties and driving forces of the interaction are of interest, titration calorimetry can yield simultaneous determination of the binding constant, standard enthalpy and entropy changes, and stoichiometry (see below) via

$$\Delta G^{\circ} = \Delta H^{\circ} + T\Delta S^{\circ} \tag{17.3}$$

where

$$K_d = -RT \log \Delta G^{\circ} \tag{17.4}$$

Any method for determination of K_d can in principle determine thermodynamic parameters via repetition of the measurement at various temperatures and construction of a standard van't Hoff plot (Tinoco, Sauer, Wang, & Puglisi, 2002). In favorable cases, temperature-dependent SPR measurements provide access to activation energies, in addition to standard enthalpy and entropy changes, via an Arrhenius analysis of the temperature dependence of rate constants (N. W. & C. G. H., manuscript in preparation). However, for many systems, the accessible temperature range may not be large enough to allow robust determinations of ΔH° with this technique. In addition, many RNA recognition events show a significant variation of ΔH° with temperature via a heat capacity change upon binding (ΔC_p) term. ΔC_p can be an important indicator of parameters including the burial of nonpolar surface area upon binding (Loladze, Ermolenko, & Makhatadze, 2001; Spolar & Record, 1994). For ITC, which measures ΔH° at an individual temperature, such effects are directly observable if the experiment is repeated at several temperatures, whereas for other techniques, ΔC_p is only manifest as curvature in the van't Hoff plot, which can be difficult to detect within a temperature range consistent with sample stability. The details of implementation of these techniques for the case of RNA–RNA tertiary assembly are discussed below.

2.3. RNA assembly: Analytical aspects and experimental design

The analysis of experimental binding curves generally revolves around the parameter θ, defined as the fraction of binding sites occupied by ligand:

$$\theta = \frac{[\mathrm{RL}]}{[\mathrm{L}] + [\mathrm{RL}]} \tag{17.5}$$

where [L] is the concentration of ligand, usually taken as the added component in titration experiments, [R] is the concentration of receptor, and [RL] is the concentration of the receptor–ligand complex. Measurement of θ thus depends on an assay sensitive to the state of the receptor molecules, i.e., a signal change upon conversion of R to RL that saturates when that conversion is complete. For the derivation of the familiar textbook binding isotherm

$$\theta = \frac{[\mathrm{L}]}{K_d + [\mathrm{L}]} \tag{17.6}$$

the total concentration of ligand is assumed to be much greater than the total concentration of receptor, such that a negligible fraction of ligand is present as RL and the unknown concentration of free ligand [L] can be taken as equal to the experimentally controlled total concentration of ligand $[L]_{total} = [L] + [RL]$. Under these conditions, known as "trace-receptor" or "K_d" conditions, titration data plotted as θ versus [L], in the absence of cooperative binding of multiple ligands, are described by the simple hyperbola of Eq. (17.6), and the K_d is the ligand concentration at which θ is equal to 0.5 (as demonstrated in the simulations of Fig. 17.2A). For trace-receptor conditions, the shape of the data is independent of the concentration of receptor (Eq. 17.6), and this parameter thus does not need to be precisely measured for the data to be analyzed accurately. This situation is common in studies of small molecule–large molecule interactions, where the small-molecule ligand is usually available in greater molar quantities and is more soluble than the macromolecular receptor. This equation also well describes surface-based studies such as SPR, in which the immobilized component is considered the receptor and the continuous renewal of the mobile component due to buffer flow fixes [L] at the experimentally controlled value throughout the experiment.

If the condition $[L] \gg [R]$ is not met, by contrast, the more complicated general equation of binding applies:

$$[LR] = \frac{L_T + K_d + R_T - \sqrt{(L_T + K_d + R_T)^2 - 4L_T R_T}}{2} \tag{17.7}$$

We note that Eq. (17.7) is symmetric to interchange of L and R, since the designation of one component as ligand and the other as receptor is arbitrary. In the specific case of titration through the equivalence point $[L] = [R]$, the experiment is referred to as corresponding to "stoichiometric conditions," and the half-maximum point is determined by the stoichiometry of the interaction (Fig. 17.2B). A common and entirely preventable error in binding studies is to analyze the data according to Eq. (17.6) even when trace-receptor equations do not apply, and thus to mistakenly identify K_d with the value of [L] giving $\theta = 0.5$. This error is demonstrated by the comparison between the filled and open symbols in Fig. 17.2B. For stoichiometric conditions, correct determination of K_d relies on a detailed fitting of the shape of the curve to Eq. (17.7), rather than identification of the half-maximum point, and is often experimentally difficult due to the small changes in observed data with large changes in K_d. Violations of the trace-receptor condition are particularly common for experiments in RNA assembly, where the two components are often of comparable size and solubility.

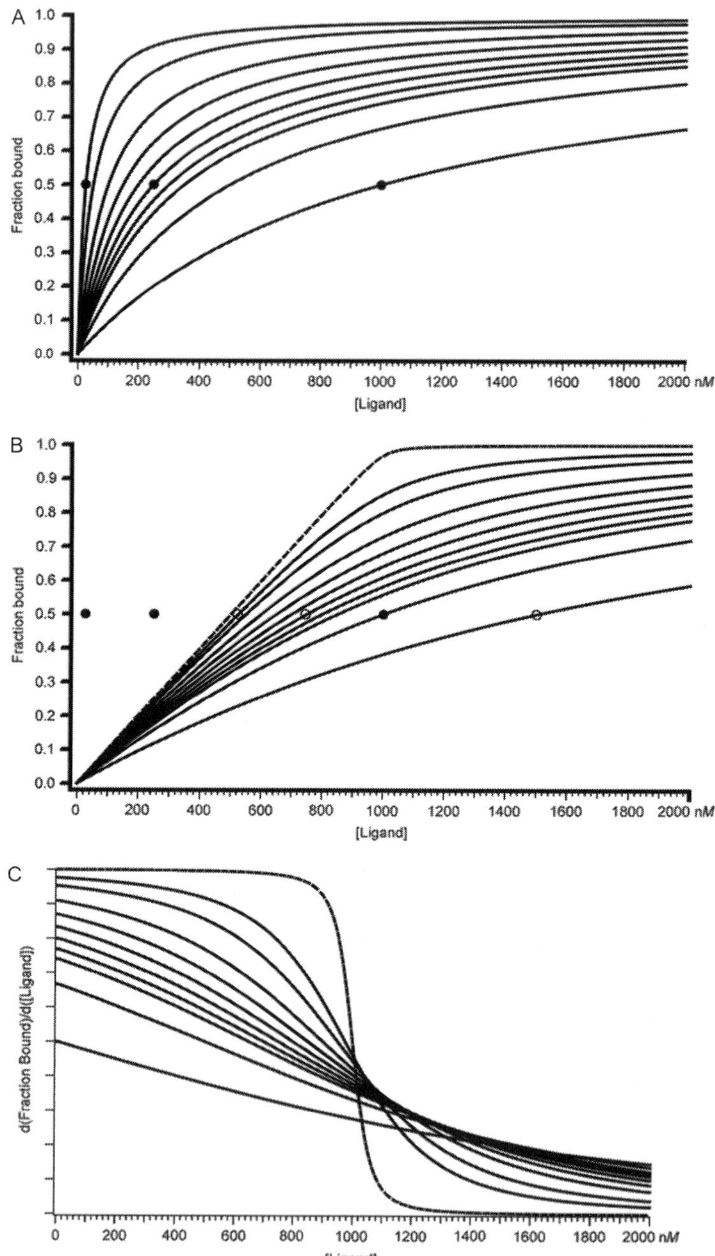

Figure 17.2 *Simulations of binding curves in different binding regimes.* All curves were simulated with the general isotherm (Eq. 17.7) assuming 1:1 stoichiometry. (A) Trace-receptor conditions: $[R]_{total} = 0.5$ n*M*, K_d varied from 25 to 1000 n*M* (top to bottom curves). For K_d values of 25, 250, and 1000 n*M*, the [L] values giving $\theta = 0.5$ are indicated as

Uniquely among the methods described here, ITC is inherently performed under stoichiometric conditions. This is fundamentally because calorimetry detects the binding event itself (via heat given off or taken up), rather than assaying the state of the receptor component; in other words, ITC data are described by the *derivative* of the curves in Fig. 17.1B, as seen in Fig. 17.1C. Thus, substantial amounts of both components are required, setting important constraints on the applicability of ITC in cases for which one component is poorly soluble or is available in limited amounts (see below).

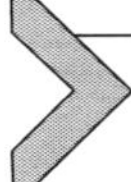

3. SPECIFIC MEASUREMENTS OF ION-DRIVEN RNA ASSEMBLY

3.1. Ion dependence of assembly: CD

The binding of ions to RNA molecules generally, and the coupling of ion-binding events to RNA structural transitions specifically, is a problem of substantial and abiding interest in the field (Draper, 2004, 2008). However, a great problem is posed by the polyanionic nature of RNA, which leads to the inevitable presence of a variety of "background" specific ion sites and nonspecific (electrostatic) ion interactions with any folded RNA, and which complicates efforts to detect the individual ion(s) bound at the site of interest or coupled to the structural transition under study (Narlikar & Herschlag, 1997). In the case of the hairpin ribozyme, a variety of di- and trivalent ions can drive the loop–loop docking process that forms the catalytically active tertiary structure. In fact, the observation of full activity of the ribozyme in cobalt hexammine provided key evidence that metal ions do not participate directly in the chemical step of the reaction (Hampel & Cowan, 1997; Nesbitt, Hegg, & Fedor, 1997; Young, Gill, & Grasby, 1997). We routinely use cobalt hexammine in studies of hairpin docking to enhance RNA stability and spectroscopic quality relative to the biological cofactor Mg^{2+}.

solid dots; this simple graphical procedure gives accurate estimates of K_d in all cases. (B) Stoichiometric conditions: $[R]_{total} = 1000$ nM, K_d varied as in (A) with an additional dashed curve for $K_d = 1$ nM indicating the near-limiting case with abrupt saturation at the equivalence point [L] = [R]. Under these conditions, the [L] values giving $\theta = 0.5$ (open symbols), if interpreted naively under the inappropriate equation (17.6), would give a very poor estimate of the true K_d values, which are shown as filled symbols reproduced from (A). (C) First derivative presentation of the data in (B), representing a technique such as ITC that detects an event rather than a state.

To probe the binding of only those ions directly coupled to the formation of tertiary structure as probed by intermolecular complex formation between loop A and loop B, we derived a novel difference assay based on CD spectroscopy. CD is sensitive to asymmetric (chiral) molecular structures, including folded protein and nucleic acid structures, and enhancement of the primary RNA CD band is usually reflective of the formation of stacked, helical structure. In our difference assay, schematized in Fig. 17.3, two spectra are constructed: an *arithmetic* sum of spectra of individual samples of loops A and B dialyzed against a desired concentration of metal ion added together, and a spectrum of a *physical* mixture of the two loops in the same cuvette. In the absence of any loop–loop interaction, these two spectra will be identical on a molar basis, since the mixed sample results in a superposition of independent spectra for the two components. In the presence of

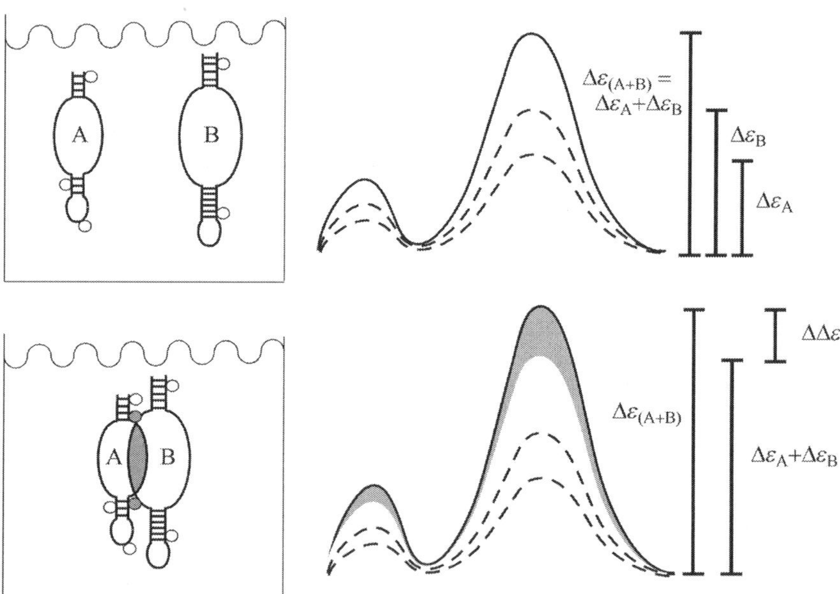

Figure 17.3 Schematic of the difference CD assay for the binding of ions linked to domain docking. In the absence of any docking, the observed CD spectrum of a mixture of loops A and B ($\Delta\varepsilon_{(A+B)}$, solid line) will be the arithmetic sum of those for the individual loops ($\Delta\varepsilon_A$ and $\Delta\varepsilon_B$, dashed lines) (top), whereas if docking occurs a change in the molar CD spectrum from that simple sum will be observed (shaded area, $\Delta\Delta\varepsilon$) (bottom). Circles indicate multivalent cations bound to RNA, shaded in the case of ions whose binding is linked to domain docking. *Reprinted from Sumita et al. (2013) by permission of Taylor & Francis, LLC, www.tandfonline.com.*

molecular interaction, however, the two spectra will differ to the extent that the CD spectrum changes upon docking, scaled by the extent of docking at the ion concentration used. Measurement of this difference as a function of free ion concentration gives a binding isotherm for those ions, and only those ions, whose interaction with RNA is coupled to the interaction of the two loops. Experimental details of this assay are given in Protocol 2. The keys to success in this experiment are careful control of free ion concentration (see Protocol 1), precise measurement of the RNA concentration in each postdialysis sample, and consistent and appropriate handling of the baseline in the CD traces. Since the difference spectrum is taken at the level of molar CD (i.e., raw CD data scaled by RNA concentration), and the final plotted value is a relatively small difference between two large numbers, any imprecision in RNA concentration will propagate into the $\Delta\Delta\varepsilon$ values and lead to strong scatter in the binding isotherm. In our hands, this assay gives highly useful results that are difficult to obtain with any other technology, but is sensitive to imperfections in RNA handling or concentration analysis. We used a comparison of difference CD analysis of docking with kinetic measurements of ribozyme function to argue that binding of metal ions plays a role in hairpin ribozyme catalysis beyond simply driving the docking process, most likely either by coupling to further conformational transitions or by long-range electrostatic transition state stabilization (Sumita et al., 2013).

3.1.1 Protocol 2

CD spectrometers report the preference of asymmetric molecules for absorbance of radiation with circularly polarized light ΔA, defined as

$$\Delta A = (A_{\mathrm{L}} - A_{\mathrm{R}}) \tag{17.8}$$

where A_{L} and A_{R} are the absorbance of left and right circularly polarized light, respectively (Gray et al., 1995). The data can be converted to molar CD ($\Delta\varepsilon$) using Beer's Law

$$\Delta\varepsilon = \varepsilon \mathrm{L} - \varepsilon \mathrm{R} = \Delta A/(C \times I) \tag{17.9}$$

where I is the path length in cm and C is the concentration of the sample in M. The shapes of the CD spectra of typical oligonucleotide helical structures, such as A-, B-, and Z-forms, are known (Bloomfield, Crothers, & Tinoco, 2000). CD spectroscopy is useful for binding studies of RNA–RNA and RNA–small molecules and for monitoring changes in overall nucleic acid conformation (Bloomfield et al., 2000). To implement the CD difference assay of Fig. 17.3 in the case of the hairpin ribozyme (Sumita et al., 2013), the following steps were followed:

Procedures

1. RNA samples of loop A, loop B, and an equimolar mixture of the two loops were prepared in the absence of $Co(NH_3)_6^{3+}$ and at a series of $Co(NH_3)_6^{3+}$ concentrations as described in Protocol 1. Final RNA concentrations in all samples varied between 2 and 3 μ*M*.
2. All CD spectra were obtained with a Chirascan CD spectrometer (Applied Photophysics) equipped with a water bath to control the temperature. Baseline-corrected spectra (200–400 nm at 30 °C) were converted to molar CD values ($\Delta\varepsilon$) using concentrations determined as described above. All CD experiments were performed multiple times to obtain consistent results.

2a. As a control, it was confirmed that the CD spectrum of buffer did not vary with the presence of high concentrations of $Co(NH_3)_6^{3+}$, eliminating these components as sources of spurious effects.

3. In the absence of $Co(NH_3)_6^{3+}$, the mathematically combined CD(loop A) + CD(loop B) and experimentally combined CD(loop A + loop B) spectra were compared and found to be essentially identical, indicating that no spectral changes were observed in the absence of ion-driven RNA interactions.
4. At each concentration of $Co(NH_3)_6^{3+}$, the extent of docking was assessed by subtracting the molar CD spectrum of the loop A–loop B mixed sample from the sum of the spectra of loop A and loop B measured separately:

$$\Delta\Delta\varepsilon = (\Delta\varepsilon_A + \Delta\varepsilon_B) - \Delta\varepsilon_{(A+B)} \tag{17.10}$$

5. The binding isotherm for those ions coupled to RNA–RNA assembly was constructed from a plot of $\Delta\Delta\varepsilon$ at 270 nm versus the concentration of free $Co(NH_3)_6^{3+}$. Apparent ion-binding dissociation constants were obtained from nonlinear fits to

$$\Delta\Delta\varepsilon = \Delta\Delta\varepsilon_{max} \frac{[L]_f}{[Co]_{1/2}^{dock} + [L]_f} \tag{17.11}$$

where $\Delta\Delta\varepsilon_{max}$ is the extrapolated $\Delta\Delta\varepsilon$ value in the limit of high [L] and $[Co]_{1/2}^{dock}$ is the concentration of $Co(NH_3)_6^{3+}$ at which $\Delta\Delta\varepsilon = 0.5 \times \Delta\Delta\varepsilon_{max}$. In this case, a standard Hill plot gave a slope indistinguishable from unity, and fits to equations incorporating cooperative binding of multiple ions were not attempted. In the general case, analysis of binding incorporating a Hill coefficient n would use the expression:

$$\Delta\Delta\varepsilon = \Delta\Delta\varepsilon_{\max}\frac{[\mathrm{L}]^n}{\left([\mathrm{Co}]_{1/2}^{\mathrm{dock}}\right)^n + [\mathrm{L}]^n} \qquad (17.12)$$

3.2. Rates of intermolecular assembly: SPR

SPR is a surface-based technique that, by detecting the accumulation of mass on a surface containing an immobilized component as a buffer containing a mobile component flows across the surface, followed by the loss of that mass as buffer alone flows through the apparatus, allows direct measurement of on- and off-rates for the molecular interaction of interest. The measurement is performed with an optical apparatus under total internal reflection conditions, in which electromagnetic fields from light reflecting off the optical surface opposite the chemically treated side of a gold chip penetrate a short distance into solution. The angle of reflection will change slightly with variations in the index of refraction near the surface, indicating accumulation and loss of the mobile component. The physical principles of SPR have been described (Schuck, 1997), and the factors involved in obtaining accurate SPR results for biomolecular systems have been reviewed in detail (Myszka, 1999; Myszka, He, Dembo, Morton, & Goldstein, 1998; Rich & Myszka, 2010, 2011). Injections are repeated at varying concentration of mobile component and interspersed with blank injections to remove baseline effects (Myszka, 1999). For RNA molecules prepared via solid-phase synthesis, immobilization is straightforward via 5′-biotin labeling combined with chemically immobilized avidin molecules on the optical surface. In our hands, chemical immobilization of streptavidin using 1-ethyl-3-(3-dimethylamino propyl) carbodiimide hydrochloride (EDC)–*N*-hydroxysuccinimide (NHS) coupling (see below) immediately prior to use provides more consistent results than commercially available avidin surfaces. Since many repeated injections are performed on a single surface, one key experimental parameter is the so-called regeneration step, in which remaining (undissociated) mobile component molecules are removed prior to buffer reequilibration and repeat injection. A set of solution conditions must be found that will completely disrupt remaining intercomponent interactions without disrupting the surface or degrading or irreversibly denaturing the stationary component. Widely separated injections of identical concentrations of mobile component are advisable, as reproducibility provides a critical control for stability of the surface. The specific procedures followed in our work on the hairpin ribozyme (Sumita et al., 2013) are detailed in Protocol 3; adaptations to other systems will include, at a minimum, empirical adjustments of association and dissociation times and regeneration conditions and the choice of an appropriate concentration series for the mobile component.

3.2.1 Protocol 3

All measurements described here were performed on a Reichert SR7000DC two-channel instrument equipped with an autosampler. SPR instruments are available from several suppliers that are constructed on similar principles but vary in the details of operation. 5′-Biotin-labeled loop A (immobilized phase) samples were purchased from Dharmacon (GE Healthcare) and deprotected according to the manufacturer's instructions; loop B (mobile component) samples were prepared by *in vitro* transcription and purified as described in Protocol 1 with a final free $Co(NH_3)_6^{3+}$ concentration of 250 μ*M*. All samples were carefully degassed and filtered through 0.22 μm membranes. The flow cell and sapphire optical surface were carefully cleaned and prepped according to Reichert protocols. The sensor chip used was a 90% PEG-terminated alkanethiol/10% carboxyl-terminated alkanethiol self-assembled monolayer (Reichert #13206061).

Procedures

1. Surface preparation: The chip was primed by treatment with 0.1% SDS (1 min), 50 m*M* glycine–HCl, pH 2.2 (10 min), 2 *M* NaCl (10 min), and 10 m*M* NaOH (10 min). All steps were performed at a flow rate of 100 μL min^{-1}. The surface was regenerated with running buffer (20 m*M* HEPES, pH 7.5 with 20 μ*M* Na_2EDTA; 5 min), 2 *M* NaCl/10 m*M* NaOH (5 min), and three injections of deionized (18 *M*Ω) H_2O, all at 50 μ*M* min^{-1} flow. Avidin was coupled to the monolayer surface using EDC/NHS reagents with published techniques (Fischer, 2010). Briefly, the surface was activated with a freshly prepared mixture of 0.22 *M* EDC and 0.20 *M* NHS (18 min). Streptavidin was coupled until the surface was coated with 1500–3000 μRIU protein, usually about 20 min, and the remaining reactive sites were capped using treatment with ethanolamine (18 min). The surface was then rinsed thoroughly with deionized H_2O.

2. The surface was thoroughly rinsed with running buffer. Samples of 375 μL of circa 1 μ*M* 5′-biotin-labeled wild type and G+1A mutant loop A were flowed over the right (downstream) and left (upstream) channels, respectively, resulting in typical densities of 100–125 μRIU on each channel.
3. Immediately prior to analysis, the surface was equilibrated in interaction buffer (running buffer plus 250 μ*M* $Co(NH_3)_6^{3+}$) until a level baseline was established.
4. On the same surface, a series of concentrations of the mobile component were injected in random order with multiple repeats at each concentration and periodic injections of interaction buffer to facilitate the double-referencing procedure upon data workup (Myszka, 1999). The series contained several concentrations both above and below the estimated K_d. The appropriate association time, dissociation time, and regeneration protocol must be empirically determined for each system. When possible, mass transport effects are minimized by using a sufficiently fast flow rate that the measured kinetics are independent of that flow rate. For the hairpin ribozyme system in 250 μ*M* $Co(NH_3)_6^{3+}$, slow interaction kinetics dictated relatively long, 15 min association and 10 min dissociation times at a flow rate of 10 μL min^{-1}. Regeneration was achieved by 10 min injections of 1 *M* NaCl and deionized H_2O, after which reequilibration in interaction buffer yielded a return to the original baseline.
5. Data workup was performed in Scrubber 2 (BioLogic; supplied with the Reichert instrument). For each injection, the data trace consists of the difference between the experimental and reference channels, with further subtraction of blank-injection traces to implement the double-referencing protocol introduced by Myszka (1999). In the case of the hairpin ribozyme, the difference between wild-type loop A and a point mutation (G+1A) known to be inactive for docking results in a signal corresponding to authentic docking events only. Individual injections are aligned, referenced, and subjected to a global fit procedure in which the association and dissociation curves for all concentrations of mobile component are simultaneously described by a single set of parameters (on-rate k_{on}, off-rate k_{off}, any necessary bulk shift corrections, and a global *y*-axis scaling, with K_d reported as an additional but non-independent parameter). Error limits are determined via repeats of the complete injection series on freshly prepared avidin surfaces. Representative results are shown in Fig. 17.4.

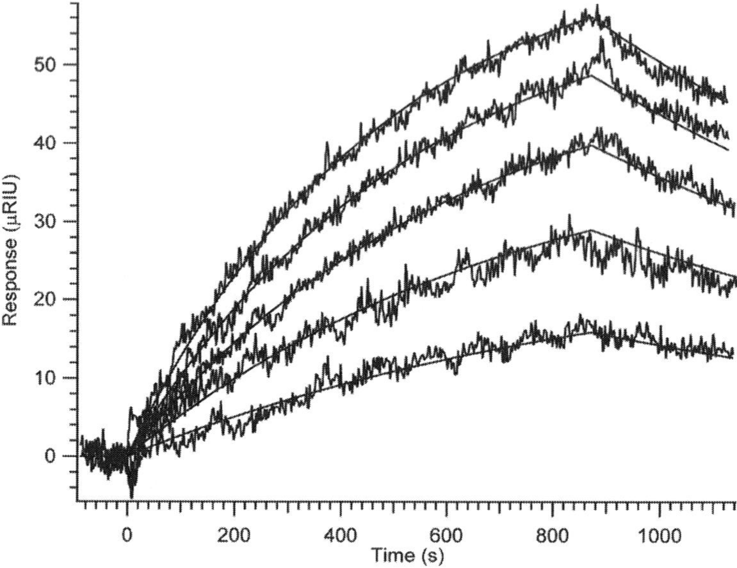

Figure 17.4 Representative data for SPR analysis of hairpin ribozyme domain docking at 250 µ*M* $Co(NH_3)_6^{3+}$ (Sumita et al., 2013). Data shown are differences between a channel with immobilized wild-type loop A and one with immobilized G+1A mutant and thus reflect only specific docking interactions. Lines are global fits to a 1:1 interaction model incorporating bulk refractive-index shift. Concentrations of loop B used: 150, 300, 450, 600, and 750 n*M*. *Reprinted from Sumita et al. (2013) by permission of Taylor & Francis, LLC, www.tandfonline.com.*

3.3. Thermodynamics of RNA assembly: ITC

Uniquely among biophysical techniques, ITC provides the measurement of $\Delta H°$, $\Delta S°$, and $\Delta G°$ (K_d), along with the binding stoichiometry if appropriate, in a single experiment at one temperature. Repetition of the experiment at a series of temperatures thus allows any dependence of the enthalpy change on temperature to be determined, and thus the robust detection of heat capacity changes upon binding via

$$\Delta C_p = \left(\frac{\partial \Delta H°}{\partial T}\right)_p \tag{17.13}$$

Physically, the ITC experiment consists of a fixed concentration of a single component in a thermally isolated sample cell, with the second component present in an injection syringe that is titrated into the cell a few microliters at a time. ITC has been used extensively to analyze the binding of small-molecule ligands to riboswitches (Gilbert & Batey, 2009; Gilbert, Stoddard, Wise, & Batey, 2006) and RNA–RNA assembly processes in ribozymes (Bouchard & Legault, 2014; Sumita et al., 2013) and the tetraloop–tetraloop receptor complex (Vander Meulen & Butcher, 2012; Vander Meulen et al., 2008). Representative results from the latter system published by the Butcher lab are shown in Fig. 17.5 to indicate the type of data obtained. In the hairpin ribozyme system, despite extensive efforts over several years, we were unable to obtain robust and reproducible ITC signals of docking. SPR analysis quickly established the reason for this, as the unusually slow kinetics of docking (Sumita et al., 2013) meant that the heat given off in any single ITC injection was spread out over a time longer than the typical response of the instrument and was very difficult to

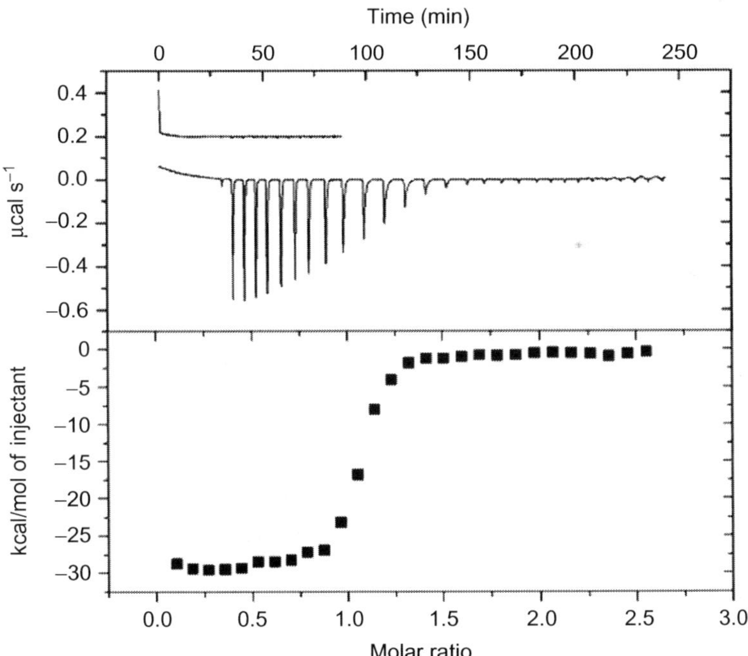

Figure 17.5 Representative ITC data for a bivalent RNA tetraloop–tetraloop receptor interaction by Vander Meulen et al. (2008). Upper panel: ITC traces of the binding reaction (lower trace) and of a reference titration of the injector component into a sample cell filled with buffer alone (upper trace; arbitrarily offset vertically for visibility). Lower panel: integrated and normalized heat for each injection. Experimental details are given in the original work. *Reprinted from Vander Meulen et al. (2008) with permission from Elsevier.*

distinguish from baseline. In this case, therefore, the availability of two complementary biophysical assays allowed not just the one that gave the best results in the system to be used, but provided a robust explanation for a poor set of results, rigorously identified a variety of artifacts in the system, and prevented the waste of further time and material.

3.3.1 ITC experimental design

As discussed above, ITC detects a binding *event*, via the evolution or uptake of heat, rather than distinguishing the bound versus unbound *state* of one component. Thus, it is inherently performed under stoichiometric-titration conditions, since the heat given off by a binding event that occurs to only a tiny fraction of ligands, such as under trace-receptor conditions, would be far too small to detect. Thus, substantial amounts of both components are needed.

With modern instrumentation, the performance of the ITC experiment itself is straightforward and highly automated. The entire data workup routine is conveniently implemented in a set of macros for the Origin software provided by the instrument manufacturer. The success or failure of an ITC experiment, in our experience, is almost wholly determined by the method and quality of sample preparation, and we therefore concentrate here on two critical aspects of experimental design and setup. Many aspects of ITC data acquisition and analysis for RNA have been discussed in detail (Salim & Feig, 2009) and Chapters 5, 10, and 18 by the Wedekind and Ferré-D'Amaré groups discuss applications to RNA–ligand interactions. The appropriate choice of experimental conditions is conventionally represented by a single unitless quantity, known as the *c*-value, which completely determines the shape of the ITC binding curve:

$$c = n \times C_{\mathrm{T}} \times K_{\mathrm{a}} \tag{17.14}$$

where n is the binding stoichiometry, C_{T} is the initial concentration of macromolecule in the sample cell, and K_{a} is the association constant for binding (equal to the reciprocal of the more commonly reported K_{d}). Figure 17.6, reproduced from the operating manual for the MicroCal VP-ITC (Malvern Instruments), shows the data curves expected for various *c*-values. These curves represent fits of the integrals of heat given off or taken up upon each repeated injection, as shown in Fig. 17.5, to the general binding equation (17.7) with appropriate corrections for sample dilution and other effects. The resemblance of these curves to the general simulations in Fig. 17.2C for stoichiometric titrations in derivative format is readily

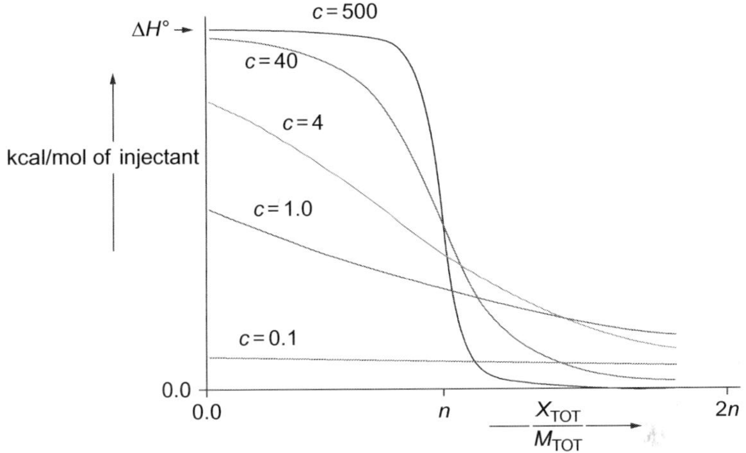

Figure 17.6 *ITC experimental design using the c-value.* ITC data fitting to datasets of the type shown in the lower panel of Fig. 17.5 as scaled by ΔH° (*y*-axis) and stoichiometry *n* (*x*-axis). The best simultaneous determination of *n*, K_d, and ΔH° is obtained at intermediate values of *c*, which for a given interaction is completely determined by the initial molecular concentration in the sample cell C_T (see main text). *Reproduced from Section 3 of the User Manual for the MicroCal VP-ITC instrument and reprinted with permission from Malvern Instruments, Ltd., www.malvern.com.*

apparent. Figure 17.6 implies that, at too low of a *c*-value (i.e., too low a concentration in the cell), the observed signals will be small and the change across the titration will be weak, making the analysis difficult. In the less common case of extremely high *c*-value, the data form a step function corresponding to complete binding at the equivalence point, making determination of ΔH° and the stoichiometry straightforward but essentially ruling out determination of K_d and therefore ΔS°. The usual rule of thumb is thus to design the experiment such that *c* is between roughly 20 and 100. If no estimate of K_d is available, some empirical adjustment of C_T will be necessary to achieve optimal data.

These considerations place strong limitations on the applicability of ITC, since they imply that both molecules must be highly soluble and available in relatively large quantities, especially for relatively weak binding. For example, in the popular MicroCal VP-ITC instrument (Malvern Instruments), the sample cell has a working volume of 1.3–1.4 mL, with approximately 2.0 mL typically prepared to allow for the volume of the cell access tube and losses in filling, whereas approximately 300 μL of the syringe component is injected over the course of a titration, with about 450 μL of material necessary to ensure that the syringe can be filled completely without the introduction of any bubbles. For a 1 μ*M* dissociation constant and 1:1 stoichiometry, a *c*-value of 50 would require a cell concentration of 50 μ*M*, which is beyond the aggregation limit of many biomolecules. Furthermore, these values would require the preparation of 100 nmol of material, which is often a prohibitive amount. Because the titration must run to at least two times stoichiometry and the working volume of the injector is much smaller than the cell, the injector component must be roughly an order of magnitude more soluble yet, and it must be available in somewhat greater quantities. Finally, it should be noted that if the experimental question is, say, the effect of various mutations, the above considerations apply to the weakest binding mutant for which data are to be analyzed quantitatively. More recently-introduced ITC instruments have smaller cell volumes and consequently somewhat lower (although still substantial) sample requirements, but at some cost in sensitivity and experimental convenience.

3.3.2 Experimental design: Buffer match

ITC is conventionally described as a "label-free" methodology, and indeed, its application requires neither a specifically detectable molecular component (fluorophore, radiolabel, etc.) nor immobilization on a surface, making it a potentially highly general technique. The good news about ITC, in a word, is that it detects everything (or, at least, every process that is not fortuitously isenthalpic). However, the bad news about ITC is also that it detects everything, including a large number of background events of considerably lesser interest if rigorous sample preparation and appropriate controls are not implemented. If the two binding components are not carefully prepared to the same solution conditions, intense background signals may occur that dominate the data. For example, a relatively minor mismatch in free monovalent ion concentration can yield what amounts to a measurement of the heat of dilution of, say, NaCl, with the process of interest a small and probably undetectable perturbation. In cases where one component requires an organic cosolvent, detergent solubilization, reconstitution in vesicles, or some other specialized condition, these effects may completely abrogate the utility of the technique. For RNA assembly studies, because of the ion depletion effects discussed above, the possibility of buffer mismatch makes careful dialysis of all macromolecular components completely *de rigueur* for trustworthy analysis. In short, titration calorimetry is a remarkable technique that uniquely permits the measurement of subtle thermodynamic properties for noncovalent interactions in robust fashion at a single temperature. The technology has equally important limits, however, notably the need for large amounts of sample for all but the tightest binding systems and the requirement for essentially perfect buffer match between the two binding components.

4. CONCLUDING REMARKS

This chapter has concentrated on those aspects of the RNA-folding problem that have been reduced to the study of intermolecular interactions, especially the formation of RNA–RNA tertiary interfaces. In this case, numerous powerful technologies with their roots in physical and biophysical chemistry can be brought to bear, allowing the dissection of a single interface, such as the loop–loop docking in the hairpin ribozyme in our group's own work, in terms of ion dependence, kinetics, detailed thermodynamics, and potentially other parameters accessible via, for example, NMR spectroscopy combined with differential isotope labeling. These experiments are in many cases quite demanding in terms of the amount and purity of material used and of careful design of the actual experiments. We have attempted to outline some of the pitfalls and keys to success of the corresponding approaches. Whichever techniques are applicable in a given system, the insights obtainable from the use of several biophysical approaches in combination with more conventional biochemical, kinetic, and structural biology methods, as well as the contemporary calculational technologies discussed in a companion volume of this Series, represent important synergies over the narrow application of a single technique or class of related techniques. The unraveling of the various aspects of the complex RNA-folding problem will demand nothing less.

ACKNOWLEDGMENTS

The authors are grateful to Kristine R. Julien for assistance in protocol development in the early stages of this work and to Michigan State University's Office of the Vice President for Research and Graduate Studies, the NIH (GM069742 to C. G. H.) and the NSF (MCB-1413356 to C. G. H.) for research support. The Reichert SPR instrument in the Hoogstraten lab was purchased with an ARRA supplement to NIH GM069742.

REFERENCES

Baldwin, R. L. (2007). Energetics of protein folding. *Journal of Molecular Biology*, *371*, 283–301.

Bloomfield, V. A., Crothers, D. M., & Tinoco, I., Jr. (2000). *Nucleic acids: Structures, properties, and functions*. Sausalito, CA: University Science Books.

Bouchard, P., & Legault, P. (2014). A remarkably stable kissing-loop interaction defines substrate recognition by the Neurospora Varkud Satellite ribozyme. *RNA*, *20*, 1451–1464.

Cate, J. H., Gooding, A. R., Podell, E., Zhou, K., Golden, B. L., Kundrot, C. E., et al. (1996). Crystal structure of a group I ribozyme domain: Principles of RNA packing. *Science*, *273*, 1678–1685.

Conn, G. L., & Draper, D. E. (1998). RNA structure. *Current Opinion in Structural Biology*, *8*, 278–285.

Correll, C. C., Freeborn, B., Moore, P. B., & Steitz, T. A. (1997). Metals, motifs, and recognition in the crystal structure of a 5S RNA domain. *Cell*, *91*, 705–712.

DeAbreu, D. M., Olive, J. E., & Collins, R. A. (2011). Additional roles of a peripheral loop-loop interaction in the Neurospora VS ribozyme. *Nucleic Acids Research*, *39*, 6223–6228.

Delano, W. L. (2002). *The PyMOL molecular graphics system*. Palo Alto, CA: DeLano Scientific.

Doherty, E. A., & Doudna, J. A. (2001). Ribozyme structures and mechanisms. *Annual Review of Biophysics and Biomolecular Structure*, *30*, 457–475.

Draper, D. E. (2004). A guide to ions and RNA structure. *RNA*, *10*, 335–343.

Draper, D. E. (2008). RNA folding: Thermodynamic and molecular descriptions of the roles of ions. *Biophysical Journal*, *95*, 5489–5495.

Esteban, J. A., Banerjee, A. R., & Burke, J. M. (1997). Kinetic mechanism of the hairpin ribozyme. *The Journal of Biological Chemistry*, *272*, 13629–13639.

Fedor, M. J. (2000). Structure and function of the hairpin ribozyme. *Journal of Molecular Biology*, *297*, 269–291.

Ferré-D'Amaré, A. R., & Doudna, J. A. (1999). RNA folds: Insights from recent crystal structures. *Annual Review of Biophysics and Biomolecular Structure*, *28*, 57–73.

Ferré-D'Amaré, A. R., & Rupert, P. B. (2002). The hairpin ribozyme: From crystal structure to function. *Biochemical Society Transactions*, *30*, 1105–1109.

Fischer, M. J. (2010). Amine coupling through EDC/NHS: A practical approach. *Methods in Molecular Biology*, *627*, 55–73.

Garst, A. D., Edwards, A. L., & Batey, R. T. (2011). Riboswitches: Structures and mechanisms. *Cold Spring Harbor Perspectives in Biology*, *3*, a003533.

Gilbert, S. D., & Batey, R. T. (2009). Monitoring RNA-ligand interactions using isothermal titration calorimetry. *Methods in Molecular Biology*, *540*, 97–114.

Gilbert, S. D., Stoddard, C. D., Wise, S. J., & Batey, R. T. (2006). Thermodynamic and kinetic characterization of ligand binding to the purine riboswitch aptamer domain. *Journal of Molecular Biology*, *359*, 754–768.

Gray, D. M., Hung, S. H., & Johnson, K. H. (1995). Absorption and circular dichroism spectroscopy of nucleic acid duplexes and triplexes. *Methods in Enzymology*, *246*, 19–34.

Hampel, A., & Cowan, J. A. (1997). A unique mechanism for RNA catalysis: The role of metal cofactors in hairpin ribozyme cleavage. *Chemistry & Biology*, *4*, 513–517.

Hoogstraten, C. G., & Sumita, M. (2007). Structure-function relationships in RNA and RNP enzymes: Recent advances. *Biopolymers*, *87*, 317–328.

Johnson, J. E., Jr., & Hoogstraten, C. G. (2008). Extensive backbone dynamics in the GCAA RNA tetraloop analyzed using 13C NMR spin relaxation and specific isotope labeling. *Journal of the American Chemical Society*, *130*, 16757–16769.

Kim, I., McKenna, S. A., Viani, P. E., & Puglisi, J. D. (2007). Rapid purification of RNAs using fast performance liquid chromatography (FPLC). *RNA*, *13*, 289–294.

Leroy, J.-L., & Guéron, M. (1977). Electrostatic effects in divalent ion binding to tRNA. *Biopolymers*, *16*, 2429–2446.

Leulliot, N., & Varani, G. (2001). Current topics in RNA-protein recognition: Control of specificity and biological function through induced fit and conformational capture. *Biochemistry*, *40*, 7947–7956.

Lilley, D. M. (2011). Catalysis by the nucleolytic ribozymes. *Biochemical Society Transactions, 39*, 641–646.
Loladze, V. V., Ermolenko, D. N., & Makhatadze, G. I. (2001). Heat capacity changes upon burial of polar and nonpolar groups in proteins. *Protein Science: A Publication of the Protein Society, 10*, 1343–1352.
Mikulecky, P. J., Takach, J. C., & Feig, A. L. (2004). Entropy-driven folding of an RNA helical junction: An isothermal titration calorimetric analysis of the hammerhead ribozyme. *Biochemistry, 43*, 5870–5881.
Misra, V. K., & Draper, D. E. (1998). On the role of magnesium ions in RNA stability. *Biopolymers, 48*, 113–135.
Misra, V. K., & Draper, D. E. (1999). The interpretation of Mg(2+) binding isotherms for nucleic acids using Poisson-Boltzmann theory. *Journal of Molecular Biology, 294*, 1135–1147.
Misra, V. K., Shiman, R., & Draper, D. E. (2003). A thermodynamic framework for the magnesium-dependent folding of RNA. *Biopolymers, 69*, 118–136.
Myszka, D. G. (1999). Improving biosensor analysis. *Journal of Molecular Recognition, 12*, 279–284.
Myszka, D. G., He, X., Dembo, M., Morton, T. A., & Goldstein, B. (1998). Extending the range of rate constants available from BIACORE: Interpreting mass transport-influenced binding data. *Biophysical Journal, 75*, 583–594.
Narlikar, G. J., & Herschlag, D. (1997). Mechanistic aspects of enzymatic catalysis: Lessons from comparison of RNA and protein enzymes. *Annual Review of Biochemistry, 66*, 19–59.
Nesbitt, S., Hegg, L. A., & Fedor, M. J. (1997). An unusual pH-independent and metal-ion-independent mechanism for hairpin ribozyme catalysis. *Chemistry & Biology, 4*, 619–630.
Noller, H. F. (2005). RNA structure: Reading the ribosome. *Science, 309*, 1508–1514.
Rich, R. L., & Myszka, D. G. (2010). Grading the commercial optical biosensor literature—Class of 2008: 'The Mighty Binders'. *Journal of Molecular Recognition, 23*, 1–64.
Rich, R. L., & Myszka, D. G. (2011). Survey of the 2009 commercial optical biosensor literature. *Journal of Molecular Recognition, 24*, 892–914.
Rupert, P. B., & Ferré-D'Amaré, A. R. (2001). Crystal structure of a hairpin ribozyme-inhibitor complex with implications for catalysis. *Nature, 410*, 780–786.
Rupert, P. B., Massey, A. P., Sigurdsson, S. T., & Ferré-D'Amaré, A. R. (2002). Transition state stabilization by a catalytic RNA. *Science, 298*, 1421–1424.
Saenger, W. (1984). *Principles of nucleic acid structure*. New York: Springer-Verlag.
Salim, N. N., & Feig, A. L. (2009). Isothermal titration calorimetry of RNA. *Methods, 47*, 198–205.
Salter, J., Krucinska, J., Alam, S., Grum-Tokars, V., & Wedekind, J. E. (2006). Water in the active site of an all-RNA hairpin ribozyme and effects of Gua8 base variants on the geometry of phosphoryl transfer. *Biochemistry, 45*, 686–700.
Schuck, P. (1997). Use of surface plasmon resonance to probe the equilibrium and dynamic aspects of interactions between biological macromolecules. *Annual Review of Biophysics and Biomolecular Structure, 26*, 541–566.
Spolar, R. S., & Record, M. T., Jr. (1994). Coupling of local folding to site-specific binding of proteins to DNA. *Science, 263*, 777–784.
Sumita, M., White, N. A., Julien, K. R., & Hoogstraten, C. G. (2013). Intermolecular domain docking in the hairpin ribozyme: Metal dependence, binding kinetics, and catalysis. *RNA Biology, 10*, 425–435.
Tinoco, I., Jr., Sauer, K., Wang, J. C., & Puglisi, J. D. (2002). *Physical chemistry: Principles and applications in biological sciences* (4th ed.). Upper Saddle River, NJ: Prentice-Hall.
Treiber, D. K., & Williamson, J. R. (2001). Beyond kinetic traps in RNA folding. *Current Opinion in Structural Biology, 11*, 309–314.

Vander Meulen, K. A., & Butcher, S. E. (2012). Characterization of the kinetic and thermodynamic landscape of RNA folding using a novel application of isothermal titration calorimetry. *Nucleic Acids Research, 40*, 2140–2151.

Vander Meulen, K. A., Davis, J. H., Foster, T. R., Record, M. T., Jr., & Butcher, S. E. (2008). Thermodynamics and folding pathway of tetraloop receptor-mediated RNA helical packing. *Journal of Molecular Biology, 384*, 702–717.

Vicens, Q., & Cech, T. R. (2006). Atomic level architecture of group I introns revealed. *Trends in Biochemical Sciences, 31*, 41–51.

Walter, N. G., & Burke, J. M. (1998). The hairpin ribozyme: Structure, assembly and catalysis. *Current Opinion in Chemical Biology, 2*, 24–30.

Williamson, J. R. (2000). Induced fit in RNA-protein recognition. *Nature Structural Biology*, 7, 834–837.

Wilson, T. J., Nahas, M., Ha, T., & Lilley, D. M. (2005). Folding and catalysis of the hairpin ribozyme. *Biochemical Society Transactions, 33*, 461–465.

Wu, M., & Tinoco, I., Jr. (1998). RNA folding causes secondary structure rearrangement. *Proceedings of the National Academy of Sciences of the United States of America, 95*, 11555–11560.

Young, K. J., Gill, F., & Grasby, J. A. (1997). Metal ions play a passive role in the hairpin ribozyme catalysed reaction. *Nucleic Acids Research, 25*, 3760–3766.

PART V

Ligand Interactions

CHAPTER EIGHTEEN

ITC Analysis of Ligand Binding to $PreQ_1$ Riboswitches

Joseph A. Liberman*[,†], Jarrod T. Bogue*[,†], Jermaine L. Jenkins*[,†,‡], Mohammad Salim*[,†], Joseph E. Wedekind*[,†,‡,1]

*Department of Biochemistry & Biophysics, University of Rochester School of Medicine and Dentistry, Rochester, New York, USA

[†]Center for RNA Biology, University of Rochester School of Medicine and Dentistry, Rochester, New York, USA

[‡]Structural Biology & Biophysics Facility, University of Rochester School of Medicine and Dentistry, Rochester, New York, USA

[1]Corresponding author: e-mail address: joseph.wedekind@rochester.edu

Contents

Abstract

Riboswitches regulate genes by binding to small-molecule effectors. Isothermal titration calorimetry (ITC) provides a label-free method to quantify the equilibrium association constant, K_A, of a riboswitch interaction with its cognate ligand. In addition to probing affinity and specific chemical contributions that contribute to binding, ITC can be used to measure the thermodynamic parameters of an interaction (ΔG, ΔH, and ΔS), in addition to the binding stoichiometry (N). Here, we describe methods developed to measure the binding affinity of various $preQ_1$ riboswitch classes for the pyrrolopyrimidine effector, $preQ_1$. Example isotherms are provided along with a review of various $preQ_1$-II (class 2) riboswitch mutants that were interrogated by ITC to quantify the

Methods in Enzymology, Volume 549
ISSN 0076-6879
http://dx.doi.org/10.1016/B978-0-12-801122-5.00018-0

energetic contributions of specific interactions visualized in the crystal structure. Protocols for ITC are provided in sufficient detail that the reader can reproduce experiments independently, or develop derivative methods suitable for analyzing novel riboswitch–ligand binding interactions.

1. INTRODUCTION

Pre-queuosine$_1$ (7-aminomethyl-7-deazaguanine or preQ$_1$) is a secondary metabolite synthesized in five steps exclusively in bacteria starting from GTP (McCarty & Bandarian, 2012). The resulting pyrrolopyrimidine is incorporated subsequently by a transglycosylation reaction that replaces guanine within tRNA(GUN) anticodons (Fig. 18.1). In two additional enzymatic steps, the hypermodified base queuosine (Q) is produced, which enhances the ability of tRNAs(QUN) to read degenerate codons (Meier, Suter, Grosjean, Keith, & Kubli, 1985). The Q modification is widely distributed in bacteria and animals (Yokoyama et al., 1979), although the latter organisms must obtain the Q-base (queuine) from dietary sources or gut flora (Farkas, 1980). PreQ$_1$ appears to be unique to the bacterial metabolome and has been found to be the ligand that affects three phylogenetically distinct riboswitches known as preQ$_1$-I (class 1), preQ$_1$-II (class 2), and preQ$_1$-III (class 3) (McCown, Liang, Weinberg, & Breaker, 2014; Meyer, Roth, Chervin, Garcia, & Breaker, 2008; Roth et al., 2007; Weinberg et al., 2007). This discovery provides a rich system to explore how evolutionarily diverse riboswitches recognize a common ligand, as well as the chemical diversity of effector binding that is accessible through the tertiary folding of RNA.

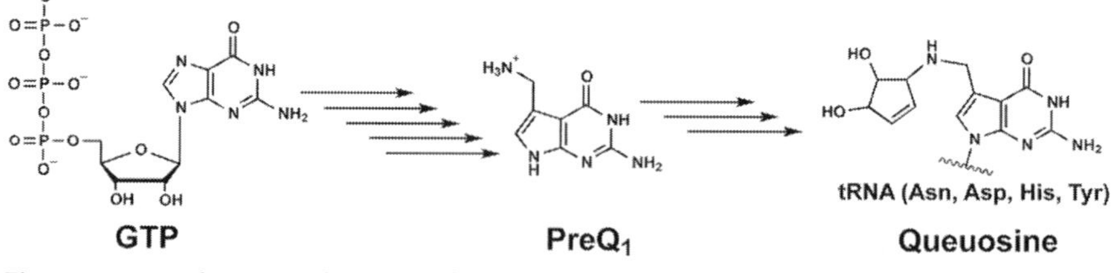

Figure 18.1 Schematic diagram of prequeuosine$_1$ (preQ$_1$) as an intermediate on the queuosine (Q) biosynthetic pathway. For a review of known enzymes, see McCarty and Bandarian (2012). Although animals must obtain Q from dietary sources or gut flora, bacteria can produce Q by *de novo* synthesis, which proceeds via preQ$_1$ formation (reviewed in Iwata-Reuyl, 2003). The procedures herein were developed to probe the binding affinity of various bacterial preQ$_1$ riboswitches for the preQ$_1$ molecule.

Significant progress has been made on crystallographic structure determinations and biophysical analysis of $preQ_1$-I and $preQ_1$-II riboswitches involved in translational regulation (Jenkins, Krucinska, McCarty, Bandarian, & Wedekind, 2011; Liberman, Salim, Krucinska, & Wedekind, 2013; Spitale, Torelli, Krucinska, Bandarian, & Wedekind, 2009; Suddala et al., 2013). Isothermal titration calorimetry (ITC) has been an integral part of this work since it provides a basis to quantify the $preQ_1$ binding affinity of various riboswitch constructs generated for crystallization trials. Moreover, once a structure has been solved, ITC can be used to corroborate the observed mode of binding of the riboswitch to $preQ_1$. To illustrate, ITC was used to measure the equilibrium dissociation constant (K_D) for $preQ_1$ binding to the wild-type $preQ_1$-II riboswitch from *Lactobacillus rhamnosus*. The resulting K_D of 17.9 ± 0.6 n*M* was then compared to individual nucleobase mutants that were designed to disrupt hydrogen bond interactions to the ligand based on the wild type structure (Liberman et al., 2013). Figure 18.2 shows the binding site and the relative changes in affinity (K_{rel}) for the respective mutants. Whereas the C30U mutant produced a K_{rel} of ~46 ($K_D = 0.81 \pm 0.12$ μ*M*), the U41C mutant produced a K_{rel} of ~90 ($K_D = 1.60 \pm 0.02$ μ*M*). The $\Delta\Delta G$ values for C30U and U41C were 2.2 and 2.6 kcal mol^{-1}, respectively, which is consistent energetically with the loss of two or three hydrogen bonds to $preQ_1$. The results not only

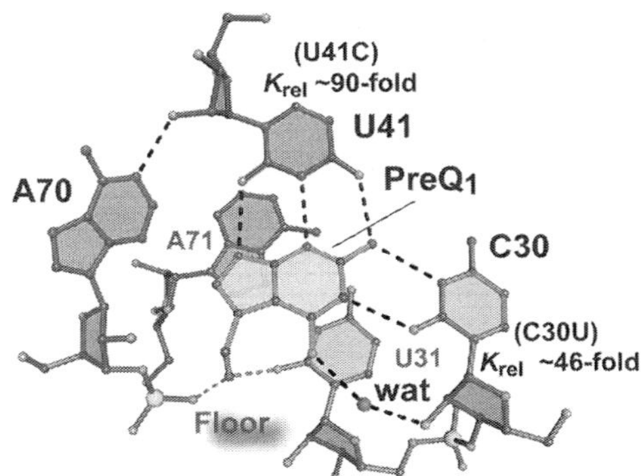

Figure 18.2 Mode of chemical recognition of $preQ_1$ by the $preQ_1$-II riboswitch as described in Liberman et al. (2013). Putative hydrogen bonds are shown as broken lines. The "floor" of the binding pocket is formed by a Hoogsteen base pair between A71·U31. The affinity of the C30U and U41C mutants for $preQ_1$ were probed by ITC and compared to wild type. K_{rel} is defined as the mutant K_D divided by the wild-type K_D. In this manner, ITC was used to quantify changes in free energy resulting from binding site mutations, which appear to corroborate the mode of ligand binding based on crystallographic observations. (See the color plate.)

support the structural observations but also suggest that each mutant causes the loss of one additional hydrogen bond between the mutated base and the ligand compared to what might be expected if the respective nucleobase mutations were isostructural with the wild-type binding pocket. Overall, this work demonstrates the general utility of ITC to interrogate the binding of ligands to riboswitches, which can be analyzed in terms of K_D and relative energetic differences. Moreover, ITC can provide insight into the cellular concentration of the metabolite required to elicit a biological response. For a broader description of ITC theory, methodology, and a general analysis of ITC-based RNA–ligand interactions, the reader is referred to several recent reviews that include analyses of RNA binding to small ligands, ions, sugars, and large molecules such as tRNA (Gilbert & Batey, 2009; Salim & Feig, 2009; Sokoloski & Bevilacqua, 2012; Zhang, Jones, & Ferre-D'Amare, 2014).

1.1. Information content in an ITC experiment

Since the purpose of this chapter is to provide a practical context for ITC, as well as pedagogical instruction for those new to the field, it is worth mentioning some of the significant properties of ITC. Some knowledge is assumed with respect to the instrument design and the reader's understanding of free energy relationships in the context of ligand binding by biological macromolecules. Importantly, ITC is a label-free method to characterize the binding thermodynamics for any (usually two) interacting molecules—such as a riboswitch and its small-molecule effector. The approach allows characterization of the thermodynamic parameters including: enthalpy (ΔH), entropy (ΔS), and free energy (ΔG) changes that result from binding interactions in solution. In addition, the heat capacity change (ΔC_p) can be measured by acquiring ΔH values at various temperatures. Such information can be useful to evaluate buried surface area, as described (Salter, Lippa, Belashov, & Wedekind, 2012). Herein, we are interested in the integrated heats of injection that directly report on the ΔH of a binding event, and allow us to extract K_A from a curve fit of the integrated heat as a function of the ligand-to-receptor molar ratio; notably, the reciprocal of K_A equals K_D. We can extract other parameters by the knowledge that $\Delta G = -RT\ln K_A$ and $\Delta G = \Delta H - T\Delta S$, where R is the gas constant and T is the absolute temperature. Although the approach can require relatively large amounts of material compared to other methods—usually mg to μg—ITC is operative over a wide range of affinities between 1 mM and 1 nM.

In practice, this range is governed by the solubility of the respective ligand and receptor. Low-affinity interactions may require very high concentrations, whereas very high-affinity interactions can have large heat changes that preclude efforts aimed at monitoring the true titration. In practice, the amount of material consumed by a single ITC experiment on a wild-type $preQ_1$ riboswitch is more than that required for a single, 96-condition crystallization screen, assuming in the latter case that one uses a liquid-handling robot at an RNA concentration of 5 mg mL^{-1}. Although the inexperienced crystallographer may be conflicted about experimental priorities, the ability to evaluate quantitatively an RNA crystallization construct for ligand binding is key to a successful crystallization outcome, because the information garnered will be necessary for designing screens that ensure a ligand concentration that is greater than the K_D measured for binding the target RNA.

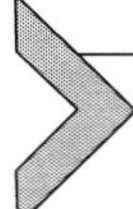

2. EXPERIMENTAL PROCEDURES FOR ITC

2.1. Assessing the feasibility of ITC experiments

Before initiating any ITC experiment, it is important to evaluate the feasibility of the proposed experiment. Apart from having sufficient amounts of pure receptor and ligand, it is helpful to know approximately how tightly the molecules will interact based on an educated guess. It is not unusual for riboswitches to bind their ligands with apparent K_D values ranging from 2 n*M* to 2 μ*M* (Jenkins et al., 2011; Rieder, Kreutz, & Micura, 2010). There are examples of exceptionally tight binding riboswitches that bind with affinities of 100 p*M* (Nelson et al., 2013) to 10 p*M* (Smith et al., 2009). Such high affinity can create difficulties for ITC experiments. Problems arise during data analysis because the isotherms resulting from these experiments will produce binding curves that are not well populated with measurements at the sigmoidal inflection point, thus yielding a curve that conforms to a step function. The resulting K_A values from fitting such curves are not reliable and should only be considered as an estimate of affinity, although the ΔH and stoichiometry values can still be reliable. When the affinity is too high, it is possible to weaken the interaction by changing the temperature, lowering the Mg^{2+} concentration, increasing monovalent ion concentration, or by the addition of a mild denaturant. Isotherms with an ideal curve will appear sigmoidal with an initial flat slope, an obvious inflection point within a gradually sloping region, and a clear point of saturation with a zero slope. Populating the curve with data points is especially important near the inflection region since these observations are needed to accurately fit the K_A.

Perhaps, the best way to establish whether an ITC experiment will yield a suitable isotherm is by calculation of the unitless parameter c, which dictates the shape of the curve. The c value is the product of the equilibrium association constant, K_A, the receptor concentration in the cell at the start of the experiment, [M], and the stoichiometry of ligand binding to the receptor, N:

$$c = K_A \cdot [\mathrm{M}] \cdot N$$

Large c values approaching 500 will result in a very steep inflection point, which precludes a proper fit of K_A. Here, values for N and ΔH can still be measured reliably, which is an important consideration if one is assessing heat capacity (ΔC_p) changes (Salter et al., 2012; Sokoloski, Dombrowski, & Bevilacqua, 2012). By contrast, c values less than 10 are associated with flat, featureless curves that do not possess the information necessary to extract K_A, N, or ΔH accurately. Such isotherms are characteristic of weak binding interactions. In practice, one should strive for the range $20 < c < 100$ (Myszka et al., 2003). Because we typically have an estimate of the K_A (i.e., $1/K_D$) for the interaction in question, we can calculate the $[M]$ value for our desired receptor concentration in the sample cell at the onset of ITC analysis. A good starting point for the ligand concentration in the syringe is ~10 times the value of [M], which is necessary to ensure saturation. For example, the experimental preparation for titration of preQ$_1$ into a new class 1 type III preQ$_1$ riboswitch from *Enterobacter cloacae* (McCown et al., 2014) was based on the knowledge of K_D (7.3 ± 2.3 nM and N value of 0.98) measured previously by ITC for a related class 1 type I preQ$_1$ riboswitch (Suddala et al., 2013). As such, the [M] value was estimated to be 0.75 μM assuming a c value of 100. In practice, the type III riboswitch was observed to possess 10-fold poorer affinity ($K_D = 72$ nM) than the type I molecule. Following the initial ITC experiment, the [M] value was adjusted accordingly to a value of 8.7 μM with an appropriate increase in the starting ligand concentration in the syringe. This resulted in a c value of 112 (Fig. 18.3). If such estimations are not possible based on known K_D values, the reader is encouraged—as with all aspects of the ITC experiment—to read the manufacturer's guidelines for the appropriate starting concentration of the receptor and ligand, which is described in the operation manual.

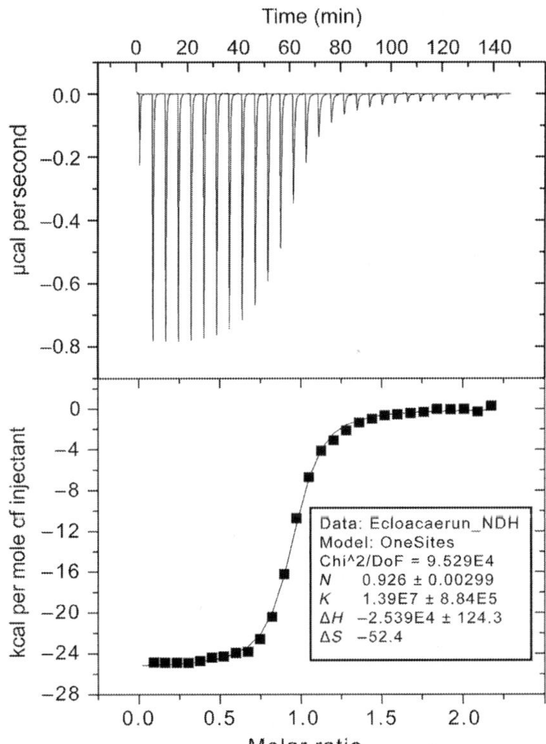

Figure 18.3 Representative isotherm and binding-model fit for a $preQ_1$-I type III riboswitch. ITC was performed at 25 °C in 0.0060 *M* $MgCl_2$, 0.10 *M* NaCl, and 0.050 *M* Na-HEPES (pH 7.0). The wild-type riboswitch was in the cell at 8.74 μ*M*; $preQ_1$ was in the syringe at a concentration that was [10-fold] higher than the RNA. The *c* value is 112. The parameters obtained from a "One Set of Sites" binding model are shown as text in the inset DeltaH window. The values are the binding stoichiometry, $N = 0.93$; $K_A = 1.39 \times 10^7\ M^{-1}$; $\Delta H = -25.39 \times 10^3$ cal mol^{-1}; and $\Delta S = -52.4$ cal(mol K)$^{-1}$.

2.2. Instrumentation, materials, and solutions for ITC

The following instruments or equivalents are required for ITC analysis: a ThermoVac (GE Life Sciences) system for solution degassing, a Nanodrop UV Spectrophotometer (Thermo Scientific), Pipettes (Gilson Inc.), an aluminum heating block with a thermostatic controller, and a VP-ITC Calorimeter (GE Life Sciences). Other ITC calorimeters in common use include the iTC-200 (GE Life Sciences), and the Nano ITC (TA Instruments).

The following stock solutions and supplies are required: RNA resuspension buffer: 0.10 *M* NaCl, and 0.050 *M* Na-HEPES (pH 7.0); dialysis buffer: 0.10 *M* NaCl, 0.050 *M* Na-HEPES (pH 7.0), and 0.0060 *M*

$MgCl_2$; a stock solution of 1.0 *M* $MgCl_2$; 3.5 K MWCO Slide-A-Lyzer (Thermo Scientific) for dialysis. All stocks should be sterile filtered through 0.2 μm cellulose acetate filters (Millipore) and prepared under ribonuclease-free conditions. UV-irradiated water with a resistivity of $\geq$18 MΩ should be used from a Barnstead NanoPure™ UV/UF system or equivalent.

2.3. RNA and ligand preparation

The RNA sample must be of the highest possible purity, such as that used for crystallization. Effective purification methods include HPLC (Spitale et al., 2009; Spitale & Wedekind, 2009; Wedekind & McKay, 2000) or denaturing polyacrylamide gel electrophoresis (Liberman et al., 2013; Lippa et al., 2012). At all stages of the experiment, the user is advised to avoid ribonuclease contamination by using approaches described in the aforementioned purification methods. Riboswitches can be folded for ITC using any protocol that has been found to be effective. For the $preQ_1$-I and $preQ_1$-II riboswitches, we developed a procedure that entails heating the RNA in a neutral pH buffer containing sodium chloride, followed by addition of magnesium chloride while the RNA is still hot with subsequent slow cooling to room temperature (details below). The volumes described herein are for the VP-ITC instrument, and should be revised accordingly if a different instrument will be used that possesses a smaller cell.

A key consideration is that the buffer used to suspend the sample in the reference cell (i.e., the receptor) is matched perfectly to that of the titrant (i.e., ligand) in the syringe. This is achieved for the small-molecule ligands that typically interact with the riboswitches by dissolving the ligand, or diluting a concentrated stock, in the same buffer used for dialysis of the riboswitch. It is essential that the ligand is of the highest purity possible; in our investigations $preQ_1$ was produced by chemical synthesis as described (Liberman et al., 2013).

The step-by-step protocol for sample preparation is as follows. First dissolve the lyophilized RNA stored at −80 °C in 2.2 mL of RNA "resuspension buffer" described in Section 2.2. Use the *c*-value calculation above to determine the starting receptor concentration, [M]. Ensure that a sufficient amount of RNA is resuspended to perform all the required titrations; at this point it is more desirable to have a slightly higher concentration than one that is too low since it is easier to dilute the sample than to concentrate it. Heat the RNA solution to 65 °C for 3 min in an aluminum heating block, then add sufficient volume from the $MgCl_2$ stock to give a final concentration of 0.0060 *M*. Return the sample to the heating block at 65 °C for 5 min. Remove the aluminum block from the heater and cool the hot RNA inside the block until it reaches room temperature. Load the RNA into 3.5 K molecular weight cutoff Slide-A-Lyzer for dialysis. Dialyze the RNA overnight against 4 L of dialysis buffer; 0.2 μm sterile filter and degas the used dialysis buffer using a vacuum-based filter bottle (Nalgene) and save it for later use. This step will help to preserve the buffer (see below), and will facilitate the removal of undesirable trapped gas that can evolve during the ITC experiment, leading to measurement artifacts. The concentration of the RNA recovered from the Slide-A-Lyzer should be determined by OD_{260} based on the calculated extinction coefficient; use the Beer–Lambert relationship. Dilute the RNA to the desired concentration using the 0.2 μm, vacuum filtered dialysis buffer above; reuse of the dialysis buffer ensures a precise solvent match, which is necessary to avoid heat-of-dilution artifacts during ITC. Although the minimum sample volume required to fill the ITC cell is 1.8 mL, a volume of 2.2 mL of RNA per experiment is recommended to ensure proper loading with no air bubbles. Dissolve the ligand in the same dialysis buffer used for the RNA dialysis (above) to ensure a proper buffer match. The ligand concentration should be ~10-fold higher than the RNA concentration. A ligand volume of 600 μL will allow facile loading of the VP-ITC syringe. Degas both the RNA and ligand solutions, respectively, for 10 min using the ThermoVac set at a temperature 1–2 °C lower than the temperature at which ITC will be conducted. Take care to avoid boiling the sample; reduce the vacuum if bubbling is observed.

2.4. The isothermal titration calorimetry experiment

Prior to conducting ITC experiments, the water in the reference cell should be changed according to the manufacturer's instructions. Additionally, after each ITC experiment the sample cell and syringe should be flushed thoroughly with at least 150 mL of degassed dialysis buffer. At the end of each day of ITC use, the sample cell and syringe should be cleaned according to the manufacturer's instructions. During all procedures, it is especially important to avoid placing mechanical stress on the tip of the loading syringe. A bent tip can cause measurement artifacts and usually necessitates a costly replacement. Review the manufacturer's instructions for proper handling and storage.

The following protocol describes how to initiate ITC measurements to analyze ligand interactions with a riboswitch, and can be adapted readily to the analysis of other RNA-small molecule complexes. First, flush the sample cell with 300 mL of 0.2 μm filtered, degassed dialysis buffer retrieved from the RNA dialysis experiment. Set the temperature of the sample cell; values of 25 or 30 °C work well for initial experiments. Notably, the VP-ITC has a temperature range of 2–80 °C but we have not been able to collect useful data higher than 60 °C due to baseline fluctuations (Suddala et al., 2013). Next, adjust the instrument settings for the VP-ITC. The reference power is set to 15 μcal s^{-1}, the mixing speed should be 300 rpm, and the feedback mode/gain is set to "high." The time allocated between injections is a critical parameter. If an injection begins before the prior injection has returned fully to baseline, the measured peak magnitudes will be inaccurate. A spacing of 300 s is a safe starting point that can be increased or decreased as necessary in subsequent experimental runs. The injection volume and duration rarely need to be changed from defaults of 10 μL and 20 s. The first injection is rarely accurate, so the initial injection volume is usually 3 μL to avoid wasting sample; this data point is discarded later in fitting of the binding model. In the computer interface, enter the concentration of RNA [M] (receptor) in the cell, and ligand in the syringe; accurate values are essential for successful analysis. Importantly, the concentration of [M] or ligand can be revised *a posteriori* if an erroneous value was entered at the onset of the experiment. Load the RNA into the cell and the ligand into the syringe following the manufacturer's instructions. Perform the purge/refill procedure three times to remove air bubbles that may be in the syringe. Carefully place the syringe into the cell and start the run. As a heuristic, one should strive for an average integrated heat of ≥5 μcal evolved (or absorbed) per injection for the first two-thirds of the injections. The sensitivity of the VP-ITC is about 0.1 μcal.

2.5. ITC data analysis

Here, we present a rudimentary protocol for data analysis using the VP-ITC associated software Origin® 7. Treatment of isotherms to arrive at high-precision measurements is described elsewhere (Keller et al., 2012). First, load the ITC data by clicking the "Read Data . . ." box under "ITC Main Control" on left side of the screen, and select the appropriate .itc file (in this protocol, the data file will be referred to as "YourFile.itc"). Under the "Window" pull-down menu, select the item that has the same name as your .itc file. Under the column labeled "NDH" select the last three cells. These are the heats of injection of the ligand into buffer in units of kcal mol^{-1}, provided that saturation was achieved. As such, these heats must be subtracted from all injections. Right click on the highlighted cells and select "statistics on column" in the menu that opens, then copy the value from the cell labeled "Mean(Y)." Return to the original window that was opened after selecting your ITC data. Ensure that no cells are selected. Open the "Math" pull-down menu and select "Simple Math...." In the "Available Data" column select "YourFile_NDH" and click the top double arrow. The box next to Y1 will now show "YourFile_NDH." In the "operator" box enter a minus sign (−). In box Y2, paste the value copied above for the Mean(Y) value, representing the last three heats of injection; press "OK." The heat of dilution of the ligand has now been removed from all data points. Open the "Window" pull-down menu and select "DeltaH." The first data point from the 3 μL injection must be removed. Select the "Remove Bad Data..." box from under "Data Control," click on the first data point, and press the "return" key.

Now we will consider the binding model for the interaction between the ligand and riboswitch. There are several possibilities, but for $preQ_1$ riboswitches the most likely model will be the "One Set of Sites..." model, which assumes all sites are equivalent. To fit this binding model, click "One Set of Sites..." under "Model Fitting" on the left side of the screen. In the window that opens, click the box that says "100 Iter."; the chi-squared value denoted "chi^2" should appear in a new dialogue box, and is an indicator of agreement between the experimental data and the binding-model curve. After the first 100 iterations of least-squares fitting, there should be an updated display that shows improvement in the agreement between the data and the trend curve, in addition to a reduced "chi^2" value. Since our goal here is to reach convergence, continue to click the "100 Iter." button until no reduction is observed in chi^2, then select the "Done" box. As a result of fitting, a new box will appear next to the isotherm. This "DeltaH" box will contain the associated binding including: the stoichiometry of binding "N," the equilibrium K_A in units of M^{-1}, designated "K," "ΔH" in calories per mole, and "ΔS" in units of calories per mole per degree, which is calculated from ΔH and K after fitting. A publication-quality figure, such as Fig. 18.3, can be generated by selecting "Final Figure" in the "ITC" pull-down menu. Be sure to adjust the spacing between units so that the values on the ordinate and abscissa do not overlap.

In our experiments so far, we have observed 1:1 binding stoichiometry between $preQ_1$ riboswitches and their ligands. As stated, the choice of binding model is "One Set of Sites" but other stoichiometries and binding models are feasible. These should be considered if the visual fit between the binding model and the data is poor. Importantly, the best choice model should improve visibly relative to other choices (also chi^2 should be reduced significantly) and the binding model should be biologically sensible.

2.6. Manual adjustment of the baseline

Origin® 7 will fit automatically the baseline of ITC data. As stated above, a sufficiently long spacing is required between injections to ensure that the baseline does not overlap with neighboring injections, which is a prerequisite for proper fitting. However, there are occasionally instances where the automatic baseline does not fit the data despite adequate separation. Here, manual intervention is recommended to obtain the best results. To conduct manual fitting, enter the "Window" pull-down, and select "RawITC." Click "Adjust Integrations..." under ITC Main Control on the left side of the screen. Click the first peak. The "≪" and "≫" arrows will advance to the previous or next peak. Here, only one peak is considered at a time. The area between the two blue lines is integrated to determine the heat of injection (Fig. 18.4A). The blue lines can be dragged to alter the window considered for integration (for example, to remove a bubble spike in the baseline region); the red line is the baseline. To adjust the baseline, click the "Baseline" button. A series of black boxes appear on the red baseline that can be dragged up or down to account for irregularities. After adjustments have been made to the baseline, click the "Integrate" button before advancing to the next peak. The integrated area will be filled with vertical black lines (Fig. 18.4B). Following manual adjustment and integration of each individual peak, click "Quit." The results should show a better fit of the data to the curve (Fig. 18.4C vs. D), which can have a subtle effect on the K_A, N, and ΔH, as well as other parameters. Notably, both the flatness of the baseline and the apparent separation between injections have improved in Fig. 18.4D. To gauge the productiveness of one's baseline adjustment efforts, the reader is encouraged to experiment with a subset of injections to ascertain whether the newly integrated data fits better to the model based on the criteria described above.

2.7. Publishing ITC results and representative analysis

As in any experimental approach, it is preferable to conduct multiple measurements to improve accuracy and generate error estimates. In this respect ITC is no exception, although the quantity of sample required often

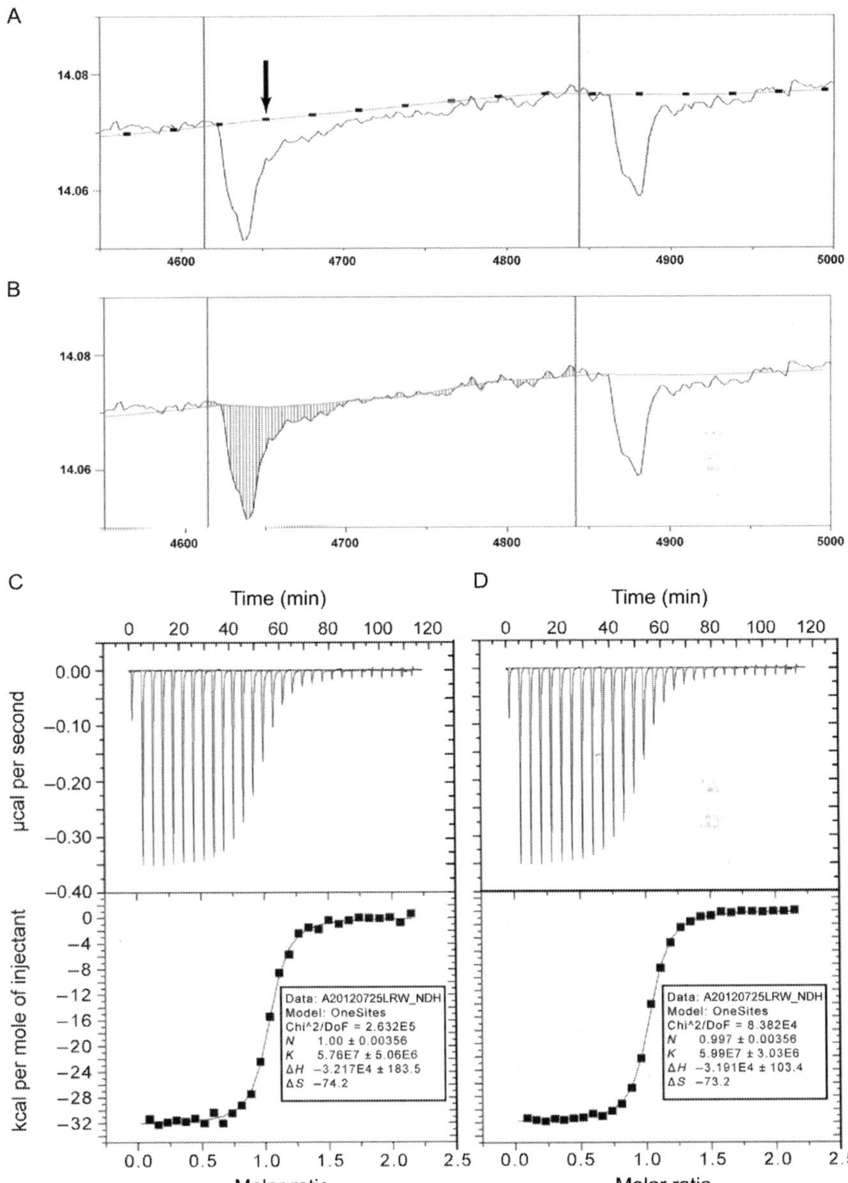

Figure 18.4 Diagrams comparing automated and manual baseline corrections of ITC data. (A) Example of a baseline that was determined automatically. The baseline shown in red (light gray in print version) (horizontal line) is too high but can be adjusted by dragging the rectangular boxes (e.g., see arrow). The area between the two blue (dark gray in print version) lines is integrated to determine the heat of a specific injection; these lines can be maneuvered to change the amount of the peak that is integrated

(Continued)

precludes numerous measurements due to the costly nature of producing the RNA and the associated ligand, such as preQ_1. At a minimum, at least two ITC experiments should be conducted per sample (preferably more), and the results should be presented as an arithmetic mean in textual, or tabular form, depending on the number of samples. The reported values should include: K_A or K_D, N, ΔH, $-T\Delta S$, and ΔG along with the associated standard deviation of each. It is recommended to always include a representative isotherm and the associated curve fit to demonstrate the quality of the data. A plot of kcal per mole of injectant versus molar ratio should be sigmoid with a visually discernable fit of the binding model to the experimental data points (Fig. 18.3). The *c* value for each experiment should also be provided, or sufficient information to calculate the *c* value and to reproduce the experiments. In cases where the *c* value is high (approaching 500), the K_A or K_D results should be described with a disclaimer that the values cannot be accurately determined, which may be the only alternative if the use of a lower [M] results in poor heats. Alternatively, a high *c* may be acceptable if the goal is to measure ΔH as part of a heat capacity measurement (Salter et al., 2012). The reader is also encouraged to explore various temperatures to improve the quality of isotherms and values of *c*. For a practical example of how systematic changes to the ITC conditions can influence binding isotherms, see Sokoloski et al. (2012). Altering a riboswitch's ligand can provide information on the chemical groups involved in aptamer binding (Gilbert, Mediatore, & Batey, 2006). Conversely, mutations of a specific aptamer can provide insight into conserved groups required for ligand recognition (Gilbert, Love, Edwards, & Batey, 2007; Gilbert, Stoddard, Wise, & Batey, 2006). For a summary of thermodynamic parameters obtained by ITC for various riboswitches, see Zhang et al. (2014).

ACKNOWLEDGMENTS

We thank Clara Kielkopf for helpful discussions and Philip Bevilacqua for critical comments on this chapter. This research was funded by NIH grants RR026501 and GM063162 to

Figure 18.4—Cont'd and the associated baseline. (B) Baseline from data in panel (A) after manual adjustment and integration (red; light gray in print version). The area filled by the vertical black lines has been integrated; note, the units of the abscissa in panels (A) and (B) are time (s). (C) ITC experiment from panel (A) in which the baseline was derived by automated selection in Origin® 7. (D) Isotherm resulting from manual baseline adjustment, shown in part as panel (B). Although the thermodynamic parameters and stoichiometry of binding have not significantly changed, the fit of the binding model is improved based on visual inspection, and the improved chi-squared value.

J. E. W. J. A. L. was funded in part by NIH T32 training grant GM068411, and an E.H. Hooker graduate fellowship. J. T. B was funded in part by a fellowship from NIH/ NCATS CTSA award TL1 TR000096 to the University of Rochester. Portions of this research were carried out at the Stanford Synchrotron Radiation Lightsource (SSRL, Menlo Park CA), a Directorate of SLAC National Accelerator Laboratory and an Office of Science User Facility operated for the U.S. DOE by Stanford University. The SSRL Structural Molecular Biology Program is supported by the DOE and NIH grants GM103393 and RR001209.

REFERENCES

Farkas, W. R. (1980). Effect of diet on the queuosine family of tRNAs of germ-free mice. *The Journal of Biological Chemistry*, *255*, 6832–6835.

Gilbert, S. D., & Batey, R. T. (2009). Monitoring RNA-ligand interactions using isothermal titration calorimetry. *Methods in Molecular Biology*, *540*, 97–114.

Gilbert, S. D., Love, C. E., Edwards, A. L., & Batey, R. T. (2007). Mutational analysis of the purine riboswitch aptamer domain. *Biochemistry*, *46*, 13297–13309.

Gilbert, S. D., Mediatore, S. J., & Batey, R. T. (2006). Modified pyrimidines specifically bind the purine riboswitch. *Journal of the American Chemical Society*, *128*, 14214–14215.

Gilbert, S. D., Stoddard, C. D., Wise, S. J., & Batey, R. T. (2006). Thermodynamic and kinetic characterization of ligand binding to the purine riboswitch aptamer domain. *Journal of Molecular Biology*, *359*, 754–768.

Iwata-Reuyl, D. (2003). Biosynthesis of the 7-deazaguanosine hypermodified nucleosides of transfer RNA. *Bioorganic Chemistry*, *31*, 24–43.

Jenkins, J. L., Krucinska, J., McCarty, R. M., Bandarian, V., & Wedekind, J. E. (2011). Comparison of a $preQ_1$ riboswitch aptamer in metabolite-bound and free states with implications for gene regulation. *The Journal of Biological Chemistry*, *286*, 24626–24637.

Keller, S., Vargas, C., Zhao, H., Piszczek, G., Brautigam, C. A., & Schuck, P. (2012). High-precision isothermal titration calorimetry with automated peak-shape analysis. *Analytical Chemistry*, *84*, 5066–5073.

Liberman, J. A., Salim, M., Krucinska, J., & Wedekind, J. E. (2013). Structure of a class II $preQ_1$ riboswitch reveals ligand recognition by a new fold. *Nature Chemical Biology*, *9*, 353–355.

Lippa, G. M., Liberman, J. A., Jenkins, J. L., Krucinska, J., Salim, M., & Wedekind, J. E. (2012). Crystallographic analysis of small ribozymes and riboswitches. *Methods in Molecular Biology*, *848*, 159–184.

McCarty, R. M., & Bandarian, V. (2012). Biosynthesis of pyrrolopyrimidines. *Bioorganic Chemistry*, *43*, 15–25.

McCown, P. J., Liang, J. J., Weinberg, Z., & Breaker, R. R. (2014). Structural, functional, and taxonomic diversity of three $preq_1$ riboswitch classes. *Chemistry & Biology*, *21*, 880–889.

Meier, F., Suter, B., Grosjean, H., Keith, G., & Kubli, E. (1985). Queuosine modification of the wobble base in tRNAHis influences 'in vivo' decoding properties. *The EMBO Journal*, *4*, 823–827.

Meyer, M. M., Roth, A., Chervin, S. M., Garcia, G. A., & Breaker, R. R. (2008). Confirmation of a second natural $preQ_1$ aptamer class in Streptococcaceae bacteria. *RNA*, *14*, 685–695.

Myszka, D. G., Abdiche, Y. N., Arisaka, F., Byron, O., Eisenstein, E., Hensley, P., et al. (2003). The ABRF-MIRG'02 study: Assembly state, thermodynamic, and kinetic analysis of an enzyme/inhibitor interaction. *Journal of Biomolecular Techniques*, *14*, 247–269.

Nelson, J. W., Sudarsan, N., Furukawa, K., Weinberg, Z., Wang, J. X., & Breaker, R. R. (2013). Riboswitches in eubacteria sense the second messenger c-di-AMP. *Nature Chemical Biology, 9*, 834–839.

Rieder, U., Kreutz, C., & Micura, R. (2010). Folding of a transcriptionally acting preQ$_1$ riboswitch. *Proceedings of the National Academy of Sciences of the United States of America, 107*, 10804–10809.

Roth, A., Winkler, W. C., Regulski, E. E., Lee, B. W., Lim, J., Jona, I., et al. (2007). A riboswitch selective for the queuosine precursor preQ$_1$ contains an unusually small aptamer domain. *Nature Structural & Molecular Biology, 14*, 308–317.

Salim, N. N., & Feig, A. L. (2009). Isothermal titration calorimetry of RNA. *Methods, 47*, 198–205.

Salter, J. D., Lippa, G. M., Belashov, I. A., & Wedekind, J. E. (2012). Core-binding factor beta increases the affinity between human Cullin 5 and HIV-1 Vif within an E3 ligase complex. *Biochemistry, 51*, 8702–8704.

Smith, K. D., Lipchock, S. V., Ames, T. D., Wang, J., Breaker, R. R., & Strobel, S. A. (2009). Structural basis of ligand binding by a c-di-GMP riboswitch. *Nature Structural & Molecular Biology, 16*, 1218–1223.

Sokoloski, J. E., & Bevilacqua, P. C. (2012). Analysis of RNA folding and ligand binding by conventional and high-throughput calorimetry. *Methods in Molecular Biology, 905*, 145–174.

Sokoloski, J. E., Dombrowski, S. E., & Bevilacqua, P. C. (2012). Thermodynamics of ligand binding to a heterogeneous RNA population in the malachite green aptamer. *Biochemistry, 51*, 565–572.

Spitale, R. C., Torelli, A. T., Krucinska, J., Bandarian, V., & Wedekind, J. E. (2009). The structural basis for recognition of the PreQ$_0$ metabolite by an unusually small riboswitch aptamer domain. *The Journal of Biological Chemistry, 284*, 11012–11016.

Spitale, R. C., & Wedekind, J. E. (2009). Exploring ribozyme conformational changes with X-ray crystallography. *Methods, 49*, 87–100.

Suddala, K. C., Rinaldi, A. J., Feng, J., Mustoe, A. M., Eichhorn, C. D., Liberman, J. A., et al. (2013). Single transcriptional and translational preQ$_1$ riboswitches adopt similar pre-folded ensembles that follow distinct folding pathways into the same ligand-bound structure. *Nucleic Acids Research, 41*, 10462–10475.

Wedekind, J. E., & McKay, D. B. (2000). Purification, crystallization, and X-ray diffraction analysis of small ribozymes. *Methods in Enzymology, 317*, 149–168.

Weinberg, Z., Barrick, J. E., Yao, Z., Roth, A., Kim, J. N., Gore, J., et al. (2007). Identification of 22 candidate structured RNAs in bacteria using the CMfinder comparative genomics pipeline. *Nucleic Acids Research, 35*, 4809–4819.

Yokoyama, S., Miyazawa, T., Iitaka, Y., Yamaizumi, Z., Kasai, H., & Nishimura, S. (1979). Three-dimensional structure of hyper-modified nucleoside Q located in the wobbling position of tRNA. *Nature, 282*, 107–109.

Zhang, J., Jones, C. P., & Ferre-D'Amare, A. R. (2014). Global analysis of riboswitches by small-angle X-ray scattering and calorimetry. *Biochimica et Biophysica Acta* in press, http://dx.doi.org/10.1016/j.bbagrm.2014.04.014.

CHAPTER NINETEEN

Facile Characterization of Aptamer Kinetic and Equilibrium Binding Properties Using Surface Plasmon Resonance

Andrew L. Chang*, Maureen McKeague†, Christina D. Smolke†,[1]

*Department of Chemistry, Stanford University, Stanford, California, USA

†Department of Bioengineering, Stanford University, Stanford, California, USA

[1]Corresponding author: e-mail address: csmolke@stanford.edu

Contents

Abstract

Nucleic acid aptamers find widespread use as targeting and sensing agents in nature and biotechnology. Their ability to bind an extensive range of molecular targets, including small molecules, proteins, and ions, with high affinity and specificity enables their use in diverse diagnostic, therapeutic, imaging, and gene-regulatory applications. Here, we describe methods for characterizing aptamer kinetic and equilibrium binding properties using a surface plasmon resonance-based platform. This aptamer characterization platform is broadly useful for studying aptamer–ligand interactions, comparing aptamer properties, screening functional aptamers during *in vitro* selection processes, and prototyping aptamers for integration into nucleic acid devices.

Methods in Enzymology, Volume 549
ISSN 0076-6879
http://dx.doi.org/10.1016/B978-0-12-801122-5.00019-2

1. INTRODUCTION

Characterization of aptamer binding properties is critical for studying aptamer molecular recognition and integrating the sensing capabilities encoded within aptamers into diverse applications. Understanding key binding properties of aptamers, including affinity, kinetics, specificity, ion dependence, and buffer sensitivity, supports aptamer design and use. Here, we describe a surface plasmon resonance (SPR)-based aptamer characterization platform for measurement of aptamer binding properties. Importantly, this characterization strategy is (a) label-free, avoiding alteration of the aptamer–ligand binding interaction or limiting its use to ligands with specific intrinsic properties or functional groups suitable for labeling; (b) scalable, allowing testing of a wide range of binding conditions and aptamer–ligand pairs; (c) sensitive, enabling binding measurement of low molecular weight, small-molecule ligands; (d) capable of measuring both binding kinetics and equilibrium affinities; and (e) able to monitor and adjust for the presence of nonspecific interactions (Chang, McKeague, Liang, & Smolke, 2014).

SPR is an optical detection method that has gained widespread use for characterizing biomolecular interactions. One interacting partner is immobilized onto the sensor surface and its binding interactions to other molecules in solution is measured (Fig. 19.1). Changes in mass concentration

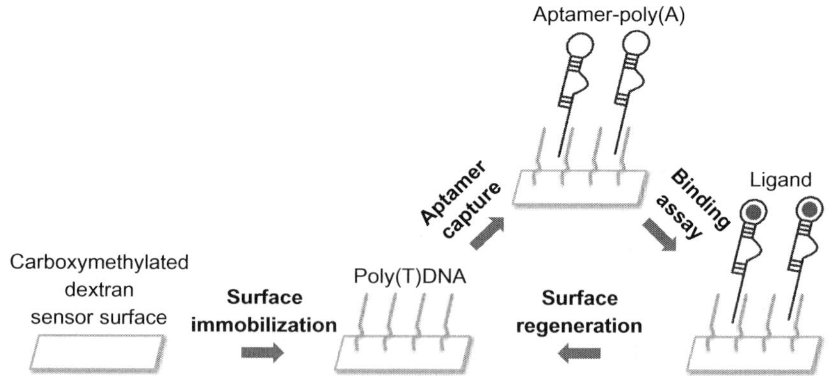

Figure 19.1 Surface plasmon resonance platform for aptamer binding characterization. A poly(T) DNA linker is covalently immobilized onto the sensor surface, enabling capture of aptamers with a corresponding poly(A) tail and real-time monitoring of ligand binding. Regeneration of the sensor surface removes aptamer and ligand and allows reuse of the surface for other aptamers, ligands, or conditions. *Adapted, with permission, from Chang et al. (2014).*

near the sensor surface result in a change in refractive index and are recorded in real time as sensorgrams in resonance units (RU). In our SPR setup, we covalently immobilize a 24-mer poly(T) single-stranded DNA linker directly to a high-capacity, carboxymethylated dextran sensor chip. Hybridization-based capture of an aptamer with a corresponding poly(A) tail onto the sensor surface allows monitoring of its interaction with ligands of interest flowed over the sensor surface. Surface regeneration enables testing of different aptamer–ligand pairs and binding conditions using the same sensor chip, without exposing either binding partner to repeated regeneration cycles. The sensor surface includes two flow cells: a reference flow cell (FC1) and a sample flow cell (FC2). Both flow cells contain the immobilized DNA linker, but the reference flow cell lacks the aptamer and is used to monitor the presence of nonspecific interactions between the sensor surface and ligand.

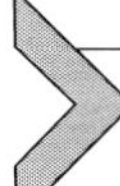

2. MATERIALS

2.1. Instrumentation

1. Biacore X100 instrument (GE Healthcare, Uppsala, Sweden) or similar SPR instrument. If using other systems, check for system compatibility of reagents and materials listed.
2. Biacore X100 Evaluation Software version 2.0 (GE Healthcare) or similar data processing software.

2.2. Sensor surface immobilization

1. CM5 sensor chip (GE Healthcare): CM5 chips contain a carboxymethylated dextran matrix on a gold surface and provide high binding capacity and surface stability, increasing the observable signal, particularly from small-molecule binding, and allowing many cycles to be run on a single chip.
2. DNA linker strand (5′-AmMC6-TTTTTTTTTTTTTTTTTTTTT TTT) with an amino-modified 6-carbon linker on the 5′-end (Integrated DNA Technologies, Coralville, IA): The DNA linker is covalently immobilized to the sensor surface through an amide bond-forming reaction at its 5′-end.
3. 10× HBS-N (100 m*M* HEPES, 1.5 *M* NaCl, pH 7.4) (GE Healthcare): Dilute with RNase-free water to 1× concentration and supplement with $MgCl_2$ as appropriate for binding buffers.

4. 1-Ethyl-3-(3-dimethylaminopropyl) carbodiimide (EDC) (GE Healthcare): Activates sensor surface in coupling reaction with DNA linker, in conjunction with *N*-hydroxysuccinimide (NHS).
5. NHS (GE Healthcare): Activates sensor surface in coupling reaction with DNA linker, in conjunction with EDC.
6. Hexadecyltrimethylammonium bromide (CTAB > 99%) (Sigma-Aldrich, St. Louis, MO): Surfactant that forms positively charged micelles in buffer and carries the negatively charged DNA linker to the negatively charged sensor surface during pre-concentration assays and immobilization reactions.
7. 1 *M* HEPES buffer (Sigma-Aldrich): Dilute to a concentration of 10 m*M* HEPES in RNase-free water and use to dissolve the CTAB and DNA linker.
8. 1 *M* ethanolamine, pH 8.5 (GE Healthcare): Blocks excess EDC/NHS-activated carboxylate groups on sensor surface after immobilization reaction.
9. 50 m*M* NaOH (GE Healthcare): Dilute in RNase-free water as appropriate for regeneration solutions.
10. NaCl (Sigma-Aldrich): Dissolve and dilute as appropriate for regeneration solutions.
11. RNase-free water: Purchase (Life Technologies, Carlsbad, CA) or prepare using diethyl pyrocarbonate (DEPC) (Sigma-Aldrich). DEPC inactivates RNase enzymes in water. Treat water with 0.1% vol/vol DEPC for at least 2 h at 37 °C and autoclave to inactivate excess DEPC.
12. 0.2 μm pore size membrane filter (Pall Corporation, Port Washington, NY, or Nalgene, Thermo Scientific, Waltham, MA): Use to filter all buffers and ligand solutions before use.

2.3. Aptamer binding assay

1. DNA template oligonucleotides: Design and synthesize as described in Section 4.1.
2. Biacore-fwd primer (5′-TTCTAATACGACTCACTATAGGG), where the T7 promoter sequence is underlined: For PCR amplification or run-off transcription of aptamer DNA templates.
3. Biacore-rev primer (5′-TTTTTTTTTTTTTTTTTTTTTTTTGGGG): For PCR amplification of RNA aptamer DNA templates.

4. PCR purification spin columns: Can also use ethanol precipitation to remove unincorporated nucleotides and DNA polymerase from PCR amplification products.
5. MEGAshortscript T7 kit (Life Technologies) or similar RNA transcription kit: The MEGAshortscript kit is designed for high yield transcription of RNAs between 20–500 nucleotides.
6. RNA Clean & Concentrator kit (Zymo Research, Irvine, CA) or similar RNA purification kit: For removal of unincorporated nucleotides and RNA polymerase from *in vitro* transcription products.
7. 1 *M* $MgCl_2$ (Life Technologies): Dilute as appropriate for binding buffers.
8. TES buffer (10 m*M* Tris–HCl, pH 8, 1 m*M* EDTA, 0.1 *M* NaCl): Annealing buffer for run-off transcription.
9. Ligand (small molecule or protein): Serially dilute in binding buffer. For small-molecules ligands, dissolve in binding buffer and filter.

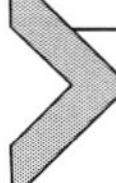

3. SENSOR SURFACE IMMOBILIZATION

3.1. Pre-concentration assay

Pre-concentration refers to the process of obtaining a high local concentration at the sensor surface. For the aptamer binding assay, higher immobilization levels of the DNA linker are preferred to maximize the sensor surface's capacity to capture aptamer and increase the observable response from ligand binding. Before running the immobilization reaction, it is helpful to run a pre-concentration assay to verify or optimize the levels of DNA linker that interact with the sensor surface and are available for immobilization. To overcome the electrostatic repulsion between the sensor surface and DNA linker, both of which are negatively charged under immobilization conditions, a positively charged carrier, here a CTAB micelle, can shield the negatively charged DNA linker and bring the DNA linker into contact with the sensor surface.

1. Dock a new CM5 sensor chip into the Biacore instrument. Prime instrument with 1 × HBS-N buffer to equilibrate the system.
2. Prepare three solutions: 0.6 m*M* CTAB in 10 m*M* HEPES buffer, 0.6 m*M* CTAB and 20 μ*M* DNA linker in 10 m*M* HEPES buffer, and 40 m*M* NaOH and 1 *M* NaCl in RNase-free water.

3. Inject solution of 0.6 m*M* CTAB in 10 m*M* HEPES for 3 min at a flow rate of 5 μL/min over a single flow cell (either reference flow cell FC1 or sample flow cell FC2).
4. Regenerate sensor surface with solution of 40 m*M* NaOH and 1 *M* NaCl in RNase-free water for 30 s.
5. Inject solution of 0.6 m*M* CTAB and 20 μ*M* DNA linker in 10 m*M* HEPES for 3 min at a flow rate of 5 μL/min over the same flow cell used in step 3.
6. Regenerate sensor surface as in step 4.

Typically, we observe a response of approximately 2500–3000 RU for CTAB and 8000–18,000 RU for the CTAB and DNA linker solution (Fig. 19.2). The solution containing both surfactant and DNA linker should produce a higher response. Pre-concentration parameters such as concentration of surfactant or DNA linker, ratio of surfactant to DNA linker, and surfactant used (e.g., CTAB or others such as dodecyltrimethylammonium bromide, DTAB) can be optimized to maximize the potential response observed. The pre-concentration assay is a measurement of interaction between the DNA linker and CTAB micelle with the sensor surface but not of the covalently conjugated DNA linker levels produced in the immobilization reaction. Therefore, optimized conditions for the pre-concentration assay are not necessary equivalent to optimized conditions for the immobilization reaction but can provide a useful starting point for optimization without irreversibly altering the sensor surface.

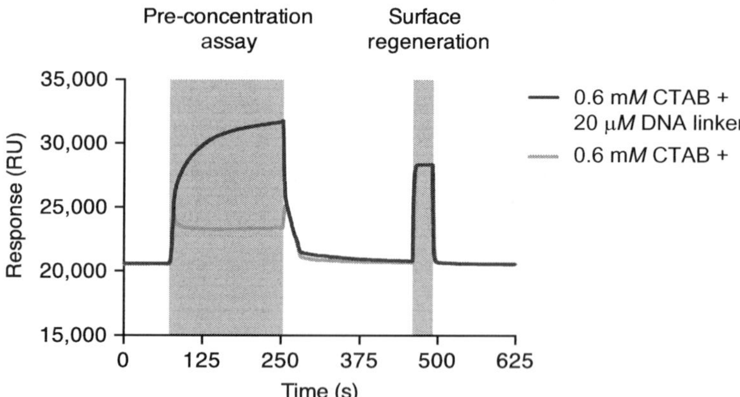

Figure 19.2 Pre-concentration assay for observing interactions with the sensor surface. CTAB forms micelles that carry the DNA linker to the sensor surface, resulting in a measurable binding response.

3.2. DNA linker immobilization

If sufficient interaction is observed in the pre-concentration assay, run an immobilization reaction to immobilize DNA linker covalently onto both flow cells.

1. Dock a new CM5 sensor chip, or a chip used for pre-concentration assays, into the Biacore instrument. Prime instrument with 1 × HBS-N buffer.
2. Activate carboxylate groups on chip surface with 1:1 volume ratio of 0.4 *M* EDC and 0.1 *M* NHS for 7 min at a flow rate of 10 μL/min. The activation reaction results in an observed increase in response of approximately 200 RU (Fig. 19.3).
3. Dilute DNA linker and CTAB in 10 m*M* HEPES buffer in a 1:30 molar ratio to a final concentration of 20 μ*M* and 0.6 m*M*, respectively, and inject over the activated surface for 10 min at a flow rate of 5 μL/min.
4. Block excess activated groups with an injection of 1 *M* ethanolamine, pH 8.5, for 7 min at a flow rate of 10 μL/min.
5. Perform immobilization reaction (steps 2–4) sequentially on both flow cells (FC1 and FC2). Immobilization reactions yield approximately 3700–4400 RU of the DNA strand covalently attached to the sensor surface, typically with less than 5% difference between the two flow cells.

As with the pre-concentration assay, the immobilization reaction can be optimized by testing different concentrations of surfactant or linker, ratios of surfactant to DNA linker, surfactant used, and duration or flow rate of

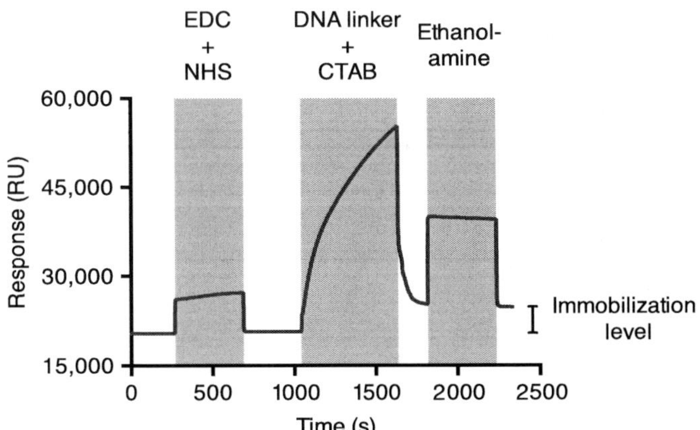

Figure 19.3 Sensor surface immobilization with poly(T) DNA linker. Amino-modified DNA linker is covalently coupled to carboxylate groups on the sensor surface through an amide bond-forming immobilization reaction.

injection. While solutions of EDC can be stored frozen, use freshly prepared solutions of EDC if low immobilization levels are observed. Immobilized sensor chips remain stable for at least 500 regeneration cycles, with a slight, steady decrease in aptamer capture levels over the lifetime of the chip.

4. CHARACTERIZATION OF APTAMER BINDING PROPERTIES

4.1. Aptamer design and preparation

Aptamers are designed with a 3′ 24-mer poly(A) sequence that is complementary to the DNA linker immobilized on the sensor surface. Check designed aptamer-poly(A) sequences for correct aptamer folding using a secondary structure prediction software, such as RNAstructure. For DNA aptamers, perform steps 1 and 5; for RNA aptamers, perform either step 2 or 3, followed by steps 4 and 5.

1. DNA aptamers can be synthesized and directly used in the binding assay. For instance, a DNA aptamer for adenosine triphosphate (Huizenga & Szostak, 1995) was designed and synthesized as 5′-CCTGGGGGAGTATTGCGGAGGAAGGAAAAAAAAAAAAAAAAAAAAAAAA (Chang et al., 2014), where the 24-mer poly(A) tail is underlined.
2. For RNA aptamers, synthesized DNA template sequences contain a 5′ T7 promoter sequence ending with three guanines for RNA transcription and include a short spacer of four cytosines between the aptamer and poly(A) sequences. For example, the DNA template of the RNA aptamer for theophylline (Jenison, Gill, Pardi, & Polisky, 1994) was designed and synthesized as 5′-**TTCTAATACGACTCACTATAGGG**AAGTGATACCAGCATCGTCTTGATGCCCTTGGCAGCACTTCCCCCAAAAAAAAAAAAAAAAAAAAAAAA, where the forward primer constant region is in bold, the reverse primer constant region is underlined, and the transcription start site is underlined twice. DNA template oligonucleotides for RNA aptamers must be transcribed into RNA before use. PCR amplify aptamer DNA template using forward and reverse primers, Biacore-fwd and Biacore-rev, respectively, and purify PCR products using a spin column or ethanol precipitation to remove unincorporated nucleotides and DNA polymerase. Check PCR products on an agarose gel for successful amplification and correct product length. Use the purified double-stranded PCR product as a template for preparing RNA aptamers by transcription.

3. As an alternative to step 2, prepare RNA aptamers by run-off transcription from a synthetic DNA template. For the same theophylline aptamer described in step 2, synthesize the complementary antisense strand, 5′-TTTTTTTTTTTTTTTTTTTTTTTTTGGGGGAAGTGCTGCCA AGGGCATCAAGACGATGCTGGTATCACTTCCCTATAGTG AGTCGTATTAGAA, and anneal with the Biacore-fwd primer, which hybridizes to the underlined sequence. Anneal the aptamer antisense strand with the promoter primer by resuspending both in TES buffer at a concentration of approximately 10–50 μ*M* in an equimolar ratio or slight excess of primer (e.g., 5:4 ratio of primer to antisense strand), denature at 95 °C for 5 min, and cool to room temperature directly before use. Use this partially double-stranded template for transcription, as only the promoter sequence of the template is required to be double-stranded for transcription. This strategy allows bypassing of the PCR amplification and purification steps in step 2. If low transcription yields are observed, design and synthesize longer, aptamer-specific primers that partially extend into the aptamer sequence to stabilize promoter hybridization during annealing.
4. Purify RNA transcription products. A minimum yield of 0.5 nmol is required to perform a new aptamer binding experiment (approximately 70 pmol per cycle). Purification methods that remove unincorporated nucleotides and RNA polymerase and enable buffer exchange are preferred and provide more consistent capture levels between experimental runs compared to not purifying the RNA. Resuspend purified RNA in RNase-free water or binding buffer. DNase treatment to remove DNA template prior to RNA purification is optional, as neither the fully double-stranded template from PCR amplification nor the partially double-stranded template from run-off transcription should bind to the sensor surface.
5. Resuspend aptamer in binding buffer, denature at 65 °C for 5 min, and cool to room temperature directly before use.

4.2. Startup cycles

Prior to running the aptamer binding assay, startup cycles stabilize the sensorgram baseline to produce more consistent runs. Typically, three to five startup cycles are run and include injection and regeneration steps. Either binding buffer or aptamer can be injected. Aptamer injection provides a means to verify sufficient aptamer capture before starting the binding assay and allows a user to stop or modify the run if capture levels are too low. To conserve the amount of aptamer used per experiment, particularly for previously verified preparations, buffer injections can equilibrate the system without aptamer consumption.

Startup cycles also allow observation of successful regeneration conditions. A regeneration solution of 25 m*M* NaOH is capable of fully dissociating aptamer and ligand from the DNA linker on the sensor surface (Fig. 19.4). If complete regeneration is not observed, test other bases, acids, denaturants, or salts; modify their concentrations; or adjust the flow rate or duration of the injection to optimize regeneration conditions. Complete regeneration occurs when cycles begin and end at the same response level.

1. Dock CM5 sensor chip immobilized with DNA linker into Biacore instrument and prime system with binding buffer, typically 1 × HBS-N, pH 7.4, supplemented with 5 m*M* $MgCl_2$, unless another $MgCl_2$ concentration is desired.
2. Inject binding buffer or aptamer solution over sample flow cell (FC2) for 40 s at a flow rate of 5 μL/min. Approximately 70 pmol (1–2 μg) of aptamer per run is sufficient for observing small-molecule binding and should yield aptamer capture levels of approximately 2000–5000 RU. Extend injection duration or increase flow rate for dilute RNA samples or low molecular weight ligands to achieve higher capture levels. For

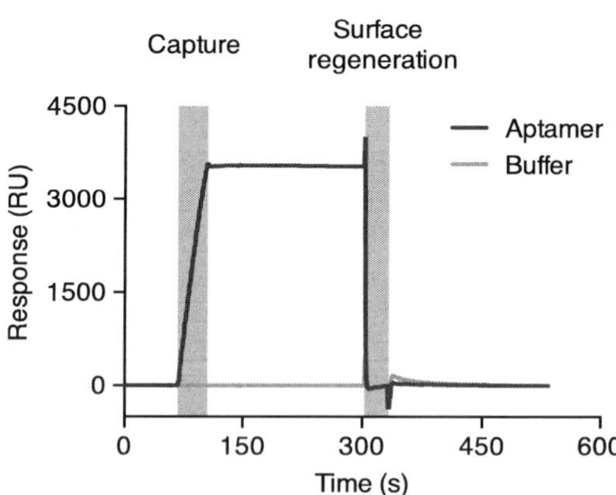

Figure 19.4 Overlaid startup cycle sensorgrams for aptamer capture and a binding buffer control, followed by regeneration of the binding surface. Sensorgram *y*-axes have been adjusted to set capture baseline levels to $y = 0$. Sensorgrams exhibit complete regeneration and stable baselines, with cycles starting and ending at the same response level.

protein ligands, less aptamer needs to be captured, as protein ligands produce a much larger binding response.

3. Regenerate sensor surface with 25 m*M* NaOH for 30 s at a flow rate of 30 μL/min.
4. Repeat steps 2 and 3 two to four more times, or until successful regeneration and stable sensorgram baselines are observed. If binding assays for multiple aptamer sequences are run within a single experiment, each startup cycle can inject a different aptamer.

4.3. Aptamer binding assay

The aptamer binding assay consists of aptamer capture, ligand association and dissociation phases, and surface regeneration (Fig. 19.5). The SPR-based characterization platform is capable of measuring both binding kinetics and equilibrium affinities (Chang et al., 2014) through multi-cycle kinetics, where each ligand concentration is run in a separate cycle with its own dissociation phase. Alternatively, single-cycle kinetics may be used, wherein increasing concentrations of ligand are injected without surface regeneration

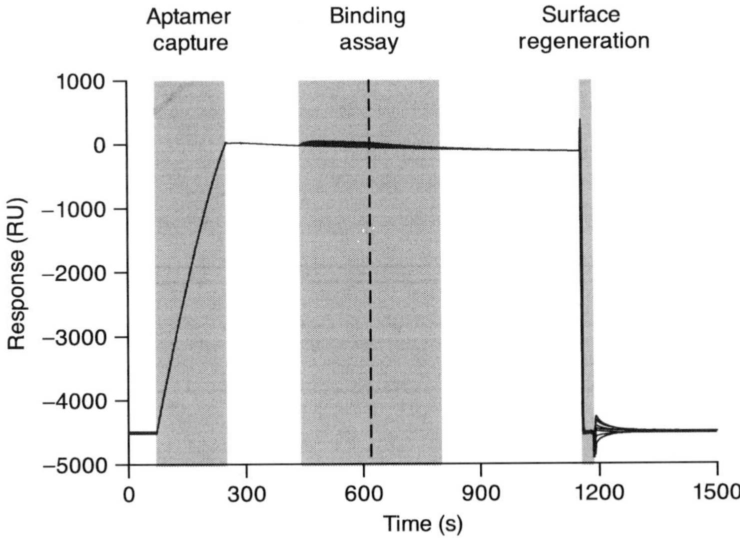

Figure 19.5 Full-length, multi-cycle aptamer binding assay. Overlaid sensorgrams for seven ligand concentrations are shown. Dashed line indicates transition from association phase to dissociation phase. Data shown are for the theophylline aptamer–ligand pair. Sensorgram *y*-axes have been adjusted to set aptamer capture level to $y=0$.

in a single cycle with a single dissociation phase. Optimization of association and dissociation phase lengths and ligand concentrations tested are necessary for accurate measurement. Association phase lengths depend on the time needed to reach equilibrium, which can range from less than 5 s to greater than 180 s at a flow rate of 30 μL/min (Chang et al., 2014). Reaching equilibrium in the ligand association phase is necessary for determining K_D through steady-state affinity but not for determining binding kinetics; whether equilibrium is reached may depend on the maximum injection volume of the instrument used, which for the Biacore X100 instrument limits the injection length to 180 s at a flow rate of 30 μL/min. Dissociation phase lengths are chosen so that substantial ligand dissociation is observed, generally with at least a 10-fold greater signal-to-noise ratio for the decrease in ligand binding response. For aptamers with very slow dissociation rates ($<10^{-3}\ s^{-1}$), dissociation phase lengths greater than 10 min may be necessary and single-cycle kinetic analysis should be considered as described in Section 4.4 (Fig. 19.7). For aptamer–ligand complexes that reach equilibrium, ligand concentrations tested should span approximately 10-fold below and above the K_D and cover the 0.2–0.8 binding saturation range. This is readily achievable using 6–8 concentration points serially diluted by 2–2.5-fold. For aptamer–ligand complexes that do not reach equilibrium in the experimental timeframe, higher concentrations of ligand will be required to provide sufficient sensorgram curvature for fitting to a 1:1 kinetic binding model.

Previously uncharacterized aptamers can be rapidly screened to determine the relevant experimental conditions for characterization. Initial association and dissociation phase lengths of 90–120 s can be subsequently extended or decreased based on the observed approach to equilibrium and dissociation rate. Running a few concentration points, for example, 3–5 concentrations at a 10-fold serial dilution, can quickly determine the relevant binding concentration range. Previously reported properties can guide initial screening; for instance, if an aptamer's binding affinity has previously been reported, ligand concentrations spanning 10-fold below and above the reported K_D can initially be tested.

1. Immediately after startup cycles are run, capture aptamer onto the sensor surface for 40 s at a flow rate of 5 μL/min.
2. Prepare filtered serial dilution of ligand in binding buffer. Inject binding buffer or ligand solution at a flow rate of 30 μL/min for a ligand association phase length relevant for the aptamer–ligand pair being characterized.

3. Dissociate ligand by injecting binding buffer at a flow rate of 30 μL/min for a ligand dissociation phase length relevant for the aptamer–ligand pair being characterized.
4. Regenerate sensor surface with 25 m*M* NaOH for 30 s at a flow rate of 30 μL/min over both flow cells. Surface regeneration should fully remove aptamer and ligand so that beginning and end response levels of all runs are the same (Fig. 19.5).
5. Two binding buffer runs are recommended, one before and one after the ligand serial dilution, to check for baseline drift or in case one buffer trace is unsuitable for use as a reference as described in Section 4.4.

4.4. Analysis of aptamer binding properties

Kinetic and equilibrium binding characterization provide two methods for determining aptamer binding affinities. When possible, both kinetic and equilibrium analyses should be conducted as an internal check for confidence; K_D obtained through both methods should differ by no more than approximately twofold (Chang et al., 2014).

1. Select runs for analysis. Double-reference all data by calculating the difference between the response from the reference flow cell (FC1) and the response from the sample flow cell (FC2), and then subtracting the reference-subtracted blank injection of binding buffer from reference-subtracted injections of ligand. Check that the resulting aptamer capture baselines (section 1 in Fig. 19.6B) are flat with a binding response of 0 for all analyzed sensorgrams after double referencing. Similarly, for aptamer–ligand pairs that fully dissociate during the ligand dissociation phase, sensorgrams should end with a binding response of 0 and not have a negative value (section 4 in Fig. 19.6B). Most small-molecule binding results in maximal response greater than 10 RU; therefore, a non-zero value of ±0.8 RU is acceptable for both the capture baseline and final binding response. This minor variation is due to noise and will not interfere with the following analysis.
2. For kinetic analysis, fit a 1:1 binding model to selected sensorgrams (Fig. 19.6B). Fitted parameters include the association rate, k_a, and the dissociation rate, k_d. The dissociation constant, K_D, is calculated as k_d/k_a.
3. For equilibrium analysis, plot the binding response averaged over a time window of 5 s versus ligand concentration and fit to a steady-state affinity model. The time window should be selected in the region where the

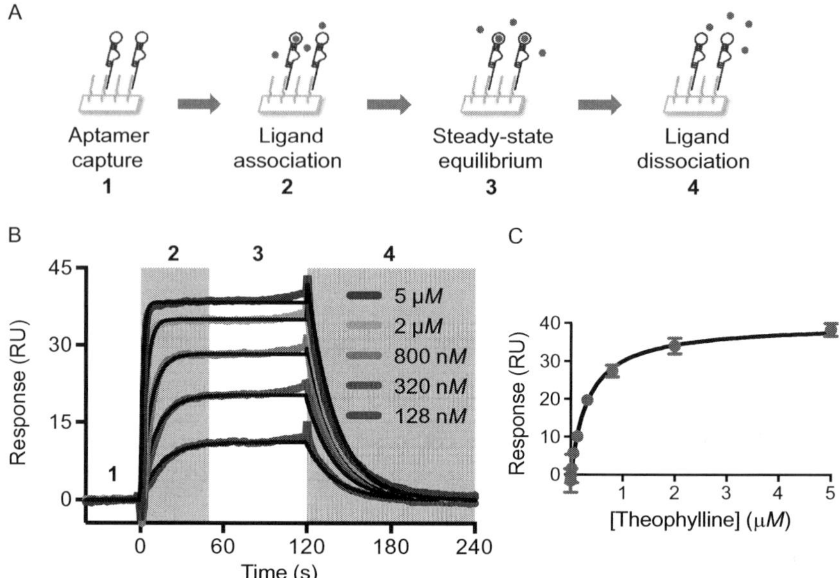

Figure 19.6 Kinetic and equilibrium binding characterization of aptamers. (A) Schematic diagram of SPR-based aptamer binding characterization. (B) Multi-cycle kinetic analysis of theophylline aptamer binding. Overlaid sensorgrams for five concentrations of theophylline are shown and fit to a 1:1 kinetic binding model. Overlaid signals are the same as those shown in Fig. 19.5. (C) Equilibrium binding analysis of theophylline aptamer binding fit to a steady-state affinity model. *Adapted, with permission, from Chang et al. (2014).* (See the color plate.)

response has fully plateaued and the binding has reached equilibrium (section 3 in Fig. 19.6B, subsegment 3). If a plateau is not present, the association phase length should be increased or only kinetic analysis should be performed. Ligand concentration range should nearly reach binding saturation (Fig. 19.6C).

For aptamer–ligand interactions with very slow dissociation rates ($<10^{-4}\ s^{-1}$), single-cycle kinetic analysis may be preferred over multi-cycle analysis. The long timeframe required for observing significant ligand dissociation (>20 min) would lead to excessively long experimental run times for multi-cycle analysis and more baseline variation, which can negatively affect kinetic analysis. Single-cycle kinetics enables a single, long dissociation phase to be run for multiple ligand concentrations (Fig. 19.7). As for all kinetic analyses, it is critical that the aptamer capture baselines are flat with a binding response of 0 after double referencing.

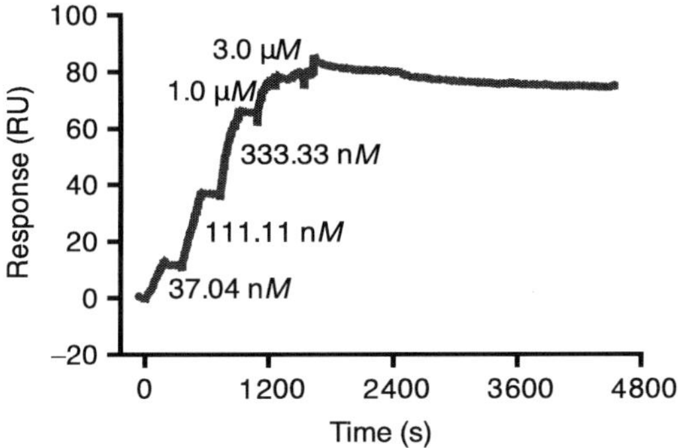

Figure 19.7 Single-cycle kinetic analysis of the cyclic di-GMP class I aptamer. For aptamers with very slow dissociation rates, single-cycle kinetics can be used to reduce the length of runs and minimize baseline variability. *Adapted, with permission, from Chang et al. (2014).*

5. CONCLUSION

The SPR-based platform for aptamer characterization outlined here is broadly useful for studying and prototyping aptamer function. This method has recently enabled the first side-by-side comparison of aptamer binding properties under consistent characterization conditions for a diverse range of previously reported aptamers (Chang et al., 2014). The aptamers so far characterized using this platform span natural and *in vitro* selected sources, are composed of RNA or DNA, range from 25 to 96 nucleotides in length, and exhibit K_D covering over five orders of magnitude, from 890 pM to 200 μM (Chang et al., 2014).

This characterization platform is a useful tool for comparing aptamer properties and rapidly testing aptamer binding under varying conditions. SPR enables facile control over multiple binding conditions and aptamer and ligand properties, allowing detailed study of the effects on aptamer binding of pH, temperature, or ion dependence; ligand specificity; ligand structure–activity relationships using ligand analogues; and aptamer sequence–activity relationships using introduced point mutations. In addition, this method is directly extendable to protein ligands and aptamers containing either modified nucleotides or expanded genetic alphabets. This experimental flexibility contrasts with other methods that require specific characterization conditions or intrinsic ligand properties (Chang et al., 2014). For studying and designing aptamers and aptamer-based gene-regulatory devices (Chang, Wolf, & Smolke, 2012) for *in vivo* use, testing relevant physiological conditions is important for understanding aptamer behavior and for measuring quantitative parameters that can be incorporated into computational models of aptamer function (Beisel & Smolke, 2009). The broad screening capabilities of this platform make it compatible with *in vitro* selection processes (McKeague & Derosa, 2012; Ozer, Pagano, & Lis, 2014) for monitoring binding enrichment of bulk sequence libraries and for prototyping candidate aptamer sequences, where functional sequences can be identified, characterized, truncated, and coupled with methods for constructing synthetic RNA regulatory switches or other nucleic acid devices (Liang, Chang, Kennedy, & Smolke, 2012). This robust and rapid aptamer characterization platform provides a versatile tool that can be readily combined with other methods for advancing the study, design, and engineering of functional nucleic acids.

ACKNOWLEDGMENTS

We thank J. Liang for contributions to assay development and aptamer characterization.

REFERENCES

Beisel, C. L., & Smolke, C. D. (2009). Design principles for riboswitch function. *PLoS Computational Biology*, *5*(4), e1000363.

Chang, A. L., McKeague, M., Liang, J. C., & Smolke, C. D. (2014). Kinetic and equilibrium binding characterization of aptamers to small molecules using a label-free, sensitive, and scalable platform. *Analytical Chemistry*, *86*(7), 3273–3278.

Chang, A. L., Wolf, J. J., & Smolke, C. D. (2012). Synthetic RNA switches as a tool for temporal and spatial control over gene expression. *Current Opinion in Biotechnology*, *23*(5), 679–688.

Huizenga, D. E., & Szostak, J. W. (1995). A DNA aptamer that binds adenosine and ATP. *Biochemistry*, *34*(2), 656–665.

Jenison, R. D., Gill, S. C., Pardi, A., & Polisky, B. (1994). High-resolution molecular discrimination by RNA. *Science*, *263*(5152), 1425–1429.

Liang, J. C., Chang, A. L., Kennedy, A. B., & Smolke, C. D. (2012). A high-throughput, quantitative cell-based screen for efficient tailoring of RNA device activity. *Nucleic Acids Research*, *40*(20), e154.

McKeague, M., & Derosa, M. C. (2012). Challenges and opportunities for small molecule aptamer development. *Journal of Nucleic Acids*, *2012*, 748913.

Ozer, A., Pagano, J. M., & Lis, J. T. (2014). New technologies provide quantum changes in the scale, speed, and success of SELEX methods and aptamer characterization. *Molecular Therapy Nucleic Acids*, *3*, e183.

CHAPTER TWENTY

The AdoCbl–Riboswitch Interaction Investigated by In-Line Probing and Surface Plasmon Resonance Spectroscopy (SPR)

Michelle F. Schaffer, Pallavi K. Choudhary, Roland K.O. Sigel[1]

Department of Chemistry, University of Zurich, Zürich, Switzerland

[1]Corresponding author: e-mail address: roland.sigel@chem.uzh.ch

Contents

Abstract

The unique feature of riboswitches is to control selected gene expression by specific recognition of a cognate ligand. AdoCbl (adenosyl cobalamin, coenzyme B_{12}) riboswitches regulate the expression of enzymes and transporters involved in bacterial AdoCbl biosynthesis or uptake on a transcriptional and/or translational level. The analysis of ligand recognition and the induced conformational changes requires a detailed knowledge of the kinetics and thermodynamics of ligand binding and of the secondary structure rearrangements. This chapter describes the investigation of coenzyme B_{12} binding to the *btuB* riboswitch from *Escherichia coli* by in-line probing assays and surface plasmon resonance spectroscopy. The experimental conditions, requirements, and performance of both methods are presented together with the evaluation of the experimental data to determine the associated conformational changes of the RNA and the kinetic and thermodynamic parameters of ligand binding. Owing to the light sensitivity of the cobalt(I)′—carbon bond, these methods were specifically modified to ensure the chemical integrity of AdoCbl.

Methods in Enzymology, Volume 549
ISSN 0076-6879
http://dx.doi.org/10.1016/B978-0-12-801122-5.00020-9

1. INTRODUCTION

The *btuB* riboswitch in *Escherichia coli* consist of a 202 nucleotide aptamer region containing the highly conserved B_{12}-box that is necessary for the binding of coenzyme B_{12} (AdoCbl) (Lundrigan, Koster, & Kadner, 1991; Nahvi, Barrick, & Breaker, 2004; Nahvi et al., 2002; Richter-Dahlfors & Andersson, 1992; Richter-Dahlfors, Ravnum, & Andersson, 1994). The expression platform with the ribosome binding site (RBS) is located between nucleotides 203 and 240 (Nou & Kadner, 2000), completing the 5′-untranslated region (5′-UTR). The downstream *btuB* gene encodes for an outer membrane receptor that is responsible for the transport of the B_{12} molecule into the periplasmic space (Heller & Kadner, 1985; Lundrigan et al., 1991; Nou & Kadner, 2000; Ravnum & Andersson, 2001). At low coenzyme B_{12} concentration, the RBS is accessible for the binding of the ribosome to the mRNA, thereby enabling *btuB* transcription and translation. If AdoCbl is present in adequate concentration, its specific binding leads to a conformational change of the riboswitch. This structural rearrangement results in the formation of an intrinsic terminator masking the RBS in a newly formed helical region, thus inhibiting gene expression (Fig. 20.1; Gallo, Oberhuber, Sigel, & Krautler, 2008; Lundrigan et al., 1991; Mandal & Breaker, 2004; Nahvi et al., 2004, 2002; Perdrizet, Artsimovitch, Furman, Sosnick, & Pan, 2012; Ravnum & Andersson, 2001; Vitreschak, Rodionov, Mironov, & Gelfand, 2003).

In-line probing experiments are a convenient method to follow the metabolite-induced conformational changes and were thus employed to prove AdoCbl binding to its riboswitch. This method uses the spontaneous cleavage rate of RNA, which is strongly dependent on the flexibility and local geometry of the internucleotide linkage (Regulski & Breaker, 2008; Soukup & Breaker, 1999). The nucleophile for phosphodiester cleavage is the adjacent 2′-OH, which needs to be activated and positioned opposite the leaving group, forming ideally a 180° angle at the central phosphorus atom. Alternatively, also a water molecule positioned at the equivalent position as the 2′-OH and activated by a metal ion can lead to hydrolytic strand cleavage. A specific change in the cleavage pattern of the riboswitch is visible upon binding of coenzyme B_{12}, suggesting a structural reorganization (Nahvi et al., 2004, 2002) of the RNA. The application of different B_{12} derivatives and observed changes in the in-line cleavage pattern, thus allow

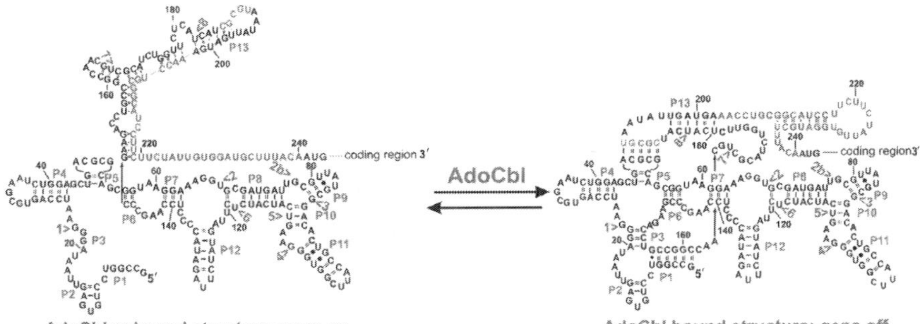

Figure 20.1 Proposed secondary structure of the *btuB* riboswitch from *Escherichia coli* in the "gene on" (left) and "gene off" (right) form. The riboswitch binds coenzyme B_{12} (AdoCbl) in the aptamer region (black) and controls the access for the ribosome by the expression platform (green). In the unbound form (left), an anti-aptamer is formed through interaction of the expression platform with the aptamer. Thereby, the ribosome binding site (RBS), situated shortly 5′ of the start codon AUG (purple), is accessible for the ribosome. At high AdoCbl concentrations (right), a pseudoknot (brown) is formed that leads to the sequestration of RBS and thus prevents the binding of the ribosome. The nine cleavage sites observed in in-line probing experiments, that demonstrate an altered cleavage pattern in presence of AdoCbl, are indicated with red numbers. (See the color plate.)

a detailed understanding of the riboswitch–ligand interaction. For example, these experiments suggest that the corrin ring and its side chains are the main determinants for the conformational alteration in the RNA structure, in particular the top β-side of the corrin ring (Gallo, Mundwiler, Alberto, & Sigel, 2010; Gallo et al., 2008). By the same method, the crucial role of Mg^{2+} for the recognition of AdoCbl could be shown (Choudhary & Sigel, 2014). Recent crystal structures of B_{12} riboswitches confirmed the ligand-induced structural changes obtained from in-line probing experiments (Johnson, Reyes, Polaski, & Batey, 2012; Peselis & Serganov, 2012), and thus prove the significance of in-line probing for accurately determining structural alterations in RNA.

In-line probing also provides a means to determine the apparent dissociation constant (K_D) of the ligand (Choudhary, Gallo, & Sigel, 2014; Gallo et al., 2008; Mandal & Breaker, 2004; Nahvi et al., 2002; Nou & Kadner, 2000; Regulski & Breaker, 2008). Newest data show that the *btuB* riboswitch from *E. coli* binds coenzyme B_{12} with a K_D of 89 ± 6 n*M*, but that it loses affinity by about three orders of magnitude if the adenosyl moiety is replaced by cyanide (Gallo et al., 2008).

Kinetic or thermodynamic control provides two modes for the regulation of gene expression by riboswitches (Serganov & Patel, 2012; Zhang, Lau, & Ferre-D'Amare, 2010). The kinetic mode of regulation is influenced by the relative speeds of transcription, ligand association, and the cotranscriptional folding of the aptamer, whereas the thermodynamic mode is controlled by the equilibrium between ligand association and dissociation and by the height of the activation barrier. In the case of the *btuB* riboswitch, transcriptional pausing by the polymerase allows cotranscriptional folding of the aptamer for appropriate gene regulatory response in the absence and presence of AdoCbl (Perdrizet et al., 2012).

The determination of the regulatory mode of gene expression in riboswitches requires the analysis of the kinetic and thermodynamic parameters of riboswitch–ligand interaction. Surface plasmon resonance (SPR) analysis has become an important technique for investigation and quantification of macromolecular interactions to determine affinity, binding enthalpy, and binding kinetics (Cosnier & Mailley, 2008; Homola, 2003; Sipova & Homola, 2013; Tseng & Chu, 2005; Wilson, 2002). SPR offers the advantage to investigate the time-resolved interaction of label-free biomolecules (except the surface-attachment). Examples are the investigation of RNA-binding proteins involved in the regulation of translation (Kim et al., 2011) and protein binding to mRNA (Jankowska-Anyszka, Piecyk, & Samonina-Kosicka, 2011; Mori, Sasagawa, Kino, & Ishiura, 2008; Ptushkina et al., 1998), tmRNA (Metzinger, Hallier, & Felden, 2008), and rRNA (Lamichhane, Abeydeera, Duc, Cunningham, & Chow, 2011). In addition, interactions between metabolites and riboswitches have also been studied by SPR (Jenkins, Krucinska, McCarty, Bandarian, & Wedekind, 2011; Mayer, Raddatz, Grunwald, & Famulok, 2007).

SPR does not provide any information on conformational changes induced by the ligand, but instead is used to determine kinetic parameters of ligand binding and dissociation. However, one of the partners needs to be surface-immobilized, e.g., with a biotin. In the case of riboswitches, in-line probing experiments can then be used to ensure correct functioning despite the modification.

Any experiments with AdoCbl are complicated by the light-sensitivity of this metabolite: upon exposure of AdoCbl to light, the cobalt(I)—carbon bond is cleaved within seconds (Bond, Lees, & Enever, 1972). Here, we describe the complementarity of in-line probing and SPR, as well as the special precautions to ensure the chemical integrity of AdoCbl, to analyze in detail the kinetics, thermodynamics, and ligand-induced conformational changes in B_{12} riboswitches.

2. IN-LINE PROBING EXPERIMENTS

2.1. Mechanism of the in-line probing reaction

In-line probing uses the inherent chemical instability of RNA due to a trans-esterification reaction leading to the spontaneous cleavage of its phosphodiester bonds. By an S_N2-mechanism, a ribose 2′-OH attacks the adjacent phosphorus center and yields the 5′-fragment with a 2′,3′-cyclic phosphate and the 3′-fragment with a 5′-hydroxyl terminus (Fig. 20.2; Soukup & Breaker, 1999). Alternatively, also an activated water molecule, i.e., bound to a divalent metal ion, can act as nucleophile.

The in-line conformation of this nucleophilic substitution is determined by the torsion angles between the three bonds C3′—O3′ (ε), O3′—P (ζ), and C2′—C3′ (υ_2) around the phosphodiester linkage. In an optimal in-line conformation, the 2′-oxygen, the phosphorus, and the leaving 5′-oxygen form a 180° angle. As in any RNA cleavage reaction, trans-esterification is accelerated by (i) a shorter interatomic 2′-O–P distance, (ii) increasing the nucleophilicity of the 2′-OH (e.g., by metal ion coordination), (iii) a stabilization of the five-coordinate transition state, and (iv) protonation of the 5′-leaving group. This general overall-strategy is equivalent to the one employed by ribozymes or RNA-cleaving enzymes such as ribonuclease A (RNase A) (Thompson et al., 1995).

The RNA backbone of a regular A-form helix has no in-line configuration and resists cleavage. Local structures capable of in-line cleavage occur in noncanonical regions, tertiary contacts, and/or relatively unstructured regions. Hence, structural rearrangement of RNA leads to a different cleavage pattern and makes this method suitable to monitor ligand binding to riboswitches (Mandal & Breaker, 2004). It is important to note that the intensity of the cleavage band is primarily dependent on the local geometry

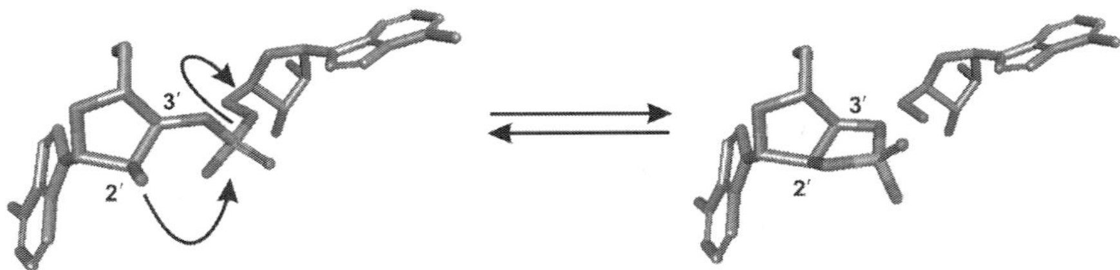

Figure 20.2 Mechanism of an in-line attack, leading to phosphodiester cleavage. The activated 2′-OH attacks the central phosphorous in a nucleophilic S_N2 substitution reaction. The opposite 5′-O as the leaving group gets protonated and a 2′3′-cyclic phosphate is left on the attacking side. (See the color plate.)

and *not* on the local ligand affinity. A change in ligand concentration then leads to either increased or decreased intensity of the cleavage bands.

In the following, we will use the *btuB*–AdoCbl system as a practical example to describe an in-line probing experiment in detail. However, in-line probing experiments are widely applicable to all different kinds of RNA.

2.2. Performing an in-line probing experiment

2.2.1 Overview and general remarks

^{32}P-labeled RNA is prepared and purified as described earlier (Hilario, 2002; Porecha & Herschlag, 2013). Here, we use 5′ end labeled *btuB* riboswitch with increasing metabolite concentrations. After the in-line probing reaction, the spontaneous cleavage products are separated by denaturating gel electrophoresis and visualized on a PhosphoImager. The intensities of the cleavage bands are then quantified and plotted against the metabolite concentration to determine the K_D value (Choudhary et al., 2014).

In-line probing assays are mostly straightforward if the following points are carefully considered:

1. To get accurate kinetic and structural data, it is essential to prevent nuclease contamination by preparing all solutions with autoclaved bidistilled water that is additionally filtered.
2. The integrity of the RNA must be confirmed in every experiment by running a RNase T1 ladder, an alkaline hydrolysis ladder, and unreacted RNA along with the experimental samples on the same gel as controls.
3. To obtain optimal intensity changes in the cleavage pattern, the experimental conditions, e.g., temperature, pH, buffer concentration, and reaction time, need to be optimized. Metal ion concentrations also need to be optimized to ensure proper RNA folding and ligand binding.

2.2.2 Equipment for in-line probing

Any lab will have its own equipment; the following is a list of equipment we use in our laboratory:

- home-made classical gel apparatus for denaturating PAGE gels of up to 80 cm in lengths
- gel dryer (Unequip, Germany)
- Whatmann™ Chromatography paper
- imaging system, such as Storage Phosphor Screens (GE Healthcare) and a Typhoon PhosphoImager with ImageQuant software (GE Healthcare)
- amber-colored microcentrifuge tubes (Eppendorf)
- data analysis and graphical software (OriginPro 9.0)

2.2.3 Buffers and solutions for in-line probing

- solutions of AdoCbl in ddH_2O (10 ×): stored at −20 °C and in the amber-colored microcentrifuge tubes
- 1 × TBE gel-running buffer diluted with ddH_2O from commercial available 10 × TBE buffer (National Diagnostic, UK)
- denaturating (7 *M* urea) 8% polyacrylamide gel solution for a gel with dimension of 30 cm × 45 cm × 0.5 mm. The percentage of the polyacrylamide solution is chosen according to the length of the RNA under investigation to ensure optimal resolution (Sambrook & Russell, 2001)
- formamide loading buffer: 82% (v/v) formamide, 0.16% (w/v) xylene cynol, 0.16% (w/v) bromophenol blue, 10 m*M* EDTA (pH 8.0)
- colorless gel loading solution: 82% formamide and 10 m*M* EDTA (pH 8.0)
- 10× sodium carbonate (Na_2CO_3) buffer: 0.5 *M* Na_2CO_3 (pH 9.0), 10 m*M* EDTA (pH 8.0)
- 10× sodium citrate buffer: 0.25 *M* trisodium citrate (pH 5.0). pH is adjusted by addition of concentrated HCl
- RNase T1-solution: RNase T1-solution was diluted to a final concentration of 1 U/μL in 50 m*M* Tris–HCl (pH 7.4) and 50% (v/v) glycerol.

2.2.4 In-line probing reaction and PAGE analysis

To obtain a good signal-to-noise ratio, 5–7 n*M* labeled RNA per reaction is used, while the total RNA concentration, i.e., including the unlabeled one can be higher (depending on the imaging sensitivity, a ^{32}P activity of 20,000–200,000 cps per lane should be considered). To determine the K_D value of AdoCbl accurately, titration experiment with at least 10 different metabolite concentrations 0 n*M*–1 m*M* are performed. We do not recommend to use metabolite concentrations higher than 1 m*M*, as nonspecific interactions may occur. To prevent misfolding of the RNA, we suggest to refold the RNA prior to the experiment. As coenzyme B_{12} is light sensitive and decomposes within a few seconds all the following steps must be performed under red light in a dark room:

1. *Incubation*: Samples of 5–7 n*M* ^{32}P-labeled RNA in 50 m*M* Tris (pH 8.3) and 100 m*M* KCl are heated at 90 °C for 1 min in amber-colored microcentrifuge tubes. After cooling to room temperature, $MgCl_2$ (final concentration of 20 m*M*) and AdoCbl in increasing concentration range (e.g., 0.03–100 μ*M*) are added, and supplemented with ddH_2O to a final volume of 10 μL each. All samples are incubated at 25 °C in the dark for 40 h.

2. *Preparation of nonreacted RNA, RNase T1, and alkaline hydrolysis*: All control samples are loaded on the gel next to the reaction samples. The concentration of the RNA corresponds to the concentration in the in-line probing reaction.

Nonreacted RNA	^{32}P-labeled RNA filled up with ddH_2O to 10 μL
	10 μL formamide loading buffer
RNase T1 ladder	^{32}P-labeled RNA
	1 μL sodium citrate buffer (0.25 *M*)
	1 μL RNase T1 (1 U/μL)
	Fill up to 10 μL with colorless gel loading solution
	Incubate at 55 °C for 5 min and quench by adding 3 μL formamide loading buffer and 7 μL ddH_2O
Alkaline hydrolysis ladder	^{32}P-labeled RNA
	1 μL Na_2CO_3 buffer (0.5 *M*)
	Fill up with ddH_2O to 10 μL
	Incubate at 90 °C for 5 min and quench by adding 10 μL formamide loading buffer

3. *Quenching of the in-line probing reaction and PAGE*: The in-line probing reaction is terminated by adding 10 μL formamide loading buffer. The samples are then loaded on a 8% denaturating (7 *M* urea) polyacrylamide gel and the gel is run at 20 W for approximately 4 h.
4. *Drying*: The gel is transferred carefully to a Whatmann™ chromatography paper, covered with plastic wrap, and dried under vacuum at 90 °C for 60–90 min and cooled to 40 °C afterward.
5. *Screening and visualization*: The gel is exposed to a PhosphoImager screen overnight and scanned the next day on the PhosphoImager.

2.2.5 Data analysis and calculation of K_D values

Titration with the metabolite allows one to determine the affinity constant K_A (or the respective $K_D = 1/K_A$) of a metabolite for its riboswitch by analyzing the intensity changes at the individual cleavage sites as a function of ligand concentration. The K_D value thereby indicates the required concentration of the metabolite to convert 50% of the riboswitch to the ligand-bound form.

1. *Assigning individual cleavage bands*: The nonreacted control RNA (Fig. 20.3, lane c) ideally should not show any degradation bands, which would otherwise interfere with interpretation of the cleavage pattern. The positions of the specific cleavage sites (1–8) (Fig. 20.1) are determined by using the RNase T1 ladder, which cleaves at each guanine residue, and by the alkaline hydrolysis ladder, which produces cleavage products at each nucleotide.
2. *Analyzing intensities of the individual cleavage sites*: By using the ImageQuant TL software (GE Healthcare), equal volume rectangles are drawn around the bands of the same cleavage site in each lane. For background correction, two areas that do not exhibit any metabolite dependent change in intensity are chosen and designated as R_1 and R_2 in all lanes of interest (Fig. 20.3A).
3. *Background correction* (Table 20.1): For each lane in R_1 and R_2, the ratio of the determined intensity relative to the intensity of the strongest lane X is calculated to get R_{r1} and R_{r2}.

$$R_{r1/2} = \frac{R_{1/2}}{X}$$

The average of R_{r1} and R_{r2} for this ratios results in the correction factor R for each lane of interest.

$$R = \frac{(R_{r1} + R_{r2})}{2}$$

The previous defined intensities I of each bands are corrected by dividing them with the correction factor R to get I_{corr}.

$$I_{corr} = \frac{I}{R}$$

4. *Determination of K_D value*: The background corrected changes in intensity I_{corr} for the nine specific nucleotide positions within the RNA chain are plotted versus the coenzyme B_{12} concentration. An appropriate fitting, such as a classical 1:1 binding isoterm, is applied separately to the data at each of the nine sites (Sigel, Freisinger, & Lippert, 2000). Root-mean-square fitting is performed in Origin Pro 9.0 to obtain the corresponding K_A values for each site (Fig. 20.3B). The mean of all obtained K_A values results in a single affinity constant K_{av} for ligand binding to the RNA.

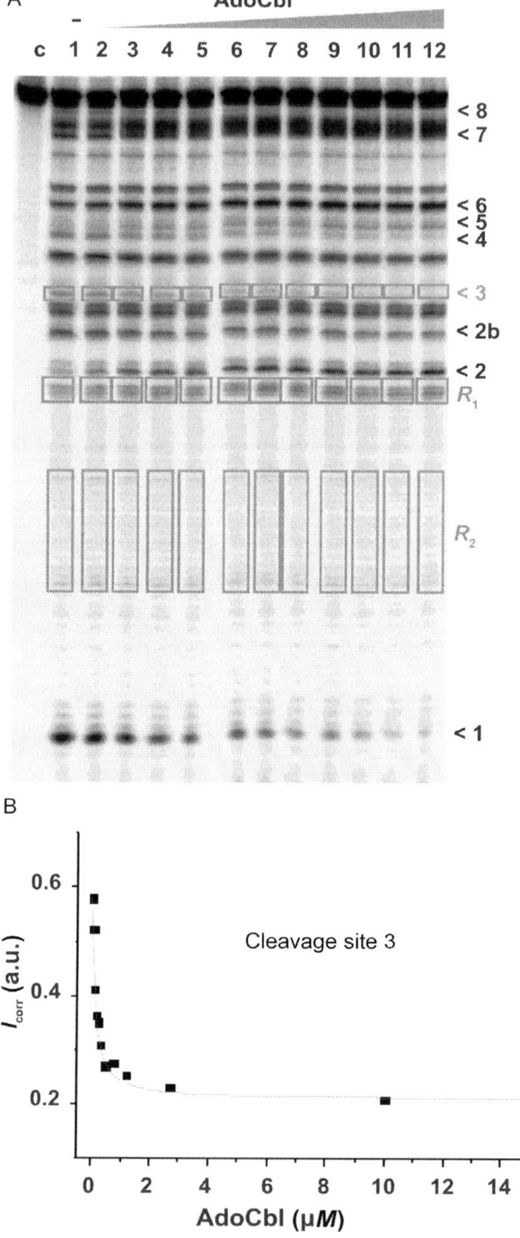

Figure 20.3 Quantitative analysis of an in-line probing titration experiment. (A) The evaluation of the PAGE of the *btuB* aptamer incubated with coenzyme B_{12}. Lane c is the nonreacted RNA. The AdoCbl concentration is increasing from lane 1 to 12 (Gallo et al., 2008). The nine cleavage sites changing their intensity are indicated on the right side. The rectangles for R_1 and R_2 show the regions used for background correction. (B) The change in intensity at cleavage site 3 for increasing amounts of AdoCbl is representative for all cleavage sites. A K_A of 10.43 ± 1.82 m*M* is obtained by a 1:1 binding model (red line (gray line in the print version)) (Gallo et al., 2008).

Table 20.1 Representative evaluation of the concentration dependent in-line probing experiments of the *btuB* riboswitch with increasing AdoCbl concentration at cleavage site 3

Lane: X	Ratio of R_1 to the strongest lane: R_{r1}	Ratio of R_2 to the strongest lane: R_{r2}	$R=(R_{r1}+R_{r2})/2$	I	$I_{corr}=I/R$
1	0.709	0.997	0.853	0.495	0.580
2	0.758	1	0.879	0.459	0.522
3	0.810	0.965	0.888	0.365	0.411
4	0.882	0.982	0.932	0.341	0.365
5	0.780	0.825	0.803	0.282	0.351
6	0.850	0.889	0.870	0.268	0.308
7	1.000	0.987	0.993	0.270	0.271
8	0.890	0.836	0.863	0.238	0.276
9	0.964	0.917	0.940	0.238	0.253
10	0.822	0.825	0.823	0.191	0.232
11	0.817	0.687	0.752	0.158	0.210
12	0.923	0.702	0.816	0.145	0.178

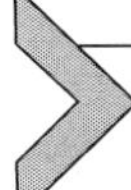

3. SPR SPECTROSCOPY

3.1. The method of SPR

SPR sensors measure refractive index changes occurring at the sensor surface during a course of biomolecular interaction (Fagerstam, Frostell-Karlsson, Karlsson, Persson, & Ronnberg, 1992; Fisher & Fivash, 1994; Jonsson et al., 1991; Malmqvist, 1993; Malmqvist & Karlsson, 1997; Morton & Myszka, 1998; Myszka, 2000; Szabo, Stolz, & Granzow, 1995; Torreri, Ceccarini, Macioce, & Petrucci, 2005). SPR spectroscopy involves immobilization of one of the binding partners (a ligand, i.e., RNA) on the sensor surface, while the other binding partner (an analyte, i.e., coenzyme B_{12}) remains in solution (de Mol & Fischer, 2010). The interaction of an analyte with a ligand increases the refractive index at the surface and is directly proportional to the amount of bound analyte. This change in refractive index is expressed in terms of Response Units (RU) (Wilson, 2002). The interaction between an analyte and the ligand is monitored in real time and is represented by a plot or sensorgram (Fig. 20.4) of RU versus time (de Mol & Fischer, 2010; Torreri et al., 2005; Wilson, 2002).

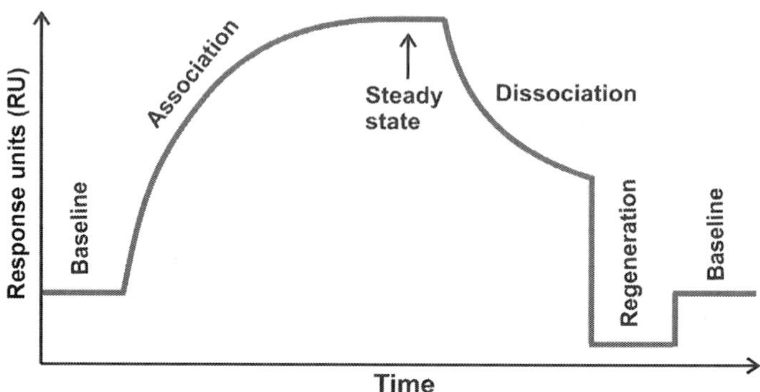

Figure 20.4 Schematic representation of an ideal SPR sensorgram: the baseline indicates a continuous flow of buffer on the sensor surface. The signal (RU) increases as analyte binds the ligand (association) and reaches saturation (arrow) with increased concentration of the bound analyte. Stopping the analyte addition, the buffer flow facilitates dissociation of the analyte from the bound complex. Following dissociation, the sensor surface is regenerated to regain the baseline before a new experimental run begins.

To study the kinetics of a biomolecular interaction, a typical SPR experiment consists of the following steps (a) immobilization of the ligand, (b) injection of a concentration series for an analyte and recording of the interaction at real time, (c) regeneration of the sensor surface if necessary, and (d) fitting the experimental data to an appropriate interaction model to extract kinetic (k) and equilibrium (K) constants. It is important to measure the background noise in the experiments using one of the flow cells from a sensor surface as a control or reference cell (Tanious, Nguyen, & Wilson, 2008).

3.2. Practical example: Studying the AdoCbl–*btuB* riboswitch interaction by SPR

3.2.1 Overview and general remarks

The first step in SPR consists of choosing one of the binding partners as an immobilized ligand on the sensor surface. In case of the AdoCbl–*btuB* riboswitch interaction, the preferred ligand for immobilization on the SPR sensor would be AdoCbl as it has a lower molecular weight than the *btuB* riboswitch. Moreover, considering the mass dependence of the SPR response (Biacore n.d.a), the signal generated from binding of the RNA to AdoCbl attached to surface would be much larger than the vice versa binding of AdoCbl to the RNA. However, using AdoCbl as an immobilized ligand poses a problem since this metabolite is known to interact with the *btuB* riboswitch using an extensive network of hydrophobic and electrostatic interactions (Johnson et al., 2012; Peselis & Serganov, 2012; Souliere, Haller, Santner, & Micura, 2013). Furthermore, modification of AdoCbl side chains leads to altered interactions with the *btuB* riboswitch (Gallo et al., 2010). Therefore, to keep the biomolecular interaction as ideal as possible, the *btuB* riboswitch is used as an immobilized ligand in the SPR experiments. The expression platform of the *btuB* riboswitch serves the purpose of immobilizing the *btuB* riboswitch to the sensor surface, since it is not involved in the direct interaction with AdoCbl (Johnson et al., 2012; Nahvi et al., 2002; Peselis & Serganov, 2012).

The immobilization of the *btuB* riboswitch is followed by injecting a concentration series of AdoCbl on the sensor surface. The acquired sensorgrams are then fitted to an interaction model to obtain the associated kinetic parameters. The reproducibility of results is confirmed by repeating the kinetic measurements under same experimental conditions.

3.2.2 Equipments for SPR

- Streptavidin (SA)-coated sensor chip from Biacore.
- Biacore T100 or similar SPR instrument.

3.2.3 Buffers and solutions for SPR

Filter all buffers through 0.2 μm filters before use.

Running buffer for the experiments: 50 m*M* Tris–HCl (pH 7.5), 100 m*M* KCl, 20 m*M* $MgCl_2$. The volume of the running buffer depends on the time of the experimental run, i.e., the number of analyte injections. The wizard in *Biacore control software* calculates the volume of buffer needed for a given experiment.

Biotinylated DNA oligo solution: A 25-mer DNA oligonucleotide complementary to the 3′ end of the *btuB* riboswitch and carrying a biotin moiety at its 5′ end is required for immobilization. A 10-μ*M* stock solution of the PAGE-purified biotinylated DNA oligo in filtered ultrapure water is prepared.

btuB riboswitch solution: A stock solution of ~10–20 μL of (at least) 50 μ*M* RNA in filtered ultrapure water is required. The *in vitro* transcribed RNA should be purified by PAGE, electroelution and concentrated by *Vivaspin* before use (Gallo, Furler, & Sigel, 2005).

AdoCbl solutions: A 10 m*M* (w/v) stock solution of AdoCbl in filtered ultrapure water is prepared. The concentration of the stock solution is determined by the absorption of the UV–vis spectrum. A series of

AdoCbl concentrations is obtained by serially diluting the stock solution in the running buffer. Prepare all AdoCbl solutions in a dark room under red light.

Conditioning solution for SA sensor chip: 1 *M* NaCl, 50 m*M* NaOH.

Regeneration solution: 1 *M* NaCl.

3.2.4 Sample preparation

Biotinylated DNA oligo: The biotinylated DNA oligo is diluted to a final concentration of 1 μ*M* in a buffer containing 50 m*M* Tris–HCl, pH 7.5, 100 m*M* KCl, 20 m*M* $MgCl_2$. 50 μL of the sample is needed for a single injection.

RNA–DNA oligo adduct: A 0.1 μ*M* RNA in 50 m*M* (final concentration) Tris–HCl (pH 7.5) is prepared. The sample is heated to 90 °C for 1 min. Biotinylated DNA (final concentration 1 μ*M*; RNA:DNA = 1:10), 100 m*M* KCl, and 20 m*M* $MgCl_2$ (all final concentrations) are added to the sample. The sample is further kept at 55 °C for 2 min, followed by incubation at 37 °C for 15 min to allow proper RNA folding and strand annealing. In total, 50 μL of the sample is needed for a single injection.

Pure RNA: 30 μ*M* RNA is prepared with filtered ultrapure water and 50 m*M* Tris–HCl (pH 7.5). The sample is heated to 90 °C for 1 min followed by the addition of KCl and $MgCl_2$ to reach final concentrations of 100 and 20 m*M*, respectively. The sample is further kept at 37 °C for 15 min to allow folding of the RNA. 10–30 μL of the sample is needed depending upon a single injection/multiple injections.

3.2.5 Immobilization of the RNA on sensor surface

The immobilization levels of the ligand (RNA) depend upon the relative molecular weights of the analyte (AdoCbl) and ligand in the assay. The theoretical ligand immobilization levels (R_L) can be calculated using the following formula (Biacore n.d.a):

$$R_{max} = \frac{\text{Analyte Molecular Weight}}{\text{Ligand Molecular Weight}} \times R_L \times S_m$$

R_{max} is the maximum analyte binding capacity of the surface and S_m = Stoichiometry of binding (usually $S_m = 1$ for riboswitches). Note that the theoretical R_{max} is mostly higher than the experimental R_{max} since it assumes 100% active surface (Biacore n.d.a).

The immobilization of the *btuB* riboswitch to the sensor surface is enabled by using a 25 nucleotide long 5′-biotinylated DNA oligo complementary to the expression platform (i.e., the 3′ end of the riboswitch) (Fig. 20.5A). When a SA-coated sensor surface is used, the high-affinity interaction between the biotinylated DNA oligo and SA sensor surface helps to immobilize the *btuB* riboswitch. However, studying the interaction between the *btuB* riboswitch and AdoCbl by SPR requires a higher surface density of the immobilized ligand (e.g., RNA) since the binding of small molecule (e.g., AdoCbl) to the sensor surface is detected as a low response by the instrument (Tanious et al., 2008).

Immobilization of the *btuB* riboswitch on the sensor surface requires the following steps:

1. Open the Biacore control software (italics indicates instrument commands).
2. Place the running buffer in the buffer compartment of Biacore system.
3. Place all required samples at the appropriate positions in the sample rack (sample holder in the Biacore system).
4. *Insert* the SA chip in the sensor chip compartment of the system and *dock* the chip.
5. Set the temperature of the system at 25 °C.
6. *Prime* the Biacore system with the running buffer. This step is important and is required to flush the running buffer through the system (Biacore n.d.a).

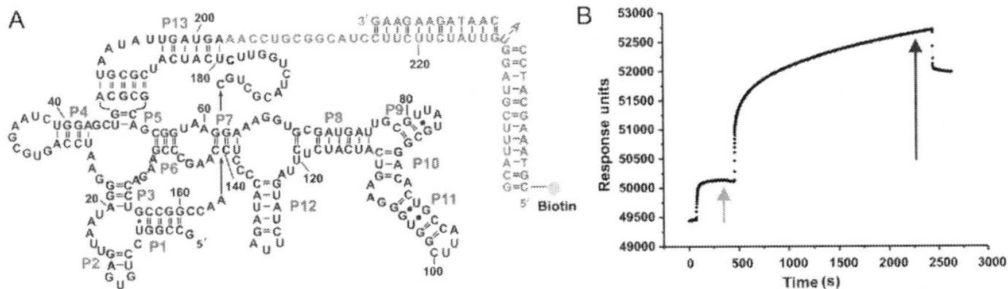

Figure 20.5 Immobilization of the *btuB* riboswitch for an SPR experiment. (A) Secondary structure of the *btuB* riboswitch construct used for SPR experiments. Immobilization on the streptavidin sensor surface is achieved by hybridizing a 25 nucleotide long DNA oligo (pink) carrying biotin (yellow) at its 5′ end to the complementary nucleotides at the 3′ end of the expression platform (green) in the *btuB* riboswitch. (B) The *btuB* riboswitch is immobilized on the sensor surface in two steps. First step (gray arrow) involves the injection of a hybridized DNA–RNA adduct. This is followed by an injection of pure RNA (black arrow) to bind to unbound DNA oligos on the sensor surface and thereby raise the surface density of the RNA. (See the color plate.)

7. Begin the *manual run* on flow cells 1 and 2 or the flow cells 3 and 4 or all of the flow cells, depending upon the experimental set up. If the interaction between one ligand and one analyte is to be studied, then two flow cells are needed for the experiment, one as a control and another for immobilization.
8. *Condition* the SA chip on the selected flow cells by injecting conditioning solution (1 *M* NaCl, 50 m*M* NaOH) at the flow rate of 30 μL/min for 60 s. Perform this step three times.
9. End the manual run.
10. Begin a new *manual run* only on one of the flow cells that serves as a control (e.g., flow cell 1). Inject sample (A) (biotinylated DNA oligo) on the control flow cell at the flow rate of 10 μL/min for 5 min. The immobilization levels on the control surface should be similar to the surface with the ligand (RNA). Therefore, injection of sample (A) can be repeated if needed. The biotinylated DNA oligo acts as a control in the experiment and helps in monitoring nonspecific interaction(s) as well as the background response.
11. End the *manual run* on the control flow cell.
12. Begin the new *manual run* on a new flow cell (e.g., flow cell 2) where the ligand (RNA) is to be immobilized.
13. *Inject* sample (B) (complex of biotinylated DNA–RNA) on flow cell 2 at the flow rate of 10 μL/min for 5 min.
14. Change the *flow rate* to 1 μL/min.
15. *Inject* sample (C) (RNA only sample) on flow cell 2 for 10 min. This sample utilizes excess of unbound/free biotinylated DNA oligo (from step 13) and the slower flow rate (i.e., 1 μL/min) will facilitate the hybridization of the DNA oligo to the RNA. This step further increases the density of RNA on the sensor surface (Fig 20.5B).
16. Check for immobilization levels and repeat injection of sample (C) until the required immobilization level (R_L) is reached.
17. End the *manual run* on flow cell 2.
18. This procedure completes immobilization of the RNA sample on the SA sensor chip.

3.2.6 SPR measurements

The concentrations of an analyte (AdoCbl) to be used in the experiment generally should span a range of at least 100-fold, well above and below the known K_D value (Tanious et al., 2008). The K_D values estimated from the in-line probing experiments can be taken as a reference. Before performing kinetics, it is important to check the RNA surface using a trial injection of an appropriate concentration of analyte to confirm significant binding levels on the surface. The following procedure describes the experimental set up for studying kinetics:

1. Select "*Run*" in the *Biacore control software* and then select "*Wizard.*"
2. Choose "*Kinetics/Affinity*" from "*Assay*" and select "*New-Flow path*" 2-1 or 4-3 depending upon the flow cells in use (2-1 or 4-3 indicates the control (1 or 3) subtracted from the ligand surface (2 or 4)).
3. Run at least 8–10 "*Start-up cycles*" with the running buffer. The start-up cycles are important for the stabilization of response from a newly docked sensor chip before the first analysis begins. Although three start-up cycles are generally recommended for most assays (Biacore n.d.a), it is advisable to run higher number of start-up cycles at least for the initial set of experiments.
4. Enter the *flow rate*, *contact time* of an analyte, *stabilization period*, and *dissociation time*. For kinetics with AdoCbl, a contact time of 120 s with a flow rate of 30 μL/min can be observed. After a stability period of 300 s, the running buffer can be injected at a flow rate of 30 μL/min for 1200 s to allow dissociation.
5. Enter the concentration series of analyte(s) in the wizard including the zero concentration (i.e., running buffer only). For each analyte under study, at least four nonzero concentrations are required, and one of the concentrations should be run in duplicate (Biacore n.d.a). To confirm reproducibility of the binding response on the surface, the concentration series of an analyte can be run twice in a single experiment but in reverse order: from zero to higher concentration and then from higher to zero concentration.
6. The regeneration of the surface can be achieved by injecting 1 *M* NaCl for 1 min at the flow rate of 30 μL/min after every injection of AdoCbl. The regeneration step helps to completely dissociate the analyte from the surface before new injection of an analyte begins.
7. Fill the vials with appropriate solutions and place them in the sample rack as suggested by the wizard template. Dark conditions should be observed while working with AdoCbl samples. Switch off the "*rack illumination*" in the Biacore system when working with light-sensitive compounds such as AdoCbl and cover the top window of the Biacore system (above the rack holder) externally (by aluminum foil or any other suitable cover) throughout the experiment.
8. Run kinetics at 25 °C.

3.2.7 Data analysis

1. Open the *Biacore evaluation software.*
2. Open the acquired kinetics data and choose for "*Kinetics/Affinity-Surface bound.*"
3. Select the sensorgrams to be included in the evaluation and then confirm that the sensorgrams are "*Blank subtracted.*"
4. Select "*Kinetics*" and then choose the interaction models from a number of predefined models in the evaluation software. It is advisable to use simple kinetic models first, e.g., Langmuir model (1:1 binding model) before exploring the more complex interaction models.
5. Perform the "*Fit*" and analyze the fit first by visual inspection to confirm, if the lines of the fit pass through the experimental sensorgrams. Further analysis is done by following the tabs that appear below the fitted sensorgrams (Biacore n.d.a):
   - *Quality control*: Validates the quality of the data.
   - *Report*: Indicates the calculated parameters, association rate constant (k_a), dissociation rate constant (k_d), equilibrium dissociation constant (K_D), R_{max}, and Chi^2 value.
   - *Residuals*: The residual plot shows the difference between the experimental and fitted data points. This plot is useful for analyzing the closeness between the fit and the experimental data and helps to indicate systematic deviations of the experimental data from the theoretical fit, i.e., possibly indicating a different binding mode.
   - *Parameters*: Gives the values of all parameters in the fitting equation along with the standard error (SE). SE indicates the significance of a fitted parameter.

The kinetic measurements should be repeated to confirm reproducibility of the calculated parameters.

4. CONCLUSION

Riboswitches are fascinating but complex systems that are used to regulate metabolite concentrations in the cell. Their mechanism of metabolite docking and subsequent structural change of the RNA three-dimensional structure, *the switch*, is characterized by a complex network of inter- and intramolecular dynamics between different structures of the RNA alone and the RNA–metabolite complex. To characterize and understand such complex interplay of kinetics and thermodynamics at various stages, is rather challenging, especially when larger systems such as the B_{12} riboswitches are considered. In most cases, X-ray structures are difficult to obtain, and NMR is not yet advanced enough to investigate >100 nucleotide long complex RNA architectures on an atomic basis.

The combination of in-line probing and SPR experiments yields a rich and informative picture of metabolite binding, the structural change of the RNA, as well as the metabolite affinity, and its kinetics of binding and dissociation. In-line probing provides a view on the regions affected by the ligand binding and in combination with further footprinting techniques can offer valuable insights into structural features of riboswitches. One drawback of in-line probing is the long reaction time of usually 40 h, which precludes any kinetic investigation, but reflects a time-averaged equilibrium state. Instead, SPR spectroscopy can be used to monitor the RNA–ligand interaction in real time, providing both kinetic rates and the equilibrium constant for the interaction. Both together, and ideally in combination with further biochemical and biophysical methods, these methods help to understand the complete mechanism of metabolite-induced RNA folding and metabolite–RNA interaction.

ACKNOWLEDGMENTS

Financial support to RKOS by the European Research Council (ERC Starting Grant), the Swiss State Secretariat for Education, Research, and Innovation and COST Action CM1105 the Swiss National Science Foundation, and the University of Zurich is gratefully acknowledged. We are grateful to Dr. Sofia Gallo for providing a figure, and we want to thank her and Dr. Richard Börner for helpful discussions and careful reading of the manuscript.

REFERENCES

Biacore (n.d.a). *Biacore sensor surface handbook*, BR-1005-71 Edition AB.

Biacore (n.d.b). *Biacore T100 software handbook*, GE Healthcare *BR-1006-48 AE 07/2008*.

Bond, C. M., Lees, K. A., & Enever, R. P. (1972). Photolytic decomposition of 3 cobalamins: A quantitative study. *Journal of Pharmacy and Pharmacology*, *24*(Suppl. 143).

Choudhary, P. K., Gallo, S., & Sigel, R. K. O. (2014). Monitoring global structural changes and specific metal-ion-binding sites in RNA by in-line probing and Tb(III) cleavage. *Methods in Molecular Biology*, *1086*, 143–158.

Choudhary, P. K., & Sigel, R. K. O. (2014). Mg(2+)-induced conformational changes in the btuB riboswitch from E. coli. *RNA*, *20*, 36–45.

Cosnier, S., & Mailley, P. (2008). Recent advances in DNA sensors. *Analyst*, *133*, 984–991.

de Mol, N. J., & Fischer, M. J. (2010). Surface plasmon resonance: A general introduction. *Methods in Molecular Biology*, *627*, 1–14.

Fagerstam, L. G., Frostell-Karlsson, A., Karlsson, R., Persson, B., & Ronnberg, I. (1992). Biospecific interaction analysis using surface plasmon resonance detection applied to kinetic, binding site and concentration analysis. *Journal of Chromatography*, *597*, 397–410.

Fisher, R. J., & Fivash, M. (1994). Surface plasmon resonance based methods for measuring the kinetics and binding affinities of biomolecular interactions. *Current Opinion in Biotechnology, 5*, 389–395.

Gallo, S., Furler, M., & Sigel, R. K. O. (2005). In vitro transcription and purification of RNAs of different size. *Chimia, 59*, 812–816.

Gallo, S., Mundwiler, S., Alberto, R., & Sigel, R. K. O. (2010). The change of corrin-amides to carboxylates leads to altered structures of the B_{12}-responding *btuB* riboswitch. *Chemical Communications, 47*, 403–405.

Gallo, S., Oberhuber, M., Sigel, R. K. O., & Krautler, B. (2008). The corrin moiety of coenzyme B12 is the determinant for switching the btuB riboswitch of E. coli. *Chembiochem, 9*, 1408–1414.

Heller, K., & Kadner, R. J. (1985). Nucleotide sequence of the gene for the vitamin B12 receptor protein in the outer membrane of Escherichia coli. *Journal of Bacteriology, 161*, 904–908.

Hilario, E. (2002). End labeling procedures. An overview. *Methods in Molecular Biology, 179*, 13–18.

Homola, J. (2003). Present and future of surface plasmon resonance biosensors. *Analytical and Bioanalytical Chemistry, 377*, 528–539.

Jankowska-Anyszka, M., Piecyk, K., & Samonina-Kosicka, J. (2011). Synthesis of a new class of ribose functionalized dinucleotide cap analogues for biophysical studies on interaction of cap-binding proteins with the 5′ end of mRNA. *Organic and Biomolecular Chemistry, 9*, 5564–5572.

Jenkins, J. L., Krucinska, J., McCarty, R. M., Bandarian, V., & Wedekind, J. E. (2011). Comparison of a preQ1 riboswitch aptamer in metabolite-bound and free states with implications for gene regulation. *Journal of Biological Chemistry, 286*, 24626–24637.

Johnson, J. E., Jr., Reyes, F. E., Polaski, J. T., & Batey, R. T. (2012). B_{12} cofactors directly stabilize an mRNA regulatory switch. *Nature, 492*, 133–137.

Jonsson, U., Fagerstam, L., Ivarsson, B., Johnsson, B., Karlsson, R., Lundh, K., et al. (1991). Real-time biospecific interaction analysis using surface plasmon resonance and a sensor chip technology. *Biotechniques, 11*, 620–627.

Kim, H. S., Wilce, M. C., Yoga, Y. M., Pendini, N. R., Gunzburg, M. J., Cowieson, N. P., et al. (2011). Different modes of interaction by TIAR and HuR with target RNA and DNA. *Nucleic Acids Research, 39*, 1117–1130.

Lamichhane, T. N., Abeydeera, N. D., Duc, A. C., Cunningham, P. R., & Chow, C. S. (2011). Selection of peptides targeting helix 31 of bacterial 16S ribosomal RNA by screening M13 phage-display libraries. *Molecules, 16*, 1211–1239.

Lundrigan, M. D., Koster, W., & Kadner, R. J. (1991). Transcribed sequences of the Escherichia coli btuB gene control its expression and regulation by vitamin B12. *Proceedings of the National Academy of Sciences of the United States of America, 88*, 1479–1483.

Malmqvist, M. (1993). Biospecific interaction analysis using biosensor technology. *Nature, 361*, 186–187.

Malmqvist, M., & Karlsson, R. (1997). Biomolecular interaction analysis: Affinity biosensor technologies for functional analysis of proteins. *Current Opinion in Chemical Biology, 1*, 378–383.

Mandal, M., & Breaker, R. R. (2004). Gene regulation by riboswitches. *Nature Reviews. Molecular Cell Biology, 5*, 451–463.

Mayer, G., Raddatz, M. S., Grunwald, J. D., & Famulok, M. (2007). RNA ligands that distinguish metabolite-induced conformations in the TPP riboswitch. *Angewandte Chemie, 46*, 557–560.

Metzinger, L., Hallier, M., & Felden, B. (2008). The highest affinity binding site of small protein B on transfer messenger RNA is outside the tRNA domain. *RNA, 14*, 1761–1772.

Mori, D., Sasagawa, N., Kino, Y., & Ishiura, S. (2008). Quantitative analysis of CUG-BP1 binding to RNA repeats. *Journal of Biochemistry, 143*, 377–383.
Morton, T. A., & Myszka, D. G. (1998). Kinetic analysis of macromolecular interactions using surface plasmon resonance biosensors. *Methods in Enzymology, 295*, 268–294.
Myszka, D. G. (2000). Kinetic, equilibrium, and thermodynamic analysis of macromolecular interactions with BIACORE. *Methods in Enzymology, 323*, 325–340.
Nahvi, A., Barrick, J. E., & Breaker, R. R. (2004). Coenzyme B12 riboswitches are widespread genetic control elements in prokaryotes. *Nucleic Acids Research, 32*, 143–150.
Nahvi, A., Sudarsan, N., Ebert, M. S., Zou, X., Brown, K. L., & Breaker, R. R. (2002). Genetic control by a metabolite binding mRNA. *Chemistry and Biology, 9*, 1043.
Nou, X., & Kadner, R. J. (2000). Adenosylcobalamin inhibits ribosome binding to btuB RNA. *Proceedings of the National Academy of Sciences of the United States of America, 97*, 7190–7195.
Perdrizet, G. A., 2nd., Artsimovitch, I., Furman, R., Sosnick, T. R., & Pan, T. (2012). Transcriptional pausing coordinates folding of the aptamer domain and the expression platform of a riboswitch. *Proceedings of the National Academy of Sciences of the United States of America, 109*, 3323–3328.
Peselis, A., & Serganov, A. (2012). Structural insights into ligand binding and gene expression control by an adenosylcobalamin riboswitch. *Nature Structural Biology, 19*, 1182–1184.
Porecha, R., & Herschlag, D. (2013). RNA radiolabeling. *Methods in Enzymology, 530*, 255–279.
Ptushkina, M., von der Haar, T., Vasilescu, S., Frank, R., Birkenhager, R., & McCarthy, J. E. (1998). Cooperative modulation by eIF4G of eIF4E-binding to the mRNA 5′ cap in yeast involves a site partially shared by p20. *EMBO Journal, 17*, 4798–4808.
Ravnum, S., & Andersson, D. I. (2001). An adenosyl-cobalamin (coenzyme-B12)-repressed translational enhancer in the cob mRNA of Salmonella typhimurium. *Molecular Microbiology, 39*, 1585–1594.
Regulski, E. E., & Breaker, R. R. (2008). In-line probing analysis of riboswitches. *Methods in Molecular Biology, 419*, 53–67.
Richter-Dahlfors, A. A., & Andersson, D. I. (1992). Cobalamin (vitamin B12) repression of the Cob operon in Salmonella typhimurium requires sequences within the leader and the first translated open reading frame. *Molecular Microbiology, 6*, 743–749.
Richter-Dahlfors, A. A., Ravnum, S., & Andersson, D. I. (1994). Vitamin B12 repression of the cob operon in Salmonella typhimurium: Translational control of the cbiA gene. *Molecular Microbiology, 13*, 541–553.
Sambrook, J., & Russell, D. W. (2001). *Molecular cloning: A laboratory manual.* 4 ed. New York: CSHL Press.
Serganov, A., & Patel, D. J. (2012). Metabolite recognition principles and molecular mechanisms underlying riboswitch function. *Annual Review of Biophysics, 41*, 343–370.
Sigel, R. K., Freisinger, E., & Lippert, B. (2000). Effects of N7-methylation, N7-platination, and C8-hydroxylation of guanine on H-bond formation with cytosine: Platinum coordination strengthens the Watson-Crick pair. *Journal of Biological Inorganic Chemistry, 5*, 287–299.
Sipova, H., & Homola, J. (2013). Surface plasmon resonance sensing of nucleic acids: A review. *Analytica Chimica Acta, 773*, 9–23.
Soukup, G. A., & Breaker, R. R. (1999). Relationship between internucleotide linkage geometry and the stability of RNA. *RNA, 5*, 1308–1325.
Souliere, M. F., Haller, A., Santner, T., & Micura, R. (2013). New insights into gene regulation—High-resolution structures of cobalamin riboswitches. *Angewandte Chemie, 52*, 1874–1877.

Szabo, A., Stolz, L., & Granzow, R. (1995). Surface plasmon resonance and its use in biomolecular interaction analysis (BIA). *Current Opinion in Structural Biology*, *5*, 699–705.

Tanious, F. A., Nguyen, B., & Wilson, W. D. (2008). Biosensor-surface plasmon resonance methods for quantitative analysis of biomolecular interactions. *Methods in Cell Biology*, *84*, 53–77.

Thompson, J. E., Kutateladze, T. G., Schuster, M. C., Venegas, F. D., Messmore, J. M., & Raines, R. T. (1995). Limits to catalysis by ribonuclease A. *Bioorganic Chemistry*, *23*, 471–481.

Torreri, P., Ceccarini, M., Macioce, P., & Petrucci, T. C. (2005). Biomolecular interactions by surface plasmon resonance technology. *Annali Dell Istituto Superiore di Sanita*, *41*, 437–441.

Tseng, M. C., & Chu, Y. H. (2005). Using surface plasmon resonance to directly identify molecules in a tripeptide library that bind tightly to a vancomycin chip. *Analytical Biochemistry*, *336*, 172–177.

Vitreschak, A. G., Rodionov, D. A., Mironov, A. A., & Gelfand, M. S. (2003). Regulation of the vitamin B12 metabolism and transport in bacteria by a conserved RNA structural element. *RNA*, *9*, 1084–1097.

Wilson, D. W. (2002). Analyzing biomolecular interactions. *Science*, *295*, 2103–2105.

Zhang, J., Lau, M. W., & Ferre-D'Amare, A. R. (2010). Ribozymes and riboswitches: Modulation of RNA function by small molecules. *Biochemistry*, *49*, 9123–9131.

CHAPTER TWENTY-ONE

Assessing RNA Interactions with Proteins by DRaCALA

Darshan K. Patel*, Margo P. Gebbie[†,‡], Vincent T. Lee[*,‡,1]

*Department of Cell Biology and Molecular Genetics, University of Maryland, College Park, MD, USA
[†]Department of Chemistry and Biochemistry, University of Maryland, College Park, MD, USA
[‡]Maryland Pathogen Research Institute, University of Maryland, College Park, MD, USA
[1]Corresponding author: e-mail address: vtlee@umd.edu

Contents

Abstract

Discovery of RNA elements, including riboswitches and regulatory RNAs, has revealed additional regulatory mechanisms for transcript stability, transcript termination, and translational initiation. These regulatory RNA molecules act through direct binding to cellular targets including other RNA molecules, proteins, and low molecular weight metabolites. RNA–RNA interactions based on complementarity can be identified through bioinformatic analysis. However, identification of novel interactions between these regulatory RNA molecules and their partners other than complementary sequences is more challenging. We have developed a technique called *D*ifferential *Ra*dial *C*apillary *A*ction of *L*igand *A*ssay (DRaCALA) to facilitate the detection of direct binding between RNA elements to proteins or low molecular weight ligands. Previously, we have described the adaptation of this technique to detect the binding interaction

Methods in Enzymology, Volume 549
ISSN 0076-6879
http://dx.doi.org/10.1016/B978-0-12-801122-5.00021-0

between Vc2 riboswitch to a signaling cyclic dinucleotide called cyclic-di-GMP. Here, we describe the adaptation of DRaCALA for identifying sequence-specific RNA-binding proteins directly from *E. coli* cell lysates expressing the recombinant binding protein. DRaCALA can be used to qualitatively and quantitatively assess RNA–protein interaction in whole cell lysate, determine the kinetics of the binding, and test for competitors. Using DRaCALA in a high-throughput format has the potential to rapidly identify sequence-specific RNA-binding proteins.

1. INTRODUCTION

Small RNA (sRNA) elements play an important role in posttranscriptional regulation by base pairing with the target mRNA or by directly binding to sequester regulatory proteins (Masse, Majdalani, & Gottesman, 2003; Storz, Vogel, & Wassarman, 2011; Waters & Storz, 2009). Additionally, RNA riboswitches located at the 5′-UTR of transcripts can interact with low molecule weight ligands to alter RNA folding and thereby alter terminator formation and ribosome accessibility. For each of these classes of RNAs, identification of their cellular partners and targets can reveal the underlying basis for regulation. While mechanisms of regulation by antisense RNAs have been characterized in depth, few examples of interaction between proteins and sequence-specific sRNAs have been identified. Nonetheless, these interactions have potential to regulate bacterial physiology and virulence as demonstrated by the CsrA/RsmA RNA-binding proteins (Babitzke & Romeo, 2007). Bioinformatics approaches have revealed many sRNAs (Raghavan, Groisman, & Ochman, 2011) and a subset of these elements have the potential to bind proteins. However, the protein partners for these sRNAs remain uncharacterized. Thus, identification of direct interaction between sRNAs and protein-binding partners represents an opportunity for discovery. There are many methods to identify protein–RNA interactions based on biochemical or genetic/molecular biology approaches. Biochemical-based approaches use either candidate protein or candidate RNA as baits to pull-down associated partners. Pull-down experiments using biotinylated RNA can isolate proteins (Iioka, Loiselle, Haystead, & Macara, 2011) that can be identified by mass spectrometry. Alternatively, crosslinking and immunoprecipitation of a known protein can isolate associated RNA species that can be identified by high-throughput sequencing (Jensen & Darnell, 2008; Murigneux, Sauliere, Roest Crollius, & Le Hir, 2013). In both cases, subsequent prioritization and characterization of the large number of candidate proteins and RNAs can be time consuming. A genetic/molecular biological approach utilizes the yeast three-hybrid system to detect protein–RNA interactions (Putz, Skehel, & Kuhl, 1996; SenGupta et al., 1996). The system consist of three components: the hook, which is the fusion protein between a sequence-specific RNA-binding domain and a DNA-binding domain; the bait, which is the hybrid RNA containing the specific binding sequence for the hook and a target RNA sequence of interest; and the prey, which is a fusion protein consisting of an activation domain and candidate proteins that bind the target RNA sequence. When the bait RNA binds both the hook and the prey proteins, the activation domain triggers the expression of the reporter gene. Despite successes, yeast three-hybrid systems face similar challenges of false positives as the yeast two-hybrid systems (Martin, 2012). The field has been limited, in part, by the lack of an easy to perform assay that have both high sensitivity of detection and allows rapid follow-up studies. Here, we describe the application of *D*ifferential *Ra*dial *C*apillary *A*ction of *L*igand *A*ssay (DRaCALA) for the rapid detection of RNA–protein interactions.

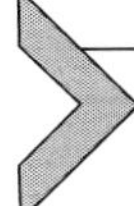

2. DRaCALA-BASED DETECTION OF PROTEIN–LIGAND INTERACTIONS

We have developed DRaCALA as a method to qualitatively and quantitatively determine protein-ligand interactions. We have utilized DRaCALA to detect interaction between various nucleic acids and purified proteins. Interactions between signaling nucleotides, such as cyclic AMP (Roelofs, Wang, Sintim, & Lee, 2011), cyclic-di-GMP (c-di-GMP) (Roelofs et al., 2011), and cyclic-di-AMP (c-di-AMP) (Corrigan et al., 2013), and their protein receptors were quantitatively assessed by DRaCALA. In addition to the detection of protein–ligand interactions, DRaCALA was able to detect the interaction of the Vc2 riboswitch and c-di-GMP (Sudarsan et al., 2008) with sensitivity that is similar to electrophoretic mobility shift assay (Donaldson, Roelofs, Luo, Sintim, & Lee, 2011). DRaCALA also allowed detection between purified proteins and larger DNA molecules, including DNA oligonucleotides, PCR products, and linearized DNA plasmids (Donaldson et al., 2011). Similarly, binding between RNA and protein was detected. EutV, the protein response regulator of the ethanolamine utilization operon, binding to the 5′-leader region of *eutP* mRNA was demonstrated using DRaCALA (Ramesh et al., 2012). In addition to direct detection of protein–ligand interactions, competition experiments have demonstrated binding specificity (Corrigan et al., 2013;

Donaldson et al., 2011; Roelofs et al., 2011). Further modification of DRaCALA for high-throughput screening allowed identification of ebselen as an inhibitor of c-di-GMP binding to receptor proteins (Lieberman, Orr, Wang, & Lee, 2013). DRaCALA represents a rapid method to detect interactions between protein and nucleic acid ligands.

More importantly, DRaCALA can allow detection of protein–ligand interaction in whole cell lysates, thereby eliminating the necessity of protein purification. DRaCALA allowed for the discovery of novel interacting partners through screening of individual *E. coli* extracts expressing each gene within an open reading frame library (ORFeome) of an organism. C-di-AMP is a recently discovered nucleotide in Gram positive organisms that appears to be essential for viability, suggesting that c-di-AMP regulates important biological processes (Corrigan, Abbott, Burhenne, Kaever, & Grundling, 2011; Mehne et al., 2013; Witte et al., 2013). However, c-di-AMP receptor proteins remained unknown in Gram positive organisms. DRaCALA screening of *E. coli* whole cell lysates expressing each of the genes within the *Staphylococcus aureus* ORFeome permitted the identification of three c-di-AMP binding proteins: KtrA, PstA, and KdpD (Corrigan et al., 2013). Identification of these receptor proteins represents an important advance in the understanding of c-di-AMP regulation.

Here, we describe the use of DRaCALA for detection of interactions between RNA and sequence-specific binding protein expressed in whole cell lysates using the most well-characterized sequence-specific RNA-binding protein, CsrA (carbon storage regulator). CsrA, first discovered in *E. coli* (Liu et al., 1997), regulates many phenotypes such as carbon metabolism, motility, and biofilm development (Babitzke & Romeo, 2007; Romeo, 1998). CsrA binds the 5′-UTR of target mRNAs at sequences that overlap the Shine–Delgarno sequence to inhibit translation initiation (Dubey, Baker, Romeo, & Babitzke, 2005; Liu & Romeo, 1997; Schubert et al., 2007). Free CsrA can be sequestered by the expression of sRNAs, CsrB and CsrC (Dubey et al., 2005; Weilbacher et al., 2003). A common feature of these sRNAs is the presence of multiple short stem loops that contain GGA sequence that specifically bind to CsrA (Dubey et al., 2005). As a consequence of CsrA sequestration by sRNAs, the Shine–Delgarno sites of mRNAs targets are no longer occluded and available for translation. CsrA homologs and homologs of the sRNAs exist in many bacteria (Babitzke & Romeo, 2007). For example, in *Vibrio cholerae*, CsrA is regulated by three functionally redundant sRNAs: CsrB, CsrC, and CsrD (Lenz, Miller, Zhu, Kulkarni, & Bassler, 2005). In *Pseudomonas aeruginosa*, the CsrA homolog is called RsmA, while the sRNAs are called RsmY and RsmZ (Valverde, Heeb, Keel, & Haas, 2003). In comparison to the *V. cholerae* CsrB, CsrC, and CsrD, RsmY and RsmZ are shorter. Despite the difference in length, the *P. aeruginosa* sRNA also contains repeat GGA motifs in short stem loops. The methods and results are described for DRaCALA-based detection of protein–RNA interaction in whole cell lysate using *V. cholerae* CsrA and *P. aeruginosa* sRNA, RsmY and RsmZ.

3. PRINCIPLE OF DRaCALA

DRaCALA relies on the differential mobility of the unbound ligand and the protein–ligand complex when applied on dry nitrocellulose. In general, the radiolabeled ligand is incubated with the protein of interest to allow the protein–ligand complex to reach equilibrium. A small aliquot of the equilibrated reaction mixture is applied to dry nitrocellulose paper. By means of capillary action, the reaction mix spreads out on the nitrocellulose radially, leading to a uniform distribution of the unbound ligand while the protein–ligand complex is immobilized at the center of the spot (Fig. 21.1A, taken with permission from Roelofs et al., 2011). Afterwards, the spot is exposed on to a phosphorimager screen and is visualized using a phosphorimager. The resulting image consists of a single spot composed of an inner circle and an outer circle (Roelofs et al., 2011). We have adapted DRaCALA for detection of the Vc2 RNA riboswitch with c-di-GMP. In this particular case, both the macromolecular receptor and the low molecular ligand are nucleic acids and both molecules can be mobilized on nitrocellulose (Donaldson et al., 2011). To immobilize the RNA riboswitch, we biotinylated the 3′-OH of the Vc2 RNA and allowed the modified RNA to bind streptavidin. The streptavidin-biotinylated RNA complex is retained at the site of application and can be used to detect binding to radiolabeled c-di-GMP (Donaldson et al., 2011). Similarly, RNA may be sequestered using sequence-specific RNA-binding protein such as the MS2 phage coat protein.

4. DETERMINATION OF FRACTION BOUND BY DRaCALA

The fraction bound can be determined by measuring the intensity of the inner circle (I_{inner}), the area of the inner circle (A_{inner}), the intensity of the total spot (I_{total}), and the total area of the spot (A_{total}). Calculating the signal intensity sequestered in the inner circle divided by the total signal

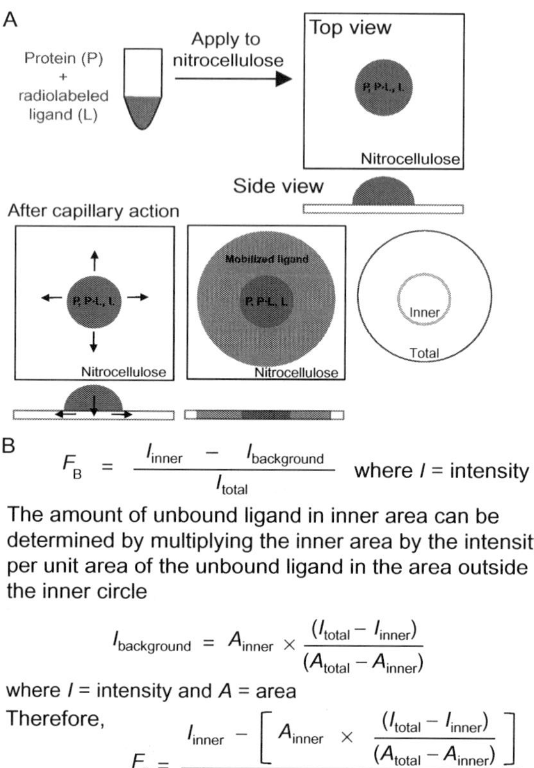

Figure 21.1 Principle of Differential Radial Capillary Action of Ligand Assay (DRaCALA). (A) Schematic representation of DRaCALA assay upon application of protein–ligand mixture onto nitrocellulose and subsequent capillary action. Protein (P), ligand (L), and protein–ligand complexes (P·L) distribution during the assay is shown. (B) Equations used to analyze DRaCALA data for fraction bound (F_B) for purified proteins. *Image is taken with permission from Roelofs et al. (2011).*

intensity of the entire sample (I_{total}) gives the fraction bound. However, the intensity in the inner circle represents the sum of both the bound ligand and unbound ligand that is evenly distributed throughout the entire spot. In order to correctly determine the intensity that is sequestered by proteins in the inner circle, the background intensity ($I_{background}$) of the unbound ligand in the area of the inner circle must be subtracted. Assuming that the unbound ligand is uniformly distributed, the background intensity per unit area can be calculated by equation shown in Fig. 21.1B. Multiplying this background density to the area of the inner circle yields the background intensity within the inner circle ($I_{background}$). The total ligand bound by the protein can be calculated by subtracting the $I_{background}$ from I_{inner}, which can be divided by the total intensity (I_{total}) to determine the fraction of ligand bound (Fig. 21.1B).

5. STEPS FOR PERFORMING DRaCALA TO DETECT PROTEIN INTERACTION WITH RNA

1. Generation of whole cell lysates (or purified proteins)
2. Generation of RNA ligand
3. Labeling of RNA ligand
4. DRaCALA assay
   a. Qualitative assessment of binding
   b. Relative affinity
   c. Binding specificity by competition

5.1. Procedure: Preparation of expression vector

DRaCALA detection of RNA–protein interactions can utilize proteins of varying purity. Rapid analysis of binding can be performed in whole cell lysates, although detection by DRaCALA requires that the protein concentration within whole cell lysates be above K_d. Typically, this is accomplished by utilizing IPTG-inducible T7 plasmids such as the pET vectors (Novagen). Genes can be placed into these plasmids by restriction, recombination, or Gibson cloning. Below are the procedures for recombination cloning to generate CsrA expression plasmids.

5.1.1 Reagents

- LR Clonase enzyme mix (Invitrogen)
- DONR vectors containing the ORF of interest
- pDEST expression vectors with the desired N- or C-terminal tags
- LB agar plates with appropriate antibiotics
- LB with 20% glycerol

5.1.2 Method

1. Gateway DONR plasmid containing sequence-verified CsrA was miniprepped from *E. coli* strain within the *V. cholerae* ORFeome library.
2. Recombination of ORFs into pDEST vectors (shown here pVL791-GW and pVL847-GW) was accomplished by mixing purified plasmid DNA, pDONR-CsrA, and LR recombinase enzyme mix (Invitrogen). The reaction was incubated for 2 h at room temperature.

3. Recombined plasmids were transformed in chemically competent *E. coli* T7 express I^q strain (NEB) and plated on selective agar plates supplemented with the appropriate antibiotics.
4. Strains were frozen in LB with 20% glycerol at −80 °C.

5.2. Procedure: Preparation of whole cell lysates

5.2.1 Reagents

- LB agar plates with appropriate antibiotics
- Sterile 96 deep well plates
- 96-well round bottom plates
- LB-M9—Na_2HPO_4 (7.0 g/l), KH_2PO_4 (2.0 g/l), NaCl (0.5 g/l), NH_4Cl (1.0 g/l), glucose (2.0 g/l), sodium succinate hexahydrate (1.0 g/l), tryptone (10 g/l), Yeast Extract (5 g/l); pH to 7.2 before autoclaving. Add sterile-filter 1 *M* $MgSO_4$ to a final concentration of 2 m*M* immediately before use
- Lysis buffer—1 m*M* PMSF, 10 μg/ml DNaseI, and 25 μg/ml lysozyme in 10 m*M* Tris, pH 8, 100 m*M* NaCl, and 5 m*M* $MgCl_2$
- 12% SDS-PAGE gel

5.2.2 Method

1. Strains were streaked out from frozen stocks on appropriate selective plates.
2. Single colonies were grown overnight at 30 °C in LB-M9 with constant shaking (~150 rpm).
3. Overnight cultures were subcultured in 1:50 in deep well plate containing 1.5 ml LB-M9 for 4 h at 30 °C. Cultures were then induced for protein expression by addition of 1 m*M* IPTG for 4 additional hours at 30 °C.
4. Following induction, the cells were pelleted by centrifugation and the culture supernatant was decanted.
5. The pellets were concentrated 10-fold by adding 150 μl of lysis buffer. *Note*: Lysozyme binds RNA and concentrations of lysozyme higher than indicated above will result in nonspecific binding to RNA.
6. The pellets were resuspended by shaking the plate on a plate shaker for 1 min. Shake longer if necessary.
7. Plates were sealed with aluminum plate seals.
8. Cells were lysed by two rounds of freeze–thaw. Plates were placed in the −80 °C to freeze the whole cell lysate for at least 1 h and then

thawed in a water bath at room temperature for 20 min. Repeat once more.

9. After the lysates were thawed, 20 μl of lysate was transferred to round bottom 96-well plates. *Note*: 6 plate aliquots can be generated from 150 μl of lysate. The remaining lysate was analyzed by denaturing SDS-PAGE gel to confirm protein overexpression. Typically, protein that can be visualized by Coomassie staining is sufficient for detection of interactions with K_d that are 10 μ*M* or lower. Quantitative measurements by DRaCALA should be subsequently performed with purified proteins.
10. The round bottom plates were stored at −80 °C until use.

5.3. Procedure: Template generation

Detection of protein–ligand binding interactions using DRaCALA requires the ligand to be radiolabeled. For protein–RNA interaction detection, the RNA of interest must be radiolabeled. *In vitro* transcription is suitable method for generating of a wide array of RNA species of varying length. *In vitro* transcription requires T7 RNA polymerase and the DNA template with a T7 promoter (5′-TAATACGACTCACTATAGGG-3′) and the coding sequence of the RNA of interest. The template can be generated by chemical synthesis or by PCR amplification of the target sequence. We used PCR amplification to generate the template for *in vitro* transcription of RsmY and RsmZ.

5.3.1 Reagents

- Primers for RNA of interest
- Template DNA
- Thermocycler
- PCR reagents—polymerase, buffer, dNTPs, and $MgCl_2$
- PCR clean-up column
- Agarose gel
- Spectrophotometer

5.3.2 Method

The template can be generated by using primers to amplify the sequence encoding the RNA directly from genomic DNA. The 5′-primer consists of the promoter sequence of T7 RNA polymerase followed by the target sequence. The 3′-primer is the reverse complement of the 3′-end of the target sequence. We used this method to generate the template for *in vitro* transcription of RsmY and RsmZ RNA. Due to high GC content of *P. aeruginosa* genome, the templates for RsmY and RsmZ were generated by sequential nested PCRs.

1. Primers were used to amplify and clone the RsmY and RsmZ regions consisting of the RsmY and RsmZ sequence flanked by ~100 additional bases on each side of the sequence.
   Option: The PCR product can be cloned and sequence verified.
2. The template for *in vitro* transcription was generated using a nested PCR. The 5′-primer was designed with a T7 promoter sequence and the target sequence. The 3′-primer is the reverse complement of the 3′-sequence of the target. These primers were used to amplify the target specific sequence from the plasmid.
3. Product was visualized by separation on agarose gel.
4. A Wizard minicolumn (Promega) was used to clean and concentrate the PCR product.
5. The product concentration was determined using a spectrophotometer and the product was stored at −20 °C.

5.3.3 Consideration for template generation

For sRNA species, annealing DNA oligonucleotides can be used. If one does not have genomic DNA for the sequence of interest, gBlocks (IDT) can be commercially ordered that include a T7 promoter and DNA sequence of interest. These gBlocks can be directly used for *in vitro* transcription.

5.4. Procedure: *In vitro* transcription of RNA

5.4.1 Reagents

- DNA template
- *In vitro* transcription reagents—T7 RNA polymerase, Transcription buffer, and NTPs
- 8 *M* Urea-PAGE gel for gel purification of RNA
- UV lamp
- Thin-layer chromatography (TLC) plate with fluorescent indicator
- Crush-soak solution—200 m*M* NaCl, 10 m*M* Tris–HCl, pH 7.5, and 1 m*M* EDTA, pH 8.0
- 2× RNA loading solution—18 *M* Urea, 20% w/v sucrose, 0.1% SDS, 0.05% bromophenol blue, 0.05% xylene cyanol FF, 90 m*M* Tris, 90 m*M* borate, 1 m*M* EDTA, pH 8.0
- Saran wrap

- Microcentrifuge
- 3 *M* Sodium acetate, pH 5.2
- 100% Isopropanol
- 70% cold ethanol
- Spectrophotometer

5.4.2 Method

1. For the transcription of RsmY and RsmZ, the following reaction was performed in a total volume of 50 μl:

Reagents	**Volume (μl)**
Template	Volume for 50 pmol
10 × Transcription buffer	5 (1 ×)
20 m*M* NTP Mix	5 (2 m*M*)
T7 RNA polymerase	6 (300 units)
Nuclease-free ddH_2O	Fill to 50 μl
Total	50 μl

2. The reaction was incubated for 2 h at 37 °C.
3. After incubation, 50 μl of 2 × RNA loading solution was added to the reaction and the entire sample was separated on a denaturing 6% PAGE gel with 8 *M* urea.
4. Following electrophoresis, the gel was wrapped in Saran wrap and placed above the TLC plate with fluorescent indicator.
5. A UV lamp was placed above the gel to visualize a shadow of RNA product on the TLC plate. A successful *in vitro*-transcribed RNA product will be visualized as a purple-black band at the position of the expected size of the RNA.
6. The band corresponding to the RNA of interest was excised, cut into 1 mm pieces, and placed in the crush-soak solution. Enough crush-soak should be used to cover all the gel pieces.
   Note: Use a fresh razor blade for each RNA species to avoid cross contamination.
7. The RNA was eluted from the gel by incubation of the gel pieces in the crush-soak solution for at least 2 h with constant shaking at room temperature or overnight at 4 °C.

8. The supernatant of the crush-soak solution was transferred into a new microcentrifuge tube.
9. RNA (equal 1 volume) was precipitated using 2 volume of isopropanol and 1/10 volume of 3 *M* sodium acetate (pH 5.2). Incubate at room temperature for 10 min.
10. RNA was pelleted by centrifugation at 15,000 rpm for 15 min at 4 °C. Supernatant was discarded. Be careful since the pellet is likely invisible at this point.
11. RNA pellet was washed with 200 μl of 70% cold ethanol.
12. RNA was pelleted by centrifugation at 15,000 rpm for 7 min at 4 °C to pellet RNA. Supernatant was discarded.
13. The RNA pellet was resuspended in nuclease-free water and stored at −20 °C for short-term storage or −80 °C for long-term storage.
14. The concentration of RNA was determined using a spectrophotometer. The A260/280 ratio can be used to gauge sample purity. A ratio of ~2.0 signifies clean RNA.

5.5. Procedure: 5′-end labeling of RNA

Once the RNA was generated, the RNA was radiolabeled for detection. Radiolabeled RNA is appropriate for DRaCALA since we have found that fluorescent dyes are not mobile on nitrocellulose (Donaldson et al., 2011). *In vitro* synthesized RNA has a 5′-triphosphate that must be removed prior to 5′-end label. Removal of the triphosphate can be performed using any 5′-phosphatase. For our experiments, the triphosphate was removed by Antarctic Phosphatase (AnP). AnP-treated RNA was then 5′-end labeled using T4 Polynucleotide Kinase (T4 PNK) and γ-^{32}P-ATP.

5.5.1 Reagents

- AnP and 10× buffer (NEB)
- Phenol:chloroform:isoamyl alcohol (25:24:1, v/v)
- Chloroform
- 3 *M* Sodium acetate, pH 5.2
- 100% Isopropanol
- 70% cold ethanol
- T4 PNK and 10× buffer (NEB)
- γ-^{32}P-ATP (3000 Ci/mmol; 10 mCi/ml)
- NucAway Spin Column (Life Technologies)
- Nitrocellulose (GE Healthcare Life Sciences)

- Phosphorimager, phosphorimager sheet, cassettes, and quantification software
- TLC chamber
- TLC plate
- TLC buffer (1:1.5 v/v of saturated $(NH_4)_2SO_4$ and 1.5 *M* KH_2PO_4)

5.5.2 Method: AnP treatment to remove 5′-triphosphate

1. The following reaction was performed to remove the triphosphate from the RsmY and RsmZ RNA:

Reagents	Volume (μl)
5 μg RNA	Volume for 5 μg RNA
10× AnP Buffer	2
AnP	2
ddH_2O	Fill to 20 μl
Total	20

2. The reaction was incubated at 37 °C for 15 min.
3. After the incubation, the AnP was heat inactivated by incubation at 70 °C for 5 min.
4. AnP was removed by phenol:chloroform extraction. 180 μl of ddH_2O was added to the reaction, followed by 20 μl of 3 *M* sodium acetate (pH 5.2) and 200 μl of phenol:chloroform:isoamyl alcohol. Invert several times.
5. The aqueous and organic phases were separated by centrifugation for 8 min at 15,000 rpm. 200 μl of the aqueous layer (top) was placed into a new 1.7-ml microcentrifuge tube. The remaining tube was discarded.
6. 200 μl of chloroform was added, inverted several times, and 200 μl of the aqueous layer (top) was placed into a new microcentrifuge tube. The remaining tube was discarded.
7. RNA was precipitated by adding 2.5 volumes of isopropanol and incubating for 10 min at room temperature.
8. RNA was pelleted by centrifugation at 15,000 rpm for 15 min at 4 °C.
9. Supernatant was removed and 200 μl of cold 70% ethanol was added to wash the pellet.
10. RNA was pelleted by centrifugation at 15,000 rpm for 7 min at 4 °C.

11. Supernatant was removed and dephosphorylated RNA was resuspended in 20 μl of ddH_2O.
12. RNA was stored at −20 °C until use.

5.5.3 Method: 5′-end labeling of RsmY and RsmZ

1. For the 5′-end labeling of RsmY and RsmZ, the following reaction was performed in a 20 μl total volume:

Reagents	Volume (μl)
25 pmol of RNA (AnP treated)	Volume for 25 pmol RNA
γ-^{32}P-ATP	4
10 × T4 PNK Buffer	2
T4 PNK	2
ddH_2O	Fill to 20 μl
Total	20

2. The reaction was incubated at 37 °C for 1 h.
3. After the incubation, the T4 PNK was heat inactivated by incubation at 65 °C for 20 min.
4. The reaction was applied to a NucAway column equilibrated with ddH_2O to recover radiolabeled RNA and to remove free phosphates, ADP, and γ-^{32}P-ATP.
   Option: If RNA degradation is a concern, the radiolabeled RNA can be PAGE gel purified to remove any degraded RNA.
5. The recovered RNA was stored at −20 °C until use.
6. The transfer of γ-^{32}P from γ-^{32}P-ATP to the RNA was observed using TLC. One microliter of the sample was removed prereaction, post-reaction, and post-NucAway column and diluted 1:10. 0.6 μl was spotted 1 cm from the bottom of an 8-cm TLC plate. Sample was dried and then separated in TLC chamber equilibrated with the TLC buffer. TLC plate was dried, exposed to phosphorimager screen and scanned in a phosphorimager. Successful transfer of the radiolabeled γ-phosphate from the radiolabeled ATP to the RNA resulted in a decrease in radioactivity signal corresponding to the ATP spot and an increase in radioactivity signal corresponding to the RNA spot.

7. The activity of the labeled RNA was determined by spotting a 1:10 diluted sample on nitrocellulose, exposing the nitrocellulose to a phosphorimager sheet for 10 min, and measuring the resulting signal.

Note: It is advised that the RNA be used within a month. Radiolabeled RNA stored for more than a month will yield poor results from radioactive decay, spontaneous cleavage of the ^{32}P label and in-line cleavage of RNA backbone.

5.5.4 Consideration for labeling of RNA ligand

As an alternative to end labeling, the RNA could also be body labeled. Body labeled RNA is generated using *in vitro* transcription by including a radioactive nucleotide (such as α-^{32}P ATP) into an alternative free nucleotide mix. As the RNA is being synthesized, the radiolabeled ATP will become incorporated into the RNA multiple times. Body labeling presents the advantage of high specific activity since multiple radiolabeled phosphates are present within the length of the RNA as compared to single radiolabeled phosphate in the 5′-end-labeled RNA. As a result, less of the body-labeled RNA can be used as a probe. This advantage can be particularly useful when detecting RNA and protein interactions with high affinity. However, body-labeled RNA must be PAGE gel purified in order to visualize RNA generation and remove other reaction components. Gel purification requires a designated gel-running apparatus for radiation use and proper handling of the radioactive waste.

5.6. Procedure: Determining protein–RNA interaction

DRaCALA can be used to determine protein–RNA interaction by simply combining the whole cell lysate and the radiolabeled RNA and spotting a portion of the reaction onto dry nitrocellulose paper. The ability of DRaCALA to detect protein–RNA interaction is demonstrated here by the binding of RsmY and RsmZ to CsrA.

5.6.1 Reagents

- Pin tool wash buffer (0.05% Tween 20 in deionized water)
- Pin tool applicator (V&P Scientific)
- 96-well round bottom plates
- Binding buffer (10 m*M* Tris, pH 8.0, 100 m*M* NaCl, 10 m*M* $MgCl_2$)
- Radiolabeled RNA
- Whole cell lysates (or purified proteins)

- Yeast total RNA (Ambion) as a nonspecific competitor (the selection of nonspecific RNA is an important consideration)
- Nitrocellulose
- Saran wrap
- Phosphorimager, phosphorimager screen, cassettes, and quantification software

5.6.2 Method: Binding reaction and spotting of DRaCALA spots

1. Whole cell lysate plate was removed from −80 °C freezer and allowed to thaw at room temperature for 10 min.
2. Stock radiolabeled RNA was removed from −20 °C freezer and diluted 1:25 in 1 × Binding buffer.
   Note: The concentration of the RNA is dependent on the specific activity of the radiolabel, which decays with time.
3. While the reagents were thawing, the pin tool was washed in the pin tool wash buffer by placing the pin side into the wash liquid and moving the pin tool back and forth several times.
4. Pin tool was placed onto the paper towels to wick away the wash buffer.
5. Repeat steps 3 and 4 at least four times before use, between samples, and after use to prevent cross contamination.
   Note: If using pipette tips, change tips between samples.
6. The following reaction was performed with whole cell lysate of the empty vectors (pVL791 and pVL847) and vectors containing CsrA (pVL791-CsrA and pVL847-CsrA):

Reaction component	Volume (μl)
Lysate	10
1 × Binding buffer or competitor in 1 × Binding buffer	5
1:25 ^{32}P-RNA Mix	5
Total	20

The total reaction volume is 20 μl and the final dilution of the radiolabeled RNA was 1:100. This volume is enough to allow spotting by the pin tool. The 1:100 dilution (concentration = 4 n*M*; specific activity = 400 nCi) allowed the RNA to stay well below K_d and allowed a strong signal to be detected in a reasonable time frame (~3 h).

7. The reaction was mixed by pipetting several times. If using round bottom plate, reactions were mixed by shaking on a plate shaker set on a gentle setting for 1 min.
8. The pin tool was placed into well and held for 10 s as capillary action draws the reaction mixture into the notches of the pin tool.
9. Pin tool was positioned vertically above the nitrocellulose at the intended spotting area and pressed onto the nitrocellulose in a single motion.
10. Gentle and even pressure was applied to ensure contact required to initiate capillary action. The pin is held in place for 10 s to allow complete diffusion of the liquid.
    Note: Should observe the liquid spreading from the point of contact.
    Note: If using pipette, place tip on nitrocellulose and the liquid should wick out of the tip. If the wicking process is not occurring, slowly depress plunger to place liquid onto dry nitrocellulose
11. Nitrocellulose membrane is allowed to air dry at room temperature. This takes about 5–10 min depending on the humidity of the room.
12. Dried nitrocellulose was wrapped completely in Saran wrap.
    Note: Make sure the Saran wrap is flat and without any wrinkles above the nitrocellulose.
13. Nitrocellulose was exposed to phosphorimager screen. The screen was scanned in a phosphorimager using the highest sensitivity setting.
14. For each spot, an inner and outer circle was drawn manually using the Fuji Multi Gauge software v3.0. For spots that lacked an inner circle, an inner circle was copied and pasted from another spot and centered within the outer circle. Area and intensity for inner and outer circle for each spot was determined. The equation in Fig. 21.1B was used to calculate the fraction bound for each spot (Roelofs et al., 2011). For large number of spots spaced uniformly, the plate function was used. For each image, the appropriate columns, rows, circle diameter, and spacing between circles need to be defined for the outer circle. A second plate function is used to define the inner circles.

Note: DRaCALA can also be performed using single- or multi-channel pipettes. For best results, volume used should be between 1 and 2.5 μl. The use of pin tool is not necessary, but accelerates sample processing time.

Visually, binding can be seen by the localization of the radioactivity signal in the inner circle of the DRaCALA spot. For the whole cells lysates that harbor CsrA on the plasmid, the majority of the radioactive signal is localized in the inner circle for pVL791-CsrA and pVL847-CsrA indicating binding

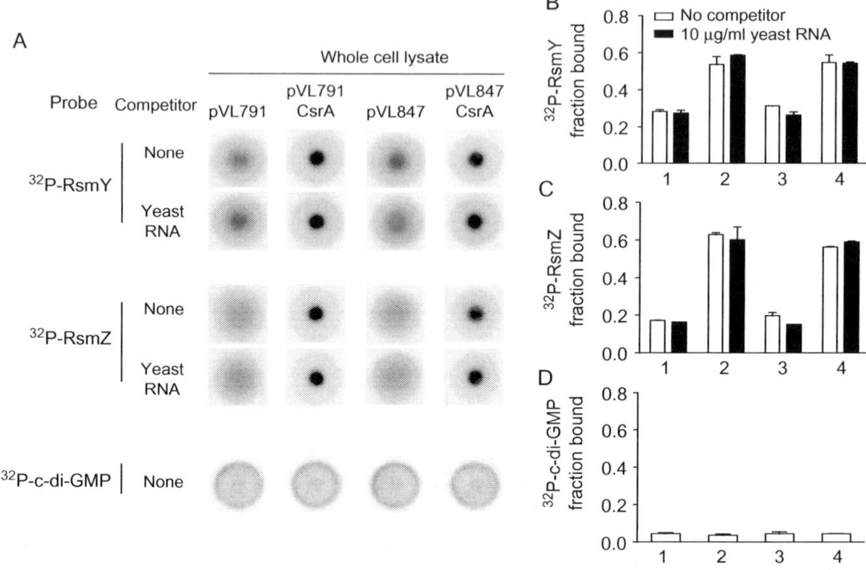

Figure 21.2 CsrA binds RsmY and RsmZ in whole cell lysate. (A) DRaCALA images of ^{32}P-RsmY and ^{32}P-RsmZ binding in empty vector whole cell lysate (pVL791 or pVL847), and CsrA expressing whole cell lysate (pVL791-CsrA or pVL847-CsrA) with no competitor or 10 μg/ml nonspecific total yeast RNA competitor. ^{32}P-c-di-GMP binding in whole cell lysate is shown to demonstrate nonspecific probe binding. (B, C, and D) Quantification of DRaCALA spots shown in (A). (1 = pVL791, 2 = pVL847, 3 = pVL791-CsrA, and 4 = pVL847-CsrA).

of RsmY and RsmZ (Fig. 21.2A). In contrast, less signal is localized in the inner circle of DRaCALA spots for whole cell lysate with the empty vector, indicating that less binding in the absence of heterologous CsrA expression. C-di-GMP, which does not bind CsrA, is not sequestered by whole cell lysates harboring either vector alone or vector expressing CsrA. Quantitation of the fraction bound can be determined using the equation in Fig. 21.1B. The fraction bound of RsmY in the pVL791 and pVL847 whole cell lysate was 0.28 and 0.31, respectively, while the fraction bound of RsmY in the pVL791-CsrA and pVL847-CsrA was 0.54 and 0.55, respectively (Fig. 21.2B). Similarly, the fraction bound of RsmZ in the pVL791 and pVL847 whole cell lysate was 0.17 and 0.20, respectively, while the fraction bound of RsmZ in the pVL791-CsrA and pVL847-CsrA was 0.63 and 0.56, respectively (Fig. 21.2C). The competition with nonspecific total yeast RNA had no effect on the fraction bound between RsmY and RsmZ to CsrA (Fig. 21.2B and C). Quantitation of the c-di-GMP spots showed no binding to any of the whole cell lysate (Fig. 21.2D). DRaCALA enables detection of CsrA binding to RsmY and RsmZ.

5.7. Procedure: Determining relative affinity

DRaCALA can be used to determine the amount of binding activity in a given whole cell lysate. By assaying serially diluted whole cell lysates, the relative binding activity can be determined by plotting the fraction bound value against the dilution. Below, the use of DRaCALA is demonstrated by twofold serial dilution of pVL791 lysate and pVL791-CsrA lysate in buffer followed by the addition of radiolabeled RsmY or radiolabeled RsmZ.

5.7.1 Method

1. Pin tool was cleaned as described above.
2. Whole cell lysate of empty vector (pVL791) and vector with CsrA (pVL791-CsrA) was removed from −80 °C and thawed for 10 min at room temperature.
3. While the lysates were thawing, 10 μl of buffer was added to each well of a round bottom plate except the wells of the 1st column.
4. To the wells in the 1st column, 20 μl of the appropriate thawed lysate was transferred.
5. Starting from the first well, 10 μl of the lysate was removed and added to the subsequent well and mixed by pipetting the mixture several times. A total of 11 twofold serial dilutions were performed. The first well contained 10 μl of undiluted lysate and each subsequent well was consisted of 10 μl of twofold diluted lysate from the previous well. The last well consisted only of buffer.
6. To each well 5 μl of buffer and 5 μl of 1:25 diluted radiolabeled RsmY or RsmZ was added.
7. The mixture was incubated for 1 min on the plate shaker.
8. The reaction was spotted on nitrocellulose and processed as described previously.
9. The fraction bound was calculated and plotted using Prism. The curve was fitted using a one-site total binding assumption.

Note: A more accurate determination of affinity can be determined with purified active protein.

The results show that diluting the lysate led to a reduction in the fraction bound for each dilution. The decrease in fraction bound can be discerned visually by the decreased localization of the signal in the inner circle of the DRaCALA spot as well as qualitatively by calculating the fraction bound.

The fraction bound can be plotted for each dilution to generate a graph that is similar to a dissociation curve. The fraction bound of RsmY and RsmZ to empty vector whole cell lysate and CsrA whole cell lysate was plotted using a one-site total binding assumption. For both RsmY and RsmZ, dilution of whole cell lysates that overproduced CsrA resulted in a decrease of binding activity until it reached 0. The CsrA containing lysate had approximately 16-fold more CsrA required for 1/2 maximal binding. The low level binding activity of RsmY/Z by the whole cell lysates containing empty vector lysate observed in Fig. 21.2A–C is also titratable. This is not surprising since *E. coli* encodes and expresses CsrA. Comparing the two curves, this suggests that there is approximately 16 × amount of CsrA binding activity when recombinant CsrA is overexpressed.

However, this method can only provide a relative measure of affinity since the CsrA protein concentration in the lysate is not determined. To determine the K_d accurately, the protein must be purified and assayed for binding using the same protocols as described in this section.

5.8. Procedure: Determining specificity of binding through competition

DRaCALA can be used to determine the specificity of binding competing the binding of the protein and radiolabeled ligand in the presence of excess, unlabeled RNA. We demonstrate the specificity of RsmY and RsmZ binding to CsrA by competing away binding of radiolabeled RsmY and RsmZ to CsrA in the presence of excess, unlabeled yeast total RNA, RsmY, and RsmZ.

5.8.1 Method

1. Pin tool was cleaned as described previously.
2. Whole cell lysate of empty vector (pVL791) and vector with CsrA (pVL791-CsrA) was removed from −80 °C and thawed for 10 min at room temperature.
3. The pVL791 lysate and pVL791-CsrA lysates were diluted 1:8 from the undiluted lysate. The dilution reflects the point at which pVL791-CsrA lysate binding to RsmY and RsmZ approached saturation as determined by the titration curve (Fig. 21.3).
4. To 10 μl of the diluted lysate, 5 μl of 40 μg/ml of unlabeled, total yeast RNA, 1.6 m*M* unlabeled RsmY, or 1.6 m*M* unlabeled RsmZ was

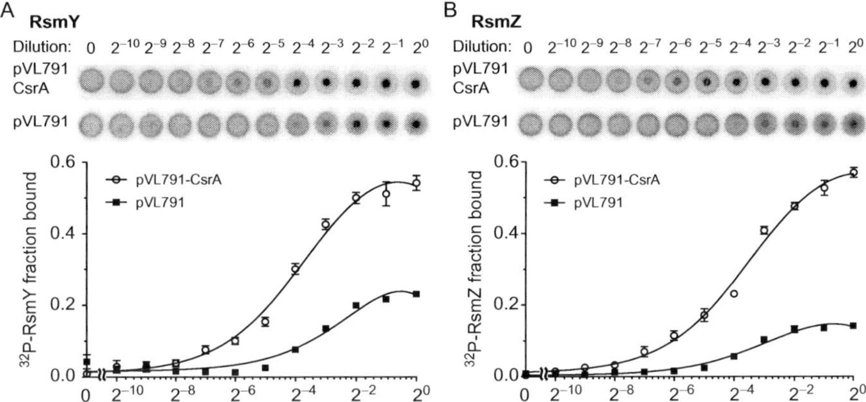

Figure 21.3 Both RsmY and RsmZ binding to CsrA are titratable. DRaCALA images (above) and quantification (below) of binding to ^{32}P-RsmY (A) or ^{32}P-RsmZ (B) by two-fold serially diluted pVL791 or pVL791-CsrA whole cell lysates.

added. To the control binding reaction, 5 μl of buffer was added in place of a competitor. After the addition of the competitors, 5 μl of 1:25 radiolabeled RsmY or RsmZ was added.

5. The spots were spotted on nitrocellulose and processed as described above.

6. CsrA BINDS SPECIFICALLY TO RsmY AND RsmZ

DRaCALA can be used to determine binding specificity by assaying RNA binding in the presence of competitors. To observe good competition, the protein or lysate concentration should be at 2 × the concentration required for 1/2 maximal binding. Whole cell lysates of vector alone and overexpressing CsrA were both diluted 1:8 to reflect this concentration (Fig. 21.3A and B). We assayed binding of radiolabeled RsmY and RsmZ in the presence of no competitor, nonspecific competitor (10 μg/ml of total yeast RNA) or specific competitor (400 n*M* of RsmY or 400 n*M* of RsmZ). Nonspecific total yeast RNA does not compete for the binding of CsrA to RsmZ (Fig. 21.4B), whereas excess RsmY or RsmZ RNAs were able to compete away binding of radiolabeled RsmY and RsmZ from CsrA. The competition assay reveals that CsrA binds specifically to RsmY and RsmZ.

Interestingly, the fraction bound for CsrA to RsmY and RsmZ in the presence of excess RsmY or RsmZ is less than even the binding in the empty vector lysate. These observations agree with the idea that binding of RsmY

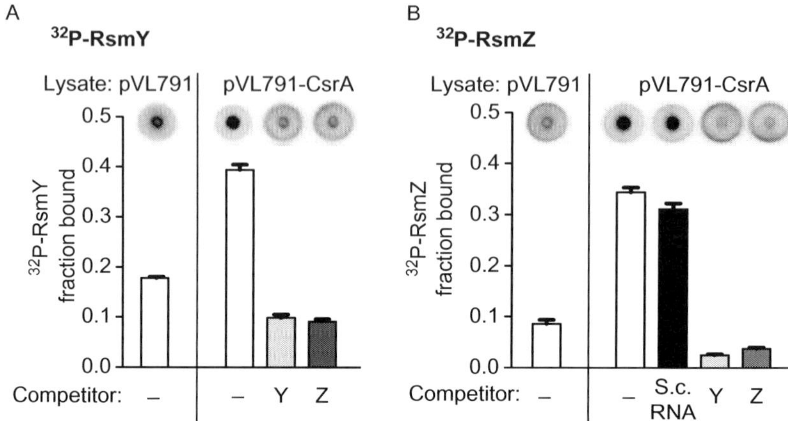

Figure 21.4 Unlabeled RsmY/Z can compete with CsrA binding to ^{32}P-RsmY and ^{32}P-RsmZ. DRaCALA images and quantification of ^{32}P-RsmY (A) and ^{32}P-RsmZ (B) binding to whole cell lysate containing an empty vector (pVL791) (diluted 1:8) with no competitor or whole cell lysate overexpressing CsrA (pVL791-CsrA) (diluted 1:8) in the presence of the indicated competitor: "–": no competitor; "Y": 400 n*M* unlabeled RsmY; "Z": 400 n*M* unlabeled RsmZ; and "S.c. RNA": 10 μg/ml total Yeast RNA competitor that serves as a nonspecific competitor.

and RsmZ to whole cell lysates harboring vector alone is due to endogenous *E. coli* CsrA. DRaCALA can be used to determine specificity of binding in whole cell lysate through the addition of specific and nonspecific competitors.

7. OTHER MODIFICATIONS OF DRaCALA FOR RNA–PROTEIN INTERACTIONS

DRaCALA can be modified in several ways to allow for systematic detection of binding proteins for a known RNA. We described here the assay for one single ORF (CsrA), but it is possible to array the entire ORFeome in a 96-well format to mediate high-throughput screening of sequence-specific RNA-binding partners. Once an interaction pair is identified, disruption of this interaction by screening a library of RNA (mRNAs) can reveal the regulated targets of the RNA-binding protein. Furthermore, screening of chemical libraries for compounds that can disrupt the protein–RNA interaction can yield useful inhibitors to further interrogate the RNA–protein regulation *in vivo*.

REFERENCES

Babitzke, P., & Romeo, T. (2007). CsrB sRNA family: Sequestration of RNA-binding regulatory proteins. *Current Opinion in Microbiology*, *10*(2), 156–163.

Corrigan, R. M., Abbott, J. C., Burhenne, H., Kaever, V., & Grundling, A. (2011). c-di-AMP is a new second messenger in Staphylococcus aureus with a role in controlling cell size and envelope stress. *PLoS Pathogens*, 7(9), 1002217.

Corrigan, R. M., Campeotto, I., Jeganathan, T., Roelofs, K. G., Lee, V. T., & Grundling, A. (2013). Systematic identification of conserved bacterial c-di-AMP receptor proteins. *Proceedings of the National Academy of Sciences of the United States of America*, *110*(22), 9084–9089.

Donaldson, G. P., Roelofs, K. G., Luo, Y., Sintim, H. O., & Lee, V. (2011). A rapid assay for affinity and kinetics of molecular interactions with nucleic acids. *Nucleic Acids Research*, *40*(7), e48.

Dubey, A. K., Baker, C. S., Romeo, T., & Babitzke, P. (2005). RNA sequence and secondary structure participate in high-affinity CsrA-RNA interaction. *RNA*, *11*(10), 1579–1587.

Iioka, H., Loiselle, D., Haystead, T. A., & Macara, I. G. (2011). Efficient detection of RNA-protein interactions using tethered RNAs. *Nucleic Acids Research*, *39*(8), e53.

Jensen, K. B., & Darnell, R. B. (2008). CLIP: Crosslinking and immunoprecipitation of in vivo RNA targets of RNA-binding proteins. *Methods in Molecular Biology*, *488*, 85–98.

Lenz, D. H., Miller, M. B., Zhu, J., Kulkarni, R. V., & Bassler, B. L. (2005). CsrA and three redundant small RNAs regulate quorum sensing in Vibrio cholerae. *Molecular Microbiology*, *58*(4), 1186–1202.

Lieberman, O. J., Orr, M. W., Wang, Y., & Lee, V. T. (2013). High-throughput screening using the differential radial capillary action of ligand assay identifies ebselen as an inhibitor of diguanylate cyclases. *ACS Chemical Biology*, *9*(1), 183–192.

Liu, M. Y., Gui, G., Wei, B., Preston, J. F., 3rd., Oakford, L., Yuksel, U., et al. (1997). The RNA molecule CsrB binds to the global regulatory protein CsrA and antagonizes its activity in Escherichia coli. *Journal of Biological Chemistry*, *272*(28), 17502–17510.

Liu, M. Y., & Romeo, T. (1997). The global regulator CsrA of Escherichia coli is a specific mRNA-binding protein. *Journal of Bacteriology*, *179*(14), 4639–4642.

Martin, F. (2012). Fifteen years of the yeast three-hybrid system: RNA-protein interactions under investigation. *Methods*, *58*(4), 367–375.

Masse, E., Majdalani, N., & Gottesman, S. (2003). Regulatory roles for small RNAs in bacteria. *Current Opinion in Microbiology*, *6*(2), 120–124.

Mehne, F. M., Gunka, K., Eilers, H., Herzberg, C., Kaever, V., & Stulke, J. (2013). Cyclic di-AMP homeostasis in bacillus subtilis: Both lack and high level accumulation of the nucleotide are detrimental for cell growth. *Journal of Biological Chemistry*, *288*(3), 2004–2017.

Murigneux, V., Sauliere, J., Roest Crollius, H., & Le Hir, H. (2013). Transcriptome-wide identification of RNA binding sites by CLIP-seq. *Methods*, *63*(1), 32–40.

Putz, U., Skehel, P., & Kuhl, D. (1996). A tri-hybrid system for the analysis and detection of RNA–protein interactions. *Nucleic Acids Research*, *24*(23), 4838–4840.

Raghavan, R., Groisman, E. A., & Ochman, H. (2011). Genome-wide detection of novel regulatory RNAs in E. coli. *Genome Research*, *21*(9), 1487–1497.

Ramesh, A., DebRoy, S., Goodson, J. R., Fox, K. A., Faz, H., Garsin, D. A., et al. (2012). The mechanism for RNA recognition by ANTAR regulators of gene expression. *PLoS Genetics*, *8*(6), e1002666.

Roelofs, K. G., Wang, J., Sintim, H. O., & Lee, V. T. (2011). Differential radial capillary action of ligand assay for high-throughput detection of protein-metabolite interactions.

Proceedings of the National Academy of Sciences of the United States of America, 108(37), 15528–15533.

Romeo, T. (1998). Global regulation by the small RNA-binding protein CsrA and the non-coding RNA molecule CsrB. *Molecular Microbiology, 29*(6), 1321–1330.

Schubert, M., Lapouge, K., Duss, O., Oberstrass, F. C., Jelesarov, I., Haas, D., et al. (2007). Molecular basis of messenger RNA recognition by the specific bacterial repressing clamp RsmA/CsrA. *Nature Structural and Molecular Biology, 14*(9), 807–813.

SenGupta, D. J., Zhang, B., Kraemer, B., Pochart, P., Fields, S., & Wickens, M. (1996). A three-hybrid system to detect RNA-protein interactions in vivo. *Proceedings of the National Academy of Sciences of the United States of America, 93*(16), 8496–8501.

Storz, G., Vogel, J., & Wassarman, K. M. (2011). Regulation by small RNAs in bacteria: Expanding frontiers. *Molecular Cell, 43*(6), 880–891.

Sudarsan, N., Lee, E. R., Weinberg, Z., Moy, R. H., Kim, J. N., Link, K. H., et al. (2008). Riboswitches in eubacteria sense the second messenger cyclic di-GMP. *Science, 321*(5887), 411–413.

Valverde, C., Heeb, S., Keel, C., & Haas, D. (2003). RsmY, a small regulatory RNA, is required in concert with RsmZ for GacA-dependent expression of biocontrol traits in Pseudomonas fluorescens CHA0. *Molecular Microbiology, 50*(4), 1361–1379.

Waters, L. S., & Storz, G. (2009). Regulatory RNAs in bacteria. *Cell, 136*(4), 615–628.

Weilbacher, T., Suzuki, K., Dubey, A. K., Wang, X., Gudapaty, S., Morozov, I., et al. (2003). A novel sRNA component of the carbon storage regulatory system of Escherichia coli. *Molecular Microbiology, 48*(3), 657–670.

Witte, C. E., Whiteley, A. T., Burke, T. P., Sauer, J. D., Portnoy, D. A., & Woodward, J. J. (2013). Cyclic di-AMP is critical for Listeria monocytogenes growth, cell wall homeostasis, and establishment of infection. *MBio, 4*(3).

AUTHOR INDEX

Note: Page numbers followed by "*f*" indicate figures and "*t*" indicate tables, "*np*" indicate footnotes, and "*s*" indicate schemes.

A

B

D

G

H

I

J

K

L

M

Q

R

S

X

Y

Z

SUBJECT INDEX

Note: Page numbers followed by "*f*" indicate figures and "*t*" indicate tables, "*np*" indicate footnotes, and "*s*" indicate schemes.

F

G

H

Q

R

X

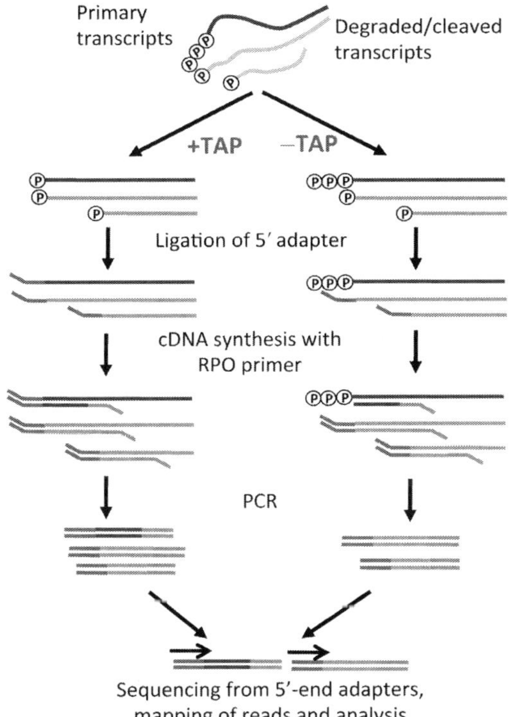

Isabelle Rosinski-Chupin *et al.*, Figure 1.2 TSS mapping by dRNA-seq.

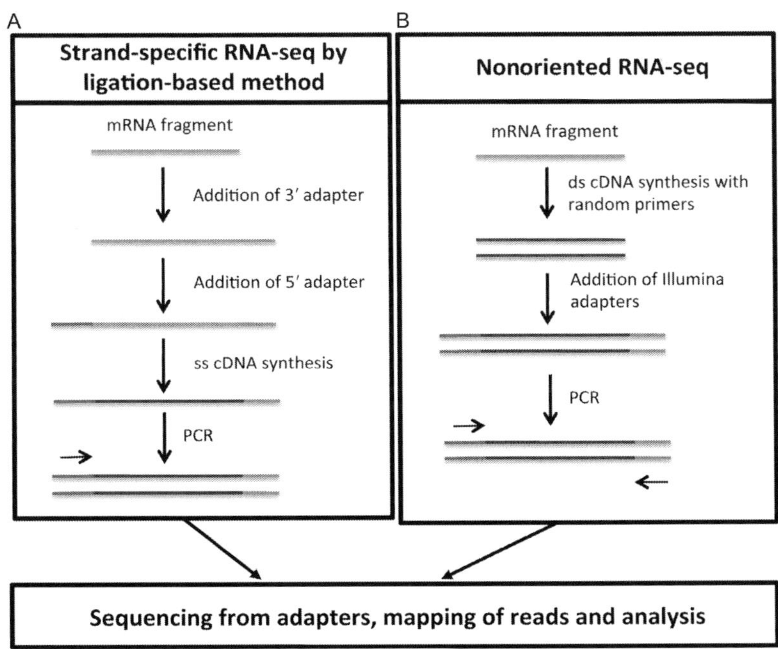

Isabelle Rosinski-Chupin *et al.*, Figure 1.3 Whole-transcript sequencing by (A) strand-specific RNA-seq and (B) nonoriented RNA-seq.

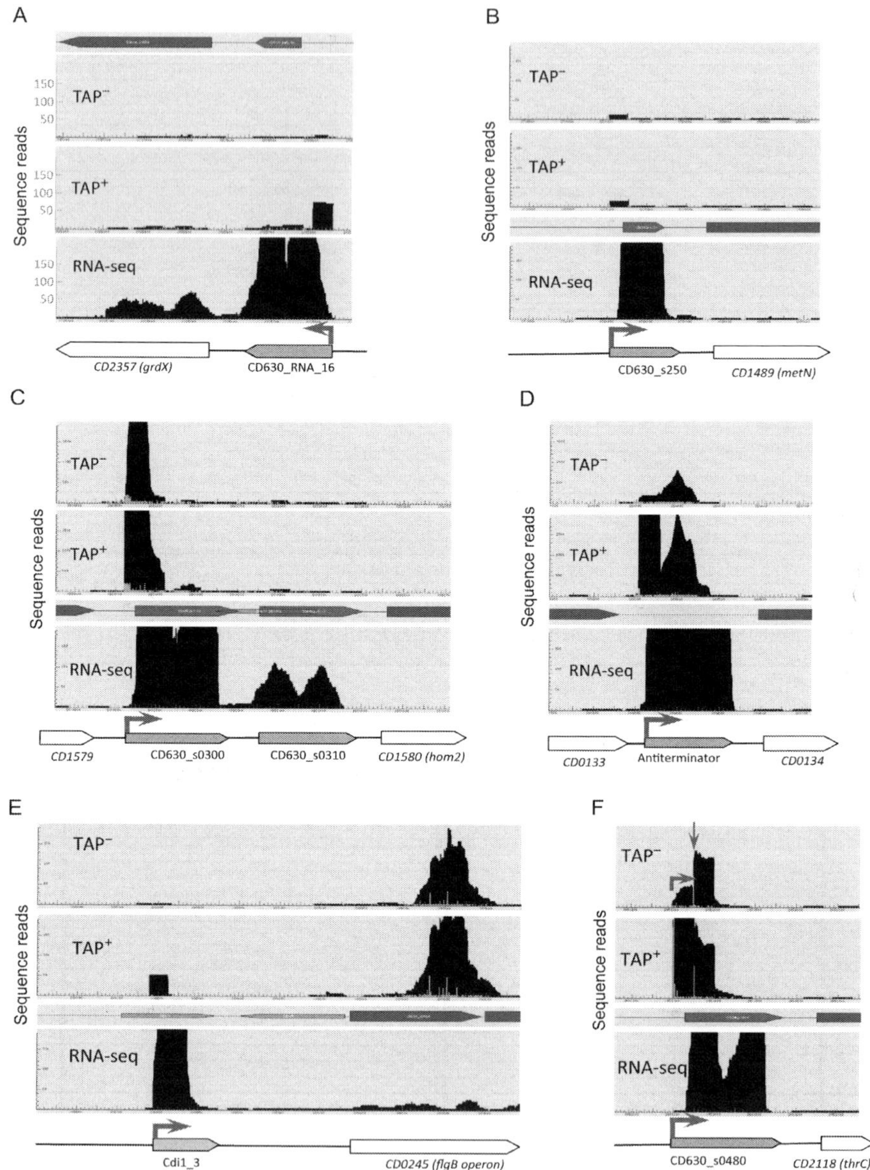

Isabelle Rosinski-Chupin *et al.*, Figure 1.6 Characteristic riboswitch patterns in *C. difficile*. (A) Glycine-responsive riboswitch; (B) S-box; (C) two T-boxes in tandem; (D) PTS antiterminator; (E) c-di-GMP-responsive riboswitch; (F) cleavage site of T-box (Thr). The riboswitches are indicated by gray arrows. The TSS and processing sites are pointed out by red broken arrows and vertical arrows, respectively.

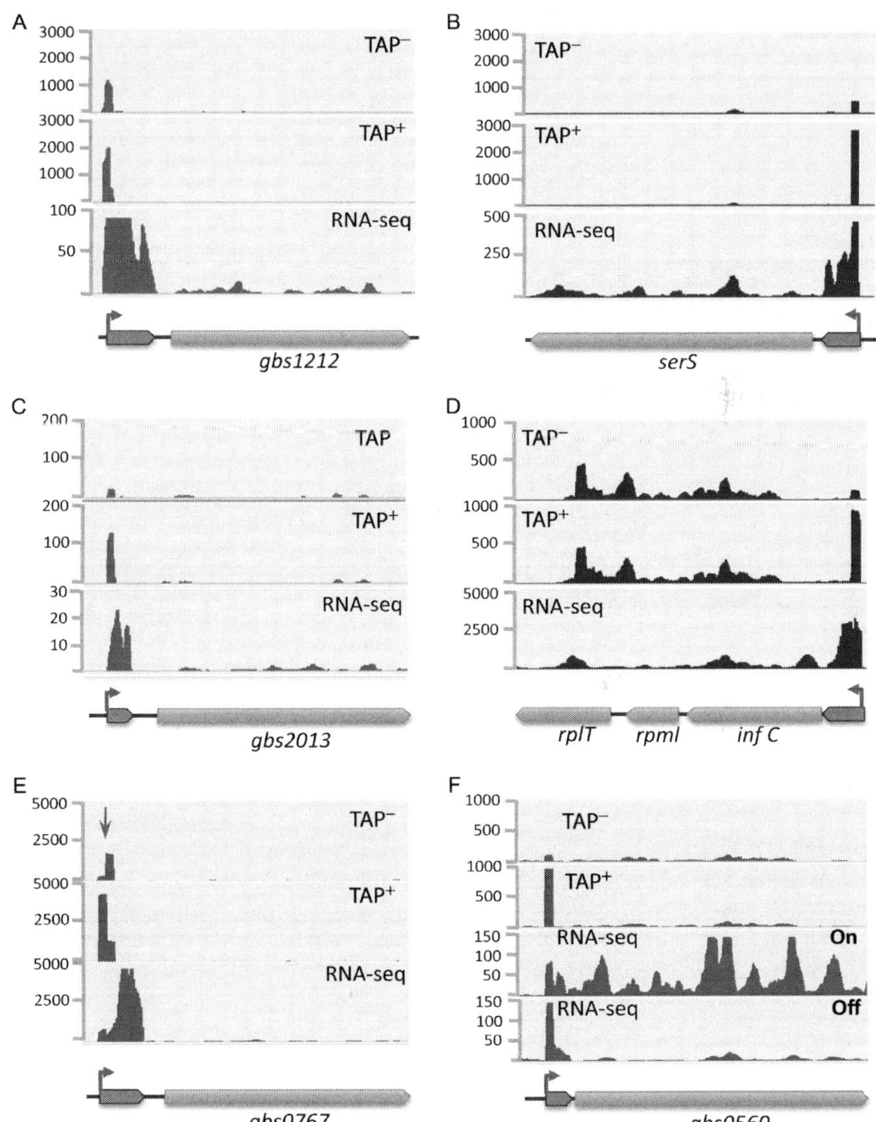

Isabelle Rosinski-Chupin *et al.*, Figure 1.7 Riboswitch profiles in *S. agalactiae*. (A) Glycine-responsive riboswitch; (B) T-box; (C) PyrR-binding site; (D) L20 leader; (E) FMN riboswitch with internal cleavage; (F) *yybP–ykoY* leader in on/off state.

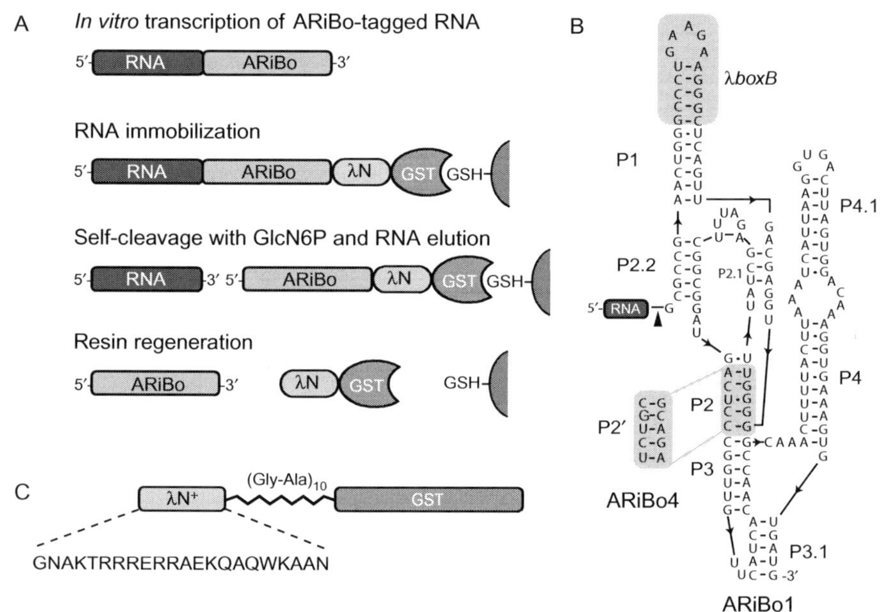

Geneviève Di Tomasso *et al.*, Figure 3.1 Affinity purification of RNA using a 3′-ARiBo tag. (A) Schematic of the basic procedure. (B) The ARiBo-fusion RNA, showing the ARiBo1-tag sequence that corresponds to the *B. anthracis glmS* ribozyme sequence in which the P1 stem has been modified to include the *boxB* RNA from bacteriophage λ. The ARiBo4 tag was obtained by modifying the P2 stem of the ARiBo1 tag. (C) Diagram of the λN^{+}-L^{+}-GST fusion protein.

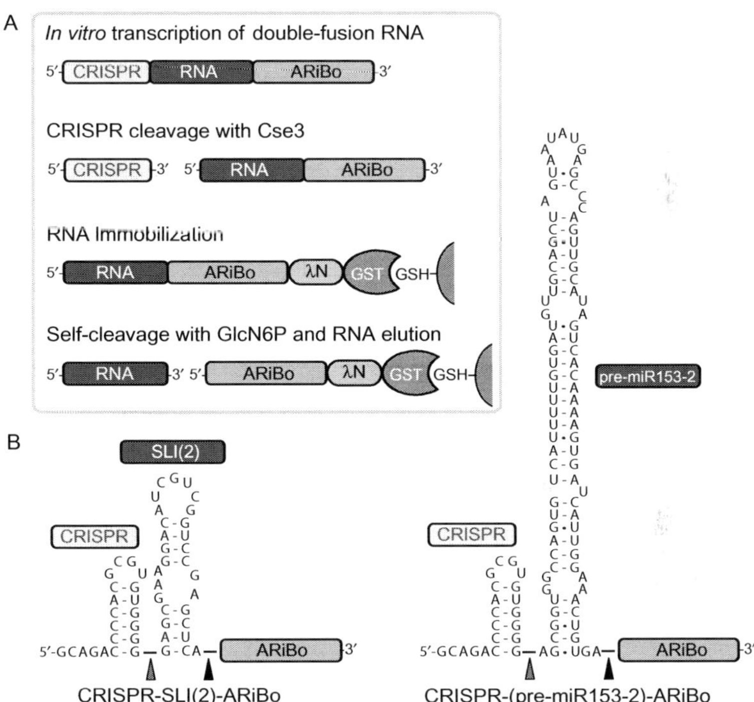

Geneviève Di Tomasso *et al.*, Figure 3.4 Affinity purification of RNA using a 5′-CRISPR tag and a 3′-ARiBo tag. (A) Schematic of the procedure. (B) Partial sequence and proposed secondary structures of CRISPR-RNA-ARiBo precursors for affinity purification of SLI(2) and pre-miR153-2.

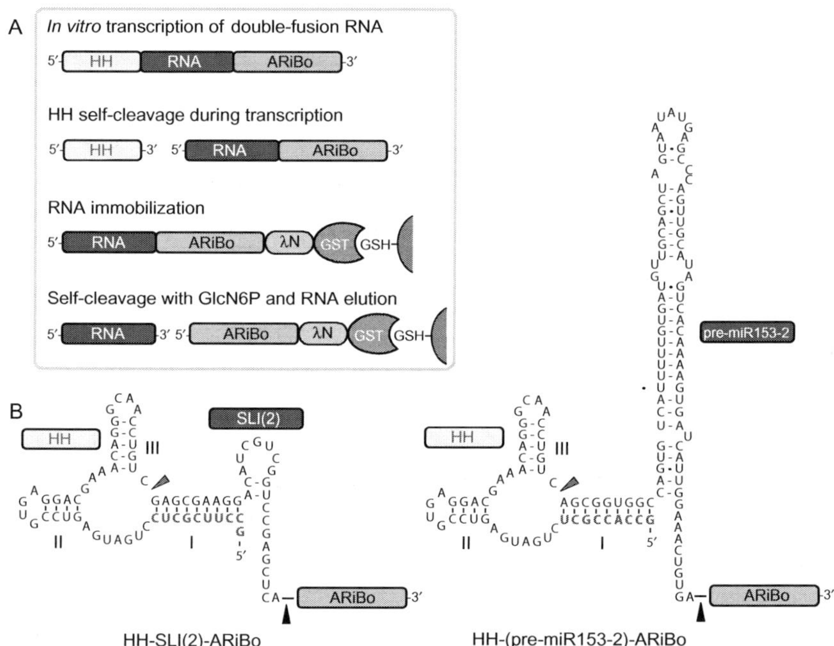

Geneviève Di Tomasso *et al.*, Figure 3.5 Affinity purification of RNA using a 5′-HH tag and a 3′-ARiBo tag. (A) Schematic of the procedure. (B) Partial sequence and proposed secondary structures of HH-RNA-ARiBo precursors for affinity purification of SLI(2) and pre-miR153-2. The 5′-HH tag contains three helical domains (numbered in roman numerals) and its variable 5′-sequence (burgundy) needs to be tailored to the RNA sequence of interest.

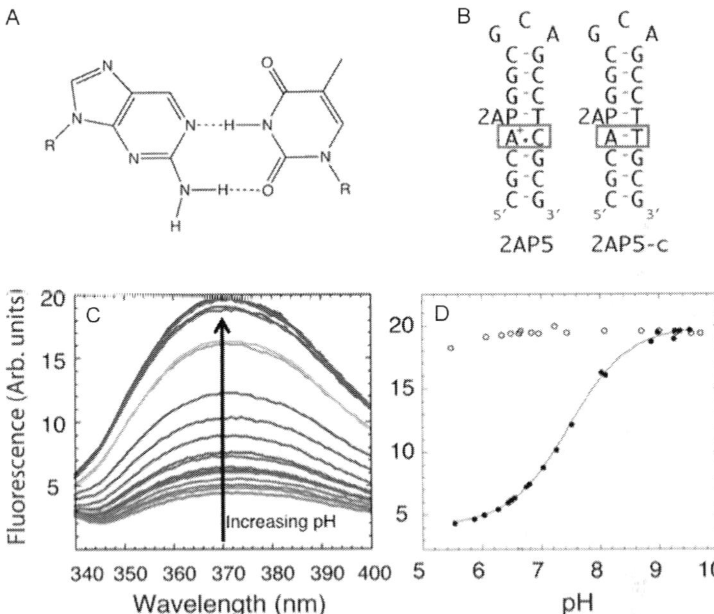

Pallavi Thaplyal and Philip C. Bevilacqua, Figure 9.6 Fluorescence-based determination of pK_a using 2AP-substituted oligonucleotides. (A) 2AP is structurally similar to adenine and is able to form a two-hydrogen bond base pair with thymine. (B) DNA constructs containing the A^+·C wobble (2AP5) and the control construct containing an AT Watson–Crick (2AP5-c) base pair. The signal change for the 2AP substitution was optimal when 2AP was positioned directly above the wobble base pair. (C) Fluorescence spectra at different pH for 2AP5 construct, with pink corresponding to low pH and blue to high pH. (D) Plot of observed fluorescence as a function of pH for 2AP5 (solid circles) and 2AP5-c (hollow circles). 2AP5-c shows no change in fluorescence with pH, whereas the 2AP5 shows a fourfold change in fluorescence. *Adapted with permission from Wlicox and Bevilacqua (2013). Copyright (2013) American Chemical Society.*

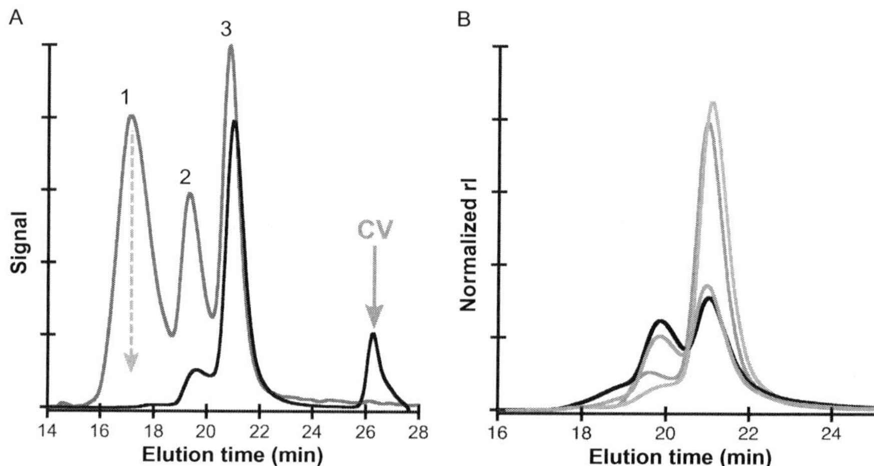

Francis E. Reyes *et al.*, Figure 11.2 Size exclusion chromatographic (SEC) separation of SAM-I riboswitch under varying annealing conditions. (A) Elution profile of SAM-I riboswitch monitored by refractive index (concentration detector, black) and light scattering (mass detector, red). Cyan and gray arrows mark the void and column volumes, respectively. Peak 1 is an aggregate peak given by the high light scattering at very low concentration. Peak 2 is an RNA dimer. Peak 3 corresponds to the RNA monomer. (B) Elution profile (refractive index) of SAM-I riboswitch annealed using four different refolding strategies. RNA was heated (85 °C) and either snap- or slow cooled in the presence and absence of Mg^{2+} under dilute conditions (~0.1 mg/mL). In the absence of Mg^{2+}, snap cooled using prechilled buffer (cyan) performed better than slow cooling (orange) which performed better than snap cooling (green) and slow cooling (black) in the presence of Mg^{2+}. Annealing in the presence of Mg^{2+}, results in severe material loss of monomeric RNA. RNA was concentrated to 5 mg/mL using a 5-kDa cut-off spin concentrator at 18 °C.

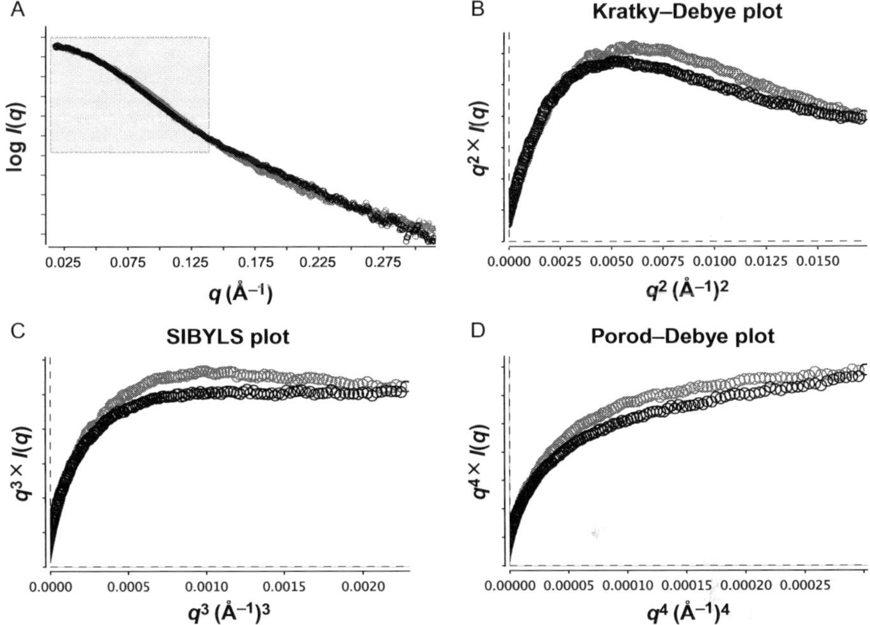

Francis E. Reyes *et al.*, Figure 11.5 Flexibility plots for the SAM-I riboswitch in the presence (red) and absence (black) of ligand. (A) SAXS data plot as log $I(q)$ versus q. Boxed region defines limits for the plots in B–D. (B) Kratky–Debye plot ($q^2 \cdot I(q)$ vs. q^2). A plateau would indicate the data could be approximated using the Debye approximation for a Gaussian chain with a P_E near 2. (C) SIBYLS plot ($q^3 \cdot I(q)$ vs. q^3). A plateau would indicate a P_E near 3. (D) Porod–Debye plot ($q^4 \cdot I(q)$ vs. q^4). A plateau would indicate a P_E near 4 and that the data could be approximated using the Porod–Debye approximation for particles with a defined surface and contrast. For the SAM-I riboswitch, the (+) ligand state has a P_E near 4, whereas the (−) ligand state would be near 3. These plots clearly demonstrate a change in state of the riboswitch in the presence of ligand. Figures were prepared using the program ScÅtter available at www.bioisis.net.

A

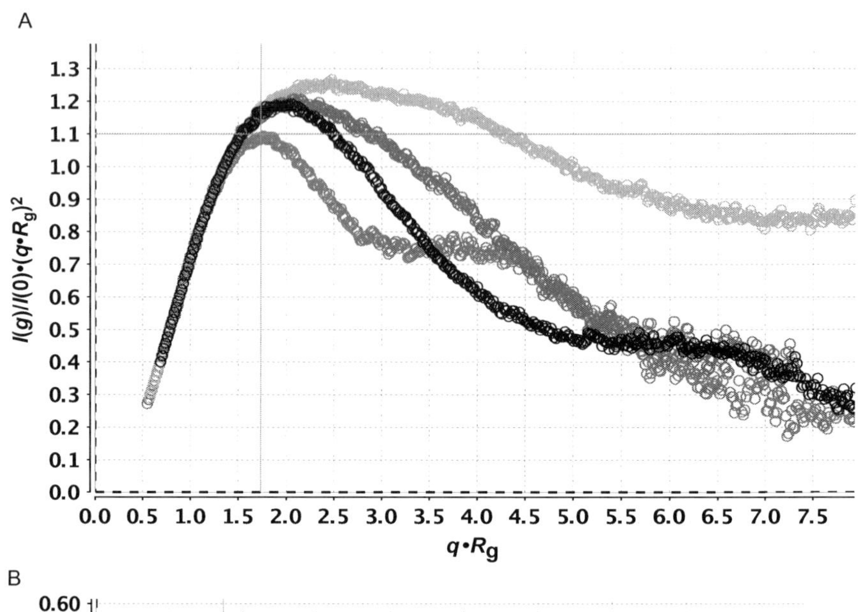

B

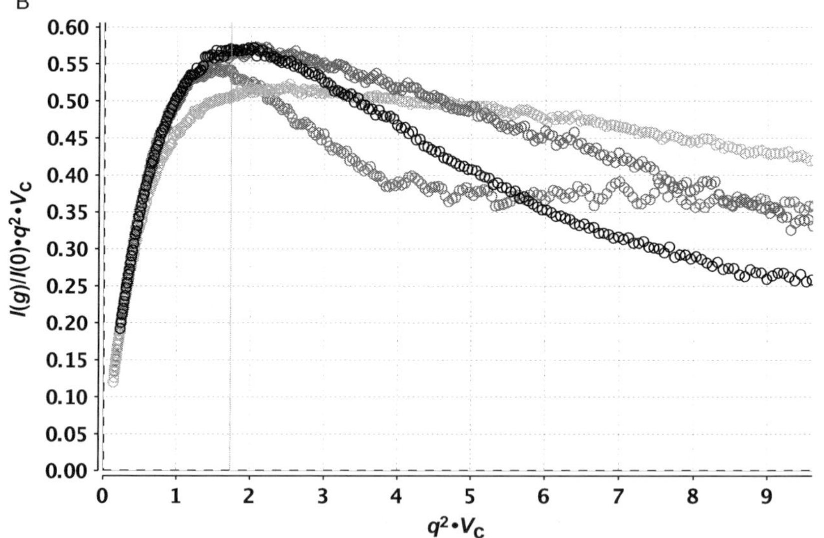

Francis E. Reyes *et al.*, Figure 11.6 Dimensionless Kratky plots. P4–P6 domain (black), $tRNA^{phe}+Mg^{2+}$ (red), $tRNA^{phe}-Mg^{2+}$ (cyan), and TyMV UDP (purple). (A) R_g-based plot, cross hair (gray) marks the position of the peak for an ideal, compact, globular particle at $q{\cdot}R_g=\sqrt{3}$. Less compact or nonglobular particles will have a peak shifted upward and to the right. (B) V_c-based plot, vertical line represents $\sqrt{3}$. Peak height is inversely proportional to the particle's surface-to-volume ratio with the maximum occurring for a sphere at 0.85. Changes in peak height reflect changes to the particles surface to volume ratio. Similar peak heights for P4–P6 domain and $tRNA^{phe}+Mg^{2+}$ V_c-based plots suggest similar surface-to-volume ratios. Dimensionless plots will be sensitive to the accuracy of the Guinier region or real space transforms. Figures were prepared using the program ScÅtter available at www.bioisis.net.

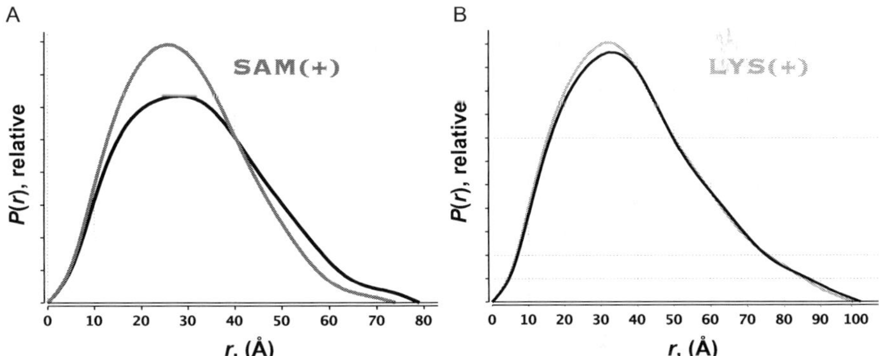

Francis E. Reyes *et al.*, Figure 11.7 Normalized $P(r)$-distributions demonstrating conformational differences. Each distribution is scaled by $I(0)^{-1}$ and normalizes for RNA concentration and volume. (A) SAM-I riboswitch in the presence (red) and absence (black) of ligand. Large increase in peak height and narrowing of the distribution suggests significant compaction of the RNA in the presence of ligand. (B) LYS riboswitch in the presence (blue) and absence (black) of ligand. Overlay shows small but significant differences suggesting a small conformational change occurs upon binding.

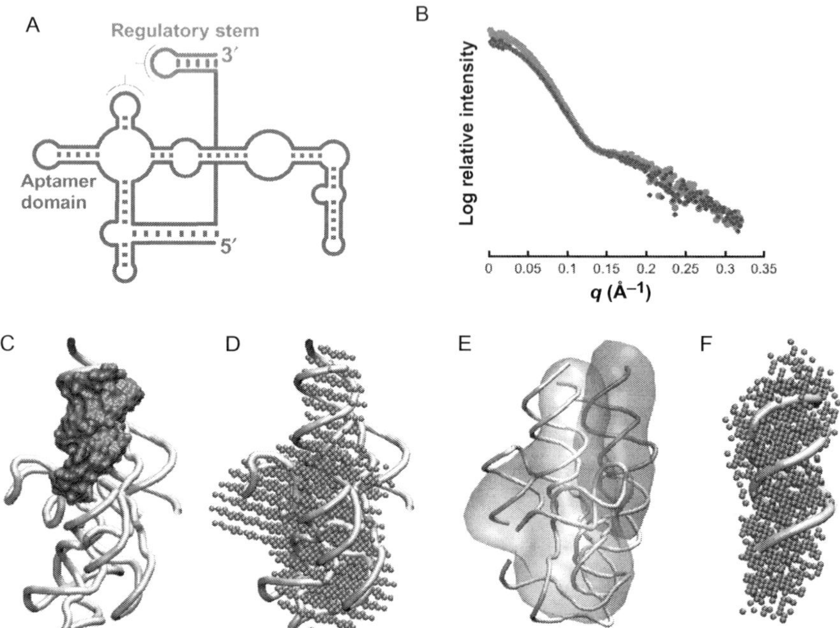

Francis E. Reyes *et al.*, Figure 11.8 Secondary structure identification within volumetric model using MONSA. (A) Secondary structure of B_{12} riboswitch (Johnson et al., 2012). Full-length RNA (WT) is divided into two independent domains: (1) aptamer domain (APT, gray) and (2) regulatory P1,3 stem. (B) Simulated SAXS data with noise for WT (purple) and APT (gray). Data were simulated with CRYSOL (Svergun et al., 1995) using default parameters. Noise was transposed onto the simulated datasets from real SAXS data using a Gaussian sampling algorithm. (C) Atomistic model (PDB 4GMA) showing orientation of regulatory stem (purple) and APT (gray). (D) Averaged volumetric model (beads) of the APT volume calculated using MONSA from the SAXS data in B. (E) Averaged volumetric model of the APT domain (gray) and regulatory stem (purple). Relative orientation of the two volumes was determined by MONSA during the *ab initio* modeling using the SAXS data in B. (F) Alignment of the regulatory stem within the MONSA volume. In this example, only the APT volume (V_P^{APT}) was constrained during the MONSA modeling. V_P^{APT} was determined as the Porod volume using the program ScÅtter available at www.bioisis.net. In practice, the final model will be an average of 15–20 MONSA runs with the volume of each phase (APT domain and P13 stem) constrained during the MONSA modeling. All atomistic models were superimposed using SUPCOMB (Kozin & Svergun, 2001).

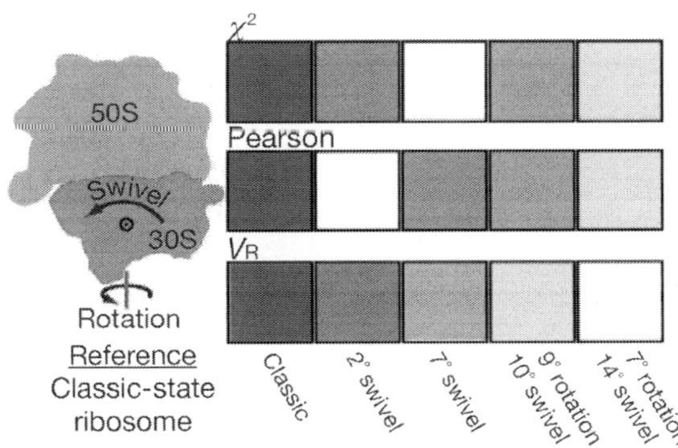

Francis E. Reyes *et al.*, Figure 11.9 SAXS applied to measure structural similarity. χ^2, Pearson correlation coefficient and V_R scores were assigned a gradient color from red (high similarity) to white (low similarity). Comparison of ribosomal structures solved with the 30S subunit rotated about two axes (annotated by rotation and swivel degree) relative to the 50S subunit. Left to right: Protein Data Bank reference structures 3R8T:4GD2, 3I21:3I22, 3I1O:3I1P, 3R8S:4GD1, and 3UOQ:3UOS. *Adapted from Hura, Budworth, et al. (2013).*

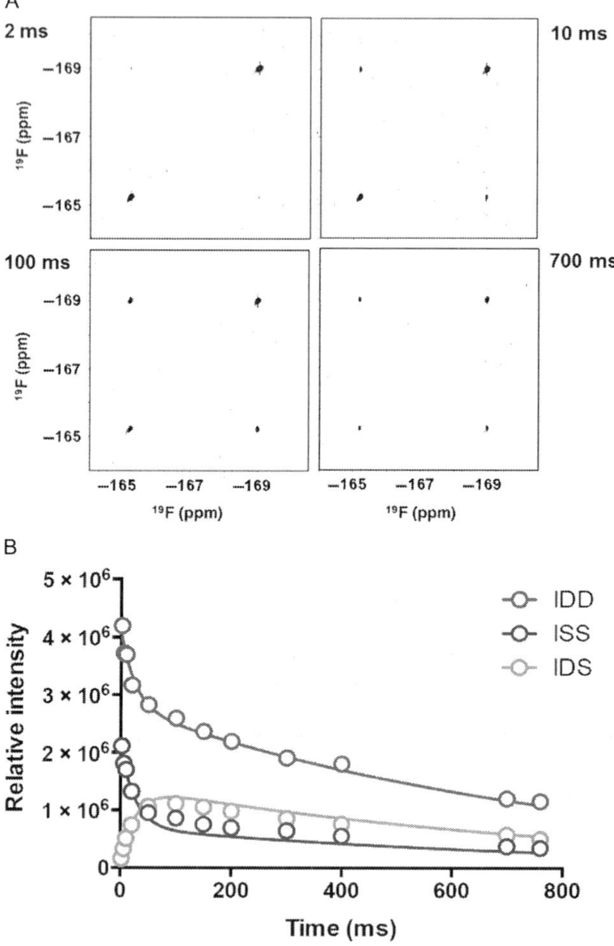

Caijie Zhao *et al.*, Figure 12.2 (A) Regions of two-dimensional ^{19}F–^{19}F EXSY spectra at mixing times of 2, 10, 100, and 700 ms, as marked. Spectra were acquired at 470.22 MHz. The ^{19}F excitation pulse was 15 μs and relaxation delay was 2.5 s. 4096 × 200 points and 10,527.7 Hz spectral width were used in acquisition. (B) Plot of the intensities of exchange peaks versus the mixing times (2–760 ms) from which exchange values were calculated. In this figure, I_{DD} represents the intensity of the auto peak for double-stranded 5-^{19}F-U, I_{SS} represents the intensity of the auto peak for single-stranded 5-^{19}F-U, I_{SD} and I_{DS} represent the intensities of exchange peaks from "*S*" to "*D*" and vice versa. The curves fit to the data points for I_{SD} and I_{DS} are essentially identical and overlap fully; therefore, only the curve for I_{DS} is shown. Fitting of the curve was achieved using Prism 6 software suite (GraphPad Software Inc.) with in-house written scripts.

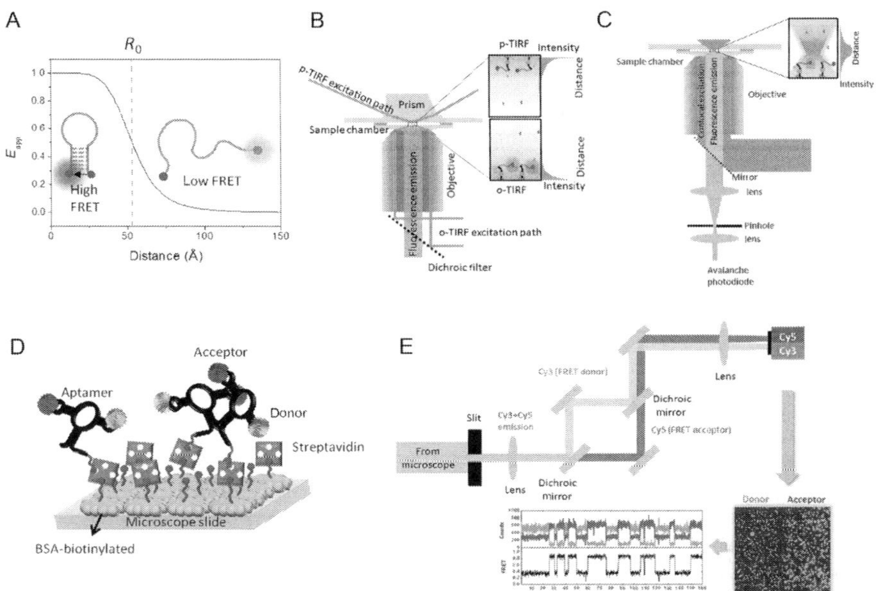

Euan Shaw *et al.*, Figure 14.2 Principle of single-molecule FRET (sm-FRET). (A) Efficiency of FRET as a function of interdye separation, *R*. E_{FRET} depends on the inverse of the sixth-power of the distance, making changes in FRET-sensitive indicators of conformational changes in fluorescently labeled RNA molecules. (B) Schematic of the excitation pathway for prism-type total-internal reflection fluorescence (p-TIRF) and objective-type TIRF (o-TIRF). In p-TIRF, the excitation laser is focused onto the upper face of the sample chamber through a quartz prism, while in o-TIRF, it is coupled onto the lower face through the extreme edge of the microscope objective using a dichroic mirror. In confocal microscopy (C), the objective focuses the excitation beam as in ordinary confocal microscopy. In all cases, dye fluorescence is collected by a high numerical aperture microscope objective (water-immersion for p-TIRF and oil-immersion for o-TIRF). Residual excitation light is filtered or directed away from the detection optics. The intensity of the evanescent wave generated at the quartz microscope slide/water interface (p-TIRF) or at the glass coverslip/water interface decays exponentially with the distance from the surface. This allows excitation of a very thin layer within the sample chamber, immediately adjacent to the surface where the RNA is immobilized. (D) Schematics of sample immobilization using the noncovalent interactions between biotinylated bovine serum albumin (BSA) and streptavidin or neutravidin. Sixty microliters of a 1 mg/mL solution of biotinylated BSA (bi-BSA) is injected into the sample chamber and incubated for 10 min to allow nonspecific binding to the slide. After washing the unbound bi-BSA another 60 μL of a 0.2 mg/mL solution of streptavidin is injected into the chamber and allowed to incubate for 10 min. After washing the unbound streptavidin, a 100–200 p*M* solution of biotinylated RNA is injected into the sample chamber and allowed to incubate for 5 min. (E) Schematic of the optical emission pathway common to p-TIRF and o-TIRF. The fluorescence emission from the sample is collected by the objective and directed onto a slit to select an appropriate image size that fills half of the EMCCD chip. The fluorescent signal containing Cy3 (FRET donor, green) and Cy5 (FRET acceptor, red) is separated into its two components using a dichroic mirror and then recombined using a second dichroic mirror to allow simultaneous imaging of each signal into each half of the camera. A representative image and single-molecule trace showing donor and acceptor variations in fluorescence intensity as a function of time for a nucleic acid sample exhibiting two-state dynamics are shown. FRET efficiency can be calculated from the Cy3 (green) and Cy5 (red) intensities (see main text), resulting in a single-molecule trajectory of E_{app} versus time, as shown in the bottom panel (black).

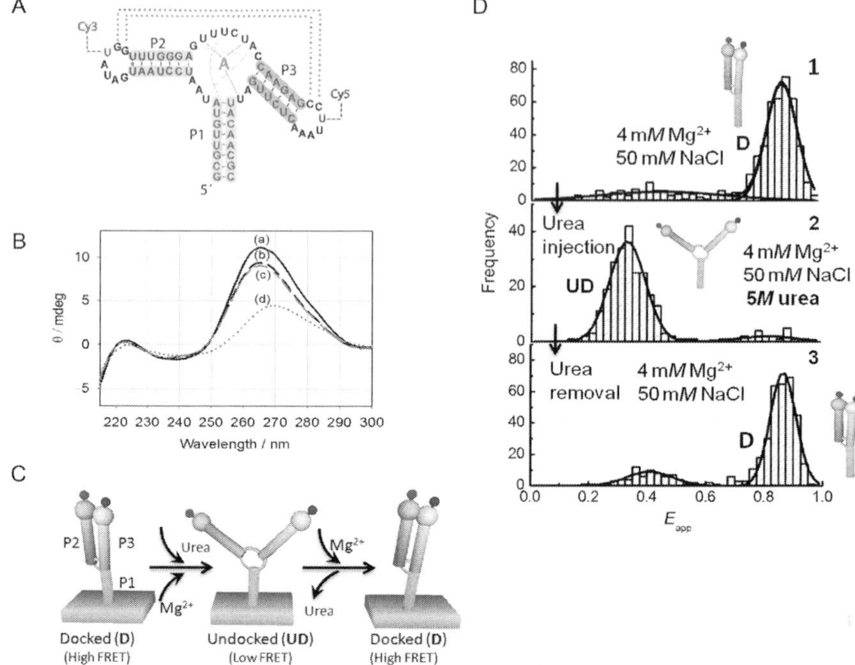

Euan Shaw *et al.*, Figure 14.4 (A) Secondary structure of the add adenine riboswitch showing the network of interactions within the aptamer core that are involved in ligand sensing (orange) and in the stabilization of the tertiary structure. The G–C base pairs responsible for the formation of the loop–loop interaction are also shown. The locations of the donor (Cy3) and the acceptor (Cy5) dyes used as FRET pair in single-molecule studies are also displayed. (B) Urea-induced denaturation is specific to the tertiary structure. Circular dichroism (CD) spectra of the adenine aptamer plotted as ellipticity (millidegrees) versus wavelength (nm). [RNA] = 12 μ*M*. (a) 50 m*M* Tris–HCl, pH 7.8, 50 m*M* NaCl, 4 m*M* Mg^{2+}, (b) 50 m*M* Tris–HCl, pH 7.8, No NaCl, No Mg^{2+}, (c) 50 m*M* Tris–HCl, pH 7.8, 50 m*M* NaCl, 4 m*M* Mg^{2+}, 5 *M* urea, (d) 50 m*M* Tris–HCl, pH 7.8, No NaCl, No m*M* Mg^{2+}, 7 *M* urea. (C) Schematic of the folding/unfolding/refolding cycles performed on the add adenine aptamer from *Vibrio vulnificus* to test the reversibility of single-molecule denaturation processes. Surface-immobilized adenine aptamers labeled with an FRET pair as indicated in (A) are placed in an initial docked state characterized by the formation of the loop–loop interaction (high-FRET state). In a first denaturing cycle, the loop–loop interaction is disrupted by the addition of urea (undocked state, low FRET). Subsequent replacement of urea by Mg^{2+} restores the docked state. (D) Single-molecule FRET histograms corresponding to the cycles described in (C). (1) In a background of 4 m*M* Mg^{2+} and 50 m*M* Na^{+} most of the aptamer molecules are in the docked conformation as indicated by the histogram centered at E_{app} ~0.9. (2) Addition of 5 *M* urea while maintaining the concentrations of mono- and divalent ions shifts the sm-FRET histogram completely to the undocked conformation (E_{app} ~0.3). (3) An additional refolding cycle removing urea restores the aptamer molecules to the high-FRET docked state and confirms the reversibility of the denaturation process. *Adapted from Dalgarno et al. (2013).*

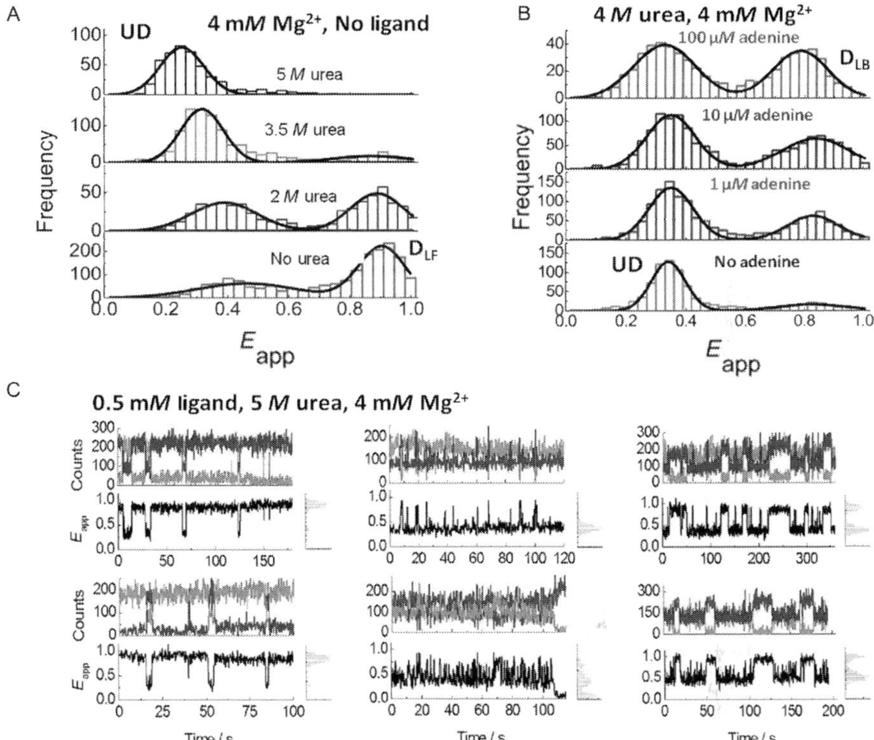

Euan Shaw *et al.*, Figure 14.5 Dynamic heterogeneity in the presence of ligand. (A) Single-molecule histograms of FRET efficiency as a function of the indicated urea concentrations obtained in the absence of ligand. (B) Single-molecule FRET histograms obtained as a function of adenine concentration in the presence of 4 *M* urea and 4 m*M* Mg^{2+} showing the relative variation in the population of docked (E ~0.9) and undocked states (E ~0.3). (C) Single-molecule trajectories obtained for adenine aptamers in the presence of 500 μ*M* adenine ligand, 4 m*M* Mg^{2+} and 5 *M* urea grouped according to the dynamic pattern observed for the fluctuation between the **D** and **UD** states. Left panel: long-lived docked state (**D_{LB}**) with occasional fluctuations to a short-lived undocked (**UD**) conformation. Mid-panel: **r**apid fluctuations between short-lived ligand-free docked states (**D_{LF}**) and undocked states (**UD**). Right panel: combination of transitions between short-lived (**D_{LF}**) and long-lived (**D_{LB}**) docked states to short-lived **UD** states. *Adapted from Dalgarno et al. (2013).*

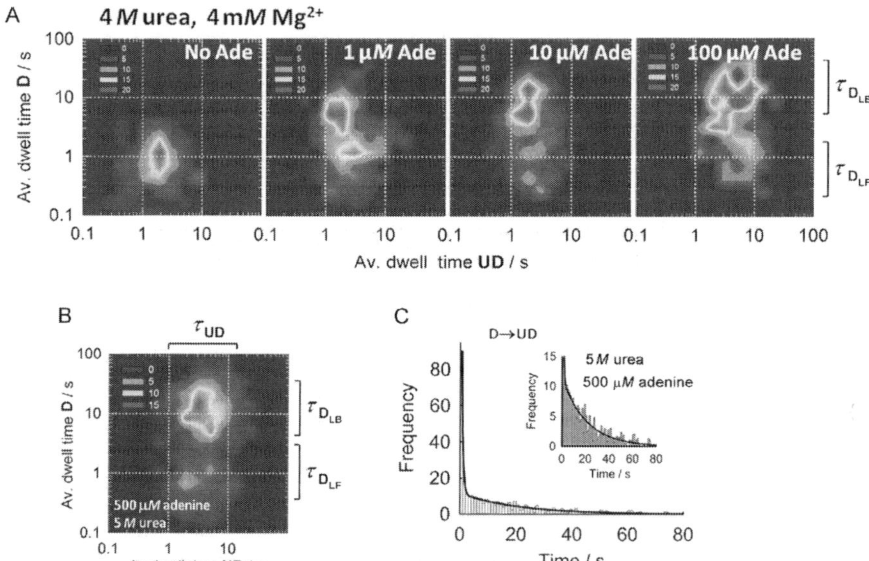

Euan Shaw *et al.*, Figure 14.6 Differentiating ligand-free (A) and ligand-bound docked states (B, C) based on their stability against urea-induced denaturation. (A) 2D contour plots of average dwell times on the docked (**D**) and undocked state (**UD**) obtained at the indicated concentrations of adenine ligand in a background of 4 *M* urea and 4 m*M* Mg^{2+}. The stabilization of the docked state can be clearly seen from the shift in the contour map without ligand (short $\tau_{\mathbf{D_{LF}}}$) and with ligand (long $\tau_{\mathbf{D_{LB}}}$). (B) Contour map showing the distribution of average dwell times of the docked and undocked states at 5 *M* urea, 500 μ*M* ligand, and 4 m*M* Mg^{2+}. (C) Exponential distribution of dwell times for the undocking transition at the conditions indicated in (B). The decay was fitted to a biexponential function (solid line) with a fast component with a value of $2.1 \pm 0.1\ s^{-1}$ (minor contribution) and a slow component with a value of $0.045 \pm 0.003\ s^{-1}$ (major component), corresponding to undocking events taking place from ligand-free and ligand-bound states, respectively. *Adapted from Dalgarno et al. (2013).*

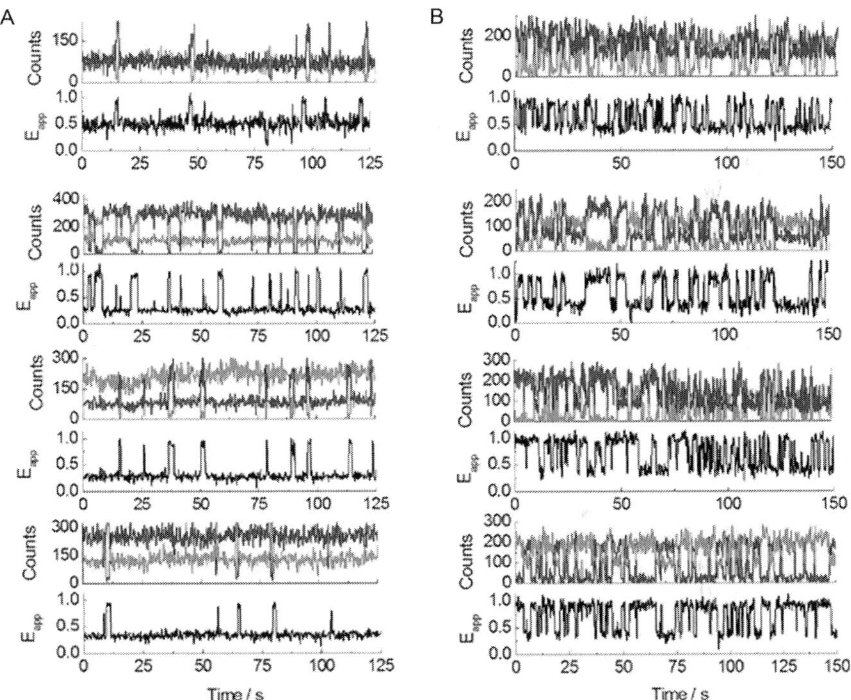

Euan Shaw *et al.*, Figure 14.8 Representative single-molecule intensity trajectories (top panels) and FRET traces (bottom panels) obtained in the presence of 100 μ*M* adenine ligand, 100 μ*M* Mg^{2+}, and 2 *M* urea concentration (A) and in the absence of urea (B). A comparison between both groups of trajectories clearly reveals a pronounced urea-induced deceleration of the docking process in the presence of adenine ligand. The dwell time of the docked state reflects the **UD** → **D** transition, which becomes much longer lived in the presence of adenine and urea (A). *Adapted from Dalgarno et al. (2013).*

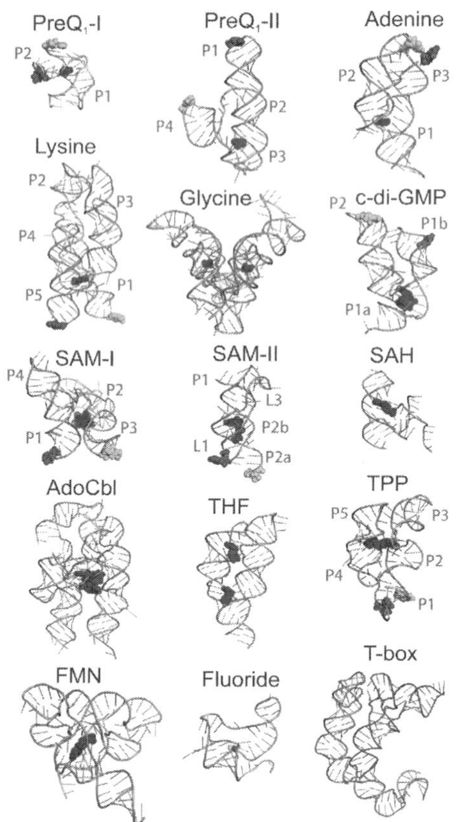

Krishna C. Suddala and Nils G. Walter, Figure 15.1 Structures of different riboswitch classes. Structures of the preQ$_1$-I (PDB: 2L1V;Kang, Peterson, & Feigon, 2009), preQ$_1$-II (PDB: 4JF2; Liberman, Salim, Krucinska, & Wedekind, 2013), adenine (PDB: 1Y26; Serganov et al., 2004)), lysine (PDB: 3D0U; Garst, Heroux, Rambo, & Batey, 2008), glycine (PDB: 3P49; Butler, Xiong, Wang, & Strobel, 2011), c-di-GMP (PDB: 3IWN; Kulshina, Baird, & Ferre-D'Amare, 2009), SAM-I (PDB: 3IQR; Stoddard et al., 2010), SAM-II (PDB: 2QWY; Gilbert, Rambo, Van Tyne, & Batey, 2008), SAH (PDB: 3NPQ; Edwards, Reyes, Heroux, & Batey, 2010), AdoCbl (PDB: 4GMA; Johnson, Reyes, Polaski, & Batey, 2012), THF (PDB: 4LVV; Trausch & Batey, 2014)), TPP (PDB: 2GDI; Serganov, Polonskaia, Phan, Breaker, & Patel, 2006), FMN (PDB: 2YIE; Vicens, Mondragon, & Batey, 2011), Fluoride (PDB: 4ENC; Ren, Rajashankar, & Patel, 2012), and the T-box (PDB: 4LCK; Zhang & Ferre-D'Amare, 2013) riboswitches are shown. Riboswitch RNAs are shown in cartoon representation in gray with their ligands in blue. Green and red spheres indicate nucleotides labeled with Cy3 and Cy5 fluorophores, respectively, in the preQ$_1$-I (Suddala et al., 2013), preQ$_1$-II (Souliere et al., 2013), adenine (Lemay, Penedo, Tremblay, Lilley, & Lafontaine, 2006), lysine (Fiegland, Garst, Batey, & Nesbitt, 2012), c-di-GMP (Wood, Ferre-D'Amare, & Rueda, 2012), SAM-I (Heppell et al., 2011), SAM-II (Haller, Rieder, Aigner, Blanchard, & Micura, 2011; Haller, Souliere, & Micura, 2011), and TPP (Haller, Altman, Souliere, Blanchard, & Micura, 2013) riboswitches that were studied using smFRET microscopy. The *xpt* guanine riboswitch (Brenner, Scanlan, Nahas, Ha, & Silverman, 2010, not shown) is very similar to the adenine riboswitch. In smFRET studies of riboswitches where multiple constructs were used, only one of them is shown here for clarity. Structures are not drawn to scale.

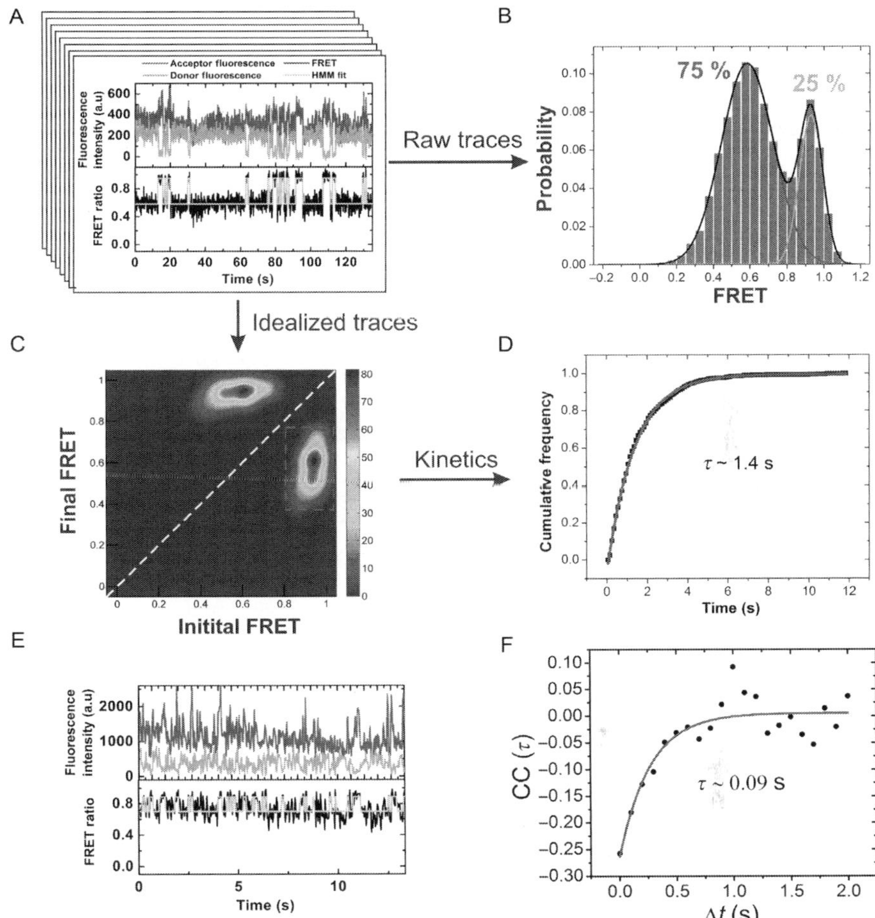

Krishna C. Suddala and Nils G. Walter, Figure 15.3 Analysis of smFRET data. (A) Raw single-molecule time trace showing anticorrelated donor (green) and acceptor (red) intensities for the *Bsu* preQ$_1$-I riboswitch in the presence of 100 n*M* preQ$_1$ and no Mg^{2+} (60 ms time resolution, unpublished data). The FRET trace (black) idealized with a two-state HMM fit (cyan) is shown in the lower plot. (B) FRET histogram showing two major populations and their equilibrium distribution. (C) Transition density plot (TDP) showing as heat maps the transitions from initial to final FRET states and their frequency. The dwell times of all the molecules in a given FRET state (~0.9 in this example, red broken box) can be extracted from this plot. (D) Cumulative dwell time distribution of the dwell times in the ~0.9 FRET state fit with a single-exponential function. (E) An smFRET trace of the ligand-free *Bsu* preQ$_1$-I riboswitch with very fast dynamics (33 ms time resolution, unpublished data). (F) Cross-correlation curve of the trace shown in panel E fit with a single exponential to obtain the combined rate of transitions ($k_{1,2}+k_{2,1}=1/\tau$, for a two-state process).

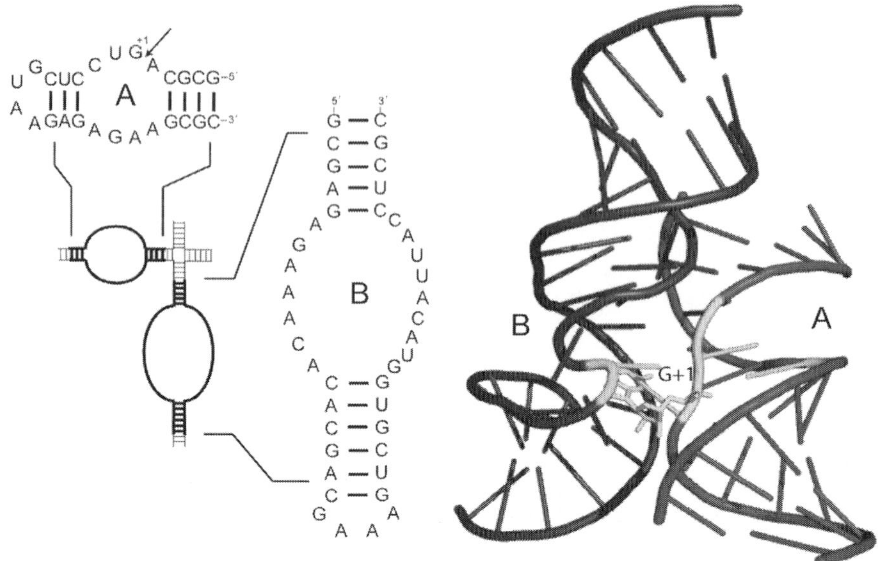

Charles G. Hoogstraten *et al.*, Figure 17.1 Left: Schematic secondary structure of the native four-way junction form of the hairpin ribozyme with the constructs used to represent loop A and loop B in our binding work in the system shown. In three dimensions, the two internal loops interact ("dock") to form an intricately structured interface. The arrow indicates the site of self-cleavage. Right: Three-dimensional structure of the docked form (Salter, Krucinska, Alam, Grum-Tokars, & Wedekind, 2006) (PDB: 2OUE), with the G+1 residue that forms a key part of the tertiary interface highlighted. *Figure prepared with PyMol (Delano, 2002).*

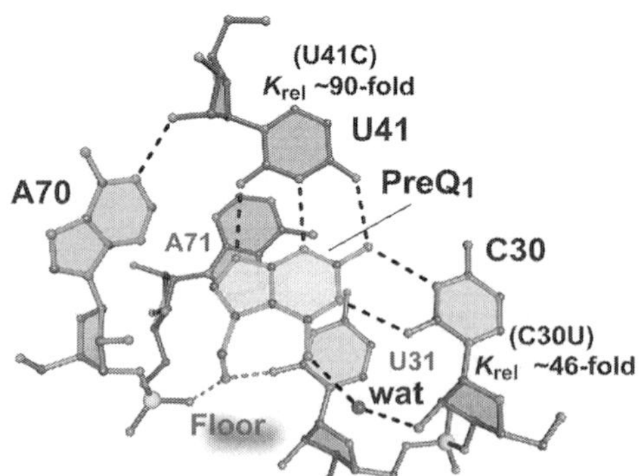

Joseph A. Liberman *et al.*, Figure 18.2 Mode of chemical recognition of $preQ_1$ by the $preQ_1$-II riboswitch as described in Liberman et al. (2013). Putative hydrogen bonds are shown as broken lines. The "floor" of the binding pocket is formed by a Hoogsteen base pair between A71·U31. The affinity of the C30U and U41C mutants for $preQ_1$ were probed by ITC and compared to wild type. K_{rel} is defined as the mutant K_D divided by the wild-type K_D. In this manner, ITC was used to quantify changes in free energy resulting from binding site mutations, which appear to corroborate the mode of ligand binding based on crystallographic observations.

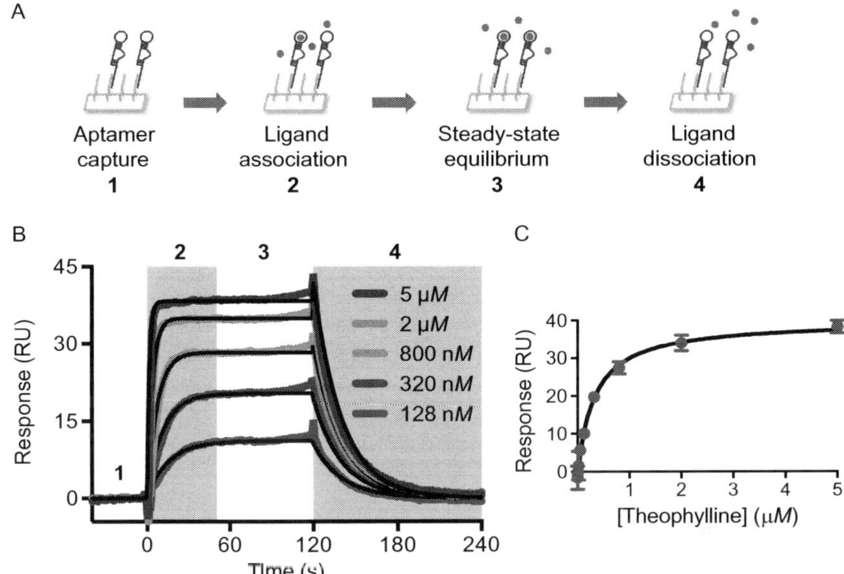

Andrew L. Chang *et al.*, Figure 19.6 Kinetic and equilibrium binding characterization of aptamers. (A) Schematic diagram of SPR-based aptamer binding characterization. (B) Multi-cycle kinetic analysis of theophylline aptamer binding. Overlaid sensorgrams for five concentrations of theophylline are shown and fit to a 1:1 kinetic binding model. Overlaid signals are the same as those shown in Fig. 19.5. (C) Equilibrium binding analysis of theophylline aptamer binding fit to a steady-state affinity model. *Adapted, with permission, from Chang et al. (2014).*

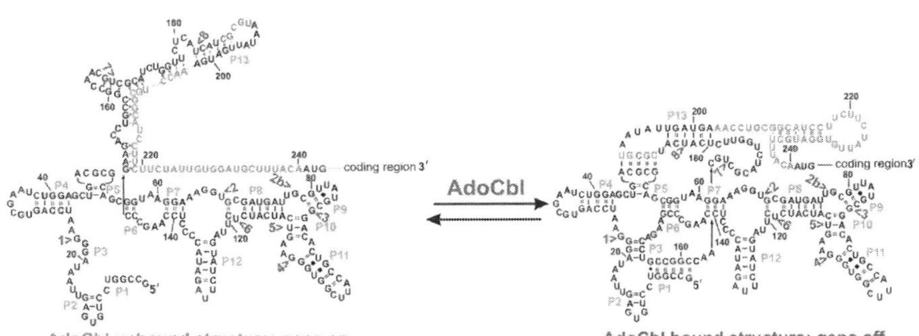

Michelle F. Schaffer *et al.*, Figure 20.1 Proposed secondary structure of the *btuB* riboswitch from *Escherichia coli* in the "gene on" (left) and "gene off" (right) form. The riboswitch binds coenzyme B_{12} (AdoCbl) in the aptamer region (black) and controls the access for the ribosome by the expression platform (green). In the unbound form (left), an anti-aptamer is formed through interaction of the expression platform with the aptamer. Thereby, the ribosome binding site (RBS), situated shortly 5′ of the start codon AUG (purple), is accessible for the ribosome. At high AdoCbl concentrations (right), a pseudoknot (brown) is formed that leads to the sequestration of RBS and thus prevents the binding of the ribosome. The nine cleavage sites observed in in-line probing experiments, that demonstrate an altered cleavage pattern in presence of AdoCbl, are indicated with red numbers.

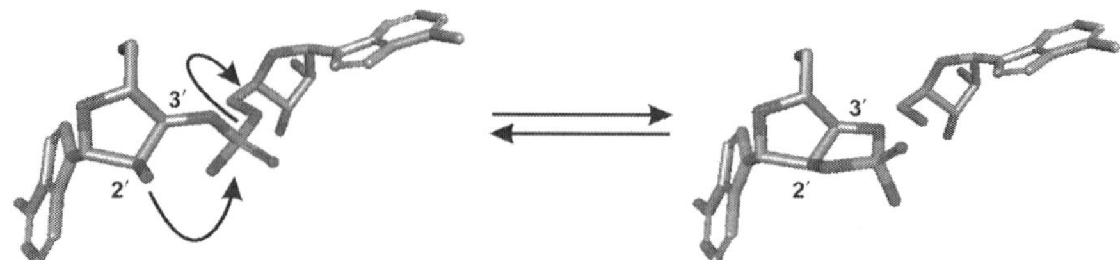

Michelle F. Schaffer *et al.*, Figure 20.2 Mechanism of an in-line attack, leading to phosphodiester cleavage. The activated 2′-OH attacks the central phosphorous in a nucleophilic S_N2 substitution reaction. The opposite 5′-O as the leaving group gets protonated and a 2′3′-cyclic phosphate is left on the attacking side.

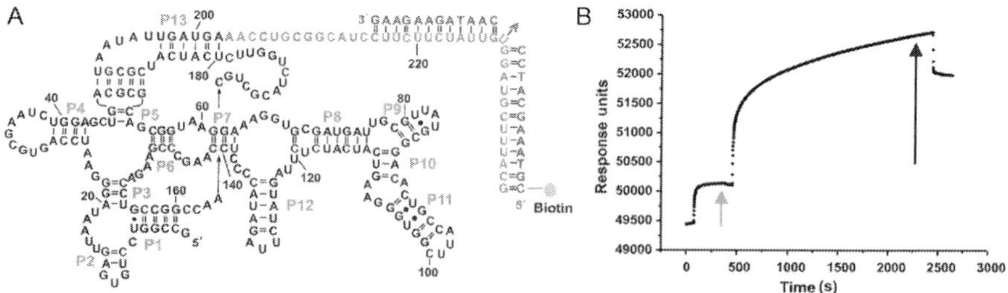

Michelle F. Schaffer *et al.*, Figure 20.5 Immobilization of the *btuB* riboswitch for an SPR experiment. (A) Secondary structure of the *btuB* riboswitch construct used for SPR experiments. Immobilization on the streptavidin sensor surface is achieved by hybridizing a 25 nucleotide long DNA oligo (pink) carrying biotin (yellow) at its 5′ end to the complementary nucleotides at the 3′ end of the expression platform (green) in the *btuB* riboswitch. (B) The *btuB* riboswitch is immobilized on the sensor surface in two steps. First step (gray arrow) involves the injection of a hybridized DNA–RNA adduct. This is followed by an injection of pure RNA (black arrow) to bind to unbound DNA oligos on the sensor surface and thereby raise the surface density of the RNA.

CPI Antony Rowe
Eastbourne, UK
March 31, 2015